HANDBOOK OF RESEARCH ON FAMILY BUSINESS, SECOND EDITION

T0329911

Handbook of Research on Family Business, Second Edition

Edited by

Kosmas X. Smyrnios

Professor of Family Business Entrepreneurship, School of Management, RMIT University, Melbourne, Australia

Panikkos Zata Poutziouris

Professor of Entrepreneurship and Family Business and Head, Business and Management School, UCLan Cyprus

Sanjay Goel

Associate Professor of Strategic Management and Entrepreneurship, Labovitz School of Business and Economics, University of Minnesota Duluth, USA

Edward Elgar
Cheltenham, UK • Northampton, MA, USA

Published by
Edward Elgar Publishing Limited
The Lypiatts
15 Lansdown Road
Cheltenham
Glos GL50 2JA
UK

Edward Elgar Publishing, Inc.
William Pratt House
9 Dewey Court
Northampton
Massachusetts 01060
USA

A catalogue record for this book
is available from the British Library

Library of Congress Control Number: 2012943181

This book is available electronically in the ElgarOnline.com
Business Subject Collection, E-ISBN 978 1 78100 938 3

ISBN 978 1 84844 322 8 (cased)

Typeset by Servis Filmsetting Ltd, Stockport, Cheshire
Printed and bound by MPG Books Group, UK

Contents

Contributors

Diane Arijs (PhD) is Professor of Entrepreneurship, Family Businesses and Research Methodology at the Faculty Economics and Management at the Hogeschool-Universiteit Brussel (HUB). She is senior researcher at the Research Centre for Entrepreneurship. Her current research interests include family business succession, gender, leadership styles and entrepreneurship policy.

Blanca Arosa (PhD) is Senior Lecturer of Business Administration at Faculty of Business and Economics, University of the Basque Country, UPV/EHU, Spain. Her academic area of expertise is in corporate governance and family business. She is co-author of several academic peer-reviewed articles in corporate governance and family business research.

Patricia Bachiller is Lecturer at the Department of Accounting and Finance, University of Zaragoza (Spain). Her research interests include privatization and liberalization. She has published in journals including *Management Decision, Public Money and Management, Global Economic Review, International Journal of Health Planning and Management*, among others. She has been Visiting Professor at the University of Tampere (Finland) and the University of Siena (Italy).

Sihem Ben Mahmoud-Jouini, Orange Chair holder, Associate Professor at HEC Paris, where she is the programme director of Innovation and Entrepreneurship at the Executive MBA. Her main topics of research are managing exploration within new ventures and established firms.

Alain Bloch, Graduate of Saint-Cyr French Military Academy (PhD) in Information Systems and Management (University of Paris–Dauphine), is Full Professor at the French Conservatoire National des Arts et Métiers (CNAM). He is also an affiliate Faculty member (Entrepreneurship Department) of HEC Paris School of Management. His research focus is on innovation, entrepreneurship, family business and leadership.

Anna Blombäck has a PhD in Business Administration and holds a position as Assistant Professor at Jönköping International Business School. Blombäck's research revolves around the notion of companies as societal actors, related to marketing and management. Specifically, her focus is on corporate communications, branding, identity and societal responsibility.

Isabel C. Botero (Aubry Group LLC) obtained her PhD in Organizational Communication Michigan State University. Dr Botero's research interests include communication in and about family firms, influence processes in the organization, information sharing in groups and crisis communication. Her work has appeared in *Communication Monographs, Communication Yearbook, Management Communication Quarterly, Corporate Communications: An International Journal, Journal of Management Studies* and *Journal of Cross-Cultural Psychology*.

Laura Cabeza-García is Associate Professor of Business Administration at the University of Leon, Spain. She graduated in Business Administration and obtained her PhD at the University of Oviedo (Spain). Her research interests include privatizations, corporate governance, family firms and corporate social responsibility.

Donella Caspersz (PhD, University of Western Australia) is an Assistant Professor in Management and Organisations at the University of Western Australia Business School. Her current research interests in family business studies include the efficacy of managerial interventions in enhancing management capabilities of family business owners and managers, and successful management transitions.

Sooduck Chang is Associate Professor of Business Administration at Hannam University in Korea. Dr Chang teaches courses on organizational behaviour, strategic management and entrepreneurship. He received his MBA and PhD in Organization and Strategy from Kyungpook National University. His current research interests are in strategic management, entrepreneurship and organization theory.

James J. Chrisman (PhD, University of Georgia) is Professor of Management and Director of the Center of Family Enterprise Research at Mississippi State University. He also holds a joint appointment as a Senior Research Fellow with the Centre for Entrepreneurship and Family Enterprise at the University of Alberta, Canada.

Guido Corbetta is AIdAF-Alberto Falck Professor of Strategic Management in Family Business and Professor of Corporate Strategy at Bocconi University, and Senior Faculty Member of SDA Bocconi School of Management (Italy). He is a Fellow of the International Family Enterprise Research Association (IFERA). He has 25 years of experience in the family business field and he is a consultant and board member to many family companies. He is an editorial board member of *Entrepreneurship Theory and Practice* and *Family Business Review*.

Léo-Paul Dana is at Groupe Sup de Co Montpellier Business School, Montpellier Research in Management, Montpellier, France, on leave from the University of Canterbury in New Zealand, where he has been tenured since 1999. He has served on the faculties of McGill University and INSEAD. Professor Dana earned BA and MBA degrees at McGill University, and a PhD from the Ecole des Hautes Etudes Commerciales.

Sharon M. Danes (PhD) is a Professor in the Family Social Science Department at the University of Minnesota and one of the authors of the sustainable family business theory. She has authored over 150 refereed research articles, book chapters and outreach publications emphasizing the intersection of economic and social decision-making. She is a Past Chair of the Family Business Section of the US Association for Small Business and Entrepreneurship.

Alexandra Dawson is Assistant Professor of Management at Concordia University's John Molson School of Business, Montreal, Canada. She received her PhD in Management from Bocconi University, Milan, Italy in 2007. Her research focuses on growth and entrepreneurial behaviour in family firms, with the aim of understanding how the individual and social features that are typical of this type of organization can become antecedents of competitive advantage.

Bart J. Debicki is Assistant Professor of Management in the College of Business and Economics at Towson University, Maryland. He received his PhD from the Mississippi State University.

Francesca di Donato is a researcher in Business Economics at Luspio University of Rome. She is Lecturer in Business Administration at Luspio University of Rome. She is Lecturer in Accounting at LUISS – Guido Carli University of Rome. During the period 2004/2008 she was Research Fellow at LUISS.

Eduardo L. Giménez is Associate Professor at Universidade de Vigo (Galiza, Spain). His research interests lie in the application of general equilibrium theory to financial economics, family economics, monetary economics, environmental economics and real business cycles.

Maria-Cleofe Giorgino is Research Fellow at the Department of Business and Social Studies of the University of Siena (Italy). She obtained her PhD in Business Administration at the University of Salento (Italy) and she is also public accountant and registered auditor. Her research interests are financial accounting, insolvency prediction models and cultural enterprise management.

Luca Gnan is Associate Professor of Family Business and Organizational Behaviour at the University of Rome Tor Vergata, Italy and Vice-President and Executive Director of EURAM (European Academy of Management). He has published on topics related to family business governance, corporate and public governance, with a special interest in boards of directors, governance structures and mechanisms.

Sanjay Goel is Associate Professor of Strategic Management and Entrepreneurship at University of Minnesota Duluth and President of the International Family Enterprise Research Association (IFERA). His current teaching, research and training interests include entrepreneurship, governance and strategy in family business firms, development of strong business families, and effect of family ownership on social wealth. His research has been published in many journals dedicated to these broad topics.

Silvia Gómez-Ansón graduated in Economics at the Complutense University of Madrid, Spain, holds a Masters in International Economics from the University of Constance, Germany and a PhD in Economics from the University of Oviedo, Spain. She is Full Professor of Finance and Accountancy at the University of Oviedo. Her research interests include corporate governance, family firms and privatizations.

José Luis Calvo González is a member of the Economic Analysis Department at Spanish UNED. His studies have focused on technological innovation and the effects of brands on fashion consumer behaviour. He has published articles in national and international books and reviews.

Toshio Goto is Professor at the University of Economics in Tokyo, Japan. He obtained a BA from Tokyo University and an MBA from Harvard Univesity. His main research interests are business strategies focusing on innovation, succession and longevity of family businesses. He contributed 'Longevity of Japanese family firms' to the *Handbook of Research on Family Business* (2006). He has authored various books and articles in

English, Japanese and Chinese. His most recent book is *Family Business: Its Unrecognized Power and Potential* (in Japanese). Professor Goto pioneered research and recognition of family business in Japan.

Vipin Gupta (PhD, Wharton School) is Professor and Co-director of the Global Management Center at the California State University San Bernardino. His research includes the science of culture, strategic and international management, organizational and technological development, and entrepreneurial and women's leadership.

Elias Hadjielias is Lecturer in Business and Management at UCLan Cyprus. Elias's research interests revolve around entrepreneurship and entrepreneurial learning, family businesses, and cooperation and learning in organizations. He is involved in teaching at both the undergraduate and postgraduate levels.

Eleanor Hamilton (PhD) is Associate Dean for Enterprise Engagement and Impact at Lancaster University Management School, UK. She teaches Entrepreneurship, Small Business and Family Business at both the undergraduate and postgraduate levels. Her research interests include the influence and impact of intergenerational learning in family businesses, entrepreneurial learning and entrepreneurship education.

Carole Howorth is Professor of Entrepreneurship and Family Business at Bradford University School of Management, UK. She researches and teaches various topics related to entrepreneurship, performance and family businesses.

Tuuli Ikäheimonen is a doctoral student of Management and Organization at the Lappeenranta University of Technology (LUT) School of Business, Finland. She also works as a training manager in the LUT Centre for Training and Development. Her research interests include family business governance, especially board of directors, and succession.

Markku Ikävalko (PhD) is Director of the LUT Centre for Training and Development, Finland. He specializes in entrepreneurship and small business management, and has long experience in SME development and consultancy. His research interests include SME management, entrepreneurship education, ownership issues and family businesses.

Txomin Iturralde is Senior Lecturer in Finance and Business Administration and Director of Family Business Centre of the University of the Basque Country, UPV/EHU (Spain). His current research interests include cash management, international finance, corporate governance and family business.

Juha Kansikas is Associate Professor of Entrepreneurship at the University of Jyväskylä, Finland, and Adjunct Professor at the Mendel University, the Czech Republic. His research interests are entrepreneurship education and family entrepreneurship.

Franz W. Kellermanns is a Professor of Management in the College of Business at the University of Tennessee, USA. He holds a joint appointment with the INTES Center at the WHU–Otto Beisheim School of Management (Germany). He received his PhD from the University of Connecticut. His research interests include strategy process and entrepreneurship, with a focus on family business research.

Antti Kirmanen (MSc, University of Jyväskylä, Finland) has acted as a research assistant at the Jyväskylä University School of Business and Economics.

Alexander Koeberle-Schmid (PhD, WHU–Otto Beisheim School of Management, INTES-Consulting for Family Business, Germany) is a family business consultant and a lecturer at WHU. He advises business-owning families in strategic and structural issues. He is a supervisory board member of a family business. He has published several books and articles on the most relevant issues of family business governance.

Rania Labaki (PhD) is Associate Professor of Management Sciences at the University of Bordeaux IV and researcher at the Family Business Research Centre (IRGO) and the INSEEC Research Centre, France. Her PhD dissertation examined the antecedents and outcomes of the quality of family relationships in French listed family businesses. She currently teaches and conducts research on finance and family businesses, especially governance, financial policies, family relationships and emotions in decision-making.

Isabelle Le Breton-Miller is Associate Professor of Management and Chair of Succession and Family Enterprise at HEC Montreal, Canada and is Senior Research Fellow at the University of Alberta. She earned her PhD at Imperial College, London and serves on the editorial boards of *Entrepreneurship Theory & Practice, Family Business Review* and *Journal of Family Business Strategy*. Her most recent book with Danny Miller is *Managing for the Long Run* (Harvard Business School Press), now in six languages. Her research examines the strategies, organization designs and governance structures of family businesses.

Jangwoo Lee (PhD, Korea Advanced Institute of Science and Technology) is a professor and Director of The Research Institute of Creative and Cultural Industries at Kyungpook National University. His research focuses on technological entrepreneurship, family enterprises and strategic management. He has served as a chairman of Korean Association of Small Business Studies and Korean Society of Strategic Management. Dr Lee was born and resides in Korea.

Nancy M. Levenburg (PhD) is Associate Professor of Management at Grand Valley State University. Her research includes family business, small business management and strategic applications of information technologies to improve operations. She serves on the editorial review board of *Family Business Review* and the board of the North American Case Research Association (NACRA).

Corinna M. Lindow (PhD, HHL–Leipzig Graduate School of Management, Germany) is a Research Fellow at Loyola University Chicago Family Business Center (USA). She has been a visiting researcher at the Cox Family Enterprise Center at Kennesaw State University (USA). Her main research interests are strategic management and corporate entrepreneurship within the context of family businesses.

Shanan R. Litchfield is a doctoral candidate at Mississippi State University, USA. Her studies have focused on behaviour in family firms. Her dissertation explores the successful use of human resource practices to maximize beneficial family behaviours in the family firm.

Amaia Maseda is Senior Lecturer in Business Administration and Accounting at the University of the Basque Country, UPV/EHU (Spain). Her academic area of expertise is cash management, corporate governance and family business. She is co-author of several academic peer-reviewed articles in corporate and management research.

Curtis F. Matherne III (PhD, Mississippi State University) is Assistant Professor of Management in the B.I. Moody III College of Business Administration at the University of Louisiana at Lafayette.

Nava Michael-Tsabari is a PhD candidate at the Technion–Israel Institute of Technology. Since 2007 she has been teaching the first and only course on family businesses at the Tel-Aviv University. She is a researcher on family businesses and a third-generation member of a multinational family business, enabling her to combine personal insights with scholarly skills on family businesses.

Sophie Mignon, former student of ENS Cachan, PhD in management. She is an associate professor and a PhD supervisor at the University of Montpellier II (MRM), France. Her research examines the sustainability, exploration and capitalization processes of family firms.

Danny Miller is Research Professor at HEC Montreal and Chair Professor of Strategy and Family Business at the University of Alberta, Canada. He earned his PhD from McGill University. His research examines the strategies, organization designs and governance structures of family and other types of businesses.

Alessandro Minichilli is Assistant Professor in the Department of Management and Technology at Bocconi University, Italy. His research interests are family-controlled firms, focusing on the intersection between corporate governance, top management teams (TMTs) and family business literatures, with emphasis on gender issues. He is editorial review board member of *Family Business Review* and *Corporate Governance: An International Review*.

Fabio Matuoka Mizumoto is Professor of Business Administration at Insper Institute of Education and Research, and Professor at the School of Economics of São Paulo's Getulio Vargas Foundation (FGV–EESP), Brazil. He holds a doctorate in Business Administration from the University of São Paulo (FEA–USP) and was a visiting PhD scholar at Olin Business School at Washington University in St Louis, USA.

Daniela Montemerlo is Associate Professor of Business Administration and Family Business at University of Insubria, Professor of Strategic Management in Family Business at Bocconi University and Senior Faculty Member of SDA Bocconi School of Management (Italy). She is a Fellow of IFERA and was a member of the IFERA Board from 2001 to 2011. She has been actively involved in family business research, teaching, governance and consulting since 1990, with a special focus on family agreements, family and corporate governance, teams at the top, generational transitions and gender issues.

Mattias Nordqvist is Professor of Business Administration and The Hamrin International Professor of Family Business at Jönköping International Business School (JIBS) in Sweden. He is founding associate editor of the *Journal of Family Business Strategy*.

Jose Antonio Novo (PhD in Economics, Universidade of A Coruña) is Associate Professor at the Universidade of A Coruña (Spain). He also serves as the Director of the Family Business Chair, Universidade of A Coruña. His research area is family firms, banking theory and industrial organization.

Sergio Paternostro is Research Fellow at the Department of Business and Social Studies, University of Siena (Italy). He has been visiting PhD student at IESE Business School (University of Navarra, Barcelona, Spain) and visiting scholar at the Faculty of Economics (University of Castilla La Mancha, Spain). His research interests include corporate social responsibility, social disclosure and family business.

Atilano Pena-López (PhD in Economics) is Associate Professor at the Department of Applied Economics of the University of A Coruña (Spain). His research has focused on business ethics, socioeconomics and social capital.

Timo Pihkala (PhD) is Professor of Management and Organization, specializing on entrepreneurship and small business management at the Lappeenranta University of Technology (LUT) School of Business and he is the director of the LUT Lahti School of Innovation, Finland. His research interests include entrepreneurship, innovativeness, strategic management and family businesses.

Daniel Pittino is Assistant Professor in Organization and Human Resource Management at the University of Udine (Italy). His main research interests include governance and management issues in family firms and entrepreneurial ventures. He is author of several articles and research papers on the topics of corporate governance and organization in the family business.

Panikkos Zata Poutziouris (PhD) is Professor of Entrepreneurship and Family Business and Head of the Business and Management School at UCLan Cyprus – the Enterprising British University in Cyprus. Previously, for almost two decades, he served on the faculty of Manchester Business School, University of Manchester, and Cyprus International Institute of Management, where he led a number of research, educational and consulting initiatives. Professor Poutziouris is the Past President of IFERA and has served on the advisory board of IFB (UK) and as a board member on the UK Institute for Small Business Entrepreneurship (ISBE). In 2011, the Family Firm Institute honoured him with the FFI International Award in recognition of his contribution to the development of family business initiatives across the globe.

Francisco Negreira del Río (PhD in Business Administration, University of Santiago de Compostela, Spain (2002)). His current position is full-time Business Management Lecturer at Novacaixagalicia Business School, Vigo, Spain. His research is based on family business and he is co-author of various books and academic articles on this subject.

Jesús Negreira del Río (PhD in Pharmacy, University of Santiago de Compostela, Spain (1997)). Since 2000 he has been full-time Marketing Lecturer at Novacaixagalicia Business School. His current research is focused on family business topics.

María Sacristán-Navarro graduated in Economics at the Complutense University of Madrid, Spain where she also obtained her PhD in Economics. She is Associate Professor of Strategy at Rey Juan Carlos University, Madrid. Her research interests are associated with the strategy field, corporate governance and family firms.

Maria Sylvia Macchione Saes holds a Doctorate in Economic Sciences and Habilitation in Business Administration from the School of Business Administration at the University of São Paulo (FEA–USP). She is currently Professor of Business Administration at FEA–USP, Coordinator of the Center for Organizational Studies (CORS) at USP, and the President of FEA–USP's research committee.

José Manuel Sánchez-Santos (PhD in Economics) is Associate Professor at the Department of Applied Economics of the University of A Coruña (Spain). His research has focused on socioeconomics, monetary policy and sports economics.

Pramodita Sharma (PhD) is the Sanders Professor at the School of Business Administration, University of Vermont, USA. She holds a joint appointment at Babson College where she is the Academic Director for the Global STEP project. Sharma is the editor of FBR and a fellow of the Family Firm Institute. She is a co-founder of the Family Enterprise Research Conference and the Family Enterprise Case Competition.

Kosmas X. Smyrnios (PhD, MAPS) holds the position of Professor of Family Business Entrepreneurship, School of Management, RMIT University, Melbourne, Australia. He is a former Foundation Board Member of the International Family Enterprise Research Academy (IFERA) and Associate Editor of *Family Business Review*. He is a foundation Associate Editor of the *Journal of Family Business Strategy*. Kosmas has developed an extensive applied research record with over 100 international and national refereed publications in different disciplines including business management, marketing, entrepreneurship, accounting, physics and psychology. Professor Smyrnios is frequently called upon to provide expert media commentary on SMEs, family business and fast-growth firms.

Lucrezia Songini is Associate Professor of Family Business and Managerial Control at the Eastern Piedmont University, Novara, Italy and Senior Professor at Bocconi School of Management, Milan, Italy. She is the Chair of the Entrepreneurship SIG of EURAM. She has published on topics related to strategic planning and managerial control systems in family businesses, female entrepreneurship and the role of women in family firms.

Kathryn Stafford (PhD) is Associate Professor at The Ohio State University in the Department of Consumer and Textile Sciences. She teaches a course on business-owning families and conducts research on the management practices of business-owning families and family businesses.

Emma Su has an MS in Business Administration from the University of British Columbia and an MS in Knowledge Management from NanYang Technological University, Singapore. Her research covers various issues related to family businesses: family business succession, conflicts in family businesses, strategic planning, knowledge management in family businesses, and Chinese family businesses.

Riccardo Tiscini is Full Professor in Business Economics at Universitas Mercatorum of Rome. He also teaches Business Economics and Family Business Management at

Luiss Guido Carli University and La Sapienza University in Rome. His main research interests are accounting, corporate governance and family business.

Giovanni Valentini is Assistant Professor of Strategy at Bocconi University, Milan. He holds a PhD in Management from IESE Business School. His research examines how firms' innovation and technology strategy can lead to sustainable competitive advantage. More specifically, he is interested in the effects of M&A on technological performance, the relationship between innovation and export, and the organization of R&D.

Álvaro Gómez Vieites (PhD in Economy and Business Administration (2009), Bachelor in Business Administration, Telecommunications Engineering and Computer Science Engineering). His research has been focused on innovation and the effect of new technologies on marketing and commerce. He has published 28 books and several articles in scientific reviews.

Francesca Visintin is Associate Professor in Organization and Human Resource Management at the University of Udine (Italy). Her main fields of study are the management of innovation and the comparative technological performance of the systems of capitalism. She is author of several articles on the topics of human resource management and performance in the family business setting.

Ramona Kay Zachary (PhD) is the Academic Director of the Lawrence N. Field Programs of Entrepreneurship and the Jonas Chair of Entrepreneurship in the Department of Management of the Zicklin School of Business at Baruch College, New York. Professor Zachary teaches and conducts research related to family businesses and the owning family's internal social and economic dynamics, and the effects of the family on the family business viability over time, as well as entrepreneurship issues and research.

Victor Zheng (PhD) is currently Associate Director of Social and Political Development Studies, HKIAPS, The Chinese University of Hong Kong. His research interest includes Chinese family business and the equal inheritance system, and social and commercial history in Hong Kong and Macao.

Acknowledgements

The publishers wish to thank the following who have kindly given permission for the use of copyright material.

Palgrave Macmillan via the Copyright Clearance Centre for the chapter:
  Danny Miller, Jangwoo Lee, Sooduck Chang and Isabelle Le Breton-Miller (2009), 'Filling the institutional void: the social behavior and performance of family versus non-family technology firms in emerging markets', *Journal of International Business Studies*, **40**(5), 802–17.
Sage Publications via the Copyright Clearance Centre for the chapter:
  Bart J. Debicki, Curtis F. Matherne III, Franz W. Kellermanns and James J. Chrisman (2009), 'Family business research in the new millennium: an overview of the who, the where, the what, and the why', *Family Business Review*, **22**(2), 151–66.

Every effort has been made to trace all the copyright holders but if any have been inadvertently overlooked the publishers will be pleased to make the necessary arrangements at the first opportunity.

Introduction: trends and developments in family business research

Kosmas X. Smyrnios, Panikkos Z. Poutziouris and Sanjay Goel

The second edition of the *Handbook of Research on Family Business* extends Poutziouris et al. (2006) by delivering a series of contemporary scholarly conceptual and empirical research papers that advance our critical thinking and identify recent advances in the field.

A considerable amount of water has passed under the bridge since Craig Aronoff's (1988) article on the megatrends in family business almost a quarter of century ago. Since this time, the family business glacier has not only responded to climatic changes, but is now attracting researchers identified with other disciplines including sociology, anthropology, psychology, economics, finance, law, management, strategy, marketing and accounting, *inter alia*. Researchers are gaining a heightened appreciation of family business, challenging and contributing to our collective wisdom. As a result, the field is charting new waters and terrains.

These influences are having a fundamental impact not only on our thinking, but also on our research and practice. Family business scholarship has moved beyond what might be regarded as emergent to a phase of rapid growth, admittedly from a relatively low baseline (Astrachan, 2010). Recently, Stewart and Miner (2011) reported that an interrogation of the ProQuest's scholarly *Business* journal's section between 1985 and 2009 shows an annual growth rate of 12.4 per cent, significantly higher than the overall rate of growth in publications. Similarly, Astrachan and Pieper (2010) stated that bibliometric research carried out by Elsevier indicated a 17 per cent annual growth rate over the previous 12 years in the number of papers dedicated to family business.

In 2009, Bart Debicki and colleagues undertook a content analysis of 394 family business articles published across 30 management journals between 2001 and 2007. Chapter 2 of this Handbook extends their research to cover the period from 2001 to 2009. This examination identifies strategy implementation and control, including the sub-themes of structure, evolution and change, leadership and change, and corporate governance as being the most popular topics of investigation.

Despite these trends, the development of family business related theory is lagging to the point that this deficiency can be regarded as one of the main contributors retarding the emergence of the family business as a respected scholarly field in its own right. As Stewart and Miner (2011) stated, this lacuna has created a window of opportunity 'for theoretical development, an important requirement for a core presence in research universities' (p. 3). Research published in top-tier journals and doctoral student numbers also remain at the margins.

The International Family Enterprise Research Association (IFERA) has come a long way since its inception in the late 1990s, with its subsequent foundation in 2001, when about 30 colleagues met in Amsterdam. At that time, this cohort functioned as an informal community banded together by shared interest in promulgating family business research. Similarly, according to Alden Lank, the inaugural FBN conference involved only five paper presentations to an audience of fewer than 20 participants. We can only marvel at its standing in the international community now. Other conferences dedicated solely to family business are the Family Firm Institute (FFI), established in 1985, and another key conference dedicated solely to family business research – the more recently founded Family Enterprise Research Conference (FERC).

We have three peer-reviewed journals dedicated specifically to the field: *Family Business Review* and the recently established *Journal of Family Business Strategy* and the *Journal of Family Business Management*. How far the discipline has moved since these formative years! The family business field has shifted, and is gradually gaining acceptance as part of the mainstream. It can be said that our field now strives to address relatively sophisticated research questions, aiming to underpin these questions by established theory, albeit that the methods that have driven investigations in other disciplines, structural equation modelling and multivariate methods, are all being used as a matter of course – far removed from opinion pieces, anecdotes and reporting of merely descriptive statistics. There is yet also room for methodologies to be more robust, whether qualitative, quantitative or mixed, and data analytic techniques, including sophisticated case studies, qualitative data analytic programs such as N-vivo, and causal network modelling need to be used judiciously rather than indiscriminately or thoughtlessly. In line with the speed of socioeconomic changes and the influx of emerging and established researchers across different disciplines, so-called traditional views and established notions concerning family business need to be put to the test through more rigorous questioning and robust research methodologies. In other words, significant work remains to be done for the next generation of scholars to make family business research proportionately as important in the academic world as family businesses are in the economic world.

There are a number of identifiable streams of research published in peer-refereed journals, including the financial performance of publicly listed companies (Anderson and Reeb, 2003; Villalonga and Amit, 2006), governance issues of family businesses (including the unique role of external directors) (Carney, 2005; Steier, 2003; Randøy and Goel, 2003; Dumas et al., 2000; Goel, Voordeckers et al., forthcoming), social performance of family businesses (Berrone et al., 2010; Dyer and Whetten, 2006), family business best practice (Ward, 2004; Dana and Smyrnios, 2010), long-lived family businesses (Goto, 2009), kinship (Stewart, 2003) and clans (Moores and Mula, 2000), stakeholder-based research (Zellweger and Nason, 2008), to mention only a few. In addition, there are a number of sound studies that contextualize issues such as governance, entrepreneurship and leadership to family businesses, for example, by investigating family business leadership in different generations (Miller and Le Breton-Miller, 2011; Miller et al., 2011). Special issues, in association with IFERA conferences, reflect a wide variety of theoretical approaches, and many thought-provoking ideas (e.g. see Goel, Mazzola et al., forthcoming, for a recent introduction to a special issue).

An exploratory examination of principal themes of research emanating from the 2007–2011 IFERA conferences reveals a relatively small number of major themes, with

---

BOX I.1   PRINCIPAL THEMES OF RESEARCH EMANATING
FROM THE 2007–2011 IFERA CONFERENCES

- Family influence (cohesion, power, culture, family values, psychology, emotions)
- Financial behaviour and performance (capital structure MBOs, M&A, VC-PE, IPO, value)
- Succession
   1. Cross-sectional perspective (attitudes, successor attributes, mentoring, executive training, grooming)
   2. Process perspective (life stage, longevity, socialization)
- Strategy (decision-making, strategic thinking)
- Marketing (branding, family branding, family and corporate brand identity)
- Gender (top management, copreneurs, female leaders)
- Governance and performance (differences between family businesses and non-family businesses, family governance practices, life cycle and financial performance, board composition)
- Family business entrepreneurship (entrepreneurial behaviour, corporate entrepreneurship)
- Sustainability and longevity, long-lived family businesses
- Theoretical papers (resource-based view, dynamic capabilities, evolutionary economics, evolutionary theory, systems approach, stewardship perspective, behavioural approach)
- Social responsibility, environment and culture, philanthropy
- Internationalization, globalization
- Methodology (narrative)
- Organizational behaviour and cultural paradigms (organizational change, social exchange and commitment, sibling partnerships, culture and dynamic capabilities)
- Regional family businesses and ethnicity (Japan, Asia, Chinese, Italian, Bulgarian)
- Family business case studies (internationalization, joint ventures, transgenerational succession)
- Innovation (business models)

---

research in the areas of financial behaviour and performance, succession, governance and performance, family influence and strategy standing out (Box I.1). In line with what we alluded to earlier, is the limited research on theory, theorizing and modelling, not to mention methodology.

To where is the field heading? If only we had a crystal ball. It is clear that the field has moved towards shared theoretical frameworks, albeit from other disciplines, application of diverse and robust methodologies, and leaders supportive of emerging researchers who provide a climate of heightened interest, passion and exuberance. For Stewart and Miner

(2011), the family business field needs to develop 'richer theories of the business enterprise' (p. 5). To some extent this process has been demonstrated in debates, replication studies, and support of and failures to support the F-PEC scale (Astrachan et al., 2002; Klein et al., 2005), and 'familiness' and other constructs.

Debate relating to definitional matters and appropriate theories, and comparisons between family and non-family firms, no longer receive the same level of prominence. We are moving towards the establishment of a top-tier journal, defining pluralistic boundaries, particularly in relation to entrepreneurship and management in general, undertaking rigorous scholarship, and developing large international databases, such as that relating to the STEP (Successful Transgenerational Entrepreneurship Practices) project that is accessible to international family business researchers. This project involves over 33 partner universities (http:// www3.babson.edu/eship/step/).

To some extent, it can be argued that the field is at the stage of conceptual model formulation, development and testing. The same goes for the development of family business constructs and scales, a preliminary step necessary for advancing basic family business theory, and associated scientific inquiry and discovery. Researchers have moved away from the sole reliance on so-called hard financial measures of firm performance to the application of idiosyncratic performance metrics and goals (Zellweger and Astrachan, 2008) and multiple dimensions such as firm survival, family financial benefit, family non-financial benefit (emotional well-being), and societal benefits (Astrachan, 2010; Astrachan and Pieper, 2012). Investigators now have the tools to test for non-recursivity between family and business dimensions.

STRUCTURE OF THE *HANDBOOK*

The *Handbook of Research on Family Business* comprises 31 major contributions, two of which are key reprints published in leading journals. The *Handbook* is divided in ten sections: Recent Developments in Family Business Research; Corporate Governance; Family Governance; Social Capital; Women in Family Business; Leadership and Human Resource Management in Family Firms; Knowledge Management; Family Business Sustainability; Family Enterprises from a Macroeconomic Perspective; and Broad-based Issues in Family Firms. See the Contents page for the titles of each of these major research papers.

1   Family Business Research in the New Millennium: An Assessment of Individual and Institutional Productivity, 2001–2009

In their analysis of 394 family business articles published across 30 management journals between 2001 and 2009, Curtis Matherne, Bart Debicki, Franz Kellermanns and James Chrisman report on the contributions of individual scholars and academic institutions to family business research. A network analysis of co-author relationships has led to an understanding of the who, where and what of family business research, the reasons why the developmental trends have occurred and how the field's momentum can be maintained and directed towards productive ends.

2 Filling the Institutional Void: The Social Behavior and Performance of Family versus Non-Family Technology Firms in Emerging Markets

Danny Miller, Jangwoo Lee, Sooduck Chang and Isabelle Le Breton-Miller examine a most challenging emerging-market sector, namely Korean high-technology businesses, arguing that (1) relationships of cohesive internal community and connection (i.e. deep relationships with outside stakeholders) will be more common in FBs than in non-FBs; (2) these relationships will enhance performance in emerging-market high-technology sectors, which, because of their competitive, complex and ever-changing nature, rely on significant expert knowledge and social capital within and outside the organizational community; (3) the performance of FBs will benefit more from these community and connection relationships than the performance of non-FBs, because in these personally intimate settings employees and external partners will be especially likely to return the generosity of a visibly active owning family, or to penalize its selfishness. These authors hold that such social linkages might compensate for the lack of capital, product and labour institutional infrastructures in dynamic emerging economies. Significant empirical support was found for most of these hypotheses.

3 The Effects of Family Involvement and Corporate Governance Practices on Earnings Quality of Listed Companies

Although it is not uncommon for family firms to set incentives to extract private benefits (entrenchment effects), family enterprises can also contribute to high levels of alignment between owners' and managers' interests (alignment effects). Riccardo Tiscini and Francesca di Donato's investigation of relationships between family involvement in the governance of Italian listed companies and earnings quality (EQ) reveals that EQ is affected by the distribution of power and control set by governance systems.

4 Analysis of Social Performance and Board of Directors in Family Firms: Evidence from Quoted Italian Companies

Patricia Bachiller, Maria-Cleofe Giorgino and Sergio Paternostro examine qualitative board characteristics that influence the social performance of Italian family versus non-family firms listed on the FTSE MIB Index 40. Results show that relationships between family board representation and social performance is weak. However, organizational, structural and cultural factors, such as generation of the firm, age, size and business sector, affect social aptitude. While board principles defined for non-family firms do not appear suitable for family firms, social performance depends on the effectiveness and efficiency of a board's decision-making process, and on the corporate and individual culture of directors.

5 Board of Directors and Generational Effect in Spanish Non-Listed Family Firms

Blanca Arosa, Txomin Iturralde and Amaia Maseda investigate the effect of external boards of directors (affiliated, independent) on multi-generational family SME performance. Overall, findings demonstrate that when compared with independent directors, affiliated directors have a positive impact on performance, with the influence of independent board members being evident in first-generation entities. Interestingly, affiliated directors appear to have a negative affect on the performance of second-generation firms. External advice and counsel seems to decrease as the knowledge and family experience accumulates with successive generations, reducing the likelihood of engaging outside expertise.

6   Family Governance Bodies: A Conceptual Typology

Diffusion of ownership, differing personal interests and geographical separation threaten family firm sustainability, posing challenges to family firm governance. Alexander Koeberle-Schmid and Donella Caspersz discuss the different types of family governance options available to family firms, suggesting their suitability in responding to different scenarios, describing both the task and procedures involved in pursuing these options. These authors conclude that the literature is somewhat circumspect about the merits associated with different types of family governance bodies, along with their appropriateness in different settings.

7   Using the Configuration Approach to Understand the Reasons for and Consequences of Varied Family Involvement in Business

Pramodita Sharma and Mattias Nordqvist explore the diversity in the extent and mode of family involvement in family firms and consequent implications. Using tenets of the configuration approach, Pramodita and Mattias argue that the chosen involvement of family in the ownership and management of a business is guided by dominant values. The extent of family involvement in business has consequences for governance mechanisms that are likely to lead to aspired performance objectives on business and family dimensions.

8   Other Large Shareholders in Family Firms: Do They Monitor?

María Sacristán-Navarro, Silvia Gómez-Ansón and Laura Cabeza-García report on the relationship between ownership structures, family involvement in corporate governance and company performance. Findings suggest that non-family-managed and non-family-chaired firms tend to outperform those that are family controlled, and that this duality can have a negative effect, particularly when the two largest shareholders are families or individuals.

9   The Evolution of the Family Business Board: A Case Study

In the light of an empirical case, Tuuli Ikäheimonen, Timo Pihkala and Markku Ikävalko develop a framework of evolution of the family business board. These authors conclude that successsion, as a turning point of both the family and the business, offers a fruitful opportunity to widen our understanding of the important role and activities played by boards in family businesses.

10 The Singularities of Social Capital in Family Business: An Overview

Entrepreneurial networks, family values, altruism, personal attitudes, family commitment, interpersonal dynamics, knowledge transfer, corporate culture and emotional costs are regarded as components of social capital. Atilano Pena-López, José Manuel Sánchez-Santos and José Antonio Novo argue that social capital is a useful analytical construct that contributes to our understanding of family firms and helps to establish mechanisms that connect family and business systems to each other. These authors provide a deconstructive analysis of the fundamental components of social capital, identifying and analysing three dimensions of social capital: cognitive, structural and relational or values, and networks and trust.

11 Strategy in Family Businesses: The Analysis of Human Capital and Social Capital

Utilizing estimation methods that control for self-selection problems between two choices, strategy choice and the transaction–governance choice, Fabio Matuoka Mizumoto and Maria Sylvia Macchione Saes reveal that multigeneration family businesses outperform first-generation businesses. Family businesses demonstrating strong family ties show a significantly higher probability of change strategy. Enduring relationships allow agents to trade on the spot market and, thus, minimize costs associated with negotiating, designing and enforcing contracts.

12 Towards a Comprehensive Model of Sustainable Family Firm Performance

In the light of two types of business sustainability, sustainability of power (control, management) and sustainability of the project (business, organization), how do family enterprises (controlled by the same family) achieve organizational sustainability? Drawing upon theories of ambidexterity and organizational reliability, Sihem Ben Mahmoud-Jouini, Alain Bloch and Sophie Mignon demonstrate that the cultural characteristics of family companies (stable values, stewardship) and taking a long-term time horizon help these companies to capitalize on past experience while also thinking outside the box to change. Being geared towards sustainability and connected to their external environment, along with an intensity of internal relations, makes family enterprises naturally vigilant to environmental threats.

13 Network Capital and the Rise of Chinese Banks in Hong Kong: A Case Study on the Bank of East Asia Limited

Victor Zheng explores the interrelationship between network capital and family control: the intangible resources of personal ties and business connections. An in-depth case study analysis of the Bank of East Asia Limited indicates that in order to secure family control and domination over the bank, different kinds of network capital such as intermarriage, interlocking directorships and sociopolitical appointments play key roles. Notwithstanding, the pervasiveness and indispensable nature of network capital can still become a liability when there is a loss of mutual trust and loyalty.

14   The Determinants of Women's Involvement in Top Management Teams: Opportunities or Obstacles for Family-Controlled Firms?

Despite the increasing participation of women in family businesses and the valuable contributions that they make, an apparent 'glass ceiling' seems to prevent them from attaining top-level responsibilities. Daniela Montemerlo, Alessandro Minichilli and Guido Corbetta explore the role of family and female CEOs in top management teams (TMTs) based on a representative sample of medium and large Italian family firms. Results show that family ownership positively predicts female presence in TMTs; family CEOs and female CEOs positively predict the presence of family women within the TMTs; and family CEOs also negatively predict the presence of non-family women in TMTs. Results are interpreted in the light of agency and resource-based view theories.

15.   Women and the Glass Ceiling: The Role of Professionalization in Family SMEs

Luca Gnan and Lucrezia Songini focus on the multifaceted role of women and professionalization in family firms, examining whether the so-called 'glass ceiling' prevents women from advancing to governance and managerial positions in family SMEs. Luca and Lucrezia suggest that while most research on the role of women in family firms has focused on expectations, values, objectives, leadership styles, and on the decision-making processes, it appears that relatively few studies concentrate on strategy formulation, design of organizational structures, and the implementation of managerial mechanisms and managerial control systems.

16   Women in Family Business: Three Generations of Research

Although women are an integral part of the family, their role and contribution within family businesses are often invisible – in practice as well as in the literature. In this chapter, Vipin Gupta and Nancy Levenburg review two generations of research, the first focusing on the forces contributing to the historical invisibility of women in business, and the second on the characteristics of women's roles in family businesses. Using the articles from the CASE project pertaining to gender in family business, Vipin and Nancy then discuss a third generation of findings. Prototypes of women in family business across various worldwide cultures are presented to illustrate the diversity of gender solutions.

17   Exploring Human Resource Management in Family Firms: A Summary of What We Know and Ideas for Future Development

The effective management of human resources (HRM) is playing an increasingly important role in knowledge-based economies. Perhaps surprisingly, to date, there appears to be limited family business research in this area. In addressing this apparent gap, Isabel Botero and Shanan Litchfield highlight a number of pertinent considerations and summarize relevant family business research on this topic.

18 The Adoption of High-Performance Work Systems in Family versus Non-Family SMEs: The Moderating Effect of Organizational Size

Daniel Pittino and Francesca Visintin investigate whether the size of an organization moderates the extent to which high-performance work systems (HPWS) in human resource management are adopted by small and medium family and non-family firms. Results indicate that family firms are less inclined to employ HPWS compared to their non-family counterparts, especially in the fields of recruitment and selection, teamwork, training, and when utilizing formal involvement tools. As well, adoption of HPWS is more likely to occur when an organizational structure does not impose too many restrictions on the choice of a dominant coalition.

19 Measuring and Comparing Leadership Styles of Male and Female Chief Executive Officers in Businesses with a Varying Family Intensity

In the light of family intensity of business, Diane Arijs reviews the inconsistent findings on gender differences associated with the full-range leadership theory (FRLT). Within the context of a mixed design involving 16 in-depth interviews across five heterogeneous family businesses and telephone surveys of 188 female and 208 male CEOs, MIMIC models reveal that family intensity of the business is a much stronger explanatory variable of a person's leadership style than his/her gender or the gender composition of the leadership team. Diane concludes that typical female person-oriented leadership appears pronounced when a higher proportion of women are participating in a leadership team.

20 Entrepreneurial Learning in the Family Management Group: A Social Organizational Learning Perspective

According to Elias Hadjielias, Eleanor Hamilton and Carole Howorth, research within family business entrepreneurship needs to move beyond static and individualistic perspectives and adopt approaches more suited to the real-world context of families in business. Elias Hadjielias and his colleagues argue that social theoretical frameworks, such as situated learning, and social capital and activity theory, capture the social character, collective nature and informality that often characterizes learning in family enterprises. The family management group is viewed as an appropriate unit of analysis for helping researchers to explain entrepreneurial learning practices within the family business context, capturing transgenerational entrepreneurial practices that are crucial to securing family firm profitability, growth and longevity.

21 Strategy Formulation in Family Businesses: A Review and Research Agenda

Corinna Lindow provides a comprehensive and systematic review of empirical work on family business strategy formulation. Her in-depth review explores scholarship in the area, and identifies key issues and specific gaps, culminating in locating promising areas for future research.

22   The Impact of Knowledge Sharing on the Growth of Family Businesses in China: The Role of Chinese Culture

Emma Su investigates the interrelationships between knowledge sharing among Chinese family businesses and the role played by Chinese culture on knowledge sharing. Within the context of a mixed-methods design, Emma demonstrates that knowledge sharing is instrumental in the growth of Chinese family businesses and certain components of Chinese culture, and that the absence of trust between family and non-family members is not conducive to the sharing of knowledge.

23   Extensions of the Sustainable Family Business Theory: Operationalization and Application

This chapter focuses on the conceptual and operational aspects of Sustainable Family Business Theory (SFBT), summarizing its components, major theoretical propositions and application. Owing to its systems orientation and comprehensiveness, Ramona Kay Zachary, Sharon Danes and Kathryn Stafford argue that this theory enhances the understanding of family in the business and business in the family. Unlike many other models that take a comprehensive approach to the study of the family business, SFBT emphasizes the interaction of the family and business systems while recognizing the different characteristics of each.

24   Secrets of Family Business Longevity in Japan from the Social Capital Perspective

In a series of studies of long-lived Japanese family businesses, Toshio Goto reveals significant factors contributing to their longevity. Constitutions and precepts of century-old Japanese family firms are analysed from philosophical and institutional aspects. Their longevity is also discussed from a social capital perspective. Evidence of their practices to foster longevity is presented in support of his argument.

25   The Push–Pull of Indigenous Sámi Family Reindeer Herding Enterprises: A Metaphor for Sustainable Entrepreneurship

In this ethnographic study, Léo-Paul Dana and Kosmas Smyrnios explore the indigenous family business entrepreneurship activities of Sámi reindeer (*Rangifer tarandus*) herders. Family-based community entrepreneurship exemplifies Sámi reindeer herding, a traditional practice passed down primarily from fathers to sons. Freedom is a primary motivating factor and herding represents a sustainable exploitation of marginal natural resources, providing a cultural basis for small tribal societies comprising at least 20 ethnic minorities spread across the northern circumpolar region. Indigenous family business entrepreneurship provides an important metaphor for environmentally friendly long-practised sustainable capitalism.

26 Small Family Business Contributions to the Economy: An Enterprise Population Level Study

Antti Kirmanen and Juha Kansikas examine the contribution of small family versus non-family businesses to the Finnish economy, utilizing data derived from a random sample of 2004 enterprises across eight different industries. Contributions to the Finnish economy are discussed in relation to turnover, employment, and products and services.

27 The Microeconomics of Family Business

The application of a wide variety of instruments, tools and frameworks derived from microeconomics is useful for characterizing and differentiating family business from their non-family business counterparts, as well explaining under what conditions a number of distinctive features of family firms hold. Eduardo Giménez and José Antonio Novo develop an analytical framework incorporating the microeconomic literature of family firms, focusing on three sets of works: family firms as owner-managers; agency theory to study relationships among family business members; and the influence of legal and financial imperfections on family firm decision-making.

28 Reputational Capital in Family Firms: Understanding Uniqueness from the Stakeholder Point of View

In this chapter Anna Blombäck and Isabel Botero argue that an increased understanding of how family firms brand themselves and reference family association can represent a complementary approach to understanding uniqueness and benefit. Anna and Isabel argue that a focus on brand management provides scholars with an opportunity to recognize unique resources, involving external stakeholders' views on family businesses. Moreover, family business reputation and reputational capital can be viewed as sources of competitive advantage for family business.

29 A Study of Innovation Activities and the Role Played by Ownership Structure in Spanish Industrial Companies

Álvaro Gómez Vieites, Francisco Negreira del Río, Jesús Negreira del Río and José Luis Calvo González develop and test a model of R&D and innovation activities in a cohort of Spanish industrial firms. Factors included in their model are: ownership structure; organizational factors; R&D activities; information management; technological resources; innovation results; and firm performance. Perhaps surprisingly, findings demonstrate that family ownership has no significant influence on R&D activities but impacts negatively on innovation.

30 Acquisition and Diversification Behaviour in Large Family Firms

In their investigation of the acquisition and diversification behaviour of large family firms, Alexandra Dawson and Giovanni Valentini conclude that acquisition propensity is not linked to being a family firm, but rather to whether an enterprise is publicly listed, highly profitable and large. Family firms are more likely to acquire entities in non-correlated sectors.

31   Emotional Dimensions within the Family Business: Towards a Conceptualization

Rania Labaki, Nava Michael-Tsabari and Ramona Kay Zachary examine emotions within different systems and at different stages of family business development, contending that an almost exclusive focus on emotions in family systems has prevented researchers from examining the nature of emotions in and at the interface between family and business systems. Conceptually, this chapter considers, possibly for the first time, theoretical and empirical studies exploring this construct in the family business area, suggesting ways of incorporating emotions into an understanding of family business behaviour. Three major propositions are outlined and several theories underpin their research.

CONCLUSION

In closing, we would like to thank the authors for their outstanding scholarship and the reviewers for their dedication, valuable guidance, and direction to both the authors and editors. We are grateful to Edward Elgar Publishers for their ongoing interest in family business entrepreneurship. We hope that readers will not only enjoy reading this compilation of original family business research papers but also employ the knowledge contained within, helping to forge strong links between theory, research, practice and policy.

REFERENCES

Anderson, R.C. and Reeb, D.M. (2003), 'Founding-family ownership and firm performance: evidence from the S&P 500', *Journal of Finance*, **58**(3), 1301–28.
Aronoff, C. (1988), 'Megatrends in family business', *Family Business Review*, **9**(3), 181–5.
Astrachan, J.H. (2010), 'Strategy in family business: toward a multidimensional research agenda', *Journal of Family Business Strategy*, **1**(1), 6–14.
Astrachan, J.H. and Pieper, T.M. (2010), 'Introduction to Volume 1', *Journal of Family Business Strategy*, **1**(1), 1–5.
Astrachan, J.H. and Pieper, T.M. (2012), 'Family business research – past accomplishments and future developments', in M.R. Marvel, *Encyclopedia of New Venture Management*, Thousand Oaks, CA: Sage, pp. 189–92.
Astrachan, J.H., Klein, S.B. and Smyrnios, K.X. (2002), 'The F-PEC scale of family influence: a proposal for solving the family definition problem', *Family Business Review*, **15**(1), 45–58.
Berrone, P., Cruz, C., Gómez-Mejía, L.R. and Larraza-Kintana, M. (2010), 'Socioemotional wealth and corporate responses to institutional pressures: do family-controlled firms pollute less?', *Administrative Science Quarterly*, **55**, 82–113.
Carney, Michael (2005), 'Corporate governance and competitive advantage in family-controlled firms', *Entrepreneurship Theory and Practice*, **29**(3), 249–65.
Dana, L. and Smyrnios, K.X. (2010), 'Family business best practices: where from and where to?', *Journal of Family Business Strategy*, **1**(1), 40–53.
Debicki, B.J., Matherne, C.F., III, Kellermanns, F.W. and Chrisman, J.J. (2009), 'Family business research in the new millennium: an overview of the who, the where, the what, and the why', *Family Business Review*, **22**, 151–66.
Dumas, C., Goel, S. and Zanzi, A. (2000), 'Through the eyes of the beholder: determinants of positive percep-

tion of board contribution in family-owned firms', *International Journal of Entrepreneurship and Innovation*, October, 151–61.

Dyer, W.G., Jr and Whetten, D.A. (2006), 'Family firms and social responsibility: preliminary evidence from the S&P 500', *Entrepreneurship Theory and Practice*, **30**(6), 785–802.

Goel, S., Mazzola, P., Phan, P.H., Pieper, T.M. and Zachary, R.K. (Forthcoming), 'Strategic, ownership, governance, and socio-psychological perspectives on family businesses from around the world', *Journal of Family Business Strategy*.

Goel, S., Voordeckers, W., Van Gils, A. and Van den Heuvel, J. (Forthcoming), 'Family business as emotional arenas: the family CEO's empathy, the board of directors, and family-oriented goals', *Entrepreneurship and Regional Development*.

Goto, T. (2009), 'How can long-lived family firms enhance entrepreneurship in Japan? Implications of adoption of succession into a family', paper presented at the 9th Annual IFERA World Family Business Research Conference, held in Limassol, Cyprus, 24–27 June 2009.

Klein, S.B., Astrachan, J.H. and Smyrnios, K.X. (2005), 'The F-PEC scale of family influence: construction, validation, and further implication for theory', *Entrepreneurship Theory and Practice*, **29**, 321–39.

Miller, D. and Le Breton-Miller, I. (2011), 'Governance, social identity, and entrepreneurial orientation in closely held public companies', *Entrepreneurship Theory and Practice*, **35**, 1051–76.

Miller, D., Le Breton-Miller, I. and Lester, R.H. (2011), 'Family and lone founder ownership and strategic behaviour: social context, identity, and institutional logics', *Journal of Management Studies*, **48**, 1–25.

Moores, K. and Mula, J. (2000), 'The salience of market, bureaucratic, and clan controls in the management of family firm transitions: some tentative Australian evidence', *Family Business Review*, **13**(2), 91–106.

Poutziouris, P.Z., Smyrnios, K.X. and Klein, B.S. (eds) (2006), *Handbook of Research on Family Business*, Cheltenham, UK and Northampton, MA, USA: Edward Elgar.

Randøy, T. and Goel, S. (2003), 'Ownership structure, founder leadership, and performance in Norwegian SMEs: implications for financing entrepreneurial opportunities', *Journal of Business Venturing*, **18**(5), 619–38.

Steier, L. (2003), 'Variants of agency contracts in family-financed ventures as a continuum of familial altruistic and market rationalities', *Journal of Business Venturing*, **18**(5), 597–618.

Stewart, A. (2003), 'Help one another, use one another: toward an anthropology of family business', *Entrepreneurship Theory and Practice*, **27**, 383–96.

Stewart, A. and Miner, A.S. (2011), 'The prospects for family business in research universities', *Journal of Family Business Strategy*, **2**(1), 3–14.

Villalonga, B. and Amit, R. (2006), 'How do family ownership, control and management affect firm value?', *Journal of Financial Economics*, **80**(2), 385–417.

Ward, J.L. (2004), *Perpetuating the Family Business: 50 Lessons from Long-Lasting Successful Families in Business*, New York: Palgrave Macmillan.

Zellweger, T.M. and Astrachan, J.H. (2008), 'On the emotional value of owning a firm', *Family Business Review*, **21**(4), 347–63.

Zellweger, T.M. and Nason, R.S. (2008), 'A stakeholder perspective to family firm performance', *Family Business Review*, **21**(3), 203–16.

PART I

RECENT DEVELOPMENTS IN FAMILY BUSINESS RESEARCH

.

1 Family business research in the new millennium: an assessment of individual and institutional productivity, 2001–2009[1]

Curtis F. Matherne III, Bart J. Debicki,
Franz W. Kellermanns and James J. Chrisman

INTRODUCTION

In 1997, Shane published a study on the contributions of authors and institutions to the development of the field of entrepreneurship. His analysis was timely, since the field of entrepreneurship was growing rapidly and was beginning to gain prominence among management scholars. Family firm research, a field whose domain significantly overlaps that of entrepreneurship, has experienced similar growth in recent years (cf. Katz, 2003; Sharma et al., 2007). Indeed, scholarly articles on family firms have started to appear in premier journals (e.g. Gómez-Mejía et al., 2007; Schulze et al., 2001) and a host of special issues have been published (e.g. Chrisman et al., 2007; Chrisman et al., 2008a; Heck and Mishra, 2008; Rogoff and Heck, 2003). Since family firms appear to dominate the world economy (Cromie et al., 1995; Donckels and Frölich, 1991; Westhead and Cowling, 1998), the growth in research is overdue. As a result, a need has emerged to systematically evaluate the contributions of researchers and universities to family business research, to show the interconnectedness of those contributions, and take stock of the content of the articles in question (see also Casillas and Acedo, 2007; Chrisman et al., 2005; Sharma, 2004).

This chapter addresses this need by identifying the researchers who have contributed to the field of family business and the institutions where the research has been conducted. The chapter also analyzes the content areas that have been studied over the period 2001–2009. Finally, by analyzing the network relationships among the authors, we are able to provide a more nuanced understanding of why certain scholars and institutions have been productive and why some topics have received greater attention than others. We concentrate on the publications in 30 leading 'management' journals because most of the scholars who conduct family business research publish their work in those outlets.

Our chapter contributes to the field of family business in several ways. First, this study identifies the scholars whose work has made the largest contribution to the recent development of the family business literature based on their number of contributions, adjusted by the quality of the outlets in which they have published and the number of co-authors with whom they have worked. As our analysis will show, research in the field has been dominated by a relatively small number of scholars who appear to be connected in terms of backgrounds, institutional affiliations and interests.

Second, we provide a listing of the academic institutions that have been the most active in contributing to family business research. Our findings suggest that factors such as critical mass, resource availability and administrative support are important in developing an institutional focus on emerging research fields whose importance may not be apparent to those committed to more mature research disciplines. By presenting evidence of the contributions to knowledge that the institutions which have invested in family business research have made, we hope to provide justification for continuing investments and perhaps stimulate the interest of external stakeholders to provide additional investments in the future (Shane, 1997).

Third, we conducted a network analysis to gain a better understanding of the extent to which family firm scholars are collaborating, the relationships among the individual scholars, and how the nomological net of family firm research has developed (Acedo et al., 2006). Although the family business research community is growing, it remains small and closely knit, which suggests both that knowledge diffusion will be rapid in the years to come and that further efforts are needed to expand that community. Because the network analysis illustrates the importance of scholarly networks to the advancement of research, we hope to encourage other scholars and institutions to link with those networks as well as build new networks of their own.

Finally, by analyzing the topic areas that have been covered in family business research and comparing that coverage with prior periods, we are able to identify research trends and areas that deserve further investigation. Since these trends and gaps are related to the individuals, institutions and networks involved in family business research, we hope to stimulate scholars in existing and emerging networks to build upon the momentum gained in particular areas of inquiry as well as to incorporate new topic areas into their repertoire in order to fill the gaps in knowledge identified in this chapter.

METHOD

To conduct the analysis, we reviewed articles published in 30 management journals between 2001 and 2009. We derived our initial list of journals from earlier studies that focused on journal outlets appropriate for entrepreneurship research (MacMillan, 1993; Shane, 1997). In addition to the journals identified in the aforementioned studies, we included journals that were either family firm specific (e.g. *Family Business Review*) or published numerous family firm articles in the time period of our investigation (e.g. *Journal of Business Research*). Finally, we added journals that a survey of scholars suggested were appropriate outlets for publishing family business research (Chrisman et al., 2008b).[2] Additionally, we reviewed *Business Ethics Quarterly*, as its editors have indicated an interest in family business research as evidenced by their announcement of a special issue on family firms.

Publications considered relevant to this study included peer-reviewed articles, invited publications, substantive editorials and research notes. Book reviews were not considered, nor were family-firm-related books or book chapters in edited volumes. Applying a lenient definition of family firms (i.e. firms where there was significant family involvement or support) to the journal articles, the two lead authors of this chapter identified 394 family business articles. To categorize the articles, their titles, key words and abstracts were examined. In cases where a clear determination could not be made from the initially obtained information, the entire article was reviewed. For example, in cases where the terms 'family business' or 'family enterprise' were not used explicitly, but the context indicated that the paper was part of the nomological network of family businesses research, the article was classified as a family firm article. In cases of disagreement, the third author reviewed the article and made a final assessment, which was necessary for 12 articles.

Individual and Institutional Research Productivity

We determined the research productivity of individuals and institutions in the following ways. In the first step, the two lead authors counted the number of articles that each individual authored or co-authored. A list of all authors with two or more family business publications during the time period analyzed is provided in the Appendix. As the publication counts do not take the number of co-authors associated with the article into consideration, we calculated the adjusted number of appearances for each scholar using the following formula: weights of one were assigned for each sole-authored article, weights of one-half were assigned for each article with two co-authors, weights of one-third were assigned for each article with three co-authors and so on. This formula has been used in previous studies of the contributions of authors in entrepreneurship (Shane, 1997), finance (Heck and Cooley, 1988) and international business (Morrison and Inkpen, 1991).

To account for the quality of the publications, the mean SSCI impact factors between 2007 and 2009 were utilized.[3] The journals' average impact factors and number of family business articles published are provided in Table 1.1. Of the 394 family business articles published during the time period analyzed, 46.2 percent were published in *Family Business Review*, the only dedicated family business journal in existence. Another 30.7 percent of the articles were published in three entrepreneurship journals: *Entrepreneurship Theory and Practice, Journal of Business Venturing* and *Journal of Small Business Management*.

Finally, we established institutional productivity scores by aggregating the individual journal publications, which were adjusted by co-authorship and journal quality to the university level. To do so, we recorded the primary institutional affiliation of the authors at the time at which the article was published.[4]

Network Analysis

Co-authorship of research articles can also be analyzed in terms of networks formed by scholars, as well as the central positions certain authors might occupy in such networks (Acedo et al., 2006). To understand a scholar's influence, importance, or value of their social capital, it is necessary to analyze that individual's position in the network. To carry out this analysis, we used the concepts of degree centrality (the number and strength of an author's connections to others), betweenness centrality (the number of an author's connections without regard to strength), and neighborhood size (an author's impact and importance in the network), which connote different facets of an individual's network position (Freeman, 1979). All three indices have been employed in previous research (Acedo et al., 2006) to evaluate an individual's position in scholarly networks in organizational studies. We utilized UCINET 6 (Borgatti et al., 2002) to establish the

*Table 1.1   Journal list: mean Social Science Citation Index (2007–2009) impact factors
and number of family business articles published*

Journal	Mean SSCI impact factor (2007–2009)	Number of family business articles
Academy of Management Journal	5.9	4
Academy of Management Review	6.1	1
Administrative Science Quarterly	3.2	3
Business Ethics Quarterly	1.1	0
California Management Review	1.3	0
Corporate Goverance	1.6	15
Entrepreneurship & Regional Development	1.1	2
Entrepreneurship Theory and Practice	1.7	70
Family Business Review	1.3	182
Harvard Business Review	1.6	2
Human Relations	1.4	2
International Small Business Journal	1.4	13
Journal of Applied Psychology	3.6	0
Journal of Business Ethics	0.9	4
Journal of Business Research	1.0	16
Journal of Business Venturing	2.1	25
Journal of Management	3.2	0
Journal of Management Studies	2.4	7
Journal of Organizational Behavior	2.1	1
Journal of Small Business Management	0.9	26
Leadership Quarterly	2.1	1
Long Range Planning	1.6	1
Management Science	2.2	0
Organization Science	2.9	2
Organization Studies	2.0	4
Organizational Dynamics	0.5	0
Sloan Management Review	1.0	1
Small Business Economics	1.3	8
Strategic Management Journal	3.5	1
Strategic Organization[1]	4.1	3
TOTAL		394

Note: [1] Listed in the SSCI for 2009 only. The 2009 impact factor used instead of the 3-year mean.

various indices and the plotting software to map the networks of scholars. A detailed interpretation of the indices is provided in the results section.

Content Analysis

The two lead authors reviewed the articles and coded them based on six broad topic areas and 21 sub-categories, which were based on previous research (Chrisman et al., 2003). The categories included: (1) goals and objectives with three sub-categories; (2) strategy formulation and content with nine sub-categories; (3) strategy implementation and control with six sub-categories; (4) management with three sub-categories; (5) other topics relevant to strategic management; and (6) non-strategic management topics. To provide a more detailed assessment, the content of each article was coded based on their primary topics.[5] Disagreements in coding were resolved by discussions with the third author. This was necessary for 30 articles.

RESULTS

Ranking of Authors

Table 1.2 presents the ranking of the most productive scholars in family business after adjustments for co-authors and journal quality. The final scores were calculated by multiplying appearances, adjusted by number of co-authors, by the journal quality ratings (for a detailed description of the calculation see Shane, 1997). After adjustments for co-authors and journal quality, the most productive scholar between 2001 and 2009 was

Table 1.2   Most published authors adjusted by number of co-authors and SSCI measure of journal quality

Author	Adjusted publications
Lloyd Steier	14.77
James J. Chrisman	14.07
Jess H. Chua	13.40
Franz W. Kellermanns	10.44
Danny Miller	10.01
Isabelle Le Breton-Miller	9.36
Pramodita Sharma	9.33
Joseph H. Astrachan	8.22
Kimberly A. Eddleston	6.92
W. Gibb Dyer, Jr	6.53
Shaker A. Zahra	6.34
Michael H. Lubatkin	5.89
William S. Schulze	5.54
Michael Carney	5.27
Mattias Nordqvist	5.19
Luis Gómez-Mejía	5.13
Paul Westhead	4.44
Sabine B. Klein	4.23
Frank Hoy	3.97
Richard Dino	3.92
Justin Craig	3.69
Ramona K.Z. Heck	3.49
Carlo Salvato	3.41
Carole Howorth	3.38
Sharon M. Danes	3.37

Steier, followed by Chrisman, Chua, Kellermanns and Miller. Not surprisingly, some of these scholars were frequent collaborators on studies of family firms, as shown in our network analysis reported below. It should also be apparent that to a great extent these scholars (as well as other scholars on the list in Table 1.2) share present or past primary or secondary institutional affiliations and are connected in other ways such as journal editorships and involvement in conferences and professional organizations.

Ranking of Institutions

Ranking of institutions according to their contributions to scientific fields has previously been established in fields such as accounting (Andrews and McKenzie, 1978; Bazley et al., 1975), marketing (Henry and Burch, 1976) and entrepreneurship (Shane, 1997). Similar reviews have been done to assess the impact of institutions on other disciplines. For instance, Eisenberg and Wells (1998) have ranked the scholarly contributions of law schools.

We follow the aforementioned approach by analyzing contributions to family business research by different academic institutions. As outlined above, to address the argument that the scholarly impact might, in fact, depend both on the number of co-authors and the quality of journals in which the research is published, we incorporated both of those adjustments in the rankings that appear in Table 1.3. As this table shows, when adjusting for both co-authors and journal quality, Mississippi State University is the top-ranked institution followed by University of Alberta, Jönköping International Business School, University of Calgary and Kennesaw State University.[6] As with the scholars themselves, institutional relationships appear to exist among the top-rated universities. For example, Mississippi State University, the University of Alberta and the University of Calgary are co-sponsors of the Theories of Family Enterprise Conference.

Co-authorship Network Analysis

The position of an author in the network of scholars was first evaluated using the number of connections an author had to others (degree centrality), including multiple connections between specific co-authors who worked on several articles together. Degree centrality considers the number of scholars an author cooperates with, which determines the options and possibilities of collaboration on projects, as well as potential access to information or data. Degree centrality also reflects an author's autonomy, which means that network members are linked to other scholars using different paths (Acedo et al., 2006). As shown in Table 1.4, Chrisman and Chua have the highest degree centrality scores, followed by Sharma, Danes, Kellermanns and Astrachan.

Another measure of a scholar's position in a network is 'neighborhood size' (Acedo et al., 2006). This measure is designed to reflect the number of scholars with whom a specific author has worked, without regard to the 'strength' of connection (i.e. treating each link as one, even if authors worked together on several projects). Here, we find roughly the same set of authors, albeit in a somewhat different order: Chrisman, Astrachan, Sharma, Zahra, Danes and Smyrnios. This classification method introduces several changes in the positioning of the authors on the list. For instance, Kellermanns falls from the fifth spot in the degree centrality ranking to a significantly lower position

Table 1.3   Most active institutions adjusted by number of co-authors and SSCI measure of journal quality

Institution	Adjusted publications
Mississippi State University	33.63
University of Alberta	32.45
Jönköping International Business School	17.02
University of Calgary	16.88
Kennesaw State University	15.25
Arizona State University	10.92
University of Minnesota	10.76
University of Connecticut	10.62
Concordia University	9.62
HEC Montreal	9.57
Northeastern University	9.04
Nottingham University Business School	8.97
National University of Singapore	8.90
Brigham Young University	8.06
Babson College	8.04
Case Western Reserve University	7.87
Wilfrid Laurier University	7.67
Rensselaer Polytechnic Institute	7.49
Grand Valley State University	6.30
Harvard University	6.17
Nanyang Technological University	5.98
Bocconi University, Italy	5.79
Oregon State University	5.69
Universidad de Jaen	5.67
Baruch College	5.17

according to neighborhood size, which indicates in his case that he has worked with fewer co-authors.

Finally, we assessed 'betweenness centrality', which assesses an individual's impact and importance in the network (Acedo et al., 2006; Cross and Cummings, 2004). This measure illustrates to what extent an author is able to connect others within the network (Cross and Cummings, 2004; Newman, 2005). Members of a network who would otherwise have no connection can potentially link with each other through another individual to whom they are both connected. Acedo et al. (2006) refer to those individuals who perform such a connecting role in a network as 'brokers'. As shown in Table 1.4, Chrisman has the highest betweenness centrality score, followed by Steier. The next four positions are held by Sharma, Astrachan, Heck and Zahra. It is instructive that all of these scholars have contributed to the field as journal editors, associate editors, special issue editors and/or conference organizers. In effect, these roles have allowed them to develop connections with one another and with other scholars. Furthermore, their activities in these roles appear to have led to connections among other scholars, as shown below.

Because the overall network diagram was too complex and dense to present, we prepared a reduced diagram to provide a more transparent picture of the interrelationships

Table 1.4   Top authors according to network measures

Degree centrality		Neighborhood size		Betweenness centrality (normalized)	
James J. Chrisman	32	James J. Chrisman	12	James J. Chrisman	0.243
Jess H. Chua	21	Joseph H. Astrachan	12	Lloyd Steier	0.194
Pramodita Sharma	14	Pramodita Sharma	10	Pramodita Sharma	0.172
Sharon M. Danes	13	Shaker A. Zahra	10	Joseph H. Astrachan	0.152
Franz W. Kellermanns	12	Sharon M. Danes	10	Ramona K.Z. Heck	0.120
Joseph H. Astrachan	12	Kosmas X. Smyrnios	8	Shaker A. Zahra	0.099
Shaker A. Zahra	11	Luis Gómez-Mejía	8	Jess H. Chua	0.068
Lloyd Steier	11	Jess H. Chua	7	Patricia D. Olson	0.063
Danny Miller	9	Ritch Sorenson	7	Franz W. Kellermanns	0.062
Michael H. Lubatkin	9	Alvin N. Puryear	6	Kosmas X. Smyrnios	0.060
Luis Gómez-Mejía	9	Franz W. Kellermanns	6	Sharon M. Danes	0.051
William S. Schulze	8	Lloyd Steier	6	Peter Jaskiewicz	0.033
Justin Craig	8	Peter Jaskiewicz	6	Allison W. Pearson	0.026
Kosmas X. Smyrnios	8	Ramona K.Z. Heck	6	Justin Craig	0.023
Ritch Sorenson	7	A. Frank Adams III	5	Daniel L. McConaughy	0.022
Isabelle Le Breton-Miller	7	David Pistrui	5	Danny Miller	0.021
Kimberly A. Eddleston	7	James Marshall	5	Carlo Salvato	0.016
Paul Westhead	7	Justin Craig	5	Kimberly A. Eddleston	0.016
Peter Jaskiewicz	6	Michael H. Lubatkin	5	Jon C. Carr	0.009
Ramona K.Z. Heck	6	Patricia D. Olson	5	Erick Chang	0.009
Carole Howorth	6	Paul Karofsky	5	Leif Melin	0.008
Alvin N. Puryear	6	Allison W. Pearson	4	Peter S. Davis	0.008
David Pistrui	5	Andrew D. Keyt	4	Sabine B. Klein	0.008
Allison W. Pearson	5	Carlo Salvato	4	Reginald Litz	0.007
Sabine B. Klein	5	Danny Miller	4	Pietro Mazzola	0.006
A. Frank Adams III	5	Eleni T. Stavrou	4	Ritch Sorenson	0.004
James Marshall	5	Erick Chang	4	Michael H. Lubatkin	0.002
Kathryn Stafford	5	George A. Tanewski	4	Eric Gedajlovic	0.002
Carlo Salvato	5	Greg McCann	4	Lars-Goran Sund	0.002
Paul Karofsky	5	Jeremy C. Short	4	Luis Gómez-Mejía	0.002
Ajay Bhalla	5	Kimberly A. Eddleston	4		
Patricia D. Olson	5	M. Scholes	4		
Wen-Hsien Tsai	5	Mary Winter	4		
Pietro Mazzola	5	Matthew W. Rutherford	4		
		Nancy Upton	4		
		Pietro Mazzola	4		
		Sabine B. Klein	4		
		William S. Schulze	4		
Network mean values	1.757				0.003

among the most active scholars in the field (see Figure 1.1). The reduced network focuses on the connections between scholars who have published four or more family business articles. Some of these authors may have worked with more individuals, but if those co-authors published fewer than four family firm articles, they are excluded from the

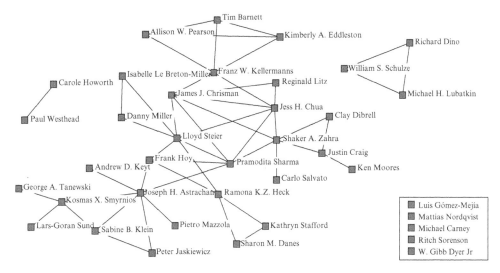

Figure 1.1　Family business research co-authorship network (four or more publications per author)

diagram. The picture also includes scholars who have published four or more family business articles but have no connections to other individuals with similar productivity (four or more articles). These are portrayed on the upper left corner in the figure. Again, these authors may have worked with co-authors who are not portrayed in the diagram.

Our network approach shows distinct clusters of scholars. The primary cluster includes 28 scholars. As this diagram shows, authors like Chrisman, Steier, Sharma and Astrachan have important linking positions in the network and are connected with many authors such as Hoy, Klein, Smyrnios, Zahra, Chua and Kellermanns, who, in turn, have multiple additional connections. As noted above, Chrisman, Steier, Sharma and Astrachan's connections to one another and to other individuals that link the upper and lower portions of the largest network illustrate their high levels of betweenness centrality (see Figure 1.1).

Aside from the dominant network, the diagram indicates that there are two smaller networks that are not directly connected. Of course, these smaller networks (i.e. Howorth and Westhead; Dino, Lubatkin and Schulze) may have connections to the larger network in ways that cannot be depicted in the diagram restricted to scholars with at least four family business publications. Furthermore, the lack of connections in the diagram does not mean that these scholars do not frequently interact at conferences or build upon one another's work. For example, the series of articles on agency and altruism in family firms by Schulze, Lubatkin and colleagues (e.g. Schulze et al., 2001) has been instrumental in shaping the work of scholars in the other networks depicted in Figure 1.1 (e.g. Chrisman et al., 2004).

Content Analysis

Research activities in the six research categories taken from Chrisman et al. (2003) varied widely by category (see Table 1.5). The overall activity with regard to primary topics of

Table 1.5   Topic areas in family business research

Strategic management topic classification		Current study (n = 394)		Chrisman et al., 2003 (n = 190)		Δ % *
		No.	%	No.	%	
Goals and	1.1 Economic goals	7	1.8	5	2.6	−31.7
objectives	1.2 Non-economic goals	4	1.0	5	2.6	−61.0
	1.3 Goal formulation process	2	0.5	1	0.5	1.5
Strategy	2.1 Strategic planning	12	3.1	6	3.2	−4.8
formulation	2.2 Resources and competitive advantage	28	7.1	11	5.8	22.5
and content	2.3 Environment opportunity and threats	6	1.5	4	2.1	−27.5
	2.4 Corporate strategy	4	1.0	3	1.6	−36.6
	2.5 Business strategy	5	1.3	2	1.1	15.4
	2.6 Functional strategy	8	2.0	7	3.7	−45.1
	2.7 International strategy	8	2.0	6	3.2	−36.6
	2.8 Entrepreneurship and innovation	18	4.6	10	5.3	−13.8
	2.9 Stakeholders, ethics, social responsibility	10	2.5	4	2.1	20.9
Strategy	3.1 Corporate governance	65	16.5	18	9.5	73.7
implementation	3.2 Structure	13	3.3	3	1.6	106.2
and control	3.3 Systems, processes, and networks	11	2.8	5	2.6	7.4
	3.4 Behaviors and conflict	22	5.6	12	6.3	−11.4
	3.5 Culture and values	14	3.6	9	4.7	−24.4
	3.6 Evolution and change	19	4.8	3	1.6	201.4
Management	4.1 Leadership and ownership	54	13.7	14	7.4	85.2
	4.2 Professionalization	11	2.8	4	2.1	33.0
	4.3 Succession	47	11.9	42	22.1	−46.0
Other	5 Other topics relevant to strategic mgt	38	9.6	19	10.0	−3.6
Non-strategy	6 Non-strategic mgt topics	36	9.1	43	22.6	−59.6

Note: * Represents the change in the percentage of articles on each topic in comparison with Chrisman et al. (2003) as shown in the following formula:

[Percentage of total articles on topic (current study) – Percentage of total articles on topic (prior study)] ÷ Percentage of total articles on topic (prior study)

the articles is as follows: goals and objectives (3.3 percent); strategy formulation and content (25.1 percent); strategy implementation and control (36.6 percent); management (28.4 percent); other topics relevant to strategic management (9.6 percent); and non-strategic management topics (9.1 percent).

In addition to the six main categories, there were 21 sub-categories (two of the main categories had no sub-categories), which are displayed in the left-hand column of Table 1.5. The work associated with the sub-categories is diffuse, as would be expected among scholars who pursue their own unique research agendas.

Research focal points

The most attention in the period of time covered by our review in terms of primary topic areas was given to family business issues associated with corporate governance, which was classified as part of strategy implementation and control. Specifically, this category included investigations of agency theory stewardship theory and other governance concerns. Indeed, corporate governance was the primary topic of 65 (16.5 percent) of the family firm articles published in the twenty-first century.

Consistent with earlier reviews (Chrisman et al., 2003), matters of leadership and ownership, as well as succession, both constituted significant portions of family business research in the time period investigated. Leadership and ownership issues were primary topics for almost 14 percent of the examined family business articles, while 11.9 percent were focused on succession-related subject matters. Furthermore, in keeping with the emerging importance of the resource-based view in the domain of family business (e.g. Habbershon and Williams, 1999), the resources and competitive advantage sub-category of strategy formulation and content constituted a significant portion of research: 7.1 percent of the articles had this area as a primary research topic.

Family firm behavior and conflict also received substantial attention as primary topic of research (5.6 percent). Although this research area has a long history in the family firm domain (e.g. Levinson, 1971), the continued interest in this topic suggests that processes leading to the occurrence and resolution of conflict in family firms are still not fully understood.

Research gaps

By contrast, it is also instructive to examine the topic areas that have received little research attention. Among the most striking is the lack of attention to the economic and non-economic goals of family firms, as well as the process in which goals are formulated. The lack of attention to non-economic goals is especially surprising for at least two reasons. First, concepts such as altruism (Schulze et al., 2001) and socioemotional wealth (Gómez-Mejía et al., 2007) are considered to be important drivers of family firm behavior and both have a pronounced non-economic element. Second, the recent work of Basco and Rodríguez (2009) suggests that family firm performance will be better when attention is given to the governance of the family, which is likely to pursue non-economic goals, as well as the governance of the firm.

Other areas of note that have received relatively little research attention include family firm strategy (corporate, business, functional and international), stakeholders, ethics and social responsibility, and professionalization. A substantial gap can also be observed in studies examining the opportunities and threats in the family firm's environment.

Research trends

The rightmost column of Table 1.5 provides comparative statistics with regard to trends in research between this study and the period covered by Chrisman et al. (2003).[7] Although their classification of articles published from 1996 to 2003 and our classification of articles published between 2001 and 2009 have overlaps, the comparison is still instructive. Thus, among areas that have received significant attention as primary topic areas it is interesting to note that the relative proportion of studies that have focused on evolution and change in family firms has increased by over 200 percent. Similarly, the content of papers pertaining to structure, relative to the overall number of articles, has more than doubled. Furthermore, the emphasis on corporate governance and leadership and ownership issues has increased substantially, with the portion of total articles focusing on these topics increasing by 73.7 percent and 85.2 percent respectively.

By contrast, while still constituting a significant percentage of published articles, the relative attention to succession issues has declined by nearly half. However, an even more substantial decrease was observed in the percentage of studies focusing on non-strategic management issues, which indicates that specific management topics are generating more interest than before.

Excluding work using the resource-based view, there seems to have been a small absolute increase in the number of family business, corporate, functional and international strategy articles. However, with the exception of business strategy articles, the relative attention to strategy seems to have declined. Conversely, the relative emphasis on professionalization and stakeholders, ethics and social responsibility has increased by 33 percent and 20.9 percent respectively and more than doubled in absolute numbers, but this belies the fact that not much work has been produced on either of these sets of topic areas.

Again, the more troubling statistic is the sharp decline in studies that consider goals, especially of a non-economic variety, all the more since the numbers of studies conducted were so few to begin with. If we do not understand what the goals of family firms are, we will be less able to understand their behavior and how it might be adapted to achieve the desired ends.

DISCUSSION AND CONCLUSIONS

Our study identified the individuals and academic institutions that have contributed the most to family business research in the past nine years as well the topics of interest that these authors investigated. As expected, the publication of family business research is heavily skewed towards journals that specialize in family business or entrepreneurship, particularly *Family Business Review, Entrepreneurship Theory and Practice, Journal of Business Venturing* and *Journal of Small Business Management*.

Although we reported the adjusted contributions of scholars and institutions, the rankings shown in Tables 1.2 and 1.3 are generally consistent with the unadjusted lists shown in Appendix Table 1A.1 and 1A.2.[8] Thus it appears at this point in the field's development that family business research is dominated by a relatively small number of scholars from a small number of schools. These small clusters suggest that continued efforts to expand the field through exposure to family firm research at mainstream conferences such as the Academy of Management and at specialized conferences such as the Family Enterprise Research Conference (FERC), International Family Enterprise Research Academy (IFERA), Eiasm Family Business Workshop and Theories of the Family Firm Conference are needed. While currently scholars seem to work together in relatively stable groups and publish their work in the same set of outlets, as the field grows this will undoubtedly change. In the meantime, however, the relative concentration of scholarship at this stage of the field's development does seem to suggest that progress will be rapid and that the opportunity to build a research paradigm for the field is reasonably high.

These conclusions are supported by our network analysis of the patterns of authorship among the scholars involved in the field. Although the overall network density was low in absolute terms at 0.0018, this density was substantially higher than the network density of 0.0002 reported in Acedo et al. (2006) for management research. The nine-times greater network density trends suggest that the family firm network would allow for more rapid knowledge diffusion throughout the research community and that scholars would be more aware of each other's research than in the overall management literature. In this respect, it is important to note that the roles of journal editors and conference organizers appear especially important owing to the early stage of development and small size of the field.

Our analysis also has implications for both universities and scholars alike. For universities, our research suggests that family firm research centers should be encouraged. As many of the successful universities in our study had established centers and a significant proportion of the most prolific researchers were located at universities providing this infrastructure, centers appear to have a reinforcing effect on family business research. For example, research shows that such centers facilitate collaborations within the university (Boardman and Corley, 2008). This is of particular relevance to junior faculty since the ability to develop a research program and work with other faculty will be a key to their progress toward promotion and tenure. As such, centers serve as important mechanisms to promote a common research agenda as well as in attracting new faculty, since they may enhance the positive effects of departmental research productivity on early career research productivity (Williamson and Cable, 2003).

However, functioning research centers are not easily created. As the number of family firm centers has increased and competition has become more pronounced (Sharma et al., 2007), it is even more important now that universities provide an environment conducive to these centers. Particularly, sufficient funding for these centers is necessary (Stahler and Tash, 1994). Not only will this facilitate the attraction of a core group of faculty necessary to create the above mentioned research benefits, but it will also ensure the legitimacy of the research center. Specifically centers that are aligned with the university's mission and leadership stand to benefit and enhance their survivability over time (Sharma et al., 2007).

We want to mention, however, that while hiring a 'star' to create a center may be beneficial in attracting other faculty and that while championing and mentoring behavior is important to make research groups successful in the long run, this can only be one step of many. Buy-in of colleagues and the recruitment of faculty interested in the subject area to create a critical mass remain essential. In fact, our experience has suggested that a critical mass of researchers is more important than funding and infrastructure in developing a research program in family business. Furthermore, building a critical mass can be accomplished without funding or infrastructure, although having all three components is obviously the most desirable situation.

However, not all universities have centers or a core group of faculty interested in family firm research. Here, family firm research conferences and university support facilitating the attendance at such conferences become important to the individual researcher. As the field is small and still developing, these conferences will often provide developmental activities led by senior scholars (e.g. *Family Business Review* editors started hosting paper development sessions at some of the abovementioned conferences). Moreover, family-firm-specific conferences provide opportunities to forge relationships with researchers holding similar interests. Such opportunities are important because collaboration on research projects tends to increase knowledge, improve quality and facilitate idea generation (Melin, 2000). This effect is nicely highlighted by our network portrayed in Figure 1.1, which shows research links between productive scholars within and across universities.

With regard to the content analysis of the study, our review of research areas using Chrisman et al.'s (2003) strategic management topic classification revealed the most widely investigated issues in the family business domain. Corporate governance, leadership and ownership, succession, resources and competitive advantage, and behavior and conflict were the most common themes. Conversely, our analysis revealed areas that have not been sufficiently examined such as the general aspects of strategy formulation and content, professionalization, and stakeholder, ethics and social responsibility issues. More importantly from our vantage point, family business goals have received scant attention in the literature. Gaining an understanding of how non-economic goals affect behavior and performance seems critical for the development of a theory of the family firm.

Finally, our comparison of the topic areas covered in recent family business research with those covered in an earlier period indicates that the relative attention given to evolution and change, structure, corporate governance, leadership and ownership in family firms has increased while family firm succession and goals have received relatively less attention than in prior periods. Furthermore, while there does appear to be some growth in research on professionalization, stakeholder, ethics and social responsibility topics, that growth has been relatively insignificant as evidenced by the scant attention those topics have been given in the literature. Of course, it should come as no surprise that the most productive scholars and institutions are among the leaders in the emerging emphasis on corporate governance and family involvement and influence as a source of competitive advantages and disadvantages in family firms. Noteworthy also is the overall decline in relative attention given to issues related to family corporate, functional and international strategies.

Limitations

This chapter documents the contributions of scholars to family business research. Our approach to assess individual and institutional contributions to the field of family business was adapted from earlier approached in entrepreneurship (Shane, 1997). However, there are several limitations to this study.

First, scholarly work is not limited to journal publications (Shane, 1997). Activities such as journal editorship, book authorship, organization of conferences, and doctoral student training are alternative and perhaps equally effective ways to support the development of the field (Sharma et al., 2007). Since these activities are not reflected in our chapter, a detailed investigation of how these activities contribute to the development of family firm research is needed.

Second, while this study focused on measuring contributions based on the number of published articles, the extent of co-authorship and the quality of the journals in which the work was published, we did not consider the impact of the authors' individual publications. Future studies using citation counts and co-citations are therefore needed to more fully understand the contributions of authors and their work to the development of the field (for recent examples see Casillas and Acedo, 2007; Chrisman et al., 2010; Podsakoff et al., 2008).

A third limitation of this study is that we focused solely on research published in the twenty-first century. Given the early stage of development of the field of family business, this appeared appropriate. However, the scope of our inquiry does exclude a number of influential studies published before 2001. Future research could correct this limitation by considering longer time periods and providing a more detailed analysis of research trends.

Fourth, the results of our study are further influenced by the journals we selected to analyze. Our study started and expanded upon an initial list of journals identified for entrepreneurship research (MacMillan, 1993; Shane, 1997), which has a management bias. Our focus on management journals should not be construed, however, as an attempt to diminish the important contributions made by scholars in other research fields. Rather, management journals were selected because most family business research is published in such journals. Inclusion of additional journals, however, may have slightly shifted the rank order of some authors or institutions (e.g. the study by Schulze et al., 2002 published in *Managerial and Decision Economics* was not counted, as the journal was not on our journal list). We believe, however, that a representative picture of the state of the field was provided.

Finally, the classification of articles according to topics was driven by Chrisman et al.'s (2003) scheme, which is biased toward strategic management topics. While our approach allowed comparisons with their prior work, our use of strategic management topics is not meant to imply that research grounded in other management or business disciplines has not been conducted in the study of family business. Indeed, we could have selected another way to organize our discussion of topic areas (e.g. Sharma, 2004) and this would have of course provided a somewhat different, although equally valid, perspective on the research being conducted in the field.

Future Research Directions

Aside from studies that correct the limitations of the current study by including a wider range of journals over a longer period of time, analyzing scholarly contributions using citations, and presenting alternative representations of the literature, our content analysis revealed topic areas that appear to warrant more extensive assessments in future research. While it would exceed the scope of our chapter to comment on all of the specific areas that have potential as future research topics, we nevertheless would like to highlight the following.

First, based on our analysis, non-economic goals remain an underresearched topic in the family firm literature. Recent research has made an attempt to systematize the emotional aspects of family firm performance (e.g. Astrachan and Jaskiewicz, 2008; Basco and Rodríguez, 2009; Zellweger and Astrachan, 2008). However, more research on non-economic goals and performance seems necessary to develop a complete theory of the family firm (Klein and Kellermanns, 2008). According to Chrisman et al. (2005), family firms often pursue goals – such as family well-being and providing jobs for family members – that differ from those pursued by non-family organizations. Therefore non-economic goals are likely to be important to many family businesses and indeed some of the differences in behaviors and performance between family and non-family firms appear to be tied to the greater pursuit of non-economic goals in the former versus the latter (e.g. Gómez-Mejía et al., 2007). The process by which these goals are formulated may help explain the success or failure of family firms, particularly since the types and importance of non-economic goals may differ among family members. How family firms deal with the trade-offs between economic and non-economic goals and avoid potential relational conflicts that goal incompatibilities might entail deserves much more research attention than it has received heretofore.

Second, as noted by Chrisman et al. (2005), agency theory and the resource-based view of the firm appear to be the dominant theoretical perspectives in the literature in the new millennium. This is further emphasized by our findings that studies of corporate governance and resources and competitive advantage account for substantial portions of the studies conducted and that the relative attention paid to those topic areas is growing rapidly. Since these perspectives represent two important bases for the distinctiveness and within-group variations in the behavior and performance of family firms, this attention appears warranted and will, we hope, continue. We also believe, however, that this work could be augmented by the application of related theoretical approaches such as stewardship, stakeholder salience and transaction cost economics.

Third, agency theory and the resource-based view should also be applied to other topics of importance to family firms such as professionalization and succession. The former is especially in need of good empirical work because little has been done. Furthermore, succession continues to receive significant attention in the literature but that topic area would also benefit from a more systematic application of theory to its study. Related to this, with the exception of the study by Howorth et al. (2004), selling out as an alternative to intra-family succession has received almost no attention in the literature. Additional work is needed in this area because it is clear that intra-family succession is not always a viable option (DeMassis et al., 2008). Likewise, more work along the lines of Lambrecht and Lievens's (2008) article on how the involvement of family members or certain branches of the family is reduced over time to preserve the advantages of the family, ensure continuity and/or reduce conflicts is also needed.

Finally, although not analyzed in this study, we need to mention that about half the papers were not empirical, and of the empirical papers many were case studies. A diversity of approaches in a young field is welcomed and should continue. However, we also need to re-emphasize the need for greater methodological rigor and multi-level analyses (Chrisman et al., 2007), definitional convergence (Chrisman et al., 2005), and a fuller reporting of sample characteristics (e.g. family firm size) and descriptive statistics (e.g. means, standard deviations and complete correlation matrices). More sophisticated and stringent statistical analysis techniques should also be encouraged where appropriate (e.g. structural equation modeling or hierarchical linear modeling).

Conclusion

This study examined individual and institutional contributions to family business research and the scholarly networks that have emerged in the early years of the twenty-first century. The content of the journal articles was also analyzed and compared to that reported in a previous study (Chrisman et al., 2003). Through our findings and a discussion of their implications we hoped to provide a reference point for doctoral students and faculty who are interested in this field of study by identifying who is doing family business research and where, as well as what questions researchers are trying to answer. Our study also provides useful productivity and journal quality benchmarks for scholars and institutions that are already so engaged. Our network analysis indicates that the field exhibits a relatively high degree of connectivity among scholars and suggests that knowledge generation and diffusion are likely to be purposeful and rapid in the years to come. Finally, our analysis of the coverage of topic areas in the field provides an illustration of research trends and helps to identify the major gaps in our knowledge. Our hope is that this study will serve as an acknowledgment of the research on family business already done and serve to encourage future work that builds on those foundations.

NOTES

1. An earlier version of this chapter reviewing the period of 2001–2007 was published in *Family Business Review* (B.J. Debicki, Matherne, C.F., Kellermanns, F.W. and Chrisman, J.J. (2009), 'Family business research in the new millennium: an overview of the who, the where, the what, and the why', *Family Business Review*, **22**(2), 151–66). The current version has updated the review to include 2008 and 2009; otherwise the content remains essentially unchanged.
2. The journals included were: *Corporate Governance, Human Relations, International Small Business Journal, Journal of Business Ethics, Leadership Quarterly, Long Range Planning* and *Strategic Organization*.
3. *Strategic Organization* is only listed in the 2009 SSCI reports. For that journal we used the single-year impact factor (4.1) instead of the 3-year mean.
4. In determining institutional rankings, the institution where an author worked when the article was published is credited for the publication even if the researcher subsequently changed his or her affiliation. However, we did not consider the secondary affiliations of scholars in the analysis. Although only a few scholars had a secondary affiliation, this decision should be noted because it affects our results, particularly for the highest-rated institutions.
5. It should be noted that an article might have more than one primary topic. Thus the totals do not equal the number of articles examined.
6. The overall counts of article authorship by scholars at different institutions before adjustments are provided in the Appendix. It should be noted that the unadjusted counts are based solely on author affiliations; an institution could receive multiple credits for a single article if it was co-authored by several scholars from that school. However, since we were primarily interested in institutional involvement as measured by the contributions of scholars at that institution, this appeared to be a reasonable method.
7. These statistics were calculated as the proportional growth in the percentage that each topic area constituted of the articles published during the time period. The following formula was utilized: [Percentage of total articles on topic (current study) − Percentage of total articles on topic (prior study)] ÷ Percentage of total articles on topic (prior study).
8. We also used the assessments of journal quality found in Chrisman et al. (2008b) to determine the robustness of our rankings of scholars and institutions. Despite some minor variations in the rankings of top scholars and institutions, the results for both were highly consistent using the alternative approach.

REFERENCES

Acedo, F.J., Barroso, C., Casanueva, C. and Galan, J.L. (2006), 'Co-authorship in management and organizational studies: an empirical and network analysis', *Journal of Management Studies*, **43**(5), 957–83.

Andrews, W.T. and McKenzie, P.B. (1978), 'Leading accounting departments revisited', *Accounting Review*, **53**(1), 135–9.

Astrachan, J. and Jaskiewicz, P. (2008), 'Emotional returns and emotional costs in privately-held family businesses: advancing traditional business valuation', *Family Business Review*, **21**(2), 139–50.

Basco, R. and Rodríguez, M.J.P. (2009), 'Studying the family enterprise holistically', *Entrepreneurship Theory and Practice*, **33**(1), 82–95.

Bazley, J.D., Nikolai, L.A. and De Coster, D.T. (1975), 'A comparison of published accounting research and qualities of accounting faculty and doctoral programs', *Accounting Review*, **50**(3), 605–10.

Boardman, P.C. and Corley, E.A. (2008), 'University research centers and the composition of research collaborations', *Research Policy*, **37**, 900–913.

Borgatti, S.P., Everett, M.G. and Freeman, L.C. (2002), *UCINET for Windows: Software for Social Network Analysis*, Harvard, MA: Analytic Technologies.

Casillas, J. and Acedo, F. (2007), 'Evolution of the intellectual structure of family business literature: a bibliometric study of FBR', *Family Business Review*, **20**(2), 141–62.

Chrisman, J.J., Chua, J.H. and Sharma, P. (2003), 'Current trends and future directions in family business management studies: toward a theory of the family firm', Cole Whiteman Paper Series.

Chrisman, J.J., Chua, J.H. and Litz, R. (2004), 'Comparing the agency cost of family and non-family firms', *Entrepreneurship Theory and Practice*, **28**, 225–54.

Chrisman, J.J., Chua, J.H. and Sharma, P. (2005), 'Trends and directions in the development of a strategic management theory of the family firm', *Entrepreneurship Theory and Practice*, **29**(5), 555–76.

Chrisman, J.J., Sharma, P. and Taggar, S. (2007), 'Family influences on firms: an introduction', *Journal of Business Research*, **60**(10), 1005–11.

Chrisman, J.J., Steier, L.P. and Chua, J.H. (2008a), 'Toward a theoretical basis for understanding the dynamics of strategic performance in family firms', *Entrepreneurship Theory and Practice*, **32**(6), 935–47.

Chrisman, J.J., Chua, J.H., Kellermanns, F.W., Matherne, C.F. and Debicki, B.J. (2008b), 'Management journals as venues for publication of family business research', *Entrepreneurship Theory and Practice*, **32**(5), 927–34.

Chrisman, J.J., Kellermanns, F.W., Chan, K.C. and Liano, K. (2010), 'Intellectual foundations of current research in family business: an identification and review of 25 influential articles', *Family Business Review*, **23**(1), 9–26.

Cromie, S., Stephenson, B. and Montieth, D. (1995), 'The management of family firms: an empirical investigation', *International Small Business Journal*, **13**(4), 11–34.

Cross, R. and Cummings, J.N. (2004), 'Tie and network correlates of individual performance in knowledge-intensive work', *Academy of Management Journal*, **47**(6), 928–37.

Debicki, B.J., Matherne, C.F., Kellermanns, F.W. and Chrisman, J.J. (2009), 'Family business research in the new millennium: an overview of the who, the where, the what, and the why', *Family Business Review*, **22**(2), 151–66.

DeMassis, A., Chua, J.H. and Chrisman, J.J. (2008), 'Factors preventing intra-family succession', *Family Business Review*, **21**(2), 183–99.

Donckels, R. and Frölich, E. (1991), 'Are family businesses really different? European experiences from STRATOS', *Family Business Review*, **4**(2), 149–60.

Eisenberg, T. and Wells, M.T. (1998), 'Ranking and explaining the scholarly impact of law schools', *Journal of Legal Studies*, **27**(2), 373–414.

Freeman, L.C. (1979), 'Centrality in social networks: conceptual clarifications', *Social Networks*, **1**, 215–39.

Gómez-Mejía, L.R., Hynes, K.T., Núñez-Nickel, M. and Moyano-Fuentes, H. (2007), 'Socioemotional wealth and business risk in family-controlled firms: evidence from Spanish olive oil mills', *Administrative Science Quarterly*, **52**, 106–37.

Habbershon, T.G. and Williams, M. (1999), 'A resource-based framework for assessing the strategic advantage of family firms', *Family Business Review*, **12**, 1–25.

Heck, J.L. and Cooley, P.L. (1988), 'Most frequent contributors to the finance literature', *Financial Management*, **17**, 100–108.

Heck, R.K.Z. and Mishra, C.S. (2008), 'Family entrepreneurship', *Journal of Small Business Management*, **46**(3), 313–16.

Henry, W.R. and Burch, E.E. (1976), 'Market shares of space in marketing journals', *Journal of the Academy of Marketing Science*, **4**(2), 473–83.

Howorth, C., Westhead, P. and Wright, M. (2004), 'Buyouts, information asymmetry and the family management dyad', *Journal of Business Venturing*, **19**(4), 509–34.

Katz, J.A. (2003), 'The chronology and intellectual trajectory of American entrepreneurship education: 1876–1999', *Journal of Business Venturing*, **18**(2), 283–300.

Klein, S.B. and Kellermanns, F.W. (2008), 'Understanding the non-economic motivated behavior in family firms: an introduction', *Family Business Review*, **20**(2), 121–5.

Lambrecht, J. and Lievens, J. (2008), 'Pruning the family tree: an unexplored path to family business continuity and family harmony', *Family Business Review*, **21**(4), 295–313.

Levinson, H. (1971), 'Conflicts that plague family businesses', *Harvard Business Review*, **49**, 90–98.

MacMillan, I.C. (1993), 'The emerging forum for entrepreneurship scholars', *Journal of Business Venturing*, **8**, 377–81.

Melin, G. (2000), 'Pragmatism and self-organization: research collaboration on the individual level', *Research Policy*, **29**, 31–40.

Morrison, A.J. and Inkpen, A.C. (1991), 'An analysis of significant contributions to the international business literature', *Journal of International Business Studies*, **22**(1), 143–52.

Newman, M.E.J. (2005), 'A measure of betweenness centrality based on random walks', *Social Networks*, **27**(1), 39–54.

Podsakoff, P.M., MacKenzie, S.B., Podsakoff, N.P. and Bachrach, D.G. (2008), 'Scholarly influence in the field of management: a biliometric analysis of the determinants of university and author impact in the management literature in the past quarter century', *Journal of Management*, **34**(4), 641–720.

Rogoff, E.G. and Heck, R.K.Z. (2003), 'Evolving research in entrepreneurship and family business: recognizing family as the oxygen that feeds the fire of entrepreneurship', *Journal of Business Venturing*, **18**(5), 559–66.

Schulze, W.S., Lubatkin, M.H., Dino, R.N. and Buchholtz, A.K. (2001), 'Agency relationships in family firms: theory and evidence', *Organization Science*, **12**(2), 99–116.

Schulze, W.S., Lubatkin, M.H. and Dino, R.N. (2002), 'Altruism, agency, and the competitiveness of family firms', *Managerial and Decision Economics*, **23**(4, 5), 247–59.

Shane, S.A. (1997), 'Who is publishing the entrepreneurship research?', *Journal of Management*, **23**, 83–95.

Sharma, P. (2004), 'An overview of the field of family business studies: current status and directions for future', *Family Business Review*, **17**(1), 1–36.

Sharma, P., Hoy, F., Astrachan, J.H. and Koiranen, M. (2007), 'The practice-driven evolution of family business education', *Journal of Business Research*, **60**(10), 1012–21.

Stahler, G.J. and Tash, W.R. (1994), 'Centers and institutes in the research university', *Journal of Higher Education*, **65**(5), 540–54.

Westhead, P. and Cowling, M. (1998), 'Family firm research: the need for a methodological rethink', *Entrepreneurship Theory and Practice*, **23**(1), 31–56.

Williamson, I.O. and Cable, D.M. (2003), 'Predicting early career research productivity: the case of management faculty', *Journal of Organizational Behavior*, **24**, 25–44.

Zellweger, T. and Astrachan, J. (2008), 'On the emotional value of owning a firm', *Family Business Review*, **21**(4), 347–63.

APPENDIX

Table 1A.1 Published authors by total number of articles, 2001–2009 (≥2)

Author	Art.	Author	Art.	Author	Art.	Author	Art.
James J. Chrisman	27	Peter Jaskiewicz	4	Claudio A. Romano	4	Louise Cadieux	2
Jess H. Chua	25	Pietro Mazzola	4	Curtis F. Matherne III	4	Manuel Núñez-Nickel	2
Lloyd Steier	18	Reginald Litz	4	Daniel L. McConaughy	4	Marc Cowling	2
Franz W. Kellermanns	16	Richard Dino	4	David Pistrui	4	Margaret A. Fitzgerald	2
Joseph H. Astrachan	13	Tim Barnett	4	Dean A. Shepherd	4	Marianna Makri	2
Pramodita Sharma	13	David G. Sirmon	3	Deborah L. Murphy	3	Matti Koiranen	2
Danny Miller	10	Eleni T. Stavrou	3	Donald Getz	3	Miguel Angel Gallo	2
Isabelle Le Breton-Miller	9	Eric Gedajlovic	3	Donald O. Neubaum	3	Monder Ram	2
Kimberly A. Eddleston	9	Erick Chang	3	Edward G. Rogoff	3	Mustafa R. Yilmaz	2
Shaker A. Zahra	8	Jill Thomas	3	Ercilia Garcia-Elvarez	3	Nancy J. Miller	2
Sharon M. Danes	8	Katiuska Cabrera-Suarez	3	Ernesto J. Poza	3	Nancy M. Levenburg	2
Justin Craig	7	Leif Melin	3	Francesco Chirico	3	Nigel Nicholson	2
Michael H. Lubatkin	7	Lorraine Uhlaner	3	G.T. Lumpkin	3	Panikkos Poutziouris	2
Paul Westhead	7	Manuel Carlos Vallejo	3	Gaia Marchisio	3	Patricia D. Olson	2
Carole Howorth	6	Matthew W. Rutherford	3	Garry D. Smith	3	Paul Karofsky	2
Sabine B. Klein	6	Michael A. Hitt	3	Glenn Muske	3	Peter S. Davis	2
W. Gibb Dyer Jr	6	Michael D. Ensley	3	Greg McCann	3	Phillip H. Phan	2
William S. Schulze	6	Mike Wright	3	Guido Corbetta	3	Pier A. Abetti	2

Name	Count
Carlo Salvato	5
Kathryn Stafford	5
Kosmas X. Smyrnios	5
Mattias Nordqvist	5
Ramona K.Z. Heck	5
Ritch Sorenson	5
Allison W. Pearson	4
Andrew D. Keyt	4
Clay Dibrell	4
Frank Hoy	4
George A. Tanewski	4
Ken Moores	4
Lars-Goran Sund	4
Luis Gómez-Mejía	4
Michael Carney	4
Nancy Upton	3
Per-Olof Bjuggren	3
ThomasZellweger	3
Timothy Habbershon	3
Wim Voordeckers	3
Yan Ling	3
A. Frank Adams III	2
Ajay Bhalla	2
Alex Stewart	2
Anita Van Gils	2
Annika Hall	2
Bart J. Debicki	2
Bernard Yeung	2
Chamu Sundaramurthy	2
Chris Graves	2
Harold Welsch	3
Holly Schrank	3
Jean-Luc Arregle	3
Jean Lee	3
Jennifer E. Cliff	3
Johan Wiklund	3
Johnben Teik-Cheok Loy	2
John James Cater III	2
John Ward	2
Jon C.Carr	2
Jordi López-Sintas	2
Jung-Hua Hung	2
Keith Brigham	2
L.A.A. Vanden Berghe	2
Lai Si Tsui-Auch	2
Randall Morck	2
Robert Millen	2
Samuel Seaman	2
Shaheena Janjuha-Jivraj	2
Sharon L. Oswald	2
Steven Carchon	2
Steven Henderson	2
Thomas M. Hubler	2
Thomas V. Schwarz	2
Timothy Blumentritt	2
Torsten M. Pieper	2
Trond Randøy	2
Wen-Hsien Tsai	2
Yi-Chen Kuo	2

Table 1A.2   Most active institutions according to total appearances,
2001–2009 (≥3)

Institution	App
Mississippi State University	59
University of Alberta	36
University of Calgary	30
Kennesaw State University	25
University of Minnesota	24
Jönköping International Business School	22
Northeastern University	16
Nottingham University Business School	15
Oregon State University	13
Texas Tech University	12
University of Connecticut	12
Wilfrid Laurier University	12
Baruch College	11
Case Western Reserve University	11
Concordia University	11
Arizona State University	10
HEC Montreal	10
Baylor University	9
Bocconi University, Italy	9
Iowa State University	9
Babson College	8
Brigham Young University	8
European Business School	8
Monash University	8
Rensselaer Polytechnic Institute	8
University of Manitoba	8
Bond University	7
Grand Valley State University	7
San Diego State University	7
University of Cyprus	7
Auburn University	6
Erasmus University	6
Hasselt University	6
National University of Singapore	6
Ohio State University	6
Texas A&M University	6
Universidad de Jaen	6
University of Las Palmas de Gran Canaria	6
University of Navarra	6
University of St Thomas	6
Nanyang Technological University	5
National Cheng Kung University	5
Not given	5
RMIT University	5
University of Adelaide	5

Table 1A.2　(continued)

Institution	App
Antwerp, Belgium	4
California State University	4
Harvard University	4
Loyola University Chicago	4
Oklahoma State University	4
Southampton Business School	4
Universita IULM	4
University of St Gallen	4
University of Texas at El Paso	4
Alfred University	3
Cass Business School	3
Edhec Business School	3
George Mason University	3
Indian Institute of Management	3
Indiana University	3
Instituto de Empresa, Spain	3
Lancaster University Management School	3
Lausanne, Switzerland	3
London Business School	3
National Sun Yat-Sen University	3
Purdue University	3
Simon Fraser University	3
Stetson University	3
Universidad Autònoma de Barcelona	3
Universidad Carlos III	3
Universita Cattaneo	3
Université du Québec à Trois-Rivières	3
University of Alicante, Spain	3
University of Burgos, Spain	3
University of Jyväskylä	3
University of New England, Australia	3
University of Oviedo	3
University of Pennsylvania	3
University of Southern Mississippi	3
University of Victoria	3
Vienna University of Economics and Business Administration	3
Wake Forest University	3
Wendell International Centre for Family Enterprise	3

2 Filling the institutional void: the social behavior and performance of family versus non-family technology firms in emerging markets[1]

Danny Miller, Jangwoo Lee, Sooduck Chang and Isabelle Le Breton-Miller

INTRODUCTION

This chapter first argues that family businesses (FBs) are more apt than non-FBs to form close relationships with employees and external stakeholders that enable them to outperform in the most turbulent sectors of emerging markets. It suggests that such ties may be especially useful in such economies because they fill what Khanna and Palepu (1997) have termed an 'institutional void' in capital, product and labor markets. The chapter then develops hypotheses about the relative prevalence and performance implications of these relationships in family versus non-family firms, and tests them on a sample of Korean high-technology firms. It concludes with a discussion of results.

Family firms account for about half of the US gross national product, employ over half of the workforce, and create more than 85 percent of all new jobs (Shanker and Astrachan, 1996). Although many are small, they make up about one-third of Fortune 500 companies (Anderson and Reeb, 2003). Their presence in Asia is greater still, accounting for over 60 percent of the mid-cap public firms in Hong Kong, Singapore and South Korea (LaPorta et al., 1999). Yet family firms remain negatively portrayed and poorly understood (Miller and Le Breton-Miller, 2005).

This becomes clear from an apparent contradiction that has begun to surface only recently. Much of the theory on FB has emphasized its shortcomings – succession problems, nepotism, inadequate capital, family conflicts and a lack of professional management (Chandler, 1990; Gersick et al., 1997; Miller et al., 2007; Schulze et al., 2001). Recent studies, however, have shown that some family firms out-survive their peers, and also reap higher returns and richer market valuations (Anderson and Reeb, 2003; Mackie, 2001; Villalonga and Amit, 2006). Despite the vital role that family firms play in the economy, we know little about their distinctive resources, or the competitive advantages that might cause their outperformance.

We believe that one reason for the confusion surrounding FBs and their performance is that current theories view them as being mired in the past. They have been portrayed as being traditional, overly humane, paternalistic in relationships with their employees (Bertrand and Schoar, 2006; Chandler, 1990; Landes, 1949; Lazonick, 1986), and excessively sentimental, subject to cronyism, and too cooperative in their long-term associations with outside stakeholders (Morck et al., 2005). Thus most scholars have deemed such organizations as 'businesses of yesterday' – too stagnant or poorly performing, especially in dynamic environments (Chandler, 1990; Morck et al., 2005).

On the other hand, some scholars have argued that cohesive clan cultures in which employees are hired for the long run, and are generously and well treated, are central to competitive advantage in the industries of the future (Collins, 1995; Davis and Meyer, 1998; Koch, 2007; Miller, 2003; Miller and Le Breton-Miller, 2005). So are ongoing, partnering relationships with external stakeholders – suppliers, advisors, collaborators – who provide resources needed to enhance the effectiveness of innovative ventures and enable the firm to focus on its core competencies (Adler and Kwon, 2002; Bubolz, 2001; Nahapiet and Ghoshal, 1998). It is perhaps an irony, then, that some of these denigrated FB 'ways of the past' might be useful in the high-technology industries of the future.

This may be especially true in emerging markets, where the close social connections that some family firms are able to build can make for 'institutional voids' – the relative lack of intermediary firms, regulatory systems and contract-enforcing mechanisms. Khanna and Palepu (1997) have argued that these voids may hamper economic exchange in the capital, labor and product markets of emerging economies. Moreover, Khanna and Palepu (1999, 2000) and Khanna and Rivkin (2000) have shown that business groups in emerging economies such as South Korea and India outperform unaffiliated companies because the connections within such groups help to fill the institutional void by providing superior access to human, financial and technological resources. We shall argue that the close connections that family firms may build with stakeholders inside and outside the firm also may help fill that institutional void. Specifically, close ties with employees and with external parties who provide financing, professional advice and training may well provide an institutional context that makes up for gaps in the political, social and economic infrastructures of emerging markets. This is especially true in competitive, high-technology settings, where such ties are needed to access scarce human and capital resources and to buffer firms from uncertainty (Nonaka, 1994, 1995).

Family firms in Korean high-technology industries provide ideal venues for studying the topic. First, FBs in Korea represent over one half of the economy (Nam, 2002). Second, like Brazil, Russia and China, Korea enjoys one of the most dynamic and fast-growing economies in the world, and has become a hotbed of new company creation in high-technology industries such as computers, telecommunications and specialized machinery (Lee and Chang, 1999; Lee et al., 2001). Finally, like the above countries, Korea lacks the institutional development of Europe and America (Choi, 2004; Lee and Lee, 1994). Indeed, Khanna and Palepu (1999) have argued that Korean *chaebols* such as Daewoo and Samsung have formed business groups precisely in order to overcome the institutional voids in Korea's capital, labor and product markets. Korea thus provides a useful arena for investigating whether strong ties within and outside the firm might help to fill the institutional gap (Park, 1982).

This chapter will argue that the aspects of FBs that are said to limit them to stable contexts – namely close relationships with employees and external stakeholders – are the very same characteristics that allow them to perform well in the most turbulent sectors of emerging markets. It draws hypotheses about the nature and performance implications of these relationships within family versus non-family Korean high-technology businesses.

COMMUNITY AND CONNECTION IN EMERGING-MARKET FBs

When firms are run by proprietors from the same family who view their businesses as vehicles for the security, reputation and intergenerational benefits of their kin, then the connections between these owners and their organizations are apt to be unusually close (Arrègle et al., 2007; Miller et al., 2008; Zahra et al., 2004). There is among such leaders an acute awareness that a great deal is at stake in how their organizations perform over the long haul: family fortune, family stature in society, the future careers of the children, and even the potential for the family to carry on a cherished tradition or exalted mission (Miller and Le Breton-Miller, 2005). Thus the relationship with the business, and often its employees and stakeholders, can be more lasting, generous and encompassing (Arrègle et al., 2007). By contrast, owners of non-FBs are said to be more motivated by economic rationales (Jacobs, 1991; Ward, 2004). They are driven by financial performance in the short to medium term, and are less concerned with very long-term, and often quite personal, partnerships (James, 1999). These putative differences may have significant implications for how FB versus non-FB owners act towards their employees and outside stakeholders, and how those partners in turn will benefit the business.

Some writers, for example, have suggested that FB owners build a corporate 'community' to help their firms fulfill their mission and to increase company longevity (Guzzo and Abbott, 1990; Miller and Le Breton-Miller, 2005). Community elements include loyalty to and caring for workers beyond immediate legal or bureaucratic requirements, and providing secure, satisfying jobs. Such elements may create close associations with employees that overcome talent scarcities in the tight labor markets of emerging economies (Khanna and Palepu, 1997).

FBs are also said to manifest an apparent desire to create 'connections': enduring relationships that build social capital with a wide variety of external stakeholders who supply the company with resources (Arrègle et al., 2007; Bubolz, 2001; Miller and Le Breton-Miller, 2005). These parties may include critical suppliers of knowledge, social and financial capital who can strengthen the business, afford it stability, and stretch its capabilities (Adler and Kwon, 2002; Hagel and Singer, 1999; Nahapiet and Ghoshal, 1998). Again, such relationships – alliances and joint ventures as opposed to 'one-shot' transactions – may help to compensate for the institutional voids in capital, product, knowledge and supply markets (Khanna and Palepu, 1997, 1999). The social capital of trust and loyalty engendered by these stable relationships can reduce the risks associated with a venture. Moreover, family owners and managers may have an advantage in forming and benefiting from such relationships, as they have the incentive and power to make and honor their commitments (Bubolz, 2001; Miller and Le Breton-Miller, 2005; Saxton, 1997).

Unfortunately, the prevalence of these community and connection ties in family versus non-family firms, and their performance implications for high-technology firms in emerging markets, have been neither argued nor researched. The following sections of the chapter do that.

HYPOTHESES RELATED TO COMMUNITY

Relative Prevalence of Community in FBs

The literature on organizational commitment to employees (OCE) has identified a construct that very much mirrors Miller and Le Breton-Miller's (2005) concept of community. The OCE construct is based on Eisenberger et al.'s (1986) notion of perceived organizational support, as refined and operationalized by Lee and Miller (1999) and Miller and Lee (2001). In essence, it is the degree to which an organization 'goes the extra mile' to treat its employees well. This involves generous compensation, employee security, profit sharing, and even concern for personal satisfaction and growth on the job. Some scholars have suggested that OCE can evoke employees' loyalty and motivate them to work smarter and harder (Eisenberger et al., 1990; Lee and Miller, 1999; Miller and Lee, 2001; Moorman et al., 1998; O'Reilly and Chatman, 1986). Unfortunately, OCE has not been well studied outside developed economies, or in today's most competitive environments. Yet these community approaches may be quite common among businesses operating in emerging markets to overcome scarcities and imperfections in the labor market (Khanna and Palepu, 2000, 2006; Nam, 2002). They may also be popular with high-technology firms that compete on the basis of knowledge, and must therefore attract and keep top talent (Nonaka, 1994).

As noted, whereas non-family companies tend to have an impersonal or 'professional' orientation, and a financially driven set of motives, FBs frequently act as long-term stewards of the business, its aims and its people – across the generations (Gersick et al., 1997; Ward, 2004). Within FBs, it is not only an owners' fortune and reputation at stake, but also that of their children and other family members currently or prospectively involved in the business. Here the business is not seen simply as a way of making money but as an extension of the family and its reputation in the community, as well as a means for supporting the children or other family members and their career aspirations (Miller et al., 2008). Thus there is often an unusually deep commitment to the business and its employees, and family owners are willing to invest generously in their staff (Allouche and Amann, 1997; Reid and Harris, 2002). It is the employees, after all, who must keep the business spry and creative and secure the health of the company. They therefore should be treated well by FB owners who have the greatest incentive to commit to and invest in them – that is, exhibit a high level of OCE (Guzzo and Abbott, 1990).

There is a growing body of qualitative evidence to support the strong emphasis that many American FBs place on OCE to enhance the internal community. Gersick et al. (1997) mention altruism and trust as primary factors in FBs. Dyer (1986) suggested that such 'paternalism' often encompasses non-family employees, promoting a sense of stability and commitment to the firm. Allouche and Amann (1997) and Miller and Le Breton-Miller (2005) argued that family firms would have exceptionally generous compensation packages; they also were said to train copiously and avoid layoffs. Beehr et al. (1997), Donckels and Fröhlich (1991), and Guzzo and Abbott (1990) have echoed many of these arguments. Thus we hypothesize that:

Hypothesis 1 Community, as measured by organizational commitment to employees (OCE), will be greater among family than among non-family technology firms in emerging-market economies.

Not all agree with this hypothesis. Some authors have argued that FBs are especially given to stinginess because of poor access to capital, nepotism, family conflict and sentimentality, and that they discriminate against non-family managers (see the reviews of this literature by Chandler, 1990; Morck et al., 2005; Schulze et al., 2001; Singell, 1997). Although such conditions may well prevail among some FBs, they have been argued to be far rarer among those operating in more competitive, rapidly changing environments, such as those of our study (Carney, 2005).

Effects of Community (OCE) on Performance

In high-technology environments, where employee initiative and creativity are especially important to competitive vitality, OCE may be especially important to performance. Here, consideration of employees can help to attract and keep the best people (Eisenberger et al., 1990; Lee and Lee, 1994). It takes talented staff to invent and commercialize better products and important innovations, and to leverage these across new market opportunities (Galbraith, 2000). In addition, the low levels of turnover associated with a positive corporate climate help to preserve team knowledge and tacit knowledge within the firm, and keep it away from competitors – again enhancing innovative endeavors and the collaboration that high-technology ventures require (Barney and Hansen, 1994; Nonaka, 1995). This logic has been largely ignored and implicitly disputed in many firms that have engaged in widespread downsizing and in restructuring that penalizes the workforce (Miller and Le Breton-Miller, 2005).

As noted, we expect that devotion to employees will be rewarded by a reciprocal dedication, and the resulting emotional attachment and level of motivation may serve well a high-technology business (O'Reilly and Chatman, 1986; Orpen, 1995). Indeed, a dedicated and motivated workforce may act as a valuable, scarce, inimitable resource that can help firms execute a strong innovation strategy (Barney and Hansen, 1994; Lee and Miller, 1999). It may also enhance initiative and collaboration among decision-makers – qualities vital to successful innovation (Miller and Lee, 2001).

Although Lee and Miller (1999) found only modest main effects of OCE on performance, they did not concentrate on high-technology businesses, in which innovation, knowledge creation and the preservation of organizational knowledge capital are so critical. It is in those contexts that we would anticipate OCE to contribute to performance. Indeed, the employee initiative engendered by OCE is expected to be especially rewarding in uncertain high-technology settings that demand flat organization structures, participative management styles that put a premium on employee initiative, and fast, collaborative decision-making systems to support the necessary innovation (Cooper et al., 1986; Duchesneau and Gartner, 1990; Miller and Lee, 2001).

The emerging-market context, too, may amplify the OCE advantage. According to Khanna and Palepu (1997, 1999, 2006), the institutional void in the labor market that characterizes emerging economies makes critical enduring relationships with talented employees. As the presence of intermediary organizations and contract-enforcing mechanisms is lacking, obtaining a motivated, trustworthy and stable workforce is a challenge. Thus, for example, Korean businesses blend Confucian ethics and paternalism to create a climate of commitment to employees, and to receive dedication from them in return (Lee and Lee, 1994; Shin, 1993). Here, an organization's commitment to its employees, along with the sense of dedication and community it brings, is believed to be at the very heart of organizational success (Lee and Miller, 1999). Thus OCE in the form of a 'paternalistic culture' may be an especially important source of competitive advantage.

Hypothesis 2   Community as measured by OCE will contribute positively to performance in technology firms in emerging-market economies.

Although other studies have examined and partially supported this hypothesis, they have focused neither on high-technology environments nor on emerging markets, in which OCE may be of special significance because of the importance of employee initiative, creativity and commitment in the innovative process. Nor have these studies devoted attention to smaller FBs, in which a close, personal connection between employees and owners may engender the trust and reciprocal generosity that make OCE especially effective.

Family Advantage in Community (OCE)

Although OCE might benefit all kinds of high-technology organizations (Lee and Miller, 1999; Miller and Lee, 2001), it may be especially effective within an FB involving multiple relatives. This is because of the personal relationships that so often develop between family owner-managers and their employees (Ward, 2004). Thus generosity and loyalty are credited to family members, not to an impersonal corporate entity, and so evoke reciprocity. In owner-managed FBs, OCE generosity has a clear and human source. As a result, a more personal and intimate relationship may be formed between the benevolent family and the grateful workers. Employees can see at first hand the sacrifices the family makes. They are face to face with multiple family members, get to understand their values and characters, and, when there is true consideration, begin to feel a sense of loyalty. Family managers also have the power to grant special benefits on a one-off basis: they may, for example, ignore bureaucracy and short-term financial concerns and extend generosity to exceptional employees or under exceptional circumstances. Such acts of 'outside the box' kindness may generate unusual devotion. Habbershon and Williams (1999) have argued that it is exactly such human and social resources that are keys to competitive advantage and performance in family firms, as these are so very difficult to emulate in more economically focused or impersonal corporations.

It is important to acknowledge that there is a negative side to paternalism in FBs. Issues of favoritism, nepotism, discrimination against non-family managers and disregard for merit are among these shortcomings (for reviews of these well-known criticisms see Miller et al., 2003; Morck et al., 2005; Schulze et al., 2001; Singell, 1997). Given such weaknesses, when OCE is poor, FBs may pay dearly – again making OCE a more critical variable to family than to non-FBs.

Hypothesis 3   Community (OCE) will have a stronger impact on performance in family than in non-family technology firms in emerging markets.

HYPOTHESES RELATING TO CONNECTION

Prevalence of Connection in FBs

Two archetypal modes in which a firm may interact with external stakeholders are transactions and relationships (Arrègle et al., 2007; Saxton, 1997; Sirmon and Hitt, 2003; Williamson, 1999). In the former, exchange takes place based on competitive bidding in a market context. The unit of analysis is the transaction, and the incentive is largely economic. Relationships, on the other hand, involve ongoing, social-capital-building associations – ties based on economic factors and non-economic factors alike. They represent closer, more stable, and encompassing ties.

Arrègle et al. (2007) and Miller and Le Breton-Miller (2005) argued that FBs were especially apt to form such relationship connections with outside stakeholders. Owing to their emphasis on the long-term viability of their enterprise, again because of concern that the business supports the futures of other family members, FB owners may be more apt than others to form alliances with external parties who might supply valuable knowledge, information and capital (Miller and Le Breton-Miller, 2005). The stable nature of external relationships of FBs also enables these firms to generate social capital (Nam, 2002). Such alliances help a firm to survive during the tough times that often beset uncertain, high-technology environments (Saxton, 1997). They also aid in overcoming the institutional gaps so common in emerging markets (Khanna and Palepu, 1997, 1999). Moreover, FBs are more apt to invest deeply in these alliances as they can help assure the future of the business for the next generation (Habbershon and Williams, 1999; Sirmon and Hitt, 2003).

If family owners have a greater incentive to work with outside partners, they also have an unusual ability to do so. The personal status of family owner-executives makes many of them ideal relationship partners to outsiders. Partners, quite rightly, tend to see family owner-managers as stable and powerful representatives of their organizations, with the clout to make commitments, and the staying power and incentive to honor them. Family executives tend to be there for decades, have the best long-term interests of their companies and families at heart, and so behave accordingly in relationships with outside parties. These qualities make relationships easier for FBs to form and preserve (Adler and Kwon, 2002; Bubolz, 2001; Miller and Le Breton-Miller, 2005; Sirmon and Hitt, 2003). Thus it can be argued that:

Hypothesis 4   Connections with outside partners will be more extensive among family than among non-family technology firms in emerging markets.

We should note that FBs are not expected to form the types of alliances that would threaten their control of the business (Gómez-Mejía et al., 2007). They are most apt to favor connections that provide valuable resources and develop capabilities. Relationships that would involve giving up financial control or compromise family values would be resisted (Miller and Le Breton-Miller, 2005).

Performance Effects of Connection

Given the uncertainty of high-technology environments, enduring relationships with other institutions and professionals can usefully increase organizational knowledge and reduce financial risk (Adler and Kwon, 2002). Pfeffer and Salancik (1978) and their followers have argued that firms depend for their viability on external resources, and that they need to form relationships with external stakeholders to ensure access to information, talent, capital and clients. In the context of high-technology businesses, the most important resources tend to be access to knowledge capital, technology and patents – much of which can be accessed via robust relationships with external parties (Grant, 1996; Lee et al., 2001; Nahapiet and Ghoshal, 1998; Nonaka, 1994).

Khanna and Palepu (1997, 2000) have argued that in emerging markets where there is an institutional void, business groups characterized by solid, long-term commitments outperform standalone firms. They suggest that this is because the ties between firms within business groups reduce transactions costs and provide reliable access to capital, human, reputational and technological resources that are hard to come by in such economies (Khanna and Palepu, 1997; Khanna and Rivkin, 2000). These ties are to be found not only within business groups but also in connections with suppliers, partners and others who provide managerial and technological support (Miller and Le Breton-Miller, 2005).

For uncertain emerging markets it might also be argued that the more extensive the geographic range of such ties, the more salutary they will be. Just as business groups provide support through business diversification (Khanna and Palepu, 1997, 1999), regional, national and especially international connections with business partners, clients and suppliers may counter the risks inherent in the reliance on very local political and economic conditions. Indeed, the more geographically far-reaching these connections, the greater the ability to reduce local risk.

The most relevant relationships with outsiders for high-technology companies may include joint research ventures with universities, other companies and research organizations, as well as associations with technological and management consultants, government agencies, legal experts, and technical experts (Lee et al., 2001). Joint research ventures spread risk, provide complementary knowledge, and facilitate technology transfer, which is an important source of innovation in Korea. Ties with individual experts provide firms with highly specialized knowledge that they can use to bolster their innovation projects or commercialization efforts. Links with governments and legal experts can help in funding and developing market connections (Lee et al., 2001; Lee and Chang, 1999). Thus:

Hypothesis 5 Relationships and connections with outside partners and stakeholders will contribute positively to performance in technology firms in emerging-market economies.

Family Advantage in Connection

Just as relationships between employees and owners may evoke reciprocal commitment, so may ongoing relationships with outside stakeholders and partners generate social capital (Adler and Kwon, 2002; Nahapiet and Ghoshal, 1998). Family owners are usually there for the long run, with family executive tenures often exceeding 20 years – compared with the four to five years one finds within other enterprises (Miller and Le Breton-Miller, 2005). This stability elevates family executives' accountability to partners, as they are apt to be present to answer for any problems that arise. Thus family executives have an incentive to behave reliably and honorably to stakeholders. An added inducement to such behavior is that family reputations and fortunes are at stake. Finally, family owners have the power to fulfill the commitments they undertake – they usually cannot be derailed by a high-pressure, short-sighted board. All of these things make FBs desirable partners – and therefore more likely to evoke cooperation and reciprocal generosity from their relationships with outsiders. It is hardly surprising, then, that studies have argued that FBs have a real advantage in creating social capital – which serves as a solid basis for all kinds of alliances with outsiders (Arrègle et al., 2007; Bubolz, 2001; Nahapiet and Ghoshal, 1998; Sirmon and Hitt, 2003).

Given the stability of family ownership and management, family executives can hope to harvest the fruits of relationships for years to come. The concept of social capital is central here, as ongoing, long-term relationships engender trust and goodwill, and reduce transaction costs (Adler and Kwon, 2002; Bubolz, 2001; Nahapiet and Ghoshal, 1998). Often, families can even pass on relationships across the generations: this happened in firms such as J.P. Morgan and Bechtel, where in the inner sanctums of exclusive business associations and elite social clubs family scions were introduced by an older generation to the wealthy and powerful (Miller and Le Breton-Miller, 2005). That way, the trust and credibility of one generation could be passed on to the next (Gómez-Mejía et al., 2001). This social capital and its potentially long-term payoff period are other reasons why FBs may benefit especially from relationships with alliance partners.

By contrast, in firms led by those with briefer tenures, there may be pressures for short-term performance that might induce opportunism – a favoring of bargain transactions over relationships. Managers of non-FBs sometimes have less incentive to protect reputation or make relationships pay off for the very long run. So they may not evoke as much trust and business from their partners. Non-family managers also may not have enough power to make the exceptional commitments, often reciprocated, that render relationships especially productive.

Hypothesis 6   Relationships and connections with outside stakeholders and partners will have a more positive impact on the performance of family than on non-family technology firms in emerging markets.

Table 2.1 summarizes our hypotheses and their rationales.

METHOD

Data

As noted, and consistent with Khanna and Palepu (1997, 1999), we chose South Korea as our representative emerging market. We selected as target firms all 271 independent

Table 2.1 Summary of hypotheses and rationales

	Community (OCE)	Connection
Family versus non-family prevalence	*Hypothesis 1* Higher in FBs: Family long-run perspective motivates investment in human capital (Guzzo and Abbott, 1990; Reid and Harris, 2002)	*Hypothesis 4* Higher in FBs: Family concern for later generations motivates relationship formation (Saxton, 1997; Sirmon and Hitt, 2003)
Effect on performance in high-technology, emerging-market companies	*Hypothesis 2* Positive: Community attracts good people, motivates initiative and collaboration; loyalty retains knowledge capital (Lee and Miller, 1999); fills institutional void (Khanna and Palepu, 1997, 1999)	*Hypothesis 5* Positive: Connection provides access to capital, knowledge, technology and information needed for successful innovation (Adler and Kwon, 2002; Nahapiet and Ghoshal, 1998); fills institutional void (Khanna and Palepu, 1997, 1999)
Family versus non-family relationship effects on performance	*Hypothesis 3* Higher in FBs: Family managers form more personal relationships with employees; so they get more credit and more reciprocity from their beneficence (Habbershon and Williams, 1999; Miller and Lee, 2001)	*Hypothesis 6* Higher in FBs: Family stability, power, stake engender more loyal partners, more trusting relationships with outsiders, more time to reap benefits (Bubolz, 2001; Miller and Le Breton-Miller, 2005)

companies on the Daegu High Tech Venture Guide List of 2003 (these were situated in the two high-tech zones in Daegu city). We have already discussed the relevance of Korean high-technology firms to the purpose of this study, and the two zones in Daegu city represent high concentrations of such companies to which the researchers had significant access. We approached the CEOs or highest-ranking officers of these firms, and 170 companies agreed to participate in the study (a response rate of 62.7 percent).

The top managers who agreed to participate were interviewed by telephone after they had examined our pre-mailed questionnaires. We and our trained research assistants helped the executives complete the survey, and explained any items that the executives wished to have clarified (e.g. the meaning and scope of technology transfer). We assured everyone that their responses would be kept completely confidential. Our final sample consisted of 52 computer and related firms (30.6 percent), 40 communications equipment makers (23.5 percent), 36 machine manufacturers (21.2 percent), and 42 electronic components producers (24.7 percent) (Appendix Table 2A.1 describes the sample). In order to guard against common method variance we obtained, for 35 randomly chosen firms, two independent responses from the top-most executives. This enabled us to assess inter-rater reliabilities, which we report below.

Measures

Most of our variables were measured using the previously validated scales of others. Following La Porta et al. (1999) and Miller and Le Breton-Miller (2005), family firms were defined as those in which owner-managers report that their family owns more shares than any other block holder, and in which strategic decision-making is directly influenced by multiple members of the same family.

OCE was assessed using the scales of Lee and Miller (1999) and Miller and Lee (2001). These consisted of four anchored five-point Likert scale items gauging how much the organization is committed to employee well-being, ample and fair pay, satisfaction at work, and sharing profits (Appendix Table 2A.2 presents all measurement items). The Cronbach alpha for our OCE measure in this study was 0.81. The inter-rater reliability, as assessed across our 35 pairs of executives (the top and next-to-top executives from 35 randomly chosen companies), was 0.78.

Connection was assessed by taking the mean values of two components: managerial (i.e. financial and politico-legal) and technology-related relationships. These were considered to be the types of association most relevant to our firms. High-technology companies require financial, legal, technological and knowledge resources to fund, license and undertake product and process innovation – a core capability and primary source of competitive advantage (Lee, 1998; Lee et al., 2001). The managerial connection component was assessed using five five-point Likert scales assessing the degree (from very rarely to very frequently) to which the organization pursued ongoing relationships with

(1) government agencies,
(2) venture capitalists,
(3) banks and insurance companies,
(4) lawyers, and
(5) financial experts and consultants.

The technological connection variable was assessed using three five-point Likert scales gauging the degree (from very rarely to very frequently) to which the firm pursued long-term relationships with universities or research institutes to conduct

(1) joint research and development efforts,
(2) projects involving significant technological transfer, and
(3) education and training efforts.

The Cronbach alphas for these two component variables were 0.75 and 0.87, respectively, and 0.82 for the eight-item composite connection variable. Inter-rater reliabilities were 0.78 and 0.77 respectively, and 0.84 for the eight-item composite connection variable.

A second aspect of connection, its geographic range, was assessed using three scales that gauged the geographic scope of the connections – ranging from local, to subregional, to regional, to national, to international. The Cronbach alpha for the dimension was 0.70, and the inter-rater reliability was 0.76.

Performance was measured using the measures of Gupta and Govindarajan (1984).

Table 2.2 Descriptive statistics: non-family versus family firms

Variable	Total sample (N = 170)		Non-family firms (N = 99)		Family firms (N = 71)		t-value
	Mean	Std dev.	Mean	Std dev.	Mean	Std dev.	
Size	28.34	44.56	23.49	30.46	32.06	53.81	−1.19
Age	7.43	6.76	6.35	3.93	9.11	9.30	−2.34**
Uncertainty (dummy)	0.79	0.41	0.83	0.38	0.73	0.45	1.47
Community (OCE)	3.68	0.63	3.70	0.69	3.65	0.60	0.48
Connections	2.79	0.68	2.70	0.73	2.79	0.60	−1.98**
Geographic reach of connections	2.22	1.07	2.03	1.05	2.45	1.08	−2.56**
Performance	3.74	0.70	3.72	0.56	3.76	0.87	−0.31

Note: **$p < 0.05$ (two-tailed test).

Because our sample includes companies in different industries, and whose goals and performance criteria differ, we were required to use a relative, multidimensional and subjective assessment of performance rather than a narrow financial indicator. Also, over 50 percent of the sample refused to provide financial data, as they were private companies. Six performance factors were rated by the top executives of each firm along five-point scales. Respondents were asked how well the firm had achieved its objectives concerning profitability, growth, efficiency, customer service, turnover and employee morale. The Cronbach alpha for the performance measure was 0.84, and inter-rater reliability was 0.87, suggesting excellent correspondence among independent raters. The limitations of the performance measure are that it only partly and imprecisely reflects financial performance, and is influenced by the priorities of individual companies.

Analyses

A firm was classified as an FB only if a family was the largest shareholder in the company and actively influenced decision-making. To test Hypotheses 1 and 4, Tables 2.2 to 2.4 present means comparison tests, correlation analyses and multiple regression analyses respectively, that compare community (OCE) and connection in family versus non-family firms. Table 2.4 performs this comparison controlling for firm age, size and industry (Jorissen et al., 2005). To test Hypotheses 2 and 5 concerning the impact of community and connection on performance, we conducted the correlation and hierarchical regression analyses of Tables 2.3 and 2.5, respectively. Again, all regressions control for the size and age of the firms, and also for industry, in the latter case by using dummy variables. The follow-up analyses of Table 2.6 were run to assess the generality of Hypotheses 2 and 5 across industries with differing levels of uncertainty. Finally, Hypotheses 3 and 6 on the differential impact of community and connection on performance in family versus non-FBs were tested by the interaction terms of Table 2.5. These terms were a product of a family dummy variable and either community (OCE) or connection. The significance of the interaction terms was established according to the incremental variance they explained over that of the main effects and control variables.

Table 2.3   Pearson correlations and Cronbach alphas

Variables	1	2	3	4	5	6	α
1. Size (log employees)							NA
2. Age	0.52***						NA
3. Community (OCE)	−0.07	−0.10					0.81
4. Connections	0.00	−0.07	0.17**				0.82
5. Geographic reach	0.25***	0.16**	0.10	0.14*			0.70
6. Performance	0.06	−0.01	0.37***	0.20**	0.21***		0.84
7. Family (dummy)	0.10	0.20***	−0.04	0.15**	0.16**	0.03	NA

Note: $*p < 0.10$; $**p < 0.05$; $***p < 0.01$ (two-tailed test); $N = 170$.

Table 2.4   Regression of community and connection on family dummy and controls

Dependent variable	Community	Connection	Geographic reach
Size (log employees)	−0.045	0.143	0.210**
Age	−0.127	−0.188*	0.020
Computers	−0.086	−0.014	−0.085
Telecommunication	−0.069	0.059	0.004
Machinery	0.047	−0.116	−0.031
Family (dummy)	−0.048	0.229***	0.134*
N	170	170	170
Adj. R^2	0.001	0.048	0.047
F	1.029	2.357**	2.327**

Note: $*p < 0.10$; $**p < 0.05$; $***p < 0.01$ (two-tailed test).

Table 2.5   Regression of performance on community and connections

Dependent variable	Performance		
Size (log employees)	0.147**	0.031	0.063
Age	−0.041	−0.066	−0.120
Computers	−0.125*	−0.176*	−0.188*
Telecommunication	−0.069	−0.089	−0.120
Machinery	−0.055	0.008	−0.019
Family (dummy)	0.065	−0.042	0.004
Community (OCE)	0.655***		
Connections		0.243***	
Geographic reach of Connections			0.191**
Family × Community (OCE)	0.154***		
Family × Connections		0.143*	
Family × Geographic reach			0.136*
N	170	170	170
Adj. R^2	0.466	0.047	0.046
F	18.86***	2.00**	1.97**

Note: $*p < 0.10$; $**p < 0.05$; $***p < 0.01$ (two-tailed test).

Table 2.6   Regression of performance on community and connection: effects of industry uncertainty

Dependent variable	Performance		
Size (log employees)	0.160**	0.065	0.058
Age	−0.027	−0.046	−0.085
Uncertainty (dummy)	0.018	−0.080	−0.074
Family (dummy)	0.072	−0.029	−0.003
Community (OCE)	0.694***		
Connections		0.221***	
Geographic reach of connections			0.226***
Ind. uncertainty × Community (OCE)	−0.110*		
Ind. uncertainty × Connections		0.027	
Ind. uncertainty × Geographic reach			−0.006
N	170	170	170
Adj. R^2	0.451	0.020	0.023
F	23.444***	1.549	1.616

Note: $*p < 0.10$; $**p < 0.05$; $***p < 0.01$ (two-tailed test).

RESULTS

Hypotheses 1 and 4: Community and Connection in Family versus Non-family Firms

The mean comparisons of Table 2.1 show that community (OCE) does not differ significantly between family and non-family firms, but connections are stronger in family than in non-FBs. To determine whether these findings were influenced by differences between family and non-FBs in age, size and industry (Jorissen et al., 2005), we performed the multiple regression analyses of Table 2.4, incorporating these potential differences as control variables while regressing community and connections on a family firm dummy variable (1 = family, 0 = non-family). The results confirm those of Table 2.1. Thus Hypothesis 1 is not supported, whereas Hypothesis 4 is well supported. Although our high-tech FBs are more apt to form connections with outside stakeholders than non-family companies, they are not apt to try to build an internal community by treating their employees better than their non-family counterparts – perhaps because those high-technology counterparts are also highly solicitous of their staff.

Hypotheses 2 and 5: The Impact of Community and Connection on Performance

The correlation matrix of Table 2.3 shows that community and connections both had positive correlations with performance, lending support to Hypotheses 2 and 5, respectively. More importantly, these relationships are confirmed by the multiple regression analyses of Table 2.5. Among our high-technology companies, community and connection each contribute to performance, broadly defined. The geographic breadth of the connections has the same effect. This finding is consistent with arguments that, in emerging-market high-technology industries, connections and relationships help access the resources needed for innovation and good performance (Lee, 1998; Lee and Chang, 1999; Lee et al., 2001).

In order to establish the robustness of these relationships across different levels of industry uncertainty we defined a new dummy variable. The variable took on a value of 1 for the most uncertain industries of computers and telecommunications, and a value of 0 for the least uncertain industry of machinery. This split was based on Lee's (1998) analysis of uncertainty among emerging-market high-technology firms. Firm performance was regressed against interaction terms that were the product of the uncertainty dummy and community, connection, and the geographic scope of connections, respectively. As shown in Table 2.6, these interaction results were not related to performance, nor was the uncertainty dummy variable. Thus support for Hypotheses 2 and 5 does not vary materially among the industries of our sample. We hesitate, however, to generalize this result to stable industries, as all of our firms were in the high-technology sector, and all faced a considerable degree of uncertainty.

Hypotheses 3 and 6: The Impact of Community and Connection on Performance in Family versus Non-FBs

The regression analyses of Table 2.5 predict performance. They confirm significant interactions between the dummy variable for family firm status and community, connections, and the geographic reach of those connections, respectively. The interaction analyses assess whether FBs were better able to benefit from higher levels of community or connection than non-FBs. The results show strong support for the community–family interaction, but more modest support for the two connection–family interactions. Moreover, the F values for the changes in R^2 derived from adding the interaction terms to the full models are 7.068, 3.338 and 2.934. These coefficients are significant at beyond the 0.01, 0.10 and 0.10 levels, respectively, under a two-tailed test. The results clearly support Hypothesis 3, and provide tentative support for Hypothesis 6. It thus appears that community, connection, and geographically extended connections are more useful in family than in non-FBs.

DISCUSSION, IMPLICATIONS AND LIMITATIONS

The results lend significant support to most of our hypotheses. Investment in community and connection are indeed germane to success in our emerging-market high-technology environments, and both characteristics appear to be more helpful to family than to non-FBs. Connections are also more common in family than in non-FBs. The one major surprise was that OCE was not more common in FBs than elsewhere, and that may be one major reason why performance does not vary significantly between family and non-family enterprises. Perhaps in high-technology environments, talented employees are so clearly a critical resource that all firms try to treat them well – family and non-family alike. Another reason why FBs in our sample did not outperform may be because of the unique disadvantages that beset some FBs – family conflicts, nepotism and tradition may all be especially damaging in competitive and turbulent settings. These disadvantages may offset any advantage from community or connection. Finally, our non-FBs are also high-technology companies: thus they are dynamic entities that are able to avoid the bureaucratic snares of more staid non-FBs.

This research has a number of implications. First, it suggests that OCE – a human dimension – appears to be important to the performance of both family and non-family firms in a high-tech industry. Specifically, organizations that attempt to form tighter emotional bonds with their employees by being more solicitous of their well-being may be rewarded for doing so in a fast-changing industry – but most especially if they are family firms. The resulting motivation, dedication and cooperation among employees may represent a valuable competitive resource for high-technology family firms. The formation of connections with external providers of expertise, and social and financial capital, also appears to be an important source of advantage, and one more often used in FBs. Moreover, consistent with the arguments of Khanna and Palepu (1997, 1999, 2006), the formation of community and connection ties may help to overcome the institutional void in emerging-market economies.

Limitations of the Research and Future Directions

It is important to note some of the limitations of this research. First, the findings may apply mostly to smaller companies in uncertain, high-technology environments. We cannot say whether our results would hold in more stable settings, or in very large companies. Also, whereas these Korean findings may have application to other emerging economies that are institutionally challenged, it remains to be discovered whether they are as relevant to the developed world. We hope that this study will motivate scholars to do more research on family enterprise. Future research might examine in more detail how family firms differ from non-family firms in other aspects of behavior, strategy and performance. It might be useful also to replicate this research in other countries and industries to establish its generality and limitations.

CONCLUSION

It is perhaps paradoxical that the very aspects of FBs that have caused them to be subject to criticism in the management and governance literature are the same characteristics that allow these and other businesses to perform well in dynamic, high-technology environments of an emerging market. The approach for which FBs have been criticized – affective, collective, community relationships with their employees, and intensive, ongoing connections with outside stakeholders – appears to contribute not to failure but to success. Moreover, this advantage occurs not in staid, placid environments but in the most turbulent and competitive ones. These relational, as opposed to transactional, orientations contribute to performance in FBs, and also in non-family companies, albeit less powerfully. It may well be that the close ties formed by family firms give them an edge in surmounting the institutional void so characteristic of emerging markets (Khanna and Palepu, 1997, 1999). Emerging-market executives and government policy-makers might do well to take note of the importance of FBs in high-technology settings, and pay attention to the levers that can be used to make these businesses more competitive.

ACKNOWLEDGMENTS

The authors are indebted to Professors Lorraine Eden, Shaker Zahra, Kenneth C. Craddock, the Social Sciences and Humanities Research Council of Canada, and two anonymous reviewers for their most helpful comments.

NOTE

1. This chapter originally appeared in the *Journal of International Business Studies* (2009), **40**(5), 802–17.

REFERENCES

Adler, P.S. and Kwon, S.W. (2002), 'Social capital: prospects for a new concept', *Academy of Management Review*, **27**(1): 17–40.
Allouche, J. and Amann, B. (1997), 'Le retour du capitalisme familial', *L'expansion: Management Review*, **85**(1): 92–9.
Anderson, R.C. and Reeb, D. (2003), 'Founding-family ownership and firm performance: evidence from the S&P 500', *Journal of Finance*, **58**(3): 1301–28.
Arrègle, J.L., Hitt, M., Sirmon, D. and Very, P. (2007), 'The development of organizational social capital: attributes of family firms', *Journal of Management Studies*, **44**(1): 73–95.
Barney, J.B. and Hansen, M.H. (1994), 'Trustworthiness as a source of competitive advantage', *Strategic Management Journal*, **15**(Winter Special Issue): 175–90.
Beehr, T., Drexler, J. and Faulkner, S. (1997), 'Working in small family businesses: empirical comparisons to non-family businesses', *Journal of Organizational Behavior*, **18**(3): 297–312.
Bertrand, M. and Schoar, A. (2006), 'The role of family in family firms', *Journal of Economic Perspectives*, **20**(2): 73–96.
Bubolz, M. (2001), 'Family as source, user and builder of social capital', *Journal of Socio-Economics*, **30**(1): 129–31.
Carney, M. (2005), 'Corporate governance and competitive advantage in family-controlled firms', *Entrepreneurship Theory and Practice*, **29**(2): 249–65.
Chandler, A.D. (1990), *Scale and Scope*, Cambridge, MA: Harvard University Press.
Choi, J. (2004), 'Transformation of Korean HRM based on confucian values', *Seoul Journal of Business*, **10**(1): 1–26.
Collins, J. (1995), *Built to last*, New York: Harper Business.
Cooper, A.C., Willard, G.E. and Woo, G. (1986), 'Strategies of high performing new and small firms: a reexamination of the niche concept', *Journal of Business Venturing*, **1**(2): 247–60.
Davis, S. and Meyer, C. (1998), *Blur*, New York: Warner Books.
Donckels, R. and Fröhlich, E. (1991), 'Are family businesses really different? European experiences from STRATOS', *Family Business Review*, **4**(2): 149–60.
Duchesneau, D.A. and Gartner, W. (1990), 'A profile of new venture success and failure in an emerging industry', *Journal of Business Venturing*, **5**(3): 297–312.
Dyer Jr, W.G. (1986), *Cultural Change in Family Firms: Anticipating and Managing Business and Family Transitions*, San Francisco: Jossey-Bass.
Eisenberger, R., Fasolo, P. and Davis-Lamastro, V. (1990), 'Perceived organizational support and employee diligence, commitment and innovation', *Journal of Applied Psychology*, **75**(1): 51–9.
Eisenberger, R., Huntington, R., Hutchison, R. and Sowa, D. (1986), 'Perceived organizational support', *Journal of Applied Psychology*, **71**(4): 500–507.
Galbraith, J. (2000), *Designing the Global Corporation*, San Francisco: Jossey Bass.
Gersick, K.E., Davis, J., Hampton, M. and Lansberg, I. (1997), *Generation to Generation: Life Cycles of the Family Business*, Boston, MA: Harvard Business School Press.
Gómez-Mejía, L., Haynes, K., Núñez-Nickel, M., Jacobson, K. and Moyano-Fuentes, J. (2007), 'Family owned firms: risk loving or risk averse', *Administrative Science Quarterly*, **52**(1): 106–37.
Gómez-Mejía, L., Núñez-Nickel, M. and Gutierrez, I. (2001), 'The role of family ties in agency contracts', *Academy of Management Journal*, **44**(1): 81–95.

Grant, R. (1996), 'Toward a knowledge-based theory of the firm', *Strategic Management Journal*, **17**(Special Issue): 109–22.

Gupta, A.K. and Govindarajan, V. (1984), 'Business unit strategy, managerial characteristics, and business unit effectiveness at strategy implementation', *Academy of Management Journal*, **27**(1): 25–41.

Guzzo, R. and Abbott, S. (1990), 'Family firms as utopian organizations', *Family Business Review*, **3**(1): 23–33.

Habbershon, T.G. and Williams, M.L. (1999), 'A resource-based framework for assessing the strategic advantages of family firms', *Family Business Review*, **12**(1): 1–26.

Hagel, J. and Singer, J. (1999), *Net Worth*, Boston, MA: Harvard Business School Press.

Jacobs, M.T. (1991), *Short-term America*, Boston, MA: Harvard Business School Press.

James, H.S. (1999), 'Owner as manager, extended horizons and the family firm', *International Journal of the Economics of Business*, **6**(1): 41–55.

Jorissen, A., Leveren, E., Martens, R. and Reheul, A.M. (2005), 'Real versus sample-based differences in comparative family business research', *Family Business Review*, **18**(3): 229–46.

Khanna, T. and Palepu, K. (1997), 'Why focused strategies may be wrong for emerging markets', *Harvard Business Review*, **75**(4): 41–51.

Khanna, T. and Palepu, K. (1999), 'The right way to structure conglomerates in emerging markets', *Harvard Business Review*, **77**(4): 125–34.

Khanna, T. and Palepu, K. (2000), 'Is group affiliation profitable in emerging markets? An analysis of diversified Indian business groups', *Journal of Finance*, **55**(4): 867–91.

Khanna, T. and Palepu, K. (2006), 'Emerging giants?', *Harvard Business Review*, **84**(4): 60–69.

Khanna, T. and Rivkin, J.W. (2000), 'Estimating the performance effects of business groups in emerging markets', *Strategic Management Journal*, **22**(1): 45–74.

Koch, C. (2007), *The Science of Success*, New York: Wiley.

Landes, D. (1949), 'French entrepreneurship and industrial growth in the nineteenth century', *Journal of Economic History*, **9**(1): 45–61.

LaPorta, R., Lopes-de-Silanes, F. and Shleifer, A. (1999), 'Corporate ownership around the world', *Journal of Finance*, **54**(3): 471–517.

Lazonick, W. (1986), 'The cotton industry', in B. Erbaum and W. Lazonick (eds), *The Decline of the British Economy*, Oxford: Oxford University Press, pp. 18–50.

Lee, J. (1998), 'Characteristics of successful high-technology venture companies', *The Korean Venture Management Review*, **1**(1): 101–28.

Lee, J. and Chang, S. (1999), 'Characteristics of successful high-tech ventures', *The Korean Small Business Review*, **21**(1): 105–33.

Lee, J. and Lee, M. (1994), *Korean Management in Global Competition*, Seoul: Gim-Young Sa.

Lee, J. and Miller, D. (1999), 'People matter: commitment to employees, strategy and performance in Korean firms', *Strategic Management Journal*, **20**(4): 579–93.

Lee, C., Lee, K. and Pennings, J. (2001), 'Internal capabilities, external networks, and performance: a study of technology-based ventures', *Strategic Management Journal*, **22**(4): 615–40.

Mackie, R. (2001), 'Family ownership and business survival: Kirkcaldy, 1870–1970', *Business History*, **43**(1): 1–32.

Miller, D. (2003), 'An asymmetry-based view of advantage: towards an attainable sustainability', *Strategic Management Journal*, **24**(10): 961–76.

Miller, D. and Lee, J. (2001), 'The people make the process: commitment to employees, decision making, and performance', *Journal of Management*, **27**(2): 163–89.

Miller, D. and Le Breton-Miller, I. (2005), *Managing for the Long Run: Lessons in Competitive Advantage from Great Family Business*, Boston, MA: Harvard Business School Press.

Miller, D., Steier, L. and Le Breton-Miller, I. (2003), 'Lost in time: intergenerational succession, change, and failure in family business', *Journal of Business Venturing*, **18**(3): 513–31.

Miller, D., Le Breton-Miller, I., Lester, R. and Cannella, A. (2007), 'Are family firms really superior performers?', *Journal of Corporate Finance*, **13**(5): 829–58.

Miller, D., Le Breton-Miller, I. and Scholnick, B. (2008), 'Stewardship versus stagnation: an empirical comparison of small family versus non-family businesses', *Journal of Management Studies*, **41**(1): 50–78.

Moorman, S., Blakely, G. and Niehoff, B. (1998), 'Does perceived organizational support mediate the relationship between procedural justice and organizational citizenship behavior?', *Academy of Management Journal*, **41**(2): 351–7.

Morck, R., Wolfenzon, D. and Yeung, B. (2005), 'Corporate governance, economic entrenchment, and growth', *Journal of Economic Literature*, **53**(3): 655–720.

Nahapiet, J. and Ghoshal, S. (1998), 'Social capital, intellectual capital and the organizational advantage', *Academy of Management Review*, **23**(2): 242–66.

Nam, Y.H. (2002), 'A study on the characteristics of Korean family businesses', *The Korean Small Business Review*, **24**(4): 201–24.

Nonaka, I. (1994), 'A dynamic theory of organizational knowledge creation', *Organization Science*, **5**(1): 14–37.

Nonaka, I. (1995), *The Knowledge-creating Company*, New York: Oxford University Press.

O'Reilly, C. and Chatman, J. (1986), 'Organizational commitment and psychological attachment: the effects of compliance, identification, and internalization on prosocial behavior', *Journal of Applied Psychology*, **71**(3): 492–9.

Orpen, C. (1995), 'The effects of exchange ideology on the relationship between perceived organizational support and job performance', *Journal of Social Psychology*, **78**(3): 569–83.

Park, G.D. (1982), 'A study on the family business of Korea', *Korean Management Review*, **11**(1): 39–60.

Pfeffer, J. and Salancik, G. (1978), *The External Control of Organizations*, New York: Harper & Row.

Reid, R. and Harris, R. (2002), 'The determinants of training in SMEs in Northern Ireland', *Education & Training*, **44**(1): 8–9.

Saxton, T. (1997), 'The effects of partner and relationship characteristics on alliance outcomes', *Academy of Management Journal*, **40**(2): 443–61.

Schulze, W.S., Lubatkin, M., Dino, R. and Buchholtz, A. (2001), 'Agency relationships in family firms: theory and evidence', *Organization Science*, **12**(1): 99–116.

Shanker, M.C. and Astrachan, J.H. (1996), 'Myths and realities: family business' contribution to the US economy: a framework for assessing family business statistics', *Family Business Review*, **9**(2): 107–23.

Shin, Y.K. (1993), *Korean Management: Present and Future*, Seoul: Bak-Young Sa.

Singell, L. (1997), 'Nepotism, discrimination, and the persistence of utility-maximizing, owner-operated firms', *Southern Economics Journal*, **63**(4): 894–920.

Sirmon, D. and Hitt, M. (2003), 'Managing resources: linking unique resources, management, and wealth creation in family firms', *Entrepreneurship Theory and Practice*, **27**(3): 339–58.

Villalonga, B. and Amit, R. (2006), 'How do family ownership, control and management affect firm value?', *Journal of Financial Economics*, **80**(3): 385–415.

Ward, J. (2004), *Perpetuating the Family Business*, Marietta, GA: Family Enterprise Publishers.

Williamson, O.E. (1999), 'Strategy research: governance and competence perspectives', *Strategic Management Journal*, **20**(7): 1087–108.

Zahra, S.A., Hayton, J. and Salvato, C. (2004), 'Entrepreneurship in family versus non-family firms: a resource-based analysis of the effect of organizational culture', *Entrepreneurship Theory and Practice*, **28**(4): 363–81.

APPENDIX

Table 2A.1   Characteristics of responding firms

Item	Category	Total		Non-family firms		Family firms	
		Number	%	Number	%	Number	%
Age of firm	1–2 years	13	7.7	9	5.3	4	2.4
	3–4 years	71	42.0	41	24.3	30	17.8
	5–6 years	46	27.2	29	17.2	17	10.1
	7 years and more	39	23.1	20	11.8	19	11.2
Number of	Fewer than 11	78	47.0	45	27.1	33	19.9
employees	11–20	34	20.5	20	12.0	14	8.4
	21–40	25	15.1	18	10.8	7	4.2
	41 or more	29	17.5	15	9.0	14	8.4
Industry	Computers	52	30.6	33	19.4	19	11.2
	Telecommunications	40	23.5	25	14.7	15	8.8
	Machinery	36	21.2	17	10.0	19	11.2
	Electronics	42	24.7	24	14.1	18	10.6
N valid		170	100.0	99	58.2	71	41.8

Table 2A.2   Scale items in questionnaire

Community (OCE)					
Rate the extent to which you agree with the following:	Do not agree			Strongly agree	
The organization really cares deeply about its employees' well-being 3.56 (0.72)[a]	1	2	3	4	5
The firm is profoundly concerned about paying everyone what they deserve 3.87 (0.68)	1	2	3	4	5
The firm cares deeply about employees' overall satisfaction at work 3.53 (0.77)	1	2	3	4	5
If the firm earned more profit, it would share gains by increasing salaries 3.79 (0.69)	1	2	3	4	5

Managerial connection					
Rate how regularly your firm interacts with the following entities to build strong managerial relationships:	Very rarely			Very frequently	
Government agencies 2.69 (1.04)	1	2	3	4	5
Financial experts and consultants 2.67 (0.93)	1	2	3	4	5
Lawyers 2.08 (0.94)	1	2	3	4	5
Venture capitalists 2.04 (0.89)	1	2	3	4	5
Bankers and insurers 2.54 (0.94)	1	2	3	4	5

Technological connection					
Rate the regularity with which you cooperate with universities and research institutes in the following ongoing relationships:	Very rarely			Very frequently	
Joint research and development efforts 2.99 (1.34)	1	2	3	4	5
Technical and technology transfer and information exchange 3.06 (1.22)	1	2	3	4	5
Education and training 2.79 (1.13)	1	2	3	4	5

Geographic reach: From local to regional to national to international

Please check the location of your most important connections

Business partners 2.36 (1.44)	(1) Within the existing high-tech zone and Daegu City
	(2) Kyungpook Province
	(3) Yongnam Province and Seoul area
	(4) Other national area
	(5) Foreign area

Table 2A.2   (continued)

Geographic reach: From local to regional to national to international	
Please check the location of your most important connections	
Customers 2.31 (1.43)	(1) Within the existing high-tech zone and Daegu City (2) Kyungpook Province (3) Yongnam Province and Seoul area (4) Other national area (5) Foreign area
Suppliers 1.98 (1.41)	(1) Within the existing high-tech zone and Daegu City (2) Kyungpook Province (3) Yongnam Province and Seoul area (4) Other national area (5) Foreign area

Performance						
How well has the firm achieved the following objectives *vis-à-vis* its principal competitors over the last 3 years?	Very poorly				Very well	
Profitability achievement 3.50 (0.84)	1	2	3	4	5	
Growth in business and orders 3.92 (0.78)	1	2	3	4	5	
Improvement in consumer loyalty 4.08 (0.72)	1	2	3	4	5	
Improvement in internal efficiency 3.77 (0.72)	1	2	3	4	5	
Employee turnover 3.68 (0.89)	1	2	3	4	5	
Employees' morale 3.62 (0.75)	1	2	3	4	5	

Family firm		
We classified the subjects as a family firm when they answered 'yes' to both items (1 and 2)		
1. The family owns more shares than any other blockholder:	Yes ( )	No ( )
2. Strategic decision-making is significantly influenced by family members:	Yes ( )	No ( )

Note: [a]Numbers are item means and standard deviations, respectively.

PART II

CORPORATE GOVERNANCE

3 The effects of family involvement and corporate governance practices on earnings quality of listed companies

Riccardo Tiscini and Francesca di Donato

INTRODUCTION

A growing stream of literature is studying the relation between performance and family control, but a few studies exist on comparing the quality of the financial reporting of family and non-family firms. These studies, however, do not reach unanimous findings.

It is a diffused common thinking that listed family firms are less transparent than publicly held companies, because of the excessive power of controlling shareholders and ineffective monitoring systems counterbalancing it. This is consistent with the view of family firms being a less efficient ownership structure because family behaviors can be more easily aimed at extracting private benefits at the expense of minority shareholders (Fama and Jensen, 1983a; Morck et al., 1988; Shleifer and Vishny, 1997; Bebchuk et al., 1999). Empirical evidence has been provided about that (Francis et al., 2005; Fan and Wong, 2002). This is mainly due to the 'entrenchment effect' in concentrated ownership structures.

On the other hand, companies, when owned and managed by a family, benefit from the natural alignment between management and shareholders' interests, which have the common purpose of creating value in the long run. And even if a non-family member is acting as CEO, management monitoring by family controlling shareholders is much more effective than in a large public companies (Demsetz and Lehn, 1985; Shleifer and Vishny, 1986). Families thus have higher incentives to report good earnings quality (EQ) because they need to preserve the family's name and reputation, to pass on their business to future generations, and they look for long-term profitability. This is the 'alignment effect' (Wang, 2005). This chapter discusses if and how family ownership and corporate governance practices affect earnings quality. Our theoretical explanation is that the effects depend on the attitude of the family towards corporate governance mechanisms, because this shows the family's incentives for good reputation and accountability in the long run. In particular, we explore the effects of family involvement in the board and of top management characteristics on the quality of reported earnings.

The empirical analysis is carried out using an Italian data set. Italy represents an ideal setting to address issues related to earnings management among listed family firms, because family capitalism is persistent even after important reforms in corporate and financial regulation.

The chapter is structured as follows. First, the literature on earnings quality and ownership structure is reviewed. Then the research hypothesis is developed, based on existing theoretical frameworks and new theoretical insights. A following section explains the methodology of the analysis. The presentation of empirical results, their discussion and future research directions conclude the chapter.

LITERATURE REVIEW

Earnings Quality and its Different Measures

In recent years the quality of financial reporting has become an increasingly interesting topic for the financial world. The academic literature does not present a unique definition of earnings quality. In accounting literature, various measures of earnings quality (EQ) have been proposed (Balsam et al., 2003; Bernstein, 1993; Dechow, 1994; Francis, 2003; Schipper and Vincent, 2003). The accounting literature embraces several definitions of EQ. Some of them focus on the persistence of earnings, meaning that current earnings can be considered a good indicator of future earnings (Hodge, 2003; Chan et al., 2004). Some others consider the relation between accruals and cash flows (Mikhail et al., 2003).

But what are 'high-quality' earnings? Revsine et al. (1999) consider that earnings are of higher quality when they are sustainable. According to Kirschenheiter and Melumad (2004), high-quality earnings are earnings that are more informative and closer to the long-run value of the firm. In continental European countries the practice of conservative accounting is claimed as producing higher-quality earnings, consistently with the definition of White et al. (2003), who define EQ as the degree of conservatism in a firm's reported earnings. But this is not the case in Anglo-Saxon countries, nor in the new International Financial Reporting Standards. A possible explanation for the multiplicity of those different interpretations could be that different readers use the information to make different decisions (Kirschenheiter and Melumad, 2004).

The main difficulty in treating EQ is the lack of a generally accepted measurement approach. Schipper and Vincent (2003) discussed the several classes of EQ constructs that have been used in literature. They classified them according to four categories (without being exhaustive). In line with Bernstein (1993), the persistency or sustainability of earnings and earnings management are important features of EQ.

To summarize, EQ is a broad concept encompassing many determinants. In this chapter, EQ is measured using an abnormal accruals-based approach.

Ownership Structure and Earnings Quality

Ownership structures affect the supply of financial reporting (Fan and Wong, 2002). When ownership is diffuse, agency problems stem from the conflicts of interest between managers and shareholders (Berle and Means, 1932; Jensen and Meckling, 1976; Roe, 1994). As ownership concentration increases and a single or a few owners get control of the firm, the nature of agency problems shifts from manager–shareholder conflicts to conflicts between the controlling owner and minority shareholders (Shleifer and Vishny, 1997).

In terms of both managerial ownership and concentrated ownership, prior research argues that high levels of ownership may increase or reduce earnings informativeness, depending on whether incentive effects or information effects dominate (Francis et al., 2005), so that accounting earnings have a double role.

In terms of managerial ownership, on the one hand, Warfield et al.'s (1995) argument that high levels of managerial ownership enhance earnings informativeness by aligning managers' with shareholders' interests (Watts and Zimmerman, 1986; Christie and

Zimmerman, 1994; Bushman and Smith, 2001). On the other hand, by information effects, Fan and Wong (2002) argue that managers have incentives to use earnings management to maximize private benefits at the expense of shareholders and creditors. Also, in the case of concentrated ownership, such as family firms, accounting earnings can have a double role. On the one hand, when the owner effectively controls a firm, he also controls the production of the firm's accounting information and the reporting policies even if the company is managed by non-family managers. As the controlling owner is perceived to have strong incentives to expropriate outside shareholders, the credibility of the firm's accounting information is reduced. That is, outside investors pay less attention to the reported accounting numbers because they expect that the controlling owner reports accounting information more for self-interested purposes than to reflect the firm's true underlying economic transactions. In particular, outside investors may not trust the firm's reported accounting earnings because the controlling owner may manipulate earnings for outright expropriation (Fan and Wong, 2002), even through fraudulent accounting behaviors (Tiscini and di Donato, 2005).

On the other hand, instead, a single or a few controlling shareholders, who could be family members, monitor managers more effectively and can reward them properly through direct monitoring. Since management compensation in these firms is less likely to be tied to earnings, their earnings are less likely to be manipulated (Healy and Palepu, 2001; and Fields et al., 2001).

Furthermore, the quality of reporting is important for money lenders (banks and institutional investors). In fact, since the verification of the true characteristics of the projects by outside parties may be costly or impossible because of the existence of information asymmetries, it creates incentives for good-quality reporting to obtain better financing terms and other contractual conditions (Ball and Shivakumar, 2005). This could be related to the 'signaling' power of information (Leland and Pyle, 1977). In fact, for projects of good quality to be financed, if information cannot be transferred directly, one signal to the lending market of the quality of the project is the willingness of the people with inside information to invest in the project; the attitude of investors can be different, depending on the ownership structure of the company.

Family Firms and Earnings Quality

In this context founding family ownership could affect the demand and supply of quality financial reporting, generating a twofold effect (Wang, 2005).

In general, family firms face less severe agency problems arising from the separation between ownership and control but they are characterized by more severe agency problems arising between controlling and non-controlling shareholders (Gilson and Gordon, 2003): shareholders may use their controlling position in the firm to extract private benefits at the expense of the small shareholders. Consistent with the view that family management mitigates the classic agency problem, Morck et al. (1988), Palia and Ravid (2002) and Fahlenbrach (2004) find that founder-CEO firms trade at a premium relative to other firms. On the other hand, Smith and Amoako-Adu (1999) and Pérez-González (2001) find that the stock market reacts negatively to the appointment of family heirs as managers. Many studies have been conducted on the relations between family ownership, control, management and firm value. Villalonga and Amit (2006) suggest that family ownership creates value for all shareholders only when the founder is still active as CEO, while, in the firms run by a descendant CEO, minority shareholdes are worse than they would be in non-family firms.

Stewardship is another perspective from which to view the advantages and disadvantages of a family business. This theory assumes aligned goals between owners and managers (Davis et al., 1997; Fox and Hamilton, 1994). These attitudes will be prevalent among family business in which leaders are either family members or linked to the family (Miller and Le Breton-Miller, 2006).

According to these two theories, the board of directors has a different role. In the agency theory its main function is to lower the conflict between shareholders and managers, while according to stewardship theory the main role of the board is to advise and support the management (Corbetta and Salvato, 2004; Gubitta and Gianecchini, 2002). Organization might require less control from a board when goal alignment between owners and managers is high (Luoma and Goodstein, 1999; Sundaramurthy and Lewis, 2003). For this reason, board size should be smaller in family business with high alignment of goals between owners and managers (Jaskiewicz and Klein, 2007). According to Pieper et al. (2008), firms with relatively high level of goal alignment are even less likely to have a board of directors.

These characteristics of family firms, and the role of board of directors, raise interesting issues also about their corporate disclosure practices affecting EQ. The existing literature does not come to the same results. On the one hand, family firms produce better information than non-family firms thanks to the ability of the controlling owner to directly monitor the managers (Demsetz and Lehn, 1985; Shleifer and Vishny, 1997; Anderson and Reeb, 2003b). Families tend to have much longer investment horizons as compared to those of other shareholders. Thus families help mitigate myopic investment decisions by managers (James, 1999; Kwak, 2003; Stein, 1988, 1989). This is consistent with the 'alignment effect' of family ownership.

Family firms with a founder CEO (rather than those with a descendant CEO) are primarily responsible for family firms exhibiting better disclosure practices and better disclosure-related economic consequences as compared to non-family firms (Ali et al., 2007). This is especially due to family incentives to create long-term employee loyalty (Weber et al., 2003), to preserve the family's reputation and to forgo short-term benefits from managing earnings because of the incentives to pass on their business to future generations.

On the other hand, family firms' boards tend to be less independent and are often dominated by family members (Anderson and Reeb, 2003a; Anderson et al., 2004). Controlling shareholders can seek such private benefits by freezing out minority shareholders (Gilson and Gordon, 2003; Anderson and Reeb, 2003a; Shleifer and Vishny, 1997).

This could contribute to manipulating accounting earnings, and is consistent with the 'entrenchment effect' of family ownership producing a worse EQ (Wang, 2005). Family members usually have important positions on both the management team and the board of directors. Thus these firms may have inferior corporate governance and lower accountability because of ineffective monitoring by the board. Thus, whether family firms have better or worse EQ compared to non-family firms requires empirical testing.

FAMILY FIRMS IN ITALY

The high number of big-sized family firms is traditionally one of the most typical features of Italian capitalism, in which publicly held companies are quite absent, most companies are closely held, the market for corporate control seems to be quite ineffective and entrepreneurial families play a decisive role in the economic system performance. Thus Italian listed firms' ownership structure is highly concentrated and characterized by controlling families with a strong leadership (Montemerlo, 2000; Corbetta and Minichilli, 2005).

In the last ten years, controlling ownership stakes by the state have been reduced by a wave of privatizations, and a 'coalition model' of firms' control, mainly through shareholders' agreements, has raised in importance. Moreover, some important reforms have strongly changed the features of corporate and financial market law, which can be nowadays considered as characterized, at least formally, by a high degree of investor protection. Listed companies have also widely adopted a self-regulation code aligned with international best practice. Nevertheless, these reforms have not led, at the moment, to a real shareholding fragmentation and to a decrease in family control.

Thus the Italian case is important as an example of a country in which family capitalism is persistent even after important reforms in corporate and financial regulation (and self-regulation). Italian family firms have some specific characteristics already analyzed in some research. For example, a large part of the controlling family's wealth is invested in the company (Bianchi et al., 2001; Montemerlo, 2000; Volpin, 2002; Brunello, Graziano and Parigi, 2003; Corbetta and Minichilli, 2005). For this reason, the controlling family is highly involved in the activities of the company. Moreover, the companies' ownership is highly concentrated, and institutional or other outside investors do not get significant positions in the governance mechanisms. Finally, the Italian family firms have a strong presence of family members in their governance bodies. This allows us to consider Italian capitalism as a good setting to test the effects of family governance on financial reporting quality.

RESEARCH QUESTIONS AND HYPOTHESES DEVELOPMENT

This study aims at contributing to the recently increasing stream of literature on the economic efficiency of listed family firms, in the perspective of information asymmetries and transparency. As the existing literature shows, the relation depends on the prevalence of the 'entrenchment effect' or of the 'alignment effect' and has to be demonstrated empirically.

We argue that the relation between family ownership and EQ (and thus the prevalence of the 'alignment' or of the 'entrenchment' effect) depends mainly on the existence of checks and balances between decisional and control powers. In this perspective, a higher involvement of the family in the governance of the company (i.e. board participation) would lead to higher EQ.

The rationale is that the higher is the involvement of family members in the governance, the stronger will be the management monitoring activity by the family and the more influence the 'alignment effect' will gain. On the other hand, the lower is family involvement, the stronger will be excessive CEO power and the more influence the 'entrenchment effect' will gain.

If the family is highly involved in the governance of the company, it will be more willing to protect its reputation through transparent reporting. Furthermore, it has a long-term investment horizon and lower incentives to short-term earnings management, because of incentives to pass on the business to future generations. Finally, family board members are more effective in monitoring financial information quality because they have at their disposal a large array of relational governance mechanisms based on kinship ties, that is, communication within the family and family events (Mustakallio et al., 2002; Tagiuri and Davis, 1996).

On the contrary, a lower family involvement leads to lower CEO monitoring, higher information asymmetries between the board and the CEO, and higher incentives for earnings management and short-term-oriented financial reporting.

This can be explained by the fact that family non-executive directors are much more active than other external non-executive or independent directors, thus causing family members' involvement to be stronger than the effects of external independent directors.

But we also expect the relation to be different according to the characteristics of the CEO, consistent with the hypothesis of a positive effect of power balancing on EQ.

A competing view is based on the widespread opinion that non-executive family directors are faithfully aligned to the decisions of the family CEO, due to kinship relations, implying that a higher involvement of the family in the board could increase the entrenchment of the family CEO, strengthening his or her excessive power. Nevertheless, it must also be considered that generally a high number of family directors is the result of more than one single family and more than one generation involved in the firm, and this should lead to a higher dialectical behavior on the board.

In the case of a non-family CEO, the involvement of the family in the board mitigates managerial power, leading to the prevalence of the 'alignment' effect. On the contrary, in the case of a family CEO, the board is instead more likely to be dominated by the CEO if the number of family directors is high. This indeed depends on the behavior of executive and non-executive family directors. Family directors can indeed play an active monitoring role if they have strong personality, independent judgment and distinctive competences, but they exercise a very weak influence if they only ratify the CEO's decisions, rather than challenge the uncontested authority of the boss.

The second kind of situation is more likely to happen when the time of intergenerational succession is approaching, and it generally lasts for a limited period. The founder's sons need some time to settle in and learn the decision-making mechanisms; therefore they will probably delay taking an active control role. After a short time, however, the mere presence on the board is not enough for their entrepreneurial ambitions. Board membership is rather seen as a transition to prepare the following phase in which they will take the control of the company. Consequently, later on, the family directors' role will be active and targeted to gradually balance the excessive power of the CEO, consistent with the need to assert a role for the emerging generation.

The role of family directors' involvement with a family CEO is thus more difficult to conceptualize and the relation with EQ is then a matter of empirical testing. For sure, the

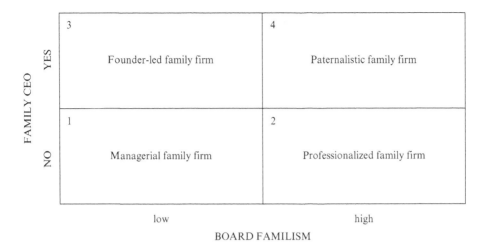

Figure 3.1   Typologies of family firm governance

relation between the familism of the company and EQ could be usefully studied not only in terms of family ownership, but also in terms of actual family involvement in the governance.

Different governance models of family firms can be distinguished, depending on two dimensions: (a) the strategic choice of hiring a professional manager (family CEO versus non-family CEO); and (b) the involvement of the family in the board.

Four different governance models can be schematized, according to the presence of the family in the board and in the CEO role:

- non-family CEO with low board familism (managerial family firm);
- non-family CEO with high board familism (professionalized family firm);
- family CEO with low board familism (founder-led family firm);
- family CEO with high board familism (paternalistic family firm).

The different models can be represented as in Figure 3.1.

The four models can ideally be put on a qualitative scale of 'familism', from the lower (the managerial family firm), to the higher (the paternalistic family firm), with the professionalized family firm and the founder-led family firm in the middle.

According to the general hypothesis of a positive correlation between 'checks and balances' and EQ, the models with lower (managerial) and higher (paternalistic) 'familism' should be associated with lower EQ, while the models in the middle (professionalized and founder-led) should be associated with higher EQ.

In fact, the two extremes are the models in which the power is more concentrated (in the hands of the managers in the managerial model; in the hands of the family in the paternalistic one). The two intermediate models are instead characterized by more balancing between decisional power and controls (the managers controlled by family directors in the professionalized model and the family CEO controlled by non-family directors in the founder-led model).

Accordingly, we formulate the following hypotheses:

Hypothesis 1   A higher family involvement in the board leads to higher earnings quality, but only when the CEO isn't a member of the family.

Hypothesis 2   The presence of family CEOs leads to higher earnings quality, but only when they are not associated with high family involvement in the board.

The explanation of the above hypotheses is that the interaction between a family CEO and strong family involvement in the board makes the 'entrenchment' effect stronger and moderates the general positive correlation between family governance and EQ.

In testing this hypothesis, it is necessary to take into consideration other variables related to corporate governance practices having effects on EQ.

The next section will explain in detail the variables and methodology used for the study.

METHODOLOGY

The Sample and the Methodology of the Analysis

The empirical data cover the period 2001–2006 and they allow the analysis of EQ measures for the period 2002–2005. The sample consists of 126 Italian companies listed on the Milan Stock Exchange Market and includes all listed companies, with the exception of banks, insurance companies, other financial intermediaries and public utilities, since in these industries the presence of family firms is absent.

The analysis was performed through the following steps. First, we confirmed the validity of the assumptions of the Dechow–Dichev (2002) EQ measurement model for our sample. Then we calculated the EQ measure as the residuals from the regression of changes in working capital on past, present and future operating cash flows. According to the model, these residuals are a proxy for the 'abnormal accruals', discretionary adjustments expressing dis-alignment between earnings and cash flows from the operations of a given year, which do not reverse in the previous or in the following years. Next, we performed two linear regression models in order to analyze the relation between the EQ measure and the independent and control variables.

In particular, our first regression model considers the following variables: family directors, representing the involvement of the family in governing bodies; board independence and CEO duality, representing the main governance practices; interlocking directorship/cross-ownership, representing the connection between banks and firms; debt/equity ratio, to control for financial pressures; ROE ratio, to control for profitability; the logarithm of number of employees, to control for size.

While the first regression model considers only the effect of family involvement on EQ, regardless of who runs the role of CEO, the second one adds the following variables:

- family CEO, to express if the CEO is a family member or not;
- family directors * family CEO, representing the interaction between a family CEO and high family involvement in the board.

This second regression is aimed at testing diversities in the effects of family involvement on EQ depending on the CEO being a family member or not.

The Dependent Variable: EQ Measures from Dechow–Dichev (2002)

According to the Dechow–Dichev (2002) method, we have derived a practical measure of working capital accrual quality using the following firm-level time-series regression:

$$\Delta WCt = \alpha_1 + \alpha_2 CFO_{t-1} + \alpha_3 CFO_t + \alpha_4 CFO_{t+1} + \varepsilon_t$$

where:
ΔWCt = change in working capital time t
CFO_{t-1} = cash flow from operation time $t - 1$
CFO_t = cash flow from operation time t
CFO_{t+1} = cash flow from operation time $t + 1$

The relevance of the model is confirmed by the data of our sample.

The R^2 is high for every year of the analyzed period and in the pooled regression (630 firm-year observations) the adjusted R^2 is 0.56.

The residuals of the regression analysis, expressing abnormal accruals, are then used as an EQ measure on a firm-year observation basis: the higher the residuals, the lower the EQ.

The Independent and Control Variables

As we argue that the influence of family ownership on EQ depends on the involvement of the family in the governance mechanisms of the company, we measure family involvement as the number of family members on the board of directors (*FAMDIR*, also referred as 'board familism').

In the second regression model we test also the effects of a family CEO (*CEOFAM*, expressed by a dummy variable equal to 1 if CEO is a family member and 0 otherwise).

The second model includes as independent variable also the interaction between family directors and family CEO (*FAMDIR*CEOFAM*), in order to check the effect of a simultaneous presence of many family directors and a family CEO.

The other independent variables expressing corporate governance practices are the following:

- board independence (*INDIR*) is the number of independent directors on the board. Board independence is expected to mitigate the 'entrenchment effect' and thus contribute to higher EQ;
- bank/firm connection (*IC/CO*) is considered to exist if at least one director is in common between the firm and a listed bank (interlocking directorate) and if there is a cross-ownership between banks and the firm for at least 2 percent shareholding (cross-ownership). This percentage is the thresold required by *CONSOB* in order to publicly declare relevant shareholding interests. *IC/CO* is a dummy variable equal to 1 if at least one of the two conditions exists or 0 otherwise. Bank/firm

connections are expected to create incentives, from a demand-side perspective, for better reporting quality.

- CEO duality (*CEODUAL*) is expressed by a dummy variable equal to 1 if it exists and 0 otherwise. CEO duality is a signal of top management entrenchment and it is expected to have a negative correlation with EQ.

Consistent with existing literature on EQ, the models control for: size, expressed by the logarithm of the number of employees (*EMPL*) and expected to be positively correlated with EQ, thanks to better internal control systems of big firms and a good balance between managers and shareholders interests; profitability, expressed by *return on equity* (*ROE*) and expected to be positively correlated with EQ, thanks to higher incentives to manipulate earnings in case of poor results; financial leverage, expressed by the net debt/equity ratio (*LEV*) and expected to be negatively correlated with EQ, thanks to greater incentives to manipulate earnings in case of high level of debt.

Sample Descriptive Statistics

Before considering the results of our analysis, we resume a few brief descriptive statistics information about the sample, divided into the two sub-samples of family and non-family firms. For the purpose of this descriptive analysis, a company is defined as a 'family firm' if two conditions are respected:

- if there is a single shareholder or a single controlling family owning at least the 20 percent of voting rights, directly, indirectly or through voting agreements and voting trust (as a device for coordination between significant shareholders);
- if there is at least one member of the family (or a relative in law) with a seat on the board of directors.

The information presented below refers to the whole period 2001–2006.

Family companies are 56 percent of the total sample. This confirms that family firms are quite widespread in the Italian stock market. We also calculated, for family and non-family firms, means, standard deviations and independent sample *t*-tests for the variables in the model. Table 3.1 reports the results.

Non-family firms got, on average, a higher level of debt (1.03) compared to family firms (0.808) but the difference is not significant. Family firms also present higher equity profitability, although the significance level is not high. Moreover, on average, family firms are smaller (the mean difference is significant) and are more characterized by CEO duality (with quite significant mean values). This is consistent with the common opinion that family control is a constraint on growth and entails a higher risk of 'entrenchment' of top management.

As expected, the number of independent directors is lower in family firms (3.014 compared to 4.040 of non-family) and the difference is statistically significant.

Finally, both family and non-family firms have more or less the same frequency of connections with the banks (0.605/0.589), which is a typical feature of Italian capitalism and confirms the pervasive power still held by banks in Italy.

Table 3.1   Descriptive statistics and t-*test**

	Mean values		SD		t	Sig.
	Family	Non-family	Family	Non-family		
Observations	281		220			
CEOFAM	0.65		0.48		−13.14	0.00
CEODUAL	0.44	0.35	0.50	0.48	−2.05	0.04
FAMDIR	2.33	0.27	1.35	0.71	−20.48	0.00
LEV	0.87	1.13	2.79	5.61	0.66	0.51
ID/CO	0.62	0.59	0.49	0.49	−0.84	0.40
ROE	5.41	0.91	37.63	32.13	−1.02	0.31
INDIR	3.02	4.09	1.80	3.20	4.75	0.00
Ln *EMPL*	3.17	3.07	0.63	0.87	−2.23	0.03

Note: * In the calculation of the *t*-test we considered the Levens test of variance homogeneity.

Finally, the average number of family CEOs in family firms is around 0.652, meaning that the large majority of family firms have a family CEO.

The Regression Models

The first linear regression model used in the analysis is the following:

$$EQ = \beta_1 + \beta_2(FAMDIR)_t + \beta_3(INDIR)_t + \beta_4(ID/CO)_t + \beta_5(CEODUAL)_t$$

$$+ \beta_6(LnEMPL)_t + \beta_7(ROE)_t + \beta_8(LEV)_t + \varepsilon_t$$

The second one is the following:

$$EQ_t = \beta_1 + \beta_2(FAMDIR)_t + \beta_3(INDIR)_t + \beta_4(ID/CO)_t + \beta_5(CEODUAL)_t$$

$$+ \beta_6(LnEMPL)_t + \beta_7(ROE)_t + \beta_8(LEV)_t + \beta_9(CEOFAM)_t$$

$$+ \beta_{10}(FAMDIR*CEOFAM)_t + \varepsilon_t$$

We also performed a robustness test through a regression analysis using, as dependent variable, the value of residuals (abnormal accruals) scaled by the revenues (residuals/revenues), rather than using the absolute value of residuals, for a better control of the size effect.

EMPIRICAL RESULTS

The regression analysis has been performed on a cross-sectional basis, on 630 firm-year observations.

Table 3.2 and Table 3.3 present, respectively, the results for first and the second

Table 3.2   First regression results

Indep. variables	Beta coefficients	t	Sig.	Tolerance	VIF
(Constant)	−296664.165	−7.690	0.000		
CEODUAL	18638.416	1.046	0.296	0.938	1.066
FAMDIR	−26086.339	−4.438	0.000	0.908	1.102
LEV	691.538	0.342	0.733	0.914	1.094
ID/CO	−9978.791	−0.566	0.572	0.963	1.038
ROE	−254.405	−1.402	0.162	0.912	1.096
INDIR	11019.670	3.227	0.001	0.892	1.120
Ln EMPL	113592.014	9.659	0.000	0.923	1.083
Adj. R^2	*0.220*				

Table 3.3   Second regression results

Indep. variables	Beta coefficients	t	Sig.	Tolerance	VIF
(Constant)	−261669.419	−7.0122	0.000		
CEOFAM	−93087.110	−3.325	0.001	0.349	2.867
CEODUAL	10469.455	0.602	0.547	0.932	1.073
FAMDIR	−40716.688	−4.122	0.000	0.296	3.379
LEV	495.102	0.221	0.824	0.912	1.096
ID/CO	−6816.632	−0.401	0.688	0.965	1.037
ROE	−299.802	−1.544	0.123	0.915	1.093
FAMDIR*CEOFAM	36369.320	2.825	0.005	0.168	5.963
INDIR	8701.711	2.559	0.011	0.888	1.126
Ln EMPL	113979.325	10.160	0.000	0.921	1.086
Adj. R^2	*0.237*				

regression models, including measures of multicollinearity. The 'model fit' for the first and the second regression models is quite good (adjusted R^2 0.220 and 0.237 respectively).

In both regression models, the regression coefficient of board familism (*FAMDIR*) is negative and highly significant (t equal to −4.438 and −4.122 respectively). Moreover, in the second regression model, the regression coefficient of family CEO (*CEOFAM*) is negative and highly significant ($t = -3.325$). The coefficient of the interaction variable *FAMDIR*CEOFAM* is positive and highly significant ($t = 2.825$). The results of the regression models confirm both Hypothesis 1 and Hypothesis 2.

As the dependent variable is an opposite measure of EQ, the results of both regressions confirm that a stronger presence of family members on the board has a positive effect on EQ; that is, the 'alignment effect' prevails. Moreover, the presence of a family CEO has also positive effects on EQ, confirming the 'alignment effect'.

But the positive effects of family directors and family CEOs are not confirmed when they are combined. The interaction variable between family CEO and family directors (*FAMDIR*CEOFAM*) shows that the positive effect of the involvement of family

Table 3.4   Third regression results

Independent variables	Beta coefficients	t	Sig.	Collinearity statistics	
				Tolerance	VIF
Constant	0.445	11.099	0.000		
CEOFAM	−0.107	−3.559	0.000	0.349	2.867
CEODUAL	−0.013	−0.717	0.474	0.932	1.073
FAMDIR	−0.022	−2.076	0.038	0.296	3.379
LEV	−0.002	−0.932	0.352	0.912	1.096
ID/CO	0.016	0.876	·0.381	0.965	1.037
ROE	0.000	−1.946	0.052	0.915	1.093
FAMDIR*CEOFAM	0.028	1.991	0.047	0.168	5.963
INDIR	0.006	1.627	0.104	0.888	1.126
LOG EMPL	−0.100	−8.259	0.000	0.921	1.086
Adj. R^2	*0.237*				

members on EQ is no longer confirmed when there is the simultaneous presence of a family CEO, showing a stronger 'entrenchment effect'. When there is a family CEO, in other words, a strong presence of family directors does not place more effective controls on the CEO, but makes it more likely that the board will be dominated by one or a few key members of the family.

It is interesting to note the result for independent directors. Both the regression models show a negative and significant correlation between EQ and board independence (expressed by the number of independent directors). The t-statistic is respectively $t = 3.227$ and $t = 2.559$.

The negative correlation between EQ and board independence is counterintuitive. According to dominant theory, a stronger presence of independent directors should affect positively firms' disclosures. This result sheds doubts on the effectiveness of Italian independent directors.

The other variables, in the second regression model, show in significant correlations with EQ. Note, however, the expected positive effects of profitability (*ROE*) ($t = -1.544$) and of bank–firm connections ($t = -0.401$) on EQ, consistent with the most important supply-side (profitability) and demand-side (bank–firm connections) incentives for good reporting, as well as the expected negative effect of debt level (*LEV*), with $t = 0.221$.

The CEO duality shows a negative correlation with EQ, consistent with the rationale that many appointments held by a single person are symptoms of the 'entrenchment effect', all other things being equal (also in this case, however, the t-statistic is not significant). The variables of the model do not show significant collinearity, except for the variables *CEOFAM, FAMDIR* and *FAMDIR*CEOFAM*, whose tolerance is quite low (respectively 0.349, 0.296 and 0.168).

In order to test the robustness of our model, in regard to controlling for the size effect, we performed a further regression analysis using the ratio residuals/revenues as a dependent variable, instead of considering the absolute value of residuals (as in the Dechow–Dichev model). Table 3.4 reports the results of this third regression.

The results confirm our hypotheses. In fact, the adjusted R^2 of the regression is the same as in the previous regression (0.237): the model confirms the positive relation between EQ and family directors and between EQ and the presence of a family CEO, but also the negative correlation between EQ and the interaction between family directors and family CEOs.

CONCLUSIONS

A general result is the existence of a positive correlation between the involvement of the family in the governing bodies of the company and EQ, but only when this does not imply an excessive and uncontested power of the family. This means that what really counts for EQ is not the 'familism' itself, but the distribution of powers and controls set by the governance system of the company.

Family governance is then good for EQ, but not when at the same time there is a family CEO and a high number of family directors on the board. This result confirms the positive effect of family directors on alignment and agency cost reduction, but it confirms the prevalence of the 'entrenchment effect' when at the same time many family directors and a family CEO join the board of the company.

This result, as far as we know, is partially novel. The results confirm the explicative power of the classification of large family firms according to family involvement in the board and in the top management of the firm. EQ is lower when the family (paternalistic model) or the top management (managerial model) dominate the board, and higher when there is more balancing of powers and controls inside the governance bodies (as in the professionalized model).

These findings have important implications for entrepreneurs and for financial reporting users (respectively from the supply side and the demand side of the financial reporting process), showing the 'family model' as an efficient model of firm, able to gain trust through transparency, thus creating a precondition for the cost of capital reduction, but also showing that this is possible only when good governance practices are put in place, in order to moderate the 'entrenchment' effects of family ownership and management.

LIMITATIONS AND DIRECTIONS OF FUTURE RESEARCH

Further improvements of the research could shed new light on the relation between family involvement in the management of the firm and earnings management. First, it could be interesting to consider the effect of different family generations on EQ, because some studies have been conducted in terms of performance showing that the first generation outperforms later generations. Moreover, studies could also consider the difference between inside, non-family directors (who are not family members but usually voting with family), and outside or family directors. Furthermore, the (somewhat counterintuitive) results on the relation between board independence and EQ should be more deeply analyzed, taking into consideration some well-known problems in defining independent directors such as the difficulties in defining independence and in monitoring their real behavior. Finally, the extension of the analysis in time and space and the consideration of some other corporate governance features, such as minorities shareholdings composition and institutional investors' shareholdings and coverage, could represent a direction for future research improvements.

REFERENCES

Ali, A., Chen, T.Y. and Radhakrishnan, S. (2007), 'Corporate disclosures by family firms', *Journal of Accounting and Economics*, **44**(1/2), 238–86.

Anderson, R.C., Mansi, S.A. and Reeb, D.M. (2003), 'Founding family ownership and the agency cost of debt', *Journal of Financial Economics*, **68**, 263–85.

Anderson, R., Mansi, S.A. and Reeb, D.M. (2004), 'Board characteristics, accounting report integrity, and the cost of debt', *Journal of Accounting and Economics*, **37**, 315–42.

Anderson, R.C. and Reeb, D.M. (2003a), 'Founding family ownership and firms' performance: evidence from the S&P 500', *The Journal of Finance*, **58**, 1301–28.

Anderson, R.C. and Reeb, D.M. (2003b), 'Who monitors the family?', Working Paper. American University and University of Alabama, http://ssrn.com/abstract=369620.

Ball, R. and Shivakumar, L. (2005), 'Earnings quality in UK private firms: comparative loss recognition timeliness', *Journal of Accounting and Economics*, **39**, 83–128.

Balsam, S., Krishnan, J. and Yang, J.S. (2003), 'Auditor industry specialization and earnings quality', *Auditing: A Journal of Practice and Theory*, **22**(2), 71–97.

Bebchuk, L., Kraakman, R. and Triantis, G. (1999), 'Stock pyramids, cross-ownership, and dual class equity: the creation and agency costs of separating control from cash flow rights', Working Paper No. 6951, NBER, http://papers.ssrn.com/sol3/papers.cfm?abstract_id=147590.

Berle, A. and Means, G. (1932), *The Modern Corporation and Private Property*, New York: NJ: Transaction Publishers, 1991; originally published by Harcourt, Brace & World.

Bernstein, L. (1993), *Financial Statement Analysis*, 5th edn, Boston, MA: Irwin Publishing.

Bianchi, M., Bianco, M. and Enriques, L. (2001), *Pyramidal Groups and the Separation between Ownership and Control in Italy*, Oxford: OUP.

Brunello, G., Graziano, C. and Parigi, B. (2003), 'CEO turnover in insider-dominated boards: the Italian case', *Journal of Banking and Finance*, **27**(6), 1027–51.

Bushman, R.M. and Smith, A. (2001), 'Financial accounting information and corporate governance', *Journal of Accounting and Economics*, **32**, 237–351.

Chan, K., Chan, L., Jegadeesh, N. and Lakonishok, J. (2004), 'Earnings quality and stock returns', *Journal of Business*, **79**, 1041–82.

Christie, A. and Zimmerman, J. (1994), 'Efficient and opportunistic choices of accounting procedures: corporate control contests', *The Accounting Review*, **69**, 539–66.

Corbetta, G. and Minichilli, A. (2005), 'Il governo delle imprese italiane quotate a controllo familiare: i risultati di una ricerca esplorativa', *Economia & Management*, **6**, 59–77.

Corbetta, G. and Salvato, C.A. (2004), 'The board of directors in family firms: one size fits all?', *Family Business Review*, **17**, 119 34.

Davis, J., Schoorman, R. and Donaldson, L. (1997), 'Towards a stewardship theory of management', *Academy of Management Review*, **22**, 20–47.

Dechow, P.M. (1994), 'Accounting earnings and cash flows as measures of firm performance. The role of accounting accruals', *Journal of Accounting & Economics*, **18**, 3–42.

Dechow, P. and Dichev, I. (2002), 'The quality of accruals and earnings: the role of accrual estimation errors', *The Accounting Review*, **77**, 35–59.

Demsetz, H. and Lehn, K. (1985), 'The structure of corporate ownership: causes and consequences', *Journal of Political Economy*, **93**, 1155–77.

Fahlenbrach, R. (2004), 'Founder-CEOs and stock market performance', unpublished working paper. Wharton School, University of Pennsylvania.

Fama, E. and Jensen, M. (1983a), 'Separation of ownership and control', *Journal of Law and Economics*, **26**, 301–25.

Fama, E. and Jensen, M. (1983b), 'Agency problems and residual claims', *Journal of Law and Economics*, **26**, 325–44.

Fan, J. and Wong, T.L. (2002), 'Corporate ownership structure and the informativeness of accounting earnings in East Asia', *Journal of Accounting and Economics*, **33**, 401–25.

Fields, T.D., Lys, T.Z. and Vincent, L. (2001), 'Empirical research on accounting', *Journal of Accounting & Economics*, **31**(1–3), 255–307.

Francis, J., LaFond, R., Olsson, P. and Schipper, K. (2003), 'The market pricing of earnings quality', Working Paper, www.ssrn.com.

Fox, M. and Hamilton, R. (1994), 'Ownership and diversification: agency theory or stewardship theory', *Journal of Management Studies*, **31**, 69–81.

Francis, J., Schipper, K. and Vincent, L. (2005), 'Earnings and dividends informativeness when cash flow rights are separated from voting rights', *Journal of Accounting and Economics*, **39**, 329–60.

Gilson, R.J. and Gordon, J.N. (2003), 'Controlling controlling shareholders', *University of Pensylvania Law Review*, **152**, 785–843.

Gubitta, P. and Gianecchini, M. (2002), 'Governance and flexibility in family-owned SMEs', *Family Business Review*, **15**, 277–97.

Healy, P. and Palepu, K. (2001), 'Information asymmetry, corporate disclosure, and the capital markets: a review of the empirical disclosure literature', *Journal of Accounting and Economics*, **31**, 405–40.

Hodge, F. (2003), 'Investors' perceptions of earnings quality, auditor independence, and the usefulness of audited financial information', *Accounting Horizons*, Supplement, 37–48.

James, H. (1999), 'Owner as a manager, extended horizons and the family firm', *International Journal of Economics of Business*, **6**, 41–56.

Jaskiewicz, P. and Klein, S. (2007), 'The impact of goal alignment on board composition and board size in family businesses', *Journal of Business Research*, **60**, 1080–89.

Jensen, Michael C. and Meckling, W.H. (1976), 'Theory of the firm: managerial behavior, agency costs and ownership structure', *Journal of Financial Economics*, **3**, 305–60.

Kirschenheiter, M. and Melumad, N. (2004), 'Earnings' quality and smoothing', Working Paper, Columbia Business School.

Kwak, M. (2003), 'The advantages of family ownership', *MIT Sloan Management Review* (Winter), 12.

Leland, H.E. and Pyle, D.H. (1977), 'Informational asymmetries, financial structure, and financial intermediation', *The Journal of Finance*, **XXXII**(2), 371–87.

Luoma, P. and Goodstein, J. (1999), 'Stakeholders and corporate bands: institutional influences on board composition', *Academic Management Journal*, **42**, 553–63.

Mikhail, M., Walther, B. and Willis, R. (2003), 'Reactions to dividend changes conditional on earnings quality', *Journal of Accounting, Auditing and Finance*, **18**(1), 121–51.

Miller, D. and Le Breton-Miller, I. (2006), 'Family governance and firm performance: agency, stewardship, and capabilities', *Family Business Review*, **XIX**(1), 73–87.

Montemerlo, D. (2000), *Il Governo delle imprese familiari. Modelli e strumenti per gestire il rapporto tra proprietà e impresa*, Milano: EGEA.

Morck, R., Shleifer, A. and Vishny R. (1988), 'Management ownership and market valuation: an empirical analysis', *Journal of Financial Economics*, **20**, 293–315.

Mustakallio, M., Autio, E. and Zahra, S.A. (2002), 'Relational and contractual governance in family firms: effects on strategic decision making', *Family Business Review*, **15**(3), 205–22.

Palia, D. and Ravid, S.A. (2002), 'The role of founders in large companies: entrenchment or valuable human capital?', unpublished working paper, Rutgers University.

Pérez-González, F. (2001), 'Does inherited control hurt firm performance?', unpublished working paper, Columbia University.

Pieper, M.T., Klein, S.B. and Jaskiewicz, P. (2008), 'The impact of goal alignment on board existence and top management team composition: evidence from family-influenced businesses', *Journal of Small Business Management*, **46**(3), 372–94.

Revsine, L., Collins, D. and Johnson, B. (1999), *Financial Reporting and Analysis*, Upper Saddle River, NJ: Prentice Hall.

Roe, M.J. (1994), *Strong Managers, Weak Owner – The Political Roots of American Corporate Finance*, Princeton, NJ: Princeton University Press.

Schipper, K. and Vincent, L. (2003), 'Earnings quality', *Accounting Horizons*, Supplement, 97–110.

Shleifer, A. and Vishny, R. (1986), 'Large shareholders and corporate control', *Journal of Political Economy*, **94**, 461–89.

Shleifer, A. and Vishny, R. (1997), 'A survey of corporate governance', *Journal of Finance*, **52**, 737–83.

Smith, B.F. and Amoako-Adu, B. (1999), 'Management succession and financial performance of family controlled firms', *Journal of Corporate Finance*, **5**, 341–68.

Stein, J. (1988), 'Takeover threats and managerial myopia', *Journal of Political Economy*, **96**, 61–80.

Stein, J. (1989), 'Efficient capital markets, inefficient firms: a model of myopic corporate behavior', *Quarterly Journal of Economics*, **106**, 655–69.

Sundaramurthy, C. and Lewis, M. (2003), 'Control and collaboration: paradoxes of governance', *Academy of Management Review*, **28**, 397–415.

Tagiuri, R. and Davis, J. (1996), 'Bivalent attributes of the family firms', *Family Business Review*, **9**(2), 199–208.

Tiscini, R. and di Donato, F. (2005), 'The relation between accounting frauds and corporate governance systems: an analysis of recent scandals', *Global Business and Finance Review*, **10**(3), 99–109.

Villalonga, B. and Amit, R. (2006), 'How do family ownership, control, and management affect firm value?', *Journal of Financial Economics*, **80**, 385–417.

Volpin, P. (2003), 'History of corporate ownership in Italy', ECGI Finance Working Paper 017/2003, retrieved from www.ecgi.com.

Wang, D. (2005), 'Founding family ownership and earnings quality', White Paper.

Warfield, T., Wild, J.J. and Wild, K. (1995), 'Managerial ownership, accounting choices, and informativeness of earnings', *Journal of Accounting and Economics*, **20**(1), 61–91.

Watts, R. and Zimmerman, J. (1986), *Positive Accounting Theory*, Englewood Cliffs, NJ: Prentice-Hall.

Weber, J., Lavelle, L., Lowry, T., Zellner, W. and Barrent, A. (2003), 'Family, Inc.', *Businessweek*, 10 November, 100–114.

White, G., Sondhi, A. and Fried, D. (2003), *The Analysis and Use of Financial Statements*, 3rd edn, New York: John Wiley and Sons.

4 Analysis of social performance and board of directors in family firms: evidence from quoted Italian companies

Patricia Bachiller, Maria-Cleofe Giorgino and Sergio Paternostro

INTRODUCTION

In literature, the firm is defined as a three-dimensional organism (Catturi, 2003). In addition to the economic dimension related to the ownership's interest, other aspects such as the social and the sociopolitical are relevant. They are respectively internal and external to the firm. According to this view, firm performance is also a multidimensional concept, as it includes a financial aspect (related to the economic dimension of the firm) and a social aspect (related to the other two dimensions). Although performance is usually structured in a hierarchical way with more attention to its financial dimension (main objective of the firm), a complete analysis of the firm performance requires considering its social aspect.

Providing a definition of the so-called 'corporate social performance' (CSP) is not easy. According to Wood (2010, p. 51), CSP 'concerns the harm and benefits that result from a business organization's interactions with its larger environment, including the social, cultural, legal, political, economic and natural dimensions'. In this context, we aim to analyse the CSP topic referring in particular to a specific type of firm that assumes particular relevance for the significant role it plays in the economic system: the family firm. In the Italian context, family firms assume in fact great importance in terms of GDP produced (80 per cent), number of firms (90 per cent) and job creation (75 per cent) (Zocchi, 2004). They have specific characteristics deriving from the strong link existing between family and firm. Some previous studies have tried to associate those characteristics with the social performance of a family firm, but they obtained contradictory results. So we need to do further investigations on CSP in family firms and in particular on a specific element of their governance system that has a crucial role in balancing family and firm interests: the board of directors (Lane et al., 2006).

The board of directors is a central mechanism of corporate governance, mainly aimed at supervising the firm activities in order to pursue objectives that are in line with the interests of its shareholders and to obtain a higher performance. To understand the importance of the board to business success, many theoretical perspectives have been formulated in order to highlight the board capacity to solve organizational problems. Thus numerous researchers try to understand its contribution to the improvement of performance.

Social performance plays a significant role in the economy and the integration of different perspectives on performance is important. Thus this chapter aims at analysing qualitative board characteristics that influence the social performance of these firms. For this purpose, an empirical study was carried out on the Italian firms included in the FTSE MIB Index 40, that is the 40 most liquid and quoted Italian firms. The sample included family and non-family firms in order to detect social behaviour differences between the two types of firm. To evaluate their performance, our research considered two social measures: the social ratings elaborated by the Agenzia Europea degli Investimenti (European Investment Agency) and the AccountAbility indicator.

This study adds new evidence to previous literature as it empirically tests the social performance of the firms analysed, while previous empirical research mainly investigated the influence of the board on financial performance. The chapter is organized as follows. First, the CSP concept and its measurements are defined. Then the antecedents of social performance are presented, moving the discussion into the specific context of family firms. The next section defines the link between CSP and the board of directors in the family business context. Then we describe the data and methodology employed and show the empirical research results. The final section discusses the results and presents the main conclusions of the study.

CORPORATE SOCIAL PERFORMANCE: CONCEPT AND MEASUREMENT

Corporate social performance (CSP) is strictly linked to the corporate social responsibility concept (CSR). CSR can be seen according to different theoretical perspectives: economic, integrative, political and ethical (Garriga and Melé, 2004). Despite the heterogeneity of the concept and the difficulty of finding a generally accepted definition, we can say that CSR is concerned with the relationship between the firm and society.

CSP is considered as an attempt to pragmatically approach CSR, trying to 'model and measure social responsibility in terms of performance' (Matten et al., 2003). Also CSP is a controversial and ambiguous field in which many scholars have developed different models and methodologies of measurement (Wood, 2010). In general, CSP 'concerns the harm and benefits that result from a business organization's interactions with its larger environment, including the social, cultural, legal, political, economic and natural dimensions' (Wood, 2010, p. 51). In literature this multidimensional view is largely acknowledged (Griffin and Mahon, 1997), but there are differences about the concept and theoretical framework.

The first conceptual model of CSP was developed by Carroll (1979). The author identified the three pillars of the CSP concept: the domains of firm's responsibility; the philosophies of responsiveness; and the social issues to manage. Carroll proposed four different responsibilities: economic, legal, ethical and discretionary (according to historical importance). In a subsequent work, Carroll (1991) introduced philanthropic responsibilities. The philosophies of responsiveness were: reactive, defensive, adaptive and proactive. The six social issues considered in the model were: consumerism, environment, discrimination, product safety, occupational safety and shareholders. Based on these three pillars, the CSP should be assessed.

From the point of view of Carroll, Wartick and Cochran (1985) developed an advanced CSP concept. They suggested that principles, processes and policies were the main components of CSP. While as regards principles and processes these authors followed the Carroll approach, the policies were the new element of their model. Policies indicate how the firm manages social issues and introduce a variable outcome into the CSP model.

Wood (1991, 1994) completed the previous approaches, emphasizing the view of CSP as an inputs–process–outcomes model. The inputs of the model were the principles of social responsibility: legitimacy, public responsibility and managerial discretion. The processes of social responsiveness were: environmental scanning, stakeholder management and issues/public affairs management. Finally, the outcomes of the model were: effects on people and organizations, effects on the natural and physical environments, effects on social systems and institutions. Swanson (1995) criticized this model, stating that it failed because it did not sufficiently consider the business ethics. To overcome this lack, she put into the model the decision-making process based on ethical values.

Clarkson (1995) emphasized the importance of stakeholders, stressing that a firm did not have a relationship with society, but with its stakeholders. In this sense, social performance could be assessed in terms of a firm's capacity to fulfil stakeholders' requests. For this reason, Wood and Jones (1995) proposed that the stakeholder theory was the key to understand the firm's societal relationship related to the outcomes of CSP concept.

Finally, the social audit approach deals with the internal and external measurement processes related to social screening used for ethical funding to identify the social impact of an organization (Johnson, 2001).

The inherent complexity of the concept associated with the different theoretical frameworks led to several measurement methods: perceptual measures and survey instruments; corporate disclosure measures; amount of particular corporate practices, behaviours and policies; ratings issued by specialized organizations.

As for the perceptual measures and survey instruments, the Fortune survey is one of the most used (Griffin and Mahon, 1997). Through this survey the opinions of senior executives, outside directors and financial analysts are gathered to build a reputation index. The reliability of this index as a CSP measure is questionable because it tends to be considered as a measure of overall management rather than being specific to CSP (Waddock and Graves, 1997). In general, the survey is not considered fully adapted to assess the CSP because of some conceptual and technical problems, such as the return rates and the limitations inherent to a perceptual measure (Waddock and Graves, 1997).

The corporate disclosure measures are based on the annual report to shareholders, social reports and so on. Although Ullman (1985) noted that social performance and social disclosure are two different concepts, this methodology is still used; for example Muñoz et al. (2008) detected some positive relationships between disclosure level and advanced social goals. However, it is not possible to know whether the social performance is underestimated or overestimated in the voluntary disclosure because it depends on the motivations to produce the document (Waddock and Graves, 1997).

Finally, another measurement method is based on the social ratings published by rating agencies. In the USA, the KLD index developed by Kinder, Lydeberg, Domini & Co. is the most used. In recent years, other social ratings were developed: CSID, ARESE, Vigeo, Accountability rating, AEI standards ethics and so on. These ratings are used by researchers because they have the advantage of being a third-party assessment (Wood, 2010). Every rating agency uses a specific methodology based on different criteria and approaches.

THE ANTECEDENTS OF SOCIAL PERFORMANCE: A FOCUS ON FAMILY FIRMS

In the literature, we find two main perspectives to explain the social performance drivers: external pressures and internal mechanisms. In the first perspective, external pressures and expectations of the social actors cause the CSP. The cultural, social, political and institutional context assumes a crucial role to explain both the level and the content of the firm social behaviour (Muller and Kolk, 2010). The pressures are mass media campaigns, stakeholders' activities (e.g. consumer boycott), market dynamics, regulatory pressures, widespread ecological sensitivity, religious beliefs and so on. According to the other perspective, CSP depends mainly on internal forces and it underlines the need to take into account the individual managerial motivations (Aguilera et al. 2007). In this sense, some studies were focused on individuals values, management commitment and organizational culture (Banerjee et al., 2003; Bansal, 2003). Also Swanson (1999) outlined the importance of conceptualizing responsibility and responsiveness as decision-based value processes, proposing four relevant fields of research: the executive's normative orientation to social policy; formal organizational decision-making; informal organizational decision-making; and external affairs management. In short, the role of the values system and ethical orientation of managers is crucial. Governance and, specifically, board structure play an important role as internal mechanisms. Therefore the specific effect of the board structure on CSP is analysed in this chapter.

This topic assumes a specific relevance in a particular kind of firm, family firms, in which the role of the family can modify previous frameworks used to understand CSR and CSP and their drivers. Family firms characteristics are associated, often in a contradictory way, with social performance. In general, two opposing perspectives can be identified: the former claims that the family firms have a natural propensity toward higher standards of ethical and social behaviour; the latter argues that the orientation of these firms is to give precedence to the good of the family, rather than to the more general social welfare (Déniz and Cabrera, 2005). As for the first perspective, one explanation is the strong link between social performance and family reputation (Dyer and Whetten, 2006). Family members are interested in building and maintaining a good family reputation, and a socially responsible behaviour may be a tool to achieve this goal. In general, the reputation effect is stronger when the name of the family is included in the firm name (Uhlaner et al., 2004). The family firm can set up a sort of 'moral capital' through social activities to reduce the effects of actions perceived as socially negative (Dyer and Whetten, 2006). Another explanation is linked to the specific organizational identity orientation of family firms (Bingham et al., 2010). Organizational identity orientation concerns the motivations that explain the relationships between a firm and its stakeholders (Brickson, 2007). In this perspective, family firms having relational and collectivist identity orientations would have a higher level of CSP, while the non-family firms characterized by an individualistic identity orientations consider stakeholders only as transactional partners in the value creation process (Bingham et al., 2010). In family firms, moreover, the financial value creation is not the only or primary goal of the firm (Chrisman et al., 2003). Moreover, a higher CSP could be explained by the more long-term orientation, leading to stronger stakeholder relationships (Sirmon and Hitt, 2003). Finally, the respect for tradition, the importance of the emotional aspects and the loyalty to the location can also explain a positive orientation towards the social issues (Déniz and Cabrera, 2005).

The second perspective, negative relation between social performance and family firms, may be also explained by different arguments. Obtaining a good reputation may not necessarily lead to a positive social performance. The family firm may avoid behaviours considered as socially irresponsible, but this does not necessarily mean acting in a socially responsible way. The family firms owners can desire to protect the family interest by adopting philosophies and practices oriented to the family good and not to the social good (Margolis and Walsh, 2003). Nepotism may be an outcome of this kind of management approach. Nepotism in family firms is negative, because it does not fit with the principle of fairness and it can lead to a distorted perception of the relationship between firm and social environment. Nepotism gives priority to the family rather than the society, giving evidence of 'amoral familism' (Dyer and Whetten, 2006). In this case, the firm can be considered as a source of employment for the family members. This can lead a family firm to act according to lower ethical standards of behaviour.

CORPORATE SOCIAL PERFORMANCE AND BOARD OF DIRECTORS

The board of directors is the body of elected or appointed members who jointly oversee the activities of a firm and has been analysed at length in the literature. Board characteristics and roles cannot be defined in a general way, because they differ widely across various countries and firm types (Charkham, 1995). The board represents one of the governance mechanisms aimed at the control and direction of firms (in addition to ownership, incentives, company law and so on) and it can have many important functions for an organization.

Researchers have used many theoretical perspectives to understand the importance and usefulness of the board of directors. According to agency theory, the board's main function is control of management in order to protect ownership interest (Jensen and Meckling, 1976). Instead, according to stewardship theory, monitoring management action is not necessary because its aim is the same as that of the organization: the improvement of firm performance through innovation, international expansion, sales growth and so on (Muth and Donaldson, 1998). Another theoretical perspective on the board is related to the resource dependence theory and to the importance of controlling critical environmental resources (such as know-how, channels for communicating information, social legitimacy and so on) in order to achieve business success (Pfeffer and Salancik, 1978). In a similar way, stakeholder theory underlines the importance of controlling a specific critical resource, for example the consensus among all stakeholders regarding organization activity. In this sense, the main board function is to resolve possible conflicting interests among the different stakeholder categories (Donaldson and Preston, 1995).

Theories presented show varying points of view adopted to understand the most important board function and, therefore, which function mainly influences board behaviours. For incorporation, board existence is required by law, but it cannot be simply considered a product of regulation. Organizations do not seem to treat the board as a deadweight cost, trying to eliminate its imposition or to maintain its size at the minimum level required by law. According to the previous theories, it is instead more reasonable to consider the board as a market solution to organizational problems, in the perspective of achieving the general objective of business success.

Assuming that the board presence is essential for a firm, many studies have tried to understand the influence the body has had on firm performance. In particular, they have tried to analyse how firm performance changed when there was a different board structure, in terms of its size and composition.

These researchers especially considered the 'financial' aspect of firm performance, probably because it could be measured more easily and objectively. So, regarding size, many studies showed that large boards were generally less effective than smaller ones, emphasizing a negative correlation between board size and firm financial performance (Jensen, 1993; Lipton and Lorsch, 1992). When a board has many directors, it is more likely that some of them take the attitude of a 'free rider' and do not participate in the others' activities. However, other studies have obtained the opposite results (Beiner et al., 2004; Coles et al., 2008).

As to board composition, the most relevant aspect is represented by board proportion of insider/outsider directors. Following Weisbach's classification scheme (1988), a director can be defined as an insider when he works for the firm on a full-time basis and his career is strongly linked to the CEO's success. Outside directors are not employees of the firm, and they do not have extensive dealings with the same firm, aside from their directorship. Thus they are independent of the CEO. Finally, the board includes affiliated or grey directors. Like outsiders, they are not full-time employees of the firm, but they have a long-standing relationship with it, for example as consultants.

Board directors can also be classified as executives, non-executives and independents, and non-executives but non-independents. The first play an important role in day-to-day management of the firm in functions in which they have specific, in-depth knowledge (finance, marketing and so on). They are full-time employees with particular responsibilities, but they are CEO subordinates, so they do not have the ability to control him. Non-executive and independent directors are assigned only if they 'demonstrate an independence of mind, independence of knowledge sources and independence of income' (McCabe and Nowak, 2008, p. 51). They cannot be a substantial shareholder, a significant supplier or a professional advisor of the firm. Finally, non-executive and non-independent directors are those non-executive directors having any form of contractual relationship with the firm (such as major shareholders). Thus they cannot be considered independent (Baysinger and Butler, 1985).

Between these categories of directors, regulators usually define a minimum number of outsiders allowed on a corporate board, on the assumption that independent directors can better resolve agency problems, more effectively acting in the interest of shareholders (Harris and Raviv, 2008). A higher number of outsiders can have a negative effect due to the 'free-rider' problem, but they also provide more expertise on a firm-strategic direction. Thus the optimal number of outsiders is balanced by the two effects. Empirical studies on the insider–outsider ratio have suggested that removing inside and affiliated directors could be harmful for the firm, as they played the important role of providing industry-specific knowledge (Fama and Jensen, 1983; Baysinger and Hoskisson, 1990).

Outsiders are usually less informed on the firm situation than insiders, since they are part-time employees and they sit on different boards.

However, researchers have usually referred to the financial aspect of firm performance. Although some authors are considered the natural link among the shareholders, managers and other stakeholders of a firm (Freeman, 1984; Pye and Pettigrew, 2005), there are few studies available to support a relationship between board of directors and CSP. In other words, a director's role consists in inducing firm policies to improve performance, and the board function aligns the interests of a firm and its stakeholders (Galbraith, Kazanjian, 1986). As firm success is strongly connected to the satisfaction of its different stakeholders, their needs have to be considered by firm leaders in the formulation of the firm strategy. In this sense, directors cover a specific social responsibility role, just favouring the meeting between firm policies and stakeholders' expectation (Hillman and Hitt, 1999; Hung, 2011).

On this assumption, some studies analyse how the board composition carries out its function as defender of stakeholders' interests. In particular, the relationship between board size and CSP was rarely studied, while some researchers have analysed this topic in reference to the board mixture of insider/outsider directors. Based on the assumption that CSP evaluates how well firms meet expectations of stakeholders and environmental concerns (Griffin, 2000), these studies tried to evaluate if insiders and outsiders could have different stakeholder orientations (Wang and Dewhirst, 1992). According to agency theory, outsiders can be more oriented to stakeholders than insiders due to conflicting interests between principals and agents. On the other hand, according to resource dependency theory, outsiders and insiders have the same stakeholder orientation because the first are co-opted by the incumbent management. An increasing outsider proportion is evident and, consequently, a higher interest in the social responsiveness orientation.

For researchers, the principal aspect to consider is the proportion of independent directors on the board. Since the board is responsible for monitoring management, it has to ensure that management's actions are correctly implemented and are in line with the needs of multiple stakeholders. On this point, some studies demonstrate a positive correlation between board independence and CSP, as firms with a higher percentage of independent directors were usually more responsible and sensitive to the different stakeholders' interests (Wang and Dewhirst, 1992; Ibrahim and Angelidis, 1995). Independent board firms exhibit greater concern for philanthropic corporate responsibility and normally obtain better social performance ratings (Coffey and Wang, 1998). However, other researches showed no relationship between board independence and CSP, as insiders and outsiders do not differ in their stakeholder orientation (Wang and Dewhirst, 1992; Chapple and Ucbasaran, 2007).

Other studies focus attention on the figure of the CEO, trying to connect him to the firm social performance. Many studies support the relationship between the CEO and CSP (Hemingway and Maclagan, 2004; Simerly, 2000), but different related aspects were considered. So, a connection between executive incentives and CSP was noted, as the first can influence managerial decisions and encourage strategies having both financial and social implications (Donaldson and Preston, 1995, Jones and Wicks, 1999). For example, forms of short-term bonus payments may lead executives to not build long-term stakeholder relations and to aim at the more immediate 'bottom line' (McGuire et al., 2003).

Other studies suggested that executives' experiences (like an international assignment experience), values and personalities could influence their strategic choices and finally both the financial and social performance of the firm (Slater and Dixon-Fowler, 2009).

THE LINK BETWEEN BOARD OF DIRECTORS AND CORPORATE SOCIAL PERFORMANCE IN FAMILY FIRMS

Considerations of the role and function of a board need further investigation for family firms. In these firms, we can find two different entities with different aims: the family and the firm, which are linked. For this reason, the success of a family firm depends on two different dimensions: business and family dimensions (Sharma, 2006). The business dimension concerns the creation of financial capital, while the family one concerns the creation of emotional capital. The business management and the family management have different governance structures. So, to better understand the management of family firms, it is therefore relevant to consider how the family influences the firm. In particular, a family firm needs to coordinate effectively the two entities to avoid conflicts of interest between them. In this sense, the role of the board is crucial because it connects property (family) and firm, and balances both entities (Lane et al., 2006).

The board role has been studied in a family business context, although often associated with the SMEs firms. The majority of research is descriptive, and empirical approach is rarely used. Despite the fact that authors often use different names to identify board roles, the results substantially differ between two principal board functions in family firms: control and service. The control role was the predominant result since it is based on agency theory, which is the primary theoretical paradigm used (Johannisson and Huse, 2000; Mustakallio et al., 2002). For these studies, board control is essential since the influence of family loyalties and the relevance of the decisions taken by family managers bring about an agency problem in family firms (Gimeno Sandig et al., 2006). Instead the service role usually includes multiple theoretical perspectives, but in particular it is based on the resource dependence perspective. In this sense, these other studies underline the importance of the advice, counsel or strategy role the board has in a family firm, and also in planning succession (Harris, 1989).

CEOs hold a responsible position in family firms, as they have a great power to direct the running of the board of directors. In the CEO perspective, the service role is probably the most important function of the board. Also, its control role is essential to negotiate the succession and to balance the owner/manager behaviour in the firm.

In family businesses, all aspects of the relationship between board structure and firm performance may be relevant, so some authors also study this topic, referring to the peculiarities that characterize this kind of firms. In particular, they try to analyse how much of a contribution the board makes to the firm performance when the firm has a family ownership and some family members form part of the board. While Huse (1994) supports the importance of finding a balance between independence and interdependence in family firms, the independent status of directors is sometimes considered less important in family businesses (Lane et al., 2006).

Some authors have analysed the added value of the board as a group (Van Den Heuvel et al., 2006; Johannisson and Huse, 2000), while others have tried to estimate the contribution of individual directors (Whisler, 1988; Schwartz and Barnes, 1991). These studies refer only to the firm's financial performance.

Several indicators can be identified to determine family representation. The most used is the number or percentage of seats held by family members. The sense of membership may lead to benefits in terms of motivation, emotional involvement and commitment of family members in management. While the presence of family members on the board could lead to greater conflict with possible non-family shareholders or other stakeholder categories, the presence of non-family members could lead to an increase of external relationships and thus to the use of additional and various types of resources (Filatotchev and Bishop, 2002). The presence of non-family members creates a greater openness due to their ability to consider issues not directly related to owner family interests.

Another indicator of family representation is the percentage of family members among the executives. A high percentage may be evidence of nepotism, which means a possible lack of professional competence with adverse consequences for the firm (Sciascia and Mazzola, 2008). In general, the use of external managers can provide family firms with greater rationality and objectivity in decision-making processes and strategic management (Ibrahim et al., 2001). Dyer (1989) argues, however, that outsiders have greater difficulty in understanding the human issues and have an excessive focus on the short term. Hall and Nordqvist (2008) argue that formal and cultural competencies play a more important role than being a family member.

To define family representation, if the chairman or CEO is a family member (or not) is another factor that should be taken into account. This aspect is also important to define the leadership in terms of relations between family and non-family members (Nicholson and Björnberg, 2006). Many empirical studies have shown that the presence of a CEO family member is positively linked with performance when the CEO was the firm founder, while it had a negative effect when he was one of the successors (Villalonga and Amit, 2006). This is usually explained by the fact that the founders are self-selected to be better than average in terms of business ability (Thomsen, 2008). The relationship between the presence of a chairman or CEO family member and social performance has not been studied; thus our study aims to contribute to the academic debate.

Finally, another variable to consider is the number of family generations on the board. The presence of multiple generations on the board could have two different explanations. On the one hand, it could be a demonstration of careful 'generation change' planning and an important sign of continuity for family involvement in the firm. This could be the manifestation of a firm's wish to preserve and transmit to succeeding generations. On the other hand, however, the presence of several generations may signal only a formal renewal that does not exist in substance, or an attempt to maintain family balance and not to improve firm performance.

HYPOTHESES OF THE RESEARCH

This chapter represents a further step to the study of the link between board structure and social performance and of differences in the behaviour of family and non-family firms. We assume that a board works differently in a family firm than in a non-family firm due to peculiarities of a family business. To develop our hypotheses, we suppose that the presence of family members on the board has a positive effect on social performance as they have a natural attention toward social issues. This is connected to the higher standards of ethical and social behaviour that usually characterize family firms – family reputation, organizational identity orientation, long-term orientation.

As for the board size, we assume that while in non-family firms the free-rider problem leads to a negative link between number of directors and social performance, in family firms this relationship is not so direct. For these firms, in fact, a larger board can mean a bigger number of both family and non-family members, leading to different effects on social performance. So our first hypothesis is:

Hypothesis 1   Board size is negatively related to social performance in non-family firms, while the two concepts are not related in family firms.

As for executive directors, we suppose that an increase of them has a negative effect on social performance in non-family firms. As they are CEO subordinates and short term oriented, executives are unlikely to build long-term stakeholder relations aiming at more immediate 'bottom-line' benefit. Instead, as seen with board size, in family firms more executives may entail a higher number of both family and non-family members, so it is not possible to suppose a correlation between the two variables. Our second hypothesis is:

Hypothesis 2   The number of executives is negatively related to social performance in non-family firms, while the two concepts are not related in family firms.

As for independent directors, we suppose that they are more oriented to stakeholders than insiders due to conflicting interests existing between principals and agents. According to our assumption, firms with a higher percentage of independent directors should be more responsible and sensitive to stakeholders' interests. Also, in family firms independents more than insiders account for the social responsibility role of favouring the meeting between firm policies and stakeholders' expectations, so our third hypothesis is:

Hypothesis 3   The number of independents is positively related to social performance both in non-family firms and in family firms.

The presence of family members on the board is a key characteristic of family firms. Considering that family members take into account social issues, we suppose that a higher family representation contributes to align better stakeholder interests and firm purposes. We analyse this characteristic in terms of percentage of seats held by family members, percentage of family members among the executives, whether or not the chairman or CEO is a family member and the number of family generations on the board. For this, our last hypothesis is:

Hypothesis 4   In family firms, family representation on the board is positively connected with social performance.

METHODOLOGY

Sample and Data Collection

The sample comprises Italian firms quoted on the S&P/MIB 40 stock market index of Borsa Italiana (the Italian national stock exchange). It should be noted that in June of 2009, the index changed its name from the FTSE MIB Index to the S&P/MIB 40 Index, which includes the 40 most liquid and quoted Italian companies. The index maintains sector weights of the Italian stock market.

From this list of companies, financial firms and those that did not have social ratings were excluded. With these restrictions, the final sample comprised 29 companies, using 2008 information, and of 25 companies, using 2009 information.

Family and non-family firms were distinguished in order to analyse the significant differences between the boards in the two types of firms. To identify the family firms, two criteria were followed: a family owning at least 30 per cent of the capital of the company; and at least one family member on the board. Both criteria reflect the two characteristics that the doctrine uses to identify family firms: ownership (with a high enough percentage to ensure control); and family involvement in management and strategic direction. The threshold of 30 per cent is significant in the Italian context because it is associated with the legal obligation to launch a takeover bid on the entire capital by a person who reaches this ownership percentage. That is, the law considers this threshold sufficient to allow for control of the firm, and if a family holds 30 per cent of the shares, it will control the firm. To avoid uncertainty in defining control of the firm, the research set as a condition that the family had to have twice the number of shares as the second-largest shareholder. The presence of at least one family member on the board should signify that the family does not view the company as a mere financial investment, but that it is involved in firm management. Considering this distinction, the sample for 2008 includes 14 family firms and 15 non-family firms, while the sample for 2009 includes 12 family firms and 13 non-family firms.

Description of Variables

Two social ratings were chosen for measuring social performance in an attempt to reduce the subjectivity of the evaluation without limiting its reliability.

The choice to use social ratings does not guarantee absolute objectivity, but it ensures that the criteria established by rating agencies, when they act with methodological rigour and transparency, are applied uniformly. To assess the social performance of Italian listed companies, the AEI standard ethics rating and accountability rating were chosen. These indicators have two different approaches to social performance, which may limit the subjectivity of the criteria chosen by the two agencies.

The Agenzia Europea degli Investimenti (AEI – European Investment Agency) is an Economic Interest European Group (EIEG) that aims to promote corporate social responsibility. The methodology adopted to develop the AEI rating is based on the evaluation of internal rules of corporate social responsibility adopted voluntarily by companies. The evaluation process focuses on three areas: competition, ownership and management. It is based on official documents issued by the European Union, the OECD and the United Nations.

The accountability rating is developed by CSRNETWORK (a consultancy dedicated to corporate social responsibility) and AccountAbility (an international institute dedicated to promoting organizational accountability). The rating evaluates companies in reference to four domains: strategic intent; governance and management; engagement; and operational performance. For each of these domains, analysts assess the firms' social behaviour. The difference from the AEI rating derives not only from the different areas investigated, but also from the fact that the accountability rating is more stakeholder-oriented. This is emphasized, in particular, by explicit reference to the concepts of 'accountability' and 'engagement'.

The two social ratings express the final assessment of the company through two different scales. The AEI rating expresses eight possible scores: EEE, EEE−, EE+, EE, EE−, E+, E, E−.[1] The Accountability rating, by contrast, uses a scale from 0 to 100. To homogenize the two assessments, both were transformed to a scale from 0 to 3.

To examine how the structure of the board affects performance, board characteristics considered to be significant were identified. With the purpose of verifying if a larger board is more or less effective than a smaller one, board dimension was analysed, expressed as the number of directors on the board. The research identified how many directors were executive, that is, whether directors have an effective role in the day-to-day management of the firm. This variable was expressed as a percentage of the board dimension (size of the board). Finally, to define board composition, the presence of independent directors was used. According to the self-discipline code of the Italian quoted companies, a director can be considered independent when:

- he does not have extensive dealings or any form of contractual relationship with the firm (or with its controlled firms or with its management) aside from their directorship;
- he is not a shareholder of the firm in which he is a director;
- he is not related to any firm executive.

According to this definition, an executive director cannot be considered independent, but not all non-executive directors are independent. This is why board composition was defined as a third variable (presence of independent directors), expressed as a percentage of the board dimension.

To provide a more in-depth analysis of family firms, other important characteristics were identified. 'Family representation' was evaluated by a number of variables in order to analyse its tendency in the sample firms.

The first is the number of family members on the board. This was defined using all the directors having the surname of the family owner. This assumption has probably led the researchers to underestimate this number. Subsequently, it was verified if the board president and/or the CEO were family members. Also considered were how many executive directors of the board were family members, as well as how many family generations were included on the board (using degree of kinship between family members of the board).

STATISTICAL ANALYSES

Multivariate Analysis

In order to test the hypotheses, linear mixed-effect models were conducted for the sample firms, where the dependent variable included one of the social performance indicators (AEI score and Accountability score).

Our database was made up of observations of 15 family firms and 16 non-family firms for two years (2008 and 2009). As our sample was small and the assumption that one of the estimators is efficient is violated if the observations are clustered or weighted, we carried out the linear mixed-effect model with both fixed and random effects. In general, a linear mixed-effects model is any model which satisfies (Laird and Ware, 1982):

$$y_i = X_i\beta + Z_i b_i + \varepsilon_i$$
$$b_i \sim N_q(0, \Psi)$$
$$\varepsilon_i \sim N_{ni}(0, \sigma^2 \Lambda_i)$$

where

- y_i is the $n_i \times 1$ response vector for observations in group i;
- X_i is the $n_i \times p$ model matrix for the fixed effects for observations in group i;
- β is the $p \times 1$ vector of fixed-effect coefficients;
- Z_i is the $n_i \times q$ model matrix for the random effects for observations in group i;
- b_i is the $q \times 1$ vector of random-effect coefficients for group i;
- ε_i is the $n_i \times 1$ vector of errors for observations in group i;
- Ψ is the $q \times q$ covariance matrix for the random effects;
- $\sigma^2 \Lambda_i$ is the $n_i \times n_i$ covariance matrix for the errors in group i.

We constructed two linear mixed-effect models, one with AEI score as the dependent variable and the other with Accountability score as the dependent variable. As independent variables, we used Dimension, Executive and Independent as proxies for the hypotheses to be tested. Consequently, the following equations were created for every dependent variable:

AEI score$_i$ / Accountability score$_i$ = β_0 + β_1 Dimension$_i$ + β_2 Executive$_i$ + β_3 Independent$_i$ + ε_i

where

- AEI score = social rating elaborated by Agenzia Europea degli Investimenti;
- Accountability score = social rating elaborated by AccountAbility;
- Dimension = number of members on the board;
- Executive = number of executive members / Total members on the board;
- Independent = number of independent members / Total members on the board.

The equations developed divided the sample into family and non-family firms in order to draw more relevant conclusions.

Complementary Analysis

Furthermore, a multivariate regression analysis was applied (using ordinary least squares (OLS) estimation algorithm with forward stepwise estimation) to more deeply understand the determinants of the board (for family firms) that influence social performance. This estimation procedure only chose variables to be included in the regression model: those that allowed for the best fit in statistical terms. Variables were added to the model one by one. At each step, the independent variable that passed the entry requirements,[2] and had a higher correlation (in absolute value) with the dependent variable, was selected for inclusion in the model. The selection of variables was concluded when no more variables passed the entry requirements. If all the variables were included, the estimated model would be as follows:

AEI score$_i$/ Accountability score$_i$ = α_0 + β_1 Number of family members on the board$_i$ + β_2 President family member$_i$ + β_3 Number of executive family member on the board$_i$ + β_4 CEO family member$_i$ + β_5 Number of family generations on the board$_i$ + u_i

RESULTS

Table 4.1 shows the results of our study for the total, family and non-family samples. These regressions were carried out in order to determine if board characteristics influenced social performance. In the first row of Table 4.1, it can be seen that the AEI score was inversely correlated with the Dimension and directly correlated with the Independent variable in the total sample. That is, firms with larger boards had lower AEI scores and those with more independent members had higher AEI scores. The non-family sub-group showed the same behaviour as the total sample but, with regard to the family firms, all board characteristics analysed were not related to the AEI score.

When the Accountability score was used as dependent variable, the Executive variable affected negatively and significantly in the total sample. The more executives on the boards, the lower the social performance, and the same occurred for the family sample. Moreover, it was found that the Dimension of the board was positively related to this social score for family firms. These results are interesting because this is the only regression for family firms that showed significant variables. The results indicate that family firms with a larger board and fewer executive members were more aware of social performance.

Table 4.2 shows the results of the complementary analysis for the family sample. It should not be surprising that only two/three variables were significant in every equation, as there were 15 family firms and the more variables introduced into a model, the fewer degrees of freedom the model has.

In the first regression, the presence of family members and executive family members

Table 4.1   Multivariate regression results

Dependent		Independents			Wald χ^2	Random-effects parameters
AEI score	Constant	Dimension	Executive	Independent		
Total sample	**2.002*****	**−0.143*****	−0.019	**0.189*****	26.31	0.5606
p-value	0.000	0.000	0.732	0.000	0.000	
AEI score						
Family firms	**1.416*****	−0.032	−0.091	0.007	4.620	0.479
p-value	0.002	0.590	0.182	0.381	0.201	
AEI score						
Non-family firms	**2.042*****	**−0.181*****	0.120	**0.224****	19.43	0.607
p-value	0.000	0.000	0.331	0.000	0.000	
Acc. score						
Total sample	**0.985*****	0.027	**−0.095****	0.038	9.660	0. 469
p-value	0.000	0.330	0.035	0.326	0.021	
Acc. score						
Family firms	−0.018	**0.108*****	**−0.122*****	0.035	32.76	0.328
p-value	0.948	0.002	0.004	0.487	0.000	
Acc. score						
Non-family firms	**1.547*****	−0.019	−0.040	0.025	0.710	0.504
p-value	0.000	0.597	0.683	0.609	0.871	

Notes:
*   Statistically significant at the 10% level.
**   Statistically significant at the 5% level.
***   Statistically significant at the 1% level.

Table 4.2   Standardized regression coefficients and statistical significance

Model		β	*F*-value	R^2	R^2 corrected
AEI score	Number of family members	0.578*	2.35	0.227	0.1306
		(0.054)	(0.127)		
	Number of executive family members	−0.436**			
		(0.046)			
Acc. score	CEO family members	1.770***	7.85	0.581	0.507
		(0.000)	(0.001)		
	President family members	−0.534***			
		(0.006)			
	Number of executive family members	−0.308***			
		(0.007)			

Notes:
p-values in parentheses.
*   Statistically significant at the 10% level.
**   Statistically significant at the 5% level.
***   Statistically significant at the 1% level.

on the board was positively and negatively related to social behaviour, respectively. That is, a board with more family members obtained a higher social performance and a lower percentage of executives on the board increased social performance. We must be cautious about these results, as the *F*-value is low.

As for the Accountability regression, CEO family member, president family member and the number of executive family members were significant variables. CEO family member was positively correlated with social performance, and a president family member and more executive family members were negatively correlated with this indicator. If the CEO was a family member, the social performance increased; however, companies with president family members obtained a lower performance. When the number of executive family members was higher, social performance decreased. For family firms, the possibility that the CEO was a family member was the only characteristic that improved social performance. The other board characteristics had no positive influence on social performance. In this regression, the *F*-value and the R^2 values indicate that there was no misspecification error.

CONCLUSIONS

Our analysis aimed to obtain new evidence about family firms, investigating the link between their board structure and social performance. The analysis shows that board dimension of non-family firms was negatively related to the AEI rating, but it was not statistically related to the Accountability rating. For the family firms, instead, board size was not related to the AEI rating and positively correlated with the Accountability rating. This means that our first hypothesis was confirmed for one rating and, coherently with previous research, the size of the non-family firm's board should not be too large to obtain better social performance (Harris and Raviv, 2008). In family firms, instead, this negative correlation was not verified, due to the presence of family members on the board and supposed positive effects on the firm' social behaviour. Our first hypothesis is only partially confirmed owing to the contradictory result obtained for the second rating. This contradiction may be explained from another perspective: the resource-based theory, which emphasizes the relevance of the degree of knowledge, relationships and other strategic resources provided by directors (Pfeffer and Salancik, 1978).

As for the number of executives on the board, the analysis showed that this variable was not related to the AEI rating for both non-family and family firms. However, this was not entirely confirmed for the Accountability rating as a negative correlation between the Executive variable and social performance is verified for the family firms. For the non-family firms, it was supposed that a higher number of executives entailed a weaker attention to social issues, but it is more important to assess the individual qualities of this kind of directors than executive numbers. The unexpected result obtained for the family firms (e.g. negative correlation with Accountability rating) may be justified as executives are frequently family members, which could be considered a negative sign of nepotism, meaning a possible lack of professional competence (Sciascia and Mazzola, 2008). For these reasons, our second hypothesis is almost never confirmed.

As for the number of independent directors, our study verified a positive correlation between the AEI score and social performance for non-family sample. This is consistent with our assumption that an independent director should guarantee the interests of all categories of stakeholders. So the improvement in social performance is not surprising when the number of independents increases. Our third hypothesis is not entirely confirmed because other factors affect this relationship. A definition to identify the status of independent director that really guarantees a formal but not necessarily a substantial independence, and theoretical requirements of independence of 'mind' and of 'knowledge sources' (McCabe and Nowak, 2008), are not verifiable in our study. Moreover, the effective fulfilment of the independents' role depends on their individual qualities and personality traits.

To try to better understand the link between board and social performance, we carried out a complementary analysis for family firms. Considering the AEI rating, we found that number of family members and executive family members on the board were significant variables. The positive correlation between number of family members and social performance showed that their presence on the board could lead to better social behaviour. As can be seen, family involvement entails the pursuit of goals linked to social reputation and also a greater focus on traditional family values, which can improve social performance. The negative relationship between the number of executive family members and social performance suggests that a high degree of professionalization is needed on boards, which cannot be always ensured by an executive director who is family member. It is not enough to incorporate social values into the organization; adequate capabilities and skills are also needed to be socially effective. The Accountability rating regression confirms a negative correlation between the number of executive family members and social performance. Moreover, we found other interesting results: the positive correlation with CEO family member and the negative correlation with president family member. The former means that although it is preferable to have a lower number of executives on the board, a board with a CEO family member can obtain a better social performance. The latter correlation means that it is more likely to have a better social performance when the president of the board is not a family member. This result can be considered surprising, but an explanation may be found in the different CEO and president roles in the Italian corporate governance system: the former is more substantial and the latter is more formal. According to this perspective, the best solution may be to incorporate a CEO family member into a board with a high percentage of professional executives. Summarizing, we can assert that the relationship between 'family representation' on the board and social performance (fourth hypothesis) is weakly verified, probably because individual, organizational, structural and cultural factors (such as the generation of the firm, the age, the size, the business sector) that characterize the firms can affect its social aptitude.

To better understand our results it is important to consider that the sample size we investigated is quite limited. For this reason our conclusions cannot be fully generalized but they remain significant as they refer to a representative sample of the most liquid and capitalized Italian firms (e.g. the firms included in the S&P/MIB 40 Index). We considered only the Italian context and its specific legal and economic characteristics; that is, an economic environment different from that used in previous research, that is, Anglo-Saxon countries.

This study contributes to the literature because it deals with the link between board structure and social performance of family firms, rarely investigated in previous studies.

So this research could have important implications for the family firms' field. First, it confirmed that the impact of the board structure on social performance is different in family and non-family firms. This implies that rules/principles of board structure defined for the non-family firms are not necessarily suitable for family firms. Second, our results showed the relevance of the qualities and capacities of directors for their specific status on the board (e.g. independent, executive and so on). Our results corroborate that social performance depends on the effectiveness and efficiency of the Board's decision-making process, as well as on the corporate culture and the individual culture of directors. The role of the board, in general, and that of administrators, in particular, may be important in shaping corporate culture and hence the sensitivity and awareness of the corporate sociopolitical dimension of management, if it is acknowledged at a leadership role level. Further studies must be conducted to expand the sample, analyse other economic and legal contexts, and study in more depth the impact of directors' individual characteristics.

ACKNOWLEDGEMENT

This study was carried out with the financial support of the Spanish National R&D Plan through research project ECO2010-17463 (ECON FEDER).

NOTES

1. EEE is the ideal, EE is the median and E is below average. The signs + and − indicate situations slightly above or below the assessment to which they are related. In case of serious violations of principles of reference, the rating of a company is suspended.
2. 'Significance criteria' were used as the entry requirement. According to these criteria, only the variables that contributed significantly to the model fit were included in the regression model. The individual contribution of a variable to the model fit was established by testing, from the partial correlation coefficients, the hypothesis of independence between that variable and the dependent variable. The significance criterion applied was that the introduced variable was significant at the 5 per cent level (10 per cent for the probability of taking the variable out of the model). Likewise, the increase in the R^2 value as a result of including the variable in the model had to be statistically different from zero.

REFERENCES

Aguilera, R., Rupp, D., Williams, C. and Ganapathi, J. (2007), 'Putting the S back in corporate social responsibility: a multilevel theory of social change in organizations', *Academy of Management Review*, **32**, 836–63.
Banerjee, S.B., Iyer, E. and Kashyap, R. (2003), 'Corporate environmentalism and its antecedents: influence of industry type', *Journal of Marketing*, **67**, 106–22.
Bansal, P. (2003), 'From issues to actions: the importance of individual concerns and organizational values in responding to natural environmental issues', *Organization Science*, **14**, 510–27.
Baysinger, B. and Butler, H. (1985), 'Corporate governance and the board of governors: performance effects of changes in board composition', *Journal of Law, Economics and Organization*, **1**, 101–24.
Baysinger, B. and Hoskisson, R. (1990), 'The composition of boards of directors and strategic control: effects on corporate strategy', *Academy of Management Review*, **15**(1), 72–87.
Beiner, S., Drobetz, W., Schmid, F. and Zimmerman, H. (2004), 'Is board size an independent corporate governance mechanism?', *Kyklos*, **17**(3), 327–56.

Bingham, J., Gibb Dyer, W. Smith, I. and Adams, G.L. (2010), 'A stakeholder identity approach to corporate social performance in family firms', *Journal of Business Ethics*, **99**, 565–85.

Brickson, S.L. (2007), 'Organizational identity orientation: the genesis of the role of the firm and distinct forms of social value', *Academy of Management Review*, **32**, 864–88.

Carroll, A.B. (1979), 'A three-dimensional conceptual model of corporate social performance', *Academy of Management Review*, **4**(4), 497–505.

Carroll, A.B. (1991), 'The pyramid of social responsibility: toward the moral management of organizational stakeholders', *Business Horizons*, **34**, 39–48.

Catturi, G. (ed.) (2003), *L'azienda universale*, Padova: Cedam.

Chapple, W. and Ucbasaran, D. (2007), 'The effects of corporate governance on corporate social responsibility', unpublished paper.

Charkham, J. (ed.) (1995), *Keeping Good Company. A Study of Corporate Governance in Five Countries*, Oxford: Oxford University Press.

Chrisman, J.J., Chua, J.H. and Litz, R. (2003), 'A unified systems perspective of family firm performance: an extension and integration', *Journal of Business Venturing*, **18**, 467–72.

Clarkson, M. (1995), 'A stakeholder framework for analyzing and evaluating corporate social performance', *Academy of Management Review*, **20**(1), 92–117.

Coffey, B.S. and Wang, J. (1998), 'Board diversity and managerial control as predictors of corporate social performance', *Journal of Business Ethics*, **17**(1), 1595–603.

Coles, J.L., Daniel, N.D. and Naveen, L. (2008), 'Boards: does one size fit all?', *Journal of Financial Economics*, **87**, 329–56.

Déniz, M. and Cabrera, M.K. (2005), 'Corporate social responsibility and family business in Spain', *Journal of Business Ethics*, **56**, 27–41.

Donaldson, T. and Preston, L.E. (1995), 'The stakeholder theory of the corporation: concepts, evidence and implications', *Academy of Management Review*, **20**(1), 65–91.

Dyer, W.G. (ed.) (1986), *Cultural Change in Family Firms*, San Francisco, CA: Jossey-Bass.

Dyer, W.G. (1989), 'Integrating professional management into a family owned business', *Family Business Review*, **2**(3), 221–35.

Dyer, W.G. and Whetten, D.A. (2006), 'Family firms and social responsibility: preliminary evidence from the S&P 500', *Entrepreneurship Theory and Practice*, **30**, 785–802.

Fama, E. and Jensen, M. (1983), 'Separation of ownership and control', *Journal of Law and Economics*, **22**(2), 301–25.

Filatotchev, I. and Bishop, K. (2002), 'Board composition, share ownership and underpricing of UK IPO firms', *Strategic Management Journal*, **23**(10), 941–55.

Freeman, R.E. (ed.) (1984), *Strategic Management: A Stakeholder Approach*, London: Pitman.

Galbraith, J.R. and Kazanjian, R. (1986), *Strategy Implementation: The Role of Structure in Process*, St Paul, MN: West Publishing.

Garriga, E. and Melé, D. (2004), 'Corporate social responsibility theories: mapping the territory', *Journal of Business Ethics*, **53**, 51–71.

Gimeno Sandig, A., Labadie, G.J., Saris, W. and Mendoza Mayordomo, X. (2006), 'Internal factors of family business performance: an integrated theoretical model', in P.Z. Poutziouris, K.X. Smyrnios and S.B. Klein (eds), *Handbook of Research on Family Business*, Cheltenham, UK and Northampton, MA, USA: Edward Elgar, pp.145–64.

Griffin, J. (2000), 'Corporate social performance: research directions for the 21st century', *Business and Society*, **39**, 479–91.

Griffin, J.J and Mahon, J.F. (1997), 'The corporate social performance and corporate financial performance debate', *Business and Society*, **36**(1), 5–31.

Hall, A. and Nordqvist, M. (2008), 'Professional management in family businesses: toward an extended understanding', *Family Business Review*, **21**(1), 51–69.

Harris, T.B. (1989), 'Some comments on family firm boards', *Family Business Review*, **2**(2), 150–52.

Harris, M. and Raviv, A. (2008), 'A theory of board control and size', *The Review of Financial Studies*, **21**(4), 1797–832.

Hemingway, C.A. and Maclagan, P.W. (2004), 'Managers' personal values as drivers of corporate social responsibility', *Journal of Business Ethics*, **5**, 33–44.

Hillman, A.J. and Hitt, M.A. (1999), 'Corporate political strategy formulation: a model of approach, participation, and strategy decisions', *Academy of Management Review*, **24**(4), 825–42.

Hung, H. (2011), 'Directors' roles in corporate social responsibility: a stakeholder perspective', *Journal of Business Ethics*, published online, 30 April.

Huse, M. (1994), 'Board–management relations in small firms: the paradox of simultaneous independence and interdependence', *Small Business Economics*, **6**(1), 55–72.

Ibrahim, N. and Angelidis, J. (1995), 'The corporate social responsiveness orientation of board members: are there differences between inside and outside directors?', *Journal of Business Ethics*, **14**(5), 405–10.

Ibrahim, A., Soufani, K. and Lam, J. (2001), 'A study of succession in a family firm', *Family Business Review*, **14**(3), 245–58.

Jensen, M. (1993), 'The modern industrial revolution, exit and the failure of internal control systems', *Journal of Finance*, **48**(3), 831–80.

Jensen, M.C. and Meckling, W.H. (1976), 'Theory of the firm: managerial behaviour, agency costs and ownership structure', *Journal of Financial Economics*, **3**, 305–60.

Johannisson, B. and Huse, M. (2000), 'Recruiting outside board members in the small family business: an ideological challenge', *Entrepreneurship and Regional Development*, **12**(4), 353–78.

Johnson, H.L. (2001), 'Corporate social audits: this time around', *Business Horizons*, **44**(3), 29–36.

Jones, T. and Wicks, A. (1999), 'Convergent stakeholder theory', *Academy of Management Review*, **24**(2), 208–21.

Laird, N.M. and Ware, J.H. (1982), 'Random-effects models for longitudinal data', *Biometrics*, **38**, 963–74.

Lane, S., Astrachan, J., Keyt, A. and McMillan, K. (2006), 'Guidelines for family business boards of directors', *Family Business Review*, **19**, 147–67.

Lipton, M. and Lorsch, J. (1992), 'A modest proposal for improved corporate governance', *Business Lawyer*, **48**(1), 59–77.

Margolis, J.D. and Walsh, J.P. (2003), 'Misery loves companies: rethinking social initiatives by business', *Administrative Science Quarterly*, **48**, 268–305.

Matten, D. Crane, A. and Chapple, W. (2003), 'Behind the mask: revealing the true face of corporate citizenship', *Journal of Business Ethics*, **45**(1–2), 109–20.

McCabe, M. and Nowak, M. (2008), 'The independent director on the board of company directors', *Managerial Auditing Journal*, **23**(6), 545–66.

McGuire, J., Dow, S. and Argheyd, K. (2003), 'CEO incentives and corporate social performance', *Journal of Business Ethics*, **45**, 341–59.

Muller, A. and Kolk, A. (2010), 'Extrinsic and intrinsic drivers of corporate social performance: evidence from foreign and domestic firms in Mexico', *Journal of Management Studies*, **47**(1), 1–26.

Muñoz, M.J., Rivera, J.M. and Moneva, J.M. (2008), 'Evaluating sustainability in organisations with a fuzzy logic approach', *Industrial Management & Data Systems*, **108**(6), 829–41.

Mustakallio, M., Autio, E. and Zahra, S.A. (2002), 'Relational and contractual governance in family firms: effects on strategic decision making', *Family Business Review*, **15**, 205–22.

Muth, M. and Donaldson, L. (1998), 'Stewardship theory and board structure: a contingency approach', *Corporate Governance: An International Review*, **6**(1), 5–29.

Nicholson, N. and Björnberg, Å. (2006), 'Critical leader relationships in family firms', in P.Z. Poutziouris, K.X. Smyrnios and S.B. Klein (eds) *Handbook of Research on Family Business*, Cheltenham, UK and Northampton, MA, USA: Edward Elgar, pp. 106–24.

Pfeffer, J. and Salancik, G. (eds) (1978), *The External Control of Organizations: A Resource Dependence Perspective*, New York: Harper & Row.

Pye, A.J. and Pettigrew, A. (2005), 'Studying board context, process and dynamics: some challenges for the future', *British Journal of Management*, **16**(1), 27–38.

Schwartz, M.A. and Barnes, L.B. (1991), 'Outside boards and family businesses: another look', *Family Business Review*, **4**, 269–85.

Sciascia, S. and Mazzola, P. (2008), 'Family involvement in ownership and management: exploring nonlinear effects on performance', *Family Business Review*, **21**(4), 331–45.

Sharma, P. (2006), 'An overview of the field of family business studies: current status and directions for the future', in P.Z. Poutziouris, K.X. Smyrnios and S.B. Klein (eds), *Handbook of Research on Family Business*, Cheltenham, UK and Northampton, MA, USA: Edward Elgar, pp. 25–55.

Simerly, R.L. (2000), 'A theoretical examination of the relationship between chief executive officers and corporate social performance', *International Journal of Management*, **17**(2), 218–23.

Sirmon, D.G. and Hitt, M.A. (2003), 'Managing resources: linking unique resources, management, and wealth creation in family firms', *Entrepreneurship: Theory and Practice*, **27**, 339–58.

Slater, D.J. and Dixon-Fowler, H.R. (2009), 'CEO international assignment experience and corporate social performance', *Journal of Business Ethics*, **89**, 473–89.

Swanson, D.L. (1995), 'Addresing a theoretical problem by reorienting the corporate social performance model', *The Academy of Management Review*, **20**(1), 43–64.

Swanson, D.L. (1999), 'Toward an integrative theory of business and society: a research strategy to corporate social performance', *Academy of Management Review*, **24**(3), 506–21.

Thomsen, S. (ed.) (2008), *An Introduction to Corporate Governance. Mechanism and Systems*, Copenhagen: DJØF Publishing.

Uhlaner, L.M., van Goor-Balk, H.J.M.A. and Masurel, E. (2004), 'Family business and corporate social responsibility in a sample of Dutch firms', *Journal of Small Business and Enterprise Development*, **11**(2), 186–94.

Ullmann, A. (1985), 'Data in search of a theory: a critical examination of the relationship among social perform-ance, social disclosure and economic performance of U.S. firms', *Academy of Management Review*, **10**(3), 540–57.

Van Den Heuvel, J., Van Gils, A. and Voordeckers, W. (2006), 'Board roles in small and medium-sized family businesses: performance and importance', *Corporate governance*, **14**, 467–85.

Villalonga, B. and Amit, R. (2006). 'How do family ownership, control and management affect firm value?', *Journal of Financial Economics*, **80**, 385–417.

Waddock, S.A. and Graves, S.B. (1997), 'The corporate social performance–financial performance link', *Strategic Management Journal*, **18**(4), 303–19.

Wang, J. and Dewhirst, H.D. (1992), 'Boards of directors and stakeholder orientation', *Journal of Business Ethics*, **11**(2), 115–23.

Wartick, S.L. and Cochran, P.L. (1985), 'The evolution of the corporate social performance model', *Academy of Management Review*, **10**, 758–69.

Weisbach, M.S. (1988), 'Outside directors and CEO turnover', *Journal of Financial Economics*, **20**, 431–60.

Whisler, T.L. (1988), 'The role of the board in the threshold firm', *Family Business Review*, **1**, 309–12.

Wood, D.J. (1991), 'Corporate social performance revisited', *Academy of Management Review*, **16**(4), 691–718.

Wood, D.J. (ed.) (1994), *Business and Society*, New York: HarperCollins.

Wood, D.J. (2010), 'Measuring corporate social performance: a review', *International Journal of Management Reviews*, **12**, 50–84.

Wood, D.J. and Jones, E.J. (1995), 'Stakeholder mismatching: a theoretical problem in empirical research on corporate social performance', *The International Journal of Organizational Analysis*, **3**(3), 229–67.

Zocchi, W. (ed.) (2004), *Il family business*, Milano: Il Sole24ore.

5 Board of directors and generational effect in Spanish non-listed family firms[1]

Blanca Arosa, Txomin Iturralde and Amaia Maseda

1 INTRODUCTION

Corporate governance is one of the topics receiving increased attention in the management research area. Despite the increasing attention of management scholars to corporate governance and boards of directors, empirical evidence on the relationship between board composition and corporate financial performance on the other hand is still equivocal (Minichilli et al., 2009).

The number of papers studying board composition is very large. Researchers have analysed the effect of board size (Eisenberg et al., 1998; Fernández et al., 1997; Huther, 1997; Yermack, 1996), board composition (Baysinger and Butler, 1985; Fiegener et al., 2000; Hermalin and Weisbach, 2003; Voordeckers et al., 2007; Jaskiewicz and Klein, 2007; Bammens et al., 2008; Sacristán-Navarro and Gómez-Ansón, 2009; Arosa et al., 2010) on corporate performance, the distinction between inside and outside boards (Finkelstein and Hambrick, 1996; Johnson et al., 1996), but despite numerous studies, the relationship between board characteristics and corporate performance remains unclear (Oxelheim and Randøy, 2003; Anderson and Reeb, 2004).

Some empirical findings regarding board composition in relation to performance finds that outside directors could improve board effectiveness and firm performance. For instance, Weisbach (1988) and McKnight and Mira (2003) find a positive and significant relationship between outsiders' proportion and firm value. However, others, for example Baysinger and Butler (1985), Hermalin and Weisbach (1991), and Agrawal and Knoeber (1996), find a negative relationship between the proportion of outside directors and firm performance. Dalton et al. (1998), De Andrés et al. (2005) and Jackling and Johl (2009) find no relation between the two variables. This lack of significant results seems to be due to two common characteristics of past research on boards of directors: the almost exclusive reliance on agency theory, and the resulting strong emphasis on board control tasks (Minichilli et al., 2009). Besides, the existence of these contradictory results may depend also on the sample, the development of the markets and measures of firm performance.

Family firms are the predominant form of business in economies around the world, and they contribute extensively to gross national product and job creation. Most of these family firms can be categorized as small or medium-sized (Corbetta and Montemerlo, 1999). However, there is little research on the effect of the role of outside directors on firm performance in privately owned family SMEs. Family firm governance and accountability differ from practices in non-family businesses (Bammens et al., 2008).

Boards of directors are a central institution in the internal governance of a company. In addition to strategic direction, they provide a key monitoring function in dealing with agency problems in the firm (Fama, 1980; Jensen, 1993). In a diffuse ownership context, the monitoring function must focus on reducing the agency problem between disperse shareholders and management (Hermalin and Weisbach, 2001). In the context of companies with high ownership concentration, the agency conflict in the firm is between controlling shareholders and minority shareholders (Lefort and Urzúa, 2008). However, there is some debate about the usefulness of agency theory in a family firm context (Westhead and Howorth, 2006), since agency theory may provide only a partial explanation of private family firms (Howorth et al., 2004).

The typical ownership pattern of small and medium-sized family firms (Forbes and Milliken, 1999) reduces the need for the board's control role, so the appearance of outside directors will reflect the service and advice needs of the CEO rather than the control role (Fiegener at al., 2000). The context of SMEs may consequently vary from a context of large Fortune 500 companies, and various ownership configurations may also address questions about board compositional definitions as that of insiders versus outsiders (Gabrielsson and Huse, 2005).

For this reason, in this study we also follow the stewardship theory perspective, which indicates that the board's primary role is to service and advise, rather than to discipline and monitor as agency theory prescribes (Hillman and Dalziel, 2003).

Over the past few years, academics have extensively studied the distinguishable characteristics of family firm governance systems (Corbetta and Montemerlo, 1999; Davis and Pett, 2000; Schulze et al., 2001; Lane et al., 2006; Miller and Le Breton-Miller, 2006; Van Den Heuvel et al., 2006; Arosa et al., 2010). However, fairly little is known about the relationship between the generation in charge of the firm and its corporate governance. Voordeckers et al. (2007) and Bammens et al. (2008) analyse the effect of generational phase on the existence of an outside board. Bammens et al. (2008) find that the likelihood of having an outside director on the board has a convex generational tend, and Voordeckers et al. (2007) indicate that the need for external advice and counsel decreases as subsequent generations run the firm. But the effect of the generation in charge and the proportion of independent and affiliated directors on the board in firm performance is not known.

The aim of the study is to analyse the effect of the presence of outsiders (affiliated and independents) on the board of directors on firm performance in family SMEs, highlighting the generational effect. For this purpose we have distinguished between first-, second- and third- or more generation family firms. To test our hypotheses that outside directors act as agents or stewards, we examined the relation between firm performance and the proportion of affiliated and independent directors on the board. Affiliate directors are directors with potential or existing business relationships to the firm, but are not full-time employees and may play an important role in any firm, and in the case of family firms their influence is likely to be greater given the more permanent and personal relationship with the firm's management (Jones et al., 2008). Independent directors are individuals whose only business relationship to the firm is their directorship.

Our findings show the existence of a positive impact of affiliated directors on firm performance in family firms. The presence of independent directors can be said not to have resulted in improved firm performance. It is also important to note the different behaviour between family firms run by the first generation and those run by second and subsequent generations. In this case, the presence of independents on the board has a positive effect on performance when the firm is run by the first generation. When the firm is run by second and subsequent generations, the presence of independents has no effect on performance. One might therefore wonder how independent they really are. If we analyse the effect of the presence of affiliated directors, the results are very different. For first-generation family firms, there is a positive relationship between the presence of affiliated directors on the board and firm performance. Nevertheless, when the firm is run by the second generation, this relation becomes negative. The knowledge and family experience in the business increase over generations, reducing the need for additional outside expertise. So the need for external advice and counsel decreases.

This study makes several contributions to the literature on the impact of board composition on firm performance. First, our findings provide a new perspective on the role that outside directors play in corporate governance of family firms, differentiating between affiliated and independent directors. Besides, we analyse the effect of the proportion of directors (affiliated and independent) on firm performance. Second, our research shows that the composition of the board changes because its needs are different depending on the generation running the firm – first, second, third or subsequent generations. Third, we focus on non-listed family SMEs because the findings of large firms may not extend to smaller ones.

In that context, the rest of the chapter is organized as follows. Section 2 describes the theoretical basis and the hypotheses to examine. Section 3 sets out the data and procedures for analysis used in undertaking this empirical study. The main results of the investigation are presented in Section 4. The next section presents and discusses the results. We conclude the chapter in Section 6 with some conclusions and implications for management theory and practice, and indicate paths for further investigation.

2   BOARD OF DIRECTORS AND FIRM PERFORMANCE: THEORETICAL BACKGROUND AND HYPOTHESES

Corporate board structure and its impact on firm behaviour is one of the most debated issues in the literature today. In recent years, the discussion has focused on the structure of the board of directors, the most outstanding governance mechanism of internal control systems (Jensen, 1993). Researchers studying corporate governance have used a diverse set of theoretical perspectives to understand the characteristics, roles and effects of boards of directors (Corbetta and Salvato, 2004). Although agency-theoretic arguments represent one explanation in describing the relation between founding families and boards of directors, stewardship theory provides an alternative explanation (Anderson and Reeb, 2004). It is not necessary to choose one theoretical perspective over another. Indeed, one can obtain a better understanding of family business boards by trying to integrate different theoretical perspectives (Corbetta and Salvato, 2004; Minichilli et al., 2009).

Board structure has relied heavily on agency theory concepts, focusing on the control function of the board. Agency theory treats the company as a nexus of contracts through which various participants transact with each other (Jensen and Meckling, 1976). Since assets are the property of the shareholders, a principal–agent problem may arise because managers have to make decisions concerning the productive use of these assets. Installing a board of directors can be an effective instrument for monitoring top managers and coping with this problem, and to reduce agency costs (Fama and Jensen, 1983). Thus agency theory is used to examine the role that the board of directors may play in contributing to the performance of the organizations they govern (Jackling and Johl, 2009). However, the agency problem seems less important in the context of family firms with high ownership concentration, given that the controlling shareholders have sufficient incentives, power and information to control top managers (Jensen and Meckling, 1976). Yet high ownership concentration can trigger other problems with corporate governance and other types of cost. If there are controlling shareholders, they are more likely to be able to use their power to undertake activities intended to obtain private profit to the detriment of minority shareholders' wealth (La Porta et al., 1999; Villalonga and Amit, 2006).

In this context, outside shareholders potentially rely on boards of directors to monitor and control family opportunism (Anderson and Reeb, 2004), reducing information asymmetry between various branches of the family or between the family and external stakeholders (Grabielsson and Huse, 2005).

Schulze and colleagues (2001) argued that family relationships tend to generate agency problems, mainly because control over firm resources enables owner-managers to be generous to their descendants and other relatives. Parental altruism is a trait that positively links the controlling owner's welfare to that of other family members. Over time, however, the economic incentive to do what maximizes personal utility can blur the controlling owner's perception of what is best for the firm or family (Schulze et al., 2003).

Nevertheless the ownership pattern typical of small and medium-sized family firms (Forbes and Milliken, 1999) reduces the need for the board's control role, so the appearance of outside directors will reflect the service and advice needs of the CEO rather than the control role (Fiegener at al., 2000).

Stewardship theory, in contrast with agency theory (Davis et al., 1997), defines situations in which managers and employers are not motivated by individual goals, but instead behave as stewards whose motives are aligned with the objectives of the organization. The board's primary role is to service and advise, rather than to discipline and monitor as agency theory prescribes (Hillman and Dalziel, 2003). Organizations might require less control from a board when goal alignment between owners and managers is high (Davis et al., 1997; Luoma and Goodstein, 1999; Muth and Donaldson, 1998; Sundaramurthy and Lewis, 2003). Arrègle et al. (2007, p. 84) maintain that 'Family members are concerned about the firm because it is part of their collective patrimony and is often the main asset of the family.' Family owners' and managers' stewardship stems from their socio-emotional attachment to the business, which can be very high since the company can serve to satisfy needs for security, social contribution, belonging and family standing (Ashforth and Mael, 1989; Gómez-Mejía et al., 2007; Lansberg 1999).

Acting as stewards, families may place outside directors on the board to provide industry-specific expertise, objective advice, or generally act as advocates for corporate health and viability. Stewardship theory, as such potentially offers an alternative explanation for observing a relation between outside directors and firm performance (Anderson and Reeb, 2004).

Agency theory and stewardship theory indicate that outside directors (affiliate and independent) can influence firm performance. Both theories suggest that independent directors exhibit a positive relation to firm performance; under agency, independent directors monitor and control insiders and/or the family. Under stewardship, independent directors provide valuable outside advice and counsel to the firm.

In this context, the first hypothesis proposes that a higher proportion of independent directors on the board will be associated with a positive impact on performance due to the role, monitor or advisor, that these directors play in firms. Accordingly, the following hypothesis is presented:

Hypothesis 1   The proportion of board independent directors of non-listed family firms is positively associated with firm performance.

Focusing on the other type of external directors (affiliates), however, provides an approach that helps to differentiate between the monitoring (agency) and counselling (stewardship) role of outside directors (Anderson and Reeb, 2004).

An agency perspective suggests that affiliate directors, in seeking to protect or enhance their business relationship with the firm, are less objective and less effective monitors of the family. Affiliate directors often have conflicts of interest due to their current and expected future business relationship with the firm, thereby impairing their ability to monitor and discipline (Baysinger and Butler, 1985; Daily et al., 1998). However, stewardship theory suggests a different perspective on the role that affiliate directors play in family firms. Families, acting as stewards of firm value, may not differentiate directors based on their affiliation with, or independence from, the family. Directors classified as affiliates often maintain skills in knowledge-based fields such as law, finance, accounting and consulting, suggesting that families seek these directors for their value-adding advice and counsel as opposed to affiliate directors' abilities in monitoring and controlling family activities. While affiliate directors may play an important role in any firm, in the case of family firms their influence is likely to be greater given the more permanent and personal relationship with the firm's management, whose tenure tends to be much longer than in the case of non-family firms. This should lead affiliate directors to accumulate stronger social capital within the family firm (Jones et al., 2008). Moreover, as generations succeed, knowledge and family experience in the business tend to increase, reducing the need for additional outside expertise.

In sum, agency theory indicates that affiliate directors are less effective monitors, while stewardship theory indicates that affiliate directors are placed on the board to provide alternative perspectives and expertise, similar to independent directors. Thus stewardship and agency theory lend different perspectives on the role affiliate directors play on the board and in the firm. Therefore we propose competing hypotheses. Under stewardship theory:

Hypothesis 2(a)   The proportion of affiliated directors on the board of non-listed family firms is positively associated with firm performance.

In contrast, under agency theory:

Hypothesis 2(b)   The proportion of affiliated directors on the board of non-listed family firms is negatively associated with firm performance.

The generational phase can be linked with the board composition. One of the main contributions of boards in family firms is the provision of advice, counsel and control. Changes in the level of family experience and conflict can affect the need for board advice and arbitration. As recent literature points out (Voordeckers et al., 2007; Bammens et al., 2008), the generational stage of the business mediates the relationships between board task needs and board composition, so we expect board composition to adjust to this situation.

According to Schulze et al. (2001), whereas the main source of agency problems is the separation between ownership and monitoring, such problems do not exist in first-generation family firms because the same person is responsible for making management and supervision decisions. Reductions in agency costs may be achieved by entirely eliminating the separation between owners and management. In such cases, the interests of principal and agent are aligned and it is assured that the management will not expropriate the shareholders' wealth (Miller and Le Breton-Miller, 2006).

As a family firm prepares to incorporate later generations, priorities and problems change (Gersick et al., 1997). The family property is shared by an increasingly large number of family members, conflicts may start to arise when the interests of the family members are not aligned, and the agency relations between the various participants in the firm are conducted on the basis of economic and non-economic preferences (Chrisman et al., 2005; Sharma et al., 2007). When more family members are active in the firm, the likelihood of opposite opinions and objectives increases, thereby increasing the need for outside arbitration (Voordeckers et al., 2007). Families age and a new generation takes over the key management positions in the firm; the risk of intra-family conflict augments (Schulze et al., 2003). Davis and Harveston (1999, 2001), found more conflict as subsequent generations run the firm.

Conflicts between family members generate the need for board control to ensure that the management team considers the preferences and interests of all family owners (Bammens et al., 2008). The new generations of family managers may be viewed as being exclusively concerned with the interests of their own nuclear household rather than the interests of the entire extended family (Raskas, 1998; Lubatkin et al., 2005). Sibling partnerships often require the installation of formal governance mechanisms to control employed siblings and this can be considered even more important for the cousin consortium generational stage (Steier, 2001; Lubatkin et al., 2005); as subsequent generations run the firm the need for outside arbitration takes place.

Independent directors are still necessary as they can offer an objective view on the resolution of family conflicts that tend to become more common over generations (García Olalla and García Ramos, 2010).

In contrast, the rise over the generations in the level of family experience may have the opposite effect. Knowledge and family experience in the business tend to increase over generations, reducing the need for additional outside expertise which could be provided by independent directors (García Olalla and García Ramos, 2010). The value of internal executive directors for the advisory board role increases with the generational stage of the company (Bammens et al., 2008).

A higher generation can be a proxy for a well-developed internal knowledge base in the firm. Higher-generation successors are often better educated than the first-generation owner-manager. Therefore the need for external advice and counsel decreases (Voordeckers et al., 2007). So, seeing that the level of family experience increases over the generations, the need for board advice can be expected to decrease. As the level of organizational knowledge develops over the generations (Astrachan et al., 2002; Miller and Le Breton-Miller, 2006), the need for complementary know-how held by outside directors should decrease.

As the result of the above, the generational phase will influence the need for board advice and control. Agency theory and stewardship theory indicate that affiliate and independent directors can influence firm performance, but have different perspectives on the role directors play on the board.

The agency perspective indicates that independent directors can offer an objective view on the resolution of family conflicts and exhibit a positive relation to firm performance. However, affiliate directors are less objective and less effective monitors of the family, so we expect a negative relationship when the family firm is run by subsequent generations.

Nevertheless, under the stewardship perspective independent and affiliated directors provide valuable outside advice and counsel to the firm, but knowledge and family experience in the business tend to increase over generations. The need for complementary knowledge decreases. So stewardship theory proposes that the proportion of independent and affiliated directors on the board and firm performance decreases in family firms run by subsequent generations. Therefore, we propose competing hypotheses. Under stewardship theory:

Hypothesis 3(a)   The relationship between the proportion of board independent directors of non-listed family firms and firm performance is lower in family firms run by subsequent generations.

Hypothesis 3(b)   The relationship between the proportion of board affiliated directors of non-listed family firms and firm performance is lower in family firms run by subsequent generations.

In contrast, under agency theory:

Hypothesis 3(c)   The relationship between the proportion of board independent directors of non-listed family firms and firm performance is higher in family firms run by subsequent generations.

Hypothesis 3(d)   The relationship between the proportion of board affiliated directors of non-listed family firms and firm performance is lower in family firms run by subsequent generations.

3   EMPIRICAL RESEARCH: METHOD AND DATA

3.1   Population and Sample

We conducted this study on Spanish firms included in the SABI (Iberian Balance Sheet Analysis System) database for 2006. We imposed certain restrictions on this group of companies in order to reach a representative set of the population. First, we eliminated companies affected by special situations such as insolvency, winding-up, liquidation or zero activity. Second, restrictions concerning the legal form of companies were imposed: we focused on private companies and private limited companies as they have a legal obligation to establish boards of directors. Third, we eliminated listed companies. Fourth, we studied only Spanish firms with more than 50 employees, that is, companies large enough to ensure the existence of a suitable management team and a controlling board to monitor their performance. Finally, companies were required to have provided financial information in 2006.

There is no official database of family firms, so there is no way of directly identifying family firms. Moreover, the lack of an agreed definition of family firm leads to the use of samples of convenience, or to firms being identified as family firms after the sample has been preselected (Daily and Dollinger, 1993; Schulze et al., 2001, 2003; Chua et al., 2003). Given these limitations, a detailed analysis of the information in databases and a survey are the only way of identifying family and non-family non-listed firms. This study has chosen a combination of these two methods of identification.

In this study, a family firm is taken to mean a firm that meets two conditions: (a) a substantial common stock is held by the founder or family members, allowing them to exercise control over the firm; and (b) they participate actively in monitoring it. We established 50 per cent as the minimum percentage of a firm's equity considered as a controlling interest (Voordeckers et al., 2007; Westhead and Howorth, 2006). To find compliance with these two conditions, we conducted an exhaustive review of shareholding structures (percentage of common stock) and composition (name and surnames of shareholders), and also examined the composition of the board of directors of each selected company in the database.

We accordingly classify a firm as a family firm if the main shareholder is a person or a family with a minimum of 50 per cent of firm equity and there are family relationships between this shareholder and directors, based on coincidence of surnames. The composition of the management was also reviewed in search of family relationships between shareholders and managers.

The original sample used in this study is a 2958-firm random sample. After sending a reminder or contacting the firm by phone, 369 family firms responded to the questionnaire, in which there were data on ownership structures, accounting variables and boards of directors.

3.2   Data

Data were collected by means of telephone interviews, a method that ensures a high response rate, and financial reporting information was obtained from the SABI database. To guarantee the highest possible number of replies, managers were made aware of the study in advance by means of a letter indicating the purpose and importance of the research. In cases where they were reluctant to reply or made excuses, a date and time were arranged in advance for the telephone interview. The final response rate was approximately 12.47 per cent, and the interviewees were persons responsible for management at the firms (financial managers in 56.48 per cent of the cases, the CEO in 31.06 per cent, the president in 1.54 per cent of the cases, and others in 10.92 per cent).

Table 5.1   Definition and calculation of variables

Panel A	
Variables obtained from the questionnaire	
Variable	Definition
Generation managing the firm (GEN1)	Dummy variable that takes the value of 1 if the firm is headed by the first generation and 0 otherwise
Generation managing the firm (GEN2)	Dummy variable that takes the value of 1 if the firm is headed by the second generation and 0 otherwise
Generation managing the firm (GEN3)	Dummy variable that takes the value of 1 if the firm is headed by the third and subsequent generations and 0 otherwise
Presence of affiliated directors on the board (AFFILIATED)	Percentage of affiliated directors in the total number of directors
Presence of independent directors on the board (INDEPENDENT)	Percentage of independent directors in the total number of directors
Board of directors size (BOARDSIZE)	Ln total members on the board of directors
Insider ownership (INSOWN)	Percentage of ownership of insider directors and CEO
Family dummy (FD)	Dummy variable that takes the value 1 if the company complies with the definition adopted and 0 otherwise

Panel B	
Variables obtained from financial statements	
Firm performance, measured by firm profitability (ROA)	EBIT/TA, where EBIT = earnings + financial expenses + tax benefit, and TA = total assets
Growth opportunity (GROWTHOP)	$Sales_0/Sales_{-1}$
Debt (LEV)	Total debt / total assets
Firm's size (SIZE)	Ln total assets
Firm's age (AGE)	Ln number of years since the establishment of the company
SECT	Dummy variables to control for sector

The questionnaire collects information on the variables required for the study that could not be obtained from the SABI database and which it was considered would be more reliably collected through a survey, in particular, information regarding the ownership structure and composition of the board and company management (see Table 5.1).

3.3   Method

We apply a cross-sectional ordinary least squares (OLS) regression model to test the hypotheses presented in the preceding section. Drawing on previous research on corporate governance, we also include seven control variables to minimize specification bias in the hypothesis testing.

To analyse the different characteristics attributed to family firms depending on the generation managing the firm it is necessary to classify family firms according to the generation managing them. Consistent with Miller et al. (2007), we have generated three GEN variables. GEN1 takes value of 1 if the firm is managed by the first generation and 0 otherwise. GEN2 takes value of 1 if the firm is managed by the second generation and 0 otherwise. And GEN3 takes value of 1 if the firm is managed by the third and subsequent generations and 0 otherwise. In this sense, we analyse whether the behaviour of family firms varies depending on which generation manages the firm.

To test for multicollinearity, the VIF (variance inflation factor) was calculated for each independent variable. Myers (1990) suggests that a VIF value of 10 and above is cause for concern. The results (not shown in this chapter) indicate that all the independent variables had VIF values of less than 10.

4   RESULTS

Table 5.2 presents descriptive statistics for the variables in the analysis. We show mean values for family firms in the sample. The significant proportion of independent directors in family firms boards of directors should be noted. These boards have a composition which, at first sight, seems efficient in order to keep family firm interests represented and separated. The evolution of this composition tends to reduce the presence of insider directors in favour of affiliated directors, maintaining also a significant presence of independent directors, regardless of which generation manages the firm. It is therefore necessary to determine the possible effect the presence of different types of directors might have on firm performance due to greater monitoring or counselling capacity. In relation to control variables, we highlight the high insider ownership, due to the CEO's

Table 5.2   Descriptive statistics of sample firms: mean values for variable measures

				Means		Std dev.
Number of observations				369		
Board of directors' composition Outsiders				0.35		0.35
	1st gen.	1st gen.	2nd gen.	2nd gen.	3rd gen.	3rd gen.
	Mean	Std dev.	Mean	Std dev.	Mean	Std dev.
Insiders	0.74	0.35	0.69	0.34	0.52	0.33
Affiliated	0.16	0.29	0.18	0.26	0.34	0.33
Independent	0.09	0.20	0.14	0.24	0.14	0.23
Control variables				Means		Std dev.
Insider ownership				0.50		0.41
Board of directors' size (number of directors)				5		2.12
Return on assets				0.06		0.07
Growth opportunity (sales$_0$/sales$_{-1}$)				1.14		1.33
Leverage (total debt / total assets)				0.62		0.18
Firm's size (Total assets)				27309.48		36454.4
Firm's age (years)				40		31.56

Table 5.3   Correlation data

Variables	1	2	3	4	5	6	7	8	9
1 Independent	1								
2 Affiliated	0.38***	1							
3 Insider ownership	−0.06	−0.07	1						
4 Board size	0.01	0.02	−0.20***	1					
5 ROA	−0.05	0.09	0.03	0.20	1				
6 Growth opportunities	−0.05	−0.01	−0.00	0.06	0.24***	1			
7 Borrowing level	−0.03	−0.03	0.12**	−0.11	−0.29***	−0.24***	1		
8 Firm size	0.03	−0.01	−0.08	0.18***	−0.02	−0.05	0.13**	1	
9 Firm age	−0.04	−0.01	−0.11**	0.16***	−0.01	−0.01	0.3	0.01	1

Note: *** Correlation is significant at the 0.01 level.

percentage of ownership, which is, on average, 20 per cent. It is also noteworthy that family firms have an average age of 40 years, suggesting that our firms are well established.

As shown in Table 5.3, the correlation coefficients are weak and do not violate the assumption of independence between the variables.

Table 5.4 sets out the results of our linear regression evaluating the influence of board composition on business performance for family firms.

In our first and third regressions we examined the influence of independent directors on firm performance (Table 5.4, columns I and III). The results were not expected. Our results show no significant relationship (β_1 = −0.022 and −0.040) between independents and firm performance. Thus firm performance seems to be insensitive to the presence of independent directors on the board. Hypothesis 1 was not supported. These results show that monitoring and counselling by independents does not necessarily imply efficiency improvements for family firms.

Hypothesis 2(a) predicted that the greater the fraction of affiliated directors in family firms, the better the performance of the firm and Hypothesis 2(b) predicted a negative effect. The coefficient (β_1 in column II) is positive and significant, so there is a positive effect between the presence of affiliated directors on the board and firm performance. The results (β_2 in column III) are similar if we include independent and affiliated directors in the same regression. The results support Hypothesis 2(a).

Columns IV, V and VI show the effect of the presence of independent directors on the board depending on which generation is running the firm. When the family firm is run by second and subsequent generations, the results are not expected. The coefficient β_1 (column IV) is positive and significant, so we can confirm the relationship between the presence of independent directors on the board and firm performance in first-generation family firms. However, the coefficient for the second- and subsequent generation family firms (β_1 in column V and β_1 in column VI) are not significant. We may therefore conclude that when the family firm is run by the first generation, the presence of independents on the board improves business performance. Nevertheless, if the family firm is run by

Table 5.4 *Relationship between board composition and firm performance*

	I	II	III	IV	V	VI	VII	VIII	IX
Constant	0.112	0.142	0.186	0.150*	0.027	0.025	0.015	0.043	0.025
INDEP	−0.022		−0.040						
INDEPENDENT*GEN1				0.067**					
INDEPENDENT*GEN2					−0.025				
INDEPENDENT*GEN3						−0.027			
AFFILIATED		0.070*	0.089*						
AFFILIATED*GEN1							0.075***		
AFFILIATED*GEN2								−0.038*	
AFFILIATED*GEN3									0.001
INSOWN	0.029	0.028	0.022	0.011	0.012	0.012	0.014	0.009	0.013
BOARDSIZE	0.002	0.002	0.002	−0.004	−0.001	−0.001	−0.004	−0.003	−0.003
GROWTHOP	0.273	0.385	0.444*	0.328***	0.206**	0.202**	0.215**	0.021**	0.208**
LEV	−0.105**	−0.109*	−0.112**	−0.115***	−0.113***	−0.110***	−0.106***	−0.114***	−0.012***
SIZE	−0.001	−0.002	−0.003	0.001	0.006*	0.006*	0.006*	0.006*	0.006*
AGE	0.009	0.008	0.009	0.002	0.003	0.003	0.004	0.002	0.003
F-value	2.15	2.17	2.3	4.51	3.2	3.2	4.16	3.39	3.1
R^2	0.18	0.19	0.21	0.16	0.12	0.12	0.16	0.14	0.12

Note: ***, ** and * indicate significance at 1%, 5% and 10%.

second and subsequent generations the presence of independents on the board has no effect on firm performance.

The results are different for affiliated directors. For first-generation family firms the coefficient (β_1 in column VII) is positive (0.075) and significant. The presence of affiliated directors, as independent ones, improves firm performance. However, if we consider second-generation family firms, the coefficient of β_1 (column VIII) is negative and significant (-0.038). And there is no relation between the presence of affiliated directors on the board and firm performance for third- and subsequent generation family firms (column IX).

The result shows a clear difference in behaviour between family firms run by different generations

5 DISCUSSION

We do not find any robust relationship between independent directors and firm performance; thus Hypothesis 1 was not supported. These results are partially consistent with those obtained for other types of firms by authors such as Baysinger and Butler (1985), Hermalin and Weisbach (1991); Mehran (1995), Klein (1998), Baghat and Black (2001), De Andrés et al. (2005) and Jackling and Johl (2009), who find no evidence relating to the proportion of outsiders on the board and different measures of business performance or market value. However, we have advanced further than these authors, since we have differentiated between the independent and affiliated directors.

These results do not support the assumption that independent directors have an important controlling and advising function, and in contrast can justify the presence of affiliated and insider directors in family firms.

The reasons put forward to explain the lack of a relationship between the presence of independent directors and performance vary. Hermalin and Weisbach (1991) suggest that both inside and outside directors may fail to perform their job of representing shareholders' interests properly; that is, it cannot be concluded that outsiders perform their activity better than insiders. Likewise, Mace (1986) and Vancil (1987) argue that inside directors facilitate the process of succession in the firm, offering advice and conveying knowledge to the CEO on the firm's day-to-day operations. The presence of insiders on the board makes it easier for the other directors to view them as potential top executives, since they can assess their skills more simply from seeing them act on the board itself (Bhagat and Black, 2000). Maug (1997) demonstrates that for firms with important information asymmetries – and this is the case of family firms – it is not optimal to increase monitoring through the incorporation of independents, since transferring specific knowledge about the firm to independents can prove costly. On the other hand, the CEO and management are characterized by their high level of commitment to the organization and by sharing its values.

It also needs to be said that each type of director has a specific role on the board (Baysinger and Butler, 1985). Inside directors have a greater knowledge of the firm than outsiders (Raheja, 2005), who are often unfamiliar with the working of the firm.

When the family firm is run by the first generation, having independent directors on the board improves firm performance, implying that independent directors potentially play an influential role in moderating family power and alleviating conflicts among shareholder groups as well as being advisors. According to affiliated directors, our findings support the stewardship predictions, confirming the positive relationship between the proportion of affiliated directors on the board of non-listed first-generation family firms and performance. In non-listed first-generation family SMEs, affiliated directors act as stewards of firm value, promoting corporate health and firm performance. Directors classified as affiliates often can maintain skills in knowledge-based fields such as law, finance, accounting and consulting, suggesting that families seek these directors for their value-adding advice and counsel (Anderson and Reeb, 2004). These findings confirm that the board's primary role is to service and advise, rather than to discipline and monitor as agency theory prescribes.

However, when the firm is run by second and subsequent generations, the presence of affiliated and independent directors has a different effect on performance. If the firm is run by second and subsequent generations, the results show no significant relation between the presence of independent directors and firm performance. These findings do not confirm the results obtained by Schulze et al. (2003). These researchers point out that agency dynamics during the sibling partnership stage mostly found in the second generation are more problematic than in the controlling owner (first-generation) or cousin consortium stage (third-generation and higher).

Taking into account the clearly differentiated behaviour of first-generation family firms and those run by subsequent generations, the reason may be that in the case of first-generation firms, independent directors really are more involved in their work on the board and perform their function effectively. First-generation family firms have a smaller proportion of independent directors than family firms run by second and subsequent generations. Although they have a smaller presence, this may be the right composition for the first phase in the life of a family firm, when the insider directors' knowledge of the firm's strategic planning is needed, given the long-term perspective of these firms. In this way, independent directors monitor insiders and/or family members and also offer important and helpful advice and counsel. These results confirm the tenets of both agency and stewardship theory.

Independents have a more moderate presence during this first phase of the firm's life, which is unsurprising, given that the company equity is in hands of a small number of people, who are properly represented on the board. It therefore appears that the outsiders have been selected appropriately for performing their function, perhaps prevailing in advice and counsel roles.

This might seem surprising, given that as the various generations succeed and the share base becomes more diverse, the presence of independent directors may become more necessary to ensure that the interests of the different shareholders are properly represented and that no decisions are taken that are detrimental to the interests of minority shareholders. The results, however, suggest that in such cases independents are probably not acting in this way. If we analyse the board composition in firms run by second and subsequent generations, we see that they have an ever greater presence but their monitoring role has no effect on firm performance. In addition, perhaps, the criteria for choosing directors can also vary, and personal friendship could play a relevant role. One might therefore consider that independents may not be acting objectively, given their many overlapping interests in the firm. This may explain why their presence on the board results in a drop in performance.

According to affiliated directors, when the firm is run by second generations, the results show a negative and significant relation between the presence of affiliated directors and firm performance.

Knowledge and family experience in the business increase over generations and the need for board advice can be expected to decrease. The value of internal executive directors for the advisory board role increases with the generational stage of the company (Bammens et al., 2008). These results, consistent with those obtained by Voordeckers et al, (2007), suggest a significant decrease in the need for complementary outside know-how from the first to the second generations.

Finally, when the firm is run by third and subsequent generations, there is no relation between the two variables, so the presence of affiliated directors is not significant for these family firms. As mentioned by Bammens et al. (2008), third and subsequent generations tend to contribute far less to this knowledge development process.

6   CONCLUSION

Our aim is to analyse the effect of the presence of outsiders (affiliated and independents) on the board of directors on firm performance in family SMEs, highlighting the generational effect. For this purpose we have distinguished between first-, second- and third- or more generation family firms. To test our hypotheses that outside directors act as agents or stewards, we examined the relationship between firm performance and the proportion of affiliated and independent directors on the board. Moreover, contrary to most previous studies, we did not focus on large listed companies but adopted a sample that includes mainly SMEs, none of which is listed. In an ownership concentration context, we used a sample of 369 family firms.

Our findings show the existence of a positive impact of affiliated directors on firm performance in family firms. The presence of independent directors can be said not to have resulted in improved firm performance. The firms in the sample showed a significant presence of affiliated directors, an aspect that may be related to their greater knowledge of the firm, with a subsequently positive effect on strategic planning decisions. This type of director provides alternative perspectives and expertise, playing an advising and counselling role.

It is also important to note the different behaviour between family firms run by the first generation and those run by second and subsequent generations. In this case, the presence of independents on the board has a positive effect on performance when the firm is run by the first generation. When the firm is run by second and subsequent generations, the presence of independents has no effect on performance. Thus one might therefore wonder how independent they really are.

If we analyse the effect of the presence of affiliated directors, the results are very different. For first-generation family firms, there is a positive relationship between the presence of affiliated directors on the board and firm performance. Nevertheless, when the firm is run by the second generation, this relation becomes negative. The knowledge and family experience in the business increase over generations, reducing the need for additional outside expertise. So the need for external advice and counsel decreases.

Our chapter contributes to the literature on the impact of board composition on firm performance. First, our findings provide a new perspective on the role that outside directors play in corporate governance of family firms, differentiating between affiliated and independent directors. Besides examining the board's role in controlling the conflicts between shareholder groups, we also consider the advising and counselling role of the board. Moreover, we analyse the effect of the proportion of directors (affiliated and independent) on firm performance. Second, our research shows that the composition of the board changes because its needs are different, depending on the generation running the firm. Third, the bulk of empirical research on the role and effect of outside directors on firm performance has mostly been conducted on large publicly held companies (Anderson and Reeb, 2004; Daily et al., 1998). There are consequently very few studies that have explored the role and contribution of outside directors in the context of SMEs family firms, and those that there are have often uncritically adapted concepts and theories developed for large firms. There consequently seem to be deficiencies in our knowledge of the role and contribution of outside directors in SMEs. We focus on non-listed family SMEs because the findings of large firms may not extend to smaller ones. Following Howorth and colleagues (2004), agency theory may provide only a partial explanation of private family firms.

Our research has some implications for family business owners and all those consultants. In family firms run by the first generation, the presence of outside (affiliated and independent) directors has a positive effect on firm performance. These results suggest that first-generation firms' outside directors' influence is an important element in monitoring and advising family activity.

In second- and subsequent generation family firms, outsiders do not add value to the firm. For affiliated directors in the second generation, the relation is negative. This indicates the need to incorporate directors who are really independent or have great knowledge and add value to the firm.

However, when the firm is managed by second and subsequent generations, there is no such oversight, so we think that the problem may be the criteria for choosing directors. Personal friendship could play a very relevant role and it may therefore be that outsiders, and in particular independents, may not be acting objectively, given their many overlapping interests with the firm. Therefore outside directors should be selected carefully for adequate qualifications to carry out the responsibilities, and to ensure that they have general knowledge about business management and its environment and knowledge of the peculiarities of the family firms.

It is also interesting that the consultants recommend that firms have a good balance between outside and inside directors because of the important and concrete role they play, exercising a more effective function on the board, leading to better performance.

This research has to deal with some limitations: first, the great difficulty of obtaining a non-listed firms database, and this is even more difficult in the case of family firms. Second, our data are cross-sectional in nature and, therefore, we cannot make causal inferences. Only a panel data sample will allow testing and complementing our findings.

Third, data were collected exclusively in Spain, thus limiting the possibility of generalizing our findings. Fourth, our analysis focuses solely on the formal independence of the board and ignores the social and psychological factors that may exist between the family and directors.

To conclude, some ideas about future research are pertinent. First, a research design based on longitudinal data would be more suitable for this kind of study in order to increase the reliability of causality directions. Second, we also want to consider the effect of CEO duality in conjunction with founding family ownership and the effect of the size of the board of directors in monitory and control activity. Third, a similar study could be conducted in countries other than Spain in order to increase the validity of our results.

NOTE

1. The authors thank Cátedra de Empresa Familiar de la UPV/EHU for financial support (DFB/BFA and European Social Fund). This research has received financial support from the UPV/EHU (Project UPV/ EHU 10/30).

REFERENCES

Agrawal, A. and Knoeber, C.R. (1996), 'Firm performance and mechanisms to control agency problems between managers and shareholders', *Journal of Financial and Quantitative Analysis*, **31**, 337–98.
Anderson, C.R. and Reeb, M.D. (2004), 'Board composition: balancing family influence in S&P 500 firms', *Administrative Science Quarterly*, **49**, 209–37.
Arosa, B., Iturralde, T. and Maseda, A. (2010), 'Outsiders on the board of directors and firm performance: evidence from Spanish non-listed family firms', *Journal of Family Business Strategy*, **1**(4), 236–45.
Arrègle, J.-L., Hitt, M., Sirmon, D. and Very, P. (2007), 'The development of organizational social capital: attributes of family firms', *Journal of Management Studies*, **44**(1), 73–95.
Ashforth, B. and Mael, F. (1989), 'Social identity theory and the organization', *Academy of Management Review*, **14**(1), 20–39.
Astrachan, J., Klein, S. and Smyrnios, K. (2002), 'The F-PEC scale of family influence: a proposal for solving the family business definition problem', *Family Business Review*, **15**, 45–58.
Baghat, S. and Black, B. (2001), 'The non-correlation between board independence and long-term firm performance', *Journal of Corporation Law*, **27**, 231–74.
Bammens, Y., Voordeckers, W. and Van Gils, A. (2008), 'Boards of directors in family firms: a generational perspective', *Small Business Economics*, **31**, 163–80.
Baysinger, B. and Butler, H. (1985), 'Corporate governance and the board of directors: performance effects of changes in board composition', *Journal of Law, Economics, and Organizations*, **1**(1), 101–24.
Chrisman, J., Chua, J. and Sharma, P. (2005), 'Trends and directions in the development of a strategic management theory of the family firm', *Entrepreneurship Theory and Practice*, **29**, 555–75.
Chua, J.H., Chrisman, J.J. and Sharma, P. (2003), 'Succession and nonsuccession concerns of family firms and agency relationship with nonfamily managers', *Family Business Review*, **16**, 89–107.
Corbetta, G. and Montemerlo, D. (1999), 'Ownership, governance, and management issues in small and medium-size family businesses: a comparison of Italy and the United States', *Family Business Review*, **12**, 361–74.
Corbetta, G. and Salvato, C.A. (2004), 'The board of directors in family firms: one size fits all?', *Family Business Review*, **17**, 119–34.
Daily, C.M. and Dollinger, M.J. (1993), 'Alternative methodologies for identifying family versus non-family managed businesses', *Journal of Small Business Management*, **31**(2), 79–90.
Daily, C.M., Johnson, J., Ellstrand, A. and Dalton, D. (1998), 'Compensation committee composition as a determinant of CEO compensation', *Academy of Management Journal*, **41**, 209–20.
Dalton, D.R., Daily, C.M., Ellstrand, A. and Johnson, J.L. (1998), 'Meta-analytic reviews of board composition, leadership structure and financial performance', *Strategic Management Journal*, **19**, 269–90.
Davis, J.H., Schoorman, D.F. and Donaldson, L. (1997), 'Toward a stewardship theory of management', *Academy of Management Review*, **22**, 20–47.
Davis, P.S. and Harveston, P.D. (1999), 'In the founder's shadow: conflict in the family firm, '*Family Business Reviews*, **12**(1), 311–23.
Davis, P.S. and Harveston, P.D. (2001), 'The phenomenon of substantive conflict in the family firm: a cross-generational study', *Journal of Small Business Management*, **39**(1), 14–31.

Davis, P.S. and Pett, T.L. (2000), 'Governance and goal formation among family businesses: a resource dependency perspective', *The International Journal of Entrepreneurship and Innovation*, 1, 137–49.

De Andrés, P., Azofra, V. and Lopez, F. (2005), 'Corporate boards in OECD countries: size, composition, functioning and effectiveness', *Corporate Governance*, 13(2), 197–210.

Eisenberg, T., Sundgren, S. and Wells, M.T. (1998), 'Larger board size and decreasing firm value in small firms', *Journal of Financial Economics*, 48, 35–54.

Fama, E.F. (1980), 'Agency problems and the theory of the firm', *Journal of Political Economy*, 88(2), 288–307.

Fama, E.F. and Jensen, M.C. (1983), 'Separation of ownership and control', *Journal of Law and Economics*, 26(2), 301–25.

Fernández, Á.I., Gómez, A.S. and Fernández, M.C. (1997), 'The effect of board size and composition on corporate performance', in M. Balling et al. (eds), *Corporate Governance, Financial Markets and Global Convergence*, Boston, MA: Kluwer, pp. 1–6.

Fiegener, M.K., Brown, B.M., Dreux, D.R. and Dennis, W.J. (2000), 'The adoption of outside boards by small private US firms', *Entrepreneurship and Regional Development*, 12, 291–309.

Finkelstein, S. and Hambrick, D.C. (eds) (1996), *Strategic Leadership: Top Executives and Their Effects on Organizations*, Minneapolis, MN: West Publishing Company.

Forbes, D.P. and Milliken, F.J. (1999), 'Cognition and corporate governance: understanding boards of directors as strategic decision-making groups', *Academy of Management Review*, 24, 489–506.

Gabrielsson, J. and Huse, M. (2005), '"Outside" directors in SME boards: a call for theoretical reflections', *Corporate Board: Role, Duties & Composition*, 1, 28–38.

García Olalla, M. and García Ramos, R. (2010), 'Family ownership, structure and board of directors effectiveness: empirical evidence from European firms', 9th Annual IFERA Conference, Lancaster, UK, 6–9 July.

Gersick, K., Davis, J., Hampton, M. and Lansberg, I. (eds) (1997), *Generation to Generation: Life Cycles of the Family Business*, Boston, MA: Harvard Business School Press.

Gómez-Mejía, L.R., Hynes, K.T., Núñez-Nickel, M. and Moyano-Fuentes, H. (2007), 'Socioemotional wealth and business risk in family-controlled firms: evidence from Spanish olive oil mills', *Administrative Science Quarterly*, 52, 106–37.

Hermalin, B.E. and Weisbach, M.S. (1991), 'The effects of board composition and direct incentives on firm performance', *Financial Management*, 20(4), 101–12.

Hermalin, B.E. and Weisbach, M.S. (2003), 'Boards of directors as an endogenously determined institution: a survey of the economic literature', *Economic Political Review*, April, 7–26.

Hillman, A.J. and Dalziel, T. (2003), 'Boards of directors and firm performance: integrating agency and resource dependence perspectives', *Academy of Management Review*, 28, 383–96.

Howorth, C., Westhead, P. and Wright, M. (2004), 'Information asymmetry in management buyouts of family firms', *Journal of Business Venturing*, 9(4), 509–34.

Huther, J. (1997), 'An empirical test of the effect of board size on firm efficiency', *Economics Letters*, 54, 259–64.

Jackling, B. and Johl, S. (2009), 'Board structure and firm performance: evidence from India's top companies', *Corporate Governance: An International Review*, 17(4), 492–509.

Jaskiewicz, P. and Klein, S. (2007), 'The impact of goal alignment on board composition and board size in family businesses', *Journal of Business Research*, 60, 1080–89.

Jensen, M.C. (1993), 'The modern industrial revolution, exit, and the failure of internal control systems', *Journal of Finance*, XLVIII(3), 831–80.

Jensen, M.C. and Meckling, W. (1976), 'Theory of the firm: managerial behaviour, agency costs and ownership structure', *Journal of Financial Economics*, 3(4), 305–60.

Johnson, J.L., Daily, C.M. and Ellstrand, A.E. (1996), 'Boards of directors: a review and research agenda', *Journal of Management*, 22(3), 409–38.

Jones, C.D., Makri, M. and Gómez-Mejía, L.R. (2008), 'Affiliate directors and perceived risk bearing in publicly traded, family-controlled firms: the case of diversification', *Entrepreneurship Theory and Practice*, 32, 1007–26.

Klein, A. (1998), 'Firm performance and board committee structure', *Journal of Law and Economics*, XLI, 275–303.

La Porta, R., Lopez-de-Silanes, F. and Shleifer, A. (1999), 'Corporate ownership around the world', *The Journal of Finance*, 54(2), 471–517.

Lane, S., Astrachan, J., Keyt, A. and McMillan, K. (2006), 'Guidelines for family business boards of directors', *Family Business Review*, 19, 147–67.

Lansberg, I. (ed.) (1999), *Succeeding Generations: Realizing the Dream of Families in Business*, Boston, MA: Harvard Business School Press.

Lefort, F. and Urzúa, F. (2008), 'Board independence, firm performance and ownership concentration: evidence from Chile', *Journal of Business Research*, 61, 615–22.

Lubatkin, M., Schulze, W., Ling, Y. and Dino, R. (2005), 'The effects of parental altruism on the governance of family managed firms', *Journal of Organizational Behavior*, **26**, 313–30.

Luoma, P. and Goodstein, J. (1999), 'Stakeholders and corporate boards: institutional influences on board composition', *Academy of Management Journal*, **42**, 553–63.

Mace, M.L. (ed.) (1986), *Directors: Myth and Reality*, Boston, MA: Harvard Business School Press.

Maug, E. (1997), 'Ownership structure as a determinant of IPO underpricing: a theory of the decision to go public', Working Paper, mimeo, Duke University.

McKnight, P.J. and Mira, S. (2003), 'Corporate governance mechanisms, agency costs and firm performance in UK firms', http://ssrn.com/abstract=460300.

Mehran, H. (1995), 'Executive compensation structure, ownership, and firm performance', *Journal of Financial Economics*, **38**, 163–84.

Miller, D. and Le Breton-Miller, I. (2006), 'Family governance and firm performance: agency, stewardship, and capabilities', *Family Business Review*, **19**, 73–87.

Miller, D., Le, I., Lester, R. and Cannella, A. (2007), 'Are family firms really superior performers?', *Journal of Corporate Finance*, **13**, 829–58.

Minichilli, A., Zattoni, A. and Zona F. (2009), 'Making boards effective: an empirical examination of board task performance', *British Journal of Management*, **20**, 55–74.

Muth, M.M. and Donaldson, L. (1998), 'Stewardship theory and board structure: a contingency approach', *Corporate Governance International Review*, **6**, 5–28.

Myers, R.H. (ed.) (1990), *Classical and Modern Regression with Applications*, 2nd edn, Boston, MA: PWS-Kent.

Oxelheim, L. and Randøy, T. (2003), 'The impact of foreign board membership on firm value', *Journal of Banking and Finance*, **27**, 2369–92.

Raheja, C.G. (2005), 'Determinants of board size and composition: a theory of corporate boards', *Journal of Financial and Quantitative Analysis*, **40**(2), 283–306.

Raskas, D. (1998), 'Familiarity breeds trust as well as contempt . . . What about familiarity? An examination of familial involvement and trust in family firms', doctoral dissertation, Columbia University.

Sacristán-Navarro, M. and Gómez-Ansón, S. (2009), 'Do families shape corporate governance structures?' *Journal of Management and Organization*, **15**, 327–45.

Schulze, W.S., Lubatkin, M.H., Dino, R.N. and Buchholtz, A.K. (2001), 'Agency relationship in family firms: theory and evidence', *Organization Science*, **12**(9), 99–116.

Schulze, W.S., Lubatkin, M.H., Dino, R.N. and Buchholtz, A.K. (2003), 'Exploring the agency consequences of ownership dispersion among the directors of private family firms', *Academy of Management Journal*, **46**, 179–94.

Sharma, P., Hoy, F., Astrachan J.H. and Koiranen, M. (2007), 'The practice-driven evolution of family business education', *Journal of Business Research*, **60**, 1012–21.

Steier, L. (2001), 'Family firms, plural forms of governance, and the evolving role of trust', *Family Business Review*, **14**, 353–67.

Sundaramurthy, C. and Lewis, M. (2003), 'Control and collaboration: paradoxes of governance', *Academy of Management Review*, **28**, 397–415.

Van den Heuvel, J., Van Gils, A. and Voordeckers, W. (2006), 'Board roles in small and medium-sized family businesses: performance and importance', *Corporate Governance: An International Review*, **14**, 467–85.

Vancil, R.F. (ed.) (1987), *Passing the Baton. Managing the Process of CEO Succession*, Boston, MA: Harvard Business School Press.

Villalonga, B. and Amit, R. (2006), 'How do family ownership, control and management affect firm value?', *Journal of Financial Economics*, **80**(2), 385–418.

Voordeckers, W., Van Gils, A. and Van den Heuvel, J. (2007), 'Board composition in small and medium-sized family firms', *Journal of Small Business Management*, **45**(1), 137–56.

Weisbach, M. (1988), 'Outside directors and CEO turnover', *Journal of Financial Economics*, **20**, 431–60.

Westhead, P. and C. Howorth (2006), 'Ownership and management issues associated with family firm performance and company objectives', *Family Business Review*, **19**, 301–16.

Yermack, D. (1996), 'Higher market valuation of companies with a small board of directors', *Journal of Financial Economics*, **40**, 185–211.

PART III

FAMILY GOVERNANCE

6 Family governance bodies: a conceptual typology
Alexander Koeberle-Schmid and Donella Caspersz

INTRODUCTION

Achieving continuity of a family business is extremely challenging, particularly when the number of family members and owners increases. On the one hand, an expanded number of owners and family members widens the pool of talent available and extends the resource base of the firm (Barney, 1991; Habbershon and Williams, 1999; Bubolz, 2001; Sirmon and Hitt, 2003; Arrègle et al., 2007), thus reducing the need to attract capabilities such as managerial or financial talent from outside the family, while simultaneously strengthening internal family resources and bonds (Sirmon and Hitt, 2003).

However, expanding the number of owners and family members also increases complexity, especially in the number of roles played by family members. The three-circle model (Davis, 1982; Tagiuri and Davis, [1982] 1996) suggests that family members can engage in one of seven sectors formed by the overlapping of the family, business and ownership systems; for instance, family members may be directors, executive officers as well as owners. This complexity signals the potential for conflicts to emerge, in particular, between non-managerial/director family owners and manager/director family owners (Schulze et al., 2003; Ng, 2005), as numbers and skills minimize the opportunity for all family owners to be involved in the firm beyond participating in an annual general meeting (AGM) (Vilaseca, 2002). From an agency perspective, this may lead to information asymmetries, which in turn can stimulate increased heterogeneity of interests (Schulze et al., 2003; Ng, 2005; Karra et al., 2006; Witt, 2008). However, this complexity can also distance owners from their firm, reduce the value of the business and, consequently, the interest of family members in the business, eventually diminishing the emotional value that family members attach to the business (Zellweger and Astrachan, 2008; Zellweger and Sieger, 2009; Björnberg and Nicholson, 2008).

The literature generally identifies family councils or family owners' committees as appropriate formal governance processes for family firms to implement in answer to these challenges (Hoy and Sharma, 2010; Sharma and Nordqvist, 2008; Lansberg, 2008; Moore and Juenemann, 2008; Gallo and Kenyon-Rouvinez, 2005). Moore and Juenemann (2008) describe a family council (or ownership committee) as a 'mechanism by which the family exercises and maintains its ownership responsibilities over a professionally governed and managed family company' (More and Juenemann, 2008, p.68). This may require non-executive directors to supervise and guide executive officers. Thus, in this instance, Moore and Juenemann (2008) suggest that a family council can assist non-family members as it helps 'achieve family consensus and serve as the channel for family communication to the board of directors' (ibid., p.67).

However, family governance bodies (such as family councils or ownership committees) are not clearly defined in terms of their tasks and composition, or how they intersect with other roles occupied by family members, such as that of a family board director, executive officer and even non-family owner. For instance, case descriptions of family councils (Lamp, 2008), their tasks (Lansberg, 2008) and empirical research of councils in Germany (Koeberle-Schmid, 2008) highlight that, in practice, there is evidence of a much broader and more differentiated task structure for family governance bodies than councils (or ownership committees) alone. We subsequently suggest that the governance options available for family firms may reflect a typology that, in addition to differentiating tasks, identifies the composition and appropriate representation of family owners and members to achieve the best fit between the family member and governance body, while minimizing potential conflicts between family members that may subsequently be transferred to those governance bodies. Given this context, the following questions guide our enquiry:

1. What are the different family governance bodies and how are they differentiated in terms of tasks?
2. How can these family governance bodies be composed to secure appropriate representation of family owners and members?

To answer these questions, the chapter begins with an overview of the different tasks associated with family governance types. This is followed by a discussion of four variables that – we argue – influence the development of the different types of family governance bodies. Our first question is directly addressed by describing different governance bodies and their associated tasks, and concludes with identifying five different family governance bodies. We then answer our second question by explaining how to determine the appropriate representation of family owners and members on these family governance bodies, and conclude by identifying further areas of research.

Our discussion is framed by the definition of family business proposed by Chua et al. (1999). In their view, family firms are 'governed and/or managed with the intention to shape and pursue the vision of the business held by a dominant coalition controlled by members of the same family or a small number of families in a manner that is potentially sustainable across generations of the family or families' (Chua et al., 1999, p. 25). This definition offers the advantages of embracing multiple generations, encompasses the different roles that family may occupy in the business (that is, as family members, owners, managers/directors), but clearly privileges the prominence of the family in managing or governing the firm. However, it is important to note that family influence varies across generations (Astrachan et al., 2002; Klein et al., 2005) and as the 'family in business' expands.

TASKS AND INFLUENCING VARIABLES OF FAMILY GOVERNANCE BODIES

The literature (see Hoy and Sharma, 2010; Lansberg, 2008; Gallo and Kenyon-Rouvinez, 2005; Lank and Ward, 2002; Aronoff and Ward, 1996; Ward, 1991) and empirical studies (see Koeberle-Schmid, 2008), suggests that family governance bodies perform five tasks. These are to:

Firm perspective   Family perspective

Family focus	Securing long-term family ownership (task β) (possible additional special task: pooling voting rights (task ε))	Promoting family cohesion and communication (task α)
Firm focus	Supervision/control and advice of the executive officers (task δ)	Influencing firm strategy (involvement in important decisions) on behalf of the AGM (task γ)

Source: Adaptation of Huse (2005).

Figure 6.1   Tasks of family governance bodies

- promote family cohesion and communication (task α);
- secure long-term family ownership (task β); (task β might include in some cases pooling/exercising voting shares (task ε) that could also be performed separately);
- influence firm strategy (involvement in important decisions) on behalf of the AGM (task γ); and
- supervise/control and advise the executives (task δ).

As depicted by Figure 6.1, the different tasks of family governance types can be grouped according to perspective (firm or family) and focus (firm or family). Perspective refers to the perspective from which the task is performed, while focus refers to the area of concern that the task is targeted at. Thus a member of a family governance body performs his or her tasks from a firm or family perspective, with the focus being either the firm or the family. For instance, from a family perspective family owners may focus on consolidating the 'family' across generations, implying that the task of a family governance body would be to promote family cohesion and communication (task α). The implications for the firm that arise from this focus are that the respective family governance body can influence firm strategy on behalf of other family owners and members (task γ). The same logic applies to the firm perspective: for instance, where the goal from a firm perspective is multigenerational family firm sustainability, thus necessitating long-term family ownership (task β), pooling voting shares (task ε) may be appropriate. From a firm perspective with a firm focus, the goal and task of a family governance body (if there is no other business governance body such as a board or directors) is to supervise and advise the executive officers of the family firm (task δ).

However, all family governance bodies do not perform all tasks as each strategy embodies a different goal and hence different task structure (in terms of perspective and focus). It is suggested that the following four variables influence this task structure and associated characteristics:

- the number of family owners;
- the type of involvement of family owners in management;
- the existence of other governance bodies (such as board of directors); and
- the presence of external, non-family owners.

Number of Family Owners

Complexity increases as the number of family members and owners expands and separate interests develop between different branches of a family tree. The imperative to coordinate the interests of these disparate family members demands a sophisticated family governance structure (Klein, 2010). Three difficulties emerge from this scenario: managing family members to retain loyalty to the firm and reduce negative conflicts (Aronoff and Ward, 1996; Lank and Ward, 2002; Gallo and Kenyon-Rouvinez, 2005); unifying heterogeneous interests (Lansberg, 1999; Gallo and Kenyon-Rouvinez, 2005); and – particularly in today's fast-moving world – strengthening decision-making by seeking relatively rapid consent on decisions of fundamental importance. These difficulties can be explained in more detail.

An increased number of owners means that all or most own only small shares in the firm's equity capital. This reduces altruistic behavior (Karra et al., 2006; Miller et al., 2008) as well as control at an AGM, which, in turn, might reduce a member's personal interest in the firm as each family owner increasingly prioritizes his/her own interests over the firm (Schulze et al., 2003). In large, publicly held family corporations, so-called rational apathy could emerge and voting rights are no longer personally executed (Dent, 1989). Therefore retaining family owners' and members' loyalty to family and firm, promoting family cohesion and securing family ownership become relevant especially when complex issues need to be decided quickly and cannot await an AGM of owners. Hence it becomes significant to have a family governance body that influences the firm strategy on behalf of the general membership (of owners) when required.

Type of Involvement of Family Owners in Management

The type of family owners' involvement in the management of the family business is crucial for the structure of family governance bodies. If this includes not only family owners and members but also executive officers from the family (namely family CEOs), a new set of challenges emerges. For instance, intra-family conflicts may arise, possibly of a principal–agent type, because there are active and passive family owners (Schulze et al., 2003). In this case, there is no loss in the identity of ownership and management; however, the diversity of owners' expectations and interests in the firm further increases (Tagiuri and Davis, [1982] 1996; Westhead and Cowling, 1997; Witt, 2008). A family governance body might unify family members and owners to ensure they 'speak with one voice' in this scenario. Furthermore, as in the case of a sibling partnership or a cousin consortium, ownership control might be exerted and exploited by family CEOs (Frankforter et al., 2000; La Porta et al., 1999). Theoretically, stewardship theory (Donaldson and Davis, 1991; Davis et al., 1997), which assumes that managers are driven by a commitment to the interests of owners and will be as diligent and committed to the prosperity of the business as owners, may not explain the behavior of family CEOs quite as well as agency theory does (Chrisman et al., 2005; Chrisman et al., 2007). An impressive array of empirical studies finds indications of principal–agent conflicts between management and family owners, even if the manager is a family CEO (Ang and Cole, 2000; Schulze et al., 2001; Chrisman et al., 2004; Karra et al., 2006; Miller and Le Breton-Miller, 2006; Chrisman et al., 2007; Koeberle-Schmid, 2008). This scenario calls for a more formal and organized type of family governance body that draws on a broader spectrum of tasks.

Existence of Other Governance Bodies

This refers to the existence of other governance bodies besides the AGM that may affect the task structure of family governance bodies, particularly corporate governance bodies such as a board of directors (Hoy and Sharma, 2010; Sharma and Nordqvist, 2008; Aronoff and Ward, 1996). For instance, if non-executives on the board of directors supervise executive members, then a family governance body is not involved in the supervisory sphere. The task of the family governance body would be to interact with the family and ensure there is a match between the expectations of the board and family owners.

External, Non-Family Owners

The presence of non-family owners in a family business also influences the type of family governance bodies that are formed. For instance, information asymmetries might emerge given that non-family owners differ from family owners in terms of their values, goals and strategies (Shleifer and Vishny, 1997; Witt, 2008). In addition, there may be a requirement to coordinate family interests *vis-à-vis* the interests of external owners. Decisions on raising equity capital, dividend levels or on strategic issues might be difficult to make if the final legal organ of decision-making is the AGM. In this case, a family governance body might serve to pool family shares so that the family can 'speak with one voice' with external owners.

TYPOLOGY OF FAMILY GOVERNANCE BODIES

Overview

The following discussion conceptualizes a typology of family governance bodies taking into account the abovementioned literature and exploratory empirical research (see Figure 6.2). This typology arranges family governance bodies into mutually exclusive, collectively exhaustive, internally homogeneous and stable categories (Chrisman et al., 1988). Each type of family governance body is named so as to allow for ease of identification. To conceptualize the different types of family governance bodies, we combine the

Types of family governance bodies

	Family council	Family owners' committee	Family business owners' committee I	Family business owners' committee II	Pooling firm
Cohesion (task α)	x	x	x	x	
Ownership (task β)		x	x	x	
Strategy (task γ)			x	x	
Control/advice (task δ)				x	
Pooling (task ε)		(x)	(x)	(x)	x

Tasks of family governance bodies

Figure 6.2   Types of family governance bodies with their respective tasks

five different tasks, their relationship to the family/firm and focus/perspective matrix (see Figure 6.1) and the four influencing variables.

As Figure 6.2 depicts, governance bodies with a family focus are typically a family council and family owners' committee. However, there are also family governance types that perform not only the tasks of family owners' committees, but also incorporate a firm focus. These are called family business owners' committees, and usually operate in cooperation with a board of directors. There is a further governance type referred to as a pooling firm that pools voting rights of family members (otherwise referred to as proxy voting).

Family Council

Family cohesion and communication decrease as the number of family owners and members' increases. This is independent of the fact that family owners are in management, but not necessarily independent of the fact that other governance bodies may be operating. For instance, a family council may be appropriate where there is a board of directors. However, in this case the family council is equipped with little decision-making power relating to the firm. Power may instead arise from informal meetings of a more active group of family owners and/or members. In the case of owners, those with more equity capital or those of high esteem representing different branches of a family tree are usually members of a family council. In these meetings, information about the family and family firm is exchanged. Before and after meetings, information is either collected within the family or the family is informed about the latest management decisions. In summary, when viewed from a family perspective with a family focus where harmony (DeNoble et al., 2007) and trust (Steier, 2001) within the family are important, promoting family cohesion and communication (task α) is the major reason for the existence of a family council.

Nonetheless, the family council has significant economic importance. This is because family cohesion can be considered as a unique resource that can influence family firm performance when framed by the resource-based view. Referred to as 'familiness' in the case of family business (Habbershohn et al., 2003), social (family) cohesion builds social capital in family firms (Lank and Ward, 2002; Bubolz, 2001; Nahapiet and Ghoshal, 1998; Habbershon et al., 2003; Arrègle et al., 2007) that 'facilitate[s] action and create[s] value' (Arrègle et al., 2007, p. 75): that is, a value that is distinctive, enduring and unique to family firms. Promoting family cohesion and communication can be achieved by organizing family meetings and educating family members, especially members of the next generation (Lansberg, 1999), to instill loyalty to the firm, become knowledgeable about their rights and obligations as future owners (Aronoff and Ward, 1996; Ward, 1991; Gersick et al., 1997), and forge a common vision and mission (Tagiuri and Davis, [1982] 1996) that synthesizes the goals and values of all family owners and members (Gubitta and Gianecchini, 2002). Cohesion of all family owners and members can be fostered if the family council promotes and regularly adopts this common vision and mission (Carlock and Ward, 2003).

Family cohesion is also promoted by identifying potential emotional conflicts early (Ward, 1991; Lansberg, 2008), avoiding their escalation and hence negative impact on the firm (Gersick et al., 1997). A family council can address these conflicts openly, thus positively affecting family and firm performance (Kellermanns and Eddleston, 2004) by providing opportunities for the interlocking family 'interests and goals to find their appropriate expression and for conflicts to be explored' (Gersick et al., 1997, p. 238). Thus we describe a family council as a group of family owners or members that acts to promote family cohesion and communication. However, the number of family owners and the existence of other governance bodies influences whether a family council is or is not implemented.

Family Owners' Committee

The goal of a family business is to sustain family ownership across generations (Tagiuri and Davis, [1982] 1996; Westhead and Howorth, 2006). Independent of the existence of corporate governance bodies, a family owners' committee might assist by performing the task of securing long-term family ownership (task β) in addition to fostering family cohesion (task α). This task becomes especially relevant if there are many family owners. By pursuing task β, a family owners' committee contributes to the sustainability of the firm (Huse, 2007) by devising rules for ownership (Gallo and Kenyon-Rouvincz, 2005) and inheritance. These rules should be incorporated into the family charter. The family owners' committee can also be charged with the task of monitoring ownership transfers (Lansberg, 1999; Lank and Ward, 2002). In particular, the committee should prevent or manage the impact of the uncontrolled exit of owners (Tagiuri and Davis, [1982] 1996) for the benefit rather than detriment of the family firm (Redlefsen and Witt, 2006).

The following example illustrates a type of family owners' committee. Schneider Ltd is a family firm in its third generation with 22 owners. The firm holds an AGM and employs a family CEO. The charter of the firm does not require a board of directors. A family owners' committee was established as the interests of the family in the AGM declined, and knowledge of the firm and industry decreased, especially in the next generation. One representative from each of the four branches of the family tree was chosen to form the committee, while the largest family owner became the chairperson. The council holds bi-annual meetings: one at the time of the AGM, which more or less resembles a family gathering. Standing agenda items at this meeting include information about the firm and its activities, taxation issues, professional development, opportunities for the younger generation and ownership issues. The goal of the council is to sustain family ownership across generations. Thus, we describe a family owners' committee as a group of family owners or members that acts to promote family cohesion and communication as well as secure long-term family ownership. Whether a family owners' committee is required or not depends on the number of family owners.

Where there is an external ownership interest in the firm, a pooling family owners' committee that pools voting rights (via voting by proxy) and the decision-making power of all family owners (task α, β plus task ε) can contribute to long-term family ownership. This 'pooled' family owners' committee acts on behalf of the family owners on matters related to the family business. The goal is to enable the family as a whole to make decisions by resolving conflicts 'in house' and exercising voting power en bloc. This strategy may also contribute to enhancing family cohesion and homogeneity and reduce the potential of agency conflicts. From the firm perspective, managers can be sure that family owners speak en bloc, thus minimizing the potential for disruption in decision-making.

For instance, the Swiss pharmaceutical company Roche AG formed a family owners' committee. The immediate descendants of the Fritz Hoffmann-La Roche family own only 50.01 percent of the equity capital of Roche AG. To protect the firm against unfriendly takeovers and therefore to ensure long-term dominant family ownership, the Hoffmann and Oerli families established a pooling contract between owners which merged their votes into a bloc when critical decisions were made. Thus a pooling family owners' committee can be described as a group of family owners or members that acts to promote family cohesion and communication, to secure long-term family ownership and to pool voting rights. We suggest that whether a pooling family owners' committee is required depends on the presence of external, non-family owners in the family firm.

A pooling firm is where 'pooling' (or voting by proxy) is the only task of that particular family governance body. This is applicable where not only interests of family owners need to be coordinated *vis-à-vis* external owners, but also where different family branches exist with each branch coordinating its own voting rights. Thus, for instance, if there were three branches, there would be three pooling firms.

Figure 6.3 shows how such a pooling firm in a family business with three family branches and external owners could be structured.

An example of this form of governance is Corporation X, which is a large family firm. There is a 44.5 percent non-family ownership of stock traded in the stock market. Part of this stock (0.8 percent) is non-voting shares, which further reduces the decision making influence of the non-family owners. Three family branches together hold 55.5 percent majority of the equity capital. Each family owns a 33.3 percent share in the pooling firm.

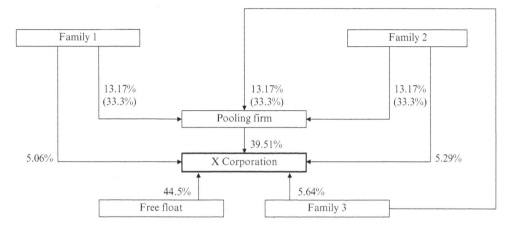

Figure 6.3   Example of a pooling arrangement

This is primarily used to assure identical voting of 39.51 percent of the equity capital owned by the three families. In addition, each family votes individually with between 5.06 percent and 5.64 percent of the equity capital. A contract on pooled voting may or may not include these shares, which is an issue of taxation and of flexibility in transferring equity to other partners. If all shares are not included in the pool yet the pooling firm needs to reach a majority decision, this would still lead to a minimum of 49.86 percent of the votes cast in the AGM of Corporation X on behalf of the owner families in agreement. The discontented family could then vote its 5.64 percent (at most). Usually, not all the voting rights from the free flow (this refers to all external shareholders that buy shares on the stock exchange) are present at the AGM. Therefore a discontented vote is unlikely to overthrow a majority decision taken by the pooling firm. Pressure to unite and assure family cohesion within one family and among the different family branches is exerted through this arrangement. Nonetheless, conflicts between different branches might arise similar to those at the lower level of the organization described before. A pooling firm can thus be described as a firm that acts only to pool voting rights. Whether it is required as part of the governance structure of a family firm is related to the number of family owners and the existence of external, non-family owners.

Family Business Owners' Committee Type I

The family council and family owners' committee are family governance bodies with a family focus. However, family governance bodies related to the business also incorporate a firm focus in addition to the family focus and respective tasks (Lansberg, 2008). In these cases, it is not only the existence of a large number of family owners and members or external owners that is relevant; the existence of other governance bodies, especially corporate governance bodies, and the representation of the family in management influence the tasks of family governance bodies.

The first family governance body with a firm focus is a family business owners' committee type I. In addition to tasks α and β, this body would, from a family perspective with a firm focus, consider the strategic goals of the family regarding the firm, and influence the firm strategy on behalf of the owners at the AGM (task γ). In this sense, the task of this body 'is to articulate the family's core values and communicate those values to the managers and directors of the business' (Lansberg, 2008, p. 63).

This family business owners' committee type I would exercise decision-making power relating to the firm. Therefore this committee has to be formalized in the firm's charter. The legitimacy assigned to this organ typically stems from the AGM, thus avoiding an overlap of activities with the tasks of the board of directors or executive committee, if applicable (Gallo and Kenyon-Rouvinez, 2005). In particular, the family business owners' committee type I will be able to respond to matters requiring quick turnaround time such as major investment opportunities; significant operational matters including devising incentive systems for management; or decisions with long-lasting effects, for instance the choice of board members (Martin, 2001; Lank and Ward, 2002; Ward, 2004). Performing these tasks effectively enhances the resource base of the firm by developing the human capital and organizational social capital among family owners (Leana and Buren, 1999; Nahapiet and Ghoshal, 1998; Sirmon and Hitt, 2003; Sirmon et al., 2007; Arrègle et al., 2007). As a prerequisite, this type of committee should attempt to unify family owners opinions about vision, mission and strategy (Lansberg, 1999; Gallo and Kenyon-Rouvinez, 2005). In the case of external owners, this can be achieved through pooling voting rights (or voting by proxy).

Where co-determined boards of directors are legislatively required, such as in Germany (this refers to a management model whereby boards are legislatively required to not only include shareholder representation, but also worker representation as per unions; see Hall and Soskice, 2001), this type of committee is highly attractive because it is not a co-determined body. However, it is not uncommon that separate meetings of the members of a family business owners' committee type I would take place prior to board meetings. Labor representatives of the board would also be able to meet separately. These meetings serve to identify interests or positions of both parties, without any immediate necessity to compromise (as would be the case in a co-determined structure). A compromised position can then be determined at the board meeting.

Franz Haniel and Cie GmbH (James, 2006) provides one example of a family business owners' committee type I. In 2006, the firm had 502 family owners of which only three owned more than 5 percent of the equity capital and only 21 owned more than 1 percent. Haniel traditionally employs non-family managers. The family owners of the business elect 30 members to a family business owners' committee type I for a period of five years at the AGM. This subsequently selects eight non-executive members of the board to represent the owners. Another eight non-executive board members are labor representatives according to co-determination laws. However, the committee is not a co-determined organ; thus it can develop the family owner perspectives while leaving the board to represent the stakeholder perspective and negotiate a compromise with all parties. Thus a family business owners' committee type I can be described as a group of family owners or members that acts to promote family cohesion and communication, to secure long-term family ownership, and influence firm strategy on behalf of the AGM (with or without the task of pooling voting rights in accordance with the presence of external, non-family owners. The requirement for a family owners business committee type 1 is related to the existence of other governance bodies, the number of family owners and the presence of external, non-family owners.

Family Business Owners' Committee Type II

The family governance body with the most far-reaching influence on the firm is the family business owners' committee type II. This only exists where there is no board with independent directors who advise and supervise the executive officers, especially where there is no or only very little family owner representation in management. The charter of the firm has to define this type, its tasks and its legitimatization as a legal organ. In addition to the tasks α, β and γ, this council makes decisions otherwise assigned to non-executive members of the board. From a firm perspective with a firm focus, this includes supervision/control and advice to executives (task δ). Thus this type of governance body considers all issues related to the family and the firm. As there are inactive owners, this committee needs to ensure that management acts in accordance with the family vision, mission and strategy. In the case of external owners, the tasks of this governance body can also be extended by pooling voting rights of the family.

The supervisory task includes monitoring and controlling the financial status of the firm as well as the appointment of executives (Gabrielsson and Winlund, 2000; Corbetta and Salvato, 2004; Huse, 2007; Randøy and Goel, 2003). From an agency perspective, control of the executive board can reduce agency threats (Gómez-Mejía et al., 2001; Steier, 2003; Chrisman et al., 2004). This applies not only to non-family managers but also family CEOs (Ang and Cole, 2000; Chua et al., 2003). Schulze et al. (2003) suggest that if there are several family managers, each will prioritize his or her own interests, while the interests of the family become secondary. These authors further highlight that if there are inactive and active family owners, the executives can use firm resources at the expense of the inactive family owners (Schulze et al., 2003; Ng, 2005; Chrisman et al., 2007), for instance the tax declaration of the family manager is done in the firm. Another threat to better performance is entrenchment, which refers to when performance by family owners on the executive board is influenced by intimate ties to their position (Schulze et al., 2001; Gómez-Mejía et al., 2001; Miller and Le Breton-Miller, 2006).

By performing an advisory task, this type of committee accumulates human capital (this refers to the knowledge and skills acquired by human beings through education activities, for instance; see Nahapiet and Ghoshal, 1998; Srimon et al., 2007), which may bestow a competitive advantage for the firm (Collis, 1994). By discussing strategic and financial issues with the executive board, the committee members communicate their knowledge and their experiences to the executives. These discussions enhance the information base of the executive board, which enables its members to better evaluate alternatives as well as to reduce uncertainty and complexity (Dooley and Fryxell, 1999). Thus a family business owners' committee type II (if there is no board of directors) is described as a group of family owners or members with additional non-family members that acts to promote family cohesion and communication, to secure long-term family ownership, influence firm strategy on behalf of the AGM, and to supervise and advise executive officers (with or without the task of pooling voting rights). The requirement for this type of governance strategy is related to the number of family owners, the presence of external, non-family owners, the type of involvement of family owners in management and the existence of other governance bodies.

Composition of Family Governance Bodies

We assumed in this chapter that there has been no pruning of family members in terms of ownership: thus the numbers of family owners increases across generations (Lambrecht and Lievens, 2008). To secure effective and efficient committee work, not every owner can nor should be a member of a family governance body. When assuming that family governance bodies should only be composed by family owners or members, it is necessary to identify a compromise that satisfies the range of owners' interests. This is a challenging task as representation in a democratic sense implies that committee members be elected at an AGM. However, minority groups may feel underrepresented at an AGM as a result of the voting procedure, particularly if potential members are elected sequentially. Therefore it is necessary to ensure proper representation of different groups. For instance, groups might be defined by different branches of a family tree, age cohorts, sizes of ownership, professional experiences or social competencies. All these factors should influence the composition of family governance bodies. However, they overlap and need to be applied simultaneously. This cannot be achieved through the election process, especially when criteria need to be considered simultaneously. Two alternatives thus emerge.

First, a patriarchal majority owner identifies the candidates for the family governance body in reference to the criteria identified above (Bernier et al., 2007). This procedure builds on the strength of this personality as well as on his or her intimate knowledge of family owners. It is fortunate if such a personality exists. However, even where this figure exists, there is no long-term guarantee that this will continue to be the case.

Second, each family owner is able to propose candidates for election to the AGM, again in reference to the criteria identified above (Johnston et al., 2008). However, only a full list of candidates or a 'ticket' can be proposed and eventually elected. Each ticket should reflect the different groups of owners. Re-election of members is also possible in this case. This election procedure can foster trust in the committee. The elected committee is independent of the board, which should help it perform its tasks. Thus a family governance body is composed of family owners and members elected at the AGM. The effectiveness of a family governance body is related to whether it reflects both identity-related diversity (for example, age, gender) as well as family-interests diversity (for example, different branches of the family).

If family owners implement a family business owners' committee type II, members need to be able to advise and supervise executive officers. However, availability of requisite expertise to perform those tasks effectively might be a scarce resource within the family and owner group. Where this is the case, family owners will consider asking non-family members to join the committee. As well as contributing their professional expertise, non-family members on the family business owners' committee type II may also enhance both impartiality and independence in decision-making, thus reducing agency costs. On the other hand, their presence may reduce the potential to strengthen cohesion within the family.

One example of such a committee composition can be seen at Dachser Ltd Logistics Group (Erker, 2008). A family business owners' committee type II with family owners and non-family members called an 'administrative board' has been in existence since 1992. The committee 'was entrusted mainly with "those tasks that are otherwise . . . the responsibility of the shareholders. A further major task . . . remains its responsibility for securing the equity ratio"' (Erker, 2008, p. 258). The non-family chairman of the committee views the committee as 'an advisory body designed to support the major shareholders in monitoring the work of the management' (ibid.). The chairman insisted on being included in the firm's communication network, to participate in the bi-annual strategy meetings of the executive officers, and to be able to place items on the agenda of those meetings in consent with the family CEO. The representation of family owners in this committee assured that the tasks of promoting family cohesion and communication, securing long-term family ownership and influencing firm strategy on behalf of the family AGM are performed.

DISCUSSION AND FUTURE RESEARCH DIRECTIONS

To assist owners develop an in-depth understanding of the appropriate family governance structure for their firm, this chapter presents a typology of family governance bodies. The selection of a type of family governance body depends on the number of owners, as well as different types of involvement of family members in the business, the existence of corporate governance bodies such as a board of directors, and the presence of external, non-family owners. When selecting a family governance body, family owners need to decide, in reference to these four variables, which tasks the committee members should perform. It has been suggested in this chapter that these tasks might be promoting family cohesion and family communication (task α), securing long-term family ownership (task β), which can be extended by pooling voting shares as proxy votes (task ε), influencing firm strategy on behalf of other family owners (task γ), and possibly supervising executive officers (task δ). Using those five tasks, we subsequently identified five different types of distinctive family governance bodies: a family council (task α), a family owners' committee (tasks α and β; if non-family owners exist also task ε), just a pooling service firm (task ε), a family business owners' committee type I (tasks α, β and γ), and a family business owners' committee type II (tasks α, β, γ and δ; only relevant if no board or directors). Concerning the appropriate representation of family owners on these bodies, we suggested that each family owner is able to propose a full list of candidates or a 'ticket' that could be elected at the AGM. Each ticket should reflect the different groups of owners.

Future research may uncover a greater variety of tasks, further variables, and effects on the economic and emotional value of such family governance bodies. In particular, little is known about the efficiency and effectiveness of task performance of the different types of family governance bodies. A further area of research is whether the family governance bodies are effective in their task performance, whether the types of election procedures are appropriate and whether alternative procedures are applied.

Another point of interest relates to organizational dynamics. Questions can be asked whether the four variables identified are sufficient to explain the transfer from one type of committee to another. For instance, is it possible that a firm begins with a family council, broadens to a family owners' committee and then extends to a family business owners' committee? The abovementioned Schneider Ltd case exemplifies this trajectory. The family owners established a family council at the same time as forming a board of directors with non-family members as non-executives. A few years later the family owners felt that the existing family council should adopt a formal role in supervising, controlling

	Ownership	
	Extended family ownership	Extended family and non-family ownership
Nuclear family management	*AGM, family council or family owners' committee*, executive board	*AGM, family owners' committee with pooling*, board of directors
Extended family-dominated management	*AGM, family owners' committee or family business owners' committee type I (if board of directors) or type II (if no board of directors)*, executive board	*AGM, family owners' committee with pooling or family business owners' committee type I with pooling*, board of directors
Non-family management	*AGM, family business owners' committee type I (if board of directors) or type II (if no board of directors)*, executive board	*AGM, family business owners' committee type I with pooling*, board of directors

Figure 6.4   Reduced typology of family firms and family governance bodies

and advising management. This led to the establishment of a family business owners' committee type II, which made the board of directors obsolete. Beside the type II committee, only an executive board is now in place.

The development of a family business across generations changes the structure of ownership, family and management (Gersick et al., 1997). This change has to be considered in any governance structure (Sharma and Nordqvist, 2008). Thus, while some governance bodies may be relevant to some generations (or at some point in time), they may be irrelevant at a different point in time to successive generations. Therefore the five types of family governance bodies could be associated with different types of family firms. Figure 6.4 depicts this typology.

In the six types of family businesses identified, an AGM where owners exercise their ownership rights is always held. We explain these options as follows:

1. In the case of extended family ownership, the firm should at least have an executive board which performs the management task. However, if there are non-family owners, a board of directors becomes crucial.
2. In the case of extended family ownership and nuclear family management, we propose a family council or a family owners' committee, because managing the family might be the main goal of family governance. In the case of extended family-dominated management, a family owners' committee would be relevant if the body deals only with family governance. If it is established to deal with corporate governance, a family business owners' committee type I (if a board of directors) or type II (if no board of directors) is the most appropriate choice.
3. If there is only non-family management, the family should be able to influence management extensively. Therefore, if there is no board of directors, a family business owners' committee of type II may be implemented; if there is a board, type I could be sufficient. Pooling interests by the governance body should be considered if coordinated voting (pooling) becomes important, particularly as an instrument to unify family interests *vis-à-vis* non-family owners and against unfriendly takeovers. This is the case in the remaining three types of family firms where the family business owners' committee type II is not applicable, because the non-executives on the board of directors supervise and advise the executive officers.

4. In the case of nuclear family management, family cohesion and securing family ownership *vis-à-vis* non-family owners are important. At the very least a family owners' committee with pooling should be implemented.
5. In the case of extended family-dominated management, the implementation of a family business owners' committee should be considered.
6. Where there is non-family management, the family should consolidate their influence in the business, which means that a family business owners' committee type I should be implemented.

In summary, the aim of this chapter has been to establish a conceptual model that can be empirically validated. This is especially in reference to unraveling the five tasks, the four variables and the appropriate composition in each strategy. This allows business-owning families to decide about the options available to deal with the question of juggling family and business in the context of governance. It is argued that it is critical for family business to continue to address this question, to safeguard sustainability beyond generations while prospering both as a family and business. Failure to do so can only be detrimental to the long-term survival of family businesses across generations.

REFERENCES

Ang, J. and R. Cole (2000), 'Agency costs and ownership structure', *Journal of Finance*, **55**, 81–106.
Aronoff, C. and J. Ward (1996), *Family Business Governance: Maximizing Family and Business Potential*, 3rd edn, Marietta, GA: Family Business Publishers.
Arrègle, J.-L., M. Hitt, D. Sirmon and P. Very (2007), 'The development of organizational social capital: attributes of family firms', *Journal of Management Studies*, **44**(1), 73–95.
Astrachan, J., S. Klein and K. Smyrnios (2002), 'The F-PEC scale of family influence: a proposal for solving the family business definition problem', *Family Business Review*, **15**(1), 45–58.
Barney, J. (1991), 'Firm resources and sustained competitive advantage', *Journal of Management*, **17**, 99–120.
Bernier, J.-F. et al. (2007), *Heraeus: Family Governance for a Global Company*, Vallendar: WHU case, Version 2007-11-21.
Björnberg, A. and N. Nicholson (2008), *Emotional Ownership – The Critical Pathway Between the Next Generation and the Family Firm*, London: Institute for Family Business.
Bubolz, M. (2001), 'Family as source, user, and builder of social capital', *Journal of Socio-Economics*, **30**(2), 129–31.
Carlock, R. and J. Ward (2003), *Strategic Planning for the Family Business: Parallel Planning to Unify the Family and Business*, Basingstoke: Palgrave Macmillan.
Chrisman, J., C. Hofer and W. Boulton (1988), 'Toward a system for classifying-business strategies', *Academy of Management Review*, **13**(3), 413–28.
Chrisman, J., J. Chua and R. Litz (2004), 'Comparing the agency costs of family and non-family firms: conceptual issues and exploratory evidence', *Entrepreneurship Theory and Practice*, **28**(4), 335–54.
Chrisman, J., J. Chua and P. Sharma (2005), 'Trends and directions in the development of a strategic management theory of the family firm', *Entrepreneurship Theory and Practice*, **29**(5), 555–75.
Chrisman, J., J. Chua, F. Kellermanns and E. Chang (2007), 'Are family managers agents or stewards? An exploratory study in privately held family firms', *Journal of Business Research*, **60**(10), 1030–38.
Chua, J., J. Chrisman and P. Sharma (1999), 'Defining the family business by behaviour', *Entrepreneurship Theory and Practice*, **23**(4), 19–39.
Chua, J., J. Chrisman and P. Sharma (2003), 'Succession and nonsuccession concerns of family firms and agency relationship with nonfamily managers', *Family Business Review*, **16**(2), 89–107.
Collis, D. (1994), 'Research note: how valuable are organizational capabilities?', *Strategic Management Journal*, **15**(8), 143–52.
Corbetta, G. and C. Salvato (2004), 'The board of directors in family firms: one size fits all?', *Family Business Review*, **17**(2), 119–34.

Davis, J. (1982), *The Influence of Life Stage on Father–Son Work Relationship in Family Companies*, Ann Arbor, MI: University Microfilms.

Davis, H., F. Schoorman and L. Donaldson (1997), 'Toward a stewardship theory of management', *Academy of Management Review*, **22**, 20–47.

DeNoble, A., S. Ehrlich and G. Singh (2007), 'Toward the development of a family business self-efficacy scale: a resource-based perspective', *Family Business Review*, **20**(2), 127–40.

Dent, G. Jr (1989), 'Toward unifying ownership and control in the public corporation', *Wisconsin Law Review*, **5**, 881.

Donaldson, L. and J. Davis (1991), 'Stewardship theory or agency theory: CEO governance and shareholder returns', *Australian Journal of Management*, **16**(1), 49–64.

Dooley, R. and G. Fryxell (1999), 'Attaining decision quality and commitment from dissent: The moderating effects of loyalty and competence in strategic decision-making teams', *Academy of Management Journal*, **42**(4), 389–402.

Erker, P. (2008), *The Dachser Logistics Company – Global Competition and the Strength of the Family Business*, Frankfurt: Campus Verlag.

Frankforter, S., S. Berman and T. Jones (2000), 'Board of directors and shark repellents: assessing the value of agency theory perspective', *Journal of Management Studies*, **37**, 321–48.

Gabrielsson, J. and H. Winlund (2000), 'Boards of directors in small and medium-sized industrial firms: examining the effects of the board's working style on board task performance', *Entrepreneurship and Regional Development*, **12**, 311–30.

Gallo, M. and D. Kenyon-Rouvinez (2005), 'The importance of family and business governance', in D. Kenyon-Rouvinez and J. Ward (eds), *Family Business: Key Issues*, Basingstoke: Palgrave Macmillan, pp. 45–57.

Gersick, K., J. Davis, M. Hampton and I. Lansberg (1997), *Generation to Generation: Life Cycles of the Family Business*, Boston, MA: Harvard Business School Press.

Gómez-Mejía, L., M. Núñnez-Nickel and I. Gutiérrez (2001), 'The role of family ties in agency contracts', *Academy of Management Journal*, **44**(1), 81–95.

Gubitta, P. and M. Gianecchini (2002), 'Governance and flexibility in family-owned SMEs', *Family Business Review*, **15**(4), 277–97.

Habbershon, T. and M. Williams (1999), 'A resource-based framework for assessing the strategic advantages of family firms', *Family Business Review*, **12**(1), 1–25.

Habbershon, T., M. Williams and I. MacMillan (2003), 'A unified systems perspective of family firm performance', *Journal of Business Venturing*, **18**(4), 451–65.

Hall, P. and D. Soskice (2001), 'An introduction to varieties of capitalism', in P. Hall and D. Soskice (eds), *Varieties of Capitalism – The Institutional Foundations of Comparative Advantage*, Oxford: Oxford University Press, pp. 1–68.

Hoy, F. and P. Sharma (2010), *Entrepreneurial Family Firms*, Upper Saddle River, NJ: Prentice Hall.

Huse, M. (2005), 'Accountability and creating accountability: a framework for exploring behavioural perspectives of corporate governance', *British Journal of Management*, **16**, S65–S79.

Huse, M. (2007), *Boards, Governance and Value Creation*, Cambridge: Cambridge University Press.

James, H. (2006), *Family Capitalism – Wendels, Haniels, Falcks and the Continental European Model*, Cambridge, MA: Harvard University Press.

Johnston, S.V. et al. (2008), *Steuler-Industriewerke GmbH – Die Zukunft als Familienunternehmen [The Future of a Family Firm]*, Vallendar: WHU, Case.

Karra, N., P. Tracey and N. Phillips (2006), 'Altruism and agency in the family firm: exploring the role of family, kinship, and ethnicity', *Entrepreneurship Theory and Practice*, **30**(6), 861–77.

Kellermanns, F. and K. Eddleston (2004), 'Feuding families: when conflict does a family firm good', *Entrepreneurship Theory and Practice*, **28**(3), 209–28.

Klein, S. (2010), *Familienunternehmen [Family Business]*, 3rd edn, Lohmar: Eul.

Klein, S., J. Astrachan and K. Smyrnios (2005), 'The F-PEC scale of family influence: construction, validation, and further implications for theory', *Entrepreneurship Theory and Practice*, **29**(3), 321–40.

Koeberle-Schmid, A. (2008), *Family Business Governance – Aufsichtsgremium und Familienrepräsentanz [Supervisory Boards and Family Councils]*, Wiesbaden: Gabler.

Lambrecht, J. and J. Lievens (2008), 'Pruning the family tree: an unexplored path to family business continuity and family harmony', *Family Business Review*, **21**(4), 295–313.

Lamp, C. (2008), 'The Eddy Family council: meeting and eating since 2000', in B. Spector (ed.), *Shareholder's Handbook*, Philadelphia, PA: Family Business Publishing Company, pp. 69–72.

Lank, A. and J. Ward (2002), 'Governing the business owning family', in C. Aronoff, J. Astrachan and J. Ward (eds), *Family Business Sourcebook: A Guide for Families Who Own Businesses and the Professionals Who Serve Them*, 3rd edn, Marietta, GA: Family Enterprise Publishers, pp. 462–9.

Lansberg, I. (1999), *Succeeding Generations: Realizing the Dream of Families in Business*, Boston, MA: Harvard Business School Press.

Lansberg, I. (2008), 'A family council elevates the family's status', in B. Spector (ed.), *Shareholder's Handbook*, Philadelphia, PA: Family Business Publishing Company, pp. 63–4.

La Porta, R., F. Lopez-de-Silanes and A. Shleifer (1999), 'Corporate ownership around the world', *Journal of Finance*, **54**, 471–518.

Leana, C. and H.V. Buren (1999), 'Organizational social capital and employment practices', *Academy of Management Review*, **24**(3), 538–55.

Martin, H. (2001), 'Is family governance an oxymoron?', *Family Business Review*, **14**(2), 91–6.

Miller, D. and I. Le Breton-Miller (2006), 'Family governance and firm performance: agency, stewardship and capabilities', *Family Business Review*, **19**, 73–87.

Miller, D., I. Le Breton-Miller and B. Scholnick (2008), 'Stewardship vs. stagnation: an empirical comparison of small family and non-family businesses', *Journal of Management Studies*, **45**(1), 51–78.

Moore, J. and T. Juenemann (2008), 'Good governance for a family and its business', in B. Spector (ed.), *Shareholder's Handbook*, Philadelphia, PA: Family Business Publishing Company, pp. 65–8.

Nahapiet, J. and S. Ghoshal (1998), 'Social capital, intellectual capital, and the organizational advantage', *Academy of Management Review*, **23**, 242–66.

Ng, C. (2005), 'An empirical study on the relationship between ownership and performance in a family-based corporate environment', *Journal of Accounting, Auditing and Finance*, **20**(2), 121–46.

Randøy, T. and S. Goel (2003), 'Ownership structure, founder leadership, and performance in Norwegian SMEs: implications for financing entrepreneurial opportunities', *Journal of Business Venturing*, **18**(5), 619–37.

Redlefsen, M. and P. Witt (2006), 'Gesellschafterausstieg in großen Familienunternehmen [Exit of Family Owners in Large Family Firms]', *Zeitschrift für Betriebswirtschaft*, **76**(1), 7–27.

Schulze, W., M. Lubatkin, R. Dino and A. Buchholtz (2001), 'Agency relationships in family firms: theory and evidence', *Organizational Science*, **12**(2), 85–105.

Schulze, W., M. Lubatkin and R. Dino (2003), 'Exploring the agency consequences of ownership dispersion among the directors of private family firms', *Academy of Management Journal*, **46**(2), 179–94.

Sharma, P. and M. Nordqvist (2008), 'A classification scheme for family firms: from family values to effective governance to firm performance', in J. Tapies and J. Ward (eds), *Family Values and Value Creation: How do Family-owned Businesses Foster Enduring Values*, Basingstoke: Palgrave Macmillan, pp. 71–101.

Shleifer, A. and R. Vishny (1997), 'A survey of corporate governance', *Journal of Finance*, **52**(2), 737–83.

Sirmon, D. and M. Hitt (2003), 'Managing resources: linking unique resources, management, and wealth creation in family firms', *Entrepreneurship Theory and Practice*, **27**(4), 339–58.

Sirmon, D., M. Hitt and R. Ireland (2007), 'Managing firm resources in dynamic environments to create value: looking inside the black box', *Academy of Management Review*, **32**(1), 273–92.

Steier, L. (2001), 'Family firms, plural forms of governance, and the evolving role of trust', *Family Business Review*, **14**(4), 353–67.

Steier, L. (2003), 'Variants of agency contracts in family-financed ventures as a continuum of familial altruistic and market rationalities', *Journal of Business Venturing*, **18**(5), 597–618.

Tagiuri, R. and J. Davis ([1982] 1996), 'Bivalent attributes of the family firm', *Family Business Review*, **9**(2), 43–62.

Vilaseca, A. (2002), 'The shareholder role in the family business: conflict of interests and objectives between nonemployed shareholders and top management team', *Family Business Review*, **15**(4), 299–320.

Ward, J. (1991), *Creating Effective Boards for Private Enterprises: Meeting the Challenges of Continuity and Competition*, San Francisco, CA: Jossey-Bass.

Ward, J. (2004), 'How governing family business is different', in U. Steger (ed.), *Mastering Global Corporate Governance*, Chichester, UK: John Wiley & Sons, pp. 135–67.

Westhead, P. and M. Cowling (1997), 'Performance contrasts between family and non-family unquoted companies in the UK', *International Journal of Entrepreneurial Behaviour and Research*, **3**(1), 30–52.

Westhead, P. and C. Howorth (2006), 'Ownership and management issues associated with family firm performance and company objectives', *Family Business Review*, **19**(4), 301–16.

Witt, P. (2008), 'Corporate governance in Familienunternehmen [Corporate Governance in Family Firms]', *Zeitschrift für Betriebswirtschaft*, **78**, Special Issue, 1–19.

Zellweger, T. and J. Astrachan (2008), 'On the emotional value of owning a firm', *Family Business Review*, **21**(4), 347–65.

Zellweger, T. and P. Sieger (2009), *Emotional Value*, Frankfurt: Ernst & Young.

7 Using the configuration approach to understand the reasons for and consequences of varied family involvement in business
Pramodita Sharma and Mattias Nordqvist

Family firms are distinguished from other organizational forms due to the significant family influence that enables pursuit of the family's vision for the business (Chua et al., 1999). However, due to an awareness of the staggering numbers and large variety in the organizational form referred to as 'family firms', researchers grapple with the fundamental question of the aspects of family involvement that helps differentiate these firms from other organizational forms, and sort out the heterogeneity within family firms (Pearson et al., 2008; Sharma and Nordqvist, 2008; Westhead and Cowling, 1998). Towards this end, two primary approaches are used in the literature which Chua et al. (1999) label as the '*components* of family involvement' and '*essence*' approaches. The first, more dominant approach captures the extent and mode of family involvement in management, ownership, governance and succession (Gersick et al., 1997; Klein et al., 2005; Westhead and Cowling, 1998); while the latter focuses on the behavioural consequences of family involvement in business (Chua et al., 1999; Klein et al., 2005).

The components approach is descriptive in its orientation as it addresses the 'what' and the 'when' questions; that is, what is the extent and mode of family involvement in management and ownership of a firm – at a particular time, and the expected or intended involvement over the longer term (Litz, 1995)? The essence approach, on the other hand, is focused on the 'how' questions or the consequences of family involvement, that is, how does the family involvement in business influence the behaviours and decision making in these firms (Chua et al., 1999; Klein et al., 2005)? Both the components and the essence approaches are integral for capturing the diversity in family firms. While the components approach is useful for providing a framework for interpreting patterns or discrepancies in empirical observations, the essence approach enables an understanding of the consequences of family involvement in business.

However, scholars assert that for the purpose of theory building and knowledge creation, the most fruitful, albeit difficult, questions are those of 'why' as they address the underlying psychological, economic or social dynamics that lead to fully understand the basis of the what, when, and how questions (Kaplan, 1964; Sutton and Staw, 1995; Whetten, 1989). According to Whetten (1989), it is the why that explains and is 'the theoretical glue that welds the model together' (p. 491). He maintains that for a field to make progress on its collective investigative journey, while avoiding degenerating into heated methodological debates, propositions should be well grounded in the whys, as well as the hows and the whats.

Greenwood and Hinings (1993) argued that elements of an organization design such as structures and systems, or the whats and hows described above, are not neutral instruments but embody the underlying sets of beliefs and values, that is, the whys. Corporate governance scholars have observed that as firms have an array of governance mecha-

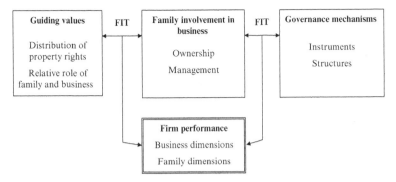

Figure 7.1   Firm performance as a function of fit between guiding values – family involvement in business – governance mechanisms

nisms to choose from, it is critical to examine the ability of firms to make these choices according to their institutional logic (cf. Coles et al., 2001; Dalton et al., 1998). From these perspectives, an understanding of the logic (i.e. the why) propelling the extent and mode of family involvement in a business (i.e. the what), and effective governance mechanisms (i.e. the how), can be gleaned through the guiding values held by the family. This 'configurational' or fit approach contends that firms with coherence between guiding values, structures, and systems enjoy performance advantages (Greenwood and Hinings, 1993; Miller and Friesen, 1984).

In this chapter, we attempt to decipher why varied levels of family involvement in a business are observed. Following the guidance of scholars such as Greenwood and Hinings (1993; 1996) and Miller and Friesen (1984), we address this question from the perspective of guiding values of a family and use tenets of configuration theory to understand the consequences of varied levels of family involvement in business. Not only does this approach enable us to begin to understand the rationale behind family involvement in business; it also helps to shed some light on the governance (how) and performance consequences (so what) of the varied levels of family involvement in business. The overarching thesis of this chapter is that family firms with good fit between guiding values, extent of family involvement in business, and governance mechanisms, are better positioned to achieve their performance objectives (Figure 7.1).

As our core interest lies in understanding the rationale behind and consequences of varied modes and extent of family involvement in business, the next section discusses related developments in the literature. The following section introduces the configuration approach. Next, we discuss the core of our configuration – values guiding family involvement in business. This is followed by a discussion of implications of varied levels of family involvement on governance and performance of firms. The concluding section shares the research and practical implications of ideas presented herein.

FAMILY INVOLVEMENT IN BUSINESS

A distinguishing feature of family firms from other organizational forms is the overlap between the family and business systems leading to their dual identity (Davis and Tagiuri,

1989; Sundaramurthy and Kreiner, 2008). Scholars use the construct of 'familiness' to capture the family–business overlaps (Habbershon and Williams, 1999; Pearson et al., 2008; Sharma, 2008). While this system overlap enables distinctive competencies, it also creates unique challenges for leaders of these firms (Levinson, 1971). A realization of the opportunities afforded and challenges brought about by the overlap in family and business systems has led researchers towards developing frameworks to capture the mode and extent of family involvement in business in the two core dimensions of business – ownership and management.

Often this is done through overlapping two- or three-circle models that capture family and non-family involvement in ownership and management of a firm (Davis, 1982; Hollander, 1983; Lansberg, 1988). Although some scholars add governance as a distinct aspect to define and operationalize family firms, most do not differentiate between governance and management (Chua et al., 1999). Still others add intergenerational transfer as a necessary component (e.g. Churchill and Hatten, 1987), but empirical studies have revealed that firms do not necessarily have to undergo generational transition to behave as family firms (Chua et al., 2004), thereby questioning whether succession is a core component distinguishing family firms from other organizational forms.

Among the proposed models, Davis's (1982) three-circle model has met with widespread acceptance as it enables a conceptual understanding of the core difference between family and non-family firms. While frustrations have been expressed at the static nature of this model (Habbershon et al., 2003), and its overemphasis on similarities between family firms while underplaying the inherent differences (Melin and Nordqvist, 2007), the model's innate appeal has led to modification efforts.

Two noteworthy extensions are the 'developmental model' (Gersick et al., 1997) and the 'F-PEC scale of family influence' (Astrachan et al., 2002). While the F-PEC scale attempts to measure family influence through ownership – power scale, management – experience scale, and 'familiness' – culture scale (Habbershon and Williams, 1999), the developmental model aims to capture the various life-cycle changes over time in ownership, management and family as more family members become involved in business and/or the business grows in size, adopting formal structures and governance mechanisms.

As firms and families go through various life-cycle stages, they change regarding the extent and mode of family involvement in the ownership and management of the firm. For example, founders of new ventures can approach family involvement in different ways. A study of over 5000 new and operating ventures in the USA suggests that while a large majority (77 per cent) of new ventures start with a significant involvement of family members in ownership and management of their ventures, another 2–3 per cent involve family in business within the first five years of operation (Chua et al., 2004). However, there are others who create ventures without any involvement of family in firm ownership or management as they choose separation between their work and family lives. For ventures that succeed during the tenure of founders, the question of family involvement in business becomes significant again as next-generation family members begin establishing their careers. At this stage, too, family firms can approach the extent of family involvement in ownership and management in different ways. The most commonly found patterns of family involvement in the ownership and management of a firm are discussed below.

Family Involvement in Firm's Ownership

Gersick et al. (1997) elaborated on the three basic forms of ownership that may develop in family firms over time – controlling owner, sibling partnership and cousin consortium. Lansberg (1999) further argues that family firms may vary in terms of whether over time they chose to recycle through the same ownership form, move to the next form, or revert to the previous form. All these ownership forms focus on variations of family ownership of a firm. However, research has indicated the presence of family firms among publicly traded firms as well, suggesting that ownership could be dispersed among family and non-family members (Anderson and Reeb, 2003; Miller and Le Breton-Miller, 2005). In order to include all these possibilities in our discussions, we find a modification of the ownership forms suggested by Gersick et al. (1997) to be useful – sole proprietor, nuclear family ownership, extended family ownership and family/non-family ownership.

The sole proprietor captures the controlling owner while clarifying that there is only one owner of the firm. Although the 'controlling ownership' form suggested by Gersick et al. (1997) is helpful to show that there is one dominant owner, it leaves open the possibility of the presence of minority owners. As the governance implications of the two forms of ownership vary, we have chosen to include the 'controlling owner' and 'sibling partnership' into the ownership form labelled as 'nuclear family ownership'. As indicated by the label, all members of a nuclear family are included in this ownership form, regardless of their being majority or minority owners, or being of same or different generations (i.e. parents and their children). 'Extended family ownership' captures the 'cousin consortium' category of Gersick et al. (1997) while including owners who are non-blood relatives and/or in-laws. The last category captures firms with a combination of family and non-family owners.

Family Involvement in Firm's Management

The management or business dimension elaborated by Gersick et al. (1997) uses three life-cycle stages of a business: start-up, extension/formalization and maturity. At each stage of life cycle, varied levels of family involvement in management are possible (Chua et al., 2004). Our focus is on management roles that have a significant influence on the strategic direction of a firm, rather than support roles performed by employees who are largely responsible for implementing decisions made by the management.

Four levels of family involvement in management of a business are prevalent. The first category aims to capture the largest segment of firms that are non-employers. According to the US Census Bureau (2007), businesses without paid employees, referred to as 'lone wolves', make up approximately 78 per cent of the nation's 26 million-plus firms. The combined receipts of these firms are in excess of $950 billion; thus they are a substantial part of the economic landscape of the USA.

Employer firms led by a CEO from the same family that owns the business fall into the second category – 'family CEO'. Although this category continues to dominate family firms, a trend towards shared leadership responsibilities between siblings or members of the extended family has been observed, as many families prefer to retain the top management of their firm within the family (American Family Business Survey, 2002). Moreover, there is a desire to utilize the talents of multiple members of the next generation, or accommodate multiple members in top management positions so as not to create sibling tensions (Barnes, 1988). Co-CEOs or 'office of presidency' are some ways in which firms attempt to operate under shared family leadership. With increasing competition, many family firms often seek non-family talent to lead the family business, as family members pursue other interests (Landes, 2006). Following these trends, four levels of family involvement in management discussed in this chapter are: 'lone wolves', 'family CEO', 'family co-CEOs' and 'non-family CEO'. In an attempt to understand factors prompting the choice for each of these levels of family involvement in management or ownership discussed earlier, we seek insights by using configuration approach and the role of guiding values of a family.

GUIDING THEORY

The 'configuration approach' derives its roots from 'contingency theory' developed in late 1960s and early 1970s (e.g. Galbraith, 1973; Lawrence and Lorsch, 1967). The two approaches share the fundamental assumptions that there is no one best way of organizing, and yet not all ways of organizing are equally effective (Scott and Davis, 2007). However, while the contingency theorists suggest that the best way to organize depends on the nature of the external environment of an organization (Galbraith, 1973; Lawrence and Lorsch, 1967), the configuration theorists focus more on the fit between the driving institutional logic of an organization and adopted structures (Greenwood and Hinings, 1993, 1996; Miller and Freisen, 1984). Attempts to reconcile these perspectives have been found in influential works such as Thompson's (1967) *Organization in Action*, or more recently Collins and Porras's (1994) *Built to Last*, as they argue to preserve the core (internal fit) while embracing progress (external fit).

While both approaches are likely to be useful in the context of family firms, over the last few years the internally focused fit approach has been used in several studies. For example, in their study of 58 large family firms with median age of 104 years, Miller and Le Breton-Miller (2005) observed that firms with coherence between their driving mission and adopted strategies enjoy significant competitive advantages over generations of industry and leadership life cycles, in comparison to other firms that lack such coherence. Later, these scholars found that, even in smaller family firms, one of the factors that distinguishes successful firms from others that fail is the extent of alignment between the resource allocation decisions and desired objectives (Miller and Le Breton-Miller, 2006).

Another study, aimed to understand what might be the most reliable ways to measure success of small family firms, revealed that measuring success on the basis of fit between the desired configuration of performance on multiple dimensions and the actual performance on these dimensions was more effective in gauging the firm performance than using any of the partial isolated measures (Hienerth and Kessler, 2006). Lubatkin et al. (2007) use the idea of fit to theorize the correspondence between various types of parental altruism and governance efficiencies. An empirical study of 92 small and medium enterprises by Ling et al. (2007) revealed that while the values of collectivism significantly influence firm performance in older and larger family firms, those of novelty exert an influence on younger and smaller firms.

Encouraged by the wide-ranging applicability of the configuration approach in the context of family firms, we use it to understand the role of guiding values in explaining the observed variations in the levels of family involvement in business, and the consequences of such variations in terms of choosing appropriate governance mechanisms, and implications on firm performance.

CORE OF THE CONFIGURATION – GUIDING VALUES

Values have been defined as a 'broad tendency to prefer certain state of affairs over others' (Hofstede, 1980, p. 2). The integral role of values in the behaviour of family members has been studied in great detail (e.g. Asakawa, 2001; Barling et al., 1991). It is understood that values are transmitted through generations and define acceptable norms of behaviours and relationships both within a family and between family members and external stakeholders (Berger and Luckman, 1967). In the context of organizations, Ranson et al. (1980) have argued that values guide our mental maps, determining what is desirable in terms of organizational domain of operations, key organizing and governing practices and performance criteria. Thus values have an inherent power to influence key behaviours and decisions in the domains of both family and business.

With an intertwinement of family and business in family firms, the powerful role of family values in guiding key decisions of a firm has been observed since the inception of family business studies (e.g. Dyer, 1986; Ward, 1987). Therefore, in order to understand key decisions such as the extent of family involvement in a business, governance mechanisms adopted, and the consequences of these decisions on firm performance, it is important to examine the underlying dominant values of a family (cf. Greenwood and Hinings, 1993).

What if all family members do not share the dominant family values? The tenacious nature of founder's values – sometimes expressed as 'founder's shadow' – has been revealed in empirical studies (e.g. Davis and Harveston, 1999; Ling et al., 2007). However, sustenance of familial values across generations requires considerable investments of family time and energy into socialization of juniors. Although families with enduring firms have been found to invest considerable resources into keeping the mission of family alive across generations (Miller and Le Breton-Miller, 2005), a variance on this dimension is likely to be found in business-owning families. As suggested by Greenwood and Hinings (1993), it is not necessary that the underlying values be supported by all actors in the organization as the commitment to these values might wane over time or the priorities of family members may differ. However, the prevailing structures and systems are likely to be guided by the dominant values held by the family at the time of inception of these mechanisms, and changing such foundational aspects of a firm is likely to face organizational tendency towards inertia (Greenwood and Hinings, 1993).

It is possible that, over time, as key stakeholders in a family change and if the dominant values held sacrosanct by them change in turn, ill fits between values and extent of family involvement in business or adopted structures may develop. These situations are likely to be fragile, as it is more efficient and effective to be a coherent whole than a combination of ill-fitting parts (Miller and Friesen, 1984). Attempts to readjust the adopted structures are likely to be made. However, given inherent inertia to change in fundamental ways, the change is likely to be slow and sometimes painful, as is the case with all major organizational changes (Greenwood and Hinings, 1996; Greiner, 1972; Hall et al., 2001). The difficulties of successfully incorporating and negotiating such foundational changes have been documented in longitudinal case studies of family firms such as a study of over 100 years of developments in the Italian Falck Group (Salvato et al., 2010), and vividly captured in interviews of later generational transformational family firm leaders such as Krister Ahlstrom of Finland's Ahlstrom Corporation (Magretta, 1998). Thus one can expect long-lasting and slow-changing influence of fundamental values held sacrosanct by leaders of family firms.

Values and norms have been shown to take many forms (e.g. Dyer, 1986; Hall et al., 2001). Our focal interest in this chapter is to understand the reason behind the observed differences in family involvement in the ownership and management of a business, and the governance and performance implications of choices made. Family values around distribution of property rights are found useful to explain the family involvement in firm's ownership, while values regarding the relative role of family and business help to explain the extent of family involvement in the management of a business.

Values regarding Distribution of Property Rights

Families vary in terms of the norms regarding distribution of property rights both within one generation and across generations. For example, families dominated by the norms of primogeniture prefer to pass ownership of business and related responsibilities of a business to the eldest son (Chau, 1991). In other families, following norms of coparcenary, all male members are expected to be equally invested in the operation of the family enterprise and property rights divided equally among these members (Chau, 1991). As liberal values become more prevalent, different norms may be emerging. For instance, norms of equality may stipulate that all next-generation members, regardless of age and gender, participate equally in the business, whereas norms of liberty and independence may encourage next-generation members to strike their own paths and not participate at all in the family firm. Research on attributes of the next generation considered desirable by senior generation leaders suggests a trend towards the decreasing importance of gender and birth order of the junior generation (Chrisman et al., 1998). While on a wane, many family firms continue to be guided by primogeniture or coparcenary.

Anthropologists have long made attempts to identify structural dimensions within families that elucidate differences in the beliefs and values regarding property rights. One such typology developed by Le Play (1875) and modified by Todd (1985) has been found useful to explain the diversity in governance and strategic decision-making in family firms (Ling, 2002; Sharma and Manikutty, 2005). This typology suggests that the relationship norms across generations (authority versus liberty) and among siblings (equality versus inequality) significantly influence the expected modes of transfer of property rights in a family (cf. Todd, 1985). While authority reinforces the power of the senior generation due to their position in the family, the liberal model emphasizes individual independence. If parental property is divided equally among all siblings, an egalitarian relationship is expressed. On the other hand, if the inheritance system in a family is based on the indivisibility of the property, with one child favoured over all others, the norm of inequality takes root (Todd, 1985). Based on these dimensions of authority–liberty and equality–inequality, the four family types identified by Todd (1985) and adopted in family business studies by Ling (2002) are summarized by Sharma and Manikutty (2005, pp. 298–9) as follows:

> *The authoritarian family* displays the values of inequality and authority. While the ultimate authority resides with the senior generation, one child is an anointed heir, who is treated more equal than others. The association between the senior generation and the chosen heir is close, while other members of the junior generation are expected to establish independent households and means of livelihood.
>
> *The egalitarian nuclear family* is characterized by the concepts of equality and liberty. While separation of households is expected, the property is divided equally among the children, who are socialized to be somewhat independent and achievement oriented.
>
> *The community family* is characterized by the values of equality and authority. Children live with their parents in extended families and all next generation members are treated equally in terms of inheritance rights. The senior generation leader has the ultimate authority in such families.
>
> *The absolute nuclear family* is liberal and inegalitarian. On reaching adulthood, children are expected to establish independent households and means of livelihood. No precise conventions of inheritance of parental property prevail as this property is viewed as belonging to one generation that may do as it wishes with it. In such families, children are socialized to be independent and achievement oriented.

We contend that firms dominated by families holding each of the above four values as sacrosanct are likely to lead to different familial norms regarding the extent and mode of family involvement in ownership of their family firm. The authoritarian families display the values of inequality between siblings with one anointed heir, who is treated more equal than other siblings. The ownership in firms of families with such beliefs is held by one individual who is the sole proprietor. Although sole proprietorship is a common form of ownership in small and new ventures, also many large family firms have been found to retain ownership with one controlling owner over time and generations (Astrachan and Shanker, 2003; Miller and Le Breton-Miller, 2005).

Egalitarian nuclear families believe in dividing the property equally among the children. Such families are likely to display ownership shared within the nuclear family as parental property including the family firm, is divided equally among the children. Community families, on the other hand, exhibit values of equality where children live with parents in extended families and all next generation members are treated equally in terms of property rights. Families guided by these beliefs of property rights are likely to exhibit firm ownership dispersed within members of an extended family. Last, the absolute nuclear families have no precise conventions of property inheritance. Property is regarded as belonging to one generation who may do as it wishes with it. Members of next generation are expected to be independent and self-sufficient. Such families are more likely to engage in a mix of family and non-family ownership. The above discussion suggests coherence between familial norms and values regarding property rights, and the varied forms of ownership of family firms.

Values regarding Relative Role of Family and Business

Although the overlap between family and business exists in all family firms, the guiding values regarding the relative role of each sub-system may vary across families, leading to one system attaining the dominant status in key decisions. Based on this observation,

Ward (1987) observed that depending on whether family or business system is the leading or trailing system, family businesses are either family-first or business-first. Whetten (2007) distinguished these two orientations as *Family* business (Fb) or *Business* family (Bf).

Ward (1987) observed a third category of firms that attempt to simultaneously balance the needs of both family and business systems, that is, *Family Business* (FB) in Whetten's (2007) terms. We argue that this is a transitional stage for businesses as they are moving from one orientation to another, or using bridge generation leadership until the next generation is ready to take over leadership roles in a business. However, the foundational orientation of the family is either towards the business or towards family systems. Theoretically, one could argue for firms where neither the family nor the business system dominates as the firm is established to pursue individual interests rather than to serve the needs of either the family or the business (*family business – fb*). However, to survive as a business for any significant length of time, they will need to make a profit and thus follow the business first orientation. For now, we focus on the two fundamental categories of family or business first, arguing that these values are likely to have a significant influence on the extent and mode of family involvement in the management of a firm.

In *Family* businesses (Fb) the values of family centrality dominate and the business is viewed as a means of livelihood for family members. Family-oriented objectives such as providing employment for family members through the business, grooming of heirs, lifestyle maintenance, accumulation of family wealth, sustaining the family's reputation and position in a community guide decision-making and setting of priorities (Tagiuri and Davis, 1992). In such firms, when the two systems collide, family interests take precedence over business interests (Sundaramurthy and Kreiner, 2008). For example, business is viewed as a source of employment for all family members regardless of their competence levels or their ability to make positive contributions to the business (Dunn, 1995; Lee and Rogoff, 1996). As observed by Reay and Hinings (2007), the dominant logic that prevails in such firms leads to a belief that retention of key leadership positions within the family is critical to the longevity and success of a firm. Thus there is a hesitation or reluctance to hire non-family members as chief executives or in other key leadership positions. Moreover, as a family grows over generations, there is a desire to balance the involvement of its different branches. As a consequence, there is a higher engagement of family members in the management of these firms leading to family CEO or family co-CEOs, depending on the number of interested and able family members. As discussed in the next section, the governance dynamics of these two forms of leadership are significantly different.

On the other hand, when business is held as central, as in *Business* families (Bf), market principles and business-related objectives such as market share, firm growth, profitability and so on guide decision-making (File et al., 1994; Reay and Hinings, 2007). As an example, hiring practices in such firms are guided by competence levels and potential contributions an individual is likely to make to the business. There is a preference to employ only the very best regardless of family membership.

In terms of the management of a firm, a large majority of new ventures start with the founder operating as the sole owner-manager of his/her firm informally supported by immediate family members (Aldrich and Cliff, 2003; Chua et al., 2004). Thus most small start-ups are likely to be non-employer firms managed by 'lone wolves'. At this stage, getting the business off the ground is the primary consideration, consuming long hours of the owner-manager (Greiner, 1972). While the guiding familial values of family or business centrality may be the prompting reasons why s/he started an independent venture, survival needs prompt business-central decision-making.

As the firm grows and the founder makes decisions on whether to engage members of his/her nuclear or extended family or hire non-family managers, the guiding values emerge. Firms guided by centrality of family in business (Fb) are more likely to employ members of immediate or extended family as managers, whereas those who regard business as central (Bf) will be more inclined to hire non-family managers.

GOVERNANCE AND PERFORMANCE IMPLICATIONS OF FAMILY INVOLVEMENT IN BUSINESS

Thus far, we have attended to the first segment of our inquiry; that is, why do we observe varied levels of family involvement in business? We have theorized that family values and norms are likely determinants of the extent and mode of family involvement in ownership and management of a firm. Specifically, we suggest that familial norms with respect to property rights lead to four variations of family involvement in ownership of a firm, while values regarding the relative role of family and business determine the four levels of family involvement in management of a firm. Next, we attend to the 'so what' question, that is, the influence of varied levels of family involvement on governance and performance of firms.

Governance Mechanisms

Incorporating the holistic principle of inquiry, scholars have argued that structural con-figurations such as governance structures in organizations are driven by the underlying values and beliefs that are the unifying enduring themes in organizations (Miller, 1981; Ranson et al., 1980). Recent research has shown that striking a well-configured balance between priorities (e.g. values and family involvement) and practices (e.g. governance structures) is a determining factor when distinguishing between high- and low-performing family firms (Miller and Le Breton-Miller, 2005, 2006).

Following a thorough review of the different facets of corporate governance literature, Coles et al. (2001) conclude that 'the most critical issue still to examine is the ability of firms to choose among a number of different governance mechanisms to create the appro-priate structure for that firm, given the environment in which it operates' (p. 23). While these authors focus on the external environmental fit of governance structures, as dis-cussed earlier, we elaborate on the internal fit between values, extent of family involve-ment in business and governance structures likely to be effective in reaching performance objectives in family firms.

The varying levels of involvement of family in the ownership and management of firm leads to unique governance challenges (Mustakallio et al., 2002; Schulze et al., 2001). In non-family firms, ownership and management are assumed to be separated into clear and distinguishable sectors generally studied under the rubric of principal–agent relations (Jensen and Meckling, 1976). In such firms, attempts to gain governance efficiencies are directed towards establishing a combination of mechanisms that align the interests of agents and principals (Jensen and Meckling, 1976), and those aimed to routinely understand the perspectives of each stakeholder group (cf. Freeman, 1984). For example, in addition to the usage of monitoring and incentive alignment structures, the management team is lead by the chief executive officer (CEO), while the owners' interests are watched by the board of directors under the leadership of its chair. The literature on the board of directors suggests that the independence of the board from the management team enables effective governance of a firm (Zahra and Pearce, 1989).

As discussed earlier, family firms are characterized by varying degrees of overlap between management and ownership systems, combined with variations in family and non-family participation along these two dimensions, leading to different nature of governance challenges (e.g. Schulze et al., 2001). Attempts to find ways to ensure that perspectives, needs and concerns of different family firm stakeholders are routinely given due consideration has prompted scholars to suggest the adoption of four types of governance bodies: 'family council' to discuss family related issues; 'executive council' for employee related issues; 'shareholder assembly' for owner-related issues; and 'board of directors/advisors' for discussions on the overall strategic direction of the business (Gersick et al., 1997; Corbetta and Salvato, 2004; Ward, 1987). In addition, given the intertwining of family and business, an array of legal instruments such as wills, partnership agreements and employment contracts may be effectively employed to clarify and monitor expectations along ownership and management dimensions (e.g. Foster, 1998; Ward, 1991).

Although one or more of these structures have been found useful in family firms (Neubauer and Lank, 1998), it is not clear whether all are necessary for governance supporting the prioritized performance goals in all family firms. In fact, a limitation of literature on family firm governance is the common assumption that all family firms should organize their governance in the same way. While prescriptions such as 'board of directors' with outsiders and 'family councils' are associated with positive outcomes for family firms' prevail, an understanding of inherent variance in family firms has prompted researchers to question whether the same governance structures are useful in all family firms (Corbetta and Salvato, 2004; Melin and Nordqvist, 2007).

The relative use of various governance structures in different types of family firms has not yet been examined. Not all governance mechanisms are likely to be helpful in all family firms. The fundamental reason for setting up these structures is to enable voicing the perspectives of stakeholders with varying levels of current and expected future involvement in the ownership and management of a firm (Gersick et al., 1997). In general, the higher the stakeholder variance in ownership and managerial roles, the greater will be the need for different governing mechanisms to ensure that the perspectives of all stakeholders are taken into consideration while making strategic decisions in a family firm (Figure 7.2).

Either too much or little support from governance mechanisms is likely to hinder the achievement of organizational objectives. When a family firm has a diversity of stakeholders involved in its ownership and management, it must be adequately supported by the shareholders' assembly and executive council to ensure that there is a forum for these legitimate and powerful stakeholders to express their perspectives (cf. Mitchell et al., 1997). In the absence of such forums, these stakeholders are likely to use their pathways of influence to express themselves, thereby obstructing or slowing down progress towards

	Values regarding distribution of property rights			
	Authoritarian *Authority* *Inequality*	Egalitarian *Liberty* *Equality*	Community *Authority* *Equality*	Absolutely nuclear *Liberty* *Inequality*
FAMILY INVOLVEMENT IN OWNERSHIP	Sole proprietor	Nuclear family ownership	Extended family owners	Family / non-family owners
Governance mechanisms needed	Will	Partnership agreement	Shareholders assembly Family council Board of directors	Shareholders' assembly Family council Board of directors
	–	Employment contract	Management team Advisory board	Executive council Advisory board
FAMILY INVOLEMENT IN MANAGEMENT	Lone wolves	Family CEO	Family co-CEOs	Non-family CEO
	Business centred fB *Business-first*	Family centred Fb *Family-first*		Business centred fB *Business-first*
	Values regarding relative role of family and business			

Figure 7.2   Guiding values, family involvement in firm ownership and management, governance mechanisms

firm objectives (cf. Frooman, 1999). On the other hand, when a firm has a simple owner-ship and management structure, too many governance bodies are likely to consume unnecessary resources leading to inefficiencies and perhaps causing frustrations for those responsible to achieve organizational objectives.

Ownership dimension

As the number of owners increases, the need for governance structures to understand owner perspectives increases. While wills can prove effective in managing transfer of property rights in the case of sole proprietor, partnership agreements can be adequately used to bring clarity to and manage ownership relationships within a nuclear family. However, as members of extended family such as cousins, in-laws, siblings from different marriages and so on become involved in the ownership of a family firm, leading to increased diversity in terms of ownership modes (active versus passive, majority versus minority, current versus potential future), mechanisms such as 'Shareholders' assembly', to understand and educate different shareholders, is likely to be helpful. As the number of shareholders increases and it becomes cumbersome to hold regular meetings, a 'family council' with members elected by the shareholders assembly is likely to be a helpful gov-ernance structure (Magretta, 1998). In addition, a mix of independent externals and internal board members can provide a good balance of continuity and fresh insights, while also being able to effectively mediate between different ownership groups within the family in discussions about objectives (Corbetta and Salvato, 2004; Zahra and Pearce, 1989).

Management dimension

In terms of management, 'lone wolves' who operate their venture without formal support of any other employees do not need any governance structures. For firms lead by a family member CEO, employment contracts may prove valuable to help define the roles, responsibilities and performance expectations of the leader, especially when ownership is dispersed among other family or non-family members. Firms in which leadership is shared between two or more family members, as in the case of co-CEOs, are likely to benefit from governance structures, such as 'management team' and 'advisory boards'. As the business gets larger and begins to grow with family and non-family members holding managerial positions, the heightened need for managerial autonomy and delegation arises (Greiner, 1972). As the number of managers increases, the need for integration and coordination escalates as well, leading to the integral role of governance structures such as 'executive council' for effective management of a firm. Figure 7.2 summarizes the governance mechanisms for each of the four levels of family involvement in ownership of a firm.

Firm Performance

In the context of family firms, high performance is a combination of family- and business-related objectives desired by the families whose firm it is (Sharma, 2004). In other words, high performance refers to family firm-specific achievements of goals both along pecuniary dimensions such as growth, profitability and so on, and non-pecuniary dimensions such as family employment, reputation, family harmony and the like (Craig and Moores, 2005; Hienerth and Kessler, 2006; Lee, 2006; Tagiuri and Davis, 1992). In some family firms, researchers have found that the achievement of family-related objectives takes precedence over the business-oriented objectives (e.g. Dunn, 1995; Lee and Rogoff, 1996), while in others business-related objectives are primary (File et al., 1994). Based on our discussion thus far, these seemingly conflicting findings seem quite understandable as family firms are heterogeneous, with some categories primarily guided by family-first orientation, while others follow business-first values. Performance aspirations of each category of these firms are likely to differ significantly.

This suggests the need for using different criteria to evaluate the success or performance of family firms as appropriate criteria for firms with different guiding values is likely to be different (cf. Greenwood and Hinings, 1988; Hienerth and Kessler, 2005). As depicted in Figure 7.1, we argue that firms with coherence between guiding values, extent and mode of family involvement, and adopted governance structures are likely to enjoy higher performance on dimensions of interest to them.

As an example, Krister Ahlstrom intimates in his interview with Joan Magretta (1998) that the Ahlstrom Corporation founded in Finland in 1851 is wholly owned by 200 descendants of the founder, although few are involved in the business. However, as the CEO of the firm, he found that to manage in the context of the widened gap between family owners and management, in addition to the formally required two-tier boards in Scandinavia, it was useful to establish a family assembly of all owners and their spouses. Five members of the assembly were then voted to form the family council, which served as the communication link between the owners, board of directors and the CEO. Such a governance structure enabled the continued high performance of Ahlstrom on both family and business dimensions.

DISCUSSION

Researchers interested in understanding the governance efficiencies in family firms question the adequacy of governance mechanisms for all family firms. 'Does one size fit all?' wonder Corbetta and Salvato (2004). An awareness of the large diversity in the organizational form referred to as 'family firms' (Astrachan and Shanker, 2003) leads to an intuitive response of 'of course not'. However, despite this common understanding and some recent efforts to distinguish between various types of family firms based on the extent of family involvement in business (Astrachan et al., 2002; Chua et al., 1999; Gersick et al., 1997; Westhead and Cowling, 1998), the issue of relative effectiveness of governance structures in different types of family firms has not yet been adequately addressed.

Following the tenets of 'fit' in the writings under the rubric of configuration approach (e.g. Miller, 1981; Miller and Friesen, 1984; Greenwood and Hinings, 1988), we have argued that the guiding values of families determine the extent of family involvement in ownership and management of their firm. In turn, the chosen mode of family involvement determines the governance structures likely to lead to desired performance outcomes (Figure 7.1). Specifically, beliefs regarding property rights of family members lead to four varied levels of ownership involvement, while beliefs regarding the relative role of business in family determine the four levels of family involvement in management of firms. The combination of ownership and management involvement prevalent in a firm determines the types of governance structures likely to be effective in achieving organizational performance goals (Figure 7.2).

The more the complexity and variance in stakeholders, that is minority/majority owners, family/non-family owners and managers, blood relatives/extended family members, the higher the need for varied governance structures to ensure that the perspectives of all stakeholders are taken into consideration when making strategic decisions in a family firm. While coherence between family values, the extent of family involvement in management and ownership of business and governance structures adopted enables sustainability and high performance, ill-fitting components retard firm progress (Miller and Le Breton-Miller, 2005, 2006). As discussion in this chapter covers as a large spectrum of firms ranging from sole proprietorships to firms with ownership dispersed between family/non-family members, it should be useful for practice and further research endeavours.

Implications for Practice

The ideas presented in this chapter have immediate as well as long-term implications for family firm owners and managers. Four commonly found variations in terms of family involvement in ownership and management of a firm are discussed. This is a first theoretical attempt to capture the reasoning behind the varied levels of family involvement in family firms. It can help provide practitioners with a basis to understand the distinctions between their firm and other family firms. This makes it easier for them to understand whether findings of a research study or advice from a consultant or management book apply to their situation or not. Further, the developed theory can provide guidance to family firm owners and managers regarding the governance structures that are more likely to contribute to their preferred performance outcomes.

The ideas developed here can be a helpful tool for teaching at different levels, ranging from undergraduate, MBA to executive education. Learning about the characteristics and differences between types of family firms should be a part of a course curriculum as natural as learning about the differences between family and non-family firms. Class discussions can be effectively structured by studying the differences in values, family involvement, governance structures and firm performance. Case studies can be developed and used to highlight the prevailing diversity among family firms, its reasons and implications. Such an understanding is likely to support students' learning and prepare them to become effective managers, owners and/or consultants to family firms.

Research Implications

This is a first attempt directed to understanding the reasons behind varied levels of family involvement in business. The theory developed in this chapter should be seen as a general conceptual framework to guide research on family firms that systematically acknowledges and build upon the diversity among these firms. The proposed ideas need to be subjected to empirical testing. A combination of qualitative and quantitative approaches is likely to generate a rich understanding of the linkages between components of our configuration – familial norms and values, components of family involvement and governance structures. A first step towards this exploration is to understand how each element of the configuration is formed and interacts in practice in different types of family firm.

Since family values and norms guide the nature of family involvement, which, in turn, determines appropriate governance for achieving high performance, researchers should first focus on how the values and norms are formed. Detailed and in-depth case studies represent an appropriate research strategy to capture these complex processes (Eisenhardt, 1989; Yin, 1994). Such a research strategy is also appropriate to address the more specific research question regarding the extent to which the fit between values, family involvement and governance structures is a deliberate versus an emergent process over time (cf. Mintzberg, 1978). Detailed empirical studies of the forces and pressures that act upon family firms to move towards fit or, indeed, out of fit, would also enhance our understanding of the performance of different types of family firms. To investigate the relationship between configurational fit and high performance in family firms, we suggest a matched-pair sampling logic where successful and unsuccessful family firms are compared (cf. Miller and Le Breton-Miller, 2005).

Even if family firms achieve a good fit between guiding familial values, family involvement in business and adopted governance structures, with time, modifications may be needed as the fit between components becomes lose due to external or internal factors. Why and how modifications in values, family involvement, or effectiveness of governance mechanisms come about is an interesting question for further research. In particular, institutional theory (e.g. Meyer and Rowan, 1977; DiMaggio and Powell, 1983) is an appropriate framework for analysing how broader societal mechanisms have an impact on these change processes at family and firm level. Further, theories of culture, identity and other frameworks from anthropology and sociology hold great potential for theorizing on the formation and change of values and the nature and impact of family involvement (e.g. Tsui et al., 2007). Family business researchers have only begun to tap this source of theoretical resources (cf. Stewart, 2003; Sundaramurthy and Kreiner, 2008).

Quantitative research approaches are suitable for testing the propositions on wider samples, including comparisons across different organizational and national settings. Since good archival data on family firms are rare, a sophisticated survey design is probably the best way to proceed for statistical testing of the propositions. In fact, reliable scales already exist for several parts of the building blocks of the configuration that facilitate the creation of a survey instrument. As evidence is gathered to verify and/or further modify the propositions in this chapter, it would be interesting to examine why and how firms move from one cell to another over time. Whether this cross-cell movement takes the form of a revolution or an evolution is another worthwhile direction to pursue in future theory building and research efforts (cf. Greiner, 1972). In summation, the ideas presented in this article open various interesting and potentially fruitful avenues for research to enable the development of scientific understanding of the broad spectrum of organizations referred to as family firms.

Beyond the family firm, we believe that the configurational approach adopted in this chapter could be used also for other forms of organizations in a more general sense. There are several categories of organizations that tend to be mistakenly seen as homogeneous in current research and practice discourses, for instance partnerships, cooperatives and public organizations (hospitals, universities etc.). It is hoped that this chapter can be a source of inspiration for researchers outside the family firm field of study where the diversity within the category is overlooked.

ACKNOWLEDGEMENT

We appreciate the funding support received from the Social Sciences and Humanities Council of Canada (SSHRC), Handelsbankens Research Foundation, Sweden and the FOBI Scholars program of the Grand Valley State University for this project. An earlier version of this chapter is published in the 2007 *Academy of Management Best Paper Proceedings*.

REFERENCES

Aldrich, H.E. and Cliff, J.E. (2003), 'The pervasive effects of family on entrepreneurship: toward a family embeddedness perspective', *Journal of Business Venturing*, **18**: 573–96.
American Family Business Survey (2002), http://www.kennesaw.edu/fec/DMD9500R.pdf.
Anderson, R.C. and Reeb, D.M. (2003), 'Founding family ownership and firm performance: evidence from the S&P 500', *Journal of Finance*, **58**: 1301–28.
Asakawa, K. (2001), 'Family socialization practices and their effects on the internalization of educational values for Asian and White American adolescents', *Applied Developmental Science*, **5**: 184–94.
Astrachan, J.H. and Shanker, M.C. (2003), 'Family businesses' contribution to the U.S. economy: a closer look', *Family Business Review*, **16**(3): 211–19.
Astrachan, J.H., Klein, S.B. and Smyrnios, K.X. (2002), 'The F-PEC scale of family influence: a proposal for solving the *Family Business* definition problem', *Family Business Review*, **15**(1): 45–58.
Barling, J., Kelloway, E.K. and Bremerman, E.H. (1991), 'Preemployment predictors of union attitudes: the role of family socialization and work beliefs', *Journal of Applied Psychology*, **76**: 725–31.

Barnes, L.B. (1988), 'Incongruent hierarchies: daughters and younger sons as company CEOs', *Family Business Review*, **2**(1): 3–12.

Berger, P. and Luckman, T. (1967), *The Social Construction of Reality*, New York: Penguin Press.

Chau, T.T. (1991), 'Approaches to succession in East Asian business organizations', *Family Business Review*, **4**(2): 161–79.

Chrisman, J.J., Chua, J.H. and Sharma, P. (1998), 'Important attributes of successors in family businesses: an exploratory study', *Family Business Review*, **11**(1): 19–34.

Chua, J.H., Chrisman, J.J. and Sharma, P. (1999), 'Defining the family business by behavior', *Entrepreneurship Theory and Practice*, **23**(4): 19–39.

Chua, J.H., Chrisman, J.J. and Chang, E.P.C. (2004), 'Are family firms born or made? An exploratory investigation', *Family Business Review*, **17**(1): 37–54.

Churchill, N.C. and Hatten, K.J. (1987), 'Non-market based transfer of wealth and power: a research framework for family businesses', *American Journal of Small Business Management*, **11**(3): 51–64.

Coles, J.W, McWilliams, V.B. and Sen, N. (2001), 'An examination of the relationship of governance mechanisms to performance', *Journal of Management*, **27**: 23–50.

Collins, J.C. and Porras, J.I. (1994), *Built to Last*, New York: Harper Business Essentials.

Corbetta, G. and Salvato, C.A. (2004), 'The board of directors in family firms: one size fits all?', *Family Business Review*, **17**(2): 119–34.

Craig, J.B.L. and Moores, K. (2005), 'Balanced scorecards to drive the strategic planning of family firms', *Family Business Review*, **18**(2): 105–22.

Dalton, D.R., Daily, C.M., Ellstrand, A.E. and Johnson, J.L. (1998), 'Meta-analytic reviews of board composition, leadership structure, and financial performance', *Strategic Management Journal*, **19**: 269–90.

Davis, J.A. (1982), 'The influence of life stage on father–son work relationship in family companies', doctoral dissertation, Harvard University.

Davis, P.S. and Harveston, P.D. (1999), 'In the founder's shadow: conflict in the family firm', *Family Business Review*, **12**(4): 311–23.

Davis, J.A. and Tagiuri, R. (1989), 'The influence of life-stage on father–son work relationships in family companies', *Family Business Review*, **2**(1): 47–74.

DiMaggio, P.J. and Powell, W.W. (1983), 'The iron cage revisited: institutional isomorphism and collective rationality in organizational fields', *American Sociological Review*, **48**: 147–60.

Dunn, B. (1995), 'Success themes in Scottish family enterprises: philosophies and practices through the generations', *Family Business Review*, **8**(1), 17–28.

Dyer Jr, W.G. (1986), *Cultural Change in Family Firms: Understanding and Managing Business and Family Transition*, San Francisco, CA: Jossey-Bass.

Eisenhardt, K.M. (1989), 'Building theories from case study research', *Academy of Management Review*, **14**(4): 287–95.

File, K.M., Prince, R.A. and Rankin, M.J. (1994), 'Organizational buying behavior of the family firm', *Family Business Review*, **7**(3): 263–72.

Freeman, E. (1984), *Strategic Management: A Stakeholder Approach*, Boston, MA: Pitman.

Foster, S. (1998), *You Can't Take it With You: The Common Sense Guide to Estate Planning for Canadians*, Toronto: John Wiley & Sons.

Frooman, J. (1999), 'Stakeholder influence strategies', *Academy of Management Review*, **24**(2): 191–205.

Galbraith, J.R. (1973), *Designing Complex Organizations*, Reading, MA: Addison-Wesley.

Gersick, K.E., Davis, J.A., Hampton, M.M. and Lansberg, I. (1997), *Generation to Generation: Life Cycles of the Family Business*, Boston, MA: Harvard Business School Press.

Greenwood, R. and Hinings, C.R. (1988), 'Organizational design types, tracks and the dynamics of strategic change', *Organiztaion Studies*, **9**: 293–316.

Greenwood, R. and Hinings, C.R. (1993), 'Understanding strategic change: the contribution of archetypes', *Academy of Management Journal*, **36**(5): 1052–81.

Greenwood, R. and Hinings, C.R. (1996), 'Understanding radical organizational change: bringing together the old and the new institutionalism', *Academy of Management Review*, **21**: 1022–54.

Greiner, L.E. (1972), 'Evolution and revolution as organizations grow', *Harvard Business Review*, July–August. Reprinted in *Family Business Review*, **10**(4): 397–409.

Habbershon, T.G. and Williams, M.L. (1999), 'A resource-based framework for assessing the strategic advantage of family firms', *Family Business Review*, **12**(1): 1–26.

Habbershon, T.G. Williams, M.L. and MacMillan, I.C. (2003), 'A unified systems perspective of family firm performance', *Journal of Business Venturing*, **18**: 451–65.

Hall, A., Melin, L. and Nordqvist, M. (2001), 'Entrepreneurship as radical change in family firms: exploring the role of cultural patterns', *Family Business Review*, **14**(3): 193–208.

Hienerth, C. and Kessler, A. (2006), 'Measuring success in family businesses: the concept of configurational fit', *Family Business Review*, **19**(2): 115–34.

Hofstede, G. (1980), *Culture's Consequences: International Differences in Work-related Values*, Sage Publishers.
Hollander, B.S. (1983), 'Family owned business as a system: a case study of the interaction of family, task, and marketplace components', doctoral dissertation, University of Pittsburgh.
Jensen, M.C. and Meckling, W.H. (1976), 'Theory of the firm, managerial behaviour, agency costs, and ownership structure', *Journal of Financial Economics*, **3**: 305–60.
Kaplan, A. (1964), *The Conduct of Inquiry*, New York: Harper & Row.
Klein, S.B., Astrachan, J.H. and Smyrnios, K.X. (2005). 'The F-PEC scale of family influence: construction, validation, and further implications for theory', *Entrepreneurship Theory and Practice*, **29**(3): 321–40.
Landes, D.S. (2006), *Dynasties: Fortunes and Misfortunes of the World's Great Family Businesses*, Penguin Books.
Lansberg, I. (1988), 'The succession conspiracy', *Family Business Review*, **1**(2): 119–43.
Lansberg, I. (1999), *Succeeding Generations: Realizing the Dream of Families in Business*, Boston, MA: Harvard Business School Press.
Lawrence, P.R. and Lorsch, J.W. (1967), 'Differentiation and integration in complex organizations', *Administrative Science Quarterly*, **12**: 1–47.
Lee, J. (2006), 'Family firm performance: further evidence', *Family Business Review*, **19**(2): 103–14.
Lee, M. and Rogoff, E.G. (1996), 'Comparison of small businesses with family participation versus small businesses without family participation: an investigation of differences in goals, attitudes, and family/business conflict', *Family Business Review*, **9**(4): 423–37.
Le Play, F. (1875), *L'organisation de la famille* [The Organization of the Family], Tours, France: Mame.
Levinson, H. (1971), 'Conflicts that plague family businesses', *Harvard Business Review*, **49**(2): 90–98.
Ling, Y. (2002), 'Parenting rationality and the diversity in family firm governance', paper presented at the Academy of Management meetings in the Entrepreneurship Division Doctoral Consortium.
Ling, Y., Zhao, H. and Baron, R.A. (2007), 'Influence of founder-CEO's values on firm performance: moderating effects of firm age and size', *Journal of Management*, **33**(5): 673–96.
Litz, R.A. (1995), 'The family business: toward definitional clarity', *Proceedings of the Academy of Management*, 100–104.
Lubatkin, M.H., Durand, R. and Ling, Y. (2007), 'The missing lens in family firm governance theory: a self-other typology of parental altruism', *Journal of Business Research*, **60**(10): 1022–9.
Magretta, J. (1998), 'Governing the family-owned enterprise: an interview with Finland's Krister Ahlstrom', *Harvard Business Review*, Jan–Feb., 112–24.
Melin, L. and Nordqvist, M. (2007), 'The reflexive dynamics of institutionalization: the case of the family business', *Strategic Organization*, **5**(4): 321–33.
Meyer, J. and Rowan, B. (1977), 'Institutionalized organizations: formal structure as myth and ceremony', *American Journal of Sociology*, **83**: 310–63.
Miller, D. (1981), 'Towards a new contingency approach: the search for organizational gestalts', *Journal of Management Studies*, **18**: 1–26.
Miller, D. and Friesen, P. (1984), *Organizations: A Quantum View*, Englewood Cliffs, NJ: Prentice-Hall.
Miller, D. and Le Breton-Miller, I. (2005), *Managing for the Long Run: Lessons in Competitive Advantage from Great Family Businesses*, Boston, MA: Harvard Business School Press.
Miller, D. and Le Breton-Miller, I. (2006), 'Priorities and strategies in successful and failing family businesses: an elaboration and test of the configurational perspective', *Strategic Organization*, **4**(4): 379–407.
Mintzberg, H. (1978), 'Patterns of strategy formation', *Management Science*, **24**(9): 937–48.
Mitchell, R.K., Agle, B.R. and Wood, D.J. (1997), 'Toward a theory of stakeholder identification and salience: defining the principle of who and what really counts', *Academy of Management Review*, **22**(4): 853–86.
Mustakallio, M., Autio, E. and Zahra, S.A. (2002), 'Relational and contractual governance in family firms: effects on strategic decision making', *Family Business Review*, **15**(3): 205–22.
Neubauer, F. and Lank, A.G. (1998), *The Family Business – its Governance for Sustainability*, London: Macmillan Business.
Pearson, A.W., Carr, J.C. and Shaw, J.C. (2008), 'Toward a theory of familiness: a social capital perspective', *Entrepreneurship Theory and Practice* (in press).
Ranson, S., Hinings, C.R. and Greenwood, R. (1980), 'The structuring of organizational structures', *Administrative Science Quarterly*, **25**: 1–17.
Reay, T. and Hinings, C.R. (2007), 'Multiple logics and strategic approach: family firms in the Canadian wine industry', paper presented at the Family Enterprise Research Conference, Monterrey, Mexico.
Salvato, C., Chirico, F. and Sharma, P. (2010), 'A farewell to the business: de-escalation strategies and business exits in family firms', *Entrepreneurship and Regional Development*, **22**(3–4).
Schulze, W.S., Lubatkin, M.H., Dino, R.N. and Buchholtz, A.K. (2001), 'Agency relationships in family firms: theory and evidence', *Organization Science*, **12**(2): 85–105.
Scott, R.W. and Davis, G.F. (2007), *Organizations & Organizing: Rational, Natural, and Open system perspectives*, Pearson Prentice Hall.

Sharma, P. (2004), 'An overview of the field of family business studies: current status and directions for future', *Family Business Review*, **17**(1): 1–36.

Sharma, P. (2008), 'Familiness: capital stocks and flows between family and business', *Entrepreneurship Theory and Practice*, **32**(6): 971–7.

Sharma, P. and Manikutty, S. (2005), 'Strategic divestments in family firms: role of family structure and community culture', *Entrepreneurship Theory and Practice*, **29**(3): 293–312.

Sharma, P. and Nordqvist, M. (2008), 'A classification scheme for family firms: from family values to effective governance to firm performance', in J. Tàpies and J.L. Ward (eds), *Family Values and Value Creation: How do Family-owned Businesses Foster Enduring Values?* Palgrave Macmillan.

Stewart, A. (2003), 'Help one another, use one another: toward an anthropology of family business', *Entrepreneurship Theory and Practice*, **27**(4): 383–96.

Sundaramurthy, C. and Kreiner, G.E. (2008), 'Governing by managing identity boundaries: the case of family business', *Entrepreneurship Theory and Practice*, **32**(3): 415–36.

Sutton, R.I. and Staw, B.M. (1995), 'What theory is not?', *Administrative Science Quarterly*, **40**(3): 371–84.

Tagiuri, R. and Davis, J.A. (1992), 'On the goals of successful family companies', *Family Business Review*, **5**(1): 263–81.

Thompson, James D. (2003) [1967], *Organizations in Action: Social Science Bases of Administrative Theory*, New Brunswick, NJ: Transaction Publishers.

Todd, E. (1985), *The Explanation of Ideology, Family Structures and Social Systems*, Oxford: Basil Blackwell.

Tsui, A.S., Nifadkar, S.S. and Ou, A.Y. (2007), 'Cross-national, cross-cultural organizational behaviour research: advances, gaps, and recommendations', *Journal of Management*, **33**(3): 426–78.

US Census Bureau (2007), 'Lone wolves boost nonemployer businesses past 20 million', News Release, 27 June, at http://www.census.gov/Press-Release/www/releases/archives/economic_census/010314.html.

Ward, J.L. (1987), *Keeping the Family Business Healthy*, San Francisco, CA: Jossey-Bass.

Ward, J.L. (1991), *Creating Effective Boards for Private Enterprises*, San Francisco, CA: Jossey-Bass.

Westhead, P. and Cowling, M. (1998), 'Family firm research: the need for a methodology rethink', *Entrepreneurship Theory and Practice*, **23**(1) 31–3.

Westhead, P. and Howorth, C. (2007), 'Types of private family firms: an exploratory conceptual and empirical analysis', *Entrepreneurship and Regional Development*, **19**(5): 405–31.

Whetten, D.A. (1989), 'What constitutes a theoretical contribution?', *Academy of Management Review*, **14**(4): 490–95.

Whetten, D.A. (2007), 'What constitutes a theoretical contribution (in family-business scholarship]?', Keynote address at the 2007 Family Enterprise Research Conference, Monterrey, Mexico.

Yin, R.K. (1994), *Case Study Research: Design and Methods*, Newbury Park, CA: Sage.

Zahra, S.A. and Pearce II, J.A. (1989), 'Board of directors and corporate financial performance: a review and integrative model', *Journal of Management*, **15**(2): 291–334.

8   Other large shareholders in family firms: do they monitor?[1]

María Sacristán-Navarro, Silvia Gómez-Ansón and Laura Cabeza-García

INTRODUCTION

Family ownership is relatively common among publicly listed firms in different countries. Indeed, many companies around the world are controlled by large shareholders, usually individuals or their families. In fact, La Porta et al. (1999) document that family control is the most widespread organizational structure, except in countries where there is strong protection of minority shareholders. In the USA, more than one-third of S&P 500 corporations can be classified as family controlled (Anderson and Reeb, 2003). In East Asia, a small number of families control firms that make up a large percentage of the stock markets (Claessens et al., 2000). For Western Europe, Faccio and Lang (2002) document that more than 44 per cent of listed companies are family controlled.

There are various forms and combinations of ownership. There may be just a single large shareholder, more than one, or none. For instance, Laeven and Levine (2008) suggest for Western economies that more than 40 per cent of public firms with one large shareholder also have two or more other shareholders who own more than 10 per cent of the shares. This is also the case for family firms (especially those that are listed). They frequently have large shareholders – families – and several minority shareholders, or families plus other significant large shareholders and minority shareholders.

The academic literature has focused on the possible conflicts of interests between large and minority shareholders (Maury, 2006). There has been less examination, with the exception of Maury and Pajuste (2005), Jara-Bertín et al. (2008) and Nieto et al. (2009), of the conflicts between families and other large shareholders. Moreover, the empirical literature usually does not refer to the typology or identity of the large shareholders. Thus very little is known, especially with regard to family firms, about how large shareholders interact with each other, how they exercise their power and control, and how their coexistence affects company performance. As Jara-Bertín et al. (2008) point out, there is a need for more research into how large shareholders interact with each other or with minority shareholders, and their impact on firm performance.

This chapter presents new empirical evidence about the influence of various combinations of large shareholders on company performance. We contribute to the literature in several ways: first, we identify the largest and second-largest shareholders within listed family firms; previous studies use samples of the whole universe of listed companies (López de Foronda et al., 2007; Nieto et al., 2009) or focus on closely held firms (Bennedsen and Wolfenzon, 2000; Gutierrez and Tribó, 2004). Second, we add new evidence about the effect of various shareholder combinations on performance. Third, we analyse how family presence in corporate governance structures may influence the way different shareholder combinations affect firm performance.

As suggested by a large body of literature, corporate rules can shape ownership structures (La Porta et al., 1998; Roe, 2000). High concentration of control rights and high diffusion of pyramidal structures, high premia of voting shares and of control block transactions, legal origin and social democracy are all recognized as indicators of low investor protection and high benefits of control (Bebchuck, 1999; Bennedsen and Wolfenzon, 2000; La Porta et al., 2000; Roe, 2000; Dyck and Zingales, 2002; Nenova, 2003) that may influence the way ownership is structured. Our empirical analysis focuses on a sample of 102 Spanish non-financial listed family companies over the period 2003–2008 (463 observations). Spain is an example of a French civil-law country that suffered a civil war during the twentieth century. Its economy ranks 93rd among 183 countries in terms of investor protection (World Bank, 2010), with listed firms presenting a high concentration of control rights and high diffusion of pyramidal structures. Moreover, banks have played an important role in the economy as both shareholders and creditors of quoted companies. Spain also has a large percentage of listed firms that are controlled by families (Sacristán-Navarro and Gómez-Ansón, 2007) who tend to exercise power not only through ownership, but also through active involvement. Therefore Spain is a good setting in which to study the issues raised in this chapter, and our empirical conclusions could be generalized to other French civil-law countries where there is a significant amount of family ownership and control.

Our results seem to suggest that the most relevant element is the control exercised by families: non-family-managed and non-family-chaired firms outperform family controlled firms. Our findings also indicate that the duality of the posts of CEO and chairman of the board of directors may harm company performance, especially when the two largest shareholders are families and individuals.

The chapter is divided into four sections. First, we analyse the theoretical framework from an agency theory point of view, then propose the hypotheses to be tested. Next, we describe the sample, the variables used and the methodology. This is followed by the results of the analyses. Finally, we present our main conclusions and their implications, with suggestions for future research.

LARGE SHAREHOLDERS IN FAMILY FIRMS: THEORETICAL BACKGROUND AND HYPOTHESES

The agency studies of the 1970s and 1980s analysed the conflicts of interest between principals and agents assuming a world with diffuse ownership. In that scenario, small shareholders lack the incentives or contractual mechanisms to align the interests of managers with those of shareholders. Consequently, managers may exert substantial discretion over company decisions and divert corporate resources for private gain. This is the classic owner-manager conflict, described by Berle and Means (1932) and Jensen and Meckling (1976). Villalonga and Amit (2006) refer to it as agency problem I.

In this context, monitoring and disciplining managers may be prohibitively expensive for small shareholders (Grossman and Hart, 1980) and monitoring will be effective only if a single party becomes large enough to internalize the costs of control. Consequently, the presence of large shareholders may be considered a corporate governance mechanism that enhances firm performance.

Nevertheless, agency problem I between owners and managers (Fama and Jensen, 1983) does not apply to a large proportion of family firms. In fact, families act as 'principals' of the agency relationship, investing their wealth in companies and protecting their interests with governance systems intended to maximize utility, and they demand market returns. However, they may also act as 'agents'. As dominant shareholders, they may dictate corporate policies, either by managing the firm directly or by appointing the management team, while the remaining shareholders may lack the power or incentives to oppose the families' decisions (Bennedsen and Wolfenzon, 2000). For example, families may be inclined to maintain control of the companies they found or acquire, to make value-reducing acquisitions that benefit the dominant family, and to see executive positions as high-paying jobs for the offspring instead of selecting the best managers that the market can provide; in this context, families as large investors may harm firm performance. Thus families may extract rents from managers *ex post* and may expropriate wealth from minority investors (Shleifer and Vishny, 1997). This issue between large and minority shareholders has been named agency problem II in the literature.

However, the ownership structure of a family firm may include other types of blockholders. In fact, listed family companies are characterized by a large owner – the family or an individual – a set of minority shareholders and sometimes other large shareholders. For instance, for Western Europe, Laeven and Levine (2008) report that other large shareholders are present in more than 40 per cent of public companies, especially when the businesses are family enterprises. The existence of other large shareholders may affect firm performance depending on their identity and the size of the stake they hold.

These other large shareholders may monitor families as controlling shareholders (Pagano and Röell, 1998; La Porta et al., 1999) and may moderate their influence and power, limiting tunnelling or private rent-seeking behaviours (Maury and Pajuste, 2005). Moreover, their presence may add professionalism and experience to the firm and contribute to better decision-taking. One has to consider, though, that bargaining problems between the large shareholders may result in corporate paralysis, reducing company efficiency and performance and minority shareholders' wealth (López de Foronda et al., 2007). Large shareholders may also form coalitions and affect firm policy (Tribó and Casasola, 2010), and their presence limits share liquidity, leading to lower performance (Randøy and Goel, 2003).[2]

Table 8.1 shows the scarce empirical evidence on the relationship between the presence of multiple large shareholders and firm performance. Studies report conclusions about the effect of the identity of the large owner on performance and about the effect on performance of the existence of other blockholders apart from the largest one, and their identity. For example, Lehmann and Weigand (2000) find that the presence of a strong large shareholder enhances profitability in German listed companies. For Europe, López de Foronda et al. (2007) report that in civil-law countries, the second-largest shareholder plays a critical role in contesting the control of the dominant shareholder, reducing the extraction of private benefits by the largest shareholder and improving firm performance, whereas in common-law countries, capital structure and managerial ownership are the most effective mechanisms of control. Nieto et al. (2009) suggest that the existence of other blockholders moderates the relationship between family ownership and performance.

Table 8.1   Literature review: owners' identity and firm performance

References	Sample	Performance measure	Methodology	Results
Panel A: Identity of the large owner				
Andres (2008)	275 German exchange-listed companies, 1998–2004	Return on assets (EBITDA), return on assets (EBIT), Tobin's Q	Multivariate analysis Panel regression (controlling endogeneity)	If families are large shareholders, the performance is not distinguishable from other firms. Family firm performance is only better in firms in which the founding family is still active (as CEO or in the supervisory board)
Leaven and Levine (2008)	1657 publicly traded firms across 13 European countries, year 2000	Tobin's Q valuation		A negative association between valuations and the dispersion of cash flow rights that becomes more pronounced when the holders of the largest cash flow rights are of different types (family, financial institutions etc.). Large shareholders are less likely to cooperate when they are of different types
Lehmann and Weigand (2000)	361 German listed companies, 1990–1996			Having financial institutions as largest shareholders improves corporate performance
Pedersen and Thomsen (2003)	214 companies from 11 European countries	Market to book (market price per common shares/ common equity)	Simultaneous estimation	Controlling for nation and industry effects, they find that ownership concentration has a positive effect on firm value when the largest shareholder is a financial institution or another corporation. If the largest is a family or an individual, there is no effect on firm value and there is a negative effect if the largest is a government organization. Owner identity matters
Panel B: Identity of other owners				
Andres (2008)	275 German exchange-listed companies, 1998–2004	Return on assets (EBITDA), return on assets (EBIT), Tobin's Q	Multivariate analysis Panel regression (controlling endogeneity)	Other blockholders either affect firm performance adversely or have no detectable influence on performance measures

Study	Sample	Measure	Method	Findings
Tribó and Casasola (2010)	Listed and unlisted firms over the period 1996–2000	Return on assets (ROA) and Tobin's Q		The effect on a firm's returns is negative when a bank buys the largest stake and forms coalitions with other banks
Jara-Bertín et al. (2008)	Data from 11 European countries, 1996–2000	Market value (market to book ratio)	Panel data model	In firms in which the largest shareholder is the family, a second family shareholder reduces firm value. Conversely an institutional investor as second shareholder increases firm value
Lehmann and Weigand (2000)	361 German listed companies, 1990–1996			The presence of a strong second-largest shareholder enhances profitability. The presence of large shareholders does not necessarily enhance profitability
López de Foronda et al. (2007)	Data from 15 European countries, 1216 firms	Market to book value ratio	Panel data model	The ownership of the second shareholder plays a critical role in contesting the control of the large one and becomes positively related to the firm's value, especially in civil-law countries
Maury and Pajuste (2005)	Finnish listed companies, 1993–2000	Tobin's Q (market value of shares and book value of debt over the book value of total assets)		Families are more prone to private benefit extraction if they are not monitored by another blockholder. A higher voting stake by *another family* is negatively related to firm value for family firms. A *financial institution* is positively related to firm value in family firms. Firm value increases when voting power is distributed equally The relation between multiple blockholders and firm value is significantly affected by the identity of these shareholders
Nieto et al. (2009)	Listed firms from 15 European Union countries, period 2004–2005	Tobin's Q (market to book ratio adj. by sector, country and year)		The existence of other blockholders jointly with the family ownership moderates the relationship between family firm and performance: *mutual and pension funds* create value; other companies as the second blockholders destroy value

Other studies, such as Andres (2008), find that other blockholders either affect firm performance or have no influence, or that the presence of second large shareholders enhances performance (Lehmann and Weigand, 2000; Sacristán-Navarro et al., 2011a).

Nevertheless, when analysing a firm's ownership structure one should consider not only the distribution of shares, but also the identity of the large shareholders (Pedersen and Thomsen, 2003). In fact, identity establishes the large owners' preferences and goals, while the size of their stakes determines their power and incentives to achieve their aims. Thus the influence of other large shareholders on company performance may vary depending on who they are and the coalitions they may establish with the controlling family.[3] Family businesses may have various large shareholders: other families or individuals, banks, non-financial and foreign companies, other types of firms (e.g. financial institutions such as insurance companies and mutual funds or nominee funds) and the state.

If families and individuals are other large shareholders, they may influence firm performance. For instance, they may reduce company value if one family has a greater propensity than the other to seek private benefits of control, and consensus between the families is more difficult (Jara-Bertín et al., 2008). The distribution of votes among large blockholders is also a factor. As Maury and Pajuste (2005) report, a more equal distribution of votes among large blockholders has a positive effect on firm value. Particularly for family-controlled businesses they find that when another family holds a bigger stake, company value is adversely affected.

Banks as large shareholders may provide financial resources to the businesses in which they invest and may actively monitor managerial performance. They also are presumed to have a lower degree of asymmetric information and, valuing the security of their loans, they may impose wealth constraints on the firms. Moreover, banks may take a long-term view and aid in company decision-making without wanting to be in control. These are all arguments that banks as large shareholders enhance firm performance. In fact, various empirical papers tend to emphasize this beneficial role, suggesting that the ownership share held by the dominant financial institutions is associated with an increase in company value (Cable, 1985; Hoshi et al., 1990; Thomsen and Pedersen, 2000; Casasola and Tribó, 2004) or with a positive influence on productivity (Nickel et al., 1997). The distribution of votes among large blockholders also plays a role. As Maury and Pajuste (2005) report for family-controlled firms, company value is positively affected when a financial institution holds a higher stake than the family's. Nevertheless, banks may also value other business relations with the company and their presence may reduce firm value. Accordingly, studies such as Tribó and Casasola (2010) report a negative effect on company returns when a bank buys the largest stake, or when it forms coalitions with other banks so that two banks become the first and second owners.

Often, non-financial and foreign companies are also large shareholders of listed companies. Both usually hold shares in other firms as part of cross-ownership structures that may function as a takeover defence to protect managerial interests or as part of company group structures. Additionally, holding shares of other firms may facilitate their access to valuable technology and other specific resources. These large shareholders with business ties to the companies in which they participate may be considered as insider owners, their cost of profit diversion being smaller, which should lead to increased firm performance (Pedersen and Thomsen, 2003). However, these blockholders may use the companies, in which they invest as part of their general strategy, for their own interests. Actually, the scarce empirical evidence regarding the relationship between non-financial and foreign companies and family firm performance is contradictory: while Nieto et al. (2009) suggest that other companies as blockholders destroy value, Randøy and Goel (2003) report that a low level of foreign ownership has a positive effect on performance.

In addition to banks, other financial institutions, such as insurance companies and mutual and nominee funds, may hold large equity stakes in family firms.[4] These large shareholders may monitor other large shareholders and prevent discretional use of corporate resources and the extraction of private benefits. Moreover, these investors are generally subject to special regulation and supervision; thus their marginal cost of value diversion is presumably high, so their presence should have a positive influence on firm performance. Accordingly, the empirical evidence suggests that institutional investors enhance performance, both as largest shareholders (McConnell and Servaes, 1990; Chaganti and Damanpour, 1991; Acker and Athanassakos, 2003) and as second large shareholders (Jara-Bertín et al., 2008). Specifically, for family firms Nieto et al. (2009) also report that institutional investors positively influence performance, although for founders' small family firms, Randøy and Goel (2003) argue that foreign institutional owners, which typically hold shares only for short periods, may not provide much benefit in terms of reducing agency costs. On the contrary, they may impose additional costly reporting requirements.

According to these arguments, we propose the following hypothesis:

Hypothesis 1 For family firms, various types of second-largest shareholder may have varying effects on performance. Family second-largest shareholders will negatively influence it, whereas non-family second-largest shareholders will have a positive effect.

Family involvement may affect ownership, management and succession (Chrisman et al., 2003). Actually, control of a family firm may be exercised by controlling the ownership (passive control) or by also assuming the posts of board chair and/or CEO (active control). As reported by Burkart et al. (2003), patterns of separation of ownership and management may vary from country to country. In the USA, founders often hire professional managers early on and by the time the founder retires, his or her family retains only marginal ownership; in Western Europe, however, significant stakes of shares typically remain with the family after the founder retires. This is also the case in Spain, where families tend to exert control by assuming a high level of ownership concentration and being actively involved in management.

When members of the owner family serve as CEO or fill other top management positions (what is called a family-owned-managed firm), the family can more readily align company interests with its own. Therefore the effect of family ownership on company performance may be magnified with the presence of a family CEO (Anderson and Reeb, 2003). Also, families may limit executive management positions to family members, restricting the labour pool from which to draw qualified and capable candidates (Anderson and Reeb, 2003). In non-family-managed firms, families may have more trouble inducing managers to pursue family interests, especially in the presence of another large shareholder, and therefore better company performance should be expected; in family-managed firms, however, owners and managers belong to the same group – the family – and this may allow them to extract private benefits of control.

Moreover, when ownership is shared among different parties, control may be crucial and the board of directors may become an important governance device. Families may use the board, for instance, to retain control or to establish family-dominated decision-making processes. Thus the board's composition may be key and may help families achieve their control aims or improve decision-making. For instance, Anderson and Reeb (2004) report that the most valuable public family firms are those where independent directors balance family representation on the board. Another issue that should be taken into account is whether a family member is the chairman; if so, family influence over company decisions presumably will increase. When that chairman is also the CEO (duality), families both manage and control the company and may extract to a larger extent private benefits of control that may harm minority shareholders' wealth.

Thus the influence of other large shareholders on firm performance may differ depending on how the dominant family exercises control through the company's corporate governance structure.

Hypothesis 2 For family-managed firms, family-chaired firms and duality firms, the effect of having a non-family second significant owner will be positive.

SAMPLE, VARIABLES AND METHODOLOGY

The initial sample comprised the whole population of firms listed on the Spanish stock exchanges over the period 2003–2008. From this initial sample, we excluded financial companies (SIC 6000–6999), companies that stopped quoting during the study period or did not fill in a corporate governance report, and non-family firms. With the application of these filters, the final sample amounts to 102 firms. The number of family firm observations amounts to 463. Sample firms show a widespread industry distribution and belong mainly to the building construction industry (SIC Code 15, 23.3 per cent), followed by the food and kindred products industry (SIC Code 20, 9.7 per cent), the communications industry (SIC Code 48, 8 per cent) and engineering and management services (SIC Code 87, 7.1 per cent) (see Table 8.2).

Our data collection process was done manually and in two steps. First, we gathered all the information about the firms' ownership and corporate governance structures; second, we collected economic and financial data for all sample firms. We obtained ownership and corporate governance data individually from the annual corporate governance report that each company completed for the Spanish securities regulator, CNMV, over the sample period (2003–2008). Financial and economic information for each company and each year was obtained from various sources: the SABI database, the Madrid Stock Exchange and CNMV.

We identified the large and/or ultimate owners of each sample firm and the percentage of common shares they held. For that purpose, we followed the standard methodology employed by La Porta et al. (1999), Claessens et al. (2000), Claessens et al. (2002), and Faccio and Lang (2002). Following La Porta et al. (1999), a large owner is a legal entity that directly or indirectly controls at least 10 per cent of the voting rights. A shareholder

Table 8.2   Family firms sample's industry and annual classification

Panel A: Sample industry classification		
Industry (SIC codes)	Number of observations	Percentage (%) of observations
1	6	1.3
12	9	1.9
14	6	1.3
15	108	23.3
16	18	3.9
17	2	0.4
20	45	9.7
22	12	2.6
23	12	2.6
24	3	0.6
26	20	4.3
28	13	2.8
31	5	1.1
32	23	5
33	16	3.5
34	6	1.3
35	12	2.6
38	12	2.6
41	10	2.2
42	1	0.2
45	2	0.4
48	37	8
49	12	2.6
50	2	0.4
51	6	1.3
70	12	2.6
72	6	1.3
73	8	1.7
79	4	0.9
80	2	0.4
87	33	7.1
Total	463	100.0

Panel B: Sample annual distribution		
Year	Number of observations	Percentage (%) of observations
2003	65	14
2004	73	15.8
2005	73	15.8
2006	80	17.3
2007	90	19.4
2008	82	17.7
Total	463	100.0

Note: The sample consists of 102 Spanish non-financial listed family firms over the period 2003–2008, with 463 observations. Family firms are those in which families and individuals are either large shareholders or the ultimate owners, and hold more than 10% of the voting rights of the firm.

Table 8.3   Variables of the study

Variables	Description
FF	Family firms: when families and individuals are either large shareholders or ultimate owners, holding more than 10% of the voting rights
FSH	The percentage of common shares held by the largest shareholder
SSH	The percentage of common shares held by the second-largest shareholder
FAMCONTROL	Dummy variable that equals 1 if the family firm has either any member of the family owner group acting as family CEO and/or as family chairman and 0 otherwise
FAMMANG	Dummy variable that equals 1 if the family firm has any member of the family owner group acting as family CEO and 0 otherwise
FAMCHAIR	Dummy variable that equals 1 if the family firm has any member of the family owner group acting as family chairman and 0 otherwise
FAMDUAL	Dummy variable that adopts value of 1 if a family CEO is the same person as the chairman of the board of directors and 0 otherwise
AVALUE	Adjusted market to book value of equity (MB – industry median each year)
AROA	Adjusted operating income over total assets (ROA – industry median each year)
AROE	Adjusted net profit over book value of equity (ROE – industry median each year)
SIZE	Total assets in €000s
AGE	$(Year_{it} - INC_i)$ where $Year_{it}$ is the corresponding period of time and INC_i is the date of incorporation of the firm

was defined as large if direct and indirect voting rights summed above 10 per cent. Since the large shareholders of corporations are sometimes corporations themselves, we identified, whenever possible, the large shareholders in these corporations. This indirect ownership chain was traced backward through numerous corporations to identify the ultimate vote holders. Using this methodology, we identified all large shareholders of each sample firm. When a large and/or ultimate owner was an individual or a family holding more than 10 per cent of the shares, the company was classified as a family firm (FF).[5]

A summary of the variables of the study is detailed in Table 8.3. We defined two variables that represent respectively the stake held by the largest (first) and second-largest shareholders (FSH and SSH). We computed the shares held by the largest and second-largest shareholders of each sample firm following the methodology described earlier and defined six types of large or ultimate shareholders: families and individuals, banks, non-financial firms, foreign firms, other financial firms and miscellaneous (that category includes a few cases such as pension or mutual funds, nominees or the state). When the largest shareholder owns the second shareholder, the latter's shares have been added to those of the largest shareholder.

Because the influence of another large shareholder on firm performance may differ depending on how the dominant family exercises control through corporate governance structures, we defined two variables: FAMCONTROL and FAMDUAL. Variable FAMCONTROL is a dummy variable that adopts value 1 when a family member occupies the post of CEO and/or chairman of the board. We decomposed this variable into two others: FAMMANG, a dummy variable that adopts value 1 when a family member is CEO and 0 in other cases; and FAMCHAIR, a dummy variable that adopts value 1 when a family member is chairman. Variable FAMDUAL is a dummy variable that adopts value 1 when a family member is both CEO and chairman.

To test the hypotheses, we defined various firm performance accounting and market value performance measures: VALUE, ROA and ROE. Ratio VALUE is defined as market value of common shares plus book value of total debt over total assets; ROA as firm return on assets; and ROE as net profit over book value of equity. Previous studies demonstrate that industry factors affect performance (King, 1966; Livingston, 1977), so to take that into account and to avoid multicollinearity problems that could arise if we included dummy variables representing firm industry, we used industry-adjusted performance indicators (AVALUE, AROA and AROE). Such measures were computed by subtracting the industry median ratio from the company's ratio.

We looked for significant differences among subsamples by employing non-parametric tests, such as the Mann–Whitney U test, as previously the Kolmogorov–Smirnov test revealed the non-normality of the variables used in the analyses.

RESULTS

Summary Statistics and Correlations

Spanish listed family firms are characterized by high ownership concentration. As can be observed in Table 8.4, the mean stake of the largest shareholder (FSH) is 40.63 per cent

Table 8.4 Summary statistics

Variables	N	Min.	Max.	Mean	St. dev.
FSH	463	10.01	97.72	40.63	22.00
SSH	451	0	36	8.74	7.09
AVALUE	434	−21.13	34.84	0.23	2.21
AROA	429	−2.3	2.7	−0.004	0.21
AROE	429	−9.35	3.7	−0.024	0.68
SIZE	449	555	54979976	2953938	7664800
AGE	453	3	115	44.52	25.43

Other variables		Number (percentage) of observations
DUMMYSSH	461	190 (41)
FAMCONTROL	461	357 (77.1)
FAMMANG	461	250 (54)
FAMCHAIR	461	334 (72.1)
FAMDUAL	461	211 (45.6)

Notes: The sample consists of 102 Spanish non-financial listed family firms over the period 2003–2008, with 463 observations. Family firms are those in which families and individuals are either large shareholders or the ultimate owners, and hold more than 10% of the voting rights of the firm. DUMMYSHH is a dummy variable that equals 1 if the family firm has a second shareholder over 10% and 0 otherwise

Table 8.5   Correlation matrix

Variables	FUSH	SSH	FAM-CONTROL	FAM-DUAL	AVALUE	AROA	AROE	SIZE
FSH	1							
SSH	−0.328***	1						
FAM-CONTROL	0.019	−0.028	1					
FAMDUAL	−0.037	−0.334***	0.029	1				
AVALUE	0.062	0.025	−0.015	−0.054	1			
AROA	0.078	0.059	−0.008	−0.020	0.809***	1		
AROE	−0.067	0.015	−0.096**	0.039	0.029	0.181**	1	
SIZE	0.052	−0.100**	−0.073	0.048	−0.041	0.010	0.044	1
AGE	−0.036	−0.114**	−0.060	0.163***	−0.096**	−0.046	−0.023	0.141***

Notes: The sample consists of 102 Spanish non-financial listed family firms over the period 2003–2008, with 463 observations. Family firms are those in which families and individuals are either large shareholders or the ultimate owners, and hold more than 10% of the voting rights of the firm. * Statistically significant at 10%; **statistically significant at 5%; ***statistically significant at 1%.

and the second-largest shareholder (SSH) owns on average 8.74 per cent of the firm's shares (the proportion of family firm observations with a second large shareholder that holds more than 10 per cent of the firms' shares amounts to 45.1 per cent). The mean industry-adjusted value (AVALUE) amounts to 0.23; the mean industry-adjusted ratio of operating income to total assets amounts to −0.004 and the mean industry-adjusted ratio of return on equity stands at −0.024. Family firms have a mean euros size (SIZE) of 2 953 938 in total assets, and a mean age (AGE) of about 44 years. In 54 per cent of the observations, a family member is CEO and in 72.1 per cent of the cases a family member is chairman of the board. Finally, in 41 per cent of the observations a family member is both CEO and chairman (FAMDUAL).

Table 8.5 shows the variable correlations. AROA is significantly and positively correlated with AVALUE and AROE (at the 0.001 level). Variables SIZE and AGE and AGE and FAMDUAL are also positively correlated (at the 0.001 level). Negative significant correlations (at the 0.001 level) are held between FAMDUAL and the shares owned by the second-largest shareholder (SSH), and between FAMCONTROL and AROE. Variable AGE is also negatively correlated (at the 0.001 level) with variable AVALUE. Finally, the amount of ownership held by the second-largest shareholder (SSH) is negatively correlated with the amount of shares held by the largest one (FSH) – at the 0.001 level – and with firm size (SIZE). These correlations suggest that older and family-controlled firms have worse performance indicators, and that family duality tends to be less frequent among family companies that have a second large shareholder (SSH).

The Identity of Large Shareholders in Family Firms

Table 8.6 shows the identity of the firms' largest shareholders and their percentage of shares. The identity of the largest shareholder is reported in Panel A, and in Panel B we report the identity from the ultimate owner perspective; that is, taking into account which

Table 8.6   Family firm's large and ultimate shareholder identity and percentage of shares held

Panel A: Large owner identity (FSH)

	No. observations	Frequency (%)	Min.	Max.	Mean	St. dev.
Families and individuals	293	63.29	10	94	37.56	20.060
Non-financial firms	156	33.7	10	98	45.31	23.22
Other financial firms	9	1.9	11	24	19.75	4.157
Foreign firm	4	0.8	21	70	33.88	24.218
Banks	1	0.2	22.51	22.51	22.51	0
Total firm's observations	463	100	10	98	39.8	21.507

Panel B: Ultimate large owner identity (FSH)

	No. observations	Frequency (%)	Min.	Max.	Mean	St. dev.
Families and individuals	463	100	10.012	97.721	40.626	22.007

Notes: The sample consists of 102 Spanish non-financial listed family firms over the period 2003–2008, with 463 observations. Family firms are those in which families and individuals are either large shareholders or the ultimate owners, and hold more than 10% of the voting rights of the firm. Although it could be confusing, as we identify owners following control chains and pyramidal structures, families and individuals are sometimes behind non-financial firms other financial firms, foreign firm or banks. Those cases have also been considered as family firms. That is why sóme large shareholders are apparently not families.

of the largest shareholders are the ultimate owners (whenever they exist). When we consider the identity and amount of shares owned by the largest shareholder (FSH) – see Panel A – families and individuals, as expected, are in most cases the largest shareholders (in 63.3 per cent of the family firm observations) with an average stake of 37.56 per cent of the shares, followed by non-financial firms[6] (33.7 per cent of cases, average stake 45.31 per cent). In fewer cases, the largest owners are financial firms other than banks, such as insurance companies (1.9 per cent of cases, average stake 19.75 per cent). Other categories are barely represented as largest shareholders (foreign companies, 0.8 per cent of cases, or banks, 0.2 per cent of cases, although when present they have significant holdings at 33.88 per cent for foreign companies and 22.51 per cent for banks). When the identity of the ultimate owners as large shareholders is taken into account – see Panel B – the results indicate that families and individuals are, obviously, the largest shareholders of all family firms, with a mean stake of 40.62 per cent.

Table 8.7 analyses the identity of the second-largest shareholder (SSH) and its stake. The number of family firm observations with a second significant shareholder drops to 190. The type of second shareholder is more diverse than the type of largest one and its average stake (15.66 per cent) is much smaller. Families and individuals are again the most frequent second-largest shareholder (in 36.8 per cent of cases, with a mean average stake of 17.32 per cent), followed by non-financial firms (32.6 per cent, mean stake 15.27 per cent), banks (15.8 per cent, average stake 13.08 per cent), foreign firms (10 per cent,

Table 8.7   Family firms' second large shareholder identity and percentage of shares held

	No. observations	Frequency (%)	SSH			
			Min.	Max.	Mean	St. dev.
Families and individuals	70	36.8	10	36	17.32	5.45
Non-financial firms	62	32.6	10	29	15.27	4.47
Banks	30	15.8	10	28	13.08	4.59
Foreign firms	19	10	10	24	14.05	4.40
Other financial firms	6	3.2	11	16	14.04	2.23
Pensions, mutual funds, nominee and state	3	1.6	10	17	12.35	4.02
Total firm's observations	190	100	10	36	15.66	5.002

Note: Family firms are those firms whose large or ultimate shareholder, if there is one, is a family or an individual holding more than 10% of the shares. From them, we have selected for observation only those family firms where the second significant shareholder owns more than 10%. When the largest shareholder owns the second shareholder, the latter's shares have been added to those of the largest shareholder. After these filters are applied, the sample comprises 58 family firms, over the period 2003–2008, with 190 observations.

average stake 14.05 per cent), other financial firms (3.2 per cent, average stake 14.04 per cent), and the miscellaneous category (1.6 per cent, average stake of 12.35 per cent). In this sense, our results differ from those reported by Nieto et al. (2009). For a sample of 15 European countries (Spain included), those authors find that the most common second shareholder in a family company is a non-financial firm (20.7 per cent of cases), whereas in our sample, the most common second shareholders are families or individuals. Thus, in Western European continental countries such as Spain, families seem to be even more important shareholders – even as second largest – than in the mean European country.

Next, we describe the most frequent combinations of largest and second-largest shareholder in family firms. As Table 8.8 (Panel A) shows, the combination that appears most often in our sample is families and individuals as first shareholders (FSH) plus families and individuals as second shareholders (SSH) – 30 per cent of the observations. The second-most frequent combination is families and individuals plus non-financial firms (18.4 per cent of cases), followed in 13.7 per cent of cases by the combination families and individuals and banks. In 12.1 per cent of cases the first and second-largest shareholders are both non-financial firms. Finally, in just 8.9 per cent of cases, we find the combination is families and individuals and foreign firms. When we consider the identity of the ultimate largest owner (Panel B), the results are somewhat different: the combination families and individuals as the largest shareholder and other families and individuals as the second-largest shareholder appears more frequently (37.9 per cent of cases versus 30 per cent in Panel A); the second-most common combination continues to be families and individuals and non-financial firms, but again this combination is more frequent when the ultimate-owner criterion is used. (32.1 per cent of cases versus 18.4 per cent in Panel A); and the same applies to the combinations of families and individuals and banks (14.7 per cent of cases versus 13.7 per cent in Panel A) and families and individuals and foreign firms (10 per cent of cases versus 8.9 per cent in Panel A). The combination of non-

Table 8.8   Shareholder combinations in family firms: the first and the second largest

Panel A: First and second large shareholder

FSH	SSH	No. of cases	%
Families and individuals	Families and Individuals	57	30
Families and individuals	Non-financial firms	35	18.4
Families and individuals	Banks	26	13.7
Non-financial firm	Non-financial firm	23	12.1
Families and individuals	Foreign firm	11	8.9
Non-financial firm	Families and Individuals	9	4.7
Families and individuals	Other financial firms	5	2.6
Other non-financial firms	Families and Individuals	4	2.1
Non-financial firm	Banks	4	2.1
Other combinations		8	4.4
Total cases		190	100.0

Panel B: First ultimate shareholder and second shareholder

FUSH	SSH	No. of cases	%
Families and individuals	Families and Individuals	72	37.9
Families and individuals	Non-financial firms	61	32.1
Families and individuals	Banks	28	14.7
Families and individuals	Foreign firm	19	10
Families and individuals	Other financial firms	5	2.6
Families and individuals	Pensions, mutual funds	3	1.6
Total cases		190	100.0

Note: See note for Table 8.7.

financial firms as largest and second-largest shareholders is not present with the ultimate-owner criterion.

Shareholder Combinations and Firm Performance

In order to test Hypothesis 2, we analyse whether there are differences in family company performance depending on the identity of the largest and second-largest shareholders. In Table 8.9 we refer only to the most frequent combinations: families and individuals plus other families and individuals, families and individuals plus banks, families and individuals plus non-financial firms, and families and individuals plus foreign companies. No significant differences are found for the combinations families and individuals plus families and individuals, and for families and individuals plus foreign firms, compared with the rest of the possible combinations (Panels A and D, respectively). Only a slight positive influence on company performance is found for the combinations families and individuals plus non-financial firms (Panel B, but only in terms of adjusted value and at the 0.10 level), and families and individuals plus banks (Panel C, in terms of AROE at the 0.05 level), compared with the rest of the firms. These results contradict those of Maury and Pajuste (2005), but are similar to those reported by Nieto et al. (2009). Therefore, as in

Table 8.9   Family firms with a second significant shareholder: differences in performance
for the most frequent first ultimate owner/second-largest shareholders

Panel A: Families and Individuals (FSH) + Families and Individuals (SSH) compared to the rest of firms with SSH

Variable	FSH + SSH				Other shareholder's combinations of family firms				Mann–Whitney U test
	N	Mean	Median	A. R.[a]	N	Mean	Median	A. R.[a]	
AVALUE	69	0.141	0	85.79	112	0.320	0.04	94.21	3504.5
AROA	69	−0.020	0	84.70	112	0.022	0	94.88	3429.5
AROE	69	−0.091	0.02	90.09	112	0.046	0	91.56	3801

Panel B: Families and Individuals (FSH) + Non-financial Firms (SSH) compared to the rest of firms with SSH

Variable	FSH + SSH				Other shareholder's combinations of family firms				Mann–Whitney U test
	N	Mean	Median	A. R.[a]	N	Mean	Median	A. R.[a]	
AVALUE	59	0.527	0.11	103.41	122	0.1186	0	85	2867**
AROA	59	0.032	0	97.08	122	−0.006	0	88.06	3240
AROE	59	0.019	0.04	99.01	122	−0.017	0	87.13	3126

Panel C: Families and Individuals (FSH) + Banks (SSH) compared to the rest of firms with SSH

Variable	FSH + SSH				Other shareholder's combinations of family firms				Mann–Whitney U test
	N	Mean	Median	A. R.[a]	N	Mean	Median	A. R.[a]	
AVALUE	28	0.085	0.02	63.86	117	0.397	0.04	75.19	1382
AROA	28	0.0007	0	63	117	0.022	0.010	75.39	1358
AROE	28	0.119	−0.01	57.79	117	0.051	0.040	76.64	1212**

Panel D: Families and Individuals (FSH) + Foreign Firms (SSH) compared to the rest of firms with SSH

Variable	FSH + SSH				Other shareholder's combinations of family firms				Mann–Whitney U test
	N	Mean	Median	A. R.[a]	N	Mean	Median	A. R.[a]	
AVALUE	19	0.042	−0.02	80.68	162	0.276	0	92.21	1343
AROA	19	0.017	0.01	97.47	162	0.005	0	90.24	1416
AROE	19	0.028	0	87.39	162	−0.009	0.01	91.42	1470

Notes:
See note for Table 8.7.
* Statistically significant at 10%; **Statistically significant at 5%; *** Statistically significant at 1%.
[a] Average range.

Table 8.10   Family firms with a second significant shareholder: the effect of family corporate governance

Panel A: Family firms with a second significant shareholder: the effect of family management

Variables	Family-managed firms				Non-family-managed firms				Mann–Whitney U test
	N	Mean	Median	A. R.[a]	N	Mean	Median	A. R.[a]	
AVALUE	101	0.101	0	83.58	79	0.466	0.02	99.35	3290**
AROA	101	−0.001	0	84.25	79	0.016	0.02	98.49	3358*
AROE	101	−0.005	0	77.08	79	−0.007	0.07	107.66	2634***

Panel B: Family firms with a second significant shareholder: the effect of family chaired firms

Variables	Family-chaired firms				Non-family-chaired firms				Mann–Whitney U test
	N	Mean	Median	A. R.[a]	N	Mean	Median	A. R.[a]	
AVALUE	115	0.168	0	85.22	65	0.426	0.02	99.85	3130*
AROA	115	0.006	0	87.10	65	0.007	0	96.51	3347
AROE	115	−0.035	0	82.64	65	0.044	0.03	104.41	2833**

Panel C: Family firms with a second significant shareholder: the effect of duality

Variables	Duality				Non-duality firms				Mann–Whitney U test
	N	Mean	Median	A. R.[a]	N	Mean	Median	A. R.[a]	
AVALUE	74	0.07	−0.020	79.42	107	0.372	0.02	99.01	3102**
AROA	74	−0.009	0	78.78	107	0.017	0.01	99.45	3054**
AROE	74	0.031	−0.015	83	107	−0.031	0.02	96.53	3367*

Notes:
See note for Table 8.7.
* Statistically significant at 10%; **Statistically significant at 5%; *** Statistically significant at 1%.
[a] Average range.

Nieto et al. (2009), our findings suggest that in general the identity of the large shareholders in family firms does not have an impact on firm performance,[7] although the results suggest that non-family second large shareholders could have an effect.

We continue to test Hypothesis 2 by analysing whether differences in family firm corporate governance structures – such as having a family member as CEO (FAMMANG) or chairman (FAMCHAIR), or having a family member hold both posts (FAMDUAL) – influence company performance for the subsample of firms with a second significant shareholder. We break down the data according to whether the businesses are family managed (Panel A), family chaired (Panel B) or have family duality (Panel C). The results in Table 8.10 indicate that companies with a second significant shareholder, family-managed and family-chaired firms have a worse showing on all performance indicators, and suggest that family duality may also play a role. These findings support Hypothesis 2.

Next, for the most common combinations of first and second shareholders we test for

Table 8.11   Family firms with a second significant shareholder: the effect of family control on performance for the most frequent first ultimate owner/second-largest shareholders

Panel A: Families and Individuals (FSH) – Families and Individuals (SSH)

Variables	Family-controlled				Non-family-controlled				Mann–Whitney U test
	N	Mean	Median	A. R.[a]	N	Mean	Median	A. R.[a]	
AVALUE	45	0.015	0	31.94	69	0.375	0.01	40.73	402.50*
AROA	45	−0.046	−0.01	29.50	69	0.028	0.030	45.31	292.50**
AROE	45	−0.192	0	28.10	69	0.099	0.10	47.94	229.50***

Panel B: Families and Individuals (FSH) – Non-financial firms (SSH)

Variables	Family-controlled				Non-family-controlled				Mann–Whitney U test
	N	Mean	Median	A. R.[a]	N	Mean	Median	A. R.[a]	
AVALUE	46	0.383	0.14	29.48	13	1.037	0.02	31.85	275
AROA	46	0.041	−0.038	28.75	13	0.002	0.02	34.42	241.5
AROE	46	0	0.01	25.83	13	0.223	0.220	44.77	107***

Panel C: Families and Individuals (FSH) – Banks (SSH)

Variables	Family-controlled				Non-family-controlled				Mann–Whitney U test
	N	Mean	Median	A. R.[a]	N	Mean	Median	A. R.[a]	
AVALUE	20	0	−0.09	12	7	0.553	0.67	19.71	30*
AROA	20	−0.009	0	13.80	7	0.026	−0.03	14.57	66
AROE	20	0.161	−0.025	13.35	7	0	0	15.86	57

Notes:
See note for Table 8.7. We only report statistical differences of the most common combinations shown in Table 8.9.
*   Statistically significant at 10%; ** Statistically significant at 5%; *** Statistically significant at 1%.
[a] Average range. We do not report the category families and individuals and foreign firms because one of the groups contains only one observation.

differences in performance depending on whether a firm is family controlled. The results for companies that are family controlled and family managed (FAMCONTROL) are summarized in Table 8.11. As can be observed, non-family-controlled firms surpass family-controlled firms in all performance indicators for the following shareholder combinations: families and individuals plus families and individuals (Panel A), families and individuals plus banks in terms of AVALUE (Panel C), and families and individuals plus non-financial firms in terms of AROE (Panel B). These findings support the results in Table 8.10 and suggest that family-controlled firms perform worst, especially when families and individuals are the second-largest shareholders.

We have also considered for each FSH–SSH combination how duality may influence firm performance. For that purpose, we divided the sample according to whether the chairman is the same person as the CEO (FAMDUAL) (see Table 8.12). The results indicate that when there is a second significant owner, performance is better if there is no duality for the following combinations: families and individuals plus families and indi-

Table 8.12   Family firms with a second significant shareholder: the effect of duality on performance for the most frequent first ultimate owner/second-largest shareholders

Panel A: Families and Individuals (FSH) – Families and Individuals (SSH)

Variables	Duality				Non-duality				Mann–Whitney U test
	N	Mean	Median	A. R.[a]	N	Mean	Median	A. R.[a]	
AVALUE	33	−0.134	−0.05	26.14	36	0.092	0	43.13	301.5***
AROA	33	−0.043	−0.020	25.55	36	0	0.025	43.67	282***
AROE	33	0.054	−0.030	31.95	36	−0.223	0.030	37.79	493.5

Panel B: Families and Individuals (FSH) – Non-financial firms (SSH)

Variables	Duality				Non-duality				Mann–Whitney U test
	N	Mean	Median	A. R.[a]	N	Mean	Median	A. R.[a]	
AVALUE	33	−0.134	−0.05	26.14	36	0.392	0	43.13	301.5***
AROA	33	−0.043	−0.02	25.55	36	0	0.025	43.67	282***
AROE	33	0.054	−0.03	31.95	36	−0.223	0.030	37.79	493

Panel C: Families and Individuals (FSH) – Banks (SSH)

Variables	Duality				Non-duality				Mann–Whitney U test
	N	Mean	Median	A. R.[a]	N	Mean	Median	A. R.[a]	
AVALUE	10	0.441	0.275	20.25	18	−0.112	−0.120	11.31	32.5**
AROA	10	−0.031	−0.030	10.25	18	0.018	0.005	16.86	47.5**
AROE	10	−0.086	−0.04	10.85	18	0.233	0.000	16.53	53.5**

Panel D: Families and Individuals (FSH) – Foreign firms (SSH)

Variables	Duality				Non-duality				Mann–Whitney U test
	N	Mean	Median	A. R.[a]	N	Mean	Median	A. R.[a]	
AVALUE	11	0.165	−0.05	9.64	8	−0.128	0.060	84	40
AROA	11	0.046	0.030	11.95	8	−0.022	−0.005	58.50	22.5*
AROE	11	0.001	−0.03	9.36	8	0.066	0	87	37

Notes:
See note for Table 8.7. We only report statistical differences of the most common combinations shown in Table 8.9.
* Statistically significant at 10%; **Statistically significant at 5%; *** Statistically significant at 1%.
[a] Average range.

viduals – Panel A – for performance indicators AVALUE and AROA, families and individuals plus banks (in terms of AROE and AROA), and families and individuals plus non-financial companies (in terms of AVALUE and AROA). Interestingly, duality seems to enhance firm value for the combination families and individuals plus banks (only for AVALUE).

Thus, overall, our results tend to suggest that the effect of other large shareholders on company performance depends on the way families exercise control, as put forth in Hypothesis 2.

CONCLUSIONS

This study describes the identity of large shareholders in a set of Spanish non-financial listed family firms over the period 2003–2008. We identify each company's two largest shareholders and assess how various shareholder combinations, in conjunction with ownership, control and duality, may influence performance using univariate analysis.

We find that in Spain, a Western continental European French civil-law economy with a great deal of ownership concentration, a high percentage of pyramidal groups and a large proportion of family firms, 40 per cent of the family companies have a second significant shareholder. Moreover, the most common shareholder combination is a family or individual as the largest, plus another family or individual as the second largest. There are other frequent combinations, however, such as families and individuals plus banks, families and individuals plus non-financial firms, and families and individuals plus foreign firms.

Although our results suggest that we should study further the role played by various types of other large shareholders, they reinforce previous findings (Villalonga and Amit, 2006; Sacristán-Navarro et al., 2011a, 2011b) and suggest how the effect on performance of the identity of the second-largest shareholder depends on their presence in the control and management of the firm; that is, what really seems to matter is corporate governance structure. In general, in all shareholder combinations, non-family-controlled firms outperform those controlled by the family, while performance decreases when the same person is both CEO and chairman of the board, except in the combination of families and individuals plus banks.

Overall, this chapter suggests that the impact of other large shareholders on firm performance depends to a great extent on the way family firms design their corporate governance structures. How different types of second shareholders influence the design could be an avenue for future research.

We are aware that analysing the firms of a single country could be considered a limitation of this study because our results may not be transferable to other institutional environments. However, single-country studies enable us to overcome a problem associated with multicountry studies: the use of samples comprising mainly large companies, and not the whole universe of traded firms.[8] Another limitation of the chapter may be the methodology, as it is mainly descriptive. We have used mean and median difference analyses; thus we have not considered the possible influence of other variables, omitted variables and possible selection biases.

Future analyses that employ regression techniques may explore these relationships and take into account these limitations. We should also study how the size of the stakes owned by the various types of shareholders may alter family firm performance; or, by considering the composition of the management team and board, how other large shareholders affect family influence in corporate control. Another interesting avenue for research could be to analyse whether the different types of shareholders are linked to particular strategic decisions, such as investment in R&D or mergers and acquisitions.

NOTES

1. We acknowledge the financial support provided by the Spanish Ministry of Science and Innovation, Projects ECO2008-01439 and ECO2009-10358. We want to thank all the suggestions made by the reviewers and the chair of the session of the 10th World Family Business Research Conference (IFERA) held in Lancaster (UK). A related version of this chapter is found in the *Journal of Family Business Strategy*, **2** (2011), 101–12.
2. Bennedsen and Wolfenzon (2000) show that the best ownership structure relies on a single large shareholder or a combination of shareholders of roughly the same size.
3. Other papers suggest the importance of analysing not only the identity of these shareholders but also the equilibrium between them and relate the presence of different types of shareholders to different stages or needs in family firms (Bennedsen and Wolfenzon, 2000).
4. The state may also be an important large shareholder of listed firms. A common view is that state ownership tends to reduce firm value: politicians have a tendency to distort managerial objectives in order to satisfy political objectives, especially excess employment, as they do not internalize the costs of diverting the objectives of firms away from profit maximization. Accordingly, Claessens et al. (1997) contend that if the state holds a majority ownership, a privatized firm is more likely to delay restructuring and maintain high levels of employment; Shleifer and Vishny (1996) argue that divested firms controlled by the state may not have incentives to assume risks, given their lesser degree of wealth diversification, and could pursue non-value-maximizing objectives.
5. For families, we added the individual voting rights held by the different members of the family. Note that although the largest shareholder may be, for instance, a non-financial firm, a bank or a foreign firm, the firm may be classified as a family firm if an ultimate owner is a family or an individual. For example, in Abengoa, the first large owner is a non-financial firm called Inversión Corporativa (55 per cent), which belongs to the Abengoa family, and the second large shareholder is Finapirsa (5 per cent), a non-financial firm which also belongs to the Abengoa family. Thus the Abengoa family is the ultimate owner of Abengoa.
6. Although it could be confusing, as we identify owners following control chains and pyramidal structures, families are sometimes behind non-financial firms, other financial firms, foreign firm or banks. Those cases have been also considered as family firms. That's why some large shareholders are not apparently families.
7. We have repeated all the analyses year by year separately and the results do not change significantly.
8. Equally important, narrowing the focus to a single country provides homogeneity in accounting measures and avoids the possible weakness of multicountry data (due to variations in financial reporting standards, for instance).

REFERENCES

Acker, L. and Athanassakos, A. (2003), 'A simultaneous equation analysis of analysts' forecast bias and institutional ownership', *Journal of Business, Finance and Accounting*, **30**, 1017–41.
Andres, C. (2008), 'Large shareholders and firm performance – an empirical examination of founding-family ownership', *Journal of Corporate Finance*, **14**, 431–45.
Anderson, R.C. and Reeb, D.M. (2003), 'Founding-family ownership and firm performance. Evidence from the S&P 300', *Journal of Finance*, **58**(3), 1301–28.
Anderson, R.C. and Reeb, D.M. (2004), 'Board composition: balancing family influence in S&P 500 firms', *Administrative Science Quarterly*, **49**(2), 209–37.
Bebchuck, L.A. (1999), 'A rent-protection theory of corporate ownership and control', NBER Working Paper 7203.
Bennedsen, M. and Wolfenzon, D. (2000), 'The balance of power in closely held corporations', *Journal of Financial Economics*, **58**, 113–40.
Berle, A. and Means, G. (1932), *The Modern Corporation and Private Property*, New York: Macmillan.
Burkart, M., Panunzi, F. and Shleifer, A. (2003), 'Family firms', *Journal of Finance*, **58**(5), 2167–201.
Cable, J. (1985), 'Capital market information and industrial performance: the role of West German banks', *The Economic Journal*, **95**(377), 118–32.
Casasola, M.J. and Tribó, J.A. (2004), 'Banks as blockholders', Universidad Carlos III Working Paper 04-01.
Chaganti, R. and Damanpour, F. (1991), 'Institutional ownership, capital structure and firm performance', *Strategic Management Review*, **12**(7), 479–92.

Chrisman, J.J., Chua, J.H. and Litz, R. (2003), 'A unified systems perspective of family firm performance: an extension and integration', *Journal of Business Venturing*, **18**, 467–72.

Claessens, S., Djankovand, S. and Pohl, G. (1997), 'Ownership and corporate governance: evidence from the Czech Republic', World Bank Working Paper 1737.

Claessens, S., Djankov, S. and Lang, L. (2000), 'The separation of ownership and control in East Asian corporations', *Journal of Financial Economics*, **58**, 81–112.

Claessens, S., Djankov, S., Fan, J. and Lang, L. (2002), 'Disentangling the incentive and entrenchment effects of large shareholdings', *Journal of Finance*, **57**(6), 2741–71.

Dyck, A. and Zingales, L. (2002), 'Private benefits of control: an international comparison', NBER Working Paper 8711.

Faccio, M. and Lang, L. (2002), 'The ultimate ownership of Western European corporations', *Journal of Financial Economics*, **65**, 365–95.

Fama, E. and Jensen, M. (1983), 'Separation of ownership and control', *Journal of Law and Economics*, **26**, 301–25.

Grossman, S. and Hart, O. (1980), 'Takeover bids and the free-rider problem and the theory of the corporation', *Bell Journal of Economics*, **11**, 42–64.

Gutierrez, M. and Tribó, J. (2004), 'Private benefits extraction in closely-held corporations: the case for multiple large shareholders', ECGI Working Paper Series, 53, October.

Hoshi, T., Kashyap, A. and Sharfstein, D. (1990), 'The role of banks in reducing the costs of financial distress in Japan', *Journal of Financial Economics*, **27**(1), 67–88.

Jara-Bertín, M., López-Iturriaga, F. and López de Foronda, O. (2008), 'The contest to the control in European family firms: how other shareholders affect firm value', *Corporate Governance: An International Review*, **16**(3), 146–59.

Jensen, M. and Meckling, W. (1976), 'Theory of the firm: managerial behaviour, agency costs and ownership structure', *Journal of Financial Economics*, **3**, 305–60.

King, B.F. (1966), 'Market and industry factors in stock price behaviour', *Journal of Business*, January, 139–90.

La Porta, R., López-de-Silanes, F., Shleifer, A. and Vishny, R. (1998), 'Law and finance', *Journal of Political Economy*, **106**, 1113–55.

La Porta, R., López-de-Silanes, F. and Shleifer, A. (1999), 'Corporate ownership around the world', *The Journal of Finance*, **54**(2), 471–517.

La Porta, R., López-de-Silanes, F., Shleifer, A. and Vishny, R. (2000), 'Investor protection and corporate governance', *Journal of Financial Economics*, **58**(1–2), 3–27.

Laeven, L. and Levine, R. (2008), 'Complex ownership structures and corporate valuations', *The Review of Financial Studies*, **21**(2), 579–604.

Lehmann, E. and Weigand, J. (2000), 'Does the governed corporation perform better? Governance structures and corporate performance in Germany', *European Finance Review*, **4**(2), 157–95.

Livingston, M. (1977), 'Industry movements of common stock', *Journal of Finance*, June, 861–74.

López de Foronda, O., López-Iturriaga, F. and Santamaría Mariscal, M. (2007), 'Ownership structure, sharing of control and legal framework: international evidence', *Corporate Governance: An International Review*, **15**(6), 1130–43.

Maury, B. (2006), 'Family ownership and firm performance: empirical evidence from Western European corporations', *Journal of Corporate Finance*, **12**, 321–41.

Maury, B. and Pajuste, A. (2005), 'Multiple large shareholders and firm value', *Journal of Banking and Finance*, **29**, 1813–34.

McConnell, J.J. and Servaes, H. (1990), 'Additional evidence on equity ownership and corporate value', *Journal of Financial Economics*, **27**, 595–612.

Nenova, T. (2003), 'The value of corporate voting rights and control: a cross-country analysis', *Journal of Financial Economics*, **68**, 325–51.

Nickel, S., Nicolistsas, D. and Dryden, N. (1997), 'What makes firms perform well?', *European Economic Review*, **41**(3), 783–96.

Nieto Sánchez, M.J., Fernández Rodríguez, Z., Casasola Martínez, M.J. and Usero Sánchez, B. (2009), 'Impacto de la implicación familiar de otros accionistas de referencia en la creación de valor', *Revista de Estudios Empresariales*, **2**, 5–20.

Pagano, M. and Röell, A. (1998), 'The choice of stock ownership structure: agency costs, monitoring and the decision to go public', *Quarterly Journal of Economics*, **113**, 187–225.

Pedersen, T. and Thomsen, S. (2003), 'Ownership structure and value of the largest European firms: the importance of owner identity', *Journal of Management and Governance*, **7**, 27–55.

Randøy, T. and Goel, S. (2003), 'Ownership structure, founder leadership and performance in Norwegian SMEs: implications for financing entrepreneurial opportunities', *Journal of Business Venturing*, **18**, 619–37.

Roe, M.J. (2000), 'Political preconditions to separating ownership from corporate control', *Stanford Law Review*, **53**, 539–606.

Sacristán-Navarro, M. and Gómez-Ansón, S. (2007), 'Family ownership and pyramids in the Spanish market', *Family Business Review*, **20**(3), 247–65.

Sacristán-Navarro, M., Gómez-Ansón, S. and Cabeza-García, L. (2011a), 'Family ownership and control, the presence of other large shareholders, and firm performance: further evidence', *Family Business Review*, **24**(1), 71–93.

Sacristán-Navarro, M., Gómez-Ansón, S. and Cabeza-García, L. (2011b), 'Large shareholders' combinations in family firms: prevalence and performance effects', *Journal of Family Business Strategy*, **2**, 101–12.

Shleifer, A. and Vishny, R.W. (1996), 'A theory of privatization', *The Economic Journal*, **106**, 309–19.

Shleifer, A. and Vishny, R.W. (1997), 'A survey of corporate governance', *Journal of Finance*, **52**, 737–83.

Tribó, J.A. and Casasola, M.J. (2010), 'Banks as firm's blockholders: a study in Spain', *Applied Financial Economics*, **20**, 425–38.

Thomsen, S. and Pedersen, T. (2000), 'Ownership structure and economic performance in the largest European countries', *Strategic Management Journal*, **21**, 689–705.

Villalonga, B. and Amit, R. (2006), 'How do family ownership, control and management affect firm value?', *Journal of Financial Economics*, **80**(2), 385–417.

World Bank and IFC (2010), 'Doing business in Spain, comparing regulation in 183 economies', The World Bank and the International Finance Corporation (http://doingbusiness.org).

9 The evolution of the family business board: a case study
Tuuli Ikäheimonen, Timo Pihkala and Markku Ikävalko

INTRODUCTION

The nature and definition of family firms remain a puzzle for researchers. The family has an influence on the firm through ownership, governance and top management. This involvement of the family in the organizational processes distinguishes family companies from non-family ones (e.g. Chrisman et al., 2005). The involvement becomes visible at all the levels of family businesses: in its long-term orientation and goal setting; in its economic and non-economic motives (e.g. job creation for family members and maintenance of family harmony); and in its culture and succession planning (Chrisman et al., 2005; Westhead and Howorth, 2006). Typical of family businesses is also the simultaneous participation of many generations in the business, the implemented or planned succession in later generations' favor and strong concentration of ownership (Churchill and Hatten, 1987; Koiranen, 1998; Chua et al., 1999; Heinonen and Toivonen, 2003; Brockhaus, 2004).

This study focuses on the relationship between the family business succession and the family business board. In family business studies the board of directors has been found to have the role as an advisor, a strategic decision-making group and, of course, it represents the owners in the management (e.g. Huse, 2000; Blumentritt, 2006; Miller and Le Breton-Miller, 2006). Boards also have roles in planning management succession, as a bridge between the family and the firm, as an additional capacity in family business management and as a mediator when there is a need to allay down disagreements and emotional conflicts within the family (Corbetta and Tomaselli, 1996; Bammens, 2008). The board roles have been studied using, for example, agency theory, stewardship theory and resource-based theory (e.g. Zahra and Pearce, 1989; Miller and Le Breton-Miller, 2006).

Besides having a strong influence on various board dimensions such as tasks (e.g. resolving family disagreements or restraining owner-managers' altruistic tendencies), the closeness of the family also affects the board's composition and processes (e.g. Ward and Handy, 1988; Voordeckers et al., 2007; Bammens, 2008). Although Ward and Handy (1988) mention that the ideal board consists only of outside directors and the CEO, they found in their survey that family businesses can design their board of directors at least in three ways. First, the family business can choose a board with directors who assume the role of representing all the owners, are business oriented and have influence on the business's future direction and decisions. Second, the board can include family members and some outside directors, whose role is to provide counsel and to mediate family business issues. Finally, the board can be an arena for owning family members to discuss and make decisions about the business's future direction and, for example, succession issues (Ward and Handy, 1988).

The assumption of continuity and generational changes is a unique feature of family businesses (Gersick et al., 1999) and as, for example, Ward (1991), Dyer (1986) and Bammens (2008) noted, these changes have influence on expectations about board activities. Hence it is crucial to consider the generational phase of the family firm in order to understand its governance system (Steier, 2001; Bammens et al., 2008). Succession between the two generations as a turning point of both the family and the business offers an opportunity to widen our understanding of board roles and activities within family businesses.

Dyer (1986) identified four basic roles for the board of directors in family business. These roles – the paper board, the rubber-stamp board, the advisory board and the overseer board – are defined from different life-cycle stages of family businesses (Dyer, 1986). Also Ward (1991) highlights the dynamic aspect of the family business board. Our reasoning is based on the assumption that the role of a family business board is not, and should not be, judged as a static *a priori* decision. We will follow the idea of Dyer (1986) that changes in the family business board interact with the development of the actual company. We will combine the idea of developed ownership structure together with that of Dyer (1986) and seek to describe the evolutionary development of family business board in the sense of the board's tasks and assumptions behind them. Furthermore, we extend the theoretical perspective of the roles of the board in family business and succession. The focus is on the relations between the family business, the board and the succession process. Our empirical aim is to make these expectations and relations more visible. Through a qualitative study, the insights of varying expectations about the board in the family business and succession will be outlined and early evidence of the empirical pilot study will be presented.

GENERATIONAL STAGES

An ambition of continuity through ownership and management succession is one of the determinant characteristics of the family business (e.g. Churchill and Hatten, 1987). As a result, there is a constant need to study the family firm transition from one generation to the next, and the family firm development as a consequence of this transition (e.g. Westhead and Cowling, 1998; Gersick et al., 1999).

Gersick et al. (1999) introduced their developmental model including the development of ownership, family and business. According to the model, the development of business progresses from start-up via expansion or formalization toward maturity. The family develops when it grows from the young business family toward the situation where several generations are working simultaneously in the firm and individuals are taking on management responsibilities by participating to the business in different roles (Handler, 1994; Gersick et al., 1999). In the model, the development of ownership moves through the controlling owner stage to sibling partnership, and further to cousin consortium. This transition model is called evolutionary transition (the ownership structure moves toward a more complex structure) (Gersick et al., 1999). 'The final destination' can thus be seen as management succession. The object of the transfer of succession can be both management, that is, the transfer of managerial responsibilities and power, and ownership, that is, the transfer of control over the company (Churchill and Hatten, 1987). In management succession transferable objects are both managerial responsibilities and management experience (knowledge) (Varamäki et al., 2008).

Changes in ownership are likely to transfer the family business from one ownership structure to another. These changes have influence on the interaction between the family and the business, the decision-making and the board's tasks.

EVOLUTION IN THE STRUCTURE OF GOVERNANCE AND MANAGEMENT

Family business governance is highly influenced by the family, and family involvement in business is one issue determining the appropriateness of specific governance structure for the family-owned firm (Sharma and Nordqvist, 2008). To study as complicated a topic as evolution of family business governance and management, we will use a simplified description of the stages and base our work on the evolutionary transition model (the ownership structure moves toward a more complex structure) by Gersick et al. (1999) to describe the process of family business development from the perspective of governance and management. As a summary, we seek to form an ideal typology of family business governance focusing on decision-making and the board of directors. While the board of directors is the main topic, board attributes such as composition, selection criteria of board members and tasks, together with participation in the strategy process of the firm and background theories of board roles (agency, stewardship and resource-based theory) are all studied more closely.

First Generation

The founders have a very influential role in the initiation and development of an organization's vision and culture (Kelly et al., 2000). In addition, they often have a deep emotional tie to their companies, as the success of their family, their personal satisfaction and public reputation are all tied to the business (Miller and Le Breton-Miller, 2006). The emotional investment they have made while creating the business differentiate founders' goals for the business from those that succeeding generations' managers have and has influence on their management style, while founders seems to have a greater need to oversee, coordinate and control the activities personally (Fiegener et al., 2000).

It has been suggested that owners of family firms prefer the CEO and other higher-level executive managers to be drawn from the family (Ward and Handy, 1988; Westhead et al., 2002). As long as there is a controlling owner as manager of the family business, the role of the other family members and the board seems to be to follow the CEO's ideas (Alderfer, 1988; Kelly et al., 2000). Founders tend to avoid being held to outside entities and typically also eschew formal planning (Kelly et al., 2000). In most cases the CEO's relatively high level of ownership gives a reason and makes it possible for him/her to actively influence the board composition and this way also to configure boards that are less inclined to threaten their discretion (Fiegener et al., 2000).

The situation is easy to understand and may often be adequate in early phases of the company; as long as there is only one person owning and managing the business, the idea behind the business, money used for developing the business and the risk included in the business are usually assumed by this same person. In this light, it is only natural to keep all the decisions in one's own hands, and in this way, implement the development as one sees fit. Thus the critical decision-maker is the controlling owner, often acting as the CEO. Miller and Le Breton-Miller (2006) point out that the negative side of the controlling owner comes to the fore if he/she views the firm as a personal playground and thus has the discretion to act without a monitoring board or top management team (Miller and Le Breton-Miller, 2006).

Very often the controlling owner seems to ensure his/her power in the company by having a dual role as a CEO and a chairman of the board. In addition, a legal control by the family and less diffuse shareholding increases the level of dependence (Feltham et al., 2005). The role of the board in the controlling owner stage seems minor; following Dyer's terminology the board is either a 'paper board' or a 'rubber-stamp board' (Dyer, 1986). At best, the central task of the board is to confirm or give a formal approval to decisions the owner has already made (regardless of the nature of the decisions, e.g. strategic decisions) (Alderfer, 1988). The board may also be quite small (the owner and only a few other persons). The selection criteria of the board members may vary, but quite often family membership seems to increase the possibility of becoming a board member. In addition, a CEO with strong ownership tends to protect discretion from board interference by selecting less independent directors for the board (Fiegener et al., 2000). The board's participation in the strategy process is modest, but this role grows when the transition to the next ownership structure becomes topical (see Table 9.1).

Transition from First to Second Generation

When the family business enters the sibling stage, the formal power of the CEO increases, but, on the other hand, there may be more equal partners in the company and more opinions to take into account. However, family harmony and sustaining family ownership are still dominant goals of business (Ward, 1991). The board is mostly composed of family members, even more than earlier when, according to Fiegener et al. (2000), inheritor CEOs tend to have larger board representation by family directors than their predecessors. (Also the decisions of the board may be made somewhere else than in the board room.) However, the members of the board can participate in the decision-making, at least if they are also working in the business. The board works at best in an advisory role (Dyer, 1986). When the business grows and more people are involved and the business itself becomes more complicated, the board tasks slowly become more diversified. A need for monitoring the CEO may increase and the support for operational management is needed (Westhead et al., 2002). (see Table 9.1).

Transition from Second to Third Generation

The transition from the sibling partnership to cousin consortium phase further increases the complexity of ownership. The role of the board is not always given and the decision-making does not always follow that of companies with a widely held ownership. In smaller firms there seems to be a tendency to have smaller boards of directors, and fewer outside directors on these boards. However, when the complexity of the family business increases, the CEO in the family business is more willing to expand the board of directors,

Table 9.1   The evolution of the family business board – a summary of the literature

	Founder		Cousins	Second cousins	Public company
Stage of ownership	Controlling owner	Sibling partnership	Cousin consortium	Shareholders (family)	Stakeholders (family and outsiders)
Critical actors in decision-making	Owner-manager	CEO	CEO<> board	Family council > board	AGM >board
The CEO's background	Owner	One of the owning siblings	One of the owning cousins or hired manager	One of the owning family or hired manager	Hired manager (or one of the owning family)
The members of the board	Owner-manager and possibly others	Owner-manager and siblings	Family members or outside expert members	Outside expert members (probably)	Professional members
Board member selection criteria	Family membership	Family membership	Family membership or expertise	Expertise, company needs	Expertise, company needs
The role of the board	To support owner-manager's decisions	To prepare and support the decisions of the management	Enforcing family owner's benefit, controlling the CEO, strategic management	Enforcing owner's benefit, controlling the CEO, strategic management	Defined by the corporate law and corporate governance
Participation in strategic management	No role	Supports the CEO in strategy work	Active participation in strategy work	Active participation in strategy work	A critical role, forming and selecting strategy
Controlling role (agency theory)	Not relevant	Some relevance – grows with the number of owners	Relevant – grows with the number of owners	Relevant – grows with the number of owners	Important
The role in steward relationship (stewardship theory)	The board members are stewards	The board is a steward along with the CEO	The board is a steward along with the CEO	The board is a steward along with the CEO	The CEO and the board are not expected to show stewardship behavior
The service role (resource-based theory)	Not relevant	Family-based competence and networks to the management	Additional competence and networks to the management	Additional expertise, competence and networks to the management	Expertise, competence and networks to the business

as well as to include more family directors. This allows different business conflicts to be resolved at board level (Fiegener et al., 2000).

While ownership becomes more diverse and the stock becomes more widely held, the power based on the legal ownership decreases. However, this does not necessarily influence the use of the power in company (Mace, 1971). Different mechanisms are needed for management and governance to protect individual shareholder interests (Westhead et al., 2002). The CEO may be chosen inside or outside the family, but in both cases the board is getting increasing power to monitor the CEO and his/her decisions. The board is active in the overseer role (Dyer, 1986). Thus the CEO is no longer the only critical actor or decision-maker in the business. New tasks also demand a new kind of knowledge from the board members, and because of that, the selection criteria for board membership may emphasize the candidates' expertise more than their family ties. In addition to monitoring the CEO, in this phase the board will be participating increasingly in the strategy process (and thus in the development of the firm), although service and giving advice to the family is also emphasized (Mace, 1971; Forbes and Milliken, 1999; Corbetta & Salvato, 2003).

Future Generations

While the complexity of ownership continues to grow, the status of owners will be more as shareholder than as family member. Yet the origins of the business may still be strongly reflected in the management. Kelly et al. (2000) hypothesized that size and age of the family firm affect a firm's strategic planning posture. In short, in the growth and development of the family business the top management group (whether family members or not) is less dominated by the founder's philosophy. Also the amount of formal planning increases (Feltham et al., 2005). Possibilities for conflict among family members reproduce as well as conflicts among managers and even between these two groups (Miller and Le Breton-Miller, 2006). The management of shareholder relations becomes more important (Ward, 1991). The AGM as the channel for the owner's voice increases its significance as a critical element of the firm and there may also be a family council as well as the board. The important role of the board is to take part in the strategy process but also to monitor the interests of owners and support operational management. Although the family council collects the expectations of the family members, there is a need for an institution that can reconcile the aims of the family (Alderfer, 1988) (see Table 9.1). Also the interest of the business needs monitoring; the growing demand for dividends from a greater number of family members may represent a drain on capital and lead to reduced capability for development and growth (Miller and Le Breton-Miller, 2006).

EVOLUTION OF FAMILY BUSINESS BOARDS FROM THE PERSPECTIVE OF AGENCY THEORY, STEWARDSHIP THEORY AND RESOURCE-BASED THEORY

Both family business research and research on boards of directors have used agency and stewardship theories to explain, for example, the advantages of family-owned and -managed organization and the tasks of boards of directors in them. The resource-based theory is also widely used as a base for the board's advisory task. All these theories are examined more closely as sources of board roles.

Agency Theory and the Family Business Board

The impact of agency theory on research into boards has been significant. It could be suggested that agency theory has been one of the major initiatives to study boards of directors (Fama and Jensen, 1983). The origin of agency theory lies in the separation of ownership and control (e.g. Jensen and Meckling, 1976). The agency relationship arises when a person (principal) delegates decision-making authority to another person (agent). Because of the delegated power and information asymmetries, the company managers (agents) have the possibility to operate opportunistically and they may also make decisions that do not serve the owners' interests. In these circumstances managers may seek compensation through non-compensatory means such as free-riding or shirking, or prefer maximization of their own interests (Jensen and Meckling, 1976; Schulze et al., 2001). The role of the board, according to agency theory, is mostly to control, and the board implements this role through specific activities like monitoring the CEO, monitoring strategy implementation, planning CEO succession and both evaluating and rewarding top management (Corbetta and Salvato, 2004).

In the controlling-owner stage of a family business the board's ability to influence the decisions of the owner-manager is limited and in the case of the single owner-manager, the board's need to guard the business from the CEO's opportunistic behavior is nonexistent (e.g. Jensen and Meckling, 1976; Corbetta and Salvato, 2004). Depending on the owner-manager, the board's role could at best be that of an advisor, supporting the decision-making of the entrepreneurial venture and providing insights into the development of the growing business. From this perspective it seems that agency theory and the need for monitoring of the controlling owner are not so relevant from the perspective of the owner, especially in small businesses. Should there be minority owners in the company, the board's monitor role would benefit mostly minority owners (Miller and Le Breton-Miller, 2006). This peculiar finding suggests that the board would be guarding minority shareholders' interests against the majority shareholders' entrepreneurial activities. In later stages, as a consequence of fragmented ownership and non-family managers, the need for monitoring increases (see Table 9.1).

Agency theory is widely used in the field of family business studies, although quite recently some scholars have started to question the applicability or adequacy of agency theory in the context of family business (Gómez-Mejía et al., 2001; Schulze et al., 2001; Corbetta and Salvato, 2004). Sharma (2004, 16) argued that 'it was expected that an alignment of ownership and management within a family would alleviate the agency problems in family firms because individual family members would engage in altruistic behavior wherein they subjugate their self-interests for the collective good of the family'. That is, agency theory would not fully apply to the family business context because of the specific character of family business. This view was supported by Brundin et al. (2005), who added that the agency theory perspective in the family business context is reductionist in its view when it excludes the non-economic dimension of relationship between the principal and the agent.

However, the introduction of agency control mechanisms could be helpful for family firms too. Schulze et al. (2001) argue that the private ownership and family-managed form of family businesses increases agency threat by freeing family businesses from the discipline imposed by the market for corporation control. This causes different agency threats (e.g. self-control problem, opportunistic behavior of the owner) that can prevent the alignment of ownership interests and thus lead to the increase of agency costs of ownership within family businesses. Thus the role of the board is to monitor managers (also the owner-manager) and the decisions they make on behalf of the owners by monitoring the conduct of the agent, gaining access to the firm's internal information flows and providing incentives that encourage agents to act in the owners' best interest (Zahra and Pearce, 1989; Schultze et al., 2001; Huse and Rindova, 2001).

It seems that the more complex the ownership structure is, the more monitoring is needed to ensure the implementation of shareholders' interests (Westhead et al., 2002) (see Table 9.1). However, although agency theory offers a good explanation to the control role of boards, there is a need for additional theoretical perspectives to explain their other roles (Daily et al., 2003).

Stewardship Theory and the Family Business Board

Stewardship theory challenges agency theory with an opposite approach. According to stewardship theory, the goals of owners and managers are congruent with each other. Managers aspire to 'higher purposes' in their jobs, and are thus more motivated to reach goals set for the organization rather than their individual ones. Reaching for the success of their organization, they can even act altruistically to achieve that goal. According to Miller and Le Breton-Miller (2006), these kinds of attitude will be especially prevalent among family businesses in which leaders are either family members or emotionally linked to the family. The manager (steward) is maximizing the benefits for owners (principals) through the performance of the company. Thus the manager is successful when the company reaches its goals, which at the same time benefits owners (Davis et al., 1997; Daily et al., 2003; Sharma, 2004).

The board can facilitate the steward's effort by acting in service and advisory roles. A corporate governance structure, which gives the steward high authority and discretion, facilitates the steward's pre-organizational actions. This is attained particularly if the CEO also chairs the board and, thus, has unlimited control over the company and its strategy processes without the fear of interference from the board (Davis et al., 1997). An overlap of goals and values between the CEO, the board and the organization is beneficial for the running of the business. In this way stewardship also has influence on the board structure by approving links and social ties between board members (Corbetta and Salvato, 2004).

Mace noticed that while the board serves as source of advice and counsel, these activities are deemed to be primarily for the benefit of the family (Mace, 1971). It could be argued that, when the board consists of family members, the manager's stewardship is directed towards the members of the board, while where the board consists of outside-family experts, the manager would feel that stewardship towards the family and the board would be assisting in fulfilling this behavior. Should stewardship concern dominantly the relationship towards the owning family, agency theory and stewardship theory do not conflict but complement each other. Furthermore, it could be suggested that the underlying assumption of collectivism behind the stewardship behavior would indicate the steward's ability to identify with the owner group. In other words, the fragmentation of the owner group would lead to diminished needs for stewardship behavior (see Table 9.1).

Resource-Based Theory and Family Business Boards

The resource-based view (RBV) for assessing the competitive advantage of family firms was first presented by Habbershon and Williams (1999). RBV highlights foremost the service role of boards. The service role of the family business board stems from resource scarcity (Wernerfelt, 1984; Barney, 1991).

The board evolution is closely related to the development of strategic management practices within growing small businesses. The myopic and careless attitudes of owner-managers towards strategy and strategic planning have attracted attention in the literature (Cooper and Dunkelberg, 1986; Wiklund, 1999). The low intensity of strategic management may stem from the educational background of owner-managers. Owner-managers often lack formal business education and the multitude of managerial tools to guide the development of their company (Gibson and Cassar, 2002). Thus the board of directors may have at least two effects on the strategic management of the family business: first, the presence of the board would require the manager to present explicitly business strategies (e.g. Lane et al., 2006); and second, the board members' expertise could be seen as the compensation for the low level of managerial knowledge within the business (e.g. Minichilli and Hansen, 2007). It could be suggested that the role of the board grows as the business becomes more complex and the more the business keeps growing, the more the CEO is likely to need new managerial expertise on the board. In other words, the selection of board members is likely to emphasize competences of the person rather than family background.

Besides managerial expertise, the board and its individual members are expected to span boundaries between the company and its environment (Huse and Rindova, 2001). The board has been seen as a strategic resource for the company, making impact an through board members and their personal connections. The task of the board is, according to this perspective, to increase knowledge of managers and advise them, offer legitimacy and reputation, and finally, act as a channel for communication between an environment and important actors as well as organizations outside the firm (Forbes and Milliken, 1999; Corbetta and Salvato, 2004). This perspective sees the board of directors as a significant resource for the company through its contacts or connections with stakeholder groups and through its prestige in these groups (Huse and Rindova, 2001; Daily et al., 2003). Sharma (2004) suggested that resource-based theory of the firm is especially important in stressing the uniqueness of resources in family firms. It is likely that in the evolution of the family business board of directors, the selection criteria of board members change largely because of these resource-based logics (see Table 9.1).

METHOD AND DATA COLLECTION PROCESS

Yin defines a case study as an empirical inquiry that investigates a phenomenon within its real-life context (Yin, 2003). The main reason for using the case study approach is the

Table 9.2   Case Style and Tailor, overview of interviews

Position of interviewee	Generation	Date	Duration
Chair of the board (first interview)	Fourth	November 2008	00.51.11
CEO	Fourth	January 2009	00.50.24
Former CEO and chair of the board	Third	January 2009	00.54.39
Former chair (during the management succession)	Third	January 2009	00.47.02
Chair of the board (second interview)	Fourth	March 2009	01.22.51
Family member (acted earlier as a manager in the business)	Third	March 2009	02.17.55

desire to understand particular complex phenomena either by learning something about the particular case itself or by using the case to accomplish a more general understanding (Stake, 1995; Yin, 2003). Within the business administration the case study approach has traditionally been used, especially when there has been a need for new theory development (e.g. Eisenhardt, 1989) and as a tool in critical early phases of new management theory, especially when key variables and their relationships are being explored (Gibbert et al., 2008).

As any other methodologies, the case study approach also has its limitations. Case study research can be criticized for its lack of statistical validity and representativeness. However, in this chapter the aim is not to search for generalization but rather to deepen the knowledge of the theme under study. As an approach to data collection and analysis, case strategy may lead to investigator-based biases. To control for these disadvantages, triangulation and constant discussion with colleagues on the analysis and its findings have been used.

As a case we have a 100-year-old family business. The case selection followed the sampling guidelines suggested by Patton (1987) for purposive sample. The criteria for selection were as follows: the case is a family-owned business; it has an actively operating board of directors; the business has gone through at least one family business succession process; and there are more than one-generation family members available for data gathering. The purpose of the presented case is to describe the development of the board and its tasks, along with the development of this family business, and preliminarily test the created framework of the evolution of family business boards. It also seeks to expose relationships between the family business, the board and the succession process.

The data were collected at the end of 2008 and the beginning of 2009 by using semi-structured theme interviews (see Table 9.2). The five interviewees represented different roles in family business, including former and present CEO, former and present chair of the board, former members of the board (who also had worked as managers in family business) and family members. The present chair was interviewed twice: the first interview created an understanding of the succession process in its entirety and the second interview concerned the governance and board activities. In addition, archival data consisting of records of board meetings and annual general meetings were collected to provide a more thorough understanding of the development of the company and its governance. Using several informants and archival records, it was possible to reach data triangulation, which supports the overall validity and reliability of the study.

The case data were analyzed using the content analysis technique (Huberman and Miles, 1994). Interviews were transcribed, and transcribed texts were managed with the Atlas.ti program. To understand the case at hand, the case was organized in the form of a chronological case history, which helps to create the relevant contextual framework for understanding individual viewpoints in the interview data. The data reduction stage was conducted with coding of the data. The codes were as follows: family, family business, board of directors, chairmanship of the board, management, ownership, succession process, leadership succession, ownership succession and business. All main code classes were divided into sub-codes. Citations of chosen codes were printed for the base of analysis. In the study at hand, the data display stage comprised a thick description of the family business succession process with its colorful insights into different participants' viewpoints in the different issues in the business, the family and the ongoing processes. Finally, the case study reflects the conclusion stage as the point of view of the evolutions of the board of directors and especially pinpointing those aspects of the case that appeared to be relevant for understanding the board evolution.

CASE OVERVIEW: FASHION HOUSE STYLE AND TAILOR LTD

Fashion House Style and Tailor is a Finnish family company. The roots of the company lie in the year 1905, when the founder started a tailoring business. The first transition to the next generation took place in the 1930s. After managing the company for over 20 years, the second-generation owner-manager suddenly died in 1960 and the third generation of family members took control over the family business. The last transition so far from the third to fourth generation began in the mid-1980s. Today Fashion House Style and Tailor is a medium-sized company employing over 70 employees and having a turnover of €7.6 million. Its business activities are located mainly in southern Finland, representing some big international fashion chains and brands. The current owners of the company represent the fourth generation of the family.

During the time of the third generation the family business grew and developed strongly. The oldest son in the third generation had a dual role in the management of the company by being both the chair of the board and working as the CEO for over 25 years after his father's death until the next transition. Two others of the five siblings had active roles in the operational management and most of the time these three (two sisters and the oldest son) together also composed the board of directors. The youngest brother became a member of the board in the 1980s. Only the eldest sister of all the siblings had no role in the family business. The idea of succession arose when two participating sisters wanted to leave the family business. At first the aim was to sell the company to outsiders, but the family decided to start a succession process in 1985.

The transfer of ownership and management were implemented separately and both of these transitions took over 20 years from beginning to end. At first the third generation founded Mode as Mode Ltd at the end of 1980s. Ownership of the new company was divided into two different kinds of stock. Most of the fourth-generation members – 11 cousins – were quite young and the third-generation family members wanted to keep control over the business, so they held back the privileged shares with higher voting rights. At the end of the ownership succession the ordinary shares with one voting right were owned by the members of the fourth generation. During a period of seven years Mode as Mode bought the shares of Fashion House from the third generation piece by piece until Fashion House was totally owned by Mode as Mode in 1995. After this, the two companies merged. However, it took over ten years more to complete the ownership succession. As late as in 2007 Fashion House bought all privileged shares from the third generation and abolished them after buying. The fourth generation was now the only owner of the company and had the full control over it.

The management succession did not become topical until many years later. The eldest son, Ian, had worked as CEO from 1960. Other siblings had left their operational roles in the company earlier, but Ian started to think about retiring only after a contact from the retirement pension insurance. The board discussed and agreed Ian's retiring in the board meeting during autumn 1999. Ian's eldest son, Michael, had worked in the company acting, for example, as a director for a chain store from 1991. Michael joined the board in 1997 and the board chose him as successor to Ian in 2000. Quite soon Ian gave way from the operational management for Michael. He also gave up his position as the chair of the board but worked for a short period as an advisor and helped Michael to absorb all the information he needed.

The role of the board in Fashion House was very modest before the latest management succession in 2000. Three of five siblings were working in the operational management of the company, and these three also composed the board of the family business at that time. The company was growing strongly. In these circumstances, decisions were mostly made just when they were needed and confirmed later at the board meeting. It was also typical to have conversations about the business 'beside the work tables', not in the board meetings. Thus the board was seen to be a typical rubber-stamp board, confirming decisions that were made before by managers, and existing mostly because it was obligatory to have one.

In the late 1990s, when the management succession was forthcoming, the meaning of the board started to become more important. More members were taken into the board from the fourth generation, the successor among them. At the time of the succession the former CEO also gave up the chairmanship of the board. His brother took his place as the chair and later he was succeeded by his son (a cousin of the new CEO). Since the year 2000 the board has had five members and it is composed of family members and outsiders as well as members working in and outside the family business.

CASE ANALYSIS: NOTIONS AND REMARKS

The selection criteria seem to vary between two generations. In the sibling stage the position in day-to-day activities or management determined participation in board activities in Fashion House. As one family member (third generation) stated: 'They who are working, they should also decide.' Ward describes sibling partnership as a stage of teamwork and harmony, which also fits this case (Ward, 1991). In the cousin consortium stage the importance of the balance between different shareholders on the board was emphasized. In a more complex ownership structure the balance would ensure trust toward board decisions by creating a feeling of a common interest of the family. 'One member from every family would ensure the balance and this prevents others seeing directors as self-seeking pirates.' This way of operating seems to deal with the agency relationship; the lack of direct control is replaced with a close controlling mechanism. It is also in line with the notions of Fiegener et al. (2000), who stated that increased complexity highlights the board's ability to solve problems.

The more complex the business, the more there is a need for expertise in family businesses. The selection of the board members was affected by the needs of the company as well as by the personal interests of the owners. In a later stage of the company, the optimal composition of the board of Fashion House seemed to be a balance of expertise needed and suitable family members from different family lines. Along with the development of the family business, resource-based thinking becomes more valid, as, for example, Sharma (2004) noted. Based on the observations of Ward (1987), Sharma and Nordqvist (2008) stated that 'family firms guided by business first values are more likely to benefit from outside boards in terms of firm performance than those guided by family first orientation', and thus pointed out that the board has a significant role in creating the fit between family, family business and the environment. Ward (1987) suggested that 'family enterprise first' firms are motivated to keep the family business within the family and are likely to invest significantly in the development of their members. This implies that a family business may benefit from governance structures aimed to improve communication with family members.

The shifting of board tasks was very visible in the case. For example, Ian acted in a dual role as the chair and CEO. He said: 'It was useful for sure [to act in both positions]. You got your own ideas through almost every time. Then it became much harder when you had five members in the board.' The main task of the board was to confirm decisions made earlier; the board was not operating as a strategic entity. 'At first we decided that we were going to do this, then we had the board meeting and then we did it.' After broadening the board, the dual role was dissolved. This also reflects wider changes in the board. When the fourth generation took over control, the position and tasks of the board changed radically. The distinction between the family and the board was made clearer. The decisions were made and kept in the boardroom, and the rest of the family was treated more as normal shareholders with no special rights.

The development of the strategy became the most important task of the board, and because of that, the expertise of potential members became the determinant selection criterion for board members. The cooperation between board members was highlighted and there was plenty of time for conversation about topical issues. One board member described the board in strategy process: 'Without the board, or if the board has only a minority role, the business is so strongly CEO driven that it can't be good for the development of the business.' This comment highlights explicitly the managerial role of the board.

The support role for the CEO also became very important. This was well reflected in the attitudes of both the CEO and the board. When the third-generation manager dominated the board, the fourth-generation manager merely got a mandate and limits for the mandate from the board. However, the fourth generation also sees the CEO as the most powerful actor in the company. The CEO himself describes the situation: 'It really gives you support. Kind of stability. That you know there really has been a conversation about the topic, the lines. It is not so wavering anymore.'

During the ownership succession, the role of the board was important as a decision-maker, but still, topics were decided somewhere else than in the boardroom. Instead, in the last stage of ownership transition, the importance of the board increased. The acquisition and abolition of the privileged shares from the third generation was made purely by the board and the role of the chair was significant during the preceding negotiations. The basis of these negotiations was to buy shares but also to ensure the capability of the business after the succession. Although the retired CEO withdrew largely because of loyalty and stewardship, the chair of the current board sees one of the board tasks as supporting the new CEO's work peace: 'Of course, if the older generation tries to command, the board has to be there as a supporter. To say that there is the CEO, and he commands, and your task is to be retired and do something else.' Therefore it can be stated that the board may also have a 'firewall' role during the succession.

Naturally the board discussed and confirmed the selection of the successor. It also worked as 'an educational platform' for the younger generation by familiarizing the new generation with the business and people around the CEO at the time of succession. This is in line with the findings of Hermalin and Weisbach (1988), who noted that forthcoming succession has an influence on the board composition while firms tend to add inside directors (possible candidates to be the next CEO) to the board. Expanding the board may also be a part of a larger process of successor training where the CEO candidates get insights into the corporate issues and make these candidates more visible to other board members (Fiegener et al., 2000; Hermalin and Weisbach, 1988).

The chair of the board had a massive role as a supporter of the successor during the management succession. This support consisted mostly of conversation between the chair and the successor and was related both to day-to-day operations and strategic decisions as well as the new role of the successor in the company and in the family. This was found to be such good practice that after the management succession the close dialogical connection has stayed alive between the CEO and the chair, even if these two positions are held by different people. This is also probably the best way for the successor to learn the steward role as the family business CEO. The learning platform can also be seen as an important element of risk management within the succession process. Ward and Handy (1988) suggested that family members could learn board processes (or this opportunity is missed) to become more bonded to the directors, which can be valuable in the case of death or disability of the CEO/owner.

In the cousin consortium stage, with 11 owners and many interested previous owners, the family had more expectations of the board activities than earlier. In addition to participation in the strategy process and supporting the CEO, the family expected the board to do two things. The monitoring of the managers and their decisions, especially in the sense of business development, was seen as important: 'The board task is to monitor the development of the business; the number of owners has increased so much. They [operational managers] can't act there like they have got used to.' The task of the board follows closely that illustrated in agency theory. Corbetta and Salvato (2004) suggest that the board can carry out their control function by, for example, monitoring the CEO, monitoring strategy implementation, planning CEO succession, and evaluating and rewarding both the CEO and top managers. The family as a whole, regardless of ownership, also wanted more information about decisions and plans related to the future of the business: 'Those families who are involved, they should know what is going on and how their share of the business is managed.' The board operates as an information channel to the owners and the family expects the board to have its impact on the business.

CONCLUSIONS FROM THE CASE ANALYSIS

The following conclusions can be drawn from our case study. The board and its tasks seem to evolve dramatically during the development of a family business through different generations. These changes reflect needs and expectations of the main owners and players in the business. In later phases of development, other expectations also seem to affect board tasks. The other purpose of our case was to preliminarily test the framework of board development created in the theoretical part of this study. The case shows that changes in ownerships structure have influence on the governance and especially of the board in the case study company. More specifically, the case illustrated the two theoretically and empirically distinguishable processes, ownership succession and management succession, having an impact on the board. These effects became visible in board composition, the CEO–board relationship, decision-making style, board tasks and processes, and, finally, in board roles.

The third-generation board was a highly dependent board composed purely of family members who in addition all were in managing roles in family businesses. This was not a coincidence: the board members were purposefully selected because of their role and position in the firm. The fourth generation selected board members by using more resource-based logic. The aim was to equip the board members with all the skills and knowledge needed, whether they were family members or not. Another criterion for selection was to ensure an adequate balance between different families and in this way to control the development of the business.

The board composition had an influence on the board's working processes. The third-generation board made most of decisions somewhere else than in board meetings and the formal parts of the processes were minimal (e.g. preparing a meeting beforehand). The fourth-generation board formalized processes a great deal. Almost all strategic decisions but also some most important operational decisions were managed in the board meeting.

The CEO–board relationship also changed over time. The third generation's CEO acted in dual role as a CEO and the chair of the board, and often he first made decisions and later asked approval for them from the rest of the board. The fourth generation's CEO separated these two roles. In addition, the CEO had a mandate to act as representative of the company. In spite of this, interestingly, it seems that the third-generation directors saw themselves as equally important for the business while the fourth-generation board members named the CEO to be (without any questions) the most important decision-maker in the company.

As the role of the third-generation board was very nominal, we may call it a rubber-stamp board. It was there because there had to be one. Although there was a family member CEO, the possibility for opportunistic behavior was large. Luckily the stewardship toward the family seemed to control this kind of behavior while the board did not control it (see, e.g., Mace, 1971; Ward, 1997). When the ownership became more complex, the role of the board was developed toward a more controlling direction. In addition, changes in the environment and the field of business demanded increasing knowledge and this gap was filled with new directors, selected for their expertise. After the succession, the close connection between the CEO and the chair was kept alive for the CEO's support. The fourth generation's board acted both in a controlling (Dyer: overseer) and strategic as well as supporting roles.

It is evident that the board assumes specific roles related to the operational context of the family business. In this study, it was possible to identify specific board roles for the ownership succession process and the management succession process. In the ownership succession process the board is expected to take part in decision-making, and most of all, to ensure the company's possibilities for development and business activities after the succession (by negotiating a reasonable compensation to the third generation about their shares). On the other hand, in the management succession process the board is expected to take part in the selection of the successor or possibly even be the main decision-maker on the issue. Furthermore, the board works as an 'educational platform' for fourth-generation family members about business and it assumes the support role for the new CEO. In practice, the support role refers to conversations between the new CEO and the chair (day-to-day operations, strategic decisions and the new role of the successor both in the company and in the family). Finally, the board plays an important role in management succession as a monitor for the development of the business on behalf of the family and operates as an information channel to the owners.

As confirmed in previous studies, the board and its tasks seem to evolve during the development of a family through different generations. The changes reflect needs and expectations of the main owners and players in business and, in that sense, the evolution is proactive – preparing for future needs. Because of the constant evolution, the board seems to have many roles in family businesses (wider mediator role, facilitator during and after the succession).

DISCUSSION, LIMITATIONS AND FUTURE STUDY POSSIBILITIES

This study contributes to family business research by modeling and testing the link between the family business succession and the board of directors, and through this, highlighting the concept of evolution in family business research. Our research suggests that the role and constellation of a board in a family business is a dynamic process with several connections to the changes and alterations in the actual company. As confirmed in previous studies, the board and its tasks seem to evolve during the development of a family through different generations. Furthermore, it seems that changes reflect needs and expectations of the main owners and players. Similarly, it was found that the board seems to have many roles in family businesses, such as wider mediator role or the role as a facilitator in the succession.

Larger family firms often have an advisory board as a collector of family opinions. This kind of role as a mediator between the family and the business could also be suitable for boards in smaller family firms. Should the level of family experience increase over the generations (Bammens et al., 2008), it would be very useful to take more advantage of this experience. Thus the board could be one part in the process, which would be built to collect and exploit ideas of the family for creating more coherent and diversified family business. This would also adapt the resource-based perspective for the family business by seeing the family as a resource for development (Habbershon and Williams, 1999). In addition, by identifying different needs the family has in respect of the family business, the board could get a clearer picture of the family's expectations. The significance of this kind of problem-preventing role would be emphasized during and after the succession. Part of the process would naturally be the communication from the board to the family.

There has been some discussion about the board role (and especially its outside directors' role) as a mediator, especially in the sense of 'peace negotiator' in conflict situations (Mace, 1971; Dyer, 1986; Bammens, 2008). In these situations its role, in short, is to find the least harmful compromise to satisfy both the family and the business or, even more often, different family members. However, the mediator role could be seen more widely and the attention could be moved from the relationship issue between family members to the family and the business.

The dual role of the CEO and the chair of the board seems problematic. Interestingly, it should be noted that the board cannot be an effective guardian of shareholder wealth unless it has the power to limit CEO pursuit of self-interest at the cost of shareholders' interest (Fiegener et al., 2000). That is, even if the agency relationship were there in a theoretical sense, the board could not carry out its control role when the CEO is acting as the chair of the controlling mechanism. However, according to our study it seems that this dual role is a temporary stage that is due to dissolve along with the growth of the business and the growing complexity of ownership.

The development models presented by Gersick et al. (1999) and Dyer (1986) seem to capture the evolution of the family business board rather well. It seems that it is useful to manage the board as a dynamic, active actor in the family business and continue to widen the evolutionary perspective to the role of family business boards. However, many more questions remain. Assuming that transitions in family businesses are mostly happening via succession, an important question is what the board is doing between these different evolutionary stages. What kind of tasks and roles does the board have in the succession? Also the separation of ownership and management succession highlights interesting questions. Finally, how can the board fulfill expectations of owners while the interests of shareholders are divided? Who will be the agent and who is managed as a principal?

Our study emphasized the importance of the ownership structure and its development in the sense of understanding the management and governance mechanism in family businesses. Based on one particular case, the study is not meant to be generalized as such. However, the purpose of the case study was to test the theoretical framework presented earlier in this chapter. Family business governance studies are criticized for ignoring the multifaceted needs of companies embedded in widely different cultural, historical and institutional settings as well as ownerships structure (Corbetta and Salvato, 2004; Sharma and Nordqvist, 2008). Our model is a highly simplified representation of a complex phenomenon. This simplification can be seen to continue the tradition of studying governance of heterogeneous family businesses as one homogeneous group. However, in this chapter the perspective is evolutionary, not one particular determined structure of governance. We suggest that our framework, combining the family business succession and family business board, contributes to the development of the theory of family business governance by offering a wider picture of the wholeness of this interesting and complicated topic.

REFERENCES

Alderfer, C.P. (1988), 'Understanding and consulting to family business boards', *Family Business Review*, 1(3): 249–61.

Bammens, Y. (2008), 'Boards of directors in family firms: generational dynamics and the board's control and advisory tasks', dissertation, Faculteit Toegepaste Economische Wetenschappen, Universiteit Hasselt.

Bammens, Y., Voordeckers, W. and Van Gils, A. (2008), 'Boards of directors in family firms: a generational perspective', *Small Business Economics*, 31: 163–80.

Barney, J. (1991), 'Firm resources and sustained competitive advantage', *Journal of Management*, 17(1): 99–120.

Blumentritt, T. (2006), 'The relationship between boards and planning in family businesses', *Family Business Review*, 19(1): 65–72.

Brockhaus, R.H. (2004), 'Family business succession: suggestions for future research', *Family Business Review*, 17(2): 165–76.

Brundin, E., Melin, L. and Florin Samuelsson, E. (2005), 'Family ownership logic – core characteristics of family controlled businesses', paper presented at the Family Business Network 16th World Conference, Brussels, September.

Chrisman, J.J., Chua, J.H. and Steier, L. (2005), 'Sources and consequences of distinctive familiness: an introduction', *Entrepreneurship Theory and Practice*, 29(3): 237–47.

Chua, J.H., Chrisman, J.J. and Sharma, P. (1999), 'Defining the family business by behavior', *Entrepreneurship Theory and Practice*, 23(4): 19–39.

Churchill, N. and Hatten, K. (1987), 'Non-market-based transfers of wealth and power: a research framework for family businesses', *American Journal of Small Business*, 11(3): 51–64.

Cooper, A.C. and Dunkelberg, W.C. (1986), 'Entrepreneurship and paths to business ownership', *Strategic Management Journal*, 7(1): 53–68.

Corbetta, G. and Salvato, C.A. (2004), 'The board of directors in family firms: one size fits all?', *Family Business Review*, 17(2): 119–34.

Corbetta, G. and Tomaselli, S. (1996), 'Boards of directors in Italian family businesses', *Family Business Review*, 9(4): 403–21.

Daily, C.M., Dalton, D.R. and Cannella Jr, A.A. (2003), 'Corporate governance: decades of dialogue and data', *Academy of Management Review*, 28(3): 371–82.

Davis, J.H., Schoorman, F.D. and Donaldson, L. (1997), 'Toward a stewardship theory of management', *Academy of Management Review*, 22(1): 20–47.

Dyer, W.G. (1986), *Cultural Change in Family Firms: Anticipating and Managing Business and Family Transitions*, San Francisco, CA: Jossey-Bass.

Eisenhardt, Kathleen M. (1989), 'Building theories from case study research', *Academy of Management Review*, 14(4): 532–50.

Fama, E.F. and Jensen, M.C. (1983), 'Separation of ownership and control', *Journal of Law and Economics*, 26: 301–25.

Feltham, T.S., Feltham, G. and Barnett, J.J. (2005), 'The dependence of family business on a single decision-maker', *Journal of Small Business Management*, 43(1): 1–15.

Fiegener, M.K., Brown, B.M., Dreux IV, D.R. and Dennis Jr, W.J. (2000), 'CEO stakes and board composition in small private firms', *Entrepreneurship Theory and Practice*, 24(4): 5–24.

Forbes, D.P. and Milliken, F.J. (1999), 'Cognition and corporate governance: understanding board of directors as strategic decision-making groups', *Academy of Management Review*, 24(3): 489–505.

Gersick, K.E., Lansberg, I., Desjardins, M. and Dunn, B. (1999), 'Stages and transitions: managing change in the family business', *Family Business Review*, 12(4): 287–97.

Gibbert, M., Ruigrok, W. and Wicki, B. (2008), 'Research notes and commentaries. What passes as a rigorous case study?', *Strategic Management Journal*, 29: 1465–74.

Gibson, B. and Cassar, G. (2002), 'Planning behavior variables in small firms', *Journal of Small Business Management*, 40(3): 171–86.

Gómez-Mejía, L., Núñez-Nickel, M. and Gutierrez, I. (2001), 'The role of family ties in agency contracts', *Academy of Management Journal*, 44(1): 81–95.

Habbershon, T.G. and Williams, M. (1999), 'A resource-based framework for assessing the strategic advantages of family firms', *Family Business Review*, 12(1), 1–25.

Handler, W.C. (1994), 'Succession in family business: a review of the research', *Family Business Review*, 12(2): 133–57.

Heinonen, J. and Toivonen, J. (2003), 'Perheyritykset suomalaisessa yhteiskunnassa', in J. Heinonen (ed.), *Quo vadis, suomalainen perheyritys?*, PK-instituutti, Turun kauppakorkeakoulu. Kirjapaino Grafia Oy, pp. 23–40.

Hermalin, B.E. and Weisbach, M.S. (1988), 'The determinants of board composition', *RAND Journal of Economics*, 19(4): 589–606.

Huberman, M.A. and Miles, M.B. (1994), 'Data management and analysis methods', in N.K. Denzin and Y.S. Lincoln (eds), *Handbook of Qualitative research*, Thousand Oaks, CA: Sage Publications.

Huse, M. (2000), 'Boards of directors in SMEs: a review and research agenda', *Entrepreneurship & Regional Development*, **12**(4): 271–90.

Huse, M. and Rindova, V.P. (2001), 'Stakeholders' expectations of board roles: the case of subsidiary boards', *Journal of Management & Governance*, **5**(2): 153–78.

Jensen, M.C. and Meckling, W.H. (1976), 'Theory of the firm: managerial behavior, agency costs and ownership structure', *Journal of Financial Economics*, **3**: 305–60.

Kelly, L.M., Athanassiou, N. and Crittenden, W.F. (2000), 'Founder centrality and strategic behavior in the family-owned firm', *Entrepreneurship: Theory & Practice*, **25**(2): 27–42.

Koiranen, M. (1998), Perheyrittäminen. Huomioita suku- ja perheyrityksistä, Tampere: Tammerpaino Oy.

Lane, S., Astrachan, J., Keyt, A. and McMillan, K. (2006), 'Guidelines for family business boards of directors', *Family Business Review*, **19**(2): 147–67.

Mace, M.L. (1971), 'Directors: myth and reality', Division of research, Graduate School of Business Administration, Harvard University, Boston, MA.

Miller, D. and Le Breton-Miller, I.L. (2006), 'Family governance and firm performance: agency, stewardship, and capabilities', *Family Business Review*, **19**(1): 73–87.

Minichilli, A. and Hansen, C. (2007), 'The board advisory tasks in small firms and the event of crises', *Journal of Management & Governance*, **11**(1): 5–22.

Patton, Q.M. (1987), *How to Use Qualitative Methods in Evaluation*, Newburg Park, CA: Sage Publications.

Schulze, W.S., Lubatkin, M.H., Dino, R.N. and Buchholtz, A.K. (2001), 'Agency relationships in family firms: theory and evidence', *Organization Science*, **12**(2): 99–116.

Sharma, P. (2004), 'An overview of the field of family business studies: current status and directions for the future', *Family Business Review*, **17**(1): 1–36.

Sharma, P. and Nordqvist, M. (2008), 'A classification scheme for family firms: from family values to effective governance to firm performance', in J. Tàpies and J.L. Ward (eds), *Family Values and Value Creation: The Fostering of Enduring Values within Family-owned Businesses*, New York: Palgrave Macmillan, pp. 71–101.

Stake, R.E. (1995), *The art of case study research*, Thousand Oaks, CA: Sage Publications.

Steier, L. (2001), 'Family firms, plural forms of governance, and the evolving of trust', *Family Business Review*, **14**: 353–68.

Varamäki, E., Pihkala, T. and Routamaa, V. (2008), 'Transferring knowledge in small family business succession', in V. Gupta, N. Levenburg, L. Moore, J. Motwani and T. Schwartz (eds), *Culturally-sensitive Models of Family Business in Nordic Europe: A Compendium using the GLOBE Paradigm*, Hyderabad: ICFAI University Press, pp. 166–83.

Voordeckers, W., Van Gils, A. and Van den Heuvel, J. (2007), 'Board composition in small and medium-sized family firms', *Journal of Small Business Management*, **45**(1): 137–56.

Ward, J.L. (1987), *Keeping the Family Business Healthy: How to Plan for Continuing Growth Profitability and Family Leadership*, San Francisco, CA: Jossey-Bass.

Ward, J.L. (1991), *Creating Effective Boards for Private Enterprises*, San Francisco, CA: Jossey-Bass.

Ward, J.L. and Handy, J.L. (1988), 'A survey of board practices', *Family Business Review*, **1**(3): 289–308.

Wernerfelt, B. (1984), 'A resource-based view of the firm', *Strategic Management Journal*, **5**(2): 171–80.

Westhead, P. and Cowling, M. (1998), 'Family firm research: the need for a methodological rethink', *Entrepreneurship: Theory & Practice*, **23**(1): 31–56.

Westhead, P. and Howorth, C. (2006), 'Ownership and management issues associated with family firm performance and company objectives', *Family Business Review*, **19**(4): 301–16.

Westhead, P., Howorth, C. and Cowling, M. (2002), 'Ownership and management issues in first generation and multi-generation family firms', *Entrepreneurship & Regional Development*, **14**(3): 247–69.

Wiklund, J. (1999), 'The sustainability of the entrepreneurial orientation–performance relationship', *Entrepreneurship: Theory & Practice*, **24**(1): 39–50.

Yin, R.K. (2003), *Case Study Research: Design and Methods*, 3rd edn, Applied Social Studies Research Methods series, vol. 5, Thousand Oaks, CA: Sage Publications.

Zahra, S.A. and Pearce II, J.A. (1989), 'Boards of directors and corporate financial performance: a review and integrative model', *Journal of Management*, **15**(2): 291–334.

PART IV

SOCIAL CAPITAL

10 The singularities of social capital in family business: an overview

Atilano Pena-López, José Manuel Sánchez-Santos and José Antonio Novo

1 INTRODUCTION

Entrepreneurial networks, family values, altruism, personal attitudes, family commitment, interpersonal dynamics, knowledge transfer, corporate culture or emotional costs are only some of the topics to which the family business literature has paid particular attention in recent years, in an effort to identify the source of the competitive advantage behind this type of firm. A common feature of these issues is that they can be analysed as components of the social capital, a concept that refers to the institutions, norms and networks that promote cooperation and enable collective action.

In our opinion, taking the social capital concept as a reference is a useful analytical device that contributes towards a better understanding of some of the singularities of family firms. The concept of social capital has acquired a growing importance in social sciences and has recently gained wider acceptance in economics and business administration. Although there is a considerable debate with regard to its nature, most of the theorists on social capital (e.g. Coleman, 1990; Putnam, 1993; Torsvik, 2000; Fukuyama, 2000; Adler and Kwon, 2002) agree to define it in terms of its three main dimensions – networks, values and trust – which make it possible for social and economic agents to achieve their goals in a more efficient way. In fact, social capital is a term used to identify the resources present in relationships between individuals. This concept emphasizes the relevance of networks of personal bonds that lay the foundations for relationships of trust, which in turn have their roots in codes of shared values. Following this line of reasoning, this chapter offers a deconstructive analysis of the aforementioned fundamental components of social capital from the perspective of its configuration and interrelation in the sphere of the family business.

With regard to the values, these configure an important dimension of social capital as a mechanism for coordination (among other reasons) as they constitute the foundations and support for the trust and the networks (Uphoff, 2000; Pearson et al., 2008). The members of the family who work in a family business can play three different roles: as members of the family, as owners, and as managers. It is precisely the superposition of these subsystems that explains the vital role played by the core values of the family business, to the extent that this superposition may create conflicts in the decision-making process (Lansberg, 1983; Davis and Tagiuri, 1989). Consequently, values and norms should be considered in order to explain the mechanism linking the family's social capital to the development of the family firm's social capital.

With respect to the networks, seen as a set of associated norms and resources that convert them into links or bonds of commitment, these facilitate cooperation and coordination between the individuals who form a part of the networks, as they reduce the uncertainty and the transaction costs (e.g. Nahapiet and Goshal, 1998, or Durlauf and Fafchamps, 2004). Due to the fact that the family business actually comprises two institutions, the family and the business, it is especially interesting to study the coexistence of two interrelated forms of social capital: a relationship-based network, and a network of commitment.

Finally, trust leads to a reduction in the uncertainty that characterizes the relationships of interdependence between individuals, and it is defined by the existence of mutuality or a link of interdependence of the utility functions. As Uzzi (1997) proposes, the heuristic process of decision-making is saved through mental resources, so that the existence of trust and relational overlaps facilitates it, reducing the transaction and information costs, and saving the resources necessary to supplement private norms (coercion, monitoring, etc.). In this sense, the fundamental question to be explored refers to how family relations generate an unusual motivation, bonds of loyalty to the business, increasing trust and contributing towards the creation of social capital.

In summary, the aim of this chapter is twofold: first, to assess the special interaction among the three components of social capital in a family firm; and second, to clarify the complementary role of family social capital and organizational social capital. The relevance of this approach based on the theory of social capital is clear because, among other things, it makes it possible to shed light on two fundamental questions: on the one hand, how the specific feedback between the social capital of families and family firms may be at the root of the fact that these have a higher endowment of this type of capital than non-family businesses; and on the other hand, taking into account the differentiation between positive and negative social capital along with its singularities in family business, to what extent it may be concluded that this is a competitive advantage for this type of firms.

The structure of the chapter is as follows. The chapter begins in Section 2 by situating the general theory of social capital among investigations on the specific resources and capabilities of family firms. In the next sections we study each of the dimensions of social capital. In Section 3 we explore the cognitive dimension of social capital, the values, and its role as a determinant of corporate culture. Section 4 examines the family firm network and its main components and interactions. Section 5 analyses the role of trust in the context of the family enterprise. Section 6 interrelates these dimensions, studying the main implications of the analysis in terms of the evolution and the intergenerational transmission of social capital in family firms, and Section 7 concludes the chapter.

2   FAMILY FIRMS, FAMILINESS AND SOCIAL RELATIONS

2.1   Family Business and Familiness

The term 'family firms' is often used to refer to a very heterogeneous set of entities, which comprises firms of different sizes and complexity, families of different sizes and various ways of implementing control, and different degrees of involvement in the business, among other factors. In other words, family business in practice is far from being a homogeneous set of firms, and includes very diverse configurations depending on the combination of variables which characterizes both the family and the firm it comprises. The difficulties of establishing an appropriate characterization and definition of family firms are evident when we consider the multiplicity of definitions, typologies and scales that the academic literature has developed in order to establish and delimit the family character of a firm (e.g. Astrachan et al., 2002; Sharma, 2004; Davis, 2008; or Westhead and Howorth, 2008).

Therefore, according to Litz (1995), the family firm is defined as one in which 'the ownership and management are concentrated in the family and it is an express desire to increase the degree of family involvement in the same'. In a similar sense Chua offers a more complete definition, according to which 'A family business is a company governed with the intention to shape and maintain it through the eyes of the dominant group, controlled by family members or a small number of it, that is sustainable over generations' (Chua et al., 1999, p. 25). In general, definitions of family firm typologies proposed by different authors 'seem to revolve around the important role of family in terms of determining the vision and control mechanisms used in a firm, and creation of unique resources and capabilities' (Sharma, 2004, p. 3). In other words, family involvement in management as a defining element of the family business is only a necessary but not a sufficient condition, because this link should be aimed at producing different types of behaviour as a result of the interaction between the family and the company (Chrisman et al., 2005). Not only ownership and management, but also intentionality and culture, underlie this process. It is at this point that the notion of familiness should be situated.

Although we can find similar applications of this notion in the literature, this concept was originally introduced by Habbershon et al. (1999) to define an idiosyncratic set of resources of the family business derived from the systemic interaction of the family, individuals integrated within the firm and the company itself. From the perspective of the resources and capabilities approach (Wernerfelt, 1984), competitive advantage is based on both the heterogeneity of the resources available to the company and its use in a particular or unique manner. Studies from this perspective, trying to establish a relation with familiness (Moores, 2009; Irava, 2009; Chrisman et al., 2003), converge on the existence of a number of specific resources that can be reduced to a set of five essential components: experience, reputation, speed of informed decision-making, learning and the availability of networks of relationships. Despite the apparent evidence of the dimensions, they all share an ambivalent character, meaning that they could provide either an advantage or a disadvantage, which leads to the potential negative familiness character and the need for it to be managed correctly. At the same time, the explanatory power of this theory is limited by causal ambiguity (King, 2007). Indeed, a resource is distinctive when it cannot be imitated, and when, by definition, it is difficult to define how it operates.

The above-mentioned resources could be integrated into a perspective focused on social relations; that is, the family's ability to sustain a long-term business adaptation lies in the social bonds between family members and business (Le Breton-Miller and Miller, 2009). The concentration of ownership in the family unit can facilitate communication and decision-making processes, adopt a long-term perspective (innovation and risk taking) and, in general, promote a reduction in transaction costs. The networks of relations inside and outside the firm and the norms and values underlying them shape the specific nature of the family firm, and have a high explanatory power that ranges from the transmission of knowledge to informing the decision-making process. However, these systems of social relations in which actors are involved can vary greatly from one family to another and can help or hinder corporate governance.

2.2   Social Relations in the Family Firm

The study of social relations as a differential resource in family business has been addressed from two perspectives. On the one hand is the agency theory, of an eminently economic nature. On the other hand, the stewardship theory constitutes a holistic attempt to incorporate the 'other' determinants of human behaviour.

The agency theory can be considered in the first instance as an appropriate approach to designing a complete theory of the family business, since, based on our first description, it has been characterized in terms of ownership and control (Fama and Jensen, 1983; Schulze et al., 2001). However, as posed by Le Breton-Miller and Miller (2009), agency assumptions have been viewed critically; it has been argued that this economic perspective reduces organizational and social reality to rationales that could, in some way, ignore social forces and relationships, and view human nature through the filters of economic rationality. These authors insist that agency theory should only be used alongside complementary theories that respect the complexity of human behaviour (Granovetter, 2005).

Stewardship theory goes beyond the assumptions of agency theory, adopting a more holistic view. This proposal supports the existence of multiple motivating factors for members of the family firm, which are not only economic, but also altruistic and connected with identity. The owning family is emotionally attached to the survival and reputation of the company, even in terms of succession; therefore it strongly invests in the business with a long-term perspective and tends to form stable relationships with stakeholders. The strengthening of these links, which we will analyse through the concept of social capital, motivates the agents to act for the benefit of the institution understood in a broad sense (Davis et al., 1997; Davis and Harveston, 2001).

This approach, taking concepts from socioeconomics, will allow us to address this reality in a more complete way. From this perspective, the study objects are the networks of relationships and not atomistic actors, so that economic behaviour becomes viewed as a social context (Cruz et al., 2010). Social networks can generate trust and perceptions, motivations, actions and, consequently, alter economic behaviour. These systems of social relations in which actors are involved can vary greatly from one family to another and can help or hinder corporate governance.

2.3   Social Capital: Definition and Dimensions

The social capital concept constitutes a suitable explanatory framework for the specificity of family firms in so far as it generates a conceptual basis that can be used to analyse the generation of social relations and the effects derived from them (Pearson et al., 2008). Using a wide definition, social capital refers to relations between individuals and organizations that facilitate action and create value (Adler and Kwon, 2002). In a more descriptive way, social capital is made up of shared norms and values (cognitive dimension), social networks (structural dimension) and social trust (relational dimension) (Winter, 2001).

First, the cognitive dimension includes values and norms, that is, representations, interpretations and systems of meanings between the members of an organization (Nahapiet and Ghosal, 1998). A unique language, history and culture ensure communications that integrate the company. As Lansberg (1999) states, the family enterprise culture and history in common grant a special sense to the activity, favouring cooperation.

Second, the structural dimension is defined by networks of social interactions, that is, the density and strength of the existing connections, linked to the ability to take advantage of these networks. In the case of a family company's 'organization', the concept of 'the appropriable organization' is particularly important. This term was coined by Coleman (1988) to express the capacity of an organization to transfer the networks from one individual to another. In our case of analysis, the structural bonds of the family make it possible to extend the links of the organization, guaranteeing their transferability and appropriation.

Finally, the relational dimension is reflected in the existing levels of particular or general trust between the set of stakeholders of the family business, and especially between those members of the family who have a higher level of involvement in the firm. The role of trust as a factor that can improve the efficiency and the performance of the institutions by reducing transaction and monitoring costs has been extensively studied in the academic literature (see Chami and Fullenkamp, 2002, section 2 for a survey). Then, in discussions on social capital, attention is usually focused on 'social connectedness', analysed in its three dimensions (values and norms, networks and trust). At the same time, we need to introduce a brief typology into this concept. In social relations we can find bonding (exclusive ties of solidarity between individuals of the same group), bridging (links between different groups) and linking (links between individual/groups and any form of institution) (Woolcock, 2001). Each type has different effects. In fact, many family firms tend to produce bonding as opposed to bridging or linking social capital. This can be seen as problematic, because in simple terms the bonding form of social capital is exclusive, whereas the bridging form is more inclusive. In other words, the family is generally recognized as playing a significant role in building bonding capital. The opportunities for bridging capital are less clear, and linking capital is likely to be more limited.

3   VALUES AND SOCIAL CAPITAL IN FAMILY BUSINESS

3.1   The Cognitive Dimension of Social Capital

When adopting a perspective based on a cognitive dimension, social capital is inextricably linked with the production and maintenance of a set of shared values or paradigms that permit a common understanding of appropriate ways of acting (Nahapiet and Ghoshal, 1998). This approach is entirely consistent with the conceptual model developed by Uphoff (2000) in which the cognitive dimension of social capital is derived from mental processes and resulting ideas, reinforced by culture and ideology, specifically, values, norms, attitudes and beliefs that contribute to cooperative behaviour and mutually beneficial collective action. More recently, Pearson et al. (2008) have argued that the cognitive dimension of social capital comprises the group's shared vision and purpose, as well as unique language, stories and culture of a collective that are commonly known and understood, yet deeply embedded. Therefore the cognitive dimension of social capital is unique in family firms, as it is often deeply embedded in the family's history.

Value systems help to shape the set of shared symbols that promote collective identity and this aspect becomes especially relevant in a family setting, because for families core values are typically one of their first priorities (Denison et al., 2004). According to Bourdieu (1994), the family is an institution that contributes towards shaping the attitudes and behaviour of its members and, therefore, it has a direct impact on the generation of social capital of the company. More specifically and in order to assess the influence of values on the interaction of family social capital and the company, it is useful to consider family businesses as a structure made of three subsystems with their own (individual) needs, expectations and responsibilities: ownership, management and family (Davis and Tagiuri, 1989). Each of these elements tends to have different goals and expectations, and individuals may belong to more than one group simultaneously. Consequently, the family members working in family businesses can play three different roles: as parents, as owners and as managers.

In family businesses, the overlap of the above-mentioned subsystems may create a conflict of values when making decisions about hiring, firing, promotion and discipline (Lansberg, 1983). This overlap explains the vital role played by the core values of the family business. Most dilemmas in family businesses arise when the needs or priorities of the family differ from the needs of the company; for example, when a family member expects people in the business to operate according to the rules used in the family realm and vice versa. In particular, Hoffman et al. (2006) argue that the manner in which family capital affects family business performance is contingent on the amount of conflict in the organization. In contrast, however, the values, ideals and sense of purpose nurtured by the owning family are potentially a vast source of strength and energy for the business. According to Aronoff and Ward (1995), a healthy owning family with strong values may in fact be the greatest resource a business can have.

To the extent that family firms are organizations characterized by a dominant family with its own values and behavioural norms, these elements must be considered in order to achieve a better understanding of the mechanism linking family social capital with the development of the family firm's organizational social capital (Arrègle et al., 2007). In particular, Arrègle et al. (2004) argue that the family has a direct impact on the establishment of corporate social capital in so far as it contributes strongly towards shaping the behaviour and thought patterns of its members. Furthermore, values, norms, attitudes and beliefs that qualify as social capital are built up over time, but can be diminished and even destroyed in a relatively short period of time. That which has been accumulated can be lost subsequently through a variety of uses or misuses. For these reasons, it is important to focus on the role of values in creating social capital which is specific to the family business, as this is an important aspect affecting the ability of family businesses to create their own competitive advantages or disadvantages.

3.2 Family Values and Corporate Culture in Family Firms

Although no unique and universal hierarchy of values exists, it is possible to assume the persistence of certain social values associated with the family. Bourdieu (1994) refers to a kind of 'family spirit' that makes family members behave as a collective agent and not as a mere aggregate of individuals. Moreover, according to the definition of Putnam (1993), norms are the unwritten rules of conduct of a certain group of people. Indeed, these types of norms are the concrete elaborations of the group's values, which are the abstract, ethical principles that lie at the roots of cultures. In fact, family norms include internalized sets of accepted behaviour for members of the family business; a common belief system that allows family members to communicate their ideas and make senses of common experiences (Adler and Kwon, 2002); and shared strategic visions, systems of meanings and normative value orientations (Nahapiet and Ghoshal, 1998). Moreover, increased family stability enhances the understanding of the values, behavioural norms and cognitive schemes used by family members. This understanding facilitates the integration, cohesion and survival of the family unit.

In order to explain family business health, it is necessary to take into account the values and goals that guide the family, business and ownership systems, as well as the overall family business system (Distelberg and Sorenson, 2009). In this line, Kepner (1983) explores different types of family systems and notes that a family can be characterized by how it manages conflicts and differences, individualism, emotional expression, the acceptance of change, separation and so on. Dyer (1986) establishes three models of family culture: patriarchal, collaborative and conflictive. Alternatively, Olson (1986) characterizes different family systems in terms of two dimensions: their cohesion and adaptability. This author distinguishes four levels (from weak to strong) of each dimension. In fact, families at the ends of each of these dimensions have problems, while more balanced families seem to work better. The importance of considering different types of families is also emphasized by Bubolz (2001), who points out that, depending on their characteristics, the family creates social capital that will have more or less beneficial effects for their members.

When exploring whether family values help shape a culture of family businesses that promotes a stronger and better performance, one of the main aspects is to verify the existence of differences in values between family and non-family firms. Following this line of analysis, Denison et al. (2004) show that family businesses are in a unique and enviable position due to their link with strong beliefs and core values. In this case, the role of the founder is crucial to establish the identity, the basic beliefs and the *raison d'être* of the organization. Specifically, according to the findings of Denison et al. (2004), two aspects of consistency – core values and agreement – appear to represent distinct advantages in family businesses. In a recent study, Duh et al. (2010) show that family as well as non-family enterprises maintain positive attitudes towards the core values with ethical content. However, their results suggest the existence of significant differences between family and non-family enterprises regarding the type and strength of culture as well as the type of ethical climate. Furthermore, Webb et al. (2010) theorize that family involvement, shaped by four key dimensions of identity, justice, nepotism and conflict, creates differences in the nature of strategic entrepreneurship between family-controlled and non-family-controlled firms.

Regarding the specific role of values in family firms, Vallejo (2008) provides some empirical evidence suggesting that the corporate culture of family businesses is different from that of non-family firms. To test this hypothesis, the author identifies the specific set of values whose presence in the family business culture becomes a distinguishing feature. First, this author concludes that the importance and weight of commitment is greater in family businesses. In particular, he distinguishes three types of commitment: affective (emotional attachment and identification with the organization), calculative (based on the recognition by employees of the costs associated with leaving the organization) and normative (a sense of loyalty to an organization and the internal conviction that loyalty is important). Second, Vallejo highlights the existence of better human relations within the company and a better working atmosphere, and that this harmony is one of the characteristic values of the family business. Third, he stresses the trend among family businesses to target their activities toward the long term (long-term orientation) in contrast to non-family businesses. Indeed, family businesses tend to have goals with a strong, intrinsic sense of security (family safety) together with the vision of the company as a legacy to be passed on to successive generations, leading to a management style that is highly geared towards the long term. Finally, the dedication and concern for the client (customer service) as a value is also considered a key element in the competitive strategy of family firms. Ultimately, the results of Vallejo (2008) indicate that a values-based model can help the company survive several generations, which is one of the most important challenges for family businesses.

The previous characterization of values as a constitutive element of family firms culture supports the idea that 'the differentiating factor lies in the fact that the behaviour of family companies emanates not from external pressure but from a deeply ingrained, learned-at-the-dinner-table sense of history and morality' (Denison et al., 2004, p. 64). Moreover, this kind of argument suggests that family values and norms can guide the family business in decision-making, improve their efficiency of action and reduce external unknowns (Hoffman et al., 2006). Furthermore, to the extent that the specific culture of the family company is usually rich in core values and is supported by its founding family which has nurtured it for generations, it is difficult to replicate and, therefore, can be a source of strategic advantage.

3.3   The Ambiguous Role of Family Values in Family Firms

The social case for family values appears to be underpinned by a presumption that the core values are a valuable asset for a family firm. However, family values are also associated with factors such as nepotism, autocracy or inflexibility (Ram and Holliday, 1993). This would be the 'dark side' of family values that matches the 'dark side' of social capital. Therefore, apart from the beneficial aspects, there are also negative aspects of social capital that are also worth mentioning (Portes and Landolt, 1996). Following Portes (1998), in general, the negative manifestations of social capital include four major types: exclusion of those outside the group; the excessive demands of solidarity and mutual aid among group members; constraints to individual freedom; and the rules that hamper the development of individual members.

Therefore it should not be overlooked that the role of values is ambiguous. On the one hand, they promote the internal cohesion of the group. However, on the other hand they hinder cooperation with those groups who do not share the same values (Parsons, 1949). According to Parsons's well-known distinction between particularistic and universalistic values, the former foster internal cohesion but hinder cooperation with out-groups. Particularistic values promote solidarity and at the same time segregation. Family values, for example, confer social cohesion and solidarity on members of one family, while segregating non-members. Indeed, people experience both types of values simply by belonging to social circles of different extents. For instance, the feeling of belonging to a businessman's family would be due to particularistic values, while the need for cooperation with the wider environment would require universalistic values.

The idea that a culture based on strong family ties may impair economic efficiency can be found in Weber (1904). This author argues that strong culturally predetermined family values may place constraints on the development of capitalist economic activities, which require a more individualistic form of entrepreneurship and the absence of nepotism. In a similar line, Banfield (1958) focuses on the concept of 'amoral familism' as one of the main reasons for the smaller average firm size and slower economic development of the south of Italy in comparison to the north. In his study of families in southern Italy, he identified a potential trade-off between trust among the narrow realm of kinship networks and trust in the society at large. A similar argument has been developed by Fukuyama (1995), who proposes that in societies where people are raised to trust their close family networks, they are also taught to distrust people outside the family, which impedes the development of formal institutions in society.

Continuing this line of reasoning, Bertrand and Schoar (2006) conclude that a culture based on strong family ties can give rise to nepotism. If founders derive utility from seeing relatives involved in the business, they may decide to hire key managers from within their kinship network rather than turn to more talented professional managers. Beyond the direct effect of these lower-quality appointments on performance, nepotism may also have adverse spillover effects, whereby it creates negative incentive effects throughout the organization (Vinton, 1998; Padgett and Morris, 2005). If lower-level employees know that promotion decisions are not tied to performance, they may be less willing to make greater efforts or to remain within the family business, thus making it more difficult to retain talent.

Family values can also create efficiency distortions if they introduce non-monetary objectives into the founder's utility maximization that go against optimal decisions for the business. Zellweger and Astrachan (2008) show that the non-financial aspects of organizational ownership are particularly relevant in the context of privately held family firms, as it is widely acknowledged that most family firms deliberately strive for a mix of pecuniary and non-pecuniary performance outcomes (Westhead and Cowling, 1997). Ward (1997), Sorenson (1999), Sharma et al. (1997), Anderson and Reeb (2003) and Corbetta and Salvato (2004) consider independence, tradition and continuity as common examples of these non-pecuniary outcomes. Moreover, most of this literature is essential in order to gain a better understanding of how these non-financial aspects are actually endowed and valued by owners within the context of the family firm.

Perhaps most symptomatic of the cultural constraints within family firms are the inheritance rules that govern many of them. These inheritance norms vary from strict primogeniture, where the oldest son inherits everything, to equal sharing rules among all the sons of the founder. The main point is that rigid inheritance rules may have direct cost for family business (Bertrand and Schoar, 2006). Furthermore, in line with the cognitive dimension of social capital, the role of codes and language in relationships development is essential (Nahapiet and Ghoshal, 1998). Therefore, what may constitute a risk factor is a situation in which the successor's 'system of representation' may differ from the standards, values and beliefs to which family members adhere.

In summary, the role of family values as a component of social capital that contributes to explaining the dynamics of the family firm can be assessed using the concept introduced by Tagiuri and Davis (1996) of the 'bivalent attribute': a unique, inherent feature of an organization that is the source of both advantages and disadvantages.

4   NETWORKS AND FAMILY FIRMS

4.1   The Structural Dimension of Social Capital

Several authors identify networks as one of the main dimensions of social capital and relate this concept to the density and stability of a social network. Nahapiet and Ghoshal (1998, p. 249) define social capital as 'the network of relationships possessed by an individual or social unit, and the sum of actual and potential resources embedded within, available through, and derived from such a network'. As indicated by Durlauf and Fafchamps (2004), social capital may be defined as resources embedded in social networks that are accessed and used by actors for actions.

A network comprises agents (individuals and/or organizations) who are connected by some type of link which allows them to exchange resources (Paldam, 2000). The ultimate goal of the network is to facilitate cooperation and coordination by reducing uncertainty and transaction costs. The networks are mainly connected with two dimensions of social capital: the relational dimension, which refers to the relationships between the network members and groups; and the structural dimension, which identifies the general or architectural characteristics of the network.

This concept has three basic components (Paldam, 2000): (i) the members of the network, that is, the possessors of social capital; (ii) the resources embedded in the network, that is, the resources exchanged or transferred through the network; and (iii) the links or kind of interactions among members, that is, the mechanism through which members are connected and interact. In an initial approach, a family firm network first includes several types of members, fundamentally family members, but also some friends and workers who may belong to the family network if a close relationship exists; second, it includes links that are mainly parental, but may also include friendship and stable professional relationships; and third, resources including a wide variety of elements such as information, specific knowledge, values and trust.

Coleman (1988) establishes a number of important dimensions of network configuration, and Salvato and Melin (2008) adapt them to the context of family firms' social capital. These dimensions are network centrality and network closure. Network centrality refers to the extent to which the 'central' individuals have ties throughout the network and thus enjoy a broad span of influence, while network closure is the extent to which all actors in a network have relationships with one another. Another important feature of the architectural dimension of social capital is appropriable organization, which captures the extent to which networks created for one purpose may be used for another. Network centrality is a concept that can be related to the concept of founder centrality. This concept was developed within a family firm by Kelly et al. (2000) (see also Athanassiou et al., 2008). These authors suggest three dimensions of centrality: 'betweenness' (central to the flow of information), closeness (direct links with the top management group); and connectivity (the ability to influence the most connected members).

This description led to the establishment of a fundamental distinction between family networks and organizational or family firm networks. In other words, family business 'constitutes family and business systems interpenetrating one another and when one looks at a family firm, one is really looking at the interaction of two complex social systems' (Lee, 2006, p. 176); or 'family firms are unique in that, although they work as a single entity, at least two forms of social capital coexist: the family's and the firm's' (Arrègle et al., 2007, p. 73).

4.2 Family Networks and Firm Networks

In the structural dimension we distinguish, on the one hand, the family network and, on the other, the enterprise or organizational network. Family networks are formed on the basis of the existing relationships between family members. As mentioned in Section 3.1, the family is the primary source of social capital by providing aspects such as education, values, information or the transfer of knowledge.

Hoffman et al. (2006) introduce the concept of family capital as a special form of social capital which is limited to family relationships. These authors point out that this concept is limited to the structural and relational components of social capital. Thus family capital refers first to network ties in terms of information channels among family members, and, second, the obligations and expectations, reputation, identity and moral infrastructure of the family. It is interesting to note that information channels are considered social networks within the family and the family business and also are the mechanisms that connect them to the outside world. In other words, family capital includes internal and external information channels.

Lee (2006) considers two specific characteristics of family relationships in order to document the influence of family relationships on the outcomes of family business: family cohesion and family adaptability. Family cohesion refers to the degree of closeness and emotional bonding experienced by the members in the family. Family adaptability is defined as the ability of a family system to change its power structure, role relationships and relationship rules in response to situational and developmental stress.

Firm networks arise as a result of the fact that entrepreneurs engage in stable exchange relations that provide a context of cooperation. Anderson and Jack (2002) point out that social capital is more than everyday interaction in the context of entrepreneurial networks: 'agents seek to build a picture of each other and use it to locate each other in some wider scheme: social capital is a relational artefact but can be described as a quality of a relationship' (p. 201). Entrepreneurial networks are a 'complex mixture of multiplex social and professional ties, all of which tend to contain both affective and instrumental elements, bonded by trust' (Anderson et al., 2006, p. 139). In this sense, 'networks can provide both, access to resources and a predictable environment for social and economic exchange activities' (Bowley and Easton, 2007, p. 274). In fact, it can be said that the survival and success of a firm often depend on an entrepreneur's ability to establish a network of relationships.

Another interesting issue in this area is the role of family firms and the behavioural effect of interlocking directorates. Only a few studies have considered this issue, such as

Salvaj et al. (2008) and Silva et al. (2006). Salvaj et al. (2008) point out that the key concept is embeddedness, that is, the actor's relative depth of involvement in the social structure. In the same direction is the study of the influence of external networks (Parada et al., 2010), for example, the role of professional associations and changing values.

Following Granovetter (1973), Anderson et al. (2006) distinguish between two types of network ties in an entrepreneurial network: strong ties and weak ties. The first type includes 'network contacts are those people with whom the entrepreneur has a close personal relationship, and with whom he or she interacts quite frequently' (p. 140) and they are family and friends. The second type 'are more distant emotionally and may be activated only infrequently' (ibid.). These authors underline the fact that strong ties have been found to provide very high-quality resources – especially information – which are often not commercially available and are focused on the specific needs of the entrepreneur and the business. However, because family and friends tend to move in the same circles as the entrepreneur, these resources may not offer much beyond the entrepreneur's own scope; that is, they may not be adequately diverse in nature. In the debate about what kind of tie is more important for a firm, Jack (2005) concludes that 'the effectiveness of the network seems to depend upon the presence of both strong and weak ties since different forms of ties are seen to provide distinct and different resources' (p. 1238).

A particularly interesting distinction for family firms can be found in Casanueva and Galán (2004). These authors differentiate between two kinds of entrepreneurial networks: those that have formed out of the explicit intentions of the firms concerned; and those that have formed without explicit intention, due to a series of historic, geographic, social and cultural circumstances that have led to a set of preferential relations between competing firms, between suppliers and their customers and between firms and institutions. The same authors emphasize the concept of embeddedness and distinguish between two types in inter-firm relations: structural and relational. The concept is connected with the cohesion of the network, 'insofar as it refers to the strength of the direct links and the mechanisms through which firms obtain specific and valuable information. The fact that firms share more direct connections implies that they possess more information in common and more knowledge about the other parties' (Casanueva and Galán, 2004, p. 121).

4.3   Interdependence between Both Types of Networks

Following Arrègle et al. (2007), overlapping social networks is one of the mechanisms that links a family's social capital to the creation of the family firm's social capital, as the firm's network is often initially based on the family member's network. These authors, and Pearson et al. (2008), examine how factors underlying the family's social capital affect this creation, and indicate four elements that act as motivational drivers of family social capital within the family firm: (i) stability as a necessary condition for strong social relations to emerge, in a double perspective: family nucleus stability independent of the firm, and the preservation of the firm in the family; (ii) interaction, meaning that frequent and diverse interactions among family members strengthen family social capital and simultaneously contribute towards the development of the family firm's organizational social capital; (iii) interdependence because the firm is often the main asset of the family's collective patrimony, which implies not only an economic interdependence but also a psychological interdependence and emotional costs; and (iv) closure, meaning that only family members can participate in the intra-group network through kinship, although the density of linkages and interactions is family-specific.

Also analysing the interdependence among different kinds of networks and ties in the entrepreneurial context, Jack (2005) shows that strong ties act as a mechanism for generating knowledge and resources, but are also used to link into wider social contexts and provide a mechanism to invoke apparently weak ties, again connected with the concept of appropriability, whereby a family member's network generates the firm's network, and at the same time the family firm's network can influence the family's network.

The characteristics of the interaction between a family's and a firm's social capital depend on both the characteristics of the family and the firm, and in this case an interaction of this kind can vary considerably from one family firm to another. For example, 'family members involved in the firm generate the firm's initial network structure that in turn influences the development of family firms organizational social capital' (Arrègle et al., 2007, p. 81). However, the intensity and directionality of this influence will be modified along time as both networks, the family's and the firm's, tend to acquire different branches and their links become increasingly complex. In this sense, it can be illustrative to think about families that have different family branches and where several generations have been involved in the business, and then, the relational and cognitive frameworks have a very high diversity, family ties have a lower intensity and personal networks are then differentiated and sparse (Arrègle et al., 2004).

The evolution of the family and particularly the arrival of new generations will lead to changes in the way in which both types of social capital establish their interaction and feedback. In this sense, it should be noted that the fact that the family grows and changes its composition does not imply that at the same time the members of the family who are involved in the firm change too. Obviously, these changes will happen sooner or later, but they can involve conflicts among the members of the family and firm networks. As we will mention again in the section on the intergenerational transfer of social capital, the design of the succession process is crucial in determining and altering the existing interdependence between both types of social capital and the stock of available family firm social capital, especially when we think about the process as a transfer of the components of the founder's network. This process could damage the density and strength of the links of the network, for example in cases of conflict among family branches, when the successor is not integrated in that network, or he (she) does not have a easy access to the type of relations and links of the existing network, or when the successor tries to create a new, different network to replace the existing one (Arrègle et al., 2004).

In a similar way, this reasoning applies to the evolution and increase of complexity of the business over time. For instance, if the firm has a certain dimension and its activity is diversified, the firm network will be complex and involve a large number of agents (some of whom are external to the family). In this sense, as the business becomes established, depending on its success, the directionality of this flow could reverse as the networks developed through the business begin to serve to the goals of family members, regardless of their involvement in the business (Sharma, 2008). Moreover, not only networks among family members are important for a firm's social capital, but also networks outside the boundaries of the firm with external agents (brought to the firm by family members), which can play an important role in determining the family firm's performance, resources, culture and so on (Anderson et al., 2005; Jack, 2005).

5　TRUST AND SOCIAL CAPITAL IN FAMILY FIRMS

5.1　The Relational Dimension of Social Capital

Despite the high number of studies which have explored the term 'trust', the concept is far from being clearly defined (Kramer, 1999). The most influential definitions consider a general attitude or expectation of the behaviour of the individuals or the social system in which these are inserted (Luhmann, 1988; Hardin, 2001). In other words, trust in the other is based on a belief in their correct intentions, whereby their commitment is to fulfil their obligations, not to adopt opportunistic behaviours and cause damage voluntarily.

From a more psychological point of view, trust is an intention to accept vulnerability on the basis of positive expectations of the intentions of the other (Rousseau et al., 1998). Therefore this concept is directly linked to feelings of security. An atmosphere can be described as secure if everything functions in the way the different actors expect, so that the individuals do not find any problem in carrying out what they do in a routine way. Distrust, on the contrary, is connected with a lack of transparency and the accompanying sense of uncertainty (Schul et al., 2008).

Trust is essential for companies and the economy in general due to its capacity to facilitate the formation of large-scale organizations with agency relations. The expansion of the activity of an organization or the economy in general supposes an increase of the interdependence between economic agents and an increase in the division of labour. Consequently, it also involves an exponential expansion of the number of agency relations. In these, a principal must trust an agent for the development of an activity within a context of strong information asymmetry. Therefore one of the alternatives for evaluating the efficiency of the economic system implies finding an effective way of solving these types of problems (La Porta et al., 1997).

If we apply these basic definitions of trust to the operations of firms, trust is a reduction of the uncertainty that characterizes the relations of interdependence between individuals (agency relations). This bond is defined by the existence of mutuality that can be expressed by the interdependence of individual utility functions between subjects (sympathy). This relation generates cooperative behaviours, even if the actions carried out are of a concealed nature. Therefore, in this situation the firm would not need to monitor behaviours nor the alignment of preferences proposed by agency theory, as the sympathetic links are able to provide it socially (Pena and Sánchez, 2006).

Given these characteristics, trust is a 'merit good' that is especially present in the family unit (Becker, 1991), and as a result, family enterprises have a comparative advantage. However, we can find diverse forms of trust that must be analysed and, at the same time, a conflictive process in their evolution that implies a necessary investment of resources for sustaining this advantage as the company expands.

5.2　Bases and Effects of Trust

According to Lewicki and Bunker (1996), trust can be built on three bases: calculation, knowledge and identification. Whereas the first is based on a fear of the consequences of the rupture, knowledge-based trust is based on the capacity to predict the behaviour of others, and therefore on the information that is available. Both kinds of trust are 'non-tuistic' or 'egoistic' and fragile sources, since the motivation is associated with the pres-ervation of one's own interests or the avoidance of some type of punishment, which would not be compensated by the force exerted by an opportunistic behaviour (Arrègle et al., 2007).

These first two types of trust make it necessary to deal with the monitoring costs of the tasks carried out by agents, or 'to align' the incentives of the principal and the agents through compensation contracts. This is the proposal of agency theory. However, this theory is a partial solution, in so far as it concentrates on the hierarchical relations between stockholders and managers, doing without the bonds between intermediate members of an organization. For these members, the strategies of this theory are expen-sive and ineffective, since for an intermediate level of organization the connection between effort and evolution of the stock value is very fuzzy. Also, these strategies can be aggressive, expensive and, in many cases, impossible (Chami and Fullenkamp, 2002; Chami et al., 2002).[1]

Nevertheless, the third base of trust or identification arises when both parts understand the intentions and preferences of the other, or in other words when an alignment of pref-erences occurs that is motivated by the existence of commonly shared values. This third or 'tuistic' expression constitutes trust in the strictest sense and has a more permanent character (Dess and Shaw, 2001; Pena and Sánchez, 2005). In these three sources of trust, rational and emotional components are combined. Nevertheless, the rational compo-nents seem to predominate in the non-tuistic expression; the emotional and moral com-ponents are essential in the third, and are especially characteristic of family bonds (Rousseau et al., 1998; Nooteboum, 2000) (see Table 10.1).

As already mentioned, the tuistic forms are built on values, norms or standards of conduct and, at the same time, on individual interactions and the constitution of com-munities rooted in cultural affinities or social bonds. However, the ethical character of this kind of trust does not mean that it is 'blind', as sympathetic relations also have a dialectic character or demand some form of reciprocity (Williams, 1988). In the same sense, this trust cannot be standardized or established contractually, and so the establish-ment of a contractual relation could even become a self-fulfilling prophecy of its destruction.

Apart from the two previous solutions, theory has traditionally relegated the capacity of ethical codes to avoid or overcome these agency problems. Ethics is a simpler and superior way of resolving economic conflicts, in so far as it supposes a reduction of

Table 10.1   Sources of trust

	Sources	Instruments
Non-tuistic	Coercion by authority	Third-party certifications, external evaluation
	Search for advantages or material interest	Systems of incentives
Tuistic	Ethics, values and norms of behaviour	Familiarity, community common culture, friendships, commitment
	Identification and sympathy bonds	

Source: Authors' own elaboration.

transaction costs, favours group cohesion and constitutes a system of pre-coordination of individual decisions which precede the market (Chami and Fullenkamp, 2002). As Habermas indicates, 'morals allow the members of a group to expect certain actions from others in given situations, and force them to fulfil the expectations of behaviour justified by the other' (Habermas, 1986, p. 51). Focusing on this concept, we refer to the dispositions and capacities that lead us to mutual understanding and agreement as basic mechanisms for the satisfaction of interests and the consensual resolution of conflicts. These shared ethical codes, as previously mentioned, are the expression of the tuistic form of trust and, to a certain extent, could more properly be denominated as a type of moral capital.

The reciprocal tuistic trust, typical of family enterprises, established in sympathy or interdependence of utility functions, can be ambivalent (Hardin, 1999). On the one hand, it makes it possible to overcome problems of cooperation caused by situations similar to the 'prisoner's dilemma', and therefore facilitates a system of social pre-coordination (Warren, 1999). However, on the other hand, it could create networks based on sympathy relations and common objectives that facilitate the breaking of norms and form stable structures of corruption. This variant can be referred to as 'particularistic trust' and creates bonds between the agents that are analogous to the generalized bond between any social agents, but with the opposite effects. We could even speak, in terms of the theory of the *raccomandazione*, of overlapping forms of corruption in the political and economic culture of the society, or 'amoral familism' (Uslaner, 2005; Lambsdorff, 2002). The difference between these expressions of reciprocal trust is rooted in the universalistic ethical principles of the first, contrasted with the particularistic ethical principles of the second.

In short, trust is a way of reducing uncertainty by generating information to tackle the problem of opportunistic behaviours, namely an informal mechanism of management and alternative government to the systems based on rewards or some form of authority (Bradach and Eccles, 1989). In the case of family-run companies, its characteristic trust corresponds to reciprocal tuistic forms, and its foundations are based on identification and sympathy relations, although it may also have an ambivalent character.

5.3   Trust, Family Systems and Firms

The basic singularity of a family company is the influence of family relations on the economic activity, specifically in the way the organization is managed, structured and transferred. In fact, family relations could generate a motivation, bonds of fidelity to the company, and increase trust, thereby reducing transaction costs (Tagiuri and Davis, 1996). In consequence, firms with a family dimension have incentives to use the trust implicit in its network's relations as a governance mechanism (Eddleston et al., 2010). Family enterprises may even be particularly capable of capitalizing on trust (Cruz et al., 2010). Consumers and employers perceive family businesses as having more trustworthy policies and practices than non-family businesses because of the long-term relationships between family and firm, and the links with reputational capital (Orth and Green, 2009).

The type of trust that is predominant in family business has a tuistic character with relevant emotional bases (Anderson and Thompson, 2004). Positive emotions linked

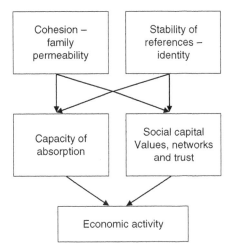

Source: Authors' own elaboration.

Figure 10.1   Family system and family enterprise

with the family founder evoke a pro-social and cooperative orientation towards others, which can affect whether individuals are seen as trustworthy and cooperative. Even when it comes to decision-making, emotions can supersede rational considerations and cognitive processes. In contrast, negative emotions may damage trust and lead to an organizational culture based on agency principles. This initial expression of trust develops over time. In a non-family firm, the trust between individuals begins with calculative trust and moves to knowledge-based trust or agency management of distrust. In family firms, the evolution of trust among family members begins with interpersonal trust based in shared values and a common history, which explains other-oriented behaviours and even altruism to ensure the firm's prosperity (Steier, 2001). The perceptions of the leader's stewardship in this case are marked by the absence of opportunism. This can motivate organizational citizenship and value-creation behaviours (Mayer and Gavin, 2005). Nevertheless, as we will see, trust tends to diminish over time, due to a lack of common values between new members, and for this reason it is necessary to cultivate competence and calculative trust based on fairness in firm governance (Eddleston et al., 2010).

A family system is characterized by cohesion, flexibility and communication (Olson and Gorrall, 2003) (Figure 10.1). Cohesion implies a certain form of closure that guarantees a strong connection between the members. Flexibility alludes to the capacity of members to interchange social and entrepreneurial roles, whereas communication expresses the existing bonds of respect and obedience that guarantee the absence of shirking and reserved utility.

Consequently, trust is an essential dimension of family firms, since its differential character lies in the presence of bonds between the members of the company, whether they are relatives or not, that go beyond economic interests. These networks of relations, obligations and expectations are translated into the generation of collective trust, that is, a convergence of expectations or a shared common code.

This common code can also be present in non-family companies, but is reinforced in this case by the reference to a model of administration of a common ancestor or background and a certain familiar identity (Corvetta and Salvato, 2004). This construction of an identity and a shared code ('we-rationality') in a more favourable context makes it possible to endow the company with a sustainable advantage that results in a greater success in the long term (Zellweger et al., 2010).

Common identity and shared values, sympathy relations and trust permit cooperation, promoting networks of relations and reducing conflicts. However, in the case of family-run companies, we find an additional benefit: absorption. This signifies an organizational routine through which the companies introduce, assimilate and adapt knowledge. This is a team-form of learning that the company can use for its objectives, and is based on the internal and external interactions of the agents. The strong bonds that are typical of a family company organization permit an almost altruistic transmission of information that provides them with a sustainable advantage in terms of creative capacity and adaptation to new contexts. Put simply, agents choose to do without their utility of reserve (Sirmon and Hitt, 2003). However, this use of the term 'identity' is excessively simplistic. It is necessary to consider the distinguishing features of the generated trust and to analyse its evolution in the organization in its process of growth and adaptation.

6   EVOLUTION AND TRANSMISSION OF SOCIAL CAPITAL IN FAMILY FIRMS

The previous deconstructive analysis of social capital does not clarify the nature and scope of the interrelation of its three dimensions. It is therefore necessary to explore the causal link between these dimensions, because in order to explain the creation and evolution of social capital, we need to explore the models of causality in detail, making every effort to avoid 'black box' explanations (Nahapiet and Ghoshal, 1998; Pearson et al., 2008).

6.1   General Interpretative Models

General models of social capital in family firms differ particularly in the proposed causality between the first two dimensions and the relational dimension. For example, Tsai and Ghoshal (1998) propose that the structural dimensions are an antecedent of the cognitive dimensions; consequently, personal interactions lead to the generation of values. In the same sense, the cognitive dimension constitutes the antecedent of the relational dimension. A cognitive shared vision, therefore, finally leads to the generation of interpersonal trust, diminishing opportunistic behaviour. In this way, the structural and cognitive dimensions are antecedent to the relational dimensions, and priority would be given to the structural features of the firm (Pearson et al., 2008) (Figure 10.2).

However, this proposal is open to criticism. From Uphoff's perspective (2000), only two major dimensions can be distinguished in social capital: structural and cognitive. Both dimensions reduce the transaction costs and facilitate cooperative behaviour. These dominions are intrinsically linked, since although the structures and the norms and values can be analysed independently, both are cognitive and the only difference lies in the

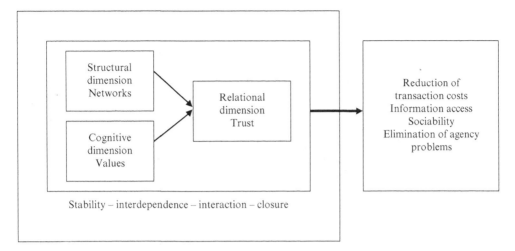

Source: Pearson et al. (2008).

Figure 10.2   Causal links between social capital dimensions

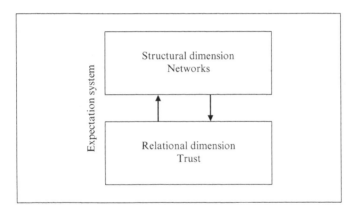

Source: Authors' own elaboration, based on Uphoff (2000).

Figure 10.3   Uphoff's proposal on social capital causal links

observability of the first. At the same time, these two dimensions are actually bound in social sciences to another subjective phenomenon: expectations (Figure 10.3). The roles and behaviours are caused by expectations and a system of values or norms that supports the structure justifying these expectations about how an individual should act within a network. Those expectations can be interpreted directly in terms of trust, which is also essentially of a cognitive nature.

Consequently, Uphoff's perspective questions the causality proposed by the previous general model. His proposal is a cognitivist interpretation of social capital, focused on the concept of expectations, where the differentiation of dimensions is exclusively in their objective character. Considering this reframing, and from our point of view, the most

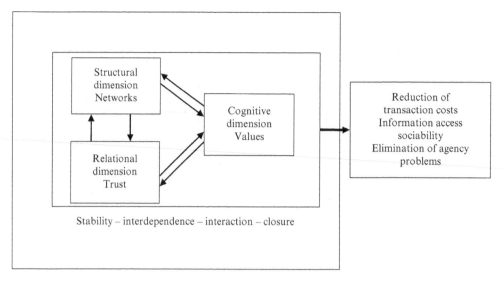

Source: Authors' own elaboration.

Figure 10.4   Circular causal links of social capital

reasonable vision of the interrelation is circularity (Figure 10.4). In this case, it is not possible to include the structures without the relational bonds of trust, and the latter without the existence of underlying value systems.

In economic terms, social capital and its expression in the family firm is also a form of cognitive economy that is mainly materialized in what we could call a 'trust economy'. As Uzzi (1997) proposes, the heuristic process of decision-making is saved through mental resources, so that it is facilitated through the existence of trust and relational overlaps, reducing the transaction and information costs, and saving the necessary resources to supplement private norms (coercion, monitoring, formation of rules etc.).

On the whole, entrepreneurial social capital is essentially a cognitive system that can be interpreted in terms of expectations and trust in the behaviour of the members of the company. This can be considered as the most important aspect of social capital. Consequently, the system can be analysed on the basis of any of its three dimensions: the formal and informal structures, the underlying values; and interpersonal trust. Obviously, the existing values and networks influence the trust levels, yet the structures cannot be included without understanding the levels and characteristics of the existing trust and the values shared by its members.

6.2   Evolution of Social Capital in Family Firms

The peculiarities of social capital within family-run firms discussed in the previous sections provide a better understanding of the parallel evolution of this form of capital and the growth and development of these companies. This parallel process is clearly reflected in the evolution of the three dimensions involved (values, networks and trust), which in turn influence the sustainability of the potential comparative advantage of these types of firms.

From a process perspective, Arrègle et al. (2007) investigate mechanisms that link a family's social capital to the creation of the family firm's social capital. Social capital developed within the context of the family can be transferred to the firm by means of four mechanisms: (i) institutional isomorphism, meaning that when a background institution is actively involved in the management of a firm, as is the case of family firms, and it is dependent on critical resources, the firm will tend to be similar to the family in structure, behavioural focus, climate and, as a consequence organizational social capital; (ii) organizational identity and rationality, because family members transmit its main characteristics to the firm; (iii) human resources practices, which in general will be determined by the values and norms of family social capital; and (iv) overlapping social networks, because family members involved in the firm generate the firm's initial network structure that in turn influences the development of the family firm's organizational social capital.

The interdependence of both kinds of social networks can also imply dysfunctional and negative consequences. Arrègle et al. (2007) point out three potential problems that can emerge from a strong family social capital for family firms: (i) overdeveloping organizational social capital as a consequence of ignoring new sources of information, causing dysfunctional power arrangements within the firm, hindering innovation as people are embedded in established practices and so on; (ii) the transfer of dysfunctional family realities to the family firm's organizational social capital, such as problems of communication or personal conflicts; and (iii) a strong family can inappropriately capture for the family the goodwill intended for the firm by external actors. As Durlauf and Fafchamps (2004) state, it is interesting to note that dense and stable networks can also have negative implications in certain contexts. These authors analyse the required conditions in order for the information sharing, group identity and explicit coordination derived from the existence of social capital to generate efficiency gains in organizations and in the economy as a whole.

The accumulation and dissipation of social capital can be seen as a dynamic process, and also as a regenerative cycle, whereby the family-run company is in a constant process of recreating the foundations over which trust, values and networks are based. According to one of Luhmann's assumptions (1979), trust and social capital, by extension, require distrust for their development. The evolutionary character of social capital can differ depending both on the company and on whether internal or external relations are considered. However, despite the differences seen in family firms, at least three different stages can generally be distinguished in the above-mentioned process. The characteristics of the different levels can be described as follows.

The first stage corresponds to the starting point of family-run companies. In this stage, these firms are endowed with high levels of social capital, essentially based on relations of an interpersonal nature (Corvetta and Salvato, 2004). In terms of trust, this phase is based on affinity or communality, a common history or a long period of common experiences between members of the company (Steward, 2003). In a general way, communality fortifies the cognitive and emotional foundations of the interpersonal trust in the predictability of the actions of the other, and in the emotional bonds that they facilitate. Individuals put themselves in the place of the other (sympathy networks) and are identified with a set of norms. As a result, this kind of trust is based on identification and interpersonal networks (Sundaramurthy, 2008). This first stage is characterized in evaluative terms by the high consistency of core values and general aims, which are also translated in a high organizational cohesion. Therefore a certain predominance of the relational family network against the firm or organizational network seems to emerge in this stage.

Family-run companies therefore begin with a high level of interpersonal trust since the family is a common factor of identification in values and in objectives, and provides a basic network of trust. Consequently, the company can count on the contribution and commitment of a substantial number of its members and even certain forms of altruism with regard to the overall well-being of the family and, by extension, of the company (Gersick et al., 1997). However, situations of this kind can give rise to forms of blind trust and 'we-rationality' that would be dysfunctional in so far as they destroy the necessary quest for profit. Supported by the initial success that the community of interests generates, the family could constantly seek consensus, which erodes the quality of the decision-making process and the ability to compete in the market. In this case we can find a paradox, whereby trust, networks and values must make it possible to reduce the transaction costs caused by the potential conflicts, but they do not have to eliminate the functional conflicts that constrain the capacity of the company in its adaptation to changes.

Moreover, stagnation in this first phase may be a serious obstacle to the growth of the company, as long as it hinders the integration of new individuals into the organization. At the same time, changes in market conditions, competitors and stakeholders call for constant changes in its activity. As the company grows, the family extends its involvement in the company to a more extensive nucleus. The lack of knowledge among the members of the structure supposes a change in the management style, and the necessity of developing a new way of trust evolving the dominant values and the firm's networks.

The second stage – competential social capital – is associated with a trust in the capacity or competence of the organization's members. Then, it is the belief that the parts involved in the development of a task are not only capable, but their will is to develop the work in an effective and efficient way (Mishra, 1996). This kind of trust starts to expand at the moment at which the family firm is opened to external influence, enabling the company to establish bonds with the exterior. This change is critical for guaranteeing the survival of the company (Ward, 2004). New agents can clarify the role of the family in order to determine which are its identitary characteristics and what the strategy of the family is. At the same time, they act as a catalyst for trust, building bridges with subordinates and within the family, and even bringing a new degree of transparency to the activities carried out by the management. This trust can also be obtained as a result of young people acquiring professional experience outside of the company. Consistently, external success and the experience gained by the employees before adhering to the company can be decisive for the growth of the family firm. In the same way, the creation of a framework of communication and collaboration in the access to information, learning and the generation of resources helps in adapting to new contexts.

In terms of networks, a potentially conflicting overlapping of systems occurs in all family companies (Tagiuri and Davis, 1996). On the one hand, some separated nuclei of the family that might prefer other managerial trajectories exist, and on the other hand, the bonds of the company with stakeholders and, in particular, the system of the employees who are not bound to the family, also exists. In this sense, clarifying the expectations of the different systems with regard to their role in the evolution of the company can be decisive, namely through clear policies in terms of admission, succession, compensation and promotion.

Finally, systemic social capital usually appears as a third stage. This evolution of familiness expresses the collective features of an administrative organization and its management, which are not reducible to individual actors and which ensure continuity when these disappear. This means that it is institutional in nature, and is linked to the trust that the individuals invest in systems and proceedings, and is practically extended to the company's stakeholders. At this point a bond may appear with the formal traditions and rules that have identified the company, as these constitute a fundamental reference at the time of establishing institutional trust (Sydow, 1998). The logical consequence is that the transparency of rules and established traditions and the supply of information to the agents, directly affected by the management of the company, is a *conditio sine qua non* for this change, as this is the base of the trust in the system.

Reaching this phase without the dissolution of the stock of family social capital depends directly on the fairness of procedures. In this sense, Heyden et al. (2005) refers to five precise and essential features in this evolution: to give voice to all the stakeholders involved, clarity of information, procedures and expectations, consistency of the decisions with the past, possibility of changes in the policies based on clear mechanisms and the existence of a 'commitment to fairness'.

Therefore family companies can enjoy competitive advantages based on trust as long as the initial interpersonal trust can be complemented by structures and procedures that maintain the systemic and competential trust, and both require the policies that are applied to be transparent and consistent (see Figure 10.5 below).

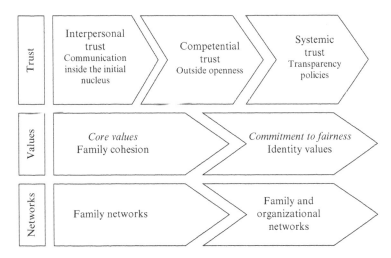

Source: Authors' own elaboration.

Figure 10.5 Evolution of social capital in the family company

6.3   Intergenerational Transfer of Social Capital

In general, firms accumulate social capital over time, and a necessary condition for accumulation is intergenerational transmission. Salvato and Melin (2008) discuss the relevant role played by family-related social capital components in shaping a family firm's transgenerational value-creation profile. Although social capital enhances value creation in any type of firm, in a family business the specificity comes from the fact that these advantages are absorbed in the social links of family members and in the configuration of the family network, and therefore can be more easily sustained over successive generations.

Prior to the succession process, the family's social capital can play a role in determining the attitude of the next generation towards the family firm. Lee (2006) highlights the fact that family relationships (more precisely the dimensions of family cohesion and family adaptability explained in the section dedicated to networks) do have a substantial influence on the attitudes and behaviours of the second generation working in family businesses. More specifically, he shows that family adaptability is a valuable asset in family businesses, as it significantly affects the work satisfaction and organizational commitment of the second generation. On the other hand, the author states that family cohesion has a limited or insignificant effect on the commitment and satisfaction levels of the second generation.

An example of this can be found in García-Álvarez et al. (2002), who studied a group of Spanish family firms. These authors observe that the founder's view of the business influences the mode and process of socialization used for the next generation of family members. Those who view their business as a means of supporting the family value the feeling of family, limit the growth of their firms and incorporate the successors at a lower position and with low levels of formal education. On the other hand, founders who view the family firm as an end in itself encourage successors to achieve high levels of formal education and experience outside the business before joining the firm.

Steier (2001) points out that in the case of firms that are already established, a central task is to pass on the key resources residing within this network to the next generation. Within the context of family firms and succession, social capital represents one of the least tangible and least fungible assets, and it is not easily traded or transferred. This can be due to several reasons. In some cases, personal and professional circumstances impede an accurate transmission and, in other cases, the agents who are involved do not implement the appropriate mechanisms to transfer it. In this sense, Cabrera et al. (2001) suggest that the performance of the next generation is likely to be based on the effectiveness with which these cognitive structures, common schemes, family and professional contacts are transferred across generations. Here it is important to note that, in general, family businesses are characterized by less formal ways of operating and generally less formalized policies and rules than non-family firms, taking into account the fact that knowledge of network structures is frequently tacit and not easily communicated. As Sharma (2004, p. 13) states, 'due to their long tenures, family firm leaders posses a significant amount of idiosyncratic or tacit knowledge related to the firm'.

Steier's work systematizes the ways in which this transfer can be made, depending on the type of succession: unplanned, sudden succession when unanticipated events call for another family member to take over a management role at short notice; rushed succession, when circumstances force the family to make previously unanticipated management changes; natural immersion, when the successor gradually assimilates the nuances of network structure and relationships; and planned succession and the deliberate transfer of social capital.

Also, the same study refers to seven ways of managing social capital: deciphering or interpreting existing network structures; deciphering the transactional content of network relationships; determining criticalities by determining which relationships are the most critical for the survival and success of the firm, and taking steps to ensure their continuation; attaining legitimacy in the new tasks and roles within the network; clarifying the optimal role of the successor in the family's and firm's networks; managing ties through delegation and division of labour; and striving for optimal network configuration and reconstituting network structure and content.

In this sense, Arrègle et al. (2004) emphasize the importance of the design of the succession process as a condition for the maintenance of a firm's social capital and the interaction between the family's and the firm's social capital. On the one hand, a succession process involving a fight for power among family branches will imply damaging or losing the links and components of the family's social configuration. On the other hand, an inadequate integration of the successor into the networks that compose the family's and the firm's systems could imply a loss in the stock of the firm's social capital. Moreover, an insufficient integration of the successor in the networks that compose the system of family and firm, or an attempt to substitute the type of relationships or the configuration itself of the founder's network, could imply a loss of the family firm's social capital. In short, although the family is a source of stability, its evolution and particularly the incorporation of new generations is a source of perturbation and alteration of the interdependence between the social capital of the family and the social capital of the firm.

Another important point in this respect is that owners derive value from passing on the legacy of the enterprising family tradition, emotional bonds between family members and nostalgia (Sharma and Manikutty, 2005). Cultural beliefs may also underlie the decision to build a family legacy, and instil the desire to ensure survival and family control at all cost. This objective may not always be in line with the most suitable long-term strategy, especially if it leads families to display an excessive aversion to risk or to forgo profitable expansion strategies or mergers with other firms (Bertrand and Schoar, 2006). Therefore suboptimal economic organization can emerge when parents put too much emphasis on keeping the business in the family, either as a result of a strong sense of duty towards other family members, or a more selfish desire to turn the business into a family legacy.

Finally, one interesting area where family firm networks can be crucial for the company's future prospects is mentoring, that is, the creation of a figure who is responsible for designing and monitoring the training process of the candidates for succession. Depending on the characteristics of the family and the firm, the mentor should be a person who has a relevant position in both networks, the firm's and the family's, as their success will largely depend on the existing credibility and trust in their actions. The capacity to improve the experience and suitability of the candidates could depend on the existence of links and relationships with other firms and institutions.

7   CONCLUDING REMARKS

This chapter reviews the components and evolution of social capital in family firms in order to establish the mechanisms that connect family and business systems. This concept constitutes an analytical instrument that integrates and sheds light on some of the singular aspects of family firms that are commonplace in the literature (values, commitment, entrepreneurial networks, trust etc.) and that can be considered as benchmarks for familiness.

Based on a deconstructive perspective, we identify and analyse three dimensions of social capital: cognitive, structural and relational or values, networks and trust. The cognitive dimension of social capital (norms and values) refers to the valorative consensus, and constitutes an agreement on what is a priority in business behaviour. This is the substrate of the organization's culture or the core values, where the founder has a determining role. In the structural dimension we distinguish, on the one hand, the family network and, on the other, the enterprise or organizational network. The former is characterized by a predominance of the strong bonds that are used to provide resources that combine high quality with low generation cost, such as information and knowledge, which are non-tradable resources linked to specific needs of the firm. Finally, trust or the relational dimension implies a reduction of the uncertainty that characterizes the agency relations between individuals. This is defined by the mutuality or interdependence of utility functions between agents, meaning that it is not necessary to monitor behaviour or the alignment of preferences.

In general, entrepreneurial social capital is essentially a cognitive system that can be interpreted in terms of networks of trust. In terms of the way in which these dimensions interact, we consider the existence of a circular causality, where values, networks and trust are expressions of a system of expectations.

Familiness, understood as family social capital, experiences a temporary evolution parallel to the vital cycle of the family–company relations. The departure point is interpersonal confidence, linked to the cohesion generated by the protagonism of the family in first stage. Later, forms of competential and systemic trust prevail, in which the nucleus is the fidelity to identity values, the establishment of norms and the balance between the familiar and enterprise networks. In these stages, the generational changes constitute a cause of modification of the interdependence between the social capital of the family and the firm, since it will affect to what extent the common values are adopted, the strength of the bonds and the level of trust between the agents.

Regarding the role of social capital in family firms, the construction of an identity and a shared code ('we-rationality') in a more favourable context of trust makes it possible to endow the company with a sustainable competitive advantage that could result in greater success in the long term. This competitive advantage can be interpreted in terms of a reduction of transaction costs, reflected in the transmission of knowledge and information and the decision-making process. Although social capital enhances value creation in any type of firm, in a family business the specificity comes from the fact that these advantages are absorbed in the social links of family networks, and reinforced by reference to a model of administration of a common ancestor or certain familiar identity. This means that it can be sustained over successive generations, making use of systemic synergies associated with the interactions between individual family members, the family unit and the business, which can become a competitive advantage.

Nevertheless, there is an ambiguous functionality in family social capital. Values closed to external influence, redundant networks and particularistic trust can unite the group but, at the same time, can isolate the family firm. Competitive advantages or disadvantages could be derived from a balanced or imbalanced flow between family social capital and organizational social capital. In other words, the characteristics of the interaction between the family and the firm, in terms of the respective values, networks and trust of each system, encourage the generation of both positive and negative social capital. In summary, the sustainability of the competitive advantage of the family firm is significantly linked to a suitable management of the dimensions in conflict of the social capital. As Sharma (2008) points out, both families and firms have stocks of social capital, and the flow of social capital from one to the other is bidirectional. The distinctiveness of the stocks of social capital in both a family and a business depend on a balanced flow between them over time.

Further research in this area could take into account the breakdown of the social capital concept, in order to first identify the specific channels that make it possible for each of these components to be provided separately in family firms in comparison to non-family firms, and second, to explore in detail the causality that exists between these components in the context of family firms. In this sense, succession decisions are an especially interesting scenario for dealing with these issues, because this is when cognitive, structural and relational components experience some type of alteration that could influence the success of the process.

ACKNOWLEDGEMENTS

The authors would like to thank the Galician Association of Family Business (AGEF), Caixanova, Inditex and the Spanish Family Enterprise Institute (IEF) for their financial support. Sánchez-Santos and Pena-López acknowledge financial support from Xunta de Galicia (Proyect 10SEC100041PR). Novo-Peteiro also acknowledges financial support from Xunta of Galicia (Proyect 10PXIB137153PR). The authors are grateful to the editors and an anonymous reviewer for their helpful comments that extended the scope of the analysis and improved the exposition of the chapter. All remaining errors are our own.

NOTE

1. Whatever the case, the solution provided by agency theory is undoubtedly preferable to establishing a coercive external mechanism.

REFERENCES

Adler, P.S. and Kwon, S. (2002), 'Social capital: prospects for a new concept', *Academy of Management Review*, **27**(1), 17–40.
Anderson, A.R. and Jack, S.L. (2002), 'The articulation of social capital in entrepreneurial networks: a glue or a lubricant?', *Entrepreneurship & Regional Development*, **14**(3), 193–210.

Anderson, A.R., Jack, S.L. and Drakopoulou, S. (2006), 'The role of family members in entrepreneurial networks: beyond the boundaries of the family firm', *Family Business Review*, **18**(2), 135–54.

Anderson, C. and Thompson, L. (2004), 'Affect from the top down: how powerful individuals' positive affect shapes negotiations', *Organizational Behavior and Human Decision Processes*, **95**, 125–39.

Anderson, R.C. and Reeb, D.M. (2003), 'Founding-family ownership and firm performance: evidence from the S&P 500', *Journal of Finance*, **58**(3), 1301–29.

Aronoff, C. and Ward, J.L. (1995), 'Family-owned business: a thing of the past or a model of the future?', *Family Business Review*, **8**(2), 121–30.

Arrègle, J.C., Durand, R. and Very, P. (2004), 'Origines du capital social et avantages concurrentiels des firmes familiales', *M@n@gement*, **7**(1), 13–36.

Arrègle, J.C., Hitt, M.A., Sirmon, D.G. and Very, P. (2007), 'The development of organizational social capital: attributes of family firms', *Journal of Management Studies*, **44**(1), 73–95.

Astrachan, J., Klein, S. and Smyrnios, K. (2002), 'The F-Pec scale of family influence: a proposal for solving the family business definition problem', *Family Business Review*, **15**(1), 45–58.

Athanassiou, N., Crittenden, W.F., Kelly, L.M. and Márquez, P. (2008), 'Founder centrality effects on the Mexican family firm's top management group', *Journal of World Business*, **37**(2), 139–50.

Banfield, E. (1958), *The Moral Basis of a Backward Society*, New York: Free Press.

Becker, G. (1991), *A Treatise on the Family*, Cambridge, MA: Harvard University Press.

Bertrand, M. and Schoar, A. (2006), 'The role of family in family firms', *Journal of Economic Perspectives*, **20**(2), 73–96.

Bourdieu, P. (1994), *Raisons Pratiques. Sur la théorie de l'action*, Paris: Seuil.

Bowley, J.L. and Easton, G. (2007), 'Entrepreneurial social capital unplugged. an activity-based analysis', *International Small Business Journal*, **25**(3), 273–306.

Bradach, J.L. and Eccles, R.G. (1989), 'Price, authority and trust: from ideal types to plural forms', *Annual Review of Sociology*, **15**, 97–118.

Bubolz, M. (2001), 'Family as source, user, and builder of social capital', *Journal of Socio-Economics*, **30**(2), 129–31.

Cabrera-Suárez, K., De Saá-Pérez, P. and García-Almeida, D. (2001), 'The succession process from a resource- and knowledge-based view of the family firm', *Family Business Review*, **14**(1), 37–48.

Casanueva, C. and Galán, J.L. (2004), 'Social and information relations in networks of small and medium-sized firms', *M@n@gement*, **7**(3), 215–38.

Chami, R. and Fullemkamp, C. (2002), 'Trust and efficiency', *Journal of Banking and Finance*, **26**(9), 1791–820.

Chami, R., Cosimano, T.F. and Fullemkamp, C. (2002), 'Managing ethical risk: how investing in ethics adds value', *Journal of Banking and Finance*, **26**(9), 1697–718.

Chrisman, J.J., Chua, J.H. and Zahra, S. (2003), 'Creating wealth in family firms through managing resources: comments and extension', *Entrepreneurship Theory and Practice*, **27**(4), 359–65.

Chrisman, J., Chua, J. and Steier, L. (2005), 'Sources and consequences of distinctive familiness: an introduction', *Entrepreneurship Theory and Practice*, **29**(3), 237–47.

Chua, J.H., Chrisman, J.J. and Sharma, P. (1999), 'Defining family business by behaviour', *Entrepreneurship Theory and Practice*, **23**(4), 19–39.

Coleman, J. (1990), *Foundations of Social Theory*, Cambridge, MA: Harvard University Press.

Coleman, J.S. (1988), 'Social capital in the creation of human capital', *American Journal of Sociology*, **94**, S95–S120.

Corbetta, G. and Salvato, C. (2004), 'Self-serving or self-actualizing? Models of man and agency cost in different types of family firms', *Entrepreneurship Theory and Practice*, **28**, 355–62.

Cruz, C.C., Gómez-Mejía, L.R. and Becerra, M. (2010), 'Perceptions of benevolence and the design of agency contracts: CEO–TMT relationships in family firms', *Academy of Management Journal*, **53**, 69–89.

Davis, J. (2008), 'Toward a typology of family business systems', in J. Tàpies and J. Ward (eds), *Family Values and Value Creation: The Fostering of Enduring Values within Family-owned Business*, New York: Palgrave Macmillan, pp. 127–54.

Davis, J.H., Schoorman, R. and Donattson, L. (1997), 'Toward a stewardship theory of management', *Academy of Management Review*, **22**(1), 20–47.

Davis, J. and Tagiuri, R. (1989), 'The advantages and disadvantages of the family business', Santa Barbara, CA: The Owner Managed Institute.

Davis, P.S. and Harveston, P.D. (2001), 'The phenomenon of substantive conflict in the family firm: a cross-generational study', *Journal of Small Business Management*, **39**(1), 14–30.

Denison, D., Lief, C. and Ward J.L. (2004), 'Culture in family-owned enterprises: recognizing and leveraging unique strengths', *Family Business Review*, **17**(1), 61–70.

Dess, G.D. and Shaw, J.D. (2001), 'Voluntary turnover, social capital, and organizational performance', *Academy of Management Review*, **26**(3), 446–56.

Distelberg, B. and Sorenson, R.L. (2009), 'Updating systems concepts in family businesses: a focus on values, resource flows, and adaptability', *Family Business Review*, **22**(1), 65–81.

Duh, M., Belak, J. and Milfelner, B (2010), 'Core values, culture and ethical climate as constitutional elements of ethical behaviour: exploring differences between family and non-family enterprises', *Journal of Business Ethics*, **97**(3), 473–89.

Durlauf, A.N. and Fafchamps, N. (2004), 'Social capital', NBER Working Paper 10485.

Dyer, W. (1986), *Cultural Change in Family Firms: Anticipating and Managing Business and Familty Traditions*, San Francisco, CA: Jossey-Bass.

Eddleston, K., Chrisman, J., Steier, Ll. and Chua, J. (2010), 'Governance and trust in family firms: an introduction', *Entrepreneurship Theory and Practice*, **36**(6), 1043–56.

Fama, E.F. and Jensen, M.C. (1983), 'Separation of ownership and control', *Journal of Law and Economics*, **26**, 301–25.

Fukuyama, F. (1995), *Trust, the Social Virtues and the Creation of Prosperity*, New York: Free Press.

Fukuyama, F. (2000), 'Social capital and civil society', IMF Working Paper, WP/00/74.

García-Álvarez, E., López-Sintas, J. and Saldaña-Gonzalvo, P. (2002), 'Socialization patterns of successors in first- and second-generation family businesses', *Family Business Review*, **15**(3), 189–203.

Gersick, K., Davis, J., McCollon, M. and Lansberg, I. (1997), *Generation to Generation*, Boston, MA: Harvard Business School Press.

Granovetter, M. (1973), 'The strength of weak ties', *American Journal of Sociology*, **78**(6), 1360–80.

Granovetter, M. (2005), 'The impact of social structure in economic outcomes', *Journal of Economic Perspectives*, **19**(1), 33–50.

Habbershon, T., Williams, M. and MacMillan, I. (1999), 'A unified systems perspective of family firm performance', *Journal of Business Venturing*, **18**(4), 451–65.

Habermas, J. (1986), *Teoría de la acción comunicativa*, Madrid: Taurus.

Hardin, Russell (1999), 'Social capital', in Alt and Margaret Levi (eds), *Competition and Cooperation: Conversations with Nobelists about Economics and Political Science*, New York: Russell Sage Foundation, pp. 170–89.

Hardin, R. (2001), 'Gaming trust', in E. Olstrom and J. Walker (eds), *Trust and Reciprocity: Interdisciplinary Lessons from Experimental Research*, New York: Russell Sage Foundation, pp. 80–101.

Heyden, L., Blondel, C. and Carlock, R.S. (2005), 'Fair process: striving for justice in family business', *Family Business Review*, **18**(1), 1–21.

Hoffman, J., Hoelscher, M. and Sorenson, R. (2006), 'Achieving sustained competitive advantage: a family capital theory', *Family Business Review*, **19**(2), 135–45.

Irava, W.J. (2009), 'Familiness qualities, entrepreneurial orientation and long-term performance advantage', PhD thesis, Queensland University.

Jack, S. (2005), 'The role, use and activation of strong and network ties: a qualitative analysis', *Journal of Management Studies*, **42**(6), 1233–59.

Kelly, L., Athanassiou, N. and Crittenden, W.F. (2000), 'Founder centrality and strategic behaviour in the family-owned firm', *Entrepreneurship Theory and Practice*, Winter, 27–42.

Kepner, E. (1983), 'The family and the firm: a coevolutionary perspective', *Organizational Dynamics*, **12**(1), 57–70.

King, A.W. (2007), 'Disentangling interfirm and intrafirm causal ambiguity: a conceptual model of causal ambiguity and sustainable competitive advantage', *The Academy of Management Review*, **32**(1), 156–78.

Kramer, R.M. (1999), 'Trust and distrust in organizations: emerging perspectives, enduring questions', *Annual Review in Psychology*, **50**, 60–98.

Lambsdorff, J. (2002), 'Corruption and rent-seeking', *Public Choice*, **113**, 97–125.

Lansberg, I. (1983), 'Managing human resources in family firms: the problem of institutional overlap', *Organizational Dynamics*, **12**, 39–46.

Lansberg, I. (1999), *Succeeding Generations*, Boston, MA: Harvard Business School Press.

La Porta, R., Lopez-de-Silanes, F., Shleifer, A. and Vishny, R. (1997), 'Trust in large organizations', *American Economic Review*, **87**(2), 333–8.

Le Breton-Miller, I. and Miller, D. (2009), 'Agency vs. stewardship in public family firms: a social embeddedness reconciliation', *Entrepreneurship Theory and Practice*, **33**(6), 1169–91.

Lee, J. (2006), 'Impact of family relationships on attitudes of the second generation in family business', *Family Business Review*, **XIX**(3), 175–91.

Lewicki, R. and Bunker, B. (1996), 'Developing and maintaining trust in work relationships', in R.M. Kramer and M. Tyler (eds), *Trust in Organizations: Frontiers of Theory and Research*, Thousand Oaks, CA: Sage, pp. 114–39.

Litz, R.A. (1995), 'The family business: toward definitional clarity', *Family Business Review*, **8**(2), 71–81.

Luhmann, N. (1979), *Trust and Power*, Chichester, UK: Wiley.

Luhmann, N. (1988), 'Familiarity, confidence and trust: problems and alternatives', in D. Gambeta, (ed.), *Trust: Making and Breaking Cooperative Relations*, New York: Blackwell, pp. 94–108.

Mayer, R.C. and Gavin, M.B. (2005), 'Trust in management and performance: who minds the shop while the employees mind the boss?', *Academy of Management Journal*, **48**, 874–88.

Mishra, A.K. (1996), 'Organizational responses to crisis: the centrality of trust', in R.M. Kramer and M. Tyler (eds), *Trust in Organizations: Frontiers of Theory and Research*, Thousand Oaks, CA: Sage, pp. 261–87.

Moores, K. (2009), 'Paradigms and theory building in the domain of business families', *Family Business Review*, **22**(2), 167–80.

Nahapiet, J. and Ghoshal, S. (1998), 'Social capital, intellectual capital and the organizational advantage', *Academy of Management Review*, **23**, 242–67.

Nooteboom, B. (2000), 'Trust as a governance device', in M. Casson and A. Godley, *Cultural Factors in Economic Growth*, Heidelberg: Springer, pp. 44–68.

Olson, D.H. (1986), 'Circumplex Model VII: validation studies and FACES III', *Family Process*, **25**(3), 337–51.

Olson, D.H. and Gorall, D.M. (2003), 'Circumplex model of marital and family systems', in F. Walsh, *Normal Family Processes*, New York: Guilford, pp. 3–28.

Orth, U.R. and Green, M.T. (2009), 'Consumer loyalty to family versus non-family businesses: the roles of store image, trust and satisfaction', *Journal of Retailing and Consumer Services*, **16**, 248–59.

Padgett, M. and Morris, K.A. (2005), 'Keeping it "All in the family": does nepotism in the hiring process really benefit the beneficiary?', *Journal of Leadership and Organizational Studies*, **11**, 34–45.

Paldam, M. (2000), 'Social capital: one or many? Definition and measurement', *Journal of Economic Surveys*, **14**(5), 629–53.

Parada, M.J., Nordqvist, M. and Jimeno, J. (2010), 'Institutionalizing the family business: The role of professional associations in fostering a change of values', *Family Business Review*, **23**(4), 355–72.

Parsons, T. (1949), *The Structure of Social Action: A Study in Social Theory with Special Reference to a Group of European Writers*, 2nd edn, Glencoe, IL: Free Press.

Pearson, A.W., Carr, J.C. and Shaw, J.C. (2008), 'Toward a theory of familiness: a social perspective', *Entrepreneurship Theory and Practice*, **32**(6), 949–69.

Pena-López, J.A. and Sánchez-Santos, J.M. (2006), 'Altruismo, simpatía y comportamientos prosociales en el Análisis Económico', *Principios: Estudios de Economía Política*, **4**, 55–70.

Portes, A. (1998), 'Social capital: its origins and applications in modern sociology', *Annual Review of Sociology*, **24**(1), 1–24.

Portes, A. and Landolt, P. (1996), 'The downside of social capital', *The American Prospect*, **26**, 18–21.

Putnam, R. (1993), *Making Democracy Work: Civic Traditions in Modern Italy*, Princeton, NJ: Princeton University Press.

Ram, M. and Holliday, R. (1993), 'Relative merits: family culture and kinship in small firms', *Sociology*, **27**(4), 629–48.

Rousseau, D., Sitkin, S.B., Burt, B.R. and Camerer, C. (1998), 'Not so different after all: a cross discipline view of trust', *Academy of Management Review*, **23**, 405–21.

Salvaj, E., Ferraro, F. and Tàpies, J. (2008), 'Family firms and the contingent value of board interlocks: the Spanish case', in J. Tàpies and J. Ward (eds), *Family Values and Value Creation*, New York: Palgrave Macmillan, pp. 236–60.

Salvato, C. and Melin, L. (2008), 'Creating value across generations in family-controlled businesses: the role of family social capital', *Family Business Review*, **21**(3), 259–76.

Schul, Y., Mayo, R. and Bursntein, E. (2008), 'The value of distrust', *Journal of Experimental Social Psychology*, **93**(3), 593–601.

Schulze, W., Lubatkin, M., Dino, R. and Buchlholtz, A. (2001), 'Agency relationships in family firms: theory and evidence', *Organization Science*, **12**(2), 99–116.

Sharma, P. (2004), 'An overview of the field of family business studies: current status and directions for the future', *Family Business Review*, **17**(1), 1–36.

Sharma, P. (2008), 'Familiness: capital stocks and flows between family and business', *Entrepreneurship Theory and Practice*, **32**, 971–77.

Sharma, P. and Manikutty, S. (2005), 'Strategic divestments in family firms: role of family structure and community culture', *Entrepreneurship Theory and Practice*, **29**, 293–311.

Sharma, P., Chrisman, J.J. and Chua, J.H. (1997), 'Strategic management of the family business: past research and future challenges', *Family Business Review*, **10**(1), 1–36.

Silva, F., Majluf, N. and Paredes, R. (2006), 'Family ties, interlocking directors and performance in business groups in emerging countries: the case of Chile', *Journal of Business Research*, **59**(3), 315–21.

Sirmon, D.G. and Hitt, M.A. (2003), 'Managing resources: linking unique resources, management, and wealth creation in family firms', *Entrepreneurship Theory and Practice*, **27**(4), 339–58.

Sorenson, R.L. (1999), 'Conflict strategies used by successful family businesses', *Family Business Review*, **12**(4), 325–39.

Steier, Ll. (2001), 'Next-generation entrepreneurs and succession: an exploratory study of modes and jeans of managing social capital', *Family Business Review*, **24**(3), 259–76.

Steward, A. (2003), 'Help one another, use one another: toward an anthropology of family business', *Entrepreneurship Theory and Practice*, **27**, 383–96.

Sundaramurthy, C. (2008), 'Sustaining trust within family businesses', *Family Business Review*, **21**(1), 89–102.

Sydow, J. (1998), 'Understanding the constitution of interorganizational trust', in I.C. Lane and R. Bachmann (eds), *Trust within and between Organizations*, New York: Oxford University Press, pp. 31–63.

Tagiuri, R. and Davis, J. (1996), 'Bivalent attributes of the family firm', *Family Business Review*, **9**(2), 199–209.

Torsvik, G. (2000), 'Social capital and economic development', *Rationality and Society*, **12**(4), 451–76.

Tsai, W. and Ghoshal, S. (1998), 'Social capital and value creation: the role of intrafirm networks', *The Academy of Management Journal*, **41**(4), 464–76.

Uphoff, N. (2000), 'Understanding social capital: learning from the analysis and experience of participation', in P. Dasgupta and I. Serageldin (eds), *Social Capital: A Multifaceted Perspective*, Washington, DC: The World Bank, pp. 215–49.

Uslaner, E. (2005), 'Trust and corruption', in J. Lambsdorff, M. Taube and M. Schramm (eds), *The New Institutional Economics of Corruption*, New York: Routledge, pp. 76–92.

Uzzi, B. (1997), 'Social structure and competition in interfirm networks: the paradox of embeddedness', *Administrative Science Quarterly*, **42**, 35–67.

Vallejo, M.C. (2008), 'Is the culture of family firms really different? A value-based model for its survival through generations', *Journal of Business Ethics*, **81**, 261–79.

Vinton, K.L. (1998), 'Nepotism: an interdisciplinary model', *Family Business Review*, **11**(4), 297–303.

Ward, J.L. (2004), *Perpetuating the Family Business*, New York: Macmillan.

Ward, J.L. (1997), 'Growing the family business: special challenges and best practices', *Family Businesses Review*, **10**(4), 323–37.

Warren, M. (1999), 'Democratic theory and trust', in M. Warren, *Democracy and Trust*, Cambridge: Cambridge University Press, pp. 310–45.

Webb, J.W., Ketchen, D.J. and Ireland, R.D. (2010), 'Strategic entrepreneurship within family controlled firms: opportunities and challenges', *Journal of Family Business Studies*, **1**(2), 67–77.

Weber, M. (1904), *The Protestant Ethic and the Spirit of Capitalism*, New York: Scribner's Press.

Wernerfelt, B. (1984), 'A resource–based view of the firm', *Strategic Management Journal*, **5**, 171–80.

Westhead, P. and Cowling, M. (1997), 'Performance contrasts between family and non-family unquoted companies in the UK', *International Journal of Entrepreneurial Behaviour and Research*, **3**, 30–52.

Westhead, P. and Howorth, C. (2008), 'Types of private family firms: an exploratory conceptual and empirical analysis', *Entrepreneurship Theory and Practice*, **19**(3), 405–31.

Williams, B. (1988), 'Formal structures and social reality', in D. Gambetta (ed.), *Trust: Making and Breaking Cooperative Relations*, Oxford: Blackwell, pp. 453–86.

Winter, I. (2001), 'Toward a theorized understanding of family life and social capital', Working Paper no. 21, Melbourne University.

Woolcock, M. (2001), *Using Social Capital: Getting the Social Relations Right in the Theory and Practice of Economic Development*, Princeton, NJ: Princeton University Press.

Zellweger, T., Eddleston, K. and Kellermanns, F. (2010), 'Exploring the concept of familiness: introducing family firm identity', *Journal of Family Business Strategy*, **1**(1), 54–63.

Zellweger, T. and Astrachan, J.H. (2008), 'On the emotional value of owning a firm', *Family Business Review*, **21**(4), 347–63.

11 Strategy in family businesses: the analysis of human capital and social capital
Fabio Matuoka Mizumoto and
Maria Sylvia Macchione Saes

INTRODUCTION

Recurring questions in strategic management literature focus on how to explain perform-ance differences and on how to predict the firms that will switch strategy positioning. Considering family businesses, what would be the family contributions to strategy change and to business performance? Although we recognize previous literature on the influence of family in strategy decisions (Habbershon and Williams, 1999; Hoffman et al., 2006; Salvato and Melin, 2008; Danes et al., 2009), little was researched on how the family changes the probability of switching strategies and its resulting performance. Moreover, in our investigation, we controlled for endogeneity problems by applying appropriate estimation methods to derive contributions to family business, entrepreneurship and strategy research fields.

From the strategy perspective, we recognize that the literature linking transaction-cost economics, the resource-based view and strategic positioning has been growing over recent years (Nickerson et al., 2001; Ghosh and John, 1999). These studies focus on the tangible resources and the associated level of specificity (Williamson, 1985) that they represent for a certain transaction, by assuming homogeneous management ability, skills and experience for all firms. However, many scholars consider the fact that human capital (Becker, 1964; Schultz, 1961, 1982) and social capital (Burt, 1992; Coleman, 1988) are positively associated to firms' performance (Hitt et al., 2001; Harrington, 2001) and competitive advantage (Ding and Abetti, 2002; Hatch and Dyer, 2004; Acqaah, 2007).

Indeed, parents are responsible for investments in the child's human capital (Becker, 1964) and, considering the family business context, the family provides human, social and financial capital to businesses (Danes et al., 2009). In this chapter, we discuss the contri-butions of family by estimating the probability of changing the strategy and the transaction–governance arrangement according to the family contributions of human capital and social capital to the business. We shed light on the investments of family on education and the experience from family background to help explain changes in business strategy and performance. In addition, we investigated the contributions of families' social capital to the business, considering the length of commercial relationship and the size of labor market hired under family relationship.

Family businesses have a particular distinction from other organizations, which is the involvement of families. Previous studies associated family involvement to the sustained competitive advantage of family business over non-family business (Habbershon and Williams, 1999; Hoffman et al., 2006) and to value creation through generations of family

(Salvato and Melin, 2008). Families provide a unique work environment that inspires greater employee care and loyalty (Donnelley, 1964; Ward, 1988). The inseparability of family and business objectives favors a long-term strategy and a commitment to accomplish it (Aronoff and Ward, 1995). Family relationships contribute to unusual motivation, and greater communication, and favor the emergence of reliable reputation (Tagiuri and Davis, 1996). In addition, it is claimed that reputation of families leads to lower overall transaction costs (Aronoff and Ward, 1995; Tagiuri and Davis, 1996).

Although we recognize advances in the family business literature, little is known about the mechanisms of positive family contributions to the business. In this sense, we concur with the Habbershon and Williams (1999) critique that existing literature on family business relies heavily on anecdotes, concepts and consultant's frameworks. Although Hoffman et al. (2006) reacted to this by proposing a family capital theory, this perspective struggled to clarify the mechanisms of family involvement, lacked empirical evidence, and provided little distinction to social capital theory. Arrègle et al. (2007) reacted to the Habbershon and Williams (1999) critique and provided a promising framework to disentangle social capital from the family and from the organization, considering that both have different contributions to a family firm's social capital, but they ignored the human capital source of advantages to family firms and, as a conceptual framework, lacked empirical evidence. Salvato and Melin (2008) provided empirical support to explain value creation through family generations by means of renewing and reshaping family-specific social interactions; however, they ignored the antecedents of competitive advantages such as firm-specific knowledge, experience and skills that a family has. Danes et al. (2009) expanded the family capital concept by introducing the idea of financial capital, human capital and social capital into the discussion of family business survivability. Their findings opened discussion about stock versus use of family capital; the non-use of family capital does not necessarily indicate absence of family capital.

Although we observed that Lovas and Ghoshal (2000) reported human capital and social capital as resources that will define how firms plan strategic initiatives, little has been examined about their implications for transaction-cost economics. In addition, Masten et al. (1989) indicated that relationship-specific human capital has a stronger influence than physical assets on the decision to vertically integrate production, but its implications on strategy have not been investigated. Our aim is to connect these isolated perspectives by applying appropriate methods that control for self-selection of transaction-governance and strategy choice (Masten, 1993; Nickerson et al., 2001). Moreover, we disentangled the sources of human capital and social capital to provide distinctive contributions for strategy choice moderated by transaction-governance choice.

Brazilian coffee production provides a good context for this analysis. First, the coffee farmer represents the main decision-maker. This fact facilitates the assessment of human capital and social capital; for comparison, consider a large corporation and the implications of making the same assessment but for different decision-makers, for instance, the owners and the managers. Second, it is possible to clearly identify the strategy alternatives if the farmer pursues a low-cost strategy or a differentiation strategy (Porter, 1991). Third, it is possible to observe that the adoption of spot-market or contract (Williamson, 2002) governs one of the most critical transactions, for instance, the coffee trade between the farmer and the coffee buyer. Fourth, it is possible to disentangle tangible and intangible resources; the former represents specific investments in assets owing to a particular strategy, while the latter are the investments in social and human capital made by a particular farmer.

There are certain implications when distinguishing tangible and intangible resources. The intangible resources are considered as firm-specific (Hatch and Dyer, 2004; Kor and Mahoney, 2004; Kor et al., 2007), task-specific (Gibbons and Waldman, 2004) or even, with regard to the empirical context, soil-specific (Laband, 1984). This perspective is different from specific investments in tangible resources owing to a certain strategy; for instance, courier firms specialized in documents invest on specific information technology to provide traceability (Nickerson et al., 2001) that loses its value if the courier firm changes the market positioning. In the case of intangible resources, expropriation of value occurs when the potential of the existing human capital and social capital are not exploited (Lovas and Ghoshal, 2000).

With regard to the coffee-production context, a farmer who had invested in sun-drying equipment (tangible resource) to accomplish the quality standards required for a differentiation strategy may have the investment expropriated if he switches to a low-cost strategy. The investment in 'the skills necessary for growing and processing agricultural products, however sophisticated and specialized, will seldom be relationship-specific and are thus unlikely to generate quasi-rents that would expose the transactors to the threat of hold ups' (Masten, 2000, p. 187). Consistent with the observation by Masten (2000), we consider that human capital and social capital are not relationship-specific, but a coffee farmer who had invested in formal education (Becker, 1964) may have his investment expropriated if a financial constrain prevents him from exploiting all his potentials (Lovas and Ghoshal, 2000).

The aim of this study is to address the importance of intangible resources provided by families, such as human capital and social capital, to improve the understanding of transaction-governance, strategy decisions and the resulting performance of the business. Although standard theories of economics and strategy convey the idea that some producers would switch to a differentiation strategy as the market grows, these theories find it difficult to predict which farmers would switch their production capacity. For instance, theories from industrial organization such as the theory of market contestability, which assumes no entry barriers or no entry costs, indicate that some farmers will switch, but these theories contribute little in indentifying which farmers will switch. Although the strategic positioning framework (Porter, 1991) identifies the opportunity for farmers to differentiate, it does not explain which farmer would adopt a differentiation strategy, especially when the technology is freely accessible and economies of scale and regulatory privileges are not sources of entry barriers, as in the case of Brazilian coffee production. Other theories of strategy, such as the resource-based view (Barney, 1991; Kor and Mahoney, 2004) and the knowledge-based view (Peteraf, 1993; Prahalad and Hamel, 1990), are not efficient in predicting the choice of differentiation. Although we agree that production of differentiated coffee may be linked to the geographical conditions or other physical resources,[1] there is little indication to predict why some farmers do not adopt a differentiation strategy even when possessing privilege-tangible resources. The information about the market, prices and production techniques is widely available and known, which reduces the likelihood that the possession of rare, inimitable information or knowledge is central to the differentiation decision. Transaction-cost economics (Williamson,

1985) is another theory in the strategy domain, which provides little information regarding which farmers would switch.

While our empirical context provides advantages toward the research objectives, we are aware of some limitations that need to be addressed initially. On considering the farmer as the main decision-maker and the relative simplicity of the farm organization, we are constrained to evaluate the existence of routines and tasks owing to the dynamic capabilities (Teece et al., 1997) of the organization. With regard to performance, our measures provide support for the comparison of firms that pursue a differentiation strategy, but not for the comparison of low-cost versus differentiation strategy. Even though we cannot provide a performance comparison on the alignment of govenance-resource-strategy alternatives (Nickerson et al., 2001; Ghosh and John, 1999), we can partially address the efficiency perspective on economizing the transaction costs (Williamson, 1985; Masten, 1993, 2002) and the performance implications owing to asymmetries of resources (Barney, 1991). In addition, differences in the performance can be predicted by the knowledge-based view of competences and capabilities (Peteraf, 1993; Prahalad and Hamel, 1990). The distinction of resources, capabilities and competences has few implications for this research, as we are interested in the effects of human capital and social capital on governance choice and strategy positioning. Previous studies have addressed the internal consistency on these perspectives: 'As the literature makes increasingly clear, a knowledge-based view is the essence of the resource-based-view perspective. The central theme emerging in the strategic management resource-based literature is that privately held knowledge is a basic source of advantage in competition' (Conner and Prahalad, 1996, p.477).

The chapter begins by adopting the perspective that assumes that farmers possess essentially equivalent physical assets and identical information about production techniques and market opportunities. Subsequently, differences in the decisions must be attributed to the way in which they process information, and their mental models and cognitive structures. While these models and structures cannot be observed directly, human capital theory (Becker, 1964; Schultz, 1961, 1982) can provide a window into these structures by exploring the relationship between formal education and the experience of the decision-maker and how these influence the firms' positioning in the market. Moreover, we have individually investigated the effects of human capital and social capital (Coleman, 1988) to overcome the constraints of the previous research that evaluated both the effects, but without distinctions (Lovas and Ghoshal, 2000).

Subsequently, background information on coffee production in Brazil is provided, followed by a discussion on the use of spot-market and contractual arrangements to trade coffee (Williamson, 1985), and the implications on tangible resources (Barney, 1991) when pursuing a low-cost or a differentiation strategy (Porter, 1991), and we also discuss family farms (Flören, 2002). After the context description, the theoretical references on transaction-cost economics, the resource-based view and strategy positioning are presented along with a discussion on the assumptions of those references and implications from the perspective of human capital and social capital theory. By considering that strategy and governance choice are interdependent (Masten, 1993; Nickerson et al., 2001), we applied a switching regression model that is presented in detail on the methods and data section. The results of the hypothesis testing, limitations and final remarks are presented in the last section.

FAMILY FARM AND COFFEE BUSINESS CONTEXT

The Family Farm

Allen and Lueck (1998) stated that the family unit has been the dominant organization in farming since the earliest days of agriculture, and referred to previous studies that indicate the presence of family farms in ancient Egypt, Israel, Mesopotamia, North America (pre-Columbian Indians), Latin America and Asia. Considering a modern approach, Flören (2002) articulated the definition of the family farm as a subsection of the entire family business population.[2] Based on his definition in the Dutch context, an enterprise is recognized as a family business if it complies one of the three criteria: (1) a single family owns more than 50 percent of the shares (with regard to ownership control by a family). However, if the business has been started less than ten years ago, then it should also employ at least one more family member of the owner(s); (2) a single family is capable of exercising considerable influence on the business strategy or succession decisions; and (3) at least two members of the board of directors or board of advisors are from one family.

By switching our analytical lenses, it can be stated that a

> farm organization can vary from a single owner or simple partnership, where labor is paid by residual claims, to a public corporation with many anonymous owners and specialized labor. A 'pure' family farm is the simplest case, where a single farmer owns the output and controls all farm assets, including labor assets. [footnote ignored] Factor-style corporate agriculture is the most complicated case, where many people own the farm and labor is provided by large groups of specialized fixed wage labor. (Allen and Lueck, 1998, p. 347)

With respect to this 'nature of the farm', Allen and Lueck argued that farmers who control the effects of nature by mitigating the effects of seasonality and external shocks have chances to turn into a large-scale corporation. The family-controlled farm organization dominates the stages of production highly exposed to the forces of nature, as a consequence of limited gains from specialization owing to seasonality. The family farmer has important choices and particular dynamics. The family farmer must decide on how to allocate resources between the family and farm (Keef and Burk, 1967), and must decide how to allocate farming time across different tasks (Allen and Lueck, 1998). With regard to family, there are endowments, investments on education (Becker and Tomes, 1986), and propensity to transfer knowledge supported by altruism and care for future generations (Murphy et al., 2008). The sample of family farms for this study complies with Flören's (2002) conceptual definition and with Allen and Lueck's (1998) perspective of farm organization. It is important to mention that our sample consists of farmers who differ with respect to generational experience (incumbents in coffee business and farmers with long tradition in the business, up to the seventh family generation) and the size of the operations (small family farms dependent on family members as labor force and 'corporate' family farms).

Coffee Business

Brazil is the largest producer of coffee in the world, primarily producing Robusta and Arabica beans. The Arabica beans contain the aroma, flavor and taste attributes that are highly valued when compared with the Robusta beans. The quality of a coffee blend prepared by the roasting industry is determined by the quality of the Arabica beans produced on the farms. With the growth of firms like Starbucks and Seattle's Best, the market for this differentiated Arabica coffee has been increasing fast over the past decade, representing about 8 percent of the world coffee production and 35 percent of the USA coffee market in 2004 (Chaddad and Boland, 2007). As this market grew, some Brazilian farmers switched some or all of their production capacity to differentiated Arabica, while some farmers remained focused on commodity Arabica. Current isolated theoretical perspectives find it difficult to determine which farmers switch to a differentiation strategy (Porter, 1991).

With regard to the Brazilian coffee producers, the strategy choice is not trivial; there are trade-offs between the commodity and differentiation strategies with respect to the investment decision (Saes, 2010). First, instead of the standard equipment for commodity production, the farmer has to invest in specific ones to guarantee post-harvest quality for specialties; examples of specific investments made for specialty coffee are as follows: (i) harvest equipments that are specific to differentiated production, because it allows the harvest of the mature beans without mixing them with the green beans, as in the case of harvest equipments for commodity production, (ii) investments to adjust the sun-drying process are specific to specialties – the adjustment is necessary to promote the migration of sugar and aroma from the fruit to the coffee beans, which will give body to the blend coffee, and which is a relevant attribute of the composition of the espresso (differentiation strategy). Second, the technical and agronomic practices to grow the coffee trees are idiosyncratic to the type of the specialty. Third, in most of the cases, yield productivity is negatively impacted by those practices to increase the coffee quality; the farmer may adopt agronomic practices to increase the quality of the coffee bean, but as a result, the volume of production may decrease – this is a typical trade-off of quantity versus quality. Fourth, in addition to the price coordination mechanism, the producer has to use certification programs and third-party evaluations.

This research investigated the effects of human capital and social capital owing to changes from low-cost strategy (commodity production) to differentiation strategy. Specifically, we investigated the farmer's choice to produce coffee that is differentiated by the quality of the drink, which is observed to have conceptual implications. First, the other types of coffee depend on tangible resources rather than on human and social capital (intangible resources). For instance, the existence of forest is a determinant resource owing to the production of 'shade-grown' type of differentiation. However, one could argue that even if the tangible resource is available, the lack of human capital or social capital would prevent the farmer from adhering to 'shade-grown' production. Nevertheless, we may underestimate the farmers with intangible resources, constrained by tangible resources. Second, although we could not distinguish the volume of each type of differentiation owing to poor statistics on the sector, market experts indicate that differentiation by the quality of drink (which takes into account aroma, taste, body and acidity) is the most widely produced among specialty coffee farmers in Brazil.

Farmers observe output from past resource allocations and learn from previous decisions. Genetic variety, level of fertilizer and agricultural practices are examples of decisions that have been improved over the years by the owner carrying out business. Although codified knowledge exists, such as manuals and recommendations from extension centers, universities and research institutions, the results depend on the adjustments that the farmer makes for the particular soil and climate conditions. Moreover, coffee trees have a natural production cycle of high-volume production in one year and low-volume production in the following year, which affects the producer's cash flow. This is important because the producer should invest when he is actually capital constrained. In the years of low production, revenue will also decrease; however, this is the technically efficient moment to invest to achieve high quality of production in the following year, when production also tends to increase with the natural condition of coffee trees. The ability to manage production fluctuations depends on the owner's knowledge about the resources that are specific to the firm. Indeed, for the farmers who adopt a differentiation strategy, this imposes an additional challenge because techniques and agronomic practices to improve the coffee quality may also reduce the yield productivity. Thus, in addition to the quasi-rent appropriation problem (Klein et al., 1978) from idiosyncratic investments, the farmers who switch to a differentiation strategy need firm-specific knowledge to manage the decrease in production volume.

THEORETICAL REFERENCE

Governance, Resource and Strategy Choice

In this section, we present the discussion about the literature on transaction-cost economics, the resource-based view and strategy positioning. In addition, we discuss the assumptions of those references and implications from human and social capital theory to derive the hypothesis that guided the empirical investigations.

The discussion on the firm's strategy to economize on transaction costs began with Coase's (1937) seminal work, 'The nature of the firm'. Williamson (1985) developed a theory to predict the efficient governance structure owing to the characteristics of specificity, frequency and uncertainty involved in the transaction. In this sense, transaction-cost economics predicts the adoption of contractual arrangements in the presence of idiosyncratic investments (Williamson, 1985) to avoid quasi-rent appropriation (Klein et al., 1978).

Saes (2005) suggested that it is unfeasible for a roasting industry to vertically integrate the supply of coffee, because the consistency of a high-quality blend depends on the mixing of coffee beans from different regions or even different countries. Hence the trade of coffee can be considered to rely on coordination by spot-market and by contracts. In a spot-market relationship, there is no commitment among the parties and nothing is specified *ex ante*: 'the negotiation evolves two steps: in the first round processing firms only signal their interest in acquiring the desired attribute. This can be done, for instance, through quality contests they conduct. The second round of the transaction may or may not take place' (Saes, 2005, p. 6). However, if the spot-market relationship frequently occurs between the parties, a relational contract emerges. While transaction is still voluntary, the coffee grower may have incentives to invest in specific assets to pursue the production of specialties.

Another coordination mechanism is the establishment of contracts, which determine the *ex ante* commitment among the parties (the contract is set before the production is made effective), define a fixed price or at least the criteria for pricing, and determine the duration of the contract (e.g. for one up to four crops). Although Masten (2000) claimed that contracting or vertical integration in the organization of agricultural transactions is driven by temporal or local specificity, this may not apply to the context of specialty coffee. Indeed, Masten's argument fits with respect to a commodity context (e.g. the temporal specificity of fruits to reach the consumer market); however, on a differentiation strategy, the investments in assets are highly specialized.

In the context of Brazilian coffee production, the choice for a differentiation strategy implies that the coffee producer makes specific investments, and, to avoid quasi-rent appropriation, should tend to set a formal contract with the coffee buyer. Indeed, these specific investments in equipment, agronomic processes and practices are tangible resources necessary to achieve the differentiated quality of Arabica beans demanded by the roast processor industry. The farmer will seek for a price premium when compared with the price paid for the commodity Arabica beans to pay back those investments. Considering that the critical transaction is on the demand side (Saes, 2010), farmers may seek for a formal contract that determines the volume of coffee and, even more importantly, the price premium. When the farmer pursues a commodity strategy, there may be no specific investment toward the demand for any particular roasting industry; thus the spot-market is the main coordination mechanism. The first hypothesis is based on the transaction-cost economics argument:

Hypothesis 1   The investment in tangible and transaction-specific resources necessary to pursue a differentiation strategy enhances the probability of adopting contracts.

By integrating different perspectives, Nickerson et al. (2001) provided empirical support by investigating the international couriers and small package services in Japan to argue that strategic positioning, resource profile and governance are interdependent. For instance, a firm that is specialized in documents transportation (strategy) may require high investments in information systems (resource profile) for tracking purposes through the transportation flow (domestic truck, international flight, international truck) and, owing to the high specificity of the investments, the firm may tend to vertically integrate (governance choice). Another illustration is the firm that is specialized in package transportation that may demand a relatively low level of information; thus the courier firm may outsource more activities because the investments are not specific.

Despite the critiques of the competence perspective (resource-based view) for its tautological definitions and lack of predictability, Williamson (1999) suggested further developments that could integrate the transaction-cost economics perspective: 'There are many respects in which the competence and transaction cost perspectives are congruent. Both take exception with orthodoxy, both are bounded rationality constructions, and both maintain that organization matters' (Williamson, 1999, p. 1098). In this sense, Conner and Prahalad (1996) suggested that the governance mode through which individuals could interact affects the knowledge that they apply to make decisions. Both the perspectives assume that individuals are boundedly rational, but Conner and Prahalad (1996) indicated that, unlike transaction-cost economics, the presence of opportunism is not a necessary assumption for the knowledge-based view.

Porter (1994) argued that the resource-based view by itself is circular and lacks a prediction framework to be considered an alternative theory of strategy. However, the integration with the competitive strategy is desirable: 'Resources are not valuable in themselves, but because they allow firms to perform activities that create advantages in particular markets' (Porter, 1994, p. 446). In this sense, firms rely on the resources that enable the adoption of competitive strategies. One generic competitive strategy is the low-cost strategy: 'A great deal of managerial attention to cost control is necessary to achieve . . . a low-cost position [that] yields the firm above-average returns in its industry despite the presence of strong competitive forces' (Porter, 1998, p. 35). Another generic competitive strategy is the differentiation strategy: 'achieving differentiation will imply a trade-off with cost position if the activities required in creating it are inherently costly, such as extensive research, product design, high quality materials, or intensive customer support' (ibid., p. 38).

From the resource-based view (Barney, 1991; Kor and Mahoney, 2004), the competitive advantage is rooted in the resources; thus the firm creates value by exploiting resources and taking action to prevent competitors from imitating or having access to valuable resources. We understand that strategic positioning and the resource-based view have complementary views once the former focuses the analysis on factors external to the firm (such as industry structure) while the latter focuses on factors internal to the firm (tacit knowledge in Penrose's perspective and resources in Barney's perspective). Indeed, 'the analysis of the growth process [includes] the expectations of a firm – the way in which it interprets its "environment" – are as much a function of the internal resources and operations of a firm as of the personal qualities of the entrepreneur' (Penrose, 1995, p. 41).

The importance of governance with regard to the performance of firms, especially on how to compare alternative governance arrangements, becomes increasingly important owing to the fact that transaction-cost economics follows the normative rationale of strategic management (Masten, 1993; Masten et al., 1989). Managers rely on the economics discipline to improve their decisions and enhance business performance; thus the methods have to provide appropriate support to findings on governance and performance of the firms. However, many scholars have failed to account for self-selection with respect to organization and strategy choice that contributes to 'incontrovertible insights into that relation' (Masten et al., 1989, p. 430). We have addressed the hypothesis on performance, despite the constraints on our measures, and have accounted for the self-selection bias by using appropriate methods.

Human Capital

When the concept of human capital was addressed by Gary Becker in 1957, there was much concern about the view of the man as a 'stock', because human is 'free' and not comparable with other forms of capital (Becker, 1964). However, when people invest more in formal education and training, they become even freer in contrast to the 'slave' criticism of human capital:

> Although it is obvious that people acquire useful skills and knowledge, it is not obvious that these skills and knowledge are a form of capital, that this capital is in substantial part a product of deliberate investment . . . and that its growth may well be the most distinctive feature of the economic system. (Schultz, 1961, p. 1)

Human capital represents the acquired knowledge, skills and capabilities of a person, which increase with the investment in formal education (Becker, 1964) and family endowments (Becker and Tomes, 1986). Sirmon and Hitt (2003) claimed that human capital in family firms is complicated because family members simultaneously participate in business and family relationships. The dual association of personal and professional relationships creates a unique context of both positive and negative human capital. In a positive sense, human capital is promoted by the extraordinary commitment of family members (Donnelley, 1964) and takes advantage of intimate relationships (Horton, 1986) to transfer deep firm-specific tacit knowledge. Moreover, the early involvement of children in family firms provides a competitive advantage over non-family firms, because tacit knowledge is difficult to codify and is transferred through direct exposure and experience (Lane and Lubatkin, 1998). In fact, people gain knowledge through formal education, by doing the job and through mentoring (Hitt et al., 2001).

However, employing family members could lead to hiring suboptimal employees (Dunn, 1995). Indeed, 'family firms frequently have trouble to attract and retain qualified managers due to exclusive succession, limited potential for professional growth, lack of perceived professionalism and limitations of wealth transfer' (Sirmon and Hitt, 2003, p. 342). Family firms are constrained to manage human capital by effective selection, but have the advantage of tacit knowledge transfer owing to the early involvement of children and intimate relations, education endowments (Becker and Tomes, 1986), and less propensity to human capital migration, which is an additional mechanism to protect from rivals' expropriation (Hatch and Dyer, 2004).

While human capital has positive effects on firms with respect to the accumulation of knowledge, skills and experience, the implications on transaction-cost economics rely on economizing the cognition and recognizing the opportunism threat. Consistent with March's (1978) idea that bounded rationality imposes limits to human decision-making by the cognitive capabilities of human beings, the transaction-economizing perspective claims: 'The attributes of human actors are centrally implicated . . . Cognitive specialization, within and between firms, is a means by which to economize on mind as a scarce resource' (Williamson, 1999, p. 1090). In fact, cognition also improves the capacity to recognize an opportunism threat: 'economic actors have the capacity to look ahead and recognize contractual hazards and investment opportunities . . . as a product of experience' (Williamson, 1999, p. 1104). This latter perspective is consistent with Simon (1987), who stated that experience and training improve the set of skills, cultivation of intuition and judgment. Considering that human capital improves the capacity to recognize threats, and that governance mechanisms economize cognition, we state the second hypothesis as follows:

Hypothesis 2 A high level of human capital, comprising investments in formal education and experience from a family background, enhances the probability of adopting formal contracts to protect specific investments.

Becker and Schultz provided empirical evidence that associates investments in formal education with more opportunities, for both work and earnings. Hatch and Dyer (2004) provided empirical evidence to support the idea that human capital is an important source of competitive advantage of firms, because it is specific to the originating firm, and even if human capital migrates to competitors, the adjustments to the new environment prevent immediate expropriation. Considering human capital as a stock of resources, which provides competitive advantage to the firms, is consistent with the resource-based view (Barney, 1991). The farmer may appropriate value from this competitive advantage by adopting efficient strategic positioning in the market, as stated by Porter (1991). The human capital of coffee farmers is enhanced by investments in formal education (Becker, 1964) and firm-specific experience (Hatch and Dyer, 2004; Kor and Mahoney, 2004; Kor et al., 2007) accumulated by the family (Sirmon and Hitt, 2003). In addition, farmers may accumulate a soil-specific (Laband, 1984) human capital that facilitates the estimation of production behavior due to adoption of new techniques. Therefore we formulate the third hypothesis:

Hypothesis 3   A high level of human capital, comprising investments in formal education, is associated with more adoption of a differentiation strategy.

However, the family may accumulate non-valuable resources that lead to inertia and suboptimal decisions (Mosakowski, 2002; Tripsas and Gavetti, 2000; Leonard-Barton, 1992). For instance, the 'internal' labor market of family business could lead to hiring suboptimally qualified employees (Dunn, 1995). In addition, a family farm may avoid switching strategies because the current orientation fits with the existing human capital. Thus we state the fourth hypothesis as follows:

Hypothesis 4   A high level of human capital, comprising experience from a family background, is associated with less adoption of a differentiation strategy.

Earlier studies associated a positive effect of human capital and firm performance (Hitt et al., 2001). Sirmon and Hitt (2003) argued that the most important resource for a family firm is its human capital, considering it as a primary predictor of new venture performance. Moreover, human capital provides deep firm-specific tacit knowledge, a type of intangible resource that is socially complex and difficult to imitate (Barney, 1991; Hitt et al., 2001). Human capital is also associated with a firm's survival, on which highly educated business owners presented greater longevity than low educated ones in the context of small business in the USA between 1976 and 1986 (Bates, 1990). It is also related to firms' diversification decision, in the sense that the firm tends to invest within the groups of industries that are related to one another in the types of human skills required in each industry (Farjoun, 1994). The human capital of family firms enhances the knowledge of firm-specific resources, thus leading to better evaluation, selection and even shedding of the firms' resources (Sirmon and Hitt, 2003).

In the coffee-production context, firm-specific human capital provides better estimations on how the farm's land will react to a certain fertilizer treatment, and how the historical climate conditions would fit a differentiated coffee production (because it largely contributes to quality attributes) or commodity production (because it increases volume productivity). Indeed 'Observed behavior reflects the beliefs and judgment of decision makers and will reflect the true performance relations only to the extent that those beliefs are accurate' (Masten, 1993, p. 120). Considering the price premium of specialty coffee as a reflection of differentiation strategy performance, we state the fifth hypothesis:

Hypothesis 5 A high level of human capital, comprising investments in formal education and experience from a family background, is associated with a higher price premium
owing to a differentiation strategy.

Social Capital

Social capital involves the relationship between individuals or organizations (Burt, 1992),
and provides access to resources embedded within, available through and derived from
the network (Nahapiet and Ghoshal, 1998). Adler and Kwon (2002) argued that social
capital affects the resource interchange, creation of intellectual capital, learning, product
innovation and entrepreneurship. The family's social capital increases by connecting
social structures of networks, improving shared language and narratives, and promoting
relational ties based on trust, norms and obligations (Sirmon and Hitt, 2003). Family ties
are important source of resources (Laird, 2006); for instance, family connections provide
access to cheap financial resources, information about new opportunities of investment,
and knowledge from other family members.

Enduring relationships lead to different interpretations from social capital and
transaction-cost economics. Considering the former, a long-term relationship is a condition for the emergence of the benefits from social capital, such as access to resources, trust
and so on. The latter perspective implies that a long-term contract specifies the terms and
conditions of future transactions *ex ante*; in this sense, the contract is salvage against
ex post problems (Joskow, 1987).

There exists an important apprehension when combining the sociological perspective
with the economizing rationale. While the existence of prior exchange (Uzzi, 1997) leads
to emergence of social ties and expectations of cooperation, cooperation at present is only
reliable with respect to the expectations of future gains from the calculative perspective of
the economists (Baker et al., 2002). To reinforce the calculative rationality and prevention
of opportunist behavior, 'Credible contracting is very much an exercise in farsighted contracting, whereby the parties look ahead, recognize hazards, and devise hazard mitigating
responses – thereby to realize mutual gain' (Williamson, 1999, p. 1090). However,
'Sometimes the risk may be reduced by use of contracts that are enforceable by law, but,
for a variety of reasons, contracts cannot always serve this purpose' (Coleman, 1990, p. 91).

Indeed, Uzzi (1997) suggested that trust plays the role of the governance structure in
the relationships where social ties overcome calculative impersonal contractual ties.
Although from contrasting perspectives, Poppo and Zenger (2002) suggested that formal
contracts and relational governance function as complements. In this sense, relational
governance enables the refinement of contracts and promotes stability in exchange
among the parties. Thus, consistent with the complementary perspective, we state the
sixth hypothesis:

Hypothesis 6 High social capital, comprising a larger labor market hired under a family
relationship and a longer relationship to the buyer, is associated with more adoption of
contracts.

Walker et al. (1997) suggested that entrepreneurial actions take place when firms utilize
the network structure to facilitate the governance of relationships and when opportunities

arise from connections between unlinked firms. In addition, these authors contrast Coleman's and Bourdieu's perspective as well as Burt's perspective regarding the emergence of trust: 'placing trust involves the trustor's voluntarily placing resources at the disposal of another party (the trustee), without any real commitment form that other party' (Coleman 1990, p. 98). In addition, Coleman assumes that trust emerges by judgment and evaluation among parties considering the future benefits of placing trust, not necessarily by previous relationships.

According to Burt (1992), social capital creates value by enabling the emergence of trust by selection of partners: 'The question is not whether to trust, but whom to trust' (Burt, 1992, p. 15). In this perspective, trust emerges as a result of a strong relationship, in which parties select each other with similar social attributes of education, income, occupation, shared background and interests. Thus an underlying condition of the emergence of trust is the relationship duration between parties; it takes time to identify similar social attributes. In addition, the selection of partners has cognition reasoning: 'Creatures of bounded rationality like ourselves have no choice but to attend selectively to the environment in which we operate and information about it. Identification with groups is the major selective mechanism controlling human attention in organizations (and elsewhere)' (Simon, 1993, p. 137).

It is expected that highly socially connected farmers pursue a differentiation strategy, facilitated by a high number of social connections (similar to Coleman's and Bourdieu's perspective) and an enduring relationship (similar to Burt's perspective). Specifically, we assume that socially connected farmers take advantage of cooperation (Uzzi, 1997) to establish contracts,[3] refine the terms of the contract, and promote its stability. However, we assume a sociological perspective for an enduring relationship that predicts the emergence of trust among the agents, and relaxes the opportunism assumption (Conner and Prahalad, 1996) – in this sense, farmers with an enduring relationship will economize on the costs of designing, negotiating and establishing contracts by adopting spot-market governance. Thus we state the hypotheses moderated by governance choice as follows:

Hypothesis 7   High social capital, comprising a larger labor market hired under a family relationship, is associated with more adoption of a differentiation strategy when contracts are established.

Hypothesis 8   High social capital, comprising a longer relationship to the buyer, is associated with more adoption of a differentiation strategy when spot-market is chosen.

Harrington (2001) confirmed the earlier studies that associated the benefits of social capital and firms' performance. His results support the idea that network ties at the individual level have a powerful impact on organizational performance. Specifically, the number of networks of one individual is considered to enhance the organization's financial performance, both directly and indirectly, through an increase in task orientation (willingness to sacrifice some degree of social cohesion for decision quality) and group heterogeneity (the larger the information pool, the better the decision-making process). Ding and Abetti (2002) indicated the utilization of the unique social capital with respect to the Chinese family entrepreneurs, to the economic development of Taiwan, and the success of firms in the electronic-hardware-manufacturing sector. The results are consistent with earlier studies that suggested that the embedded social and economic context of specific geographical regions positively influences the formation and performance of new business. By considering the price premium of specialty coffee as a proxy of performance of a differentiation strategy, we state the hypothesis:

Hypothesis 9 High social capital, comprising a larger labor market hired under a family relationship and a longer duration of the relationship to the buyer, is associated with better performance on a differentiated strategy.

DATA

The description and measures of all variables in the model are presented in Table 11.1. The data were obtained by interviewing 409 farmers over the phone from July to November 2007, following a structured questionnaire. The sample of farmers was provided by the coffee-processing industries and cooperatives. Although the data were collected from 409 coffee producers, further analysis indicated that, for some regions, access to unique resources or natural conditions would influence the strategy choice. For instance, farmers in the State of Espirito Santo cannot produce differentiated coffee because of the low altitude of the region. Another competing explanation for the heterogeneity of strategies is the social structure effects. This is the case of fair trade coffee in the city of Machado and in the State of Ceará. All those cases were excluded from our sample, for the above-mentioned reasons. The sample was reduced to 283 farmers who were in similar natural conditions and competitive environments, a context that made the test of the hypotheses valid. With respect to the missing variables in the specified model, the sample was narrowed down to 255 coffee producers.

Investment is a continuous variable that captures the amount of money (measured in R$ million – Brazilian currency reals) invested in equipment, assets and techniques that are specific to the production of differentiated coffee. This measure is consistent with the literature on transaction-cost economics, which considers the size of the initial investments as a proxy for specific investments (Masten et al., 1989). *Education* is a dummy variable, coded 1 if the farmer has a college degree. This measure is consistent with the previous study that measured the school degree as a proxy for human capital (Rauch et al., 2005; Hitt et al., 2001). *Experience* from a family background is a dummy variable, coded 1 if the current farmer has a previous family generation in the coffee business. Other studies measured experience as a proxy for human capital, for instance the founder's experience on start-up (Shane and Stuart, 2002) and manager's experience in the industry (Hitt et al., 2001). *Relationship duration* measures the number of consecutive years of relationship between the farmer and the coffee buyer. This is a proxy for Burt's perspective, which indicates that increasing social capital should enable trust with the selection of partners, and has no effect on the number of new relationships. *Family ties in the labor market* are measured by the size of the labor market comprising people who are hired under a family relationship in each county. It is a region-based proxy for social capital from Coleman's and Bourdieu's perspective, following the idea that 'some firms occupy positions that are embedded in regions filled with relationships, indicating a high

Table 11.1   Description and measures of variables

Dependent variable: measures for equations 11.1, 11.2 and 11.3	
Transaction–Governance choice (equation 11.1)	The governance of the transaction between the coffee farmer and coffee buyer is a binary variable codified as 1 for contract arrangement or 0 for market relationship
Strategy choice (equation 11.2)	The strategy variable measures the volume (metric tons) of differentiated coffee for each observation. Variable equals 0 if farmer is focused on commodity production. Variable takes any positive value in direct proportion to the differentiation strategy adopted by the farmer
Differentiation performance (equation 11.3)	Performance is measured by the price premium for the special coffee over the commodity price (%). Variable equals 0 if the farmer is focused on commodity production. Variable takes any positive value in direct proportion to the price premium over the commodity price
Explanatory variable: measure for asset specificity	
Investment	Investment is a continuous variable that captures the amount of money (measured by R$ million – Brazilian currency reals) invested in equipment, assets, and techniques that are specific to the production of specialty coffee
Explanatory variables: measures for human capital	
Education	Education is a binary variable codified as (1) for owners with college degree or (0) for owners who did not complete college
Experience	The measure is a binary variable that equals 1 if the farmer is the second or third generation in coffee production or 0 if the farmer is the founder of the coffee business
Explanatory variables: measures for social capital	
Family ties in labor market	Size of labor market comprising people who are hired under family relationship in each county (measured by the number of workers). *Source:* IBGE (Brazilian Institution of Geography and Statistics) 2006 Agricultural Census
Relationship duration	Number of consecutive years of relationship between the farmer and the coffee buyer (measured by the number of years)
Control variables	
Farm size	Farm size is measured by land dimension. All data were standardized in hectares (10 000 square meters)
Age of the owner	Owner's age is measured in years
Distance	The distance from the owner's home and the farm is measured in kilometers (each value represents 10 kilometers for rescaling purposes). In case of more than one location for home or farm, the following criteria were applied: (i) the home where the owner expends more time and (ii) farm where the owner concentrates the administrative duties
Diversification	Diversification is a binary variable codified as 1 for farmers who diversified from coffee production or 0 for farmers who are focused only on coffee production
Instrumental variable	
CPR	The use of CPR (rural product credit note) as a financing mechanism by the farmer is a binary variable codified as 1 for use of CPR as finance contract or 0 for no use of CPR

level of available social capital, but other positions are located in regions with few relationships, suggesting a low social capital' (Walker et al., 1997, p. 111).

Acqaah (2007) discussed the difficulties of obtaining performance measures in emerging economies because the data are either not available or difficult to acquire. In fact, firms may be reluctant to provide objective performance measures. However, in the context of the coffee farmer context, the difficulty of obtaining data may stem from the lack or low consistency of information given by the farmer. For instance, most of the respondents could not answer how much more the differentiated coffee cost than the commodity coffee, because they have low administrative control to support this information. While cost information is not consistent, the price premium paid for differentiated coffee is well known by the farmer. Thus we relied on this alternative measure, which allows the investigation of performance among farmers who pursue a differentiation strategy.

The summary statistics and correlations for all variables are presented in Table 11.2. With regard to explanatory variables, *Relationship duration* showed a positive correlation ($p < 0.05$) with *Strategy choice*; *Experience* inherited from family presented a positive correlation ($p < 0.05$) with *Differentiation performance*; *Investment* showed a strongly positive correlation ($p < 0.01$) with *Strategy choice*.

METHODS

One dependent variable is the *Strategy choice*, which is a continuous measure of the volume of the differentiated coffee for each observation. This measure is left-censored, because farmers who chose the commodity strategy will present zero value for the dependent variable, in contrast to any positive value for those who adopt a differentiation strategy. Hence the appropriate method of estimation is the Tobit regression.

The correlation between strategy choice and governance choice is statistically significant ($p < 0.01$; see Table 11.2). Furthermore, previous literature accounts for endogeneity in strategy choice and governance choice (Nickerson et al., 2001), as well as endogeneity in strategy choice and performance (Shaver, 1998; Masten, 1993). This indicates that strategy and governance are not independently chosen by the decision-maker, and that there is a problem that emerges when individuals self-select a strategy that provides a better match with governance. However, we cannot observe the counterfactual choice; for example, if we observe one particular farmer who produces a certain volume of differentiated coffee, given that he had settled a formal contract with the coffee buyer, we cannot observe what would be his production (the volume of differentiated coffee or even a change in the commodity strategy) if he had chosen commercialization through the spot market. To reinforce the importance of endogeneity control, 'What is needed, therefore, is an approach that combines transaction-cost economics' insights regarding the selection of governance arrangements with strategy's orientation towards performance' (Masten, 1993, p. 120).

To correct for the endogeneity problems between governance and strategy choice, we can apply an endogenous switching regression method[4] (Hamilton and Nickerson, 2003). We propose an equation to predict the value for *Transaction–Governance choice* that will be introduced in another equation to explain *Strategy choice*. By considering that *Transaction–Governance choice* is a binary variable that takes the value 1 for formal

Table 11.2 Summary statistics and correlations

Variables	Mean	Std dev.	Min.	Max.	1	2	3	4	5	6	7	8	9	10	11	12	13
1 T-Governancechoice	0.067	0.250	0	1	1.000												
2 Strategy choice	31.395	130.759	0	1320	0.186** 0.001	1.000											
3 Differ. performance	22.555	11.627	0	80	−0.037 0.710	0.006 0.952	1.000										
4 Investment	0.180	1.549	0	25	0.039 0.506	0.178** 0.002	−0.039 0.697	1.000									
5 Education	0.521	0.500	0	1	−0.025 0.668	0.044 0.454	−0.181 0.072	0.075 0.207	1.000								
6 Experience	0.373	0.484	0	1	−0.065 0.295	0.091 0.143	0.210* 0.043	−0.020 0.743	0.063 0.312	1.000							
7 Family ties labor	105.869	243.948	1.012	971	0.022 0.708	0.001 0.988	0.068 0.504	−0.030 0.610	−0.046 0.440	0.007 0.906	1.000						
8 Relationship duration	12.568	9.546	0	50	0.049 0.409	0.117* 0.047	−0.089 0.376	−0.037 0.529	−0.003 0.960	0.079 0.200	0.023 0.692	1.000					
9 CPR	0.190	0.393	0	1	0.121* 0.041	0.037 0.526	0.036 0.720	−0.027 0.644	0.043 0.470	−0.094 0.129	0.005 0.922	−0.016 0.779	1.000				
10 Farm size	86.975	170.419	0	1500	0.233** 0.000	0.734** 0.000	0.041 0.680	0.267** 0.000	0.065 0.276	−0.004 0.945	0.052 0.384	0.175** 0.003	0.035 0.557	1.000			
11 Distance	58.597	148.841	0	1400	−0.075 0.206	−0.033 0.576	−0.028 0.780	−0.019 0.740	0.217** 0.000	−0.113 0.068	−0.049 0.412	0.060 0.314	0.029 0.620	−0.009 0.879	1.000		
12 Age of the owner	51.487	12.996	22	83	−0.060 0.313	−0.065 0.271	−0.111 0.272	−0.081 0.173	−0.068 0.249	−0.169** 0.006	0.052 0.380	0.259** 0.000	0.060 0.313	0.051 0.388	0.081 0.173	1.000	
13 Diversification	0.705	0.456	0	1	−0.105 0.076	−0.004 0.946	−0.275** 0.006	0.055 0.356	0.236** 0.000	−0.018 0.767	−0.091 0.126	0.133* 0.025	0.077 0.197	0.055 0.349	0.147* 0.013	0.089 0.133	1.000

Note: $**p < 0.01$; $*p < 0.05$.

contract or 0 for the spot market, we applied a probit regression. All the explanatory variables for *Strategy choice* were also introduced into the equation to predict *Transaction–Governance choice*. In addition, we introduced an instrumental variable that affects governance choice but does not directly impact strategy choice. The rural product credit note (*CPR*) is an appropriate instrumental variable for the following reasons.

The *CPR* is a mechanism to finance the activities on the farm by selling the production in advance. It was first created by the Bank of Brazil as an alternative way to raise funds when the producers' assets, such as land and equipment, are not available as credit salvage. Instead, future production is employed to guarantee payment of the credit. The *CPR* is a title recognized by the Brazilian government since 1994. With this support, farmers can negotiate competitive funds with banks, trading companies or roasting industries. The use of *CPR* as a financing mechanism is primarily related to the *Transaction–Governance choice* and is not related to *Strategy choice*. *CPR* explains the *Governance choice* because the farmer will be willing to set a contractual arrangement with the coffee buyer to trade the *CPR* to raise funds, or the bank that accepted the farmer's *CPR* may ask for a contract of sale with the coffee buyer. In the other case, if the farmer has other sources of financing, the use of a contract with coffee buyer depends on the farmer's wiliness to hedge the coffee price or to avoid the costs of contractual arrangements. *CPR* does not relate to *Strategy choice* because, independent of the farmer's choice for commodity or differentiation strategy, the use of *CPR* fits as an adequate instrument for financing. The amount of finance raised in a *CPR* is adequate to cover the operational costs (working capital) but is not relevant for investment decisions.

$$\Pr(\textit{Governance choice}) = \Phi \, (\beta_0 + \beta_1 \, \textit{Education} + \beta_2 \, \textit{Experience} + \beta_3 \, \textit{Family ties in labor market} + \beta_4 \, \textit{Relationship duration} + \beta_5 \, \textit{Farm size} + \beta_6 \, \textit{Investment} + \beta_7 \, \textit{Farmer age} + \beta_8 \, \textit{Distance} + \beta_9 \, \textit{Diversification} + \gamma_1 \, \textit{CPR}) \tag{11.1}$$

Where: $\Phi \, (.)$: cumulative normal distribution.

$$\textit{Strategy choice} = \beta_0 + \beta_1 \, \textit{Education} + \beta_2 \, \textit{Experience} + \beta_3 \, \textit{Family ties in labor market} + \beta_4 \, \textit{Relationship duration} + \beta_5 \, \textit{Farm size} + \beta_6 \, \textit{Investment} + \beta_7 \, \textit{Farmer age} + \beta_8 \, \textit{Distance} + \beta_9 \, \textit{Diversification} + \beta_{10} \, \textit{Mills ratio} + \varepsilon \tag{11.2}$$

This procedure is known as the switching regression model in labor econometrics. First, we estimate the reduced form of governance choice via probit, and construct the inverse *Mills ratio* terms. Second, we estimate the strategy-specific governance equations via Tobit regression, including the *Mills ratio* terms as regressors, to obtain unbiased estimates (Hamilton and Nickerson, 2003). The *Mills ratio* signal indicates a positive or negative selection. In this study, the *Mills ratio* < 0 is a positive selection into formal contract as the governance choice, and *Mills ratio* > 0 is a positive selection in the spot market chosen as the governance choice. Here, a positive selection indicates that the farmer produces more differentiated coffee (as a measure of differentiation strategy) than the average under formal contract governance. Alternatively, a positive selection means that the farmer is specialized in commodity production when the spot market is chosen as the governance choice. Considering the producers who had chosen the formal contract, if *Mills ratio* > 0, then a negative selection occurs and they may produce less differentiated coffee than the average. The residual (error term) in the proposed model might capture differences in the owner's ability that are not explained by formal education or by experience inherited from the family. Similarly, the residual might capture differences in the owner's social capital not explained by family ties or by relationship duration. In addition, the residual term may also capture differences in the owner's preference for any particular governance or strategy choice. The specified model does not control for regional differences, because it does not expect any geographically concentrated condition to explain the dependent variables, given the treatment of the sample before the analysis.

Another dependent variable is the performance of differentiation strategy, which is a measure of the price premium for differentiated coffee over commodity coffee, for each observation. This measure is left-censored because farmers who chose the commodity strategy will present zero value for the dependent variable, in contrast to any positive value for those who adopted a differentiation strategy. Hence the appropriate method of estimation is the Tobit regression.

$$\begin{aligned}
\textit{Differentiation performance} = {} & \beta_0 + \beta_1 \textit{ Education} + \beta_2 \textit{ Experience} + \beta_3 \textit{ Family ties in} \\
& \textit{labor market} + \beta_4 \textit{ Relationship duration} + \beta_5 \textit{ Farm} \\
& \textit{size} + \beta_6 \textit{ Investment} + \beta_7 \textit{ Farmer age} + \beta_8 \textit{ Distance} \\
& + \beta_9 \textit{ Diversification} + \beta_{10} \textit{ Governance choice} + \beta_{11} \\
& \textit{Strategy choice} + \varepsilon \qquad\qquad\qquad\qquad\qquad\qquad (11.3)
\end{aligned}$$

RESULTS

Probit and Tobit estimations for transaction–governance choice (model 1), strategy choice (models 2 and 3) and differentiation performance (model 4) are presented in Table 11.3. Model specifications control for endogeneity[5] between the governance choice and strategy choice, by applying the *Mills_ratio* (*Mills_ratio_1* = contract; *Mills_ratio_0* = spot market), estimated in model 1 as the endogenous governance choice for estimating the strategy choice. Estimation for governance choice considered all 255 observations, while for the strategy choice the sample was split into two subsamples as a part of the method. All the 89 farmers who adopted a differentiation strategy were considered in the estimation of performance. With respect to the governance–choice equation (model 1), it is important to note that the instrumental variable *CPR* (financial contract) is statistically significant ($p < 0.05$) and its positive value indicates that the use of *CPR* as a financing mechanism increases the farmer's adoption of a formal contract to govern the relation with coffee buyers. However, all human capital and social capital explanatory variables were not statistically significant with respect to transaction–governance choice. Regarding the control variables, *Age of the owner* ($p < 0.05$) indicates that older farmers adopted less formal contracts; *Distance* ($p < 0.05$) suggests that the further the owner lives from the farm, the less willing he will be to adopt a formal contract; and *Farm size* ($p < 0.10$) was weakly significant and positive, suggesting further adoption of contracts when the operation scale increases.

Table 11.3 Probit and Tobit results

Variables	Probit *Transaction–* *Governance choice* (1 = contract; 0 = spot market)	Tobit *Strategy choice* (0 = commodity; > 0 = degree of differentiation)		Tobit *Differentiation* *performance* (price premium for specialty)
	(1) β (std dev.)	(2) Contract β (std dev.)	(3) Spot market β (std dev.)	(4) β (std dev.)
Asset specificity				
Investment	0.313[†]	54.938*	88.131*	0.997
	(0.165)	(19.497)	(36.490)	(1.859)
Human capital				
Education	−0.251	165.180*	−3.033	−4.126[†]
	(0.254)	(55.838)	(25.245)	(2.143)
Experience	−0.364	−112.581	20.31	5.762**
	(0.303)	(59.798)	(25.929)	(2.119)
Social Capital				
Family ties in labor	0.463	0.436*	−0.095[†]	0.451
market	(0.546)	(0.138)	(0.054)	(6.212)
Relation. duration	0.110	−11.183[†]	2.411*	−0.127
	(0.141)	(5.278)	(1.202)	(0.113)
Instrumental var.				
CPR	0.541*			
	(0.215)			
Mills_ratio_1		−384.999**		
		(85.958)		
Mills_ratio_0			294.183[†]	
			(160.240)	
Controls				
Farm size	1.096[†]	0.714*	0.519***	0.019
	(0.619)	(0.213)	(0.081)	(0.013)
Distance	−3.311**	0.826	0.025	4.772
	(1.288)	(1.831)	(0.077)	(5.052)
Age of the owner	−0.020**	13.540[†]	−1.110	−0.058
	(0.008)	(6.483)	(1.136)	(0.086)
Diversification	−0.281	−318.388*	1.516	−2.854
	(0.305)	(105.618)	(27.028)	(2.370)
Contract				−10.728*
				(4.636)
Differentiation				−0.021
				(0.015)
Constant	−0.504[†]	−1261.461*	−125.333	26.964***
	(0.545)	(393.540)	(79.458)	(4.773)
Observations	255	16	239	89
Prob > χ^2	p<0.001	p<0.001	p<0.001	p<0.05
Pseudo R^2	0.154	0.295	0.076	0.030

Note: *** $p < 0.001$; ** $p < 0.01$; * $p < 0.05$; [†] $p < 0.10$.

We can observe that the asset specificity proxy, *Investment*, was positive and statistically significant ($p < 0.05$), which supported Hypothesis 1: the investment on tangible and transaction-specific resources necessary to pursue a differentiation strategy enhances the probability of adopting contracts. This finding was in agreement with previous studies (Klein et al., 1978; Masten, 1993, 2002). On the other hand, investments in formal education or experience from family background were not statistically significant to explain the adoption of contracts; thus our findings did not support Hypothesis 2. Although we are not aware of previous studies claiming this relation, we expected that human capital would contribute to the assessment of hazards that would directly justify the adoption of contracts (Williamson, 1999; March, 1978). Alternatively, we speculated that social capital would also contribute to prevent hazards from opportunism. However, none of the social capital proxies supported Hypothesis 6.

With respect to strategy-choice equations (models 2 and 3), it can be observed that *Mills_ratio* was statistically significant for strategy choice if contract ($p < 0.01$) or spot market ($p < 0.10$) was chosen (subsamples[6]). Moreover, one can observe a positive selection in the contract subsample (*Mills_ratio_1* < 0), which indicated that the farmer produces more specialty coffee (as a measure of differentiation strategy) than the average under formal contract governance. A positive selection also occurred in the spot-market subsample (*Mills_ratio_0* > 0). In this case, the farmer was specialized in commodity production when the spot market was chosen as the governance choice. In addition, we observed that some control variables were statistically significant. *Farm size* can be observed to be positive and statistically significant in model 2 ($p < 0.05$) and in model 3 ($p < 0.001$), indicating a direct relationship of scale of operation and adoption of differentiation strategy. Furthermore, it was observed that *Age of the owner* was weakly significant ($p < 0.10$) while *Diversification* was statistically significant in model 2 ($p < 0.05$); its negative coefficient suggests that farmers with diversified economic activity have fewer propensities to pursue a differentiation strategy, even under the protection of contracts.

Education was the only proxy for human capital with statistical significance in the estimation of strategy choice, especially when contract was chosen (model 2). Thus Hypothesis 3, stating that a high level of human capital, comprising investments in formal education, is associated with more adoption of differentiation strategy was partially supported, because *Education* indicated significant influence on strategy choice only when contract was chosen (model 2). This result suggests that investments in formal education (Becker, 1964) help the identification and evaluation of new opportunities for profit. Although we have predicted that families would deal with suboptimal decisions (Mosakowski, 2002; Tripsas and Gavetti, 2000; Leonard-Barton, 1992) due to inertia effects, our results were not conclusive; thus Hypothesis 4 was not supported. All the social capital proxies were statistically significant in the estimations of strategy choice. The variable *Family ties in labor market* was positive and statistically significant ($p < 0.05$) in explaining the differentiation strategy when contract was chosen (model 2). Although we found a negative coefficient for the *Family ties in labor market* proxy, it was weakly significant ($p < 0.10$) in explaining the strategy when the spot market was chosen. Our findings are consistent with the idea that socially connected farmers have the advantage of cooperation to establish contracts (Uzzi, 1997), refine the terms of the contract, and promote its stability. This supported the Hypothesis 7: high social capital, comprising a number of connections in the labor market, is associated with the adoption of a differentiation strategy when contracts are established. *Relationship duration* was observed to be positive and statistically significant to explain strategy adoption when the spot market was chosen (model 3). Similar to our findings on *Family ties in labor market*, *Relationship duration* had a negative but weakly significant ($p < 0.10$) coefficient in the estimation of differentiation adoption when the contract was chosen (model 2). Our findings suggest that farmers with an enduring relationship economized on the costs of designing, negotiating and establishing contracts by adopting spot-market governance. Thus, this supported Hypothesis 8: high social capital, comprising the duration of relationship to the buyer, is associated with the adoption of a differentiation strategy when the spot market is chosen.

Differentiation performance was estimated in model 4. The Tobit regression estimated the price premium achieved by a farmer who pursued a differentiation strategy. Although there are data and measurement constraints to compare a low-cost versus differentiation strategy, this estimation provided helpful insights considering human capital proxies.

The positive and strongly significant coefficient ($p < 0.01$) for *Experience* suggested that a farmer with higher experience from family background achieves a higher premium price for specialty coffee. However, the negative coefficient for *Education* indicated the opposite, although it was weakly significant ($p < 0.10$). These findings partially supported Hypothesis 5: a high level of human capital, comprising investments in formal education and experience from a family background, is associated with a higher price premium owing to a differentiation strategy. The effects of *Experience*, the proxy for human capital with a stronger and positive effect on performance, was in agreement with earlier studies on the family as a repository of valuable firm-specific knowledge (Hatch and Dyer, 2004; Kor and Mahoney, 2004; Kor et al., 2007), which supports better use of resources (Mahoney and Pandian, 1992) and accurate estimations from judgments (Masten, 1993). Moreover, the experience from generation to generation provides a competitive advantage over non-family firms (Lane and Lubatkin, 1998) when family members promote extraordinary commitment (Donnelley, 1964) and intimate relationships (Horton, 1986).

Contract presented a negative and significant coefficient in model 4. This finding suggested that adoption of contract leads to lower prices when compared with spot-market governance, although we have applied a cross-sectional analysis that prevents us from considering a persistence of this effect over time. By assuming this limitation, our results indicated that some 'price is paid' when setting a contract that reflected the lower price premium compared to the premium achieved under spot-market governance.

Considering the results on differentiation strategy performance (model 4), we identified that *Experience* supported a higher price premium while *Education* and *Contract* lead to conservative performance. The lower price for specialty coffee may reflect a cost for establishing contracts, although we are not aware of previous studies that associate higher education and conservative performance. Hypothesis 9, that social capital would support a higher price premium, was not supported by model 4. According to Weisz and Vassolo (2004), entrepreneurs who are highly connected to family members fail to choose the adequate business partners, and these suboptimal decisions explained more failure of nascent business in the Argentine context. With regard to coffee producers, the close proximity to the coffee buyer may have resulted in a suboptimal price premium.

LIMITATIONS

To accomplish the task of integrating transaction-cost economics, the resource-based view, strategy, human capital and social capital theory, we made many simplifications. By considering the linking of human capital, social capital and the resource-based view, we limited the discussion of resources to exploitation (e.g. firms choose strategies that effectively exploit the existing human capital and social capital), while previous studies (Lovas and Ghoshal, 2000; Wernerfelt, 1984; Dierickx and Cool, 1989) have addressed concerns on the creation of resources (in this case, firms facilitate the development of new, valuable human capital and social capital). We assumed no role for the mobility of people carrying human capital and social capital across the firms, from firms to market, or coordination of this flow by any governance structure (Conner and Prahalad, 1996); however, we believe that these concerns were ameliorated on a mature technology industry, such as the production of coffee. Regarding strategic positioning, we simplified the strategies around two discrete options, although Porter (1998) predicted an intermediary alternative, which is the focus of generic competitive strategy. Although transaction-cost economics analyzes the specificity of the assets, frequency and uncertainty (Williamson, 1985) involved in a certain transaction to predict the appropriate governance structure, we focused our attention on the first attribute – in fact, many studies relied on asset specificity. We made no distinction on contract duration (Joskow, 1987) and frequency of transaction. Moreover, we assumed the emergence of trust in direct association to relationship duration, a simplification that reduces the role of the sociological dynamics (Burt, 1992; Coleman, 1990). In addition, our analysis ignored the institutional effects (Williamson, 1999), which Mesquita and Lazzarini (2008) investigated on emerging economies to conclude that firms strengthen informal ties to overcome transaction hazards and the lack of strong institutional settings.

We have made a number of simplifications to our measures. As we initially addressed in this chapter, our constrained measure of performance was an effort to overcome the challenges of obtaining objective proxies (Acqaah, 2007). Our measures on human capital and social capital had their limitations. Although we identified the farmer's level of formal education, we were not able to distinguish the quality of the school. In this respect, D'Aveni (1989) suggested that people who graduated from prestigious universities have access to privileged networks, in addition to the high quality of education. Our measures on social capital suffered from simplifications from the concepts of Burt (1992), Bourdieu (1985) and Coleman (1990). Moreover, our measures on social capital had limitations to capture the effects of cooperatives,[7] assistance bureaux and other agents that may constitute the farmer's social relationships. We acknowledge the limitations of our measures; our aim was to incorporate human and social capital theory into the analysis of the triadic decisions of governance, resource and strategy.

FINAL REMARKS

The debate about family contributions to the business is central to the current literature on family business. We accessed a unique data set to investigate how the decision to change strategy was influenced by the family's human and social capital. We estimated the probability of changing strategy by applying appropriate methods to control for endogenous effects of strategy choice and transaction–governance choice. Our findings on the probabilities provided helpful insights for family business, entrepreneurship and the strategy field of research.

Family businesses with previous generations in the same business presented a superior performance compared to first-generation businesses. Second or earlier generations may take advantage of some specific knowledge about the business, knowledge that would be hard to codify or transmit through a formal education process. This finding challenges the education programs to encourage development and entrepreneurship programs. How to transmit relevant knowledge to ensure the success of entrepreneurs new to a particular business? Considering the family business field, our results reinforced the positive effect of families to the business. We do not neglect the potential negative effects of inertia to strategy or resistance to change, but we found that most of the investigated families have overcome them. While we have estimated the contribution of generational experience to the business, we encourage future research to shed light on the mechanisms by which families deal with resistance to change and how they evaluate their experience. Indeed, strategy scholars could consider the generational experience as a valuable resource, or how a family has the discretionary knowledge to adjust resources over time to pursue new opportunities for profit.

We have investigated the level of education as another proxy for human capital. Our findings supported the hypotheses that well-educated entrepreneurs presented more propensities to change strategy. Education increases the capacity of entrepreneurs to evaluate scenarios, to recognize opportunities and risks. In fact, well-educated entrepreneurs also achieved a conservative performance on price premium.

While generational experience is embedded into the family organization, investment in education is an opportunity to increase the human capital of potentially all family businesses. An additional analysis of the interaction variables between both human capital proxies (unreported results) investigated the compensation effects (Boxman et al., 1991; Coleman, 1988), for instance whether a lack of experience inherited from the family could be compensated by investments in formal education. However, the results were not conclusive, despite the complexity of handling multiple equations and controlling for endogeneity. We estimated to what extent higher education increases the probability for a family business to change strategy and we also concluded that experience from a family background helps in achieving superior performance. Additionally, we suggest future research to investigate the compensating effects of education and experience from a family background due to strategy change and performance of the business.

Our measures on social capital reported significant results to explain the probability of switching strategy. We found that family businesses inserted into a context of high family ties in the labor market presented a higher probability to strategy change. Although our proxy captures a regional labor-market effect and not the specific number of connections for each family business, this result supported the idea that these families may access important resources such as information, the sharing of opportunity and risk assessment with their peers in a regional context. We do not neglect the importance of the number of social connections or their strength, but we found helpful insights when the regional context of family ties was investigated.

The other proxy for social capital was the duration of the relationship between the business owner and its main commercial partner. Enduring relationships allowed the agents to trade on the spot market and, thus, they economized on the costs of negotiating, designing and enforcing contracts. Moreover, in these cases, the family businesses presented more probability to change strategy. However, when contracts where chosen to govern an enduring relationship, the probability of switching strategy was reduced. This finding suggests that the family businesses became embedded in one particular relationship that prevented the seeking of new opportunities, which is consistent with previous literature on networks. Indeed, it adds to the discussion on transaction–governance choice, as the optimal governance arrangement would be the one that economizes on transaction costs and keeps the flexibility to engage into new strategies. Still in the transaction–governance perspective, it is worth noting that more use of contracts was found in the presence of specific investments, as predicted by the transaction-cost economics literature.

In conclusion, we argue that the family's human and social capital assessment provided a helpful framework by exploring its relationships to strategy change and to business performance. We encourage future research to consider the family's decision to invest in education, to take advantage from generational experience and to nurture social ties.

NOTES

1. We are aware that environmental resources and geographically concentrated and particular social conditions may explain the choice for other types of differentiated coffee, such as 'fair trade'. However, this is not the case for special coffee differentiated by the quality of the drink, which includes attributes of aroma, taste and flavor.
2. See Flören (2002, pp. 17–22) for an extensive discussion on the various definitions of family business. Definitions are aggregated into categories of: generational transfer, interdependent subsystems, multiple exclusive, voting control, family management, family ownership, multiple inclusive, family employment and ownership-management.
3. To be precise, Uzzi (1997) investigates two forms of exchange in the New York City apparel industry: 'arm's-length ties' close related to a spot-market arrangement, and 'embedded ties', closely related to relational contracts (Poppo and Zenger, 2002).
4. See Hamilton and Nickerson (2003) for a detailed treatment of the endogeneity problem, including the *Mills ratio*, instrumental variable choice and switching procedures.
5. Considering that Strategy choice and Transaction–Governance choice could be simultaneous decisions, we tested the seemingly unrelated regression (SUR) as the method of estimation, but the results indicated no significant correlation between the error terms of the equations.
6. We noticed the few observations to test *Strategy choice* (second equation) when the farmer had chosen 'formal contract' as the *Governance choice* (first equation). Alternatively, we tried another model by introducing the predicted *Governance choice* (*Governance HAT*) in the second equation considering all the observations, but the findings were similar to models that do not control for endogeneity.
7. Important remark: we accessed the coffee producers through cooperatives and associations. We tried the measures on a number of cooperatives and associations related to the coffee farmer, size of the cooperatives and associations, and proxies for the relevance of these organizations; however, none of them were promising.

REFERENCES

Acqaah, Moses (2007), 'Managerial social capital, strategic orientation, and organization performance in an emerging economy', *Strategic Management Journal*, **28**, 1235–55.
Adler, Paul S. and Kwon, Seok-Woo (2002), 'Social capital: prospects for a new concept', *Academy of Management Review*, **27**, 17–40.

Allen, Douglas W. and Lueck, Dean (1998), 'The nature of the farm', *Journal of Law and Economics*, **41**(2), 343–86.

Aronoff, Craig E. and Ward, John L. (1995), 'Family-owned businesses: a thing of the past or a model of the future?', *Family Business Review*, **8**(2), 121–30.

Arrègle, Jean-Luc et al. (2007), 'The development of organizational social capital: attributes of family firms', *Journal of Management Studies*, **44**(1), 74–95.

Baker, George et al. (2002), 'Relational contracts and the theory of the firm', *Quarterly Journal of Economics*, **117** (1), 39–84.

Barney, Jay B. (1991), 'Firm resources and sustained competitive advantage', *Journal of Management*, **17**(1), 99–120.

Bates, Timothy (1990), 'Entrepreneur human capital inputs and small business longevity', *The Review of Economics and Statistics*, **LXXII**(4), 551–9.

Becker, Gary S. (1964), *Human Capital: A Theoretical and Empirical Analysis, with Special Reference to Education*, 3rd edn, Chicago, IL: University of Chicago Press, 1993.

Becker, Gary S. and Tomes, Nigel (1986), 'Human capital and the rise and fall of families', *Journal of Labor Economics*, **4**(3), 1–39.

Bourdieu, P. (1985), 'The forms of capital', in J.G. Richardson (ed.), *Handbook of Theory and Research for the Sociology of Education*, New York: Greenwood, pp. 241–58.

Boxman, Ed A.W. et al. (1991), 'The impact of social and human capital on the income attainment of Dutch managers', *Social Networks*, **13**, 51–73.

Burt, Ronald, S. (1992), *Structural Holes: The Social Structure of Competition*, Cambridge, MA: Harvard University Press.

Chaddad, Fabio Ribas and Boland, Michael (2007), 'Cooxupé and the world coffee industry: strategies to increase producer income', *Case Studies Ibmec São Paulo*.

Coase, Ronald H. (1991), 'The nature of the firm', *Economica*, N.S. 386–405. Originally published in Oliver E. Williamson and S. Winter (eds), *The Nature of the Firm: Origins, Evolution, Development*, New York: Oxford University Press, 1937, pp. 18–33.

Coleman, James, S. (1988), 'Social capital in the creation of human capital', *American Journal of Sociology*, **94**, S95–S120.

Coleman, James S. (1990), *Foundations of Social Theory*, Cambridge, MA: Belknap Press.

Conner, Kathleen R. and Prahalad, C.K. (1996), 'A resource-based theory of the firm: knowledge versus opportunism', *Organization Science*, **7**(5), 477–501.

Danes, Sharon, M. et al. (2009), 'Family capital of family firms: bridging human, social and financial capital', *Family Business Review*, **22**(3), 199–215.

D'Aveni, Richard A. (1989), 'The aftermath of organizational decline: a longitudinal study of the strategic and managerial characteristics of declining firms', *Academy of Management Journal*, **32**, 577–605.

Dierickx, Ingemar and Cool, Karel (1989), 'Asset stock accumulation and sustainability of competitive advantage', *Management Science*, **35**(12), 1504–11.

Ding, Hung-bin and Abetti, Pier A. (2002), 'The entrepreneurial success of Taiwan: synergy between technology, social capital and institutional support', in Gary D. Libecap (ed.), *Advances in the Study of Entrepreneurship, Innovation and Economic Growth: Issues in Entrepreneurship, Contracts, Corporate Characteristics and Country Differences*, Oxford: Elsevier, pp. 91–123.

Donnelley, Robert, G. (1964), 'The family business', *Harvard Business Review*, **42**(2), 93–105.

Dunn, Barbara (1995), 'Success themes in Scottish family enterprises: philosophies and practices through the generations', *Family Business Review*, **8**(1), 17–28.

Farjoun, Moshe (1994), 'Beyond industry boundaries: human expertise, diversification and resource-related industry groups', *Organization Science*, **5**(2), 185–99.

Flören, Roberto, H. (2002), *Crown Princes in the Clay: An Empirical Study on the Tackling of Succession Challenges in Dutch Family Farms*, Assen: Van Gorcum.

Ghosh, Mrinal and John, George (1999), 'Governance value analysis and marketing strategy', *Journal of Marketing*, **63**, 131–45.

Gibbons, Robert and Waldman, Michael (2004), 'Task-specific human capital', *AEA Papers and Proceedings*, **94**(2), 203–7.

Habbershon, Timothy G. and Williams, Mary L.A. (1999), 'Resource-based framework for assessing the strategic advantages of family firms', *Family Business Review*, **12**(1), 1–26.

Hamilton, Bart and Nickerson, Jackson A. (2003), 'Correcting for endogeneity in strategic management research', *Strategic Organization*, **1**(1), 53–80.

Harrington, Brooke (2001), 'Organizational performance and corporate social capital: a contingency model', in Shaul M. Gabbay et al. (eds), *Research in the Sociology of Organizations: Social Capital of Organizations*, Oxford: Elsevier, pp. 83–106.

Hatch, Nile W. and Dyer, Jeffrey H. (2004), 'Human capital and learning as a source of sustainable competitive advantage', *Strategic Management Journal*, **25**, 1155–78.

Hitt, Michael, A. et al. (2001), 'Direct and moderating effects of human capital on strategy and performance in professional service firms: a resource-based perspective', *Academy of Management Journal*, **44**(1), 13–28.

Hoffman, James et al. (2006), 'Achieving sustained competitive advantage: a family capital theory', *Family Business Review*, **19**(2), 135–45.

Horton, T.R. (1986), 'Managing in a family way', *Management Review*, **75**(2), 3.

Joskow, Paul, L. (1987), 'Contract duration and relationship-specific investments: empirical evidence from coal markets', *The American Economic Review*, **77**(1), 168–85.

Keef, Dennis R. and Burk, Marguerite C. (1967), 'Interdisciplinary analysis of farm–home interrelationships and decision-making and action on the family farm', *The American Journal of Economics and Sociology*, **26**(1), 33–46.

Klein, Benjamin et al. (1978), 'Vertical integration, appropriable rents, and the competitive contracting process', *Journal of Law & Economics*, **21**(2), 297–326.

Kor, Yasemin Y. and Mahoney, Joseph T. (2004), 'Edith Penrose's (1959) contributions to the resource-based view of strategic management', *Journal of Management Studies*, **41**(1), 183–91.

Kor, Yasemin Y. et al. (2007), 'Resources, capabilities and entrepreneurial perceptions', *Journal of Management Studies*, **44**(7), 1187–212.

Laband, David N. (1984), 'Restriction of farm ownership as rent-seeking behavior: family farmers have it their way', *American Journal of Economics and Sociology*, **43**(2), 179–89.

Laird, P.W. (2006), *Pull: Networking and Success since Benjamin Franklin*, Cambridge: Cambridge University Press.

Lane, Peter J. and Lubatkin, Michael (1998), 'Relative absorptive capacity and interoganizational learning', *Strategic Management Journal*, **19**(5), 461–77.

Leonard-Barton, Dorothy (1992), 'Core capabilities and core rigidities', *Strategic Management Journal*, **13**, 111–25.

Lovas, Bjorn and Ghoshal, Sumatra (2000), 'Strategy as guided evolution', *Strategic Management Journal*, **21**(9), 875–96.

Mahoney, Joseph T. and Pandian, J. Rajendran (1992), 'The resource-based view within the conversation of strategic management', *Strategic Management Journal*, **13**(5), 363–80.

March, James G. (1978), 'Bounded rationality, ambiguity, and the engineering of choice', *The Bell Journal of Economics*, **9**(2), 587–608.

Masten, Scott E. (1993), 'Transaction costs, mistakes, and performance: assessing the importance of governance', *Managerial and Decision Economics*, **14**, 119–29.

Masten, Scott E. (2000), 'Transaction-cost economics and the organizations of agricultural transactions', *Industrial Organization*, **9**, 173–95.

Masten, Scott E. et al. (1989), 'Vertical integration in the U.S. auto industry: a note on the influence of transaction specific assets', *Journal of Economic Behavior and Organization*, **12**, 265–73.

Mesquita, Luiz F. and Lazzarini, Sergio Giovanetti (2008), 'Horizontal and vertical relationships in developing economies: implications for SMEs' access to global markets', *Academy of Management*, **51**(2), 359–80.

Mosakowski, Elaine (2002), 'Overcoming resource disadvantages in entrepreneurial firms: when less is more', in Michael A. Hitt et al. (eds), *Strategic Entrepreneurship: Creating a New Integrated Mindset*, Oxford: Blackwell Publishing, pp. 106–26.

Murphy, Fran et al. (2008), 'Entrepreneurial risk behavior in family firms: a family influence perspective', *Proceedings of the Academy of Management*.

Nahapiet, Janine and Ghoshal, Sumatra (1998), 'Social capital, intellectual capital, and the organization advantage', *Academy of Management Review*, **23**(2), 242–66.

Nickerson, Jackson A. et al. (2001), 'Market position, resource profile, and governance: linking Porter and Williamson in the context of international courier and small package services in Japan', *Strategic Management Journal*, **22**, 251–71.

Penrose, Edith. T. (1959), *The Theory of the Growth of the Firm*, 3rd edn, New York: John Wiley.

Peteraf, Margaret (1993), 'The cornstones of competitive advantage: a resource-based view', *Strategic Management Journal*, **14**(3), 179–91.

Poppo, Laura and Zenger, Todd (2002), 'Do formal contracts and relational governance unction as substitutes or complements?', *Strategic Management Journal*, **23**(8), 707–25.

Porter, Michael E. (1991), 'Towards a dynamic theory of strategy', *Strategic Management Journal*, Special Issue: Fundamental Research Issues in Strategy and Economics, **12**, 95–117.

Porter, Michael E. (1994), 'Toward a dynamic theory of strategy', in Richard Rumelt et al., *Fundamental Research Issues in Strategy: A Research Agenda*, Boston, MA: Harvard Business School Press, pp. 423–61.

Porter, Michael E. (1998), *Competitive Strategy: Techniques for Analyzing Industries and Competitors*, New York: The Free Press.

Prahalad, C.K. and Hamel, Gary (1990), 'The core competence of the corporation', *Harvard Business Review*, **1**, 79–91.

Rauch, A. et al. (2005), 'Effects of human capital and long-term human resources development and utilization on employment growth of small-scale businesses: a causal analysis', *Entrepreneurship Theory and Practice*, **29**(6), 681–98.

Saes, Maria Sylvia Macchione (2005), 'Relational contracts and comparative efficiency in the Brazilian specialty coffee supply', in *International Society for New Institutional Economics*, Barcelona: International Society for New Institutional Economics.

Saes, Maria Sylvia M. (2010), 'Strategies for differentiation and quasi-rent appropriation in agriculture: the small-scale production', São Paulo: Editora Annablume.

Salvato, Carlo and Melin, Leif (2008), 'Creating value across generations in family-controlled businesses: the role of family social capital', *Family Business Review*, **11**(3), 259–76.

Schultz, Theodore W. (1961), 'Investment in human capital', *The American Economic Reviews*, **51**(1), 1–17.

Schultz, Theodore W. (1982), 'Investment in entrepreneurial ability', *Sandinavian Journal of Economics*, **82**(4), 437–88.

Shane, Scott and Stuart, Toby (2002), 'Organizational endowments and the performance of university start-ups', *Management Science*, **48**(1), 154–70.

Shaver, J. Myles (1998), 'Accounting for endogeneity when assessing strategy performance: does entry mode choice affect FDI survival?', *Management Science*, **44**(4), 571–85.

Simon, Herbert, A. (1987), 'Making management decisions: the role of intuition and emotion', *The Academy of Management Executive*, **1**(1), 57–64.

Simon, Herbert A. (1993), 'Strategy and organizational evolution', *Strategic Management Journal*, **14**, 131–42.

Sirmon, David G. and Hitt, Michael, A. (2003), 'Managing resources: linking unique resources, management, and wealth creation in family firms', *Entrepreneurship Theory and Practice*, **27**(4), 339–58.

Tagiuri, Renato and Davis, John, A. (1996), 'Bivalent attributes of the family firm', *Family Business Review*, **9**(2), 199–208.

Teece, David, J. et al. (1997), 'Dynamic capabilities and strategic management', *Strategic Management Journal* (1986–1998), **18**(7), 509–33.

Tripsas, Mary and Gavetti, Giovanni (2000), 'Capabilities, cognition & inertia: evidence from digital imaging', *Strategic Management Journal*, **21** (special issue), 1147–62.

Uzzi, Brian (1997), 'Social structure and competition in interfirm networks: the paradox of embeddedness', *Administrative Science Quarterly*, **42** (1), 35–67.

Walker, Gordon et al. (1997), 'Social capital, structural holes and the formation of an industry network', *Organization Science*, **8**(2), 109–25.

Ward, John, L. (1988), 'The special role of strategic planning for family businesses', *Family Business Review*, **1**(2), 105–17.

Weisz, Natalia and Vassole, Roberto S. (2004), 'O capital social des equipes empreendedoras nascentes', *Revista de Administra fão dwe Empresas*, **4**(2), 26–37.

Wernerfelt, Birger (1984), 'A resource-based view of the firm', *Strategic Management Journal*, **5**(2), 171–80.

Williamson, Oliver E. (1985), *The Economic Institutions of Capitalism*, New York: The Free Press.

Williamson, Oliver E. (1999), 'Strategy research: governance and competence perspectives', *Strategic Management Journal*, **20**(12), 1087–108.

Williamson, Oliver E. (2002), 'The theory of the firm as governance structure: from choice to contract', *Journal of Economic Perspectives*, **16**(3), 171–95.

12 Towards a comprehensive model of sustainable family firm performance

Sihem Ben Mahmoud-Jouini, Alain Bloch and Sophie Mignon

The recent crisis has shown the potential flaws in an economic and financial system functioning solely in the interests of short-term efficiency. In the current climate of debate and questioning of modern capitalism principles, sustainable family firms (SFFs) offer several insights into company management. Certain characteristics specific to SFFs, such as long-term success, the concentration of share ownership, the search for reliability as well as intra- and inter-organizational relations are worth analysing more closely. They could indicate a currently very fashionable capacity to integrate business development into the notion of sustainability.

Considering the important role of SFFs in the economy, our aim is therefore to offer a framework to enhance the understanding of their performance. They represent a significant proportion of economic activity and offer a potential model for the development of other businesses which, while lacking intrinsic family characteristics, would do well to draw inspiration from them. Hence the framework we suggest will be useful for practitioners either operating within family business or not. Furthermore, it will offer scholars an innovative way to think about SFFs because the framework tends to mobilize concepts that were suggested in management research but have not been specifically applied to the case of family business so far.

We shall begin by specifying what we mean by family firm. We should point out that the criteria for defining what constitutes a family firm as well as the various questions it raises are many and varied (Sharma, 2004; Carney, 2005; Miller and Le Breton-Miller, 2005). Should such a definition be based on a limited or rather a broad notion of the family? Can a firm be considered a family firm as from the first generation? What is meant by family control? We will retain the generic definition proposed by Allouche and Amann (2008):

> A family firm is one in which one or several members of the same extended family or several families significantly influence its development through ownership of its capital, placing the emphasis on family ties with regard to the process for selecting company directors, whether they be family members or recruited externally, and expressing a desire to transmit the business to the next generation while understanding the importance of the business for the interests and objectives of the family.

This definition emphasizes the sustainable dimension of the business, characterized by the desire to transmit the patrimony it represents from one generation to another, in addition to the presence of the family.

Hence, as mentioned earlier, we are interested in enhancing the understanding of this sustainability considered as the main performance indicator of family business. The lit-

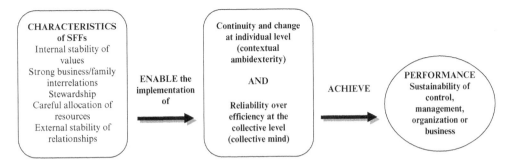

Figure 12.1 A framework for SFF performance

erature, as presented below, shows a wide variety of meanings for this concept: sustainability of control, of management, of business or of organization. Nevertheless, whatever type it is, a common attribute of these meanings is that sustainability is about adaptation and durability of the organization. How do family firms achieve this performance?

In order to shed new light on this question and renew the approach, we intend to mobilize two concepts suggested in the management literature addressing the performance of the firms and focusing on their adaptation through their life cycle: the ambidextrous organization (AO) concept put forward by Duncan (1976) and popularized by Tushman and O'Reilly (1997) and the high reliability organization (HRO) concept proposed by Weick and Roberts (1993). We argue that these concepts, presented below, can renew the sustainability notion and shed new light on it. The research developed on these concepts led to the identification of organizational attributes that enable the achievement of performance drivers such as the pursuit of conflicting demands like continuity and change or adaptation and stability in the case of AO or the pursuit of reliability over efficiency when facing unforeseen events in the case of HRO. The framework we suggest, as summarized in Figure 12.1, is based on a literature review that shows that the characteristics of sustainable family firms match these organizational attributes. This matching suggests an understanding of the sustainability source of SFFs: considering their characteristics, they have the ability to acheive ambidexterity and to pursue reliability leading to their sustainability.

The following sections will address the various components of the framework.

1 DIVERSITY OF THE CONCEPT OF SUSTAINABILITY

Sustainability immediately appears to constitute one of the fundamental characteristics of family firms and one for which their directors strive. As we shall see below, while by no means contradictory to short-term performance, sustainability constitutes the primary objective of the controlling family entity (Olson et al., 2003; Bloch et al., 2012).

However, such a theme would appear at first glance to cover a vast field of study symbolizing the very purpose of management itself, that is, the ability to create and sustain a business project (Bréchet, 1994). Paradoxically, works dealing specifically and directly with this theme are relatively rare, even if this sustainability is present implicitly: in the strategic intentions of company directors, in the speeches expressing such intentions, in the business theories underpinning them and in the conceptual frameworks supporting them. On the other hand, observation of the life span of firms shows us that non-sustainability would seem to be the rule and sustainability rather the exception.

In reality, observing sustainability raises the question of time scale: from what point can we say that a firm is sustainable?

INSEE studies[1] on the survival rates of businesses in France reveal that 65.9 per cent of companies created in 2005/6 survived for more than three years. Moreover, only a handful of companies are still around 30, 60 or even 100 years after their creation. A few famous firms such as Berretta, St Gobain and L'Oréal are among the most notable examples.

Out of the 'top 100' industrial firms listed by the American magazine *Fortune* in 1965, only 19 still exist in 2005 (Burgelman and Grove, 2007, p. 965).[2]

The various studies carried out on the subject concur that the average life span of a company is between 15 and 20 years (Collins and Porras, 2005; De Rooij, 1996; Lesourne and Stoffaës, 2001). We can therefore propose a chronological definition of the concept of sustainability as beyond 50 years of existence. As regards control, studies on the subject (Lank, 1992; Neubauer and Lank, 1998; Ward, 1997) have shown that only 15 per cent of firms surviving beyond the first five years of existence remain family firms up until the third generation. The many pitfalls characterizing the difficult transfer of power between the first, second and in particular the third generation have led us to select this additional criterion in order to define sustainability. In practice, the choice of a threshold of 50 years of existence also means that if a firm has remained a family firm, it must have demonstrated the ability to generate at least one succession.

Beyond this chronological definition, the diversity of points of view expressed by top managers questioned with regard to the definition of this term makes it possible to distinguish two major types of sustainability (Mignon, 2001):

1   The *sustainability of power*: this covers two sorts of sustainability:
    - *sustainability of ownership control* is ensured if the capital remains in the hands of the same group of shareholders (usually an individual or family);
    - *management sustainability* is achieved if the company directors belong to this same group.
2   The *sustainability of the project*: this also covers two sorts of sustainability:
    - *business sustainability* is ensured if the main business of the company is maintained despite, for example, the disappearance of the company as an autonomous entity and the breakdown of family ownership;[3]
    - *sustainability of the organization* is preserved if the company manages, throughout its life, to initiate or deal with internal or external upheavals while preserving the fundamental aspects of its identity up to the present day.

Of course, those heads of family firms who wish to render their company sustainable are for the most part concerned with sustainability of control and/or management, even if in some cases the purely patrimonial dimension is of primary importance to them.

However, sustainability of control cannot in itself be envisaged without the company's capacity to endure on one or several markets as, at the end of the day, it is this factor that will enable the survival of the company. This requires adaptation in order to preserve or create competitive advantage. Therefore, in family firms, sustainability of control very often involves pursuit of organizational longevity (Collins and Porras, 2005; De Geus, 1997; Mignon, 2001, 2009).

In this sense, the definition provided by Chua et al. (1999) is particularly representative as it includes the search for sustainability as a criterion for defining the family nature of a firm: 'We define family business as a business governed and/or managed on a sustainable, potentially cross-generational basis'.

Hence a sustainable company has to find a way to reconcile a major contradiction: that of having to both evolve while preserving its identity, of being able to seriously challenge itself while respecting its fundamental values, of being able to innovate and acquire new knowledge while at the same time exploiting existing skills. Finding how to achieve a balance between these competing orientations seems to be a key factor in analysing sustainability.

2   THE CULTURAL CHARACTERISTICS OF SUSTAINABLE FAMILY FIRMS

Based on the works of Ward (1997), Sharma (2004), Habbershon and Blank (2005), Chua et al. (1999), Arrègle et al. (2004) and Miller and Le Breton-Miller (2005), we propose to characterize the culture of SFFs based on the following five characteristics: (1) the internal stability of values; (2) the density of family–enterprise interrelations; (3) the emotional involvement of the family in the management; (4) risk management by the careful allocation of resources; and (5) the external stability of relationships.

2.1   Internal Stability of Values

A culture consists of beliefs, values, norms, traditions and so on, shared by all members of the organization (Hall et al., 2001). The transmission of these beliefs and values from one generation to another generates relatively stable cultural characteristics within both the family and the family business. These strong values are often based on the personal ethics of the directors, characterized by devotion, responsibility, a capacity for work and a sense of success (Macombe, 2003).

These values are the result of a historical process during which they are gradually accepted and internalized by members of the company. Durability therefore seems to be acquired thanks to a balance between innovation, tradition and the long-term vision of the company directors (Koiranen, 2002). This internalization of 'family standards', characterized by the same belief system and the same manner of extracting meaning from a shared experience, has several consequences: it favours the development of a set of reciprocal obligations and expectations, it dissuades potential behavioural slip-ups and it leads to the standardization of behaviour and coordination based on trust.

2.2   Strong and Dense Business/Family Interrelations

According to Hoffman et al. (2006), the close links within the family network constitute one of the fundamental aspects of family capital. They also constitute one of the characteristics of 'familiness', according to Habbershon et al. (2003), Tokarczyk et al. (2007) and Pearson et al. (2008). The family business is seen as a system composed of (i) a family subsystem based on the history and traditions of the family life cycle; (ii) a company subsystem including the strategies and structures put in place to create value; and (iii) a subsystem composed of individuals and family members characterized by their interests, aptitudes and degree of participation in the process of control and management. 'Familiness is defined as the unique bundle of resources a particular firm has because of the systems interaction between the family, its individual members and the business' (Habbershon and Williams, 1999, p. 11).

Given the positions occupied and roles performed by family members working in the family business, a transfer 'of certain "family spirit" characteristics to the business' (Arrègle et al., 2004, p. 22) takes place and consequently also an entrenchment of the management of the family business in the behaviour and ways of thinking of the family at the origin of the business.

2.3   Stewardship: Emotional Involvement of the Family in the Management

Investment by company directors/shareholders is emotional in nature as their wealth, personal satisfaction and reputation are closely linked to their business. Directors-owners of family firms are motivated by a certain sense of altruism and by a collective and long-term vision: stewardship (Davis et al., 1997; Greenwood, 2003; Miller and Le Breton-Miller, 2006; Le Bretton-Miller and Miller, 2008; Gómez-Mejía et al., 2007). Stewardship is characterized by identification with the organization and its goals, a personal commitment by the director to the company's success at the cost of significant personal sacrifice, and motivation to act for the best and for the collective and long-term interest of the shareholders, employees and stakeholders of the company (Miller and Le Breton-Miller, 2006). Several obstacles may nonetheless complicate the relationship between shareholders and directors (Schulze et al., 2001, 2003): shortsightedness (lack of vision with regard to the long-term impact); the inability to stand up for oneself against one's family; nepotism; and the juxtaposition of multiple objectives (economic and non-economic). Because it has its roots in the altruism of the directors with regard to their family, stewardship is therefore also a source of cost due to three basic factors: the manipulation exerted by children over their parents; rivalry between family members in order to obtain a greater share of the value created; and failure to accurately gauge the expectations of each member (Schulze et al., 2003). In this regard, and in line with agency theory, financial incentives are often necessary.

2.4   Careful Allocation of Resources and Risk Management

According to Carney (2005), decision-making for the long term, the involvement and loyalty of the workforce, patience in terms of return on investment expectations and a certain parsimony all constitute the specific nature of familiness. They lead to a preference for investment, enabling the consolidation of the long-term reputation of the firm, and to avoidance of those deemed to carry too much risk. This point of view is shared by Miller et al. (2008) and Gómez-Mejía et al. (2007) when they point out that the pursuit of longevity by family firms pushes them to favour the gradual implementation of innovation, social contribution and construction of a reputation rather than high-growth strategies. The growth/autonomy dilemma has also been underlined by Hirigoyen (1984): a large number of family firms thus tend to favour independence with regard to shareholders, banks and financial markets rather than growth at any cost and the pursuit of funding that this involves (Donckels and Frohlich, 1991; Daily and Dollinger, 1992; Maherault, 1998).

Nevertheless, a long-term vision also enables these firms to invest in projects the benefits of which will be felt in the long term (certain change innovations, productive investment to improve individual and collective know-how, etc.) even if their short-term profitability is not necessarily guaranteed (Miller and Le Breton-Miller, 2005). Arrègle et al. (2004) refer to the works of Dreux (1990) and De Visscher et al. (1995) and propose the notion of 'patient' capital, authorising 'investment in opportunities with long-term profitability without any short-term constraints' (p. 36).

2.5   External stability of relationships

The connection with customers, suppliers, banks and the society in general in which they exist is a significant characteristic of SFFs (Miller and Le Breton-Miller, 2005). These relationships are facilitated by the durability of the management teams, as they facilitate the building of trust and make it possible to test the fulfilment of commitments made over time. Thus the development of partnerships with suppliers involved in the value creation process, the desire to remain in contact with former customers and banks in order to maintain a network of relationships and the ability to respond to needs in a personal manner are recurrent forms of behaviour in this kind of company. They are often firmly entrenched geographically, maintaining an affective and ethical relationship with their region of origin (a desire not to relocate in order to sustain employment in the area). Ward (1997) observes and recommends alliances as a key factor in the success of family businesses. Arrègle et al. (2004) also point out that interpersonal relations with stakeholders (customers, suppliers, banks etc.) are strong and frequent in family businesses (Lyman, 1991; Yeung, 2000a, 2000b). In addition, succession within the same family makes it possible to render these relationships sustainable (Miller and Le Breton-Miller, 2005).

The cultural characteristics highlighted above and the different dimensions of sustainability identified lead to the fact that SFFs have to pursue simultaneously continuity and change. We will mobilize below theoretical frameworks from the management literature, such as the ambidexterity and the high reliability organization, that can help us develop a deeper understanding of the SFF functioning and performance. These cultural characteristics are a source of cohesion within the organization, encouraging stability in intra- and inter-organizational relations. These elements of permanence allow a firm to progress along a defined route, a guiding line sketched out over the course of the company's history that ensures that strategic decisions have a temporal coherence. Nonetheless, the search for long-term sustainability also requires renewal, questioning of old knowledge and exploration of new avenues opened up by innovation strategies.

3   AMBIDEXTERITY AND THE HIGH RELIABILITY ORGANIZATION: TWO FRAMEWORKS TO UNDERSTAND THE PERFORMANCE OF SUSTAINABLE FAMILY FIRMS

The search for sustainability and specific cultural characteristics led SFFs to develop a specific model of strategic renewal (Agarwal and Helfat, 2009) that can be characterized by the simultaneous pursuit of change and continuity. This balance between change and continuity is at the heart of the processes rendering firms sustainable (De Geus, 1997; Collins and Porras, 2005; Mignon, 2001, 2009; Schuman et al., 2010). It can moreover be seen in various fields of management science: organizational learning and its developments in single and double loops (Argyris and Shön, 1978), evolutionary theories (Nelson and Winter, 1982; Durand, 2006) analysing the development of routines as a source of innovation, dynamic capacities (Teece et al., 1997; Winter, 2003) highlighting the necessity of creating flexible capacities in order to continue to exist in the long term, punctuated equilibrium (Tushman et al., 1986) highlighting alternating major and minor reorientations. Within these existing frameworks, we have decided to focus on two areas that seem particularly promising: ambidexterity (Tushman and O'Reilly, 1997) and high reliability (Weick and Roberts, 1993). More than any other area, these fields allow us to approach change and continuity not as opposing forces that repeatedly succeed one another, but as two factors that, when they are in harmony in a firm, can be a source of durability.

3.1   Organizational Ambidexterity

Management literature has dealt with the simultaneous pursuit of continuity and change by firms through the concept of the ambidextrous organization put forward by Duncan (1976) and popularized by Tushman and O'Reilly (1997).

Our aim is to analyse how SFFs achieve organizational ambidexterity, notably through their family characteristics, enabling them to simultaneously pursue often conflicting objectives such as continuity and change, or two different types of learning such as exploration and exploitation. We shall begin by considering the manner in which SFFs, with their family characteristics, implement exploitation on the one hand and exploration on the other, before considering them jointly.

3.1.1   Capitalization and exploitation of existing knowledge

This is first and foremost facilitated in family firms by stewardship and its associated effects. Miller and Le Breton-Miller (2006, p. 78) advance the theory that the positive effects associated with this emotional involvement are a better aptitude for learning: 'CEOs continue to learn on the job for many years . . . firms with more frequent executive turnover will find such capabilities hard to match' and above all a preservation of individual and collective tacit knowledge ('Stewardship may take the form of preserving tacit knowledge . . . this farsighted, focused investment approach builds on path dependencies that keep a firm's capabilities growing cumulatively, thereby making its learning trajectory especially tough for rivals to imitate', ibid., p. 79). This farsightedness and the investments that are made as a result (in R&D, technical and human capital etc.) enable the cumulative training of key skills, which is the result of complex learning paths over a long period of time. The search for sustainability enables the transmission of tacit knowledge from one generation to another and therefore its perpetuation over time. The very strong culture present in family businesses together with the loyalty, employee trustworthiness with regard to their employer and specific HRM mechanisms such as employee profit sharing, training and job protection (Allouche and Amann, 1995, 2008; Miller et al., 2008; Arrègle et al., 2007; Ward, 1997; Tagiuri and Davis, 1996; Daily and Rueschling,

1980) all contribute to capitalizing on individual and collective skills, which, as we know, can otherwise be jeopardized by a high employee turnover (Nonaka, 1994; Girod, 2000). This stability thus enables the development of skills based on a cumulative process over a long period of time.

Finally, capitalization of market-based knowledge is facilitated by the stability of the relationships that sustainable family firms maintain with their customers and an intimate knowledge of their needs (James, 2006; Lyman, 1991; Miller and Le Breton-Miller, 2005; Miller et al., 2008). Habbershon and Blank (2005) also underline the role played by the director-owner of a family firm in the building of strong links with customers, thereby infusing their business with a philosophy oriented towards customer satisfaction. 'Clearly customer connection is related to innovation in these firms' (ibid., p. 14). However, these personal relationships also constitute a weakness in that as they are by nature informal and personalized; their sustainability can be threatened when the persons concerned leave the company. Generally speaking, good preparation for the succession of power (anticipation, early immersion in the business, selection criteria based on skills) will enable the transfer, however difficult (Szulanski, 2000) of the tacit and idiosyncratic knowledge (Cabrera-Suarez et al., 2001) developed by the directors of family firms (the creation and accumulation of which is linked to the longevity of the individuals concerned), as well as the networks and social capital (Steier, 2001) that constitute an essential condition of the firm's competitiveness (Sharma, 2004).

3.1.2 Exploration and the development of new knowledge

These are encouraged by long-term investment in training, R&D, production and marketing to a greater degree by family firms than by non-family firms (Weber et al., 2003; Kang, 2000; Miller and Le Breton-Miller, 2005, 2006; Miller et al., 2008; James, 2006). This investment underlies an innovative offering (in terms of products, business model or technology) and entry into new markets (Miller et al., 2008; Weber et al., 2003; Lyman, 1991; Gallo and Vilaseca, 1996; Morris et al., 1997):

> Stewardship over the continuity of the family business can take several forms: more emphasis on the research and development of new offerings, more attention to boosting the reputation of the business, and more emphasis on broadening the market by more deeply penetrating existing markets or expanding into new ones, again to solidify the business for the future ... these longer-term investments might be less attractive to an impatient single founder. (Miller et al., 2008, p. 54).

The experimentation required for the process of exploring new paths is facilitated by the specificity of human resources and abilities in family firms: 'the family has unique training, skills, flexibility and motivation' (Dyer, 2006, p. 259). Gudmundson et al. (2003) show that the promotion of factors favourable to creativity (autonomy granted to innovators, systems for encouraging and rewarding involvement, resources and time given to individuals testing new ideas) correlate specifically to innovation and that this context is more frequently found in family firms than in non-family firms.[4]

The involvement of family members other than the director-owners (Aldrich and Cliff, 2003; Olson et al., 2003) also facilitates the exploration of new alternatives, discussion on the risks associated with each option and a collective decision on how best to carry out the selected strategy. This hypothesis has been validated by Zahra (2005), in particular in the case of investment in radically new technology. Finally, the members of family firms develop a sense of loyalty and trust conducive to the process of understanding by trial and error. In this respect, Hall et al. (2001) specify that an open and explicit family culture can also encourage 'double loop' learning and unlearning inherent to exploratory processes. The allotment of own resources by sustainable family firms is also conducive to exploration as these firms tend to reinvest a greater share of their profits than non-family firms (Anderson et al., 2003; Daily and Dollinger, 1992; Miller and Le Breton-Miller, 2006).

However, the stability of the internal culture, the desire not to place the sustainability of the business in danger, personal attachment to the company as well as external relations all act as safeguards. In other words, the communal values at the internal level guarantee organizational cohesion. Links with partner companies and special contacts with customers provide an opportunity to verify that the innovation pursued is seen as relevant by the market: 'keep innovation efforts market relevant' (Miller and Le Breton-Miller, 2005, p. 151). Certain authors thus show that the specific culture of family firms leads to more measured risk-taking and therefore to 'careful innovation' (Zahra et al., 2004; Carney, 2005; Hatum and Pettigrew, 2004; Habbershon and Blank, 2005; Ben Mahmoud-Jouini and Mignon, 2009).

3.1.3 The simultaneous development of exploration and exploitation

It would seem that SFFs manage to protect themselves against the two areas of risk generally associated with learning through exploration and exploitation. These risks are:

- excessive exploitation, which can obstruct the acquisition of new skills and can lead to a spiral of decline;
- exploration without capitalization of associated knowledge, which can prove costly for the company while failing to provide the benefits of a well-established competitive position in the future.

In effect, excessive exploitation, meaning the continuous improvement of core skills, renders the development of new abilities more problematic. This observation reflects the metaphor of the Icarus paradox developed by Miller (1993), with the spirals of decline generated by success underlining that the blind faith and arrogance that success can inspire can be fatal to an organization. The weight of past experience and the focusing of resources on a single area of activity can lead to a certain strategic shortsightedness, heightened by a sense of invulnerability generated by the size and maturity of the company.

On the other hand, organizations engaged solely in exploration without seeking to transfer knowledge and reduce the distance between existing and newly acquired knowledge risk suffering the costs without reaping the associated competitive advantage.

Gibson and Birkinshaw (2004) suggest contextual ambidexterity as the behavioural capacity to simultaneously demonstrate alignment and adaptability. They consider that the top management is a key actor in developing an organizational context that can promote such a behavioural capacity. If context refers to the systems, processes and beliefs that shape individual-level behaviours in an organization (Bartlett and Ghoshal, 1994), they consider that top management has to develop a context where stretch and discipline need to be as strong as support and trust. Hence firms use meta-routines and create a shared vision in order to achieve ambidexterity through individuals. This form gives room for manoeuvre to the members of the firm that have big autonomy in the trade-off between conflicting demands such as exploitation and exploration.

This ambidexterity can also be achieved thanks to the existence within these SFFs of constants that in a sense pilot change, particularly major changes. Based on an in-depth case study, Mignon (2001) has shown that certain constants such as a historical culture of process innovation, human values guaranteeing a certain level of behaviour, employee loyalty, strategic decisions favouring jobs ensuring the preservation of know-how and financial management favouring investment repeatedly constituted the 'internal context' underlying strategic initiatives by the firm in question. Of course, these constants also constitute elements of inertia contributing to the restriction of firms' margin for strategic manoeuvre; however, they also contribute directly to the sustainable evolution of firms, as they make it possible to abandon certain options in favour of the most pertinent strategies. The implementation of initiatives shows that they are generally anticipated and are subject to a long process of learning by trial and error, which indicates the pugnacity of the director. Breaks with continuity are more or less radical according to the type of initiative chosen. Above all, an initiative will only be developed long term if it remains in sync with internal and/or external contexts. Consequently, stability is not only necessary for firms' sustainability (in the sense that phases of change and continuity must alternate) but these constants fulfil the role of safeguards, or filters, enabling the firm to change and evolve while pursuing sustainability. In other words, it is not so much the confrontation between change and continuity that would appear essential in order to understand sustainability, but rather how the constants, or invariants, contribute to change.

3.2   The High Reliability Organization (HRO) Literature Stream

Another hypothesis to explain the performance of SFFs can be found at the collective level and not at the level of individuals or of top management. Weick and Roberts (1993) have analysed HROs, that is, firms striving for high reliability such as a nuclear power plant or aircraft carrier, and shown that these reliability-oriented organizations adopt more elaborate collective mental processes than those of efficiency-oriented companies. In particular, the former dedicate more time and effort to the organization of data processing, to quality of attention and to vigilance in their actions. The richness of their intra-organizational interrelations therefore constitutes the strength of reliability-oriented companies and enables them to avoid making wrong decisions. The density of these interrelations is promoted by the following factors: acknowledgement of past experience, use of history as a diagnostic tool, confrontation of divergent points of view in order to improve the global understanding of phenomena, learning by trial and error, a collective system of thinking and of decision-making, shared representation of any given situation resulting in the interrelationship of activities, and measured, vigilant collective action. The greater the presence of vigilance in the collective thinking, the greater the capacity of the firm to understand and face up to unforeseen events. The stronger the interrelationships, the better the collective thinking is able to exploit past experience, imagine all the stages in a process and be capable of grasping the complexity of a situation. When interrelationships are weakened, the understanding of events diminishes, corrective processes are weakened and even minor errors can combine and grow. According to Weick and Roberts (1993), interpersonal relationships and their density are necessary features of reliable systems. When people become more individualistic and less interconnected, organizational thinking is simplified. This entails heightened vulnerability to accidents and a diminished understanding of the environment. Cooperation is essential for the development of trust, giving rise to shared ways of thinking and acting. Cooperation is what lends meaning within an organization.

This integrating concept of collective thinking and action leading to the consideration of reliability before efficiency seems perfectly relevant to the nature of family firms. According to Le Breton and Miller (2005, 2006), to cite but these researchers, family business can be defined by three distinctive traits: a strong organizational cohesion, a sense of collective spirit and farsighted decision-making.

Now Roberts and Weick point out that, in their opinion, it was Eisenberg (1990, p. 160) who best described the characteristics of the 'collective mind' in reference to jazz improvisation groups, characteristics that the authors feel are the greatest strength of HROs. Indeed Eisenberg describes these characteristics as constituting a 'nondisclosive intimacy' that 'stresses . . . mutual respect over agreement, trust over empathy, diversity over homogeneity'. Roberts and Weick make these specificities the foundations of their ideas of 'heedful interrelating' and the 'collective mind', which are the key to the viability of these atypical organizations. Yet it is difficult not to be struck by the similarities between these concepts and the existing mainstream literature on family firms, in terms of the focus on the particularities of their human resources management. A great number of authors have drawn attention to the strong culture within family firms: loyalty, faithfulness of employees to their company, and specific HR policies such as participation, training and job preservation (see Allouche and Amann, 1995, 2008; Miller et al., 2008; Arrègle et al., 2007; Ward, 1997; Tagiuri and Davis, 1996; Daily and Rueschling, 1980). These authors use a different vocabulary to describe very similar concepts. From an integrative perspective, Miller et al. sought to unite these factors under the umbrella term 'Community', first of their 'Four Cs' (the other three being Continuity, Connection and Command). They believe that these concepts cover the original configuration of family firms in the execution of their strategy. Now if we follow Roberts and Weick and agree that 'reliable performance may require a well-developed collective mind in the form of a complex, attentive system tied together by trust', then family firms are clearly eligible for this kind of performance. And if we further admit that the intelligence of highly efficient organizations, measured by their criteria of collective mind and heedful interrelating, is simply more basic than that of HROs, then the specificities concerning the human resources management of family firms would appear to place them firmly in the latter category.

Yet the specific human resources management methods of family firms do not constitute the only point of comparison with HROs. Family firms also demonstrate heedful interrelating, quite simply because for them sustainability is an objective that takes precedent over all others: this quest for sustainability makes them naturally more vigilant regarding threats from their environment. Just as on the flight deck of an aircraft carrier, all key players in family firms pay close attention to the factors that could dramatically compromise the success of their operations, and mobilize their cognitive capacities to achieve a detailed understanding of the risk factors: the inherent prudence of family firms inspires a strategic vigilance that, far from condemning them to stagnation, inspires them to connect as intelligently as possible with their environment. But, as Roberts and Weick say, 'to connect *is* to mind' (1993, p. 374).

CONCLUSION

We have reviewed the literature on the sustainability pursued by SFFs to propose a framework (see Figure 12.1) that enhances the understanding of the performance of these companies measured through their sustainability whatever its type: control, management, organization or business. Our motivation was that, apart of some exceptions such as Schuman et al. (2010), little research has pointed out the paradox that these firms encounter when they have to achieve continuity and change and reliability over short-term efficiency. The framework we suggest is based on the mobilization of concepts in management literature that address specifically these conflicting demands: the ambidextrous concept that addresses the pursuit of exploration and exploitation of knowledge simultaneously; and the high reliability stream of research that addresses the way firms pursue reliability over short-term efficiency through the collective mind concept.

Research on the ambidextrous concept highlights the benefits of setting a context that enables individuals to be ambidextrous, meaning developing new knowledge simultaneously with exploiting and capitalizing on the existing one. The analysis of the characteristics of SFFs shows a convergence between these latter and the conditions that enable individual ambidexterity. On the other hand, the research stream addressing highly reliable organizations points out the organizational attributes that lead to the settlement of a collective mind. These attributes could be enabled by SFFs characteristics.

These two streams of research have been widely studied in many fields of management, in order to address how firms reconcile efficiency and flexibility, adaptation and stability and continuity and change. However, no research has explicitly considered the case of family firms. Hence the framework we suggest (Figure 12.1), based on these streams, is an innovative one and should renew research on the performance of SFFs.

Further research on this subject should be empirical. Several research propositions can emerge from this framework and can be tested on samples. Another complementary approach could be to analyse through a fine-grained qualitative analysis of several sustainable family firm how their characteristics set up a context that enable individuals to be ambidextrous and that encourage the development of collective mind that enables the pursuit of adaptability and reliability over short-term efficiency.

NOTES

1. Insee (National Institute for Statistical and Economic Information), Sine Survey (Information System on New Businesses – 2006–2009).
2. The survivors are General Motors, Exxon, Ford Motors, General Electric, IBM, Chevron Texaco, Boeing, Procter and Gamble, Lockheed Martin, Conoco Philips, United Technologies, Dow Chemical, Caterpillar, DuPont, International Paper, Honeywell International, Alcoa, Coca Cola, Weyerhauser. (Some of them – and not necessarily the smallest – may not survive the current global crisis.)
3. However, rendering business sustainable without ensuring continuity at the human level is not easy, as the

transfer of tacit skills upon which the business is based is difficult to disassociate from the persons who have that knowledge. Promoting a more rounded business implies taking into consideration the organization into which it has been inserted.

4.   Test of the following hypothethes:

H1:   The level of innovation in small business is positively related to the level of support for innovation provided in the business.

H2:   The level of innovation in small businesses is positively related to the degree that workers are empowered to make decisions in the organizations.

H3:   The organizational culture in small non-family businesses is significantly different from the organizational culture in small family businesses.

H4:   The level of innovation in small non-family businesses is significantly greater than the level of innovation in small family businesses.

H5:   The level of innovation will be significantly higher in small businesses serving customers than in small businesses serving other businesses.

Results: H1 and H2 were supported. H3 was not supported. Not only H4 was not supported, but also the opposite was found. H5 was partially supported.

REFERENCES

Agarwal, R. and Helfat, C.E. (2009), 'Strategic renewal of organizations', *Organization Science*, **20**(2), 281–93.

Aldrich, H.E. and Cliff, J.E. (2003), 'The pervasive effects of family on entrepreneurship: toward a family embeddedness perspective', *Journal of Business Venturing*, **18**(5), 573–96.

Allouche, J. and Amann, B. (1995), *Le retour triomphant du capitalisme familial: gestionnaires et organisations*, Toulouse: Presse de l'Université des Sciences Sociales.

Allouche, J. and Amann B. (2008), 'Nature et performances des entreprises familiales', in Géraldine Schmidt (eds.), *Le management: fondements et renouvellements*, Paris: Sciences Humaines, pp. 223–32.

Anderson, R., Mansi, S.A. and Reeb, D. (2003), 'Founding family ownership and the agency cost of debt', *Journal of Financial Economics*, **68**, 263–85.

Argyris, C. and Schön, D. (1978), *Organizational Learning: A Theory of Action Perspective*, Reading, MA: Addison Wesley.

Arrègle, J.-L., Durand, R. and Very, P. (2004), 'Origines du capital social et avantages concurrentiels des firmes familiales', *M@n@gement*, **7**(1), 13–36.

Arrègle, J.-L., Hitt, M., Sirmon, D. and Very, P. (2007), 'The development of organizational social capital: attributes of family firms', *Journal of Management Studies*, **44**, 73–95.

Bartlett, C. and Ghoshal, S. (1994), 'Changing the role of top management: beyong strategy to purpose', *Harvard Business Review*, 79–88.

Ben Mahmoud-Jouini, S. and Mignon, S., (2009), 'Entrepreneuriat familial et stratégies de pérennité. Contribution au concept d'innovation prudentielle', *Management International*, **14**(1), 25–41.

Bloch, A., Kachaner, N. and Mignon, S. (2012), *La stratégie du propriétaire: enquête sur la résilience des entreprises familiales*, Paris: Editions Pearson.

Bréchet, J.-P. (1994), 'Du projet d'entreprendre au projet d'entreprise', *Revue Française de Gestion*, **99**, June–July, 5–14.

Burgelman, R.A. and Grove, A.S. (2007), 'Let chaos reign, then rein in chaos – repeatedly: managing strategic dynamics for corporate longevity', *Strategic Management Journal*, **28**, 965–79.

Cabrera-Suarez, K., De Saa-Pérez, P. and Garcia-Almeida, D. (2001), 'The succession process from a resource and knowledge-based view of the family firm', *Family Business Review*, **14**(4), 37–46.

Carney, M,. (2005), 'Corporate governance and competitive advantage in family-controlled firms', *Entrepreneurship Theory and Practice*, **29**(3), 249–65.

Chua, J.H., Chrisman, J.J. and Sharma, P. (1999), 'Defining the family business by behaviour', *Entrepreneurship Theory and Practice*, **23**(4), 19–39.

Collins, J.C. and Porras, J.I. (2005), *Built to Last: Successful Habits of Visionary Companies*, New York: Random House Business Books.

Daily, C. and Dollinger, M. (1992), 'An empirical examination of ownership structure in family and professionally managed firms', *Family Business Review*, **5**(2), 117–36.

Daily, R.C. and Rueschling, T.H. (1980), 'Human resources management in family owned companies', *Journal of General Management*, **5**(3), 49–56.

Davis, J.H., Schoorman, F.D. and Donaldson, L. (1997), 'Toward a stewardship theory of management', *Academy of Management Review*, **22**(1), 20–47.

De Geus, A. (1997), *Habits for Survival in a Turbulent Business Environment*, Cambridge, MA: Harvard Business School Press.

De Rooij, E. (1996), 'A brief desk research into the average life expectancy of companies in a number of countries', Stratix Consulting Group, August.

De Visscher, F.M., Aronoff, C.F. and Ward, J.L. (1995), *Financing Transitions: Managing Capital and Liquidity in the Family Business*, Marietta, GA: Business Owner Resources.

Donckels, R. and Frohlich, E. (1991), 'Are family businesses really different? European experiences from STRATOS', *Family Business Review*, **4**(2), 149–60.

Dreux, D.R. (1990), 'Financing family business: alternatives to selling out or going public', *Family Business Review*, **3**(3), 225–43.

Duncan, R. (1976), 'The ambidextrous organization: designing dual structures for innovation' in R. Kilmann, L. Pondy and D. Slevin (eds), *The Management of Organization Design: Strategies and Implementation*, New York: North Holland, pp. 167–88.

Durand, R. (2006), *Organizational Evolution and Strategic Management*, London: Sage.

Dyer, W.F. Jr (2006), 'Examining the "family effect" on firm performance', *Family Business Review*, **19**(4), 253–73.

Eisenberg, E. (1990), 'Jamming: transcendence through organizing', *Communication Research*, **17**, 139–64.

Gallo, M.A. and Vilaseca, A. (1996), 'Finance in family business', *Family Business Review*, **9**(4), 387–401.

Gibson, C. and Birkinshaw, J. (2004), 'The antecedents, consequences and mediating role of organizational ambidexterity', *Academy of Management Journal*, **47**(2), 209–26.

Girod-Seville, M. (2000), *Mémoire des organisations*, Paris: L'Harmattan.

Gómez-Mejía, L.R., Haynes, K.T., Núñez-Nickel, M., Jacobson, K. and Moyano-Fuentes, J. (2007), 'Socioemotional wealth and business risks in family-controlled firms: evidence from Spanish olive oil mills', *Administrative Science Quaterly*, **52**, March, 106–37.

Greenwood, R. (2003), 'Commentary on: toward a theory of agency and altruism in family firms', *Journal of Business Venturing*, **18**(3), 491–4.

Gudmundson, D., Tower, C.B. and Hartman, E.A. (2003), 'Innovation in small business: culture and ownership structure do matter', *Journal of Development Entrepreneurship*, **8**(1), 1–17.

Habbershon, T.G. and Blank, A.M. (2005), 'Innovation in dominant regional family firms: a model for assessing the familiness factor', unpublished paper, Babson College, Institute for Family Enterprising.

Habbershon, T.G. and Williams, M.L. (1999), 'A resource-based framework for assessing the strategic advantages of family firms', *Family Business Reviews*, **12**(1), 1–25.

Habbershon, T.G., Williams, W. and MacMillan, I.C. (2003), 'A unified systems perspective of family firm performance', *Journal of Business Venturing*, **18**, 451–65.

Hall, A., Melin, L. and Nordqvist, M. (2001), 'Entrepreneurship as radical change in the family business: exploring the role of cultural patterns', *Family Business Review*, **14**(3), 193–208.

Hatum, A. and Pettigrew, A. (2004), 'Adaptation under environmental turmoil: organizational flexibility in family-owned firms', *Family Business Review*, **17**(3), 237–58.

Hirigoyen, G. (1984), 'Contribution à la connaissance des comportements financiers des moyennes entreprises industrielles familiales', Thèse de Doctorat, Université de Bordeaux 1.

Hoffman, J., Hoelscher, M. and Sorenson, R. (2006), 'Achieving sustained competitive advantage: a family capital theory', *Family Business Review*, **19**(2), 135–87.

James, H. (2006), *Family Capitalism*, Cambridge, MA: Belknap-Harvard University Press.

Kang, D. (2000), 'Family ownership and performance in public corporations: a study of the U.S. *Fortune* 500, 1982–1994', *Working Paper* 00-0051, Harvard Business School, Boston, MA.

Koiranen, M. (2002), 'Over 100 years but still entrepreneurially active in business: exploring the values and firm characteristics of old Finnish family firms', *Family Business Review*, **15**, 175–88.

Lank, A. (1992), 'Les entreprises familiales européennes: espèce en voie de disparition ou puissants acteurs économiques?', *Revue Economique et Sociale*, no. 3, Lausanne, 157–68.

Le Bretton-Miller, I. and Miller, D. (2008), 'To grow or to harvest? Governance, strategy and performance in family and lone founder firms', *The Journal of Strategy and Management*, **1**(1), 41–56.

Lesourne, J. and Stoffaës, C. (2001), *La prospective stratégique d'entreprise: de la réflexion à l'action*, Paris: Edition Dunod.

Lyman, A.R. (1991), 'Customer service: does family ownership make a difference?', *Family Business Review*, **4**, 303–24.

Macombe, C. (2003), 'Ethique et pérennité chez les exploitants agricoles', Clermont I, Thèse de sciences de Gestion, Clermont-Ferrand.

Maherault, L. (1998), 'Des caractéristiques financières spécifiques aux entreprises familiales non cotées', *Revue du Financier*, **114**, 59–75.

Mignon, S. (2001), *Stratégie de pérennité d'entreprise*, Paris: Editions Vuibert.
Mignon, S. (2009), 'La pérennité organisationnelle: un cadre d'analyse', Introduction to the special issue on 'la pérennité organisationnelle', *Revue Française de Gestion*, **35**(192), 73–89.
Miller, D. (1993), *Le Paradoxe d'Icare*, Paris: Editions Eska.
Miller, D. and Le Breton-Miller, I. (2005), *Managing for the Long Run: Lessons in Competitive Advantage from Great Family Businesses*, Boston, MA: Harvard Business School Press.
Miller, D. and Le Breton-Miller, I. (2006), 'Family governance and firm performance: agency, stewardship and capabilities', *Family Business Review*, **19**(1), 73–87.
Miller, D., Le Breton-Miller, I. and Scholnick, B. (2008), 'Stewardship vs. stagnation: an empirical comparison of small family and non-family businesses', *Journal of Management Studies*, **45**(1), 51–78.
Morris, N., Williams, R., Allen, J. and Avilla, R. (1997), 'Correlates of success in family business', *Journal of Business Venturing*, **12**, 385–401.
Nelson, R. and Winter, S.G. (1982), *An Evolutionary Theory of Economic Change*, Cambridge, MA: Belknap Press of Harvard University Press.
Neubauer, F. and Lank, A.G. (1998), *The Family Business: Its Governance for Sustainability*, New York: Routledge.
Nonaka, I. (1994), 'A dynamic theory of organizational knowledge creation', *Organization Science*, **5**(1), 14–37.
Olson, P.D., Zuiker, V.S., Danes, S.M., Stafford, K., Heck, R.K.Z. and Duncan, K.A. (2003), 'Impact of family and business on family business sustainability', *Journal of Business Venturing*, **18**(5), 639–66.
Pearson, A., Carr, J.C. and Shaw, J.C. (2008), 'Toward a theory of familiness: a social capital perspective', *entrepreneurship theory and practice*, November, 949–69.
Roberts, K. and Weick, K. (1993), 'Collective mind in organizations: heedful interrelating on flight decks', *Administrative Science Quarterly*, **38**, 357–81
Schulze, W.S., Lubatkin, M.H. and Dino, R.N. (2003), 'Toward a theory of agency and altruism in family firms', *Journal of Business Venturing*, **18**(4), 473–90.
Schulze, W.S., Lubatkin, M.H., Dino, R.N. and Buchholtz, A.K. (2001), 'Agency relationships in family firms: theory and evidence', *Organization Science*, **12**(2), 99–116.
Schuman, A., Stutz, S. and Ward, J.L. (2010), *Family Business as Paradox*, New York: Palgrave Macmillan.
Sharma, P. (2004), 'An overview of the field of family business studies: current status and directions for the future', *Family Business Review*, **12**(1), 1–36.
Steier, L. (2001), 'Next-generation entrepreneurs and succession: an exploratory study of modes and means of managing social capital', *Family Business Review*, **14**(3), 259–76.
Szulanski, G. (2000), 'The process of knowledge transfer: a diachronic analysis of stickiness' *Organizational Behavior and Human Decision Processes*, **82**(1), 9–27.
Tagiuri, R. and Davis, J.A. (1996) 'Bivalent attributes of the family firm', *Family Business Review*, **9**(2), 199–208.
Teece, D.J., Pisano, G. and Shuen, A. (1997), 'Dynamic capabilities and strategic management', *Strategic Management Journal*, **18**(7), 509–33.
Tokarczyk, J., Hansen, E., Green, M. and Down, J. (2007), 'A resource-based view and market orientation theory examination of the role of "familiness" in family business success', *Family Business Review*, **20**(1), 17–31.
Tushman, M.L. and O'Reilly, C. (1997), *Winning Through Innovation*, Boston, MA: Harvard Business School Press.
Tushman, M. Newman, W. and Romanelli, E. (1986), 'Convergence and upheaval: managing the unsteady pace of organizational evolution', *California Management Reviews*, **29**(1), 29–44.
Ward, J.L. (1997), 'Growing the family business: special challenges and best practices', *Family Business Review*, **10**(4), 323–37.
Weber, J., Lavelle, L., Lowry, T., Zellner, W. and Barret, A. (2003), 'Family Inc', *Business Week*, **3857**, 10 November, 100–14.
Weick, R.E. and Roberts, K.H., (1993), 'Collective mind in organizations: heedful interrelating on flight decks', *Administrative Science Quaterly*, **39**(3), 357–82.
Winter, S.G. (2003), 'Understanding dynamic capabilities', *Strategic Management Journal*, **24**(10), 991–5.
Yeung, H.W. (2000a), 'Limits to the growth of family-owned business? The case of Chinese transnational corporations from Hong-Kong', *Family Business Review*, **13**(1), 55–70.
Yeung, H.W. (2000b), 'Strategic control and coordination in Chinese business firms', *Journal of Asian Business*, **16**(1), 95–123.
Zahra, (2005), 'Entrepreneurial risk taking in family firms', *Family Business Review*, **18**(1), 23–40.
Zahra, S.A., Hayton, J.C. and Salvato, C. (2004), 'Entrepreneuship in family vs. non family firms: a resource-based analysis of the effect of organizational culture' *Entrepreneurship Theory and Practice*, **28**(4), 363–81.

13 Network capital and the rise of Chinese banks in Hong Kong: a case study on the Bank of East Asia Limited
Victor Zheng

INTRODUCTION

On 23 September 2008, an ordinary working day, thousands of panicked depositors queued outside the various Hong Kong branches of the Bank of East Asia (hereafter, BEA) hoping to withdraw their savings due to rumour of a run on the bank. The triggering point was that the bank, which had just celebrated its 90th anniversary, had suffered a heavy loss on 'certain equity derivatives'. Before that, due to repeated negative reports, the bank's share price dropped from its highest level of HK$61.0 per share in 7 December 2007 to HK$22.0 by the middle of September 2008. As the Hong Kong SAR government took immediate measures to prevent the onset of financial instability, the rumour ultimately subsided. However, the 'financial tsunami' that swept the world shortly after the collapse of Lehman Brothers in October saw its share price plummet further to its lowest level of HK$13.2 in 28 October 2008. Worse still, in 11 November 2009, another situation greatly affected the bank and its controlling family – the David Li Kwok-po family. It was reported that the Guoco Group, a Hong Kong-listed Malaysian Chinese firm controlled by the Kuek Leng-chan family, had continuously absorbed BEA shares when their price was low. It further revealed that the Kuek has become the third-largest single shareholder of the bank. Speculation on a takeover grew up spontaneously (*The South China Morning Post*, various dates). Shares in the bank quickly changed hands and many stories about the two families appeared in the mass media.

Although many people merely see the fight for control over the bank as a soap opera, we take this case as a good example of a bank that was originally founded by a group of partners but later transformed to single family control. Throughout this chapter, the concept of network capital, a kind of capital built on the foundation of mutual benefit and mutual trust, will be used as key explanation for the bank's establishment, development and transformation. In addition, attention will also be given to explaining how the bank's controlling families used their network capital to exercise their domination, and to meet various crises and challenges.

ENTREPRENEURSHIP, NETWORK CAPITAL AND FAMILY CONTROL

When talking about capital, we generally refer to economic capital such as cash, bank deposits and property, and follow Karl Marx's idea that economic capital determines the mode of production and therefore sociopolitical relations. We seldom pay attention to intangible human capital like personality and leadership, or social capital such as personal ties, social position and cultural patterns, in determining social behaviour. In fact, although social capital is not measurable, fluid and difficult to assess, it can 'facilitate certain actions of individuals who are within the structure' (Coleman, 1990, p. 302). Its influence on day-to-day business practice, personal interaction or organization structure is fundamental and far-reaching (Bourdieu, 1986).

Although there is no unchallengeable definition of network capital, I think it is acceptable to refer the concept as stock of social trust and cultural norms that people can draw on to solve common problems. The most crucial question is why different social actors unanimously try to initiate network capital for solving problems. In explaining the rise of modern capitalism in the West, private property rights and the free market are suggested as the most unshakable foundation (Coase, 1937). However, as time goes by, other socioeconomic theories emerge to criticize the insufficiency and inadequacy of private property rights and the free market. One of them is that of Oliver Williamson (1975), who argues that the free market is not the panacea for all socioeconomic behaviours. He further points out that there are frequent market failures either due to tremendous transaction costs or unbearable business risks. In order to overcome these problems, institutional arrangements such as commercial guilds, clan associations and professional regulatory bodies were 'invented'.

Undeniably, Williamson's argument goes a big step further than free market theory. However, we may reasonably ask if institutional arrangements can better solve socioeconomic problems, why are personal ties and business connections ubiquitous, as such behaviours seem to bypass the institutional arrangements. Apparently, the deployment of network capital seems due to the defectiveness of the market mechanism on the one hand and the inadequacy of institutional arrangements on the other. In fact, if we put aside the conventional negative view on business networks, crudely linked to cronyism, we may find the concept useful in helping us understand better long-term or enduring socioeconomic behaviours.

With this theoretical background in mind, we come to another question: why the application of network capital is so common not only on the Chinese mainland, but also in highly modernized societies such as Taiwan, Hong Kong and the overseas Chinese communities. Before an explanation, some background information and argument are clearly needed. In China before 1912 (commonly called feudal China), merchants ranked far lower than the gentry, farmers and artisans in the social hierarchy. So when the economies of South Korea, Taiwan, Hong Kong and Singapore, the so-called 'four little Asian Dragons', flourished after the Second World War, people began to ask why. What caused these economic miracles is the main research question frequently asked. Some researchers argue from the perspective of the cold war and geopolitics (Dirlik, 1997), some from the angle of government intervention (Pye, 1988), while some look at it from view of the free market (Pananek, 1988). Some aim at religious motivation and emphasize Confucian ethics (Berger, 1988). Although these points of view are diverse, they all agree that firms, particularly family businesses, are the locomotives that drive economic growth. Among other things, entrepreneurs, attract most of the attention (Orru et al., 1997).

In the tradition of suppressing business activities and businessmen's social status, education for joining officialdom was treated as the only means of upward social mobility. At the beginning of the twentieth century, a tumultuous period of socioeconomic and political strife, more pragmatic approaches to running the country were adopted. Doing business as a means of supporting the family and upward social mobility became preferable, particularly for overseas Chinese societies. A common argument is that after some years of employment, when the overseas Chinese had saved a certain amount of money, collected some experience and acquired certain connections in business, they would consider that working under somebody's roof has no future, and choose to set up their own businesses. This was because they did not want to be subjugated to other people. In their minds, starting their own business of whatever size was considered a major path towards upward mobility, and it is a common belief that there is no lack of entrepreneurship in Chinese societies (Chan and Chiang, 1994; Amsden and Chu, 2003). The rise of mainland China after the introduction of economic reforms in the late 1970s further supports the argument that entrepreneurship and family business both flourish in the Chinese social and cultural context (White et al., 1996).

Although there is sufficient research examining entrepreneurship and family business in Chinese societies, especially the internal logic between them, integrated discussion on network capital in facilitating entrepreneurs is under-studied and far from satisfactory. The scholarship seldom pinpoints the critical function that network capital plays in facilitating family businesses. Since network capital can be used on the one hand to maximize efficiency to supplement the free market and institutional arrangements, and for securing prolonged family domination and in sustaining business continuous growth on the other, it is commonly manoeuvred not only in business, but also in social and political endeavours.

If we take a brief look at the current literature on network capital and Chinese family business, we may further discover that the discussion falls into three types: (1) it is generally believed that small and medium businesses rely more on network capital, and when businesses grow larger and reach a certain scale, less network capital is required; (2) family-controlled businesses rely more on network capital, and as the management team is gradually replaced by professional non-family members, network capital fades out naturally; (3) it is considered that economic capital is far more important than network capital, which therefore puts stronger emphasis on earning money instead of building personal ties and socioeconomic and sociopolitical connections (Redding, 1990; Mackie, 1992).

In-depth research even shows that network capital is commonly applied in all types of businesses – sole proprietor or joint-venture business; small or large in scale; family or non-family control. Its function and effects spread from raising capital for starting up (or further expansion) of a business to ensuring supply of key raw materials, and to acquiring market outlets for the final products or services. More importantly, network capital is generally deployed by the entrepreneur of the business for three major purposes: for exercising effective control by the family (owner); for maximizing profits; and for the business's sustainable growth and continuous domination by the family. In short, network capital is used for correcting the market mechanism and institutional arrangements to make sure that income generated is properly harvested – or, in Marxist terminology, network capital serves as the superstructure for maintaining capitalists' interest in society.

In order to achieve these goals, three types of network capital are commonly interoven. The first type is rooted in family. The second type is based on business, while the third type involves socioeconomic and sociopolitical allies. The common social behaviour

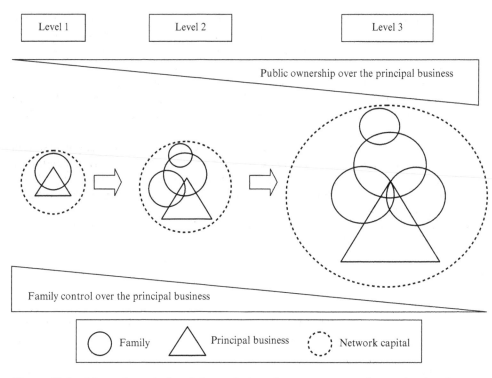

Figure 13.1   Network capital and the evolution of management and organizational structure

shown in the first type includes many of the family (kin) members, assigned to key management positions. Nepotism and intermarriages among key business partners for forging closer blood-ties are other special features. The common social behaviour in the second type of network capital is to interlock directorates among strategic businesses. Interfirm ownership and transcorporate cooperation are equally salient. The common social behaviour shows in the third type is to appoint key family members (representatives) or directors of strategic companies to political positions or actively participate in government and political affairs.

How can network capital be raised, accumulated and invested for better returns? In what way it can supplement free market and institutional arrangements for sharpening the competitive edge and for securing family control? Much research indicates that the family firm was the cornerstone of classical economics from the eighteenth to the early twentieth century (Scott and Griff, 1984). The evolution of management, organizational structure and family domination through network capital can be roughly described as a 'spade shape', which reflects the level of control by the founding family in different times. When the self-made entrepreneur sets up a business, he is usually put at the organizational helm. Extensive overlapping between family and business represents overwhelming control and power centralization (see Level 1, Figure 13.1). As the business gradually expands, ownership may spread and be shared among kin and descendants. Continuous expansion and diversification may absorb more trusted family/kin members into the management team to run different businesses/departments. A 'web of kinship' that emphasizes blood ties is usually identified (Useem, 1984).

As the business keeps on expanding, ownership by the founding family may be diluted – with the family usually no longer remaining as the major shareholder. Apart from absorbing kin and family members into the business, non-family members (business partners) and professionals who have demonstrated higher trust/loyalty will be also invited to join the management. Interfirm ownership and transcorporate networks are usually formed for exploring targeted business opportunities (Scott and Griff, 1984).

Family-based network capital and business-based network capital may be forged through intermarriage as social interaction among families and businesses intensifies and becomes more frequent. Through intermarriages, family, business and mutual trust condense, which can further reinforce each another so that large amounts of economic capital and human capital can be mobilized from within the cousinhood and social elites for minimizing risk or for maximizing return (Berkowitz, 1976; Scott and Griff, 1984).

Zeitlin and Ratcliff (1975) further point out that extensive intermarriage among potential families is not only a consequence of close mutual trust and interaction, but also serves to create reciprocal obligations and loyalties and to buttress the economic foundations of the controlling family. Clearly, in so far as the founding family is no longer the sole owner (or majority shareholder) of the business, network capital is mobilized for ensuring continuous family control mainly through intermarriage alliances (see Level 2, Figure 13.1).

Similarly, as family wealth and business interests are increasingly accumulated, and as the family name in society becomes prominent, more network capital will be deployed for protecting its wealth and interests, and for ensuring its continued influence in society. Family members actively participating in voluntary and charitable organizations are some of the ways of establishing reputation and fame. Going into politics or being appointed to a senior government position are some other common practices. Furthermore, as family leaders or representatives become more prominent, they will be invited to serve as directors for other large companies. On the other hand, they will also consider inviting other large family representatives to join their company management team to enhance mutual cooperation and control. Interlocking directorships become more frequent (Level 3, Figure 13.1). At this stage, if there is no support from the alliance, the minority shareholding family may lose control over the business. Through network capital, economic capital and human capital are translated into political domination and social influence while family control over its wealth and business interests is further cemented.

In sum, the central purpose of this chapter is to put network capital under the spotlight so that we can have a better understanding of its influence in business organization, operation and development, particularly as a provider of trust, loyalty and reputation when the free market and institutional arrangements prove to be unreliable/incapable. My main postulation is control. If a business is founded by a family and as the business continue to expand, the control mechanism may ultimately change, especially when the business becomes a publicly listed entity. Since the free market is far from perfect and institutional arrangements are far from ideal, the major shareholding family may find it difficult to maintain effective control over a business as the company share is increasingly diluted. Network capital is therefore forged accordingly as a supplement for maintaining family control. In the subsequent sections 1 examine the case of the Bank of East Asia Limited, a long-established Chinese bank in Hong Kong.

A BRIEF HISTORY OF THE BANK OF EAST ASIA LIMITED

The BEA was registered on 14 November 1918 and formally opened on 4 January 1919 by a group of Chinese business elites, '[who] not only understood modern banking, but the needs of modern Chinese business'. These business elites were from local big and wealthy families. In 1921, five more elites were absorbed as founding directors as the bank required raising more capital for expansion (Sinn, 1994, pp. 14–15). Among these founding directors, Kan Tong-po, the bank's first chief manager (later changed to chief executive officer), Li Tse-fong, a key supporter who was selected as manager, and Chow Shou-son, the bank's second chairman, were worthy of note (see discussion in later sections).

The rationale for setting up this bank was due to some founding members' thoughts that the so-called modernized Chinese banks of that day 'only had the outward form of Western banks, but not the spirit'. They considered that these banks would not be able to offer up-to-standard financial services to their people to stop the drain of China's wealth as China's capital market was still dominated by foreign banks. Because of the strong emphasis on learning 'the spirit of foreign [Western] banks' and 'good methods', BEA not only followed strict procedure in incorporating the bank, but also introduced a modern accounting and auditing system as well as modern customer-service methods. In this regard, the bank was treated as a modernized corporation that was neither a family business nor a business that was owned/control by a few families.

Notwithstanding the strong emphasis on 'the spirit of foreign banks', the most critical mechanism of separating management and control seemed to be intentionally or unintentionally overlooked. Although the mechanism of corporate governance of BEA was clearly different to that of a 'Western bank', its business did not show signs of less competitiveness even when compared with the leading Hong Kong and Shanghai Banking Corporation. For instances, not only the amount of deposits received from the public went up continuously; the number of the banks' representative offices in the world's major cities also increased gradually. Other indexes, such as the loan–deposit ratio, the return-on-assets ratio, the dividend–payout ratio and the return-on-equity ratio also increased steadily (Zheng and Ho, 2012). By the end of the 1930s, BEA emerged as the most influential Chinese bank in the colony (Sinn, 1994; *Kung Sheng Daily*, various years and dates).

In 1937, the Anti-Japanese War broke out. This prolonged war not only brought countless casualties and destruction, but also heavy losses to the bank, particularly after the fall of Hong Kong into Japanese hands. Most of the bank's assets in the Chinese mainland, Hong Kong and elsewhere were either ruined or robbed by Japanese troops. No normal business was allowed to continue locally or regionally (Sinn, 1994).

Shortly after the war, BEA reopened its doors and tried its best to regain business strength and vitality. However, civil war broke out again in the Chinese mainland between the Communist Party and the Nationalist Party. The victory of the Communists and the subsequent United Nations trade embargo on the newly established People's

Republic seriously affected the Hong Kong economy. The bank also faced another serious crisis. Not only were most of its branches on the Chinese mainland forced to close their doors; its overseas branches were also forced to restructure. The major business in Hong Kong also had to reorganize its business focus to enable it to keep up with the rapidly changing socioeconomic and political environment (Sinn, 1994).

As Hong Kong underwent a drastic transformation from a re-export trading port to an industrialized economy, the bank responded quickly to the change and its business grew continuously. Also in the 1950s, the bank adjusted its first generational succession, as many of the founding directors were old enough to step down while their successors were experienced enough to take over the reins (Sinn, 1994). Just before the succession process was complete, a territory-wide banking crisis suddenly erupted in 1965. Although many Chinese banks were hit badly, BEA was undisturbed. However, the bank became more conservative in expanding business afterwards.

In 1984, after prolonged negotiation on the future of Hong Kong between the Chinese and the British governments, the Joint Declaration was finally signed. While high autonomy to Hong Kong under the unprecedented framework of 'one-country, two-systems' was pledged, the Kan family chose to reduce their investment and retreat from Hong Kong (Chung, 2001). Kan Yuet-keung not only resigned from his post as executive and legislative councillor, but also sold the family's controlling shares in BEA. Because of this, Yuet-keung himself resigned as chairman of the bank, while his other brothers also eventually stepped down as directors.

Unlike the Kan family, the Li family thought the opposite and therefore decided to assume a bigger role after the Kans left. They absorbed more shares in the market and took both key positions – chairman and chief manager (later changed to chief executive officer). Although many influential Hong Kong companies, including a number of key long-established British *hongs* (a general term for a major trading company), changed their place of domicile from Hong Kong to Bermuda or the Virginia Islands after the 1989 June Fourth Incident,[1] the BEA insisted that its domicile in Hong Kong would remain unchanged. Furthermore, it re-emphasized its 'roots in Hong Kong' and its long-standing commitment to act as an agent in 'bringing China to the world' (Sinn, 1994, pp. 177–90), particularly after the handover of sovereignty in 1997.

Compared to many Western banks in Hong Kong, BEA put more emphasis on internal growth instead of acquisitions or mergers. Thus its pace of expansion was seen as less breathtaking. However, if we look into its basic statistics, we can see a similar stunning growth. For instance, in 1981, the bank's annual profit was only HK$88.1 million; in 2000 and 2009, it jumped to HK$1887.0 million and HK$2638.0 million respectively. In the same period, its total number of employees increased from 1381 in 1981 to 5095 in 2000 and then to 10 540 in 2009. Its local branches rose from 37 in 1981 to 100 in 2000 and then to 90 (plus 50 SupremeGold centres) in 2009, while its overseas branches rose from 2 in 1981 to 35 in 2000 and then to 115 (including 28 in the Chinese mainland, 6 overseas and 3 in Southeast Asia) in 2009 (The Bank of East Asia Limited, various years). By any standard, BEA's performance over the past two decades cannot be rated as mediocre.

From this unusual development, we can see that although the bank has faced various hurdles at different stages of development, its management has exercised its entrepreneurial spirit to weather all forms of challenges, ultimately turning the bank into a gigantic financial institution in Hong Kong. In short, although BEA stated clearly in its

Prospectus that the bank 'should not learn the outward form of the Western banks, but their spirit', in many ways bank's actual *modus operandi* is similar to that of other Western-funded local banks, but the most critical management mechanism is clearly different. Thus we can see that even though operating under the same socioeconomic and sociopolitical environment, and following the same banking and company ordinances, these two banks diverged along two different paths: one quickly became a global and truly 'publicly owned' bank, while the other retains the image of a local, 'family-owned' bank.

RAISING NETWORK CAPITAL FOR STARTING BUSINESS

From this brief introduction to the bank's development, it is not easy to identify the pervasiveness and indispensability of network capital. However, if we look into the process of incubating the business idea of forming a Chinese-funded modernized bank and mobilizing all sorts of capital in the actualizing of the idea, we may be surprised to see the ubiquitous presence of network capital in every interaction.

As indicated by Sinn (1994), Kan Tung-po seemed to be the initiator. Research clearly reveals that the formation of the bank was a typical example of an inspired entrepreneur with an idea and solid knowledge in the field but a lack of socioeconomic and sociopolitical capital for making it work. It is similar to an inventor who invents a new product but lacks funding to turn the product into something marketable. As the initiator of the bank, Kan Tung-po was born and raised in a *compradore* family. His father was a *compradore* of Yokohama Specie Bank, while Tung-po himself once worked for Kobe Bank and First National City Bank before establishing his family-controlled *yinhao* (remittance house) – a small scale and traditional-style bank. With down-to-earth knowledge in banking and also a strong entrepreneurial spirit, Tung-po was inspired to establish a bank but clearly lacked the requisite capital. He therefore sought support from friends and business associates.

Among those who supported Tong-po's proposal, the Li brothers (Li Koon-chun and Li Tse-fong) and Chow Shou-son are particularly worthy of mention. The Li brothers were from one of the wealthy and extended Chinese families in Hong Kong. This family had vast commercial interests in China, Japan, Indonesia, French Indo-China and other countries of East Asia, especially in the shipping and rice trading business (Ching, 1999). It happened that the Li family was seeking a business opportunity to upgrade its investment, and therefore gave Tung-pa their favourable and unfailing support.

If the Li family represented financial capital, then Chow Shou-son seemed to represent sociopolitical capital. Chow Shou-son was one of the students sent to study in the USA under the well-known Chinese Education Mission by the Qing government as early as the 1870s. After returning to China, he served in the Qing Court for over 30 years. Upon retirement, Chow Shou-son returned to Hong Kong and was quickly handpicked by the Hong Kong Colonial government to serve in the Urban Council (1919) and the Legislative Council (1921) because of his strong connections in mainland China. In 1926, Chow Shou-son was even knighted by the British Royal Family and admitted to the Executive Council. These were the greatest honours that a Chinese citizen could earn at that time (Zheng and Chow, 2010).

In short, it seems that although Kan Tong-po had a challenging business idea, it would be nearly impossible to execute if there was insufficient financial and sociopolitical backup. Since he could successfully get support through mobilizing network capital, his idea would be put into practice. Because of this, Tung-po himself became chief manager. He introduced many Westernized measures in transforming the *yinhao* to a modernized bank. For this he was ranked as one of China's top bankers and served in the bank for 44 years until his death. Li Tse-fong became his second in command, being appointed manager, a position he held for 34 years until his death. Chow Shou-son was elected as chairman after his appointment as a legislative councillor. He served as chairman for 34 years until his death (Sinn, 1994).

Having conducted in-depth research on Chinese family business, Redding (1990) and Hamilton (1996) unanimously argue that Chinese capitalism is first and foremost network capitalism. They further elaborate that this kind of capitalism is built from the ground up, not on the basis of legal contracts and the supervisory authority of the state, but on particularistic relationships of mutual trust. Thus personal networks are usually mobilized by Chinese entrepreneurs for investment and sociopolitical purposes in order to ensure family control and domination.

In short, we can see clearly that the formation of the bank demonstrates how network capital was deployed for mobilizing various types of resources to supplement each other in achieving a particular goal. Although the bank was registered as a modernized corporation, its nature was like a family business or a business that was controlled by few families. In other words, the formation of the bank was similar to a creation of clusters of people with intense interpersonal relations. As the bank expanded, network capital helped many of the founding members to ensure profit and control. Hence these families become increasingly prominent in Hong Kong.

ACCUMULATING NETWORK CAPITAL FOR SECURING CONTROL

As the bank gradually took root in Hong Kong and while its scale of business and market share rose, some of the controlling directors seemed to be aware that their dominant status might be at stake if they did not secure reliable and long-term alliances. Two kinds of network capital were therefore forged and mobilized in the 1930s and after the Second World War. The first kind was intermarriage while the second was political affiliation. Both of them demonstrate clearly how a particular project is mobilized or implemented while family control over this project can be exercised and secured.

About ten years after the opening of BEA, an intermarriage was arranged by matchmaker between two of the director families – the Mok Ching-kong family and the Li Koon-chun family. It was arranged that one of Li Koon-chun's younger brothers, Li Chok-chung, would marry Mok Ching-kong's daughter, Stella Mok. Not long later, another wedding that linked the Li family with another director family was arranged. This time, Li Koon-chun's eldest daughter, Li Yue-chu, newly graduated from St Paul's Girls' College, was affianced to Chow Hau-leung. Hau-leung was the grandson of Chow Chi-nam, the bank's chief cashier. Chi-nam was the cousin of Chow Shou-son, the bank's chairman.

A wedding that really cemented the bank's leading families to form a 'tri-families dominant' pattern occurred a few years later, when the twin sons of Fung Ping-shan were married in a double wedding in 1933. One son, Fung Ping-fan, married Ivy Kan, the eldest daughter of Kan Tong-po, while the other son, Fung Ping-wah, married Li Wai-yin, the eldest daughter of Li Tse-fong. This twin wedding was seen as a 'double cord' that further cemented the Kans, Lis and Fungs (Ching, 1999, pp. 72–3).

However, if we look from a larger perspective and at a longer time frame, we can see that this marriage alliance is far greater than it seems. Figure 13.2 shows some prominent families who had engaged in marriage alliances with the bank's founding families. Also in the 1930s, it was arranged that Kan Yuet-hing, son of Kan Tung-po, should marry Lee Shun-yin. Lee Shun-ying was from the Lee Hysan family. Lee Hysan emerged in the 1910s in the opium trade and was assassinated in 1928. Shun-yin's brother was Lee Ming-chak, who joined the bank as a director in the 1950s and also became a legislative and executive councillor (see later sections).

Some other prominent Hong Kong families are also linked through marriage. For instance, Li Koon-chun's sister, Sylvia Li, married Kwok Lam-po, the eldest son of Kwok Chun, who was the founder of the Wing On Department Stores in Hong Kong and Shanghai. Sylvia and Lam-po's son, Philip Kwok, who had a PhD from Harvard University, married Maxine Li, the eldest daughter of Li Shu-pui. Li Shu-pui and his elder brother Li Shu-fun were the founders of the Hong Kong Sanatorium Hospital, a first-class private hospital in Hong Kong. Li Shu-fun's family was famous for specializing in medicine. Li Shu-pui's wife was Ellen Li, the first Chinese woman legislative councillor in Hong Kong. Li Shu-fun's daughter, Li Fu-yun, married Lambert Kwok, younger brother of Kwok Lam-po.

Li Koon-chun's son, Li Fook-shu, married Woo Hey-tung's daughter, Daisy Woo. Woo Hei-tung's youngest son, Woo Pak-chun, was a senior solicitor and former legislative councillor. Koon-chun's other son, Li Fook-siu, married Low Hiu-wah, daughter of Low Min-nong, the sole distributor of British and American Tobacco (Far East) Limited. Li Koon-chun's grandson, Li Kowk-po, married Penny Poon, daughter of Poon Kam-kai. Poon Kam-kai was a meticulous businessman who specialized in retailing and department stores. Kam-kai's son, Dickson Poon, is a glamorous and energetic young entrepreneur in Hong Kong who heads one of the largest department stores in Hong Kong.

As one of the founding directors, Li Tse-fong married Tang Sau-ching, whose father once served as *compradore* of the Mercantile Bank. Tse-fong gained most of his banking knowledge and experience from his father-in-law. Li Fook-tai, son of Li Tse-fong, married Cindy Yu. Cindy Yu's father was Yu Hung-kwan, a former premier of Taiwan, Republic of China. That was why the Li family maintained close connections in Taiwan in the early days. Li Fook-kow, another son of Tse-fong, was a former secretary of home affairs and official member of the legislative and executive councils. He initiated a marriage with Woo Siu-che. Woo Siu-che was a mentor of the so-called 'Three Musketeers' of property developers, Kwok Tak-seng (founder of Sun Hung Kai Property), Lee Shau-kee (founder of Henderson Land Development) and Fung King-hei (founder of Sun Hung Kai Bank, now renamed as Fubon Bank). Woo Siu-che's daughter, Judy Woo, married Li Fook-kow's son, Andrew Li. Andrew Li was the first chief justice of the Court of Final Appeal of the Hong Kong Special Administrative Region.

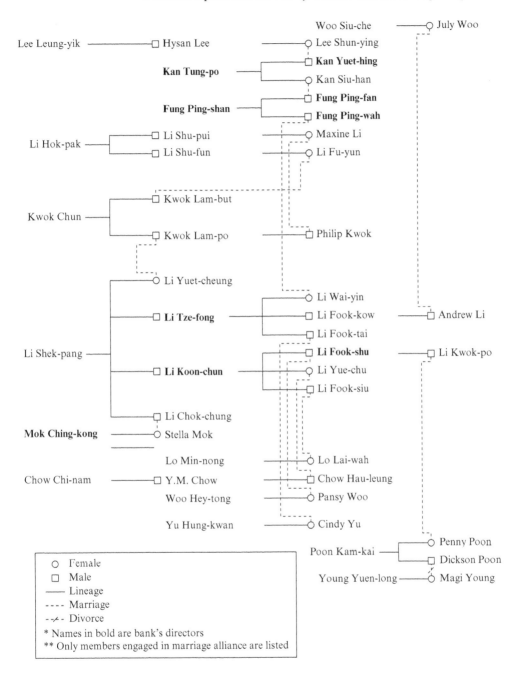

Figure 13.2   Marriage alliances of the BEA-controlling families

In short, through interconnected marriages, not only can network capital be raised and accumulated; human capital can also be diversified and family control over certain business interests can be assured. The formation of marriage alliances by the Li Koon-chun family, Kan Tung-po family, Fung Ping-shan family, Chow Shou-son family and many other prominent Hong Kong families could on the one hand secure their dominant status in BEA, but could also maintain their sociopolitical influence from the 1920s until the present time on the other. Such a phenomenon obviously follows what Scott and Griff (1984) have unanimously indicated in their studies: upper-class dynasties in Europe are maintained through cousin marriages and through cooperative business enterprises.

EXPANDING NETWORK CAPITAL TO THE SOCIOPOLITICAL SPHERE

Money and power are usually called 'twin brothers'. Both go together and interact for mutual benefit and defence. If we look at the BEA case, we can see clearly how they work together. As mentioned, when the bank was founded, the leading directors seemed keen to solicit political support. The invitation extended to Chow Shou-son to serve as one of the founding directors and later granting him the post of chairman obviously demonstrated the heavy emphasis stressed by some of the leading directors (Sinn, 1994; Ching, 1999). Although we do not have concrete evidence on what kind of benefit Chow Shou-son ultimately brought to the bank, we should not underestimate this invisible influence.

After Chow Shou-son, Li Tse-fong was invited to join the Legislative Council in 1939 on Chow Shou-son's recommendation. However, his appointment ended abruptly after 1941 when Hong Kong fell into Japanese hands. After the Second World War, as the Hong Kong Colonial government agreed to open the door slightly for political absorption, more Chinese elites were allowed to join the political arena. While the bank continued to grow, more directors of the bank were appointed into the Legislative and Executive Council. After Chow Shou-son and Li Tse-fong, key directors such as Lo Man-kam, Fung Ping-fan, Kan Yuet-keung, Li Fook-shu, Li Fook-wo, Lee Ming-chak and Li Kwok-po were appointed either as legislative councillors or executive councillors simultaneously from the late 1940s until the present. In Hong Kong history, only Hong Kong and Shanghai Bank – the quasi-central bank – could have its directors uninterruptedly appointed on to these two councils (King, 1987–91).

Apart from the intangible but unparalleled influence of some directors in politics, two more special features can be easily identified. First, many of the directors had served on the board for several decades. For instance, Wong Yun-tong had served for 59 years while Li Koon-chun, Kan Tung-po and Chow Shou-son had served 47 years, 44 years and 40 years respectively. This fits in well with Allen's (1981) finding that in the USA the average tenure of the principal officers of management-controlled firms was nearly nine years, while that for those running family-controlled firms was over 17 years, with a minor variation that the average tenure for Chinese family-controlled firms is much longer.

Second, many of the directorships were passed from father to son, older brother to younger brother, or uncle to nephew. After the resignation of Fung Ping-shan because of poor health, when his eldest son, Fung Ping-wah, came to maturity, he filled his father's shoes. However, after serving the post for several years, Ping-wah decided to quit and migrate to the USA after the Second World War. His post was later filled up by his younger brother, Ping-fan. Other directorships more or less followed the pattern of 'father's post, son inherits' pattern. For examples, Kan Tung-po's position was filled by his eldest son, Kan Yuet-keung; Li Koon-chun's post was filled by his eldest son, Li Fook-shu, while Li Tse-fong's post was succeeded by his eldest son, Li Fook-wo. Other examples include Wong Yun-tong's position filled by Wong Chung-hin, and Wong Chu-son's position taken over by Wong Chung-nam.

Other research data further indicate that many of the directors also actively participated in respectable local charitable organizations such as the Tung Wah Group of Hospitals (an influential charitable conglomerate) and Po Leung Kuk (an association for helping abducted women and orphans). Their contributions are either in the form of pecuniary donations (sometimes in-kind subsidization – by sending gifts to orphans during festivals), undertaking senior management positions of charitable organizations, or simply taking part in fundraising activities (Zheng, 2009). Through various kinds of social activities, their personal names are carved deeply into the history of these charitable organizations and their families' moral capital in society would also be raised.

If we interpret the bank's development simply from the business and management angle, we may feel that intermarriages and sociopolitical participation are irrelevant. However, if we look through lenses of network capital and family control, we may be surprised to find a number of critical and deep-rooted reasons to explain why the bank could be founded even though the initiator was not from the richest of families and why the key founding families could firmly hold the helm from generation to generation even when they were minority shareholders. More importantly, how did the bank survive all changes unscathed, whether these changes were economic, social or political?

TESTING NETWORK CAPITAL IN TIME OF CRISIS

Although the key founding families have established multi-layered networks for ensuring control over the bank, such links are not necessarily unbreakable. The weakest or most vulnerable part tested in the 1980s crisis seemed to be mutual trust and loyalty. As indicated earlier, in the early 1980s there was a 'crisis of confidence' when the Beijing government declared that it would hold Hong Kong sovereignty after 1997. Different strategies pursued by the families not only affected their destiny but also the landscape of the bank's management and control.

As the senior member of the Executive Council who accompanied the Hong Kong governor, Murray McLehose, on his visit to Beijing to meet with China's paramount leader, Deng Xiaoping, Kan Yuet-keung was believed to be the first Hong Kong citizen who had information about the firm position taken by the Chinese government on the resumption of Hong Kong sovereignty. On their return to Hong Kong after the visit, they relayed the oft-quoted message to the public from Deng, 'Tell investors to put their minds at ease' (Chung, 2001).

Since Kan Yuet-keung knew that the Chinese government would definitely take back Hong Kong and his position as the senior member of the Executive Council might bring him lot of work, so he chose to quit (Chung, 2001). The key factor was that he estimated the change of sovereignty might drastically alter Hong Kong's business environment, particularly his family's previous strong network capital invested outside China. Since he did not have too much confidence in the post-1997 Hong Kong, he chose to retreat from Hong Kong by selling his family's controlling share before the situation worsened.

After several years of repeated talks over the future of Hong Kong, both governments came to a final agreement and signed the Joint Declaration in 1984 (Chung, 2001). That year, Kan Yuet-keung further announced that he had decided to step down as chairman of BEA, while other Kan family members also subsequently resigned from the board. However, Kan Yuet-keung's pessimistic attitude towards Hong Kong's future was not shared by the Li family. The latter chose to stay and absorbed part of the controlling shares sold by the Kans to become the single controlling minority shareholder. Some of the Li family quickly filled positions on the board vacated by the Kans.

In 1986, another critical issue seriously affecting the bank's ownership structure also erupted. When the 'crisis of confidence' was at its peak, the Hong Kong stock market plummeted (Zheng and Wong, 2006). The Fung family seemed seriously affected and was believed to be on the verge of bankruptcy. Fung Ping-fan decided to sell his family's controlling shares in Chinese Estate Limited, a cash-rich and debt-free company, without discussing it with the Lis, who also played key roles in the company. This action destroyed the harmonious relations between the Lis and the Fungs.

In fact, according to Ching (1999, pp. 195–6), 'a rupture between the Lis and the Kans [had been created] in 1958'. My further research indicates that the issue that ruptured the relationship between the Lis and the Kans in 1958 was due to the 'transfer of shares without proper notification given to other controlling shareholders'. Since some of the controlling families saw the transfer of shares alter the 'balance of power' on the board, they raised their objections publicly in the 1958 annual meeting and asked for an internal investigation over the transfer of shares (*Kung Sheng Daily*, 13 March 1958). As no follow-up report was disclosed, the dispute was clearly settled privately; we do not have too much information about its development. However, we can see clearly that the foundation of mutual trust and loyalty among the controlling families was shaken.

When the 'crisis of confidence' in Hong Kong's future was at its height, many local companies chose to move their place of domicile from Hong Kong elsewhere, which caused high volatility on the stock market (Zheng and Wong, 2006). Knowing the situation early on, there was reasonable ground to believe that the Kans might want to sell their controlling shares for a better price. However, such an action might again alter the 'balance of power' on the board and lead to conflict. Although little information was leaked about the actual arrangement among the key controlling families, in the mid-1980s two things were clear. First, their multi-layered network had broken down. Second, the 'tri-families dominant' ownership structure in BEA was pruned to become a 'single-family dominant' pattern. Later, as the Fungs sold more of their BEA shares and while the Lis absorbed some of them, more Lis joined the board.

In the bank's recent annual report, we find the following fascinating information: (1) Li Kwok-po is both bank chairman and chief executive officer; (2) among eight non-executive directors, four are from the Li family; (3) of the five members of senior management, three are from the Li family; (4) the total declared controlling shares held in the hands of the Li family is not more than 15 per cent (The Bank of East Asia Limited, 2009, p. 52).

Under the full stewardship of the Lis (holding the posts of both chairman and chief executive officer) since the mid-1980s, what developmental strategy was pursued for securing family control over the bank? How did they handle this 'crisis of confidence'? In what way did the strategy initiated by the Lis in the 1990s pave the way for a hostile takeover in 2009? More interestingly, what was the key weapon used to help the controlling family defend the invaders so that they could keep their dominant position unchallenged?

INTERLOCKING DIRECTORSHIP AND TRANSCORPORATE NETWORK

Many Chinese family businesses may face the same dilemma that while they would like to expand their businesses they would also like to retain family control over their businesses (Zheng et al., 2010). In modern capitalist society, the most rapid means of expanding one's business is to go public. While other people's money can give the business more low-cost capital for bigger projects, it will inevitably reduce the controlling family's shareholding ratio. One of the critical considerations in introducing interlocking directorship – a kind of strategic business alliance that is primarily supported by network capital – is for securing the family's continuous domination.

In the case of BEA, although the Li family decided to stay in Hong Kong and bought part of the shares sold by the Kans and the Fungs, they seemed to understand clearly that they should not put all their eggs in the same basket. Although BEA was incorporated at the beginning as a publicly listed bank, its share offered to the public was minimal. The overwhelming majority of shares were in the hands of the founding directors' families. From the 1990s onwards, apart from diversifying other family investments to Europe and the USA, the Lis also chose to reduce their controlling shares in the bank. Offering more shares to the public to absorb more financial capital for strategic expansion was considered as a 'kill two birds with one stone' method, which on the one hand could provide energy for the bank's continuous growth and internationalization while on the other it could reduce investment risk or over-concentration.

As BEA pursued an aggressive expansionary strategy, the Hong Kong economy underwent a transformation from concentration in manufacturing industries to financial services. Hence the whole banking sector boomed while the bank grew at an even faster pace. The imminent merging of the mainland Chinese economy into the world economy further added impetus to the bank's continuous growth. The Lis might be driven to think about the mechanism that could ensure their family effective control as the bank kept on expanding even though the proportion of shares in their hands was largely reduced. The best options seemed to be interlocking directorships and a transcorporate network.

If we study carefully the bank's various annual reports, we can see that the Lis hold only a minor proportion of the shares but they firmly control the bank, which is valued in the multi-billions. For instance, in 1998, 2003 and 2008, the Lis' declared shareholding interests were only 7.72 per cent, 8.74 per cent and 8.14 per cent respectively. Although one could say that the undeclared shareholding interests held by other Lis are not insignificant, the percentage is rarely double. Even if it was double, the Lis are still minority shareholders. As such, strategic alliances with other friendly shareholders are a must in order to secure their control.

Second, under the leadership of Li Kwok-po, many of the bank's directors are extremely wealthy and influential tycoons in Hong Kong and elsewhere. These people are: Lee Shau-kee, Kwok Ping-kong (son of Kwok Tak-seng), Li Tzar-kai (son of Li Ka-shing, the wealthiest person in Hong Kong), Kuok Khoon-ean (son of Robert Kuok Hok-nian of Kerry Properties and *South China Morning Post*), George Ho (founder of the Hong Kong Commercial Radio), Mong Man-wai (founder of Shun Hing Group), Lo Yau-lai (son of Lo Kwee-seong of the Vitasoy International Holding), and Khoo Kay-peng (influential tycoons in Malaysia). In exchange for these tycoons sitting in the board of BEA, some of the Lis, particularly Li Kwok-po, are invited to sit on some of their flagship companies. BEA also serves as one of the principal banks for their businesses. Clearly, the Lis try to manoeuvre an interlocking directorate network for strategic alliances.

Third, each of the Lis only holds 1 to 2 per cent (seldom more than 3 per cent) of the bank's shares, which may be a result of the so-called *fengjia* (family estate division) under the traditional Chinese equal inheritance principle (Zheng, 2009). In other words, if they did not unite, they would simply become ordinary small shareholders who would have little influence over the bank's management (The Bank of East Asia Limited, various years).

A simple conclusion can be drawn here: the bank is a highly profitable cash-cow and debt-free, but the Lis are minority shareholders whose control is not only secured by economic capital but also by network capital. Opportunities for big profits clearly attract the eyes of predators and lead to takeover attempts. Back to the takeover saga mentioned at the beginning of the chapter, the day after the disclosure of Kuek Leng-chan's action, a local journalist checked with the Stock Exchange of Hong Kong about the registered shareholding interests of BEA and reported the following distributions: the Li family altogether holds 14.12 per cent of the bank's total shares, Criteria Caixa Corporation (a publicly listed company in Spain), owns 9.04 per cent, Gucco Group and Kuek Leng-chan hold 8.01 per cent, and Bank of China (Hong Kong) owns 4.94 per cent. The remaining balances of 63.89 per cent are held by public investors (*East Week*, 14 November 2009). To a certain extent, BEA may have formed a transcorporate network with Criteria Caixa Corporation and Bank of China (Hong Kong) for mutual support.

Follow-up reports indicate that a representative from Criteria Caixa Corporation, Faine Casas Isidro, was appointed a director of the BEA board in 2009 while Li Kwok-po was appointed a director of the board of Criteria Caixa Corporation. However, no representative from the Kuek Leng-chan family was invited. When asked by the media to comment on Kuek Leng-chan's action, Li Kwok-po said that he knew little about the plot but hinted that all the Lis would stand together and that many local tycoons including Li Ka-shing and Lee Shau-kee had already indicated to him their strong support (*Ming Pao Daily*, various dates and years).

The takeover saga became the talking point of the town, centring on such questions such as: would all the Lis really stand together to defend the bank? Would the strategic partners also stand behind the Lis? And would Kuek Leng-chan halt his plan for acquiring control over the bank? Some speculated that the Kueks would take whatever measures until a reasonable arrangement was reached, while some thought the Lis' network capital would be the important defensive shield that could help them secure control. There was further speculation that the Lis and the Kueks would finally form a new alliance to share in the cash-cow (*East Week*, 14 November 2009; *Ming Pao Daily*, various dates and years). Without doubt, although network capital is pervasive and highly influential, it is by no means unbreakable. Mutual trust and loyalty are critical elements that could change the whole business landscape.

CONCLUSION AND DISCUSSION

To conclude, if we unfold BEA's 90 years of remarkable development and see through the lenses of network capital and family control, we may make more interesting findings. First, although the bank flew the flag of 'learning the spirit of foreign banks', it did not put the separation of ownership and control mechanism into actual practice. Compared to most Western banks, which strictly followed the separation of management and control principle, BEA insisted on deploying insider family members on to the management team. The critical reason behind this seems to be family control, as Chinese culture and social psychology put strong emphasis on blood ties and family control. Also, loss of family domination over a business has a generally negative connotation.

Although some of the founding families were squeezed out to become ordinary shareholders, a few actually become larger and more dominant as the bank expanded. At the beginning (from the 1920s to the 1930s), the bank was jointly managed in a 'multi-families' dominant pattern (14 permanent directors from 12 families). From the mid-1930s to the 1980s, it changed to a 'tri-families' dominant pattern (the Li, the Kans and the Fungs). Then, from the mid-1980s onwards, it evolved to become a 'single-family' dominant pattern (the Lis). Such patterns of evolution reflect intense competition for control over the bank while the Chinese saying 'a mountain can't hide two tigers' appears to ring true.

Third, although the controlling share of each founding director was more or less equal and primarily calculated by their contribution of economic capital, investment in network capital was different, and it was this that determined their actual control in the bank's management. Intermarriages and other network capital used to cement relations became the core that dominated the management of the bank while those who did not invest greatly in network capital were gradually squeezed out from the management team. In other words, network capital seems to be manipulated in the service of economic capital to make sure that income generated from the latter is properly harvested. Notwithstanding the pervasiveness and indispensability of network capital in determining socioeconomic and political behaviour, this type of capital is not unchallengeable as loss of mutual trust and loyalty may turn it into liability.

ACKNOWLEDGEMENTS

This chapter is part of the Hong Kong as Financial Gateway for Taiwanese Enterprises project and the Chinese Family Business and Stock Market: A Comparative and Cooperative Study in Shanghai, Taiwan and Hong Kong project. The former project is funded by the Hong Kong Research Grants Council (Project No. HKU7549-08) while the latter project is funded by the Chiang Chiang-kuo Foundation (Project No. RG012-P-10). The author would like to thank Mr Roger Luk (former executive director of Hang Seng Bank), Professor Sanjay Goel and the anonymous reviewers for their assistance and valuable comments.

NOTE

1. This refers to a series of demonstrations for economic freedom and democracy in Beijing in 1989, which ended in a bloody military crackdown and political purgation (Tiananmen Square).

REFERENCES

Allen, M. (1981), 'Managerial power and tenure in the large corporation', *Social Forces*, **60**, 482–94.
Amsden, A. and Chu, W.W. (2003), *Beyond Late Development: Taiwan's Upgrading Policies* (trans. D.K. Zhu), Taipei: Linking Publishing.
Berger, P.L. (1988), 'In search of an East Asian model?', in P. Berger and M. Hsiao (eds), *In Search of an East Asian Development Model*, New Brunswick, NJ: Transaction Books, pp. 6–18.
Berkowitz, S.D. (1976), 'The dynamics of elite structure', unpublished PhD thesis, Brandeis University.
Bourdieu, P. (1986), 'The forms of capital', in J.G. Richardson (ed.), *Handbook of Theory and Research for the Sociology of Education*, New York: Greenwood Press, pp. 241–58.
Chan, K.B. and Chiang, C. (1994), *Stepping Out: The Making of Chinese Entrepreneurs*, Singapore: Prentice Hall.
Ching, F. (1999), *The Li Dynasty: Hong Kong Aristocrats*, Hong Kong: Oxford University Press.
Chung, S.Y. (2001), *Hong Kong's Journey to Reunification: Memoirs of Sze-yuen Chung*, Hong Kong: The Chinese University Press.
Coleman, J.S. (1990), *Foundations of Social Theory*, Cambridge, MA: Harvard University Press.
Coase, R.H. (1937), 'The nature of firm', *Economica*, **4**(16): 386–405.
Dirlik, A. (1997), *The Post-colonial Aura: Third World Criticism in the Age of Global Capitalism*, Oxford: Westview Press.
Hamilton, G.G. (ed.) (1996), *Asian Business Networks*, Berlin: Walter de Gruyter.
King, F.H.H. (1987–91), *The History of the Hong Kong and Shanghai Banking Corporation* (4 vols), New York: Cambridge University Press.
Kung Sheng Daily (various dates).
Mackie, J.A. (1992), 'Overseas Chinese entrepreneurship', *Asian-Pacific Economic Literature*, **6**(1): 41–64.
Ming Pao Daily (various dates).
Orru, M., Biggart, N. and Hamilton, G. (eds) (1997), *The Economic Organization of East Asian Capitalism*, Thousand Oaks, CA/London: Sage Publications.
Pananek, G. (1998), 'The new Asian capitalism: an economic portrait', in P. Berger and M. Hsiao (eds), *In Search of an East Asian Development Model*, New Brunswick, NJ: Transaction Books, pp. 27–80.
Pye, L.W. (1988), 'The new Asian capitalism: a political portrait', in P. Berger and M. Hsiao (eds), *In Search of an East Asian Development Model*, New Brunswick, NJ: Transaction Books, pp. 81–98.
Redding, G. (1990), *The Spirit of Chinese Capitalism*, New York: De Gruyter.
Scott, J. and Griff, C. (1984), *Directors of Industry: The British Corporate Network: 1904–1976*, Cambridge: Polity Press.
Sinn, E. (1994), *Growing with Hong Kong: The Bank of East Asia, 1919–1994*, Hong Kong: The University of Hong Kong.
The Bank of East Asia Limited (various years), *Annual Report*, Hong Kong: The Bank.
The East Week, 14 November 2009.
The South China Morning Post (various years).
Useem, M. (1984), *The Inner Circle: Large Corporations and the Rise of Business Political Activity in the US and UK*, New York: Oxford University Press.
White, G., Howell, J. and Shang, X.Y. (1996), *In Search of Civil Society. Market Reform and Social Change in Contemporary China*, Oxford: Clarendon Press.

Williamson, O.E. (1975), *Markets and Hierarchies: Analysis and implications*, New York: Free Press.

Zeitlin, M. and Ratcliff, R.E. (1975), 'Research methods for the analysis of the internal structure of dominant classes: the case of landlords and capitalists in Chile', *Latin American Research Review*, **10**(3), 5–61.

Zheng, V. (2009), *Chinese Family Business and the Equal Inheritance System: Unravelling the Myth*, London, New York: Routledge.

Zheng, V. and Chow, C.W. (2010), *The Grand Old Man of Hong Kong: Sir Shouson Chow*, Hong Kong: The University of Hong Kong.

Zheng, V. and Wong, S.L. (2006), *A History of the Hong Kong Stock Market: 1841–1997*, Hong Kong: Joint Publishing Limited.

Zheng, V., Wong, S.L. and Sun, W.B. (2010), 'Taking-off through the stock market: the evolution of Chinese family business and Hong Kong's regional financial position', in T.C. Ho and L. Cheng (eds), *Economic Dynamism in the Sinospheres and Anglospheres: Identities, Integration and Competition*, Hong Kong: The University of Hong Kong, pp. 303–32.

Zheng, V. and Ho, T.M. (2012), 'Contrasting the evolution of corporate governance models: a study of banking in Hong Kong', *Asia Pacific Business Review*, iFirst 2012, 1–17 (http://dx.doi.org/10.1080/13602381.2011.62 6156).

PART V

WOMEN IN FAMILY BUSINESS

14 The determinants of women's involvement in top management teams: opportunities or obstacles for family-controlled firms?

Daniela Montemerlo, Alessandro Minichilli and Guido Corbetta

1 INTRODUCTION

Significant efforts have been devoted so far to investigating the contribution of top management teams (TMTs) to firm performance (Hambrick and Mason, 1984; Hambrick, 2007). In this vein, the upper echelon research tradition consistently focused on characteristics and composition of top executives' circles, with emphasis on team diversity (Finkelstein et al., 2009). Diversity has been studied from different perspectives, with an increasing attention to the gender perspective and the specific contribution of women in TMTs (Kilduff et al., 2000; Klenke, 2003; Helfat et al., 2006). The reason behind this interest is that women are acknowledged to be naturally gifted with peculiar leadership and managerial skills (Bird and Brush, 2002; Van der Valt and Ingley, 2003; Krishnan and Park, 2005). The contribution of women in upper echelons has been conceptualized under various theoretical frameworks and empirically tested; evidence of positive relations between women in top positions and firm performance has created large consensus on the importance of increasing gender diversity in TMTs (Catalyst, 2004; Krishnan and Park, 2005; Joy et al., 2007). In fact, despite the evidence on positive effects of women executives, the 'glass ceiling' – that is, the apparently invisible barrier that keeps women far away from top positions – is still there. Further, although female presence in upper echelons is growing, it remains significantly scarce, especially in positions of CEOs and seconds-in-command (Daily et al., 1999; Krishnan and Park, 2005).

On the other hand, extant research on TMTs and gender diversity has been mostly conducted in the context of large, publicly listed corporations. As such, the context of family firms is virtually unexplored. Only few theoretical and empirical studies have focused on TMTs in these firms (e.g. Nordqvist, 2005; Ensley and Pearson, 2005; Minichilli et al., 2010). Empirical studies on gender diversity in family firms mostly consist of surveys on women's presence in top executive positions, focusing either on female board members and female CEOs in publicly listed family-controlled companies or on female entrepreneurs in family SMEs (Allen et al., 2007; MassMutual et al., 2007; Gnan and Montemerlo, 2008; Montemerlo and Profeta, 2009). Specific consideration of gender diversity in TMTs within the context of family-controlled firms, in essence, is confined within few partial quantitative studies as well as few anecdotal studies, largely exploratory and often based on restricted samples (Sharma, 2004; Montemerlo and Profeta, 2009). What is more, these studies deal only with women belonging to the owning family, that is with daughters and spouses of entrepreneurs. On top of that, the family nature of the company seems to play an ambivalent role in the presence of female executives. On one side, owning families seem to offer their female members unique opportunities to make careers and take care of their relatives and households at the same time; on the other side, owning families apparently make it hard for their female components to gain the required self-confidence to grow professionally, to be legitimized by peer colleagues and employees and to find a satisfactory balance between work and household requirements (Dumas, 1989, 1990, 1998; Salganicoff, 1990; Gillis-Donovan and Moynihan-Brandt, 1990; Cole, 1998; Vera and Dean, 2005). Ambivalence also seems to characterize family women's influence on gender diversity in top management. Although women may possess the right aptitudes and capabilities for their professional growth, in fact they may often be the first to constrain themselves by giving up professional challenges and choosing limited responsibilities. What is more, it is not granted that women already on top actually favour other women, including their daughters (Dumas, 1989; Cole, 1998; Vera and Dean, 2005).

Based on the arguments above, and following calls to further investigate the role of context in upper echelon research (Finkelstein et al., 2009), our contributions aims to make a preliminary step towards filling gaps in both upper echelon and gender literatures. Specifically, based on a representative sample of medium and large Italian family-controlled firms, we explore the impact of firm's family nature (measured by family ownership and family CEOs) on gender diversity, and notably on presence of both family and non-family women, in TMTs. For this purpose, we move from the following research questions: is the family nature of the firm a positive or negative determinant of women's involvement in TMTs? How important is it to have women in CEO positions to attract other women inside TMTs? Do determinants of gender diversity change for women belonging and not belonging to owning family?

Our results contribute to both theory and practice, and have implications at different levels. On the theoretical side, our study integrates upper echelon and diversity literature streams as, to the best of our knowledge, it provides the first quantitative evidence on the determinants of gender diversity in family firms' TMTs. It also contributes to family business literature as it helps to clarify the ambivalence that has emerged so far about owning families and women as possible determinants of female involvement in executive positions. Also, to the best of our knowledge, it is the first study to investigate gender diversity in terms of both family and non-family women's presence. On the practice side, the study provides some guidance for entrepreneurs and owning families on how to manage gender diversity as far as both family and non-family women are concerned. As such, it offers insights also to all people and institutions – business schools, associations and consultants – who assist family firms in their development. Our hope is to offer useful hints to better leverage female resources and, by this means, to strengthen the whole portfolio of family business resources and ultimately foster family firms' continuity.

The chapter develops as follows. Section 2 presents a literature review on TMTs, diversity and gender issues in general and in the context of family firms; along with the literature review, hypotheses are developed. Section 3 illustrates how hypotheses have been tested reporting sample characteristics, methods and findings. Section 4 discusses research findings, highlights their limitations and proposes some reflections on future studies' directions as well as on practice implications.

2   LITERATURE REVIEW

Top Management Teams (TMTs), Diversity and Gender Issues

The upper echelon perspective suggests that organizational outcomes can be predicted by certain managerial demographics, both visible (such as age, gender and race) and invisible (such as marital status, education, functional background and tenure in the office: see Hambrick and Mason, 1984). Although demographic characteristics cannot accurately capture the processes inside teams and among individuals, and although they cannot be so easily connected to cognitive characteristics like attitudes, values and norms (Pettigrew, 1992; Kilduff et al., 2000), most research on top executives and strategic leadership focuses on the former attributes because it is difficult to accurately measure the latter (Finkelstein and Hambrick, 1996).

There has been extensive debate so far on the impact of diversity, that is, of heterogeneity of relevant visible and/or invisible attributes of organization members, and particularly of TMTs' members, on firm performance.

Based on a social identity framework, some studies show how diversity may be detrimental for firm performance as it may hamper cooperation and communication, and generate conflict by means of the 'self-categorization' phenomenon (Richard and Shelor, 2002; Erhardt et al., 2003; Helfat et al., 2006).

Conversely, the resource-based and decision-making frameworks maintain that diversity may foster successful performance. According to these frameworks, being endowed with a heterogeneous portfolio of resources (competences, capabilities and relationships) enables firms to better cope with the external and internal environment and its multiple challenges such as globalization, innovation and change (Daily et al., 1999; Kilduff et al., 2000). As such, diversity is assumed to foster success for various reasons: it provides talents from a larger pool; it makes it possible to take decisions based on a richer set of alternative viewpoints; and it gives representation to a variety of stakeholders with reputational benefits (Daily and Schwenk, 1996; Van der Walt and Ingley, 2003; Helfat et al., 2006; Rose, 2007).

Still, empirical results are largely tentative as they show partial effects, both positive and negative, of TMTs' diversity on firm performance; particularly, different demographic as well as cognitive variables seem to feature different impacts on performance (Richard and Shelor, 2002). As such, there seems to be room for further investigation.

Among the different facets of diversity, the gender one is raising more and more interest. Some conceptual studies have identified a number of personal traits that distinguish women in business from male colleagues in terms of identity and behaviour; an important reference is the comprehensive and interdisciplinary work of Brush (1992), which has framed distinctive traits of the feminine style as compared to the masculine one. According to this work, feminine leadership traits seem to be: perception of the business as an integrated network of cooperative relations at family, societal and personal level; lower risk-taking; focus on interpersonal relationships and teamwork, trustworthiness, empathy; informality; care for people growth; information seeking and sharing before taking decisions (even at the expense of inefficiencies); special ability to perceive and handle conflicts; stronger commitment to family as well as more difficulties to balance family and work (Brush, 1992). It is interesting to notice that these traits are acknowledged to make TMTs' gender diversity a positive driver of firm performance under all the above-mentioned theoretical frameworks, including the social identity one, as

> the representation of women in the TMT minimizes social identity problems and increases power sharing, which increases organizational performance. In addition, a firm with greater representation of women demonstrates that is has drawn its top executives from a larger labor pool, which can further enhance organizational performance. (Krishnan and Park, 2005, p. 1714)

Extant empirical studies have shown positive correlations between female presence in boards of directors (BODs) and in TMTs and firm performances (Catalyst, 2004; Krishnan and Park, 2005; Joy et al., 2007), and also between incidence of overall female managers and firm performances (Shrader et al., 1997). When correlations are not found, explanations assume that female-specific contributions might be actually 'neutralized', even when women do reach top positions, rather than doubt the very existence of gender effects (Rose, 2007). This evidence has made scholars and practitioners take strong positions in favour of policies and actions that enhance gender diversity, possibly accelerating the erosion of the glass ceiling, which seems to be quite persistent despite the large amount of progress that has been made. In fact, a number of surveys have provided measures of female presence in top roles: for example, women accounted for 8 per cent of all TMT members and 2 per cent of second-in-command executives among the *Fortune 1000* in the year 2000; female CEOs were about 2 per cent in the *Fortune 500* in the year 2007 (MassMutual et al., 2007) and they were assumed to rise to about 6.4 per cent of all CEOs between 2010 and 2015 (Helfat et al., 2006). In general, it is underlined that progress has been made in firms' commitment to female recruitment and consequently in women's careers on one side, but that there is a long way to go, as women's presence in TMTs is still concentrated in second line and in lower levels, and especially in staff positions (Krishnan and Park, 2005; Helfat et al., 2006; Montemerlo and Profeta, 2009). Some studies even show little confidence in the future, acknowledging progress in corporate boards of directors (BODs) but observing a very limited female presence over the 1990s not only at the chief executive level, but also at the inside director level, from which many CEOs are usually selected (on top of that, this presence has not increased and sometimes it has even decreased in that decade), and thereby assuming that no significant improvements can be expected for the next decades unless strong actions are taken (Daily et al., 1999; Montemerlo and Profeta, 2009). Whatever the degree of confidence, the reasons why female presence is still scarce are classified into three main categories, that is: person-centred, individual factors; situation-centred, group and organizational factors; social system-centred factors (Powell, 1999).

Notably, gender diversity is generally investigated in large, public firms, where data are much more easily available, like the *Fortune 500* and *Fortune 1000* (Daily et al., 1999; Krishnan and Park, 2005; Helfat et al., 2006; Joy et al., 2007). Thus there is a great deal of space for further research in this stream of diversity studies. On top of that, the very nature of gender – as a biological but also as a social construct – is discussed, assuming that it may be not gender *per se*, but the gender-specific style that matters (Bird and Brush, 2002; Klenke, 2003); nevertheless, all studies conducted so far have made reference to the biological construct, again for data availability reasons, and the same has been done in the research on which the present chapter is based.

Top Management and Gender Issues in the Context of Family Firms

In family business literature, there is still quite limited research on both top management and gender topics.

First, family business literature has traditionally overlooked the investigation of distinctive traits and relevance of top executives, with few exceptions (Sharma, 2004; Minichilli et al., 2010). The main topics that have been explored so far are: the mutual advantages of managerialization for both family firms (and notably family owners) and non-family managers, the key conditions to make the most of these advantages on both sides and the basic types of non-family managers (insiders and outsiders) with their characteristic features and challenges (Dyer, 1989; Aronoff and Ward, 2000); conversely, the fragile points of the relationship between owning family and non-family managers in terms of mutual concerns and disagreements (Chua et al., 2003; Poza et al., 2004; Barnett and Kellermanns, 2006); the special challenges of recruiting non-family CEOs in family firms (Aronoff and Ward, 2000; Blumentritt et al., 2008); and last but not least, the key conditions to professionalize family members in such a way as to prepare them to top management roles (Dyer, 1989; Hall and Nordqvist, 2008).

TMTs in the upper echelon perspective are hardly considered in the family business field, apart from a few recent studies on TMTs' 'familiness', defined as the level of family involvement within the group of top executives in family firms, and on the relationship between familiness and performance (Ensley and Pearson, 2005; Minichilli et al., 2010), This scarce consideration of family firms' TMTs fails to address the predictive power of top management teams' characteristics on the performance of medium and large family-controlled firms, which are subjects of special interest for their economic relevance and also for their unique mix of distinctive features of large public companies and of the typical traits of family firms, such as family involvement (Miller and Le Breton-Miller, 2006).

Similarly, family business studies devote limited attention, although increasing, to gender issues. One group of studies aims at 'measuring' the extent to which women play leading and top management roles. Evidence from these studies portrays a minority of women in upper positions, confirming difficulties in accessing the 'inner circles' also in family firms. According to the American Family Business Survey (MassMutual et al., 2007), while 10 per cent of family firms of all sizes reported a female CEO in 2002, this proportion increased to 24.5 per cent in 2007, and it is expected to increase to 31.3 per cent over the next decade. In Italian medium and large family firms, female CEOs account for 13.9 per cent, while female leaders can be found in 9 per cent of family SMEs (AldAF-Alberto Falck Chair, 2008; Gnan and Montemerlo, 2008). As to TMTs, including both leaders/CEOs and first-line managers, data are even more difficult to find: in Italy, female members account for 20 per cent of TMTs in incorporated family SMEs, and two-thirds of them are women belonging to the owning family (Gnan and Montemerlo, 2008). Similar figures can be found in medium and large family firms (20.8 per cent of women in TMTs), although in this case family women are less numerous, accounting for about 40 per cent of total female executives (Montemerlo and Profeta, 2009).

A second group of gender studies in family business has built upon extant research on female leadership and managerial styles, analysing the characteristics of entrepreneurial and family firms owned and led by women, which account for 20 to 30 per cent of SMEs' activity worldwide (Allen et al., 2007). These studies highlight specific goals, structures and processes that differentiate these firms from men-led ones. Specifically, women-led firms show higher consideration for social and organizational goals – such as people's growth, quality of work life and customer satisfaction – than for economic ones. Further, they are generally smaller in size, with less hierarchical organizational structures, more participative and informal decision-making processes, more sharing of succession plans and a greater attention in transmitting values to the next generation (Brush, 1992; Gnan and Montemerlo, 2008). Interestingly, some works show that participative leadership styles can lead to greater family and business success (Sorenson, 2000). A number of similarities between women-led and men-led firms have also been found in terms of industries, strategic profiles, general business problems encountered over the life cycle of the firm, economic performance, and awareness of the importance of succession planning (Brush, 1992; Harveston et al., 1997; Allen and Langowitz, 2003; Gnan and Montemerlo, 2008).

A third group of family business studies looks at female family members' variety of managing and non-managing roles in both business and family. It is generally acknowledged that women belonging to the owning family also play unofficial or invisible roles, which very often are more relevant than the official ones. Although evidence is still limited and based on small, selected samples or on anecdotal experience, interesting conceptual frameworks and role classifications have been crafted (Dumas, 1989; Poza and Messer, 2001). Poza and Messer, for instance, have identified a number of roles that women may cover both inside and outside the family firm. Within the business, particularly, women may act as co-preneurs and directors of business functions, as well as keepers of values and CEOs' senior advisors (often with no official role). Co-preneurs have been dealt with by several other studies, which highlight how women may be assigned (and sometimes deliberately choose) less dominant and worse paid positions than their husband entrepreneurs, but also how they often act as peacekeepers, even after divorce (Ponthieu and Caudill, 1993; Rowe and Hong, 2000; Cole and Johnson, 2007). Spousal commitment has been analysed as a key determinant of supportive relationships and, by this means, of superior financial performance (Van Auken and Werbel, 2006).

A fourth group of family business studies investigates the grooming processes of female family members in their careers and the processes of delegation and letting go of women-in-command. Grooming processes have been analysed by Dumas (1989), who found that they can turn out to be either non-productive or healthy. If they are non-productive, they will probably feature at one extreme women dependent on others, and thereby unable to carry out top-level responsibilities autonomously and bound to remain 'daddy's little girl' forever. At the other extreme, women will grow up with a strong commitment to affirm their independence, but this commitment will be so strong as to suffocate the integration and coordination skills that are necessary to play the leadership role. Healthy processes, on the contrary, foster personal and professional development of women and enable them to manage interdependence between family and business, and particularly to take care of both and take charge of the business as well (Dumas, 1990). It should be noted that all the mentioned studies focus on female family members and that non-family women are virtually ignored.

If room exists for further research on both top management and gender issues, virtually no studies at all exist that deal with gender diversity and TMTs at the same time. The above-quoted findings about positive effects of TMTs, and notably of TMTs' gender diversity, on firm performance in other contexts stimulated us to bring an upper echelon perspective into family business studies and to explore female presence in top management teams in terms of both family and non-family women, with the purpose of investigating the determinants of this presence. So far, some of the mentioned studies on family women's roles have built on Powell's classification of 1999 and have considered various determinants of these roles, notably: the family nature of the firm and the attitudes and behaviours of the internal firm's actors at the situational level; women themselves at the individual level; society as a whole at the social system level (Salganicoff, 1990). Given the prominent role of family and the strong personal character of family firms, our attention is focused on the first and second levels, and particularly on family nature of the firm and on women as possible determinants of TMTs' gender diversity, also because an ambivalent role of both owning family and women seems to emerge from extant literature, which deserves special attention (Martinez Jimenez, 2009).

TMTs, Gender Diversity and Family Nature of the Firm: Exploring the Role of Family Ownership

Following Chua et al.'s point (1999; 2003, p. 92) that 'the combination of family involvement that makes the business unequivocally a family business is when the family both owns and manages the business', we chose to analyse family nature in terms, first, of family ownership.

In distinguished cases, family ownership is acknowledged to bring strong responsible values and commitment to the family firm. Effective compliance with responsible ownership orientation should guarantee that the best talents are provided to firms and, by this means, that firms are put in the best conditions to last beyond single individuals and/or generations. Further, owning family's values are acknowledged to include special attention to people and to the challenges of work and family balance (Aronoff and Ward, 1992). This suggests that family ownership may exercise its role by inspiring an organizational context in which talented women are selected with no gender prejudices as well as regardless of family membership, and are offered unique possibilities to pursue a professional career and manage the households at the same time, for example by means of more secure and flexible jobs than those that can be obtained in non-family firms (Salganicoff, 1990; Gnan and Montemerlo, 2008). This leads us to assume the following:

Hypothesis 1a   There will be a positive relationship between family ownership and the presence of women (family and non-family) in the firm's top management team.

On the other hand, owners' 'family-first' orientation (Montemerlo and Ward, 2005) may determine the opposite effects. If traditional, chauvinistic family values prevail on responsible ownership values, business hierarchies can often be perceived by family owners as incongruent with family typical hierarchies, and thereby inappropriate for young women should they want to climb them (Barnes, 1988). Also, in a family-first culture family relationships might be shaped in such a way as to create obstacles to female family members' professional growth. In fact, obstacles may be rooted in conflicts with fathers; mothers and siblings' rivalry; family–work conflict due to tough family expectations (Dumas, 1989, 1998; Salganicoff, 1990; Gillis-Donovan and Moynihan-Brandt, 1990; Cole, 1998; Vera and Dean, 2005). Female non-family members might be more protected from owning family's dynamics but they are also likely to find obstacles in the nepotistic consequences that often derive from a family-first culture. Thus an opposite hypothesis on family ownership's impact follows:

Hypothesis 1b   There will be a negative relationship between family ownership and the presence of women (family and non-family) in the firm's top management team.

TMTs, Gender Diversity and Family Nature of the Firm: Exploring the Role of Family CEOs

Going back to Chua et al.'s point on ownership and management as core traits of family nature (1999; 2003, p. 92), we chose to analyse family nature also in terms of family presence in top executive positions, with specific focus on the CEO position. In fact, whether or not the CEO is a family member is another important component of the family nature of the firm, as 'familiness' and its bundle of resources and capabilities are especially provided to the firm through the CEO's activity (Habbershon et al., 2003; Ensley and Pearson, 2005; Minichilli et al., 2010). In fact, the CEO is generally regarded as the most important and powerful organizational actor with responsibility for the overall structure, conduct and performance of the firm and, particularly, for the distribution of responsibilities and tasks within the TMT (Finkelstein and Hambrick, 1996; Wu et al., 2005). As a consequence, CEO dominance inside both the organization as a whole and the TMT is likely to be higher for family CEOs than for external appointees.

Given these characteristics of family CEOs, we assume they are key actors in putting family orientation into practice. Responsible ownership values might then be reflected in formulation and adoption of consistent recruitment and career policies under the CEO's leadership. Also, CEO dominance provides the family CEO with both means and motives to behave 'altruistically'. Altruism is 'a moral value that motivates individuals to undertake actions that benefit others without any expectation of external reward' (Schulze et al., 2002, p. 252). Schulze et al. (2001, 2002, 2003) suggest that in this vein the family CEO will make decisions that favour firm profits and profitability and thus benefit the owning family as well, which should include selecting the best talents independently of gender and family membership.

Hence, based on the arguments above, we hypothesized the following:

Hypothesis 2a   There will be a positive relationship between the presence of a family CEO and the presence of women (family and non-family) in the firm's top management team.

Conversely, in contexts of family ownerships' family-first and chauvinistic values, family CEO might translate them into firm policies that hamper rather than support women's careers. Asymmetrical altruism combined with such values might enhance obstacles to women: to family women in favour of male heirs; to non-family women in favour of family heirs, whatever their gender. This would bring about the following:

Hypothesis 2b   There will be a negative relationship between the presence of a family CEO and the presence of women (family and non-family) in the firm's top management team.

TMTs and Gender Diversity in Family Firms: Exploring the Role of Female CEOs

Another apparently double-edged determinant of women's careers is represented by women themselves. Specifically, we focus on women who have already achieved leadership appointments, and particularly the CEO position. In doing so, we follow research showing how the presence of a woman CEO positively influences female presence (family and non-family) in the TMT of family SMEs (Gnan and Montemerlo, 2008). Also, female CEOs are supposed to understand all the difficulties that other women may encounter and to create an organizational context that helps talents to emerge independently of gender, and that especially helps women in balancing family and career. This would especially occur if female CEOs were fully endowed with the aptitudes, skills and capabilities that a responsibility role requires, which includes gender maturity, defined as the 'individual adult's awareness of gender as an influence on behaviour and social constructs and his or her conscious integration of both gender qualities in self concept, social roles and behaviour' (Bird and Brush, 2002, p. 56). Gendered maturity, regardless of a person's biological sex, is seen as a key condition for achieving success in top positions and make the most of the female-specific talents mentioned above. Based on the previous arguments, we hypothesize the following:

Hypothesis 3a   There will be a positive relationship between the presence of a female CEO and the presence of women (family and non-family) in the firm's top management team.

On the other hand, some of the above-mentioned studies on gender issues in family business highlight that women-in-command may create more obstacles to daughter-successors than their male colleagues do, or that they may simply not help other women, either family or non-family (Dumas, 1989; Cole, 1998; Vera and Dean, 2005). Business studies not specific to family firms also assume that, given the difficulties and pressures that they need to face, family CEOs might be reluctant to put their careers at risk by selecting other women for TMT positions (Klenke, 2003). This might be enhanced in the case of women with low gender maturity and masculine, competitive styles (Bird and Brush, 2002). Thus we also formulate the opposite:

Hypothesis 3b   There will be a negative relationship between the presence of a female CEO and the presence of women (family and non-family) in the firm's top management team.

3 RESEARCH METHOD AND FINDINGS

Sample and Collection of Data

The data for this study have been collected through a questionnaire survey administered in mid-2008. This choice has been motivated by evidence that information on TMTs' characteristics and composition is not available in Italy, especially for non-publicly listed firms, which represent the vast majority of our target population. The sample frame for the survey consisted of the top 2221 industrial Italian family-controlled firms with revenues over €50 million, identified from public sources, such as AIDA (Italian Digital Database of Companies), which is part of the Bureau van Dijk European databases. To identify family firms out of the original population of all the Italian firms above €50 million in turnover, we collected data on ownership structure through the Consob (Italian Commission for the Stock Exchange) for the listed firms, and through AIDA for the non-listed. The definition of family control we adopted is the power to appoint the board of directors, both directly and through financial holdings (Minichilli et al., 2010). We consider a firm in family control where the same family owns more than 50 per cent of the shares. The threshold is reduced to 30 per cent for listed companies, which is reasonable given the specific features of the Italian Stock Exchange both in terms of average size and average stock ownership (Corbetta and Minichilli, 2006). Having both public and private firms in the same sample in the Italian context is not surprising. This is due to the very small number of public firms (fewer than 300 in total, including financial firms and high-tech ventures), and to the presence of large private firms, often family-controlled. Moreover, publicly listed family-controlled firms in Italy have strong familial characteristics: in 53.5 per cent of the family-controlled listed firms, the CEO is a family member, while the chairman is a member of the controlling family in 71.9 per cent of these firms. In 44.7 per cent of cases, both the chairman and the CEO are members of the controlling family (Corbetta and Minichilli, 2006).

Further, moving from the original list of the largest 2221 family-controlled firms over €50 million, we excluded all the sub-holdings and generally all the firms controlled by other firms included in the above list to take into account the strong presence of large business groups in Italy. Based on these criteria, the final population consisted of 1776 family-controlled firms featuring the characteristics described above.

Data Collection Procedure

In late March 2008, we sent an electronic questionnaire survey via e-mail to all chairpersons of these 1776 firms to gather information on their TMTs' characteristics. The electronic survey mode has been preferred as it reduces the possibility of mistakes in the data entry procedures. Given that most of the information required in the questionnaire refers to objective data, we considered it proper to have at least one respondent as a key informant in the TMT for each of the firms involved in the survey. Surveys on top managers suffer from low response rates (Pettigrew, 1992). For this reason, and to ensure the highest possible response, we followed some of the consolidated techniques in survey research (Groves et al., 1992; Fowler, 1993; Carpenter and Westphal, 2001): an in-depth pre-test to streamline the questionnaire with some family chairpersons, a review by a panel of academic experts on gender-related issues, a formal request for participation to sampled chairpersons emphasizing the need for further research on TMTs and women. To further encourage participation in the survey, we promised to invite all the responding chairpersons to a presentation of the most relevant results. Additionally, we sent two reminders in May and June 2008; in the meantime, we also conducted a telephone recall to persuade non-respondents to take part in the survey. Overall, the data collection procedure took four months, and it was completed by mid-July 2008.

As a result of the above procedure, we received responses from 141 different TMTs in the same number of firms, 9 of which (6.4 per cent) were publicly listed at the Milan Stock Exchange. This represents a gross response rate of 7.9 per cent. Unfortunately, a significant number of questionnaires had missing values on some of the most relevant variables. For the purposes of this study, we have been able to use at least 75 full questionnaires (77 for the first two sets of analyses), having complete observations on all the variables described in the following section. Hence the net response rate, calculated on the final population of 1776 firms defined according to the above criteria, is 4.2 per cent, which is slightly below the response rate obtained in previous survey studies on top management teams (Cycyota and Harrison, 2006). However, the sensitivity of the issue investigated (gender) may partially explain the figures we obtained.

We also collected additional archival data for firms in the larger sample frame in order to check for the non-respondent bias. Data on firm characteristics from AIDA were used to examine whether there are significant differences between respondents and non-respondents. We performed the non-parametric, two independent samples test using the Kolmogorov–Smirnov procedure on different variables, such as size, geographical distribution, generation and industry (Siegel and Castellan, 1988). This test assesses whether significant differences exist in the distribution of respondents and non-respondents for the variables we indicate, including differences in central tendency, dispersion and skewness. The results of this test indicate that respondents and non-respondents came from the same population.

Variables and Measures

Dependent variables
Both dependent and independent variables were collected via the questionnaire survey. The questionnaire survey allowed us to gather information not publicly available, especially with respect to top executives. Notably, doing the survey helped determine the number and gender of family members inside the TMTs with more accuracy than using public sources, which, for instance, estimate family membership based solely on the family name. As such, the use of publicly available information does not identify kinship relationships with people bearing a different family name from the controlling family's, thereby providing biased results (Villalonga and Amit, 2006). The dependent variables for this study are three different but related measures of women's involvement within TMTs of the family-controlled companies included in our target population. Specifically, on one hand, we computed the *TMTWomenRatio*, which is the overall ratio of female managers within the top management team of each firm. On the other hand, we calculated two additional dependent variables considering whether female managers belong to the controlling family or not. They are the *TMTfamilyWomenRatio*, that is, the ratio

between the number of women in top management positions belonging to the controlling family and the total number of TMTs' members for each firm. Conversely, the *TMT Nonfamily Women Ratio* is the ratio between the number of women in top management positions not belonging to the controlling family and the total number of TMTs' members for each of the firms in our sample. All the dependent variables have been built combining the information about gender and family membership that we collected for each TMT member in the surveyed firms.

Independent variables
The independent variables of this study are family ownership, family CEO and female CEO. All this information has been collected through the same survey following the indications above. Specifically, we asked respondents to acknowledge directly about: (i) family ownership, that is, the percentage of shares held by the controlling family; (ii) the presence of a family CEO, coded as a dummy variable with value 1 if the CEO was a member of the controlling family, and 0 otherwise; (iii) the presence of a female CEO, coded as a dummy variable with value 1 if the CEO was a woman, and 0 otherwise.

Control variables
Control variables include different measures both at the firm, family and TMT level. All these variables aim to capture other possible influences on the presence of women inside the TMT besides the predictors we identified above. Specifically, *firm age* was measured as the logarithmic transformation of the number of years the firm has operated; similarly, *firm size* has been computed as the logarithmic transformation of the annual turnover of a given firm; *listing* was coded 1 if the firm was listed at the Milan Stock Exchange, and 0 otherwise; $ROE(n-1)$ is the previous year's performance in terms of return on equity, calculated as net profit over net capital; *first generation* is a dummy variable indicating whether the family firm had still the founder active in the firm's leadership; *CEO age* has been computed as the absolute age of the firm's CEO; *TMT size* has been computed as a logarithmic transformation of the number of TMT members. All logarithmic transformations have been performed to adjust for skewed distribution of the originating variables.

Analyses and results
Table 14.1 presents the means, standard deviations, and correlations among all predictors, outcome and control variables.

The table shows reasonably low correlations among dependent variables and our predictors. The only rather high correlation emerges between *firm age* and *first generation*, as expected. Significant correlations emerge also between our three dependent variables, which, however, are never used together in the same regression models. Other significant correlations are between *TMT size* and both *firm age* (0.37**) and *firm size* (0.38**). Instead, the presence of a family CEO is negatively related to the previous variables (respectively, −0.24** with firm age, and −0.25** with firm size), which indicates how firms in our sample have experienced a managerialization process – as long as the firm has matured and 'grown up' – characterized both by a larger presence of top managers and a relatively lesser presence of family leaders. With respect to our dependent variables, then, positive correlations emerge between the overall presence of women in the TMT

Table 14.1 *Descriptives, correlations, outcome and control variables*

	Mean	S.d.	1.	2.	3.	4.	5.	6.	7.	8.	9.	10.	11.	12.	13.
1. Firm age (Ln)	3.82	0.73	1												
2. Firm size (Ln)	11.8	0.77	0.21	1											
3. Listing	0.04	0.20	0.03	0.17	1										
4. ROE (n-1)	8.25	15.1	0.11	0.37**	0.10	1									
5. First generation	0.23	0.42	-0.61**	-0.02	0.05	0.05	1								
6. CEO age	52.3	11.1	0.01	0.06	0.19	-0.06	-0.09	1							
7. TMT size (Ln)	1.6	0.75	0.37**	0.38**	0.01	0.20	-0.17	0.02	1						
8. Family ownership	90.1	18.8	0.09	-0.05	-0.30**	0.06	-0.04	0.11	0.16	1					
9. Family CEO	0.87	0.34	-0.24*	-0.25*	-0.12	-0.11	0.02	-0.19	-0.21	-0.11	1				
10. Woman CEO	0.12	0.32	-0.05	-0.28*	-0.07	-0.15	-0.10	-0.21	-0.29**	-0.12	0.14	1			
11. TMT Women Ratio	0.18	0.22	0.02	0.05	-0.07	0.21	0.02	0.01	0.22	0.29*	-0.09	0.06	1		
12. TMT Family Women Ratio	0.08	0.14	-0.04	-0.22	-0.12	0.12	0.12	-0.08	0.04	0.14	0.22	0.31**	0.54**	1	
13. TMT Nonfamily Women Ratio	0.09	0.18	0.05	0.23*	0.00	0.16	-0.06	0.07	0.23*	0.23*	-0.27*	-0.16	0.77**	-0.11	1

Note: Pearson's product-moment correlation coefficients; 2-tailed: $* < 0.05$, $** < 0.01$; $N = 75$.

and family ownership (0.29**), the presence of family women in the TMT and the presence of a woman CEO (0.31**), the presence of non-family women in the TMT and TMT size (0.23*), the presence of non-family women in the TMT and family ownership (0.23*). Instead, the ratio of non-family females in the TMT is negatively associated with the presence of a family CEO (−0.27*). Despite the low level of correlation, we also examined the variance inflation factor (VIF) of each independent variable in each of the regression models presented below in order to detect potential problems with multicollinearity. VIF values range consistently from 1 to 3, and so multicollinearity is generally not a problem in our study (Pelled et al., 1999).

Empirical analyses have been realized through hierarchical multiple regressions. Due to listwise deletion procedure, the final number of valid and complete cases considering missing values is 77 for both *TMTWomenRatio* and for *TMTFamilyWomenRatio*, and 75 for the *TMTNonfamilyWomenRatio*. However, despite the relatively low response rate with respect to our originating population, the sample size is in line with previous studies on TMTs (e.g. Wiersema and Bantel, 1992; Smith et al., 1994; Sutcliffe, 1994; Iaquinto and Fredrickson, 1997; Miller et al., 1998; Pelled et al., 1999; Simons et al., 1999; Tihanyi et al., 2000).

To test the hypotheses in this study we ran regressions in four different steps, each one corresponding to a different model (models I to IV for each of the three dependent variables). Specifically, controls were entered in model I, percentage of family ownership was entered in model II, presence of a family CEO was entered in model III, and the presence of a woman CEO was entered in model IV. The significance of each hypothesis was evaluated by examining the change in F values (ΔF) in each step and using t-values to interpret the significance of individual beta parameters. Detailed results are presented in Table 14.2.

As the table shows, results differ according to the dependent variable. When the overall ratio of women managers over TMT is considered (*TMTWomenRatio*), family ownership emerges as the most significant predictor of women's presence in TMTs (0.24* in model IV). Although the F-sign of some of the models is not significant, the F-change from model I (control variables only) to model II (considering family ownership) is shown to be significant (3.62*). Results differ when considering the ratio of family and non-family women in TMTs. The presence of family women seems to be positively influenced both by the presence of a family CEO (0.23*) and the presence of a woman CEO (0.41***). As to the control variables, they indicate that the presence of family women in TMTs is more likely in high-performing firms, and when the TMT becomes larger. Further, during the first generation it seems more likely to have women among the top managers of the firm. All the models considering the presence of family women in TMTs are strong and significant, with high R-squared and F-changes with respect to our interest variables. Conversely, when the presence of non-family women is considered, family ownership appears to exercise a positive influence (0.21+), while the presence of a family CEO seems to be an obstacle to the presence of female top managers not belonging to the controlling family (−0.22+). Although models are less significant, F-changes from model I to model II (3.46+), and from model II to model III (3.14+) indicate that our interest variables may actually have an impact on the presence on non-family women in TMTs, while all controls are shown to be not significant to our purposes.

Based on the analyses above, Hypothesis 1a about the positive influence of family ownership on women's presence in TMTs is supported; specifically, the split of women's

Table 14.2 *Regression models*

Standardized beta coefficients	Model I	Model II	Model III	Model IV	Model I	Model II	Model III	Model IV	Model I	Model II	Model III	Model IV
	DV: TMT Women Ratio				DV: TMT family Women Ratio				DV: TMT Non-family Women Ratio			
Controls												
Firm age	−0.08	−0.11	−0.12	−0.12	0.12	0.11	0.17	0.16	−0.11	−0.13	−0.19	−0.20
Firm size	−0.07	−0.04	−0.05	−0.02	−0.37**	−0.35**	−0.32*	−0.25*	0.15	0.18	0.15	0.14
Listing	−0.09	−0.01	−0.02	−0.01	−0.09	−0.06	−0.04	−0.04	−0.04	0.04	0.03	0.03
ROE(n−1)	0.21+	0.18	0.18	0.19	0.19+	0.18	0.18	0.20+	0.09	0.07	0.07	0.06
First generation	0.00	−0.02	−0.03	−0.02	0.25+	0.23+	0.27+	0.30*	−0.09	−0.11	−0.15	−0.16
CEO age	0.06	0.02	0.01	0.04	−0.05	−0.06	−0.02	0.06	0.06	0.02	−0.02	−0.03
TMT size	0.23+	0.19	0.19	0.22+	0.15	0.13	0.14	0.22+	0.18	0.14	0.13	0.11
Predictors												
Family ownership		0.23*	0.23+	0.24*		0.10	0.12	0.14		0.23+	0.21+	0.21+
Family CEO			−0.05	−0.05			0.23+	0.22*			−0.22+	−0.22+
Woman CEO				0.15				0.41***				−0.05
R^2	0.09	0.14	0.15	0.16	0.17	0.18	0.22	0.36	0.09	0.14	0.18	0.18
Adj R^2	0.01	0.04	0.03	0.04	0.08	0.08	0.12	0.26	0.00	0.04	0.07	0.06
F-sign	1.01	1.43	1.28	1.35	2.05+	1.86+	2.13*	3.67**	0.99	1.34	1.58	1.14
F-change	1.01	3.62*	0.18	1.48	2.05+	0.65	3.67+	13.91***	0.99	3.46+	3.14+	0.19
N	77	77	77	77	77	77	77	77	75	75	75	75

Note: + = 0.10 level, * = 0.05 level, ** = 0.01 level, *** = 0.001 level.

315

presence in its family and non-family components shows that such a positive impact relates to non-family women only. Conversely, Hypothesis 1b is not supported. As to Hypotheses 2a and 2b about the positive and negative effects of family CEOs on women's presence in TMTs, respectively, they are not supported in general; nevertheless, Hypothesis 2a is supported with respect to family women and Hypothesis 2b is supported with respect to non-family female presence in TMTs. Similarly, as far as Hypothesis 3a on the positive impact of a female CEO on women's presence in TMTs is concerned, our results indicate that this hypothesis is not supported in general, but only with respect to family women. Conversely, Hypothesis 3b is not supported.

4   DISCUSSION, LIMITATIONS, RESEARCH PERSPECTIVES AND PRACTICE IMPLICATIONS

Discussion

The main purpose of this study was to bring an upper echelon perspective into family business studies, investigating top management teams' composition with respect to gender diversity and its determinants as well as splitting gender diversity into family and non-family women's involvement; to the best of our knowledge, this is the first study to address these issues. The potential determinants of women's involvement that we considered, following previous research, are family nature of the firm – in terms of family ownership and family leadership – as well as female leadership. Although preliminary, our research findings provide insights for discussions, and they aim to contribute both theoretically and empirically to the hotly debated topic of women's involvement in top managerial positions.

First, family ownership appears to be a positive determinant of female representation in general, and particularly of non-family women's representation, in TMTs. On this finding, our argument is that owning family's orientation may actually feature a strong sense of responsibility towards family business continuity and thereby inspire an organizational context open to talented women in top positions, whether they belong to the family or not. In fact, family ownership seems to encourage firms to recruit managerial resources regardless of gender and family membership. In the resource-based and decision-making perspective, responsible family owners might do this in order to strengthen TMTs' diversity and thus leverage a richer pool of resources and enhance quality of organizational outcomes (Van der Walt and Ingley, 2003). Also, responsible family ownership may better understand women's special challenge to meet family and job needs, and may consequently shape an organizational context where career opportunities are supported by work conditions consistent with such a challenge. According to recent interpretations of agency relationships in family firms, this might reflect an altruistic attitude of family owners towards women (Schulze et al., 2001); what is more, altruism seems to especially address non-family women, which represents a further evidence of responsible ownership values.

On the other hand, such values do not seem to flow easily from family ownership to family CEOs' actions, as our findings show that family CEOs appear not only to favour family women's involvement in TMTs, but also to 'penalize' non-family women. In the light of agency theory, altruism might actually be operating in an uneven way; particularly, family CEOs might altruistically support family women to the detriment of non-family women (Schulze et al., 2001). In fact, family CEOs might be so committed to breaking the glass ceiling for their female relatives that they end up neglecting non-family candidates for top positions, and they might be subject to a sort of 'selection bias' as well. Social identity factors might also be present; that is, homogeneity of female TMTs' component might be privileged due to solidarity to the CEO's own family group (Richard and Shelor, 2002). Another possible explanation could be that non-family women constrain themselves even more than family women do and ultimately let the latter emerge, taking limited responsibilities and refraining from top management challenges (Salganicoff, 1990; Vera and Dean, 2005).

In essence, the two variables that we used to test the impact of firm's family nature on female involvement in TMTs partially led to diverging findings, as owning families seem to be more open to women than the CEOs they appoint, if they appoint a family one; or putting owning family's values into practice might prove to be tough. Nevertheless, the 'family-first' attitude of family CEOs that emerged from the present research is somewhat surprising and is worth further exploration in future studies.

With respect to the role of female CEOs, our findings show that female CEOs' effect on women's involvement in TMT is similar to that of family CEOs. Female CEOs actually appear to be the strongest, positive drivers of family women's presence, but they do not predict the presence of non-family women. Since all female CEOs are also family members, this shows that both family membership and gender of the CEO are important determinants of family women's representation in TMTs. In their family vest, female CEOs might be too much concentrated on family women's careers to be able to devote analogous efforts to non-family women's ones. In their female vest, female CEOs might be led by a weak gender maturity to adopt a 'masculine' approach – that is, more competitive than cooperative – towards non-family female managers and especially towards younger ones (Brush, 1992; Bird and Brush, 2002). Both asymmetric altruism (Schultze et al., 2001) and group solidarity (Richard and Shelor, 2002) might explain such attitudes towards non-family women.

In summary, gender diversity in TMTs seems to be favoured by the family nature of the firm, but at the same time to be partial in medium and large family companies, as it appears to privilege family women.

Our research suggests that the obstacles that family women may encounter in their career, including those coming from their own relatives, might be overcome by the opportunities that the family nature of the firm offers them, which contributes to clarifying the ambivalence that has so far emerged in family business literature regarding whether family firms represent a positive or negative factor for family women's careers within them. Opportunities from the firm's family nature seem to come through family ownership and family CEOs, and they can be read in the light of both the resource-based and decision-making perspectives and the agency and social identity ones.

Conversely, the presence of a family CEO seems to favour in principle, but to hamper in practice, the presence of non-family women in TMTs. In this case, agency and social identity-based factors apparently prevail over resource-based and decision-making ones, which may shrink the firm's resource pool by limiting it to family candidates.

Limitations and Perspectives for Future Research

The study has some limitations that open the way for further inquiry.

First of all, larger samples should be analysed in various countries to check whether the findings are influenced by national, cultural-specific factors.

Second, the study measures women's presence in terms of percentage of female top managers out of the total number of top managers. But what specific managerial roles do women play, and for what reasons? For example, we did not distinguish between line and staff managerial roles, and if women's presence were concentrated in staff ones the interpretation of the results might take a different light.

Third, we looked at the presence of total women in TMTs. But is there any difference between the presence of junior and senior women and related determinants? A study by Chrisman et al. (1998) found that a sample of about 480 Canadian family business members ranked gender and blood relations lowest among successors' preferred attributes, and similar results were found in an Indian sample (Sharma and Rao, 2000). So, we might expect a differentiated presence of senior and junior women in TMTs as well as more openness to junior non-family women, in particular.

Also, we do not have data on women's characteristics in TMTs. What type of women are chosen, and based on which criteria? If family women are preferred, is this the result of a meritocratic selection or of a nepotistic orientation?

Finally, there is an even larger research area to further develop the results achieved so far and to address other important questions that still deserve more attention, such as: how do women's distinctive contributions shape key business roles such as TMT ones? How is women's contribution to key roles, such as TMT ones, reflected in family business resources, behaviours and performance? (Brush, 1992; Sharma, 2004). On top of that, some thought-provoking questions are emerging from entrepreneurship studies, as mentioned above: does it make sense to deal with 'women' as a homogeneous category, while differences might be bigger within the feminine gender than between feminine and masculine genders (Bird and Brush, 2002; Ahl, 2006)?

Implications for Family Firms

As to implications for family firms, the study seems to suggest that, first, in their careers, female family members can count on favourable conditions in terms of both owning family's openness and of family CEOs' support; obstacles might also come from within the family, but the 'net effect' of belonging to the owning family appears to be positive. This is a further and important stimulus for family women not to constrain themselves to roles of minor responsibility, but on the contrary to feel free and committed to prepare themselves so as to become qualified enough to apply for top executive positions. In fact, extant literature shows that women's self-constraints can be decisive factors and even counterbalance the opportunities that the family business context seems to offer to female family members (Dumas, 1989; Salganicoff, 1990; Cole, 1998; Vera and Dean, 2005).

Second, family CEOs might want to reflect very carefully on the reasons that might lead them to behaviours inspired by asymmetric altruism as well as by non-family discrimination and on the related risks for company's viability, and thereby adopt recruiting and career systems that give real peer opportunities to high-potential women as candidates for TMT positions, not to give up valuable resources. The same would be important for female CEOs; besides, it is crucial for them to develop an adequate gender maturity (Bird and Brush, 2002) to be able to effectively groom other talented women, either family or non-family, and give them the chance not to experience the same difficulties they might have encountered.

Third, owning families might seriously consider their family education systems to make sure that both female and male heirs grow up free from gender prejudices, and they might want to check the actual consistency between the distinctive values of responsible ownership and their own values, as well as the human resource management policies that derive from such values – again, to prevent detrimental agency and social identity effects.

Finally, professionals and educators serving family firms should take the important challenges to help family women in their careers to develop mature identities and distinguished skills, to assist family CEOs and female CEOs to apply meritocratic policies and rules in human resources management, to support families in keeping and transmitting the values of responsible ownership that need to support policies and rules and also to contribute to the spreading of such values throughout the family firms' population, so that these firms enhance their capacity to attract and retain the best talents regardless of gender and blood relations, which is increasingly crucial given the environmental complexity to be coped with, at present times but also, and possibly even more, in the future.

REFERENCES

Ahl, H. (2006), 'Why research on women entrepreneurs needs new direction', *Entrepreneurship Theory and Practice,* **30**(5), 595–621.

AldAF-Alberto Falck Chair (2008), *Giovani e donne nelle aziende familiari: una ricerca esplorativa* (Youngsters and women in family firms: an exploratory study), Research Report, Università Bocconi.

Allen, I.E. and Langowitz, N.S. (2003), *Women in Family-Owned Businesses*, MassMutual and Center for Women's Leadership, Babson College.

Allen, I.E., Elam, A., Langowitz, N. and Dean, M. (2007), *Report on Women and Entrepreneurship*, Global Entrepreneurship Monitor.

Aronoff, C.E. and Ward, J.L. (1992), 'The critical value of stewardship', *Nation's Business*.

Aronoff, C.E. and Ward, J.L. (2000), *More than Family: Non-Family Executives in the Family Business*, Marietta, GA: Family Enterprise Publishers.

Barnes, L.B. (1988), 'Incongruent hierarchies: daughters and younger sons as company CEOs', *Family Business Review*, **1**(1), 9–21.

Barnett, T. and Kellermanns, F.W. (2006), 'Are we family and are we treated as family? Perceptions of justice in the family firm', *Entrepreneurship Theory and Practice*, **30**(6), 837–54.

Bird, B. and Brush, C.A. (2002), 'Gendered perspective on organizational creation', *Entrepreneurship Theory and Practice*, **26**(3), 41–65.

Blumentritt, T.P., Keyt, A.D. and Astrachan, J.H. (2008), 'Creating an environment for successful nonfamily CEOs: an exploratory study of good principals', *Family Business Review*, **XX**(4), 321–36.

Brush, C.G. (1992), 'Research on women business owners: past trends, a new perspective, and future direction', *Entrepreneurship Theory and Practice*, **16**(4), 5–30.

Carpenter, M.A. and Westphal, J.D. (2001), 'The strategic context of external network ties: examining the impact of director appointments on board involvement in strategic decision making', *Academy of Management Journal*, **44**(4), 639–60.

Catalyst (2004), *The Bottom Line: Connecting Corporate Performance and Gender Diversity*, New York.

Chrisman, J.J, Chua, J.H. and Sharma, P. (1998), 'Important attributes of successors in family businesses: an exploratory study', *Family Business Review*, **XI**(1), 19–34.

Chua, J.H., Chrisman, J.J. and Sharma, P. (1999), 'Defining the family firm by behavior', *Entrepreneurship Theory and Practice*, **23**(4), 19–39.

Chua, J.H., Chrisman, J.J. and Sharma P. (2003), 'Succession and nonsuccession concerns of family firms and agency relationship with nonfamily managers', *Family Business Review*, **XVI**(2), 89–108.

Cole, P.M. (1998), 'Women in family business', *Family Business Review*, **XI**(4), 353–71.

Cole, P.M. and Johnson, K. (2007), 'An exploration of successful copreneurial relationships after divorce', *Family Business Review*, **XX**(3), 185–98.

Corbetta, G. and Minichilli, A. (2006), 'Board of directors in Italian public family controlled companies', in P. Poutziouris, K. Smyrnios and S.B. Klein (eds), *Family Business Research Handbook*, Cheltenham, UK and Northampton, MA, USA: Edward Elgar, pp. 488–500.

Cycyota, C.S. and Harrison, D.A. (2006), 'What not to expect when surveying executives: a meta-analysis of top manager response rates and techniques over time', *Organizational Research Methods*, **92**, 133–60.

Daily, C.M. and Schwenk, C.R. (1996), 'Chief executive officers, top management teams and boards of directors: congruent or countervailing forces?', *Journal of Management*, **22**(2), 185–208.

Daily, C.M., Certo, S.T. and Dalton, D.R. (1999), 'A decade of corporate women: some progress in the boardroom', *none* in the executive suite', *Strategic Management Journal*, **20**, 93–9.

Dumas, C.A. (1989), 'Understanding of father–daughter and father–son dyads in family-owned businesses', *Family Business Review*, **II**(1), 31–46.

Dumas, C.A. (1990), 'Preparing the new CEO: managing father–daughter succession process in family businesses', *The Family Business Review*, **XIII**(2), 169–81.

Dumas, C.A. (1998), 'Women's pathways to participation and leadership in the family-owned firm', *Family Business Review*, **XI**(3), 219–28.

Dyer, W.G. Jr (1989), 'Integrating professional management into a family owned business', *Family Business Review*, **II**(3), 221–35.

Ensley, M.D. and Pearson, A.W. (2005), 'An exploratory comparison of the behavioral dynamics of top management teams in family and nonfamily new ventures: cohesion, potency, and consensus', *Entrepreneurship Theory and Practice*, **29**(3), 267–84.

Erhardt, N.L., Werbel, J.D. and Shrader, C.B. (2003), 'Board of director diversity and firm financial performance', *Corporate Governance*, **11**(2), 102–11.

Finkelstein, S. and Hambrick, D.C. (1996), *Strategic Leadership. Top Executives and Their Effects on Organizations*, St Paul, MN: West Publishing Company.

Finkelstein, S., Hambrick, D.C. and Cannella, A.A. (2009), *Theory and Research on Executives, Top Management Teams, and Boards*, Oxford: Oxford University Press.

Fowler, F.J. (1993), *Survey Research Methods*, Newbury Park, CA: Sage.

Gillis-Donovan, J. and Moynihan-Brandt, C. (1990), 'The power of invisible women in family business', *Family Business Review*, **III**(2), 153–7.

Gnan, L. and Montemerlo, D. (2008), *Le PMI familiari in Italia tra tradizione e novità* (Italian family SMEs between tradition and change), Milano: EGEA.

Groves, R.M., Cialdini, R.B. and Couper, M.P. (1992), 'Understanding the decision to participate in a survey', *Public Opinion Quarterly*, **56**, 475–95.

Habbershon, T.G., Williams, M. and MacMillan, I.C. (2003), 'A unified perspective of family firm performance', *Journal of Business Venturing*, **18**(4), 451–65.

Hall, A. and Nordqvist, M. (2008), 'Professional management in family businesses: toward an extended understanding', *Family Business Review*, **XXI**(1), 51–70.

Hambrick, D.C. (2007), 'Upper echelons theory: an update', *Academy of Management Review*, **32**(2), 334–43.

Hambrick, D.C. and Mason, P.A. (1984), 'Upper echelons: the organization as a reflection of its top managers', *Academy of Management Review*, **9**(2), 193–206.

Harveston, P.D., Davis, P.S. and Lyden, J.A. (1997), 'Succession planning in family business: the impact of owner gender', *Family Business Review*, **X**(4), 373–96.

Helfat, C.E., Harris, D. and Wolfson, P.J. (2006), 'The pipeline to the top: women and men in the top executive ranks of US corporations', *The Academy of Management Perspective*, **20**(4), 42–64.

Iaquinto, A.L. and Fredrickson, J.W. (1997), 'Top management team agreement about the strategic decision process: a test of some of its determinants and consequences', *Strategic Management Journal*, **18**(1), 63–75.

Joy, L., Carter, N.M., Wagner, H.M. and Narayanan, S. (2007), *The Bottom Line: Corporate Performance and Women Representation on Boards*, New York: Catalyst.

Kilduff, M., Angellmar, R. and Mehra, A. (2000), 'Top management-team diversity and firm performance: examining the role of cognitions', *Organization Science*, **11**(1), 21–34.

Klenke, K. (2003), 'Gender influences in decision-making processes in top management teams', *Management Decision*, **41**(10), 1024–34.

Krishnan, H.A. and Park, D. (2005), 'A few good women – on top management teams', *Journal of Business Research*, **58**, 1712–20.

Martinez Jimenez, R. (2009), 'Research on women in family firms: current status and future directions', *Family Business Review*, **XXII**(1), 53–64.

MassMutual, Kennesaw State University and Family Firm Institute (2007), *American Family Business Survey*, Massachusetts Mutual Life Insurance Company.

Miller, C.C., Burke, L.M. and Glick, W.H. (1998), 'Cognitive diversity among upper-echelon executives: implications for strategic decision processes', *Strategic Management Journal*, **19**(1), 39–58.

Miller, D. and Le Breton-Miller, I. (2006), 'Family governance and firm performance: agency, stewardship, and capabilities', *Family Business Review*, **XIX**(1), 73–86.

Minichilli, A., Corbetta, G. and MacMillan, I.C. (2010), 'Top management teams in family-controlled companies: "Familiness", "Faultlines", and their impact on financial performance', *Journal of Management Studies*, **7**(2), 205–22.

Montemerlo, D. and Ward, J.L. (2005), *The Family Constitution. Agreements to Perpetuate your Family and your Business*, Marietta, GA: Family Enterprise Publishers.

Montemerlo, D. and Profeta, P. (2009), 'La *diversity* di genere nelle aziende familiari: una risorsa da valorizzare' (Gender diversity in family firms: a resource that deserves more value), *Economia e Management*, **6**, 83–96.

Nordqvist, M. (2005), 'Familiness in top management teams: a commentary', *Entrepreneurship Theory and Practice*, **29**(3), 285–92.

Pelled, H.L., Heisenhardt, K.M. and Xin, K.R. (1999), 'Exploring the black box: an analysis of work group diversity, conflict, and performance', *Administrative Science Quarterly*, **44**(1), 1–28.

Pettigrew, A. (1992), 'On studying managerial elites', *Strategic Management Journal*, **13**, special issue, 163–82.

Ponthieu, L.D. and Caudill, H.L. (1993), 'Who's the boss? Responsibility and decision-making in copreneurial ventures', *Family Business Review*, **VI**(1), 3–17.

Powell, G.N. (1999), 'Reflections on the glass ceiling: recent trends and future prospects', in G.N. Powell (ed.), *Handbook of Gender & Work*, Thousand Oaks, CA: Sage Publications, pp. 325–45.

Poza, E. and Messer, T. (2001), 'Spousal leadership and continuity in the family firm', *Family Business Review*, **XIV**(1), 25–35.

Poza, E.J., Hanlon, S. and Kishida, R. (2004), 'Does the family business interaction represent a resource or a cost?', *Family Business Review*, **XVII**(2), 99–118.

Richard, O.C. and Shelor, R.M. (2002), 'Linking top management team age heterogeneity to firm performance: juxtaposing two mid-range theories', *The International Journal of Human Resource Management*, **13**(6), 958–74.

Rose, C. (2007), 'Does female representation influence firm performance? The Danish evidence', *Corporate Governance*, **15**(2), 404–13.

Rowe, B.R. and Hong, G. (2000), 'The role of wives in family business: the paid and unpaid work of women', *Family Business Review*, **XIII**(1), 1–13.

Salganicoff, M. (1990), 'Women in family business: challenges and opportunities', *Family Business Review*, **XIII**(2), 125–37.

Schulze, W.S., Lubatkin, M.H., Dino, R.N. and Buchholtz, A.K. (2001), 'Agency relationships in family firms: theory and evidence', *Organization Science*, **12**, 99–116.

Schulze, W.S., Lubatkin, M.H. and Dino, R.N. (2002), 'Altruism, agency, and the competitiveness of family firms', *Managerial Decision Economics*, **23**(4–5), 247–59.

Schulze, W.S., Lubatkin, M.H. and Dino, R.N. (2003), 'Toward a theory of altruism in family firms', *Journal of Business Venturing*, **18**, 473–90.

Sharma, P. (2004), 'An overview of the field of family business studies: current status and directions for the future', *Family Business Review*, **XVII**(1), 1–36.

Sharma, P. and Rao, A.S. (2000), 'Successor attributes in Indian and Canadian family firms: a comparative study', *Family Business Review*, **XIII**(4), 313–30.

Shrader, C.B., Blackburn, V. and Iles, P. (1997), 'Women in management and firm financial performance: an exploratory study', *Journal of Managerial Issues*, **9**, 355–72.

Siegel, S. and Castellan, N.J. (1988), *Nonparametric Statistics for the Behavioral Sciences*, 2nd edn, New York: McGraw-Hill.

Simons, T., Pelled, H.L. and Smith, K.A. (1999), 'Making use of difference: diversity, debate, and decision comprehensiveness in top management teams', *Academy of Management Journal*, **42**(6), 662–73.

Smith, K.G., Smith, K.A., Olian, J.D., Sims, H.P. Jr, O'Bannon, D.P. and Scully, J.A. (1994), 'Top management team demography and process: the role of social integration and communication', *Administrative Science Quarterly*, **39**, 412–38.

Sorenson, R.L. (2000), 'The contribution of leadership style and practices to family and business success', *Family Business Review*, **XIII**(3), 183–200.

Sutcliffe, K.M. (1994), 'What executives notice: accurate perceptions in top management teams', *Academy of Management Journal*, **37**(5), 1360–78.

Tihanyi, L., Ellstrand, A.E., Daily, C.M. and Dalton, D.R. (2000), 'Composition of the Top Management Team and firm international diversification', *Journal of Management*, **26**(6), 1157–77.

Van Auken, H. and Werbel, J. (2006), 'Family dynamic and family business financial performance: spousal commitment', *Family Business Review*, **XIX**(1), 49–64.

Van der Walt, N. and Ingley, C. (2003), 'Board dynamics and the influence of professional background, gender and ethnic diversity of directors', *Corporate Governance*, **11**(3), 218–34.

Vera, F.V. and Dean, A.D. (2005), 'An examination of the challenges daughters face in family business succession', *Family Business Review*, **XVIII**(4), 321–45.

Villalonga, B. and Amit, R. (2006), 'How do family ownership, control and management affect firm value?', *Journal of Financial Economics*, **80**(2), 385–417.

Wiersema, M.F. and Bantel, K.A. (1992), 'Top Management Team demography and corporate strategic change', *Academy of Management Journal*, **35**(1), 91–121.

Wu, S., Levitas, E. and Priem, R.L. (2005), 'CEO tenure and company invention under differing levels of technological dynamism', *Academy of Management Journal*, **48**(5), 859–73.

15 Women and the glass ceiling: the role of professionalization in family SMEs

Luca Gnan and Lucrezia Songini

INTRODUCTION

The chapter focuses on two topics, rarely jointly analyzed by literature: the multifaceted role of women in family firms and its quite complex relationship with the enterprise's professionalization.

First, it examines if in family SMEs the 'glass ceiling' exists and bars women from advancing to governance and managerial roles. We assume that the presence of a 'glass ceiling' in a firm implies that women are not in a position to exercise an active role in it and they do not have the opportunity to enhance their role.

Previous research on women focused on their managerial positions in large companies (Grant, 1988; Ohlott et al., 1994; Bombelli, 2000; O'Connor, 2001). The literature on family firms mainly considered women in ownership and in governance (Goffee and Scase, 1985; Moore and Buttner, 1997; Gnan and Montemerlo, 2001; Montemerlo and Gnan, 2001; Songini and Dubini, 2003). Only a few contributions explored women as top and executive managers in family firms, considering mostly how women can reach managerial roles as a consequence of the succession process (Frishkoff and Brown, 1997; Cole, 1997; Dumas, 1998; Cadieux et al., 2002; Allen and Langowitz, 2003).

The chapter analyzes women's role in both governance and managerial positions, exploring the conditions for glass ceiling removal in family SMEs. We assume that the presence of women in ownership *per se* does not assure the elimination of the glass ceiling. In family SMEs, we argue that the broader involvement of women in governance and managerial roles (Montemerlo and Gnan, 2001; Gnan and Montemerlo, 2008) can represent a better situation for glass ceiling removal (Hisrich and Brush, 1984; Aldrich, 1989; Veale and Gold, 1998).

Second, we propose that in family SMEs the broader involvement of women in governance and managerial roles can influence both company's strategy and organization (in terms of structure, processes and mechanisms). Thus women also affect the adoption of managerial mechanisms, affecting the enterprise's professionalization. In particular, the professionalization of family SMEs is associated with the presence of: (1) formal governance mechanisms, such as the board of directors, and (2) formal strategic planning and managerial control systems – MCS (Ward, 1991, 2001; Dyer, 2001; Schulze et al., 2003; Montemerlo et al., 2004; Villalonga and Amit, 2006; Songini, 2006; Songini and Gnan, 2008) and (3) non-family members in boards and management, often called professional managers (Songini, 2006).

A number of studies addressed the family firm's professionalization issue (Schulze et al., 2001; Songini, 2006; Songini and Gnan, 2008), but without analyzing the relationship between women and professionalization.

Previous research on women-owned and managed firms focused on objectives, management styles, decision-making processes and start-up strategies of female entrepreneurs (Watkins and Watkins, 1984; Hisrich and Brush, 1987; Cromie and Hayes, 1988; Carter and Cannon, 1992; Brush, 1992; Allen and Truman, 1993; Powell et al., 2002). But research said little about how women run their family firms, as managers, considering the diffusion of formal governance and managerial mechanisms, the strategy formulation processes and the organization structures (Cuba et al., 1983; Carter et al., 1997; Cliff, 1998).

Finally, literature highlighted the role of governance and top management teams in the adoption of formalized governance, strategic planning and management control systems (Zimmerman, 2006; Naranjo-Gil et al., 2009).

Accordingly, the chapter outlines, in family SMEs, the relationship between the role of women, as members of the governance and the top management teams, and the enterprise's professionalization, defined as the adoption of formal strategic planning and managerial control systems – MCS (budget, reporting system and incentives).

Three hypotheses on the presence of women in governance and managerial roles and glass ceiling removal are developed; two other hypotheses are elaborated on the relationship between the role of women and the professionalization of family SMEs. We conducted a quantitative deductive design and tested the hypotheses on the data collected through a questionnaire survey on 198 SMEs in Italy (whose 166 were family SMEs).

The findings reveal a limited number of women in governance and managerial roles in SMEs, verifying the presence of the glass ceiling also in family firms. With reference to the role of board member, family SMEs appear as a more favorable context for the glass ceiling's removal. Moreover, the functional director role shows a greater number of women than the governance ones, confirming the tendency for women to cover mostly operating and supporting roles.

As far as the link between the firms' professionalization and the role of women is concerned, we did not find a significant relationship in SMEs. Only in family SMEs is the relationship verified with respect to incentives and reporting systems.

The chapter makes theoretical as well as empirical and practical contributions to literature. The main theoretical contribution regards the presence of the glass ceiling even in family SMEs, the relationship between the involvement of women in governance and managerial roles, and the use of incentives and reporting systems in family firms. Empirically, it explores family SMEs operating in Italy, which is recognized as one of the most interesting contexts in which to study family firms. Finally, from a practical perspective, it helps family SMEs to design a consistent system of managerial mechanisms with, specifically, women's involvement in the business.

The chapter proceeds in five sections. First, the theoretical mainstream about women and family firm professionalization is outlined. Second, hypotheses are derived. In the third section, the research design and methods are described. In the fourth section, findings are presented. Finally, implications and limitations of the chapter are discussed.

THEORETICAL STREAMS

The chapter refers to different theoretical streams: literature on women's role in family firms and glass ceiling removal, literature on women's management styles and approaches to leadership, the research stream on the role of the boards and top management teams in the adoption of managerial mechanisms, and literature on family firms' professionalization.

Women's Role in Family Firms and Glass Ceiling Removal

Most of the studies on women's role in family firms dealt with the ambiguous role of family in supporting female entrepreneurship. On the one hand, the family provides a woman with financial resources and invisible assets, such as consolidated relationships based on trust, knowledge and socialization in the entrepreneurial culture; access to industries traditionally regarded as 'masculine' (e.g. construction); job security; and more chance of accessing positions of responsibility, professional challenges and opportunities for personal growth (Aldrich et al., 1989; Coleman, 2000). On the other hand, the family may be a context of constraint and economic exploitation. Relatives are recognized more with respect to their family role (entrepreneur's wife, son, daughter, nephew, sibling etc.) than their firm role (Hollander and Bukowitz, 1990; Christensen, 1995). This issue is not without consequences for women. Family firms are often characterized by the replication of the same processes of functional specialization of activities and of the typical authority model of the family, the tendency of women to cover operating and supporting roles rather than managerial ones, and the reproduction of patriarchism (Dumas, 1989). Furthermore, in family firms, involvement may be a weak entrepreneurial choice for a woman, particularly when she inherits her firm (Barnes, 1996), even though managerial mechanisms might help her to cope with the reconciliation of work and family roles (especially those of wife and mother). Finally, given both firm and home continuity, women 'should' and might manage the requested double presence (Balbo, 1979; Longstreth et al., 1988).

Many family rules are actually grounded on gender differences and they contribute to women's invisibility in family firms (Christensen, 1995; McGivern, 1978). Women's invisibility relates to: (a) the discrimination, deriving from the social bias against the female gender; and (b) the typical women's socialization process, which may cause difficulties for women in developing the needed attitudes to cope with managerial roles (Salganicoff, 1990).

As far as succession is concerned, the literature suggests that in family firms women's chances of running the company remain slim because of the primogeniture rule (the first-born son usually inherits the business) (Cole, 1997). Women's invisibility and the stereotypical roles are also evident when we analyze the processes that characterize the entry of daughters in family firms and when we explore the succession's processes, where women are rarely considered serious leader's candidates – except during a crisis or when the founder has no sons (Dumas, 1997, 1998; Cadieux et al., 2002; Curimbaba, 2002; Haberman and Danes, 2007).

Due to the ambiguity of the family role, although family firms should be an easier context for glass ceiling removal for women belonging to the owning family, literature still contests the existence of a glass ceiling in such firms (Songini and Dubini, 2003). Nevertheless, only a few studies investigate situations where women are involved not only in ownership, but also in governance and in managerial roles (Cromie and O'Sullivan, 1999; Montemerlo and Gnan, 2001; Gnan and Montemerlo, 2008). These contexts present a relatively high level of formalization of the governance system and a decision-making process based on consensus (Songini and Dubini, 2003). They reveal institutional frameworks that are more open to the presence of different actors in governance and managerial roles and they often achieve good economic performances (Kalleberg and Leicht, 1991; Gnan and Montemerlo, 2001). At the same time, some empirical studies propose that family firms offer advantages that help women progress professionally and achieve managerial positions without coming up against the glass ceiling (Iannarelli, 1992; Dumas, 1998; Jimenez, 2009).

In sum, some studies focused mainly on the difficulties and obstacles that women find when joining family firms and on the lack of recognition for their work, while more recent research has revealed the opportunities and the advantages that family firms can offer women, the pathways that they take to assume positions of management or leadership in these firms, and their achievements (Nelton, 1998; Vera and Dean, 2005; Dugan et al., 2008).

Women's Management Styles and Approaches to Leadership

Literature on women in family firms has mostly dealt with the characteristics of female entrepreneurship, but did not investigate the features of firms managed by women (Smith et al., 1982; Hamilton, 2006; Arenius and Kovalainen, 2006). Female entrepreneurs usually find their firms in the service industry and they run small firms with lower levels of profitability (Anna et al., 1999; Du Rietz and Henrekson, 2000). They pursue different objectives than pure profitability, such as company growth, personal and professional development, and satisfaction as well as employee involvement (Soldressen et al., 1998).

Early research on women-owned firms focused on employment relations, generic SME management issues and broad descriptions of managerial processes (Hisrich and Brush, 1983; Greer and Greene, 2003; Ahl, 2006). Several contributions concerned women's management styles and their approaches to leadership (Helgesen, 1990; Brush, 1992). Mutual empowerment, collaboration, information sharing, empathy and nurturing characterize management styles in women-owned firms (Allen and Langowitz, 2003).

Other research explored the gender effect on both the experience of self-employment and the performance of small businesses (Rosa and Hamilton, 1994; Rosa et al., 1996; Berg, 1997; Carter and Allan, 1997; Watson, 2002), gender differences in business financing (Buttner and Rosen, 1989; Riding and Swift, 1990; Fay and Williams, 1993; Carter and Rosa, 1998), and the use of business networks by female entrepreneurs (Smeltzer and Fann, 1989; Cromie and Birley, 1992). However, research seldom investigated the distinctive characteristics of firms owned and managed by women, such as the diffusion of formal governance and managerial mechanisms, the strategy formulation processes and the organization issues (Cuba et al., 1983; Carter et al., 1997; Cliff, 1998). Practically no contributions analyzed the leadership style of women in the family firm in depth, focusing on how women run their family firms, and what their leadership style is.

The Role of the Boards and Top Management Teams in the Adoption of Managerial Mechanisms

Family business literature has rarely analyzed the mutual influences among planning and control mechanisms and managers, either professional, non-family members, or family members. By contrast, in accounting and finance literature, managers, and in particular CFOs, are generally considered to be in charge of developing and operating management control systems. A recent research stream focused on the relationship between managerial roles and the adoption of management control systems (Zimmerman, 2006; Naranjo-Gil et al., 2009), highlighting that, ultimately, the top management team takes the decision to adopt formalized management control systems and the CFO is in charge of their formalization, development and operation (Zimmerman, 2006; Naranjo-Gil et al., 2009). In the start-up phase the hiring of a finance manager is reported to be associated with a faster adoption of MCS (Davila and Foster, 2005). Abernethy et al. (2010) found that senior management's leadership style is a significant predictor of use of the planning and control systems.

Family Firms' Professionalization

Family firms' professionalization is associated with the presence of: (1) formal governance mechanisms, such as the board of directors; (2) formal strategic planning and managerial control systems (budget, reporting system, and incentives); and (3) non-family members in boards and management, often called professional managers (Songini, 2006). Professionalization is a typical issue of SMEs, but it plays a significant role in family firms as a result of their specific features.

In literature, a general agreement about the need, the effects and the way towards family firms' professionalization has not yet been reached, notwithstanding the many theories dealing with it. Family firms' professionalization features, drivers and advantages may be analyzed following different theories: the stewardship theory (Davis et al., 1997); the resource-based view of the firm (RBV) theory (Habbershon and Williams, 1999); the organizational control theory (Hopwood, 1974; Galbraith, 1977); the agency theory (Ross, 1973; Jensen and Meckling, 1976); and the company growth theory (Rostow, 1960; Greiner, 1972; Normann, 1977). Most of them show that family firms present a lower diffusion and a lower use of formal governance, strategic planning and managerial control systems than non-family firms.

Stewardship and RBV theories suggest that their distinctive characteristics allow family firms to be effectively managed without the adoption of formal managerial mechanisms and the involvement of non-family members. These distinctive characteristics are: familiness, altruism, emotional involvement, common and unique language, and values (Van den Berghe and Carchon, 2003; Poza et al., 2004). It is noteworthy that, according to RBV theory, the board, managers, planning and managerial control systems may be considered relevant resources for family firms. In particular, the role of strategic planning and managerial control system implies: (a) identifying strategic resources, capabilities and opportunities; (b) analyzing strengths and weaknesses of the company and competitors; (c) allocating scarce strategic resources to relevant capabilities; and (d) selecting strategic decisions that better use resources and capabilities (Grant, 1991). Their goal is the optimal allocation of resources with the aim of gaining a competitive advantage that is consistent with the capabilities of the firm.

Organizational control theory reveals that, in family firms, social and individual control systems fit better than the bureaucratic–administrative ones. Family firms present shared values and languages, informal and kinship relationships, small groups of people in charge of ownership, governance and management (Daily and Dollinger, 1992).

Agency theory highlights the need for family firms to adopt agency cost control mechanisms, such as formal governance systems, strategic planning and managerial control systems, and to involve non-family members in governance and managerial roles (Morck et al., 1988; Gallo and Vilaseca, 1998; Gómez-Mejía et al., 2001; Morck and Yeung, 2003; Schulze et al., 2003; Songini and Gnan, 2008). Actually, some family firm characteristics (free-riding, ineffective managers, predatory managers, non-alignment of interests among non-employed shareholders and the top management team) may reveal peculiar agency costs (Myers, 1977; Smith and Warner, 1979; Morck et al., 1988; Bruce and Waldman, 1990; Daily and Dollinger, 1992; Schulze et al., 2001, 2003; Anderson and Reeb, 2003; Chrisman et al., 2003; Anderson et al., 2003; Chrisman et al., 2004; Villalonga and Amit, 2006). As a consequence, family firms should adopt agency cost control mechanisms, such as the board, strategic planning and managerial control systems, to deal with them.

Finally, company growth theory affirms that family firms' professionalization relates to a life-cycle model of the introduction of different mechanisms and the involvement of non-family members, connected to both business and family development (Gersick et al., 1997; Moores and Mula, 2000).

In this chapter, we focus on family firms' professionalization through the adoption of formal strategic planning and managerial control systems (budget, reporting system, and incentives).

HYPOTHESES

Different literature streams have been discussed in the theoretical discussion: literature on women's role in family firms and glass ceiling removal, literature on women's management styles and approaches to leadership, the research stream on the role of the boards and top management teams in the adoption of managerial mechanisms, and literature on family firms' professionalization. Based on these research streams, our conceptual development is as follows:

1. Family SMEs should be a more favorable context for glass ceiling removal than non-family ones, as women are more probably involved not only in ownership, but also in governance and in managerial roles.
2. When women hold governance (i.e. as chairman and/or as board members) and managerial roles, they can influence the strategy and the organization (in terms of structure, processes and mechanisms) of the firm. Therefore they can influence the adoption of managerial mechanisms (strategic planning and managerial control systems – MCS – and the budget, the reporting system and the incentives system) too.
3. In family firms, and in family SMEs as well, the adoption of managerial mechanisms increases the professionalization of the firm.
4. According to literature, the board and top management teams take the decision to adopt formalized strategic planning and management control systems.
5. Accordingly, it is interesting to investigate both whether family firms are really a

more favorable context for glass ceiling removal and how the presence of women in governance and top management roles influence the professionalization of family firms.

Women in Governance and Managerial Roles and the Glass Ceiling

Literature and empirical evidence revealed that women's presence in ownership does not guarantee a significant influence on decision-making processes. Nevertheless, the simple presence of women in governance and managerial roles does not entail glass ceiling removal, even in family firms, that are expected to be a more favorable context (Songini and Dubini, 2003).

Literature on corporate governance (Milliken and Martins, 1996; Huse and Solberg, 2006; Huse, 2007) tackles the complex issue of glass ceiling removal in organizations, particularly in SMEs. The stakeholder approach suggests the presence of a variety of stakeholders with firm-specific stakes (Freeman and Reed, 1983). This situation occurs, for example, in family firms with women who have inherited shares, who do not play an active role in management, and who count on distributed dividends as an important source of income. Furthermore, the stakeholder approach emphasizes an active management of the business environment, suggesting that governance systems and mechanisms are instrumental to the company's success. Therefore glass ceiling removal may take place only when women are not just formally in power, as shareholders, but rather when they are actively involved in running the firm, as members of the board of directors and of the top management team. Thus we state that owning shares in the family firm is a facilitating element for women willing to play a 'public' role within the company in addition to the traditional 'private' one, but is not a sufficient condition for the removal of the glass ceiling, which requires the possibility to influence the strategy and organization and to actively run the company. Consequently the presence of the glass ceiling is associated with the fact that women cannot exercise their power in the firms, even in family ones, because they usually are shareholders, but do not hold powerful positions in governance and management. Thus the presence of women in ownership, governance and managerial positions should be investigated not only in start-ups, but also in ongoing companies, particularly at times of institutional discontinuity (as in the case of entrepreneurial succession), when potentially conflicting views of different stakeholders may be more evident and when the existence of an effective governance structure and mechanisms is more critical.

We hypothesize that family SMEs allow removing the glass ceiling more than non-family ones. In other words, women in governance and managerial roles in SMEs are less numerous than men, even though they are more numerous in family firms than in non-family ones. However, this removal is not an intrinsic trait of family firms. Invisibility and the tendency of women to be in charge of operating and supporting roles, instead of managerial ones, still characterize family SMEs (Cole, 1997). Thus the family role in supporting a wider women's presence in governance and managerial roles is ambiguous.

We define governance roles in terms of: chairman, CEO or sole CEO, and board member. The sole CEO is in charge of top management roles, as an alternative to the board of directors. The term sole CEO occurs in Italian law, due to the fact that this person does not belong to any board. Where a sole CEO is appointed, neither the board of directors nor the chairman exists. Managerial roles are analyzed with regard to three main directorships: managing director, business unit director, and functional director.

According to literature, the chapter investigates if a more extensive involvement of women, as we may suppose in family firms (Montemerlo and Gnan, 2001; Gnan and Montemerlo, 2008), not only in ownership, but also in governance and managerial roles, may represent a condition for glass ceiling removal.

Accordingly, we propose:

Hypothesis 1A (H1A)   In SMEs, the proportion of women in governance and managerial roles is smaller than that of men.

Hypothesis 1B (H1B)   In SMEs, the proportion of women in managerial roles is greater than in governance roles.

Hypothesis 1C (H1C)   In family SMEs, the proportion of women in governance and managerial roles is greater than in non-family ones.

Women and Professionalization of Family Firms

Following agency theory, agency cost control mechanisms, such as strategic planning and managerial control systems (budget, reporting system and incentives), play a significant role in the professionalization of family firms. Strategic planning may help to cope with interests and critical issues of both the company and the family (Ward, 1991, 2001; Schwenk and Shrader, 1993; Rue and Ibrahim, 1996; Gnan and Montemerlo, 2006). Budget and reporting systems may ensure a wider delegation of responsibilities, not only to family members, but also to professional managers (Songini and Gnan, 2008). In addition, according to RBV, the adoption of governance and managerial mechanisms usually increases the managerial consciousness of a firm (Songini, 2006).

Literature focuses mostly on the role of women in family firms, in terms of their expectations, values, objectives, decision-making processes and leadership styles (Kaplan, 1988). Few contributions explore how women participate in strategy formulation, in organization structure design, in implementing and using managerial mechanisms (Gundry and Ben-Yoseph, 1998; Verheul et al., 2002). According to literature, the board and top management teams take the decision to adopt formalized governance, strategic planning and management control systems. Thus we hypothesize that women in governance and managerial roles can influence the adoption of managerial systems, and therefore the firm's professionalization.

We define professionalization as related to the adoption of strategic planning and managerial control systems (budget, reporting system and incentives). Accordingly, we propose:

Hypothesis 2A (H2A)   SMEs with a greater proportion of women in governance and managerial roles present higher levels of professionalization.

Hypothesis 2B (H2B)   In family SMEs with a greater proportion of women in governance and managerial roles the level of professionalization is higher than in non-family-owned firms.

RESEARCH DESIGN

We used a quantitative deductive design and tested the hypotheses through a questionnaire survey of 198 family SMEs in Italy. The deductive approach helped us make general inferences beyond the setting of Italian SMEs. In most cases, the company CEO was the respondent.

The sample was drawn from the AIDA database (by Bureau Van Dijk Electronic Publishing), which contains: (i) balance sheet data of incorporated SMEs, representative of the Italian population and operating both in manufacturing and non-manufacturing industries; (ii) data about the ownership structure (shareholders), the governance system (chair and board members) and some information about management (CEO). We used both primary (from questionnaires) and secondary data[1] (from the AIDA database). This approach helped us to avoid from the outset common methods bias related to survey studies.

Sampling Frame

The initial sample consisted of 1526 manufacturing SMEs in the Milan and Brescia provinces, Italy, at the four-digit level of the ATECO91 Classification System. We adopted the European definition of SMEs[2] in use when our data collection procedure took place, which defined SMEs as firms that: (i) have fewer than 250 employees; (ii) have either an annual turnover not exceeding €40 million, or an annual balance-sheet total not exceeding €27 million; and (iii) are independent enterprises.[3] The Milan and Brescia provinces assure a high level of internal homogeneity for the sample and they are representative of the Italian population of SMEs in general.[4] The 1526 companies covered a range of turnover, employees and industry contribution.

Primary Data Collection Procedure

The primary data collection procedure consisted of three phases. First, a single researcher pre-tested the preliminary version of the questionnaire with some senior SME executives attending training programs in a major Italian business school. The pre-tests led to item revision as well as the introduction of some new items. Next, 15 on-site interviews with CEOs or executives of SMEs shaped the questionnaire final version. In the third phase, the survey was mailed to 1526 companies included in the sampling frame. Following Dillman (1978), two follow-up letters and one replacement questionnaire were mailed after the initial mailing. A single informant was used for each firm.[5] The key methodological solution in using a single respondent approach is to find the most appropriate one. The questionnaire-covering letter requested that it should be filled in either by the CEO or by a senior executive with overall responsibility for strategic management issues and this was checked.

Achieved Sample

A total of 198 completed questionnaires were returned. The 13 percent response rate is comparable with those of large-scale surveys involving executives (Powell and Dent-Micallef, 1997; Robertson et al., 1995), but higher than those normally obtained in Italy (Corbetta and Montemerlo, 1999; Giacomelli and Trento, 2005). It is a reasonable result given the setting of the survey (small firms), firm diversity, the positions of the respondents (CEO or equivalent position), and the sensitivity of the information.

A total of 166 firms (83.7 percent) were family firms. This finding is consistent with the average weight of family firms in the Italian context. Italy is characterized by a very relevant presence of small and medium-sized family firms and our proportion of family SMEs as compared to non-family SMEs is similar to that of other Italian studies (e.g. Gnan and Montemerlo, 2008). Italian businesses are regulated by the civil law and actually they can be incorporated or unlimited. The first type includes joint stock companies and companies with limited liability, while the latter features unlimited liability of owners. We made our survey by addressing a questionnaire to Italian incorporated SMEs, as these are more likely to feature articulated governance and managerial control systems and they represent a significant actor in the Italian economy (49.1 percent of total Italian employment; ISTAT, 2004). We define a family firm as an enterprise meeting at least one of the following requirements: (i) 51 percent or more of the equity is owned by the family; (ii) the family owns less than 51 percent, but controls the company in partnership with friends, other entrepreneurs, employees; (iii) respondents perceive the firm as a family firm, whatever the family share, which actually happened in six cases (Greenwald & Associates, 1995).

Non-response biases were evaluated by comparing industries in the sample achieved with the initial one. No differences were found. We also compared early respondents (first half) with late respondents (second half), following the Armstrong and Overton procedure (1977). No significant differences were found on key characteristics such as age of the company, size (employees and turnover), market conditions or industry characteristics, suggesting that non-response bias may not be a problem. The sample achieved represents a wide range of industries, firms and types of the firm, as shown in Tables 15.1–15.3. In order to account for potential biases, we controlled for sources of heterogeneity in the sample, as discussed below. The sample achieved presents a distribution fairly similar to the initial one.

Control for Sources of Sample Heterogeneity

Industry
Whilst the focus of the study is on women in governance and managerial roles and on the professionalization in family SMEs, there may be various degrees of relatedness within these issues among different industries. ATECO91 measures, even at a four-digit level, are likely to suffer from aggregation biases. For example, two firms from the same ATECO91 category may be direct competitors with very similar products and markets, or be qualified as 'complementors'. This situation may influence the level of competitive and economic performance. Again, different industries may be in different economic phases at the same time. It seems likely that belonging to different

Table 15.1   Industries

Industry	Number of responses	%
Chemical	32	16.2
Food	29	14.6
Electronic	41	20.7
Textile	24	12.1
Mechanical	21	10.6
Raw material transformation	51	25.8
Total	198	100.0

Table 15.2   Turnovers

Turnover	Number of responses	%	Cumulative %
From €4 to 8 million	91	46.0	46.0
From €8 to 20 million	75	38.1	84.1
From €20 to 40 million	32	15.9	100.0
Total	198	100.0	

Table 15.3   Employees

Employees	Number of responses	%	Cumulative %
Up to 15 employees	25	12.5	12.6
From 16 to 50 employees	98	49.4	62.7
From 51 to 100 employees	47	23.5	86.5
Over 100 employees	26	13.3	100.0
Total	196	98.8	
Missing	2	1.2	
Total	198	100.0	

industries has different effects on women in governance and managerial roles and on professionalization.

Relative size of the firm

Only a few authors have studied gender-related issues in SMEs (Brush, 1992; Cliff, 1998), and whether women's presence in SMEs relates to firm size still remains an open issue.

As far as professionalization is concerned, in non-family firms the adoption of managerial control systems is relatively independent of firm size, while in family ones size relates to the professionalization (Speckbacher and Wentges, 2007). Exclusively owner-managed firms are more centralized and they adopt formalized managerial control systems to a lesser extent. In partly owner-managed firms, a large impact of size is ascertained. Partly owner-managed firms more frequently adopt managerial control systems when the number of employees increases and/or when the level of decentralization of the decision-making processes rises (Speckbacher and Wentges, 2007).

Age of the firm
A small firm passes through different phases of development (Churchill and Lewis, 1983; Scott and Bruce, 1987), until it comes to a critical stage, requiring a more professional approach, characterized by the adoption of planning and managerial control systems. Following this perspective, we controlled for the influence of an eventual temporal heterogeneity in the sample.

Although we used standard control variables in the study, our list of control variables was not as extensive as desired. For example, in contrast to Schulze et al. (2001), we did not control for capital intensity and industry growth. Although it is impossible to tell how a more extensive set of controls might have affected our results, we do note that aside from the above control variables, the study conducted by Schulze et al. (2001) shows that the additional controls were either insignificant or mixed in their impacts on governance systems.

Measures

Women in governance and managerial roles
We distinguish the governance roles (chairman, CEO/sole CEO and board member) from the managerial ones (managing director, BU director and functional director), which are related to roles more involved in operational concerns. We use six variables: CHAIRMAN, CEO/SOLE CEO, BOARD MEMBER, MANAGING DIRECTOR, BU DIRECTOR and FUNCTIONAL DIRECTOR. They are dichotomous variables based on responses to questions whether the incumbent of the post is a male or a female. For each variable, we use a twofold version (a male one and a female one), where a score of '1' denotes the presence of a man/woman in each role, and a score of '0' otherwise. Literature reveals a difference in the glass ceiling experienced by a woman, according to the considered role: owner, member of a governance mechanism and manager. Most studies deal with the glass ceiling for women managers (Veale and Gold, 1998). With regard to family firms, research focused mostly on ownership and governance (Montemerlo and Gnan, 2001; Songini and Dubini, 2003; Gnan and Montemerlo, 2008).

Professionalization
We use four variables: STRATEGIC PLANNING, BUDGET, REPORTING and INCENTIVES. They are dichotomous variables based on responses to questions whether the firm adopts each managerial mechanism. For each variable, a score of '1' denotes the presence of the managerial mechanism; a score of '0' otherwise. Recent research reports a relationship between professionalization of family firms and the presence of agency cost control mechanisms (Songini and Gnan, 2008).

FINDINGS

In this section, we report and comment on the results regarding women's presence in governance and managerial roles in SMEs (in general and in family SMEs), and its relationship with professionalization.

Table 15.4   Women in governance and managerial roles

Roles	Male	Female	Sig.
	%	%	
Chairman	97.0	3.0	***
CEO/sole CEO	95.4	4.6	***
Board member	95.3	17.8	***
Managing director	39.6	1.4	***
BU director	24.5	0.6	***
Functional director	77.8	33.1	***

Note: *** t is significant at the 0.01 level (2-tailed).

Women in Governance and Managerial Roles

As far as Hypothesis H1A is concerned (see Table 15.4), for the entire sample of SMEs we compared the male and female percentages of presence in each governance and managerial role. Table 15.4 reports the percentages and the significances of differences. In SMEs, men are mostly in charge of governance and managerial roles. Consequently, Hypothesis H1A is verified, confirming that the glass ceiling is an issue characterizing not only large companies, but also SMEs.

The above results are also confirmed after controlling for sources of sample heterogeneity (industry, company size and age of the firm), although some effects should be pointed out for BU and functional directors. The industry does not affect the presence of women in governance and managerial roles. Our results confirm those studies that describe a limited involvement of women in traditional manufacturing industries. We did not find a relationship between company age and the presence of women in governance and managerial roles, while there is a quite limited relationship between male managerial roles (BU and functional directors) and company size.

As far as Hypothesis H1B is concerned, which states a greater proportion of women in managerial roles than in governance ones, for the entire sample of SMEs we compared each managerial role with each governance role covered by women. We tested nine differences (managing director versus chairman, managing director versus CEO/sole CEO, managing director versus board member, BU director versus chairman, BU director versus. CEO/sole CEO, BU director versus board member, functional director versus chairman, functional director versus CEO/sole CEO, and functional director versus board member). Hypothesis H1B (see Table 15.5) is verified only for the functional director role, which presents a greater percentage of women than the governance roles. The control variables do not have any effect on women in governance and managerial roles. These results confirm the tendency of women to be in charge of mostly operating and supporting roles (Grant and Tancred, 1992; Ufuk and Ozgen, 2001).

As far as Hypothesis H1C is concerned (see Table 15.6), for each governance and managerial role we compared the percentages of women in family SMEs and non-family ones. We did not find any significant difference (ANOVA tests for each female role between non-family SMEs and family ones). Family SMEs seem to be a more favorable

Table 15.5   Women in managerial roles compared with women in governance roles

Managerial roles (female percentages)/governance roles (female percentages)		Managerial roles		
		Managing director	BU director	Functional director
Governance roles	Chairman	1.4 / 3.0	1.0 / 3.0	33.1 / 3.0***
	CEO/sole CEO	1.4 / 4.6	1.0 / 4.6**	33.1 / 4.6***
	Board member	1.4 / 1.8***	1.0 / 1.8***	33.1 / 1.8***

Note: *** t is significant at the 0.01 level (2-tailed); ** t is significant at the 0.05 level (2-tailed).

Table 15.6   Women in governance and managerial roles in family and non-family firms

Women in governance and managerial roles	Non-family firms (%)	Family firms (%)	Sig.
Chairman	0.0	3.6	
CEO/sole CEO	0.0	5.5	
Board member	6.7	20.2	†
Managing director	0.0	1.7	
BU director	0.0	0.7	
Functional director	23.2	34.8	

Note: † F is significant at the 0.10 level.

context only with regard to the involvement of women on the board ($F = 3.066$ – sig. 0.082). Therefore Hypothesis H1C is only partially verified, confirming the ambiguous role of family in supporting the involvement of women in governance and in managerial roles. Moreover, the glass ceiling is more evident in managerial than in governance roles. These results are confirmed also after controlling for sources of sample heterogeneity (industry, company size and age of the firm).

Women and Professionalization

The second part of our research aimed at validating the relationship between women in governance and managerial roles in SMEs and the level of professionalization. In more detail, Hypothesis H2A states that SMEs with a greater proportion of women in governance and managerial roles present higher levels of professionalization. This hypothesis is not verified (see Table 15.7). In 42.8 percent of firms that have a woman in at least a governance role or a managerial one, the results do not show significant differences in the adoption of different managerial mechanisms, with the exception of incentives ($F = 2.884$ – sig. 0.091). In any case, the presence of incentives is less diffused in firms with women in governance and managerial roles. The results remained stable after including the control variables.

Hypothesis H2B affirms that in family SMEs with a greater proportion of women in governance and managerial roles, the level of professionalization is higher than in non-

Table 15.7 Professionalization and SMEs with women in governance and managerial roles

Managerial mechanisms	Firms with women in governance and managerial roles		Sig.
	No (%)	Yes (%)	
Strategic planning	45.3	47.7	
Budget	69.9	71.8	
Reporting	68.3	62.2	
Incentives	39.2	27.7	†

Note: † *F* is significant at the 0.10 level.

Table 15.8 Professionalization and family and non-family SMEs with women in governance and managerial roles

Professionalization mechanisms	Firms with women in governance and managerial roles		Sig.
	Non-family firm (%)	Family firm (%)	
Strategic planning	46.9	55.9	
Budget	70.8	83.5	
Reporting	59.3	93.5	**
Incentives	25.1	55.9	*

Note: ** *t* is significant at the 0.05 level (2-tailed); * *t* is significant at the 0.10 level (2-tailed).

family ones. Hypothesis H2B is partially verified regarding the adoption of reporting systems ($t = 3.004$ – sig. 0.012) and incentives ($t = 1.774$ – sig. 0.080; see Table 15.8). These results confirm that in family SMEs a woman needs to affirm her leadership as a manager by using a management system focused on actual results. This certifies woman's contribution and allows her not to be perceived as merely the entrepreneur's daughter, mother or wife. The results remained stable after including the control variables.

DISCUSSION AND CONCLUSIONS

The findings reveal a limited number of women in governance and managerial roles in SMEs, verifying the presence of the glass ceiling not only in large companies. The functional director role shows a greater proportion of women than the governance roles, confirming the tendency for women to cover more operating and supporting roles than top management ones. These findings are similar to those of previous studies that explained women's invisibility and their presence in operating and supporting roles in family firms as a consequence of the replication of the same process of functional specialization of activities and of the typical authority model of the family (Grant and Tancred,

1992). Literature and case studies on women in management yield similar evidence in big enterprises.

Family SMEs and non-family ones present no significant differences as regards the role of women in governance and management, except for the role of board member. Thus family SMEs seem to be a more favorable context only with regard to the involvement of women on the board. Therefore the glass ceiling is more evident in managerial roles than in governance ones. Our findings confirm theories and research evidencing the ambiguous nature of the family role in supporting women entrepreneurship (Salganicoff, 1990). In particular, consistent with early research on the glass ceiling, they highlight more difficulties and obstacles found by women when joining their family firms than opportunities offered by family firms to women, as evidenced by recent literature (Nelton, 1999; Vera and Dean, 2005; Dugan et al., 2008).

As far as the relationship between the firm's professionalization and the role of women is concerned, we did not find any significant relationship in SMEs. Only in family SMEs is the relationship verified regarding incentives and reporting systems. This result reveals that in family SMEs women need to legitimate their roles and competencies through mechanisms that can formally, objectively and systematically measure and monitor a manager's results and evaluate and reward his/her performance. Especially in family SMEs, a woman has to affirm her leadership as a manager in order not to be merely perceived as the entrepreneur's daughter/mother/wife. These findings are consistent with Vera and Dean's study (2005), which evidenced the problems that daughters have to face once the succession is completed and they have taken over the running of the firm. This study stressed the problem of work–family compatibility and the fact that these women must make great efforts to prove their ability to run the firm, not only to other family members but also – and especially – to workers and managers not belonging to the family.

Our findings highlight an ambiguous relationship between family SMEs' professionalization and women's role. On the one hand, when women are in charge of governance and managerial roles, they adopt managerial mechanisms, such as reporting and incentives systems, influencing the firm's professionalization. On the other hand, results also revealed that the low level of professionalization of family SMEs could explain the low presence of women in governance and managerial roles. In family SMEs, the limited adoption of managerial mechanisms and, as a consequence, the low managerial consciousness may lead to an unfavorable context regarding the involvement of all people, regardless of gender, in governance and managerial roles. Actually, previous studies highlighted that family firms with a relatively higher level of formalization of governance systems and consensus-based decision-making processes have better economic performance and they partially remove the glass ceiling (Songini and Dubini, 2003).

From a theoretical point of view, the main contributions of this chapter find both the presence of the glass ceiling in family SMEs, mostly with regard to managerial roles, and the evidence of a relationship between the presence of women in governance and managerial roles and the use of incentives and reporting system in family SMEs. The last finding represents an issue under-investigated in family firms, that has to be analyzed in more depth in future research.

Other relevant empirical contributions concern the characteristics of the sample studied, which mostly consists of family SMEs operating in Italy, which is recognized as one of the most interesting contexts to study family firms.

Practical implications for managerial purposes and for policy-makers of our study can be summarized as follows:

- Companies, particularly family-owned ones, could favor female active participation through a careful planning of governance structures and managerial mechanisms; the family board seems to be a particularly effective structure in which different expectations can converge and be aligned for the family as well as for the company's best interest.
- Breakage of the glass ceiling requires an active involvement of women, not just as co-owners, but also in governance and management. If their involvement is to be real and not just formal, it is necessary for women to be eager and prepared to deal with the discipline that running a company requires.
- Women pursuing a professional or an entrepreneurial career should ask for a higher level of involvement in governance and managerial roles, knowing that mere ownership – although very important – does not automatically grant equal opportunities. In fact, family SMEs' professionalization does not necessarily pass through women's involvement, but it can be managed by professional managers, with appropriate competencies and capabilities, with no regard to gender (Songini and Gnan, 2008).
- According to organizational control theory, as the environmental and organizational complexity increases, it becomes necessary for a company to define more formalized and clear managerial responsibility to be delegated to specialized managers who are in charge of different organizational departments. In this situation, firm performance is a consequence of both the ability of each manager, male or female, to cope with the specific challenges and risks of his/her activities and the ability of top management/entrepreneurs to use the appropriate managerial mechanisms to cope with and exploit their human and social capital.
- Policy-makers interested in developing equal opportunities measures should encourage companies to carefully plan their governance structures and to manage succession processes in order to let women have the same opportunities as men in occupying managerial roles. On the other hand, they should encourage women entrepreneurs to acquire a level of managerial capabilities and skills that can allow them to reach governance and top management positions.

As far as the limitations of the research are concerned, the redemption rate appears to be quite low if compared with North American and other countries' surveys. However, it is noteworthy to underline that it is in line with rates normally obtained in Italy and other European countries. A second limitation relates to the fact that the research was conducted on Italian SMEs. Studies on other countries might show different patterns of presence of women and/or they might give different results for hypothesis testing, due to the influence of national culture (Hofstede and Bollinger, 1987; Davidson and Burke, 2004; Gupta et al., 2008). Third, the sample, focusing on manufacturing firms (although many different manufacturing industries were in it), limits the possibilities for generalization of results. Studies also including non-manufacturing firms could extend our findings. Finally, several issues concerning the role of women and the family firm's professionalization would merit more detailed scrutiny.

Future research could further test our results by investigating the relationship between the perceived measures of the family's female members' involvement and the adoption of the managerial mechanisms used in this research. Second, although heterogeneity in a sample is a condition for empirical generalization, industry- or country-level studies would be useful to validate these results. For example, additional research could usefully compare the relevance of the theories of women's presence in large family firms and services. On this latter aspect, many studies suggest that large family firms are different from small ones. More attention should be paid to sources of differences. Then, further investigation might elaborate on the relationships between the importance and effectiveness attributed to managerial systems and the role of women.

As a final point, future research should take into account different family and ownership characteristics, composition and dynamics, the generation involved in the business, the features of succession process (if any), in order to consider different kinds of family firms' context and evolution.

At a more theoretical level, it would be useful to extend the analysis on how firms renew and recombine their resources by adopting alternative managerial mechanisms. Such research would consider different ways by which firms change their set of human resources, both male and female, including internal development, discrete resource enlargement, and governance mechanisms' evolution. The aim would be to identify systematic influences that lead managers to choose among these paths of change and to measure their effectiveness on family firms' ability to change.

NOTES

1. Unfortunately the AIDA data were not available for all the firms in the sample. Therefore we decided to collect data via a questionnaire on ownership, governance and management, and to check them against the reports available in the AIDA database.
2. European Commission Recommendation 96/280/EC.
3. Independent enterprises have no more than 25 percent of the capital or the voting rights owned by an outside enterprise or jointly by several enterprises (European Commission Recommendation 96/280/EC).
4. With more than 520 000 firms, incorporated and not incorporated, manufacturing and non-manufacturing, these two provinces cover a notable role in the Italian economy, assuring the largest contribution to GDP, with a value over 16 percent.
5. Although the use of multiple respondents would have reduced concerns about potential response biases, respondents had to be knowledgeable about the firm and its competitive environment (Campbell, 1955).

REFERENCES

Abernethy, M.A., Bouwens, J. and van Lent, L. (2010), 'Leadership and control system design', *Management Accounting Research*, **21**(1), 2–16.
Ahl, H. (2006), 'Why research on women entrepreneurs needs new directions', *Entrepreneurship Theory and Practice*, **30**(5), 595–621.
Aldrich, H. (1989), 'Networking among women entrepreneurs', in O. Hagan, C. Rivchum and D.L. Sexton (eds), *Women-owned Businesses*, New York: Praeger, pp. 103–32.
Aldrich, H., Dubini, P. and Ray Reese, P. (1989), 'Women on the verge of a nervous breakdown: networking among entrepreneurs in the US and Italy', *Entrepreneurship and Regional Development*, **1**(4), 339–56.
Allen, S. and Truman, C. (1993), 'Women and men entrepreneurs: life strategies, business strategies', in S. Allen and C. Truman (eds), *Women in Business: Perspectives on Women Entrepreneurs*, London: Routledge, pp. 1–13.

Allen, I.E. and Langowitz, N.S. (2003), 'Women in family-owned businesses', Center for Women's Leadership, Babson College, Mass Mutual Financial Group, August.

Anderson, R.C. and Reeb, D.M. (2003), 'Founding-family ownership and firm performance: evidence from the S&P 500', *The Journal of Finance*, **58**(3), 1301–28.

Anderson, R.C., Mansi, S.A. and Reeb, D.M. (2003), 'Founding-family ownership and the agency cost of debt', *Journal of Financial Economics*, **68**, 263–85.

Anna, A.L., Chandler, G.N., Jansen, E. and Mero, N.P. (1999), 'Women business owners in traditional and non-traditional industries', *Journal of Business Venturing*, **15**(3), 279–303.

Arenius, P.M. and Kovalainen, A. (2006), 'Similarities and differences across the factors associated with women's self-employment preference in the Nordic countries', *International Small Business Journal*, **24**, 31–59.

Armstrong, J.S. and Overton, T.S. (1977), 'Estimating non-response bias in mail surveys', *Journal of Marketing Research*, **14**, 396–402.

Balbo, L. (1979), 'La doppia presenza', *Inchiesta*, no. 32, 3–11.

Barnes, L.B. (1996), 'Incongruent hierarchies: daughters and younger sons as company CEO', *The Best of Family Business Review*, Boston, MA: The Family Firm Institute, pp. 38–43.

Berg, N.G. (1997), 'Gender, place and entrepreneurship', *Entrepreneurship and Regional Development*, **9**(3), 259–68.

Bombelli, M.C. (2000), *Soffitto di vetro e dintorni*, Milano: Etas.

Bruce, N. and Waldman, M. (1990), 'The rotten kid meets the Samaritan's dilemma', *Quarterly Journal of Economics*, **105**, 155–65.

Brush, C. (1992), 'Research on women business owners: past trends, a new perspective and future directions', *Entrepreneurship Theory and Practice*, **16**(4), 5–30.

Buttner, E.H. and Rosen, B. (1989), 'Funding new business ventures: are decision-makers biased against women entrepreneurs?', *Journal of Business Venturing*, **4**, 249–61.

Cadieux, L., Lorrain, J. and Hugron, P. (2002), 'Succession in women-owned family businesses: a case study', *Family Business Review*, **15**(1), 17–30.

Campbell, D.T. (1955), 'The informant in quantitative research', *American Journal of Sociology*, **60**, 339–42.

Carter, N. and Allan, K.R. (1997), 'Size determinants of women owned businesses: choice or barriers to resources?', *Entrepreneurship and Regional Development*, **9**(3), 211–20.

Carter, N.M., Williams, M. and Reynolds, P.D. (1997), 'Discontinuance among new firms in retail: the influence of initial resources, strategy, and gender', *Journal of Business Venturing*, **12**(2), 125–45.

Carter, S. and Cannon, T. (1992), *Women as Entrepreneurs*, London: Academic Press.

Carter, S. and Rosa, P. (1998), 'The financing of male- and female-owned businesses', *Entrepreneurship and Regional Development*, **10**(3), 225–41.

Chrisman, J.J., Chua, J.H. and Sharma, P. (2003), 'Current trends and future directions in family business management studies: toward a theory of the family firm', Coleman Foundation White Paper Series, available at: http: www.usasbe.org/knowledge /whitepapers/index.asp.

Chrisman, J.J., Chua, J.H. and Litz, R.A. (2004), 'Comparing the agency costs of family and non-family firms: conceptual issues and exploratory evidence', *Entrepreneurship Theory and Practice*, **28**(4), 335–54.

Christensen, L.T. (1995), 'Buffering organizational identity in the marketing culture', *Organization Studies*, **16**(4), 651–72.

Churchill, N.and Lewis, V. (1983), 'The five stages of small business growth', *Harvard Business Review*, **61**(3), 30–50.

Cliff, J.E. (1998), 'Does one size fit all? Exploring the relationship between attitudes towards growth, gender and business size', *Journal of Business Venturing*, **13**(6), 523–42.

Cole, P. (1997), 'Women in family business', *Family Business Review*, **10**, 353–71.

Coleman, S. (2000), 'Access to capital and terms of credit: a comparison of men owned and women owned small businesses', *Journal of Small Business Management*, **38**(3), 17–52.

Corbetta, G. and Montemerlo, D. (1999), 'Ownership, governance and management issues in small and medium sized family businesses: a comparison of Italy and the United States', *Family Business Review*, **12**, 361–74.

Cromie, S. and Birley, S. (1992), 'Networking by female business owners in Northern Ireland', *Journal of Business Venturing*, **7**(3), 237–51.

Cromie, S. and Hayes, J. (1988), 'Towards a typology of female entrepreneurship', *The Sociological Review*, **36**(1), 87–113.

Cromie, S. and O'Sullivan, S. (1999), 'Women as managers in family firms', *Women in Management Review*, **14**(3), 76–88.

Cuba, R., Decenzo, D. and Anish, A. (1983), 'Management practices of successful female business owners', *American Journal of Small Business*, **82**(2), 40–45.

Curimbaba, F. (2002), 'The dynamics of women's roles as family business managers', *Family Business Review*, **15**, 239–52.

Daily, M. and Dollinger, M.J. (1992), 'An empirical examination of ownership structure in family and professionally managed firms', *Family Business Review*, **2**, 117–36.

Davidson, M. and Burke, R. (2004), *Women in Management Worldwide*, Aldershot, UK: Ashgate.

Davila, A. and Foster, G. (2005), 'Management accounting systems adoption decisions: evidence and performance implications from early-stage/startup companies', *The Accounting Review*, **80**(4), 1039–68.

Davis, J.H., Schoorman, F.D. and Donaldson, L. (1997), 'Toward a stewardship theory of management', *Academy of Management Review*, **22**(1), 20–47.

Dillman, D. (1978), *Mail and Telephone Surveys: The Total Design Method*, New York: Wiley.

Dugan, A.M., Krone, S.P., LeCouvie, K., Pendergast, J.M., Kenyon-Rouvinez, D.H. and Schuman, A.M. (2008), *A Woman's Place: The Crucial Roles of Women in Family Business*, Marietta, GA: Family Business Consulting Group.

Dumas, C. (1989), 'Understanding of father–daughter and father–son dyads in family-owned businesses', *Family Business Review*, **2**(1), 31–46.

Dumas, C. (1997), 'Preparing the new CEO: managing the father–daughter succession process in family business', in C.E. Aronoff, J.H. Astrachan and J.L. Ward (eds), *Family Business Sourcebook II. Business Owner Resources*, Marietta, GA: Family Enterprise Publishers, pp. 434–41.

Dumas, C. (1998), 'Women's pathways to participation and leadership in the family-owned firm', *Family Business Review*, **12**, 215–28.

Du Rietz, A. and Henrekson, M. (2000), 'Testing the female underperformance hypothesis', *Small Business Economics*, **14**(1), 1–10.

Dyer, W.G. (2001), 'Integrating professional management into a family owned business', *The Best of Family Business Review*, Boston, MA: The Family Firm Institute, pp. 38–43.

Fay, M. and Williams, L. (1993), 'Gender bias and the availability of business loans', *Journal of Business Venturing*, **8**(4), 363–76.

Freeman, R.E. and Reed, D.L. (1983), 'Stockholders and shareholders: a new perspective on corporate governance', *California Management Review*, Spring, 20–56.

Frishkoff, P.A. and Brown, B.M. (1997), 'Women on the move in family business', in C.E. Aronoff, J.H. Astrachan and J.L. Ward (eds), *Family Business Sourcebook II. Business Owner Resources*, Marietta, GA: Family Enterprise Publishers, pp. 446–51.

Galbraith, J.R. (1977), *Organization Design*, Reading, MA: Addison Wesley.

Gallo, M. and Vilaseca, A. (1998), 'A financial perspective on structure, conduct, and performance in the family firms: an empirical study', *Family Business Review*, **11**, 35–47.

Gersick, K.E. et al. (1997), *Generation to Generation: Life Cycles of the Family Business*, Boston, MA: Harvard Business School Press.

Giacomelli, S. and Trento S. (2005), 'Proprietà, controllo e trasferimenti nelle imprese italiane: cosa è cambiato nel decennio 1993–2003?', Bank of Italy Working Papers, No. 550, June.

Gnan, L. and Montemerlo, D. (2001), 'Structure and dynamics of ownership, governance and strategy: role of family and impact on performance in Italian SMEs', Research paper DIR, SDA Bocconi School of Management, Milan.

Gnan, L. and Montemerlo, D. (2006), 'Family-firm relationships in Italian SMEs: ownership and governance issue in a double-fold theoretical perspective', in P. Z. Poutziouris, K.X. Smyrnios and S.B. Klein (eds), *Handbook of Research on Family Business*, Cheltenham, UK and Northampton, MA, USA: Edward Elgar, pp. 501–16.

Gnan, L. and Montemerlo, D. (2008), *Le PMI familiari tra tradizione e novità*, Milan: EGEA.

Goffee, R. and Scase, R. (1985), *Women in Charge. The Experiences of Female Entrepreneurs*, London: Allen & Unwin.

Gómez-Mejía, L., Núñez-Nickel, M. and Gutiérrez, I. (2001), 'The role of family ties in agency contracts', *Academy of Management Journal*, **44**, 81–95.

Grant, J. (1988), 'Women as managers: what they can offer to organisation', *Organizational Dynamics*, **16**, 56–63.

Grant, R.M. (1991), 'The resource-based theory of competitive advantage: implication for strategy formulation', *Califoria Management Review*, **33**(3), 114–35.

Grant, J. and Tancred, P. (1992), 'A feminist perspective on state bureaucracy', in A. Mills and P. Tancred (eds), *Gendering Organizational Analysis*, London: Sage, pp. 112–28.

Greenwald & Associates (1995), *1995 Research findings*, Massachussets Mutual Life Insurance Company.

Greer, M. and Greene, M. (2003), 'Feminist theory and the study of entrepreneurship', in J. Butler (ed.), *New Perspectives on Women Entrepreneurs*, Charlotte, NC: IAP, pp. 1–24.

Greiner, L.E. (1972), 'Evolution and revolution as organization growth', *Harvard Business Review*, **50**(4), 37–46.

Gundry, L.K. and Ben-Yoseph, M. (1998), 'Women entrepreneurs in Romania, Poland, and the U.S: cultural and family influences on strategy and growth', *Family Business Review*, **11**(4), 61–75.

Gupta, V., Levenburg, N., Moore, L., Motwani, J. and Schwarz, T. (eds) (2008), *A Compendium on the Family Business Models Around the World* (10 vols), Hyderabad: ICFAI University Press.

Habbershon, T.G. and Williams, M. (1999), 'A resource-based framework for assessing the strategic advantages of family firms', *Family Business Review*, **12**, 1–25.

Haberman, H. and Danes, S.M. (2007), 'Father–daughter and father–son family business management transfer comparison: family FIRO model application', *Family Business Review*, **20**, 163–84.

Hamilton, E. (2006), 'Whose story is it anyway? Narrative accounts of the role of women in founding and establishing family businesses', *International Small Business Journal*, **24**(3), 253–71.

Helgesen, S. (1990), *The Female Advantage: Women's Ways of Leadership*, New York: Doubleday.

Hisrich, R.D. and Brush, C. (1983), 'Women entrepreneurs: problems and prescriptions for success in the future', in O. Hagan, C. Rivchun and D. Sexton (eds), *Women-owned Businesses*, New York: Praeger, pp. 3–32.

Hisrich, R.D. and Brush, C. (1984), 'The woman entrepreneur: management skills and business problems', *Journal of Small Business Management*, **22**(1), 30–7.

Hisrich, R.D. and Brush, C. (1987), 'Women entrepreneurs: a longitudinal study', in N.C. Churchill, J.A. Hornaday, B.A. Kirchoff, O.J. Krasner and K.H. Vesper (eds), *Frontiers of Entrepreneurship Research*, Wellesley, MA: Babson College, pp. 187–99.

Hofstede, G. and Bollinger, D. (1987), *Les différences culturelles dans le management*, Paris: Les Editions d'Organisation.

Hollander, B.S. and Bukowitz, W.R. (1990), 'Women, family culture and family business', *Family Business Review*, **3**(2), 139–51.

Hopwood, A.G. (1974), *Accounting and Human Behaviour*, London: Haymarket Publishing.

Huse, M. (2007), *Boards, Governance and Value Creation: The Human Side of Corporate Governance*, Cambridge: Cambridge University Press.

Huse, M. and Solberg, A.G. (2006), 'Gender related boardroom dynamics: how women make and can make contributions on corporate boards', *Women in Management Review*, **21**, 113–30.

Iannarelli, C. L. (1992), 'The socialization of leaders in family business: an exploratory study of gender', unpublished doctoral dissertation, University of Pittsburgh, PA.

Irwin, D. (2000), 'Seven ages of entrepreneurship', *Journal of Small Business and Enterprise Development*, **7**(3), 255–60.

ISTAT (2004), 'Struttura e dimensione delle imprese', *Archivio statistico delle imprese attive*, Roma: ISTAT Ufficio di Comunicazione.

Jensen, M.C. and Meckling, W.H. (1976), 'Theory of the firm: managerial behaviour, agency costs and capital structure', *Journal of Financial Economics*, **3**, 305–60.

Jimenez, R.C. (2009), 'Research on women in family firms. Current status and future directions', *Family Business Review*, **22**(1), 53–64.

Kalleberg, A.L. and Leicht, K.T. (1991), 'Gender and organizational performance: determinants of small business survival and success', *Academy of Management Journal*, **34**(1), 136–61.

Kaplan, E. (1988), 'Women entrepreneurs: constructing a framework to examine venture success and business failures', in B.A. Kichoff, W.A. Long, W.E. McMullan, K.H. Vesper and W.E. Wetzel (eds), *Frontiers of Entrepreneurship Research*, Wellesley, MA: Babson College, pp. 625–37.

Longstreth, M., Stafford, K. and Mauldin, T. (1988), 'Self-employed women and their families: time use and socio-economic characteristics', *Journal of Small Business Management*, **25**(3), 30–7.

McGivern, C. (1978), 'The dynamics of management succession', *Management Decision*, **16**, 32–46.

Milliken, F.J. and Martins, L.L. (1996), 'Searching for common treads: understanding the multiple effects of diversity in organizational groups', *Academy of Management Review*, **21**, 402–33.

Montemerlo, D. and Gnan, L. (2001), 'Proprietà e governo nelle PMI italiane familiari e non familiari: il ruolo delle donne', Research Paper DIR, SDA Bocconi School of Management, Milan.

Montemerlo, D., Gnan, L., Schulze W. and Corbetta, G. (2004), 'Governance structures in Italian family SMEs', in S. Tomaselli and L. Melin (eds), *Family Firms in the Wind of Change. Research Forum Proceedings – FBN 15th World Conference*, IFERA Publications.

Moore, D. and Buttner, H. (1997), *Women Entrepreneurs. Moving beyond the Glass Ceiling*, Thousand Oaks, CA: Sage.

Moores, K. and Mula, J. (2000), 'The salience of market, bureaucratic, and clan controls in the management of family firm transitions: some tentative Australian evidence', *Family Business Review*, **13**(2), 91–106.

Morck, R. and Yeung, B. (2003), 'Agency problems in large family business groups', *Entrepreneurship Theory and Practice*, **27**, 367–83.

Morck, R., Shleifer, A. and Vishny, R. (1988), 'Management ownership and market valuation: an empirical analysis', *Journal of Financial Economics*, **20**, 293–316.

Myers, S. (1977), 'The determinants of borrowing', *Journal of Financial Economics*, **5**, 147–75.

Naranjo-Gil, D., Maas, V.S. and Hartmann, F.G.H. (2009), 'How CFOs determine management accounting innovation: an examination of direct and indirect effects', *European Accounting Review*, **18**(4), 667–95.

Nelton, S. (1999), 'Why women are chosen to lead', *Nation's Business*, **87**(4), 48–51.

Normann, R. (1977), *Management for Growth*, Chichester, UK: John Wiley & Sons.

O'Connor, V.J. (2001), 'Women and men in senior management – a "different needs" hypothesis', *Women in Management Review*, **16**(8), 400–404.

Ohlott, P.J., Ruderman, M.N. and McCauley C.D. (1994), 'Gender differences in managers' development job experiences', *Academy of Management Journal*, **37**(1), 46–67.

Powell, G.N., Butterfield, D.A. and Parent J.D. (2002), 'Gender and managerial stereotypes: have the times changed?', *Journal of Management*, **28**(2), 177–93.

Powell, T.C. and Dent-Micallef, A. (1997), 'Information technology as competitive advantage: the role of human, business, and technology resources', *Strategic Management Journal*, **18**, 375–405.

Poza, E.J., Hanlon, S. and Kishida, R. (2004), 'Does the family business interaction factor represent a resource or a cost?', *Family Business Review*, **17**(2), 99–118.

Riding, A. and Swift, C. (1990), 'Women business owners and terms of credit: some empirical findings of the Canadian experience', *Journal of Business Venturing*, **5**(5), 327–40.

Robertson, T.S., Rymon, T. and Eliashberg, J. (1995), 'New product announcement signals and incumbent reactions', *Journal of Marketing*, **59**, 1–15.

Ross, S. (1973), 'The economic theory of agency: the principal's problem', *American Economic Review*, **63**, 134–39.

Rosa, P. and Hamilton, D. (1994), 'Gender and ownership in UK small firms', *Entrepreneurship Theory and Practice*, **18**(3), 11–28.

Rosa, P. et al. (1996), 'Gender as a determinant of small business performance: insights from a British study', *Small Business Economics*, **8**, 463–78.

Rostow, W.W. (1960), *The Stages of Economic Growth*, Cambridge: Cambridge University Press.

Rue, L.W. and Ibrahim, N.A. (1996), 'The status of planning in smaller family owned businesses', *Family Business Review*, **9**, 29–43.

Salganicoff, M. (1990), 'Women in family business: challenges and opportunities', *Family Business Review*, **3**(2), 125–37.

Schulze, W.S., Lubatkin, M.H., Dino, R.M. and Bucholtz, A.K. (2001), 'Agency relationships in family firms: theory and evidence', *Organization Science*, **12**, 99–116.

Schulze, W.S., Lubatkin, M.H. and Dino, R.N. (2003), 'Toward a theory of agency and altruism in family firms', *Journal of Business Venturing*, **18**(4), 473–90.

Schwenk, C.R. and Shrader, C.B. (1993), 'Effects of formal strategic planning on financial performance in small firms: a meta-analysis', *Entrepreneurship Theory and Practice*, **17**, 53–64.

Scott, M. and Bruce, R. (1987), 'Five stages of growth in small business', *Long Range Planning*, **20**(3), 45–52.

Smeltzer, L.R. and Fann, G.L. (1989), 'Gender differences in external networks of small business owners/managers', *Journal of Small Business Management*, **27**(2), 25–32.

Smith, C. and Warner, J. (1979), 'On financial contracting; an analysis of bond covenants', *Journal of Financial Economics*, **7**, 117–61.

Smith, N.R., McCain, G. and Warren, A. (1982), 'Women entrepreneurs really are different: a comparison of constructed ideal types of male and female entrepreneurs', *Frontiers of Entrepreneurship Research*, Wellesley, MA: Babson College, pp. 68–77.

Soldressen, L.S., Fiorito, S.S. and He, Y. (1998), 'An exploration into home-based businesses: data from textile artists', *Journal of Small Business Management*, **36**(2), 33–44.

Songini, L. (2006), 'The professionalization of family firms: theory and practice', in P.Z. Poutziouris, K.X. Smyrnios and S.B. Klein (eds), *Handbook of Research on Family Business*, Cheltenham, UK and Northampton, MA, USA: Edward Elgar, pp. 269–97.

Songini, L. and Dubini, P. (2003), 'Glass ceiling in SMEs: when women are in command', paper presented at the Annual Academy of Management Meeting, Washington, Seattle, August.

Songini, L. and Gnan, L. (2008), 'Family involvement and agency cost control mechanisms in family firms', paper presented at the Annual Academy of Management Meeting, Anaheim, August.

Speckbacher, G. and Wentges, P. (2007), 'The impact of firm size and family ownership on management control systems in small and medium-sized enterprises', Working Paper, Wirtschaftsuniversität, Wien.

Ufuk, H. and Ozgen, O. (2001), 'Interaction between the business and family lives of women entrepreneurs in Turkey', *Journal of Business Ethics*, **31**(2), 95–106.

Van den Berghe, L.A.A. and Carchon, S. (2003), 'Agency relations within the family business system: an exploratory approach', *Corporate Governance*, **11**(3), 171–9.

Veale, C. and Gold, J. (1998), 'Smashing into the glass ceiling for women managers', *Journal of Management Development*, **17**(1), 17–26.

Vera, C.F. and Dean, M.A. (2005), 'An examination of the challenges daughters face in family business succession', *Family Business Review*, **18**, 321–46.

Verheul, I., Risseeuw, P. and Bartelse, G. (2002), 'Gender differences in strategy and human resource management', *International Small Business Journal*, **20**(4), 443–76.

Villalonga, B. and Amit, R. (2006), 'How do family ownership, control and management affect firm value?', *Journal of Financial Economics*, **80**, 385–417.

Ward, J.L. (1991), *Creating Effective Boards for Private Enterprises*, San Francisco, CA: Jossey-Bass.

Ward, J.L. (2001), 'The special role of strategic planning for family businesses', *The Best of Family Business Review*, Boston, MA: The Family Firm Institute, pp. 140–46.

Watkins, D.S. and Watkins, J. (1984), 'The female entrepreneur: her background and determinants of business choice, some British data', *International Small Business Journal*, **2**(4), 21–31.

Watson J. (2002), 'Comparing the performance of male- and female-controlled business: relating outputs to results', *Entrepreneurship Theory and Practice*, **26**, 91–100.

Zimmerman, J.L. (2006), *Accounting for Decision Making and Control*, New York: McGraw-Hill.

16 Women in family business: three generations of research

Vipin Gupta and Nancy M. Levenburg

I INTRODUCTION

In the family business context, women often play an important role in leading families and businesses into new business contexts. However, a number of reasons are offered in the literature for the scarcity of women in top leadership positions. These reasons include stereotyping, which leads to resistance to women's leadership, discriminatory treatment that contributes to differential outcomes for men and women, the challenges of dealing with persistent double-binds, and the difficulties associated with work and family integration.

Jimenez (2009) reviewed 48 articles, 23 books and three doctoral dissertations published since 1985 on the involvement of women in family business. She identified two generations of contributions. The first generation of contributions in the 1990s (e.g. Dumas, 1989; Salganicoff, 1990) analyzed 'the difficulties or obstacles that women have found when joining their family firms or on the lack of recognition for their work' (Jiminez, 2009, p. 53). These contributions also highlighted the positive interaction between the family businesses and women. Research pointed to how family businesses may help women gain the confidence and skills necessary for them to assume leadership roles. Some studies showed women were better poised to serve in leadership roles within a family business context than in a non-family business context (Salganicoff, 1990). Cole (1997) found that women were able to achieve high positions in their family firms, and were not held back by the glass ceiling. Family business offered them significant career opportunities, responsibility and respect, and generated a positive self-concept of their careers and a sense of personal fulfillment.

The second generation of contributions over the 2000s (e.g. Rowe and Hong, 2000; Vera and Dean, 2005) discussed 'the opportunities or advantages that family firms can offer women, the pathways that these women take to assume positions of management or leadership in these firms, and their achievements' (Jiminez, 2009, p. 53). Research showed that women enjoyed a supportive and cooperative environment, where they could combine their professional responsibilities with childcare, access sectors traditionally regarded as 'masculine' (e.g. construction), and achieve satisfaction by working for themselves or for their families (Jiminez, 2009). In addition, Vera and Dean's (2005) study underscored the importance of acquiring previous experience outside the family firm for building their self-confidence and credibility in dealing with other family members, employees and outsiders.

In this work, we first review the two generations of research on the obstacles and pathways to leadership for women in family business. Then we rely on the Culturally sensitive Assessment System and Education (CASE) project (Gupta et al., 2008a) to identify a third generation of contributions that provide a foundation for discourse over the next decade. The broader purpose of the CASE research program is to develop culture-specific models of family business in cultural and geographic regions of the world, with the ultimate goal of enabling genuine cross-cultural comparisons. The CASE research program comprised ten volumes on different cultural regions, plus one volume on gender that 'contains 10 articles selected by the editors depicting women's experience in geographically diverse family business settings, including Thailand, Spain, the United States, and the Netherlands. There are also three fascinating chapters on immigrant women's experience as participants in business ventures in their new cultural environment' (Hampton, 2009, p. 368). These articles were selected because they offer a useful and interesting perspective on women's experiences as leaders in family businesses. Of the 100 articles included in the regional volumes, 30 (30 percent) of the articles included gender as a factor in the family business (see Appendix for a listing of these research articles).

Using insights from the articles included in the CASE project, we point to the conditions required for engaging women's leadership in family business. We also discuss a diverse range of global forces that both surround these conditions and serve to enable a growing cadre of women leaders. Prototypes of women in family business across various cultures worldwide are presented to illustrate the diversity of gender solutions.

II   TRADITIONAL 'INVISIBILITY' AND RECENT 'VISIBILITY' OF WOMEN

First Generation: Forces Contributing to 'Invisible' Women

The first generation of research over the 1990s highlighted how women's roles in the family business have traditionally been 'invisible' (Gillis-Donovan and Moynihan-Bradt, 1990). In a family business context, many women as mothers, wives, daughters and daughters-in-law served in an unpaid, informal role, without formal positions of authority, influence and compensation. The gender-specific identity and responsibility of women has traditionally been subtle, as mothers and wives typically focused more on the family aspect than as business professionals (Ward and Sorenson, 1989). This perception draws on the ideology of demarcating work and home roles, and responsibilities based on gender (Rowe and Hong, 2000).

Societies around the world are still overwhelmingly governed by the patriarchal norms of family. Men are considered heads of the family, and primary bread-winners. Such cultural traditions confer authority and prestige on men. Women, on the other hand, 'own' a disproportionate responsibility for family care. They receive little or no support from men in family care responsibilities (Moen, 1992). Help from other family members or hired help is often not an option, because of the availability, cost, quality, or even personal, family or social value factors. Many wives and daughters are socialized to believe that family business roles are not suited for them (Galiano and Vinturella, 1995). The result in many cases is an 'outward division of labor' (Frishkoff and Brown, 1993), where men take care of the family business and women take care of the family, so that the family business can be run and sustained through succession.

Family hierarchy of patriarchal norms is carried over to the family business, where men hold virtually all formal positions of power and decision-making. In patrilineal succession systems, the property succeeds to male children, following the primogeniture criterion that gives a priority to the first-born male child (Llano and Olguin, 1986). Bloom and Van Reenen (2007) found about 15 percent of the sampled family businesses in France and the UK follow primogeniture criterion, versus only 3 percent in Germany and the USA. Even where the daughters have rights to succeed, they may not be given equity in the family business, and instead may be given other types of property, including estate jewelry or other tangible assets – or their share of equity in the family business may be given to their husbands.

Men's identity, on the other hand, is typically predicated upon individuality. Beginning at a very early age, sons are socialized into the family business and its network of relationships, giving them an edge over daughters in assuming leadership positions. Sons often receive superior opportunities to study at institutions away from their homes (including abroad), to prepare for visible transformative and change initiatives in the family business. Hollander and Bukowitz (1990) found that the family businesses implicitly followed primogeniture in their decision-making process, even if they were not from a patrilineal society. Iannarelli (1992) found that families socialized daughters to care for their children, husband and home, and daughters spent less time in the firm, and learnt fewer skills, than sons.

Research shows that when daughters are appropriately socialized, they are more likely to become effective family business successors. Dumas (1998) interviewed 702 women who had significant managerial roles in family businesses, and had the potential to be successors. She found that these women had been socialized by their parents (since childhood) to work for and participate actively in the firm. Positive initiation experience comprising family and business values, and relevant technical, interpersonal and managerial skills and knowledge, steadily increased daughters' commitment to, and interest in, joining the family business, and their aspirations for leadership. This initiation experience increased the likelihood of daughters being chosen as successors, especially when their involvement was needed in the face of family-related factors (e.g. illness or death of the founder, exit of a family member, or absence of brothers), or the firm's (e.g. a moment of crisis or an expansion). Women with formative experiences were also more likely to be chosen as successors, particularly when their brothers were not strong leaders and when these women had limited family responsibilities (no husband, no children), according to a study conducted among 15 males and 15 females in second-generation family businesses (Iannarelli, 1992).

In practice, though, the gender-differentiated socialization of the family is the norm in most societies and carries over into the family business culture. Women are socialized to see their identity through their connections with other family members, while men are socialized in differentiation of self from other family members. Nelton (1997) found that many daughters of the founders work full-time during their vacations, although they are unpaid, or part-time during their studies, because they see this as helping their families. Similarly, Salganicoff's (1990) study of 91 women found that only 27 percent wanted to join the family business, although they tended to see their work in the family firm as 'just another job' (rather than as a professional career) and did not aspire to assume leadership or ownership. They were simply interested in helping the family or filling a position that no other relative wanted. While working in the family business, they received conflicting messages, such as 'Devote yourself to the firm' and 'Give me a grandchild soon'. In another study, 90 percent of women saw their participation in the family firm as being only temporary (Dumas, 1989).

In patriarchal family systems, children take their father's family name as their surname, even if their parents are divorced and they reside with their mothers. Women have an implicit role in the preservation and transmission of family culture and tradition, even within a patriarchal system in which the husband's family culture and tradition are considered most relevant. Consequently, it is a woman who joins the family business of her husband, rather than a husband joining the family business of his wife's parental family. A woman's point of entry into family business is generally through marriage, whereas it is through inheritance and professional choice for a man. And a woman is expected to join the family and social networks of her husband, more so than husbands are expected to join pre-marital networks of their wives. All of this makes it more challenging for women to navigate the new relationships after their marriage, and to stake rights to meaningful positions within the preexisting power relationships of the family business, in which the husband's extended family may also be involved.

In many societies, women may have strong relationships with other women, but not with other men who are not members of their immediate family. Women in business find this challenging because men overwhelmingly hold managerial and leadership positions in the business. Also, the behaviors of businessmen and women are influenced by society's gender stereotypes. Women are expected to organize their involvement in the family business in ways that do not take away from their family responsibilities. Women's primary loyalties are typically assumed to revolve around family care; they have less time for business and for socializing with business associates, which excludes them from important business relationships.

Men usually perform the businesses' execution roles, as well as the strategic decision-making, grounded in the emergent realities. Based on interviews with 23 women and men in nine family businesses, non-family members – particularly customers and suppliers – did not recognize the work women were doing (Cole, 1993). Two possible explanations have been offered in the literature. Marshack (1993) found that the wives performed mostly internally oriented (i.e. less outwardly visible) roles of accounting and secretarial, along with the household tasks, whereas their husbands performed externally oriented roles of equipment maintenance and contract negotiation. Galiano and Vinturella (1995) suggest that women's roles are relegated to those perceived as 'feminine' (e.g. human resources or customer service issues. Marshack (1993) found many wives accepted less visibility of their roles, and sacrificed their own career prospectives, simply to avoid or mitigate potential gender role conflicts.

Many women are involved in their family's firm for schedule flexibility reasons, so that they may work without sacrificing their family roles. In other cases, even if they are uninterested in the family business, women are asked to work in it because the family business needs their assistance. In either case, the norms of role differentiation, hierarchy, succession identity and relational spaces tend to carry over from the family system to the family business; consequently, they may work primarily in supporting roles, rather than in a CEO-level position. For instance, they may work as assistants, informal advisers, or mediators between the members of the family who formally run the company (Francis, 1999). Women are also expected to behave in a gendered manner – being ready to listen and to respond to others' needs, refraining from criticism, caring for others and, above all, being the mother figure for the employees (Lyman, 1988). These conditions generate role conflict for women, as social cues push them to 'do gender' (i.e. assume traditional roles and sacrifice career goals, threaten recrimination from their families and business employees if they don't, and impose higher expectations for succeeding in professional careers) (Freudenberger et al., 1989).

In general, women are considered unfit for the frontline leadership roles, and are often given varying roles at different times, depending on the specific needs of the family business. They may be asked to help identify, conceptualize, plan and design major change initiatives, but if these endeavors prove to be promising in the pilot phase, the charge for their further development may be transferred to men. At home, discussions about the business may dominate conversations, resulting in women's higher stress and guilt levels about family responsibilities. At work, their need for performing the family role may result in a lower credibility and self-confidence, and a reluctance to assume visible leadership roles. In the end, they may become a 'jack of all trades but master of none', thereby reinforcing the basis for their invisibility in the business and enabling males to receive a disproportionate share of credit and visibility. This is despite the fact that these roles of women are integral to both the well-being of the family and the daily operation of the business (Jimenez, 2009).

Few organizations recognize that gender gaps may be associated with the implicit male-centered assumptions about work, which results in an exclusion of women, even if there is no intended discrimination against women. Fathers are often skeptical of the business competence and knowledge of their daughters, and seek to protect them by disallowing their participation in challenging roles and formative experiences (Barnes and Kaftan, 1990). Consequently, a double standard exists when higher expectations prevail about women's qualifications or the number of years they must work in the family business before becoming eligible for visible leadership positions. Further, fathers' skepticism of daughters carries over to the sons, making employees reticent to accept commands from and work under a female boss (Dumas, 1989).

Women's work in the family business tends to be informal and unpaid, for which they do not receive the same consideration as their male counterparts (Hollander and Bukowitz, 1990). They tend to perform tasks that the other members of the family are unable or ill equipped to perform because of time or expertise factors, and for which professional managers are not available due to cost or trust factors. For instance, the family may not have sufficient funds to pay for professional managers, or may not trust externally hired professional managers in matters involving financial or strategic roles. In such cases, women may not be given market rate compensation for their contributions. Further, their labor in the family business may be deemed as the joint property of the family, while the labor of the male family members is generally considered as their personal property. In a study conducted among 498 family business households, Rowe and Hong (2000) found that women who were working in family firms sometimes did not earn salaries, and when they did, their salaries were lower than the men's. Further, some women, who had other jobs, did a 'triple shift' in the family business at low – or no – salary and as a result, they were able to contribute only 30 percent to the family income.

Following from the aforementioned, society, family and even women may underestimate the level of women's involvement and influence in family business (Iannarelli, 1992).

Second Generation: Positive Aspects of Women's Visibility in Family Business

The second generation of research over the 2000s has underlined several positive aspects of women's visibility in leadership roles in family business. What distinguishes women within family businesses most is their behind-the-scenes 'emotional leadership' (Jiminez, 2009). Poza and Messer (2001, p. 34) note that whether 'in formal or informal positions, recognized or unrecognized for their contributions, they often adopt a role that seeks to preserve and strengthen family unity and the feasibility of family business continuity'. By virtue of being connected through several intimate relationships, they help to preserve peace and harmony, resolving conflicts among various family members, and between the family and the business system. Their mediation role is usually particularly noticeable with regard to the owner/father and the successor/son (Dumas, 1989). All this contributes to the resilience of the family business, and to the strength of its critical relationships.

As 'chief emotional officers' (Salganicoff, 1990) in the family and the family business, women play an important role derived from their socialization as wives and mothers. Their distinctive emotional discourse enriches conversations about the business system, and complements the pragmatic discourse of male family members' focus on planning, prioritizing and balancing the interests of different stakeholders. Because of their psychological and behavioral characteristics, and socialization, women adopt a holistic perspective, and demonstrate behaviors such as loyalty to the company, concern for other family members, and sensitivity to the needs of others (Salganicoff, 1990). As 'nurturer of the next generation of leaders' (Dugan et al., 2008), they prepare the successors by transmitting values that are vital to the business' endurance and success – values such as performance orientation, caring about employees' welfare, and appreciating that the family is a steward for the business, and should neither abuse nor exploit it. Lyman et al. (1985) observe that as family caretakers and as the main confidantes of the family business leaders, women gain a unique knowledge about both the family and the business. Thus women are able to focus on issues and goals that transcend the interests of their particular constituencies, and can identify common threads necessary for both systems' survival and subsequent development.

According to the second generation of gender literature, women tend to rely on a multiplicity of social influence, support networks and relational resources in their decision-making and execution. In many contexts, they do find it necessary to 'over-justify' these linkages in the family sphere, and are constantly preoccupied with preserving strong and durable linkages with their families (Schmoll, 2005). In a meta-analysis of leadership studies, Eagly et al. (2003, p. 573) concluded that, compared to men, women tend to adopt a transformational leadership style, because otherwise 'confirming to their gender role can impede their ability to meet the requirements of their leader role'. Other studies have found that women are not more transformational than men (see Barbuto et al., 2007), but differ in terms of enacting transformational leadership using relational rather than a direct, power-based or authoritarian style (Komives, 1991). Rather than asserting themselves through a position of power or authority, they may use keen insights to move and mobilize social influence to negotiate barriers and stereotypes within the system.

Women tend to pursue smaller lifestyle businesses, as opposed to fast-growing businesses (Coleman and Robb, 2010). They appear less entrepreneurial, because of their preference to integrate family and business needs. But they also appear more resilient, because of their emphasis on steady growth and adaptability to market changes. In contexts where women's multiple identities are respected and supported, women are able to establish their role in the family business effectively (Barrett and Moores, 2009). In such situations, on average and over time, the growth and profitability of the women-owned family businesses may be on par with that of the men-owned family businesses. In their research, Allen and Langowitz (2003) found female-owned family businesses were 1.7 times more productive than were male-owned family firms.

Women's approach is often part of a business/family livelihood, adaptation and success strategy, and they attempt to fit everything holistically into this strategy. Frishkoff and Brown (1993) note that women are important stakeholders in terms of risk, effort and commitment to the family business, even if they do not have a formal role as an employee or stockholder. Their stake derives from their unconditional support and sacrifice of money, time and effort for the well-being of a family member's involvement in the business. Women consider it important to allocate enough time for both business and family; therefore they select business activities that are less scale-intensive. For instance, they may choose seasonal activities, and seek to organically extend these activities in ways that do not conflict with their family's priorities. These less scale-intensive activities also tend to be less risky, and allow women to maintain control over their lives in both family and business systems.

While men's actions tend to be driven by a 'sense of freedom', women feel a 'sense of obligation or responsibility' to help the family or the business adapt to the changing situation or the needs of the family or the business (Perkins and DeMeis, 1996). The sense of obligation may, if supported by the context, lead them to help, for instance, by cultivating new lines of diversification, new customer segments, or new technological applications and usage. At the same time, an acute sense of the current needs and capabilities of the family and the business often make them strong supporters of tradition. Consequently, Allen and Langowitz (2003) discovered that the family firms owned by women experienced higher levels of family loyalty and business goal agreement, and lower rates of family member departure from the business.

The challenge of developing and perpetuating the culture of both the family and the family business, and integrating and balancing the role of the family system, frequently leaves women with little time for themselves. Women are often expected and obligated to take charge in a context of insufficient resource support, minimal division of labor, and a lack of confidence by family members in their abilities. However, when conditions promote their visible leadership, women tend to find that the integration and challenge actually energizes them; they experience high self-worth from their contributions to developing and revitalizing both current and succeeding generations.

Research suggests that when their leadership is supported by organizations and societies, women are able to carve a space for themselves within the bounds of their complex responsibilities. The terrain for carving out a personal space is often very difficult. But, even on smoother terrain, women's leadership journeys are marked by role modeling and diligent, creative self-reinvention. Women often achieve 'small wins' by renegotiating the conditions required for their successful enactment of multiple roles and responsibilities. Their division of labor, responsibilities and position within the family/family business system evolves as a result of their navigations, generating a complementary shift within that system. Greater understanding and cooperation with the spouse, other members of the family and members of the family business is cultivated, as such opportunities may offer them constructive developmental growth opportunities to foster personal respect and recognition.

Research also suggests that if suitable conditions exist for visible leadership by women, then women are able to assume leadership roles from their fathers in a non-conflicting and harmonious manner, as, in general, cross-gender successions appear to proceed more smoothly than with the same-gender successions (Jiminez, 2009). In same-gender succession, the successor tends to be in the shadow of the predecessor, and is constantly compared with the predecessor (Vera and Dean, 2005).

Several societal and organizational conditions influence the ability of women to negotiate and achieve more fully vested involvement and leadership in the family firm. We explore this issue next.

III   CONDITIONS FOR ENGAGING WOMEN AND ENABLING TRENDS

Conditions for Successful Engagement of Women

The literature identifies several conditions that foster women's success in the family business context. First, to avoid the feelings of guilt over neglecting the family, women in family businesses need to renegotiate the gender-specific division of labor. Sometimes, flexible gender role arrangements may be formed, allowing sharing of work with the husband. Or a support system may be nurtured for some of the family roles that could be distributed or delegated, such as by taking advantage of professional services, family members and the community. For instance, paid nannies may be hired, or parents or neighbors may assist.

Moreover, it is a mistake to assume that women in family business can perform 100 percent of family roles that at-home mothers might assume, and 100 percent of the business roles that men focused exclusively on business might embrace. Women must develop a strategy of how they will have a major impact in each system, given a reasonable investment of time and energy. When they give a greater priority to business, women face unique challenges related to the functioning of their families. They may, for instance, find themselves not being able to maintain family harmony, leading to dysfunctional family dynamics and dysfunctional business dynamics. Conversely, when they give a greater priority to family, they may find themselves being taken for granted by the family members who are trying to run the family business according to their priorities and preferences.

There is often a great deal of skepticism about women's willingness and ability to attend to business, without being diverted by family responsibilities, and to perform family roles, without being influenced by business matters. Women may use collaborative and distributed approaches, along with strong communication, to gain the support of business associates. Similarly, they could become strong role models for their children and family members, to help enhance family functionality and success. For example, daughters are more likely to be interested in joining family businesses in which their mothers are leaders. Allen and Langowitz (2003) found that 31 percent of the firms run by women had female successors, as compared to only 7 percent of the firms run by males.

Many women find family businesses offer unique freedom to balance their family and business roles. In a family business context, it is easier to perform family roles (e.g. helping children study while they are on the business premises), and to perform business roles (e.g. contacting an important client while they are at home, in between their family chores). However, when the family and business systems are not well differentiated, it is difficult to contain the conflicts and stresses in one system. Also, fluid boundaries between the family and the business result in a transfer of traditional gender role stereotypes and practices from the family to the business domain, making it difficult for women to negotiate positions and roles that are appropriate to the business system. Consequently, the business system fails to leverage the full benefits of their involvement, and the family system similarly fails to benefit fully from the positive synergies of changes in gender roles that might have otherwise taken place in the business system.

Women participating in family businesses typically have to deal with a hierarchy of gender roles built into the family system before they can make significant contributions and maximize their potential. As a first step, they may build upon the role specializations they are already adept at in the family system, to secure quick, small wins in the business system. For instance, they may have a persuasive but participative approach to management, because of their experience in interacting with children. Designating distinct areas of responsibility also tends to help women develop a sense of equality, confidence and satisfaction, even when men hold top leadership positions. Role specialization also makes it more likely that they will be permitted to perform specific roles, and that conditions will be fostered for positive and intensive communication with men. Such conditions then open communication channels about additional roles, responsibilities and opportunities suggested by the business environment, which, in turn, can be transferred to the family system in the form of new, more meaningful roles for women and greater gender role flexibility for both women and men. For instance, women could be tasked with developing a promotional plan to increase awareness about the family business, thereby learning new marketing and business management skills, and how to shape the culture of the family business, which previously may not have emerged as opportunities.

The specific context of a family business influences the conditions for successful engagement of women's power. For instance, when a woman has several brothers, she may be sidetracked for the leadership roles. She may still be able to leverage her areas of 'feminine' strength, helping to develop the family business as a steward for the family and the future generations, but her role may not be seen as essential to the family business. In contrast, when she has few brothers, she may be obliged to play an entrepreneurially oriented anchor role, helping to build and leverage the innovative capacities of the business (Curimbaba, 2002).

In summary, focused interventions are required to clear blocked pathways, and adapt and modify existing realities, for full engagement of women in family businesses. Otherwise, the contributions of women are likely to remain invisible, their journeys may remain difficult, and family businesses may fail to thrive.

Trends Enabling Women's 'Engagement'

In recent years, several forces have been generating a greater visibility of the roles women play in family businesses, and are helping to advance women into more visible and meaningful leadership roles. In the USA in 2007, for instance, 24 percent of the family businesses were led by a woman CEO, versus 15.6 percent in 2002 (Mass Mutual American Family Business Survey, 2007). Nearly 60 percent of the family businesses in the USA have women in their top leadership ranks. The enabling forces include transformation in family structures, the pace of technological change, a scarcity of managerial talent, global supply chains integrating home-based businesses, legal and social policy reforms, and women-focused national economic development agendas.

Traditional family structures have been rapidly transforming within many societies worldwide. Extended family systems have loosened, the number of children born per couple has declined, the acceptance of daughters as the only child(ren) has grown, and single parenthood has gained social sanction. With fewer male family members upon which to rely, and with more educationally well-prepared female family members available and interested, families are expecting women to work in the family businesses. Many women now have alternative work options, at least in the short term, and consider entry into the family business attractive only if they are given meaningful roles that are consistent with their potential, skills and identity.

Women now have a greater range of options to assist them with quality childcare and family care. In many societies, elderly parents are able to provide their daughters or daughters-in-law with childcare and help in family care. Alternatively, professionally run day care centres and after-school care are becoming popular. Hired nannies are yet another option. Men are also sharing family and childcare roles, by opting for flexible time and off-site work arrangements. The cost of quality care may be quite high, but their rising educational level is providing women with sufficient earning power to afford this care as well as save enough to contribute substantially to their children's future education. Family businesses may, in fact, be seen as a place where alternative care arrangements may be tapped with the least sacrifice, given greater flexibility and accommodation by family members in senior management.

Contemporary businesses and economies are driven by rapid technological change. Family businesses find rapid technological change particularly problematic, because their emphasis on trust and loyalty makes them reluctant to rely on outsiders to champion change. Because women tend to have highly creative insights, tend to be patient and diligent learners, and demonstrate the interpersonal skills required for successful change, they can be highly effective change agents. Men, on the other hand, tend to focus on the business's immediate success and are less tolerant of the possibility of minimal rewards if the change is not successful. Consequently, this suggests that women may be more willing and able to assume the responsibility for more long-term, strategic business development.

Such opportunities allow women to develop and maintain their identity, and to have a sense of fulfillment, even though their initiatives, once successful, may be expropriated by male leadership. Since the need for championing change is frequently ongoing, these opportunities may ultimately lead to women's assuming meaningful leadership positions in the family business.

The pressures for managerial talent have intensified with the globalization of competition and professionalism of businesses. Many families are choosing to create a team of siblings to share the leadership and ownership, and include both men and women to cope with these pressures (Aronoff, 1998). Like non-family businesses, family firms are simultaneously finding it difficult to attract high-performing women executives to their ranks, unless they have women in their senior leadership. Women in the family are a readily accessible resource for filling gaps in the leadership team, with their distinctive competencies related to their differing formative education and experiences, as well as their gender.

One unique opportunity for women exists within household-type family businesses, which now employ a significant percentage of women around the world (e.g. textiles and footwear). These businesses are operated from home, and the work is scheduled around the family demands, with considerable mobility between the family and work sphere, and vice versa. They may receive inputs from global suppliers who contract with several such micro family businesses, and may then supply the processed products back to the global firms for their worldwide distribution.

Another avenue for women occurs with home-based Internet family businesses. With such firms, women take primary charge of the family business with their own labor and investment, as well as the caretaking of their children and their spouses (and sometimes extended family members). When men hold other jobs, they may work in these businesses on a part-time basis, or they may perform more externally oriented roles, such as scouting for suppliers or customers.

Gender non-discrimination laws, and the social and public scrutiny of the percentage of women at different levels of management and leadership, have also fostered awareness about the masculine nature of work norms. Further, alternative advancement systems have been adopted, such as allowing women to continue work in special consulting positions without losing their seniority when they choose to reprioritize their time towards their family roles. All of these factors have created pressures for the family businesses to adopt similar practices and, in fact, to pioneer the best practices.

An active and fuller involvement of the 'other' half of the society is high on the development agenda of many nations. Efforts are being made to increase the representation of women in decision-making roles in the government, non-government and semi-government sectors. In many emerging markets, gender mainstreaming projects are seeking to train women and to build their capacities for participation in the local and national planning efforts. Gender-based national budgeting and accounting systems are seeking to: (a) allocate special funds for women's employment and businesses; (b) offer fiscal and monetary policy concessions to women, and explicitly account for the contribution of women in the household sector; and (c) provide better guidance to economic analysis and policy formulation.

The aforementioned factors suggest that families in many societies see the active involvement of women in their businesses as an indication of their social and economic status, and for their contributions to national development. With their economic contributions becoming more visible, women in family business are being seen as a strategic asset and, in fact, a source of distinct advantage.

Prototypes of Women in Family Business Across Cultures

Several non-Anglo prototypes of women's engagement in family businesses prevail across different regional cultures of the world. Some are the vestiges of patriarchal family traditions, while others are the products of more contemporary and emergent trends (e.g. egalitarianism and inclusiveness). Most are hybrid forms, reflecting some aspects of traditional roles and identities, and other aspects of contemporary social, political and economic change. Based on the CASE research (Gupta et al., 2008a, 2008b), we identify below some dominant prototypes across cultures.

Latin America/Latin Europe prototype (Gupta and Levenburg, 2010)
In many Latin heritage societies, inheritance laws require gender non-discrimination during estate transfer, but the property rights do not necessarily translate into visible roles for women in the family business. In Latin American societies, daughters generally do not inherit a share in family business unless their husbands are part of the firm. Further, the shares given to the daughters tend to be peripheral and involve less lucrative parts of the family business.

Wives may be in charge of the hospitality for business relations, and for participation in business clubs. Increasingly, however, married or unmarried couples may jointly own, found and manage a family business. To assure success, they often maintain written, albeit flexible, job descriptions, shared values for the business, synergistic cooperation and effective communication.

In Latin European societies, on the other hand, women have a more substantial presence as the owners of family businesses, and are actively involved as the directors on the board, functional directors and general managers – more so than in the non-family businesses. Yet male successors are favored for the primary leadership position of CEO, and women family managers are expected to prove their credentials as deserving and respectworthy leaders. Often father and sons have very limited education and have experience only within the family business, while the daughters are well educated yet are deprived of the family business and are excluded from the succession.

Confucian prototype (Gupta et al., 2009)
With increasing competition and business expansion, many family businesses are witnessing a shortage in the number of male family members who are available, prepared and willing to join the family firm. This is because Confucian societies are witnessing a breakdown of family-centered values, and Western-educated male children often refuse to join the family businesses. Consequently, a growing tendency in the Confucian region is to involve women family members in family business senior management positions.

Confucian daughters may feel obligated to join a family business to fulfill filial piety. Those who have been brought up in a strong family business culture may feel a need to demonstrate their capability and to express themselves and their identity through business. This is particularly true if they are the only or eldest child, or the most appropriate candidate in the family. Often given precedence over non-family executives, they enter their family's businesses directly as executives and are given fairly substantial opportunities in senior and visible positions. For them, there is seemingly no need to work their way up through the ranks or gain experience within other companies before joining the family firm.

In addition, Confucian wives often assist their husbands in managing the family business, to help enhance the business's success, and to secure family resources for educating children and supporting the family. Women are perceived of as the keepers of the family fortune, and are entrusted with the tasks of keeping accounts, saving money and business growth. Thus they hold a position of power by virtue of their in-depth knowledge of the firm's finances. However, among the immigrant Confucian enterprises, language barriers sometimes result in men taking over the financial management role in both business as well as home domains.

Southern Asian prototype (Gupta et al., 2007)

In Southern Asian cultures, the daughters are traditionally not involved in family business, though the son-in-law and the male spouses of aunts may be involved as consultants. While the wives are often included as co-owners of the family business, they tend to have limited involvement, with their husbands exercising decision-making rights as their proxies. Wives, however, assume leadership roles in cases in which their husband has died and their sons have not yet matured. Other immediate women family members, such as the founder's sister, sister-in-law, daughter and daughter-in-law, may also be included as silent directors on the board.

Changes are, however, occurring. With increased opportunities in the marketplace, families are increasingly looking for new types of successors, including daughters and daughters-in-law – not just younger sons. Often, daughters and wives take up the role of developing new business lines (e.g. technology-based) or new sector businesses or distribution channels, which help to renew the family businesses and more effectively compete in a dynamic market environment.

Middle Eastern prototype (Gupta et al., 2010)

In the Middle East, women are increasingly joining family businesses in management roles. Particularly in Gulf nations, minority nationals are seeking to advance women to preserve their cultural identity and to promote their national development. The Islamic law of Shari'a mandates that wives share one-eighth of business ownership, with the remainder being divided among siblings, and sons receiving twice the share of daughters. When the family business is facing difficulties or the father has grown old and has no other successor, this allows women to join senior leadership.

Daughters are also increasingly marrying husbands who share similar interests in allowing them to work in the family business. Wives gain particular visibility among the ladies' circles, and organize social events for prominent men in their husbands' circles. In most cases outside the Middle East's Gulf region, women in the family, if involved in the business, are assigned roles such as budgetary planning and control that do not require outside interaction. They have limited decision-making authority even within their assigned roles and must defer key decisions to the senior male leaders. In most businesses, daughters are not visible to the outside world.

Eastern European prototype (Gupta and Levenburg, 2010)
In the Eastern European region, partnerships and joint ownership of a family business by a single husband–wife team, or with another couple who are friends, are common. Usually, the husband is the CEO, while the wife works as an accountant or functional manager. Sometimes, especially in younger families and in instances where she is either older than her husband or better educated and trained, the wife may be the leader. In such cases, husbands are generally responsible for externally oriented functions, and for relationships with the partners and suppliers. But when the wife is clearly better educated and trained, and where the husband has no alternative employment option, husbands may work as employees and follow the leadership of their wives. Many single mothers also operate family businesses, with their daughter or son assisting them as accountants, and appreciating the flexibility to take care of the family while also earning a living. Even where women play an important role in running family businesses as only informal co-preneurs, they may become official owner-managers of the family businesses after the death of their parents or spouse, or after their own divorce. They may also provide resilience to the family business by working in another established business, while their spouse and other family members work in the family business. Such a model helps augment the financial resources of the business, and provides valuable 'weak ties' with the externally employed wife's more diverse set of skills and relationships.

Nordic prototype (Gupta et al., 2011)
Although the states in the Nordic region generally offer legal frameworks for equal opportunity, the roles of husbands and wives (or sons and daughters) in a family business fall into gender stereotypes. The males lead and take part in the line activities of purchasing, production and marketing, while women play a supporting role. Women tend to be the supporters of continuity, and of using traditional technology, products, markets and organizational solutions in the family business. They also perform a supporting role when necessary to augment the family business's competitiveness, such as by learning and performing tasks for which they had little previous training or interest, and helping the business adapt to changing needs, technologies or markets. Alternatively, when the husband must adopt new technology because of severe client pressure, the wife is often expected to have a fixed job, providing stable income for the family. Thus spouses enhance the resilience and change capability of the family business.

Germanic prototype (Gupta et al., 2011)
Social systems institutionalized in the Germanic region during the Second World War to engage women in running businesses have influenced men's perceptions of women's active participation in the family business as enhancing their social prestige, and assuring the firm's success. It is common for a husband and wife team to be at the core. Wives serve as a sounding board, adviser and confidante, besides performing managerial responsibilities. The couple model makes it more likely for daughters to join the family business, and for leaders to be successful for a longer period of time without early succession. Typically, the husband leads crafts-based production, and the wife looks after retailing/trading, thereby combining the benefits of craft apprenticeship with the trusting image of family business. Within this region, many larger corporations seek exclusive franchisees and dealers who are not only family businesses but also have a family image,

and are jointly operated by a couple with one of the spouses specializing in sales and the other in services. In families where the potential and contribution of women is appreciated and integrated, the family business shows greater resilience, with constant renewal, gradual diversification, professionalism or deliberate exit strategies. Women may help open related diversified lines for the family business, or engage in other types of innovation. If needed, paid help is hired to do the household work, freeing women to make innovative contributions, which are often subsequently furthered by men.

Sub-Saharan prototype (Gupta et al., 2010)

A home-based form of family business operated as a micro-enterprise, and linked to the global supply chain, has exploded around the world. This is an important form of family business in many regions, including among the indigenous population of Sub-Saharan Africa. Micro-enterprises founded by regional immigrants are yet another widely pervasive form of family business. Many immigrant micro-enterprises are founded and managed by a couple, sometimes assisted by their children, with women generally responsible for customer service and men for external activities. Women and their capabilities play an equally important role as their husbands in the strategic decision-making, including decisions about the type of industry in which to compete. As a husband and a wife work together, family work (e.g. cooking and studying) is done at work, and work is done in the home domain.

IV   CONCLUSIONS

In this work, we investigated the 'invisible role' of women in family businesses that is well documented in the literature. While several factors traditionally contributed to making the role of women an invisible one, and their pathways to success have often been tumultuous and difficult, the environment has changed considerably in recent years. Women are now playing an active role in contemporary family businesses. It is important to recognize, acknowledge and further investigate these new roles and contributions of women. Such an explicit recognition will help us celebrate the successes that many women have enjoyed in what appears to be a relatively short period of time. More importantly, it will help build women's confidence to negotiate and navigate their entry, advancement and requisites for success in family business.

A family business – as commonly understood – is a business characterized by family involvement (Miller and Rice, 1967; Chua et al., 1999; Astrachan et al., 2002; Klein et al., 2005). Inclusion of gender identity can substantially enrich the family business literature. Anecdotal evidence, for instance, suggests that women in many cultures become part of the husband's family after marriage, which gives them a shorter time window (as compared to their husbands) to become assimilated into the family business. Moreover, since women's interpretation of cultural practices and priorities is often a blend of learning from their own and their husband's families, the emphasis by a family business on the culture of the husband's family diminishes the wife's value-added set of experiences. However, to be effective, family involvement needs to address the involvement of both men and women in their varying roles. Family involvement also needs to include the experiences of both, as women's experiences may also help the family businesses extend their individualized resources into new, innovative and value-accruing directions. Finally, family involvement also needs to include the cultural interpretations of women.

As demonstrated by the CASE project's findings, family firms – and women's roles and responsibilities within them – are best examined within their cultural contexts. Whereas the first generation of gendered research focused on women's invisibility in family-owned businesses (and various promulgating forces), the second generation delved into their contributions when their roles are more visible. The third generation extends prior work by examining women's roles and opportunities in family firms within their cultural contexts, such as the impact of inheritance laws (i.e. legal environment) in Latin America or the technological environment in Southeast Asia. By expanding our understanding and appreciation of these cross-cultural differences, the body of knowledge with respect to both the opportunities presented to women and the challenges they face in family businesses may be enhanced.

Increased globalization, competition and operational professionalism confront family businesses around the world. By placing confidence in the roles and contributions of women, families should be able to draw upon their 'other half', whose power has traditionally remained undervalued and underutilized. One example occurs with respect to emerging technologies, and the male family business members are simply too preoccupied with the present configurations and business activities. Here, women may be particularly adept in helping the family business cultivate new capabilities and integrate them with the firm's prior core capabilities, while also preserving stability within family relations.

Yet policy-makers, in general, have not devoted sufficient attention to the unique issues facing family businesses, and the potential contributions they may make to the vibrancy and resilience of their local communities and the positive impact of gender mainstreaming on local, regional and global economies. Family businesses are uniquely poised to strengthen and regenerate the entire value-adding chain in local communities. Carefully crafted and targeted interventions, based on cultural and gender sensitivity, may transform family businesses into powerful and sustainable forms of organizations for successive generations of women, and the families and businesses they support.

REFERENCES

Allen, I.E. and N.S. Langowitz (2003), *Women in Family-Owned Businesses*, Boston, MA: MassMutual Financial Group and Center for Women's Leadership at Babson College.

Aronoff, C.E. (1998), 'Megatrends in family business', *Family Business Review*, 11(3), 181–5.

Astrachan, J.H., S.B. Klein and K.X. Smyrnios (2002), 'The F-PEC scale of family influence: a proposal for solving the family business definition problem', *Family Business Review*, 15(1), 45–58.

Barbuto Jr, J.E., S.M. Fritz, G.S. Matkin and D.B. Marx (2007), 'Effects of gender, education, and age upon leader's use of influence tactics and full range leadership behaviors', *Sex Roles*, 56 (January), 71–83.

Barnes, L.B. and C. Kaftan (1990), *Organizational Transitions for Individuals, Families and Work Groups*, Englewood Cliffs, NJ: Prentice Hall.

Barrett, M. and K. Moores (2009), 'Fostering women's entrepreneurial leadership in family firms: ten lessons', Management Online Review, ro.uow.edu.au, 1–11.

Bloom, N. and J. Van Reenen (2007), 'Measuring and explaining management practices across firms and countries', *The Quarterly Journal of Economics*, 122(4), 1351–408.

Chua, J.H., J.J. Chrisman and P. Sharma (1999), 'Defining the family business by behavior', *Entrepreneurship Theory and Practice*, 23, 19–39.

Cole, P.M. (1993), 'Women in family business: a systemic approach to inquiry', unpublished doctoral dissertation, Nova Southeastern University, Fort Lauderdale, FL.

Cole, P.M. (1997), 'Women in family business', *Family Business Review*, **10**(4), 353–71.

Coleman, S. and A. Robb (2010), 'Sources of funding for new women owned firms', *Western New England Law Review*, **32**, 497–514.

Curimbaba, F. (2002), 'The dynamics of women's roles as family business managers', *Family Business Review*, **15**(3), 239–52.

Dugan, A.M., S.P. Krone, K. LeCouvie, J.M. Pendergast, D.H. Kenyon-Rouvinez and A.M. Schuman (2008), *A Woman's Place: The Crucial Roles of Women in Family Business*, Marietta, GA: Family Business Consulting Group.

Dumas, C. (1989), 'Understanding of father–daughter and father–son dyads in family-owned businesses', *Family Business Review*, **2**(1), 31–46.

Dumas, C. (1998), 'Women's pathways to participation and leadership in the family-owned firm', *Family Business Review*, **11**(3), 219–28.

Eagly, A.H., M.C. Johannesen-Schmidt and M.L. van Engen (2003), 'Transformational, transactional, and laissez-faire leadership styles: a meta analysis comparing women and men', *Psychological Bulletin*, **129**, 569–91.

Francis, A.E. (1999), *The Daughter Also Rises: How Women Overcome Obstacles and Advance in the Family-Owned Business*, San Francisco, CA: Rudi.

Freudenberger, H.J., D.K. Freedheim and T.S. Kurtz (1989), 'Treatment of individuals in family business', *Psychotherapy*, **26**(1), 47–53.

Frishkoff, P.A. and B.M. Brown (1993), 'Women on the move in family business', *Business Horizons*, March–April, 66–70.

Galiano, A.M. and J.B. Vinturella (1995), 'Implications of gender bias in the family business', *Family Business Review*, **8**(3), 177–88.

Gillis-Donovan, J. and C. Moynihan-Bradt (1990). 'The power of invisible women in the family business', *Family Business Review*, **3**(2), 153–67.

Gupta, V. and N. Levenburg (2010), 'The Catholic spirit and family business: contrasting Latin America, Eastern Europe and Southern Europe', *Advances in Entrepreneurship, Firm Emergence & Growth*, vol.12, Bingley, UK: Emerald Group, pp.185–228.

Gupta, V., N. Levenburg, L. Moore, J. Motwani and T. Schwarz (2007), 'Organizational model of the Southern Asia cluster family businesses', *The South East Asian Journal of Management*, **1**(2), 125–42.

Gupta, V., N. Levenburg, L. Moore, J. Motwani and T. Schwarz (2008a), *Culturally Sensitive Models of Family Business: A Compendium Using the GLOBE Paradigm*, Hyderabad, India: ICFAI University Press.

Gupta, V., N. Levenburg, L. Moore, J. Motwani and T. Schwarz (2008b), 'Exploring the construct of family business in the emerging markets', *International Journal of Business and Emerging Markets*, **1**(2), 189–208.

Gupta, V., N. Levenburg, L. Moore, J. Motwani and T. Schwarz (2009), 'Anglo vs. Asian family business: a cultural comparison and analysis', *Journal of Asian Business Studies*, **44**, 46–55.

Gupta, V., N. Levenburg, L. Moore, J. Motwani and T. Schwarz (2010), 'Family Business in Sub-Saharan Africa vs. Middle East', *Journal of African Business*, **11**(2), 146–62.

Gupta, V., N. Levenburg, L. Moore, J. Motwani and T. Schwarz (2011), 'The spirit of family business: a comparative analysis of Anglo, Germanic and Nordic nations', *International Journal of Cross-cultural Management*, **11**(3), in press.

Hampton, M.C. (2009), 'Book Review', *Family Business Review*, **22**(4), 366–9.

Hollander, B.S. and W.R. Bukowitz (1990), 'Women, family culture and family business', *Family Business Review*, **3**(2), 139–51.

Iannarelli, C.L. (1992), 'The socialization of leaders in family business: an exploratory study of gender', unpublished doctoral dissertation, University of Pittsburgh, PA.

Jimenez, R.M. (2009), 'Research on women in family firms: current status and future directions', *Family Business Review*, **22**(1), 53–64.

Klein, S.B., J.H. Astrachan and K.X. Smyrnios (2005), 'The F-PEC scale of family influence: construction, validation, and further implication for theory', *Entrepreneurship Theory and Practice*, **29**(6), 321–40.

Komives, S.R. (1991), 'Gender differences in the relationship of hall directors' transformational and transactional leadership and achieving styles', *Journal of College Student Development*, **32**, 155–65.

Llano, C. and F. Olguin (1986), 'La Sucesión en la Empresa Familiar', in V.F. Pascual (ed), *La Empresa Familiar 2*, Barcelona, Spain: Universidad de Navarra, IESE, pp.36–66.

Lyman, A.R. (1988), 'Life in the family circle', *Family Business Review*, **1**(4), 383–98.

Lyman, A., Salganicoff, M. and Hollander, B. (1985), 'Women in family business: an untapped resource', *SAM Advanced Management Journal*, **50**(1), 46–9.

Marshack, K.J. (1993), 'Copreneurial couples: a literature review on boundaries and transitions among copreneurs', *Family Business Review*, **6**(4), 355–69.

Mass Mutual American Family Business Survey (2007), http://www.massmutual.com/mmfg/pdf/afbs.pdf, retrieved 25 July 2011.

Miller, E.J. and A.K. Rice (1967), *Systems of Organization: Task and Sentient Systems and Their Boundary Control*, London, UK: Tavistock Publications.

Moen, P. (1992), *Women's Two Roles*, Westport, CT: Auburn House.

Nelton, S. (1997), 'A different message for daughters', *Nation's Business*, **85**(5), 62.

Perkins, H. and D.K. DeMeis (1996), 'Gender and family effects on the "second-shift" domestic activity of college-educated young adults', *Gender & Society*, **10**, 78–93.

Poza, E.J. and Messer, T. (2001), 'Spousal leadership and continuity in the family firm', *Family Business Reviews*, **14**(1), 25–35.

Rowe, B.R. and G.S. Hong (2000), 'The role of wives in family businesses: the paid and unpaid work of women', *Family Business Review*, **13**, 1–13.

Salganicoff, M. (1990), 'Women in family businesses: challenges and opportunities', *Family Business Reviews*, **3**(2), 125–37.

Schmoll, C. (2005), 'Moving "on their own"? Mobility strategies and social networks of migrant women from Maghreb in Italy', paper presented at Conference on Alternative Narratives for Globalization? New Theorisations of Migrant Women's Global Networks, Trinity College, Dublin, Ireland.

Vera, C.F. and M.A. Dean (2005), 'An examination of the challenges daughters face in family business succession', *Family Business Review*, **18**, 321–46.

Ward, J.L. and L.S. Sorenson (1989), 'The role of mom', *Nation's Business*, **11** (77), 40–41.

APPENDIX

Table 16A.1   Description of CASE sample of gender-focused articles on family businesses

Author(s)/title of paper	Focus	Country	Methodology
John Davis, Elye Pitts and Keely Cormier, 'Challenges facing family companies in the Gulf region'	Effect of globalization and liberalization on family businesses	Gulf	Grounded theory
Josiane Fahed-Sreih, 'The unique approaches of the family businesses in the Middle East'	Factors influencing longevity of family businesses	Middle East	Grounded theory
Nidal Sabri, 'Performance and succession in Palestinian family businesses'	Discriminating advantages and disadvantages of family businesses	Palestine	Survey
Khalid Nadvi, 'Shifting ties of family businesses: the surgical instrument cluster of Sialkot, Pakistan'	Issues when a regional cluster comprises family businesses, linked via generations of coexistence and family relations	Pakistan	Qualitative
Wim Vijverberg, 'Returns to schooling in non-farm self-employment in Ghana'	Impact of educational attainment on income from family business	Ghana	Secondary data set
Fomba Emmanuel Mbebeb, 'Managing human resources in the familistic family business in Cameroon'	Effect of householder model on the human resource management in family businessses	Cameroon	Grounded theory
Lucrezia Songini and Luca Gnan, 'Women in Italian family firms and professionalization'	Role of women in family businesses	Italy	Survey
Ana María Presta, 'Migratory rationality, marriage strategies and business in early Bolivia: the Paniagua de Loaysa family'	Role of marriage and migratory strategies, and local connections and political agendas, in the development of family business	Bolivia	Historical analysis
Roberto Kertesz, Clara Atalaya and Jorge Kammerer, 'Psychosocial issues of family businesses in Argentina'	Psychosocial issues involving small and medium family businesses	Argentina	Clinical interventions
Thomas Glauben, Hendrik Tietje and Christoph Weiss, 'Intergenerational succession in farm households: evidence from Upper Austria'	Role of farm and family resources in intergenerational succession planning in family farms	Austria	Survey
Willem Burggraaf, Roberto Flören and Jurgen Geerlings, 'Righteousness in ownership transfer: a cultural perspective'	How cultural context sustains solidarity in the face of egalitarian transfer of family business ownership	Netherlands	Grounded theory

Table 16A.1   (continued)

Author(s)/title of paper	Focus	Country	Methodology
Katerina Sarri and Anna Trichopoulou, 'Female entrepreneurship, self-starting entrepreneurs and family business successors'	Informal role of women in family businesses, except in push conditions	Greece	Survey
Mary Barrett and Ken Moores, 'Women learning business leadership: journeys in the family firm'	Varying pathways of women to family business leadership	Multiple nations	Interviews
Sharon M. Danes, Heather R. Haberman and Donald McTavish, 'Gendered discourse about Euro-American family business'	Use of an emotional discourse by women, and of a more pragmatic discourse by men, in conversations on family business management	European immigrants into the USA	Interviews, content analysis
Min-Jung Kwak, 'Work in family business and gender relations: recent Korean immigrant women in Toronto'	Effects of women's participation in family business on traditional gender relations	Korean immigrants into Canada	Interviews, participant observation
Saijja Katila, 'The gendered moral order of Chinese immigrant business families in Finland'	Effects of culture and of context on gender relations in family business	Chinese immigrants into Finland	Biographical interviews
Bettina B. Bock, 'Gender, diversification and family farming in the Netherlands'	How women organize family farm diversification activities around their traditional gender identity to facilitate change and continuity simultaneously	Netherlands	Interviews
Ghadeer Nassar, 'Effect of father–daughter relation on daughter's role in Egyptian family businesses'	Effect of inclusion versus control relation with daughter on her integration into the father's family business	Egypt	Interviews
Jenny White, 'Gender and the lifecycle of a family atelier in Turkey'	Neighborhood of families linked together in a value-adding subcontracting chain	Turkey	Ethnographic study
Khalid Kanoo, 'The house of Kanoo: foundations of succession and success'	Effect of nationalistic and futuristic ethos on family business	Bahrain	Case study
Alma Kadragic and Marsha Ludwig, 'Al Fahim group: developing a long term business in a young country'	Functioning of a mega-professionally managed multi-generation family business	UAE	Case study

Table 16A.1   (continued)

Author(s)/title of paper	Focus	Country	Methodology
Christine Blondel and Ludo Van der Heyden, 'Niraj: successor's dilemma in an Indian family firm'	Developing successors, and differences in the aspirations of the successors, when a successor enjoys alternative career options	India	Case study
Ole Bruun, 'Household businesses and local bureaucracy in Sichuan, China'	Operations of micro-household enterprises	China	Ethnographic study
Eric Tsang, 'Organizational learning in the expansion of Singapore family businesses to China'	Knowledge management dynamics in foreign direct investments of family businesses	Singapore	Case studies
Shaheena Janjuha-Jivraj and Adrian Woods, 'Encounters of culture in intergenerational succession of Asian family firms in Kenya'	Role of cultural and migratory influences in intergenerational succession	Kenya	Interviews
Su Fei Tan and Bara Gueye, 'Resilience of family farming in West Africa'	Resilience of resource acquisition and development in family farms	Ghana/ Senegal/ Mali	Case studies
Åge Mariussen, Jane Wheelock and Susan Baines, "Family into business" model in Norway: modernization and reinvention?'	Issues when family identity and labor are closely integrated with the business, and viewed as giving independence	Norway	Interviews and survey/ fishing families
Tiina Silvasti, 'Gendered division of labour on Finnish farms'	Issues in transfer of a male-oriented business to the daughter	Finland	Multiple case
Simone Ghezzi, 'Strategies of shareholding exclusion in northern Italian family workshops'	Role of masculine attitudes in succession and family in business	Italy	Ethnographic study
Carole Howorth and Zahra Assaraf Ali, 'Family business succession in Portugal'	Dynamics of succession in cousin consortia model	Portugal	Case study
Larissa Lomnitz and Marisol Lizaur, 'Family enterprise in Mexico: a case study of an elite family'	How the family business organization, management and goals are structured as an extension of family structure	Mexico	Historical Case
Ruth Rossier, 'Role models and farm development options: a comparison of seven Swiss farm families'	How flexible gender role models facilitate farm renewal and development	Switzerland	Interviews

Table 16A.1   (continued)

Author(s)/title of paper	Focus	Country	Methodology
Norbert Dannhaeuser, 'The family-operated firm: survival of a traditional institution in a developed setting'	Role of couple leadership and cultural idealism in enabling continued viability of family businesses	Germany	Field study
Nonna Barkhatova, 'Russian families in small business'	Behaviors of Russian families in business, against the backdrop of transitional economic context	Russia	Interview
Justin Craig and Ken Moores, 'Australia's Dennis family corporation professionalizes'	How formal systems are developed to professionalize a family firm	Australia	Case study
Natenapha Wailerdsak (Yabushita), 'Women executives in Thai family businesses'	Wake-up call – glass ceiling does exist at the management and leadership level!	Thailand	Analysis of corporate reported data
Silvia Gómez Ansón and María Sacristán Navarro, 'Women board of directors in Spanish family firms'	Family businesses have more women on their boards, and they represent the owning families	Spain	Analysis of corporate reported data
Matthew C. Sonfield and Robert N. Lussier, 'Women in the U.S. family business ownership and management'	Impact of women in family business leadership team on family business strategic decision making	USA	Regional survey
Margaret A. Fitzgerald and Cathleen Folker, 'Women's leadership in the U.S. family businesses: role of family vs. business priorities'	Impact of family business women priorities on family versus business on family functionality and business effectiveness	USA	National survey
Marilyn F. Reineck, 'Role carryover between spouses in U.S. family businesses: development of a model'	Impact of communication behaviors on role carryover problems between couples in family businesses	USA	Interviews, content analysis, surveys

PART VI

LEADERSHIP AND HUMAN RESOURCE MANAGEMENT IN FAMILY FIRMS

17 Exploring human resource management in family firms: a summary of what we know and ideas for future development
Isabel C. Botero and Shanan R. Litchfield

As a result of the technological revolution and other changes in the twentyfirst century, the importance of human capital and human resources for organizations has changed. While 100 years ago companies were creating standardized products and viewed employees as expendable, organizations today are more specialized and depend on the intellectual capital of their employees to succeed (Cascio, 2009). Thus attracting, retaining and managing human resources is critical for the success of organizations in today's economy (Rynes and Cable, 2003). In the last two decades, the importance of people to organizations and their success has been highlighted by both the academic (Birdi et al., 2008; Wright et al., 2001) and popular press (Pfeffer, 1998; Senge, 2006). In general, the belief is that employees and their performance have implications for firm-level outcomes (Barney, 1991; Barney and Wright, 1998; Huselid, 1995). Rooted in this belief there has been an interest in understanding how organizations manage their human resources to support business strategy and provide value to the firm.

Human resource management (HRM) has been the area of research that has explored the management of people in the organization. HRM is the process and activities organizations use to attract, develop and maintain their workforce with the intention of supporting and helping advance the mission, the objectives and the strategies of the organization (Cascio, 2009; Schermerhorn, 2001). HRM is often seen as a 'micro' oriented approach that looks at management practices that affect employee behaviors and performance (Lengnick-Hall et al., 2009; Wright and McMahan, 1992). Given the importance of human resources (HR) for organizations, in the last 15 years there has been a growing body of research devoted to exploring the role of HR in supporting business strategy and firm performance (Becker and Huselid, 2006; Birdi et al., 2008; Wright et al., 2001). This research has been described under the label of strategic human resource management (SHRM). SHRM represents the 'patterns of planned organizational activities that enable an organization to achieve its overall goals' (Wright and McMahan, 1992, p. 298). While HRM has a micro focus, SHRM takes a 'macro'-oriented approach and is concerned with how the HR practices and their management fit into the overall strategy of the firm and affect their overall performance (Lengnick-Hall et al., 2009).

Although HRM and SHRM issues have received extensive attention in the literature, the focus has primarily been on large firms (Hornsby and Kuratko, 2003); less research attention has been given to HRM/SHRM in small and medium-sized enterprises (SMEs) (Heneman et al., 2000) and family firms (Reid and Adams, 2001; Reid et al., 2000; Sharma, 2004). This is interesting, because it is estimated that, at least in the USA, the majority of organizations are small or medium enterprises (SMEs), understood as employing 500 or fewer employees (SBA, 2008), and that many of these organizations are also family firms, understood broadly as organizations in which there is some participation of family members and the family has control over the economic strategic directions in the business (Astrachan and Shanker, 2003). We believe that the focus on understanding HRM practices based on the practices of large organizations is problematic because there are theoretical and empirical reasons why SMEs differ from larger firms (Barber et al., 1999; Hayton, 2003; Tocher and Rutherford, 2009) and why family firms differ from non-family firms (De Kok et al., 2006; Dyer, 2006; Reid et al., 2000). With this in mind, this chapter has three purposes. First, we explain the unique considerations for human resource research in SMEs that are family owned. Second, we summarize published research on HRM and SHRM that has been conducted in SMEs and family firms. Third, we conclude by summarizing what we currently know about HR in family firms and we then outline areas for future research.

To achieve our purpose we have structured the chapter as follows. We begin by explaining the importance of HRM for productivity and financial performance of organizations; we then turn to explaining the unique considerations for conducting research in HR in family firms. After this, we summarize published research about HR in small and medium family firms. We conclude the chapter by explaining what we know about HRM in small and medium family firms and outlining future research in this area.

IMPORTANCE OF HUMAN RESOURCE MANAGEMENT FOR PRODUCTIVITY AND FIRM PERFORMANCE

The way in which organizations manage their human resources has increasingly been recognized as an important factor for executing the firm's strategy (Hambrick et al., 1989; Koch and McGrath, 1996). The argument advanced is that the use of high-performance work practices (e.g. comprehensive employee recruitment and selection procedures, incentives in compensation and performance management systems, and extensive employee involvement and training, to mention a few) can improve the knowledge, skills and abilities of the employees in a firm, can improve motivation, and reduce employee shirking (Huselid, 1995; Jones and Wright, 1992). The idea is that HRM practices can help in the creation of sustained competitive advantage (Barney and Wright, 1998; Wright et al., 2001).

Drawing on the resource-based view (RBV) of the firm (Barney, 1991), researchers have argued that human resources can become a source of sustained competitive advantage when four requirements are met (Barney and Wright, 1998; Huselid, 1995; Wright et al., 2001; Wright and McMahan, 1992). First, employees (i.e. human resources) must add value to the firm's production processes by assuring that the level of individual performance matters. This value can be added by the quality and quantity of work that employees perform. Second, the skills that the organization looks for in their human resources must be rare. This can be achieved by attracting applicants with unique characteristics that can help the organization. Third, the human resources that an organization has cannot be easily imitated. One of the ways to achieve this difficulty of imitation is through opportunities for employees and a culture that cannot be copied by other organizations. And, fourth, an organization should not be able to easily substitute their human resources. That is, employees who work for the organization should offer unique knowledge that can help the organization succeed. Thus, to achieve these four requirements in their employees, organizations need to develop HRM practices that will influence their human capital by developing individual employees and ensuring that the organizational environment is conducive for employees to benefit from these developments (Birdi et al., 2008). In turn, HRM practices can also influence performance by providing structures that enable and encourage employee participation, and allow employees to improve the way they do their job (Huselid, 1995).

Empirical research supports the impact that HRM practices have on firm performance. For example, Huselid (1995) presented evidence that HR practices are economically and statistically related to employee outcomes and short- and long-term measures of corporate and financial performance. Findings from Koch and McGrath (1996) also provide evidence that HR practices (i.e. HR planning, recruitment and staffing) are significantly related to labor productivity, and that this relation is stronger for capital intensive organizations. The work of Pfeffer (1998) also provides evidence that in large companies from multiple industries the way that people are managed is directly related to the economic results they achieve. And, more recently, the work of Birdi and colleagues (2008) has also supported the idea that in manufacturing organizations HR practices (i.e. empowerment, extensive training and adoption of teamwork) have an impact on organizational performance. Similar support for the effects of HR practices on performance has also been found for SMEs (Buller and Napier, 1993; Chandler and McEvoy, 2000; Hayton, 2003; Rowden, 2002) and family firms (Astrachan and Kolenko, 1994; Carlson et al., 2006).

Given the effects of HRM practices on firm performance, in this chapter we argue that understanding HRM in small and medium family firms can help family business researchers and practitioners better understand performance in family firms and why the performance of these organizations may differ from that of other organizations. Before summarizing the research that has been conducted in the area of HRM in small and medium family firms, we present four important considerations that we believe are necessary when conducting HR research in small and medium family firms.

CONSIDERATIONS FOR HR RESEARCH IN SMALL AND MEDIUM FAMILY FIRMS

Although there is an extensive body of research exploring HR issues, our knowledge of HRM practices and their effects on performance is primarily based on research that explores large organizations (Kotey and Sheridan, 2004; Wilkinson, 1999). Recent works exploring the management of human resources in SMEs has suggested that HR practices in these firms differ from those of larger organizations (Buller and Napier, 1993; Deshpande and Golhar, 1994; Golhar and Deshpande, 1997; Heneman et al., 2000). In particular, two factors that influence the use of HRM practices in organizations are: firm size and development phase of the firm (Cardon and Stevens, 2004). It is believed that both firm size and level of development of a firm are two factors that present unique challenges for the management of human resources for small and medium enterprises. Thus, to understand the unique challenges of HR research in small and medium family firms we first need to understand the role that firm size and firm development play in the management of human resources.

Research in entrepreneurship has supported the idea that organizational size affects the way organizations operate (Deshpande and Golhar, 1994), and in particular small organizations are more likely to be flexible and informal in the way they operate when compared to larger firms (De Kok and Uhlaner, 2001; Gibb, 1997). Thus some researchers argue that the liability of smallness is tied to the lack of resources which affect the opportunities that organizations can seek out and the ability to deal with difficult economic times and/or heavy competition (Cardon and Stevens, 2004; Ranger-Moore, 1997; Wilkinson, 1999). To support this idea, past research has found that organizational size is positively related with the use of traditional HRM practices, HRM planning in general and HRM sophistication (Barber et al., 1999; Hill and Stewart, 1999; Hornsby and Kuratko, 1990, 2003; Koch and McGrath, 1996; Kotey and Sheridan, 2004; Kotey and Slade, 2005; Nguyen and Bryant, 2004). In particular, smaller firms are less likely to use formal practices and use fewer practices than bigger firms. The reason behind this is that, in smaller firms, the person who is the manager often plays multiple roles at the same time and needs to divide their time at work between the multiple roles. Therefore firms with fewer employees are less likely to use HR practices in the same way as larger firms. Additionally, because smaller firms have fewer people to manage they often do not need to use the same practices that larger firms use to keep track of their human resources (Rutherford et al., 2003).

The development phase of the organization represents the second factor that we need to consider to understand the management of human resources in SMEs that are family firms (Cardon & Stevens, 2004). Baird and Meshoulam (1988) argue that HRM practices should fit the business needs of a firm and that these needs differ based on the firm's life cycle. While it is common that firms in the start-up phase have owners who are responsible for executing all the management functions, as the business grows there are more HR issues that need to be dealt with and the demand will exceed the owner's/founder's capability to manage effectively. In a similar way, when firms are in a high-growth stage their use of HRM practices shifts from focusing on attracting and hiring the right kind of people to managing them (Baird and Meshoulan, 1988). Thus the organization will need to develop a more formal HRM approach as it develops.

Because of the challenges that firm size and firm development have on the way organizations function, we believe, similar to other researchers (e.g. Cardon and Stevens, 2004; Heneman and Tansky, 2002), that the study of human resources in SMEs is different than in larger firms. In particular, SMEs face unique HR challenges which include issues such as difficulty in attracting and retaining key talent and skills (Barber et al., 1999; Williamson et al., 2002), lack of legitimacy as employer organizations (Williamson, 2000; Williamson et al., 2002), and difficulty in developing sustainable human resource policies that endure market and organizational fluctuations (Cardon and Stevens, 2004).

We believe that SMEs that are family owned or managed have two additional characteristics which affect how they manage their human resources: the presence of family and non-family employees, and the level of influence that family members have on the firm and its members. Having employees, at managerial and non-managerial levels, who are family members makes the management of the human resources more challenging because family membership can contribute to the blurring of boundaries among the three different systems in family firms (i.e. family membership, management and ownership systems of the firm). That is, family employees can sometimes be more difficult to manage because for them family patterns and dynamics can override the logic of business management (Poza, 2010). For example, family employees may choose not to report employment violations of other family members to avoid family conflict, while they may report a similar violation from a non-family employee. Thus the presence of family members in the business will most likely affect how human resources are managed in small and medium family firms.

In a similar way, the degree to which the family is involved and able to influence the firm and its members is an important consideration when exploring HR in family firms. Research indicates that the family influence has three components: power (i.e. ability to control the firm through ownership), experience (i.e. family memory available in the firm) and culture (i.e. values and commitment of family members introduced into the firm) (Astrachan et al., 2002; Klein et al., 2005). Using this framework, Barnett and Kellermanns (2006) define three descriptive levels of family influence: dormant family influence (i.e. low influence), facilitating family influence (i.e. moderate to moderately high levels of influence) and restrictive family influence (i.e. excessive influence). Barnett and Kellermanns argue that different levels of family influence can affect the HRM practices that are used in family firms and how non-family employees may view these practices. For example, when there is a low level of family influence the use and perceptions of HRM practices will be similar to those of non-family firms, but as family influence increases there may be more special considerations given to family members when compared to non-family members. Thus we argue that family influence is an important factor when exploring HR in family firms.

Given the arguments presented above, we contend that the management of human resources in small and medium family firms poses challenges that are distinct from those in larger firms and SMEs that are not family owned, managed or operated. And, similar to other researchers (Cardon and Stevens, 2004; Carlson et al., 2006; Heneman and Tansky, 2002), we believe that the management of HR has an important effect on the ability of the organization to address challenges and therefore it can affect the effectiveness and survival of family firms (see Figure 17.1).

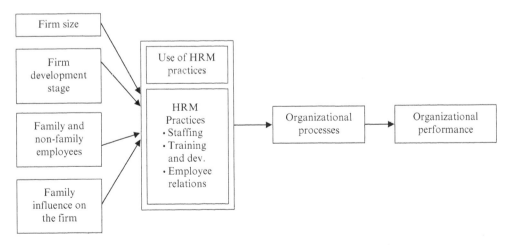

Figure 17.1   Considerations for human resource research in small and medium family firms

---

BOX 17.1   INITIAL LIST OF JOURNALS USED IN THE INITIAL REVIEW

Academy of Management Journal
Academy of Management Review
Administrative Science Quarterly
Business Ethics Quarterly
California Management Review
Corporate Governance
Entrepreneurship & Regional Development
Entrepreneurship Theory and Practice
Family Business Review
Harvard Business Review
Human Relations
Human Resource Management
International Journal of Human Resource Management
International Small Business Journal
Journal of Applied Psychology
Journal of Business Ethics
Journal of Business Research
Journal of Business Venturing
Journal of Management
Journal of Management Studies
Journal of Organizational Behavior
Journal of Small Business Management
Leadership Quarterly
Long Range Planning
Management Science
Organization Science
Organization Studies
Organizational Dynamics
Personnel Psychology
Sloan Management Review
Small Business Economics
Strategic Management Journal
Strategic Organization

To better understand what we know about the management of human resources in family firms, we looked for empirical and conceptual articles published about human resource management in SMEs and family firms. To obtain the articles for our review we first conducted a series of searches using Proquest, Psychinfo, Business Source Complete and Academic Search Premier databases. In this first stage we focused our search on the top-tier management journals and journals that publish studies on SMEs and family firms primarily (see Box 17.1 for a complete list). Our search focused on the following terms or a combination of these terms: family firms, family-owned businesses, human resources management, and strategic HRM. We collected 74 articles in this initial search. Once we had read all the articles we retained 52 that directly examined HR in SMEs or family firms. These articles served as the basis for our review.

SUMMARIZING HR RESEARCH IN SMALL AND MEDIUM FAMILY FIRMS

After collecting all the articles about HR research in SMEs and family firms, we divided the studies based on two topics. The first group of studies explored which HRM practices are used in SMEs and family firms; the second group explored how specific HRM practices are used and the effects this has on the organization. Thus our review is outlined based on these two broad issues. Before we present our review, it is important to note that when trying to understand how people are managed in organizations, researchers tend to group HR practices in different ways. For organizational purposes, in this project we focus on three broad HR practices to structure this review. The first HR practice that we discuss is staffing. Staffing practices are generally defined as the set of activities that managers follow to identify work requirements within the organization, to determine the number of people and skills necessary to do the work, and the recruitment, selection and promotion of qualified employees (Cascio, 2009). First we summarize findings of articles that explain how family firms and SMEs recruit, select and assign employees into positions. The second HR practice that we summarize is the training and development of human resources. Employee development and personal growth is a major concern for organizations (Cascio, 2009). In HRM, development practices often group activities such as employee training and development, performance management (i.e. goal setting, performance appraisal and rewards) and compensation. Thus, in this section we summarize research that we found in these areas. The third, and final, group of HR practices reviewed describes issues regarding employee relations. Employee relations groups HR activities that the organization engages in to keep people working together and happy at work. These activities include the management of organizational culture, and the interactions between employees and between the organization and the employee. Therefore, in this section we summarize research that explains how SMEs and family firms manage relationships with their employees. Later in the chapter we summarize the research that we found about HRM issues in SMEs and family firms.

Use of HR Practices in SMEs and Family Firms

To begin our review we first wanted to examine what we currently know about the use of HR practices in SMEs and family firms. As can be seen in Table 17.1, although we found 19 articles in this section, only nine of those articles compared the use of HRM practices in both SMEs and family firms, and only two articles explored the use of HRM practices in family firms exclusively. Based on the results of these studies, it can be concluded that, in general, SMEs are less likely to use formal and traditional HR practices when compared to larger firms (Cardon and Stevens, 2004; Tocher and Rutherford, 2009). Additionally, when exploring family firms in particular, results from

Table 17.1 Summary of studies that explore the use of HR practices in SMEs and FF by year of publication

Authors	Research question/ purpose	Sample	Variables	Key HR results
Hornsby and Kuratko (1990)	At what level of growth will particular HR issues become a concern for small business owners? The focus was SMEs in the USA	247 firms – 1/3 for each size	DV – importance of HR practice (job analysis and description, recruitment and selection (R&S), T&D, compensation and benefits, and performance appraisal (PA)) IV – firm size (1–50, 51–100, 101–50) Controls – Type of business, age, existence of personnel dept	Industry type affects the use of benefits and PA. Size did not affect use of observation and interviews in job analysis. For R&S, smaller firms were more likely to use less expensive advertising. The size of a company affects the sophistication of methodology used to construct wages & benefit packages. As size increases, more use of performance appraisal.
Astrachan and Kolenko (1994)	(1) Which are the most used HR practices in FF? (2) Do HR practices contribute to FF success? (3) Which owner characteristics (sex, edu, age) predict use of HRMP? The focus was on FF in the USA	600 family firms	DV – family firms success & survival IV – HRM practices (written job descriptions, formal compensation plans, employee performance review, written employee manual, succession plan, specific entry requirements) Control – size, generation	FFs were more likely to use ee reviews, compensation plans, written ee policy manuals and written job descriptions. FFs did not have formal entry requirements for family members. In general, HR practices were positively related to success/survival: 0.16 to income, 0.20 to full-time employees, firm gross revenues (0.21), & access to capital (−0.14).

Author (Year)	Description / Objectives	Sample	Variables	Findings
Cromie et al. (1995)	Comparison between HR practices used by FF and NFF. The focus was on SMEs in Northern Ireland	382 Firms	DV – not clear IV – FF vs NFF Controls – age, size, turnover, growth in turnover & location, public or private	FFs were less likely to be professionally managed. The roles of top management for FF are less specified that those for NFF. 85% of FFs reported that promotion at work was based on expertise. 23% of FF and 40% of FFs mentioned that they hired graduates straight from university. FFs are less keen on formal training. FFs were more likely than NFF to have appraisal systems.
Golhar and Deshpande (1997)	This study compares the use of HRMP in both SMEs and large firms and their relationship to firm performance. The location was Canada.	143 firms – 110 small & 33 large firms	DV – HR practices (importance of workforce characteristics, recruitment strategies, selection instruments, T&D, compensation other HRM practices) IV – firm size (small vs. large)	Job posting and bidding was the preferred recruitment method for both small and large firms. There was no significant difference between small and large firms in the use of HR practices.
Heneman et al. (2000)	(1) Identify gaps in HRMP research for SMEs (2) HRMP perceived as important by SME leaders This study was conducted in the USA.	156 entre. & 173 CEOs		Some areas that need further development are: how to develop high-potential employees and the matching of people to org. culture.
Reid et al. (2000)	(1) Identify HRM practices within SMEs (10–100 employees) (2) Compare between FF and NFF use of these practices. Study conducted in Ireland.	219 firms – FF = 133 NFF = 86	DV – use of HR practice IV – size and ownership	More NFF had unions in comparison to FF. NFF were also more likely to keep HR records than FF. NFF were also more likely to have used appraisal systems for managers and employees. FF reported spending less on training even though they reported training as their

Table 17.1 (continued)

Authors	Research question/ purpose	Sample	Variables	Key HR results
				biggest HR challenge. 65% of the family businesses reported that family managers received mgt training. Only 27% of the FF reported using formal performance systems to assess FM.
De Kok and Uhlaner (2001)	Identify the underlying explanations for the variability in use of HRM practices in small firms. Study conducted in the Netherlands.	4 firms	DV – formalization of HR practices IV – collective labor agreement, org. size, large firm associate, & growth strategy	Collective labor agreement was not sig. related to formal use of HRM practices. Size was sig. related to the formalization of training programs. There was also a sig. relationship between growth strategy and formalization of HRM practices.
King et al. (2001)	Exploring the use of stratified systems theory to HRM in FF	1 FF – four plants	DV – job performance IV – manager's potential capability (PC) level	Manager's PC is correlated with manager's performance
Reid and Adams (2001)	Same study and data as Reid et al. (2000)			Same as Reid et al. (2000).
Rowden (2002)	(1) Identify perceptions of successful manufacturing SMEs regarding their high performance and HR practices. Study conducted in the USA.	31 firms		Less than 50% of the firms included an identifiable HR function in their plants. High-performance practices included: training (job rotation, cross-training) quality circles, TQM, employee participation, selective staffing and compensation.
Hayton (2003)	How can HRM practices promote entrepreneurial performance in SMEs? Study conducted in the USA.	99 SMEs	DV – entrepreneurial performance. IV – HCM practices & HRM practices Control – resources available for the firm, slack resources, type of industry	HRM practices can be understood in 2 broad categories: traditional HR practices & discretionary HR. Discretionary HRMP were significantly related to entrepreneurial performance of SMEs

Study	Description	Sample	Variables	Findings
Hornsby and Kuratko (2003)	Replication of Hornsby and Kuratko 1990 study Study conducted in the US.	262 firms	DV – importance of HR practice (job analysis & description, recruitment & selection, T&D, compensation and benefits, & performance appraisal) IV – firm size (1–50, 51–100, 101–150)	Changes in recruitment include decrease in use of agencies that are public and more radio. For that are private, and more radio. For selection, decline is use of ref checks, increase in drug testing. In compensation, payment is based on market rates, performance appraisal, job requirements changed. Concerns for owners of small business have not changed in one decade.
Rutherford et al. (2003)	What are the specific HR problems that SMEs face across their life cycle? This study explored both SMEs and FFs in the USA.	2903 firms	DV – life-cycle stage IV – HR problems over firm life cycle (hiring, retention, and training)	Training problems highest in high-growth firms; lowest in low-growth firms. Compensation problems existed in high-growth stages. Recruiting problems highest in no-growth firms and lowest in low-growth firms. Low-growth firms reported the lowest levels of training and recruitment problems.
Kotey and Sheridan (2004)	How do HRM practices change with firm size, and what are the implications of these changes? This study focused on SMEs in Australia.	371 firms – 84 micro, 211 small, 76 medium	DV – rate of adoption of HRM practices (recruitment & selection, training, perf appraisal, HRM policies and records) IV – firm	As organizational size increases, more formal recruitment sources were used, multiple selection methods were used, the training and performance appraisal responsibilities were shifted to middle mgt, the development of managerial staff is given more attention, more documentation of HR practices occur, and tend to change more towards prescribed HR practices.

Table 17.1 (continued)

Authors	Research question/ purpose	Sample	Variables	Key HR results
Nguyen and Bryant (2004)	(1) What HRMP do Vietnamese SMEs use? (2) What factors influence level of formality of HRMP? (3) How does level of HRMP formality affect performance? The focus was on SMEs and FFs in Vietnam.	89 firms	DV – HR formality, performance, IV – firm size Controls – company age & industry	Firm size is positively related to HR formality; HR formality is positively associated with owners' perceptions of firm performance. The only two practices were significantly related to performance were written criteria for hiring & written criteria for performance appraisal.
Kotey and Slade (2005)	Extent to which HRM practices become formal as firms progress in size, and the implications of these changes for competitive advantage. This study was conducted in Australia with focus on SMEs.	371 firms – 84 micro, 211 small, 76 medium	DV – rate of adoption of HRM practices (recruitment & selection, training, perf appraisal, HRM policies and records) IV – firm size: micro, small, medium Control – number of business locations, age, sector (private vs public)	Adoption of HRMP increased with firm size. Formal practices are incorporated early in the growth process. Greater range of formal recruitment sources was employed with growth. Screening grew too. Word of mouth was main recruitment source in micro and small. Interview was the predominant selection method. At the manager level this applied too. On-the-job training is predominant; other training methods are adopted with increase in size.
Carlson et al. (2006)	What are the effects of firm performance on HRM practices (recruitment, perf. appraisal, compensation and benefits, maintaining morale, & T&D)? The focus of this study was on SMEs and FF in the USA.	168 firms	DV – sales growth performance IV – T&D, appraisal, morale, compensation & recruitment Control – firm age, tenure of CEO, sales in $, growth index	Low-performance firms paid more base salary. Firms that performed better placed more imp. on T&D. There was also a positive relationship of importance of performance appraisal and performance, of competitive comp and performance, maintaining morale and performance. Additionally the use of cash incentives was positively related to performance.

Author	Research question/context	Sample	Variables	Findings
De Kok et al.(2006)	Why do family-owned and operated firms use fewer professional HRM practices than other SMEs? The study was conducted in Australia and the Netherlands.	736 firms responded (either CEO or employee directly under CEO)	DV – use of professional HRM practices (recruitment, selection, compensation, T&D, appraisal) IV – organizational complexity (size, HRM specialization, formal business plan, export strategy) & family firm (no, owner, manager) Control – firm age, sector, % of employees belonging to union.	FF had less HRM specialization (−0.40, $p<0.01$) This was also supported with a regression. The reason for this may be FF have less time for monitoring of mgt by owner & ees by mgt. A second factor is firm size which indicates complexity.
Tocher and Rutherford (2009)	What are the HRM problems faced by SME owners? This study was conducted in the USA.	1693 SMEs	DV – HRM problems mentioned by SME owners IV – firm size, age, growth & financial performance Controls – industry, location	More experienced & educated SME owners are more likely to perceive acute HRM problems. Owners and managers of larger SMEs were more likely to perceive HRM problems as acute. Owners/managers of lower-performing SMEs were more likely to perceive HR problems as acute.

the studies included in this review suggest that family firms are less specialized in their use of HRM practices when compared to non-family firms (De Kok et al., 2006; Reid and Adams, 2001; Reid et al., 2000), and they are also less likely to use HRM practices in general when compared to non-family firms (Harris et al., 2004).

There are some important issues to highlight about the research on the use of HR practices by SMEs and family firms. First, it is important to note that most of the research included in this section was conducted in multiple countries and similar results were found between studies. Second, although family firms used fewer HRM practices in general, the four practices that were most commonly used by family firms were: formal and regular employee performance review (59 percent), compensation plans (57 percent), written employee manual (56 percent), and written job descriptions (53 percent) (Astrachan and Kolenko, 1994).

In these studies, we also found research that explored the relationship between the use of HR practices and performance of SMEs and family firms. There were two studies that linked HR practices and performance in SMEs. Results from both of these studies indicate that successful small firms were more likely to provide training to employees, good compensation and benefit packages, and selective staffing (Rowden, 2002). Additionally, results also support that the use of these HR practices is only significantly related to performance in mature firms (Buller and Napier, 1993). Two studies explored the link between HRM practices and firm performance in family firms in particular. Astrachan and Kolenko (1994) found a positive association between HRM practices and gross firm revenues and the CEO's personal income level. They argue that this shows that better practices yielded significant payoffs for family firms. Finally, in a more recent study Carlson and colleagues (2006) found that high-performing family firms placed greater importance on issues of training and development, performance appraisals, recruitment package, maintaining morale and competitive compensation levels when compared to low-performing family firms.

Review of Specific HRM Practices in SMEs and Family Firms

As mentioned earlier, the second group of articles for this review focused primarily on the exploration of specific HRM practices in SMEs and family firms. The three HRM practices that we found research for were staffing, training and development and employee relations. In this section we review research on these practices.

Staffing in SMEs and family firms

Past research has indicated that in order for an organization to be successful, it must engage in HR practices designed to attract high quality applicants (Rynes and Barber, 1990). The rise of knowledge-based organizations has created a need for companies to attract and select employees with diverse skill sets and proven achievement (Trank et al., 2002). Attracting employees who are capable of seeing and furthering the organizational vision is a key factor in achieving organizational effectiveness (Allen et al., 2007; Barber, 1998; Breaugh and Starke, 2000). Thus organizations today have started devoting more resources to HR practices which help them attract, select, hire and retain qualified employees (Trank et al., 2002). In this section we summarize research that talks about all of these issues in SMEs and family firms.

In our review we found 12 articles that addressed one of two primary issues: what are the HRM practices used by family firms and SMEs to attract, recruit, select and retain employees? And what are the perceptions that applicants have about SMEs and family firms as places of employment? (See Table 17.2.) In response to the first question, results from the studies indicate that as the size of the organization increases, firms were more likely to use formal practices for their recruitment and selection (Barber et al., 1999; Deshpande and Golhar, 1994; Hausdorf and Duncan, 2004; Heneman and Berkley, 1999; Hornsby and Kuratko, 1990, 2003). In particular, smaller firms were more likely to rely on word of mouth and informal practices to attract employees (Kotey and Sheridan, 2004; Kotey and Slade, 2005) instead of using more formal activities like newspapers, Internet, recruitment agencies and recruiting from schools (Barber et al., 1999; Hornsby and Kuratko, 2003). This tendency differed when comparing operational and managerial positions (Kotey and Sheridan, 2004; Kotey and Slade, 2005), such that recruitment for managerial positions was more formal than recruitment for operational positions. Additionally, smaller firms primarily used recruiting sources and practices that were convenient, inexpensive and directly controlled by the company (Heneman and Berkley, 1999). In general, the most common recruitment practices for smaller firms were advertisements, employee referrals and walk-ins, and in general small firms offer a wide array of attraction practices (Carroll et al., 1999; Deshpande and Golhar, 1994; Heneman and Berkley, 1999; Hornsby and Kuratko, 1990, 2003). It is important to note that there were only two studies that focused on HRM practices used by family firms to attract and select applicants (Cromie et al., 1995; Reid et al., 2000). Results from these studies found that family firms are less likely to recruit and hire straight out of college (Cromie et al., 1995), and that family firms were less likely to engage in HRM practices that showed preference for a 'business first' approach to management (Reid et al., 2000).

Regarding the arguments used to describe the perceptions that job seekers have about working in family-owned businesses and SMEs there seems to be two extremes (Wilkinson, 1999). On one side there is a perception that 'small is beautiful', which suggests that small firms lead to close and harmonious working relationships (see Kotey and Sheridan, 2004). On the other hand, proponents of the 'bleak house' perspective argue that small firms can be dangerous for employees because these firms are managed in a dictatorial way and offer poor working conditions (Wilkinson, 1999). The research that we found suggested that, in general, job seekers express intentions to search for positions in larger organizations more often than in smaller organizations (Barber et al., 1999). One of the reasons for this is that job seekers often use information about organizational size as a heuristic to determine the legitimacy of the organization and the availability of resources to them (Nguyen and Bryant, 2004; Williamson, 2000). And often, job seekers perceive that smaller firms are less legitimate because they do not engage in the same formal practices as large organizations (Williamson, 2000), and they have fewer resources available to them (De Kok and Uhlaner, 2001). In particular, Froelich (2005) found that one of the difficulties for small firms in attracting job applicants is the perceptions that job seekers have regarding the ability of small firms to fulfill job choice factors and characteristics that they find important. Additionally, it is also difficult for small firms to retain employees because they are more likely to break the promises they make to employees and this is strongly related with turnover intentions (Kickul, 2001).

When examining the perceptions about family firms in particular, we found only one

Table 17.2   Summary of studies that explore staffing issues in SMEs and FF by year of publication

Authors	Research Question/ Purpose	Sample	Variables	Key HR Results
Covin (1994)	(1) What life history & job characteristic factors distinguish between individuals indicating preference for working in FF? (2) Do these 2 factors differ between undergraduate and graduate students? This study was conducted in the USA.	222 individuals	DV – attitudes toward FF IV – life history predictors & job characteristic predictors Control – school year, sex	100 respondents indicating preference to work in their FF, 72 NF, and 2 someone else's FF. Those with strong preference to work in FF are more likely to have started their business, have worked for FFs, worked for more companies, and be female. Additionally those that prefer FF have higher need for job variety, independent work, continuous development, salary, & feeling of accomplishment. There was a difference btw undergraduate and graduate.
Deshpande and Golhar (1994)	Comparison between SMEs and large firms regarding workforce characteristics, sources of recruitment, selection, compensation, T&D & retention. Study conducted in the USA.	100 firms – 21 large firms & 79 small firms	DV – HRM practice (workforce characteristic, source of recruitment, selection tests, compensation, T&D & retention) IV – firm size	Job posting and bidding was the preferred recruitment method for both small and large firms, and employee reference, and there was no significant dif between small and large firms. For small firms the preferred selection test was interview, followed by a job tryout, and interviews were used by the majority of small and large firms.

Barber et al. (1999)	(1) Differences in recruitment practices as a function of firm size. (2) Whether search behavior changes as a function of the type of employer they prefer. Study conducted in the USA.	Study 1 – 119 small & 189 large firms Study 2 – 585 students	Study 1 DV – use of recruitment activities, selection and attraction practices IV – firm size Study 2 DV – level of search activity & sources used IV – size preference & actively searching for size	Study 1 – Larger firms were more likely than SF to use HR staff and small firms were more likely to use line mgt in recruitment. Larger firms initiate recruiting farther in advance, flex start date, sources of campus placement. Small firms are more likely to use internal sources, external employment agencies, and advertisements to recruit. Larger firms attach more imp to academic record, while smaller firms to motivation and interpersonal skills. Study 2 results – 266 prefer large, 226 no pref, 93 prefer small. Those interested in large should engage in earlier searches and rely on campus recruitment.
Carroll et al. (1999)	The aim of this project is to compare how recruitment practices of SMEs and compare them with prescriptive procedures of selection. Study conducted in the UK.	40 firms	DV – type of recruitment used (job analysis, type of vacancy that needs to be filled, job description, person description) IV – org size (0–24, 25–49, 50–99, 100+) and industry (hotel & catering,	No evidence of job analysis, job descriptions used in the majority of the firms. These firms had few formalized procedures and systematic procedures used for recruitment which are prescribed in textbooks. Tend to rely on tried and trusted techniques for each industry.

Table 17.2 (continued)

Authors	Research Question/ Purpose	Sample	Variables	Key HR Results
			road haulage, nursing homes, printing, & solicitors)	
Heneman and Berkley (1999)	This study explores the nature and effectiveness of employee attraction practices of SMEs. Study conducted in the USA.	117 small busi-nesses – 83 < than 50, & 34 = 50 to 99	DV – attraction outcomes: applicant's vacancy, days-to-fill, acceptance rate, & retention rate IV – applicant attraction practices Controls – HR dept, industry, location	Small businesses use a wide variety of attraction practices. Use of HR practices also varied by size and presence of HR dept. Use of newspaper ads and recruitment sources resulted in fewer days to fill vacancies. New employee training resulted in higher acceptance rates. When HR managers evaluated applicants the retention rates were higher.
Williamson (2000)	This is a conceptual paper that uses institutional theory to explain how SMEs can improve recruiting practices.			This paper suggests that employer legitimacy is an important factor in attracting potential applicants. To the extent that org. recruitment procedures & HR policies are seen by applicants as proper and appropriate, the org. will be seen as a legitimate employer. Larger firms are more likely to be seen as legitimate by applicants because norms of evaluation are based on larger organizations. Thus, to the extent that small firms mirror recruitment practices of larger firms they are more likely to be seen as more legitimate.

Gudmundson and Hartenian (2000)	This study explores the relationship between workforce diversity in small firms, as well as the owner/manager's motivation to diversify. Study conducted in the USA.	207 services firms	DV – workforce diversity in small firms; IV – owner's motivation to diversity; owner ethnic group; gender; age; education; no. of family members employed	Owner characteristics are significant predictors of firm's level of workforce diversity.
Leung (2003)	Why do entrepreneurial firms use network ties to facilitate the acquisition of the core mgt team during start-up phases? This study using a sample of SMEs from Singapore.	4 firms	DV – business network recruitment; IV – social network recruitment; Controls – revenue, size, growth phase, age	Results show that organizations at different phases of development face different constraints/resource needs leading to different network strategies. At the start-up phase entrepreneurs rely mainly on social network for recruiting, during growth phase they focus on the business network. In both stages the ties used are strong and direct.
Hausdorf and Duncan (2004)	What is the role of firm size in the use of Internet recruiting? Study focused on SMEs and was conducted in Canada.	175 firms	DV – use of Internet recruiting; IV – firm size: small, medium, large	Large companies (91%) were more likely to have their own website than small firms (77%). All sizes of organizations were equally likely to use online recruitment. Smaller firms were less aware of Internet recruiters, and were less likely to use them. Online recruitment messages btw small and large firms varied on the amount of information about the company that was offered. In general 53% of the organizations included in this study used their websites for recruitment.

Table 17.2 (continued)

Authors	Research Question/ Purpose	Sample	Variables	Key HR Results
Ibrahim et al. (2004)	Explore the qualities that are perceived as critical to effective successor and the role of education and training. The project focused on SMEs and FFs in Canada.	42 CEOs	DV – effective succession IV – leadership, management skills, & commitment	Three factors: capacity to lead, management skills/ competencies, and willingness/commitment are related to effective selection of successor. Additionally form size hinders the ability to develop a systematic HRM strategy to select a successor.
Froelich (2005)	What are the job factors that affect applicant job choice? This study focused on perceptions of SMEs in the USA.	476 individuals	DV – importance of job choice factors IV – year of graduation	The most important factors in job choice for the respondents were: challenge and variety of work, health insurance benefits, opportunity to use education, preference of spouse/partner, stability of org, job security, salary level, friendly & supportive co-workers, pension/retirement plan, level of autonomy, safety. This offers a way to frame the info to applicants.
Arrègle et al. (2007)	This conceptual paper explores how organizational social capital is created within family firms. This project is a conceptual paper.			Organizational social capital is defined and supported by the organizations employment practices such as recruitment and selection.

study that addressed the perceptions about family firms as places to work for. In this study, Covin (1994) found that the large majority of the participants indicated a strong preference for working in their own family firm, and that life history and job characteristic variables predicted individuals' interest in working for family firms. The findings indicate that those who owned a business in the past, who have worked for a family firm in the past, and those who were females were more likely to indicate a preference for working in family firms. Additionally, participants who preferred jobs that provided variety, liked to work independently, wanted continued development of knowledge and skills and a job that provides a feeling of accomplishment were also more likely to express interest in working for family firms.

Training and development in SMEs and family firms

The ability of organizations to develop employees has been rated as one of the most important factors when considering employment and attraction to organizations in general (Chapman et al., 2005; Ehrhart and Ziegert, 2005; Rynes and Cable, 2003). Continuous employee development has become critical to maintaining a competitive advantage in today's market (London and Moore, 1999; Smith-Jentsch et al., 2001; Thayer, 1997). Thus, we explored what research was conducted in SMEs and family firms that was related to employee training and development. Here we include research on activities such as workplace training, performance and career management, and pay and rewards.

Past research indicates that one of the biggest liabilities that SMEs and family firms possess is the perception of smallness (Cardon and Stevens, 2004; Nguyen and Bryant, 2004; Williamson, 2000). When potential employees perceive that organizations are small they engage in cognitive isomorphism. That is, they believe that small organizations always have fewer resources, have more problems with HR practices, and as a consequence they view SMEs and family firms in a negative light. This is one of the reasons why understanding the development of human resources is important. To the extent that we know more about what family firms do to develop their employees, it will also be easier to communicate messages that counter act the liability of smallness. As can be seen in Table 17.3, we found nine studies that can be summarized in this section. We begin by addressing issues of training, given that eight of the nine studies refer to this topic.

Today, more than ever, organizations rely on training as a form of organizational learning and improvement. Previous research defines training as 'the systematic acquisition of skills, rules, concepts, or attitudes that result in improved performance in another environment' (Goldstein and Ford, 2002, p. 1). Training programs are designed to produce specific outcomes contingent on the instruction of new information presented. The function of a training program is to utilize training methods that will encourage and enable participants to learn what they are being trained on and to maximize the transfer of this information into different contexts (Kontogiannis and Sheperd, 1999).

There are several reasons why organizations should train employees (Bryan, 2006). At a micro level, training helps employees learn new skills and abilities which can help them perform better at their job and in turn contribute to the sustained competitive advantage of an organization (Koch and McGrath, 1996). At a macro level, employee training is expected to influence the level of human capital available in the organization, which in turn should impact the performance of employees and the capability for economic growth

Table 17.3   Summary of studies that explore employee training and development in SMEs and FF by year of publication

Authors	Research Question/ Purpose	Sample	Variables	Key HR Results
Handler (1991)	Succession training from the perspective of the next generation family member. Study conducted in the USA.	32 individuals	DV – effectiveness of succession IV – life stage of successor & phase of succession process	Level of mutual respect and understanding between current and next generation was the most important part of the succession success. The second factor is the accommodation of siblings to the succession process.
Loan-Clarke et al. (1999)	Enhance the understanding of management training and development (MTD) in SMEs and FFs. With emphasis on differences on investment in MTD. This study was conducted in the UK.	551 firms	DV – business success IV – industrial sector, ownership, size, age, turnover financial, growth, HR policy	22% of the organizations did not spend any time on mgt T&D, and 21% spent no money. Sector had an influence on the amount of MTD offered. Family businesses with no family member in mgt spent more money on MTD than those that still had a family member. As size increased, organizations spent more money in MTD, but there was no difference between groups 3 and 4.
Chandler and McEvoy (2000)	To examine the idea that effective organizations adapt their HR practices to fit their strategies. Study conducted in the USA.	66 firms	DV – org. profitability IV – firm size Moderator: training and compensation practices. Control: company age	More training was helpful in the implementation of TQM. Results also support the idea of fit between HRMP and firm to obtain the most strategic benefits. Compensation strategies are more likely to work when they do not perceive that management will change the promise.
Matlay (2002)	What are the attitudes towards training family vs non-family employees in family SME's? Study conducted in the UK.	6000 firms	DV – attitudes toward training IV – firm size and firm ownership	Size predicted who would make decisions about training and HR. In FF the training of non-f employees was viewed strictly as an HR development issue while the training of family members was seen as individual career development. Succession issues affected owners overall training and HRD strategies.

Author (Year)	Description	Sample	Variables	Findings
De Kok (2002)	What are the effects of firm size on firm-provided training? Study conducted in the Netherlands	173 firms	DV – returns to firm-provided training IV – firm size	Support found for existence of HRM effect: training support/worker/day has positive influence on benefits of training; however, small firms provide less training support/worker/day
Peters and Buhalis (2004)	This project explores management behavior in family SMEs and identifies education and training requirements. Study conducted in Austria.	156 FF	DV – performance & growth IV – planning, strategy development & behavior	Most family business owners strive to keep the family together and plan for the future. However, not many are qualified to manage. Some training areas that need further development are strategy development and planning, mgt of cooperation and partnerships, development of new products and services, & empowerment of employees.
Bryan (2006)	This paper explores the relationship between training and growth in small manufacturing businesses. Study conducted in Wales and England.	114 firms	DV – growth/sales performance IV – type of training (in-house vs outside) Control – sector, location, age	In-house training is more common than out of house training with this sample.
Ensley et al. (2007)	This study explores the issue of pay dispersion in family and non-family top management teams (TMTs) Study conducted in the USA.	200 executive teams, 88 NFF & 112 FF	DV – growth index – revenue & employment growth IV – stock dispersion & pay dispersion Mediator – potency, cohesion, & conflict	Pay dispersion creates negative behavioral consequences in both family and non-family firms, but produces very strong neg. behavioral dynamics in fam. firms. Pay dispersion generally increases conflict and diminishes cohesion and potency. These dynamics are known to influence DM of employees and in turn it may affect performance.
Kotey and Folker (2007)	We examine the main and interaction effects of size and type of firm (FF vs NFF) on training programs in SMEs. Study conducted in Australia.	918 firms	DV – training programs IV – size & type of firm	On-the-job training is the predominant form of training in SMEs. As size increases the adoption of formal training increases. These results were not evident for FF. For FF increases in formal training only occurred for early growth.

of the firm (Aguinis and Kraiger, 2009). Based on the results of the studies included in this review, we can conclude that smaller firms often provide less formal training than larger firms (De Kok, 2002; Kotey and Folker, 2007). In particular, SMEs predominantly use on-the-job training and other training methods tend to be more common as organizational size increases, particularly at the managerial level (Hornsby and Kuratko, 1990, 2003; Kotey and Slade, 2005). Additionally, as firms grow they are more likely to provide external training for managers (Kotey and Folker, 2007).

When exploring training in family business, the five studies we found suggest that in family firms the training for non-family and family employees is viewed differently and the training process is more reactive than proactive in nature (Matlay, 2002). In general, the most common form of training in family firms was on-the-job training (Kotey and Folker, 2007). Additionally, the training of family employees in managerial positions is critical for the success of the organization and sometimes it is not emphasized enough (Ibrahim et al., 2004; Loan-Clarke et al., 1999; Peters and Buhalis, 2004). Finally, similar to other HR practices, the formality of training increased with the size of the organization and the greatest increase in formal training happened during different growth stages (Kotey and Folker, 2007).

The additional study that we found in this section explored the idea of pay dispersion in top management teams for family firms. In general, pay is one of the most important factors for the satisfaction of employees (Rynes, 1991; Rynes and Barber, 1990). Pay is important because it helps the employee feel valued and that their work is worthwhile. One of the issues that is important when thinking about pay in family firms is understanding how being a family member affects employee pay (Poza, 2010). The study that we found explored the idea of pay dispersion in top management teams (TMT). This study found that in family firms perceptions of pay dispersion in TMTs produce very strong negative behavior dynamics that will influence the decision-making of employees and in turn their performance.

Employee relations in family firms
In recent years the concepts of human and social capital have been used to identify the unique characteristics that differentiate family from non-family businesses (Sirmon & and Hitt, 2003). As originally defined, human capital represents the knowledge, skills and capabilities that allow a person to engage in unique and novel actions (Coleman, 1988), while social capital involves the relationship between individuals or between organizations (Burt, 1997). In this section we summarize research on how HR practices affect employee relations, particularly in the areas of employee commitment and organizational justice. We argue that how firms manage their HR practices will affect both the social and the human capital of the organization and in turn its performance. For this section we found five articles, which are summarized in Table 17.4.

Research on HRM practices emphasizes that the strategic benefits of HRM emerge through the benefits that occur once an organization meets employee needs and enables workers to control their lives (Kaman et al., 2001). One of the critical issues for employee performance is employee commitment. The research that we found supports the idea that SMEs that have very formal HR practices are perceived as more bureaucratic and thus are less likely to have employees that are committed (Kaman et al., 2001). In particular, family firms are often perceived by employees as having lower levels of communication

Table 17.4 Summary of studies that explore employee relations in SMEs and FF by year of publication

Authors	Research Question/ Purpose	Sample	Variables	Key HR Results
Matlay (1999)	How does size affect the professionalism of mgt style and HR decision-making (DM)? This study focused on SMEs in the UK.	6000 firms	DV – locus of DM in HR IV – firm size	As size increased, organizations were more likely to have different person from the owner make HR decisions. As size increased, so did the formality of mgt style. Micro businesses focused primarily on manager for recruitment. These informal preferences were also encountered in the training and HR development. Those managers who preferred informal mgt styles were also more likely to use informal pay bargaining. Finally, to deal with grievances, the managers primarily used informal discussions or meetings. The choice of MGT style also affected interpersonal relationships.
Kaman et al. (2001)	This article describes how small firms address issues about commitment and bureaucracy in HRM practices. This study included SMEs and family firms from the USA.	283 individuals	DV – business outcomes IV – firm size, bureaucratic HRM practices, high commitment practice	Larger firms use bureaucratic practices to a greater extent than smaller firms, and report more concern for attracting and motivating workers. The use of high-commitment practices was not related to firm size, but HC practices were related to lower turnover and absenteeism, less litigation and fewer concerns for motivating workers. Even after controlling for size bureaucratic practices are associated with concern about motivating employees and higher absenteeism.
Harris et al. (2004)	How does communication with employees and consultation with employees in FF affect performance? Study conducted in the UK.	Data from 1998 Workplace Employee Relations Survey	DV – performance IV – communication procedures, type of business (FF vs NFF) Control – firm size	FF use fewer HRM practices and are less likely to target product quality. FF are less likely to be unionized, FF were more stable and less likely to be innovative. No difference in the type of profit pay offered. FFs were less likely to be involved and communicate to employees. There was no evidence of difference in performance between FF and NFF.

395

Table 17.4 (continued)

Authors	Research Question/ Purpose	Sample	Variables	Key HR Results
Barnett and Kellermanns (2006)	This paper explores the processes that influence the justice perceptions of non-family employees within the family firm.		DV – non-family employee's attitudes & behavior IV – family influence Control – family firm HRM practices Mediators – non-family employee justice perceptions	Perceptions of justice will affect non-family employees' perceptions of pay, promotion, value-creating attitude, etc. IMPORTANT: Family influence can have both a + and – effect on the fairness of HR practices in different ways, and HR practices may have differential effects on NF employees. This article addresses 2 issues: (1) How does family influence affect HR practices? (2) How do family influence and HRP affect non-family employee perceptions of justice?
Beehr et al. (2007)	This study explores the potential advantages and disadvantages of working for a family firm. The data were collected in the USA.	34 firms – 17 matched	DV – job satisfaction & organizational commitment IV – inter-role conflict, interpersonal conflict, personal advantages of being member of owning family	Results showed that, contrary to most studies, conflict in family firms was not significantly greater than in non-family firms in this sample. Additionally, being an employee of a small FF does not differ from being an employee of an NFF.
Vallejo (2008)	Does the commitment of non-family employees differ between FF and NFF? This study was conducted in Spain.	126 total – 90 FF & 36 NFF	DV – profitability & survival IV – identification, involvement, & loyalty	The ID level of non-family employees was positively related to profitability and survival of FF. The involvement level of non-family employees was positively related to survival and profitability.

and consultation, which leads to lower employee involvement (Harris et al., 2004). Additionally, research also supports that the employee's level of commitment and involvement is positively related to the survival and profitability of family firms (Vallejo, 2008).

Organizational commitment may be difficult, especially for non-family employees, if perceptions of decision outcomes, decision processes and decision-makers are not seen as fair (Barnett and Kellermanns, 2006). In their work, Barnett and Kellermanns (2006) suggest that family influence plays a key role in the way employees create perceptions about fairness of HRM practices. They address two main issues: (1) how does family influence affect HR practices? and (2) how do family influence and human resource practices affect non-family employee perceptions of justice? These authors argue that the justice perceptions of non-family employees are often a consequence of specific HR decisions (i.e. pay, promotion or discipline), and will be affected by perceptions of distributive justice. Perceptions of procedural justice will have an effect on non-family employees' attitudes and behaviors. Furthermore, perceptions of interactional justice will affect non-family employees' attitudes and behaviors through perceptions of trust and identification with one's supervisor. The authors conclude that family influence can have both a positive and a negative effect on perceptions of fairness of HR practices, and these HR practices may have differential effects on non-family employees.

The last study that we want to discuss in this section explores the advantages and disadvantages of working for a family firm based on the perceptions of conflict in different organizations. One of the main concerns that non-family employees have about working for family firms is that these organizations have high levels of conflict that a person has to deal with (Litchfield, 2008). In this study, Beehr and colleagues (1997) found that, contrary to people's perceptions in their study, conflict in family firms was not significantly greater that in non-family firms. In this study the researchers also found that the higher the perceived conflict in the organization, the lower the satisfaction and the higher the turnover intentions.

WHAT DO WE KNOW ABOUT HRM IN SMALL AND MEDIUM FAMILY FIRMS?

After summarizing the research on HRM in SMEs and family firms, we now want to present a broad picture of what we currently know about HRM in small and medium family firms (SMFFs). In general, SMFFs are less likely to have formal and specialized HR practices when compared to other organizations, but as size increases their use of formal HRM practices also increases. The reason for this may be tied to agency theory. Based on agency theory (Chrisman et al., 2004; Eisenhardt, 1989), the management of human resources can be more informal in situations in which employees belong to the same family as the owner or manager (Heneman et al., 2000; Randøy and Goel, 2003). In these situations, coordination may be more efficient because of the communication systems in place that enable the alignment of interests between managers and employees (De Kok et al., 2006). However, in situations in which family employees are not loyal to the family or in situations in which performance is diminished, family managers may be reluctant to take action against non-performing family employees (Schulze et al., 2001).

One aspect that is important to highlight is that organizations that have formal HRM practices are more likely to perform better, especially when the firm is more mature. It may be that having formal practices provides structure to the organization, and family and non-family employees can use this structure to communicate and follow up on organizational goals and their achievement.

When exploring HRM practices in particular, the results from our review indicate that when exploring staffing practices, SMFFs are more likely to focus on informal practices (e.g. word of mouth and employee references) to recruit and attract employees for non-managerial positions, and more formal (e.g. Internet postings and use of agencies or head hunters) for managerial positions. Additionally, these organizations are less likely to recruit applicants directly from college. The reasons for this may be centered on the impressions that applicants are believed to have about family firms and small and medium enterprises. That is, family firms are often seen as small organizations (Carrigan and Buckley, 2008; Orth and Green, 2009), and these perceptions of smallness may affect the perceptions that non-family applicants have about the opportunities that organizations and resources that these organizations have. And, given that perceptions of opportunities and availability of resources for employees are two of the most important factors predicting attractiveness to a firm (Chapman et al., 2005), it may be difficult to attract applicants who have just graduated from college and are looking for greater opportunities and resources.

Similar to staffing practices, training and development activities are less formal in small and medium family firms. In these types of organizations, smaller firms are more likely to train directly on the job, especially those employees who are non-family members. At the same time, there is more emphasis on the training of family employees because they are more likely to stay in the firm and, thus, more benefit can be obtained from training them. Finally, when exploring HR practices focusing on employee relations, there are three important issues to note. First, small and medium family firms are seen as providing lower levels of communication and consultation to non-family employees. Thus these employees are less likely to have feelings of involvement and commitment to the firm, which in turn affects their satisfaction. Second, family involvement is likely to affect how non-family employees perceive the fairness of HR practices. As mentioned earlier, Barnett and Kellermanns (2006) suggest that as family involvement increases, non-family employees are more likely to perceive preferential treatment for family members and this will affect their perceptions of fairness. Finally, small and medium family firms can also be seen as organizations with higher levels of conflict compared to other organizations. The presence of family and business issues in the organization may lead to these perceptions.

Earlier in this chapter we commented on the considerations that are necessary when studying HRM issues in small and medium family firms. From our perspective it seems that most of the research that we found focuses primarily on issues of size, while considerations on level of development of the firm, the presence of family and non-family employees, and family involvement have received very little attention. The lack of research focusing on these considerations provides only a partial picture of HRM practices in small and medium family firms. In the final section of this chapter we conclude by suggesting some areas of research that can help academics and practitioners better understand the relationship between HRM practices and performance.

FUTURE DIRECTIONS FOR HRM RESEARCH IN SMALL AND MEDIUM FAMILY FIRMS

Although the research summarized in this chapter provides some initial thoughts about HRM practices in small and medium family firms, there has been very little research that has explored the unique factors that affect our understanding of HR in these types of organizations. As presented in Figure 17.1, in this chapter we argue that there are four important factors that need to be considered to effectively understand HRM and its effects on the performance of family firms. These factors are: firm size; level of development of the firm; the presence of family and non-family employees; and family involvement. Based on the published literature, it seems that most of the research on HRM in SMEs and family firms has centered on issues of size; thus in this section we provide ideas for future research that incorporate the other three factors and help us better understand the uniqueness of family firms, and how HRM can affect their performance. Our ideas for future directions are presented based on the two major issues addressed in the review: (1) the use of HRM practices in small and medium family firms, and (2) HRM practices in particular.

Future Research in the Use of HRM Practices

To better understand the use of HRM practices in small and medium family firms we believe that it is first necessary to explore the relationship between family involvement and the use of HRM practices. In particular, we believe it is important to explore how the levels of family involvement affect the use of HRM practices. This is an issue that can be explored theoretically and empirically. Building on the theoretical work of Barnett and Kellermanns (2006), researchers can explore theoretically how different levels of family involvement can affect the likelihood of using HRM practices. It may be that as family involvement increases, there is a lesser need to use formal HRM practices because the family structure and norms will be more likely to influence the structure and culture of the firm, and this structure will help in managing human resources. Empirically, this can also be explored by measuring the level of family involvement in different firms and exploring their use of HRM practices.

A second aspect that needs to be explored is the different HRM practices that are used for family and non-family employees. It would be interesting to explore this for managerial and non-managerial positions. Given that HRM practices provide the official guidelines on how to manage human resources in the organization (Cascio, 2009); it would be interesting to explore whether similar principles and practices are followed for family and non-family employees, and the consistency with which these practices are followed for each type of employee. Again, this research can have theoretical (i.e. why should HRM practices be used in a similar way for family and non-family employees? why should they be different?) and empirical (i.e. what are the practices that family businesses have?) components and will help to broaden our understanding of HRM research in family firms.

A third aspect that needs to be explored is how these unique factors (i.e. size, level of development, family involvement and type of employee) interact to affect the use of HRM practices in family firms and the effects these practices have on firm performance.

In other words, if you consider size and type of employee, do these factors combine to explain the use of HRM practices in family firms? Or do level of family involvement and organizational size interact to affect the use of HRM practices? Does the combination of size, level of family involvement and level of firm development influence the effects that HRM practices have on firm performance? We believe that all of these are important questions for which there is no current answer or understanding.

Future Research on Specific HRM Practices

Similar to the research on the use of HRM practices in general, we believe that research on specific HRM practices is biased toward the exploration of the effect that organizational size has on the specific practice. Thus in this section we also suggest that future research should explore how the level of development of the firm, family involvement and type of employee (i.e. family versus non-family) affect specific HRM practices. For example, in the area of staffing and training it would be interesting to explore how family and non-family members are recruited and trained for managerial and non-managerial positions and how this affects the perceptions that other employees have about fairness and opportunities in the organization. Understanding both of these issues could also shed light on how non-family employees and applicants may view employment opportunities and professional careers in family firms. At the same time, a better understanding of unique HRM practices can also help researchers and practitioners understand the advantages and disadvantages that family firms have when compared to non-family firms when attracting, retaining and developing qualified non-family talent.

Another area that needs better development and understanding is the variety of HRM practices explored. In this project, we limited our review to three HRM practices: staffing; training and development, and employee relations. One of the reasons for using these three practices is that we could not find research on other practices. With this in mind, we suggest that future research should explore how other HRM practices work in family firms given the four important considerations that we explained earlier. For example, it was difficult for us to find published research about employee compensation in family firms and SMEs, performance management (e.g. promotion of family and non-family employees), practices regarding organizational change and issues about labor relations. These HRM practices represent traditional views of HR in the organization, and there was very little research that explored them in family firms.

A third and final area for future research in specific HR practices could focus on exploring the organizational challenges that small and medium family firms have as a consequence of how family firms currently use that practice. For example, research can explore how the HRM practices family firms follow regarding staffing or compensation affect issues such as perceptions of legitimacy, sustainability, flexibility, or the skills and capabilities of the firm. This is an important area that has currently has very little attention and can greatly help HR practitioners in family firms when communicating with non-family talent to join family firms.

CONCLUSIONS

The importance of HRM research is based on the premise that HRM practices have been related to the performance of the firm and, in particular, the belief that the development of organizational human resources can be transformed into a source of competitive advantage. That is, developing a qualified and satisfied workforce can lead to motivated and committed employees who will be more likely and perform better. Thus it is possible to believe that family firms can have a unique advantage when they are able to develop and motivate their family and non-family talent using their HRM practices. With this assumption in mind, this chapter was developed with three objectives. First, we wanted to explain the unique considerations necessary to explore HR research in family firms. To fulfill this purpose, Figure 17.1 presents a model of four factors that influence the use of HRM practices in family firms in general, and specific HRM practices like staffing, training and development, and employee relations. Our second objective was to summarize what we currently know about HRM research in family firms and SMEs. Tables 17.1, 17.2, 17.3 and 17.4 summarize the published research that we found on HR issues in our target area. When combined, the results and ideas from these studies provide a broad understanding of HRM research in small and medium family firms. Although this is a good start, there still is much research that needs to be conducted to fully understand HRM in family firms, and its effect on performance. The third and final objective of our study was to present some ideas for future research. We do this by emphasizing the need for research that explores the effects of family involvement, development of the firm, type of employee (family versus non-family) and the combination of these factors (including size) on the use of HRM practices in general, and specific HRM practices. We believe that better understanding HRM practices in family firms can complement the current understanding that we have about the difference in performance between family and non-family firms.

REFERENCES

Aguinis, H. and Kraiger, K. (2009), 'Benefits of training and development for individuals and teams, organizations, and society', *Annual Review of Psychology*, **60**, 451–74.

Allen, D.G., Mahto, R.V. and Otondo, R.F. (2007), 'Web-based recruitment: effects of information, organizational brand, and attitudes toward a web site on applicant attraction', *Journal of Applied Psychology*, **92**(6), 1696–708.

Arrègle, J.-L., Hitt, M.A., Sirmon, D.G. and Very, P. (2007), 'The development of organizational social capital: attributes of family firms', *Journal of Management Studies*, **44**(1), 73–95.

Astrachan, J.H. and Kolenko, T.A. (1994), 'A neglected factor in explaining family business success: human resource practices', *Family Business Review*, **7**(3), 251–62.

Astrachan, J.H. and Shanker, M.C. (2003), 'Family businesses' contribution to the U.S. economy: a closer look', *Family Business Review*, **16**, 211–19.

Astrachan, J.H., Klein, S.S. and Smyrnios, K.X. (2002), 'The F-Pec scale of family influence: a proposal for solving the family business definition problem', *Family Buisness Review*, **15**(1), 45–58.

Baird, L. and Meshoulam, I. (1988), 'Managing two fits of strategic human resource management', *Academy of Management Review*, **13**(1), 116–28.

Barber, A.E. (1998), *Recruiting Employees: Individual and Organizational Perspectives*, Thousand Oaks, CA: Sage.

Barber, A.E., Wesson, M.J., Roberson, Q.M. and Taylor, M.S. (1999), 'A tale of two job markets: organizational size and its effects on hiring practices and job search behavior', *Personnel Psychology*, **52**(4), 841–67.

Barnett, T. and Kellermanns, F.W. (2006), 'Are we family and are we treated as family? Nonfamily employees' perceptions of justice in the family firm', *Entrepreneurship Theory and Practice*, **30**(6), 836–54.

Barney, J.B. (1991), 'Firms' resources and competitive advantage', *Journal of Management*, **17**(1), 99–120.

Barney, J.B. and Wright, P.M. (1998), 'On becoming a strategic partner: the role of human resources in gaining competitive advantage', *Human Resource Management*, **37**(1), 31–46.

Becker, B.E. and Huselid, M.A. (2006), 'Strategic human resources management: where do we go from here?', *Journal of Management*, **32**(6), 898–925.

Beehr, T.A., Drexler, J.A. and Faulkner, S. (1997), 'Working in small family businesses: empirical comparisons to non-family businesses', *Journal of Organizational Behavior*, **18**(3), 297–312.

Birdi, K., Clegg, C., Patterson, M., Robinson, A., Stride, C., Wall, T. et al. (2008), 'The impact of human resources and operational management practices on company productivity: a longitudinal study', *Personnel Psychology*, **61**(3), 467–501.

Breaugh, J.A. and Starke, M. (2000), 'Research on employee recruitment: so many studies, so many remaining questions', *Journal of Management*, **26**(3), 405–34.

Bryan, J. (2006), 'Training and performance in small firms', *International Small Business Journal*, **24**(6), 635–60.

Buller, P.F. and Napier, N.K. (1993), 'Strategy and human resource management integration in fast growth versus other mid-sized firms', *British Journal of Management*, **4**(2), 77–90.

Burt, R.S. (1997), 'The contingent value of social capital', *Administrative Science Quarterly*, **42**, 339–65.

Cardon, M.S. and Stevens, C.E. (2004), 'Managing human resources in small organizations: what do we know?', *Human Resource Management Review*, **14**(3), 295–323.

Carlson, D.S., Upton, N. and Seaman, S. (2006), 'The impact of human resource practices and compensation design on performance: an analysis of family-owned SMEs', *Journal of Small Business Management*, **44**(4), 531–43.

Carrigan, M. and Buckley, J. (2008), 'What is so special about family business? An exploratory study of UK and Irish consumer experiences of family businesses', *International Journal of Consumer Studies*, **32**, 656–66.

Carroll, M., Marchington, M., Earnshaw, J. and Taylor, S. (1999), 'Recruitment in small firms: processes, methods and problems', *Employee Relations*, **21**(3), 236–50.

Cascio, W.F. (2009), *Managing Human Resources: Productivity, Quality of Work Life, Profits*, 8th edn, Boston, MA: McGraw-Hill Irwin.

Chandler, G.N. and McEvoy, G.M. (2000), 'Human resource management, TQM, and firm performance in small and medium-sized enterprises', *Entrepreneurship Theory and Practice*, **25**(1), 43–57.

Chapman, D.S., Uggerslev, K.L., Carroll, S.A., Piasentin, K.A. and Jones, D.A. (2005), 'Applicant attraction to organizations and job choice: a meta-analytic review of the correlates of recruiting outcomes', *Journal of Applied Psychology*, **90**(5), 928–44.

Chrisman, J.J., Chua, J.H. and Litz, R. (2004), 'Comparing the agency costs of family and non-family firms: conceptual issues and exploratory evidence', *Entrepreneurship Theory and Practice*, **28**, 335–54.

Coleman, J.S. (1988), 'Social capital in the creation of human capital', *American Journal of Sociology*, **94**(Supplement), S95–S120.

Covin, T.J. (1994), 'Profiling preference for employment in family firms', *Family Business Review*, **7**(3), 287–96.

Cromie, S., Stephenson, B. and Montieth, D. (1995), 'The management of family firms: an empirical investigation', *International Small Business Journal*, **13**(4), 11–34.

De Kok, J.M.P. (2002), 'The impact of firm-provided training on production: testing for firm-size effects', *International Small Business Journal*, **20**(3), 271–95.

De Kok, J.M.P. and Uhlaner, L.M. (2001), 'Organization context and human resource management in the small firm', *Small Business Economics*, **17**(4), 273–91.

De Kok, J.M.P., Uhlaner, L.M. and Thurik, A.R. (2006), 'Professional HRM practices in family owned-managed enterprises', *Journal of Small Business Management*, **44**(3), 441–60.

Deshpande, S.P. and Golhar, D.Y. (1994), 'HRM practices in large and small manufacturing firms: a comparative study', *Journal of Small Business Management*, **32**(2), 49–56.

Dyer, W.G. (2006), 'Examining the "family effect" on firm performance', *Family Business Review*, **19**(4), 253–73.

Ehrhart, K.H. and Ziegert, J.C. (2005), 'Why are individuals attracted to organizations?', *Journal of Management*, **31**(6), 901–19.

Eisenhardt, K. (1989), 'Agency theory: an assessment and review', *Academy of Management Review*, **14**(1), 57–74.

Ensley, M.D., Pearson, A.W. and Sardeshmukh, S.R. (2007), 'The negative consequences of pay dispersion in family and non-family top management teams: an exploratory analysis of new venture, high-growth firms', *Journal of Business Research*, **60**(10), 1039–47.

Froelich, K.A. (2005), 'Attracting today's educated workforce: opportunities and challenges for small business firms', *Journal of Small Business Strategy*, **15**(2), 1–17.

Gibb, A.A. (1997), 'Small firms' training and competitiveness: building upon the small business as a learning organisation', *International Small Business Journal*, **15**(3), 13–29.

Goldstein, I.L. and Ford, J.K. (2002), *Training in Organizations*, 4th edn, Belmont, CA: Wadsworth.

Golhar, D.Y. and Deshpande, S.P. (1997), 'HRM practices of large and small Canadian manufacturing firms', *Journal of Small Business Management*, **35**(3), 30–38.

Gudmundson, D. and Hartenian, L. (2000), 'Workforce diversity in small business: an empirical investigation', *Journal of Small Business Management*, **38**(3), 27–36.

Hambrick, D.C., Fredrickson, J.W., Korn, L.B. and Ferry, R.M. (1989), 'Preparing today's leaders for tomorrow's realities', *Personnel*, August, 23–6.

Handler, W.C. (1991), 'Key interpersonal relationships of next-generation family members in family firms', *Journal of Small Business Management*, **29**(3), 21–32.

Harris, R.I.D., Reid, R.S. and McAdam, R. (2004), 'Consultation and communication in family business in Great Britain', *The International Journal of Human Resource Management*, **15**(8), 1424–44.

Hausdorf, P.A. and Duncan, D. (2004), 'Firm size and internet recruiting in Canada: a preliminary investigation', *Journal of Small Business Management*, **42**(3), 325–34.

Hayton, J.C. (2003), 'Strategic human capital management in SMEs: an empirical study of entrepreneurial performance', *Human Resource Management*, **42**(4), 375–91.

Heneman, H.G. and Berkley, R.A. (1999), 'Applicant attraction practices and outcomes among small businesses', *Journal of Small Business Management*, **37**(1), 53–74.

Heneman, R.L. and Tansky, J.W. (2002), 'Human resource management models for entrepreneurial opportunity: existing knowledge and new directions', in J. Katz and T.M. Welbourne (eds.), *Managing People in Entrepreneurial Organizations*, Vol. 5, Amsterdam: JAI Press, pp. 55–82.

Heneman, R.L., Tansky, J.W. and Camp, S.M. (2000), 'Human resource management practices in small and medium-sized enterprises: unanswered questions and future research perspectives', *Entrepreneurship Theory and Practice*, **25**(1), 11–26.

Hill, R. and Stewart, J. (1999), 'Human resource development in small organizations', *Human Resource Development International*, **2**(2), 103–24.

Hornsby, J.S. and Kuratko, D.F. (1990), 'Human resource management in small business: critical issues for the 1990s', *Journal of Small Business Management*, **28**(3), 9–18.

Hornsby, J.S. and Kuratko, D.F. (2003), 'Human resource management in U.S. small businesses: a replication and extension', *Journal of Developmental Entrepreneurship*, **8**(1), 73–92.

Huselid, M.A. (1995), 'The impact of human resource management practices on turnover, productivity, and corporate financial performance', *Academy of Management Journal*, **38**(3), 635–72.

Ibrahim, A.B., Soufani, K., Poutziouris, P. and Lam, J. (2004), 'Qualities of an effective successor: the role of education and training', *Education & Training*, **46**(8/9), 474–80.

Jones, G.R. and Wright, P.M. (1992), 'An economic approach to conceptualizing the utility of human resource management practices', in K. Rowland and G. Ferris (eds), *Research in Personnel and Human Resource Management*, Vol. 10, Greenwich, CT: JAI Press, pp. 271–99.

Kaman, V., McCarthy, A.M., Gulbro, R.D. and Tucker, M.L. (2001), 'Bureaucratic and high commitment human resource practices in small service firms', *Human Resource Planning*, **24**(1), 33–44.

Kickul, J. (2001), 'Promises made, promises broken: an exploration of employee attraction and retention practices in small business', *Journal of Small Business Management*, **39**(4), 320–35.

King, S.W., Solomon, G.T. and Fernald, L.W. Jr (2001), 'Issues in growing a family business: a strategic human resource model', *Journal of Small Business Management*, **39**(1), 3–13.

Klein, S.S., Astrachan, J.H. and Smyrnios, K.X. (2005), 'The F-Pec scale of family influence: construct validation, and further implications for theory', *Entrepreneurship Theory and Practice*, **29**(3), 321–39.

Koch, M.J. and McGrath, R.G. (1996), 'Improving labor productivity: human resource management policies do matter', *Strategic Management Journal*, **17**(5), 335–54.

Kontogiannis, T. and Sheperd, A. (1999), 'Training conditions and strategic aspects of skill transfer in a simulated process control task', *Human–Computer Interaction*, **14**, 355–93.

Kotey, B. and Folker, C. (2007), 'Employee training in SMEs: effect of size and firm type – family and nonfamily', *Journal of Small Business Management*, **45**(2), 214–38.

Kotey, B. and Sheridan, A. (2004), 'Changing HRM practices with firm growth', *Journal of Small Business and Enterprise Development*, **11**(4), 474–85.

Kotey, B. and Slade, P. (2005), 'Formal human resource management practices in small growing firms', *Journal of Small Business Management*, **43**(1), 16–40.

Lengnick-Hall, M.L., Lengnick-Hall, C.A., Andrade, L.S. and Drake, B. (2009), 'Strategic human resource management: the evolution of the field', *Human Resource Management Review*, **19**, 64–85.

Leung, A. (2003), 'Different ties for different needs: recruitment practices of entrepreneurial firms at different development phases', Human Resource Management, **42**(4), 303–20.

Litchfield, S.R. (2008), 'Exploring customer perceptions regarding products, services and job opportunities of 'family-owned businesses', paper presented at the 8th Annual IFERA Conference, July.

Loan-Clarke, J., Boocock, G., Smith, A. and Whittaker, J. (1999), 'Investment in management training and development by small businesses', *Employee Relations*, **21**(3), 296–310.

London, M. and Moore, E.M. (1999), 'Continuous learning', in D.R. Ilgen and E.D. Pulakos (eds), *The Changing Nature of Performance*, San Francisco, CA: Jossey-Bass, pp. 119–53.

Matlay, H. (2002), 'Training and HRD strategies in family and non-family owned small businesses: a comparative approach', *Education & Training*, **44**(8/9), 357–69.

Nguyen, T.V. and Bryant, S.E. (2004), 'A study of the formality of human resource management practices in small and medium-size enterprises in Vietnam', *International Small Business Journal*, **22**(6), 595–618.

Orth, U.R. and Green, M.T. (2009), 'Consumer loyalty to family versus non-family business: the roles of store image, trust and satisfaction', *Journal of Retailing and Consumer Services*, **16**, 248–59.

Peters, M. and Buhalis, D. (2004), 'Family hotel businesses: strategic planning and the need for education and training', *Education & Training*, **46**(8/9), 406–15.

Pfeffer, J. (1998), *The Human Equation*, Boston, MA: Harvard Business School Press.

Poza, E.J. (2010), *Family Business*, 3rd edn, Mason, OH: Cenegade Learning.

Randøy, T. and Goel, S. (2003), 'Ownership structure, founder leadership, and performance in Norwegian SMEs: implications for financing entrepreneurial opportunities', *Journal of Business Venturing*, **18**, 619–37.

Ranger-Moore, J. (1997), 'Bigger may be better, but is older wiser? Organizational age and size in the New York life insurance industry', *American Sociological Review*, **62**, 903–20.

Reid, R.S. and Adams, J.S. (2001), 'Human resource management: a survey of practices within family and non-family firms', *Journal of European Industrial Training*, **25**(6/7), 310–20.

Reid, R.S., Morrow, T., Kelly, B., Adams, J.S. and McCartan, P. (2000), 'Human resource management practices in SMEs: a comparative analysis of family and non-family businesses', *Irish Business and Administrative Research*, **21**(2), 157–81.

Rowden, R.W. (2002), 'High performance and human resource characteristics of successful small manufacturing and processing companies', *Leadership & Organization Development Journal*, **23**(1/2), 79–83.

Rutherford, M.W., Buller, P.F. and McMullen, P.R. (2003), 'Human resource management problems over the life cycle of small to medium-sized firms', *Human Resource Management*, **42**(4), 321–35.

Rynes, S.L. (1991), 'Recruitment, job choice, and post-hire consequences: a call for new research directions', in M.D. Dunnette and L.M. Hough (eds), *Handbook of Industrial and Organizational Psychology*, Vol. 2, Palo Alto, CA: Consulting Psychologists Press, pp. 399–444.

Rynes, S.L. and Barber, A.E. (1990), 'Applicant attraction strategies: an organizational perspective', *Academy of Management Review*, **15**(2), 286–310.

Rynes, S.L. and Cable, D.M. (2003), 'Recruitment research in the twenty-first century', in W.C. Borman, D.R. Ilgen and R.J. Klimoski (eds), *Handbook of Psychology: Industrial and Organizational Psychology*, Vol. 12, Hoboken, NJ: John Wiley & Sons, pp. 55–76.

SBA (2008), 'Frequently asked questions', retrieved September 2009 from www.sba.gov.

Schermerhorn, J.R. (2001), *Management Update 2001*, 6th edn, New York: John Wiley and Sons.

Schulze, W.S., Lubatkin, M.H., Dino, R.N. and Buchholtz, A.K. (2001), 'Agency relationships in family firms: theory and evidence', *Organization Science*, **12**(2), 99–116.

Senge, P.M. (2006), *The Fifth Discipline: The Art and Practice of the Learning Organization*, New York: Currency Double Day.

Sharma, P. (2004), 'An overview of the field of family business studies: current status and directions for the future', *Family Business Review*, **17**(1), 1–36.

Sirmon, D.G. and Hitt, M.A. (2003), 'Managing resources: linking unique resources, management, and wealth creation in family firms', *Entrepreneurship Theory and Practice*, **27**(4), 339–58.

Smith-Jentsch, K.A., Salas, E. and Brannick, M.T. (2001), 'To transfer or not to transfer: investigating the combined effects of trainee characteristics, team leader support, and team climate', *Journal of Applied Psychology*, **86**(2), 279–92.

Thayer, P.W. (1997), 'A rapidly changing world: some implications for training in the year 2001 and beyond', in M.A. Quiñones and A. Ehrenstein (eds), *Training for a Rapidly Changing Workplace: Applications of Psychological Research*, Washington DC: APA, pp. 15–30.

Tocher, N. and Rutherford, M.W. (2009), 'Perceived acute human resource management problems in small and medium firms: an empirical examination', *Entrepreneurship Theory and Practice*, **33**(2), 455–79.

Trank, C.Q., Rynes, S.L. and Bretz, R.D., Jr (2002), 'Attracting applicants in the war for talent: differences in work preferences among high achievers', *Journal of Business and Psychology*, **16**(3), 331–45.

Vallejo, M.C. (2008), 'The effects of commitment of non-family employees of family firms from the perspective of stewardship theory', *Journal of Business Ethics*, **87**, 379–90.

Wilkinson, A. (1999), 'Employment relations in SMEs', *Employee Relations*, **21**(3), 206–17.

Williamson, I.O. (2000), 'Employer legitimacy and recruitment success in small businesses', *Entrepreneurship Theory and Practice*, **25**(1), 27–42.

Williamson, I.O., Cable, D.M. and Aldrich, H.E. (2002), 'Smaller but not necessarily weaker: how small businesses can overcome barriers to recruitment', in J. Katz and T.M. Welbourne (eds), *Managing People in Entrepreneurial Organizations*, Vol. 5, Amsterdam: JAI Press, pp. 83–106.

Wright, P.M., Dunford, B.B. and Snell, S.A. (2001), 'Human resources and the resource based view of the firm', *Journal of Management*, **27**(6), 701–21.

Wright, P.M. and McMahan, G.C. (1992), 'Theoretical perspectives for human resource management', *Journal of Management*, **18**(2), 295–320.

18 The adoption of high-performance work systems in family versus non-family SMEs: the moderating effect of organizational size

Daniel Pittino and Francesca Visintin

INTRODUCTION

Several arguments in the field of family business research suggest that human resource management (HRM) practices are one of the fundamental drivers for the success and longevity of family companies (e.g. Astrachan and Kolenko, 1994; Sirmon and Hitt, 2003; Miller et al., 2008; Miller et al., 2009; Astrachan, 2010). Family businesses are often believed to treat their employees with high consideration, building cohesive internal communities and fostering extraordinary motivation and commitment. But how do these attitudes towards employees relate to the so-called 'high-performance' human resource management systems that have been increasingly identified as a fundamental driver of competitive advantage by the organization and management literature in the past two decades? And how does the family influence on the business affect the rate of adoption of these HRM systems?

Empirical evidence and theoretical reflection on these topics are still relatively scarce in comparison to other themes in the field of family business studies; more extensive research is therefore needed on the way human resource policies and practices are developed in family businesses (Astrachan, 2010).

The research on HRM practices in family firms presents significant degrees of overlap with the studies on human resource management in small and medium enterprises (SMEs). In these researches, the emphasis is on the use of 'professional' human resource practices aimed at achieving employees' motivation and commitment (e.g. Reid and Adams, 2001; Reid et al., 2002, Harris et al., 2004; De Kok et al., 2006). These researches suggest that family SMEs, compared to their non-family counterparts, tend to adopt a more informal approach to human resource management and are more reluctant to employ professional techniques to promote employee involvement and commitment.

On the one hand, this may be due to the prevalence of a stewardship attitude in the family firm employees, who develop 'naturally' a strong sense of commitment and a feeling of identification with the goals of the organization and the family (e.g. Pearson and Marler, 2010). On the other hand, this also may be due to the 'paternalistic' structure of the family firm's organization, where often the responsibilities are not clearly defined, the leadership is authoritative and the decisional processes are highly concentrated in the hands of the entrepreneur and his family members (e.g. Cromie et al., 1995; Harris et al., 2004). Paternalism has also often been related to nepotism or altruism in human resource practices, leading to the prevalence of 'family principles' over the 'business principles', with possible negative consequence in terms of fairness in the treatment of non-family employees compared to family members (Lansberg, 1983; Lubatkin et al., 2005; Barnett and Kellermanns, 2006).

We may argue, however, that the effect of these traits in differentiating family firms from non-family firms in their human resource practices is not equally important across firms of different size. In other words, we may assume that organizational size is an important contingent variable that moderates the effect of family control on the adoption of professional HRM practices. The studies within the 'organizational contingencies' tradition (e.g. Pugh et al., 1968; Blau, 1970) posit that the size of the organization is positively related to the organizational complexity; higher degrees of organizational complexity require, in turn, higher levels of formalization and constrain managerial discretion (Pondy, 1969; Hall et al., 1967). Since family influence on management and organization requires some degree of discretion and strategic choice by decision-makers, we argue that constraints in managerial discretion may lead to a reduced impact of the family dimension on management decisions; in our particular case, as organizations grow in size, choices on human resource management practices are less likely to follow entirely the goals and preferences of the dominant coalition and are more likely to be determined by structural contingencies. Organizational size may affect the family influence also through its impact on entrepreneurial attention (Gifford, 1992). Entrepreneurial attention is a limited resource that is allocated to employee direct supervision and other coordination activities (Kaldor, 1934; Simon, 1976). When the organization grows in size, time and effort of the entrepreneur must shift from the direct monitoring of activities to the indirect coordination. Thus, in larger organizations, the entrepreneurial family, to effectively implement its goals, must delegate the decision power to lower-level employees and managers. To work properly, delegation requires effective coordination and control systems. In family firms coordination and control of lower-level employees may occur partially through a value-based alignment of interests, but above a certain degree of complexity effective coordination may require the establishment of formal human resource management practices.

In this study we aim at providing further evidence of the different rates of adoption of 'professional' HRM practices among family and non-family SMEs, focusing on a specific subset of HRM policies that have been the object of interest and lively debate over the last two decades in organization and management studies, namely the so-called high-performance work systems (HPWS). According to the concept of HPWS, an organization can obtain superior performance by adopting a given set of human resource management practices that emphasize employee involvement and commitment, even for lower level workers, extensive training and development, reliance on pay for performance, flexible and broadly defined job responsibilities, emphasis on teamworking and employee participation in organizational decision-making (Huselid, 1995; Delaney and Huselid, 1996; Delery and Doty, 1996; Huselid et al., 1997).

Moreover, we aim at providing an additional insight in to the literature on HRM in family business, assessing the moderating effect of organizational size on the relationship between family business status and HPWS adoption.

Our expected contribution is therefore twofold: we add to the family business literature, presenting further evidence in the emerging stream of research on HPWS in family firms and shedding also some light on one of the possible contingencies (i.e. organizational size) that may moderate the family influence in management decisions and practices; we also contribute to the mainstream management and organization literature by discussing a form of structural constraint affecting the decisions of organizations' dominant coalition.

We focus our analysis on SMEs to allow comparability with previous studies on the topic and also because we assume that the most significant effects of changing organizational size on managerial discretion and complexity occur within the range 0–250 employees.

The chapter is structured as follows. In the first section we highlight the main findings of the empirical literature on human resource management practices and HPWS in small and medium family and non-family firms; in the second section we develop the hypotheses of the research with particular reference to the moderating effect of organizational size as a source of structural constraint; in the third section we present the sample and the method of the research; in the fourth section we present the results; in the fifth section we discuss the findings; the sixth section concludes.

HUMAN RESOURCE MANAGEMENT AND HPWS IN FAMILY AND NON-FAMILY SMEs

Empirical research on human resource management practices in family and non-family SMEs seems to have reached consensus on two points: (1) SMEs make less use of 'formal' or 'professional' HRM practices than larger firms. For example, smaller companies are less likely to adopt HRM planning systems and formal training, have less formalized performance appraisal systems, and less sophisticated recruitment and selection practices (e.g. Aldrich and Langton,1997; Westhead and Storey 1997, 1999; De Kok and den Hartog, 2006; Reid and Adams, 2001; Reid et al., 2002; Harney and Dundon, 2006). (2) Among SMEs, family firms are less likely to adopt professional HRM practices than non-family firms (De Kok et al., 2006; Harris et al., 2004; Kotey and Folker, 2007). Various explanations have been proposed for this result. De Kok et al., (2006), for example, assume that, since formal HRM practices are often used to promote the alignment of interests between managers and employees, family firms do not require formal systems to commit the employees to the company goals, since they are able to create an organizational culture of stewardship where all employees feel loyal to the family and the firm, and, in turn, the business family develops a sense of commitment towards the workforce (Miller et al., 2009; Vallejo, 2009; Pearson and Marler, 2010). Other authors suggest that family firms make less use of formal HRM practices because these practices often require formal employee involvement and significant degrees of decentralization of decision power, and these requirements may be in conflict with the attitudes of family business leaders, who often prefer a paternalistic command-and-control approach over the employees (Dyer, 1986; Harris et al., 2004). According to Carney (2005, p. 255), 'owner–managers of family firms may be unwilling to abide by formalized human resources management practices that inhibit their ownership prerogatives'.

Among the 'formalized' and 'professional' human resource practices, growing attention has been devoted in the last decade to the diffusion of the high-performance work systems (HPWS).

We define HPWS as a set of distinct but interrelated HRM practices that together select, develop, retain and motivate employees with the goal of achieving superior performance and sustainable competitive advantage (Huselid, 1995; Guthrie, 2001; Way, 2002). Other terms have been used in the literature to identify people management systems that privilege commitment over control, for example 'employee empowerment techniques' (e.g. Pfeffer, 1998; Argyris, 1998), 'high involvement work systems' (e.g. Walton, 1985; Lawler, 1992), 'high commitment management practices' (e.g. Wood and De Menezes 1998; Wood and Wall, 2002). For the purpose of this chapter these terms can be understood as synonyms for HPWS, since they all refer to similar sets of techniques aimed at increasing employee motivation through increased commitment.

Given the growing popularity of these notions, several attempts have been made to test the relationship between the adoption of HPWS and actual organizational performance. Many studies have shown a positive and significant effect on performance (e.g. Appelbaum et al., 2000; Becker and Gerhart, 1996; Huselid and Becker, 1996; Huselid, 1995; Delaney and Huselid, 1996; Guthrie, 2001) and in a recent review Paauwe concludes that, despite significant theoretical and methodological challenges, empirical evidence shows that HPWS are 'at least weakly related to firm performance' (Paauwe, 2009, p. 133).

Although in literature there are some differences in the specification of the components of the HPWS, there seems to be an established consensus around some practices (e.g. Arthur, 1994; Bae and Lawler, 2000; Huselid, 1995; Huselid et al., 1997; MacDuffie, 1995; Ichniowski et al., 1997; Guthrie, 2001).

In particular, in research on SMEs in the USA, Way (2002) has defined the HPWS as comprising seven categories of practices, namely: (1) staffing: to what extent a firm's staffing process uses information gathered from several selection devices to evaluate job candidates; (2) group-based performance pay: to what extent the employees' compensation is related to collective performance and is seen as a way in which firms can align the desired goals of employees with those of the firm; (3) above-average compensation level: the firm decides to pay salaries above the market average to attract the best employees; (4) flexible job assignments: to what extent the firm uses job rotation techniques to broaden the skills spectrum of the employees; (5) teamwork: to what extent the workforce is organized in self-directed teams, in order to enhance employees' abilities and motivation; (6) formal training: opportunities for the employees to follow off-the-job training programs to improve their abilities and knowledge; (7) communication: formal processes where employees can both provide their opinions and receive relevant information about work organization and firm performance.

Some recent studies have explored the use of HPWS in family firms and their impact on performance. For example Carlson et al. (2006) show that the use of human resource practices such as training and development, recruitment package, maintaining morale, performance appraisals and competitive compensation are positively associated to sales growth in a sample of small UK-based family firms.

In a study on Taiwanese family companies, Tsao and colleagues (2009) show that the family firms adopting HPWS are able to outperform non-family firms, whereas family firms not adopting such practices are significantly underperforming. Kidwell and Fish (2007) carry out an exploratory study on family businesses in the Australian wine industry and find that the adoption of HPWS is positively related to perceived improvements in business performance.

This preliminary evidence is in line with the observation by Astrachan and Kolenko (1994), who point out that HRM practices are an important element in a successful family business strategy, and with the argument put forward by Zahra et al. (2008), that the combination of the stewardship attitude with formal high commitment to human resource practices may lead to superior performance.

It appears, therefore, important to provide further evidence on the use of HPWS in the family business setting, in comparison with non-family business companies, introducing also contextual factors that could influence their adoption.

THE HYPOTHESES OF THE RESEARCH

Our basic assumption is that the family influence over the business decisions impacts on the rate of adoption of HPWS. According to the definition by Astrachan et al. (2002), family influence comprises power, experience and culture. Power refers to the ability of the family to control the business through ownership and/or management. Experience refers to family intergenerational commitment, providing a 'memory' that is available to the organization. Culture refers to the systems of values that family members transfer to the firm.

According to the previously highlighted findings, the components of family influence are likely to impact on relevant dimensions of human resource management choices. The power dimension may be reflected in highly hierarchical structures, with low propensity to decentralization and concentration of authority in the hands of the family members at the expense of non-family managers and employees, thus discouraging the adoption of formal high-involvement work practices.

The experience dimension, which reflects the intergenerational commitment of the family, is likely to impact on the 'community ties' of family firms. Family firm leaders are usually aware of the importance of their organization's performance in the long term, since it affects family wealth, family reputation, the future of the children, and the continuity of the family business tradition and mission (Miller et al., 2009; Schneper et al., 2008). Therefore some family business owners aim at building a corporate community to increase company longevity and to help the accomplishment of company's mission (Miller et al., 2009, p. 804). Community dimensions include altruism, loyalty and caring for workers, which create motivation and commitment among employees without the need of professional and formal practices.

Finally, the culture dimension contributes to the transfer of family values to the firm, thus supporting the establishment of a stewardship culture towards the employees and, on the other hand, the development of a stewardship attitude among the employees towards family values. This stewardship relation helps the establishment of a value-based coordination and alignment of the goals between owner-managers and employees. Thus the dimensions of family influence may contribute to a lower rate of adoption of HPWS in family SMEs compared to non-family ones – on the one hand because they may drive the management decisions of the dominant coalition towards the accomplishment of family values and principles, and on the other hand because they may directly facilitate the use of more informal and value-based coordination practices.

Therefore we propose the following:

Hypothesis 1   On average, family SMEs have a lower degree of adoption of HPWS compared to non-family SMEs.

However, according to Barnett and Kellermanns (2006, p. 841), 'The level of family influence actually exerted is the result of a political process of value determination, goal setting, and strategy formulation by the dominant coalition of family members and the extent to which the values, goals, and strategies are successfully implemented'. We assume that the implementation of family goals and values in the organization is influenced by the managerial discretion available to the dominant coalition. One of the most relevant factors that impact on managerial discretion is the size of the organization. Larger organizations impose higher constraints on the discretion of strategic decision-makers (Hall et al., 1967; Child, 1972; Bourgeois, 1984). These constraints manifest themselves mainly through: (1) the need to increase the specialization of the organization in order to increase the efficiency of the activity; and (2) the need to decentralize the control system, in order to effectively monitor people.

Increased levels of specialization are likely to require higher structural differentiation among heterogeneous and increasingly autonomous sub-units. The effective coordination of the activity of the sub-units forces the top management to adopt a system of impersonal controls through the use of norms, formal procedures and routines. Moreover, managing a larger number of employees and activities makes it difficult to employ a personalized and centralized decision-making setting. This happens because entrepreneurial attention is a limited resource; limited attention limits the span of control of the entrepreneur: 'as firm size increases, the attention of the entrepreneur becomes spread so thin that control of operations is diminished' (Gifford, 1990, p. 268). Therefore direct supervision of activities must be increasingly replaced by organizational routines or delegated to middle-level managers (Simon, 1976), and this reduces the influence of the entrepreneur's personal style and values in firms' decision-making.

Thus, although the dominant coalition can maintain various degrees of freedom of choice, even in larger organizations (Child, 1972), growth in size always results in a reduced influence of the top management on firms' organization and strategy. What are the implications of these size-related constraints on the adoption of HPWS in family firms? We may identify two main consequences: (1) the constraints to the dominant coalition limit the influence of the personal values of the decision makers on the selection of strategies, practices and policies. Thus the family influence on the choice of specific HRM practices turns out to be reduced as firm grows in size; (2) the structure itself, through increasing needs of specialization and decentralization, has a direct impact on the adoption of more formalized HRM practices, regardless of the dominant coalition's values and preferences.

If we apply these considerations to the adoption of HPWS in family firms compared to non-family ones, we can formulate the following:

Hypothesis 2   Organizational size moderates the family influence on the adoption of HPWS.

The theoretical arguments underlying Hypothesis 2 can be further developed and refined with reference to different groups of organizations according to the number of employees.

First we focus on the firms with fewer than 25 employees, since this limit in the studies on small firms has often been considered as a critical threshold in terms of growing organizational complexity and effectiveness of entrepreneurial direct supervision (e.g. Hall et al., 1967; Moreno and Casillas, 2008; Wolff and Pett, 2000). In very small firms the decisions of the entrepreneur are not constrained by extensive bureaucratic structures, thus there are broad margins of discretion in strategic choices, including the adoption of HRM practices. At the same time, however, direct supervision is almost the exclusive coordination mean, and also the most efficient and effective. In very small organizations the centralization of the decision-making structure, the direct communication with the employees, and the involvement of the entrepreneur(s) in both strategic and day-to-day business activities can be considered common features in the management of employees both for family and non-family firms. Thus family influence should not lead to a distinctive behavior in human resource management of family firms compared to non-family ones.

Hypothesis 2a   In very small enterprises (fewer than 25 employees), there is no significant difference between family and non-family firms in the adoption of HPWS.

In larger firms, between 25 and 100 employees, effective coordination usually cannot be achieved exclusively through direct supervision, and additional mechanisms must be established. Organizational size, however, still allows for a consistent degree of discretion in the choice of the coordination mechanisms, with the possibility to realize a different and equally effective combination of coordination mechanisms. We assume that family firms differ from non-family ones in the choice of mechanisms that supplement or substitute entrepreneurial direct supervision, and this has direct effects on the adoption of HRM practices.

Non-family firms may rely more on formal systems to coordinate, control and motivate the employees. On the other hand, family firms, given their relative reluctance to delegate power and given the possibility to rely on employees' stewardship as a mean of interest alignment, will make less use of formal practices, HPWS being among them.

Hypothesis 2b   In small enterprises (between 25 and 100 employees), family firms have a significantly lower degree of adoption of HPWS.

Beyond the limit of 100 employees, structural constraints become important in management choices, and this contributes to narrowing the gap between family and non-family SMEs in the use of HPWS. Growing organizational dimension pushes towards an increase in hierarchical levels, in structural differentiation and division of labor, and in formalization (Hall et al., 1967; Pugh et al., 1969; Blau, 1970). Moreover, the control over highly differentiated activities and the need to control a large number of people make it impossible to employ a personalized, entrepreneurial-centered style of management. Thus family firms' dominant coalitions over certain dimensions and level of complexity face a significant management constraint (Carney, 1998), and are somewhat 'forced' by structural requirements to choose more formal human resource management practices; the scope of the coordination based on stewardship is also narrower in large organizations and may be limited to upper-level employees, or, if it applies to all employees, it involves only a small portion of work behaviors. We might therefore assume that the attitude towards the adoption of HPWS is more similar in family and non-family firms of over 100 employees compared with their smaller counterparts.

Hypothesis 2c   In medium enterprises (between 100 and 250 employees) the difference in the adoption of HPWS between family and non-family firms is less pronounced compared to small firms (between 25 and 100 employees).

METHOD

Sample and Data Set

Hypotheses were tested on a data set that comes from a survey on human resource management practices carried out on a randomly selected sample of SMEs operating in the north-east of Italy. To identify the firms to be included in the study we employed the number of employees criterion adopted by the European Union that defines SMEs as companies employing fewer than 250 people.

An initial sample of 500 manufacturing firms has been randomly drawn from the population of firms listed on a local chamber of commerce data set (Udine Chamber of Commerce). The selected firms were first contacted to assess their willingness to participate to the survey; 312 enterprises agreed to participate. The data on the participants have been collected using a structured questionnaire administered through phone interview in the period September–October 2008 by team of three MBA students.

The questionnaire was made up of three sections: the first was devoted to the collection of general data about the firm, with questions on products, markets and management structure; the second was about the existence and the organization of the human resource management department/function; the third was about the adoption of specific human resource management practices.

Non-respondent bias was assessed through an analysis on 23 additional firms that agreed to participate after a second round of calls. No significant differences were found between this group and a matched sample of the firms participating in the first round. The final sample was therefore made up of 335 firms; for the purposes of this research 34 questionnaires were excluded due to missing or inconsistent answers. The analysis was thus performed on 301 firms. For the purposes of the research firms we divided the sample into three groups according to the employment levels that are considered critical thresholds in terms of growing organizational complexity (e.g. Hall et al., 1967; Wolff and Pett, 2000; Moreno and Casillas, 2008): up to 25 employees; from 25 to 100 employees; more than 100 employees.

The sample distribution according to organizational size and family control is presented in Table 18.1.

Variables

Dependent variables
Since our focus is on SMEs, we follow mainly the approach adopted by Way (2002) in his research on HPWS in smaller firms, with some adjustments due to the nature of

Table 18.1   Distribution of the SMEs of the sample according to organizational size and family firm status

	Non-family firms (%)	(n)	Family firms (%)	(n)	Total (%)	(n)
(1) Up to 25 employees	47.9	(34)	52.1	(37)	100	71
(2) 25 to 100 employees	41.0	(50)	59.0	(72)	100	122
(3) More than 100 employees	38.8	(42)	61.2	(66)	100	108
						301

information gathered and to the characteristics of our sample. In particular, the component 'flexible job assignments' was replaced by a variable capturing the degree of formal employee participation in decisions on job design and work planning. This measure has already been employed in previous research on HRM in SMEs (e.g. Patel and Cardon, 2010). Other minor changes compared to Way's dimensions concern the specification of single components of the indicators.

Thus dependent variables are seven components of the HPWS measured on scales normalized to 1. In particular:

(1)   *Extensiveness of staffing/selection devices*   The combination of different devices may result in the selection of individuals who possess superior competencies that, in turn, produce superior employee output (e.g. Ployhart, 2004). The measure is an additive score of the extent to which different selection devices are used to evaluate job candidates; each of the selection devices is on a scale ranging from 0 to 5 according to the number of employees categories to which it is applied. The normalized score is therefore interviews + tests + work samples + references from previous employers + assessment centres/25. Maximum score equals 1.

(2)   *Group-based pay for performance*   Group-based performance plays an important role in aligning the desired goals of employees with those of the organization (e.g. Guthrie, 2001). The measure is a dichotomous variable assuming value 1 if the firm adopts variable pay schemes based on the evaluation of group performance.

(3)   *Pay level*   Firms paying salaries above the market level may attract and retain workers with superior abilities (e.g. Becker and Huselid, 1998). The measure is a dichotomous variable assuming value 1 if the firm salary level is above the industry's average.

(4)   *Self-directed teams*   Team empowerment (e.g. in terms of task autonomy, impact and meaningfulness) helps the development of employee motivation, satisfaction and, ultimately, enhances employee performance (e.g. Kirkman and Rosen, 1999). The measure is the share of non-managerial and non-supervisory employees involved in self-managed teams. Maximum score equals 1.

(5)   *Formal off the job training*   Formal training may have an impact both on employee motivation and skills (e.g. Kirkpatrick, 1998). The measure is the share of front-line employees who received formal training in the previous three years. Maximum score equals 1.

(6)   *Extensiveness of communication to the employees*   The availability of information

on a wide range of firm-related topics may contribute to improving the organizational climate and enhance the degree of identification of the employees with the goals of the firm (e.g. Smidts et al., 2001). The measure is an additive score of the extent to which information on different topics is transferred to the employees. Each of the topics is on scale ranging from 0 to 5 according to the number of employee categories to which it is transferred. The normalized score is information on: (work organization + training + compensation + general firm performance + quality of products and processes)/25.

(7) *Involvement in meetings discussing work-related issues*   Formal systems that allow employees to have their points of view considered in work related decisions will have a positive impact on the perceptions of fairness (e.g. Locke et al., 1997). Share of non-managerial and non-supervisory employees involved in regularly scheduled meetings to discuss work-related issues. Maximum score equals 1.

Independent variables

For the purposes of this study, our explanatory variables are the firm's size and the family business status. However, in the multivariate estimation we also employed a number of control variables.

- *Family business*   Family business status is a dichotomous variable assuming value 1, according to the definition by Westhead and Cowling (1999), if a family controls the company through the majority of voting shares and the family is represented in the entrepreneurial and management team.
- *Organizational size*   Organizational size was measured by the number of employees. The number of employees has been widely used as a proxy for the structural complexity of an organization (e.g. Pugh et al., 1968; Blau, 1970).

We also used as *control variables* the following:

- *Firm's strategy*   Following Porter's definition of competitive strategies, we employed a dichotomous variable assuming value 1 if the firm pursues its competitive advantage mainly through innovativeness and product quality or value 0 if the firm pursues its competitive advantage mainly through efficiency; the use of Porter's strategy as a variable influencing HRM practices traces back to Schuler and Jackson (1987).
- *Firm's age*   Firm age is the number of years since the firm was founded and, similarly to size, may have an impact on institutionalization of norms and habits (Baker and Cullen, 1993).
- *Industry's technological intensity*   This is a categorical variable that follows the OECD definition in low technology sectors, low-to-medium-technology sectors, and medium-to-high-technology sectors. Technological intensity may also have an impact on human resource requirements (e.g. Lepak et al., 2003).

Descriptive statistics and correlations among variables are shown in Table 18.2 and Table 18.3.

Table 18.2   Descriptive statistics and correlations among variables

	Mean	SD	1	2	3	4	5	6	7	8	9	10	11	12
1 Family firm	0.61	0.49	1.00	−0.07	−0.13	−0.13	0.05	−0.11	−0.08	−0.16	−0.15	−0.17	−0.01	−0.07
				0.23	0.07	0.06	0.35	0.07	0.18	0.01	0.01	0.00	0.87	0.35
2 Organizational size	58.3	28.1	−0.07	1.00	−0.19	−0.06	0.07	0.20	−0.08	0.15	0.17	0.05	−0.06	0.35
			0.23		0.01	0.44	0.23	0.00	0.18	0.01	0.00	0.37	0.35	0.00
3 Technological intensity	1.64	0.59	−0.13	−0.19	1.00	−0.22	−0.02	0.01	−0.10	−0.18	−0.20	−0.15	−0.17	−0.16
			0.07	0.01		0.00	0.80	0.87	0.16	0.01	0.00	0.04	0.02	0.02
4 Strategic posture	0.55	0.50	−0.13	−0.06	−0.22	1.00	0.09	0.04	0.06	0.16	0.05	0.03	−0.08	0.08
			0.06	0.44	0.00		0.22	0.59	0.44	0.02	0.52	0.68	0.26	0.27
5 Age	34.2	22.2	0.05	0.07	−0.02	0.09	1.00	0.13	−0.02	0.02	0.02	0.07	−0.04	0.08
			0.35	0.23	0.80	0.22		0.03	0.80	0.77	0.76	0.26	0.55	0.25
6 Staffing	0.51	0.20	−0.11	0.20	0.01	0.04	0.13	1.00	0.04	0.19	0.21	0.09	−0.10	0.14
			0.07	0.00	0.87	0.59	0.03		0.47	0.00	0.00	0.13	0.09	0.05
7 Work teams	0.36	0.36	−0.08	−0.08	−0.10	0.06	−0.02	0.04	1.00	0.15	0.13	0.22	0.08	0.13
			0.18	0.18	0.16	0.44	0.80	0.47		0.01	0.04	0.00	0.18	0.06
8 Communication	0.41	0.25	−0.16	0.15	−0.18	0.16	0.02	0.19	0.15	1.00	0.73	0.27	−0.05	0.27
			0.01	0.01	0.01	0.02	0.77	0.00	0.01		0.00	0.00	0.38	0.00
9 Meetings	0.44	0.25	−0.15	0.17	−0.20	0.05	0.02	0.21	0.13	0.73	1.00	0.27	−0.09	0.21
			0.01	0.00	0.00	0.52	0.76	0.00	0.04	0.00		0.00	0.13	0.00
10 Training	0.24	0.25	−0.17	0.05	−0.15	0.03	0.07	0.09	0.22	0.27	0.27	1.00	0.02	0.31
			0.00	0.37	0.04	0.68	0.26	0.13	0.00	0.00	0.00		0.75	0.00
11 Pay level	0.28	0.45	−0.01	−0.06	−0.17	−0.08	−0.04	−0.10	0.08	−0.05	−0.09	0.02	1.00	0.11
			0.87	0.35	0.02	0.26	0.55	0.09	0.18	0.38	0.13	0.75		0.10
12 Group-based pay	0.26	0.44	−0.07	0.35	−0.16	0.08	0.08	0.14	0.13	0.27	0.21	0.31	0.11	1.00
			0.35	0.00	0.02	0.27	0.25	0.05	0.06	0.00	0.00	0.00	0.10	

Note: Correlations higher than 0.14 and lower than −0.14 are significant at the 0.05 level.

Data Analysis Techniques

The hypotheses were tested through multivariate analysis of variance (MANOVA) aimed at identifying the influence of family firm status and size on the adoption of the various components of the HPWS. This approach has been applied because the high-performance work system should be seen as a set of practices that complement each other and act synergistically (Becker and Huselid, 1998; Delery, 1998); therefore it does not seem appropriate to consider each component separately. However, to provide a more comprehensive picture, we also present the univariate analysis of variance between family and non-family firms at different sizes according to the single HPWS component.

The analysis is similar to the one performed by Kotey and Folker on the diffusion of formal training techniques among SMEs. At first we perform a multivariate analysis of variance on the entire sample, estimating the main effects of size and family/non-family firm status on the adoption of HPWS; we also introduce in the MANOVA an interaction effect, namely family firm interacted with size, to assess whether the family firm effect on HPWS adoption is moderated by organizational size. Finally, we consider separately the effect of family/non-family firm status within each size group of firms (micro, small and medium). All the models include also the control variables.

RESULTS

Multivariate analysis of variance was used at first to test the influence of the family firm variable over the entire sample (Table 18.3). Results confirm that being a family firm has a negative impact on the rate of adoption of the whole set of HPWS; at the same time, firm size is also positively and significantly related to the adoption of HPWS. Both values of Wilks' lambda are significant at p level < 0.01.

If we introduce the interaction effect (family firm $\times$ size), we also observe that the effect of family firm status depends significantly on the size of the firm ($p = 0.02$). Hypothesis 1 and Hypothesis 2 are thus supported.

Table 18.3   MANOVA analysis for the effects of independent variables on HPWS adoption, entire sample

Effect	Wilks' lambda value	F-value	Sig.
Intercept	0.225	180.679	0.000
Family firm	0.917	4.752	0.000
Organizational size	0.924	4.323	0.001
Family firm $\times$ Organizational size	0.951	2.681	0.022
Technological intensity	0.940	2.359	0.042
Strategy	0.931	2.715	0.023
Firm's age	0.925	2.992	0.013

Note: Design: intercept + family firm + organizational size + technological intensity + strategy + firm's age + family firm $\times$ organizational size.

Table 18.4   Univariate analysis of variance of the effect of family firm status on the single components of HPWS, entire sample

	Family firms	Non-family firms	*F*-value	Sig.
Staffing	0.42	0.50	12.097	0.001
Work teams	0.28	0.36	4.881	0.003
Communication	0.36	0.42	0.924	0.337
Meetings	0.32	0.47	8.977	0.009
Training	0.23	0.36	6.865	0.028
Pay level	0.26	0.27	0.147	0.788
Group-based pay	0.29	0.34	0.713	0.308

Table 18.5   MANOVA analysis for the effects of independent variables on HPWS adoption, comparison of the effects for each subsample.

Effect	Very small firms (up to 25)			Small firms (25 to 100)			Medium firms (100 to 250)		
	Wilks' lambda Value	*F*	Sig.	Wilks' lambda	*F*	Sig.	Wilks' lambda	*F*	Sig.
Intercept	0.343	10.863	0.000	0.343	27.196	0.000	0.363	27.196	0.000
Family firm	0.940	1.153	0.338	0.497	9.913	0.000	0.803	1.009	0.399
Technological intensity	0.819	3.139	0.013	0.916	3.894	0.093	0.819	3.139	0.013
Strategy	0.799	3.578	0.006	0.911	4.215	0.016	0.799	3.578	0.006
Firm's age	0.807	3.405	0.008	0.697	4.253	0.003	0.807	3.480	0.007

Note: Design: intercept + family firm + technological intensity + strategy + firm's age.

Among the control variables, all the dimensions proved also to be significant for the whole sample.

If we look at the univariate analysis of the single components of the HPWS, we observe that over the entire sample the significant differences at $p < 0.01$ and $p < 0.05$ between family and non-family firms are in the use of staffing procedures in personnel selection, in the establishment of work teams, in the formalization of meetings with non-executive employees and in the use of formal training programmes.

The significance of the interaction terms supports the breakdown of the sample into three groups; we observe the multivariate and univariate effect of family firm status in each size group (Table 18.5 and 18.6).

In firms with fewer than 25 employees, as predicted by Hypothesis 2a, there is no significant difference between family and non-family firms in the adoption of HPWS ($p = 0.338$). Technological intensity, innovation-led strategy and age of the firm are all significant discriminants in explaining the adoption of HPWS in very small firms.

Univariate comparison (Table 18.6) shows that the only difference within very small

Table 18.6   *Univariate analysis of variance of the effect of family firm status on the single components of HPWS, comparison of the differences between family and non-family firms in each subsample*

	Very small firms (up to 25)				Small firms (25 to 100)				Medium firms (100 to 250)			
	Family firms	Non-family firms	F	Sig.	Family firms	Non-family firms	F	Sig.	Family firms	Non family firms	F	Sig.
Staffing	0.26	0.40	8.46	0.004	0.43	0.55	18.63	0.000	0.43	0.55	18.63	0.000
Work teams	0.07	0.10	0.01	0.977	0.39	0.48	42.88	0.000	0.39	0.48	42.88	0.000
Communication	0.30	0.33	0.24	0.628	0.38	0.45	11.09	0.001	0.38	0.45	11.09	0.001
Meetings	0.32	0.47	0.28	0.599	0.32	0.47	8.98	0.000	0.32	0.47	8.98	0.000
Training	0.25	0.45	9.08	0.504	0.25	0.38	9.08	0.004	0.25	0.38	9.08	0.004
Pay level	0.37	0.31	0.75	0.572	0.22	0.27	0.75	0.572	0.22	0.27	0.75	0.572
Group-based pay	0.17	0.22	2.09	0.152	0.21	0.31	3.52	0.066	0.21	0.31	3.52	0.066

firms is in the adoption of extensive recruitment and selection practices ($p = 0.00$), which is more frequent among non-family companies.

In the 25 to 100 employees group, as expected according to Hypothesis 2b, significant differences emerge between family and non-family SMEs in the adoption of HPWS (Table 18.5) with family firms less inclined to adopt formal high involvement practices ($p = 0.00$).

Significant differences at $p < 0.01$ emerge for all components except the dimension of the above-average pay level, which does not show significant differences, and group-based pay (See Table 18.6).

In the group of medium-sized enterprises (100 to 250 employees), the gap between family and non-family SMEs narrows again. No significant difference emerges ($p = 0.399$) (Table 18.5). Hypothesis 2c is thus supported. Age, technological intensity and strategy continue to be significant predictors of HPWS adoption.

Univariate comparisons highlight that no significant difference emerge in any of the components (Table 18.6).

DISCUSSION

The results of the empirical analysis provide rather robust support for our hypotheses. On average, family SMEs make less use of HPWS compared to non-family ones; the strength of the results is enhanced since family firm status proves to be a significant discriminant, controlling also for firms' strategy, technological intensity and age.

This may be due both to the preference for informal management tools of family enterprises and to the easier access of family SMEs to value-based coordination, which creates employee commitment and involvement, leveraging the stewardship attitude of workers.

The results are in line with the previous findings on human resource practices in family business compared to non-family enterprises (e.g. De Kok et al., 2006; Kotey and Folker, 2007). Significant differences emerge in particular: (1) in the use of 'professional' recruitment and selection tools, where family firms are probably more likely to rely on the personal perceptions of the entrepreneurial family members and on network-community considerations rather than on strictly technical and impersonal procedures; (2) in the diffusion of work teams, which may involve a significant degree of formal empowerment towards the employees in the self-management of the groups and thus may be in contrast with the propensity towards centralized decision-making (Harris et al., 2004); it may also be possible that formal employee empowerment techniques such as self-managed work teams are perceived as unnecessary in an organizational environment with high degrees of stewardship; (3) in the involvement of the workers in formal meetings to discuss work-related issues; in this case the difference may be explained either by the paternalistic attitude of the family leadership or by the stewardship orientation that suggests other approaches in the discussion of work-related issues; (4) in the extensiveness of formal training programs; the result is in line with the findings by Kotey and Folker (2007), and may be attributed to the greater emphasis that family firms place on the tacit knowledge and training on the job and to the reliance on family members' competences rather than on more codified knowledge and practices. No relevant differences emerge in the variables related to pay level and remuneration schemes.

Our results, however, indicate that family influence on the adoption of HPWS is particularly important in firms with a number of employees ranging from 25 to 100, whereas in very small firms (fewer than 25) and in larger ones (more than 100) the differences are not significant. This seems to suggest that family influence on human resource management practices is more likely to occur (1) when it is appropriate to use different coordination mechanisms other than direct supervision, and (2) when structural constraints are 'loose' enough to allow a choice of the mechanisms by the dominant coalition.

In very small organizations we do not observe differences between family and non-family enterprises because direct supervision and close direct contact with the employees are the most appropriate coordination mechanism for workforce management, and HPWS would be unnecessary given the small size of the organization and the prevalence of a personal management style. In larger organizations (medium-sized firms with 100 to 250 employees) we do not observe any significant difference because organizational size imposes structural constraints on the choices of the dominant coalition, pushing towards the adoption of formal practices. In organizations of intermediate size (between 25 and 100 employees) the previous conditions (1) and (2) are both verified: direct supervision of employees needs to be supplemented by other mechanisms and family influence is free enough from structural constraints to choose more informal mechanisms over professional ones.

CONCLUSIONS, LIMITATIONS AND DEVELOPMENTS

In this research we analyzed the adoption of HPWS by family firms compared to non-family firms, assessing also the role played by organizational size as a source of constraint on family influence over HRM practices.

We provided further evidence to the emergent empirical literature on HPWS in family SMEs, supporting also the view that family firms are less inclined to employ formal HRM practices compared to non-family ones, especially in the fields of recruitment and selection, teamworking, training and formal involvement tools. The results indicate also that the family business impact on the adoption of HPWS is more likely to occur when organizational structure does not impose too many restrictions on the choices of the dominant coalition. Thus, in this research organizational size appears to be an important variable that may reduce the impact of the family component on business decisions. This finding could inspire further studies within the family business field in order to assess the role of structural contingencies in the distinctive family business behavior.

Our study moves from the family business context to provide also a contribution to the classic organization studies literature (Blau, 1970; Child, 1972), shedding additional light on the role of size as a source of constraint on the decisions of the dominant coalition. Results indicate that structural determinism exists to some extent in SMEs over 100 employees.

Of course the research has a number of limitations. In our opinion the most important is the lack of data on performance; we were not able to assess whether and to what extent the adoption of HPWS leads to superior organizational performance in family and non-family firms (as previous studies have suggested, e.g. Tsao et al., 2009). The evaluation of performance levels associated with the adoption of HPWS could help to discover whether the adoption of such practices is merely formal and exclusively imposed by structural (and environmental) requirements or if it is justified by expectations of superior performance. Future research should address this issue, evaluating also to what extent the combination of HPWS and family firm status is unique in terms of employee involvement leading to superior performances.

Another important topic that should be addressed in future studies is the relative importance of the two 'rival' explanations of the distinctive behavior of family firms in the management of human resources. To what extent is the lack of HPWS inspired by a paternalistic logic and to what extent is it due to a stewardship attitude? The question is important because the prevalence of a paternalistic logic may create perceptions of unfair treatment among the non-family employees, with negative consequences in terms of motivation and commitment (Barnett and Kellermanns, 2006) and consequent drawbacks in performance.

Another important issue that should be explored in future studies is the impact on HPWS of various degrees of family influence on the side of the family, for example assessing the impact of generations involved and configuration of family ownership and management.

REFERENCES

Aldrich, H. and Langton, N. (1997), 'Human resource management practices and organizational life cycles', in P.D. Reynolds, W.D. Bygrave, N.M. Carter, P. Davidsson, W.B. Gartner, C.M. Mason and P.P. McDougall (eds), *Frontiers of Entrepreneurship Research*, Wellesley, MA: Babson College Center for Entrepreneurship, pp. 349–57.

Appelbaum, E., Bailey, T., Berg, P. and Kalleberg, A.L. (2000), *Manufacturing Advantage: Why High Performance Work Systems Pay Off*, Ithaca, NY: Cornell University Press.

Argyris, C. (1998), 'Empowerment: the emperor's new clothes', *Harvard Business Review*, **76**(3), 98–105.

Arthur, J.B. (1994), 'Effects of human resource systems on manufacturing performance and turnover', *Academy of Management Journal*, **37**, 670–87.

Astrachan, J. (2010), 'Strategy in family business: towards a multidimensional research agenda', *Journal of Family Business Strategy*, **1**(1), 6–14.

Astrachan, J.H. and Kolenko, T.A. (1994), 'A neglected factor explaining family business success: human resource practices', *Family Business Review*, **7**, 251–62.

Astrachan, J.H., Klien, S.B. and Smyrnios, K.X. (2002), 'The F-PEC scale of family influence: a proposal for solving the family business definition problem', *Family Business Review*, **15**(1), 45–58.

Bae, J. and Lawler, J. (2000), 'Organizational and HRM strategies in Korea: impact on firm performance in an emerging economy', *Academy of Management Journal*, **43**, 502–17.

Baker, D.D. and Cullen, J.B. (1993), 'Administrative reorganization and configurational context: the contingent effects of age, size, and change in size', *Academy of Management Journal*, **36**(6), 1251–77.

Barnett, T. and Kellermanns, F.W. (2006), 'Are we family and are we treated as family? Nonfamily employees' perception of justice in the family firm', *Entrepreneurship Theory and Practice*, **30**(6), 837–54.

Becker, B.E. and Gerhart, B. (1996), 'The impact of human resource management on organizational performance: progress and prospects', *Academy of Management Journal*, **39**, 779–801.

Becker, B.E. and Huselid, M.A. (1998), 'High performance work systems and firm performance: a synthesis of research and management implications', in G.R. Ferris (ed.), *Research in Personnel and Human Resources*, Stamford, CT: JAI Press, pp. 53–101.

Blau, P.M. (1970), 'A formal theory of differentiation in organizations', *American Sociological Review*, **35**: 201–18.

Bourgeois, J. (1984), 'Strategic management and determinism', *Academy of Management Review*, **9**(4), 586–96.

Carlson S., Upton, N. and Seaman, S. (2006), 'The impact of human resource practices and compensation design on performance: an analysis of family-owned SMEs', *Journal of Small Business Management*, **44**, 531–43.

Carney, M. (1998), 'A management capacity constraint? Barriers to the development of the Chinese family business', *Asia-Pacific Journal of Management*, **15**, 1–25.

Carney, M. (2005), 'Corporate governance and competitive advantage in family-controlled firms', *Entrepreneurship Theory and Practice*, **29**, 249–66.

Child, J. (1972), 'Organizational structure, environment and performance: the role of strategic choice', *Sociology*, **6**, 1–22.

Cromie, S., Stephenson, B. and Monteith, D. (1995), 'The management of family firms: an empirical investigation', *International Small Business Journal*, **13**(4), 11–34.

De Kok, J.M.P. and den Hartog, D. (2006), 'High performance work systems, performance and innovativeness in small firms', *SCALES paper, EIM Business and Policy Research Reports*.

De Kok, J.M.P., Uhlaner, L.M. and Thurik, A.R. (2006), 'Professional HRM practices in family owned-managed enterprises', *Journal of Small Business Management*, **44**(3), 441–60.

Delaney, J.T. and Huselid, M.A. (1996), 'The impact of human resource management practices on perceptions of organizational performance', *Academy of Management Journal*, **39**, 949–69.

Delery, J. and Doty, D. (1996), 'Modes of theorizing in strategic human resource management: tests of universalistic, contingency, and configurational performance predictions', *Academy of Management Journal*, **39**, 802–35.

Dyer, W.G. Jr (1986), *Cultural Change in Family Firms: Anticipating and Managing Business and Family Transactions*, San Francisco, CA: Jossey-Bass.

Gifford, S. (1992), 'Allocation of entrepreneurial attention', *Journal of Economic Behavior and Organization*, **19**, 265–84.

Guthrie, J.P. (2001), 'High-involvement work practices, turnover, and productivity: evidence from New Zealand', *Academy of Management Journal*, **44**, 180–90.

Hall, Richard H., Haas, J. Eugene and Johnson, Norman J. (1967), 'Organizational size, complexity and formalization', *American Sociological Review*, **32**, 903–12.

Harney, B. and Dundon, T. (2006), 'Capturing complexity: developing an integrated approach to analyzing HRM in SMEs', *Human Resource Management Journal*, **16**(1), 48–73.

Harris, R.I.D., Reid, R.S. and McAdam, R. (2004), 'Employee involvement in family and non-family-owned businesses in Great Britain', *International Journal of Entrepreneurial Behaviour and Research*, **10**(1/2), 49–58.

Huselid, M.A. (1995), 'The impact of human resource management practices on turnover, productivity, and corporate financial performance', *Academy of Management Journal*, **38**, 635–72.

Huselid, M. and Becker, B. (1996), 'Methodological issues in cross-sectional and panel estimates of the human resource–firm performance link', *Industrial Relations*, **35**, 400–22.

Huselid, M., Jackson, S. and Schuler, R. (1997), 'Technical and strategic human resource management effectiveness as determinants of firm performance', *Academy of Management Journal*, **40**, 171–88.

Ichniowski, C., Shaw, C. and Prennushi, G. (1997), 'The effects of human resource management practices on productivity: a study of steel finishing lines', *American Economic Review*, **87**(3), 291–313.

Kaldor, N. (1934), 'The equilibrium of the firm', *Economic Journal*, **44**, 60–76.

Kidwell, R.E. and Fish, A. (2007), 'High-performance human resource practices in Australian family businesses: preliminary evidence from the wine industry', *International Entrepreneurship and Management Journal*, **3**(1), 1–14.

Kirkman, B.L. and Rosen, B. (1999), 'Beyond self-management: antecedents and consequences of team empowerment', *Academy of Management Journal*, **42**, 58–74.

Kirkpatrick, D.I. (1998), *Evaluating Training Programs: The Four Levels*, 2nd edn, San Francisco, CA: Berrett-Koehler.

Kotey, B. and Folker, C. (2007), 'Employee training in SMEs: effect of size and firm type – family and non-family', *Journal of Small Business Management*, **45**(2), 214–38.

Lansberg, I. (1983), 'Managing human resources in family firms: problem of institutional overlap', *Organizational Dynamics*, **12**(1), 39–46.

Lawler, E. (1992), 'The ultimate advantage: creating the high-involvement organization', San Francisco, CA: Jossey-Bass.

Lepak, D.P., Takeuchi, R. and Snell, S.A. (2003), 'Employment flexibility and firm performance: examining the interaction effects of employment mode, environmental dynamism and technological intensity', *Journal of Management*, **29**, 681–703.

Locke, E.A., Alavi, M. and Wagner, J. (1997), 'Participation in decision making: an information exchange perspective', in G. Ferris (ed.), *Research in Personnel and Human Resources Management*, Vol. 15, Greenwich, CT: JAI Press, pp. 293–331.

Lubatkin, M.H., Schulze, W.S., Ling, Y. and Dino, R.N. (2005), 'The effects of parental altruism on the governance of family-managed firms', *Journal of Organizational Behavior*, **26**(3), 313–30.

MacDuffie, J.P. (1995), 'Human resource bundles and manufacturing performance: organizational logic and flexible production systems in the world auto industry', *Industrial and Labor Relations Review*, **48**, 197–221.

Miller, D., Le Breton-Miller, I. and Scholnick, B. (2008), 'Stewardship versus stagnation: an empirical comparison of small family vs non-family businesses', *Journal of Management Studies*, **41**(1), 51–78.

Miller, D., Lee, J., Chang, S. and Le Breton-Miller, I. (2009), 'Filling the institutional void: the social behavior and performance of family vs. non-family technology firms in emerging markets', *Journal of International Business Studies*, **40**, 802–17.

Moreno, A.M. and Casillas, J.C. (2008), 'Entrepreneurial orientation and growth of SMEs: a causal model', *Entrepreneurship Theory and Practice*, **32**(3), 507–28.

Paauwe, J. (2009), 'HRM and performance: achievements, methodological issues and prospects', *Journal of Management Studies*, **46**(1), 129–42.

Patel, P.C. and Cardon, M.S. (2010), 'Adopting HRM practices and their effectiveness in small firms facing product market competition', *Human Resource Management*, **49**(2), 265–90.

Pearson, A.W. and Marler, L.E. (2010), 'A leadership perspective of reciprocal stewardship in family firms', *Entrepreneurship Theory and Practice*, **34**(6), 1117–24.

Pfeffer, J. (1998), *The Human Equation*, Cambridge, MA: Harvard Business School Press.

Ployhart, R.E. (2004), 'Organizational staffing: a multilevel review, synthesis, and model', *Research in Personnel and Human Resources Management*, **23**, 121–76.

Pondy, Louis R. (1969), 'Effects of size, complexity, and ownership on administrative intensity', *Administrative Science Quarterly*, **14**, 47–60.

Pugh, D.S., Hickson, D.J., Hinings, C.R. and Turner, C. (1968), 'The context of organizational structures', *Administrative Science Quarterly*, **14**, 91–114.

Reid, R.S. and Adams, J.S. (2001), 'Human resource management – a survey of practices within family and non-family firms', *Journal of European Industrial Training*, **25**(6), 310–20.

Reid, R., Morrow, T., Kelly, B. and McCartan, P. (2002), 'People management in SMEs: an analysis of human resource strategies in family and non-family business, *Journal of Small Business and Enterprise Development*, **9**, 245–59.

Schneper, W.D., Celo, S. and Jain, N.K. (2008), 'Agents, altruism, and corporate governance: the impact of family ownership on non-executive compensation and training', *Proceedings of ASBBS*, **15**(1), 1340–52.

Schuler, R.S. and Jackson, S.E. (1987), 'Linking competitive strategies with human resource management practices', *Academy of Management Executive*, **1**(3), 209–13.

Simon, H.E. (1976), *Administrative Behavior*, New York: The Free Press.

Sirmon, D.G. and Hitt, M.A. (2003), 'Managing resources: linking unique resources, management and wealth creation in family firms', *Entrepreneurship Theory and Practice*, **27**(4), 339–58.

Smidts, A., Pruyn, A.T.H. and van Riel, C.B.M. (2001), 'The impact of employee communication and perceived external prestige on organizational identification', *Academy of Management Journal*, **44**(5), 1051–62.

Tsao, C.W., Shyh, J.C. and Hyde, W. (2009), 'Funding family ownership and firm performance. The role of high performance work systems', *Family Business Review*, **22**(4), 319–32.

Vallejo, M.C. (2009), 'The effects of commitment of non-family employees of family firms from the perspective of stewardship theory', *Journal of Business Ethics*, **87**, 379–90.

Walton, R. (1985), 'From control to commitment in the workplace', *Harvard Business Review*, **63**(2), 76–84.

Way, Sean A. (2002), 'High performance work systems and intermediate indicators of firm performance within the US small business sector', *Journal of Management*, **28**, 765–85.

Westhead, P. and Cowling, M. (1999), 'Family firm research: the need for a methodological rethink', *Entrepreneurship Theory and Practice*, **23**(1), 31–56.

Westhead, P. and Storey, D.J. (1997), 'Training provision and the development of small and medium-sized enterprises', *DfEE Publications Research Report* No. 26.

Westhead, P. and Storey, D.J. (1999), 'Training provision and the development of small and medium-sized enterprise: a critical review', *Scottish Journal of Adult and Continuing Education*, **5**(1), 35–41.

Wood, S. and De Menezes, L. (1998), 'High commitment management in the UK: evidence from the workplace industrial relations survey, and employers' manpower and skills practices survey', *Human Relations*, **51**(4), 485–515.

Wood, S.J. and Wall, T.D. (2002), 'Human resource management and business performance', in P.B. Warr (ed.), *The Psychology of Work*, Harmonsworth: Penguin, pp. 351–74.

Wolff, J.A. and Pett, T.L. (2000), 'Internationalization of small firms: an examination of export competitive patterns, firm size and export performance', *Journal of Small Business Management*, **38**(2), 34–47.

Zahra, S.A., Hayton, J.C., Neubaum, D.O., Dibrell, C. and Craig, J. (2008), 'Culture of family commitment and strategic flexibility: the moderating effect of stewardship', *Entrepreneurship Theory and Practice*, **32**(6), 1035–54.

19 Measuring and comparing leadership styles of male and female chief executive officers in businesses with a varying family intensity
Diane Arijs

INTRODUCTION

The question whether women and men differ in leadership styles has been largely discussed in academic as well as popular literature (Eagly and Carli, 2007). However, an overview of the past 30 years of research on gender and leadership still yielded mixed findings on the existence of gender differences in leadership behaviour (Barbuto et al., 2007). These inconsistent findings persist even when focusing only on the new paradigm leadership styles, the so-called 'full-range leadership theory' (FRLT).

The FRLT is academically acknowledged to adequately assess leadership behaviour because it assesses a 'full range' of leadership styles (Avolio and Bass, 2004). The FRLT is mostly measured with the extensively psychometrically tested measure 'the Multifactor Leadership Questionnaire', covering effective transformational leadership, transactional leadership and ineffective *laissez-faire* leadership. Roughly sketched, a transformational leader intrinsically motivates co-workers to contribute to the realization of the organization's goals whereas a transactional leader falls back on trade-offs to make sure that the targets are met. A *laissez-faire* leader fails to assume leadership responsibility.

Thus far the family intensity of the business has never been taken into consideration as an explanatory variable of the FRLT, nor its interaction effect with gender (Vallejo, 2009). Within family business literature, we do find indications that family businesses are more considerate in the relationship with and well-being of co-workers than non-family businesses thanks to their ingrained family values and vision (Lievens and Lambrecht, 2007). This brings us to the question what a family business is and, more precisely, whether all family businesses integrate the family's values and vision in the business. Chrisman et al. (2003) in their theoretical definition make a distinction between family businesses in components-of-involvement terms and essence family businesses. Components family businesses relate to businesses where family members have a controlling influence on the business mostly in terms of ownership and leadership, or sometimes governance. Essence family businesses behave as genuine family businesses as the involved family shapes and pursues a vision of the business that is sustainable across generations. That is why our study will make a distinction between family businesses in components-of-involvement and in essence terms. With regard to gender in family businesses, women are claimed to be relation-oriented and caretakers of values and co-workers, whereas men are traditionally associated with the rational business side (Haberman and Danes, 2007; Lyman, 1988). Hence this study aims to find out whether the inconsistency in gender differences in leadership styles, still tormenting general leadership theory, can be further clarified by explicitly taking into account the family intensity of the business when comparing the full range leadership styles of male and female chief executive officers (CEOs).

For that purpose our study combined a qualitative and a quantitative approach. First, the qualitative study, consisting of 16 in-depth interviews with various family business leaders, enabled us to study the development of a person's leadership style in a family business context. These insights were a valuable input to adequately measure the leadership styles of male and female CEOs in family and non-family businesses on a large-scale basis. In total, 396 CEOs of Belgian businesses with an upper limit of 49 employees were interviewed by phone.

This study enables us to contribute extended insights into the FRLT by applying it to the family business context. Our results revealed that the family intensity of the business can no longer be omitted as an explanatory variable of the FRLT, and that gender differences can be further clarified by controlling for the family intensity of the business. Our study demystified the person-oriented leadership attributed to family business leaders and advises family business leaders and practitioners to get acquainted with the benefits of a transformational leadership style. Furthermore, ignorance about the leadership potential of female relatives in family businesses (Jimenez, 2009) is addressed.

The chapter will first clarify the FRLT, why it is used and what the most important explanatory variables are. Next, the research design is presented with the qualitative and the quantitative approach. The third part discusses the measures used for family intensity of the business and for the full range leadership styles. The fourth part addresses the statistical procedures and gives the detailed results of the multiple indicators multiple causes (MIMIC) models. Finally, the results are discussed in a larger context with recognition of the limitations of this study and giving suggestions for future research. To conclude, implications for practice and education are formulated.

LITERATURE REVIEW

The Full-Range Leadership Theory (FRLT)

The theoretical framework of the 'new paradigm' leadership model consists of a full range of leadership behaviour (Alimo-Metcalfe and Alban-Metcalfe, 2005). The basic idea is that to assess leadership styles adequately, it is necessary to include a 'full range' of leadership styles, ranging from charismatic and inspirational to avoidant, *laissez-faire* leadership styles (Avolio and Bass, 2004). The three main leadership styles that can be distinguished are transformational leadership, transactional leadership and *laissez-faire* leadership.

A transformational leader motivates and intellectually stimulates co-workers so that they are intrinsically motivated to develop their own capabilities, not in order to maximize their own self-interest but to contribute to the realization of the organization's vision and goals. Hence the extra efforts that co-workers make are not because of promised incentives or feared reprimands, but because they want to contribute to the realization of the organization's vision as articulated by the respected and trustworthy leader (Avolio and Bass, 2004; Eagly et al., 2003; Yukl, 2002).

Second, transactional leaders think of their relationships with co-workers in terms of deals or reward trade-offs (Burke and Collins, 2001; Eagly et al., 2003). Transactional leadership covers contingent reward leadership and management-by-exception leadership. A leader displaying contingent reward leadership communicates objectives and motivates co-workers by promising rewards for achieving these goals. Leaders with a management-by-exception leadership style tend to exercise power grounded on their position in the organization. They actively (active management-by-exception) or passively (passive management-by-exception) monitor effort and only intervene to identify and penalize subpar efforts or mistakes.

Third, a *laissez-faire* style is characterized by a total lack of taking responsibility. This type of 'leaders' fails to intervene or to take decisions.

The advantage of using the full range leadership model is the consistent cross-cultural evidence on the effectiveness of each leadership style. Many studies from the late 1980s up to now provide evidence for the so-called 'augmentation effect' of transformational leadership (Avolio and Bass, 2004; Goodwin et al., 2001; Heinitz et al., 2005; Hinkin and Schriesheim, 2008; Lowe et al., 1996; Rowold and Heinitz, 2007). In general, these results demonstrate that transactional leadership provides a basis for effective leadership, but more positive and lasting positive outcomes are possible when the leader augments this transactional leadership with transformational leadership. Passive management-by-exception and *laissez-faire* leadership have strong negative significant relationships with leadership effectiveness and satisfaction with the leader (Avolio and Bass, 2004; Hinkin and Schriesheim, 2008).

A second advantage of using the FRLT is the existence of the Multifactor Leadership Questionnaire (MLQ), which is the most widely used measure for assessing full range leadership styles (Avolio and Bass, 2004). Since its development in 1985 by Bass, the MLQ has been subjected to considerable psychometric scrutiny (see, e.g., Antonakis et al., 2003; Hinkin and Schriesheim, 2008).

Main Effect of Gender on FRLT

Some researchers have detected small but significant gender differences, with female leaders scoring higher on transformational leadership (especially individualized consideration) and on the contingent reward dimension, and significantly lower on the passive-avoidant leadership styles than males (Antonakis et al., 2003; Burke and Collins, 2001; Eagly et al., 2003). Komives (1991) found no significant differences between female and male leaders' self-ratings of transformational leadership, except for intellectual stimulation, which was significantly more exhibited by male leaders. Other studies point to the lack of any significant gender differences in the use of full range leadership behaviour (Barbuto et al., 2007; van Engen et al., 2001). These diverging results on the existence of gender differences persist even in studies using the same measure, the Multifactor Leadership Questionnaire (Antonakis et al., 2003; Barbuto et al., 2007; Eagly et al., 2003).

Main Effect of Family Intensity of the Business on FRLT

Vallejo (2009), who only measured transformational leadership by means of the Global Transformational Leadership Scale, found empirical evidence for family business leaders to be more transformational than non-family business leaders. Except for the recent study of Vallejo (2009), there is no empirical evidence on the influence of family intensity of the business on the adoption of full range leadership behaviour. In fact, we can only fall back on suggestions of researchers and practitioners on how family and non-family businesses might differ in their behaviour towards co-workers.

On the one hand, family businesses may exhibit more of the transformational aspects 'being considerate for individual co-workers' and 'having and communicating a compelling vision as respected leader' as they are said to be more considerate of the relationship with and well-being of employees than non-family businesses thanks to their ingrained family values and long-term vision (Aronoff and Ward, 1995; Donckels and Fröhlich, 1991; Lievens and Lambrecht, 2007). However, we would like to draw attention to the fact that a shared and pursued vision by the owning family and ingrained family values in the business system are only applicable to family businesses in *essence* terms and not to family businesses in *components-of-involvement* terms (Chrisman et al., 2003). Consequently, the question presents itself whether businesses that are only family businesses in components-of-involvement terms would also score better on being considerate of individual co-workers and on having and communicating an enthusiastic vision by a respected leader.

On the other hand, Sorenson (2000) claims an autocratic leadership style to be most prevalent in family businesses, as she associates this leadership style with the most prevalent paternalistic culture in family businesses. This might point to family businesses scoring lower on transformational behaviour, in the sense of less intellectual stimulation and a bigger focus on mistakes, than non-family businesses.

Interaction Effect of Gender and Family Intensity of the Business on FRLT

Combining the previous two main effects brings us to our leading question: can family intensity of the business explain any gender differences in leadership styles? Unfortunately, there is no large-scale empirical evidence on the comparison of male and female familial CEOs on adopting the full range leadership behaviour in family businesses (Jimenez, 2009).

Qualitative research and practitioners agree on female relatives being more relation-oriented by taking into account facts and feelings before taking decisions in their family's business (Frishkoff and Brown, 1993; Galiano and Vinturella, 1995; Haberman and Danes, 2007). Women are labelled 'keepers of the family values', 'caretakers of co-workers' or 'chief emotional officers' (Aronoff, 1998; Lyman, 1988; Poza and Messer, 2001).

In addition, there is only one empirical study partly addressing the interaction effect of gender of the leader and family link of the leader with the owning family of the business on a person's 'leadership' style. Cromie and O'Sullivan (1999) concluded on the basis of the self-image of 80 familial[1] and 62 non-familial[2] female managers in the UK that the management profile of female relatives managing the family firm turned out to be more feminine (e.g. organizer, honest communicator, people-person and team worker) than that of female managers in general. The latter have a management profile more in line with the male managerial profile (e.g. independence, task orientation and competitiveness). According to Cromie and O'Sullivan (1999), the different profiles reflect the different goals both groups of female managers face. Female relatives pursue family objectives and business goals, whereas non-familial female managers strive to succeed in a business environment directed by economic rules. Cromie and O'Sullivan's study does not provide evidence on whether male leaders are influenced by leading their family's business or a non-family business. It could be that male leaders are equally influenced by family values and goals and are more people oriented in their family's business than elsewhere. It might equally make sense that the traditional family role for male relatives to be strong and rational (Hollander and Bukowitz, 1990) makes them as masculine leaders in family as in non-family businesses.

Other Explanatory Variables of the FRLT

In order to test reliably the main and interaction effect of gender and family intensity of the business, we have to control for other relevant determinants of the FRLT that have been detected in previous research: size of the business (Mühlebach, 2005), educational level of workforce (Maccoby, 2007), educational level of the leader (Barbuto et al., 2007), gender ratio of the sector (Gardiner and Tiggemann, 1999; van Engen et al., 2001), seniority (Gardiner and Tiggemann, 1999) and hierarchical level of the leader (Rowold and Heinitz, 2007).

Based on this literature overview we formulate the following propositions we aim to test:

Proposition 1 After controlling for other relevant explanatory variables of the FRLT, gender *might* have a significant effect.

Proposition 2 After controlling for other relevant explanatory variables of the FRLT, family intensity of the business split up according to the components-of-involvement and essence approach will have a different but significant effect.

Proposition 3 Female and male leaders will significantly differ in their full range leadership styles depending on the family intensity of the business.

RESEARCH DESIGN

Our research design combines a qualitative study and a large-scale quantitative study. The qualitative part consists of 16 in-depth interviews with 7 female and 6 male family business leaders, 1 female former family business leader, 1 former non-family interim manager and 1 employee each from 5 heterogeneous family businesses. By including different perspectives for each case, we enhanced the credibility of our results by means of the interpretive case study research approach as put forward by Hall et al. (2005). The selected family businesses varied in terms of number of workforce (4 to 4687 full-time employees), sector, ownership and leadership structure (controlling owner, sibling partnership, cousin consortium), highest generation involved in the business (second to fourth), stage in succession process (in progress to fully finished), years in leadership of the family business (from 2 to 46 years) and years in family business before in lead (ranging from directly in lead to waiting for 27 years). This heterogeneity allowed us to study the impact of these context effects and improved the transferability of the qualitative results (Hall et al., 2005; Seale, 1999). These case studies were necessary to gain an in-depth insight into how a person's leadership style evolves over time and especially in a family business context due to inter- and intragenerational factors.[3] The case study approach provided us with very valuable insights into how to measure a person's leadership on a large-scale basis. For example, our case studies show that it makes sense to question a leader on his/her most dominant leadership style, that the extent of consultation with co-workers is the most situational aspect of a person's leadership style and that some items of our large-scale leadership measure, the MLQ, needed to be reconsidered (see below).

Second, in order to be able to compare the leadership styles of female and male leaders on a large-scale basis, we carried out a phone survey among 396 CEOs of Belgian businesses. Our target and realized sample was stratified with equal strata for gender of CEO, business size (3 to 9 employees and 10 to 49 employees) and sector (one-third in industry, in services and in trading). The business size was limited to 49 employees to control for the influence of the number and level of employees to whom the leader gives leadership. In addition, with these business size classes, we cover the large majority of Belgian and European businesses.[4] The public sector was excluded because previous research revealed that public or private sector could affect the construct validity of the MLQ (Antonakis et al., 2003). We opted for a phone survey because of the higher response rate (Saunders et al., 2008) and because we had a complex and different routing of questions depending on the family intensity of the business. The target and realized sample size of about 400 was necessary to be able to do confirmatory factor analysis[5] (see below).

MEASURES

Family Intensity of the Business: Five Gradations

The operationalization of the concept 'family business' should allow us to distinguish several gradations of family businesses. To be precise, we want to be able to distinguish three groups of family businesses: controlling owners, family businesses in components-of-involvement terms; and family businesses in essence terms. The reason is that these three groups of family businesses might differ in terms of leadership styles, with the first group, 'controlling owner', being more autocratic (Sorenson, 2000), and the third group, 'essence family business', being more value and people oriented compared to the second group, 'components family business'. For that purpose, our family business definition will integrate the components and essence approach as put forward by Chrisman et al. (2005) and the most important and tangible items of the F-PEC scale.[6]

Regarding the components of involvement, we questioned the percentage of ownership in family hands, the number of family members among all highest-level leaders, the number of family members involved as members of the board of directors or board of counsellors, the number of family members involved as members of the family council or involved as employees. These questions are partly in line with the power scale of F-PEC (our questions on percentage of ownership and leadership in family hands) and partly with the experience subscale of F-PEC (our questions on number of actively involved relatives). We consider a business as a family-owned and -managed business in components terms when ownership and top leadership of the business is shared among at least two family members, in such a way that the family has the largest stock or ownership representation. A controlling owner is defined as follows in components terms: one person who owns majority of the business and is involved in the daily leadership, with no other relatives involved in ownership and in top leadership.

In line with Klein et al. (2005), we did not question the self-perception of being a family business because of the possible confounding results. We suggest being careful with questioning the self-perception of being a family business as the concept 'family business' might be misunderstood by the respondent in the sense of a business where leaders and employees have an informal and companionable contact. It is more consistent to assess whether a business behaves as a family business by means of assessing the essence of the family business.

We will assess the essence of a family business by explicitly questioning to what extent (on a five-point Likert scale with 1: not at all and 5: very strongly) the family has a tangible influence on the business vision and direction. We formulated the following questions to capture the essence of businesses that yet fulfill the components-of-involvement criteria:

- To what extent are the values and the vision of involved family members clearly tangible in the business?
- To what extent do involved family members have an influence on the strategic direction of the business?
- To what extent do involved family members strive to keep the business under family control?

If family businesses fulfilling the components-of-involvement criteria and if controlling owners scored at least 4 on these three essence criteria, they were classified as essence family business respectively essence controlling owner.[7]

In sum, we could distinguish five categories of businesses combining the components-of-involvement and the essence approach:

- family intense/essence family-owned and -managed businesses: $n = 75$;
- family-owned and -managed businesses (only in components terms): $n = 137$;
- family intense/essence controlling owners: $n = 9$;[8]
- controlling owners (only in components terms): $n = 77$;
- non-family businesses: $n = 98$.

Leadership Styles and Effectiveness

Our leadership measure to assess the full range leadership styles was based on the widely used MLQ 5X (Avolio and Bass, 2004), but fine-tuned to (family) business reality (based on our case studies) and to recent empirical findings on the content and measurement validity of the MLQ 5X (e.g. Hinkin and Schriesheim, 2008; Rowold and Heinitz, 2007). Appendix Table 19A.1 gives a detailed overview of which original MLQ items are preserved (indicated by 'MLQ_number'), which changed (indicated by 'MLQ_number'), which deleted and which own items are added (indicated by 'I_number'). First, our case studies made omitted aspects of leadership in the MLQ visible, such as taking into account the feelings of co-workers before acting (I_16), giving personal compliments on good work (I_15) and creating a culture of treating mistakes as chances for improvement (I_13) (Arijs, 2009). The first two aspects (own items I_15 and I_16) are also put forward by Rafferty and Griffin (2004) as key dimensions of the effective transformational leadership scale. In addition, as suggested by Hinkin and Schriesheim (2008) interchangeable (e.g. item MLQ_22) or unclear items (e.g. MLQ_17, MLQ_20 and MLQ_33), especially on the passive-avoidant scale, were removed to shorten the questionnaire and to ensure content validity respectively. Finally, the results of pilot tests of the questionnaire requested adaptations especially in an attempt to reduce the complexity of the wording of certain items. For example, the pilot tests and the case studies revealed that the notion of 'power' had a strong negative and unrealistic connotation, especially among female leaders. To have a gender-neutral measure, we reformulated power in the neutral aspect of 'influence'. Furthermore, this 'influence' is linked with self-confidence of the leader and trust in the leader by co-workers, which is less heroic than instilling pride in co-workers (motivation of deletion of MLQ_10 and MLQ_18) (Waldman et al., 2006). The heroic connotation of charismatic leadership is dropped because it is likely to be pernicious for an organization over time (Yukl, 1999) and we wanted to have a clear link of each leadership style with effectiveness. The result of this critical screening of the MLQ 5X consisting of 36 items measuring the full range of leadership styles was a transformation into 28 items. To ensure reliable results, we changed the word 'others' into 'co-workers' in all items because the way clients or peers are treated might be very different from co-workers (employees). In line with the best practices for applying the MLQ 5X Leader Form (Avolio and Bass, 2004), respondent-leaders had to answer to what extent they applied each leadership item on a five-point scale, with 1 = never, 2 = seldom, 3 = sometimes, 4 = often and 5 = almost always. Earlier empirical findings claim a five- to seven-point scale with verbal labels to yield the highest data quality in terms of reliability and validity (Krosnick and Fabrigar, 1997).

To conclude, our adapted MLQ leadership measure consisted of eight leadership factors. Unlike the traditional nine-factor MLQ 5X, we meet recent research suggestions to combine idealized influence behaviour and inspirational motivation into one factor, idealized influence behaviour-inspirational motivation (Avolio and Bass, 2004) and to integrate passive management-by-exception and *laissez-faire* into one factor, passive-avoidant leadership (Heinitz et al., 2005; Hinkin and Schriesheim, 2008). In addition, in line with recent research (Goodwin et al., 2001; Rafferty and Griffin, 2004), we split up the factor 'contingent reward' into a transformational component, 'personal recognition' (giving personal compliments for and acknowledge achievement of specified goals), and a transactional component, 'exchange negotiation' (making clear what co-workers can expect in exchange for the realization of clearly defined goals).

For each of our leadership factors, we can fall back on previous research to gain an indication of its effectiveness (predictive validity). For the first four factors (idealized influence attributed, idealized influence behavior-inspirational motivation, intellectual stimulation and individualized consideration) we can rely on Rowold and Heinitz (2007), who confirmed the positive outcomes of these factors in terms of motivated co-workers and in terms of profit. For our fifth transformational scale, 'personal recognition', we can use the findings of Rafferty and Griffin (2004) and of Hinkin and Schriesheim (2008), both indicating a positive effect of this factor on satisfaction and effectiveness. 'Exchange negotiation' is positively related to satisfaction (Hinkin and Schriesheim, 2008) but unrelated to Goodwin et al.'s (2001) organizational citizenship behaviour[9] and performance.[10] Active management-by-exception is negatively related to the three MLQ outcome measures, although this correlation is of a small magnitude (Avolio and Bass, 2004). Passive management-by-exception and *laissez-faire* combined in the passive-avoidant leadership factor both have strong negative relationships with effectiveness and satisfaction (Avolio and Bass, 2004; Hinkin and Schriesheim, 2008). Given these relationships between our leadership styles and a leader's effectiveness, we will not explicitly link the leadership outcomes with financial outcomes. Furthermore, family businesses themselves do not always define their ultimate goal and success in traditional financial terms (Chrisman et al., 2003; Nordqvist, 2005).

STATISTICAL PROCEDURES AND RESULTS

Our leadership measure, comprising 28 leadership items and 8 first-order factors, had a satisfactory empirical fit (in terms of upper limit 90 per cent confidence interval (c.i.) RMSEA < 0.06, SRMR < 0.06, CFI and NNFI > 0.95). However, item MLQ_6' has a very low reliability of only 0.036, which is much lower than the 0.25 cut-off value (Sharma, 1996). A model in which the loading of MLQ_6' was fixed to zero yielded a significant worse fit (ΔSatorra-Bentler scaled chi^2 = 7.801, Δdf = 1, p < 0.01). Nonetheless, if we take a close look at the wording of item MLQ_6', we see that this item concerns the personal values of the leader he/she has to talk about as opposed to the collectivist tone of the other items. Given the possible individualistic or heroic connotation of item MLQ_6', it makes sense to remove item MLQ_6' from the factor idealized influence behaviour-inspirational motivation to ensure a positive link of this factor with leadership effectiveness. Another argument in favour of removing item MLQ_6' is that it was the only item for which willing respondents and respondents likely close to the refusers' profile differed significantly. In addition, after controlling for gender, this nonresponse bias turned out to be significant only for male leaders. Hence we decided to remove MLQ_6'. The internal consistency of our 8 leadership factors with Cronbach's alpha values ranging between 0.52 and 0.75 is comparable to the original MLQ 5X factors (between 0.61 and 0.78) (Avolio and Bass, 2004). Later a multigroup confirmatory factor analysis (CFA) among 188 female and 208 male leaders revealed that our measure was in the strictest sense metrical invariant (Wicherts and Dolan, 2004) across female and male leaders.

We note that a multi-sample CFA for different gradations of family intensity of the business does not work out because of too few observations per group. MIMIC models serve as an alternative technique to test for the main effect of family intensity of the business on a person's leadership behaviour. An advantage of using a MIMIC model is that we can meanwhile control for gender of the leader and for any other relevant determinants of a person's leadership style. In previous research (e.g. Antonakis et al., 2003; Barbuto et al., 2007) MANOVA was used to test for the effect of covariates on the full-range leadership behaviour with the latter being measured by its latent factor scores. As the latent factor scores are estimations (indicators) of the real latent factor values, there is still some measurement error involved (Bollen, 1989). To avoid the latter and to control for the measurement error induced by using the 28 indicators instead of the 8 first-order factors, it is better to use MIMIC models that simultaneously assess the measurement part and the structural part of a model.

Testing the Main Effect of Gender and Family Intensity of the Business

To capture the influence of the different gradations in family intensity of the business on the FRLT, our first MIMIC model includes three dummies: one for controlling owner; one for components family business; and one for essence family business. Hence a non-family business leader is the reference category in our first MIMIC model in which we also control for gender of the leader (female = reference category). MIMIC 1 has an appropriate fit as the standardized root mean square residual (SRMR) is below 0.10 and the upper 90 per cent c.i. limit of RMSEA is below 0.08. CFI and NNFI also point to an appropriate fit. Appendix Table 19A.2, with the structural effects of MIMIC 1, reveals that controlling owners and components family businesses behave quite similarly and are significantly less transformational compared to leaders in non-family businesses. Controlling owners score significantly worse on the transformational factors idealized influence behaviour-inspirational motivation ($p < 0.001$), individualized consideration ($p < 0.01$), intellectual stimulation ($p < 0.10$) and exchange negotiation ($p < 0.001$) than non-family business. Familial leaders in family-owned and -managed businesses in components terms are significantly (p at least < 0.01) worse performing for all of these trans-formational scales too, and in addition for personal recognition. Furthermore, the difference between the essence and components family businesses is illuminating. Familial leaders in family-intense family-owned and -managed businesses (in essence terms) only score significantly ($p < 0.01$) lower on intellectual stimulation and exchange negotiation than non-family business leaders. The comparison of male and female leaders yields only one significant difference ($p < 0.10$), with male leaders scoring higher on ideal-ized influence attributed, thus being more respected and having more influence and self-confidence than female leaders. Inspection of the significant standardized structural regression coefficients highlights that the effect of family intensity in components terms is of a much greater magnitude (between 0.20 and 0.26 in absolute terms) than that of gender.

Testing the Interaction Effect of Gender and Family Intensity of the Business

In order to investigate whether male and female leaders behave differently toward co-workers in function of the family character and intensity of the business, we have to include several interaction effects in subsequent MIMIC models which all had an appropriate to good empirical fit.

Comparison of male and female leaders in components family businesses versus non-family businesses

First, we compare leaders in family businesses (meeting the components[11] definition) versus non-family businesses. We can distinguish four groups (dummies): male leader in family business; male leader in non-family business; female leader in family business; and female leader in non-family business. A first MIMIC model treats the first group (male leader in components family business) as reference category by including the three remaining dummies (interaction effects) as covariates. This finds that male leaders exhibit significantly more idealized influence behaviour-inspirational motivation ($p < 0.05$), more intellectual stimulation ($p < 0.05$), more individualized consideration ($p < 0.05$), more exchange negotiation ($p < 0.001$) and significantly less active management-by-exception ($p < 0.10$) and passive-avoidant leadership ($p < 0.05$) in a non-family business than in their own family's business. A second MIMIC model treats female leaders in components family businesses as reference category, which allows the comparison of female leaders in components family businesses and in non-family businesses. Female leaders score significantly higher on idealized influence behaviour-inspirational motivation ($p < 0.001$), intellectual stimulation ($p < 0.01$), exchange negotiation ($p < 0.05$) and active management-by-exception ($p < 0.10$) in a non-family business than in their own family's business. Thus we find that female leaders do not show more individualized consideration in their family's business than in a non-family business. In addition, female leaders opposed to male leaders focus significantly less on mistakes in their family's business than in a non-family business. The general trend of leaders being more transformational in a non-family business than in a family business holds even more explicitly for male leaders than for female leaders.

Comparison of male and female leaders in essence family businesses versus non-family businesses

Next, we repeat this analysis for the essence family businesses compared to non-family businesses. For that purpose, we have to leave out the family businesses that meet only the components criteria but not the essence criteria, and hence we can make four groups: male leader in essence family business; male leader in non-family business; female leader in essence family business; and female leader in non-family business. A first MIMIC model treats male leader in essence family business as reference category by including the other three groups as covariates. Male leaders in essence family businesses do not differ significantly in their full-range leadership behaviour compared to male leaders in non-family businesses A second MIMIC model treating female leader in essence family business as reference category reveals that female leaders exhibit significantly less idealized influence behaviour-inspirational motivation ($p < 0.05$), intellectual stimulation ($p < 0.01$) and exchange negotiation ($p < 0.10$) in their essence family business than in a non-family business. Thus, when comparing only essence family businesses with non-family businesses, we equally find female leaders not to show more individualized consideration in their essence family's business than in a non-family business. Thus male leaders in essence family businesses are not less transformational than non-family business leaders, whereas female leaders are less transformational by emphasizing to a lesser extent the importance of a shared mission and by being less intellectually stimulating in essence family businesses than in non-family businesses.

In sum, we find support for Proposition 3, claiming a significant interaction effect of gender of the leader and family intensity of the business on a person's leadership style, with male leaders showing less transformational leadership and more active management-by-exception and passive-avoidant leadership in components family businesses than in non-family businesses. But this less effective leadership for male familial leaders does not hold in essence family businesses compared to non-family businesses. In addition, female leaders are also less transformational in components family businesses than in non-family businesses but to a lesser extent than males. However, female leaders in essence family businesses still perform worse on communicating a collective mission, intellectual stimulation and clarifying goals and positive rewards than in non-family businesses.

Comparison of male and female leaders in components family businesses versus essence family businesses

To compare components with essence family businesses, we have to estimate MIMIC models within the group of family businesses only. We note that essence family businesses score significantly higher ($p < 0.05$) on the motivation- and person-oriented leadership styles: idealized influence behaviour-motivational inspiration, individualized consideration and personal recognition. This more effective leadership in essence family businesses is partly attributable to male familial leaders scoring significantly ($p < 0.05$) higher on idealized influence behaviour-motivational inspiration in essence than in components family businesses and partly to female familial leaders who give significantly ($p < 0.10$) more personal recognition in essence than in components family businesses.

Testing the Robustness of the Effect of Family Intensity on the FRLT

In a final MIMIC model we included, based on previous research findings (see above) and insights from our case studies, other relevant determinants of a person's leadership style to test the robustness of the effects of gender and family intensity of the business. The following covariates were included: gender of the leader; gender of the interviewer (to test for a gendered interviewer effect); educational level of the leader; educational level of co-workers; sum of male leaders beyond respondent-leader (to test for the influence of other team leadership members, inspired by our case studies); sum of female leaders beyond respondent-leader; years in leadership; years in business before taking the lead; and the dummies controlling owner, essence family business leader and components family business leader to grasp the family intensity of the business. We refer to Arijs (2009) for an extended discussion of each covariate. Here it suffices to indicate that this final MIMIC model has a good fit with all three criteria fulfilled for RMSEA [0.0457, 90 per cent c.i. (0.0412,0.0502), p(upper limit < 0.05) $= 0.944$], and also in terms of SRMR ($= 0.0632$), CFI ($= 0.949$) and NNFI ($= 0.932$). When controlling for all these covariates, the main effect of male leaders showing more idealized influence attributed is not longer significant, which rejects Proposition 1 (see Appendix Table 19A.5 for an overview of the structural effects). We would like to draw attention to the striking finding of the effect of number of female and male leaders in case of team leadership, further clarifying Proposition 1. For each additional woman in the leadership team, the exhibition of individualized consideration increases with 0.084 (in standardized terms, $p < 0.10$), while the effect of one additional man in leadership causes a decrease in giving personal recognition with 0.133 (in standardized terms, $p < 0.05$). Hence the gender stereotype of people-oriented leadership of women becomes more pronounced when more women and fewer men are involved in leadership. Even when controlling for all these relevant covariates, the main effects of the dummies assessing the family intensity of the business re-emerge (see Appendix Table 19A.5) which confirms Proposition 2. In addition, we can conclude that family intensity of the business (measured by its three dummies) is the strongest explanatory variable in terms of size of standardized effects compared to other covariates (see Appendix Table 19A.6). This MIMIC model can explain between 5.3 per cent (of IIA) and 13.1 per cent (of PA) of the variance in the full range leadership behaviour (see Appendix Table 19A.4), which are small but realistic amounts of explained variance in leadership research (Eagly and Johnson, 1990). With all these extra covariates beyond gender and family intensity of the business, we can explain considerably more of the active management-by-exception and passive-avoidant leadership styles but not of the transformational leadership behaviour (comparison of Appendix Table 19A.4 with 19A.3).

DISCUSSION

In agreement with other studies (e.g. Barbuto et al., 2007; van Engen et al., 2001), we found that after controlling for all other relevant determinants of a person's leadership style, gender differences become petty. We found only an indication that male leaders exhibit more idealized influence attributed than female leaders, which means that female leaders still feel less confident than male leaders and, hence, gain less respect from co-workers. A recent European study similarly concludes that women are still less assertive than men with regard to their skills and achieved success (Desvaux et al., 2007). We note that studies that did find significant gender differences, such as Antonakis et al. (2003), used sample sizes of more than 1000 female and more than 1000 male leaders. This explains why very subtle differences like women being slightly more individually consid-erate or showing more personal recognition might not be detected in our sample consist-ing of about 200 male and 200 female leaders. More importantly, our study puts the gender debate in leadership theory in another light. First, we found empirical evidence for typical female person-oriented leadership becoming more pronounced when more women and fewer men are participating in the leadership team. In addition, our results reveal that the family intensity of the business is a much stronger explanatory variable of a person's leadership style than his/her gender or gender composition of the leadership team. Thus it is important to separate family businesses in components-of-involvement terms from family businesses in essence terms. We found that leaders in components family businesses score significantly worse on almost all transformational leadership factors than non-family business leaders, whereas leaders in essence family businesses score significantly worse only in performing intellectual stimulation and exchange nego-tiation. The more ineffective leadership in components family businesses and to a lesser extent in essence family businesses might be partly explained by the conviction many family business leaders put forward in case studies that 'it is their money and so they decide' (Arijs, 2009). The more person-oriented leadership in essence family businesses than in components family businesses might be attributable to the ingrained family values in the running of the essence family business.

We would like to contrast our results with the conclusion of Vallejo (2009), pointing to family businesses being more transformational than non-family businesses. There are three likely explanations for the differing results. First, Vallejo (2009) questioned only

Spanish family firms from the automobile dealer sector with fewer than 250 employees. Hence the generalizing power of his finding beyond the automobile sector may be a first concern. Second, Vallejo used the Global Transformational Leadership Scale, comprising only seven items to measure transformational leadership, and three of these relate to leaders leading by example, expressing their values and instilling pride and respect in co-workers. This might explain why Vallejo found that family firms scored higher on 'transformational leadership', as the dimension of idealized influence is strongly overrepresented in his measure. Third, Vallejo's definition of family firms relates to essence family firms as a single family must have sufficient stockholding to dominate the decisions and there should be the desire or intention to maintain the business in the hands of the following generation. Our research design has the advantage that we could distinguish three gradations of family businesses.

Furthermore, our findings make clear that the effect of the family intensity of the business works differently for male and female leaders. In short, male leaders are significantly and considerably less effective leaders in components family businesses than in non-family businesses. Female leaders are as person oriented in components family businesses as in non-family businesses, and are, as opposed to male leaders, less focused on mistakes and are less passive leaders when integrated in components family businesses than in non-family businesses. Male leaders do not differ in essence family businesses and in non-family businesses, whereas female leaders communicate less about a compelling vision and are less intellectually stimulating in essence family businesses compared to in non-family businesses. Thus male leaders tend to exhibit more masculine leadership in components family businesses than in non-family businesses, whereas female relatives score lower on the masculine leadership styles in components and essence family businesses than in non-family businesses. Within the group of family businesses, we note that female familial leaders are also more feminine leaders by giving more personal recognition in essence family businesses than in components family businesses. These results make it clear that gender differences in the full-range leadership styles can only be understood if, besides the gender of the CEO the family intensity of the business is also taken into account.

LIMITATIONS AND SUGGESTIONS FOR FUTURE RESEARCH

A first limitation of our study is that we did not investigate the effect of leadership styles on economic performance of the business. However, this effect is likely to be biased in family businesses as they may have other goals than creating economic wealth, such as family harmony (Chrisman et al., 2005; Habbershon et al., 2003; Nordqvist, 2005). In addition, since all but one adaptation to our leadership measure is based on recent research that re-tested the link with outcome criteria, we have at least clear indications of the predictive validity of a leader's effectiveness. For family business researchers, it might make more sense to investigate what the impact of this female leadership is on the health of the family system. The sustainable family business model (SFB) underscores that besides business success, good family relationships are necessary for sustainable family business success (Heck et al., 2006). Arijs (2009) has partly addressed this research question and found a female advantage in investing and realizing cognitive family cohesion (link with internal social capital). Future research should further assess the female leadership potential for family businesses by additionally focusing on how female familial leaders contribute to external social capital, financial and human capital of the family business.

A second limitation is that we only used self-ratings of leaders. Including several evaluations by subordinates on the same leader could have increased the reliability and validity of our results, as Burke and Collins (2001) detected that especially male leaders tend to overestimate their own leadership skills. Hence our obtained MLQ scores might be slightly overestimated for male leaders. However, our case studies and prior research (Antonakis et al., 2003; Yukl, 2002) revealed that factors like gender combination of follower–leader, intrinsic motivation, self-discipline, educational degree, family bond and hierarchical level of the subordinate may equally affect the perception on the leader. Furthermore, the selection of subordinates may introduce a new source of bias. MLQ scores given by subordinates tend to be inflated by one unit because subordinates may fear for their work security (Avolio and Bass, 2004; Vallejo, 2009). That is why we opted for only self-ratings, which additionally allowed us to obtain 200 different surveys of male and 200 of female leaders.

Since investigation of the non-response revealed that especially higher-generation family businesses are non-respondents, our conclusions on the comparison of family and non-family businesses might hold only for younger family businesses. Family business researchers should further investigate why transformational leadership is so poorly adopted in family businesses and which types of family businesses need to become acquainted with the advantages of exhibiting transformational leadership. Furthermore, our conclusions on leadership styles should be extrapolated only to businesses employing at least 3 to maximum 49 employees.

Finally, we hope our results have convinced leadership researchers to no longer ignore family intensity of the business as an explanatory variable of the FRLT as it is not only a very strong explanatory variable compared to other relevant determinants, but it also enables the research community to further unravel inconsistent results on gender differences in leadership styles. Besides family intensity of the business, the gender composition of the leadership team should be taken into account in future research to get a more profound and valid insight into the often subtle differences found between male and female leaders in prior research.

IMPLICATIONS FOR PRACTICE AND EDUCATION

First, the poor score of family business leaders on effective transformational leadership compared to non-family business leaders revealed the need for family business leaders and their advisors to get more in touch with aspects of transformational leadership. The changing workforce wanting their say and being more educated to have their say (Maccoby, 2007) is not a phenomenon that bypasses family businesses. Family business leaders should transcend the traditional leadership behaviour and should integrate the voice of subordinates in their decision-making. They may not be blind to the fact that it is their money that circulates in the business and, hence, they decide on business issues. Furthermore, the vision on the strategic direction of the business should not only be shared among involved relatives but should be enthusiastically communicated and reconfirmed to all employees, no matter what their seniority. We note that family businesses that manage to integrate the family values in the business can more easily benefit from taking into account the individual concerns and emotions of co-workers, which enhances the motivation and commitment of workers and employees.

Second, our study might help transferors to make sound leadership succession decisions. Researchers and practitioners fear that the loss of so much leadership talent by ignoring women as successor candidates might be a trap for the continuity of family businesses (Aronoff and Baskin, 2005; Galiano and Vinturella, 1995; Heck, 2002). Since our study results point to female leaders as more effective leaders of co-workers than male leaders in components family businesses versus in non-family businesses, and to be almost as effective in essence family businesses as in non-family businesses, we can only advise transferors and family business advisors to take into account female leadership potential. Nevertheless, female relatives themselves should become aware of their capabilities and have more self-confidence. In addition, family business education and training programs have to play a role. The male discourse when talking about entrepreneurship (Ahl, 2006) is equally present in the context of family business leadership and succession. It might be fruitful to integrate examples of female family business leaders in our courses with focus on their strengths and weaknesses, so that family business transferors and successors become aware of the full leadership potential for family business leadership succession.

ACKNOWLEDGEMENTS

The author is grateful to the Research Centre for Entrepreneurship at the Hogeschool-Universiteit Brussel for funding this doctoral research and to Professor Johan Lambrecht for his thoughtful comments.

NOTES

1. 'Familial' refers to the family link the leader has with the family that owns the business.
2. 'Non-familial' female leader applies to both female leaders in family businesses who do not belong to the owning family and female leaders in non-family businesses.
3. We refer to Arijs (2009) for a detailed discussion of the intra- and intergenerational factors influencing the leadership style and its development of a family business leader.
4. The quarterly published figures of the Rijksdienst voor Sociale Zekerheid for the first quarter of 2005 confirm a large number of small firms and a small number of large firms for the Belgian private sector: 178 647 micro firms (fewer than 10 employees), 28 860 small firms (10 to 49 employees) compared to 6137 medium-sized and large firms (more than 50 employees). A total of 99 per cent of European businesses are micro (92 per cent have 0 to 9 employees) or small (7 per cent have 10 to 49 employees) (Recommendation from the Commission 2003/361/EC from 6 May 2003).
5. Our measure consisted of 28 items, requiring a sample size of at least $(28*29)/2 = 406$ observations, taking into account the possibility that the data are not normally distributed and hence requiring the calculation of the asymptotic covariance matrix (Garson, 1998–2009).
6. We have not questioned the items of the culture subscale dealing with feelings of pride in being associated with the family business and of loyalty in supporting the business toward others, as we do not question other family members than the leader. We especially focused on the items referring to the extra effort family members are willing to make to realize the goal of the business, and their support of this business goal and decisions.

7. Essence controlling owners could only be classified as such if at least one other family member was involved in the business as employee, director or advisor (thus not as owner or leader) and for which the essence scores were at least 4.
8. Given the small number of family-intense controlling owners, we had to combine this group with the components controlling owners in our analyses.
9. Organizational citizenship behaviour relates to followers exhibiting extra-role behaviours that exceed the requirements of in-role expectations (Goodwin et al., 2001).
10. Subordinate performance was judged by the leader on the basis of quality of work, quantity of work and promotability to the next level (Goodwin et al., 2001).
11. Given the similar scores of controlling owners and of family businesses in components terms on our 8 leadership factors (see above), it makes sense to combine those two groups into 'components family businesses' in subsequent analyses.

REFERENCES

Ahl, H. (2006), 'Why research on women entrepreneurs needs new directions', *Entrepreneurship Theory and Practice*, September: 595–621.

Alimo-Metcalfe, B. and Alban-Metcalfe, J. (2005), 'Leadership: time for a new direction?', *Leadership Research and Development*, **1**(1): 51–71.

Antonakis, J., Avolio, B.J. and Sivasubramaniam, N. (2003), 'Context and leadership: an examination of the nine-factor full-range leadership theory using the Multifactor Leadership Questionnaire', *The Leadership Quarterly*, **14**(3): 261–95.

Arijs, D. (2009), 'The dynamic process of a female family member toward and in the daily executive leadership of the family business and its impact on family business success' (doctoral dissertation, final version publicly defended 24 September 2009), Brussels: Hogeschool-Universiteit Brussel.

Aronoff, C.E. (1998), 'Megatrends in family business', *Family Business Review*, **11**(3): 181–5.

Aronoff, C.E. and Baskin, O.W. (2005), 'Effective leadership in the family business', *Family Business Leadership Series*, 21, Marietta, GA: Family Enterprise Publishers, pp. 1–67.

Aronoff, C.E. and Ward, J.L. (1995), 'Family-owned businesses: a thing of the past or a model for the future?', *Family Business Review*, **8**(2): 121–30.

Avolio, B.J. and Bass, B.M. (2004), 'Multifactor Leadership Questionnaire. Manual and Sampler Set', 3rd edn [WWW]. Mind Garden, Inc: URL: htpp://www.mindgarden.info/files/MGI_Arijs_MLQ7475.pdf (3 September 2008).

Barbuto, Jr, J.E., Fritz, S.M., Matkin, G.S. and Marx, D.B. (2007), 'Effects of gender, education, and age upon leader's use of influence tactics and full range leadership behaviors', *Sex Roles*, **56**(January): 71–83.

Bollen, K.A. (1989), *Structural Equations with Latent Variables*, New York: Wiley.

Burke, S. and Collins, K.M (2001), 'Gender differences in leadership styles and management skills', *Women in Management Review*, **16**(5): 244–56.

Chrisman, J.J., Chua, J.H. and Litz, R. (2003), 'A unified systems perspective of family performance: an extension and integration', (Discussion), *Journal of Business Venturing*, **18**: 467–72.

Chrisman, J.J., Chua, J.H. and Steier, L. (2005), 'Sources and consequences of distinctive familiness: an introduction', *Entrepreneurship Theory and Practice*, May: 237–47.

Cromie, S. and O'Sullivan, S. (1999), 'Women as managers in family firms', *Women in Management Review*, **14**(3): 76–88.

Desvaux, G., Devillard-Hoellinger, S. and Baumgarten, P. (2007), 'Women matter', (Research Paper), McKinsey & Company, Inc.: http://www.europeanpwn.net/files/mckinsey_2007_gender_matters.pdf (10 January 2008).

Donckels, R. and Fröhlich, E. (1991). 'Are family businesses really different? European experiences from STRATOS', *Family Business Review*, **4**(2): 149–60.

Eagly, A.H. and Carli, L.L. (2007), 'Women and the labyrinth of leadership', *Harvard Business Review*, **85**(9): 62–71.

Eagly, A.H. and Johnson, B.T. (1990), 'Gender and leadership style: a meta-analysis', *Psychological Bulletin*, **108**(2): 233–56.

Eagly, A.H., Johannesen-Schmidt, M.C. and van Engen, M.L. (2003), 'Transformational, transactional, and laissez-faire leadership styles: a meta-analysis comparing women and men', *Psychological Bulletin*, **129**(4): 569–91.

Frishkoff, P.A. and Brown, B.M. (1993), 'Women on the move in family business', *Business Horizons*, March–April: 66–70.

Galiano, A.M. and Vinturella, J.B. (1995), 'Implications of gender bias in the family business', *Family Business Review*, **8**(3): 177–88.

Gardiner, M. and Tiggemann, M. (1999), 'Gender differences in leadership style, job stress and mental health in male and female dominated industries', *Journal of Occupational and Organizational Psychology*, **72**: 301–15.

Garson, G.D. (1998–2009), 'Structural equation modeling', in *Statnotes: Topics in Multivariate Analysis*, retrieved 9 October 2008 from http://faculty.chass.ncsu.edu/garson/PA765/structur.htm.

Goodwin, V.L., Wofford, J.C. and Whittington, J.L. (2001), 'A theoretical and empirical extension to the transformational leadership construct', *Journal of Organizational Behavior*, **22**: 759–74.

Habbershon, T.G., Williams, M. and MacMillan, I.C. (2003), 'A unified systems perspective of family firm performance', *Journal of Business Venturing*, **18**: 451–65.

Haberman, H. and Danes, S. (2007), 'Father–daughter and father–son family business management transfer comparison: family FIRO model application', *Family Business Review*, **20**(2): 163–84.

Hall, A., Nordqvist, M. and Melin, L. (2005), 'Qualitative research in family business studies: the usefulness of the interpretive approach', paper presented at FBN 16th Annual Summit 2005, 'Responsible Ownership!', 15 September, Brussels, Belgium.

Heck, R., Danes, S., Fitzgerald, M., Haynes, G., Jasper, C., Schrank, H., Stafford, K. and Winter, M. (2006), 'The family's dynamic role within family business entrepreneurship', in P.Z. Poutziouris, K.X. Smyrnios and S.B. Klein (eds), *Handbook of Research on Family Business*, Cheltenham, UK and Northampton, MA, USA: Edward Elgar, pp. 80–105.

Heck, R. (2002), '*The Daughter also Rises: How Women Overcome Obstacles and Advance in the Family-owned Business*, by Anne E. Francis [book review]', *Family Business Review*, **15**(2): 155–8.

Heinitz, K., Liepmann, D. and Felfe, J. (2005), 'Examining the factor structure of the MLQ: recommendations for a reduced set of factors', *European Journal of Psychological Assessment*, **21**(3): 182–90.

Hinkin, T.R. and Schriesheim, C.A. (2008), 'A theoretical and empirical examination of the transactional and non-leadership dimensions of the Multifactor Leadership Questionnaire (MLQ)', *The Leadership Quarterly*, **19**: 501–13.

Hollander, B.S. and Bukowitz, W.R. (1990), 'Women, family culture, and family business', *Family Business Review*, **3**(2): 139–51.

Jimenez, R.M. (2009), 'Research on women in family firms. Current status and future directions', *Family Business Review*, **22**(1): 53–64.

Klein, S.B., Astrachan, J.H. and Smyrnios, K.X. (2005), 'The F-PEC scale of family influence: construction, validation, and further implication for theory', *Entrepreneurship Theory and Practice*, May: 321–39.

Komives, S.R. (1991), 'Gender differences in the relationship of hall directors' transformational and transactional leadership and achieving styles', *Journal of College Student Development*, **32**: 155–65.

Krosnick, J.A. and Fabrigar, L.R. (1997), 'Designing rating scales for effective measurement in surveys', in ch. 6. Lyberg et al. (eds), *Survey Measurement and Process Quality*, New York: John Wiley & Sons.

Lievens, J. and Lambrecht, J. (2007), *Met uw familiebedrijf naar de Champions League*, Roeselare: Roularta Books.

Lowe, K.B., Kroeck, K.G. and Sivasubramaniam, N. (1996), 'Effectiveness correlates of transformational and transactional leadership: a meta-analytic review of the MLQ literature', *The Leadership Quarterly*, **7**(3): 385–425.

Lyman, A.R. (1988), 'Life in the family circle', *Family Business Review*, **1**(4): 383–98.

Maccoby, M. (2007), *The Leaders we Need and What Makes us Follow*, Boston, MA: Harvard Business School Press.

Mühlebach, C. (2005), *Familyness as a Competitive Advantage*, Bern, Stuttgart and Wien: Haupt Berne.

Nordqvist, M. (2005), 'Familiness in top management teams: commentary on Ensley and Pearson's "An exploratory comparison of the behavioral dynamics of top management teams in family and nonfamily new ventures: cohesion, conflict, potency and consensus"', *Entrepreneurship Theory and Practice*, May: 285–91.

Poza, E.J. and Messer, T. (2001), 'Spousal leadership and continuity in the family firm', *Family Business Review*, **14**(1): 25–36.

Rafferty, A.E. and Griffin, M.A. (2004), 'Dimensions of transformational leadership: conceptual and empirical extensions', *The Leadership Quarterly*, **15**: 329–54.

Rowold, J. and Heinitz, K. (2007), 'Transformational and charismatic leadership: assessing the convergent, divergent and criterion validity of the MLQ and the CKS', *The Leadership Quarterly*, **18**: 121–33.

Saunders, M., Lewis, P. and Thornhill, A. (2008), *Methoden en technieken van onderzoek*, 4th edn, Amsterdam: Pearson Education Benelux.

Seale, C. (1999), *The Quality of Qualitative Research*, London, Thousand Oaks, CA and New Delhi: SAGE Publications.

Sharma, S. (1996), *Applied Multivariate Techniques*, New York: John Wiley & Sons.

Sorenson, R.L. (2000), 'The contribution of leadership style and practices to family and business success', *Family Business Review*, **13**(3): 183–200.

van Engen, M.L., van der Leeden, R. and Willemsen, T.M. (2001), 'Gender, context and leadership styles: a field study', *Journal of Occupational and Organizational Psychology*, **74**: 581–98.

Vallejo, M.C. (2009), 'Analytical model of leadership in family firms under transformational theoretical approach', *Family Business Review*, **22**(2): 136–50.

Waldman, D.A, Siegel, D.S. and Javidan, M. (2006), 'Components of CEO transformational leadership and corporate social responsibility', *Journal of Management Sciences*, **43**(8): 1703–25.

Wicherts, J.M. and Dolan, C.V. (2004), 'A cautionary note on the use of information fit indexes in covariance structure modeling with means', *Structural Equation Modeling: A Multidisciplinary Journal*, **11**(1): 45–50.

Yukl, G. (1999), 'An evaluation of conceptual weaknesses in transformational and charismatic leadership theories', *The Leadership Quarterly*, **10**(2): 285–306.

Yukl, G. (2002), *Leadership in organizations*, 5th edn, Englewood Cliffs, NJ: Prentice-Hall.

APPENDIX

Table 19A.1   Overview of adaptation of original MLQ 5X short items to our measure of the full range of leadership styles

First-order factor*	Original MLQ 5X short items	Adapted MLQ 5X short items	Deleted MLQ 5X short items	Own items
Idealized influence attributed	MLQ_ 21 (respected)	MLQ_ 25' "I have influence on co-workers because I am self-confident and co-workers trust me"	MLQ_ 10 (instill pride) MLQ_ 18 (beyond self-interest)	
Idealized influence behaviour+ Inspirational motivation	MLQ_ 14 (purpose), MLQ_34 (mission) MLQ_ 9 (optimistic future) MLQ_ 13 (enthusiastic) MLQ_ 26 (compelling vision) MLQ_ 36 (confidence in goals)	MLQ_ 6: 'I talk about my most important values to co-workers'	MLQ_ 23 (moral and ethical)	
Intellectual stimulation	MLQ_ 8 (differing perspectives) MLQ_ 30 (different angles) MLQ_ 32 (new ways)		MLQ_ 2 (scrutinize critical assumptions)	I_13: 'I consider mistakes as an opportunity for learning'
Individualized consideration	MLQ_ 15 (coaching), MLQ_ 29 (individual needs), MLQ_ 31 (develop others)		MLQ_ 19 (not merely member of group)	I_16: 'I take co-workers' feelings into consideration before taking action'
Personal recognition*	MLQ_ 35 (express satisfaction)			I_15: 'I give personal compliments to co-workers who put up a performance beyond expectations'

Table 19A.1   (continued)

First-order factor*	Original MLQ 5X short items	Adapted MLQ 5X short items	Deleted MLQ 5X short items	Own items
Exchange negotiation*	MLQ_ 11 (indicate responsibilities), MLQ_ 16 (clarify rewards)		MLQ_ 1 (assistance)	
Active management-by-exception	MLQ_ 24 (tracking mistakes) MLQ_ 27 (focusing on failures)	MLQ_ 4: 'I focus attention on co-workers' mistakes'	MLQ_ 22 (focus on mistakes)	
Passive management-by-exception + laisser-faire	MLQ_ 3 (fail to intervene) MLQ_ 12 (action after problems) MLQ_ 5 (not involved) MLQ_ 28 (no decisions)		MLQ_ 17 (if it ain't broke, don't fix it) MLQ_ 20 (chronic problem before action) MLQ_ 7 (absent when needed) MLQ_ 3 (delay responding)	

Note: * These leadership aspects are the first-order factors of our measure and have the same name as in the MLQ 5X short leader form, except 'personal recognition' and 'exchange negotiation', which are collapsed in the MLQ 5X into what Avolio and Bass (2004) call the factor 'contingent reward'. We note that the full wording of the original MLQ items cannot be published because it is copyrighted. Nevertheless, we label each item by means of some substantive words to provide the reader with an idea of the content of the items. The prefix 'MLQ_' indicates that this item concerns the original MLQ item. The prime (') means that the original MLQ item has been slightly adapted. The prefix 'I_' refers to an own item.

Table 19A.2   Structural effects of gender and of family intensity of business on leadership factors

Loading estimate Critical ratio	Gender	Controlling owner	FB_essence	FB_components
IIA	0.117	0.067	0.029	−0.093
	1.746°	0.830	0.338	−1.252
IIBM	−0.006	−0.232	−0.101	−0.263
	−0.100	*−3.229****	−1.537	*−3.943****
IS	0.023	−0.178	−0.278	−0.333
	0.308	*−1.897°*	*−2.778***	*−4.007****
IC	−0.018	−0.200	−0.045	−0.218
	−0.305	*−2.651***	−0.632	*−3.214***
PR	−0.059	0.007	−0.030	−0.232
	−0.938	0.094	−0.432	*−3.113***
ExchN	−0.082	−0.437	−0.356	−0.428
	−0.864	*−3.434****	*−3.088***	*−4.324****
MBEA	−0.051	0.035	0.021	0.045
	−0.581	0.333	0.193	0.473
PA	0.007	0.103	−0.027	0.064
	0.086	1.063	−0.268	0.781

Notes: $° p < 0.10$; $* p < 0.05$; $** p < 0.01$; $*** p < 0.001$.

Table 19A.3   Squared multiple correlations for structural equations of MIMIC model with gender and family intensity as covariates

IIA	IIBM	IS	IC	PR	ExchN	MBEA	PA
0.024	0.096	0.102	0.068	0.052	0.159	0.003	0.008

Table 19A.4   Squared multiple correlations for structural equations of final MIMIC model

IIA	IIBM	IS	IC	PR	ExchN	MBEA	PA
0.053	0.078	0.118	0.082	0.076	0.103	0.064	0.131

Table 19A.5   *Structural effects of final MIMIC model with other covariates besides gender and family intensity of the business*

	Education of leader	Gender of leader	Sum male leaders excl. respondent	Sum female leaders excl. respondent	Gender of interviewer	Education of co-workers	Years before in lead	Years in lead	Control-ling owner	FB essence	FB components
IIA	-0.007	0.101	-0.001	-0.021	0.049	-0.030	-0.011	0.004	0.023	0.004	-0.116
	-0.218	1.389	-0.022	-0.364	0.709	-0.857	-1.323	1.070	0.229	0.040	-1.318
IIBM	0.017	-0.019	-0.011	0.005	0.041	0.066	-0.014	0.002	-0.222	-0.072	-0.239
	0.631	-0.296	-0.301	0.122	0.701	2.087*	-1.672°	0.826	-2.576*	-0.933	-3.128**
IS	0.049	0.036	0.048	0.040	0.208	0.048	-0.026	-0.005	-0.081	-0.222	-0.296
	1.403	0.459	1.039	0.727	2.678**	1.165	-3.208**	-1.184	-0.718	-1.935°	-3.103**
IC	0.030	-0.034	-0.302	0.074	0.095	0.024	-0.017	0.002	-0.176	-0.045	-0.216
	1.099	-0.551	-0.047	1.754°	1.563	0.648	-2.599**	0.511	-1.926°	-0.530	-2.893**
PR	-0.019	-0.070	-0.081	0.001	0.094	-0.006	-0.004	-0.004	-0.037	0.004	-0.236
	-0.612	-1.026	-2.253*	0.021	1.495	-0.144	-0.560	-1.163	-0.383	0.046	-2.678**
ExchN	0.008	-0.071	0.082	0.038	0.216	-0.020	-0.020	-0.004	-0.350	-0.337	-0.410
	0.202	-0.669	1.483	0.547	2.252*	-0.424	-1.483	-0.826	-2.320*	-2.328*	-3.309***
MBEA	0.089	-0.041	-0.017	0.065	0.204	0.000	-0.021	-0.002	0.038	0.023	0.010
	2.082*	-0.385	-0.248	0.733	2.199*	-0.006	-2.186*	-0.460	0.252	0.147	0.076
PA	0.032	-0.033	0.018	0.086	-0.294	0.003	-0.003	0.015	0.056	-0.152	0.024
	0.783	-0.347	0.328	0.821	-3.523***	0.081	-0.313	2.843**	0.431	-1.064	0.198

Notes: ° $p < 0.10$; * $p < 0.05$; ** $p < 0.01$; *** $p < 0.001$

Table 19A.6 *Standardized regression coefficients for final MIMIC model*

	Education of leader	Gender of leader	Sum male leaders excl. respondent	Sum female leaders excl. respondent	Gender of interviewer	Education of co-workers	Years before in lead	Years in lead	Controlling owner	FB essence	FB essence components
IIA	-0.015	0.098	-0.001	-0.023	0.047	-0.058	-0.098	0.073	0.019	0.003	-0.106
IIBM	0.038	-0.018	-0.017	0.006	0.040	0.127	-0.126	0.046	-0.182	-0.054	-0.221
IS	0.089	0.029	0.062	0.036	0.164	0.076	-0.189	-0.069	-0.054	-0.136	-0.223
IC	0.067	-0.034	-0.003	0.084	0.094	0.048	-0.162	0.029	-0.147	-0.034	-0.204
PR	-0.043	-0.071	-0.133	0.001	0.094	-0.012	-0.038	-0.070	-0.031	0.003	-0.225
ExchN	0.013	-0.048	0.090	0.029	0.145	-0.027	-0.123	-0.051	-0.198	-0.176	-0.263
MBEA	0.153	-0.031	-0.020	0.055	0.153	0.000	-0.144	-0.032	0.024	0.013	0.007
PA	0.059	-0.027	0.024	0.080	-0.237	0.006	-0.021	0.231	0.038	-0.095	0.018

PART VII

KNOWLEDGE MANAGEMENT

20 Entrepreneurial learning in the family management group: a social organizational learning perspective
Elias Hadjielias, Eleanor Hamilton and Carole Howorth

INTRODUCTION

Entrepreneurship within the family business context can be best understood by moving beyond the individual entrepreneur to consider the joint practices of a number of individuals. Collective units, therefore, offer a more valid representation of the reality for family businesses, providing an opportunity to understand the joint contribution of a number of business members in family business entrepreneurship (Dyer and Handler, 1994; Fitzgerald and Muske, 2002; Habbershon and Pistrui, 2002; Kellermanns and Eddleston, 2006).

Since entrepreneurs tend to develop their skills and understanding of entrepreneurship through a process of entrepreneurial learning (Rae, 2000; Minniti and Bygrave, 2001; Cope, 2003, 2005), it is important to understand how this learning takes place within a context where co-participation in entrepreneurship is apparent. Organizational learning perspectives, drawing upon theories such as situated learning (Brown and Duguid, 1991; Hamilton, 2005, 2011), social capital (Granovetter, 1985; Burt, 2000; Lin, 1999; Adler and Kwon, 2002; Taylor and Thorpe, 2004; Andersson et al., 2005), and activity theory (Engeström, 1987; Engeström and Middleton, 1996; Engeström, 1999) offer an opportunity for exploring entrepreneurial learning practices within the family business context under a collectivist lens. We term this 'collective entrepreneurial learning' and argue that it is a central element of collective entrepreneurial practices within family businesses. Although there is increased acceptance of the collective participation of business members in family business entrepreneurship (Dyer and Handler, 1994; Fitzgerald and Muske, 2002; Habbershon and Pistrui, 2002; Kellermanns and Eddleston, 2006), there is limited understanding of how they learn as a result of engaging themselves within collective entrepreneurial practices. A better understanding of the collective entrepreneurial learning process (Rae, 2000; Minniti and Bygrave, 2001; Cope, 2003, 2005) will help family businesses to design systems and routines that improve the co-participation of business members in family business entrepreneurship.

Research in the field suggests that family members can have a critical impact on entrepreneurial decisions and practices (Salvato, 2004; Kellermanns, et al., 2008) and their joint participation determines the opportunities to be considered (Discua Cruz, 2009; Discua Cruz et al., 2009; Discua Cruz and Howorth, 2010). We suggest that researchers should specifically focus on the family members who are actively engaged in the everyday management and strategic direction of their business(es). This 'family management group' (FMG) is an important unit of analysis that has received very little research attention but it is most appropriate to the study of entrepreneurial action.

Social theories can potentially help in capturing collective entrepreneurial learning within the FMG. Social approaches capture process-related and dynamic phenomena such as the learning of a particular practice (Rae, 2000; Dess et al., 2003; Fletcher, 2006; Rae, 2006). Further, social frameworks acknowledge the importance of collectivity in human actions, which stems from joint participation in a particular practice (Brown and Duguid, 1991; Lave and Wenger, 1991; Hamilton, 2005, 2011) or the embeddedness of individuals within social networks (Granovetter, 1985; Burt, 2000; Lin, 1999; Adler and Kwon, 2002; Andersson et al., 2005). Social theoretical perspectives can also explain human interactions within informal groups such as the FMG, which are not formally sanctioned or recognized within the organizational hierarchy (Brown and Duguid, 1991; Lave and Wenger, 1991). Such perspectives enable the study of the way that members of the FMG collectively learn the practices of opportunity discovery, evaluation and exploitation, across the generations.

This chapter has a dual aim: first, to highlight the combined use of social theories and organizational learning perspectives to extend our understanding of entrepreneurial learning in family businesses; second, to introduce the FMG as a new unit of analysis for helping researchers to explain entrepreneurial learning practices within the family business context, in a transgenerational manner.

In the following sections we discuss and explain the concepts associated with collective entrepreneurial learning in FMGs. We begin with the use and importance of social theories in understanding entrepreneurial learning within family businesses. We then make a case for the use of organizational learning perspectives that draw upon social theoretical frameworks to explain collective entrepreneurial learning practices within the family business context. Last, we introduce a new unit of analysis, the FMG, calling for the utilization of social organizational learning theories to explain how family members interact to learn collectively the way family business entrepreneurship should be approached.

ENTREPRENEURSHIP AS A LEARNING PROCESS – THE USE OF SOCIAL THEORIES TO EXPLAIN ENTREPRENEURIAL LEARNING

For family firms, ongoing entrepreneurship is a key element of business survival across generations (Kellermanns and Eddleston, 2006), since it promotes business profitability and growth (Salvato, 2004), as well as transgenerational wealth (Habbershon and Pistrui, 2002).

Entrepreneurship is increasingly seen as a process that leads to a number of important outcomes for individuals and businesses (Gartner, 1988; Shane and Venkataraman, 2000), including the creation of new ventures, strategic renewal and restructuring, innovation and adoption of new technologies, new product development, diversifying markets and new business alliances. Research that examines entrepreneurship within the family business context tends to draw primarily on hypothetico-deductive perspectives to test the impact of CEO, team and business-related characteristics on new venture establishment and entrepreneurship-related outcomes (Miller, 1983; Dyer and Handler, 1994; Fitzgerald and Muske, 2002; Salvato, 2004; Kellermanns and Eddleston, 2006;

Kellermanns et al., 2008). The positivist paradigm, however, that dominates this research (Howorth et al., 2005; Jennings et al., 2005) restricts understanding of the process itself and the way that entrepreneurs develop knowledge that enables them to recognize and act upon new opportunities (Politis, 2005). In order to understand the essence of the entrepreneurial process and dynamic activities such as learning entrepreneurial practices, different epistemological and methodological approaches are needed that move beyond the static and outcome-based view of entrepreneurship. Dess et al. (2003) argue that organizational renewal and innovation are not static phenomena, and need to be captured using approaches that acknowledge the process nature of these practices. These perspectives must be in a position to explain the dynamism, complexity and collaboration that is apparent within the process of entrepreneurship, acknowledging at the same time the element of learning that is embedded within opportunity identification and realization.

The need to understand entrepreneurship and shed light on the ongoing learning that takes place throughout this process has led a number of researchers to shift their attention towards social theoretical perspectives. These frameworks can capture complex and dynamic activities within the entrepreneurial process, such as entrepreneurial learning. Social theories illuminate active processes and events, where social experience and human interactions are highly valued (Rae, 2000; Dess et al., 2003; Fletcher, 2006; Rae, 2006; Anderson et al., 2007; Fletcher, 2007; Jack, 2010; Leitch et al., 2010). Situated learning (Brown and Duguid, 1991; Hamilton, 2005, 2011) and social capital (Granovetter, 1985; Burt, 2000; Lin, 1999; Adler and Kwon, 2002) are social theories that have recently been used to explain entrepreneurship and entrepreneurial learning. Within these perspectives, entrepreneurial learning is seen as one embedded within social systems, organizational structures and social interactions in informal groups and networks (Hinrichs et al., 2004; Taylor and Thorpe, 2004; Hamilton, 2005; Fletcher, 2006; Hamilton, 2011; Dimov, 2007). It is viewed as a collaborative (social) process, and one that stems from the relationality of people's actions and their respective sociocultural context (Taylor and Thorpe, 2004; Downing, 2005; Fletcher, 2006; Dimov, 2007). The social context and audience with which individuals engage to exchange ideas, information, and resources and enaction of entrepreneurship are the ones that eventually shape the learning of the entrepreneurial practice (Rae, 2000, 2006; Dimov, 2007).

Situated learning has been the only social theoretical stance used to explain entrepreneurial learning within the family business field to date (Hamilton, 2005, 2011). Research shows that a situated learning approach offers fertile ground for the study of family business entrepreneurship from a different perspective – one where individualism is not the norm and entrepreneurial practices are learned as part of co-participation in social communities. A situated learning perspective can explore the dynamics of the entrepreneurial process to understand how family business members, as part of a broad community, acquire learning that is essential for acting entrepreneurially within the family business context. In this sense, entrepreneurial learning becomes a process that governs (informal) learning of the entrepreneurial practice by a collection of family business members rather than the lonely journey of a single entrepreneur, often the owner-manager (Hamilton, 2005, 2011). This can help research within the family business field to shift from an individualistic to a collectivistic understanding of entrepreneurship and entrepreneurial learning within the family business.

Other theoretical viewpoints could be employed in an effort to explore and explain the dynamic nature of entrepreneurial learning within the family business context. Social capital is a relatively modern concept that is becoming increasingly popular within the field of entrepreneurship (De Carolis and Saparito, 2006; Anderson, et al., 2007; Bowey and Easton, 2007; Casson and Della Giusta, 2007). While still very limited, a number of studies have explored the links between social capital and entrepreneurial learning (e.g. Hinrichs et al., 2004; Taylor and Thorpe, 2004; Dimov, 2007; Ettl and Welter, 2010). The personal network within which entrepreneur is embedded can also be an important source of learning for this entrepreneur. Using this framework, entrepreneurial learning within the family business can acquire a social character and can be seen as a process that is shaped by the ongoing interactions of family business members within networks 'of domestic, voluntary, commercial and professional relations' (Taylor and Thorpe, 2004, p. 203).

Activity theory (Engeström, 1987) can also be utilized to explain entrepreneurial learning within family businesses. Despite not employed within the context of entrepreneurial learning, it is highly considered by scholars in the field of organizational learning (Blackler and McDonald, 2000; Engeström, 2000; Virkkunen and Kuutti, 2000). Having a heavily social orientation, activity theory can help explain the co-engagement of family members in the activity of entrepreneurship and the learning that can stem from the plurality and diversity of views and roles in the context of this practice (Engeström and Middleton, 1996; Engeström and Miettinen, 1999; Engeström, 1999).

FROM AN INDIVIDUALISTIC TO A COLLECTIVISTIC UNDERSTANDING OF ENTREPRENEURIAL LEARNING

Another important trend in the field of entrepreneurship is a shift from an individualistic to a more collectivistic understanding of entrepreneurship and entrepreneurial learning. Recently, entrepreneurship researchers have acknowledged that an individual perspective is inadequate to describe the complexity, dynamism (Howorth et al., 2005; Hamilton, 2006) and plurality of the entrepreneurial process (Fletcher, 2006; Hamilton, 2006; Dimov, 2007; Leitch et al., 2010). Entrepreneurship might be better understood as a collective process that encompasses joint efforts of a number of organizational members, such as copreneurs (Dyer and Handler, 1994), top management teams (Ensley et al., 2002) and entrepreneurial founding teams (Ucbasaran et al., 2003).

Viewing entrepreneurship in the conventional sense, most scholars researching entrepreneurial learning still focus on the individual, attempting to explain how the key entrepreneur develops the necessary entrepreneurial capabilities and knowledge for recognizing, evaluating and exploiting entrepreneurial opportunities (Shane, 2000; Baron, 2004; Ward, 2004; Corbett, 2007; Mitchell et al., 2007; Holcomb et al., 2009). Such a focus, however, appears to be anachronistic since it ignores the social character of learning within organizations. Entrepreneurs do not learn in isolation, but the very essence of their learning often depends on their interaction with other individuals within and outside the organizational context (Taylor and Thorpe, 2004; Hamilton, 2005; Dimov, 2007). At the same time, an explicit attention on the single entrepreneur diminishes any efforts to understand how a collection of individuals and the organization as a whole learn to be entrepreneurial through time.

Acknowledging the collective nature (Eisenhardt and Schoonhoven, 1990; Ensley et al., 2002; Dyer and Handler, 1994) and social character of entrepreneurship (Dess et al., 2003; De Carolis and Saparito, 2006; Anderson et al., 2007) and entrepreneurial learning (Taylor and Thorpe, 2004; Hamilton, 2005, 2011), this chapter calls for the study of entrepreneurial learning within the family business context under a collectivist lens. We call this 'collective entrepreneurial learning'. It refers to the process that helps a collection of individuals to acquire knowledge that is essential for thinking and acting entrepreneurially. Entrepreneurial learning in this sense can be understood as a social activity that is jointly practised by a number of organizational members.

Recognizing that the survival and success of family businesses depend on the collective entrepreneurial efforts of business members (Dyer and Handler, 1994; Fitzgerald and Muske, 2002; Habbershon and Pistrui, 2002; Dyer, 2003; Kellermanns and Eddleston, 2006; Ling and Kellermanns, 2010), researchers within the family business field have begun to explain entrepreneurship as a collective effort. Habbershon and Pistrui (2002), for example, claim that within the family business, topics such as entrepreneurial orientation and entrepreneurial performance can be best understood via a focus on the family ownership group. Other family business researchers focus on entrepreneurial founding teams in an effort to explain entrepreneurial action within the family business context as a collective phenomenon (Discua Cruz and Howorth, 2010). Moreover, a number of scholars attempt to provide an understanding of family business entrepreneurship by focusing on top management teams (TMTs) and group decision-making (Kellermanns and Eddleston, 2006).

We argue that entrepreneurial learning within the family business should be examined within the collective. Collective units of analysis allow a more thorough understanding of joint entrepreneurial learning practices, including the way that family business members collectively learn how new opportunities are discovered, assessed and exploited. Collective entrepreneurial learning as a concept can help explain the interactions that are apparent between individuals within family business entrepreneurship and the learning that stems from this co-engagement. In this sense, entrepreneurial learning within the family business can be understood as a social process that enables a group of business members or the organization as a whole to acquire essential knowledge through social interaction.

AN ORGANIZATIONAL LEARNING PERSPECTIVE IN UNDERSTANDING COLLECTIVE ENTREPRENEURIAL LEARNING

The shift to a collective understanding of entrepreneurial learning in family businesses moves the focus from an individual to an organization. The organizational context is one where collective actions are apparent (Edmondson and Moingeon, 2004; Popper and Lipshitz, 2004) and organizational learning perspectives provide a framework for using levels of analysis beyond the single entrepreneur (Lumpkin, 2005; Rae, 2006; West, 2007; Blatt, 2009).

Learning at the organizational level is no longer an individual phenomenon but a collective action or organizational schema that is practised and shared by organizational members (e.g. Fiol and Lyles, 1985; Nonaka, 1994; Hayes and Allinson, 1998; Brown and Duguid, 1991). Taking the organization as a unit of analysis, studies examine how this entity learns to change and adapt (Levitt and March, 1988; Edmondson and Moingeon, 2004; Popper and Lipshitz, 2004), either as a result of entity-level cognitive learning capacities (Friedman et al., 2005) or changes in organizational systems, structures, routines and processes (Shrivastava, 1983; Pentland and Feldman, 2005) that can help organizational members to learn (Fiol and Lyles, 1985). Other researchers conceive organizational learning as a result of individual practices and they examine how collective learning of individuals within organizations takes place (Edmondson and Moingeon, 2004; Popper and Lipshitz, 2004). The collective learning approach suggests that organizations change and adapt as a result of collective learning of organizational members that brings along new organizational knowledge and capabilities (Argyris and Schön, 1978; Brown and Duguid, 1991; Nonaka, 1994).

The importance of co-participation in identifying and realizing entrepreneurial opportunities within family businesses (Dyer and Handler, 1994; Fitzgerald and Muske, 2002; Habbershon and Pistrui, 2002; Dyer, 2003; Kellermanns and Eddleston, 2006) indicates that organizational learning perspectives could be useful in explaining how collective entrepreneurial learning experiences emerge and evolve within the family business context. It is worth considering, therefore, how the concept of organizational learning can best be utilized to shed light on the process that underpins collective entrepreneurial learning within family businesses. Since family businesses are a social arena and entrepreneurial learning is a complex and dynamic process (Minniti and Bygrave, 2001; Cope, 2005), social perspectives on organizational learning will be most useful as they capture both the vibrant nature of entrepreneurial learning and the collective character of human learning experience within family businesses.

'SOCIAL ORGANIZATIONAL LEARNING' THEORIES AND COLLECTIVE ENTREPRENEURIAL LEARNING

Social constructionist perspectives such as situated learning (Brown and Duguid, 1991) and activity theory (Engeström, 1986; Engeström and Middleton, 1996) provides an understanding of how individuals within organizations interact to commit themselves in collective learning. These perspectives explain organizational learning through the social practices in which individuals are engaged. They tend to view learning as something that takes place informally within organizational communities and groups that are not always explicitly recognized. The section following this considers what these groups might be within a family business context. The important point here is that social learning perspectives capture the learning that takes place through social interactions, which are often informal.

Entrepreneurship tends to be learned informally, as part of everyday practice and experience (Cope and Watts, 2000; Taylor and Thorpe, 2004; Hamilton, 2005, 2011). This is particularly so within family businesses (Discua Cruz, 2009). We argue that social perspectives, such as situated learning (Brown and Duguid, 1991; Hamilton, 2005, 2011), social capital (Granovetter, 1985; Taylor and Thorpe, 2004; Burt, 2000; Lin, 1999; Adler and Kwon, 2002), and activity theory (Engeström 1987; Engeström and Middleton, 1996) are in a position to capture collective entrepreneurial learning experiences within the family business context. A situated perspective (Brown and Duguid, 1991; Lave and Wenger, 1991), for example, is a useful way of understanding how informal communities within the family business nurture family business members on the entrepreneurial practices and socialize them into the family way of doing business. Understanding how entrepreneurial learning within these informal groups tends to be shared and become collective is crucial in comprehending how family businesses, in turn, might benefit from such collective engagements. Social capital views entrepreneurial learning as stemming from social experience and human interactions within networks of relational practices in which people are embedded (Hinrichs et al., 2004; Taylor and Thorpe, 2004; Dimov, 2007; Ettl and Welter, 2010). This theoretical framework can be used to delve into network structures and relationships within which family business members are embedded in an effort to understand how they influence collective entrepreneurial learning practices within the family business. Activity theory views human activities as governed by co-participation, common objectives, shared tools, performance rules and role-distribution. The presence of multiple actors with different views becomes an instrument of change, which transforms the activity itself and promotes learning of how to cope with the new way of conducting the activity (Engeström and Middleton, 1996; Engeström and Miettinen, 1999; Engeström, 1999). This perspective can be useful in explaining how the collaborative engagement of family business members within entrepreneurship-related activities can help them learn collectively how to think and act entrepreneurially through time.

Although social perspectives have been used within the organizational context to explore entrepreneurial learning (Rae and Carswell, 2001; Taylor and Thorpe, 2004; Hamilton, 2005, 2011), they have not addressed collective entrepreneurial learning, despite these frameworks being implicitly collective by nature. Social perspectives on organizational learning are, thus, ideal for examining collective entrepreneurial learning such as that observed in family businesses. Such a perspective, which we call 'social organizational learning' could explore the way that collective entrepreneurial learning of organizational members can help the family business (or other organizations) to acquire new organizational knowledge and capabilities and foster ongoing business innovation. Given the applicability of social theories to situations where informality and social interactions are often apparent, social organizational learning could be particularly useful in explaining how this informal co-participation triggers collective learning within business families.

Complemented by appropriate data collection methods such as in-depth, longitudinal interviews and ethnographic studies, social organizational learning theories could allow family business scholars to move beyond the measurement of cause–effect relationships towards an understanding of what actually goes on during the entrepreneurial process and within the relationships in which entrepreneurs are embedded. The study of social experiences and human interactions could give a better understanding of how these inter-relationships and collective learning underpin opportunity identification, evaluation and exploitation within family businesses.

Studies that take this approach, however, need to be aware that social learning perspectives emphasize that learning often takes place in organizational communities or groups that are not formally recognized. Therefore researchers should consider what is the most appropriate group to study within the family business context. The following section argues that studies should move away from the firm level of analysis and identify key groups that are core to the functioning of family businesses.

ENTREPRENEURIAL LEARNING AT THE GROUP LEVEL: THE 'FAMILY MANAGEMENT GROUP'

Organizational learning researchers suggest that studies should move away from the individual or the firm level of analysis to identify new, more appropriate units of analysis (Easterby-Smith et al., 2000) or to use approaches that can bridge multiple levels of learning (Grey and Antonacopoulou, 2004; Casey, 2005). A number of scholars emphasize the significance of examining learning processes at the group or team level (Edmondson, 1999; Vince et al., 2002) to understand how a group of key individuals acquires knowledge that is critical for business survival (Easterby-Smith et al., 2000; Vince et al., 2002). An organizational group is a set of individuals who are interdependent in their tasks; share responsibility for outcomes; and perceive themselves, and are recognized as, a group (Alderfer, 1977; Hackman, 1987). Focusing on the group level of analysis, it is possible to identify the potential contribution that group learning can make to organizational learning, for example the family business as a whole (Easterby-Smith et al., 2000).

Entrepreneurship at the group level has mainly been studied within entrepreneurial (founding) teams (Eisenhardt and Schoonhoven, 1990; Ensley et al., 2002; Cooney, 2005). An entrepreneurial team is a group of individuals involved in the establishment of a firm in which they have a financial interest and a direct influence on the strategic choice of the firm (Gartner et al., 1994; Ensley et al., 1998). Entrepreneurial teams may include copreneurs (i.e. entrepreneurial couples) (Dyer and Handler, 1994; Fitzgerald and Muske, 2002), individuals sharing similar family ties (Ucbasaran et al., 2003), and unrelated experts (Ucbasaran et al., 2003; Forbes et al., 2006). Although important in terms of researching collective entrepreneurial actions, research within entrepreneurial teams tends to take a rather static and short-term perspective to the study of collective entrepreneurship. These studies tend to neglect the dynamism and evolutionary aspects of team formation and development (Vanaelst et al., 2006). They focus instead on examining entrepreneurial outcomes, such as new venture creation and entrepreneurial performance (Ensley et al., 2002; Cooney, 2005). There is clear potential to study collective entrepreneurial learning within entrepreneurial teams, and family business researchers might examine teams comprising different combinations of family and non-family members.

A parallel stream of research claims that entrepreneurial action in the course of business functioning is essentially tied to the top management team (TMT) (Srivastava and Lee, 2005; Vanaelst et al., 2006; Escriba-Esteve et al., 2009). However, studies that focus on the importance of TMTs on organizational innovation again tend to take a static perspective, ignoring the process nature of team functioning and evolvement, as well as the learning character of the entrepreneurial process. Research on TMTs is also primarily positivistic, focusing on cause and effect relationships and the measurement of the impact of TMT characteristics on entrepreneurship-related outcomes within the organization.

Acknowledging the importance of family in family business entrepreneurship, family business scholars tend to focus on groups at the core of business functioning and dominated by family members. Thus they emphasize that family business survival and continuity depend on the entrepreneurial practices of the family ownership group (Habbershon and Pistrui, 2002), entrepreneurial founding teams (EFTs) (Dyer and Handler, 1994; Fitzgerald and Muske, 2002) and top management teams (TMTs) (Kellermanns and Eddleston, 2006; Ling and Kellermanns, 2010). In a similar way to the approaches that researchers use to study collective entrepreneurship, the focus has been on teams of individuals who are the ultimate owners of the family business.

A focus on the entrepreneurial team, the top management team or the family ownership group seems inadequate to capture fully the essence of family businesses' entrepreneurial functioning. Such foci exclude members of the owning family that may not have top managerial positions or voting rights (yet) but may have an influence on decisions concerning entrepreneurial action (Salvato, 2004; Kellermanns et al., 2008). This is the case of the younger generation or in-laws who, despite not being active owners of the business, are expected to participate in decisions pertaining to entrepreneurship within the family business (Discua-Cruz, 2009). Research shows that entrepreneurial decision-making may be a closed practice within the family business, restricted to members of the controlling family (Discua-Cruz, 2009). Thus family business entrepreneurship may often be practised by family members rather than non-family executives (Habbershon and Pistrui, 2002; Astrahan, 2003; Salvato, 2004; Kellermanns et al., 2008; Discua-Cruz, 2009). Another limitation with current units of analysis is the failure to examine changing group composition over time, which limits efforts to capture fully the impact of family on business phenomena such as entrepreneurship across the generations.

Since family members essentially control the everyday management and strategic direction of family businesses (Westhead and Cowling, 1998), a focus on family members who are involved in the business would be a good starting point for understanding collective entrepreneurial learning within family businesses. The 'family management group' (FMG) includes actors from the core family that controls one or a portfolio of businesses. These are individuals related by blood or marriage, originating from different (family) generations, and are fully employed in the family business(es). The FMG is an informal group, in the sense that it is not usually recognized formally within the organization or hierarchy of the family business, and it does not favour explicit recognition by business stakeholders. It is a group likely to include family actors from different generations that occupy managerial and non-managerial positions, at different hierarchical levels, and from different business units or even businesses. Individual members of the FMG could have varying levels of ownership from zero to 100 per cent.

In contrast to the EFT, TMT or the family shareholders as units of analysis, a focus on the FMG could help researchers to capture the dynamism and evolutionary aspects of team formation and development, as well as the entrepreneurial learning and practices within the family business context, across the generations. This group has an intergenerational character and does not face the threat of dilution of group composition through time, since it will always be composed of family members. Understanding how members of this group learn to identify, evaluate and exploit entrepreneurial opportunities, through generations, is critical in shedding light on the way that family businesses succeed in developing and sustaining an entrepreneurial orientation over time. We would argue that family business researchers should focus on the FMG as actors within this group essentially control strategic decision-making and entrepreneurship-related decisions within the family business. We now consider how to use the FMG as a unit of analysis to examine collective entrepreneurial learning by employing social organizational learning perspectives.

SOCIAL ORGANIZATIONAL PERSPECTIVE AND ENTREPRENEURIAL LEARNING AT THE FMG LEVEL

We have argued that a focus on formally sanctioned groups, such as the top management team, the entrepreneurial founding team or the team of family business shareholders, may inadequately capture the social character of family business entrepreneurship and the learning process that is embedded in its core functioning. Entrepreneurship within a business context is a collaborative process, and individuals, irrespective of their hierarchical position within the organization, can be core players in opportunity identification and exploitation (Dess et al., 2003). Thus research approaches that can capture the interactions between individuals at different levels within the organization may be more appropriate in understanding the process that leads to entrepreneurial action. Such approaches would assign less emphasis to formal teams and attribute more importance to informal groups and communities, and the social practices that generate ongoing entrepreneurial action.

The FMG is an informal (organizational) group, in the sense that it is not a formally sanctioned organizational team, such as a production team or a group recognized by its position in the business hierarchy, such as a top management team (TMT), nor a group that favours explicit recognition by business stakeholders. Furthermore, entrepreneurial learning itself is a practice that evolves implicitly and informally (Cope and Watts, 2000; Taylor and Thorpe, 2004; Hamilton, 2005, 2011). Social organizational learning approaches are thus ideal for capturing this informality and draw meaning out of informal practices within informal spaces. Further, social theoretical perspectives acknowledge the co-participation of individuals and can thus help to explain collective entrepreneurial learning experiences of FMG members. Using qualitative research approaches and theoretical frameworks such as situated learning, social capital and activity theory, researchers could build a good understanding of how members of the FMG learn to think and act entrepreneurially within the collective.

Situated learning (Brown and Duguid, 1991; Hamilton, 2005, 2011), for example, can be used to explain the everyday interactions of FMG members within and outside the business context in the course of their co-participation in collective entrepreneurial practices. This perspective can capture the collective learning that stems from collaborative engagement in family business entrepreneurship. The FMG can be conceptualized as a group where younger family members are nurtured, intergenerationally, by the incumbents in the entrepreneurial opportunity processes. The interactions among FMG members of different generations may be important in terms of promoting collective entrepreneurial learning of all participating family members. Social capital theories (Granovetter, 1985; Lin, 1999; Burt, 2000; Adler and Kwon, 2002), in turn, might view members of the FMG as embedded within networks of personal relations, which can be essential sources of entrepreneurial learning. Family members can be seen as a closed group (i.e. the FMG), characterized by high interdependency (Granovetter, 2005), and knowledge sharing through cooperative action (Andersson et al., 2005). Each family member can be viewed as an agent of the promotion of new knowledge within the FMG through his/her embeddedness in open network structures, which represent personal relations that other family members do not share (Burt, 1992; Andersson et al., 2005). These may include, for example, personal relations of a family member with a friend who is an entrepreneur maintaining his/her own business and can offer useful advice. The participation of different FMG actors in different personal networks can, therefore, become a source of learning about how to practise entrepreneurship within the family business. At the same time, the interdependency and collectivism among FMG actors can allow the sharing of this new knowledge within the FMG, thus creating a group-specific shared capital concerning the way family business entrepreneurship should be approached.

Finally, under the lenses of the activity theory (Engeström, 1987; Engeström and Middleton, 1996; Engeström and Miettinen, 1999; Engeström, 1999), FMG members can be seen as jointly interacting within an activity that can help them through time to acquire collective entrepreneurial learning. Such an activity can be the practice of entrepreneurship itself. The joint practice of entrepreneurship by FMG members can be seen as a system in its own right that includes a community of multiple points of view, traditions and interest. Younger family members can be seen as those socialized and trained by senior members to acquire understanding of how entrepreneurship is routinely carried out within the business. The presence of a number of family members and their diverse viewpoints can eventually trigger change to the way that entrepreneurship is practised. Internalization of the new approach to entrepreneurship can therefore become a source of collective learning of FMG members.

CONCLUSIONS

In this chapter, we have argued that organizational learning perspectives can be used to explain entrepreneurial learning within the family business context under a collectivistic lens. Collective entrepreneurial learning can be seen as a central element of collective entrepreneurial practices within family businesses. Given the increased emphasis on collective units for understanding family business entrepreneurship, such as copreneurs (Dyer and Handler, 1994; Fitzgerald and Muske, 2002) family ownership groups (Habbershon and Pistrui, 2002) and family management teams (Kellermanns and Eddleston, 2006; Ling and Kellermanns, 2010), it might be useful to understand how family business members learn as a result of engaging themselves within collective entrepreneurial practices. An understanding of the process that exposes individuals within collective entrepreneurial learning experiences can help family businesses to set up structures and procedures for encouraging business members to participate in collective entrepreneurial practices within the family business.

It was argued that social organizational learning perspectives that draw upon social theories, such as situated learning (Brown and Duguid, 1991; Hamilton, 2005, 2011), social capital (Granovetter, 1985; Burt, 2000; Lin, 1999; Adler and Kwon, 2002; Taylor and Thorpe, 2004), and activity theory (Engeström, 1987; Engeström and Middleton, 1996; Engeström, 1999) can be useful in understanding collective entrepreneurial learning practices within the family business context. These perspectives view learning as taking place informally within organizational communities and groups that are not always formally recognized. Since entrepreneurship tends to be learned informally (Cope and Watts, 2000; Taylor and Thorpe, 2004; Hamilton, 2005, 2011), social organizational learning perspectives can be useful in terms of capturing collective learning experiences within family business entrepreneurship.

Understanding the importance that family has on business entrepreneurship, we have argued that collective entrepreneurial learning should be studied at the level of the 'family management group', which includes the group of family members who are engaged within everyday business practices. Since family members are essentially those that shape the direction of the family business and entrepreneurial action is often tied to controlling family members (Salvato, 2004; Kellermanns et al., 2008), this group becomes the most relevant when attempting to study family business entrepreneurship. The FMG can offer better possibilities for understanding entrepreneurship within family businesses, due to its transgenerational character.

The FMG is an informal group and entrepreneurial learning also takes place informally as part of everyday practice (Cope and Watts, 2000; Taylor and Thorpe, 2004; Hamilton, 2005, 2011). This chapter argued that social organizational learning perspectives are best suited to understanding collective entrepreneurial learning within the FMG. Socially derived organizational learning perspectives, such as situated learning (Brown and Duguid, 1991; Hamilton, 2005, 2011), social capital (Granovetter, 1985; Burt, 2000; Lin, 1999; Adler and Kwon, 2002; Taylor and Thorpe, 2004) and activity theory (Engeström and Middleton, 1996; Engeström, 1999) capture social interactions within informal groups such as the FMG, and can be important in explaining collective entrepreneurial learning experiences of family members within their business.

We hope this chapter will encourage researchers within the family business field to explore further the links between organizational and entrepreneurial learning, as well as to consider the use of the FMG as a unit of analysis. Research within family business entrepreneurship needs to move beyond static and individualistic perspectives and adopt approaches that acknowledge the process nature, learning character and collective manner of entrepreneurial practices. Social organizational learning perspectives are ideally situated to contribute to a more nuanced understanding of the realities of entrepreneurial learning in family businesses.

Since entrepreneurship within the family business is crucial to securing family firm profitability, growth and longevity (Rogoff and Heck, 2003; Salvato, 2004), and entrepreneurial action is often tied to controlling family firm members (Salvato, 2004; Kellermanns et al., 2008), the study of entrepreneurial learning at the FMG level could help facilitate stronger links between the fields of entrepreneurship and family business and capture transgenerational entrepreneurial practices within the family business context.

REFERENCES

Adler, P. and Kwon, S. (2002), 'Social capital: prospects for a new concept', *Academy of Management Review*, **27**(1), 17–40.

Alderfer, C. (1977), 'Group and intergroup relations', in J.R. Hackman and J.L. Suttle (eds), *Improving Life at Work*, Santa Monica, CA: Goodyear, pp. 227–96.

Anderson, A., Park, J. and Jack, S. (2007), 'Entrepreneurial social capital: conceptualizing social capital in new high-tech firms', *International Small Business Journal*, **25**, 245–72.

Andersson, U., Blankenburg-Holm, D. and Johanson, J. (2005), 'Opportunities, relational embeddedness, and network structure', in P. Ghauri, A. Hadjikhani and J. Johanson (eds), *Managing Opportunity Development in Business Networks*, Basingstoke: Palgrave Macmillan, pp. 27–48.

Argyris, C. and Schön, D. (1978), *Organizational Learning: A Theory of Action Perspective*, Reading, MA: Addison Wesley.

Astrahan, J. (2003), 'Commentary on the special issue: the emergence of a field', *Journal of Business Venturing*, **18**, 567–72.

Baron, R. (2004), 'The cognitive perspective: a valuable tool for answering entrepreneurship's basic "why" questions', *Journal of Business Venturing*, **19**(2), 169–72.

Blackler, F. and McDonald, S. (2000), 'Power, mastery and organizational learning', *Journal of Management Studies*, **37** (6), 833–51.

Blatt, R. (2009), 'Tough love: how communal schemas and contracting practices build relational capital in entrepreneurial teams', *Academy of Management Review*, **34** (3), 533–51.

Bowey, J. and Easton, G. (2007), 'Entrepreneurial social capital unplugged: an activity-based analysis', *International Small Business Journal*, **25**, 273–306.

Brown, J. and Duguid, P. (1991), 'Organizational learning and communities of practice: toward a unified view of working, learning, and innovation', *Organizational Science*, **2** (1), 40–57.

Burt, R.S. (2000), 'The network structure of social capital', in R.I. Sutton and B.M. Staw (eds), *Research in Organizational Behavior*, Greenwich, CT: JAI Press, pp. 345–423.

Casey, A. (2005), 'Enhancing individual and organizational learning: a sociological Model', *Management Learning*, **36**(2), 131–47.

Casson, M. and Della Giusta, M. (2007), 'Entrepreneurship and social capital: analysing the impact of social networks on entrepreneurial activity from a rational action perspective', *International Small Business Journal*, **25**, 220–44.

Cooney, T. (2005), 'Editorial: what is an entrepreneurial team?', *International Small Business Journal*, **23**(3), 226–35.

Cope, J. (2003), 'Entrepreneurial learning and critical reflection: discontinuous events as triggers for higher-level learning', *Management Learning*, **34**(4), 429–50.

Cope, J. (2005), 'Toward a dynamic learning perspective of entrepreneurship', *Entrepreneurship Theory and Practice*, **29**(4), 373–97.

Cope, J. and Watts, G. (2000), 'Learning by doing: an exploration of experience, critical incidents and reflection in entrepreneurial learning', *International Journal of Entrepreneurial Behaviour and Research*, **6**(3), 104–24.

Corbett, A. (2007), 'Learning asymmetries and the discovery of entrepreneurial opportunities', *Journal of Business Venturing*, **22**, 97–118.

De Carolis, D.M. and Saparito, P. (2006), 'Social capital, cognition, and entrepreneurial opportunities: a theoretical framework', *Entrepreneurship Theory and Practice*, **30**, 41–56.

Dess, G., Ireland, D., Zahra, S., Floyd, S., Janney, J. and Lane, P. (2003), 'Emerging issues in corporate entrepreneurship', *Journal of Management*, **29**(3), 351–78.

Discua Cruz, A. (2009), 'Collective perspectives in portfolio entrepreneurship: a study of family business groups in Honduras', doctoral thesis, Lancaster University Management School.

Discua Cruz, A. and Howorth C. (2010), 'Family entrepreneurial teams: a vehicle for portfolio entrepreneurship', Lancaster University Management School Working Paper.

Discua Cruz, A., Howorth C. and Hamilton, E. (2009), 'Portfolio entrepreneurship as a solution to the succession crisis: a case study of women's successors in Honduras', in J. Astrachan, K. MacMillan, T. Pieper and P. Poutziouris (eds), *Family Business Casebook 2008–2009*, Kennesaw: Cox Family Enterprise Centre, pp. 25–48.

Dimov, D. (2007), 'Beyond the single-person, single-insight attribution in understanding entrepreneurial opportunities', *Entrepreneurship Theory and Practice*, **31**(5), 713–31.

Downing, S. (2005), 'The social construction of entrepreneurship: narrative and dramatic processes in the coproduction of organizations and identities', *Entrepreneurship Theory and Practice*, **29**(2), 185–204.

Dyer, W.G. (2003), 'The family: the missing variable in organizational research', *Entrepreneurship Theory and Practice*, **27**(4), 401–16.

Dyer, W.G. and Handler, W. (1994), 'Entrepreneurship and family business: exploring the connections', *Entrepreneurship Theory and Practice*, **19**(1), 71–84.

Easterby-Smith, M., Crossan, M. and Nicolini, D. (2000), 'Organizational learning: debates past, present and future', *Journal of Management Studies*, **37**(6), 783–96.

Edmondson, A. (1999), 'Psychological safety and learning behavior in work teams', *Administrative Science Quarterly*, **44**(2), 350–83.

Edmondson, A. and Moingeon, B. (2004), 'From organizational learning to the learning organization', in C. Grey and E. Antonacopoulou (eds), *Essential Readings in Management Learning*, London: Sage Publications, pp. 21–36.

Eisenhardt, K. and Schoonhoven, C.B. (1990), 'Organizational growth: linking founding team, strategy, environment, and growth among U.S. semiconductor ventures 1978–1988', *Administrative Science Quarterly*, **35**, 504–29.

Engeström, Y. (1987), *Learning by Expanding: An Activity Theoretical Approach to Developmental Research*, Helsinki: Orienta Konsultit.

Engeström, Y. (1999), 'Activity theory and individual and social transformation', in Y. Engeström, R. Miettinen and R.-L. Punamaki (eds), *Perspectives on Activity Theory*, New York: Cambridge University Press, pp. 19–38.

Engeström, Y. (2000), 'Activity theory as a framework for analyzing and redesigning work', *Ergonomics*, **43**(7), 960–74.

Engeström, Y. and Middleton, D. (1996), *Cognition and Communication at Work*, Cambridge: Cambridge University Press.

Engeström, Y. and Miettinen, R. (1999), 'Introduction', in Y. Engeström, R. Miettinen and R.-L. Punamaki (eds), *Perspectives on Activity Theory*, New York: Cambridge University Press, pp. 1–16.

Ensley, M., Pearson, A. and Amason, A. (2002), 'Understanding the dynamics of new venture top management teams: cohesion, conflict, and new venture performance', *Journal of Business Venturing*, **17**, 365–86.

Ensley, M.D., Carland, J.C. and Carland, J.W. (1998), 'The effects of entrepreneurial team skill heterogeneity and functional diversity on new venture performance', *Journal of Business and Entrepreneurship*, **10**(1), 1–11.

Escriba-Esteve, A., Sanchez-Peinado, L. and Sanchez-Peinado, E. (2009), 'The influence of top management teams in the strategic orientation and performance of small and medium-sized enterprises', *British Journal of Management*, **20**, 581–97.

Ettl, K. and Welter, F. (2010), 'Gender, context and entrepreneurial learning', *International Journal of Gender and Entrepreneurship*, **2**(2), 108–29.

Fiol, M. and Lyles, M. (1985), 'Organizational learning', *Academy of Management Review*, **10**(4), 803–13.

Fitzgerald, M. and Muske, G. (2002), 'Copreneurs: an exploration and comparison to other family businesses', *Family Business Review*, **15**(1), 1–16.

Fletcher, D. (2006), 'Entrepreneurial processes and the social construction of opportunity', *Entrepreneurship & Regional Development*, **18**(5), 421–40.

Fletcher, D. (2007), '"Toy Story": the narrative world of entrepreneurship and the creation of interpretive communities', *Journal of Business Venturing*, **22**, 649–72.

Forbes, D., Borchert, P., Zellmer-Bruhn, M. & Sapienza, H. (2006), 'Entrepreneurial team formation: an exploration of new member addition', *Entrepreneurship Theory and Practice*, **30**(2), 225–48.

Friedman, V., Lipshitz, R. and Popper, M. (2005), 'The mystification of organizational learning', *Journal of Management Inquiry*, **14**(1), 19–30.

Gartner, W. (1988), '"Who is an Entrepreneur?" is the wrong question', *Entrepreneurship Theory and Practice*, **13** (14), 47–68.

Gartner, W.B., Shaver, K.G., Gatewood, E. and Katz, J.A. (1994), 'Finding the entrepreneur in entrepreneurship', *Entrepreneurship Theory and Practice*, **18**(3), 5–10.

Granovetter, M.(1985), 'Economic action and social structure: the problem of embeddedness', *The American Journal of Sociology*, **91**(3), 481–510.

Granovetter,M.(2005), 'The impact of social structure on economic outcomes', *Journal of Economic Perpectives*, **19**(1), 33–50.

Grey, C. and Antonacopoulou, E. (2004), 'Introduction', in C. Grey and E. Antonacopoulou (eds), *Essential Readings in Management Learning*, London: Sage Publications pp. 1–17.

Habbershon, T. and Pistrui, J. (2002), 'Enterprising families domain: family-influenced ownership groups in pursuit of transgenerational wealth', *Family Business Review*, **15**(3), 223–38.

Hackman, J.R. (1987), 'The design of work teams', in J. Lorsch (ed.), *Handbook of Organizational Behaviour*, Englewood Cliffs, NJ: Prentice-Hall, pp. 315–42.

Hamilton, E. (2005), 'Situated learning in family business: narratives from two generations', doctoral thesis, Lancaster University Management School.

Hamilton, E. (2006), 'Whose story is it anyway? Narrative accounts of the role of women in founding and establishing family businesses', *International Small Business Journal*, **24**(3), 253–71.

Hamilton, E. (2011), 'Entrepreneurial learning in family business: a situated learning perspective', *Journal of Small Business and Enterprise Development*, **18**(1), 8–26

Hayes, J. and Allinson, C. (1998), 'Cognitive style and the theory and practice of individual and collective learning in organizations', *Human Relations*, **51**(7), 847–71.

Hinrichs, C., Gillespie, G. and Feenstra, G. (2004), 'Social learning and innovation at retail farmers' markets', *Rural Sociology*, **69**(1), 31–58.

Holcomb, T., Ireland, D., Holmes, M. and Hitt, M. (2009), 'Architecture of entrepreneurial learning: exploring the link among heuristics, knowledge, and action', *Entrepreneurship Theory and Practice*, **33**(1), 167–92.

Howorth, C., Tempest, S. and Coupland, C. (2005), 'Rethinking entrepreneurship methodology and definitions of the entrepreneur', *Journal of Small Business and Enterprise Development*, **12**(1), 24–40.

Jack, S. (2010), 'Approaches to studying networks: implications and outcomes', *Journal of Business Venturing*, **25**(1), 120–37.

Jennings, P., Perren, L. and Carter, S. (2005), 'Guest editors' introduction: alternative perspectives on entrepreneurship research', *Entrepreneurship Theory and Practice*, **29**(2), 145–52.

Kellermanns, F. and Eddleston, K. (2006), 'Corporate entrepreneurship in family firms: a family perspective', *Entrepreneurship Theory and Practice*, **30**(6), 809–30.

Kellermanns, F., Eddleston, K., Barnett, T. and Pearson, A. (2008), 'An exploratory study of family member characteristics and involvement: effects on entrepreneurial behavior in the family firm', *Family Business Review*, **21**(1), 1–14.

Lave, J. and Wenger, E. (1991), *Situated Learning: Legitimate Peripheral Participation*, New York: Cambridge University Press.

Leitch, C., Hill, F. and Harrison, R. (2010), 'The philosophy and practice of interpretivist research in entrepreneurship: quality, validation, and trust', *Organizational Research Methods*, **13**(1), 67–84.

Levitt, B. and March, J. (1988), 'Organizational learning', *Annual Review of Sociology*, **14**, 319–40.

Lin, N. (1999), 'Building a network theory of social capital', *Connections*, **22**, 28–51.

Ling, Y. and Kellermanns, F. (2010), 'The effects of family firm specific sources of TMT diversity: the moderating role of information exchange frequency', *Journal of Management Studies*, **47**(2), 322–44.

Lumpkin, G.T. (2005), 'The role of organizational learning in the opportunity-recognition process', *Entrepreneurship Theory and Practice*, **29**(4), 451–72.

Miller, D. (1983), 'The correlates of entrepreneurship in three types of firms', *Management Science*, **29**(7), 770–91.

Minniti, M. and Bygrave, W. (2001), 'A dynamic model of entrepreneurial learning', *Entrepreneurship Theory and Practice*, **25**(3), 5–16.

Mitchell, R., Busenitz, L., Bird, B., Gaglio, C.M., McMullen, J., Morse, E. and Smith, B. (2007), 'The central question in entrepreneurial cognition research', *Entrepreneurship Theory and Practice*, **31**(1), 1–27.

Nonaka, I. (1994), 'A dynamic theory of organizational knowledge creation', *Organization Science*, **5**(1), 14–37.

Pentland, B. and Feldman, M. (2005), 'Organizational routines as a unit of analysis', *Industrial and Corporate Change*, **14**(5), 793–815.

Politis, D. (2005), 'The process of entrepreneurial learning: a conceptual framework', *Entrepreneurship Theory and Practice*, **29**(4), 399–424.

Popper, M. and Lipshitz, R. (2004), 'Organizational learning: mechanisms, culture, and feasibility', in C. Grey and E. Antonacopoulou (eds), *Essential Readings in Management Learning*, London: Sage Publications pp. 37–54.

Rae, D. (2000), 'Understanding entrepreneurial learning: a question of how?', *International Journal of Entrepreneurial Behaviour & Research*, **6**(3), 145–59.

Rae, D. (2006), 'Entrepreneurial learning: a conceptual framework for technology based enterprise', *Technology Analysis & Strategic Management*, **18**(1), 39–56.

Rae, D. and Carswell, M. (2001), 'Towards a conceptual understanding of entrepreneurial learning', *Journal of Small Business and Enterprise Development*, **8**(2), 150–58.

Rogoff, E.G. and Heck, R.K.Z. (2003), 'Evolving research in entrepreneurship and family business: recognizing family as the oxygen that feeds the fire of entrepreneurship', *Journal of Business Venturing*, **18**(5), 559–66.

Salvato, C. (2004), 'Predictors of entrepreneurship in family firms', *Journal of Private Equity*, **7**(3), 68–76.

Shane, S. and Venkataraman, S. (2000), 'The promise of entrepreneurship as a field of research', *Academy of Management Review*, **25**(1), 217–26.

Shane, S. (2000), 'Prior knowledge and the discovery of entrepreneurial opportunities', *Organization Science*, **11**(4), 448–69.

Shrivastava, P. (1983), 'A typology of organizational learning systems', *Journal of Management Studies*, **20**, 7–28.

Srivastava, A. and Lee, H. (2005), 'Predicting order and timing of new product moves: the role of top management in corporate entrepreneurship', *Journal of Business Venturing*, **20**, 459–81.

Taylor, D. and Thorpe, R. (2004), 'Entrepreneurial learning: a process of co-participation', *Journal of Small Business and Enterprise Development*, **11**(2), 203–11.

Ucbasaran, D., Lockett, A., Wright, M. and Westhead, P. (2003), 'Entrepreneurial founder teams: factors associated with member entry and exit', *Entrepreneurship Theory and Practice*, **28**(2), 107–28.

Vanaelst, I., Clarysse, B., Wright, M., Lockett, A., Moray, N. and Jegers, S. (2006), 'Entrepreneurial team development in academic spinouts: an examination of team heterogeneity', *Entrepreneurship Theory and Practice*, **30**(2), 249–71.

Vince, R., Sutcliffe, K. and Olivera, F. (2002), 'Organizational learning: new directions', *British Journal of Management*, **13**, S1–S6.

Virkkunen, J. and Kuutti, K. (2000), 'Understanding organizational learning by focusing on "activity systems"', *Accounting, Management and Information Technology*, **10**, 291–319.

Ward, T.B. (2004), 'Cognition, creativity, and entrepreneurship', *Journal of Business Venturing*, **19**(2), 173–88.

West, P. (2007), 'Collective cognition: when entrepreneurial teams, not individuals, make decisions', *Entrepreneurship Theory and Practice*, **31**(1), 77–102.

Westhead, P. and Cowling, M. (1998), 'Family firm research: the need for a methodological rethink', *Entrepreneurship Theory and Practice*, **23**(1), 31–56.

21 Strategy formulation in family businesses: a review and research agenda
Corinna M. Lindow

INTRODUCTION

The effect of family on strategic firm behavior is a growing field of interest in the family business literature. Issues of family business strategy are considered an important area for future research (Harris et al., 1994), because this contributes to the development of a strategic management theory of the family business (Chrisman et al., 2008). The prime goal of scholars interested in this area is to understand whether the strategic behavior of family businesses is different from non-family businesses as well as different from diverse types of family businesses and, if so, how and why they differ (Chrisman et al., 2008). The underlying supposition therein is that the family significantly impacts the business and, therefore, its strategic behavior (Ward, 1987). The influence of family on strategy is seen as so central to the firm that Chua et al. (1999) chose to define family businesses in terms of the family domination of strategic decision-making. In particular, several researchers suggest that strategy formulation, that is, the 'strategy process' (e.g. Cromie et al., 1995; Sharma et al., 1997; Carlock and Ward, 2001) and 'strategy content' of firms (e.g. Aronoff and Ward, 1997; Sharma et al., 1997), are importantly influenced by the family (Dyer, 2003).

Reviewing the existing literature on family business strategy serves as a starting point for promoting future research. There have been a number of review articles on family business strategy by scholars (e.g. Harris et al., 1994; Wortman, 1994; Sharma et al., 1996; Sharma et al., 1997; Chrisman et al., 2003; Chua et al., 2003; Chrisman et al., 2005; Chrisman et al., 2008; Ibrahim et al., 2008; Astrachan, 2010). Among them, the review by Sharma et al. (1997) proposed a review framework along the lines of the strategic management process of goal setting, strategy formulation, implementation and evaluation/control. The authors suggested that family considerations affect every step in the strategic management process and, with their framework, offered a revolutionary approach to analyzing research on family business strategy. Written in 1997, this review alongside others presented an important new basis for researchers and, subsequently, an enormous growth in scholarly activity has occurred (see Harris et al., 1994; Wortman, 1994), especially in empirical research (see Sharma et al., 1997). The largest body of emerging empirical literature currently deals with strategy formulation as an integral part of the strategic management process. However, with the field gaining momentum – specifically in the area of strategy formulation – no in-depth review in the acknowledged literature focuses along these specific lines. In fact, Sharma et al. (1997) themselves as well as authors of other reviews (Sharma et al., 1996; Sharma et al., 1997; Chrisman et al., 2003; Chrisman et al., 2008) pointed towards an insufficient understanding of family influence on strategy along the process and content dimensions of strategy formulation in family businesses. For example, Sharma et al. (1997) put forward that it was yet unknown what role the family plays in the strategic planning process and whether family businesses followed different corporate, business or functional level strategies compared to non-family businesses.

The present chapter provides information along these lines. It aims to advance the review by Sharma et al. (1997) and respond to other respective calls by systematizing extant empirical works under the heading of strategy formulation. It is hoped that such a review will serve both as a record of the scholarly ground that has already been traversed and as an exercise in evaluating the state of our current knowledge of the area. Furthermore, it aims to identify specific gaps in that knowledge and to pinpoint promising areas for future research.

This chapter is organized as follows. In the next section, the dimensions of strategy formulation on which the classificatory framework for categorizing research on family business strategy formulation in this chapter is based are delineated and described. The next sections present a critical literature review along this framework. Directions for future research are suggested consecutively, and then three key 'needs' are specifically identified. Finally, a summary section concludes.

A FRAMEWORK FOR CLASSIFYING RESEARCH ON FAMILY BUSINESS STRATEGY FORMULATION

Family influence in the firm is what makes family businesses unique entities (Chua et al., 1999). This is because in family business, as in no other organizational form, the family and the business are 'inextricably intertwined' (Pearson et al., 2008, p. 966). Family influence results from the overlap of family and business social systems, with consequences for the overall family business system. More specifically, if decisions are made in family businesses, they are made within a dual system of family and business. Therefore the strategic management process – including the formulation of strategy – is significantly influenced by the family (Harris et al., 1994; Sharma et al., 1997). Circumstances surrounding and influencing the decision-making, such as the family's influence, interests and values, form what can be called the 'strategy context', that is, 'the where' of strategy formulation. Within this strategy context, strategy formulation can be seen from two perspectives: the process focus, which is primarily concerned with the how of strategy formulation, and the content focus, which is primarily concerned with the what of strategy formulation (Acar et al., 1985). Figure 21.1 proposes a framework for classifying the literature on strategy formulation in family businesses. As illustrated, the strategy context is arranged around both perspectives and, for family businesses, particularly assumes that the family's influence, interests and values significantly surround and affect strategy formulation.

Strategy process can be understood as three partly overlapping issues: strategic thinking, strategic planning and strategic change (De Wit and Meyer, 2010). As illustrated on the left in Figure 21.1, the processes of strategy are arranged in sequential order from left to right, each focusing on a different stage in the strategy development process. Strategic thinking emphasizes synthesis, referring to 'a systemic way to recognize opportunities'

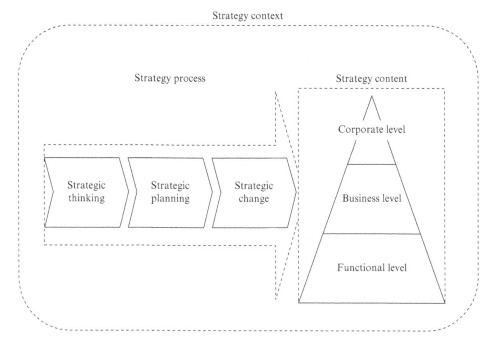

Strategy context

Strategy process

Strategy content

Strategic thinking

Strategic planning

Strategic change

Corporate level

Business level

Functional level

Source: Author, based on De Wit and Meyer (2010) and Carlock and Ward (2001).

Figure 21.1   Framework for classifying research on family business strategy formulation

(Carlock and Ward, 2001, p. 30). Strategic planning is a process that occurs after strategic thinking. Compared to strategic thinking, strategic planning is about analysis rather than synthesis (Mintzberg, 1994). It deals with the articulation, elaboration and formalization of strategies. Strategic change is the subsequent process of altering an organization's strategy (Spector, 2007).

Unlike the strategy process, strategy content can be understood as a three-level categorization: corporate, business and functional. As illustrated on the right in Figure 21.1, the contents of strategy are arranged in hierarchical order from top to bottom, ranging from the most general concept, corporate-level strategy, to the least general concept, functional strategy. Strategies at the corporate level are concerned with what businesses the firm should be in. They refer to the top level of the organization and determine the firm's different product/market combinations. Corporate strategies can be grouped into two main strands: (i) internationalization and (ii) concentration or diversification (Analoui and Karami, 2003). Strategies at the business level are concerned with how the firm should compete within a business line. They refer to single product market arenas (Schendel and Hofer, 1979). Business strategies can be grouped according to different sources of sustainable competitive advantage, such as cost or differentiation (Porter, 1980), product/market aggressiveness (Miles and Snow, 1978) or vertical integration (Dsouza, 1990). Strategies at the functional level are more detailed strategies dealing with how each functional area and unit will carry out its functional activities to implement the business strategies. Major functional strategy areas include marketing, finance, research and development (R&D), as well as human resource management (HRM) (Analoui and Karami, 2003).

In order to gain a better understanding of strategy formulation in family businesses, the following sections review extant research along both dimensions of strategy formulation: strategy process and strategy content, answering the question of what we know so far about strategy formulation in family businesses and what potential areas of future research are.

In all, publications reviewed included 118 peer-reviewed articles appearing in 44 journals from 1980 to 2010. Articles were identified in various databases such as Wiley InterScience, EBSCO Business Source Elite, Emerald, Informaworld, JSTOR, using combinations of terms such as *strategy, strategic, thinking, planning, change, corporate, international, concentration, diversification, business, competitive, functional, finance, financial, marketing, research and development, (R&D), HR, human resources* and *family, family-owned, family-controlled, family-run business/firm/company/enterprise* in the title, abstract and/or keywords. The articles had to be based on empirical research. They are listed in Appendix Table 21A.1. Each article was classified according to the scheme portrayed in Figure 21.1. Although some works may be missing, I am confident that this list includes the most relevant research over the period of interest. In the following, the main contributions within each category are synthesized and critically considered.

STRATEGY PROCESS IN FAMILY BUSINESSES: STRATEGIC THINKING, PLANNING AND CHANGE

Strategic Thinking

A capability for strategic thinking is essential in allowing firms to create a competitive advantage. Family businesses are likely to differ in their adoption of strategic thinking. On the one hand, aspects such as the families' shared vision and common language might foster strategic thinking. Moreover, family businesses seem to benefit from techniques that enhance strategic thinking (Drozdow and Carroll, 1997). On the other hand, the thinking in day-to-day issues and centralization of control might limit strategic thinking to family managers (Sirmon et al., 2008). According to Bonn (2001), strategic thinking on the individual level is generally determined by three characteristics: a holistic understanding of the organization and its environment; creativity; and a vision for the future of the firm. At the organizational level, strategic thinking attributes are structures, processes and systems that foster ongoing dialog among the top management team and an environment in which employees are encouraged to participate in the development of innovative ideas and strategies.

Despite the potential differences among family businesses and within non-family businesses in strategic thinking, insufficient attention has been devoted to this line of research. Among two current studies, Robins (1991), based on a family firm case study, found that strategic thinking in this company was 'limited to the totally informal' (p.338). On the other hand, O'Regan et al. (2010) showed that strategic thinking in family businesses differs across generations, hence indicating contingency relationships. While firms in second generations focus more on everyday operational aspects and hence did not have a holistic understanding of their business, firms in third generations had an increased focus on strategic aspects. Among the second- and third-generation family businesses, the authors also found different linguistic and cognitive perceptions of strategic thinking.

We know almost nothing about the ways in which individuals in family businesses think strategically and whether the family business context supports strategic thinking. Clearly, more attention needs to be directed towards factors that facilitate or hinder strategic thinking in family businesses (at both individual and organizational levels). In this regard, a contingency perspective seems particularly promising. For example, there is a need to understand how family control, generational involvement and culture contribute to or impede sustainable strategic thinking. Further, strategic thinking understood as strategic learning (Birdthistle and Fleming, 2005), that is, the process of learning about the firm in which one is involved, points toward an interesting area for future research.

Strategic Planning

The term 'strategic planning' refers to the process of developing strategy. As it has to manage and balance family and business concerns, strategic planning is of vital importance for family business survival (Carlock and Ward, 2001). Consistent with the long-term view of family businesses, strategic planning centers on setting long-term objectives and developing and implementing plans to achieve these objectives. Yet family businesses, for example, prefer to remain informal with respect to structures and policies, or have family considerations dominating business realities – all of which suggest the opposing hypothesis of reacting rather than planning. Characteristics of strategic planning include planning focus (i.e. participative versus restrictive), formality (i.e. formal versus informal planning), diversity (i.e. small versus broad variety of individuals involved) and intensity (i.e. frequent versus infrequent) (Dutton and Duncan, 1987). Moreover, strategic planning modes can be distinguished based on the time horizon (short, medium and long term) and the orientation toward the origin of data (internal versus external) (Brock and Barry, 2003).

The limited research on family business strategic planning has focused primarily on understanding the 'planning formality'. Most research indicated that family businesses have fairly formalized planning processes. For example, Trostel and Nichols (1982) showed that family businesses are not less formalized in their planning than non-family businesses. Rue and Ibrahim (1996) showed that family businesses engage in more planning than previously thought, with over half of the firms in the sample reporting written long-term plans and 97 percent reporting some specific plans related to growth. Upton et al. (2001) and Mazzola et al. (2008) found that the majority of their sampled firms had formalized strategic plans. On the other hand, Moores and Mula (2000) found that relatively few family business CEOs use formal strategic planning processes.

On the other hand, planning diversity, frequency and focus have received only limited attention in previous family business research. In regard to 'planning diversity', Malone (1989) found that a high correlation exists between outsider-dominated boards and business planning. In the same vein, Blumentritt (2006) found that boards play an important role in strategic planning. More specifically, family businesses with either boards of directors or advisory boards were found to be much more likely to engage in formal planning than were those without such bodies. In accordance with Blumentritt (2006), Nordqvist and Melin (2010), in analyzing three Swedish family businesses, found that executive board members but also non-family and non-executive board members played an important role in the strategic planning process. With regard to 'planning frequency', Rue and Ibrahim (1996) reported that strategic plans are mostly reviewed monthly. According to Upton and colleagues (2001), written plans had a long-term planning horizon of three to five years. Finally, with regard to 'planning focus', Malone (1989) could not confirm his hypothesis according to which the locus of control is related with strategic planning in family businesses. Similarly, the study by Peters and Buhalis (2004) showed that employee integration in planning is pursued to a medium degree.

As is evident from this account, at this point in time a limited amount of research focused on family business' strategic planning process. Thus future research is needed, in particular with respect to the planning characteristics of formality, diversity, frequency and focus, and planning modes of time horizon and origin of data. The question arises whether, in line with a contingency view, planning characteristics are dependent on family factors. For example, are more or less formalized or shorter- or longer-term planning used and useful in certain situations? Moreover, the question arises whether and in what ways varying degrees and dimensions of family influence affect strategic planning.

Strategic Change

Firm survival and performance, especially those of family businesses, rest on their ability to be responsive to changes in competitive and environmental threats (Zahra et al., 2008). Strategic change is about people, organizational structures and systems. Having been described as conservative and resistant to change, family businesses may be distinctive in how they respond to changes. Also, family members may face unique exit barriers that restrict them from refocusing the business (e.g. Sharma and Manikutty, 2005). According to Aronoff and Ward (1997), such inhibitors include, for example, long tenures of leaders, autocratic/paternalistic management styles, or the tendency to be risk- and debt-averse. Family businesses may further have certain structures and systems that promote or hinder strategic reorientation (Rüsen, 2011). On the other hand, family businesses are characterized by qualities such as 'independent command' (Miller and Le Breton-Miller, 2003, p. 129), indicating that leaders may be more free to initiate changes.

So far, several research contributions have focused on family business governance aspects in relation to strategic change. For example, Sirmon et al. (2008) showed that family businesses are less rigid in their strategic response than non-family businesses. Accordingly, when faced with the threat of imitation, family businesses maintain higher levels of R&D investment and internationalization. However, this is true only at lower ownership levels as risk aversion increases. Moreover, Le Breton-Miller and Miller (2006) demonstrated that linkages exist between CEO tenure and strategy sustainability for family businesses. Again indicating contingency relations, this linkage was moderated by factors such as conflict in the family businesses executive team. Extending these results, Ensley (2006) showed that family businesses with long-tenured CEOs tend to maintain the same strategy in the presence of high levels of executive team task conflict.

Another stream of limited research focuses on cultural aspects in relation to strategic change. Based on case research, Hall et al. (2001) showed that certain cultural patterns facilitate strategic changes in family businesses. Accordingly, to encourage and foster radical change, firms need to have explicit and open cultures. In the same line of thought, Zahra et al. (2008) identified that higher levels of family and stewardship culture are associated with strategic flexibility.

Overall, the limited research addressing strategic change in family businesses is dominated by governance and cultural antecedents of strategic change. Consistent with Salvato et al. (2010), more research is needed that investigates factors that constrain or facilitate strategic change in family businesses. This advances our knowledge of family business renewal capabilities. As has become evident, contingency relations seem to be a particularly fruitful path for future research. More specifically, how do individual (e.g. owner-manager characteristics and cognitions), group (e.g. power dynamics/CEO dominance in the top management team or heterogeneity, size, role interdependence of the top management team) and/or organizational factors (e.g. formal versus informal planning, reward systems) impact strategic change? Moreover, with extant research exploring family businesses' responsiveness to changes in the competitive environment, future efforts could build on these works by exploring processes of crisis management and restructuring; for example, how do family businesses deal with different crisis situations (i.e. immediate emerging and sustained crisis) and different levels of time pressure, control and uncertainty? How are response options evaluated? Consistent with Zahra et al. (2008) and Sirmon et al. (2008), different degrees and dimensions of family influence provide one needed step in building knowledge related to strategic change in family businesses.

STRATEGY CONTENT IN FAMILY BUSINESSES: CORPORATE, BUSINESS AND FUNCTIONAL STRATEGIES

Corporate Strategies

'Internationalization' refers to the firm's actions in one or several foreign markets. Thus international strategies concern the choice of foreign markets, products and services offered in select foreign markets as well as the mode of market entry (i.e. via subsidiary, foreign branch, joint venture, franchising, license or export). Internationalization can be beneficial for family businesses, as it may provide competitive advantages or protect them from competitive disadvantages (Gallo and Sveen, 1991). However, an internationalization strategy requires a significant amount of risk taking, which might be incompatible with the family businesses characteristic of being conservative and risk-averse (e.g. Zahra, 2005). Moreover, family members may fear losing control when internationalizing (e.g. Donckels and Fröhlich, 1991). As another barrier, family businesses might be faced with difficulties in accessing the resources and managerial capabilities essential to internationalize successfully (Graves and Thomas, 2004, 2006, 2008).

Research has found that family influence plays an important role in the degree of internationalization (e.g. Casillas and Acedo, 2005). Nearly a dozen studies assess this topic but provide mixed results. Several studies support negative associations between family involvement and internationalization (Donckels and Fröhlich, 1991; Gallo and

Garcia-Pont, 1996; Okoroafo, 1999; Fernández and Nieto, 2005; Thomas and Graves, 2005; Fernández and Nieto, 2006). On the other hand, opposing results have been found by some scholars (Davis and Harveston, 2000; Zahra, 2003). As a consequence of the mixed findings, Marchisio et al. (2010) recently tested for and found non-linear associations between family ownership and internationalization, where moderate levels of family ownership enhanced internationalization. Besides, studies have also considered several other aspects, such as the speed and level of internationalization or factors specific to family businesses. Olivares-Mesa and Cabrera-Suarez (2006) found that family businesses internationalize later and much more slowly than do their non-family counterparts. Further research found contingency relations in observing that multigenerational (Gallo and Garcia-Pont, 1996) and descendant-led family businesses (Fernández and Nieto, 2005; Menendez-Requejo, 2005) achieve higher levels of internationalization. Zahra (2003) showed that contingency relations are most likely present between family ownership, CEO tenure and internationalization.

More research is available with regard to the mode of internationalization, again indicating that contingency relations exist. According to Claver et al. (2009), long-term vision and the presence of non-family managers increased the likelihood of foreign direct investment, including joint ventures and wholly owned subsidiaries, whereas a preference for family funds increased the likelihood of entering new markets via contractual agreements or exports. In terms of partnering, Abdellatif et al. (2010) indicated that family businesses establish fewer joint ventures than do non-family businesses.

Overall, there has been high research activity. Yet there is no clear prediction in the literature as to the effect of family on internationalization. From earlier studies, it appears that mixed results might derive from inadequate attention to non-linear associations. Thus future research should move from past simple univariate to non-linear modeling. Moreover, the findings suggest that contingency effects on the internationalization of family businesses ought to be studied in more detail.

Concentration and diversification refer to the diversity of the firm's activities. Concentration strategies within existing industries can be divided into vertical integration (i.e. the firm expands forward or backward in the value chain) and horizontal integration (i.e. the firm moves into activities related to current activities). Diversification strategies into other lines of business or industry can be divided into related (concentric) and unrelated (conglomerate) diversification. Each of the resulting four core categories of strategy alternatives can be achieved internally (organically), through investment and development, or externally (inorganically), through mergers and acquisitions and/or strategic alliances. Concentration strategy has yet to be subject to scholarly discussion, even though it has been proposed as an effective strategy for family businesses, especially in emerging markets (Poza, 1995). Being the only empirical study available to date, Donckels and Fröhlich (1991) indicated that family businesses would be less involved in production subcontracting or collaboration.

Diversification strategy has been the subject of a handful of empirical family business studies. Arguments point toward both family businesses favoring and avoiding diversification strategies. For example, based on the risk aversion argument (Gallo et al., 2004), families with large portions of their wealth invested in one firm may desire to diversify business risk. On the other hand, the aversion to risk and loss of control may lead to avoiding diversification. Empirical research on the level of diversification includes several comparative studies. Anderson and Reeb (2003) found that family ownership reduced corporate diversification, whereas family management or control concurrently did not affect diversification. Hagelin et al. (2006) and Jones et al. (2008), on Swedish and American samples respectively, did not find associations between family ownership and diversification. Highlighting negative associations again, Gómez-Mejía et al. (2010) found that family businesses diversify less than non-family businesses, both domestically and internationally, with a higher likelihood of diversifying into culturally close regions. Finally, consistent with Gómez-Mejía et al. (2010), Ducassy and Prevot (2010) found that French family businesses are on average less diversified than their non-family counterparts. The authors highlight that the divergent results to previous studies may be based on contingencies. In fact, Upton et al. (2003) found that although there were no significant differences in product market strategies between low, medium and high family-ownership groups, the use of a market penetration (concentration) strategy increased with family ownership, whereas the use of diversification strategy decreased.

Although the level of diversification in family businesses has received at least some scholarly attention, studies addressing the type and mode of diversification are rarer. In terms of type of diversification, from a portfolio-theoretical point of view, unrelated (conglomerate) versus related (concentric) diversification should effectively reduce the risk exposure of family wealth. In fact, Kim et al. (2004) highlighted the prevalence of family business conglomerates, especially in emerging markets. The study identified factors that would promote a strategy of unrelated diversification. These factors include, for example, the incidence of a first-mover advantage, the alliance with business partners, and increases in home market competitive intensity. Analyzing the association between family ownership and type of diversification, Ducassy and Prevot (2010), based on a sample of French family and non-family businesses, could not confirm an association with the type of diversification. In terms of the mode of diversification, logic suggests that if family businesses follow a more risk-averse growth strategy, *ceteris paribus*, they should prefer organic over inorganic diversification strategies. In that respect, Shim and Okamuro (2010), based on a Japanese data set, found that family businesses merge less frequently than non-family businesses. However, the higher the level of family ownership, the more ready to merge were the family members.

To date, there are few studies on the concentration strategies of family businesses. An extensive amount of research is needed on the impact of family on concentration strategy. The vast amount of research done outside of the family business context presents numerous research opportunities to conduct interesting and useful research. Future areas include, for example, family businesses' level of (supply chain) integration and relevant determinants or the choice of vertical integration over strategic outsourcing. Moreover, we know too little about the diversification and de-diversification strategies of family businesses. The limited research examining the effect of family on the level of diversification strategy so far has been equivocal. Examination of how different degrees and dimensions of family influence relate to the level of diversification would provide a promising extension of previous research. Such examinations could also reveal contingency relations that were not in focus previously.

Business-Level Strategies

Business-level strategies are concerned with how a company can gain a competitive advantage through a distinctive way of competing. Family businesses, for example, having been described as being generally more risk averse (McConaughy et al., 2001; Naldi et al., 2007), conservative (Zahra et al., 2004) and long-term oriented (Kets de Vries, 1996). Thus they may adopt different business strategies than non-family businesses and may differ even among equals. So far, family business research has mainly used the typology of competitive strategies by Miles and Snow (1978) to assess the business strategies. Accordingly, four business strategies are viable: the prospector (competition based on innovation and exploration of new market opportunities); the defender (competition based on focusing on a smaller number of products and services); the analyzer (competition based on evaluating the successes of competitors); and the reactor (competition based on unsystematic responses to industry changes). Overall, the studies show inconclusive results. Daily and Dollinger (1991, 1992, 1993) found that family businesses were highly concentrated in defender strategies. According to McCann et al. (2001), however, family businesses tend to be mainly concentrated in defender and prospector strategies. Still other studies did not find any significant association between family and business strategy (e.g., Gudmundson et al., 1999; Jorissen et al., 2005; De Lema and Durendez, 2007). In assessing various degrees and dimensions of family influence, Pittino and Visintin (2009) found evidence that the strategies differed significantly for different levels of family ownership and management.

Compared to the extensive research on Miles and Snow's business level strategies, research addressing Porter's (1980) generic strategies are rarer. Porter (1980) identified three basic strategies of creating a competitive advantage: cost leadership (competition based on the costs associated with manufacturing the product or providing the service); differentiation strategy (competition based on providing products or services that are thought to be distinctive); and focus (competition based on concentrating on and serving a narrow segment of the market). Upton et al. (2001) used a US sample and found the majority of sampled family businesses pursued a differentiation strategy, whereas only a small percentage pursued a low-cost strategy. Van Gils et al. (2004), based on a Belgian sample, showed that a combination of cost leadership and differentiation strategy was pursued more often than a cost leadership strategy or a differentiation strategy alone. Furthermore, it was shown that nearly one-third of all firms pursued neither a cost nor a differentiation strategy, but rather remained unclear regarding their competitive strategy.

Finally, a single study addressed business strategy based on Dsouza (1990), according to whom three primary strategies exist (build strategy, i.e. competition based on vertical integration; expand strategy, i.e. competition based on resource allocation and product differentiation; and maintain strategy, i.e. competition based on market dominance and/or efficiency). This study was conducted by Daily and Thompson (1994) and did not find statistically significant differences between family and non-family companies.

Overall, while most family business studies have studied Miles and Snow's (1978) business strategies, the majority of all studies in this stream assess comparative analyses based on simple partition. That is, most research did not account for various degrees and dimension of family influence on firms. However, considering the overall mixed findings and the promising results by Pittino and Visintin (2009), this stream of research could benefit from adopting a heterogeneity view of family business, which makes for a more accurate and complete differentiation between family businesses.

Functional-Level Strategies

Marketing strategies

Inadequate marketing can have detrimental consequences for the family business (e.g. Rubenstein, 1990; File and Prince, 1996). Marketing strategies deal with pricing, selling and distributing a product; they mainly address issues regarding customer acquisition, service and retention. Family businesses, because of their trustworthy reputation (e.g. Tagiuri and Davis, 1996), positive customer perceptions (Aronoff and Ward, 1995) and obsession with quality (Robins, 1991), are in a unique position to convert those attributes into strategic advantages (Ward and Aronoff, 2002), for instance, by using appropriate branding, customer service or relationship management strategies (e.g. Miller and Le Breton-Miller, 2005).

Limited research exists on marketing strategies in family businesses. With regard to pricing, selling and distributing strategies, Teal et al. (2003) found that for older firms in the sample, significant differences exist with regard to market timing. Findings also revealed that family businesses, as they age, tend to set prices for products and services at rather higher levels than the average market price. Kotey and Meredith (1997) found that family businesses make use of marketing means such as branding, customer service or pricing, depending on the firms' performances.

With regard to branding strategies, two studies provide important findings. First, Craig et al.'s (2008) study concerns a company's brand image that can significantly influence customer decisions and how family businesses can leverage their brand images with family names. The authors demonstrated that family businesses' brand images facilitate a customer-centric orientation and, in turn, enhance firm performance. Second, Kashmiri and Mahajan (2010) found that family businesses place greater emphasis on marketing than on innovation, and this emphasis varied with family ownership.

With regard to customer service strategies, Lyman (1991) found that family businesses are much more customer oriented and that respective policies reflect the owner rather than the business. In addition, compared to their non-family counterparts, family businesses are more likely to have unwritten and informal policies on how to conduct customer service. Cooper et al. (2005) found that these firms are less likely to pursue customer relationship management initiatives than are non-family businesses. Finally, Ellington et al. (1996) showed that family businesses probably disregard quality management practices, even though this strategy is related to lower performance levels.

Overall, somewhat inadequate research exists that addresses important aspects of marketing in family business, particularly pricing, branding, bonding and quality control. Clearly, more research is needed on market strategies and tactics. Previous research indicated that contingency relations might exist. Thus further application of contingency models could be helpful in examining linkages between family influence and marketing strategic choice.

Financial strategy

Funding is one of the main challenges faced by family businesses. Many of these firms fail or forego growth opportunities because of a lack of capital (e.g. De Visscher et al., 1995). The finance gap exists because in order to preserve family ownership, control and financial independence from outsiders, family businesses often rely heavily on internally generated funds. Moreover, family businesses often face limited access to capital sources and/or have an aversion to capital sources that go beyond the traditional bank loan, such as venture capital or initial public offerings (IPOs) (e.g. Poutziouris et al., 1998; Poutziouris, 2001). In addition to capital structure, because of their long-term horizons, special governance structures and characteristics, family businesses also seem to have different investment, payout and hedging strategies compared to non-family businesses.

With regard to the financing strategies, family businesses' capital structures have been addressed by quite a few studies to date, with miscellaneous results. In an exploratory study, Gallo and Vilaseca (1996) observed that family businesses have a low debt/equity ratio. Also, Mishra and McConaughy (1999) showed that family businesses use less debt than non-family businesses. While Anderson and Reeb (2003) indicated similar findings, the Setia-Atmaja et al. (2009) study indicated higher debt in the capital structures of family businesses, respectively. The latter study, however, showed a non-linear (inverse U-shaped) relationship between family ownership and debt balance (an inflection point at 30 percent of family voting rights). Moreover, in terms of sources of finance, according to Romano et al. (2001), unlike larger family businesses, smaller family businesses typically have a substantial amount of their funding provided by internally generated funds such as owner capital and funds from other members of the management team, family and friends. Consistent with the idea that the source of financing is contingent on firm size, Poutziouris (2001) indicated that family businesses have a propensity to finance their operations in a hierarchical fashion, first using internally available funds, followed by debt and, finally, external equity. With regard to the type of finance, according to Dreux (1990) and Harvey and Evans (1995), numerous financing alternatives are available to family businesses that go far beyond IPOs. However, an IPO as a public equity type of financing has been specifically shown to be advantageous for family businesses because it provides for long-lasting growth (Mazzola and Marchisio, 2002). As Mahérault (2000) showed, whereas private family businesses are limited to self- and debt-financing and are thus unable to finance their growth due to that lack of capital, family businesses that went public did not face investment constraints. Thus going public appears to be a worthwhile financing strategy to overcome capital constraints. In addition, using cluster and discriminant analyses, Mahérault (2004) found four distinct types of IPOs. Consistent with a contingency view, the authors showed that family businesses differ in making strategic choices to be publicly listed.

In terms of investment strategies, Dunn (1995) found that it was not uncommon for family businesses to accept lower returns or longer payback periods on their investments or to sustain a lifestyle rather than maximizing profits or obtaining personal revenues. Consistent with the lower agency costs in family businesses (e.g. Jensen and Meckling, 1976), Anderson et al. (2003) found that the agency costs of debt are lower in family-controlled businesses. Considering the longer-term investment horizons and, consequently, the lower capital costs of family businesses, Zellweger (2007) proposed two generic investment strategies and therewith likely strategic alternatives of family businesses.

In terms of dividend payout strategies, Chen et al. (2005) did not find statistically significant associations between family ownership and dividend payouts. On the other hand, Setia-Atmaja et al. (2009) found significant relationships between family ownership and dividend payout ratio of Australian family businesses. The relationship was, however, non-linear; it first increased until reaching a maximum at a family ownership of 39 percent and subsequently decreased.

Finally, in terms of financial risk management strategies, Hagelin et al. (2006) found that family businesses with higher venture capital ratios were less prone to implement risk management programs (e.g. hedging).

Despite the progress made, further research on finance strategies in family businesses must be conducted. While there have been studies on financing, capital investment and dividend issuance, those studies did not give a conclusive picture. Moreover, they rarely address aspects such as working capital management, financial risk management and investment banking. Questions that remain include, for example, how family businesses differ from non-family businesses in terms of short-term financing, cash or inventory management; how they differ concerning management buy-outs and buy-ins; and how they differ with regard to risk management and hedging strategies. Moreover, as has been shown, much more work is required on non-linear associations between family influence and finance strategies as well as higher focus on contingency relations.

R&D strategies

Research and development (R&D) is a key factor for firms to achieve competitive advantages and profits. An R&D strategy is geared to maintain a flow of new products that will deliver sustained business growth in the short, medium and long term (i.e. product innovation and process improvement). Typically, in manufacturing and product design companies, a specific percentage of revenue is invested in R&D in order to enable innovation. Because R&D is an investment in new technologies, products or services involving high uncertainty and a certain risk of failure, risk-averse family businesses may be inclined toward lower R&D investments. On the other hand, one may argue that family businesses favor higher investments in R&D due to the long-term orientation of family businesses. Overall, Craig and Moores (2006) observed that family businesses place strong emphasis on innovation practices and strategy. However, supporting both the risk-aversion argument and family contingencies, Chen and Hsu (2009) found a negative association between family ownership and R&D investment, with CEO duality and board independency negatively and positively moderating the relationship, respectively. Similar contingency relations were found by Anderson et al. (2009),[1] indicating a significant negative association, with founder firms and heir firms with descendant CEOs devoting significantly less to R&D spending than either founder CEOs or professional-manager CEOs. Such contingency relations may be the reason why Miller et al. (2008) found no significant differences in R&D spending between family and non-family businesses. Adopting a contingency perspective, Miller et al. (2010) in fact indicated that different types of family owners and managers may affect R&D spending. They argued that lone founders are much more inclined toward a growth strategy (with high R&D spending, advertising spending, investment and leverage) than family-founder businesses.

The preceding makes abundantly clear the importance of family influence on R&D strategy. As the results propose, future research needs to put more emphasis on family contingencies. Moreover, with previous research having primarily addressed the level of R&D intensity, there is no research on other interesting aspects of examining issues such as R&D physical location (domestic versus offshore), cooperation (with competitors, suppliers, clients or universities) or outsourcing (internal versus external).

HR strategy

To be successful, firms must continually enhance their human capital through HRM practices such as hiring (including recruitment and selection), development (including training, employee involvement and performance appraisal), and retention (including compensation and a stimulating work environment) (Dess et al., 2002). However, the special relationship between the family and the business creates a volatile situation in such practices (Astrachan and Kolenko, 1994). Due to the institutional overlap of family and business, contradictions in norms and principles seem to interfere with effective human resource management, and they are thus likely to affect personnel selection, development and retention (Lansberg, 1983). For instance, Welsch (1993) observed that family businesses less clearly formulate criteria for management selection and that they rely less heavily on past performance as a selection criterion.

According to McCann et al. (2001), management, as well as family talent and resources, are ranked at the top in terms of important business practices. However, a negative relationship is generally found between family involvement and the use of professional HRM practices (see De Kok et al., 2006). Astrachan and Kolenko (1994) found significant differences in HRM practices for family versus non-family employees. Specifically, employee reviews, compensation plans, written employee policy manuals and written job descriptions were used more frequently for non-family than for family members. Additionally, as Harris et al. (2004) showed, employee involvement practices differ significantly for family businesses. Many of the findings of Reid et al. (2000), Reid and Adams (2001) and Reid et al. (2002) echo the findings of Astrachan and Kolenko. With respect to employee development, Matlay (2002) highlighted training and human resource development differences between family and non-family businesses. For instance, for family firms, training decisions relating to family members were resolved proactively, while other training interventions were of a rather reactive nature. Moreover, Miller et al. (2008) showed that family businesses conduct more training of their employees. Yet, as has been shown, HRM practices are dependent on contingencies, such as firm growth and size. More specifically, Leon-Guerrero et al. (1998) found that HRM practices (e.g. formal employee reviews or training) were utilized more as family businesses grow, Rutherford et al. (2003) documented challenges in personnel training, compensation and recruiting to vary significantly with firm growth and size. Kim and Gao (2010) also documented associations between family business size and HRM formality.

In terms of compensation, salaries of managers who are not family members have been found to be significantly lower than the salaries of managers in comparable positions in non-family-owned businesses (Werner and Tosi, 1995; Poza et al., 2004), and, adopting a more differentiated view, McConaughy (2000) and Gómez-Mejía et al. (2003) found that family CEOs receive lower than total compensation of professional managers. The former study found that family CEOs receive less incentive-based pay, whereas the latter study demonstrated the relative pay disadvantage increases with family ownership. Different pay mixes in family-owned and -managed businesses versus non-family and professionally managed family businesses were also detected by Upton et al. (2003) and Carrasco-Hernandez and Sánchez-Marín (2007). The former study found that high family-ownership businesses paid higher base salaries and fewer cash and non-cash incentives compared to low family-ownership businesses. Similarly, the latter study found that family-owned and -managed businesses paid more fixed components, whereas professionally managed family businesses paid more variable components. Lastly, Combs et al. (2010) added that differences in CEO compensation can be contingent on how the family is represented in the firm.

Finally, with regard to employee layoffs (downsizing), two studies documented that family businesses are less likely to lay off personnel than non-family businesses (Stavrou et al., 2007; Block, 2010).

So far, significant research efforts have been devoted to the topic of HR strategy. Yet earlier results point to the importance of contingencies. Future research on this topic would benefit from taking into account family considerations, such as the dependencies between family culture and employee turnover, the number of family successors and top management career opportunities.

CONCLUSIONS AND DIRECTIONS FOR FUTURE RESEARCH

This chapter has provided an overview of research on strategy formulation in family businesses with a particular focus on empirical works in that area. A framework is offered for both categorizing the existing literature and suggesting areas for future research. Overall, an impressive volume of work has grown around the topic of strategy formulation. Yet the findings of this vast body of research continue to be fragmentary and controversial. One of the general conclusions that can be drawn is that empirical research in strategy formulation research has only begun to accumulate in the more recent years (see Appendix Table 21A.1) and that there are still tremendous opportunities for research on family business strategy formulation. The review suggests that works regarding the content of strategy outnumber those dealing with the process of strategy formulation. We are aware of only two empirically based works dealing with strategic thinking. Moreover, the topic of strategic change remains largely unstudied. Conversely, three of the most pervasive content themes in the empirically based literature include internationalization strategy, finance strategy and HR strategy. Yet, even in the strategy content literature, there are still many gaps. There appear to be at least two major areas where research is scant: concentration/diversification and R&D strategy.

The review of the extant research in the strategic process and content areas revealed that many areas require extensions and further research questions need to be asked. Based on the previous section, three specific key needs can be identified and highlighted.

Need for a Heterogeneity View

Although the topic of strategy formulation has stimulated a slew of research studies exploring various themes, a substantial body of the work appears to put most attention on comparative studies, while only limited literature differentiates between family businesses. It is the opinion of the author that there is a future need to add to this present research with studies addressing the heterogeneity of family business as captured by varying degrees and dimensions of family influence.

As Klein et al. (2005) proposed, family businesses differ on a range of dimensions and, as Naldi et al. (2007) note, it is possible that different types of family businesses exhibit different patterns of firm behavior. Recently, proponents of this heterogeneity view have highlighted the need for prospective research to distinguish among different types of family businesses rather than comparing family to non-family businesses. Specifically, Barnett et al. (2009) emphasized that despite the tendency of researchers to distinguish between family and non-family businesses, there is an urgent need for future research to distinguish among family businesses. Moreover, several scholars, including Sharma and Manikutty (2005) and Chrisman et al. (2007), have called for a more fine-grained distinction between different types of family businesses, arguing that the bivariate characterization of firms in extant studies is too simplistic and therefore problematic. Future research attention must, therefore, focus explicitly on considering the heterogeneity among family businesses. In this sense, continuous and multidimensional definition of family businesses is useful.

Need for a Contingency Perspective

There is also a need to shift the focus from a universal to a contingency perspective. Accordingly, rather than assuming a single strategy to be pursued, in family businesses strategies may be assumed to vary with certain contextual factors, specifically family-related ones. Some recent works have focused on different contingency relations between family influence and variables of strategy formulation and offered intriguing results. In fact, Sharma et al. (1997) noted that family business research could make more progress if contingencies were identified and taken into account. Furthermore, Franz Kellermanns[2] highlighted a potential neglect of the contingency view in past family business research. Moreover, Cliff and Jennings (2005) noted that family influence should be treated as a moderator in future research, therewith unquestionably hinting towards potential contingency relations. Essentially, contingency relations have been suggested also in other areas of family business research. For example, Corbetta and Salvato (2004) applied the concept of contingency to family business boards. Salvato (2004) considered the idea while examining family business entrepreneurship behavior. Moreover, Mertens (2009) considered contingency theory in his study of succession and internationalization of family businesses. Finally, Eckert (2008) based his argumentation about structural adaptation in family businesses on contingency argumentation. This chapter recommends studies using a situational approach in the belief that such studies will provide richer results.

Need for Non-Linear Assessment

The review identified that a considerable amount of previous studies on strategy formulation was based largely on bivariate group comparisons. It is encouraging to see scholars start to focus on the assessment of non-linear effects of family on the business, with some non-linear associations detected. We need to learn more about linear versus quadratic or curvilinear associations between family influence and strategy formulation, using continuous measures of family influence. Exploring non-linear effects will positively contribute to our understanding of the nature of family strategy relationships.

ACKNOWLEDGMENTS

I am grateful for the detailed suggestions and comments provided by the anonymous reviewer on an earlier draft of this chapter. Thanks also to Joseph Astrachan and Sanjay Goel for their encouragement and support.

NOTES

1. Note that the study by Anderson et al. (2009) is an empirical working paper.
2. Source: Professor Franz Kellermanns, Keynote speech, 'Creating a culture of productive processes in family firms' at the EIASM 6th workshop on family firm management research, 8 June 2010, Barcelona, Spain

REFERENCES

Abdellatif, M., Amann, B. and Jaussaud, J. (2010), 'Family versus nonfamily business: a comparison of international strategies', *Journal of Family Business Strategy*, **1**(2), 108–16.
Acar, W., Chaganti, R. and Joglekar, P. (1985), 'Modes of strategy formulation: the content-focused and process-focused modes can and must meet!', *American Business Review*, **1**(9), 1–9.
Analoui, F. and Karami, A. (2003), *Strategic Management in Small and Medium Enterprises*, London: Thomson Learning.
Anderson, R.C. and Reeb, D.M. (2003), 'Founding-family ownership, corporate diversification, and firm leverage', *Journal of Law & Economics*, **46**(2), 653–84.
Anderson, R.C., Duru, A. and Reeb, D.M. (2009), 'Family preferences and investment policy: evidence from capital expenditures and R&D spending', Working Paper, American University.
Anderson, R.C., Mansi, S.A. and Reeb, D.M. (2003), 'Founding family ownership and the agency cost of debt', *Journal of Financial Economics*, **68**(2), 263–85.
Aronoff, C.E. and Ward, J.L. (1995), 'Family-owned businesses: a thing of the past or a model for the future?', *Family Business Review*, **8**(2), 121–30.
Aronoff, C.E. and Ward, J.L. (1997), *Preparing your Family Business for Strategic Change*, Marietta, GA: Business Owner Resources.
Astrachan, J.H. (2010), 'Strategy in family business: toward a multidimensional research agenda', *Journal of Family Business Strategy*, **1**(1), 6–14.
Astrachan, J.H. and Kolenko, T.A. (1994), 'A neglected factor explaining family business success: human resource practices', *Family Business Review*, **7**(3), 251–62.
Barnett, T., Eddleston, K. and Kellermanns, F.W. (2009), 'The effects of family versus career role salience on the performance of family and nonfamily firms', *Family Business Review*, **22**(1), 39–52.
Basly, S. (2007), 'The internationalization of family SME: an organizational learning and knowledge development perspective', *Baltic Journal of Management*, **2**(2), 154–80.
Bhalla, A., Lampel, J., Henderson, S. and Watkins, D. (2009), 'Exploring alternative strategic management paradigms in high-growth ethnic and non-ethnic family firms', *Small Business Economics*, **32**(1), 77–94.
Birdthistle, N. and Fleming, P. (2005), 'Creating a learning organisation within the family business: an Irish perspective', *Journal of European Industrial Training*, **29**(9), 730–50.
Block, J. (2010), 'Family management, family ownership, and downsizing: evidence from S&P 500 firms', *Family Business Review*, **23**(2), 109–30.
Blumentritt, T. (2006), 'The relationship between boards and planning in family businesses', *Family Business Review*, **19**(1), 65–72.

Bonn, I. (2001), 'Developing strategic thinking as a core competency', *Management Decision*, **39**(1), 63–71.

Brock, D.M. and Barry, D. (2003), 'What if planning were really strategic? Exploring the strategy–planning relationship in multinationals', *International Business Review*, **12**(5), 543–61.

Carlock, R.S. and Ward, J.L. (2001), *Strategic Planning for the Family Business: Parallel Planning to Unify the Family and Business*, Basingstoke: Palgrave Macmillan.

Carlson, D.S., Upton, N. and Seaman, S. (2006), 'The impact of human resource practices and compensation design on performance: an analysis of family-owned SMEs', *Journal of Small Business Management*, **44**(4), 531–43.

Carr, C. and Bateman, S. (2009), 'International strategy configurations of the world's top family firms', *Management International Review*, **49**(6), 733–58.

Carrasco-Hernandez, A. and Sánchez-Marín, G. (2007), 'The determinants of employee compensation in family firms: empirical evidence', *Family Business Review*, **20**(3), 215–28.

Casillas, J. and Acedo, F. (2005), 'Internationalisation of Spanish family SMEs: an analysis of family involvement', *International Journal of Globalisation and Small Business*, **1**(2), 134–51.

Chen, H.-L. and Hsu, W.-T. (2009), 'Family ownership, board independence, and R&D investment', *Family Business Review*, **22**(4), 347–62.

Chen, Z., Cheung, Y.-L., Stouraitis, A. and Wong, A.W.S. (2005), 'Ownership concentration, firm performance, and dividend policy in Hong Kong', *Pacific-Basin Finance Journal*, **13**(4), 431–49.

Child, J., Ng, S. and Wong, C. (2002), 'Psychic distance and internationalization', *International Studies of Management and Organizations*, **32**(1), 36–56.

Chrisman, J.J., Chua, J.H. and Sharma, P. (2003), 'Current trends and future directions in family business management studies: toward a theory of the family firm', Coleman Foundation White Paper Series. Madison, WI: Coleman Foundation and US Association of Small Business and Entrepreneurship, http://www.usasbe.org/knowledge/whitepapers/index.asp, retrieved 09.06.2009.

Chrisman, J.J., Chua, J.H. and Sharma, P. (2005), 'Trends and directions in the development of a strategic management theory of the family firm', *Entrepreneurship Theory and Practice*, **29**(5), 555–75.

Chrisman, J.J., Sharma, P. and Taggar, S. (2007), 'Family influences on firms: an introduction', *Journal of Business Research*, **60**(10), 1005–11.

Chrisman, J.J., Steier, L.P. and Chua, J.H. (2008), 'Toward a theoretical basis for understanding the dynamics of strategic performance in family firms', *Entrepreneurship Theory and Practice*, **32**(6), 935–47.

Chua, J.H., Chrisman, J.J. and Sharma, P. (1999), 'Defining the family business by behavior', *Entrepreneurship Theory and Practice*, **23**(4), 19–39.

Chua, J.H., Chrisman, J.J. and Steier, L.P. (2003), 'Extending the theoretical horizons of family business research', *Entrepreneurship Theory and Practice*, **27**(4), 331–8.

Claver, E., Rienda, L. and Quer, D. (2007), 'The internationalisation process in family firms: choice of market entry strategies', *Journal of General Management*, **33**(1), 1–14.

Claver, E., Rienda, L. and Quer, D. (2008), 'Family firms' risk perception: empirical evidence on the internationalization process', *Journal of Small Business and Enterprise Development*, **15**(3), 457–71.

Claver, E., Rienda, L. and Quer, D. (2009), 'Family firms' international commitment: the influence of family-related factors', *Family Business Review*, **22**(2), 125–35.

Cliff, J.E. and Jennings, P.D. (2005), 'Commentary on the multidimensional degree of family influence construct and the F-PEC measurement instrument', *Entrepreneurship Theory and Practice*, **29**(3), 341–7.

Coleman, S. and Carsky, M. (1999), 'Sources of capital for small family-owned businesses: evidence from the national survey of small business finances', *Family Business Review*, **12**(1), 73–84.

Combs, J.G., Penney, C.R., Crook, T.R. and Short, J.C. (2010), 'The impact of family representation on CEO compensation', *Entrepreneurship Theory and Practice*, **34**(6), 1125–44.

Cooper, M.J., Upton, N. and Seaman, S. (2005), 'Customer relationship management: a comparative analysis of family and nonfamily business practices', *Journal of Small Business Management*, **43**(3), 242–56.

Corbetta, G. and Salvato, C. (2004), 'The board of directors in family firms: One size fits all?', *Family Business Review*, **17**(2), 119–34.

Craig, J.B., Dibrell, C. and Davis, P.S. (2008), 'Leveraging family-based brand identity to enhance firm competitiveness and performance in family businesses', *Journal of Small Business Management*, **46**(3), 351–71.

Craig, J.B. and Moores, K. (2006), 'A 10-year longitudinal investigation of strategy, systems, and environment on innovation in family firms', *Family Business Review*, **19**(1), 1–10.

Craig, J.B. and Moores, K. (2010), 'Strategically aligning family and business systems using the balanced scorecard', *Journal of Family Business Strategy*, **1**(2), 78–87.

Crick, D., Bradshaw, R. and Chaudhry, S. (2006), '"Successful" internationalising UK family and non-family-owned firms: a comparative study', *Journal of Small Business and Enterprise Development*, **13**(4), 498–512.

Cromie, S., Stephenson, B. and Monteith, D. (1995), 'The management of family firms: an empirical investigation', *International Small Business Journal*, **13**(4), 11–34.

Daily, C.M. and Dollinger, M.J. (1991), 'Family firms are different', *Review of Business*, **13**(1/2), 3–5.

Daily, C.M. and Dollinger, M.J. (1992), 'An empirical examination of ownership structure in family and professionally managed firms', *Family Business Review*, **5**(2), 117–36.

Daily, C.M. and Dollinger, M.J. (1993), 'Alternative methodologies for identifying family-versus nonfamily-managed businesses', *Journal of Small Business Management*, **31**(2), 79–90.

Daily, C.M. and Thompson, S.S. (1994), 'Ownership structure, strategic posture, and firm growth: An empirical examination', *Family Business Review*, **7**(3), 237–49.

Danes, S., Loy, J. and Stafford, K. (2008), 'Business planning practices of family-owned firms within a quality framework', *Journal of Small Business Management*, **46**(3), 395–421.

Davis, P.S. and Harveston, P.D. (2000), 'Internationalization and organizational growth: the impact of internet usage and technology involvement among entrepreneur-led family businesses', *Family Business Review*, **13**(2), 107–20.

De Kok, J.M.P., Uhlaner, L.M. and Thurik, A.R. (2006), 'Professional HRM practices in family owned managed enterprises', *Journal of Small Business Management*, **44**(3), 441–60.

De Lema, D. and Durendez, A. (2007), 'Managerial behaviour of small and medium-sized family businesses: an empirical study', *International Journal of Entrepreneurial Behaviour & Research*, **13**(3), 151–72.

De Visscher, F.M., Aronoff, C.E. and Ward, J.L. (1995), *Financing Transitions: Managing Capital and Liquidity in the Family Business*, Marietta, GA: Family Enterprise Publisher.

De Wit, B. and Meyer, R. (2010), Strategy Process, Content, Context: An International Perspective, 4th edn, Hampshire: Cengage.

Dess, G., Lumpkin, G. and Eisner, A. (2002), *Strategic Management: Creating Competitive Advantages*, Boston, MA: McGraw-Hill.

Donckels, R. and Fröhlich, E. (1991), 'Are family businesses really different? European experiences from STRATOS', *Family Business Review*, **4**(2), 149–60.

Dreux, D.R. (1990), 'Financing family business: alternatives to selling out or going public', *Family Business Review*, **3**(3), 225–43.

Drozdow, N. and Carroll, V.P. (1997), 'Tools for strategy development in family firms', *Sloan Management Review*, **39**(1), 75–88.

Dsouza, D. (1990), 'Strategy types and environmental correlates of strategy for high-growth firms: an exploratory study', dissertation, Georgia State University.

Ducassy, I. and Prevot, F. (2010), 'The effects of family dynamics on diversification strategy: empirical evidence from French companies', *Journal of Family Business Strategy*, **1**(4), 224–35.

Dunn, B. (1995), 'Success themes in Scottish family enterprises: philosophies and practices through the generations', *Family Business Review*, **8**(1), 17–28.

Dutton, J.E. and Duncan, R.B. (1987), 'The influence of the strategic planning process on strategic change', *Strategic Management Journal*, **8**(2), 103–16.

Dyer, W.G. (2003), 'The family: the missing variable in organizational research', *Entrepreneurship Theory and Practice*, **27**(4), 401–16.

Eckert, M. (2008), *Evolution von Familienunternehmen: Organisationsstruktur, Marktumfeld und Unternehmenserfolg*, Lohmar: Eul.

Ellington, E.P., Jones, R.T. and Deane, R. (1996), 'TQM adoption practices in the family-owned business', *Family Business Review*, **9**(1), 5–14.

Ensley, M. (2006), 'Family businesses can out-compete: as long as they are willing to question the chosen path', *Entrepreneurship Theory and Practice*, **30**(6), 747–54.

Fernández, Z. and Nieto, M.J. (2005), 'Internationalization strategy of small and medium-sized family businesses: some influential factors', *Family Business Review*, **18**(1), 77–89.

Fernández, Z. and Nieto, M.J. (2006), 'Impact of ownership on the international involvement of SMEs', *Journal of International Business Studies*, **37**(3), 340–51.

File, K.M. and Prince, R.A. (1996), 'Attributions for family business failure: the heir's perspective', *Family Business Review*, **9**(2), 171–84.

Gallo, M.A. and Garcia-Pont, C. (1996), 'Important factors in family business internationalization', *Family Business Review*, **9**(1), 45–59.

Gallo, M.A. and Sveen, J. (1991), 'Internationalizing the family business: facilitating and restraining factors', *Family Business Review*, **4**(2), 181–90.

Gallo, M.A. and Vilaseca, A. (1996), 'Finance in family business', *Family Business Review*, **9**(4), 387–401.

Gallo, M.A., Tàpies, J. and Cappuyns, K. (2004), 'Comparison of family and nonfamily business: financial logic and personal preferences', *Family Business Review*, **17**(4), 303–18.

George, G., Wiklund, J. and Zahra, S.A. (2005), 'Ownership and the internationalization of small firms', *Journal of Management*, **31**(2), 210–33.

Gómez-Mejía, L.R., Larraza-Kintana, M. and Makri, M. (2003), 'The determinants of executive compensation in family-controlled public corporations', *Academy of Management Journal*, **46**(2), 226–37.

Gómez-Mejía, L.R., Makri, M. and Kintana, M.L. (2010), 'Diversification decisions in family-controlled firms', *Journal of Management Studies*, **47**(2), 223–52.

Graves, C. and Thomas, J. (2004), 'Internationalisation of the family business: a longitudinal perspective', *International Journal of Globalisation and Small Business*, **1**(1), 7–27.

Graves, C. and Thomas, J. (2006), 'Internationalization of Australian family businesses: a managerial capabilities perspective', *Family Business Review*, **19**(3), 207–24.

Graves, C. and Thomas, J. (2008), 'Determinants of the internationalization pathways of family firms: an examination of family influence', *Family Business Review*, **21**(2), 151–67.

Gudmundson, D., Hartman, E.A. and Tower, C.B. (1999), 'Strategic orientation: differences between family and nonfamily firms', *Family Business Review*, **12**(1), 27–39.

Hagelin, N., Holmén, M. and Pramborg, B. (2006), 'Family ownership, dual-class shares, and risk management', *Global Finance Journal*, **16**(3), 283–301.

Hall, A., Melin, L. and Nordqvist, M. (2001), 'Entrepreneurship as radical change in the family business: exploring the role of cultural patterns', *Family Business Review*, **14**(3), 193–208.

Harris, D., Martinez, J.I. and Ward, J.L. (1994), 'Is strategy different for the family-owned business?', *Family Business Review*, **7**(2), 159–74.

Harris, R., Reid, R. and McAdam, R. (2004), 'Employee involvement in family and non-family-owned businesses in Great Britain', *International Journal of Entrepreneurial Behaviour & Research*, **10**(1/2), 49–58.

Harvey, M. and Evans, R. (1995), 'Forgotten sources of capital for the family-owned business', *Family Business Review*, **8**(3), 159–76.

Hatum, A. and Pettigrew, A. (2004), 'Adaptation under environmental turmoil: organizational flexibility in family-owned firms', *Family Business Review*, **17**(3), 237–58.

Haynes, G.W., Walker, R., Rowe, B.R. and Hong, G.-S. (1999), 'The intermingling of business and family finances in family-owned businesses', *Family Business Review*, **12**(3), 225–39.

Ibrahim, N.A., Angelidis, J.P. and Parsa, F. (2008), 'Strategic management of family businesses: current findings and directions for future research', *International Journal of Management*, **25**(1), 95–110.

Jensen, M.C. and Meckling, W.H. (1976), 'Theory of the firm: managerial behavior, agency costs and ownership structure', *Journal of Financial Economics*, **3**(4), 305–60.

Jones, C.D., Makri, M. and Gómez-Mejía, L.R. (2008), 'Affiliate directors and perceived risk bearing in publicly traded, family-controlled firms: the case of diversification', *Entrepreneurship Theory and Practice*, **32**(6), 1007–26.

Jorissen, A., Laveren, E., Martens, R. and Reheul, A.-M. (2005), 'Real versus sample-based differences in comparative family business research', *Family Business Review*, **18**(3), 229–46.

Kashmiri, S. and Mahajan, V. (2010), 'What's in a name? An analysis of the strategic behavior of family firms', *International Journal of Research in Marketing*, **27**(3), 271–80.

Kets de Vries, M.F.R. (1996), *Family Business: Human Dilemmas in the Family Firm*, London: Thomson.

Kidwell, R. and Fish, A. (2007), 'High-performance human resource practices in Australian family businesses: preliminary evidence from the wine industry', *International Entrepreneurship and Management Journal*, **3**(1), 1–14.

Kim, D., Kandemir, D. and Cavusgil, S.T. (2004), 'The role of family conglomerates in emerging markets: what western companies should know', *Thunderbird International Business Review*, **46**(1), 13–38.

Kim, Y. and Gao, F.Y. (2010), 'An empirical study of human resource management practices in family firms in China', *The International Journal of Human Resource Management*, **21**(12), 2095–119.

Klein, S.B., Astrachan, J.H. and Smyrnios, K.X. (2005), 'The F-PEC scale of family influence: construction, validation, and further implication for theory', *Entrepreneurship Theory and Practice*, **29**(3), 321–39.

Kotey, B. and Folker, C. (2007), 'Employee training in SMEs: effect of size and firm type–family and nonfamily', *Journal of Small Business Management*, **45**(2), 214–38.

Kotey, B. and Meredith, G. (1997), 'Relationships among owner/manager personal values, business strategies, and enterprise performance', *Journal of Small Business Management*, **35**(2), 37–64.

Lansberg, I.S. (1983), 'Managing human resources in family firms: the problem of institutional overlap', *Organizational Dynamics*, **12**(1), 39–46.

Le Breton-Miller, I. and Miller, D. (2006), 'Why do some family businesses out-compete? Governance, long-term orientations, and sustainable capability', *Entrepreneurship Theory and Practice*, **30**(6), 731–46.

Leon-Guerrero, A.Y., McCann, J.E., III and Haley, J.D., Jr (1998), 'A study of practice utilization in family businesses', *Family Business Review*, **11**(2), 107–20.

Lindow, C.M., Stubner, S. and Wulf, T. (2010), 'Strategic fit within family firms: the role of family influence and the effect on performance', *Journal of Family Business Strategy*, **1**(3), 167–78.

Littunen, H. and Hyrsky, K. (2000), 'The early entrepreneurial stage in finnish family and nonfamily firms', *Family Business Review*, **13**(1), 41–53.

Lyman, A.R. (1991), 'Customer service: does family ownership make a difference?', *Family Business Review*, **4**(3), 303–24.

Mahérault, L. (2000), 'The influence of going public on investment policy: an empirical study of French family-owned businesses', *Family Business Review*, **13**(1), 71–9.

Mahérault, L. (2004), 'Is there any specific equity route for small and medium sized family businesses? The French experience', *Family Business Review*, **17**(3), 221–35.

Malone, S.C. (1989), 'Selected correlates of business continuity planning in the family business', *Family Business Review*, **2**(4), 341–53.

Marchisio, G., Mazzola, P., Sciascia, S., Miles, M. and Astrachan, J. (2010), 'Corporate venturing in family business: the effects on the family and its members', *Entrepreneurship & Regional Development: An International Journal*, **22**(3), 349–77.

Matlay, H. (2002), 'Training and HRD strategies in family and non-family owned small businesses: a comparative approach', *Education and Training*, **44**(8/9), 357–69.

Mazzola, P. and Marchisio, G. (2002), 'The role of going public in family businesses' long-lasting growth: a study of Italian IPOs', *Family Business Review*, **15**(2), 133–48.

Mazzola, P., Marchisio, G. and Astrachan, J. (2008), 'Strategic planning in family business: a powerful developmental tool for the next generation', *Family Business Review*, **21**(3), 239–58.

McCann, J.E., III., Leon-Guerrero, A.Y. and Haley, Jr J.D. (2001), 'Strategic goals and practices of innovative family businesses', *Journal of Small Business Management*, **39**(1), 50–59.

McConaughy, D.L. (2000), 'Family CEOs vs. nonfamily CEOs in the family-controlled firm: an examination of the level and sensitivity of pay to performance', *Family Business Review*, **13**(2), 121–31.

McConaughy, D.L., Matthews, C.H. and Fialko, A.S. (2001), 'Founding family controlled firms: performance, risk, and value', *Journal of Small Business Management*, **39**(1), 31–50.

Menendez-Requejo, S. (2005), 'Growth and internationalisation of family businesses', *International Journal of Globalisation and Small Business*, **1**(2), 122–33.

Mertens, C. (2009), *Herausforderungen für Familienunternehmen im Zeitverlauf*, Erlangen-Nürnberg: Eul.

Miles, R.E. and Snow, C.C. (1978), *Organizational Strategy, Structure, and Process*, New York: McGraw-Hill.

Miller, D. and Le Breton-Miller, I. (2003), 'Challenge versus advantage in family business', *Strategic Organization*, **1**(1), 127–34.

Miller, D. and Le Breton-Miller, I. (2005), Managing for the Long Run: Lessons in Competitive Advantage from Great Family Businesses, Boston,MA: Harvard Business School Press.

Miller, D., Le Breton-Miller, I. and Lester, R.H. (2010), 'Family and lone founder ownership and strategic behaviour: social context, identity, and institutional logics', *Journal of Management Studies*, http://dx.doi.org/10.1111/j.1467-6486.2009.00896.x, OnlineFirst 02.11.2009, retrieved 03.06.2010.

Miller, D., Le Breton-Miller, I. and Scholnick, B. (2008), 'Stewardship vs. stagnation: an empirical comparison of small family and non-family businesses', *Journal of Management Studies*, **45**(1), 51–78.

Mintzberg, H. (1994), 'The fall and rise of strategic planning', *Harvard Business Review*, **72**, 107–14.

Mishra, C. and McConaughy, D. (1999), 'Founding family control and capital structure: The risk of loss of control and the aversion to debt', *Entrepreneurshi: Theory and Practice*, **23**(4), 53–64.

Moores, K. and Mula, J. (2000), 'The salience of market, bureaucratic, and clan controls in the management of family firm transitions: some tentative Australian evidence', *Family Business Review*, **13**(2), 91–106.

Moores, K. and Mula, J.M. (1998), 'Strategy diversity in Australian family owned businesses: impact of environment induced constraints', *Bond Management Review*, **5**(2), 25–33.

Naldi, L., Nordqvist, M., Sjöberg, K. and Wiklund, J. (2007), 'Entrepreneurial orientation, risk taking, and performance in family firms', *Family Business Review*, **20**(1), 33–47.

Nordqvist, M. and Melin, L. (2010), 'The promise of the strategy as practice perspective for family business strategy research', *Journal of Family Business Strategy*, **1**(1), 15–25.

O'Regan, N., Hughes, T., Collins, L. and Tucker, J. (2010), 'Strategic thinking in family businesses', *Strategic Change*, **19**(1–2), 57–76.

Okoroafo, S.C. (1999), 'Internationalization of family businesses: evidence from northwest Ohio, U.S.A.', *Family Business Review*, **12**(2), 147–58.

Olivares-Mesa, A. and Cabrera-Suarez, K. (2006), 'Factors affecting the timing of the export development process: does the family influence on the business make a difference?', *International Journal of Globalisation and Small Business*, **1**(4), 326–39.

Pearson, A.W., Carr, J.C. and Shaw, J.C. (2008), 'Toward a theory of familiness: a social capital perspective', *Entrepreneurship Theory and Practice*, **32**(6), 949–69.

Peters, M. and Buhalis, D. (2004), 'Family hotel businesses: strategic planning and the need for education and training', *Education + Training*, **46**(8/9), 406–15.

Pinho, J.C. (2007), 'The impact of ownership: location-specific advantages and managerial characteristics on SME foreign entry mode choices', *International Marketing Review*, **24**(6), 715–34.

Pittino, D. and Visintin, F. (2009), 'Innovation and strategic types of family SMEs: a test and extension of Miles and Snow's configurational model', *Journal of Enterprising Culture*, **17**(3), 257–95.

Porter, M.E. (1980), *Competitive Strategy: Techniques for Analyzing Industries and Competitors*, New York: Free Press.

Poutziouris, P. (2001), 'The views of family companies on venture capital: empirical evidence from the UK small to medium-size enterprising economy', *Family Business Review*, **14**(3), 277–91.

Poutziouris, P., Chittenden, F. and Michaelas, N. (1998), 'The financial affairs of private companies', Tilney Fund Management, Liverpool, **5**, 87–90.

Poutziouris, P. and Wang, Y. (2004), 'The views of UK family business owners on flotation', *International Journal of Entrepreneurial Behaviour & Research*, **10**(1/2), 106–26.

Poza, E.J. (1995), 'Global competition and the family-owned business in Latin America', *Family Business Review*, **8**(4), 301–11.

Poza, E.J., Hanlon, S. and Kishida, R. (2004), 'Does the family business interaction factor represent a resource or a cost?', *Family Business Review*, **17**(2), 99–118.

Reid, R. and Adams, J. (2001), 'Human resource management: a survey of practices within family and non-family firms', *Journal of European Industrial Training*, **25**(6), 310–20.

Reid, R., Morrow, T., Kelly, B., Adams, J. and McCartan, P. (2000), 'Human resource management practices in SMEs: a comparative analysis of family and non-family businesses', *Irish Journal of Management*, **21**(2), 157–80.

Reid, R., Morrow, T., Kelly, B. and McCartan, P. (2002), 'People management in SMEs: an analysis of human resource strategies in family and non-family businesses', *Journal of Small Business and Enterprise Development*, **9**(3), 245–59.

Robins, F. (1991), 'Marketing planning in the larger family business', *Journal of Marketing Management*, **7**(4), 325–41.

Romano, C., Tanewski, G. and Smyrnios, K. (2001), 'Capital structure decision making: a model for family business', *Journal of Business Venturing*, **16**(3), 285–310.

Rubenstein, C. (1990), 'Power and priorities', *Family Business Magazine*, **2**(2), 37.

Rue, L.W. and Ibrahim, N.A. (1996), 'The status of planning in smaller family-owned business', *Family Business Review*, **9**(1), 29–43.

Rüsen, T.A. (2011), *Familienunternehmen erfolgreich sanieren*, Berlin: Erich Schmidt Verlag.

Rutherford, M.W., Buller, P.F. and McMullen, P.R. (2003), 'Human resource management problems over the life cycle of small to medium-sized firms', *Human Resource Management*, **42**(4), 321–35.

Salvato, C. (2004), 'Predictors of entrepreneurship in family firms', *The Journal of Private Equity*, **7**(3), 68–76.

Salvato, C., Chirico, F. and Sharma, P. (2010), 'A farewell to the business: championing exit and continuity in entrepreneurial family firms', *Entrepreneurship & Regional Development: An International Journal*, **22**(3), 321–48.

Schendel, D.E. and Hofer, C.W. (1979), *Strategic Management: A New View of Business Policy and Planning*, Boston MA: Little, Brown.

Scholes, L., Wright, M., Westhead, P., Bruining, H. and Kloeckner, O. (2009), 'Family-firm buyouts, private equity, and strategic change', *Journal of Private Equity*, **12**(2), 7–18.

Setia-Atmaja, L., Tanewski, G.A. and Skully, M. (2009), 'The role of dividends, debt and board structure in the governance of family controlled firms', *Journal of Business Finance & Accounting*, **36**(7–8), 863–98.

Sharma, P., Chrisman, J.J. and Chua, J.H. (1996), A Review and Annotated Bibliography of Family Business Studies, Boston, MA: Kluwer Academic Publishers.

Sharma, P., Chrisman, J.J. and Chua, J.H. (1997), 'Strategic management of the family business: past research and future challenges', *Family Business Review*, **10**(1), 1–35.

Sharma, P. and Manikutty, S. (2005), 'Strategic divestments in family firms: role of family structure and community culture', *Entrepreneurship Theory and Practice*, **29**(3), 293–311.

Shim, J. and Okamuro, H. (2010), 'Does ownership matter in mergers? A comparative study of the causes and consequences of mergers by family and non-family firms', *Journal of Banking & Finance*, OnlineFirst: DOI: 10.1016/j.jbankfin.2010.07.027, http://www.sciencedirect.com/science/article/B6VCY-50M6XG1-2/2/1ecf8f4476a31b37f69a87126adf6b5a.

Sirmon, D.G., Arregle, J.L., Hitt, M.A. and Webb, J.W. (2008), 'The role of family influence in firms' strategic responses to threat of imitation', *Entrepreneurship Theory and Practice*, **32**(6), 979–98.

Spector, B. (2007), Implementing Organizational Change: Theory and Practice, Eaglewood Cliffs, NJ: Prentice Hall.

Stavrou, E., Kassinis, G. and Filotheou, A. (2007), 'Downsizing and stakeholder orientation among the Fortune 500: Does family ownership matter?', *Journal of Business Ethics*, **72**(2), 149–62.

Tagiuri, R. and Davis, J. (1996), 'Bivalent attributes of the family firm', *Family Business Review*, **9**(2), 199–208.

Teal, E.J., Upton, N. and Seaman, S.L. (2003), 'A comparative analysis of strategic marketing practices of high-growth US family and non-family firms', *Journal of Developmental Entrepreneurship*, **8**(2), 177–95.

Thomas, J. and Graves, C. (2005), 'Internationalization of the family firm: the contribution of an entrepreneurial orientation', *Journal of Business & Entrepreneurship*, **17**(2), 91–13.

Trostel, A.O. and Nichols, M.L. (1982), 'Privately-held and publicly-held companies: a comparison of strategic choices and management processes', *Academy of Management Journal*, **25**(1), 47–62.

Tsang, E.W.K. (2001), 'Internationalizing the family firm: a case study of a Chinese family business', *Journal of Small Business Management*, **39**(1), 88–94.

Tsang, E.W.K. (2002), 'Learning from overseas venturing experience: the case of Chinese family businesses', *Journal of Business Venturing*, **17**(1), 21–40.

Tsao, C.-W., Chen, S.-J., Lin, C.-S. and Hyde, W. (2009), 'Founding-family ownership and firm performance: the role of high-performance work systems', *Family Business Review*, **22**(4), 319–32.

Upton, N., Teal, E.J. and Felan, J.T. (2001), 'Strategic and business planning practices of fast growth family firms', *Journal of Small Business Management*, **39**(1), 60–72.

Upton, N., Teal, E.J. and Seaman, S.L. (2003), 'Growth goals, strategies and compensation practices of US family and non-family high-growth firms', *The International Journal of Entrepreneurship and Innovation*, **4**(2), 113–20.

Van Gils, A., Voordeckers, W. and Van den Heuvel, J. (2004), 'Environmental uncertainty and strategic behavior in Belgian family firms', *European Management Journal*, **22**(5), 588–95.

Ward, J.L. (1987), Keeping the Family Business Healthy: How to Plan for Continuing Growth, Profitability, and Family Leadership, San Francisco, CA: Jossey-Bass.

Ward, J.L. and Aronoff, C.E. (2002), 'Trust gives you the advantage', in C.E. Aronoff, J.H. Astrachan and J.L. Ward (eds), Family Business Sourcebook: A Guide for Families who Own Businesses and the Professionals who Serve Them; Marietta, GA: Family Enterprise Publishers, pp. 19–20.

Welsch, J.H.M. (1993), 'The impact of family ownership and involvement on the process of management succession', *Family Business Review*, **6**(1), 31–54.

Werner, S. and Tosi, H.L. (1995), 'Other people's money: the effects of ownership on compensation strategy and managerial pay', *Academy of Management Journal*, **38**(6), 1672–91.

Wortman, M.S. (1994), 'Theoretical foundations for family-owned business: a conceptual and research-based paradigm', *Family Business Review*, **7**(1), 3–27.

Yeung, H.W. (2000), 'Limits to the growth of family-owned business? The case of Chinese transnational corporations from Hong Kong', *Family Business Review*, **13**(1), 55–70.

Zahra, S.A. (2003), 'International expansion of U.S. manufacturing family businesses: the effect of ownership and involvement', *Journal of Business Venturing*, **18**(4), 495–512.

Zahra, S.A. (2005), 'Entrepreneurial risk taking in family firms', *Family Business Review*, **18**(1), 23–40.

Zahra, S.A., Hayton, J.C., Neubaum, D.O., Dibrell, C. and Craig, J.B. (2008), 'Culture of family commitment and strategic flexibility: the moderating effect of stewardship', *Entrepreneurship Theory and Practice*, **32**(6), 1035–54.

Zahra, S.A., Hayton, J.C. and Salvato, C. (2004), 'Entrepreneurship in family vs. non-family firms: a resource-based analysis of the effect of organizational culture', *Entrepreneurship Theory and Practice*, **28**(4), 363–81.

Zellweger, T. (2007), 'Time horizon, costs of equity capital, and generic investment strategies of firms', *Family Business Review*, **20**(1), 1–15.

APPENDIX

Table 21A.1   Reviewed empirical strategy formulation research on family businesses

Strategic thinking
  Drozdow and Carroll (1997) (MIT *SMR*)
  O'Regan et al. (2010) (*SC*)
Strategic planning
  Trostel and Nichols (1982) (*AMJ*)
  Malone (1989) (*FBR*)
  Rue and Ibrahim (1996) (*FBR*)
  Moores and Mula (2000) (*FBR*)
  Upton et al. (2001) (*JSBM*)
  Peters and Buhalis (2004) (*E&T*)
  Blumentritt (2006) (*FBR*)
  Mazzola et al. (2008) (*FBR*)
  Danes et al. (2008) (*JSBM*)
  Bhalla et al. (2009) (*SBE*)
  Craig and Moores (2010) (*JFBS*)
  Nordqvist and Melin (2010) (*JFBS*)
Strategic change
  Hall et al. (2001) (*FBR*)
  Hatum and Pettigrew (2004) (*FBR*)
  Ensley (2006) (*ET&P*)
  Le Breton-Miller and Miller (2006) (*ET&P*)
  Sirmon et al. (2008) (*ET&P*)
  Zahra et al. (2008) (*ET&P*)
  Scholes et al. (2009) (*JPE*)
  Salvato et al. (2010) (*ERD*)
  Abdellatif et al. (2010) (*JFBS*)
  Concentration/Diversification
    Donckels and Fröhlich (1991) (*FBR*)
    Moores and Mula (1998) (*BMR*)
    Upton et al. (2003) (*E&I*)
    Anderson and Reeb (2003) (*JLE*)
    Kim et al. (2004) (*TIBR*)
    Hagelin et al. (2006) (*GFJ*)
    Jones et al. (2008) (*ET&P*)
    Ducassy and Prevot (2010) (*JFBS*)
    Gómez-Mejía et al. (2010) (*JMS*)
    Shim and Okamuro (2010) (*JBF*)
Business-level strategies
  Daily and Dollinger (1991) (*RBJ*)
  Daily and Dollinger (1992) (*FBR*)
  Daily and Dollinger (1993) (*JSBM*)
  Daily and Thompson (1994) (*FBR*)
  Gudmundson et al. (1999) (*FBR*)
  McCann et al. (2001) (*JSBM*)
  Upton et al. (2001) (*JSBM*)*
  Van Gils et al. (2004) (*EMJ*)
  Jorissen et al. (2005) (*FBR*)

Corporate-level strategies
  Internationalization
    Gallo and Garcia-Pont (1996) (*FBR*)
    Okoroafo (1999) (*FBR*)
    Davis and Harveston (2000) (*FBR*)
    Yeung (2000) (*FBR*)
    Tsang (2001) (*JSBM*)
    Tsang (2002) (*JBV*)
    Child et al. (2002) (*IMO*)
    Zahra (2003) (*JBV*)
    Graves and Thomas (2004) (*IJGSB*)
    Casillas and Acedo (2005) (*IJGSB*)
    Fernández and Nieto (2005) (*FBR*)
    George et al. (2005) (*JOM*)
    Menendez-Requejo (2005) (*IJGSB*)
    Thomas and Graves (2005) (*JB&E*)
    Crick et al. (2006) (*JSBED*)
    Fernández and Nieto (2006) (*JIBS*)
    Graves and Thomas (2006) (*FBR*)
    Olivares-Mesa and Cabrera-Suarez (2006) (*IJGSB*)
    Basly (2007) (*BJM*)
    Claver et al. (2007) (*JoGM*)
    Pinho (2007) (*IMR*)
    Claver et al. (2008) (*JSBED*)
    Graves and Thomas (2008) (*FBR*)
    Carr and Bateman (2009) (*MIR*)
    Claver et al. (2009) (*FBR*)
Functional-level strategy
  Marketing strategy
    Lyman (1991) (*FBR*)
    Ellington et al. (1996) (*FBR*)
    Kotey and Meredith (1997) (*JSBM*)
    Littunen and Hyrsky (2000) (*FBR*)
    Teal et al. (2003) (*JDE*)
    Cooper et al. (2005) (*JSBM*)
    Craig et al. (2008) (*JSBM*)
    Miller et al. (2008) (*JMS*)
    Kashmiri and Mahajan (2010) (*IJRM*)
  Financial
    Dunn (1995) (*FBR*)
    Gallo and Vilaseca (1996) (*FBR*)
    Coleman and Carsky (1999) (*FBR*)
    Haynes et al. (1999) (*FBR*)
    Mishra and McConaughy (1999) (*ET&P*)
    Mahérault (2000) (*FBR*)
    Poutziouris (2001) (*FBR*)

Table 21A.1 (continued)

Business-level strategies	*Financial*
De Lema and Durendez (2007) (*IJEBR*)	Romano et al. (2001) (*JBV*)
Pittino and Visintin (2009) (*JEC*)	Anderson and Reeb (2003) (*JLE*)*
Lindow et al. (2010) (*JFBS*)	Anderson et al. (2003) (*JFE*)
Setia-Atmaja et al. (2009) (*JBFA*)	Mahérault (2004) (*FBR*)
Shim and Okamuro (2010) (*JBF*)*	Poutziouris and Wang (2004) (*IJEBR*)
R&D strategies	Chen et al. (2005) (*PBFJ*)
Craig and Moores (2006) (*FBR*)	Hagelin et al. (2006) (*GFJ*)*
Miller et al. (2008) (*JMS*)*	Zellweger (2007) (*FBR*)
Anderson et al. (2009)[1]	Gómez-Mejía et al. (2003) (*AMJ*)
Chen and Hsu (2009) (*FBR*)	Rutherford et al. (2003) (*HRM*)
Miller et al. (2010) (*JMS*)	Upton et al. (2003) (*IJEI*)*
HRM strategy	Harris et al. (2004) (*IJEBR*)
Welsch (1993) (*FBR*)	Poza et al. (2004) (*FBR*)
Astrachan and Kolenko (1994) (*FBR*)	De Kok et al. (2006) (*JSBM*)
Werner and Tosi (1995) (*AMR*)	Carlson et al. (2006) (*JSBM*)
Leon-Guerrero et al. (1998) (*FBR*)	Carrasco-Hernandez and Sánchez-Marín
McConaughy (2000) (*FBR*)	(2007) (*FBR*)
Reid et al. (2000) (*IJM*)	Kidwell and Fish (2007) (*IEMJ*)
Reid and Adams (2001) (JEIT)	Kotey and Folker (2007) (*JSBM*)
McCann et al. (2001) (*JSBM*)*	Stavrou et al. (2007) (*JBE*)
Reid et al. (2002) (*JSBED*)	Miller et al. (2008) (*JMS*)*
Matlay (2002) (*E+T*)	Tsao et al. (2009) (*FBR*)
	Block (2010) (*FBR*)
	Combs et al. (2010) (*ET&P*)

Key: The parenthetical notations indicate journal names. *AMJ = Academy of Management Journal, BJM = Baltic Journal of Management, BMR = Bond Management Review E&I = Entrepreneurship and Innovation, E&T = Education + Training, EMJ = European Management Journal, ERD = Entrepreneurship & Regional Development, ET&P = Entrepreneurship Theory & Practice, FBR = Family Business Review, GFJ = Global Finance Journal, HRM = Human Resource Management, IJEBR = International Journal of Entrepreneurial Behaviour & Research, IJEI = The International Journal of Entrepreneurship and Innovation, IJGSB = International Journal of Globalisation and Small Business, IJHRM = International Journal of Human Resource Management, IJM = Irish Journal of Management, IMO = International Studies of Management & Organization, IJRM = International Journal of Research in Marketing, IMR = International Marketing Review, JB&E = Journal of Business & Entrepreneurship, JBE = Journal of Business Ethics, JBF = Journal of Banking & Finance, JBFA = Journal of Business Finance & Accounting, JBV = Journal of Business Venturing, JDE = Journal of Developmental Entrepreneurship, JEC = Journal of Enterprising Culture, JEIT = Journal of European Industrial Training, JFBS = Journal of Family Business Strategy, JFE = Journal of Financial Economics, JIBS = Journal of International Business Studies, JLE = Journal of Law & Economics, JMS = Journal of Management Studies, JOM = Journal of Management, JPE = Journal of Private Equity, JSBED = Journal of Small Business and Enterprise Development, JSBM = Journal of Small Business Management, MIR = Management International Review, MIT SMR = Sloan Management Review, PBFJ = Pacific-Basin Finance Journal, RBJ = Review of Business Journal, SBE = Small Business Economics, SC = Strategic Change, TIBR = Thunderbird International Business Review.*

Note: * Listed more than once.

22 The impact of knowledge sharing on the growth of family businesses in China: the role of Chinese culture
Emma Su

INTRODUCTION

Private firms have played an important role in the rapid growth of China's economy in the past two decades. As some scholars have argued, China's economic success in the past two decades has been the result of fast growth by an increasing number of non-state-owned firms (Tsui et al., 2006). As Wu (2006) stated, non-state-owned firms contributed more than 66.7 per cent of the share of GDP in China in the past decade. Certainly various factors have contributed to the fast growth of the private firms and we have yet to understand these factors, especially from a knowledge-management perspective.

According to Barney's (1991) resource-based view of the firm, resources form competitive advantage for the firm when such resources are valuable, rare, inimitable and non-substitutable. Knowledge can be considered as one type of such resources. As Argote and Ingram (2000) pointed out, knowledge sharing among employees can form the source of competitive advantage for a firm.

However, so far little research has been conducted on understanding how knowledge can be a source of competitive advantage for family firms in China (Li and Yang, 2006). Nor do we know how Chinese culture affects the process of knowledge sharing. Chinese culture, to a large extent, is derived from Confucian traditions, which influence people's behaviour and code of conduct. For example, Chinese culture is often characterized as 'collectivism', which means that Chinese people often focus on the collective interest rather than individual interest.

Therefore this chapter sets out to address the following two research questions: (1) How does Chinese culture affect the process of knowledge sharing among employees in family businesses in China? (2) How does knowledge sharing among employees relate to the growth of Chinese family businesses? Drawing on the data collected from survey and in-depth case study, I analyzed the impact of Chinese culture on knowledge sharing in Chinese family businesses and how knowledge sharing relates to the growth of Chinese family firms. I found that certain elements of Chinese culture are not conducive to knowledge sharing in Chinese family businesses and knowledge sharing is critical to the growth of family firms in China.

This study has important implications for the family business literature and practices. First, this study enhances our understanding of the factors that affect the growth of family firms in China from a knowledge-management perspective. Second, it also enhances our understanding of how Chinese culture affects the process of knowledge sharing in Chinese family firms.

THEORETICAL BACKGROUND

Family Businesses in China

Although there is no consensus on the definition of family businesses (Chua et al., 1999), researchers generally define family businesses based on the following three perspectives (Handler, 1989). First, family businesses are defined based on the degree of ownership and/or management by family members in the business (Dyer, 1986; Lansberg et al., 1988; Stern, 1986). Second, family businesses are defined based on the degree of family involvement in the business (Davis, 1983; Lansberg, 1983). Third, family businesses are defined based on whether there is potential for transferring the business to the next generations (Churchill and Hatten, 1987; Ward, 1987).

Family firms in China have their own unique characteristics. Private enterprises in China usually take two forms – 'individual/household businesses' (*Ge Ti Hu*) and 'private enterprises' (*Si Ying Qi Ye*) (Wu, 2006). The difference between individual/household businesses and private enterprises lies in the number of employees that the firm employs. Individual/household businesses usually hire fewer than eight employees, while private enterprises usually hire eight or more employees.

In this chapter, I refer to family firms as those that are owned and managed by family members and hire more than eight employees (*Si Ying Qi Ye*).

Chinese Culture

Chinese culture is largely influenced by Confucian traditions, which influence code of conduct between adults and children, loyalty to a hierarchical structure of authority and trust between people. Chinese people tend to trust close friends, relatives and family members as in traditional Chinese culture (Weidenbaum, 1996). People tend to engage in relationships with those who share the same culture – people from the same clan or village or people who speak the same dialect (Weidenbaum, 1996). Many relationships are formed based on informal networks or *guanxi*. Many business transactions are completed through such informal relationships. Lack of a formal documentation system can be seen as another character of Chinese family firms. As Weidenbaum (1996) indicated, a great deal of work in Chinese family firms is completed in an informal way.

Knowledge-Based View of the Firm and Knowledge Sharing in Family Firms

Knowledge is believed to have two dimensions – tacit and explicit dimension (Polanyi, 1966; Nonaka, 1994). Explicit knowledge is knowledge that can be put into words and expressions, while tacit knowledge is knowledge that cannot be expressed and is difficult to be communicated and formalized (Polanyi, 1966; Nonaka, 1994). In recent years, scholars have started to investigate organizational capability from an organizational learning perspective and have proposed that organizational learning is a key factor in building dynamic organizational capability and achieving sustainable competitive advantage of the firm (Grant, 1996; Kogut and Zander, 1992; Easterby-Smith et al., 2000; Easterby-Smith et al., 1998; Chirico and Salvato, 2008). Organizational learning can be achieved through knowledge sharing, recombining and creating. As Kogut and Zander (1992) argued, organizations can have better performance by sharing/transferring their knowledge, recombining it into different forms of knowledge or creating new knowledge. Knowledge sharing that happens between different departments within a firm can contribute to the performance of the firm (Epple et al., 1996; Baum and Ingram, 1998). Knowledge sharing can also happen among employees on the individual level. As Argote and Ingram (2000) argued, much of tacit knowledge can be shared through sharing knowledge among colleagues on the individual level. For example, in research institutions and law firms most of the organization's knowledge is embedded in individual members (Starbuck, 1992); thus it is especially important to engage people to share knowledge with each other. Moreover, in understanding the process of knowledge sharing in firms, Szulanski (2003) proposed a framework that involves four factors that affect knowledge sharing – the knowledge source's characteristics, the knowledge recipient's absorptive capability, the relationship between knowledge source and knowledge recipient, and the context in which knowledge sharing happens.

In recent years, family business scholars have started to apply organizational learning theory to the study of family businesses. For example, Cabrera-Suárez and colleagues (2001) suggested that in order to ensure a successful family business transition, knowledge should be transferred from the predecessor to the successor; this is because much valuable knowledge in family businesses was likely to be embedded in the founder entrepreneur and thus it is important to transfer such knowledge. Moreover, Chirico and Salvato (2008) proposed that the capability of family firms can be improved by integrating family members' specialized knowledge and sharing it across the business.

In this chapter, I define knowledge sharing as the activity of sharing knowledge among employees who may be family members and non-family members working in the business. By utilizing Szulanski's (2003) knowledge-sharing framework (below), I examine the phenomenon of knowledge sharing in family businesses in China to see how Chinese culture affects the process of knowledge sharing:

1. The knowledge source's knowledge-sharing capability (i.e. how Chinese culture affects the knowledge source's knowledge-sharing capability)
2. The knowledge recipient's learning predisposition (i.e. how Chinese culture affects the knowledge recipient's learning disposition)
3. The relationship between the knowledge source and the recipient (i.e. how Chinese culture affects the relationship between the knowledge source and knowledge recipient)
4. The organizational environment in which knowledge sharing happens (i.e. how Chinese culture interacts with the organizational environment, and hence facilitates or inhibits knowledge sharing)

I investigate how Chinese culture affects each of the above-mentioned four dimensions. In other words, through this framework I investigate whether Chinese culture plays a role in facilitating or inhibiting the process of knowledge sharing, as Chinese culture may motivate or oblige individuals to share knowledge.

METHODS

This study uses a qualitative methodology to address its two research questions. Qualitative methods are appropriate to answer the research question 'how' and are suited for studying issues from the participant's perspective rather than from the researcher's perspective (Maitlis, 2005). To be specific, this study uses survey and in-depth case study. This design offers a strong foundation for elaborating theory: the similarity of the participating firms allows for meaningful comparisons on how Chinese culture affects knowledge sharing in Chinese family firms. Also, the multi-method approach allowed me to perform between-method triangulation, which can enhance the credibility of research findings by looking for 'convergence' of research findings (Greene et al., 1989).

The aim of this study is theory elaboration, drawing on and extending Szulanski's knowledge-sharing framework. As Maitlis (2005) explained, through a purely inductive approach we can elaborate theory when pre-existing ideas provide the foundation for a new study.

Research Context

This study was carried out in 22 family firms in the city of Wenzhou, China. Wenzhou is well suited for research on family businesses for several reasons. First, Wenzhou located in the south-east of China, has the most active and developed private economy in China. Hence it is a unique living lab to study family businesses as it is hotbed for the growth of many family firms. Second, the author, as a native of Wenzhou, was born and raised there, which provides a unique opportunity to identify, access and probe these family firms. The selected firms range across different industries including the printing industry, glass manufacturing, and the automobile industry. All the selected firms were founded between 1995 and 1998. Firms ranged in size from 23 to 412 employees.

Survey Questionnaire Design

The questionnaires were designed to probe the relationship between culture and knowledge sharing, and the relationship between knowledge sharing and the growth of family businesses in China. Apart from general background questions, the survey covered queries on the four elements that affect knowledge sharing proposed by Szulanski (2003). The questionnaire was pilot-tested on a few targeted firms before the actual surveys were conducted.

The questionnaires include Likert-type scales, a single 'yes–no', 'multiple-choice' answer, or open-question format. The questionnaires were designed in English, and subsequently translated into Chinese. Some of the sensitive wording was taken care of and adjusted in light of the unique Chinese culture and traditions. The questionnaires were sent to the top executives who were members of the family in control of these firms.

Data Collection

The data were collected during a period of six months from the summer of 2007 to the spring of 2008. The interviewed family firms were selected using snowball and opportunistic sampling methods through friends or relatives. While identifying family firms, I used the following four criteria: (1) the family business has more than eight employees; (2) the business was founded by a family; (3) the control and ownership belonged to one family; (4) family members were involved in the management.

Data collection can be broken down into two phases. During the first stage I interviewed the 22 family firms to gain preliminary data on the two research questions. The interviews were semi-structured and became increasingly focused over the course of the study. In total I conducted 22 formal interviews with the top executives of the family firms and nine informal interviews, carrying out repeat interviews with key informants. The purpose of these interviews was to find similarities between cases rather than differences. During the second stage I selected two family firms for in-depth case study to verify the data that were collected through interviews.

To study the impact of knowledge sharing on the growth, or lack thereof, of the surveyed companies, two representative family firms were selected for an in-depth case study and analysis. The criteria for selecting these two firms representing fast-growing and slow-growing firms were a function of their growth rate. It is worth mentioning that the period between 2002 and 2007 saw tremendous economic growth in China, so that all companies, big and small, grew. Some firms grew faster than others. In China, revenue information on family firms was not available in the public domain. Thus I used the staff growth rate of the firm in the last five years (i.e. from 2002 to 2007) to measure the growth rate of the firm. The detailed case studies were conducted through in-depth interviews and site visits. In the two representative family firms, I interviewed the top executive of each firm.

Data Analysis

Data analysis involved two stages. During the first stage, I sought to answer the first research question: How does Chinese culture affect the knowledge-sharing process in family businesses in China? During the second stage, I sought to answer the second research question: How does knowledge sharing among employees relates to the growth of family businesses in China.

RESULTS

Findings from the Survey Study

I used descriptive and analytic matrices to analyse the data (Miles and Huberman, 1984). I mapped my findings to the four knowledge-sharing dimensions discussed earlier. Although this analysis was descriptive in nature, these basic findings provided an empirical foundation from which to develop further analysis.

How does Chinese culture affect the knowledge source's knowledge-sharing capability?

Researchers have argued that the knowledge source's credibility and intent were important factors that could affect the process of knowledge sharing (Szulanski, 2003). The results of the surveyed questions indicated that there was a misperception about the value of knowledge, which made employees less motivated to share knowledge with others. Some regarded what they knew as insignificant; however, others regarded their know-how as a source of power and extremely valuable. The possession of knowledge as a symbol of power and position was commonly found in these surveyed firms. This finding was consistent with prior research, which found that employees usually regarded certain areas of their knowledge as part of their power base within the firm; thus their willingness to share was limited (Probst et al., 2000).

A large number of surveyed firms reported that knowledge was exclusively held by top management. Knowledge was considered as a symbol of position and power of the senior management team, and the knowledge held by the large number of front-line employees was widely neglected. Knowledge sharing was unilateral and restricted to sharing knowledge from supervisors to subordinates. This finding was consistent with traditional Chinese practice, which respects the elderly and superior without any questioning. The exclusive nature of such a knowledge source could create problems for the process of knowledge sharing.

Moreover, knowledge hoarding was commonly seen in these surveyed firms. For example, in some of the printing firms, experienced technicians were unwilling to share what they knew with the novices. While a novice technician approached a senior one for a solution, a typical answer given was 'Boy, do not worry; you will know how to do it after a while'. Knowledge hoarding by knowledge source may be explained by fear of power distribution, as per Zack's (1999) argument that sharing knowledge, especially proprietary or individual knowledge, could result in power redistribution. Another reason for knowledge hoarding might be that some employees do not have enough understanding of the value of their knowledge for their co-workers.

We found that in these surveyed family firms, family members tended to share knowledge with people who were from the same clan or village, or people who speak the same dialect. This is not instrumental for the knowledge source to become motivated to share knowledge with others. This is in line with the literature that says that the amount of knowledge transferred to others depends on the level of trust you have of others (Weidenbaum, 1996).

I also found that motivation of knowledge sharing with others was also lacking in non-family members. These family members are not motivated to share their knowledge and skills with others, as they do not see the benefits of such knowledge sharing and they do not see that they can have high authority in the business even if they possesses much knowledge. The impact of Chinese culture on knowledge source is summarized in the following proposition:

Proposition 1   Such elements of Chinese culture as 'lack of trust' and 'respect for elders without questioning' is not conducive for the knowledge source to share knowledge with others in family firms in China.

How does Chinese culture affect the knowledge recipient's learning predisposition?
The knowledge recipient's learning predisposition may include his/her motivation to learn, absorptive capacity (Cohen and Levinthal, 1990), availability of time and prior experience of learning, because these are important for the process of knowledge sharing.

The survey results suggested that in the majority of the surveyed firms the employees were not motivated to learn. One of the reasons is long working hours, so that employees hardly find time to learn from others. Long working hours have been a notorious labour issue in many firms in China (Liu, 2002). Based on my conversations with the employees in some of the surveyed firms, I found that employees were heavily overworked, which prohibits them from sharing their knowledge with other employees. An organization needs to provide employees with slack time to work on new ideas, and this would enhance knowledge transfer (Davenport and Prusak, 2000).

Another reason for employees' lack of motivation to learn is that seeking knowledge meant acknowledging an inferior position. This is why the junior workers or technicians did not take the risk of losing their jobs by seeking help. The unique composition of the workforce in the majority of the surveyed firms was that the migrant workers accounted for the bulk of the labour force; this might also explain why employees are not motivated to learn and seek knowledge from others.

They also lacked absorptive capacity to realize and absorb the transferred knowledge. Cohen and Levinthal (1990) argued that a recipient with a limited stock of prior related knowledge was less likely to see the value of new knowledge. The majority of the surveyed firms did not pay attention to improving employees' absorptive capacity by providing training programmes. As Kostova (1999) argued, knowledge recipients' internalization of knowledge is more important compared to the knowledge communication itself. Instead, the majority of surveyed firms held that employee training or education programmes meant training the employees for competitor firms. A common saying is: 'Employee training is to make bridal clothes for competitor firms.' Lastly, learning from others was considered as '*Shi Mian Zi*' (to lose face). '*Mianzi*' is considered as important for Chinese people. We also found that, due to lack of trust between people who are from different clans or speak different dialects, the knowledge recipients are not motivated to seek knowledge from others. The impact of Chinese culture on the knowledge recipient is summarized in the following proposition:

Proposition 2   Such elements of Chinese culture as 'fear of losing face in seeking knowledge from others' and 'lacking slack time to learn' are not conducive to motivating the knowledge recipient to seek knowledge from others in family firms in China.

How does Chinese culture affect the relationship between the knowledge source and the knowledge recipient?

Prior studies have indicated that the strength of relationship between knowledge recipient and source could affect knowledge sharing (Hansen, 1999). The results of the survey indicated that a good relationship between knowledge source and knowledge recipient is absent because of a lack of trust between family members and non-family members. This finding is in line with Tsang's finding (2001) that Chinese businesses were perceived as essentially a family possession, where the head of the family had the final say in decision-making. Again, the firms reported that the unique composition of the labour source proved to be a problem in building relationships between local employees (i.e. employees from Wenzhou) and migrant employees (i.e. employees are from parts of China other than Wenzhou). Such a unique composition of the labour force affects smooth knowledge sharing and transfer. Most of the migrant workers came from inland and remote areas of China. China is a huge country with a diverse local culture and uneven economic development across different regions. The local workers were likely to form their own work groups, while the migrant workers were more likely to seek help from their own home mates. This kind of segregation was not conducive to facilitating knowledge sharing between local workers and migrant workers.

The findings also revealed that there is lack of trust between family members and non-family members in the majority of the surveyed firms. This finding was highly in line with Fukuyama's (1995) argument that Chinese culture does not place much trust in unrelated others. Since one party must rely upon trust in the other party throughout the exchange of knowledge (Cummings, 2003), trust is an essential element in facilitating knowledge sharing in family firms. The impact of Chinese culture on the relationship between the knowledge source and knowledge recipient is summarized in the following proposition:

Proposition 3   Such elements of Chinese culture as 'lack of trust between employees' is not conducive to maintaining a good relationship for knowledge sharing among employees in family businesses in China.

How does Chinese culture affect the organizational environment in which knowledge sharing happens?

The surveyed questions in this category focused on understanding how the factors associated with organizational environment under which these surveyed firms operated affected knowledge sharing.

The findings showed that open discussion was generally not allowed. The non-family members were not given the chance to have their opinions and views heard, or even challenge others' ideas. This finding was consistent with Confucian thinking, that a harmonious relationship is the most important element of governance and therefore should be retained at any cost, and individuals need to avoid conflict and maintain harmony (Kirkbride and Tang, 1992). However, this was not conducive to knowledge sharing, because an environment of questioning and knowledge exchange is important to ensure an organizational learning environment, or the formation of a '*Ba*' environment (Nonaka and Konno, 1998).

Moreover, the collected data revealed that there was not enough attention given to the importance of knowledge sharing for the growth of the business. The majority of the surveyed firms were found to lack an environment conducive to organizational learning and knowledge sharing.

Although *guanxi* has many advantages for family businesses, it imposes certain constraints as well. Since these networks are informal, most knowledge is not captured during the transaction process. *Guanxi* is not conducive to knowledge sharing in these family businesses. This will be problematic when employees leave the company. Since *guanxi* rules out the opportunity of having formal contracts that capture the knowledge, it is problematic for the purpose of knowledge sharing.

As Weidenbaum (1996) argued, key information is obtained through conversations with key *guanxi* members, and stored in the memory of the persons involved in the conversation; thus the need for formal reporting and capturing the information is eliminated. Therefore, from this perspective, *guanxi* is not conducive to knowledge sharing among employees in the family businesses.

I also found that, due to lack of formalization and documentation systems in place, this practice is not conducive to knowledge sharing. It requires more face-to-face interactions, which is more time-consuming. The impact of Chinese culture on the organizational environment is summarized in the following proposition:

Proposition 4   Certain elements of Chinese culture such as '*guanxi*' are not conducive to forming a knowledge-sharing environment in family firms in China.

Findings from Two In-Depth Case Studies

In identifying the two suitable firms for in-depth case study, I accentuated their differences by comparing the fastest-growing firm (the top member of the list with 48 per cent employee growth rate) with the slowest-growing firm (the bottom member of the list with 7 per cent employee growth rate).

Both these firms were established in 1998 in the printing industry; however, they grew into very different firms in terms of business success. A brief background of these two firms might be helpful to shed light on their management style and corporate culture.

After ten years of growth, Firm A has expanded to a big firm with a wide market presence and seemingly a large market share. It had successfully explored the domestic market, including 31 provinces, as well as international markets including North America, South-East Asia, the European Union and the Middle East. Moreover, Firm A has also been granted a range of awards by government and industry associations, such as 'China Printing Leading Firm', 'China Trustworthy Firm', 'Wenzhou Top 100 Enterprises', and so on.

There were a few reasons contributing to the success of Firm A. With respect to knowledge sharing, I found the positive influence of knowledge sharing on the growth of this firm. Under the leadership of Mr Goh (the CEO), Firm A had been striving to overcome the negative influence of traditional Chinese culture and working to build a learning-conducive corporate culture as a core advantage. Moreover, Firm A had been emphasizing the value of knowledge to the growth of the firm. This was indicated by the various training and learning opportunities provided to the employees. They have initiated a knowledge database that captures the knowledge of employees and then makes this accessible to other employees. This knowledge database is proving useful for their over 500 sales team to learn and exchange knowledge with each other.

The finding shows that knowledge was perceived to be owned by employees in the firm rather than by a few key top management family members. This was proved by the management's efforts to retain personnel in the firm. Also, the firm used different forms of incentive systems including bonus reward and title reward such as 'excellent sales manager' to motivate employees to develop innovative ideas.

Moreover, Firm A was actively cooperating with the local university to develop innovative printing technology. Training and further education programmes were made available to the employees with the assistance of the local university. They subsequently set up an R&D department for further innovation. Moreover, they learnt management experience from other successful companies such as '*Haier*' and implemented what was learnt from other companies in Firm A.

Firm A was attempting to create an open and learning-conducive environment for their employees. Employees were given the chance to study further and gain knowledge. Moreover, there was an internal publication to facilitate knowledge and information sharing within the company. Regular morning meetings were held every day to locate assignments and review yesterday's work. Moreover, 'reading meetings' were held regularly to motivate the employees to learn.

Mr Goh's value of knowledge is also found to be critical to the growth of Firm A. He indicated a strong eagerness to make good use of his training and skills to keep on learning. He cited Confucian thinking by saying 'When you know a thing, to recognize that you know it, and when you do not know a thing, to recognize that you do not know it. That is knowledge.'

The factors related to knowledge sharing that contributed to the success of Firm A are summarized below:

1. Firm A created an open and learning-conducive environment for its employees
2. Employees were given the chance to further study and learn
3. Firm A perceived that knowledge is owned by every employee rather than by a few key top management members
4. Communication took place between various layers of organizations

Firm B started from a household factory. After ten years, Firm B had seen little progress. The factors that impeded the development of Firm B were many. With respect to knowledge sharing, we saw the negative impact of lack of knowledge sharing on the growth of Firm B.

The founder and the current CEO of Firm B, Mr Ding, had been playing the central role in the firm. Employees were not encouraged to share knowledge with each other. There was a clear absence of trust in the company. Knowledge is considered as power. The factors related to knowledge sharing that led to the failure of Firm B are summarized below:

1. Management treated knowledge as a source of power and leverage to keep employees under control
2. Learning was often regarded as a liability and an expense
3. The company never attempted to expose the employees to new knowledge, for example providing on-the-job training programmes
4. Knowledge was considered to be held by family members
5. Communication often took the form of decrees, commands and rules

A quick look at the differences between Firm A and Firm B shows the important role of knowledge sharing in the growth of these firms. It is apparent that Firm A recognized the value of knowledge sharing and as such moved systematically towards creating a learning organization where knowledge was viewed as an asset and as a source of competitive advantage.

In contrast, Firm B's management regarded knowledge as a control instrument. Chinese culture, as many cultures of antiquity, is full of contradictions. It has great progressive elements, as well as serious backward drags.

Therefore the relationship between knowledge sharing and the growth of family firms in China is summarized in the following proposition:

Proposition 5   Knowledge sharing among employees is positively related to the growth of family firms in China.

CONCLUSIONS

In this chapter, I studied the linkage between knowledge sharing and the growth of family business in China, and how Chinese culture has affected knowledge sharing in such firms. Based on collected data, I found preliminary evidence that knowledge sharing might be instrumental in the growth of family business. This study also found that certain elements and components of Chinese culture such as absence of trust between family members and non-family members were not conducive to the free flow and exchange of knowledge within a family business. In other words, the Chinese value system created barriers for individuals in their desire to share information/knowledge related to the day-to-day affairs of a family-run business. These cultural factors were not conducive to the growth of the business. The data demonstrated that fast-growing firms were likely to promote knowledge sharing and take initiatives to build a learning corporate environment that facilities knowledge sharing.

This study has the following implications. Given the relative youth of the surveyed firms, it appears highly likely that these newly emerging family firms will face increased difficulties under the competitive pressures from rapid growth of the small-to-medium enterprises (SME) sector in China and globalization. It is critical for these firms to realize the value of knowledge sharing to the growth of the firm and to sustain the competitive advantage of the firm.

This study has contributed by providing an initial step towards empirically studying the relationship between knowledge sharing and the growth of family business under the influence of traditional Chinese culture. However, this study also has some limitations.

First, the sample size of this study is too small. The data collected from 22 firms may not be generalizable to a larger setting. Second, this study was conducted in the city of Wenzhou. The findings may not be generalizable to other parts of China, because China is a vast country with many different cultures, people and environments. Future studies may consider expanding to different localities. Third, future research might consider dimensions over and beyond the five contexts that were used to map my results.

Implications for Research

First and foremost, this study raises important questions for future research on knowledge sharing in Chinese family firms. In future, researchers can investigate how knowledge sharing among employees and creating a knowledge-sharing environment relate to the growth of family firms in China. Another question concerns how Chinese culture affects the knowledge-sharing process in family firms in China. In future, researchers can investigate how other dimensions of Chinese culture such as uncertainty avoidance affects knowledge sharing.

Implications for Practice

This study also has several important practical implications. The first stems from the connection between knowledge sharing and the growth of family firms in China. The preliminary findings drawn from this study show the positive relationship between knowledge sharing and the growth of Chinese family firms. Therefore Chinese family firms' owners/managers should pay increased attention to the importance of knowledge sharing in their firms. They are recommended to create a knowledge-sharing environment that motivates employees to share knowledge with each other, and hence help to grow the firm. A second practical implication of this study is for family firm managers to seek to promote knowledge sharing in their firms. The findings presented here suggest that certain elements of Chinese culture are not conducive to the free flow of knowledge sharing in family firms. Family firm managers/owners need to be cautious in leveraging culture and hence promote knowledge sharing in their firm.

REFERENCES

Argote, L. and Ingram, P. (2000), 'Knowledge transfer: a basis for competitive advantage in firms', *Organizational Behaviour and Human Decision Processes*, **82**(1), 150–69.

Barney, J.B. (1991), 'Firm resources and sustained competitive advantage', *Journal of Management*, **17**, 99–120.

Baum, J.A.C. and Ingram, P. (1998), 'Survival-enhancing learning in the Manhattan hotel industry, 1898–1980', *Management Science*, **44**, 996–1016.

Cabrera-Suárez, K., De Saa-Pérez, P. and García-Almeida, D. (2001), 'The succession process from a resource- and knowledge-based view of the family firm', *Family Business Review*, **14**(1), 37–46.

Chirico, F. and Salvato, C. (2008), 'Knowledge integration and dynamic organizational adaptation in family firms', *Family Business Review*, **21**(2), 169–81.

Chua, J.H., Chrisman, J.J. and Sharma, P. (1999), 'Defining the family business by behavior', *Entrepreneurship Theory and Practice*, Summer, 19–39.

Churchill, N.C. and Hatten, K.J. (1987), 'Non-market-based transfers of wealth and power: a research framework for small businesses', *American Journal of Small Business*, **11**(3), 51–64.

Cohen, W.M. and Levinthal, D.A. (1990), 'Absorptive capacity: a new perspective on learning and innovation', *Administrative Science Quarterly*, **35**, 128–52.

Cummings, J. (2003), *Knowledge Sharing: A Review of the Literature*, Washington, DC: World Bank.

Davenport, T.H. and Prusak, L. (2000), *Working Knowledge: How Organizations Manage what they Know*, Boston, MA: Harvard Business School Press.

Davis, P. (1983), 'Realizing the potential of the family business', *Organizational Dynamics*, **12**(1), 47–56.

Dyer, W.G. (1986), *Cultural Changes in Family Firms: Anticipating and Managing Business and Family Transitions*, San Francisco, CA : Jossey-Bass.

Easterby-Smith, M., Snell, R. and Gherardi, S. (1998), 'Organizational learning and learning organization: diverging communities of practice?', *Management Learning*, **29**, 259–72.

Easterby-Smith, M., Crossan, M. and Nicolini, D. (2000), 'Organizational learning: debates past, present and future', *Journal of Mangagement Studies*, **37**(6), 783–96.

Epple, D., Argote, L. and Murphy, K. (1996), 'An empirical investigation of the micro structure of knowledge acquisition and transfer through learning by doing', *Operations Research*, **44**, 77–86.

Fukuyama, F. (1995), *Trust: The Social Virtues and the Creation of Prosperity*, New York: Simon and Shuster.

Grant, R.M. (1996), 'Toward a knowledge-based theory of the firm', *Strategic Management Journal*, **17**, 108–22.

Greene, J.C., Caracelli, V.J. and Graham, W.F. (1989), 'Toward a conceptual framework for mixed method evaluation designs', *Educational Evaluation and Policy Analysis*, **11**, 255–74. Handler, W.C. (1989), 'Methodological issues and considerations in studying family businesses', *Family Business Review*, **2**(3), 257–76.

Hansen, M. (1999), 'The search-transfer problem: the role of weak ties in sharing knowledge across organization subunits', *Administrative Science Quarterly*, **44**(1), 82–111.

Kirkbride, P.S. and Tang, S.F.Y. (1992), 'Management development in the Nanyang Chinese societies of South-east Asia', *Journal of Management Development*, **11**(2), 54–66.

Kogut, B. and Zander, U. (1992), 'Knowledge of the firm, combinative capabilities and the replication of technology', *Organization Studies*, **3**, 383–97.

Kostova, T. (1999), 'Transnational transfer of strategic organizational practices: a contextual perspective', *Academy of Management Review*, **24**, 308–24.

Lansberg, I.S. (1983), 'Managing human resources in family firms: the problem of institutional overlap', *Organizational Dynamics*, **12**(1), 39–46.

Lansberg, I.S., Perrow, E.L. and Rogolsky, S. (1988), 'Family business as an emerging field', *Family Business Review*, **1**(1), 1–8.

Li, J.T. and Yang, J.Y. (2006), 'China's domestic private firms: a literature review and directions for future research', in A.S. Tsui, Y. Bian and L. Cheng (eds), *China's Domestic Private Firms: Multidisciplinary Perspectives on Management and Performance*, New York: M.E. Sharpe, pp. 206–29.

Liu, K.M. (2002), *The Migrant Workers*, Beijing: Xinhua Press.

Maitlis, S. (2005), 'The social processes of organizational sensemaking', *Academy of Management Journal*, **48**(1), 21–49.

Miles, M.B. and Huberman, M.A. (1984), *Qualitative Data Analysis*, Newbury Park, CA: Sage.

Nonaka, I. (1994), 'A dynamic theory of organizational knowledge creation', *Organization Science*, **5**(1), 14–37.

Nonaka, I. and Konno, N. (1998), 'The concept of *Ba*', *California Management Review*, **40**(3), 40–54.

Polanyi, M. (1996), *The Tacit Dimension*, London: Routledge & Kegan Paul.

Probst, G., Raub, S. and Romhardt, K. (2000), *Managing Knowledge: Building Blocks of Success*, Chichester: Wiley.

Starbuck, W. (1992), 'Learning by knowledge intensive firms', *Journal of Management Studies*, **29**, 713–40.

Stern, M.H. (1986), *Inside the Family-Held Business*, New York: Harcourt Brace Jovanovich.

Szulanski, G. (2003), *Sticky Knowledge: Barriers to Knowing in the Firm*, London: Sage.

Tsang, E. (2001), 'Internationalizing the family firm: a case study of a Chinese family business', *Journal of Small Business Management*, **39**(1), 88–94.

Tsui, A.S., Bian, Y. and Cheng, L. (eds) (2006), *China's Domestic Private Firms: Multidisciplinary Perspectives on Management and Performance*, New York: M.E. Sharpe.

Ward, J.L. (1987), *Keeping the Family Business Healthy: How to Plan for Continued Growth, Profitability, and Family Leadership*, San Francisco, CA: Jossey-Bass.

Weidenbaum, (1996), 'The Chinese family business enterprise', *California Management Review*, **38**(4), 141–56.

Wu, X.G. (2006), 'Family businesses in China, 1978–96: entry and performance', in A.S. Tsui, Y., Bian and L. Cheng (eds), *China's Domestic Private Firms: Multidisciplinary Perspectives on Management and Performance*, New York: M.E. Sharpe, pp. 40–64.

Zack, M. (1999), 'Managing codified knowledge', *Sloan Management Review*, summer, 45–58.

PART VIII

FAMILY BUSINESS SUSTAINABILITY

23 Extensions of the Sustainable Family Business Theory: operationalization and application

Ramona Kay Zachary, Sharon M. Danes and Kathryn Stafford

INTRODUCTION

Sustainable Family Business Theory (SFBT) is delineated herein by summarizing its components, systems orientation and its major theoretical propositions as well as exploring its operationalization and application. SFBT posits entrepreneurship and the business within the social context of the family and its community. Moreover, its unique comprehensive approach to the study of the family business emphasizes the interaction of the family and business systems while recognizing the different characteristics of each. The SFBT suggests testable relationships between and among independent and dependent variables in its propositions. Furthermore, Sztompka (1974) indicated that a theory's propositions need to have been tested to truly be designated a theory. That research is described in this chapter.

While the business enterprise is integral to the long-run sustainability of the family firm, the family brings together and creates the forces behind emerging and sustained entrepreneurial behavior. Any family business theory must embrace a comprehensive, multidisciplinary view of the complex and dynamic phenomenon of business that is owned and operated by family members. The *family*, with its own dynamics, is an important and fundamental entity for creating and sustaining behaviors described in the literature as entrepreneurial behavior or experience (Cramton, 1993; Danes et al., 2008a; Rogoff and Heck, 2003; Sharma, 2004; Stafford et al., 1999; Zachary, 2011). Family capital, the total resources of owning family members, is the fodder for short-term family business success and long-term sustainability (Danes et al., 2009c).

Throughout history and across countries, families and business have always existed to a large extent in tandem (Heck et al., 1992, 1995; Morck and Yeung, 2004; Narva, 2001; Rogoff and Heck, 2003; Zachary, 2011). The economic necessity of earning a living and supporting a family is often the underlying motivation for starting and growing a business (Winter et al., 1998). Among other motivators, lifestyle and wealth accumulation goals play an important role in whether a particular family member or members choose to start a business. At the same time that the business supplies income to the family, the family may supply paid and unpaid labor, as well as contribute additional resources such as money, space, equipment and other factors of production to the business.

Both conceptual and operational considerations of the SFBT (Danes et al., 2008a; Stafford et al., 1999) will be the focus of this chapter. A comprehensive and flexible theory such as the SFBT can enhance our understanding of the dynamic role of the family in family business entrepreneurship as well as demonstrate integration of the family, business and community. Astrachan (2003) has commented that the SFBT both conceptually and empirically 'exemplifies what is at the heart of the family business field: the study of the reciprocal impact of family on business' (p. 570). The initial version of SFBT was put forward in 1999 (Stafford et al., 1999). After using SFBT in empirical analyses for a decade, an amplified version was published in 2008 (Danes et al., 2008a) and that is the version portrayed in Figure 23.1. Then Danes and Brewton (2012) applied the theory to a case study and clearly delineated the propositions of the theory.

Rogoff and Heck (2003) have noted that 'the growing body of research points to the fundamental guiding principle that the combustion of entrepreneurship cannot ignite and grow without the mobilization of family forces' (p. 560). Here are just a few examples of the recent studies affirming this proposition. As empirically shown by Olson et al. (2003), both business outcomes and family outcomes are simultaneously determined by factors from and within *both* the family and firm system. In a study investigating the contribution of family capital to family firms in the short term, all types of family capital explained 13.5 percent of variance in gross revenue and 4 percent of variance in owner's perception of success. In the long term, all types of family capital explained 26.7 percent of variance in gross revenue and 11.6 percent of variance in owner's perception of success (Danes et al., 2009c). As another example, in a longitudinal study of spousal capital as a resource for couples starting a business, Matzek et al. (2010) found that spousal capital had implications for both the business sustainability of a new venture and for couple relationship quality.

The purposes of this chapter are threefold. First, it will highlight trends in entrepreneurship and family business research and provide a summary of the conceptualizations and theories used to study family businesses. Second, conceptualizations and propositions of the expanded SFBT (Danes et al., 2008a) will be reviewed. And, third, measurement of the constructs in SFBT will be discussed along with its applications. Our intent is to assist researchers in understanding the current theoretical choices in light of the unique nature of the SFBT and how it can be operationalized for in-depth study of the family and the business and their interactions. Thus we will first survey the previous and current research. Then we will fully discuss the SFBT along with the formulation of selected research propositions. The operationalization of the SFBT is illustrated by sharing a myriad of research analyses completed to date. Finally, suggestions for future research and application of the SFBT are offered. The 'value added' in total to the reader/researcher is the combination of the unique SFBT and the added discussions of: (1) possible extensions of SFBT; (2) SFBT propositions; (3) theory selection decisions; (4) operationalization; and (5) application.

PREVIOUS RESEARCH

Trends in Entrepreneurship Research

Only a few researchers have noted the connections between entrepreneurship and the family (Danes et al., 2010; Gartner, 2001; Upton and Heck, 1997; Zachary and Mishra, 2011). Moreover, previous entrepreneurship research literature and, in some cases, family business research have given little attention to the interrelatedness of families and businesses (e.g. Danes et al., 2010; Davidsson and Wiklund, 2001; Dimov, 2007; Rothausen,

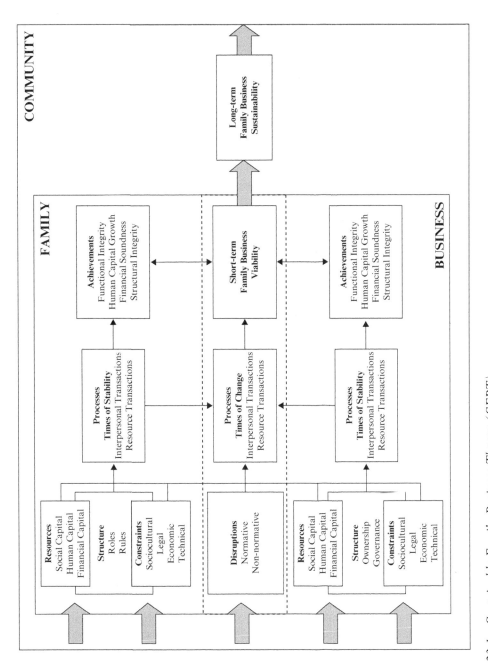

Figure 23.1 Sustainable Family Business Theory (SFBT)

509

2009; Van Auken and Werbel, 2006). In particular, entrepreneurship research rarely acknowledges the underlying effects of the owning family, as well as the founder, on the business. Some recent attention has been given to family ownership and its relationship to the ongoing performance of extant businesses (Anderson and Reeb, 2003; Weber et al., 2003). Yet, in this recent surge of interest in family business, the family itself often does not receive much notice (Zachary, 2011; Zachary and Mishra, 2011). Further, the effects of the business on the family have been entirely omitted by most entrepreneurship researchers (Aldrich and Cliff, 2003; Cramton, 1993; Rogoff and Heck, 2003; Upton and Heck, 1997).

In contrast, SFBT has been developed conceptually (Danes et al., 2008a; Stafford et al., 1999) and tested empirically (Danes et al., 2009c; Olson et al., 2003) to encompass the family perspective relative to the business enterprise and vice versa. Both the family and the business are equal systems that overlap and simultaneously move towards the sustainability of both. Families and businesses, according to Olson et al. (2003), tend to move in parallel, with success in one leading to success in the other. Similarly, problems or changes in one result in problems or changes in the other. Furthermore, SFBT recognizes that the family business interacts with its community host. A positive interdependence between the family business and its community host is more productive for both the firm and the community (Fitzgerald et al., 2010).

Early entrepreneurship research often utilized psychological attribute models which are now considered to be limiting (Ibrahim and Ellis, 2006). The rational economic model has been employed to examine entrepreneurship and family firms by integrating the profit maximization function of the firm into the monetary constraint on the household (Lopez, 1986). SFBT was the first to recognize the importance of profit maximization in the entrepreneurial venture or the family firm by recognizing the interdependence of resources, and extending the theoretical argument beyond the objective measures employed in a typical profit function (factors that produce profits or revenues) (Danes et al., 2008b). SFBT distinguishes between family capital stocks and processes that draw upon those stocks. In a longitudinal study of family capital (property, resources, money etc.) effects, Danes et al. (2009c) found family capital stock and the use and management of that capital stock had different effects on firm success.

Trends in Family Business Research

In general, family business research has consistently employed a systems approach, but attention has been focused on the business system without adequate consideration of the family system. Major topical areas of research consist of succession, professional management, boards of directors, strategy, conflict management, growth and performance (Upton and Heck, 1997). More recently, family business researchers have brought equal focus to both family and business with mutual sustainability between them as embodied in the SFBT (Danes et al., 2008a; Stafford et al., 1999). These researchers also have empirically examined the performance of the family and the business systems underlying the family business entity by analyzing resource transfers between systems and overlap management processes via the SFBT (Danes et al., 2009c; Heck and Stafford, 2001; Olson et al., 2003).

Subsequently, the family dimensions that may relate to development of a new business, including recognition of an opportunity and the mobilization of resources, are being considered and investigated (Aldrich and Cliff, 2003; Danes et al., 2010; Steier, 2003). A few entrepreneurship researchers (who typically take a business-focused approach) are taking a renewed, more in-depth, look at the family in its relation to emerging businesses (e.g. Aldrich and Cliff, 2003). In particular, Aldrich and Cliff (2003) have identified socio-historical changes in the family such as household counts, size and composition as well as roles and relationships within the family that impinge on the family and its possible motivations to create new businesses. These researchers note that previous literature in areas of emergence and recognition of opportunities, along with the decisions that create the new venture, does not include the family conceptually or empirically.

A recent research study on spousal context during venture creation framed venture creation as a dynamic, iterative and socially embedded process by using SFBT and its central tenets to integrate the Conservation of Resources theory of family stress and the Family FIRO Model (Fundamental Interpersonal Relations Orientation) of family change dynamics to explicate the iterative relationship between couple strength and venture creation (Danes et al., 2010). In this study, couple relationship strength provided a stock of resilience capacity composed of spousal resources which the entrepreneur drew upon to combat stresses created by the liability of newness in venture creation. The process of drawing upon spousal resources created a change in that stock of spousal resources (either enhancement or reduction) that, when added to the original level, became the current period's output, which was then input for the next time period, analogous to the relationship between family capital and family business success in Danes et al. (2009c). Thus, over time, spousal resources could contribute to or detract from the liabilities of newness associated with new venture creation before its launch, during the first year of launch and continually thereafter.

OVERVIEW OF PREVIOUS CONCEPTUAL FRAMEWORKS

The family is a critical element in the mix of resources that the entrepreneur needs at every stage of a venture (Rogoff and Heck, 2003). Over time, the mutual sustainability between the business and the family becomes an important goal of each system. This section will offer an overview of family and business system frameworks. These two conceptual orientations have provided important contributions to the study of family businesses upon which SFBT was built. SFBT integrates concepts of these approaches to provide a basis for integrating the results of disparate empirical studies into a single, multidimensional vision of family business functioning.

Both entrepreneurship and family business researchers view the business system as important and examine traditional topics such as strategy, management, production, labor, performance and business stages such as start-up, growth, maturity and exit (Rogoff and Heck, 2003). Although the family business is often delineated by ownership, management involvement and multiple generations, entrepreneurship more narrowly focuses on new venture opportunities and emergence. Moreover, family firm research uses systems theory while entrepreneurship is rooted in economics, management, strategy, finance, psychology and sociology. Systems theory has been especially important to business researchers in their attempts to understand the importance of culture in underpinning formal institutions, which, in turn, underpin societal business systems (Whitley, 1999). Systems theory is key to empirically analyzing the linkage between family and business systems (Danes et al., 2008a; Stafford et al., 1999).

Family systems theory acknowledges the significance of developmental change at both the individual and group levels. This theory locates behavior in hierarchically organized relationships. Therefore, families are not simply a group of individuals; rather, these individuals through intra-family interactions and transactions create unique attributes that are more than the sum of individuals and their attributes. Family systems theory suggests that the family group will operate to maintain an emotional equilibrium. When change occurs as the result of either developmental processes or external events, it disturbs the equilibrium and activates regulating mechanisms. Within the family system, both behavioral and non-behavioral responses to change occur. The theory proposes effects of members on one another and on the system itself. Family systems theory also illuminates such processes as the mechanisms of loss and replacement, the family life span, the creation of role relationships such as spouses, parent–child, or siblings, and communication strategies such as triangulating (Kepner, 1983). Systems theory is equally useful in understanding the business.

In contrast to family systems theory, family resource management theory has viewed families as having functional subsystems, analogous to the human body having functional subsystems such as the cardio-vascular system or an organization having a human resource management function (Deacon and Firebaugh, 1988; Stafford and Avery, 1993). Examples of these functional subsystems for families would be child rearing and feeding of family members. Family members select and organize these functional subsystems by combining their abilities with other resources to create activities that result in outputs. As in family systems theory, the combination of these functional subsystems results in a family system that is greater than the sum of its subsystems and their attributes, and the family is viewed as acting to maintain an emotional equilibrium. Consistent with general systems theory, family resource management theory has outputs that parallel inputs and processes represent changes in states. Some of these processes represent minor changes in states that do not disrupt the emotional equilibrium, and some of these processes represent major changes in states that can disrupt the emotional equilibrium.

Several paradigms have focused on the role of the business within the context of the family business. The concept of success has been an integral part of these frameworks. Success, however, can also be defined to include not only financial success of the firm but also other factors that may be of value to the family system such as independence, family security, and being able to choose where the family will live (Kuratko et al., 1997). In other words, success within a firm helps families meet goals other than just those connected to financial well-being, or making a profit (Danes et al., 2009c). Conversely, success within the owning family helps the firm meet its goals (Danes et al., 2002; Danes et al., 1999). Two different approaches have evolved to examine determinants of success within the firm. One approach is to examine a firm as part of the larger economy. The other approach is to examine the role of the individual as entrepreneur within the firm.

The business within the economy approach is exemplified by the work of Davidsson (1991) and Greenburger and Sexton (1987). Davidsson (1991) contended that business growth is the result of the sum of three factors – ability, need and opportunity; however, in studying these factors, Davidsson found that they only explained 25 percent of the variance in business growth. Greenberger and Sexton (1987) developed a model of business success that focused on the role of the entrepreneur and how that role changed depending on the extent of the business success. They contend that business success depends on the capabilities of individuals within the business but also on such aspects as organizational vision and empowerment of subordinates. Clearly, this approach to the study of the family business has resulted in limited understanding. Entrepreneurs may start businesses for lifestyle reasons, too (Davis-Brown and Salamon, 1987; Winter et al., 2004). Although growth and profits are important to business owners, they may want more time with family and friends, more leisure time and more control over the time they spend at work.

The individual within the business approach is exemplified by the work of Becker (1993) and others (Ehrenberg and Smith, 1997; Zuiker, 1998), who note that individuals within family businesses bring their own human capital (i.e. education, skills, experience) to a business. In this context, human capital was defined as the amount of skills, knowledge, intelligence and health that an individual brings to a business. They contend that this human capital varies from individual to individual and often determines the success of the business. This human capital can be used to gain both monetary and non-monetary resources for the individual as well as the business. This approach assumes that the individual as entrepreneur is economically mobile and that as the amount of human capital grows, so do the rewards associated with it.

Utilizing both family systems theory and business system conceptual frameworks enables researchers to study the owning family and the business entity as well as the overlap between these two major systems. Exploring the family firm from a broader vista offers richer understanding. SFBT offers a means to explore this richness and provide more satisfying answers to questions about the nature of family business.

EXTANT CONCEPTUALIZATIONS AND THEORIES OF FAMILY FIRMS

Family business researchers can now choose a number of conceptualizations and theories of the family firm. The current frameworks include, alphabetically: (a) the Bulleye model of an open-system approach (Pieper and Klein, 2007); (b) Family Embeddedness Perspective (FEP) (Aldrich and Cliff, 2003); (c) Resource-Based Framework (RBF) (Habbershon and Williams, 1999); (d) Sustainable Family Business Theory (SFBT) (Danes and Brewton, 2012; Danes et al., 2008a; Heck et al., 2006; Stafford et al., 1999); (e) Theory of Agency and Altruism in Family Firms (TAA) (Schulze et al., 2003); and (f) Unified Systems Perspective of Family Firm Performance (USP) (Habbershon et al., 2003).

Researchers have identified the need to adapt some of these major frameworks in specific areas. However, at some level of specificity both family and business systems must be identified and related to each other in any family business theory. To do otherwise limits its future usefulness (Danes et al., 2008a; Dimov, 2007; Jennings and McDougald, 2007; Heck et al., 2006; Rogoff and Heck, 2003; Rosenblatt et al., 1985).

Similar to the early disciplinary roots of the family business field, some frameworks, for example the TAA, have deeply rooted disciplinary ties that may facilitate detailed representation of specific phenomenon under study while limiting their overall scope (Schulze et al., 2003). Greenwood (2003) has suggested that economics alone as a framework, as in the TAA, is not enough. Mitchell et al. (2003) have suggested a model consisting of a business with two subsystems, similar to Cramton's (1993) pioneering research. Today's researchers demand a more comprehensive and multidisciplinary model for examining the complexities of family businesses.

Cramton (1993) was the first to conceptually move the field ahead dramatically with her groundbreaking, detailed study of one family business. With her comprehensive investigative fieldwork, she identified the discrepancy between a firm's private and public history and concluded that there was an analogous discrepancy between conceptual and actual family businesses. In the latter case, the major discrepancy was the importance of the owning family to the family business. She urged the use of family systems theory to inform research, education and practice of the family business. Others began to challenge existing research by using a broader conceptualization of the business (Dyer and Handler, 1994; Stafford et al., 1999; Upton and Heck, 1997).

In sync with Cramton's (1993) conclusions, the Family Business Research Group (FBRG) began their conceptualization of family firms to guide data collection from the first nationally representative sample of US family businesses using a household sampling frame, namely the 1997 National Family Business Survey (1997 NFBS) (Stafford et al., 1999; Winter et al., 1998). This initial survey was later paneled with surveys in 2000 and 2007. This conceptualization, published as *Sustainable Family Business Theory*, was hailed as innovative, particularly for delineating both functional families and profitable firms (Trent and Astrachan, 1999). Using a household sampling frame was deemed 'one of the biggest methodological breakthroughs since the founding of the family business field' (Astrachan and Kurtz, 1998, p. v). Researchers then had both conceptual and empirical capabilities to study family firms more comprehensively.

The open-system Bulleye model (Pieper and Klein, 2007), the Unified Systems Perspective (Habberson et al., 2003; Habbershon and Williams, 1999) and others (Klein et al., 2005) conceptualize firm-level concepts and associated measures which are really derived from family phenomena. These frameworks fail to recognize that the family system is separate from, though certainly related to, these family business constructs (Zachary, 2011). In simple terms, these frameworks fail to model completely the family system and the business system in tandem with each other (Zachary, 2011). They also only address one family type, open families, when there are many other types of families. Early research by Owen et al. (1992) showed both conceptually and empirically that family systems are varied in their family types, meaning how family members interaction with one another. Open families exist but so do closed and random family types, and the family types are related to processes and outcomes (Owen et al., 1992).

Other frameworks have sought to integrate multiple perspectives along with greater detail, namely, FEP (Aldrich and Cliff, 2003) and SFBT (Danes et al., 2008a; Heck et al., 2006; Stafford et al., 1999). Among the frameworks considered above, only these latter two have delineated details within the family system and in relation to the family business entity, though they each conceptualize these systems in very different ways.

EXTENDING THE SUSTAINABLE FAMILY BUSINESS THEORY

SFBT (Figure 23.1) describes a dynamic, behavior-based, multidimensional theory of family businesses that accommodates complex family/firm interactions (Danes et al., 2008a). Theories are abstract depictions of interconnected constructs. Thus theories have propositions that outline how the constructs are connected so that measures can be created to study the relationships that are the essence of theory (Sztompka, 1974). Theories often have underlying assumptions and SFBT has two general assumptions that distinguish it from many other theories that have been applied to family businesses: (a) family is a rational versus an irrational system; and, (b) family is not in competition with business. This section will briefly explain the various conceptual components of SFBT, and, as a way to transition from a theoretical focus to an operational focus, the section will end with a listing of the core SFBT theoretical propositions.

Guided by general systems theory, SFBT is capable of addressing, both theoretically and empirically, the behavioral complexities of family firm sustainability (i.e. mutual good among multiple systems) (Dahlhamer, 1998; Danes et al., 2009c; Olson et al., 2003). In contrast to traditional models of firm and entrepreneurial success that focus on the business and portray the family as a component of the firm's environment, in SFBT, family and firm are represented in equal detail, as is their interplay in achieving mutual sustainability. SFBT then locates entrepreneurship, both the business and the owning family, within the social context of community (Danes et al., 2008a).

Much of the traditional business performance literature is plagued by the underlying assumption that individuals make economic decisions in a social vacuum (Aldrich and Zimmer, 1986; Cramton, 1993). In contrast, the SFBT locates entrepreneurship of the business within the social context of the family, indicating that this social network is the milieu out of which the family business initiates, grows and encounters transitions. The appropriateness of locating entrepreneurship within the family context is substantiated by Aldrich's work (1999) on social networks of family-owned firms.

The current literature on family-owned business success and performance primarily emphasizes business system issues. For example, a number of authors have indicated that family tasks and values often are placed in opposition to those of the business (Danes et al., 2005; Danes and Olson, 2003; Whiteside and Brown, 1991). There is a tendency to consider the family as a system that impedes the functioning of the business (Borwick, 1986; Danes et al., 2002; Merkel and Carpenter, 1987; Ward, 1997), and the family is seen as the part of the situation that must be managed (Budge and Janoff, 1991; Hollander and Elman, 1988; Whiteside and Brown, 1991).

SFBT, however, permits a neutral approach and does not assume that family is in competition with or in conflict with business. Rather, the SFBT recognizes that disruptions created by change are normal and occur at the intersection of family and business. It further suggests that management of conflict evolving from disruptions may serve to project the family or business into needed constructive change that fosters sustainability rather than assuming conflict progresses only into destructive conflict that negatively influences survivability and sustainability (Danes and Morgan, 2004; Danes et al., 1999; Kaye, 1991).

Resources, Structures and Constraints

Resources, in general, are stocks of want-satisfying capacity. Resources in SFBT are clas-sified by their form. Families provide resources to entrepreneurial endeavors of their family members in the form of social capital, human capital and financial capital (Figure 23.1). Social capital is the stock of good will, trust and confidence in family members or their business that are the results of interactions with family members. Family entrepreneurship has an advantage over non-family entrepreneurship settings due to the increased probability of trust among family members. Human capital refers to the attributes of individuals such as knowledge and energy of the entrepreneur. Whereas social capital is created and used via human interaction, requiring at least two people, human capital requires only one person. Financial capital includes property, money, credit and financial investments of all kinds (Danes et al., 2008a).

Family capital is captured in SFBT operationally by both stock (i.e. values at one point in time) and flow (i.e. values over time) measures over time (Danes et al., 2009c). Understanding the flows as well as the stock of owning family capital is critical to under-standing long-term sustainability because Danes et al. (2009c) found that access to and utilization of family social capital over time was more important for sustainability than the level of family capital.

Families also have constraints that impose limits on resource use. These constraints may be classified as sociocultural, legal, economic and technical in nature (Figure 23.1) (Danes et al., 2009c). Sociocultural constraints refer to the informal norms and mores of the community, violation of which imposes informal social sanctions. Legal constraints are the laws and regulations imposed by political entities. Economic constraints are limi-tations imposed by finite resources and markets. Technical constraints are the laws of biology, chemistry and physics that processes must abide by (Danes et al., 2008a).

Family members often work in the business system and are a good illustration of the dual empowering and constraining aspects of capital. This human capital (as depicted in Figure 23.1) can be a resource or constraint depending on the life-cycle stage of either the family or the business. For example, during the early years of a family venture, the family often provides the firm with a steady supply of trustworthy human resources (Ward, 1997). In fact, Chrisman et al. (2002) stated that new family firms might not face the same liability of newness because of the labor provided by family members. In their formative years, family firms benefit from social and human capital transfers between family and business systems because family social capital fosters commitment and a sense of identi-fication with the founder's dream (Haynes et al., 1999; Van Auken and Neeley, 2000; Van Auken, 2003; Winborg and Landström, 2001). The human capital stock of the owning family may be limited or eventually outstripped by the demands of a growing business. Succession remains a tremendous challenge to family businesses as they transition between generations, and it clearly demonstrates the importance of family as a key source of capital.

Family structure refers to roles and rules of the family system (Figure 23.1). In family firms, owning families may need additional structures such as a family council to handle or manage a variety of family matters. Family structure changes over the life course as family members age and marry, have children or leave home. Ethnic groups may define family roles differently (Danes et al., 2008a; Gollnick and Chinn, 1990).

SFBT suggests that resource transactions (e.g. utilization or transformation of time, energy and money) and interpersonal transactions (e.g. communication or relationship and conflict management) from the business and family may facilitate or inhibit the sustainability of family businesses. For instance, interpersonal transactions among family members have been depicted as an obstacle to successful ownership transfer of family businesses (Lansberg and Astrachan, 1994; Rodriguez et al., 1999). Yet family interpersonal transactions may also be a source of support that helps a family business overcome adversity and social change (Sirmon and Hitt, 2003). Van Auken and Werbel (2006) suggest that family members may provide financial resources through outside sources of earned income (see also Haynes et al., 1999), emotional support in the form of encouragement, and instrumental support in the form of knowledge or physical assistance in helping the family business to survive (Matzek et al., 2010).

Disruptions

Disruptions in SFBT have been classified as normative and non-normative. Normative disruptions are those that may occur because of changes in family structure or events such as holidays or ceremonies. Non-normative disruptions are those that are not foreseeable or are highly unusual. An example would be a natural disaster that forced temporary or permanent closure of the business (Danes et al., 2008a). Change and the disruptions resulting from change are positioned within the overlap of family and business because dynamic and interdependent relationships that are needed to successfully maneuver through change require the resources and interpersonal interactions of both systems (Danes and Morgan, 2004). During times of change, resources that contribute to creative problem solving around disruptions are garnered from each system to manage their response to change. Other models in the family business field do not explicitly recognize that processes are different in times of change versus times of stability. Nor do they acknowledge explicitly that processes within each system must be reconstructed during times of change to incorporate the adaptations that each system has made to accommodate the disruptions.

How the family members utilize resources and processes during times of disruption caused by change may facilitate or inhibit the sustainability of the family business (Danes, 1999; Danes et al., 2002). Using the metaphor of stock and flow in economics and system dynamics modeling, a stock of resilience capacity can be built in either the family or business, and that capacity can flow across permeable boundaries when it is needed (Brewton et al., 2010). If families have built a stored capacity for resilience, when they encounter a disruption, the store of trust and creativity in problem solving can be more easily and quickly tapped and adapted to the new situation (Danes et al., 2002). Although sustainability of the family firm depends, in part, upon how it adapts to change, it is important to understand in detail the resource and interpersonal transactions that increase the probability of successfully responding to change (Stafford et al., 2010).

Processes

Processes in SFBT differ during times of stability and times of change (Danes et al., 2002; Stewart and Danes, 2001). Ward (1997) indicated that the long-term sustainability of any family business depends on its ability to anticipate and respond to change. Modified processes are needed for a family business to remain healthy when responding to changes that occur during disruptions in either the family or the business system (Danes, 1999; Danes et al., 2002). During times of change, interpersonal and resource transactions are adjusted at the intersection of the family and business systems (Danes et al., 2002; Stafford et al., 1999).

SBFT processes transform inputs into achievements in the short run and sustainability in the long term, given structure and constraints. In the short run, processes use capital to create other capital or enhance and increase existing capital. Short-run processes, which entail capital flows, result in transformed capital stocks that are available inputs for future periods' processes, determining long-term sustainability. In other words, resource change in the present affects the available resources at a later time (Danes et al., 2009c). For example, if a credit card or loan is incurred now, this will reduce the income of the family in the future by the amount of the payments made to the credit card or loan. Families and firms are affected by environmental and structural change. Different processes occur in each system during periods of stability and change (Danes et al., 2002). Danes et al. (2009a) concluded that resilience processes may be more important to achievements and sustainability than capital availability. Stress in SFBT evolves when resources are threatened, lost, or believed to be unstable, or where people cannot see a path to fostering and protecting resources through joint or individual efforts (Hobfoll, 2001).

Capital Adjustments to Change

Business disruptions can require the business and family to pool resources to sustain the family business. Further, business disruptions caused by natural disasters, labor actions, cyber or virus attacks and other major disruptions can be especially serious and place the business and family at risk (Haynes et al., 2011; Keating, 2001). These types of disruptions not only impact the business and family, but they have very serious ramifications for the host community. If the business community finds itself unable to recover from these disruptions, these communities face the dual challenges of reduced business and agency services and increased social and economic needs. Businesses leave because they are unprofitable and agencies depart because they are serving too few people, while those remaining in the community grapple with the challenges of a declining community. Internal to the family business, tensions resulting from the disruptions of change affect the interdynamics of spouses who own family businesses. The tensions that occur between spouses at the intersection of the family and business systems often center around resources, such as the allocation of finances, the distribution of time across the family and business, or the energy and commitment provided to either or both systems (Danes and Morgan, 2004; Danes et al., 1999).

In family businesses, spousal commitment to the business underscores the nature of the marital relationship and affects the health and achievements of the family business (Danes et al., 2010). Few studies have examined the role or impact of spousal relationships on family business performance (Danes et al., 2010; Matzek et al., 2010; Poza and Messer, 2001). Even though some studies have examined the impact of family business on the marital relationship (Miller et al., 1999), little is known about the simultaneous trade-offs to achieve both family and business goals. Strong spousal commitment can be a source of competitive advantage (e.g. a supportive spouse affects the likelihood a business will succeed) and facilitate the success of family businesses (Danes et al., 2010; Harris et al., 1994). Spouses can provide active support in the form of personal or temporal resources (Danes and Olson, 2003). Alternatively, spouses can provide emotional support that ameliorates financial stresses (Van Auken and Werbel, 2006). Many spouses are even 'copreneurs' or otherwise active business partners (Fitzgerald and Muske, 2002; Ponthieu and Caudill, 1993). Whether the spouse makes direct work contributions or not, the extent to which the spouse listens, offers ideas and makes suggestions about the business can positively influence the quality of the owner's decision-making.

Achievements

Family firm achievements are current year's outcomes; they are revenue, profit, goods and services produced, perceived success, jobs created and so on. Viability is the result of family/firm achievements in the current year. Achievements are multiple and must be evaluated multidimensionally for a complete outcome assessment (Cooper and Artz, 1995; Cooper et al., 1988a, 1988b). Financial outcomes are traditional achievements in firm and economic literature. Using multidimensional outcomes leads to greater understanding of the entire payoff to owners' investments (Danes et al., 2007). Family firm sustainability is the outcome of multiple years of viability, and is also evaluated multidimensionally. SFBT posits that sustainability is a function of both firm success and family functionality (Danes et al., 2009c; Olson et al., 2003). Sustainability also encompasses how family members exchange resources across systems (Danes and Brewton, 2012). Viability is an outcome of the family and business achievements in the current year, whereas sustainability of both systems mutually interlocked occurs in the longrun or over time (Danes and Brewton, 2012).

In the natural disaster context, sustainability is the ability to 'tolerate damage, diminished productivity, and reduced quality of life from an extreme event without assistance' (Mileti, 1999, p. 4). Rate of hazard onset confounds operationalization of sustainability because slow-onset hazards such as droughts are sometimes referred to as pressures or stressors. Slow-onset events allow systems to modify their behavior as the event occurs. The SFBT has been utilized to examine family and business characteristics and processes that affect both survival and success of family businesses in areas suffering natural disasters as well as the effects of federal disaster assistance (Haynes et al., 2011; Stafford et al., 2010).

Family Firm within the Community Context

SFBT recognizes that the firm is part of a larger system by placing the family business within its community context (Danes et al., 2008a). Members of the family and business system may interact with the community; the impetus for the manner and degree to which that interaction occurs is rooted in the meanings that family members give to that activity. The owning family provides a fertile environment of values, attitudes and beliefs that serve as inputs into the family business culture. One of the attitudes from the family that often transfers into the business through its family employees is responsibility to the community. Success of the family business depends on whether the firm is managed in harmony with the local community culture (Astrachan, 1988; Niehm et al., 2008). A positive symbiosis between the family business and its community host is more productive for both the firm and the community compared to a situation where there is not a good match between the two cultures.

SFBT Propositions

One of the advantages of SFBT is that it is a family business theory that addresses the complexities of family businesses, especially at the intersection of family and business. However, a theoretical advantage such as this one can create challenges. In this case, the challenge is to describe conceptual components in enough detail to set the stage for a discussion of its operationalization. Sztompka (1974) stated that a theory's propositions outline how constructs are connected so that measures can be created to study the relationships among the theory's constructs. The following are central propositions of SFBT but they are not all inclusive:

(a)   An individual in either family or business may affect parts of both systems (family and business).
(b)   The family or business system can die if the boundaries are too diffuse.
(c)   Family capital (composed of human, social, and financial capital in form of skills, relationships and money as examples) from both family and business are inputs that can be used to solve problems of the collective interaction of family, business and community.
(d)   Resources (e.g. property, wealth, assets) can have simultaneous positive or negative effects on firm performance, depending on the circumstances.
(e)   Constraints (i.e. restrictions or controls) impose limits on alternatives available, alternative resources, processes and achievements.
(f)   The process of drawing upon family capital stock creates a change in that capital stock (either enhancement or reduction), which, when added to the original level, becomes the current period's output, which will be input for the next time period.
(g)   Owning families manage both family and business system resources together to meet overlapping needs instead of each apart from the other.
(h)   The degree of overlap between family and business adjusts depending upon demands emanating from either internal or external demands.
(i)   Out of the overlap of family and business evolves a culture that assumes (either intentionally or unintentionally) some of the values, attitudes and beliefs of the owning family.
(j)   Systems interact by exchanging capital (resources and constraints) at their boundaries during times of disruption and those resources can be tracked.
(k)   Processes in the family and business are composed of interpersonal transactions (e.g. communication, personal relationships, conflict management) and resource transactions (utilization or transformation of social, human or financial capital) that can be thought as routine, or standard operating, procedures.
(l)   After disruptions, processes must be reconstructed to ensure sustainability over time.

(m)   Conflicts arise when there is a mismatch between demands and resources that can be used to meet those demands.

(n)   Patterns of resource and interpersonal transactions in firm and family systems during times of stability create a resilience capacity that serves as a foundation for addressing stresses during time of change and disruption.

(o)   Family and business are affected by environmental and structural change that can be normative and non-normative.

(p)   Capital transactions in firm or community may facilitate or inhibit firm sustainability.

(q)   Sustainability is a function of both business success and family functionality.

(r)   Owning families manage family and firm jointly to optimize achievements.

(s)   Family firms outcomes (results or products) include both short-term viability (feasibility) and long-term sustainability (mutual good among multiple systems).

(t)   A positive symbiosis between family, firm and its community host is productive for both firm and community.

Thus, as a way to transition from the description of SFBT in its theoretical form to its operationalization, a number of core SFBT propositions are identified. Many of the propositions have been tested in the research that is described and cited in this chapter.

THE OPERATIONALIZATION OF SFBT

Given the great need for more research specific to the internal family dynamics of family firms, small or large, including Fortune 500 companies, SFBT provides a detailed framework to do so. This section presents major concepts or constructs within SFBT and discusses their measurement.

SFBT was developed specifically to inform and coordinate a stream of empirical research on family businesses. Because SFBT is a specific social systems theory, the components and their relationships have been portrayed in a manner that is consistent with the general theory of social systems. The business and family have been portrayed with parallel constructs at equivalent levels of theoretical specificity. This consistency facilitates coordination of research that focuses on either the family or business or the intersection of the two, and can yield a more complete model of a complex social system such as a family business than would otherwise be possible.

The most basic of all the relationships in SFBT is that between inputs, processes and outcomes. Inputs precede processes; in other words, inputs explain processes. Inputs and processes precede outcomes and, therefore, explain them in empirical models. Processes may occur simultaneously and their simultaneity may affect the way they are modeled empirically. The same issue exists for achievements. Having said this, empirical researchers have to think about the implications of their data for these relationships. With cross-section data, inputs are given; they are independent variables rather than dependent variables. Only processes and outcomes can serve as dependent variables. However, with panel data or time series data, later time period inputs can depend on processes and outcomes of previous time periods.

Researchers must be clear about whether their purpose is descriptive or normative.

Like all systems models, SFBT is descriptive. However, general systems theory proposes that all systems must efficiently organize themselves to achieve their purpose. SFBT is consistent with normative theories in economics and psychology, and these theories can be subsumed seamlessly within SFBT. The mid-level of detail and focus on resources in SFBT facilitates integration with normative theories. For example, family processes can be conceived and modeled as household production functions (i.e. creation of products and services within families such as prepared meals to well-adjusted children), and business processes can be conceived and modeled as firm production functions (i.e. creation of products and services). Coefficients derived from such models or firm records can be embedded in linear or non-linear programs to find optimally efficient levels of production. They can also be embedded in 'What if' analysis on an Excel spreadsheet, if desired. Similarly, cognitive traps for business managers can be identified within SFBT.

SFBT can be used to explain both large and small business owner behavior; however, family business researchers need to be cognizant of the scale of firms within their data when operationalizing SFBT. Businesses have a greater range of size than families, so businesses are usually the determining unit in this decision. Relevant measures for small firms may be irrelevant for large or very large firms, and vice versa. In contrast, Habbershon and Williams (1999) have proposed a model in which the influence of the owning family declines as firm size increases. The F-PEC familiness scale (Astrachan et al., 2002) was developed for use with data on relatively large family businesses; whereas the family orientation index (FOI) (Uhlaner, 2005) developed as a familiness scale for use with small and very small businesses. Measures for families usually do not differ with scale. Some measures may differ for families with and without children, but family scholars view this as a structural difference rather than a scale difference.

For both families and businesses, researchers need to decide the level of aggregation in which they are interested and the focal unit. Then researchers need to keep that decision in mind when designing data collection, selecting measures for constructs and choosing methods of estimation or hypothesis testing. Both business and family scholars agree that organizations (families) and their members are not synonymous, and a single member cannot be relied upon to give reliable information about the organization. Care needs to be taken when using data from one person as an indicator of an organizational construct. Some researchers refer to the failure in addressing this measurement issue adequately as the mono-method problem or the ecological fallacy. When designing data collection, ask the questions about the focal unit. Researchers cannot interview families or businesses, only their members. When reliability of data is important, thought should be given to interviewing more than one member. When researchers are interested in the effect of a community attribute, thought should be given to obtaining data from more than one organization within that community.

STATA software has the capability of allowing for sophisticated sampling schemes to adequately address this issue. Repeated measures techniques are prevalent in statistical software. Even Excel has this capacity. Estimation of hierarchical linear models is another means of addressing this issue.

So far, in this section, reference has been made to measures of constructs. Measures are numerical information that results from measurement. Measurement includes ascertaining the presence of an attribute as well as ascertaining how much of an attribute is present.

Thus measures include both quantitative variables and non-quantitative variables, sometimes called indicators. Measures also include the indicators of latent variables. Components of some of the constructs in SFBT are important, but not observable. For example, family social capital may not be directly observable; researchers may only be able to observe a transaction that is evidence of the existence of family social capital. Inability to observe a construct in SFBT or some of the specific components does not prohibit operationalization of SFBT. Statistical techniques exist for index construction and use of observable responses to construct indicators of latent constructs.

Resource inputs to families and firms in SFBT are in the form of capital, and capital is an inherently stock concept. In other words, capital is a supply reservoir rather than a flow of services. It is the lake, not the water flowing through turbines in the dam. However, both stock of capital available and the rate of flow and use of capital are relevant measures in SFBT. Processes in SFBT are about the use of available capital. Sometimes when modeling processes, researchers may know only capital available, not the actual use of the capital in the process. Emotional support provided is a flow measure of social capital stock that provides evidence of the existence of the social capital stock. Researchers reviewing studies and designing questionnaires need to keep this distinction between flow measures and stock measures in mind. It is best to avoid using flow measures for one form of capital and stock measures for another form of capital. When modeling processes, it is also best to use the same type of measures for each input into the process.

Family Resources

Family social capital

In general, family social capital is good will among family members and between owning family members and their communities that can be input to the family and its firm to facilitate action (Danes et al., 2009c). Social capital is embodied in relationships among people and formal institutions. Social capital can be relied upon to uphold social norms and reciprocate favors (Danes et al., 2008a). Cultural knowledge is a form of social capital that plays a prominent part in management of many ethnic family firms such as trade credit from co-ethnic suppliers, training opportunities form co-ethnic owners and, in some cultures, negotiating competition through informal politics (Danes et al., 2008a).

Level of concept abstraction is an important concern when measuring family social capital, and being clear about that level is critical in family social capital research. For instance, concepts such as trust and love, the essence of family-firm-owning couple relationships, are theoretical forms of social capital because transactions between spouses act as an accumulation of resources that entrepreneurs can draw upon to help achieve family and business goals (Matzek et al., 2010). But those theoretical concepts cannot be directly measured. Instead, indicators of trust and love are what can be measured, as in Matzek et al. (2010) and Danes et al. (2010). Family social capital might include, for example, the level of spousal resource contribution measured by spousal involvement in the business or it might include interpersonal transactions such as development of guidelines about acceptable and unacceptable behaviors of family members related to the business. Social capital measures might include emotional support, calculative or moral commitment to the business, resource transference across family/business boundaries during hectic times in the firm, sharing in firm decision-making processes, or representing the family firm in the community.

The family's social capital includes such concepts as trust, love and altruism, as well as in-kind exchanges of all types. Trust among family members develops from shared experiences and a willingness to allow family members to learn and grow together. One working definition of trust has been provided by Mayer et al. (1995) as 'the willingness of a party to be vulnerable to the actions of another party based on the expectation that the other will perform a particular action important to the trustor, irrespective of the ability to monitor or control that other party' (p. 712). Several researchers have specifically explored the existence and the fostering of trust within the context of the family firm and, in particular, relative to governance (Steier, 2001a; Sundaramurthy, 2008) as well as the mechanism of trust in financial arrangements among family members in family firms (Steier, 2003).

Empirically, respondents and/or family members could be asked to rate or rank the levels of trust with every other family member via Likert scales. Then the level of trust within a particular family could be additively measured and correlated with other variables or employed as an independent variable within an explanatory model based on the SFBT. Love and altruism are equally intangible commodities exchanged between and among individuals with families and other groups or networks. Such components of social capital are somewhat more difficult to measure than trust itself, and perhaps love and altruism could be deciphered from more qualitative interviews with family members. On the other hand, love and altruism could be inferred from appropriately measured trust levels (Becker, 1993).

Families are lovingly notorious for in-kind exchanges of all types; that is, money rarely changes hands in the constant flow of activities that are embedded in the myriad of relationships and interactions within families. For example, one spouse may disengage from full-time employment but contribute unpaid labor to the specific and general production within the family. An unpaid spouse may perform work activities from rocking infants, to cleaning house and clothes for the entire family, to shopping and preparing meals.

Emotional support among family members is also vital to the mental health and physical health of the individuals involved therein (Kepner, 1983). Olson et al. (2003) empirically showed an effect of business variables on the emotional health of the family and the effect of family variables on the business. In fact, a family APGAR measure of the functional integrity of the family has been used widely by researchers using the National Family Business Panel (NFBP) (Heck et al., 2006).

In a longitudinal study of family capital's impact on family firm performance (Danes et al., 2009c), stock and flow measures of social capital were identified. The authors incorporated a detailed discussion in their article on the measurement issues involved in such an analysis. In acknowledging the importance of culture in family social capital, Danes et al. (2008a), in an article focusing on effects of ethnicity, families and culture on the entrepreneurial experience, identified the most prominent ethnic and cultural values, beliefs, norms and practices that are characteristic of a number of cultures that are the essence of family social capital in those cultures. The authors also identified some research hypotheses that could be tested in the future about some of the social capital characteristics about these cultures. Danes and Stafford (2011) provided two tools to be used by family business educators and consultants that are based on two of their social capital research measures used in Danes et al. (2009c).

Of all the family capital types, the context in which the family business owner is grounded (family) (Danes et al., 2010; Dimov, 2007), and the context in which the family firm is grounded (community) (Astrachan, 1988), are of critical importance and need to be measured. For example, in a longitudinal study of spousal context during the venture creation process, Danes et al. (2010) approached venture creation as a dynamic, iterative and socially embedded process, with the couple relationship being the focal social context within the process. This study provides specific measures for both spousal enabling resources and spousal constraining resources and examines the interrelationship of these resources measures with couple relationship strength over a year during the venture creation process.

Fitzgerald et al. (2010) include a number of measures that might be used for measuring social capital shared between family firms and their communities. Community social capital's effect can vary by firm location. In comparing urban and rural family firm resilience, Brewton et al. (2010) found that social capital measures had a significant impact on the firm resilience of rural family firms.

Gender of the family business owner also makes a difference in the use of social capital. In a study of family firm resilience after a natural disaster, females used more social capital resources in maintaining family firm resilience than did males (Danes et al., 2009a). In fact, the constraining characteristics of social capital were the ones that were statistically significant.

Another SFBT contribution is the acknowledgment that resources can have either enabling or constraining characteristics or simultaneous enabling and constraining characteristics. An example of the simultaneous characteristics can be found in the Gudmunson et al. (2009) study of work–family balance where the effects of emotional spousal support on work–family balance were confounded until a satisfaction-with-business-communication measure was introduced, revealing competing direct and indirect effects on work–family balance in launching a new family business. Business owners who sensed that spousal emotional support for business-related concerns was productive were found to be more satisfied with communication about the business contributing to their sense of work–family balance. On the other hand, once these positive effects of spousal support through satisfying communication were accounted for, it was also discovered that the receipt of spousal support could detract from a sense of work–family balance for business owners.

These findings provided support for the SFBT tenet that social support flowing from a stock of social capital is a conditional resource dependent on context and circumstances, and can have both enabling and constraining characteristics. That is one of the reasons that resources and constraints were separated in the revision of the SFBT in 2008. It is important to note, however, that in order to obtain these results in Gudmunson et al. (2009), the researchers had data from more than one point in time, measures from multiple informants (entrepreneur and spouse), and measures about the business and the interface of the business and family.

Another concern in measuring family social capital is the nature of implied boundaries between family capital components. For example, boundaries between one's human capital and a group's social capital accessed by an individual can be fuzzy. For example, an argument could be made that an owner's value of the reason for having a family business could be a human capital measure rather than a social capital one, as operationalized in Danes et al. (2009c). On the other hand, values are rooted in the business owner who traverses the permeable boundaries of the family and firm. Thus the critical point to be made here is that when reviewing research or doing empirical research, it is important to pay careful attention to the operationalization of theoretical concepts such as the family capital components in both the firm and family systems in family business research. Furthermore, it is important to be aware of whether a family capital variable is measured as a stock available or if it is treated as the use of the stock.

Family human capital

In part, the accumulation of social capital within families has its roots in the human capital or attributes of its individual family members. Human capital is considered the most fundamental form of capital. Ethnicity, education, time and energy are examples of human capital present within families. Ethnicity embodies common values, beliefs and practices related to nationality, common ancestry and/or common immigration experiences (Hill et al., 2005). And although it sometimes is associated with race, ethnicity embodies more than race as well as being an important input into a family's culture, which is the result of interpersonal interaction (Gollnick and Chinn, 1990).

Education most often refers to formal education and the level of attainment such as high school and higher education degrees. It is also the case that family members provide informal education via mentoring and modeling behaviors exemplified among elders within families with their younger members. Measures of education for each family member would be the level of education attained. Informal education might be measured in terms of the number of years a particular skill-related activity was engaged in or experienced by a particular family member.

Researchers using the NFBP data chose to measure family human capital by the education and gender of the family manager rather than the family head. Use of family manager's human capital as an indicator of the family's human capital makes sense for several reasons. Males are more likely to marry down than are females. Mother's education also has more implications for children's human capital development than does father's education. Mother's education is more highly correlated than father's education with children's education. Measures such as number of family members with a given level of education have not been used because of insufficient variance in such measures for relatively small families.

More often, age or education level of the children has been used as a measure of family structure than a measure of family human capital. For example, having high school age children affects how families function. The degree that family labor is available to the firm also affects how families function. In other words, family human capital resources and constraints inevitably change with structure in obvious ways. Families change with varied structures in less obvious ways as well. For instance, access to human capital of family members is greater and more reliable in married couples than in unmarried couples (Bryant and Zick, 2005).

Time and energy contributions by family members to their families have nearly endless possibilities, sometimes only limited by the individual contributors themselves. Time use research studies have long documented the hours and minutes of contributions of family members to the needs and wants of the family in general (Juster and Stafford, 1985; Walker and Woods, 1976). Parents playing with their children is a vital component to that child growing into a balanced and well-adjusted adult. Siblings cooperating with each other to build a snowman in the front yard is essentially a peer laboratory where young children learn to collaborate there and later as adults (Friedman, 1991). Time can be measured in the number of hours spent in various activities in the home and energy levels might be inferred from the intensity level of the particular activity engaged in during the period of time examined.

Because human capital consists of skills and abilities vested in people, human capital is not only genetically determined; it can be augmented via investment over time. These endowments or stocks can be taken as given in cross-section data, but not in panel data. Because human capital is vested in individuals, thought should be given to the desired measure of human capital for a group of people such as a family or a firm. Care needs to be taken to delineate between human and social capital when measuring human capital of a group. For a group of people, human capital can be measured by counting the number of people with a skill or ability, or by using a measure of central tendency for a skill possessed by members of the group.

A major societal function of the family is building the human capital of its members. Optimal investment requires consideration of the capacities of family members and the prospective use of the accrued capital. Current distribution of human capital within the family determines the time allocation of family members, but future use of capital determines current investments in family human capital. This investment is subject to technological and cultural changes. For families, human capital has frequently been measured by the human capital of the 'household head'. For male household heads, this has not been problematic. Measuring the human capital of females is more problematic because of their more diverse life paths. Family human capital includes the education and experience of family members or the average education of the parents.

Family financial capital

Financial capital is composed of physical assets (i.e. property and houses) and financial assets (i.e. money, stocks and bonds). Assets are anything tangible or intangible that one possesses which is considered applicable to the payment of one's debts. Financial assets are cash or assets that are readily converted into cash. Physical assets are less readily converted into cash. Historically, more attention has been paid to family financial capital than to other forms of family capital. Family financial capital includes such tangibles as money, credit, assets and investments of all kinds. Such forms of capital are necessary and critical to the well-being of the family and have long been studied by many researchers examining money via the income levels of families and their associated credit use. Assets and investments are routinely counted in national surveys such as the Panel Study of Income Dynamics (Duncan, 1984) and surveys of consumer finances and others. Wealth is important and often counted and measured to show the financial health of families.

Measures of family assets also are usually available, although they may not be updated as often as firm net worth statements. Families' greatest asset is usually their home, and for this reason home ownership may be the only asset measure included for a family. Business-owning families are the exception to the rule about homes, but their home will usually be the second-biggest asset owned. For a group of business-owning families, such as ranchers and farmers, disentangling the value of the business's property from the family home is essentially impossible. For other business-owning families, the practice is to measure the business assets and attribute them to the business and measure non-business assets of the family and attribute them to the family. The form of measurement for families is analogous to that for firms.

Other than disentangling family and business physical assets, financial intermingling practices of owning families pose the greatest challenge in obtaining good measures of assets for both the family and the business. Financial intermingling is an example of a flow measure of assets as well as the transfer of resources between systems. In NFBP data, 9.7 percent of the owning families used personal assets as collateral for business loans and 3.7 percent used business assets as collateral for personal loans (Haynes et al., 1999). In the NFBP, researchers could tell that owning families had intermingled assets because the questions were asked. However, if the survey is only about the business, researchers may not be able to tell whether the mortgage on an asset was for personal reasons or whether property in the name of the business was purchased with a personal mortgage.

Business Resources

Note that resources within the business are identical to the family resources (Figure 23.1). And throughout the litany of business resources including social capital human capital and financial capital within the business, the measures of business resources would be similar to those used in the family. The only difference would be that the respondents would simply be workers, managers or leaders as opposed to family members rating or ranking each other.

Business social capital
In business, as in the family, social capital exists in the form of trust, caring, altruism and in-kind exchanges between and among employees, managers and leaders within the business. It may be the case that families who foster and grow their human capital may be more able to germinate, transfer and/or grow this social capital within their businesses. For example, family members who trust each other may simply transfer that trust to their business setting, whether or not a particular family member is in or out of the business arena. Those working in the business may be able to allow more freedoms and less control over each other and over their non-family employees.

Caring and altruism surely exist within businesses as well as within families from the standpoint of treating your co-worker as a good friend and providing benefits to each other as you might family members. For example, co-workers might offer gifts or accolades to each other at business functions and relative to their work activities or performance. Co-workers also might help each other to meet deadlines or deal with stressful times within the businesses.

In-kind exchanges relative to the family firm transpired via family members are frequently unpaid workers who make contributions to the business. Basic frequencies from the NFBP data showed that 27 percent of unpaid extended-family workers versus 25 percent paid extended-family workers made labor contributions to their respective family firms (Winter et al., 1998). Further, employees most certainly support each other emotionally. In fact, little work or output could be produced either in the family or the business unless individuals were willing to support each other with encouragement and understanding as well as empathy and camaraderie as they work together toward achieving their common goals.

Business human capital

Human capital in the business is defined similarly to the human capital in the family, meaning the specific human attributes of individuals. Human capital such as ethnicity and education is possessed by workers within the business setting as opposed to the family setting. The same is true for time and energy use. These forms of human capital are manifested by workers within their business setting and offered to the work at hand. As an employee, one might work overtime and expend great energy in meeting deadlines or major projects for the business.

Human capital measures are among the most frequently included firm attributes. For example, number of employees is a measure of firm human capital. By extension, the number of full-time and the number of part-time employees are also firm human capital measures. Man-hours employed or hours of overtime are additional human capital measures. Conversely, measures of hours not available also measure human capital stock. For example, an owner having a second or third job limits the time available for a small family business, and thus measures limits on human capital available.

Human capital is considered the most fundamental capital form consisting of skills and abilities vested in people that are not only genetically determined but augmented via investment over time. These endowments or stocks can be taken as given in cross-section data, but not in panel data. Because human capital is vested in individuals, thought should be given to the desired human capital measure for a group of people such as a family or a firm. Care needs to be taken to delineate between human capital and social capital when measuring human capital of a group. For a group of people, human capital can be measured by counting the number of people with a skill or ability or using a measure of central tendency for a skill possessed by members of the group.

Including human capital measures for the firm and the family in analyses of small family firms may be problematic. One problem is how to account for human capital stock available for use by the firm and the family. Danes et al. (2009b) handled this issue by using number of non-family employees to measure firm size and number of family employees to capture the family human capital available to both systems. Another is the high correlation between the spouses' human capital. For estimation purposes, researchers may have to include only one spouse's human capital in the equation(s). Education of spouses is usually more highly correlated than experience, and experience is domain specific while education is less domain specific. Fortunately, flow measures of human capital are not as closely correlated as stock measures. Measures such as weekly hours of employment or holding another job are less highly correlated because some spouses function as complements, while others function as substitutes.

Human capital theory posits a positive correlation between human capital and productivity. Consequently, measures of human capital are often used as proxy measures of people's productivity (Zuiker et al., 2002). For example, Bates (1985, 1987) contends that the better educated, more productive, subset of ethnic entrepreneurs is concentrated in businesses outside the retail and service industries where the profit is greater.

The link between human capital and productivity has been difficult to demonstrate for family firms. Most analyses using the NFBP data have not found owner's education to be significant in empirical analyses. The lack of significance in these studies for what is proposed to be an important predictor of productivity may be explained by the relatively small variance in education in that data set. Variables cannot explain a dependent variable without a sufficient amount of variance themselves.

Business financial capital
Financial capital within the firm also includes such tangibles as money, credit, assets and investments of all kinds. Classical production functions within firms have included land and capital in addition to labor. Certainly money, credit and financial investments feed the gristmill of the firm within and between/among a particular business to other businesses. The difference here again is that financial capital is defined within the business entity as opposed to the family.

Business assets, other than rights that give a business an advantage in the market, are quite readily available. The balance sheet of a firm records the monetary value of the assets owned. Rue and Ibrahim (1996) found that the majority of very small business owners use *pro forma* net worth statements and update them regularly. The more challenging problem in measuring assets' is the fact that they are applicable to the payment of debts, thus making assets and liabilities positively correlated and raising the question about whether the more desirable measure to include is assets or non-obligated assets, net worth. If the intention is to include a measure of capital available for use, then net worth would be better. The argument could be made that physical assets should be excluded from the net worth calculation. For the purpose of inclusion in empirical analyses, assets, liabilities and net worth are usually logarithmically transformed to better account for their heteroskedasticity. As the size of a firm increases, so does the variance in the assets and liabilities.

Business and family finances are linked within family-owned businesses, especially in the early stages of the business (Aldrich and Cliff, 2003; Haynes et al., 1999; Steier and Greenwood, 2000). In general, the small business finance research has overlooked the intermingling of family and businesses finances in business-owning families. It has concentrated on models of profit maximization and risk tolerance preferences of the owner/manager or the financial and regulatory structure of corporate financial markets. Family business research has frequently used samples from the upper bounds of what constitutes a 'small' business (Haynes and Avery, 1997; Scherr et al., 1993). Investigating the intermingling of finances between the family and business, Haynes et al. (1999) found that two-thirds of family businesses intermingled household and business finances, indicating that those finances are inextricably intertwined. Business to family intermingling was more likely to occur when the location of the business was a rural or small town as opposed to an urban area or if the business borrowed money or operated as a C or S corporation (with implications for tax). Sole proprietorships were more likely to use family resources in the business than other types of businesses, as were those who borrowed money, were younger owners and were owners without children.

The intermingling of financial resources is not necessarily completely positive and without cost. A potential negative is the inability to capture these interchanges in the financial records of either the family or the business. The lack of such data, while confusing for the family's financial picture, may be catastrophic to a business. Simply put, the business may not know if it is making a profit and may be jeopardizing its long-term future. The need to establish and maintain separate financial accounts is crucial to business management (Burns and Bolton, 2001). Separation of business and personal records remains a key in helping the business plan and respond to bankers and governmental entities. Separation of accounts is recommended by such entities as the United States Small Business Administration and the United States Internal Revenue Service. Another potential negative includes the inability to repay the debt at the time needed; when borrowing business capital, the lending agency assumes that the money will be used in the business venture. Intermingling the financial resources makes it virtually impossible to predict the impact that the loan transaction has on business financial results and success.

Family Constraints

Family constraints often serve to limit and control resources within the family, and other constraints may be created to manage resources. These constraints are sociocultural, legal, economic and technical in nature.

Family sociocultural constraints

These constraints consist of norms, mores and ethics within families. Norms relate to standards, measurements and judgments about circumstances within families. The standards agreed upon by family members might represent their regular or customary way of doing things within the family such as cleanliness of the home, well-balanced meals, or amount of time spent together as a family. In each case, resources in the forms of shelter, food and time are all in play.

Mores are represented by traditions, customs or way of living manifested in families. Over the life span/course, families usually engage in traditional ceremonies and customs such as marriages and divorces, christenings, coming of age, launching, retirements and, of course, funerals. Such life events affect the family, and how it endures and can be measured by instruments like the Holmes and Rahe (1967) scale, which simply counts the frequency of life events that have occurred during a 12-month period and magnifies this frequency via a weighting system. The sum is then correlated with mental and physical health (Holmes and Rahe, 1967). Patterns or ways of living manifested in families might include living in a socially conscious way or in harmony with our environment via 'green' technology or approaches. It might also include living less materialistically and more naturally, meaning that the family itself is more important than the business that it might own. Of course, in many business-owning families the business may be paramount, including the family itself. In any of these cases, families could simply be asked what is most important in their family life or what their core values are. Such choices will either enhance or limit the family in its processes and achievements.

Ethics are manifested in principles, morals and beliefs embodied by individuals and their associated families. Principles of working hard, devotion to family or contributions to one's society might come into play for many families and their members. Morals relate to such behaviors as faithfulness to family members including spouses, children and extended family members. Beliefs reflect our attitudes, ideas or viewpoints. Families often hold similar or harmonious beliefs among family members. Attitudes often are central to the well-being of individuals and their families. A positive attitude can enable an individual or a family to survive the worst of circumstances or events. Thus family ethics such as principles, morals and beliefs may either enhance or limit family life and achievements, depending on their nature. Measures for such concepts might be a Likert scale relative to a chosen list of concepts or phrases that represent various principles, morals and beliefs.

Family legal constraints
Family legal constraints include laws and regulations pertaining to families. Laws and regulations are often intended to control various behaviors and activities. Speed limit laws, if enforced, will affect the time it takes to drive from one location to another. Family law related to marriage, divorce and child custody will serve to provide legal guidance in these areas of family life. Tax laws will dictate the amount of taxes due the particular government unit levying the tax rate. Regulations are sets of laws, rules or policies. Laws and regulations may vary over time and among federal, state and local governing units. Measures of the laws and regulations pertaining to family life might simply indicate whether the law exists or not and when it was enacted. Federal estate laws now encompass the notion of a family business and garner for such businesses more favorable tax treatment for the owning family (Tauer and Grossman, 2002). Again, laws and regulations may either enhance or limit family life and achievements, depending on their nature.

Family economic constraints
The mechanisms of supply and demand within our capitalistic system as well as the general notions of scarcity and abundance form the basis of our economic constraints. During periods of economic recession or depression, families may be strained by such downturns. Traditional labor market jobs may be scarce and therefore family income may be reduced, in some cases drastically. Starting a business and its resulting business revenues may be one strategy to compensate for the loss of traditional wage and salary employment. In contrast, times of abundance or plenty may provide economic opportunities of many kinds, such as increased income, a promotion, an expansion of a business venture, among others. Economic constraints might be measured by rather standard economic indicators such as the unemployment/employment rates, gross family incomes, the growth of the GDP and the like. Such economic constraint measures usually vary over time but also are likely to vary by geographic locations and by rural/urban differences.

Family technical constraints
Constraints of a technical nature refer to the laws of nature related to physics, chemistry and natural sciences, and result in such phenomena as climate, weather and natural disasters of all kinds (Hammond, 2003). Such technical constraints will limit activities at a very basic level and may either enhance or limit family life and achievements, depending on their nature. The Eskimo families have very different lives from those in the tropics. Families who survived Hurricane Katrina in New Orleans may now live in another state or have rebuilt or remodeled where they once were, but the disaster has probably changed their lives forever. Measures of technical constraints pertaining to family life might simply indicate whether the particular natural event occurred, when it occurred, and its short- and long-run effects on the family.

Business Constraints

Similar to families, businesses face constraints as well (Figure 23.1). Relative to the various constraints within the business, including sociocultural, legal, economic and technical, the measures of business constraints would be similar to those used in the family. The only difference would be that the respondents would simply be workers, managers or leaders identifying constraints for the business, as opposed to family members denoting similar constraints but relative to their family life. Constaints also serve to limit and control resources within the business. Other constraints may be created to manage resources.

Business sociocultural constraints
Similar to the situation within families, business sociocultural constraints consist of norms, mores and ethics. Similar to families, norms relate to standards, measurements and judgments about circumstances within the business. The standards agreed upon by employees, managers and leaders usually represent their regular or customary way of doing something within the business such as production line work, the delivery of services or the completion of projects. Relative to each production activity the business may have standards of quality or quality control measures, for example.

Mores are represented by traditions, customs or way of doing business. Over the business life span/course, traditional ceremonies and customs may emerge, such as the entry of new workers and related training, employee development activities and, of course retirements or exits. Such business events affect the business and how it endures and grows over time. Patterns or ways of doing business manifested within businesses might include living in a socially conscious way or in harmony with the environment via 'green' technology or approaches. The importance of the business relative to the family will determine priorities within the business and the family and in relationship to each other. Is the business more important than the family's needs or demands? Again, business managers could simply be asked what is most in important in their business or what their core values are. Such choices will either enhance or limit the business in its processes and achievements.

Business legal constraints
Laws and regulations pertaining to businesses are often intended to control various behaviors and activities. Similar to families, tax laws will dictate the amount of taxes due. Relative to businesses, laws and regulations also may vary over time and among federal, state and local governing units. Measures of the laws and regulations relevant to the business might simply indicate whether the law exists or not and when it was enacted. Again, laws and regulations may either enhance or limit a business and its achievements, depending on their nature.

Business economic constraints
The mechanisms of supply and demand within our capitalistic system as well as the general notions of scarcity and abundance affect businesses. Just as families may be stressed or strained during periods of economic recession or depression, so can businesses suffer. Established markets and consumer demand may be reduced and therefore business

income may be reduced, in some cases drastically. Regenerating or constricting a business and its resulting business revenues may be one strategy to compensate for the lower demand for a business's standard products and services. In contrast, and similar to the effects on families, times of abundance or plenty may provide economic opportunities of many kinds such as increased business income, or an expansion of a business venture, among others. Economic constraints might be measured by rather standard economic indicators such as the unemployment/employment rates, number of employees, gross business incomes and the growth of the GDP. As stated for families, these measures will usually vary over time but are also likely to vary by geographic locations and by rural/urban differences.

Business technical constraints

Such constraints will also limit business activities at a very basic level and may either enhance or limit business processes and achievements, depending on their nature. Businesses in different climates will naturally differ in the products and services offered; that is, air conditioning businesses are more plentiful in hot and humid climates, and heating businesses meet demand in colder climates. Businesses that survived natural disasters may be forced into extreme measures and adjustments in their ongoing activities. Measures of technical constraints pertaining to business might simply indicate whether the particular natural event occurred, when it occurred, and its short- and long-run effects on the business.

Family and Business Structure

Family roles and rules

Within families, individuals embody, assume or are assigned specific roles such as household manager, parent, spouse, child or sibling, among others. These roles make up major subsystems within the family system (Kepner, 1983). And most scholars suggest that while roles change over time, individuals in various roles within the family can be most effective when roles are well defined with boundaries known and respected by all family members. For example, the parental role will most effectively be implemented if the parent can assume some level of authority and leadership for helping the child. When an older child is sometimes asked to parent other younger children, the harmony and well-being in the family may be stressed as well as the individual family member in his or her role. Rules include such phenomena as inclusion, integration, boundaries, commitment and core values (Danes, 2006).

Family capital is grounded in a structure that is composed of family roles and rules. Family roles and rules are a state and not a process (Danes et al., 2008a). Family roles and rules clarify membership, organization and bonding (Danes et al., 2002; Stewart and Danes, 2001). They clarify who leads, specify how members manage or distribute family resources, and limit the effect of constraints. Roles are often measured as a dummy variable such as if a spouse of an entrepreneur is working in a family business.

However, it is possible to measure the level of such a variable as Danes and Olson (2003) did when measuring spousal involvement in the family firm. The authors not only measured the concept with a dummy variable, but also measured it through the number of hours worked in the business and the degree to which spouses were involved in making major business decisions. With a more informative measure of the role characteristics when investigating the relationship between family structure and processes, the researcher can be more specific about the implication and applications of the research findings.

Roles and rules also cover how the business defines itself in relation to the outside world (Danes and Olson, 2003). Family structure with its roles and rules is an important dimension of culture, particularly in ethnic minority family businesses (Danes et al., 2008a). Family structure with its roles and rules influences processes and achievements in both family and firm. An example of the effect of family structure on processes is its effect on the quantity and nature of resource transfers between a business and the owning family (Danes et al., 2009c).

Shared meanings are core to family roles and rules, and these include values, norms and beliefs of the family's culture (Haberman and Danes, 2007). Decision inclusion and authority patterns also are a part of family roles and rules (Danes and Morgan, 2004). Some of these roles and rules are evident to every member of the family, but some may be so deeply engrained within the family culture that members count on them unconsciously (Haberman and Danes, 2007).

Business roles and rules

Business structures include ownership and governance. Business ownership is as varied as the business-owning families who make that choice. Historically, ownership starts with a founder who resides within a family which is frequently tapped for managers and/or employees for the business. This founder ownership signifies a closely/privately held business held by one person. As the family grows, the business grows as a result; the family ownership mix may increase and become more spread among several generations and branches of the expanding owning family. Outsiders or non-family owners might be allowed minority ownership and/or become shareholders while the majority control remains within the family. In some families businesses, 'in-laws' will join the firm while others will be systematically excluded both for the management of business conflicts and for family financial stability.

The definition of a family business has been tied to ownership in combination with other criteria such as management and control. Heck and Trent (1999) investigated most recognized definitions in the field at the time and found that family ownership of 51 percent was nearly always included as the first criterion for such definitions and sometimes the only criterion included. On the other hand, Heck and Trent (1999) were adamant that ownership alone does not define a family firm. The dimensions of management and involvement by family members were equally important in defining a family business.

Family ownership has also been shown to be related to performance. Anderson and Reeb (2003) as well as Weber et al. (2003) have shown family-owned businesses to outperform non-family businesses in annual shareholders return, return on assets, annual revenue growth and income growth. However, few researchers have modeled performance in a comprehensive way (Heck et al., 2006; Gnan and Montemerlo, 2006; Rogoff and Heck, 2003). In other words, family firms strive to achieve business performance simultaneously with family performance. Using the SFBT, Olson and her co-authors (2003) have definitively and empirically shown that to be the case. Family variables significantly contributed to explaining variations in business performance and vice versa.

Governance within the family business often starts with the notion of professionaliza-tion or, in other words, incorporating more formal business practices into the business operations. Because family businesses are likely to evolve from the informality of the family unit, sometimes the associated family business must formalize its structures inter-nally so that effective operations can be promoted and implemented (Gallo and Tomaselli, 2006; Songini, 2006). Nonetheless, the family leader, intergenerational commitment and core values engender the level of trust and respect among family members to each other and to the business (Steier, 2001a; Sundaramurthy, 2008) and helps them strategically plan and manage together (Hall et al., 2006; Sharma et al., 1997; Ward and Handy, 1988).

As they grow, mature and increase in size, some family businesses establish a board of directors while still privately held and by necessity (i.e. in the USA) when they go public (Ibrahim and Ellis, 2006; Ward, 1988). The best practice relative to board structure is around seven members who are both family and non-family and who facilitate the values and goals of the family relative to themselves and their business (Astrachan et al., 2006; Corbetta and Salvato, 2004; Corbetta and Minichilli, 2006; Ward, 1988). Blumentritt (2006) has reconfirmed the relationship between the existence of boards and the preve-lance of planning in the family-owned business, both strategic planning and succession planning. Hall et al. (2006) have identified four theoretical perspectives for strategizing in family businesses – that is, values, role, arena and legitimacy.

Business roles and rules can be measured by examining the involvement of the owners in the business. The percentage of ownership and number of family employees involved in the business were utilized by Heck and Trent (1999) in defining family businesses of various types. Boards of directors varying by size (number of members), type (mostly insiders versus mostly outsiders), ownership (nature and percentage), background (expe-rience and education) and function (e.g. strategic planning, performance, succession planning) were delineated in detail by Ward and Handy (1988) and later studied in detail by others (e.g. Corbetta and Salvato, 2004).

Family Processes in Times of Stability and Change

A unique contribution of SFBT is that it acknowledges that standard operating proce-dures used in normal, stable times need to be adjusted in times of change. SFBT stipulates that during stable periods, family and firm are managed within their boundaries. During periods of disruptions, the other system's resources are used. Those adjustments are most often made at the interface of the family and firm, where interpersonal and resource transactions occur that utilize the total family capital base from both family and firm. Business and family managers must perceive, process and respond to a changing environment and reconstruct processes to ensure sustainability over time.

SFBT recognizes that internal or external change can create disruptions that are either normative or non-normative. Normative disruptions are those such as peak season of the business when firm processes can become overwhelming to the system. Normative dis-ruptions can evolve from either system (family or firm) such as a family member having the flu and being unable to perform their business duties for a week or a myriad of norma-tive firm problems as the index operationalized by Danes et al. (2009b). Non-normative disruptions are those that are unexpected or highly unusual such as a natural disaster that forces temporary firm closure (Brewton et al., 2010).

Responses to normative disruptions are changes made in one system (firm or family) to accommodate needs of the other when unusually heavy demand exists. The NFBP included measures of six categories of adjustments to normative disruptions that occur at the family–business intersection: (a) personal time reallocation (Miller et al., 2000), (b) obtaining additional help (Fitzgerald et al., 2001), (c) adjusting family resources (Miller et al., 1999), (d) adjusting business resources (Miller et al., 1999), (e) intertwining tasks (Fitzgerald et al., 2001) and (f) intermingling of family and firm finances (Haynes et al., 1999). These response patterns to normative disruptions are often referred to as standard operating procedures. From a measurement standpoint, for purposes of parsimony, starting with Danes et al. (2007), a reduced number of variables was utilized in analyses that were the adjustment strategies significant in Olson et al. (2003).

The patterns of adjustment behaviors during normal but hectic times and the stock of family capital (composed of human, financial and social capital) creates a resilience capacity that tends to automatically kick in when encountering a non-normative disruption such as a natural disaster or the death of a family member. The owning family is the repository of this resilience capacity (Danes et al., 2009c; Danes and Stafford, in press). The family's resilience capacity is the ability of the owning family to adapt and respond to stressful event and to problem-solve effectively (Danes et al., 2009b).

The family firm's capacity to access human, financial and social capital resources and effectively plan for predictable, as well as unforeseen, circumstances is positively related to family firm continuity (Danes et al., 2007; Danes et al., 2009b; Danes and Stafford, in press; Hammond, 2003). Danes et al. (2009c) and Danes and Stafford (in press) have identified family firm resilience measures: family functional integrity, family structural integrity and the family's pattern of adjusting to normative disruptions.

Since the adjustment pattern measures have already been described, the measures of family functional and structural integrity will be described here. Family functional integrity represents the stability of the family and is measured by family APGAR, which has five components: adaptation, partnership, growth, affection and resolve (Smilkstein, 1978; Smilkstein et al., 1982). Each component has a unique function, yet is related to the whole (Danes and Morgan, 2004). It connotes a sense of trust, creativity and openness that brings a family's interactions to a higher level of responsiveness (Danes and Morgan, 2004; Stewart and Danes, 2001). It was developed to assess the capacity of a family to respond to a health emergency and help take care of a family member. It has been found to distinguish between families that hold together and families that fall apart (Sawin and Harrigan, 1995).

Family APGAR provides business owners with a valid, reliable, confidential means of monitoring family functional integrity that is also fast and easy to score. The instrument is a self-report measure, which means that it can be self-administered and the results kept confidential (Danes and Stafford, in press). It can be used with owning families with and without children and with ethnic minorities.

The family structural measure (Danes et al., 2009c), also referred to as family/business congruity (Danes et al., 2008b), is composed of the seven most prevalent family business tensions generated in home life over firm issues (role clarity, decision authority, ownership equality, fairness of compensation, failure to resolve firm conflicts, unfair workloads, and competition for resources between family and firm) using a scale of 1 (no tension at all) to 5 (a great deal of tension). The questions were reverse-coded and summed. This summed index indicates with higher scores that the owning family has structured its interactions around the firm so as to result in harmony and congruity, creating an environment to problem-solve effectively (Stafford and Avery, 1993). Low congruity scores create a family environment that undermines efficiency, and reduces cooperation and resilience. Congruity between family and firm can affect long-term family firm sustainability (Danes et al., 2008b).

Primary measurement concerns with this category of measures are those of distinguishing stocks and flows and distinguishing family capital inputs, processes of accessing family capital resources, and outputs over time. In cross-sectional research, most of the time family capital measures are a stock measure, a resource amount available for use. However, in longitudinal research, care must be taken in distinguishing between a family capital stock at one point in time, and the actual use of that family capital stock, which is a process either creating or depleting future family capital stocks. The output of these processes added to the original Time 1 resource stock is the resource input for future management operations.

Furthermore, based on the family capital research findings of Danes et al. (2009c), care must also be taken in the assumptions made about family capital stocks. Their findings indicated that it was the use of family capital rather than the level of stock available that was most important to firm performance. These findings indicate that it is critical to establish both family capital stock available and the actual stock used, rather than assuming that family capital stock available is used. It is also important not to assume that non-use of family capital necessarily indicates absence of family capital. The assumptions made about family capital may misspecify research models in empirical analyses or discount resilience capabilities in family business consultations during times of change.

Business Processes in Times of Stability and Change

Small business management research overall has shown that business planning leads to better financial performance (Ibrahim et al., 2004), but a closer examination of that relationship reveals a more complex picture focusing primarily on type, nature and extent of management (Danes et al., 2008b). Danes et al. (2007) identified ten business management questions representing routine management practices that were factored into three classifications of business management: quality management, financial management and personnel management. That same study provided measures of three types of business innovations that can be incorporated in firms.

In a study of an integrated, interfunctional approach to quality management (Danes et al., 2008b), not only the business management measures used in Danes et al. (2007) were captured but also measures for entrepreneurial management and firm owner values. Those measures sought to determine whether the firm manager placed the family or firm first, whether the business represented a way of life or a way to earn income, or whether the owner had an outward focus on customers or an inward focus on operations.

Olson et al. (2003) found that the effect of family on business ventures is significant. In fact, in that study of the impact of family and business on family business sustainability, family and family/firm interface management accounted for 22 percent of gross revenue variance and 33 percent of perceived business success. However, family firms vary greatly in the involvement of family members and there is not agreement in the literature just how to measure the 'familiness' of family firms. Danes et al., (2007), in their study of gender, firm management and family business performance, introduced a measure of familiness that incorporated the five most common criteria in the definitional literature on family businesses, which were: (a) owner perceived their business to be a family business; (b) at least one other family member was a major business decision maker; (c) at least one other family member was an owner; (d) at least one other family member worked in the business; and (e) future family ownership was considered likely.

Theories of family business growth have been tied to the life cycle (span) of the generations within the owning family (Ibrahim and Ellis, 2006; Peiser and Wooten, 1983). In other words, anchored to the family, family business growth is often propelled forward by the growth in the family over time. Overall, the family business life course starts with its founding, initial growth, maturity and then further change and growth forward and upward or, in some cases, decline and exit. Harvey and Evans (1994) delineated six specific phases of development for entrepreneurial organizations and showed the family dimension of these phases. These developmental phases were identified based on the major conflict events in each and named: (1) creative/definition; (2) enterprising phase; (3) stabilization; (4) early growth; (5) sustained growth; and (6) plateau/maturity. With each stage, both family and external events along with the business dimension must be addressed for continuation.

Simultaneously with these growth phases or trajectories, the family business faces the unique challenge of succession between generations. Ibrahim and Ellis (2006) have identified the stages of a family business from the perspective of succession tasks and processes. These stages include: (1) owner-managed business; (2) training and development of the new generation; (3) partnership between the generations; and (4) transfer of power (Ibrahim and Ellis, 2006). Many earlier succession writings exist, starting with Longenecker and Schoen (1978), that focused exclusively on the father and son transition. They identified seven distinct stages with the suggestion that complete succession planning might take from 15 to 20 years. More recent scholarship studied the unique succession experiences and challenges for daughters as well as copreneurs (Cole, 1997; Danes and Olson, 2003; Dumas 1989, 1998; Fitzgerald and Muske, 2002; Frances, 1999; Haberman and Danes, 2007).

The classic examination of the succession process which was first detailed by Lansberg's (1988) simplistic examination and view of the family business as three overlapping systems of the family, the management, and the ownership, produced five stakeholder groups including: the founder, the family, the managers, the owners and the environment. These stakeholders often unconsciously and naturally interacted as the 'the succession conspiracy', which sought to keep things the same and resisted change. Subsequentially, Handler (1992) offered a fresh examination of succession processes and dynamics from the viewpoint of the successor rather than the founder. Via detailed qualitative field interviews, she discovered both individual influences (e.g. personal need fulfillment or career interests of possible successors) and relational influences (e.g. mutual respect and understanding between generations or sibling accommodation) associated with successful succession experiences between generations.

Barach and Ganitsky (1995) specified the critical factors in the succession process which either favored or inhibited its success and which were contributed by the current owner, the possible successors, other participants and the firm. Chrisman et al. (1998)

took this a step further and investigated the desired characteristics of possible successors. They identified 30 such characteristics, with the top three including integrity, commitment to the business and respect for employees. Today, many scholars continue to address succession. For example, Rosenfeld (2008) has explored the succession process and identified it as the primary process facing the family business with unique, challenging and intricate subprocesses vital to its continuation and effectiveness.

Achievements, Short-term Family Business Viability, and Long-term Sustainability

Both the achievements within the family system and the achievements of the business system join and interact to create short-term family business viability. This short-term family business viability is represented by the separate but related well-being of the family and of the business because family and business are inextricably interconnected. One cannot achieve well-being in either system without achieving the well-being in the other system.

Well-being of the family denotes a general sense of met needs and wants as well as attained goals within a fully functioning family unit which is in harmony with itself. Measures of such states of well-being are difficult; however, indicators of well-being might be how well the family reacts to major family events or crises of a variety such as the birth of new family members, premature death of family members and sudden changes or disasters. Such happenings place the family squarely in the midst of needing to change and grow together. Families in states of well-being are simply better able to handle change and growth. Others are not and the family ceases to operate and function as it once did.

Sustainability is a function of both firm success and family functionality. A constant over time in measuring achievements of family businesses has been financial measures of business success (e.g. income, profit, growth); those types of measures have long been the gold standard against which family businesses have been measured. More recently, however, the multidimensionality of firm success has been recognized (Danes et al., 2008b; Paige and Littrell, 2002). Examples where authors have simultaneously tested firm performance with financial and non-financial measures are Olson et al. (2003), Danes et al., (2008b) and Danes et al. (2009c). Doing so addresses measurement issues associated with the use of solely financial data (Kotey and Meredith, 1997). Subjective, non-pecuniary measures of firm success provide more insight into the owner's commitment to or passion for the firm (Stanforth and Muske, 2001).

SFBT has always recognized the multidimensionality of family firm achievement and sustainability. However, in the first version of the theory, objective and subjective measures were viewed as different measures of the same construct, business success. Considering empirical results from consequent analyses incorporating human, financial and social family capital and their influence on family firm performance, Danes et al. (2008b) and Danes et al. (2009c) have suggested that rather than objective and subjective measures of the same construct, results indicated that family firm owners have financial and non-financial objectives for their firms. The qualitative nature of differences (different significant variables in the two equations or different variable signs) that specific types of family capital had in the two dependent variables (gross revenue or perception of success) indicated true multiple firm objectives (financial and non-financial) for family firms. This finding created the research need to account for these multiple firm objectives rather than treating these objective and subjective indicators as a unidimensional construct, success. Utilizing multidimensional measures of firm success in family firm research would lead to a greater understanding of the entire context in which owners invest their time and money. Doing so would also address Gimeno's (2005) argument that family firms must meet owner expectations as well as financial criteria to be considered successful.

Besides the multidimensionality of family firm achievements, another change introduced into SFBT in its 2008 revision (Danes et al., 2008a) was the distinction between short-term viability and long-term sustainability. This aspect of the theory revision came as a result of analyzing panel data with direct measures of both viability and sustainability. In SFBT, viability is the result of the overlap between what the family and firm achieved during the current year (Danes et al., 2008a). Sustainability is the outcome from multiple years of viability.

For example, viability could be measured by perceived success in the current year. Sustainability, then, would be measured by perceived success at least one year later than the achievement measures. Using panel methodology language, if resources, constraints, disruptions and processes were measured in Wave 1, achievements and short-term viability would be also measured in Wave 1, and long-term sustainability would be measured in Wave 2 or later. Danes et al. (2009c) is an example of a study set up in such a manner to study family capital's relative contribution to short-term achievements and long-term sustainability. In that study, the 2000 sustainability models performed better than the 1997 achievement models, and family capital explained more variance in sustainability.

In another study of spousal capital as a resource for couples in venture creation (Matzek et al., 2010), the authors found support for mutual firm sustainability and couple relationship measured by months to break even and relationship quality, respectively. However, in this study, even though the dependent variables were derived from Wave 2, the nature of the data (Wave 1 coming early in the business start-up phase to Wave 2 following a year later) and the nature of the research question dictate that the dependent variables would be measures of short-term viability. The point here is that theoretical constructs and their respective measures are co-created based on a number of interrelated research concerns such as sampling, unit of analysis, research questions posed and the manner in which questions are asked of respondents. So, care must be taken to read the methodology of studies carefully if you are digesting research literature, and to write about your methodology carefully if you are writing about research that you have performed.

Community Context of Family Firms

SFBT recognizes the premise in organizational behavior literature that one of the explanations for the birth, growth and death of businesses is the environment in which they are located (Tigges and Green, 1994) by placing the family business within the community in which it resides. Community is defined in SFBT as a collective interaction rather than simply a group that shares a few common characteristics (Kulig, 2000) because families act as mortar that connects communities, individuals and firms, and makes them function effectively. Members of the family firm may interact with the community, and the community, in turn, may provide various inputs to help sustain the firm (Danes et al., 2009a). The impetus for the manner and degree to which that firm/community interaction occurs is rooted in the meanings family business members give to that activity. The owning family provides a fertile environment of values, attitudes and beliefs that serve as inputs into the family firm culture, one of which is business social responsibility to the community. The firm/community interaction plays a prominent part in the management of many ethnic-family businesses (Danes et al., 2008a).

Niehm et al. (2008) and Fitzgerald et al. (2010) provide measures of such constructs as commitment to the community, community support and sense of community, along with the questions that compose those indexes. The processes of community social responsibility of these family firms are composed of interpersonal transactions in the form of community leadership and holding an elected or appointed office and resource transactions in the form of providing financial or technical assistance in community development and providing donations to local programs (Fitzgerald et al., 2010).

Fitzgerald and colleagues (2010) found that a symbiotic relationship between a firm and its community host was productive for both firm and community (a central SFBT tenet). Firm owners who felt that their communities possessed a high level of collective action, where people in the community supported local businesses, and where firm owners had a positive attitude toward the community, were more likely to have contributed time and money to the community. On the other hand, firm owners in more economically vulnerable communities were more likely to assume responsibility to fill leadership positions in the community and make substantial contributions of financial and technical assistance. These findings indicate that family firms do not make economic decisions in a social vacuum, but rather in the social context of their community host (Danes et al., 2009a).

MOVING FORWARD

The applications of SFBT are myriad and vital to advancing our understanding of the family business relative to the owning family and its business enterprise. The family business as an entity is both necessary and ubiquitous worldwide, yet few have studied its internal dynamics from an in-depth perspective of a sustainable family business. This perspective means that both the owning family and its business are present with equal vigor and fortitude. Indeed, one cannot be fully understood without the other. Both the family and the business contribute to the family business with each sustaining the other, and a family business would not be truly successful if the family system faltered while the business system blossomed. Nonetheless, sustainability is much more than survival, and the family and the business systems will not only survive but flourish if they are mutually intertwined and allow each other to grow.

As researchers, educators and practitioners focus on the family business, it is imperative that such professionals recognize, understand and convey this comprehensive view espoused in the SFBT. The purpose of this chapter was to provide a detailed examination of the SFBT as well as possible measures of its major concepts or components. Many specific conceptual and empirical choices have already been discussed in detail. This section will discuss the development of further applications of the SFBT for research, education and practice.

Research

Mainstream business research has long ignored family businesses relative to all aspects of research such as conceptualization, theories, samples, surveys, analytical procedures, and inferences and applications. Traditional research areas such as strategic planning and management, governance, organization structure, operations, growth and performance have been investigated without acknowledgment of the widespread existence of family businesses worldwide. Aldrich and Cliff (2003), Anderson and Reeb (2003), Olson et al. (2003), Steier (2003) and Morck and Yeung (2004) are notable, yet recent, exceptions, with their inclusions in widely recognized business research journals. These acceptances into the mainstream business research outlets hail a new era of family business research and hold great promise for future research. Innovative approaches in other journals include the simultaneous inclusion of family and business process measures by a study of family capital of family firms that bridged human, social and financial capital investigating its impact on family business viability (Danes et al., 2009c).

Within the general emerging family business research, many have failed to examine or even include the family dimension when examining the dynamics and nature of the entity under study. Few have offered the detailed and comprehensive view of the business-owning family and its enterprise (Danes et al., 2008a; Heck et al., 2006). The SFBT stands alone with its rigor and focus on the both the family system and the business system as well as their relationship with each other. The theory focuses on processes as well as roles and structures; it follows the resources of the family and business systems and emphasizes the managerial processes of those resources within each system and as those resources cross boundaries for the goal of sustainability of the family business system with functional families and businesses.

Early family business researchers hailed from an eclectic group of academic areas and family business research often suffered from the sometimes limited view of the researchers' disciplinary roots. Similar shortsightedness was also true for the family studies and family sociology fields of study. Early family studies researchers and those who studied families, in general, rarely incorporated the contributions of business ownership and assets into their modeling or samples. Milestones in the family business field of study have been chronicled elsewhere, from research, education and practitioner foci (Heck et al., 2008; Hoy and Sharma, 2006; Poutziouris et al., 2006; IFBPA, 1995). Of note is the early recognition of the owning family's importance to the family business. Cramton (1993) first suggested that family systems theory would inform our research, education and practice within the family business field of study. The SFBT further developed in this chapter continues to challenge researchers to broaden our conceptual base beyond the business itself (Danes et al., 2008a; Heck et al., 2006; Stafford et al., 1999; Upton and Heck, 1997; Dyer and Handler, 1994).

Heck et al. (2008) identified five major research challenges for the future: '(1) optimal integration of family and business subsystems; (2) alternative research methodologies; (3) micro-level collection and alternative data sources; (4) macro-level data collection; and (5) mastering the relationships between researchers, practitioners, sponsors, and policy makers' (p. 325). The SFBT meets the challenge of 'optimal integration' of both the family and the business within its comprehensive modeling of all relevant subsystems and recognizing the interrelationships and overlaps among the major subsystems. Along with comprehensive research theories such as the SFBT, operationalization will be required for the research concepts and variables identified within the family system such as: composition and structure; communication patterns; management styles; and many others. We may need to face the additional challenge of exploring alternative research methodologies such as qualitative research via case studies and ethnographic research. Subsequent to broader and more comprehensive theory building and alternative methodologies, we will need to continue to explore high-quality data sources and primary data collection at both the micro and macro levels.

Today researchers also have a number of data sets available, including large national databases which are usually void of detailed information, especially for the family and business concurrently. Smaller industry specific data sets may lack national representativeness (Puryear et al., 2008). Most data sets vary with respect to strengths and weaknesses, and comparative assessments concerning the data sets' size (small to large), breadth (individual populations to multiple populations), and studied variables (limited versus comprehensive) (Puryear et al., 2008). The NFBP data are unique relative to the longitudinal interviews of the household managers and the business managers of the same family businesses over three waves, namely, 1997, 2000 and 2007.

Philip Aminoff and Jesus Casado of GEEF-European Group of Owner Managed Family Enterprises presented an overview session at the 2009 Annual Conference Policy Forum of the International Family Enterprise Academy in Cyprus and offered their perspectives on what initiatives are needed to ensure the long-term development of the family business economy (Aminoff and Casado, 2009). Although the European community has begun to survey and track family businesses with greater consistency and detail, researchers fall short of collecting critical information about the family and its dynamics.

Research applications of the SFBT have only begun to emerge, and both the conceptual and the empirical understandings of researchers will continue to take shape. Rarely could a researcher fully conceptually embrace the family firm without the utilization of the SFBT in part or in full.

Education and Practice

Currently few American universities and colleges offer family business courses and none offer programs focused exclusively on family business. Worldwide, most academic programs are centered in Europe. In general, business education ignores the family dimension relative to the business.

Early efforts by family business practitioners focused on practice-based articles and case studies, as noted by Donnelley (1964), and Barnes and Hershon (1976). A number of membership-based professional associations emerged, consisting mainly of individuals and organizations with family business constituents or clienteles, specifically, the FFI in 1986 and the FBN-I in 1990. Later the International Family Enterprise Research Academy (IFERA) began in 2001 in connection with FBN-I. These international organizations encouraged academics and practitioners to conduct research investigations to identify findings and best practices that could bolster new educational programs and support services as well as consulting services to family firms.

Still other larger and established organizations began to expand by including conference segments and standing divisions devoted to and encompassing the family business focused research, education and practice. The United States Association of Small Business and Entrepreneurship (USASBE) and its Family Business Interest Group as well as USASBE's parent organization, the International Council for Small Business, began to recognize the study of family firms worldwide. Moreover, the Academy of Management's Entrepreneurship Division now encompasses family business research.

The SFBT offers an enlightened and comprehensive framework for the development of educational programs and practitioner approaches that are multidisciplinary in nature and scope. Students and practitioners must understand not only the business enterprise but also the internal dynamics of the owning family and how they interact. The family dimension must be presented in view of the ongoing and simultaneous workings of the business. For example, when ownership, governance or succession decisions are made relative to the business, students must ask what underlying family dynamics influence these important business decisions. How do the leadership roles and structures within the family relate to the business? How do the business governance roles and structures parlay into the family dynamics? How are conflicts played out or agreements achieved within the family relative to the business and the business relative to the family? Again, the family system is intricately tied to the business system and this vital link must be identified, understood and honored.

Summary, Conclusions and the Future

The conceptual (Danes et al., 2008a; Heck et al., 2006; Stafford et al., 1999) and operational (Danes et al., 2009c; Olson et al., 2003) aspects of the SFBT have been the focus of this chapter. This comprehensive theory enhances the understanding of family in the business and business in the family through its systems orientation. SFBT locates entrepreneurship and the business within the social context of the family and its community. Unlike many other theories that take a comprehensive approach to the study of the family business, it emphasizes the interaction of the family and business systems while recognizing the different characteristics of each.

In addition to the detailed conceptual explanation of the SFBT, possible measures for its major concepts have been identified, and an examination was made of the usefulness of SFBT's constructs and measures for possible future research, education and practice. We must bring family business realities to the forefront of research, education, practice and policy. We emphasize the important role of the family enterprise in the corporate world globally by recognizing and acknowledging family business contributions worldwide.

Future family business research grounded in a family business theory such as SFBT will: (a) emphasize managerial processes of family and business resources and not just roles and structures; (b) give recognition to mutual functionality of family and business systems; (c) recognize that processes are different in times of stability and times of change; (d) identify that family firm success is inclusive of both short-term viability and long-term sustainability; and (e) recognize that a positive symbiosis between family, firm and its community host is productive for both the firm and community. When grounded in such a theory, certain methodological criteria are necessary in operationalizing the theoretical principles. Many of those methodological principles were utilized in the collection of the National Family Business Panel data (Winter et al, 1998; Winter et al., 2004).

Both family and business system variables are needed. Multi-informants are much better than single informants using such a theory because the family and business management variables are best asked of the person who primarily oversees those system processes. Longitudinal data are necessary to capture processes in times of stability and change. If a researcher is to study factors influencing short-term viability and long-term sustainability, again longitudinal data are necessary.

Some measures that vary by certain family firm characteristics may not be consistent for all family firm types. For example, when size of the family firm is taken into consideration, many measures remain the same because processes are not affected by size. But, in other cases, measures may need to be tailored to characteristics of a particular sample. Minority family businesses, where culture of the family system or the culture of the host community is vital to its sustainability, is another example where unique or additional measures may need to be utilized.

For family business research to progress in the future, the complexities of the family business system need to be captured in the data that are used to do the research. This means that research teams need to be multidisciplinary. It means that funding sources will have to be pooled because such research is expensive. It means that researchers need to prepare their students for meeting the challenges of conducting such research both theoretically and methodologically with the intent of enhancing knowledge within our field of study concerning family businesses worldwide.

ACKNOWLEDGMENTS

This material is based upon work partially supported by the National Science Foundation under Grant No. CMS-0625326. Any opinions, findings and conclusions or recommendations expressed in this material are those of the authors and do not necessarily reflect the views of the National Science Foundation. The results reported in this chapter also use data collected by Cooperative Regional Research Project NC-1030, partially supported by the Cooperative States Research, Education and Extension Service (CSREES); USDA, Baruch College, the experiment stations at the University of Hawaii at Manoa, University of Illinois, Purdue University (Indiana), Iowa State University, Oklahoma State University, University of Minnesota, Montana State University, Cornell University (New York), North Dakota State University, The Ohio State University, Utah State University and the University of Wisconsin-Madison. Any opinions, results and conclusions are solely those of the authors.

REFERENCES

Aldrich, H.E. (1999), *Organizations Evolving*, London: Sage Publications.
Aldrich, H.E. and J.E. Cliff (2003), 'The pervasive effects of family on entrepreneurship: toward a family embeddedness perspective', *Journal of Business Venturing*, **18**, 573–96.
Aldrich, H.E. and C. Zimmer (1986), 'Entrepreneurship through social networks', in D.L. Sexton and R.W. Smilor (eds), *The Art and Science of Entrepreneurship*, Cambridge, MA: Ballinger, pp. 3–23.

Aminoff, P. and J. Casado (2009), 'Panel Presentation for GEEF–European Group of Owner Managed Family Enterprises', The Global Forum on Family Business Policy: The Policy Agenda, Annual Conference of the International Family Enterprise Research Academy (IFERA), Cyprus, Limassol, 24–27 June.

Anderson, R.C. and D.M. Reeb (2003), 'Founding-family ownership and firm performance: evidence from the S&P 500', *Journal of Finance*, **58**(3), 1301–28.

Astrachan, J.H. (1988), 'Family firm and community culture', *Family Business Review*, **1**(2), 165–89.

Astrachan, J.H. (2003), 'Commentary on the special issue: the emergence of a field', *Journal of Business Venturing*, **18**(5), 567–72.

Astrachan, J.H. and A.M. Kurtz (1998), 'Editors' notes', *Family Business Review*, **11**, v–vi.

Astrachan, J.H., S.B. Klein and K.X. Smyrnios (2002), 'The F-PEC scale of family influence: a proposal for solving the family business definition problem', *Family Business Review*, **15**(1), 45–58.

Astrachan, J.H., A. Keyt, S. Lane and K. McMillan (2006), 'Generic models for family business boards of directors', in P.Z. Poutziouris, K.X. Smyrnios, and S.Klein (eds), *Handbook of Research on Family Business*, Cheltenham, UK and Northampton, MA, USA: Edward Elgar Publishing in association with International Family Enterprise Research Academy (IFERA), pp. 317–42.

Barach, J.A. and J.B. Ganitsky (1995), 'Successful succession in family business', *Family Business Review*, **8**(2), 131–55.

Barnes, L.B. and S.A. Hershon (1976), 'Transferring power in the family business', *Harvard Business Review*, July/August, 105–14.

Bates, T. (1985), 'Entrepreneur human capital endowments and minority business viability', *The Journal of Human Resources*, **20**(4), 540–54.

Bates, T. (1987), 'Self-employed minorities: traits and trends', *Social Science Quarterly*, **68**, 539–51.

Becker, G.S. (1993), *Human Capital: A Theoretical and Empirical Analysis with Special Reference to Education*, 3rd edn, Chicago, IL: University of Chicago Press.

Blumentritt, T. (2006), 'The relationship between boards and planning in family business', *Family Business Review*, **19**(1), 65–72.

Borwick, I. (1986), 'The family therapist as business consultant', in L.C. Wynne, S.H. McDaniel and T.T. Weber (eds), *Systems Consultation: A New Perspective for Family Therapy*, New York: Guilford Press, pp. 423–40.

Brewton, K., S.M. Danes, K. Stafford and G. Haynes (2010), 'Determinants of rural and urban family firm business resilience', *Journal of Family Business Strategy*, **1**(3), 155–66.

Bryant, W.K. and C.D. Zick (2005), *The Economic Organization of the Household*, New York: Cambridge University Press.

Budge, G.S. and R.W. Janoff (1991), 'Interpreting the discourses of family business', *Family Business Review*, **4**(4), 367–81.

Burns, M.M. and C.B. Bolton (2001), *Business Savvy for Today's Entrepreneur*, Stillwater, OK: New Forums Press.

Chrisman, J.J., J.H. Chua and P. Sharma (1998), 'Important attributes of successors in family businesses: an exploratory study', *Family Business Review*, **11**(1), 19–34.

Chrisman, J.J., J.H. Chua and L.P. Steier (2002), 'The influence of national culture and family involvement on entrepreneurial perceptions and performance at the state level', *Entrepreneurship Theory and Practice*, **26**(4), 113–29.

Cole, P.M. (1997), 'Women in family business', *Family Business Review*, **10**(4), 353–71.

Cooper, A.C. and K.W. Artz (1995), 'Determinants of satisfaction for entrepreneurs', *Journal of Business Venturing*, **10**(6), 439–57.

Cooper, A.C., W.C. Dunkelberg and C.Y. Woo (1988a), 'Survival and failure: a longitudinal study', in Center for Entrepreneurial Studies (ed.), *Frontiers of Entrepreneurship Research*, Wellesley, MA: Babson College, pp. 225–37.

Cooper, A.C., C.Y. Woo and W.C. Dunkelberg (1988b), 'Entrepreneurs' perceived chances for success', *Journal of Business Venturing*, **3**, 97–108.

Corbetta, G. and A. Minichilli (2006), 'Board of directors in Italian public family-controlled companies', in P.Z. Poutziouris, K.X. Smyrnios and S. Klein (eds), *Handbook of Research on Family Business*, Cheltenham, UK and Northampton, MA, USA: Edward Elgar Publishing in association with International Family Enterprise Research Academy (IFERA), pp. 488–500.

Corbetta, G. and C.A. Salvato (2004), 'The board of directors in family firms: one size fits all?', *Family Business Review*, **17**(2), 119–34.

Cramton, C.D. (1993), 'Is rugged individualism the whole story?: Public and private accounts of a firm's founding', *Family Business Review*, **6**(3), 56–61.

Dahlhamer, J.M. (1998), 'Rebounding from environmental jolts: organizational and ecological factors affecting business disaster recovery', PhD dissertation, Disaster Research Center, University of Delaware, Newark, DE.

Danes, S.M. (1999), *Change: Loss, Opportunity, and Resilience*, St Paul, MN: UMES.

Danes, S.M. (2006), 'Tensions within family business-owning couples over time', *Stress, Trauma and Crisis*, **9**(3–4), 227–46.

Danes, S.M. and K.E. Brewton (2012), 'Follow the capital: benefits of tracking family capital across family and business systems', in A.L. Carsrud and M. Brännback (eds), *Understanding Family Businesses: Undiscovered Approaches, Unique Perspectives, and Neglected Topics*, New York: Springer, pp. 227–50.

Danes, S.M. and E.A. Morgan (2004), 'Family business-owning couples: an EFT view into their unique conflict culture', *Contemporary Family Therapy*, **26**(3), 241–60.

Danes, S.M. and P.D. Olson (2003), 'Women's role involvement in family businesses, business tensions, and business success', *Family Business Review*, **16**(1), 53–68.

Danes, S.M. and K. Stafford (2011), 'Family social capital as family business resilience capacity', in Richard Sorenson (ed.), *Family Business and Social Capital*, Cheltenham, UK and Northampton, MA, USA: Edward Elgar, UK, pp. 79–105.

Danes, S.M., V.S. Zuiker, R. Kean and J. Arbuthnot (1999), 'Predictors of family business tensions and goal achievement', *Family Business Review*, **12**(3), 241–52.

Danes, S.M., M.A. Rueter, H.-K. Kwon and W. Doherty (2002), 'Family FIRO model: an application to family business', *Family Business Review*, **15**(1), 31–43.

Danes, S.M., H.R. Haberman and D. McTavish (2005), 'Gendered discourse about family business', *Family Relations*, **54**, 116–30.

Danes, S.M., K. Stafford and J.T. Loy (2007), 'Family business performance: the effects of gender and management', *Journal of Business Research*, **60**, 1058–69.

Danes, S.M., J. Lee, K. Stafford and R.K.Z. Heck (2008a), 'The effects of ethnicity, families and culture on entrepreneurial experience: an extension of sustainable family business theory', *Journal of Developmental Entrepreneurship*, **13**(3), 229–68.

Danes, S.M., J.T. Loy and K. Stafford (2008b), 'Management practices of small private firms within a quality framework', *Journal of Small Business Management*, **46**, 395–421.

Danes, S.M., J. Lee, S. Amarapurkar, K. Stafford, G.W. Haynes and K. Brewton (2009a), 'Determinants of family business resilience after a natural disaster by gender of business owner', *Journal of Entreprenuerial Development*, **14**(4), 333–54.

Danes, S.M., K. Stafford, G.W. Haynes and K. Brewton (2009b), 'Business experiences with disasters and disaster assistance, 1997–2007', Paper presented at the NSF-CMMI Research and Innovation 2009 Conference, Honolulu, Hawaii, 22–25 June.

Danes, S.M., K. Stafford, G. Haynes and S. Amarapurkar (2009c), 'Family capital of family firms: bridging human, social, and financial capital', *Family Business Review*, **22**(3), 199–215.

Danes, S.M., A.E. Matzek and J.D. Werbel (2010), 'Spousal context during the venture creation process', in J.A. Katz and G.T. Lumpkin (series eds) and A. Stewart, G.T. Lumpkin and J.A. Katz (vol. eds), *Advances in Entrepreneurship, Firm Emergence and Growth: Vol. 12*, New Milford, CT: Emerald, pp. 113–62.

Davidsson, P. (1991), 'Continued entrepreneurship: ability, need, and opportunity as determinants of small firm growth', *Journal of Business Venturing*, **6**(6), 405–29.

Davidsson, P. and J. Wiklund (2001), 'Levels of analysis in entrepreneurship research: current research practice and suggestions for the future', *Entrepreneurship Theory and Practice*, **25**(3), 81–99.

Davis-Brown, K. and S. Salamon (1987), 'Farm families in crisis: an application of stress theory to farm family research', *Family Relations*, **36**, 368–73.

Deacon, R.E. and F.M. Firebaugh (1988), *Family Resource Management: Principles and Applications*, Boston, MA: Allyn and Bacon.

Dimov, D. (2007), 'Beyond the single-person, single-insight attribution in understanding entrepreneurial opportunities', *Entrepreneurship Theory and Practice*, **31**(5), 713–31.

Donnelley, R.G. (1964), 'The family business', *Harvard Business Review*, **42**, 93–105.

Dumas, C. (1989), 'Understanding of father–daughter and father–son dyads in family-owned businesses', *Family Business Review*, **11**(1), 31–46.

Dumas, C. (1998), 'Women's pathways to participation and leadership in the family-owned firm', *Family Business Review*, **11**(3), 219–28.

Duncan, G.J. (1984), *Years of Poverty, Years of Plenty*, Ann Arbor, MI: University of Michigan, Institute for Social Research, Survey Research Center.

Dyer, G.W. Jr and W. Handler (1994), 'Entrepreneurship and family business: exploring the connections', *Entrepreneurship Theory and Practice*, **19**(1), 71–83.

Ehrenberg, R.G. and R.S. Smith (1997), *Modern Labor Economics: Theory and Practice*, 6th edn, Reading, MA: Addison-Wesley.

Fitzgerald, M.A. and G. Muske (2002), 'Copreneurs: an explanation and comparison to other family businesses', *Family Business Review*, **15**(1), 1–16.

Fitzgerald, M.A., M. Winter, N.J. Miller and J.J. Paul (2001), 'Adjustment strategies in the family business: implications of gender and management role', *Journal of Family and Economic Issues*, **22**, 265–91.

Fitzgerald, M., H. Schrank, G.W. Haynes and S.M. Danes (2010), 'Socially responsible processes of small family business owners: evidence from the National Family Business Survey', *Journal of Small Business Management*, **48**(4), 524–51.

Frances, A.E. (1999), *The Daughter Also Rises: How Women Overcome Obstacles and Advance in the Family-owned Business*, San Francisco, CA: Rudi Publishing.

Friedman, S.D. (1991), 'Sibling relationships and intergenerational succession in family firms', *Family Business Review*, **4**(1), 3–20.

Gallo, M.A. and S. Tomaselli (2006), 'Formulating, implementing and maintaining family protocols', in P.Z. Poutziouris, K.X. Smyrnios and S. Klein (eds), *Handbook of Research on Family Business*, Cheltenham, UK and Northampton, MA, USA: Edward Elgar Publishing in association with International Family Enterprise Research Academy (IFERA), pp. 298–316.

Gartner, W.B. (2001), 'Is there an elephant in entrepreneurship? Blind assumptions in theory development', *Entrepreneurship Theory and Practice*, **25**(3), 27–39.

Gimeno, A. (2005), 'Performance in the family business: a causal study of internal factors and variables', PhD dissertation, ESADE Universitat Ramon Llull, Spain.

Gnan, L. and D. Montemerlo (2006), 'Family-firm relationships in Italian SMEs: ownership and governance issues in double-fold theoretical perspective', in P.Z. Poutziouris, K.X. Smyrnios and S. Klein (eds), *Handbook of Research on Family Business*, Cheltenham, UK and Northampton, MA, USA: Edward Elgar Publishing in association with International Family Enterprise Research Academy (IFERA), pp. 501–16.

Gollnick, D.M. and P.C. Chinn (1990), *Multicultural Education in a Pluralistic Society*, Columbus, OH: Charles E. Merrill.

Greenberger, D.B. and D.L. Sexton (1987), 'A comparative analysis of the effects of the desire for personal control on new venture initiations', *Frontiers of Entrepreneurship Research. 1987: Proceedings of Seventh Annual Babson College Entrepreneurship Research Conference*, Wellesley, MA: Babson College, pp. 239–53.

Greenwood, R. (2003), 'Commentary on: altruism in family firms', *Journal of Business Venturing*, **18**(4), 491–4.

Gudmunson, C.G., S.M. Danes, J.T. Loy and J.D. Werbel (2009), 'Spousal support and work/family balance in launching a family business', *Journal of Family Issues*, **30**(8), 1098–121.

Habbershon, T.G. and M.L. Williams (1999), 'A resources-based framework for assessing the strategic advantages of family firms', *Family Business Review*, **12**, 1–25.

Habbershon, T.G., M.L. Williams and I.C. MacMillan (2003), 'A unified systems perspective of family firm performance', *Journal of Business Venturing*, **18**(4), 451–65.

Haberman, H.R. and S.M. Danes (2007), 'Father–daughter and father–son family business management transfer comparison: family FIRO model application', *Family Business Review*, **20**(2), 163–84.

Hall, A., L. Melin and M. Nordqvist (2006), 'Understanding strategizing in the family business context', in P.Z. Poutziouris, K.X. Smyrnios and S. Klein (eds), *Handbook of Research on Family Business*, Cheltenham, UK and Northampton, MA, USA: Edward Elgar Publishing in association with International Family Enterprise Research Academy (IFERA), pp. 253–68.

Hammond, C.H. (2003), 'Response of family businesses to a natural disaster: a case study approach', unpublished doctoral dissertation, Oregon State University.

Handler, W.C. (1992), 'The succession experience of the next generation', *Family Business Review*, **5**(3), 283–307.

Harris, D., J.I. Martinez and J.L. Ward (1994), 'Is strategy different for the family-owned businesses', *Family Business Review*, **7**(2), 159–74.

Harvey, M. and R.E. Evans (1994), 'Family business and multiple levels of conflict', *Family Business Review*, **7**(4), 331–48.

Haynes, G.W. and R.J. Avery (1997), 'Family businesses: can the family and the business finances be separated? Preliminary results', *Entrepreneurial and Small Business Finance*, **5**(1), 61–74.

Haynes, G.W., R. Walker, B.S. Rowe and G.-S. Hong (1999), 'The intermingling of business and family finances in family-owned businesses', *Family Business Review*, **12**(3), 225–39.

Haynes, G.W., S.M. Danes and K. Stafford (2011), 'Influence of federal disaster assistance on family business survival and success', *Journal of Contingencies and Crisis Management*, **19**(2), 86–98.

Heck, R.K.Z. and K. Stafford (2001), 'The vital institution of family business: economic benefits hidden in plain sight', in G.K. McCann and N. Upton (eds), *Destroying Myths and Creating Value in Family Business*, Deland, FL: Stetson University, pp. 9–17.

Heck, R.K.Z. and E.S. Trent (1999), 'The prevalence of family business from a household sample', *Family Business Review*, **12**(3), 209–24.

Heck, R.K.Z., M. Winter and K. Stafford (1992), 'Managing work and family in home-based employment', *Journal of Family and Economic Issues*, **13**(2), 187–212.

Heck, R.K.Z., A.J. Owen and B. Rowe (eds) (1995), *Home-based Employment and Family Life*, Westport, CT: Auburn House.

Heck, R.K.Z., S.M. Danes, M.A. Fitzgerald, G.W. Haynes, C.R. Jasper, H.L. Schrank, K. Stafford and M. Winter (2006), 'The family's dynamic role within family business entrepreneurship', in P.Z. Poutziouris, K.X. Smyrnios and S.B. Klein (eds), *Handbook of Research on Family Business*, Cheltenham, UK and Northampton, MA, USA: Edward Elgar Publishers, pp. 80–105.

Heck, R.K.Z., F. Hoy, P.Z. Poutziouris and L.P. Steier (2008), 'Emerging paths of family entrepreneurship research', *Journal of Small Business Management*, **46**(3), 317–30.

Hill, N.E., V.M. Murry and V.D. Anderson (2005), 'Sociocultural contexts of African American families', in V.C. McLoyd, N.E. Hill and K.A. Dodge (eds), *Diversity in African American Family Life: context, Adaptation, and Policy*, New York: Guilford, pp. 21–44.

Hobfoll, S.E. (2001), 'The influence of culture, community, and the nested-self in the stress process: advancing conservation of resources theory', *Applied Psychology*, **50**, 337–421.

Hollander, B.S. and N.S. Elman (1988), 'Family-owned businesses: an emerging field of inquiry', *Family Business Review*, **1**(2), 145–64.

Holmes, T.H. and R.H. Rahe (1967), 'The social readjustment rating scale', *Journal of Psychomatic Research*, **11**(2), 213–18.

Hoy, F. and P. Sharma (2006), 'Navigating the family business education maze', in P.Z. Poutziouris, K.X. Smyrnios and S. Klein (eds), *Handbook of Research on Family Business*, Cheltenham, UK and Northampton, MA, USA: Edward Elgar Publishing in association with International Family Enterprise Research Academy (IFERA), pp. 11–24.

Ibrahim, A.B. and W.H. Ellis (2006), *Family Business Management: Concepts and Practice*, 2nd edn, Dubuque, IA: Kendall/Hunt Publishing Company.

Ibrahim, N.A., J.P. Angelidis and F. Parsa (2004), 'The status of planning in small businesses', *American Business Review*, **22**(2), 52–60.

International Family Business Program Association (IFBPA) (contributors/authors: R.K.Z. Heck, N.B. Upton, W. Bellet, B. Dunn, P. Parady and J. Powell) (1995). 'Family business as a field of study', *Family Business Annual*, **I**(Section II), 1–8.

Jennings, J.E. and M.S. McDougald (2007), 'Work–family interface experiences and coping strategies: implications for entrepreneurship research and practice', *Academy of Management Review*, **33**(3), 747–60.

Juster, F.T. and F.P. Stafford (1985), *Time, Goods, and Well-Being*, Ann Arbor, MI: University of Michigan, Institute for Social Research, Survey Research Center.

Kaye, K. (1991), 'Penetrating the cycle of sustained conflict', *Family Business Review*, **4**(1), 21–41.

Keating, R. (2001), *Small Business Survival Index 2001: Ranking the Policy Environment for Entrepreneurship Across the Nation*, Washington, DC: Small Business Survival Committee.

Kepner, E. (1983), 'The family and the firm: a coevolutionary perspective', *Organizational Dynamics*, **12**(1), 57–70.

Klein, S.B., J.H. Astrachan and K.X. Smyrnios (2005), 'The F-PEC Scale of family influence: construction, validation and further implication for theory', *Entrepreneurship Theory and Practice*, **18**, 321–39.

Kotey, B. and G.G. Meredith (1997), 'Relationships among owner/manager personal values, business strategies, and enterprise performance', *Journal of Small Business Management*, **35**(2), 37–64.

Kulig, J.C. (2000), 'Community resiliency: the potential for community health nursing theory development', *Public Health Nursing*, **17**(5), 374–85.

Kuratko, D.F., J.S. Hornsby and D.W. Naffziger (1997), 'An examination of owners' goals in sustaining entrepreneurship', *Journal of Small Business Management*, **35**(1), 24–33.

Lansberg, I.S. (1988), 'The succession conspiracy', *Family Business Review*, **1**(2), 119–43.

Lansberg, I.S. and J.H. Astrachan (1994), 'Influence of family relationships on succession planning and training: the importance of mediating factors', *Family Business Review*, **7**(1) 37–57.

Longenecker, J.G. and J.E. Schoen (1978), 'Management succession in the family business', *Journal of Small Business Management*, **16**(3). Reprinted in C.E. Aronoff, J.H. Astrachan and J.L. Ward (eds) (2002), *Family Business Sourcebook*, Detroit: Omnigraphics, pp. 61–6.

Lopez, R. (1986), 'Structural models of the farm household that allow for interdependent utility and profit maximization decisions', in I. Singh, L. Squire and J. Straus (eds), *Agricultural Household Models: Extensions, Applications and Policy*, Baltimore, MD and London: The Johns Hopkins University Press, pp. 306–25.

Matzek, A.E., C.G. Gudmunson and S.M. Danes (2010), 'Spousal capital as a resource for couples starting a business', *Family Relations*, **59**, 58–71.

Mayer, R.C., J.H. Davis and F.D. Schoorman (1995), 'An integrative model of organizational trust', *Academy of Management Review*, **20**, 709–34.

Merkel, W.T. and L.J. Carpenter (1987), 'A cautionary note on the application of family therapy principles to organized consultation', *American Journal of Orthopsychiatry*, **57**(1), 111–15.

Mileti, D.S. (1999), *Disasters by Design: A Reassessment of Natural Hazards in the United States*, Washington, DC: Joseph Henry Press.

Miller, N.J., M.A. Fitzgerald, M. Winter and J. Paul (1999), 'Exploring the overlap of family and business demands: household and family business managers adjustment strategies', *Family Business Review*, **12**(3), 253–68.

Miller, N.J., M. Winter, M.A. Fitzgerald and J.J. Paul (2000), 'Family microenterprises: strategies for coping with overlapping family and business demands', *Journal of Developmental Entrepreneurship*, **5**(2), 87–113.

Mitchell, R.K., E.A. Morse and P. Sharma (2003), 'The transacting cognitions of nonfamily employees in the family businesses setting', *Journal of Business Venturing*, **18**(4), 533–51.

Morck, R. and B. Yeung (2004), 'Family control and the rent-seeking society', *Entrepreneurship Theory and Practice*, **28**(4), 391–409.

Narva, R.L. (2001), 'Heritage and tradition in family business: how family-controlled enterprises connect the experience of their past to the promise of their future', in G.K. McCann and N. Upton (eds), *Destroying Myths and Creating Value in Family Business*, Deland, FL: Stetson University, pp. 29–38.

Niehm, L.S., J. Swinney and N.J. Miller (2008), 'Can community social responsibility be used as a strategy for generating family business success?', *Journal of Small Business Management*, **46**(3), 331–50.

Olson, P.D., V.S. Zuiker, S.M. Danes, K. Stafford, R.K.Z. Heck and K.A. Duncan (2003), 'Impact of family and business on family business sustainability', *Journal of Business Venturing*, **18**(5), 639–66.

Owen, A.J., B.R. Rowe and J.E. Gritzmacher (1992), 'Building family functioning scales into the study of at-home income generation', *Journal of Family and Economic Issues*, **13**(3), 299–313.

Paige, R.C. and M.A. Littrell (2002), 'Craft retailers' criteria for success and associated business strategies', *Journal of Small Business Management*, **40**(4), 314–31.

Peiser, R.B. and L.M. Wooten (1983), 'Life-cycle changes in small family businesses', *Business Horizons*, May/June. Reprinted in C.E. Aronoff, J.H. Astrachan and J.L. Ward (eds) (2002), *Family Business Sourcebook*, Marietta, GA: Family Enterprise Publishers, pp. 373–81.

Pieper, T.M. and S.B. Klein (2007), 'The bulleye: a systems approach to modeling family firms', *Family Business Review*, **20**(4), 301–19.

Ponthieu, L.D. and H.L. Caudill (1993), 'Field theory: an alternative to systems theory in understanding the small family business', *Journal of Small Business Management*, **31**, 66–78.

Poutziouris, P.Z., K.X. Smyrnios and S.B. Klein (2006), 'Introduction: the business of researching family enterprises', in P.Z. Pontziouris, K.X. Smyrnios and S.B Klein (eds), *Handbook of Research on Family Business*, Cheltenham, UK and Northampton, MA, USA: Edward Elgar, pp. 1–8.

Poza, E.J. and T. Messer (2001), 'Spousal leadership and continuity in the family firm', *Family Business Review*, **14**(1), 25–35.

Puryear, A., E. Rogoff, M.-S. Lee, R.K.Z. Heck, E.B. Grossman, G.W. Haynes and J. Onochie (2008), 'Sampling minority business owners and their families: the understudied entrepreneurial experience', *Journal of Small Business Management*, **46**(3), 422–55.

Rodriguez, S.N., G.J. Hildreth and J. Mancuso (1999), 'The dynamics of families in business: how therapists can help in ways consultants don't', *Contemporary Family Therapy*, **21**(4), 453–68.

Rogoff, E.G. and R.K.Z. Heck (2003), 'Evolving research in entrepreneurship and family business: recognizing family as the oxygen that feeds the fire of entrepreneurship', *Journal of Business Venturing*, **18**(5), 559–66.

Rosenblatt, P.C., L. De Mik, R.M. Anderson and P.A. Johnson (1985), *The Family in Business: Understanding and Dealing with the Challenges Entrepreneurial Families Face*, San Francisco, CA: Jossey-Bass.

Rosenfeld, E.S. (2008), 'Privately held business succession planning – a crucial process', *Journal of Retirement Planning*, March–April, 15–23.

Rothausen, T.J. (2009), 'Management work – family research and work – family fit', *Family Business Review*, **22**(3), 220–34.

Rue, L.W. and N.A. Ibrahim (1996), 'The status of planning in smaller family-owned business', *Family Business Review*, **9**(1), 29–43.

Sawin, K.J. and M.P Harrigan (1995), *Measures of Family Functioning for Research and Practice*, New York: Springer.

Schulze, W.S., M.H. Lubatkin and R.N. Dino (2003), 'Toward a theory of agency and altruism in family firms', *Journal of Business Venturing*, **18**(4), 473–90.

Scherr, F.C., T.F. Sugrue and J.B. Ward (1993), 'Financing the small firm start-up: determinants of debt use', *Journal of Small Business Finance*, **3**(1), 17–36.

Shane, S. and S. Venkataraman (2000), 'The promise of entrepreneurship as a field of research', *Academy of Management Review*, **25**(1), 217–26.

Sharma, P. (2004), 'An overview of the field of family business studies: current status and directions for the future', *Family Business Review*, **17**(1), 1–36.

552 *Handbook of research on family business*

Sharma, P., J.J. Chrisman and J.H. Chua (1997), 'Strategic management of the family business: past research and future challenges', *Family Business Review*, **10**(1), 1–35.

Sirmon, D. and M. Hitt (2003), 'Managing resources: linking unique resources, management, and wealth creation in family firms', *Entrepreneurship Theory and Practice*, **27**(4), 339–58.

Smilkstein, G. (1978), 'Family AGPAR: a proposal for family function test and in use by physicians', *Journal of Family Practice*, **6**, 1231–9.

Smilkstein, G., C. Ashworth and D. Montano (1982), 'Validity and reliability of the family APGAR as a test of family function', *The Journal of Family Practice*, **15**(2), 303–11.

Songini, L. (2006), 'The professionalization of family firms: theory and practice', in P.Z. Poutziouris, K.X. Smyrnios and S. Klein (eds), *Handbook of Research on Family Business*, Cheltenham, UK and Northampton, MA, USA: Edward Elgar Publishing in association with International Family Enterprise Research Academy (IFERA), pp. 269–97.

Stafford, K. and R.J. Avery (1993), 'Scheduling congruity theory of family resource management: a basis for cross cultural analysis', in R. von Schweitzer (ed.), *Cross Cultural Approacher to Home Management*, Boulder, CO: Westview Press, pp. 17–41.

Stafford, K., K.A. Duncan, S.M. Danes and M. Winter (1999), 'A research model of sustainable family businesses', *Family Business Review*, **12**(3), 197–208.

Stafford, K., V. Bhargava, S.M. Danes, G.W. Haynes and K.E. Brewton (2010), 'Factors associated with long-term survival of family businesses: duration analysis', *Journal of Family and Economic Issues*, **31**(4), 442–57.

Stanforth, N. and G. Muske (2001), *An Exploration of Entrepreneurship*, Stillwater, OK: Oklahoma State University, Department of Design, Housing and Merchandising.

Steier, L. (2001a), 'Family firms, plural forms of governance, and the evolving role of trust', *Family Business Review*, **14**(4), 353–67.

Steier, L. (2001b), 'Next-generation entrepreneurs and succession: an exploratory study of modes and means of managing social capital', *Family Business Review*, **14**(3), 259–76.

Steier, L. (2003), 'Variants of agency contracts in family-financed ventures as a continuum of familial altruistic and market rationalities', *Journal of Business Venturing*, **18**(5), 597–618.

Steier, L. and R. Greenwood (2000), 'Entrepreneurship and the evaluation of angel financial networks', *Organizational Studies*, **21**(1), 163–92.

Stewart, C.C. and S.M. Danes (2001), 'The relationship between inclusion and control in resort family businesses: a developmental approach to conflict', *Journal of Family and Economic Issues*, **22**, 293–320.

Sundaramurthy, C. (2008), 'Sustaining trust within family businesses', *Family Business Review*, **21**(1), 89–102.

Sztompka, P. (1974), *System and Function: Toward a Theory of Society*, New York: Academic Press.

Tauer, L.W. and D.A. Grossman (2002), *Estate and Succession Planning for Small Business Owners*, Extension Bulletin 2002–05, Department of Applied Economics and Management, Cornell University.

Tigges, L.M. and G.P. Green (1994), 'Small business success among men- and women-owned firms in rural area', *Rural Sociology*, **59**(2), 289–310.

Trent, E.S. (guest ed.) and J.H. Astrachan (ed.) (1999), 'Editors' notes: family businesses from the household perspective', *Family Business Review*, **12**, v–vi.

Uhlaner, L.M. (2005), 'The use of the Guttman scale in development of a family orientation index for small-to-medium-sized firms', *Family Business Review*, **18**(1), 41–56.

Upton, N.B. and R.K.Z. Heck (1997), 'The family business dimension of entrepreneurship', In D.L. Sexton and R.W. Smilor (eds), *Entrepreneurship: 2000*, Chicago, IL: Upstart Publishing Company, pp. 243–66.

Van Auken, H. (2003), 'An empirical investigation of bootstrap financing among small firms', *Journal of Small Business Strategy*, **14**(2), 22–36.

Van Auken, H. and L. Neeley (2000), 'Pre-launch preparations and the acquisition of capital', *Journal of Developmental Entrepreneurship*, **5**, 169–82.

Van Auken, H. and J. Werbel (2006), 'Family dynamic and family business financial performance: spousal commitment', *Family Business Review*, **19**(1), 49–63.

Walker, K.E. and M.E. Woods (1976), *Time Use: A Measure of Household Production of Family Goods and Services*, Washington, DC: Center for the Family of the American Home Economics Association.

Ward, J.L. (1988), 'The special role of strategic planning for family business', *Family Business Review*, **1**(2), 105–17.

Ward, J.L. (1997), *Keeping the Family Business Healthy: How to Plan for Continuing Growth, Profitability, and Family Leadership*, Marietta, GA: Business Owner Resources.

Ward, J.L. and J.L. Handy (1988), 'A survey of board practices', *Family Business Review*, **1**(3), 289–308.

Weber, J., L. Lavelle, T. Lowry, W. Zeller and A. Barrett (2003), 'Family, inc.', *Business Week*, 10 November, pp. 100–114.

Whiteside, M.F. and F.H. Brown (1991), 'Drawbacks of a dual systems approach to family firms: can we expand our thinking?', *Family Business Review*, **4**(3), 383–95.

Whitley, R. (1999), *Divergent Capitalisms*, Oxford: Oxford University Press.

Winborg, J. and H. Landström (2001), 'Financial bootstrapping in small business: examining small business managers' resource acquisition behaviors', *Journal of Business Venturing*, **16**(3), 235–54.

Winter, M., S.M. Danes, S.-K. Koh, K. Fredericks and J.J. Paul (2004), 'Tracking family businesses and their owners over time: panel attrition, manager departure, and business demise', *Journal of Business Venturing*, **19**, 535–59.

Winter, M., M.A. Fitzgerald, R.K.Z. Heck, G.W. Haynes and S.M. Danes (1998), 'Revisiting the study of family businesses: methodological challenges, dilemmas, and alternative approaches', *Family Business Review*, **11**(3), 239–52.

Zachary, R.K. (2011), 'The importance of the family system in family business,' *Journal of Family Business Management*, **1**(1), 26–36.

Zachary, R.K. and Mishra, C.S. (2011), 'The future of entrepreneurship research: calling all researchers,' *Entrepreneurship Research Journal*, **1**(1–1), 1–13. [http://www.bepress.com/erj/vol1/iss1/1/].

Zuiker, V.S. (1998), *Hispanic Self-employment in the Southwest Rising above the Threshold of Poverty*, New York: Garland.

Zuiker, V.S., Y.G. Lee, P.D. Olson, S.M. Danes, A.N. VanGuilder-Dik and M.J. Katras (2002), 'Business, family, and resource intermingling characteristics as predictors of cashflow problems in family-owned businesses', *Financial Counseling and Planning*, **13**(2), 65–81.

24 Secrets of family business longevity in Japan from the social capital perspective

Toshio Goto

INTRODUCTION

This chapter focuses on century-old Japanese family firms in order to explore the key factors for their longevity, starting with an analysis of their family constitution. Despite the importance of longevity, its sources are not well understood (Astrachan and Pieper, 2010). Another area missing in this research is Japan itself, even though it is known as the home of many century-old family firms and the average age of family firms there is more than double that of the USA.

The chapter reveals Japanese family firms' commitment to perpetuation and, more importantly, their devotion to the public welfare as the most relevant factors for their longevity, which is discussed in the social and economic context under which they have striven to uphold these values as documented in the constitution. The *ie* (household) institution is presented as the most relevant factor in the social context, while business ethics, called *Shingaku*, are presented as a base for their public welfare orientation.

The social capital theory is employed to further analyze the mechanism that has facilitated the longevity of Japanese family firms from both the network and value perspectives. The involvement of non-family players is viewed as a unique characteristic of family social capital. The interaction of family social capital and the family firm's organizational social capital (Arrègle et al., 2007) is carefully examined. Community-level social capital (Lester and Cannella, 2006) is also viewed as relevant to the achievement of longevity.

Using an inductive approach, a framework is presented, composed of a network block and a value block. Within the network block, the interaction is examined of family social capital, the family firm's organizational social capital and community-level social capital. Within the value block, hierarchical structure is examined. Finally, bidirectional influence is examined between the network and value blocks. A set of propositions is presented for further research.

There are several contributions expected in this research. First, the research sheds light on the constitutions of long-lived family firms in Japan to the largest extent ever, and addresses the key factors for their longevity, which no preceding research has revealed. Second, the research contributes to enriching the theory of social capital regarding the bidirectional interactions of family social capital, the family firm's organizational social capital and the community-level social capital. Interaction of the network and value components of the social capital is also addressed.

The remainder of the chapter is composed of the literature review, research method and the results, discussion, implications and the conclusion.

LITERATURE REVIEW

Longevity is without a doubt a subject of keen interest for every family firm worldwide. The importance of longevity has been repeatedly emphasized since the birth of family business in the world. Family firms in general are said to be notoriously short-lived due to their very complex form of business organization (Neubauer and Lank, 1998). It is often quoted that only 30 percent of family firms reach the second generation (Beckhard and Dyer, 1983), while less than 16 percent survive to the third generation (Applegate, 1994).

Succession has been one of the main subjects for both practitioners and researchers in the family business field. Perpetuating a family business is the ultimate management challenge and two-thirds of the family businesses, having survived beyond 60 years, were not growing (Ward, 2004).

'Hidden champions' are mostly family-owned (76.5 percent) and 31.1 percent have survived 75 years. They are determined to achieve a market leader position and long-term results. They grow more slowly and the CEO's tenure is longer than in ordinary firms (Simon, 1996). Major keys to the enduring success of family firms include respect for the challenge, common issues and different solutions, communication, planning and commitment. The four Ps (policy, purpose, process and parenting) are important to reduce family business conflicts. Stage three (cousin collaboration) faces a balance between freedom and commitment, and cultural and strategic adaptability as a major challenge for longevity (Ward, 2004), since the potential for intergenerational conflicts is enormous (Schwass, 2006).

Miller and Le Breton-Miller (2006) argue that family-controlled businesses do best when they take advantage of the lower agency costs and elicit attitudes of stewardship, which is typically the case under the control of the founder, but these conditions erode in the second generation and beyond. Unusual financial stewardship and superior investments in reputation, alliances, tacit knowledge transfer and corporate culture all contribute to capabilities that rivals cannot match (Teece et al., 1997).

Some other research focuses on the continuously successful family businesses to address the key factors in their success. Analysis of nine IMD-LODH Family Business Award[1] recipients, comparing the entrepreneurial family business model to ephemeral ones, identifies the following two factors relevant to remaining continuously entrepreneurial: an evolutionary 'wise growth' strategy based upon a coherent family vision, and growth of the individual in the business (phase two), for which professional work experiences outside of the family provides opportunities. Very long-term leadership tenure harbors the risk of focusing too much on historically proven success at the expense of innovation (Schwass, 2006).

Research on 40 large family-controlled firms with leading market shares for at least 20 years shows that their median age is 104 years, with more than half having survived for over a century. Their financial policy is conservative, with low debt, high liquidity ratios and higher survival rates. Leaders generally have every desire to act in the long-term interests of the enterprise. They guard against doing anything in the short run that might compromise the future of the business (Miller and Le Breton-Miller, 2006).

Due to the importance of family cohesion (Pieper and Astrachan, 2008), management of the conflicting factors, such as family and non-family, as well as innovation and conservatism, should deserve more research focusing on the several generations after the founder has gone. While longevity is an important and emerging subject, century-old long-lived family businesses (LLFBs) have rarely been researched. One exception is O'Hara (2004), who surveyed 20 LLFBs including two in Japan to identify the following as recurring principles and practices: family unity; a product catering to basic human needs; primogeniture; a role for women; a commitment to continue the legacy; the use of adoption as a means to perpetuate family ownership; allowing the business, rather than the family, to come first; an obligation to community and customer service; conflict arrangement; plans in writing; and a system of governance (p. 318). O'Hara, in an interview with Karofsky (2003), also remarks on the importance of an ability to change without forsaking basic family values.

The landscape of family business in Japan is different from its Western counterparts. Japan has 1146 family firms[2] in operation for two centuries or longer, significantly surpassing Germany (856), the Netherlands (240), and Austria (167), among others (Goto, 2006). The average age of family firms in Japan is 52 years (Goto, 2005), which more than doubles that of the USA, where the average life span of a family firm is 24 years (Lansberg, 1983). Therefore it seems reasonable to shed more light on the LLFBs in Japan to find the key factors for their longevity.

Various studies have been made related to the longevity of Japanese firms, including those by Bellah (1957) on the value system that came into being during the Tokugawa period, Fruin (1983) on Kikkoman Company, Hirschmeier and Yui (1975) on the development of the merchant philosophy, and Roberts (1973) on the Mitsui family business. Analyzing the House of Mitsui, one of the world's oldest large-scale business enterprises in operation since 1683, Horide (2000) concludes that Mitsui's longevity can be attributed to several factors, including an organization system for the maintenance of entrepreneurship for generations, which will be discussed later in this chapter.

Analyzing a LLFBs database, Goto (2006) identifies three important factors for their longevity: the steady economic growth of Japan; the management skills; and the philosophical background. As for the last factor, the teaching of *Shingaku* was recognized as an integral part of the spirit of the merchant houses since the mid-eighteenth century and contributed significantly to the longevity of family firms. This aspect will be later analyzed in depth.

Adachi (1970, pp. 6–7) analyzes precepts of long-lived firms in Kyoto Prefecture and identifies the following factors contributing to longevity: succession of the family name; worship of ancestors and a religious outlook; filial devotion to parents; a healthy life; honesty; diligence; patience; complacence and fulfillment of one's duty; prudence; propensity; compliance; foresight and caution; secretive beneficence; and harmony.

In addition, there is a collection of precepts of long-lived firms analyzed mostly by business historians, including Bokutei (1902), Hatakeyama (1988), Irie (1968), Kitahara (1921), Mitsui Bunko (1974), and 'Yasuda-hozensha to sono kankei jigyo-shi' henshu-iinkai (1974). These serve as useful resources for this chapter.

In-depth analysis of LLFBs' precepts and family constitutions may provide better understanding of the business family's value system and institutional provision to foster their longevity, which is the core issue of this chapter.

As one of the early research projects on family constitutions, Neubauer and Lank (1998) analyze family constitutions as a part of the corporate governance of family firms.

They address the importance of the family governance function, especially when the firm has reached the cousins' confederation stage, and suggest that, above a certain size, many of these (family) firms have a constitution (p. 66) to determine the tasks to be handled by the different organs, the distribution of power, the extent and the limitations of that power, the composition of these organs and their relationship to each other as well as the mechanism to resolve conflicts and so on. The Mogi family[3] constitution is described as having strong philosophical and religious overtones compared to its Western counterparts (p. 93), which will be examined later in this chapter.

This chapter aims to reexamine the business historians' research on Japanese LLFBs from the family business point of view, and to address the factors attributable for the LLFBs longevity, with a special emphasis on the social capital perspective.

RESEARCH METHOD AND RESULTS

In order to focus on the fundamental driving forces that foster the longevity of LLFBs in Japan, the LLFB Database3 was prepared by the author, which contains more than 18 000 LLFBs founded in or prior to 1909. Information covered includes the LLFBs' name, location, year of the foundation, type of industry, number of generations involved, and related notes including the precepts. In parallel to the analysis of LLFB Database3, the constitutions and precepts appearing in the above-mentioned literature were also analyzed after excluding duplication.

The LLFB Database3 in Excel format was sorted by 'precept' and its synonyms in Japanese as keywords to identify 168 cases. The preceding literature was manually searched with the same keywords to identify 94 cases excluding duplication. In total, 262 family constitutions, family precepts or codes, including both written and unwritten ones, are available, which is the largest collection of this type of document ever surveyed.

The earliest one was documented in about 1610, while many were prepared in the early part of the eighteenth century and later (see Table 24.1), and the date of issuance of many remains unknown.

They are mostly titled as a precept, memorandum or testament, while 32 (12.2 percent) are titled as a family constitution, the majority of which, however, are just like precepts in that they look only to their ancestors to provide direction. Out of 262 family constitutions or precepts, 16 relatively lengthy and systematic constitutions were chosen for a preliminary analysis of the content to avoid subjective interpretation as much as possible to assure validity and inter-rater reliability.

Table 24.1 summarizes the 16 family constitutions, with the date of the issuance and the major contents according to the categorization of Adachi (1970). The table is the most comprehensive collection of data of this type compared to among the preceding literature. Two more categorical items were added, which are house rules and social contribution. In order to assure validity, coding was done twice with a one-week interval in between. Discrepancies were settled after careful reading of the contents. The survey identifies the most often stated item as 'longevity and succession of the family name' (in 14 cases), followed by 'filial devotion to parents' (12), 'diligence' (12), 'prudence' (12) and 'propensity' (12). Honesty, harmony and house rules also appear in 11 cases.

As for the house rules, the most comprehensive one is the House Code of Mitsui

Table 24.1   Summary of the major family constitutions

Name	Date	1	2	3	4	5	6	7	8	9	10	11	12	13	14	15	16
Kikuchi	c. 1700	x	x	x	x	x	x	x	x	x	x		x		x		
Sumitomo	1721	x			x	x			x	x	x		x			x	
Mitsui	1722	x	x	x		x	x	x	x	x	x	x	x	x	x	x	
Konoike	1723	x		x			x	x		x	x				x	x	
Fukuda	1776	x	x	x	x	x	x	x	x	x	x	x	x		x		
Nishikawa	1844	x		x		x	x	x		x	x		x				
Sumitomo	1882	x	x			x	x			x		x	x			x	
Mageo	1886	x		x	x	x	x			x	x				x	x	x
Yasuda	1887																
Konoike	1889	x	x	x			x								x	x	
Shibusawa	1891	x	x	x	x	x	x	x	x	x	x	x	x	x	x	x	x
Mitsui	1900	x	x	x	x	x	x	x	x	x	x	x	x		x	x	
Handa	1903	x	x	x	x	x	x	x	x	x	x	x			x	x	x
Honma	n.a.	x	x	x		x	x	x	x	x	x	x		x	x	x	x
Hayashi	n.a.	x	x	x								x			x	x	
Total		14	10	12	7	11	12	9	8	12	12	7	8	3	11	11	4

Note: Numbers in the heading refer to the following:

1. Longevity and succession of family names
2. Worship of ancestors and religious mind
3. Filial devotion to parents
4. Healthy life
5. Honesty
6. Diligence
7. Patience
8. Complacence and fulfillment of one's duty
9. Prudence
10. Propensity
11. Compliance
12. Foresight and caution
13. Secretive beneficence
14. Harmony
15. House rules
16. Social contributions

Source: Prepared by the author based upon the literature and database analysis.

(revised in 1900), which is composed of ten chapters and 109 articles in total. The chapters are titled as follows: 1 Family structure; 2 Family obligation; 3 Family assembly and family council; 4 Marriage, adoption and branch family; 5 Guardian, quasi-incompetent and incompetent; 6 Inheritance; 7 Executive committee; 8 Property; 9 Sanction; and 10 Supplementary rules. Other elaborate ones include the Shibusawa family house rules (87 articles), the Yasuda family Hozen-sha Rules (66 articles),[4] the Konoike constitution of 1723 (54 articles),[5] Mageo (49 articles), Koyama (22 articles), Hayashi (49 articles)[6] and Miki constitution (42 articles).[7] The Sumitomo constitution of 1882 has 19 chapters composed of 170 articles. While most of the elaborate ones were prepared in the early twentieth century, the earlier documents were simple and philosophical. The Mitsui

Constitution of 1722, one of the early ones, spends most of the 51 articles on solidarity, harmony, rectitude and protocols among family members while allotting articles 8, 11, 12, 26, 36, 40, 41 and 48 to the governance system (see the Appendix).

These precepts promote the importance of conducting a legitimate business and ethical conduct, reiterating 'virtue is the root and wealth is the result', as shown below. This goes without saying, but every act of work should be performed wholeheartedly (Sumitomo Masatomo); Those who put justice first and profit second will prosper (Shimomura Hikoemon of Daimaru Department Stores); Never pursue frivolous profit (Hirose Saihei of Sumitomo); Waste nothing and work hard (Omi merchant creed for living); Do not think of yourself but what is best for everybody, do not expect high profits . . . place great importance on those to whom you will sell (Nakamura Jihei); When employing other people's children, merchant house masters must see it as their duty to teach them the way of business, make each a man and send them into society (Yao Kihei); Even when distressed after selling, be content that it is the secret of a merchant (Tonomura Yozaemon).

A large number of precepts and constitutions also emphasize self-sacrifice and dedication to society, as depicted in the following: Devote all effort to contribute to the social welfare and never spare wealth for that endeavor (Honma); Never spend wealth privately; Wealth must be akin to virtue (Shimomura Hikoemon).

Similar descriptions are observed repeatedly in the precepts of families, such as Yasuda (p. 136), Ichijima (p. 136), Fujita (p. 182), Ito (p. 192), Nozaki (p. 198), Katakura (p. 206), Wakao (p. 216), Horikiri (p. 265), Okaya (p. 276), Doi (p. 284), Jinno (p. 289), Furuya (p. 305), Handa (p. 315), Uematsu and Yamada.[8] All emphasize efforts to dedicate themselves to the public welfare.

These documents remain relevant to the family firms only when the family members continue to uphold the core value as documented. Therefore, in the next section, those emphasized values are discussed in the social context that sustains the relevance of these values. Major practices that serve longevity are also examined as evidence of the family members' commitment. The social capital theory is employed to identify the implications for the longevity of long-lived family firms.

DISCUSSION

Social Capital

Among a family's social, human and financial capital, family social capital best distinguishes family from non-family businesses (Sorenson and Bierman, 2009, p. 193). Among the various definitions of social capital, this chapter stays with Nahapiet and Ghoshal (1998, p. 243), which defines it as the network of relationships possessed by an individual or social unit, and the sum of actual and potential resources embedded within, available through, and derived from, this network. Social capital is distinguished from other types of capital, such as economic capital and human capital, by focusing on the relationships in between as a source of added value creation.

The term 'social capital' was first mentioned in the early twentieth century to refer to social cohesion and personal investment in the community. It evolved to highlight the importance of the networks of personal relationships to provide the basis for trust,

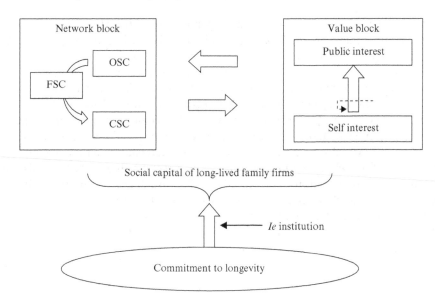

Figure 24.1   Conceptual model of the social capital of long-lived family firms

cooperation and collective action (Jacobs, 1965). In the late 1990s, the concept gained popularity, in which sociologists Pierre Bourdieu and James Coleman, among others, were instrumental.

As a source, user and builder of social capital (Bubolz, 2001), the family together with its business composes a network to share the family value system as described in their precept. Levie and Lerner (2009) suggest that family firms are stronger than other types of businesses in terms of social capital, offsetting the weaknesses in human and financial capital to show the same or even superior performance. From the founding generation to the succeeding ones, family values are transferred, during which process the value system becomes condensed if properly managed. In parallel, the network expands from the sibling to the cousin consortium, which becomes consolidated, again subject to proper management.

Family capital significantly contributes to firm achievements and sustainability (Danes et al., 2009). A strong family social capital (FSC) is suggested to facilitate a family firm's organizational social capital (OSC), as addressed by Arrègle et al. (2007). Furthermore, it is proposed that community-level social capital (CSC) is an important reason for the survival and persistence of family firms (Lester and Cannella, 2006). Therefore long-lived family firms have likely developed their OSC and CSC via FSC to effectively foster their longevity. This mechanism is analyzed hereafter in both the network and value aspects. Prior to the analysis, the *ie* institution is reviewed as a fundamental social system in which all families and their businesses have historically functioned in Japan

The conceptual model of this chapter is presented in Figure 24.1. Commitment to longevity is deeply connected with the social context of the society built around the *ie* institution. The social capital of long-lived family firms is examined in both the network and value blocks. The network block is composed of family social capital (FSC), family firm's organizational social capital (OSC), and community-level social capital (CSC), among which interaction is later examined. Within a value block, a set of values is hierarchically presented and its structure is also examined. Finally, bidirectional influence is examined between the two blocks.

The *Ie* Institution and the Social Context of the Family Constitution

The social context of the early part of the eighteenth century, when the majority of the family precepts and constitutions was documented, was critical for the survival of merchants due to two major crises. First, facing the depression after the burst of *Genroku* bubble economy, they had to tighten their belts for survival. Second, and more importantly, the Tokugawa government started a hostile policy against the merchant class, fearing the possible turmoil of the hierarchic social class structure composed of warriors, farmers, craftsmen and merchants, in that order. Observing the economic prosperity of the merchant and the decline of the warrior class, the government confiscated the assets of the two wealthiest merchants to make them scapegoats. In this context, merchants were desperate for the preservation of both *ie* and the business.

Since the beginning of the seventeenth century, the *ie*, usually translated as 'house' or 'household', was the basic unit of Japanese society, and this was legally authorized under the Meiji Constitution in 1890. In this social context, the perpetuation of *ie* as well as its business was the top priority of all parties involved.

Unlike in Western nations, Japanese law and society were not based upon the concept of the individual, but on that of *ie*. *Ie* is defined by the Meiji Civil Code as a group of persons with the same surname (Article 746), and members of *ie* other than its head were called 'family'.[9] Therefore *ie* was legally based on kinship,[10] which was established by relation by blood, adoption or marriage.

Under the *ie* system, the eldest male in a family line was vested with exclusive rights, including the right to approve a marriage, decide the place of residence of married family members, and manage and inherit the family property. Upon marriage, the husband acquired the right to the possession and management of his wife's property and to the enjoyment of rents and profits therefrom (Article 801), although he did not acquire the title to his wife's property.[11]. Every 'house' was headed by a *koshu* or household head and other members of the 'house' were the head's spouse and relatives by consanguinity or affinity (Article 725). The head of a 'house' had the duty to support the members of his 'house' (Article 747). In the family inheritance, the eldest son becomes the household head (Article 970). *Katoku Souzoku* or head-of-the-household succession[12] was a system as well as a law in the old Japanese Civil Code concerning property succession from an old head of the household to the new one. Primogeniture was enforced in the Meiji era. Prior to Meiji, there also existed other inheritance practices.[13]

Three remarks deserve special attention from the perspective of this chapter. First, *ie* formed an institutionalized household, a corporate body; therefore its preservation was essential in Japan. Second, its membership was actually extended to non-blood-related subordinates such as employees and servants as well as their relatives. This is considered unique character of Japanese *ie* (Mito, 1991, p. 313), due to the importance of the preservation of *ie* over blood continuity. This is in sharp contrast to China and Korea, where blood pureness was considered sacred. Third, Japanese society based on the *ie* institution is called a 'vertical society', and this remains unchanged according to the anthropology theory and despite the change of the political and legal systems (Nakane, 1967, p. 24). The *ie* institution legally ceased at the end of the Second World War, but the vertical structure and mentality are still dominant in present-day Japanese society.

A family firm played an important role in the *ie* institution. First, composing a part of the *ie*, the firm was a necessary means to ensure the continued existence of the capital-owning family. Second, it was therefore considered as an entity to endure eternally through profit-making. Third, eternal preservation of both the *ie* and its business was considered to be the most important obligation of the household head and subordinate members.

The growth in size and complexity of the family business with the passage of time required the good management and structure of the greater houses for the eternal growth of the family and its business. As a foundation of LLFBs, a *dozokudan* was created in the sizable merchant houses. This is an organization of greater houses composed of *honke* or main house(s), *renke* or associate house(s), *bunke* or branch houses, and *bekke* or distant houses, which were listed in descending order of their authority. While *bunke* were formed by the family's descendants, *bekke* were granted to the non-family senior managers, both with the permission of the main house executives. Mitsui, as a typical example, had six *honke* and three *renke* in 1722, which composed the core of the Mitsui *Dozokudan*. In the very center, Hachiroemon's house was positioned as the *so-honke* or senior main house, as specified by the Mitsui House Rules of 1722. The number of core houses was tightly controlled to avoid diffusion of the assets and stock.

Every possible practice was used to keep the *ie* prospering not only in the current generation but also perpetually. Two of those practices are introduced below to aid better understanding of the implications of the *ie* institution from the social capital perspective. One is the *bekke* and *noren-wake* system and the other is successor adoption.

Bekke and *noren-wake* system

Bekke or distant houses, composing a part of the *dozokudan*, were destined to support the prosperity of the main house in return for the various protections of the main house. In order not to conflict with the main house, they carry on the same line of the business in a remote location as a branch of the main house, or carry on a totally different business as *noren-wake*.

Noren originally means a traditional Japanese fabric divider used by shops and restaurants in doorways as a means of blocking out sun, wind and dust. But it is more than that, because it is a synonym for the house, as a permanent symbol and representation of management philosophy, and manifestation of the corporate brand. Merchants display their pride for the trust and goodwill extended by the stakeholders.

Noren-wake is a practice to distribute goodwill to the senior employees, as a kind of franchising. Swearing loyalty to the main house, the senior employees are granted the right to set up their own store under the same or a similar name. Franchisees are allowed not only to use the trade know-how, but also enjoy the former master's protection such as financial support.

Noren-wake is nowadays popular among various industry segments such as the restaurant and distribution business. To look at the soba noodle shop sector as an example, there are several groups of *noren-wake*, such as in the Sunaba association (156 member shops) and the Chojuan association (340 composed of four subgroups), among others.

Founded in the Bunka Era (1804–17), Tomoecho Sunaba has been owned and managed by the Hagiwara family since its foundation, and its current owner is the fifteenth generation. One of the factors contributing to longevity is *noren-wake*, according to Kojimachi-7chome-Sunaba Tokichi (current Minami-Senju Sunaba), which first appeared in a document published in 1813 and it is currently managed by the fourteenth generation. It set up Hongokucho Sunaba (current Muromachi Sunaba) and Konpiracho Sunaba (current Toranomon Sunaba). Sunaba Choeikai (Association of Sunaba for longevity) was organized in 1933 among Sunaba owner families. The association was reorganized as Sunaba Kai in 1955, and it has 156 members (Iwasaki, 2003, p. 131).

As illustrated above, *bekke* is instrumental in fostering the LLFBs' longevity by intensifying the unity of the *dozokudan* network as a non-family member. It also contributes to reducing strategic simplicity by introducing heterogeneous culture, which contributes to longevity as well.

Successor adoption

Adoption has been a common practice ever since the ancient era in Japanese history as a means to keeping a 'house' or family from extinction.[14] Merchants adopted not only relatives but also those who were totally unrelated by blood as their successors. It was quite natural and common to choose an adopted successor from among the employees, since the family head can evaluate the candidates' personality, behavior and business capability through their daily contacts. From the employees' perspective, this process works as an internal competition for promotion to top management and owner position, spurring the employees' motivation. After adopting an heir, some families adopted a husband for a younger daughter as a contingency for the worst-case scenario.

Under the Meiji Civil Code of 1898, the adoptee became a legitimate child of the adoptive parent upon adoption (Article 860) and entered his 'house' (Article 861); the same relationship as between blood-relatives was established between an adoptee and an adopter and his blood-relatives (Article 727). As a consequence thereof, the adoptee acquired the right of succession as well as all rights and duties that existed between parent and child, such as the duty of mutual support, the adopter's right to exercise parental power and so on. An adopted child assumes the surname of the parent by adoption. An adopted husband entered his wife's 'house' (Article 788-2).

Dissolution of an adoption was possible either by mutual consent or judicial decision (Article 862). A judicial dissolution could only be applied for if several grounds were given, which included the following: the adoptee having acted in a way that disgraced the name of the 'house' or endangered the 'house' property (Article 866-5), or in the case of the dissolution or annulment of the marriage of an adopted husband (Article 866-9).

Successors adopted from outside of the family's business are often expected to bring in a new type of assets, which are not available or are difficult to obtain within the family. These include but are not limited to state-of-the-art technology, human networks, outside working experiences, trade know-how and wealth.

The adoptee's position is not protected well, since adoption is subject to dissolution due to misconduct or poor performance, as stipulated in the Civil Code. Dissolution or annulment of the marriage also leads to dissolution of the adoption. Adopted successors are destined to work for the fortune of the adoptive family and its business to reduce agency costs to its minimum.

It is important to note that successor adoption should not be simply considered as a last resort for the continuity of a family and its business. Some families choose to adopt an outsider as a successor even if they have natural heirs. As typified in the case of the Nakamura family and its business, Nakasho, their precept prohibits succession to the blood-related heir, stating that natural sons should either establish their branch family or be adopted into another family, and that all successions were restricted to adoptees only.

Mehrotra et al. (2008) modestly estimate that 21 percent of long-lived family firms have practiced adoption in post-Second World War Japan. As an example, among world-famous long-lived listed firms, Suzuki Motor (founded in 1907) and Kikkoman (traced back to 1603) have adoptees as their top executives today. Osamu Suzuki, the current CEO of Suzuki Motor, was adopted and joined the firm in 1958. After 20 years of strenuous effort to prove his talent and the loyalty, he assumed the presidency in 1978 to expand the firm tenfold into a US$35 billion automotive manufacturer. His style is financially conservative and aggressive in marketing. He is committed to the family's business to show the adoptee's pride to the adoptive family and to its firm.

Goto (2009) indicates the three major strengths of successor adoption to be as follows. First, successor adoption overcomes the shallow talent pool of family firms, without increasing agency cost. Second, successor adoption is an effective recruiting strategy to get the best available human resources from the market. Third, successor adoption is a unique hybrid system combining the strength of both a direct heir and a professional manager. The last point needs further explanation from both the resource-based view and the organization ecology aspect.

From the resource-based view, adopted successors can assimilate into the inimitable and untransferable culture of the adoptive family and its business, which is recognized as its competitive advantage (Barney, 1986). At the same time, coming from the outside, they are relatively free from organizational inertia (Hannan and Freeman, 1984) that long-lived firms are liable to have. In this manner, they can lead innovative activities that the adoptive family had a hard time putting into practice.

Network Block of OSC and its Internal Structure

The network block is composed of family social capital (FSC), the family firm's organizational social capital (OSC) and community-level social capital (CSC) components. The first component, FSC, is social capital developed among family members (Arrègle et al., 2007, p. 76). From childhood, the family provides the foundation of moral behavior for cooperation, which is trust in a mutual manner to build FSC as enduring and powerful forms of social capital. Due to the intimacy and altruistic environment of a family, FSC is probably the most powerful social capital and highly likely to contribute to the perpetuity of the family.

The second one, OSC, as a critical resource for organization, reflecting the character of social relations within a firm (Leana and Van Buren, 1999, p. 538). Among the relatively limited resources available for a family firm, OSC is one of the most powerful resources contributing to its prosperity. Arrègle et al. (2007) propose that FSC influences the development of OSC through isomorphic pressures, organizational identity and rationality, human resource practices and social network overlaps (pp. 80–82).

The third component, CSC, is social capital captured at a community level and functions as an important mechanism thorough which family owners protect and nurture their family businesses (Lester and Cannella, 2006). The idea of CSC is noted by Bourdieu (1983) and Putnam (1993), but research on it is relatively new. The intercorporate network of family-controlled businesses is focused on as typical CSC by Lester and Cannella (2006). The norm of behavior and access to resources, such as mutuality, trust and respect for one another, is viewed as yielding corporate well-being (ibid., p. 758).

Below, I propose that family firms in Japan, and most significantly the long-lived family firms, have taken advantage of their social capital in intimacy, versatility and interactivity. First, intimacy is significant in the creation of FSC. Built upon the *ie* institution, families in Japan have traditionally enhanced the understanding of the common values, behavioral norms and cognitive schemes (Arrègle et al., 2007, p. 73) in an intimate manner. Various virtues have not only been emphasized in the family constitutions but also in the actual practices as introduced later, which include filial devotion to parents, honesty, harmony, diligence, prudence and propensity. Shared understanding of such values as a firm's goal is expected to substantiate a cohesive relationship (Pieper and Astrachan, 2008) among the relevant members. Enhancing the strength of FSC increases the probability of the family's survival and helps its members prosper. Intimacy is witnessed in the most formidable OSC or *dozokudan*. Very intimate and reciprocal relationships between the main and subordinate houses, and also between the family and non-family members, have been mentioned above. *Dozokudan* is a cohesive institution composed of houses to support the perpetuity of their family business. Therefore, it is proposed:

Proposition 1 The level of the cohesiveness developed in a family firm is correlated to the firm's longevity.

Second, versatility is typically observed in the successor adoption, *bekke* and *noren-wake* system, as discussed above. Prioritizing the longevity of both the family and its business, families in Japan often adopt non-blood-related successors from outside the family. Such a membership expansion beyond the kinship relation brings in not only precious assets difficult to obtain within the family and *dozokudan*, but, more importantly, heterogeneity.

The value of versatility can be well understood by introducing the concept of weak and strong ties as presented by Granovetter (1973). Adopted successors can be viewed as a hybrid system to combine embedded ties and arm's-length ties to realize an optimal network. Strong ties, embedded in an organization, are effective in reaching integrative agreements and in achieving complex adaptations (Uzzi, 1996), while they may limit access to new information. Adopted successors, taking advantage of the strong ties embedded in an adoptive family, can act as a bridge to a new type of information, utilizing the weak ties of the adopted son.

The homogeneous culture of long-lived family firm, as observed in *dozokudan*, is a double-edged sword, since it works to solidify the members on one hand but also builds a strong inertia against introducing anything new on the other hand. Therefore it requires significant energy to promote entrepreneurship under such a conservative and inward culture. Modernization, diversification or globalization requires a heterogeneous culture and a wider perspective, which adopted successors are expected to bring with them.

It can be argued that an adopted successor functions to combine the strengths of both the direct heir and professional management. On one side, he is relatively free from the strategic simplicity to follow the success experienced in the past (Miller, 1993), the tendency to follow the industry tradition (Hambrick and Finkelstein, 1987), and information filtering (Finkelstein and Hambrick, 1996), all of which are detrimental to entrepreneurship. On the other hand, his commitment to the fortune of the family and its business and assimilating to the culture and values of the family are counted as his strength, equivalent to that of the direct heir. The possibility of dissolution severely restricts him from any betrayal behaviors. He is destined to align his own goal with that of the adoptive family and its firm to mitigate agency costs. His high education, wide perspective, human network and wealth are better than those of professional managers on many occasions, which is expected to positively influence the firm's performance and sustainability. Therefore it is proposed:

Proposition 2a   An adopted successor outperforms a direct heir in the longevity of the family firm.

Proposition 2b   An adopted successor outperforms a professional manager in the longevity of the family firm.

Versatility is also observed in CSC. In addition to the inter-company social capital as addressed by Lester and Cannella (2006), other types of stakeholders also constitute an important part of CSC surrounding the family firms, which includes the employee, customer and vendor segments. This is also the case with family firms outside of Japan, but versatility is consciously pursued in Japan as a source of successor adoption.

Among the firm's CSC, customers are one of the most important stakeholders in family firms. Ishida Baigan's works emphasize the importance of customer satisfaction in the mid-eighteenth century, as already quoted. Many firms not only prioritized customer satisfaction in their precept, as exemplified in Nakamura' case, but also practiced it in their daily operation. Customers appreciated the trustworthiness of the family firms by experiencing the product or service provided and the behavior of the store clerks. In this manner, social capital exists to play an important role between the family firms and its customers.

By the same token, family firms' surrounding community, as one of their stakeholders, constitutes the family firms' network. The family firms' members are born and raised in the surrounding community, participate in community activities, and contribute to the community in various ways. It is this series of daily contacts through which trustworthiness is transmitted to and appreciated by the community members as the core value of the family and its firm.

Once it has understood the impeccable value of LLFBs, the surrounding community not only accepts them as their legitimate members but even extends various support as needed. A typical example is Morihachi, one of the major confectionery business since 1625 in Kanazawa City. In 1996, Morihachi's mismanagement resulted in 6 billion yen debts and brought it to the brink of bankruptcy when the Kanazawa municipality and the community extended financial support to the company by sacrificing some portion of their loans to it. The eighteenth head of the family, together with his wife and employees, made desperate efforts to restructure the operations and management style to improve customer satisfaction, and, as a result, completed paying back all outstanding debts in 2004.

Besides the firm's CSC, the family has its own CSC, which includes but is not limited to community leaders, dignitaries and politicians, as well as artists. Such a family's CSC is often extended to casual and informal associations with a loose membership. These groups, often called *ko* or *ren*,[15] vary in purpose, ranging from financial, religious and entertainment to cultural ones. Members voluntarily organize themselves, conduct regular meetings, cement mutual friendships to share the same values that are reflected in the mission of the association, and save a certain amount of money to give financial support to group activities, such as shrine visits. Fuji ko is one of the most popular associations and is organized in many local communities for the purpose of climbing Mt Fuji, which was traditionally perceived as a holy mountain to climb.

These types of casual and informal associations are organized independently of the business purposes, but in practice they often serve to develop new business partnerships or to get a novel idea for starting a new business. This is typically the case with cultural networks, in which upper-class merchants not only participate but also financially sponsor in order to fulfill both prestigious and commercial purposes.

Toward the center of the concentric *dozokudan* network, homogeneity increases while heterogeneity decreases. Heterogeneity of an adopted successor, however, exists at the very center. *Bekke* and non-family employees also substantiate heterogeneity. The *ie* institution and the *dozokudan* network are viewed essential as fostering the LLFBs' longevity by orchestrating the heterogeneous membership of families, extended families and non-family employees. Such a network is vital for LLFBs to effectively solidify the membership, which is more complicated than the cousin collaboration. It also functions as an important infrastructure to facilitate communication to share a coherent vision and the four Ps (policy, purpose, process and parenting), to foster the LLFBs' longevity in the long run.

The *dozokudan*'s inter-house network among the main house, associate, branch and distant houses is characterized by homogeneous membership and frequent contacts, and hence is categorized as a strong tie. The external network shared with the customer and the community is categorized as a weaker tie. Finally, the network extended to informal associations is characterized by loose and casual contacts and heterogeneous membership, and hence is categorized as the weakest tie.

Strong ties are effective as a source of power to solidify the *ie* institution and the *dozokudan* network. Overwhelming dependence upon such an inward-oriented power, however, brings the risk of keeping the family and its business exclusive and insensitive to environmental changes. Weak ties are effective for countering such an inward orientation by facilitating a bridging effect to assimilate external information and revitalize the family.

More homogeneity is productive in stable environments, whereas more heterogeneity is productive in dynamic conditions (Priem, 1990). It can be assumed that century-old families, equipped with strong and weak ties, relied more on strong ties in stable environments and weak ties in dynamic conditions. Such connecting functions as a powerful CSC are a source not only of adoption but also of recruiting investors and employees as well as an information source for risk management. Therefore:

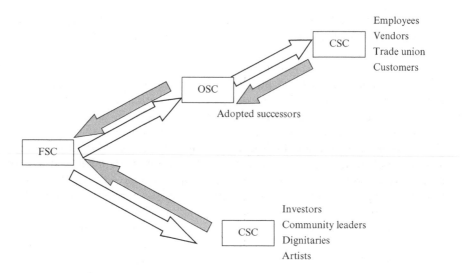

Employees
Vendors
Trade union
Customers

Investors
Community leaders
Dignitaries
Artists

Figure 24.2   Interactions among family, family firm and community social capital

Proposition 3   The level of versatility of OSC correlates to the firm's longevity.

Third, interactivity is considered to be a strength of social capital often observed among family firms in Japan. In parallel to the influence of FSC over the development of OSC as proposed by Arrègle et al. (2007), reverse influence is also observed between the two social capitals as far as family firms in Japan are concerned. A typical example is the case of adopting a senior manager of a family firm into a family as its successor. Through this transaction, OSC influences the development of additional FSC. Interactivity is also observed between CSC and FSC when a family adopts its successor from one of the community's leading family or a dignity through its connection. Due to the importance of succession, not only a family head but also key personnel of a family maintain serious efforts to develop the family's CSC to prepare for the best possible adoption. CSC is valuable not only for adoption but also for various other purposes. Recruiting of new employees and investors thorough CSC of either the family or the family firm is another purpose, which also influences the development of OSC. This is another case of reverse influence if we assume it is normal for FSC to develop OSC and CSC.
   Proposed:

Proposition 4a   The family firm's organizational social capital influences the development of the family social capital.

Proposition 4b   The organizational social capital of long-lived family firms more effectively influences the development of the family social capital than other family firms.

To conclude this part of the network block of OSC, family firms in Japan, especially the long-lived ones likely take the most advantage of their network within a family, its family firm and in the community, all of which contribute to foster the firm's longevity

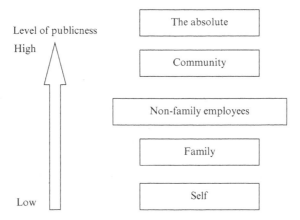

Figure 24.3   Hierarchical structure within the value block

through intimacy, versatility and interactivity of its social capitals. Long-lived family firms in Japan have developed a unique cohesion and homogeneity with a very tightly connected *ie* institution based family and close business linkages with stakeholders on the one hand. On the other hand, they enjoy heterogeneity by introducing outside blood into a family through a successor adoption and assimilating non-family members into *dozokudan* via *bekke* and *noren-wake* without diluting the unity.

The Value Block of OSC and its Hierarchical Structure

A unique value stated in the family constitution and related documents is the pursuit of the public welfare. Not only do they state their commitment to the public welfare in their family constitution, but quite a large number of LLFBs denounce their self-interest and take good care of non-family employees, customers and local community. Their promise was proven by their actual conduct, which fostered the good will and trust of the stakeholders.

The value block of OSC is structured hierarchically, starting with self-interest at the bottom, followed by family, non-family employees, community and finally the absolute (see Figure 24.3). Pursuit of the higher value goes along with the strong commitment for the perpetuity of both a family and its business in parallel. As already described, this became popular especially in the historic and social context of the early eighteenth century, when Japan experienced a major depression after the rapid economic expansion period of the Genroku Era (1688–1703). Since it was not an easy time for merchants, they carried through their retrenchment policy to tighten their own morality and to apply themselves even more vigorously to legitimate business (Bellah, 1957, p. 145). As a part of such efforts, precepts and family constitutions were documented to protect their business for perpetual growth.

It was not by accident that three great merchant houses in the Tokugawa Era established their house rules almost simultaneously shortly after the Genroku bubble economy burst. Sumitomo established their constitution (house rules) in 1721, Mitsui in 1722 and the Konoike in 1723. Many of the other constitutions and precepts also emphasized the importance of honesty, diligence and morality in practicing ethical conduct and build a strong *ie* system even though the language and the magnitude vary.

While those documents compiled the ancestors' instructions and their value system for self-discipline, some of them detailed the family governance system. As for the 16 elaborate constitutions with more than 20 articles, the main contents include the families' structure, interrelationships, ownership concentration, distribution of profits and the settlement of disputes in a harmonious manner. All are for the families' perpetual prosperity. These constitutions were prepared to define the family governance structure, which is critical for the perpetual growth of the family and its business. Some constitutions cover family business governance, but business governance is often described in a separate document such as business operation rules, employee regulations and so on, which will be covered in later work.

Neubauer and Lank (1998) overlooked the existence of such elaborate constitutions in Japan which specify family governance structure in detail, and generalized family constitutions in Japan as religious and philosophical. Such a misunderstanding is quite natural since many family precepts and constitutions were kept confidential in Japan.

Business ethics and public welfare advocated by Ishida Baigan

Shortly after the Genroku bubble economy, Ishida Baigan (1685–1744), one of the most influential business philosophers, emerged to advocate the importance of the merchant vocation and its ethics. In 1740, he published his first book, *Toi-mondo* (*City and Country Dialogues*) and another book, *Seikamon* (*Essay on Household Management*) in 1744 to present his theory of *Shingaku* as a result of amalgamating Confucianism, Buddhism and the Japanese Shinto religion.

The essence of Baigan's thought was summarized by Bellah (1957) as follows:

> Baigan, assimilating the merchants to the model of the *samurai* (warrior as a ruling class), insists that their function is to be of assistance to the empire and that profit they receive is but the just reward for their services, comparable to the stipend of the *samurai*. (p. 158)
> While taking an honest profit will lead to prosperity, taking an unjust one will lead to ruin. (p. 161)
> One of the themes on which Baigan is most insistent is knowing one's occupation and practicing it diligently. One's occupation is what heaven has decreed. It is the basis of one's service to one's nation and its ruler and it is the basis for continuing the family.
> It is within the context of occupation that a just profit, honesty and economy have meaning. The idea of occupation is closely linked to the central values of loyalty and filial piety. (p. 164)

The following quotations from Baigan's *Toi-mondo* are added for the better understanding of his idea:

> Never disrespect the customer for he sustains us.
>   Frugality is, for the good of the world, to make two sufficient when three is necessary.
>   True merchants seek a way to respect others while respecting themselves.
>   Kindness is not for a return.
>   Obey the law and respect yourself.
>   Any wrongdoing construed as correct should never be tolerated, even if it is a master who does so.

Preaching the importance of righteous conduct and just profit, *Shingaku* insisted that business is not for the private family's sake but for the public welfare. Baigan stated that 'the owner of the wealth is a citizen in the society' (*Toi-mondo*, 1–4) and that 'wealth is the treasure which belongs to the society' (*Toi-mondo*, 5–4). Pursuit of public welfare is traceable to Tejima Toan, one of the highest pupils of Baigan. Tejima released a book titled *Akindo Yawaso* (*Night Talks for Merchants*) (1727), which was written by Tejima's father. Strongly condemning selfish interest, the book praised the pursuit of the public interest, including that of family and employees.

Pursuit of public welfare is documented in the family constitution of quite a large number of long-lived family firms; therefore it may be worthwhile to examine the relationship between a public interest orientation and the longevity of the relative firms. Hence, it is proposed:

Proposition 5a   The level of value correlates to the longevity of the family firm.

Proposition 5b   The magnitude of the practice to serve the public welfare correlates to the longevity of the family firm.

Even though Baigan's real interest was in preaching Shinto, Confucianism was the greatest influence on his thinking. The concept of heart and nature, which are the foundation of his theory, were directly taken from Mencius (372–289 BCE) and the explanation for them derived largely from Sung neo-Confucianism (Bellah, 1966, pp. 142–3). He was also influenced by Buddhism, both through his teacher Ryoun and Sung Confucians who themselves were influenced by Buddhism.

Many of Baigan's ideas are traceable to the classical works of Confucius (551–479 BCE), some of which are excerpted below:

> The Master said, 'The mind of the superior man is conversant with righteousness; the mind of the mean man is conversant with gain.' (Analects, 04–16); The Master said, 'Riches and honors are what men desire. If they cannot be obtained in the proper way, they should not be held. Poverty and meanness are what men dislike. If they cannot be avoided in the proper way, they should not be avoided; if a superior man abandons virtue, how can he fulfill the requirements of that name? The superior man does not, even for the space of a single meal, act contrary to virtue. In moments of haste, he cleaves to it. In seasons of danger, he cleaves to it (Analects, 04–5); Virtue is the root; wealth is the result (The Great Learning, 7).

While Baigan crystallized his theory of righteousness and orderly society based on Confucianism, he introduced reciprocity and benevolence from Buddhism. Merchants are expected to be faithful to their duty in their vocation no more or less than craftsmen, farmers and the ruling-class warriors. His business ethics emphasizes the importance of pursuing just profit in a righteous manner. Business relationships are based on mutual trust, benevolence and reciprocal help, which are in contrast to the contractual relationships in Western society.

Baigan's idea is echoed in many family precepts. There are quite a few precepts that were directly influenced by *Shingaku*. By the mid-nineteenth century, *Shingaku* gained momentum nationwide and its scholars were invited by merchant families to prepare their precepts. Baigan documented a prototype of a family constitution of ten articles (Tsuchiya, 2002, pp. 166–8). His disciples further developed it and evidence remains that they assisted merchants in preparing their constitutions (Takenaka, 1977, pp. 142–71).

On the other hand, the author assumes that Baigan assimilated the conducts and beliefs of merchants to formulate his theory. The Mitsui House Constitution of 1722 is a typical example of the latter case; it was formalized as a compilation of the will of the founder Mitsui Takatoshi (1622–94) three decades after his death. As an ardent lay preacher of Buddhism (Nakada, 1959, pp. 218–21 and 243), he instructed the pursuit of righteous business for eternity. The Mitsui House prospered in the business of clothing and money exchange, and was respected among the merchant community and trusted by the Tokugawa Shogunates. Mitsui's success was well known nationwide. Baigan preached in Kyoto, where Mitsui's main family was also located. Therefore it is no wonder that Baigan assimilated Mitsui's conduct and beliefs into his theory.

This chapter perceives Baigan as a pioneering advocate of business ethics in the most systematic manner, superseding the preceding scholars, three of whom are briefly introduced below.

Suzuki Shōsan (1579–1655) was a warrior who later became a Zen Buddhist monk. He preached that diligent service in an ordinary person's work is no more or less than a religious service in its value (Nakamura, 1965, p. 123). He also insisted that being a merchant is a religious vocation just like any other occupations (p. 125).

Nishikawa Joken (1648–1724), an astronomer, compiled practical advice to merchants titled *Chonin Bukuro* in 1719; it is recognized as the first systematic theory of merchant ethics in Japan, and Ihara Saikaku (1642–93), a well-known poet and novelist, published several books on the rise and fall of merchant houses. In *Nippon Eitaigura* (*The Eternal Storehouse of Japan*) (1688), he praised righteous business conduct as typified by the practices of the Mitsui House. A merchant's strong pride and belief in his own occupation is built upon religious belief and Confucian ethics (Tsuchiya, 1964, p. 90).

Business ethics advocated by Baigan were well received by the merchants, who were desperate to preserve the longevity of both the family and its business. In order to act in their long-term self-interest, LLFBs chose public welfare by sacrificing self-desire, which resulted in gaining legitimacy as a highly acclaimed family business and support from stakeholders for the perpetuity of the business.

The following overview of the religious and philosophical background of the Tokugawa era is offered for the better understanding of the business ethics advocated by Baigan.

Buddhism

Originating in India in the sixteenth century BCE, Buddhism consists of the teachings of the Buddha. Japan first learned Buddhism from Korea, from where it was introduced in 552 CE, but the subsequent development of Japanese Buddhism and Buddhist sculpture was primarily influenced by China. Of the main branches of Buddhism, it is the Mahayana or 'Greater Vehicle' Buddhism which found its way to Japan. In contrast to Theravada Buddhism (with its emphasis on monastic life), Mahayana holds that not only priests (those having taken the Buddhist vows) but also the laity can attain enlightenment. One of the characteristics of Mahayana is the priority it puts on the altruistic activity, which is relevant to the merchant ethics.

In the Tokugawa Era, the feudal government placed primary importance on Buddhism. In those days, Buddhism was virtually a spiritual support for the common people, of which the essence was *Ji-Hi*, the virtue of compassion of Buddha, which was extended even to animals. *Ji-Hi* was one of the three virtues along with honesty and wisdom in ancient Japan (Horide, 2009, p. 5). Working diligently for the public benefit in the spirit of *Ji-Hi* was nothing but the Buddhist practice.

Confucianism

Confucianism is a Chinese ethical and philosophical system developed from the teachings of the Chinese philosopher Confucius (551–479 BCE). It has had tremendous influence on culture and history throughout East Asia, and Japan is no exception. Confucianism was first introduced to Japan in AD 513. Neo-Confucianism, introduced to Japan in the twelfth century, is an interpretation of nature and society based on metaphysical principles and is influenced by Buddhist and Taoist ideas, which brought the idea that family stability and social responsibility are human obligations.

In the Tokugawa Era, the Japanese nation was profoundly influenced and almost remolded by Confucianism, since its teachings were consolidated into an authentic ground for political ideas among the ruling class, and the ethical norm for daily life among the commoners. Confucian government was to be a moral government, hierarchical and benevolent to the ruled classes. Confucianism also provided a hierarchical system in which each person was to act according to his or her status to create a harmoniously functioning society and ensure loyalty to the state. The teachings of filial piety and humanity continued to form the foundation for much of social life and ideas about family and nation.

Loyalty to superiors was regarded as a sacred duty, which was regarded as an absolute obligation required for religious salvation. At the level of the family, filial piety is equivalent to the devotion and obligation to one's parents. It should also be remarked that reciprocal obligations were important, since Neo-Confucian ethics also stresses that superiors owe obligations to inferiors for benefits derived from them. A failure to repay obligations can undermine the position of the superior.

Virtues such as submissiveness, frugality and modesty were also emphasized by Confucianism. Another central value of Neo-Confucian ideology concerns the need for honesty and morality in dealing with others.

Analects, also known as the *Analects of Confucius*, are considered a record of the words and acts of the central Chinese thinker and philosopher Confucius and his disciples, as well as the discussions they held. Written during the Spring and Autumn Period in Warring States Period (*c.* 479–221 BCE), the *Analects* is the representative work of Confucianism and continues to have a tremendous influence on Chinese and East Asian thought and values today.

Shinto

Shinto is the natural spirituality of Japan and the Japanese people, which incorporates spiritual practices derived from many local and regional prehistoric traditions, emerging in the sixth century. Characterized by the worship of nature, ancestors, polytheism and animism, with a strong focus on ritual purity, its theory is not as systematic as Buddhism and Confucianism.

Shinto's practice of ancestor worship was instrumental in placing a strong religious dimension on filial piety. Since Shinto theology stresses the common ancestry of all Japanese, filial piety could easily be extended to embrace devotion and obligation to the emperor since the imperial family was considered as the main house of which all Japanese families are branches.

Major Practices of the LLFBs to Foster their Longevity

Various managerial systems were created and put into practice, which are attributable to the perpetuity of the family/business entity, including undivided inheritance and single succession, greater house cluster and managerial delegation and owner-control (Gaens, 2000, p. 208). This section presents five practices that contribute to the LLFBs' longevity: separation of management and ownership; joint ownership; consensus management; *oshikome* as a governance system; and social contribution.

Before giving an overview of these practices, three points need to be mentioned. First, these practices were designed to control the private interest of the family members and to encourage them to pursue the public interest, the interests of the employees and customers, and furthermore those of the community, at the sacrifice of the family's short-term interests.

Second is the driving force to implement the practices. They were introduced to assure the perpetuity of the family and its business for the long term rather than the financial interest for the short term. To this end, many families codified the family constitutions and precepts to prioritize the public interest and to discipline themselves.

Third is the fact that many of these practices are still pursued despite the major change of the legal system. Under the current Constitution which replaced the Meiji Constitution in 1947, the basic unit of the society nowadays is the individual, and the household head no longer exists. Despite this legal change, many practices derived from the *ie* institution are still observed, especially among LLFBs. This fact alone tells of the effectiveness of those practices to foster LLFBs' long-term prosperity.

Separation of management and ownership

Since the middle of the Tokugawa Period, large business families moved toward entrusting their management to non-family managers due to the growth of the *ie* enterprise, the expansion and the geographical spread of subsidiary stores and offices, and the branching out of business (Gaens, 2000, p. 213). As a natural consequence of this, there began to be a separation of ownership and management as a practical mechanism for fostering the prosperity and continuity of the household (Horie, 1984, pp. 47–8).

This tendency shifted the orientation of the family firm more toward public welfare, which will be discussed later in this chapter as relevant to current corporate responsibility. The *banto*, literally translated as a head clerk, is a senior and capable employee who mostly oversees operation of the business on behalf of top management, also supports the house head in his business decisions, and educates the young head (son of the house head) as well. It is also among their duties to smoothly transfer the corporate culture and value system to the next generation. It is in Mitsui that the *banto* system was most fully developed, but among other large houses the same type of mechanism was employed.

Founded in 1560 as a traditional foundry by Okamoto Taemon, Nabeya has diversified its business to high-technology fields including the production of aircraft components. The firm, together with four affiliated firms, currently has 370 employees and 12 billion yen in annual revenue. The Okamoto family has implemented two systems: to adopt successors from outside of the family almost every other generation, and to entrust the *banto* to oversee the business operations. Tomohiko Okamoto was married to the daughter of the fifteenth Okamoto as his adoptee, and assumed the presidency when he was 28 years old. When joining the firm, he had three suggestions from his father-in-law: do not start an entertainment business; do not get involved in politics, and entrust the business to his *banto*.

The fifteenth head Okamoto let Tomohiko start a new factory with a 4 billion yen investment, even though his failure was foreseen. The fifteenth Okamoto took this as a good opportunity for the young president to learn the mechanism of the *banto* system. The project turned out to be a failure, as anticipated, but Tomohiko recovered from it in ten years, working jointly with his *banto*. Nowadays, the factory produces more than half of the firm's profit (Gifu Shimbun, 2006). Tamio Miyawaki, the former *banto*, remarks that a trustful relationship between the executive and the *banto* is essential for an effective *banto* system. The current *banto* reveals his respect for Tomohiko despite his young age (Hinshitsu hosho kenkyukai, 2008). *Banto* is an institution to facilitate smooth management transfer between generations through supporting and educating the young head.

The *banto* may look similar to a non-family executive in Western family firms. The major difference, however, is the fact that *banto* not only serves as a professional manager on behalf of the family, but also monitors the family head and rectifies his misconduct whenever necessary. Separation of management and ownership functions to pursue the public interest by hampering the family from trying to maximize its short-term financial gain. This serves to get support from the public and, in the long run, to foster the longevity of LLFBs.

Joint ownership

One of the earliest joint ownerships in Japan can be traced back to 1615, when a contract was drawn up between Bungoya Shojiro, the investee, and Shimai Tokuzaemon, the investor, for the amount of 1-kan and 100-me (4.125 kg) silver for a vessel shipment, under the condition that the investee pay back the investor 1-kan and 650-me (6.1875 kg) after the completion of the shipment, while the investee would not be responsible for any shipwreck (Yasuoka, 1998, p. 17).

This is similar to *commenda*, a business organization of medieval Italy, in the sense that it is a limited partnership and the investor is liable only for debts incurred by the firm to the extent of their registered investment and has no management authority. At least 24 contracts of this kind remain in Japan, which are dated up to 1641, which is the time when overseas trade was prohibited by the Tokugawa government.

Ohmi merchants practiced various types of joint ownership. In 1741, an anonymous trade union was organized among 21 Ohmi merchants to transport dry seafood from the Matsumae clan to Nagasaki. The participants shared the profit and loss according to their respective ownership share, and management was solely taken care by one of the investors, Nishikawa Denji (Kanno, 1961, pp. 240–42).

The above-mentioned type of joint ownership was introduced in the earlier Tokugawa Period in order to take advantage of economies of scale by accumulating capital while averting financial risk, just like *commenda* of medieval Italy. Later in Japan, more joint ownerships that continued for a longer period of time were practiced, without splitting the capital. Sometimes, the joint ownership took place among non-kindred, but the majority were among a big house cluster.

The Inanishi Corporation was formed in 1813 as an equal partnership between Inamoto Riemon and Nishimura Jurobei, as the firm name implies (Kanno, 1961 pp. 247–8). The firm remains active in Osaka as a major clothing wholesaler. Several other partnership cases that remained for a limited time were also reported (Yasuoka, 1998, p. 18).

Headquartered in Ohmi, the Nakai family was in a wide variety of trades including finance, *sake* brewing, casting, and vegetable oil production almost nationwide. Each unit of the operation had its own capital under independent management. Some of them took the form of a limited partnership, while others were a limited partnership with investors from outside the family (Egashira, 1965, pp. 37–61).

Among family partnerships, the Mitsui family is the best known and most strict. Mitsui Takatoshi, the founder, left his will 'Soju Isho', to have the inherited property jointly owned by the heirs, and to distribute the business gains to the Mitsui families in proportion as designated (Nakada, 1959, pp. 245–52). This framework of unlimited partnership among Mitsui families was elaborated in the 'Sochiku Isho' of 1722 and further in the Mitsui House Constitution of 1900, which remained Mitsui's business framework until its dissolution in 1945.

Mitsui established an *Omotokata*, or great main headquarters, to regulate the affairs of the group of houses that came to be known later as Mitsui-gumi, which was a joint stock corporation of limited liability. Business assets were concentrated in the *Omotokata* for its control. Dividends were paid in proportion to the ownership share, but splitting the collective assets was prohibited.

While Mitsui is extreme in its restriction of the disposal of property (Yasuoka, 1998, p. 175), other cases of joint ownership are also observed, such as Yasuda, Sumitomo and Iwasaki. The Yasuda family is quite similar to Mitsui, which established Hozensha as a holding company with a family office function. The Hozensha Rules specify that the 500 000 yen of stock owned by Hozensha is bestowed by the ancestors, and that this shall be maintained by the six member houses collectively. The splitting of this is prohibited (Article 43).

Despite the fact that business assets were formally co-owned, in actuality they were collectively owned, since none of the members of the 11 families was allowed to dispose of the co-owned property. Although the Sochiku Isho of 1722 stipulated the allotment rules for business offices and the property in the Mitsui Family Code, the ownership was *de facto* collective because allotment was never pursued. Articles 12 and 13 prescribed the behavior of the family members. The Mitsui family possessed family properties held by 11 families collectively and business assets jointly managed by the these families; Article 92 set the terms for these business assets. As seen above, no member of the Mitsui family was allowed to engage in political or economic activities at their own will to avoid the risk of damaging the prosperity of the business.

Such joint ownership is understood as a type of co-tenancy, which is a concept in property law, particularly derived from the common law of real property. Yasuoka (1981) defines this type of joint ownership either as *Soyu* (*Gesamteigentum*) or a combination of *Soyu* and *Goyu* (*Gesamthandseigentum*) according to the German classification. *Soyu* is the most collective ownership in which individual shares of the ownership are not recognized, while *Goyu* recognizes each individual's share but splitting of the assets is tightly controlled. Such a practice of collective ownership is considered as one of the factors for fostering longevity by preserving the family assets (Yasuoka, 1998, pp. 180–82; Takeda, 1995, pp. 79–84).

Consensus management

As illustrated in the preceding section, the Konoike House Constitution of 1889 clearly prohibits the family head from sole control of the family assets or expenses.

> Every family asset shall be controlled by the senior manager so that the house head is not allowed to handle them alone (Article 12).
>
> Any official expenses of the family shall be consulted with the senior manager, without the approval of which the house head is not allowed to execute (Article 14).

The Sumitomo House Constitution prescribes the house head to consult with the general director and directors beforehand (Article 7), even for private matters occurring within an individual house (Article 11). Honma house's precept specifies that several members, more than ten members in some cases, are involved in the approval of expenditures before getting the final authorization of the house head.

This is a measure to make a decision through consensus management by avoiding authoritative decisions made arbitrarily by the house head in a subjective manner. By limiting the authority of the house head, this practice promotes business orientation more toward the public interest. Consensus management is viewed as a measure to secure the prosperity of the family and its business by avoiding any powerful house head who may make wrong decisions.

Oshikome as a governance system

Oshikome, or forced retirement, is a means to secure the family's continuity, in which the family's stakeholders and *banto* give a strong warning to the house head against his misconduct, and if he does not behave properly, he will be forced into retirement as the last resort, as crisis management to ensure survival of the family and its business.

Jingoro Nishikawa, the eighth generation head of a well-known Ohmi merchant family since 1566, was not interested in the business, wasted the family assets, and ran away from home. His father, who was the top manager and his guardian and adviser, together with the relatives and the branch family members, all expressed their objection to Jingoro. Eventually, 11 years later, he was forced to return the family assets he inherited in 1802 to the rest of the family. The Nishikawa family's House Law established in 1799 clearly prescribes *Oshikome* as a legitimate measure to ensure the prosperity of the family and its business. Many of the Ohmi merchant families prescribed *Oshikome* in their family constitution, which include but are not limited to: the Family of Zensuke Ono documented in 1714 and 1728; Genzaemon Nakai in 1823, and Ginemon Kobayashi between 1848 and 1854 (Suenaga, 2004).

Preventing the misconduct of the house head from bringing the family and its business to ruin, *Oshikome* is considered to be a kind of governance system of both the family and its business.

Social contributions

Numerous family firms were eager to donate schools, hospitals and other facilities to the society for the well-being of the people. To name a few, the Hazama family, the origin of which can be traced back to 1601, started the current brewery business in 1892. In the Meiji Era, the ancestor was instrumental in establishing the Nakatsu School for Women, which is currently named the Nakatsu High School and is run by Gifu Prefecture.

Ryuichiro Hazama, the current president of the Brewery, serves as a councilor on the school council.

Yamasa Soy Sauce, founded in 1645 by Hamaguchi Gihei, contributed to the community in various ways. Hamaguchi Goryo, the seventh head of the house, saved thousands of citizens from the big earthquake and *tsunami* of 1854 by giving alarm in advance, and later by providing residences and fishing equipment for the refugees. Starting in 1855, he invested 352 kg of silver to construct a large bank in four years. In 1858, a training school was built for the young generation to catch up with Western scientific advancement, and this school is currently the Taikyu High School run by Wakayama Prefecture.

In 1927, Kano Jiroemon of the Kikumasamune Brewery, founded in 1659, and Kano Jihei (from a branch of the Kikumasamune's family) of the Hakutsuru Brewery (1743) took the initiative to organize the Nada Scholarship Association in order to establish the Nada Junior High School in Nada district, Hyogo Prefecture. Yamamura Tazaemon of the Sakuramasamune Brewery (1717) also joined. The school has grown to the present Nada Junior and Senior High Schools, both highly acclaimed for their quality of education. Takehito Kano, the eleventh President of Kikumasamune Brewery, serves as the Chairman of the Association. Doi Mitchihiro assumed the presidency as the ninth adopted head who contributed significantly to the modernization of the brewery as well as to the recovery of the Nada district from damage sustained during the Second World War.

Ichirikitei was founded as a traditional restaurant in 1703 by Sugiura Jiroemon. The ninth Sugiura Jiroemon established one of the first elementary schools in Kyoto in 1869 and served as its first principal. The school remains as Yaei Junior High School run by Kyoto Prefecture.

Zohiko is a lacquerware manufacturer founded in 1661 and a pioneer of exporting to Western countries. Nishimura Hikobei, the eighth head, established the School of Lacquer Art in Kyoto to preserve the traditional craftsmanship.

Since Buddhism praises secretive virtues, social contribution can be logically interpreted as a practice of reciprocity and benevolence rather than a display of the donor's loyalty to society. In any event, trustworthiness is expected to be a credential for the continuity of the business operation in the long run.

To conclude this section, the major practices covered broad areas including human resource management, organization, financial management and the governance system. These practices, together with the *ie*-institutional *dozokudan* network and the value system as codified in the family precept, were instrumental in fostering the longevity of the long-lived family and its business in an integrated manner. Most importantly, it was the effort of LLFBs' self-discipline and pursuit of righteous business that prompted them to emphasize business for the public welfare and not for their private desire. As a consequence, the requisite conditions for longevity were met, which includes but is not limited to an obligation to the stakeholders, business first and family second, family unity, coherent family vision, commitment to continue the legacy, planning and commitment.

Interactions between the Network and the Value Block

In conclusion, this section analyzes the interactions between the network and the value block of social capital. The author proposes that the network and the value of the OSC interact bidirectionally (see Figure 24.4).

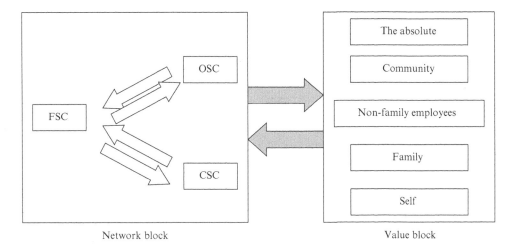

Figure 24.4   Bidirectional interaction of the network and the value block

Orientation toward the public welfare is scaled in accordance with the distance from self-interest. In other words, starting with self-interest at the bottom, the degree of publicness expands as it goes to the family, employee, the community, and finally to the absolute at the top. The higher the LLFBs aspire, the larger the group of stakeholders with which they will likely establish good will and trust. The lower down LLFBs serve, the deeper LLFBs are likely to develop OSC with the same category of the stakeholder. Hence, it is proposed:

Proposition 6a   The level of the value influences the development of the OSC.

Proposition 6b   Correlation between the value and the OSC development is higher in the long-lived family firm than in other family firms.

Through such a series of interactions with relative stakeholders, OSC is developed as proposed by Arrègle et al. (2007). According to Nahapiet and Ghoshal (1998), four dynamic factors influence the development of OSC: stability, interaction, interdependence and closure. The magnitude of the influence may vary among the stakeholders depending upon their degree of contact with the family firm, as well as their relationship, but it is highly likely that LLFBs are in a better position in the development of OSC than other family firms because of the long-time relationship during which stability, an interactive relationship, interdependence and closure have been fostered. Hence it is proposed:

Proposition 7   In the LLFBs, FSC influences the development of OSC more effectively than in other types of family firms.

To conclude the discussion, the longevity of LLFBs has been attributable to the effective management of various social capitals both in the value system and the network for centuries, and without this they could not have survived until today. The network is characterized by intimacy, versatility and interactivity to substantiate cohesion among the relative members. Most importantly, the promotion of the public welfare by LLFBs as the core value is essential to substantiate cohesiveness.

IMPLICATIONS

Focusing on the longevity of Japanese LLFBs from the social capital perspective, this research presents both theoretical and practical implications. Theoretically, the research presents six sets of propositions which might be tested through future studies, addressing the factors influencing the family firm's longevity and internal structure of social capital. This research is expected to spur additional theoretical as well as empirical studies in the following three respects. First, the research sheds light on the social capital aspects of long-term survival and sustainability, especially the continuity of century-old family ownership. Research has recently started on the cohesiveness of family firms (Pieper and Astrachan, 2008), a synthesis between family and business values (Pieper, 2007). *Ie* institution, successor adoption and *noren-wake* among others may appear to be specific to the historical and social context of Japan, but the author views this as universally valid in this chapter's findings, at least to some degree. An adopted successor may be analogous to a non-family executive, for example.

Second, the research addresses the internal structure and interaction within a given social capital. The internal structure of the network and value block, and interactions of the two blocks, have seldom been highlighted in the literature. Within the network block, the relationships among FSC, OSC and CSC are presented in an integrated manner. A bidirectional influence among the three social capitals is proposed. Within the value block, the hierarchical structure is addressed. These propositions, together with the last one regarding the interaction of the network and values, are expected to be discussed not only in the family firm research field but also more broadly.

Third, the findings of this research are expected to have implications for the discussion of the Japanese management model. The uniqueness of the Japanese management model was addressed first by Abegglen (1958), and Theory Z (Ouchi, 1981) focused on its commonality. Despite a history of more than half a century for this discussion, the most fundamental philosophical aspect has not been fully addressed. The author assumes the pursuit of public welfare as addressed by this research is central to the Japanese management model, which is characterized by long-term relationships among the stakeholders, consensus management and other factors.

As for the practical implications, the major implications reside in the value factor or the business ethics originally advocated by Ishida Baigan and practiced by merchants in the past, since this is considered as the origin of the concept of the 'corporation as a social public organ', which is popular in Japan among the business society and relevant to the present CSR (corporate social responsibility).

This approach of viewing a corporation as a public organ and not a private one has been emphasized by many philosophers and executives in Japan up to today. The contributions of Ninomiya Sontoku, Mishima Chushu, Shibusawa Eiichi and Matsusita Konosuke are relevant in this respect.

First, Ninomiya Sontoku (1787–1856), was a prominent nineteenth-century Japanese agricultural leader, philosopher, moralist and economist. Combining Buddhism, Shintō and Confucianism, he transformed them into practical ethical principles that matured out of his experiences as so-called *Ho-toku* (virtue and reward). He often had *Shingaku* scholars give lectures before his own preaching.

Second, Mishima Chushu (1830–1919) was a scholar of Japanese philosophy. Supporting his teacher, Yamada Hokoku, at the end of Tokugawa Period, he was instrumental in the reform of the Matsuyama clan. Mishima advocated '*Gi-Ri goitsu-setsu*', or a parallel quest of economic activities and ethical conduct.

Third, Shibusawa Eiichi (1840–1931) was a leading figure in the development of Japan's modern society. He was involved in the founding of more than 500 enterprises and economic organizations and another 600 non-profit organizations for social welfare, education and international exchange. As probably the most famous advocator of Neo-Confucianism of his era, he published *Rongo to Soroban* (*Analects of Confucius and the Abacus*), by adopting the *Analects* as standards of moral education.

His theory was called '*Keizai Dotoku Goitsu-setsu*' ('Harmony of morality and the economy'), which was an extension of the theory of his teacher, Mishima. Stimulating discussion about moral capitalism, he not only advocated the importance of honest profit, but also actually practiced it. His words and practices clearly show that he was conscious of social welfare and corporate social responsibility in the early twentieth century (Tsuchiya, 1964, p. 31).

Shibusawa argued that the traditional Japanese scorn for profit-making was based on an erroneous interpretation of the Confucian *Analects* because humanity has been prone to seek gain.

Fourth, Konosuke Matsushita (1894–1989) was the founder of Panasonic, a Japanese electronics giant which used to be called Matsushita Electric. For many in Japan as well as overseas, he is known as 'the god of management'. He is one of the pioneers who emphasized the concept of 'corporation as a social public organ' in a clear-cut manner.

The following is excerpted from Panasonic's official homepage:[16]

> The founder, Konosuke Matsushita, said 'since all those things necessary to a company – people, money, land, and goods – come from society, then the company itself is something entrusted to us by society, and is actually of the society, and is thus a public entity'. He also stated that 'as a public entity of society, companies should contribute to society through business activities in a variety of forms, and thus it is the company's social responsibility to improve the quality of life of society.'
>
> It was back in 1946 that he first described the company as a 'public entity.' It was the first post-war meeting amongst the people in charges of Panasonic's sales offices. In a time when most major cities in Japan had been burnt to the ground, he was talking about the company's mission and philosophy that seems to reflect the concept of corporate social responsibility (CSR) as we have come to know it.

The basic management objective set forth by Konosuke Matsushita in March 1929 states that it is the responsibility of industrialists to contribute to the progress and development of the society and the well-being of the people through their business activities, thereby enhancing the quality of life throughout the world. The idea that industrialists should contribute through their business activities meant that they should take compliance seriously and carry out their corporate activities diligently in their role as a public entity of the society.

Therefore corporations should prosper not alone, but together with the society. A corporation cannot prosper alone for long, even if it can do so for short period. This is a rule of nature and society. Peaceful coexistence and mutual prosperity is the proper form of nature and human society.

Matsushita believed that enterprises did not belong to any individuals, instead, a corporation is a 'public entity' and it can exist only if it receives support from society and therefore must contribute to society.

Nowadays, 'corporation as a public organ' remains as a major management concept in Japan and this is viewed as a Japanese model of corporate social responsibility. As explained, its origin can be traced back to *Shingaku* and its advocate, Ishida Baigan, who amalgamated three Asian philosophies in the early eighteenth century, even though the actual influence of *Shingaku* upon Matsushita's philosophy is not clearly identified. They, however, share a strong belief that merchant activity is for the sake of the public welfare and that their wealth should be devoted to this endeavor. Since the public interest is synonymous with the public good, he is considered to be keen on the importance of social responsibility (Tsuchiya, 1974, p. 172).

In English, 'going public' means listing a company on a stock market so that its stocks can be available to the public. This is related to a popular question of who owns a company. A more essential question to ask, however, should be whom a company serves. Baigan's *Shingaku* gives a clear-cut answer by emphasizing a righteous business for the public welfare taking precedence over private desire. A corporation, legally owned by the stockholders, should strive not only for the benefit of the stakeholders but also, and more importantly, for the general public and society. This is the best solution in the long run not only for the general public but also for the stockholders, including the founding family, by achieving longevity. The concept of 'corporation as a social public organ', which originated centuries ago, and remains popular in Japan, gives an important clue to address this issue in regard to both family firms as well as other types of firms worldwide.

CONCLUSION

This chapter offers three contributions to enrich the research of family businesses especially in regard to their longevity. First, this chapter identifies 262 family precepts and constitutions of long-lived family firms in Japan for analysis, which surpasses any preceding research in scope. Second, it presents three major factors for the longevity of family firms in operation for centuries, including the strong commitment to perpetual growth, business ethics and the *ie* institution as codified in the precept. These unique factors are analyzed from the social capital perspective both from the network and the value viewpoint. The quest for the public welfare is emphasized as important to achieve longevity.

The chapter proposes several theoretical implications addressing the family firm's longevity, social capital theory and Japanese management model. Practical implications are presented in regard to family firms and non-family firms worldwide in relation to the origin of the concept of 'the corporation as a social public organ' as a Japanese model of corporate social responsibility.

This chapter has several limitations, which include generalizability and single-country setting. The empirical research is preliminary. Further study, therefore, is required to cover quantitative analysis of the precepts and constitutions, and international comparative study in the East Asian region.

NOTES

1. The IMD-LODH Family Business Award sets seven criteria for qualification, which includes having survived at least three generations and achieved a solid long-term record of financial performance and stability, among others.
2. The figure was updated to 3792 as of this writing.
3. The Mogi family was one of the founding families of the present Kikkoman Corporation.
4. 'Yasuda-hozenshato sono kankei jigyo-shi' henshu-iinkai (1974, pp. 114–20).
5. Yasuoka (1998, pp. 98–104).
6. Mageo, Koyama and Hayashi are from Iwasaki (1908).
7. LLFF Database3.
8. Sources: Kitahara (1921) for Uematsu (p. 568) and Yamada (p. 570). All the rest are from Iwasaki (1908) and the page of the text is shown in parentheses.
9. Such members of a 'house' were relatives of a current or former head of the 'house' and relatives who entered a 'house' with its head's consent, such as adopted children or daughters-in-law (Article 732).
10. Relatives were defined, after various alterations, as blood-relatives within the sixth degree of relationship, husband and wife, and relatives by affinity within the third degree of relationship (Article 725).
11. The Civil Code stipulated that a wife enters the *ie* of a husband by marriage (Article 788-1) and bears the husband's family name (Article 746). Marriage in the Meiji Era literally meant a union of two families, or, more precisely, absorption of a wife by a husband's family. Women were viewed as a means to bring offspring to the *ie*.
12. Succession of family property refers to all the rights and obligations of a household head, including inheritance money, the family name, ancestral-worship objects and obligations and so on.
13. For example, the northern part of Japan, namely Iwate, Miyagi and Akita prefectures, observed inheritance by the eldest son or daughter of the parent's wealth. In Kyūshū and some other areas of Japan, property was traditionally apportioned by a modified version of ultimogeniture known as *masshi souzoku*. An estate was distributed equally among all sons, except that the youngest son received a double share as a reward for caring for the elderly parents in their last years.
14. In ancient Japan, the adoption system can be traced as far back as in the Yōrō Code of the early eighth century, but the legal adoption of the successors into a family became popular after the establishment of the shogunate government in 1192. In the feudal society of Japan, which was governed by the shogunate until 1867, reigns of the family and estate ownership were considered almost equivalent and, as a result, adoption became popular as a family succession practice.
15. *Ko* and *ren* literally mean organization and association respectively.
16. http://ex-blog.panasonic.co.jp/exhibition/en/2008/12/eco08_040.html.

REFERENCES

Abegglen, J. (1958), *The Japanese Factory: Aspects of its Social Organization*, New York: Free Press.
Adachi, M. (1970), 'Long-lived firms and their tradition', in *Long-lived Firms and Their Family Precepts*, Kyoto-Fu (in Japanese).
Applegate, J. (1994), 'Keep your firm in the family', *Money*, **23**, 1301–28.
Arrègle, J., Hitt, M., Sirmon, D. and Very, P. (2007), 'The development of organizational social capital: attributes of family firms', *Journal of Management Studies*, **44**(1), 73–95.
Astrachan, J. and Pieper, T. (2010), 'Welcome from the Editor', *Journal of Family Business Strategy*, available online at http://www.elsevierscitech.com/lm file/other format/main.pdf.

Barney, J. (1986), 'Organizational culture: can it be a source of sustained competitive advantage?', *Academy of Management Review*,. **11**(3), 656–65.

Beckhard, R. and Dyer, G. (1983), 'Managing continuity in the family-owned business', *Organizational Dynamics*, **12**(1), 5–12.

Bellah, R. (1957), *Tokugawa Religion: The Values of Pre-Industrial Japan*, Glencoe, IL: The Free Press.

Bokutei, I. (1902), *Family constitutions of millionaires of current Japan*. Daigakukan.

Bourdieu, P. (1983), 'The forms of capital', in J. Richardson (ed.), *Handbook of Theory and Research for the Sociology of Education*, Westport, CT: Greenwood Press, pp. 241–58.

Bubolz, M. (2001), 'Family as source, user, and builder of social capital', *The Journal of Socio-economics*, **30**, 129–31.

Danes, S., Stafford, K., Haynes, G. and Amarapurkar, S. (2009), 'Family capital of family firms: bridging human, social, and financial capital', *Family Business Review*, **22**, 199–215.

Egashira, T. (1965), *Ōmi shōnin Nakai-ke no kenkyū (Study of Nakai Family, an Ōmi Merchant)*, Yūzankaku (in Japanese).

Finkelstein, S. and Hambrick, D. (1996), *Strategic Leadership: Top Executives and their Effects on Organizations*, Minneapolis/St Paul, MN: West Publishing Company.

Fruin, M. (1983), *Kikkoman Company, Clan and Community*, Cambridge, MA: Harvard University Press.

Gaens, B. (2000), 'Family, enterprise, and corporation: the organization of Izumiya-Sumitomo in the Tokugawa Period', *Japan Review*, **12**, 205–30.

Gifu Shimbun (2006), 'Gifu heisei jinkokuki Dai-go-bu Atotsugi-no-sugao', *Gifu Shimbun*, 16 July.

Goto, T. (2005), 'Perspectives and issues of current family business', *Bulletin of Shizuoka Sangyo University*, **7**, 225–337 (in Japanese).

Goto, T. (2006), 'Longevity of Japanese family firms', in P. Poutziouris, K. Smyrnios and S. Klein (eds), *Handbook of Research on Family Business*, Cheltenham, UK and Northampton MA, USA: Edward Elgar, pp. 517–34.

Goto, T. (2009), 'How can long-lived family firms enhance entrepreneurship in Japan? Implications of adoption of successors into a family', in P. Poutziouris and E. Hadjilias (eds), *Book of Proceedings: Global Perspective on Family Business Developments: Theory–Practice–Policy*, Cyprus International Institute of Management, pp. 40–41.

Granovetter, M.S. (1973), 'The strength of weak ties', *American Journal of Sociology*, **78**(6), 1360–80.

Hambrick, D. and Finkelstein, S. (1987), 'Managerial discretion: a bridge between polar views of organisational outcomes', *Research in Organisational Behaviour*, **9**, 369–406.

Hannan, M. and Freeman, J. (1984), 'Structural inertia and organizational change', *American Sociological Review*, **49**(2), 149–64.

Hatakeyama, H. (1988), *Research on the History of Sumitomo Zaibatsu Establishment*, Dobunkan shuppan.

Hinshitsu hosho kenkyukai (2008), 'Dai-31-kai Kengakukai hokoku', 62, *QASG News*.

Hirschmeier, J. and Yui, T. (1975), *The Development of Japanese Business, 1600–1973*, Cambridge, MA: Harvard University Press (2nd edn 1981).

Horide, I. (2000), 'The House of Mitsui: secrets of its longevity', *Journal of Marketing Theory and Practice*, **8**(2), 31–6.

Horide, I. (2009), *The Ethics of Buddhism and the Ethos of the Japanese Management: The Spirit of Ji-Hi* (available online 16 March 2010) http://papers.ssrn.com/sol3/papers.cfm?abstract_id=1423823.

Horie, Y. (1984), *Nihon keieishi ni okeru 'ie' no kenkyu (Study of ie in Japanese Management History)*. Rinsen Shoten (in Japanese).

Irie, H. (1968), 'Kinsei Shouka Kaho-ni-okeru Tokumoku-no Kozo – "Kagyo" keieitai-no Kachi-taikei-to Ningen-kankei', *Jinmon Ronkyu*. 28. Hokkaido University of Education (in Japanese).

Iwasaki, S. (1908), *Family Constitution of Millionaires of Current Japan*, Hakugakukan.

Iwasaki, S. (2003), *Family Tree of Noodle Restaurants*, Kobunsha.

Jacobs, J. (1965), *The Death and Life of Great American Cities*, New York: Penguin Books.

Kanno, W. (1941), *Ōmi shōnin no kenkyū (Study of Ōmi Merchants)*, Yūhikaku (in Japanese).

Karofsky, P. (2003) 'Interview with Dr. William O'Hara', *Family Business Review*, **16**(3), 221–3.

Kitahara, T. (1921), *Family Constitution*, Kaken Seiteikai.

Lansberg, I. (1983), 'Managing human resources in family firms: the problem of institutional overlap', *Organizational Dynamics*, **12**(1), 39–46.

Leana, C. and Van Buren, H. (1999), 'Organizational social capital and employment practices', *The Academy of Management Review*, **24**(3), 538–55.

Lester, R. and Cannella, A. (2006), 'Interorganizational familiness: how family firms use interlocking directorates to build community-level social capital', *Entrepreneurship Theory and Practice*, **30**: 755–75.

Levie, J. and Lerner, M. (2009), 'Resource mobilization and Performance in Family and nonfamily businesses in the United Kingdom', *Family Business Review*, **22**, 25–38.

Mehrotra, V., Morck, R., Shim, J. and Wiwattanakantang, Y. (2008), 'Adoptive expectations: rising son tournaments in Japanese family firms' (available online: 2009 16 March) http://www.isb.edu/Faculty/upload/Doc1322008419.pdf.

Miller, D. (1993), 'The architecture of simplicity', *The Academy of Management Review*, **18**(1), 116–38.

Miller, D. and Le Breton-Miller, I. (2006), 'Family governance and firm performance: agency, stewardship, and capabilities', *Family Business Review*, **19**(1) 73–87.

Mito, T. (1991), *Ie no ronri* (*The Theory of ie*), Bunshindo (in Japanese).

Mitsui Bunko (1974), *History of Mitsui Businesses, Appendix 3*, Mitsui Bunko.

Nahapiet, J. and Ghoshal, S. (1998), 'Social capital, intellectual capital, and the organizational advantage', *The Academy of Management Review*, **23**(2), 242–66.

Nakada, Y. (1959), *Mitsui Takatoshi*, Yoshikawa Kobunkan.

Nakamura, H. (1965), *Critical Spirit of Modern Japan* (reprinted as Nakamura Hajime Senshu ketteiban (1998), Shunju-sha.

Nakane, C. (1967), Tate-shakai no ningen kankei. Kodansha.

Neubauer, F. and Lank, A. (1998), *The Family Business: Its Governance for Sustainability*, New York: Routledge.

O'Hara, W.T. (2004), *Centuries of Success*, Avon. MA: Adams Media.

Ouchi, W. (1981), *Theory Z: How American Business can Meet the Japanese Challenge*, New York: Avon.

Pieper, T. (2007), *Mechanisms to Assure Long-term Family Business Survival: A Study of the Dynamics of Cohesion in Multigenerational Family Business Families* New York: Peter Lang.

Pieper, T. and Astrachan, J. (2008), *Mechanisms to Assure Family Business Cohesion: Guidelines for Family Business Leaders and their Families*, Cox Family Enterprise Center Coles College of Business, Kennesaw State University.

Priem, R. (1990), 'Top management team group factors, and firm performance', *Strategic Management Journal*, **11**, 469–78.

Putnam, R. (1993), *Making Democracy Work: Civic Traditions in Modern Italy*, Princeton, NJ: Princeton University Press.

Roberts, J. (1973), *Mitsui: Three Centuries of Japanese Business*, New York and Tokyo: Weatherhill.

Schwass, J. (2006), *Wise Growth Strategies in Leading Family Businesses*, New York: Palgrave Macmillan.

Shibusawa, E. (1927), *Analects of Confucius and the Abacus.* Reprinted 2008, Kadokawa Gakugei Shuppan.

Simon, H. (1996), *Hidden Champions: Lessons from 500 of the World's Best Unknown Companies*, Boston, MA: Harvard Business School Press.

Sorenson, R. and Bierman, L. (2009), 'Family capital, family business, and free enterprise', *Family Business Review*, **22**(3), 193–5.

Suenaga, K. (2004), *Ohmi-shonin-gaku nyumon: CSR no genryu: Sanpo-yoshi* (*Introduction to Ohmi Merchant Study: The Origin of CSR: Three-way Satisfaction*), Sun-rise Shuppan (in Japanese).

Takeda, H. (1995), *Zaibatsu no jidai.* Sin'yo-sha.

Takenaka, Y. (1977), Nihonteki keiei no genry: shingaku no keieirinen wo megutte. Minerva shobo.

Teece, D., Pisano, G. and Shuen, A. (1997), 'Dynamic capabilities and strategic management', *Strategic Management Journal*, **18**(7), 509–33.

Tsuchiya, T. (1964), *History of Business Philosophy*, Nihon keizai Shinbunsha (in Japanese).

Tsuchiya, T. (1964), *Nihon keiei rinenshi; Nihon keiei tetsugaku kakuritsu no tame ni* (*History of Japanese Management Philosophy*), Nihon Keizai, Shimbun (in Japanese).

Tsuchiya, T (2002), *Nihon Keiei Rinen Shi* (*The History of Japanese Philosophy of Management*), Reitaku Daigaku. Shuppan Kai (in Japanese).

Uzzi, B. (1996), 'The sources and consequences of embeddedness for the economic performance of organizations: the network effect', *American Sociological Review*, **61**(4), 674–98.

Ward, J. (2004), *Perpetuating the Family Business: 50 Lessons Learned from Long-Lasting, Successful Families in Business*, Basingstoke: Palgrave Macmillan.

'Yasuda-hozenshato sono kankei jigyo-shi' henshu-iinkai (1974), *History of Yasuda-hozensha and its businesses*, Yasuda Real Estate (in Japanese).

Yasuoka, S. (1981), *Dozoku-kigyo ni okeru shoyu to keiei* (*Ownership and Management of Family Business*), Kokuren Daigak (in Japanese).

Yasuoka, S. (1991), *Ownership and Management of Family Firms.* Kokusai Rengo Daigaku.

Yasuoka, S. (1998), *Research on zaibatsu establishment*, Minerva Shobo (available online), http://d-arch.ide.go.jp/je_archive/english/society/wp_unu_jpn57.html (in Japanese).

APPENDIX: MITSUI CONSTITUTION OF 1722 (EXCERPT)

1. This Family Constitution being based on the written testament of the founder (Hachirobe) must be observed by all descendants.
2. Always bearing in mind the many benefits received from the ancestors, everyone must work diligently for the greater prosperity of the House.
3. The laws of the Shogunates must be carried out to the letter by the family members.
4. They should respect those in authority and show kindness to subordinates.
5. Be diligent and watchful, or your business will be taken away by pursuing trivial ones close at hand. One must be painstaking. Farsightedness is essential to the career of a merchant. In pursuing small interests close at hand, one may lose huge profits in the long run.
6. Employee selection and training must be given the greatest care. Special emphasis is to be put on the selection and treatment of the chief clerks, whose designated role is to guard the business of the House, give appropriate advice when necessary, and correct blunders made by their masters.
8. The head of the senior main family, Hachiroemon, shall be regarded as head of the House and obeyed as if he were a parent.
11. When there is no competent heir to succeed Hachiroemon, a son may be adopted from among other members of the House, or a female may succeed as head.
12. The shares of house assets shall be allotted to member families as specified, but 10 of the 220 shares shall be set aside for deserving offspring other than the heirs. Daughters of the families are to be married to sons of Mitsui clan members whenever possible, but are to be given suitable dowries otherwise.
26. Second and younger sons shall be allowed to establish families at about thirty years of age, if they are considered sufficiently capable; in such cases they may use the business name Echigoya, but not the surname Mitsui without special permission. It will not be necessary to establish any more branch or associate families.
36. Three capable older members are to be appointed as chief directors of the House to oversee all the branch shops. Monthly meetings with the managers of all shops are to be held for discussion of important business.
40. New types of enterprises must not be started, even if others should do so, notably, money lending to daimyo (lords) and other speculative investments should be avoided.
41. Boys of the families are to be apprenticed at the age of twelve or thirteen, serving at Kyoto, Edo, and Osaka to learn the rudiments of the business until the age of twenty-five. By the age of thirty, they are expected to be capable of managing a shop.
42. House members are not encouraged to enter government service because it might cause them to neglect family affairs.
47. Revere Buddha and the Gods, do some studies in Confucianism, but within limits. Instead of wasting gold and silver on temples and shrines, you should make appropriate contributions to the poor and suffering, and you will be rewarded ten-thousandfold.

48.   The number of hired managers was to be limited to six or seven – three from Kyoto, two from Edo, and one (or perhaps two) from Osaka– presumably to prevent any local clique from gaining too much influence.

25 The push–pull of Indigenous Sámi family reindeer herding enterprises: a metaphor for sustainable entrepreneurship

Léo-Paul Dana and Kosmas X. Smyrnios

INDIGENOUS PEOPLE AND REINDEER HERDING

In Norway, the Sámi[1] comprise 96 per cent of the population of Guovdageaidnu[2]/ Kautokeino, 94 per cent of Kárášjohka/Karasjok, 75 per cent of Unjárga/Nesseby, and 53 per cent of Deatnu/Tana. A Salish chief referred to Indigenous peoples as the Fourth World (Manuel and Posluns, 1974). According to Paine (1984), Fourth World refers to '(a) ethnicity within a minority context, but (b) a minority context different from that of immigrant groups' (p. 213). Paine (1985) emphasized that these peoples were once free, but disqualified by foreign forces of nationalism.

Although reindeer (Rangifer tarandus[3]) herding has traditionally been central to the entrepreneurship sector of Norway's Indigenous people, recent changes have transformed this occupation. In former times, a herder had approximately 250 reindeer. A greater number of animals meant more wealth and power. The reindeer were useful throughout their lives, and when harvested every part was used; there was no waste. Technological changes transformed this sector; the snowmobile and the helicopter facilitated herding, and in theory it became easier to manage more animals than ever before, but this gave rise to a cash society. Increasing state intervention has been complicating matters, applying food industry norms to the handling of animals and their meat. Mainstream business strategy attempts to view herding as an industry. This sector, however, is more successful when animals are not managed in farms, but when man follows the herd in a natural setting. According to the Norwegian Reindeer Husbandry Administration, about 3000 Sámi in Norway own almost 200 000 reindeer. For these people, the reindeer remains a traditional symbol. Given the nature of reindeer herding, cooperation has been and continues to be essential; this form of self-employment is thus community-based, and an expression of traditional local culture. This picture corresponds to what Peterson (1988) described as the Communitarianism Prototype: 'The community is more than the sum of the individuals in it . . . The relatedness of all things is recognized' (p. 2).

As the trend toward modernization increases the need for cash, cultural traditions risk being replaced by money-driven enterprises. This chapter reveals findings indicating that while reindeer herders are attracted or pulled to this traditional form of self-employment, many are forced or pushed into secondary enterprises. Where the Indigenous population's traditions and forms of production meet the institutions of the market economy, conflicts are on the rise. Examining Sámi entrepreneurship in Norway, this chapter shows that entrepreneurship means different things to people from unlike cultures. Although 'entrepreneurship scholars have generally focused on either individual entrepreneurial behavior or the activity of entrepreneurial (new) firms' (Reynolds, 1991, p. 48), there has been increasing interest in comparing entrepreneurs from different cultures. As Dybbroe (1999, p. 19) articulated, 'Culture is typically in focus where we find cultural differences politicized.'

Scheinberg and Macmillan (1988) found significant differences across cultures in motivations to launch new businesses. A problem identified by Davidson and Delmar (1992) is that most studies have concentrated on entrepreneurs, ignoring the general population from which these entrepreneurs emerged. A comparative study relevant to Indigenous and non-Indigenous entrepreneurs revealed that perceptions of opportunity are a function of culture (Dana, 1995). Findings showed that people from different ethnic backgrounds had been exposed to dissimilar cultural values, as reflected in their respective entrepreneurship models. Accordingly, entrepreneurship is *not* homogeneous around the world. Indigenous entrepreneurship does not necessarily fit into a box created by the industrialized West. Yet mainstream systems often pressure minorities to conform to models that ignore cultural variables. Hindle and Lansdowne (2005, p. 79) stated:

> Indigenous entrepreneurship is the creation, management and development of new ventures by Indigenous people for the benefit of Indigenous people. The organizations thus created can pertain to the private, public or the non-profit sectors. The desired and achieved benefits of venturing can range from the narrow view of economic profit for a single individual to the broad view of multiple, social and economic advantages for entire communities. Outcomes and entitlements derived from Indigenous entrepreneurship may extend to enterprise partners and stakeholders who may be non-Indigenous.

THE SÁMI

Until the late twentieth century, the Sámi people were commonly referred to as Lapps; the term Lapp is no longer in use, as it showed a lack of respect. Whitaker (1955) noted, 'a Lapp was defined as a person of Lappish origin whose father or mother, or one of their parents, was a full-time reindeer breeder' (p. 25). The Sámi people are the Indigenous nation of Sápmi (formerly known as Lapland), covering northern Finland, Norway and Sweden, and Russia's Kola Peninsula. Clarke (1824b) reported, 'Perhaps their cunning may be principally due to the necessity they are under constantly upon their guard, lest they be maltreated; the people considering them as an inferior order of beings in the creation, and thinking it lawful to make them the objects of contempt and ridicule, using their very name, *Lapp*, as a term of degradation' (p. 169).

Müller-Wille (2001) explained, 'Originally, the various Sámi populations, living by hunting, fishing, gathering and herding in maritime and terrestrial ecosystems, obtained their food with high protein and fat contents from edible mammals' (p. 91). In time, these people evolved from being a food-extracting society to a food-producing society. There is debate, however, as to when this happened. Storli (1993) suggested 'that reindeer pastoralism was well established by A.D. 900' (p. 1).

As of the 1950s, the Sámi people became increasingly dependent on imported fuel, and the introduction of snowmobiles into reindeer herding in 1962 exacerbated the situation (Müller-Wille and Pelto, 1971; Pelto, 1973). Pelto and Müller-Wille (1972/3) explained that cash became increasingly important: 'Before 1963, the costs for equipment to work in reindeer herding were essentially zero ... Full participation in mechanized reindeer herding, on the other hand, means cash outlays for the snowmobile' (p. 136). As noted by Turi (2000), 'The importance of reindeer breeding in the Arctic areas cannot be over-stated' (p. 131). Today, there are over 80 000 Sámi people, of whom more than half reside in Norway (Sara, 2000). The Sámi people are not homogeneous.

Central to Sámi life is the reindeer, and the language reflects this. Whitaker (1955) explained the importance of reindeer from a perspective of traditional culture: 'Marriage is not undertaken until it is deemed that one has sufficient property in the form of reindeer with which to support a family. This is usually set at about 200 the combined herd of husband and wife' (p. 40). Given the centrality of reindeer to Sámi life, Collinder (1949) asserted the existence of thousands of words describing reindeer herding.

The traditional Sámi way of life stresses the need to live in harmony with nature, refraining from leaving physical marks on the land. In the words of Lehtola (2002, p. 88),

> Nature has provided the sources for both their material and spiritual culture. This base sets Sámi culture apart from industrial or agricultural civilizations ... A common thread for all Sámi groups is the adaptation of their way of life to the yearly cycle of nature and to the specific local natural environment ... Because their way of life is based on respect for Nature, Sámi have been very frugal in their use of natural resources ... Sámi religious belief reflected this close link with nature. According to the traditional Sámi beliefs, the world was inhabited by spirits. Human beings could only successfully make their living by cooperating ... It was essential not to damage nature.

As the Sámi people did not mark the territories upon which they lived, government authorities acted as if these lands were unclaimed. Non-Indigenous farmers took possession of land traditionally used by the Sámi people, reducing the area available for reindeer.

For self-employed Sámi reindeer herders, life traditionally revolved around reindeer, while the extended families were the work units; there were long discussions during which parents transmitted expertise to their children. This form of production involved sharing and specializing, but without markets and without right of ownership defined by modern Western society. A single individual did not need to know everything, since it was group knowledge that was important, as discussed by Freeman (1985). Nevertheless, decisions were often made by individuals on behalf of others. When people had plenty (e.g., more food than they could consume before it lost its freshness), a common practice was to share, without accepting monetary compensation.

THEORETICAL FRAMEWORK AND CONCEPTUALIZATION

It is important to understand the context of Sámi family business enterprises, and the epistemology that surrounds these people. When René Descartes proclaimed, 'I think, therefore I am', he articulated a premise central to European and Euro-American episte-mology: the individual mind is the source of existence and knowledge; for other people, the individual's existence is contingent upon relationships[4] with others (Ladson-Billings, 2003). Likewise, the sense of identity and of land ownership reveals much about internal logic. An American says, 'I am American', and Europeans say that they 'are' European;

a Sámi person typically says, 'I belong to the Sámi people'. While a Norwegian might say, 'I own this land', a Sámi living in Norway is likely to say, in the plural, 'My people belong to Lapland'. So, too, self-employed reindeer herders refer to their entrepreneurship as community-based. A harsh climate contributes to uncertainty, and the Sámi people have learned to tolerate risk, mastering the art of herding, largely by following cues from the animals, rather than by taking dominion over them. Collinder (1949) elaborated: 'The life of the reindeer nomads is regulated by the migrations of their reindeer' (p. 105). Yet Sámi people generally do not like risks. As the domain of the lynx has spread north, reindeer husbandry entails an increase in risks, and Sámi herdsmen therefore diversify in secondary enterprises to reduce risks.

Indigenous Family Business Entrepreneurship

A decade has past since Helander (1999) argued, 'the time is ripe for a new paradigm when looking at the issues of Indigenous people' (pp. 26–7). However, as suggested by Anderson and Giberson (2003), it is a challenge to find a theoretical approach that is appropriate in the context of Aboriginal[5] people.

According to Lindsay (2005), indigenous entrepreneurship is more holistic than mainstream entrepreneurship theories as it focuses on both economic and non-economic goals to incorporate dimensions of cultural values. Such non-economic goals pertain to the pursuit of social/cultural self-determination (Anderson et al., 2006) and the preservation of heritage (Hindle and Lansdowne, 2005). Moreover, indigenous entrepreneurship differs conceptually (Peredo and Anderson, 2006, p. 260) from other forms of entrepreneurship in terms of the context of the entrepreneurship, the types of goals and outcomes towards which indigenous entrepreneurship is focused, and/or the form and organization of the enterprise (Cahn, 2008, p. 1). When comparing case studies across cultures, Morris (2004) noted that indigenous entrepreneurship takes similar forms across cultures, observing that in the two cases, neither of the two samples placed much emphasis on wealth generation (p. 2). In light of these claims, mainstream entrepreneurship theory needs must accommodate idiosyncrasies associated with indigenous entrepreneurship (Lindsay, 2005). Table 25.1 compares key elements across entrepreneurship and indigenous entrepreneurship literature.

Table 25.1   Comparing the conceptualizations, goals and value creation across entrepreneurship and indigenous entrepreneurship literature

Element	Entrepreneurship	Indigenous entrepreneurship
Conceptualization	• Focused	• Holistic
Goals	• Economic	• Economic and non-economic
	• Growth-oriented	• Non-growth-oriented
	• Autonomous	• Community-based
Value creation	• Value for customers	• Community survival
	• Value for shareholders	• Environmental sustainability
	• Firm growth	• Preservation of heritage
	• Financial gain and wealth creation	• Social/cultural self-determination

Recently, Peredo and Anderson (2006) emphasized that cultural adaptation is needed to foster indigenous entrepreneurship. Over ten years earlier, Anderson (1995) noted that success of indigenous entrepreneurship is contingent upon ethnic minority groups' abilities to accommodate for changes in the global economy. Anderson (1995) concluded that Canadian indigenous groups acknowledged the necessity of participating in the global economy and creating modes of development, such as partnerships and alliances with other indigenous and non-indigenous businesses that are in line with their goals and cultural values.

In light of this discussion, the present study holds that contingency theory (Lawrence and Lorsch, 1967; Burns and Stalker, 1961) has an important role to play in the development of indigenous entrepreneurship theories. The general model implicit in contingency theory assumes that, for organizations to be effective, there must be an appropriate fit between structure (Fincham and Rhodes, 2005) and/or strategy (Lee and Miller, 1996) and environmental context. That is, the appropriate management style and organizational structure depend on the environmental context of the organization concerned. Yet contingency theorists (Drazin and Van de Ven, 1985) propose that there is no one best way to organize different enterprises working in different industries and conditions. Consistent with other indigenous populations (Morris, 2004), the primary goal of the Sámi people is neither growth nor wealth creation. Success centres upon the preservation of cultural traditions and the environment. However, it is important for the Sámi to at least achieve minimal fit with their external environments in order to survive (Miles and Snow, 1984). As a working example of adaptive fit (cultural adaptation), the Sámi appear open to implementing new technologies into their herding processes.

Sullivan and Margaritis (2000) noted the role played by policy makers in developing (or hindering) indigenous entrepreneurship. Similarly, as the present case reveals, the success of Sámi operations (i.e. the preservation of Sámi traditions) appears contingent upon governmental regulations. Regulation theories form part of the contingent approach to economic development. The process of regulation involves the 'dynamic formation of rules, norms and institutions which are . . . constantly altered as we progress. The contingent process of regulation reflects the contingent nature of what is regulated' (Torfing, 1991, p. 73). Robbins (2003), however, noted that indigenous groups often harbour incapacity to change when cultural traditions are threatened or at stake. Organizations incapable of withstanding change, according to contingency theory, face failure. As regulations surrounding reindeer herding change, the Sámi people are faced with an ominous threat to cultural traditions. We observe these threats in relation to the change from subsistence economies developed around the domestication of reindeer to community-based herding, to market-oriented entrepreneurship. A discussion of these elements follows.

A Symbiotic Relationship

Winters in Sápmi are long and cold. Weber (1939) observed, 'Reindeer thrive under conditions and on fare that would quickly exterminate less hardy animals' (p. 481). Well adapted to the harsh environment, these animals eat snow rather than drink water in winter. Ruotsala (1999) explained, 'Growing up in a particular environment we receive as a "legacy" the knowledge of how to benefit from the resources of that environment.

We also receive the cultural pattern of how to experience, appreciate and interpret our own living environs' (p. 41).

The Sámi people thus developed a subsistence economy,[6] around the domestication of reindeer. Paine (1988) explained that reindeer have their own social organization. Beach (1990) elaborated, 'Herders sensitive to these aspects of reindeer social life are able to use them to control the deer . . . Traditional herders do not force the reindeer if need be, but they often know how to achieve the desired result by utilizing the herd's own propensities and instilling in it the desired behaviour pattern' (p. 258). Fisher (1939) suggested, 'Here we find the usual order of things reversed, man's life being ruled by an animal's needs' (p. 641). In this context, humans benefit best from respecting an animal's needs. Central to traditional reindeer herding is a symbiotic relationship between man and reindeer. Paine (1994) elaborated, 'A process of reciprocal learning occurs between animals and herder' (p. 29). The Sámi economy depended on the reindeer, and the latter were offered protection from wolves and other predators.

The Nature of Community-Based Reindeer Herding

Whitaker (1955) explained, 'The natural basic unit of Lappish society is the elementary family' (p. 37). The family is in turn central to the family business. In the words of Jääskö (1999), 'it should be noted that the most effective and durable economic unit in reindeer herding is not the reindeer woman or reindeer man, but the family' (p. 36). Turi (2002) elaborated that a crucial element in the organization of reindeer herding is that working community consists of one or more families; this is what the Sámi language defines as *sii'dâ*.

Whitaker (1955) described the *sii'dâ* as 'the herding unit; it is basically a group of reindeer owners who cooperate for the purposes of maintaining their herds together as a single working entity and dividing the work of herding among themselves, but the term is also used to connote the tents and persons as well as their herd' (p. 54). He explained 'that the individuals retain all property rights over their reindeer, and their right to leave the unit at any time' (ibid.). Helander (1999) called this a kinship group. More recently, Bjørklund (2004) explained the term as referring 'to a group of reindeer owners who live and migrate together, and to the herd of reindeer owned and herded by them' (p. 125). He added, 'the *siida* represents a flexible cooperative unit between people and animals' (Bjørklund, 2004, p. 126). In summary, the *sii'dâ* is an informal institution uniting people for symbiotic interdependence. It does not claim to be democratic; rather, solutions are reached by consensus and for this reason cooperation is essential.

Intergenerational Family Business Succession

Ruotsala (1999) explained: 'Often an important factor is that this is a profession passed down from generation to generation, primarily from father to son, which is carried on in the same place as the previous generation' (p. 43). Bjørklund (2004, p. 133) elaborated:

> Traditionally, Saami cultural arrangements had taken care of recruitment into pastoral society. Animals were allocated to children during certain ritual occasions . . . Along with the gift also came the responsibility of being a reindeer owner. Children learned how to take care of their

animals and were thus socialized into the world of reindeer pastoralism. When the time came to marry, both spouses were in possession of knowledge and enough animals – together with the animals given to them as wedding gifts – to make it possible to establish themselves as their own husbandry and perhaps herding unit.

Helander (1999) discussed how reindeer herders were trained on the job.

Riseth (2003) listed the regulatory principles of Sámi herding society: (i) the autonomy of the husbander, in 'that all husbanders are their own masters' (p. 232); (ii) the social bonds of the extensive kinship system, resulting in 'a network of mutual obligations through genetic and social kinship' (p. 232); (iii) partnership and *sii'dâ* solidarity; (iv) dialogue and consensus; and (v) responsibility toward the land and the spirits.[7] While the *sii'dâ* is the traditional unit of reindeer herding, the husbandry unit (*driftsenhet*) is the legal basis of husbandry organization in modern Norway. The individual is still interconnected with society and nature, to this day.

Why have reindeer herders specialized in this occupation? Anderson (1983) suggested one explanation: 'the reindeer still functions as a cultural focus with which all Saami identify' (p. 180). Among the causal variables motivating Sámi people to be reindeer herders is 'for the freedom' (Bergsmo, 2001, p. 132). 'The position of reindeer breeding in the northern areas is unique. No other land-based agricultural branch in northern areas has such long traditions in the Arctic as this economic activity . . . Domestic reindeer breeding represents not only sustainable exploitation of the marginal nature resources in the North, but is also the cultural basis of the many small tribal societies of the North' (Turi, 2000, p. 131). Unlike entrepreneurs who compete against one another in other cultural contexts, the success of each Sámi reindeer herder has traditionally been dependent on the mutual cooperation of reindeer herders.

Change from Subsistence Pastoralism to Motorised and Market-Oriented Entrepreneurship

Almost two centuries ago, Clarke (1824a) wrote: 'The *manufactures* of the *Lapps* are limited to their daily necessaries: the *men* make *sledges, skates, ladles, horn spoons, troughs,* and porringers: the *women,* besides their more necessary apparel, manufacture *pelisses, boots, shoes and gloves,* some of which send to the fairs for sale' (p. 505). The system was stable, but changes were taking place.

Today, external rules are being imposed on these people, reducing efficiency. Socially, this also causes tension between different groups of people. Traditionally, reindeer herding was prominent among the Sámi people, and 'Indigenous land use was based on locally available resources' (Müller-Wille, 1987, p. 352). Burgess (1999) mentioned that reindeer herding, fishing, hunting, berry picking 'have supported whole societies and their cultures, yet their impact on the landscape has been minimal' (p. 43).

Paine (1964) portrayed Sámi pastoralists in the 1960s. Müller-Wille (1978) wrote, 'one can refer to the modification of the reindeer economy in northern Fennoscandia with the use of the snowmobile and the motorcycle between 1962 and 1968; this meant a considerable financial outlay for the Lapp reindeer herder and led to a reindeer meat industry oriented to a market economy' (p. 110). Thus traditional subsistence herding yielded to a cash sector. As discussed by Ruotsala (1999), until the 1970s, the reindeerman was directly dependent on reindeer, fishing, hunting and picking berries. However, traditional occupations 'can no longer support the population growth' (Anderson, 1977, p. 368).

In 1978, the Norwegian government passed the Reindeer Management Act. The new Norwegian law made it necessary to have a permit in order to own reindeer, and in the 1980s, authorities stopped issuing new permits. Paine (1994) studied the impact of legislation such as the Reindeer Management Act and analysed attempts by non-Sámi people to regulate and rationalize Sámi pastoralism.

During the 1980s, conservationists and Sámi reindeer pastoralists allied against hydroelectric development, new roads and military installations, which disrupted natural patterns of migration, and land-use conflicts arose (Minde, 2003). Viewing the tundra[8] as wilderness, conservationists were critical of Sámi use of new technology such as landingcraft ferries, and all-terrain vehicles that could inflict ecological damage. Conservationists claimed that the Sámi people could claim a special relationship with nature and a distinctive ethnical status only if they used traditional techniques (Paine, 1994).

Anderson (1977) summarized changes: 'Where the herder's life once revolved entirely around the reindeer, which provided not only meat and milk but also materials for garments and tools, now the animals more and more are handled as a cash crop. Today the reindeer Lapp needs folding money to buy ever more abundant processed foods, readymade clothing, automobiles, television sets, and radios' (p. 371). Pelto (1978) described such change as the de-localization of resources. As was the case with other Indigenous people, activities 'became dependent on goods produced outside their sphere of influence, and introduced into their area of residence by external forces' (Müller-Wille, 1978, p. 112). In the words of Riseth (2003), 'The production system changed from subsistence pastoralism to a motorized and market-oriented industry, moving away from a nearcomplete dependence on animal and human muscle power to a degree of dependence on motorized vehicles' (p. 231).

Methodological Theoretical Underpinning

When attempting to understand culture and society, Crozier and Friedberg (1977) suggested a research strategy involving an inductive approach with qualitative interpretation. Leaning toward the naturalistic–ecological perspective, in which actions are influenced by the setting in which they occur, this study relied on naturalistic inquiry (Lincoln and Guba, 1985). With a methodological mandate to be contextually sensitive, the technique of being a participating observant (Spradley, 1997) enables an understanding of entrepreneurship and its social context. This approach seeks to comprehend the catalysts of various activities. Rather than observe an environment from outside, researchers interact with, observe and record their respective behaviours of players. Being immersed in the same host environment in which the entrepreneur functions, a researcher can fully understand motivations and responses to stimuli. 'Learning takes place through participatory activities in work' (Helander, 1999, p. 25). Participatory observation is consistent with Sámi epistemology, according to which an individual is a part of society and an individual's survival is dependent on society. As explained by Whitaker (1955), a 'requirement of this method of research is that the field-worker shall not merely observe, but shall also participate' (p. 11).

Participants

For the purposes of this study, Sámi identity was based on self-identification. Notwithstanding, on the subject of self-identification, Eythórsson (2003) noted 'the relatively sudden "disappearance" of the coastal Sámi from the census records ... when people who had classified themselves as Sámi in the pre-war census classified themselves as Norwegians in the first post-war census' (p. 151). Interviewees were identified via snowball sampling. As explained by Müller-Wille and Hukkinen (1999), 'In snowball sampling of interviewees, those already interviewed identify who else they think should be interviewed' (p. 47). As discussed by Goodman (1961), interviewing stops only when the last respondent can suggest individuals already named by others.[9]

Interview Schedule

An awareness of the Sámi concept of knowledge is very useful when asking questions among these people. The concept of knowledge in their culture is society-based and it is formed by means of discussions. The culture often has many truths within a given topic, with no right or wrong answers. Rather than giving one's personal opinion, Sámi individuals often use the term 'we', rather than 'I' or 'you'. A Sámi interviewee tends to provide a consensus of knowledge, based on previous discussions.

In describing Sámi people, Whitaker (1955) wrote, 'there are several cases of daughters being given a handsome number of reindeer as a sort of dowry by wealthy parents; the actual amounts involved are however seldom divulged' (p. 40). A big herd provided people with security, but actual numbers[10] were not discussed with strangers. In fact, asking a Sámi person how many reindeer he has may be perceived as socially insensitive. Indeed, 'Asking questions and getting answers is a much harder task than it may seem at first' (Fontana and Frey, 2003, p. 61).

Procedure

Interviews were conducted by the first author. Interviews lasted between two and 12 hours. Sámi reindeer herder Elen Solbritt Eira translated between Sámi and English, while Elin M. Oftedal of the Bodø Graduate School of Business translated between Norwegian and English. Interviewees were helpful in identifying entrepreneurs, their roles in the community, the nature of entrepreneurial activities and their products as perceived by consumers. As the research team became accepted into the community, individuals became increasingly open. Direct on-sight observations were supplied by several sources of data. Triangulation was used to cross-validate these (Patton, 1990).

FINDINGS AND DISCUSSION

The reindeer is central to Sámi culture whether or not it is a primary source of income. Reindeer herding is embedded in the cultural and social heritage of society. Four decades ago, Paine (1964) wrote that 'capable herding bestows general esteem on a person' (p. 85). Jernsletten and Klokov (2002) stated that 'reindeer husbandry forms a "way-of-life" more than a "way of production"'. The same appears to be true today. Indeed, subsistence resource harvesting has a traditional value that is not measured in currency.

Examining the division of labour, Barth (1960) noted that in Norway 'the male and female roles are defined in terms of efficacy, and may be violated on the same grounds' (p. 87). A generation later, Anderson (1983, p. 175) wrote:

> In many subsistence societies, women carry out primary subsistence chores closer to home than do men, leading to appellations of 'woman the gatherer' of basic calories and 'man the hunter' of protein. In Saami society in Norwegian Lapland, women, once hunters, then herders of reindeer alongside men, now manage long-distance networks of trade and politics in reindeer-breeding households. Contemporary Saami women in more sedentary subsistence groups, such as farmers and fishers, market their foraging surpluses and their time to busy nomadic women and to non-Saami settlers.

Findings of this study indicate that Sámi women[11] continue to be economically independent from men; while herding is a communal activity, each individual of the community – including young girls – owns reindeer. Paine's (1964, p. 84) description still holds:

> the responsibilities of husbandry are *not* shared, they are those of the married man, and his wife, of each family herd. Married men do not interact as husbanders. Unmarried children execute the orders of their parents but do not themselves take husbandry decisions. The responsibilities of the head of the family herd are grave ones for he is not the owner of the herd but its senior custodian. The family lives off its herd and one can say they take wages from it, but the herd is also a capital asset which is redistributed in the next generation. Thus the parent, the husbander, should each year select animals to be ear-marked in favour of each of his children.

Although entrepreneurial firms tend to be growth-oriented, this phenomenon does not appear to be the case among any of the Sámi respondents interviewed for this research. While Sámi reindeer herders act on account of their families, and they create jobs for family members and express interest in their children's futures, there appears to be less concern about growth of their enterprises. Findings also indicate that Sámi respondents are less likely to express interest in growth-oriented strategies than mainstream Norwegians. It is not surprising, therefore, that herding by Sámi people involves less debt than other activities, such as fishing. Sámi maintain their traditional orientation around the family.

Sámi interviewees emphasized, instead, Sámi culture and tradition. A common comment was, 'I follow the footsteps of my father'. Fathers are very much looked up to for the skills. In contrast to non-Indigenous entrepreneurs, Sámi entrepreneurs focused discussions on the observation that they 'belonged' to their people, and that being self-employed was a requirement in order to remain on their traditional homeland and to preserve their cultural heritage.

Young respondents were fascinated by the migrations. Every spring each family of reindeer herders travels to round up its reindeer and to earmark the calves; as the sun sets only for a little while (if at all), work is done day and night, with short rest periods in a tent. Each migration has its reason. Summer grass is better along the coast than inland. From June until August, the reindeer pasture is unattended. A problem expressed by interviewees, however, was that policy-makers are encouraging the culling of what the state considers to be 'excess' males that are not needed for reproduction; although older males might not be required for breeding, they serve a purpose in the herd, especially during the winter when the ground is covered with snow. In the search for food below the snow-cover, female reindeers are poor diggers when compared to their male counterparts. When there is an equal number of males and females in a herd, females can access food where males have dug through the snow. Consequently, as the ratio of males to females decreases, the accessibility of food for females decreases.

As noted by respondents, reindeer herding cannot be managed effectively in the same way as commercial cattle breeding. The eldest male reindeers, which policy-makers consider to be economically useless, serve as leaders for the less experienced animals. Several interviewees expressed frustration as outsiders telling Sámi herders what to do, with little understanding of local culture, tradition and practice.

Lee et al. (2000) observed, 'Reindeer herding is an important source of income for the Sámi, bringing in between half and three-quarters of their gross earnings. However, this income has to be supplemented by agricultural and forestry work, as well as cash-earning jobs' (p. 101). The present findings support their observations. Interviews indicate that, with a preference for work within the natural portion of the value chain, self-employed Sámi people have been pulled to reindeer herding because of social conditioning (including a close relationship with animals), but pushed into secondary enterprises in order to make a living without leaving Sápmi. Furthermore, Sámi reindeer herders claim that they are not seeking risks and that they create secondary enterprises to reduce existing risks. Secondary new ventures are often related to existing skills.

In March and April, animal hides are nailed onto walls for drying, a process that takes about two weeks. Once tanned, the hides are sold. Other secondary enterprises include selling of handicrafts, and services provided to the tourism industry. While the unit of interest in herding might be the collectivity, entrepreneurship in secondary enterprises often takes place at the level of the individual. As stated by Ingold (1980), a 'social opposition is between production for subsistence and production for the market' (p. 3). Interviewees emphasized that, nowadays, there is a perceived need for cash; traditional income is supplemented by other sectors, such as tourism. In addition, spouses often have a salary. This observation supports Jääskö (1999), who wrote, 'Mechanization and other general developments in the last decades have led to the situation where women's formerly unremunerated work has lost its importance . . . The reindeerman no longer even needs a "peski" (fur coat) or fur boots to keep him warm on the tundra' (p. 37).

Discussing women who are self-employed in the reindeer industry, Jääskö (1999) noted that they are often engaged in auxiliary occupations, such as meat preparation, making handicrafts or servicing tourism. Bjørklund (2004) added, 'a fast-growing supply of consumer goods only contributed to an expanding cash economy and its stresses' (p. 127). Direct dependence on nature and on the traditional family business has thus been reduced. Burgess (1999) found that although no Sámi lives exclusively from fishing, this activity provides a supplementary source of income and food. A problem today is that commercial fishing has been substantially overconducted. Some Sámi people must now buy fish and meat.

Sámi herders indicated that, unlike Western-style meat production, they viewed herding as an expression of traditional and cultural values. For them, Indigenous entrepreneurship was different from other forms of self-employment in that Sámi herding is a communal activity revolving around the family. Ownership is established by cutting notches into the ears of a calf, and, in spring, when it is time to identify reindeer calves with a notch on the ear, the whole family takes part in the separation. A small group is separated from the herd and chased into a small enclosure. A lasso is coiled by hand, before throwing; this enhances its reach, as well as its velocity. Although the reindeer gallop at 20 kilometres per hour, the herders seldom miss their target. Children are keen to catch and to carry calves to be marked. Small children are given reindeer, as parents are happy to share their assets with the new generation. During interviews there were frequent references to family, respect of elders and love of children. The extended family was described as a functional collectivity, with less reference to the nuclear family. Asceticism, frugality and thrift were raised on several occasions.

A number of interviewees expressed concerns about the state, which was causing changes in herding, reducing efficiency. There was bitterness about hunters being permitted to kill moose in the wild, while herders were required to send reindeer to distant slaughter-houses, resulting in expense and waste. This shift in animal husbandry reflects Jääskö (1999), who wrote: 'the commercialisation and centralization of meat processing (including slaughtering) causes a decrease in numbers of people practising a reindeer economy as well as a decrease in opportunities for other local people to benefit from raw materials from reindeer. Not only does it result in reduction of jobs, but in impoverishment of the culture as well' (pp. 37–8). As stated by Riseth (2003), 'the historical record is that the internal system has been functioning well for centuries and that the problems faced by the herders have had external causes' (p. 233). Among these external causes are new requirements for meat processing. One interviewee explained, 'The governments are doing some good and some not so good things. They don't understand reindeer herding really. They restrict our opportunities. The strict laws on how to butcher, for example. That shows that they really do not know what they are talking about. Nothing would be better than butcher the animals on the spot, rather than sending them onto the butcheries.'

Other Sámi entrepreneurs complained to the interviewer and said that they were suffering from Finland and Sweden becoming increasingly integrated into the European Union. Sámi entrepreneurs also complained about regulations[12] and about bookkeeping requirements imposed by the state. None expressed any interest in aggressive American-style marketing campaigns.

In the competitive global environment, reindeer herding is not as profitable as other sectors. Neither are young reindeer owners supported in any way, resulting in shifts to other occupations or emigration. Turi (2002) estimated that there remained only 100 000 reindeer herders. Pastoralists find themselves in a difficult dilemma. Bjørklund (2004, p. 135) concluded, 'He might either become a criminal, legally speaking, because laws and regulations often exclude established and well-proven forms of management, or he may be punished economically because the policy of subsidies only pays for those who manage their herds the way the state wants them to – and that is a way contrary to most Sámi values and customs.'

Much literature has focused on modernization (Rostow, 1953, 1957, 1960) and dependency perspectives, both of which equate development with economic growth and industrialization, and assume that evolution from a traditional to a modern society is essential, but problematic. In his discussion of modernization theories, Brohman (1996) suggested the existence of cultural barriers to modernization, and Tucker (1999) wrote, 'Other cultural formations were viewed primarily as forms of resistance to modernization which had to be overcome' (p. 3). Yet the Sámi have modernized smoothly, adopting the newest communications and positioning technologies, and in some cases using helicopters to herd reindeer. One interviewee stated in English, 'We use cell phones and snow scooters and four wheel drive, and there is some new technology on the way . . . a little chip that we can transplant into the reindeer and then herd them just sitting with our computers. We'll invest in such equipment when it is here.'

For some time, the world has been experiencing a shift to a flexible regime of accumulation (Komninos, 1989). Sensitive to variations in demand, the flexible regime of accumulation calls for increasingly specialized workplaces and a greater reliance on subcontracting and networks. This set coincides with a decrease in hierarchical control (Wright and Dana, 2003), and an increase in cooperation. In modern Western society, this process has been dubbed the 'new economy'. For the Sámi people, cooperation has traditionally been the essence of enterprise. 'The most important characteristic of pastoralism is that it is a predominant economic activity in which the whole family participates' (Tuisku, 2002, p. 101).

In Sámi society, 'individual decisions are valued . . . especially when it comes to reindeer husbandry' (Bjørklund, 2004, p. 134). In contrast to some peripheral communities that have been excluded from capitalism, the Sámi people have long practised sustainable capitalism in an environmentally friendly way. Whitaker (1955) noted that a Sámi by the name of N.M. Fjällström reported that 'a family of 3 would require 20 reindeer for their own personal needs (i.e., food), apart from those sold to bring in income' (p. 35). Siuruainen and Aikio (1977) calculated that a family would need to own 250–300 registered reindeer to exist without other income. In contrast, a shepherd would require many more sheep, and much land. Over a century ago, Wrightson (1905) wrote, 'A flock of a thousand ewes is unquestionably a valuable property. Such a large flock . . . is maintained upon about 1,000 acres of land . . . Where 1,000 stock ewes are kept 1,100 lambs may be reasonably looked for' (p. 195).

In contrast to Norwegian fishermen and industrialists, who tend to obtain considerable financing from banks, reindeer herders tend to avoid large loans. The average equity held by herders is 80 per cent, considerably higher than is the case in other industries. Only Innovation Norway (formerly the Norwegian Industry Development Fund) gives loans on herds.

Recommendations

During the nineteenth century, Spooner (1874) wrote, 'The management and selection of any breed of sheep must after all become a matter of pounds, shillings, and pence' (p. 137). Reindeer herding at the time was less focused on the cash economy. However, cash has gained a great deal of importance with the relatively recent introduction of new 'necessities' such as snowmobiles, mobile telephones, GPS technology and Internet access. Therefore it could be highly beneficial to improve profitability in the sector, through increased value creation and vertical integration. Downstream integration would allow herders to profit from a greater portion of the value chain. A value-adding programme was introduced in 2001, governed by a committee comprising representatives from the National Reindeer Herders' Organization, from the Royal Department of Agriculture, and from the Sámi Parliament. Managed by the Norwegian Industrial and Regional Development Fund, the programme focuses on sustainable processing with the use of technology, and without degrading pasture resources. The programme was evaluated by the Nordland Research Institute, Norut-NIBR Finnmark and the Norwegian Agricultural Economics Research Institute, and found to be successful (Rønning et al., 2004). Such programmes should be continued.

Emphasis on marketing also appears to be appropriate. It appears, however, that some decision-makers do not fully understand the environment of the Sámi. New requirements have caused unnecessary difficulties. A policy writer appears to have neglected the fact that cockroaches cannot live outdoors in Arctic winters. Rather than transport reindeer to the south (at a financial cost to the herder and to the discomfort of the animals), it appears to make more sense for reindeer to be processed in Sápmi. It also seems that government has assumed wrongly that reindeer meat should not be smoked in a lavvu tent, for hygienic reasons. Sámi experts say this is unjustified, because the lavvu provides a sterile environment.

Toward the Future

Sámi reindeer herders interviewed for this research are concerned that community-based, pastoral self-employment might soon be phased out in favour of an agricultural-based reindeer business leading to the demise of community-based entrepreneurship as practised by the Sámi for centuries. As argued by Beach (1990, pp. 295–6),

> in the Soviet Union large-scale reindeer ranching already exists, but in Fennoscandia growth toward ranching can be painful for the Saami. They face a difficult dilemma: large market-oriented ranching businesses seem to promise the best economic return (especially in the light of state policies fostering this development), and, with a rapidly rising cost of living, increased profits are most attractive. At the same time, traditional Saami social relations, with private ownership of reindeer . . . do not support such a move.

Reindeer are sensitive with regards to what they eat. They prefer fresh natural food, and they have traditionally travelled looking for new fresh food supplies; hence they have not stayed in one place. On a ranch, they can be fed with expensive pellets,[13] but there is still an issue of space. When crowded, reindeer catch diseases from one another. It is therefore preferable for them to be given more space per head than is the case with other animals. Judge (1983) observed, 'Faced with differing national policies, the Saami, or Lapps, of Sweden, Norway, and Finland have had difficulty in forging a united front to protect traditional activities undermined by the resource-development projects of their governments' (p. 149).

Until relatively recently, there were, between Sámi people and others, 'limitations on shared understandings, differences in criteria for judgment of values and performance and a restriction of interaction to sectors of assumed common understanding and mutual interest' (Barth, 1969, p. 15). Although groups have been learning from one another, mainstream society still has much to learn from the Sámi people; in particular, a wealth of information lies in the elders. A prerequisite to understanding, however, is open-mindedness. If Sámi entrepreneurship is analysed through Western thinking, actions risk being interpreted incorrectly. Family business entrepreneurship and enterprise development take on different forms, and are motivated by a variety of factors. Some generalizations have been made for entrepreneurs in the industrialized West; yet these are not necessarily applicable to Indigenous peoples. The Western approach is not the only way of understanding; there are indeed other valid ways of knowing, but we risk losing them. Perhaps this research provides an appropriate metaphor for sustainable entrepreneurship, particularly in the light of global and climate change.

Indigenous family business entrepreneurship transcends typical entrepreneurial paradigms by adding a degree of complexity (i.e. cultural values). However, as the present research shows, cultural values can prevail when aligned with public policy, or vice versa. Accordingly, a contingency perspective is imperative for the development of indigenous entrepreneurship paradigms.

Future research might investigate how family business entrepreneurs could best cope with government regulation in a traditional occupation such as reindeer herding. Another research focus could be to analyse the impact of recent change on Sámi culture and identity. In the words of Morris (1968), 'An ethnic group is a distinct category of the population in a larger society whose culture is usually different from its own. The members of such a group are, or feel themselves, or are thought to be, bound together by common ties of race or nationality or culture' (p. 167). As explained by Barth (1969), 'Ethnic groups only persist as significant units if they imply marked difference in behaviour, i.e., persisting cultural difference' (pp. 15–16).

NOTES

1. Sámi is sometimes spelt, in English, Saami or even Sami.
2. Guovdageaidnu was formerly known as Guov'dageai'dno.
3. *Rangifer tarandus* in Eurasia refers to reindeer; in North America, the Micmac word 'caribou' has become the standard (Anderson, 2004)
4. Barth wrote, 'the entrepreneur must initiate and coordinate a number of inter-personal relationships in a supervisory capacity to effectuate his enterprise' (1963, p. 5).
5. Morse defined Aboriginal people as 'people who trace their ancestors in these lands to time immemorial' (1985, p. 1).
6. For discussions of subsistence self-employment, see Barth (1952), Cole and Fayissa (1991), and Dana (1995).
7. Man, society and nature are viewed as interconnected. For a discussion of the land and the spirits of the Lule Sámi, see Rydving (1993).
8. The English word 'tundra' comes from the Sámi *duottar*.
9. Sámi reindeer herder Elen Solbritt Eira translated between Sámi and English, while Elin M. Oftedal of the Bodø Graduate School of Business translated between Norwegian and English.
10. Usually, between 10 per cent and 20 per cent of the herd consisted of draught reindeer.
11. See also Joks (2007).
12. The reindeer sector in Norway was regulated by the Royal Ministry of Foreign Affairs until jurisdiction was passed on to the Royal Ministry of Agriculture. All herding became regulated by the Norwegian Reindeer Herding Act, and the Norwegian Reindeer Husbandry Association was made to report to the Royal Ministry of Agriculture. More recently, the Royal Ministry for the Environment has been involved. Several of the present Sámi interviewees said that they resented that their livelihood was controlled by non-Sámi reindeer administrators who did not fully understand the local culture and who governed in accordance with interests of mainstream society. The respondents claimed that agriculture was in competition with herding, thereby resulting in a conflict of interest.
13. One herder told the interviewer, 'It is the reindeer who feed me; the day that I have to feed the reindeer then I'll quit.'

REFERENCES

Anderson, D.G. (2004), 'Reindeer, caribou and "fairy stories" of state power', in D.G. Anderson and M. Nutall (eds), *Cultivating Arctic Landscapes: Knowing and Managing Animals in the Circumpolar North*, New York and Oxford: Berghahn, pp. 1–16.

Anderson, M. (1983), 'Woman as generalist, as specialist, and as diversifier in Saami subsistence activities', *Humboldt Journal of Social Relations*, **10**(2), 175–97.

Anderson, R.B. (1995), 'The business economy of the first nations in Saskatchewan: a contingency perspective', *The Canadian Journal of Native Studies*, **15**(2), 309–46.

Anderson, R.B. and Giberson, R.J. (2003), 'Aboriginal entrepreneurship and economic development in Canada: thoughts on current theory and practice', in C.H. Stiles and C.S. Galbraith (eds), *Ethnic Entrepreneurship: Structure and Process*, Oxford: Elsevier, pp. 141–67.

Anderson, S. (1977), 'Norway's reindeer Lapps', *National Geographic*, **152**(3), 364–79.

Anderson, T., Benson, B. and Flanagan, T. (2006), *Self-determination: The Other Path for Native Americans*, Stanford, CA: Stanford University Press.

Barth, F. (1952), 'Subsistence and institutional system in a Norwegian mountain valley', *Rural Sociology*, **17**, March, 28–38.

Barth, F. (1960), 'Family life in a central Norwegian mountain community', in T.D. Eliot and A. Hillman (eds), *Norway Families*, Philadelphia, PA: University of Pennsylvania Press, pp. 81–107.

Barth, F. (1969), 'Introduction', in F. Barth (ed.), *Ethnic Groups and Boundaries: The Organisation of Cultural Difference*, Oslo: Universitetsforlaget, pp. 9–38.

Beach, H. (1990), 'Comparative systems of reindeer herding', in J.G. Galaty and D.L. Johnson (eds), *The World of Pastoralism: Herding Systems in Comparative Perspective*, New York: Guilford Press, pp. 253–98.

Bergsmo, T.I. (2001), *Four Seasons with the Reindeer People*, Oslo: Pantagruel Forlag.

Bjørklund, I. (2004), 'Saami pastoral society in northern Norway: the national integration of an indigenous management system', in D.G. Anderson and M. Nuttall (eds), *Cultivating Arctic Landscapes: Knowing and Managing Animals in the Circumpolar North*, New York and Oxford: Berghahn, pp. 124–35.

Brohman, J. (1996), *Popular Development: Rethinking the Theory and Practice of Development*, Oxford: Blackwell.

Burgess, P. (1999), *Human Environmental Interactions in Upper Lapland, Finland*, Rovaniemi, Finland: Arctic Centre, University of Lapland.

Burns, T. and Stalker, G.M. (1961), *The Management of Innovation*, London: Tavistock.

Cahn, M. (2008), 'Indigenous entrepreneurship, culture and micro-enterprise in the Pacific Islands: case studies from Samoa', *Entrepreneurship and Regional Development*, **20**(1), 1–18.

Clarke, E.D. (1824a), *Travels in Various Countries of Europe Asia and Africa: Scandinavia*, Vol. 9, London: T. Cadell.

Clarke, E.D. (1824b), *Travels in Various Countries of Europe Asia and Africa: Scandinavia*, Vol. 10, London: T. Cadell.

Cole, W.E. and Fayissa, B. (1991), 'Urban subsistence labor force: towards a policy-oriented and empirically accessible taxonomy', *World Development*, **19**(7), 779–89.

Collinder, B. (1949), *The Lapps*, Princeton, NJ: Princeton University Press, for the American Scandinavian Foundation.

Crozier, M. and Friedberg, E. (1977), *L'acteur et le système*, Paris: Seuil.

Dana, L.P. (1995), 'Entrepreneurship in a remote sub-Arctic community: Nome, Alaska', *Entrepreneurship Theory and Practice*, **20**(1), 55–72. Reprinted in N. Krueger (ed.), *Entrepreneurship: Critical Perspectives on Business and Management*, Vol. IV. London: Routledge, 2002, pp. 255–75.

Davidsson, P. and Delmar, F. (1992), 'Cultural values and entrepreneurship', *Frontiers of Entrepreneurial Research*, Wellesley, MA: Babson College, pp. 444–58.

Drazin, R. and Van de Ven, A.H. (1985), 'Alternative forms of fit in contingency theory', *Administrative Science Quarterly*, **30**(4), 514–39.

Dybbroe, S. (1999), 'Researching knowledge: the terms and scope of a current debate', in F. Sejersen (ed.), *Changes in the Circumpolar North: Culture, Ethics and Self-Determination* Copenhagen: International Arctic Social Sciences Association, pp. 13–26.

Eythórsson, E. (2003), 'The coastal Sámi: a "pariah caste" of the Norwegian fisheries? A reflection on ethnicity and power in Norwegian resource management', in S. Jentoft, H. Minde and R. Nilsen (eds), *Indigenous Peoples: Resource Management and Global Rights*, Delft, The Netherlands: Eburon Academic, pp. 149–62.

Fincham, R. and Rhodes, P. (2005), *The Principle of Organizational Behavior*, 4th edn, New York: Oxford University Press.

Fisher, C. (1939), 'The nomads of Arctic Lapland: mysterious little people of a land of the midnight sun live off the country above the Arctic circle', *National Geographic*, **76**(5), 641–76.

Fontana, A. and Frey, James (2003), 'The interview: from structured questions to negotiated text', in N.K. Denzin and Y.S. Lincoln (eds), *Collecting and Interpreting Qualitative Materials*, 2nd edn, Thousand Oaks, CA: Sage, pp. 61–106.

Freeman, M.M.R. (1985), 'Appeal to tradition: different perspectives on Arctic wildlife management', in J. Brøsted, J. Dahl, A. Gray, H.C. Gulov, G. Henricksen, J.B. Jorgensen and I. Kleivan (eds), *Native Power: The Quest for Autonomy and Nationhood of Indigenous Peoples*, Bergen, Norway: Universitetforlaget.

Goodman, L.A. (1961), 'Snowball sampling', *The Annals of Mathematical Statistics*, **32**(1), 148–70.

Helander, E. (1999), 'Traditional Sámi knowledge', in L. Müller-Wille (ed.), *Human Environmental Interactions: Issues and Concerns in Upper Lapland, Finland*, Rovaniemi: Arctic Centre, University of Lapland, pp. 25–7.

Hindle, K. and Lansdowne, M. (2005), 'Brave spirits on new paths: toward a globally relevant paradigm of indigenous entrepreneurship research', *Journal of Small Business and Entrepreneurship*, **18**(2), 131–42.

Ingold, T. (1980), *Hunters, Pastoralists and Ranchers*, Cambridge: Cambridge University Press.

Jääskö, O. (1999), 'Women's position in reindeer herding economy: an environmental factor', in L. Müller-Wille (ed.), *Human Environmental Interactions: Issues and Concerns in Upper Lapland, Finland*, Rovaniemi: Arctic Centre, University of Lapland, pp. 35–40.

Jernsletten, J.-L. L. and Klokov, K. (2002), *Sustainable Reindeer Husbandry*, Tromsø: University of Tromsø Centre for Saami Studies.

Joks, S. (2007), 'Women's Position in the Sámi Reindeer Husbandry', in L.P. Dana and R.B. Anderson (eds), *International Handbook of Research on Indigenous Entrepreneurship*, Cheltenham, UK and Northampton, MA, USA: Edward Elgar, pp. 246–56.

Judge, J. (1983), 'Peoples of the Arctic', *National Geographic*, **163**(2), 144–49.

Komninos, N. (1989), 'From national to local: the janus face of crisis', in M. Gottdiener and N. Komninos (eds), *Capitalist Development and Crisis Theory*, New York: St Martin's Press, pp. 348–64.

Ladson-Billings, G. (2003), 'Racialized discourses and ethnic epistemologies', in N.K. Denzin and Y.S. Lincoln (eds), *The Landscape of Qualitative Research: Theories and Issues*, 2nd edn, Thousand Oaks, CA: Sage, pp. 398–432.

Lawrence, P.R. and Lorsch, J.W. (1967). *Organization and Environment: Managing Differentiation and Integration*, Boston, MA: Graduate School of Business Administration, Harvard University.

Lee, J. and Miller, D. (1996), 'Strategy, environment and performance in two technological contexts: contingency theory in Korea', *Organization Studies*, **17**(5), 729–50.

Lee, S.E., Press, M.C., Lee, J.A., Ingold, T. and Kurttila, T. (2000), 'Regional effects of climate change on reindeer: a case study of the Muotkatunturi region in Finnish Lapland', *Polar Research*, **19**(1), 99–105.

Lehtola, V.-P. (2002), *The Sámi People: Traditions in Transition*, Inari: Kustannus-Puntsi.

Lincoln, Y.S. and Guba, Egon (1985), *Naturalistic Inquiry*. Beverley Hills, CA: Sage.

Lindsay, N.J. (2005), 'Toward a cultural model of Indigenous entrepreneurial attitude', *Academy of Marketing Science Review*, **5**, 1–15.

Manuel, G. and Posluns, M. (1974), *The 4th World: An Indian Reality*, New York: Free Press.

Miles, R.E. and Snow, C.C. (1984), 'Fit, failure and the hall of fame', *California Management Review*, **26**(3), 10–28.

Minde, H. (2003), 'The challenge of indigenism: the struggle for Sámi land rights and self-government in Norway 1960–1990', in S. Jentoft, H. Minde and R. Nilsen (eds), *Indigenous Peoples: Resource Management and Global Rights*, Delft, The Netherlands: Eburon Academic, pp. 75–104.

Morris, H.S. (1968), 'Ethnic groups', in D.L. Sills (ed.), *International Encyclopedia of the Social Sciences*, London and New York: Macmillan, Vol. 5, pp. 167–72.

Morris, M.H. (2004), 'Is entrepreneurship universal? A values perspective', paper presented at the Annual Meeting of the Academy of Management, New Orleans, LA, 6–11 August.

Morse, B.W. (1985), *Aboriginal Peoples and the Law: Indian, Métis, and Inuit Rights in Canada*, Ottawa, Ontario, Canada: Carleton University Press.

Müller-Wille, L. (1978), 'Cost analysis of modern hunting among the Inuit of the Canadian Central Arctic', *Polar Geography*, **2**(2), 104–14.

Müller-Wille, L. (1987), 'Indigenous people, land-use conflicts, and economic development in circumpolar lands', *Arctic and Alpine Research*, **19**(4), 351–6.

Müller-Wille, L. (2001), 'From reindeer stew to pizza: the displacement of local food resources in Sápmi, Northernmost Europe', *Fennia*, **179**(1), 89–96.

Müller-Wille, L. and Hukkinen, J. (1999), 'Human environmental interactions in Upper Lapland, Finland: development of participatory research strategies', *Acta Boreaia*, **2**, 43–61.

Müller-Wille, L. and Pelto, J.P. (1971), 'Technological change and its impact in Arctic regions: Lapps introduce snowmobiles into reindeer herding', *Polarforschung*, **41**, 142–8.

Paine, R. (1964), 'Herding and husbandry: two basic distinctions in the analysis of reindeer management', *Folk*, **6**(1), 83–8.

Paine, R. (1984), 'Norwegians and Saami: nation-state and Fourth World', in G.L. Gold (ed.), *Minorities and Mother Country Imagery*, St John's, Newfoundland, Canada: Memorial University, pp. 211–48.

Paine, R. (1985), 'The claim of the Fourth World', in J. Brøsted, J. Dahl, A. Gray, H.C. Gulløv, G. Henriksen, J.B. Jørgensen and I. Kleivan (eds), *Native Power: The Quest for Autonomy and Nationhood of Indigenous Peoples*, Bergen, Norway: Universitetsforlaget, pp. 49–66.

Paine, R. (1988), 'Reindeer and caribou: *Rangifer Tarandus* in the wild and under pastoralism', *Polar Record*, **24**(148), 31–42.

Paine, R. (1994), *Herds of the Tundra: A Portrait of Saami Reindeer Pastoralism*, Washington, DC and London: Smithsonian Institution Press.

Patton, M.Q. (1990), *Qualitative Evaluation and Research Methods*, Newbury Park, CA: Sage.

Pelto, P.J. (1973), *The Snowmobile Revolution: Technology and Social Change in the Arctic*, Menlo Park, CA: Cummings.

Pelto, P.J. (1978), 'Ecology, de-localization and social change', in L. Müller-Wille, P.J. Pelto, L. Müller-Wille and R. Darnell (eds), *Consequences of Economic Change in Circumpolar Regions*, Edmonton, Alberta, Canada: Boreal Institute for Northern Studies, pp. 29–36.

Pelto, P.J. and Müller-Wille, Ludger (1972/3), 'Reindeer herding and snowmobiles: aspects of a technological revolution', *Folk*, 14–15, 119–44.

Peredo, A.M. and Anderson, R.W. (2006), 'Indigenous entrepreneurship research: themes and variations', in C.S. Galbraith and C.H. Stiles (eds), *Developmental Entrepreneurship: Adversity, Risk, and Isolation*, Oxford: Elsevier, pp. 253–73.

Peterson, R. (1988), 'Understanding and encouraging entrepreneurship internationally', *Journal of Small Business Management*, **26**(2), 1–7.

Reynolds, P.D. (1991), 'Sociology and entrepreneurship: concepts and contributions', *Entrepreneurship Theory and Practice*, **16**, 47–90.

Riseth, J.Å. (2003), 'Sámi reindeer management in Norway: modernization challenges and conflicting strategies: reflections upon the co-management alternative', in S. Jentoft, H. Minde and R. Nilsen (eds), *Indigenous Peoples: Resource Management and Global Rights*, Delft, The Netherlands: Eburon Academic, pp. 229–47.

Robbins, J. (2003), 'Social exclusion and remote indigenous communities – is the "third way" the right way?', paper presented at the Social Policy Research Conference, 6–8 July.

Rønning, L., Kjuus, J., Vesterli, G. and Karlstad, S. (2004), *Verdiskapingsprogrammet for Reindrift – Følgeevaluering, Nordlandsforskning-rapport Nr. 4*, Nordlandsforkskning.

Rostow, W.W. (1953), *The Process of Economic Growth*, Oxford: Oxford University Press.

Rostow, W.W. (1957), 'The interrelation of theory and economic history', *Journal of Economic History*, **17**, December, 509–23.

Rostow, W.W. (1960), *The Stages of Economic Growth: A Non-Communist Manifesto*, London: Cambridge University Press.

Ruotsala, H. (1999), 'The reindeer herder's environment', in L. Müller-Wille (ed.), *Human Environmental Interactions: Issues and Concerns in Upper Lapland, Finland*, Rovaniemi: Arctic Centre, University of Lapland, pp. 41–7.

Rydving, H. (1993), *The End of Drum-time: Religious Change among the Lule Saami, 1670s–1740s*, Uppsala University PhD Thesis: distributed by Almquist and Wiksell.

Sara, Á. (2000), 'Interreg Sápmi Subprogram; Interreg III A Nordkalotten, 2000–2006', Kautokeino, Norway: Sámi Instituhtta.

Scheinberg, S. and MacMillan, Ian (1988), 'An 11 country study of motivations to start a business', *Frontiers of Entrepreneurship Research*, Wellesley, MA: Babson College, pp. 669–87.

Siuruainen, E. and Aikio, Pekka (1977), *The Lapps in Finland: The Population, Their Livelihood and Their Culture*, Helsinki, Finland: Society for the Promotion of Lapp Culture.

Spooner, W.C. (1874), *The History, Structure, Economy and Diseases of the Sheep*, 3rd edn, London: Lockwood and Co.

Spradley, J.P. (1997), *Participant Observation*, New York: Holt Rinehart and Winston.

Storli, I. (1993), 'Sámi Viking age pastoralism – or "the fur trade paradigm" reconsidered', *Norwegian Archaeological Review*, **26**(1), 1–47.

Sullivan, A. and Margaritis, D. (2000), 'Public sector reform and indigenous entrepreneurship', *International Journal of Entrepreneurial Behaviour and Research*, **6**(5), 265.

Torfing, J. (1991), 'A hegemony approach to capitalist regulation', in R. Bertramsen, J. Thomsen and J. Torfing (eds), *State, Economy and Society*, London: Unwin Hyman, pp. 35–93.

Tucker, V. (1999), 'The myth of development: a critique of a Eurocentric discourse', in R. Munck and D. O'Hearn (eds), *Critical Development Theory: Contributions to a New Paradigm*, London: Zed, pp. 1–26.

Tuisku, T. (2002), 'Reindeer herding', in I. Lehtinen (ed.), *Siberia: Life on the Taiga and Tundra*, Helsinki: National Board of Antiquities, pp. 100–107.

Turi, J.M. (2000), 'Native reindeer herders' priorities for research', *Polar Research*, **19**(1), 131–33.

Turi, J.M. (2002), 'The world reindeer livelihood – current situation, threats and possibilities', in S. Kankaanpää, L. Müller-Wille, P. Susiluoto and Sutinen, M.-L. (eds), *Northern Timberline Forests: Environmental and Socio-economic Issues and Concerns*, Kolari, Finland: The Finnish Forest Research Institute, pp. 70–75.

Weber, W.A. (1939), 'Antlered majesties of many lands', *National Geographic*, **76**(4), 479–510.

Whitaker, I. (1955), *Social Relations in a Nomadic Lappish Community*, Oslo: Utgitt av Norsk Folkemuseum.

Wright, R.W. and Dana, Leo P. (2003), 'Changing paradigms of international entrepreneurship strategy', *Journal of International Entrepreneurship*, **1**(1), 135–52.

Wrightson, J. (1905), *Sheep: Breeds and Management*, 5th edn, London: Vinton & Company.

PART IX

FAMILY ENTERPRISES FROM A MACROECONOMIC PERSPECTIVE

26 Small family business contributions to the economy: an enterprise population level study
Antti Kirmanen and Juha Kansikas

1   INTRODUCTION

This study aims to analyse small family firms' contribution at the Finnish economy. This contribution is measured through their share of the Finnish small enterprise population, their contribution to employment and the gross domestic product (GDP). Furthermore, their distribution among industries is examined.

In general discussion, family business is often considered as a synonym for a small business. There is, however, a plethora of large corporations that are controlled by a single business family (Family Entrepreneurship Working Group, 2005, p. 24). Nevertheless, the majority of family businesses are small and medium-sized firms (ibdi., p. 20); however, comprehensive studies, which concentrate particularly on small family businesses role in economies, are lacking. However, research on family businesses' contribution to various economies, regardless of their size, has been done. According to various research, family businesses are a significant and valuable resource for economies around the world (e.g. Flören, 1998; Shanker and Astrachan, 1996; Klein, 2000; Tourunen, 2009). Family businesses' proportion of the whole enterprise population is often stated to lie between 80 per cent and 100 per cent (FEWG, 2005, p. 9; Flören, 1998, p. 122). Consequently, family businesses have been noted to contribute remarkably to employment and GDP in various countries (e.g. Flören, 1998, p. 129; Shanker and Astrachan, 1996, pp. 110–16).

In Finland, some research and estimates of the family businesses' proportion of the enterprise sector have been made. According to Heinonen and Toivonen (2003, pp. 30–32) 72 per cent of all businesses in Finland are family businesses. More recently, Tourunen (2009) examined Finnish large and medium-sized family businesses by conducting an overall research of their contribution to the Finnish economy. According to him, 42 per cent of the Finnish large and medium-sized companies are family businesses. As mentioned above, Tourunen (2009) has previously researched the contribution of the Finnish large and medium-sized businesses. This study researches Finnish small family businesses' contribution for the Finnish economy on the population level. Since an overall study among nearly 250000 small enterprises would be impossible to manage, the research is conducted as a quantitative representative sample research. On the grounds of this sample study's results, population-level estimates are derived. The information concerning the firms is received from Statistics Finland (Tilastokeskus), whose statisticians have also derived the representative sample of 2004 small firms from the Finnish small firm population. The data were collected by a postal questionnaire (see the Appendix) and by telephone interviews. Furthermore, the calculations concerning the obtained data were made at Statistics Finland with SAS software for statistical analysis.

This study is limited to investigating small family businesses' contribution to the Finnish economy. Therefore the sample consisted of 2004 small Finnish firms that employ fewer than fifty people, but at least one person. The percentage of family businesses in the Finnish small business sector and their impact on the Finnish economy will be estimated according to this sample. However, in 2006, there were 160 986 Finnish firms that employed less than one employee (Statistics Finland, 2007), and consequently, are not represented in the sample. Nevertheless, separate estimations concerning this population are made. In this study, nearly all firms with less than one employee are defined as small family businesses (excluding 2292 units, which cannot be defined as Finnish small family businesses, such as cooperatives, foundations and foreign-owned enterprises), since it seems probable that the majority of them would fulfil this study's small family business definition. Furthermore, these enterprises have an influence on family businesses' contribution, although their influence on total added value and employment created by the Finnish enterprise sector is small.

The research sample has been derived from the register of Finnish enterprises in 2006. Consequently, the results will reflect the data and the situation in Finland in 2006. This study's focus is on small family businesses' role and significance in the Finnish economy, and their performance compared with small non-family businesses. Although it has been noted that family businesses often pursue both economic and non-economic goals (Chrisman et al., 2004, p. 348), non-economic goals, benefits and accomplishments of small family businesses are excluded from the study. Small family businesses' performance and contribution to the Finnish economy are observed in solely economic terms. The aim of the research is summarized in the research problem, which is: What are the characteristics of small family firms in a population-level study?

2   SMALL FAMILY FIRMS IN ECONOMIES

Comparison of small enterprises between different countries in absolute figures may be questioned, because national concepts are not identical (Bednarzik, 2000, p.4). Differences in sizes of the economies affect the obtained data. In addition, policies and definitions vary between countries. For example, according to Reynolds et al. (1999, p. 7), in the USA, enterprises with fewer than 500 employees are considered to be small businesses, whereas in Finland enterprises employing more than 50 people are defined as medium-sized businesses (Tourunen, 2009, p. 23). Clearly this kind of gap between definitions influences the results. However, comparisons can be made, but one should keep in mind their suggestive nature.

Despite the difficulty of comparing small business influence between economies, one aspect seems to be congruent: entrepreneurship does seem to have positive impact on economies (e.g. Acs, 1992; Bednarzik, 2000; Carree and Thurik, 2008). Entrepreneurship occurs in the form of small business creation (Reynolds et al., 1999, p. 9). Acs (1992, p. 39) has identified four critical contributions that small businesses have made to industrial markets.

1.   Small businesses are the source of considerable innovative activity. Their role in the process of technological change cannot be over-emphasized.

2. Small businesses serve as agents of change in a market economy. They are responsible for much of the market turbulence 'that not only creates an additional dimension of competition not captured in the traditional static measure of market structure, such as concentration, but also provides mechanism for regeneration'.
3. Small businesses promote international competition through newly created niches.
4. Small businesses have generated significant share of new jobs in recent years.

Kotey and Meredith (1997, p. 37) concur with Acs's view, as they state: 'In many countries, the small enterprise sector is a major source of employment revenue generation, innovation, and technological advancement'. Furthermore, Robbins et al. (2000, pp. 297–300) recognize similar contributions as Acs in the US economy. Their study examined small businesses' influence on employment, productivity and gross state product, that is, small businesses' significance on a country level. According to their research, a high level of businesses with 20 or fewer employees provide a more productive workforce and higher GDP growth than the smallest businesses with few employees. Moreover, countries that have a great many small businesses suffer less from wage inflation and show lower rates of unemployment. In addition, Reynolds et al. (1999, p. 10) support point 2 in the above list, as they state:

> The interaction between perceived entrepreneurial opportunities and the entrepreneurial capacity to pursue them will give rise to a greater number of start-up efforts, new firm births and jobs. As more new firms and jobs are created, there subsequently may be greater firm deaths and job destruction. Firm and job turbulence or 'churning' is what is often referred to as *Business Dynamics*, which usually accompanies economic growth.

Bednarzik's (2000) treatise examines entrepreneurship's influence on job growth in the USA and Europe, and provides convincing figures of small businesses' share of the whole enterprise sector's role in employment. According to his paper, in 1997, number of establishments with 500 or more employees comprised only 0.2 per cent of all of the enterprises in the USA. In contrast, the smallest businesses (1–19 employees) comprised 86.5 per cent of the whole enterprise sector. However, micro businesses' (fewer than 5 employees) share of the whole enterprise sector was 54.5 per cent, indicating that despite the multitude of small businesses, their share of total employment is not as critical as is large businesses' share. However, the US small business sector's influence on job growth is indisputable. The Small Business Administration's studies in 1998 (according to Bednarzik, 2000) revealed that small firms with fewer than 20 employees created about half of the net new jobs over the period 1990–95. In addition, the study showed that gross and net job creation diminishes as the establishment size rises (Bednarzik, 2000, p. 6).

Small businesses have an impact not only on the employment, but also on the other areas of economic growth. According to Reynolds et al. (1999, p. 7), firms that employ fewer than 500 people, that is small firms, generated 51 per cent of the US private sector GDP. However, the economy's stage of development may affect entrepreneurship's influence on GDP growth. Van Stel et al. (2005, pp. 318–19) researched 36 countries and suggested that entrepreneurship influenced GDP growth positively only in developed countries, whereas in underdeveloped countries the result was negative. Nonetheless, the authors concluded that the reason for this probably lies not in

Table 26.1   Enterprises according to employment class in Finland in 2006

Enterprise size	Number of enterprises	Share of the whole enterprise sector, %	Share of the whole employment, %	Share of the whole turnover, %
Small enterprises: fewer than 50 employees	247393	98.9	44.6	31.5
< 2 employees	163936	65.5	7.2	4.5
2–9 employees	69369	27.7	17.8	11.6
10–49 employees	14088	5.7	19.6	15.4
Medium-sized enterprises: 50–249 employees	2373	0.9	17.3	17.4
Large enterprises: min. 250 employees	612	0.2	38.1	51.1
Total	250376	100.0	100.0	100.0

Source: Finnish Ministry of Employment and the Economy (2008), p. 26.

inefficiency, but in the poor opportunities that the developing countries provide. Also Beck et al. (2005, p. 216) suggested a positive relationship between the share of SME employment in the total manufacturing employment and GDP per capita growth. Their research consisted of a sample of 45 countries. Additionally, Carree and Thurik (2008) examined the impact of the number of entrepreneurs (which were equalled by business owners) on the economic performance of OECD countries. They showed that the number of business owners and GDP growth have a positive interdependence: an increase in the number of business owners results in enhanced GDP growth (Carree and Thurik, 2008, pp. 107–8).

In Finland, small enterprises (fewer than 50 employees) comprised 98.9 per cent of the whole enterprise sector in 2006. Their share of employment was 44.6 per cent, and 31.5 per cent of the whole turnover. However, very small micro firms (fewer than 10 employees) comprised 93.2 per cent of the whole enterprise sector, but they created only 25 per cent of the whole employment and only 16.1 per cent of the turnover in aggregate (Finnish Ministry of the Employment and the Economy, 2008, p. 26; see Table 26.1).

Table 26.1 also shows that large and medium-sized businesses' share of employment is bigger than that of small enterprises, in relation their number. Furthermore, small businesses created 31.5 per cent of the turnover created by all the enterprises in Finland in 2006. Small firms with fewer than two employees comprised 4.5 per cent, firms with 2–9 employees created 11.6 per cent, and firms with 10–49 employees created 15.4 per cent. In contrast, large enterprises comprised 51.1 per cent of the whole turnover; that is 612 large companies create 19.6 percentage units more turnover than 247393 small enterprises.

The figures in Table 26.1 are derived from Finnish data, which use a slightly different definition for small and medium-sized businesses than does the EU Commission. Furthermore, the structures of interest are excluded from the EU statistics, so that they concern only actual, independent small businesses. Statistics (according to the Commission's size definition, which considers not only the number of employees, but also turnover and the balance sheet's total) show that in Finland the small enterprise sector's share of the employment is smaller than in the EU on average. However, the distribution of small enterprises is roughly the same. (Finnish Ministry of Employment and the Economy, 2008, pp. 29–31).

Also in Finland the industries dominated by small businesses were in the agriculture and services. For example, micro firms comprised 97.8 per cent of the businesses in personal services, 96.8 per cent of the businesses in the agriculture, forestry and fishing industry, and 96.4 per cent of the businesses in the social and health services. In manufacturing, the share of micro firms was the smallest at, 83.6 per cent (Finnish Ministry of Employment and the Economy, 2008, p. 28).

3 SMALL FAMILY BUSINESS DEFINITION AND HYPOTHESIS OF THE STUDY

The demands mentioned above are taken into account in the family business definition proposed by the Finnish Ministry of Trade and Industry's Family Entrepreneurship Working Group (FEWG). The group created a multi-layer definition, where the family enterprise 'functions as a kind of an umbrella' under which the concept of family company covers only the family businesses that operate in a company form. Then the concept of family company was defined. The starting point of the definition is the family's power through ownership of the firm in terms of voting shares. The FEWG's (Family Entrepreneurship Working Group, 2005, pp. 34–6; translation by the author) definition of family company is as follows

A business is a family company if:

1. The majority of the voting right is possessed by the natural person(s) who founded the company, or by natural person(s) who have acquired the capital stock of the firm, or by their spouses, parents, child or the child's direct heir.
2. The majority of the voting right may be direct or indirect.
3. At least one representative of the family or kinship group is in the company's management or governance.
4. A listed company fulfils the family company definition if the founder of the company, or the acquirer of the company (company's capital stock), or their family or descendants, possess 25 per cent of the voting right yielded by the shares of the company.

The definition's advantage is its exactness, since its purpose is to serve legislation. Thus it is a suitable definition for quantitative research. Therefore the definition of small family business used in this study is derived from the definition proposed by the FEWG, since the group recommended using the definition as a starting point in the compilation of statistics on small family businesses (Family Entrepreneurship Working Group, 2005, p. 11).

Given the issues related to the difficulty and demands of the small family business definition, the following definition was established for this research:

> A small family business is a business controlled by the founder generation or later generations of a single family or kinship group. The company form plays no role. At least half of the business must be owned by an individual or a group of individuals from a single family or kinship group. In addition, at least one family representative must be in the firm's management.

The definition above takes into account the FEWG's suggestion of separating the concepts of family enterprise and family company, since the definition allows companies to be family businesses regardless of company form. In addition, conditions 1 and 3 of the FEWG definition are included in this study's definition. Condition 2 is not mentioned separately, since the family's indirect influence is not considered in the definition, due to the nature of small businesses and the demands of questionnaire structure, which was developed to be as easy to comprehend as possible (see the Appendix). Naturally the last condition of the FEWG definition is not in this study's definition, as it was expected that none of the small firms in the sample would be a listed company. Whether small firms, which are owned, managed and controlled by only one person, can be defined as small family businesses is a question under constant debate, since they obviously do not employ many family members. However, despite the lack of the family's direct involvement in the business through management or ownership, the family probably influences the business because the small business owner-manager is likely to be affected by his family members' opinions and behaviour (Aldrich and Cliff, 2003).

Tourunen (2009, p. 103) estimates that family businesses' share of the Finnish small enterprise population is between 80 and 100 per cent, which is suggested as the share of family businesses in the whole enterprise population (Flören, 1998, p.122).

Hypothesis 1   The share of the small family firms out of the small enterprise population is from 80 to 100 per cent.

Previous family business research indicates that, in general, family businesses are smaller than non-family businesses (e.g. Klein, 2000, p. 162; Gudmundson et al., 1999, p. 32).

Hypothesis 2   Family firms are smaller than non-family businesses.

Founder generation firms are often considered as first-generation family firms which are smaller than the next generation firms (McConaughy and Phillips 1999, p. 130).

Hypothesis 3   Small family firms are founder generation firms.

Traditionally, service industries are dominated by small enterprises. This consequently leads to an assumption that small family firms are operating in services (Finnish Ministry of Employment and the Economy, 2008, p. 28; Bednarzik, 2000, p. 6).

Hypothesis 4   Small family firms operate in the services industry.

4 METHODOLOGICAL CHOICES

This chapter presents the sample, data, methodology and the descriptive results. Furthermore, the end of the chapter combines findings of this study with findings of large and medium-sized family businesses in 2005, which Tourunen published in his doctoral thesis (2009). However, the analysis of findings, their relation to earlier family business research and literature, and their implications are presented in section 4.

The Finnish enterprise register includes small enterprises that are part of concerns, which employ at least 50 people. These parent companies and subsidiaries do not belong to the framework of this research's sample, because otherwise the condition for small enterprises' independence would not be fulfilled. In other words, by including small businesses, which belong to a business structure that employs more than 50 people, to the sample, we would obtain skewed information about the small businesses' economic condition, and thus about their contribution to the economy.

The research of the Finnish small family businesses' contribution to the Finnish economy was conducted as a sample research based on the 2006 enterprise register's statistics. All the enterprise register's small enterprises (fewer than 50 employees) were at first divided into two groups: enterprises with less than one hired employee, and enterprises with at least one hired employee. The partitioned sample of 2004 observation units was directed to the latter group; that is, the research sample was derived from small enterprises that employ at least one hired employee. The sample frame of the small enterprises with at least one hired employee was derived in the following manner. First, small enterprises that are part of large or medium-sized concerns were excluded. Then, enterprises that are certainly not small family businesses were excluded as well. This group consists of units included in the enterprise register's annual statistics, but have certain juridical characteristics (e.g. enterprises, which are pension and other foundations, cooperatives and associations), have a certain ownership type (enterprises owned by the state or municipality, or foreign-owned enterprises), or operate in a certain industry (e.g. government and national defence). Nevertheless, this group is included in the data as a part of the control group.

The sample frame's cells have been chosen so that there are eight industry groups and four enterprise size groups; thus there are, in total, 32 cells in the frame. The eight industry groups are: (1) agriculture, game husbandry and fishery; (2) extractive industry, industry and energy; (3) construction; (4) commerce; (5) hotel, catering and accommodation services; (6) freighting, warehousing and data communications; (7) finance and real-estate services; and (8) education, health care and other services. The four size groups are: (I) 1–4 employees; (II) 5–9 employees; (III) 10–19 employees; (IV) 20–49 employees. There are, in total, 66 396 enterprises, which fulfil these criteria, 65 288 of which do not belong to any concern, and 1108 concern parents.

The smallest enterprises in the sample frame (1–4 employees) comprise 64.3 per cent (42 677 enterprises) of the enterprises in all the industry groups. In terms of industry group, the greatest amount of enterprises were in commerce (14 529 enterprises), but nearly as many operated in finance and real-estate services (14 001 enterprises). The sample frame according to the industry and the number of employees is presented in Table 26.2.

In 2006, there were 86 407 enterprises that employed at least one person in the Finnish

Table 26.2   Sample frame, number of small enterprises in terms of industry group and the number of employees (including all small firms in Finland)

	Total	Enterprise size group			
		I (1–4 empl.)	II (5–9 empl.)	III (10–19 empl.)	IV (20–49 empl.)
Industry groups	66 396	42 677	13 686	6668	3365
1	1696	1163	361	134	38
2	9423	4836	2192	1444	951
3	11 229	6937	2491	1254	547
4	14 529	9759	2941	1241	588
5	3685	2322	854	351	158
6	6284	4003	1311	670	300
7	14 001	10 067	2323	1043	568
8	5549	3590	1213	531	215

enterprise register. Now, there seems to be a difference between the sample frame and the enterprise register of 2006, since there are only 66 396 enterprises in the sample frame. The difference results from the conditions that determined the sample frame. These conditions were presented above, but basically the conditions were: only definite small family businesses (certain legal forms, ownership types and industries were excluded) and enterprises that are not a part of a concern structure employing more than 50 people formed the sample frame.

The actual sample was derived from the sample frame by relative random sampling. However, at least 40 enterprises were included in each cell of the sample, and all 38 enterprises in the cell 1/IV (group of enterprises that employ between 20 and 49 people in agriculture, game husbandry or fishery) were counted in the sample. In this way, a sample of 2004 enterprises was formed. After the creation of a research sample, a mail survey (see the Appendix) was sent to all 2004 enterprises in the sample during December 2008. On the basis of the survey, 731 enterprises' small family business status was identified. As this answer rate was not satisfactory, the postal survey was complemented by telephone interviews during January–March 2009. Both the mail surveys and the telephone interviews were directed to the owner, the CEO or the financial manager of the target company. In total, 1805 responses were received; that is, response rate was 90.1 per cent. Loss of responses was greatest, 16.7 per cent, in the industry group 5, hotel, catering and accommodation services; and smallest, 3.5 per cent, in the industry group 8, education, healthcare and other services. The family business definition suggested by the FEWG was applied to the recognition of small family business status. Furthermore, enterprises that were recognized as small family businesses were asked if a succession had occurred in the firm. The distribution between different ownership types and non-respondents in the sample is presented in Table 26.3.

Mail surveys' and telephone interviews' high response rate (90.1 per cent) anticipated high reliability for the estimations based on the sample of small enterprises in the sample frame. This was confirmed, as the estimates' variation coefficients remained below the critical limit; that is, the variation coefficients (C/V) were below 20.

Table 26.3   Number of enterprises and their relative share in the sample

Small family business status	Number	Share %
Family businesses owned by the first generation	1180	59
Family businesses owned by later generations	223	11
Businesses with other ownership type (non-family businesses)	402	20
No Response	199	10
Total	*n* (sample) = 2004	100%

Table 26.4   Small family businesses' (at least one hired employee) share of the whole
population of corresponding small enterprises, employment, and turnover in
2006, sample estimates

Industry	Share of population (%)	Employment (%)	Turnover (%)
1. Agriculture, game husbandry and fishery	81	69	73
2. Extractive industry, industry and energy	74	64	52
3. Construction	82	78	75
4. Commerce	74	72	54
5. Hotel, catering and accommodation services	84	78	78
6. Freighting, warehousing and data communications	85	78	57
7. Finance and real-estate services	60	52	37
8. Education, healthcare and other services	66	61	56
Average, % (*N* = 76 240)	74	68	56

5   RESULTS

The postal survey and telephone interview results were combined in Statistics Finland with the statistics of the sample enterprises' financial statements of 2006. The data were processed with SAS statistical analysis software, and because of the sample's high representativeness, the results could be generalized to the whole population of Finnish small enterprises. Therefore the figures presented in the following tables concern small enterprises that employ at least one hired employee in 2006 at the population level. The share of small family businesses in this population was 74 per cent in 2006. Furthermore, small family businesses accounted for approximately 68 per cent of employment, and approximately 56 per cent of the total turnover created by small Finnish enterprises.

   Table 26.4 presents small family businesses' share of the population of small enterprises (1–49 employees), share of employment, and share of total turnover, in the eight recognized industries. That is, family businesses form the majority of the small enterprises, yet their shares of employment and especially of total turnover are smaller than could be expected on the basis of their share of the population. However, this gap is not that large in the industry groups 1 (agriculture, game husbandry and fishery), 3 (construction), and 5 (hotel, catering and accommodation services).

Total value added created by small family businesses that employ at least one hired employee was, in this frame, €13.3 billion in 2006. Furthermore, according to the sample estimates, they employed 284 280 people in 2006.

The added value measures how much additional value the company has been able to create in its business from its products and services, and is calculated using the following formula (Committee for Corporate Analysis, 2005, p. 82):

Added value = Operating margin + Personnel expenses − Gains on sale of fixed assets included in operating income

The total added value created by the Finnish enterprise sector, that is, every enterprise in Finland, regardless of size, was €87.5 billion in 2006 (Statistics Finland, 2007). Thus small family businesses with at least one employee accounted for approximately 15 per cent of the whole Finnish enterprise sector's added value in 2006.

The added value is needed in calculating GDP. According to Statistics Finland (http://www.stat.fi/tup/verkkokoulu/data/talt/03/05/index_en.html):

> There are three different methods for calculating the GDP, because national accounts are based on the premise that value of production=income=expenditure. The first method is so called output method. Output method starts out from production: value added is obtained by deducting intermediate consumption from output. Value added is computed separately for each industrial sector, and the sums are then added together to get the GDP figure.

The output method for calculating GDP is the method in this study as well. Table 26.5 presents the relative share of small family businesses controlled by the first generation, small family businesses controlled by second or later generation, and non-family businesses of the small enterprise population in each industry in 2006. Clearly a majority of the small enterprises are small family businesses, which are controlled by the first generation (65.4 per cent). Slightly more than a quarter (26.4 per cent) of the enterprises are not small family businesses, and a clear minority are small family businesses that have conducted at least one succession (8.2 per cent). In industries 7 and 8 a small proportion of enterprises are controlled by second or later generations. Only 3.2 per cent of enterprises in education, healthcare and other services have gone through a succession, and only 4.7 per cent of enterprises in finance and real-estate services. In addition, the share of small non-family businesses in these industries is also the highest.

A total of 88.8 per cent of the small family businesses that employed at least one employee in 2006, are controlled by the founding generation. Consequently, the remaining 11.2 per cent have gone through at least one succession.

Table 26.6 shows how small Finnish family and non-family businesses are distributed among industries. The majority of the small family businesses operate in commerce (22 per cent), construction (18 per cent), and finance and real-estate services (17 per cent). An eye-catching feature of the industry distribution is that only 6 per cent of the small family businesses operate in hotel, catering and accommodation services, and only 8 per cent in the education, healthcare and other services. Furthermore, a majority of the small non-family businesses operate in finance and real-estate services (31 per cent), and commerce (22 per cent). Similarly with small family businesses, only 3 per cent of the small

Table 26.5   Different ownership types' shares of the small enterprise population in each industry in 2006, sample estimates

Industry	First-generation small family businesses (%)	Later-generation small family businesses (%)	Small non-family businesses (%)	Total (%)
1. Agriculture, game husbandry and fishery	67.8	13.1	19.1	100
2. Extractive industry, industry and energy	58.5	15.6	25.9	100
3. Construction	76.5	5.5	18.0	100
4. Commerce	64.4	9.6	26.0	100
5. Hotel, catering and accommodation services	77.4	6.2	16.4	100
6. Freighting, warehousing and data communications	73.3	11.3	15.4	100
7. Finance and real-estate services	55.5	4.7	39.8	100
8. Education, healthcare and other services	63.3	3.2	33.5	100
Average (%)	65.4 ($n = 49\,867$)	8.2 ($n = 6275$)	26.4 ($n = 20\,098$)	100 ($n = 76\,240$)

Table 26.6   Industry distribution of small Finnish family and non-family businesses in 2006, sample estimates

Industry	Distribution of small family businesses (%)	Distribution of small non-family businesses (%)
1. Agriculture, game husbandry and fishery	4	3
2. Extractive industry, industry and energy	13	13
3. Construction	18	11
4. Commerce	22	22
5. Hotel, catering and accommodation services	6	3
6. Freighting, warehousing, and data communications	12	6
7. Finance and real-estate services	17	31
8. Education, healthcare and other services	8	11
Total (%)	100 ($n = 56\,142$)	100 ($n = 20\,098$)

Table 26.7   Small enterprises with fewer than one hired employee: number, number of employees, and turnover in terms of industry in 2006

Industry	Number of small enterprises	Number of employees	Turnover: €
1. Agriculture, game husbandry and fishery	7064	4632	452 998
2. Extractive industry, industry and energy	13 902	7026	1 561 429
3. Construction	21 987	13 555	1 727 187
4. Commerce	27 418	16 374	3 800 659
5. Hotel, catering and accommodation services	5137	4510	383 566
6. Freighting, warehousing and data communications	14 288	13 848	1 452 347
7. Finance and real-estate services	39 054	19 899	3 052 517
8. Education, healthcare and other services	32 114	21 740	1 474 378
Other	22	8	14
Total	160 986	101 592	13 905 095

Sources: Statistics Finland (2007).

non-family businesses operate in the hotel, catering and accommodation industry. Nevertheless, Table 26.6 confirms the findings in prior research, as it shows that the majority of the small enterprises (65 per cent of the small family businesses and 73 per cent of the small non-family businesses) operate in the service industry, that is, in the industry groups 4–8 (Finnish Ministry of Employment and the Economy, 2008, p. 28).

In 2006, there were 160 986 Finnish small enterprises that employed fewer than one employee. In other words, 64.3 per cent of all of the Finnish enterprises employed fewer than one employee each. These enterprises contribute little to employment and total turnover; of the employment created by all of the Finnish enterprises in 2006, they accounted for approximately 7 per cent, and of the total turnover created by all the Finnish enterprises in 2006, their contribution share was approximately 4 per cent.

Table 26.7 presents the population of enterprises that employ fewer than one employee, total number of employees, and total turnover they create. However, there are 2292 units in Table 26.7 that cannot, with certainty, be categorized as small family businesses (these include cooperatives, foundations and foreign-owned enterprises). The debate whether the remaining 158 694 units are actually small family businesses or not is beyond the scope of this study. A separate sample is required to comprehensively examine the small family business status of this population. However, it may not be reasonable, since it is very likely that the majority of the 158 694 units would fulfil the conditions of the small family business definition used in this study. In this study, all the enterprises with fewer than one hired employee (excluding the above-mentioned 2292 units) are regarded as small family businesses, and their shares of employment and total turnover are added to the contributions of small family businesses with at least one hired employee.

When the above-mentioned 2292 small enterprises are excluded from the enterprise data, and the financial statements of the remaining enterprises are examined, the residual turnover is approximately €11.6 billion, residual value added €4.3 billion, and residual employment 94 000 employees in 2006. By adding these small enterprises to the small family businesses that employ at least one employee, the total share of small family businesses (among the Finnish small enterprises) increases from 74 per cent to 87 per cent.

Tourunen's doctoral thesis (2009) examined large and medium-sized family businesses' contribution to the Finnish economy. By adding the results of this study to the findings of Tourunen's doctoral thesis, we will obtain information about the total significance of the Finnish family business population in the Finnish economy. However, the results in this study concern year 2006, so we need to adjust the figures to correspond to the situation in 2005.

Small enterprises' turnover grew by 2.3 per cent between 2005 and 2006, and the number of employees increased by 5.0 per cent at the same time. (Statistics Finland, 2006, 2007). Now, if we adjust these change rates to value added (€13.3 billion) and employment (284 280 employees) created by small family businesses with at least one employee in 2006 (Table 26.7), we find that small family businesses employed an estimated 270 742 employees in 2005, and their value added was estimated at €13.0 billion. Furthermore, applying the same method and change rates to the figures presented in Table 26.7, we find that small enterprises that employed fewer than one employee in 2006 had an added value in 2005 estimated at €4.2 billion, and the number of employees was estimated at 89 500. In total, there were 236 435 enterprises in Finland in 2005. They employed 1 328 451 employees, created a total turnover of €318.5 billion, and total added value of €79.7 billion (Statistics Finland, 2006).

6   DISCUSSION

Tourunen's doctoral thesis (2009) used the same family business definition as this study. Hence, combining the findings is feasible. Without the same definition, combining would still have been possible, but the results could have been (and probably would have been) subjugated to continuous debate about their actual significance.

Large Finnish family businesses accounted for 16 per cent of the turnover, and 22 per cent of the employment created by their comparison industries in 2005. Medium-sized family businesses' share of their comparison industries' total turnover was 41 per cent, and the share of the comparison industries' employment was 49 per cent in 2003. In 2005, medium-sized family businesses' added value was estimated €3.8 billion, and the estimated number of employees was 78 000 (Tourunen, 2009, pp. 82–6). Family businesses' combined contribution to the Finnish economy in 2005 is displayed in Table 26.8.

The figures in Table 26.8 show that family businesses accounted for 42 per cent of the employment and 35 per cent of the added value created by the Finnish enterprise sector in 2005. In addition to the results that this research and Tourunen's doctoral thesis provided about family businesses' significance in the Finnish economy, a vital part of these studies' contribution is the unique family business database, which was created as a by-product. In Tourunen's thesis, all the Finnish large and medium-sized businesses were interviewed and examined. As it would be impossible and unnecessary to conduct a total survey among nearly 250 000 small enterprises, a representative sample of 2004 was derived. Combination of the data received from these studies paints an unprecedented

Table 26.8   Family businesses' contribution to the Finnish economy in 2005

Size group	Number of employees	Added value, € bn
Large family businesses	122 000	6.7
Medium-size family businesses	78 000	3.8
Small family businesses		
(a) 1–49 employees	270 700	13.0
(b) fewer than one employee	89 500	4.2
Total	560 200	27.7

picture of small family businesses in a certain economy. Studies as comprehensive as these two are also required in other economies, in order to turn beliefs and estimates into absolute figures. Furthermore, future family business researchers need reliable and accessible data of small family businesses around the world to continue the work of their predecessors (Flören, 1998, p. 131).

Family businesses are equated with small businesses (see, e.g., Carsrud, 1994, p. 39). Although it may be a prevalent assumption, it is not completely accurate, since many of large companies are defined as family businesses, and for example among the S&P 500 firms, family firms represent 35 per cent of the companies (Anderson and Reeb 2003, p. 1302). Additionally, this basic assumption has led to a situation in which family business researchers always remember to mention that large and remarkable family businesses also exist. However, estimates and research have suggested that family businesses do dominate the small enterprise sector (Heinonen and Toivonen, 2003, p. 31), and the larger the firms under examination, the smaller the share of family businesses among them (Klein, 2000, p. 160).

In spite of recognition of small family businesses' existence, no comprehensive study on their significance in the Finnish economy has been made. Heinonen and Toivonen's study (2003) aimed at clarifying the significance of the whole family business sector (large, medium and small family businesses) in the Finnish economy, and they did this by using a sample of 497 family firms. In this study, the impact of small family businesses alone was examined with a sample of 2004 small firms. Additionally, when the reader compares the results of this study with the results of Heinonen and Toivonen, he/she should also notice the differences in employed family business definitions.

In addition to expanding knowledge about the small family businesses' contribution to the Finnish economy, this study complements Tourunen's (2009) research on the significance of Finnish large and medium-sized family businesses. Adding the results of this study to the findings that Tourunen made provides the most comprehensive knowledge about the family businesses' contribution to the employment and GDP in Finland.

A sample of 2004 small firms was derived from the population of small Finnish enterprises, which employ fewer than 50, but at least one employee. In addition, establishments that are certainly not small family businesses (certain legal forms, ownership types and industries) were left out of the population. The research on small family businesses' contribution to the Finnish economy was then conducted on this sample. Separate estimates of the impact of the 160 986 small firms that employ fewer than one employee were given afterwards. Nearly all of these (158 694 firms) were defined as small family businesses, since it would be likely that they would fulfil the conditions of this study's family business definition. Consequently, their estimated contribution was added separately to the contributions of small family firms that employ at least one employee. In the following summary of the key findings of this study, results concerning small family firms with fewer than one employee are presented separately. Otherwise, the results concern small family businesses that employ at least one employee.

The first hypothesis, share of the small family firms out of the small enterprise population is from 80 to 100 per cent, was confirmed. This study indicated that, in 2006, approximately 74 per cent (56 142 enterprises) of the small businesses that employ at least one employee are small family businesses. By including the small family businesses employing fewer than one employee, the share of small family businesses in the Finnish small enterprise population rises to 87 per cent.

Hypothesis 2, family firms are smaller than non-family businesses, was confirmed. Out of the 160 986 small firms in Finland, 158 694 are family firms. Hypothesis 3, small family firms are founder generation firms, was confirmed. Out of the sample, 59 per cent of the small firms were founder generation firms, 11 per cent next-generation firms and 20 per cent non-family businesses.

Hypothesis 4, small family firms operate in the service industry, was confirmed. In this study, eight different industries were identified. From these, five can be considered as service industries (industry groups 4–8). As could be expected, small family businesses seem to operate largely in the service industry. Furthermore, there was no industry without small family businesses. In 2006, 65 per cent of the small family businesses that employ more than one employee operated in the service industries. The largest share of small family businesses operated in commerce (22 per cent), construction (18 per cent), and finance and real-estate services (17 per cent). Only 6 per cent of the small family businesses were noted to operate in the hotel, catering and accommodation services, and 8 per cent in the education, healthcare and other services.

7 CONCLUSIONS

Table 26.7 shows that the share of family businesses in the small enterprise population is rather large, but their shares in employment and especially in turnover are not as large as might be expected on the basis of their share in the population. The findings of this study show that small Finnish family businesses with at least one employee comprise 56 per cent of the turnover and 68 per cent (284 280 employees) of the employment created by the small enterprise population in 2006. Total added value of these family businesses was €13.3 billion in 2006. Furthermore, in small family businesses that employed fewer than one employee total turnover was €11.6 billion, total added value was €4.3 billion, and they employed an estimated 94 000 employees. According to these results, small family businesses with at least one employee accounted for approximately 15 per cent, and small family businesses with fewer than one employee accounted for approximately 5 per cent of the whole added value created by the Finnish enterprise sector in 2006.

Politically, small family firms are neglected when speaking about small firms and entrepreneurship in general. Small firms are seen as a key resource for growing economies, but rarely have politicians noted that small firms are family-owned firms. The family factor is neglected in entrepreneurship policies and should be discussed more actively. Small family firms are often forgotten in entrepreneurship policy-making, which is dominated by growth jargon and globalization debates. Educationally, entrepreneurship and small business management is taught nowadays in hundreds of universities and at all levels of the education system. However, small family firm courses are rare, and they are missing from many business schools. When most of the small firms are family-owned firms, the family should be also highlighted as one of the key factors in small business management among innovation, growth, business planning and business design. Scientifically, family business research has been dominated by management and strategy studies made in large or medium-sized family enterprises. However, small family businesses offer a variety of questions that need to be examined in rigorous in-depth studies. International comparative studies between small family firms would also contribute to knowledge of how small family firms differ culturally from each other.

ACKNOWLEDGMENTS

We are indebted for the following specialists for their continuous support for this study: Data Manager Jouko Rajaniemi (Statistics Finland), Dr Ismo Teikari (Statistics Finland), Dr Kalevi Tourunen (Haaga-Helia University of Applied Sciences, Helsinki, Finland) and Professor Matti Koiranen (University of Jyväskylä, Finland).

REFERENCES

Acs, Z.J. (1992), 'Small business economics: a global perspective', *Challenge*, **35**(November/December), 38–44.
Aldrich, H.E. and Cliff, J.E. (2003), 'The pervasive effects of family on entrepreneurship: toward a family embeddedness perspective', *Journal of Business Venturing*, **18**(5), 573–96.
Anderson, R.C. and Reeb, D.M. (2003), 'Founding-family ownership and firm performance: evidence from the S&P 500', *Journal of Finance*, **58**(3), 1301–28.
Beck, T., Demirguc-Kunt, A. and Levine, R. (2005), 'SME's, growth, and poverty: cross-country evidence', *Journal of Economic Growth*, **10**(3), 199–229.
Bednarzik, R.W. (2000), 'The role of entrepreneurship in U.S. and European job growth', *Monthly Labor Review*, **123**(7), 3–16.
Carree, M.A. and Thurik, A.R. (2008), 'The lag structure of the impact of business ownership on economic performance in OECD countries', *Small Business Economics*, **30**(1), 101–10.
Carsrud, A.L. (1994), 'Meanderings of a resurrected psychologist or, lessons learned in creating a family business program', *Entrepreneurship Theory and Practice*, **19**(1), 39–48.
Chrisman, J.J., Chua, J.H. and Litz, R.A. (2004), 'Comparing the agency costs of family and non-family firms: conceptual issues and exploratory evidence', *Entrepreneurship Theory and Practice*, **28**(4), 335–54.
Committee for Corporate Analysis (2005), *A Guide to the Analysis of Financial Statements of Finnish Companies*, Helsinki: Gaudeamus.
Family Entrepreneurship Working Group (2005), *Family Entrepreneurship. Family Enterprises as the Engines of Continuity, Renewal and Growth-Intensiveness*, Finnish Ministry of Trade and Industry publications 16/2005.
Finnish Ministry of Employment and the Economy (2008), *Entrepreneurship Review 2008*, Publications of the Ministry of Employment and the Economy. Employment and Entrepreneurship 25/2008.
Flören, R.H. (1998), 'The significance of family business in the Netherlands', *Family Business Review*, **11**(2), 121–34.
Gudmundson, D., Hartman, E.A. and Tower, C.B. (1999), 'Strategic orientation: differences between family and nonfamily firms', *Family Business Review*, **12**(1), 27–40.

Heinonen, J. and Toivonen, J. (2003), 'Perheyritykset suomalaisessa yhteiskunnassa', in J. Heinonen (ed.), *Quo Vadis, suomalainen perheyritys?* Turku School of Economics, PK-instituutti.

Klein, S.B. (2000), 'Family businesses in Germany: significance and structure', *Family Business Review*, **13**(3), 157–82.

Kotey, B. and Meredith, G.G. (1997), 'Relationships among owner/manager personal values, business strategies, and enterprise performance', *Journal of Small Business Management*, **35**(1), 37–64.

McConaughy, D.L. and Phillips, G.M. (1999), 'Founders versus descendants: the profitability, efficiency, growth characteristics and financing in large, public, founding-family-controlled firms', *Family Business Review*, **12**(2), 123–32.

Reynolds, P.D., Hay, M. and Camp, S.M. (1999), *Global Entrepreneurship Monitor. 1999 Executive Report*, www.gemconsortium.org/download.asp?fid=140, read 24 August 2009.

Robbins, D.K., Pantuosco, L.J., Parker, D.F. and Fuller, B.K. (2000), 'An empirical assessment of the contribution of small business employment to U.S. state economic performance', *Small Business Economics*, **15**(4), 293–302.

Shanker, M.C. and Astrachan, J.H. (1996), 'Myths and realities: family businesses' contribution to the US economy – a framework for assessing family business statistics', *Family Business Review*, **9**(2), 107–23.

Statistics Finland (Tilastokeskus) (2006), *Finnish Enterprises in 2005.*

Statistics Finland (Tilastokeskus) (2007), *Finnish Enterprises in 2006.*

Statistics Finland (Tilastokeskus) (2008), *Finnish Enterprises in 2007.*

Tourunen, K. (2009), 'Perheyritykset kansantalouden resurssina. Keskisuurten ja suurten yritysten omistajuus, toiminnan laajuus ja kannattavuus Suomessa 2000–2005', *Jyväskylä Studies in Business and Economics*, **71**, Jyväskylä University Printing House.

Van Stel, A., Carree, M. and Thurik, R. (2005), 'The effect of entrepreneurial activity on national economic growth', *Small Business Economics*, **24**(3), 311–21.

Internet Sources

http://www.stat.fi/tup/verkkokoulu/data/talt/03/05/index_en.html

APPENDIX: COVER LETTER AND THE SURVEY

Cover Letter

Arvoisa yrityksen omistaja / toimitusjohtaja / talouspäällikkö

Tämä lyhyt neljän kysymyksen kysely liittyy työ- ja elinkeinoministeriön tilaamaan tutkimukseen, jonka ensimmäisessä vaiheessa vuosina 2005 – 2008 kartoitimme Suomen kaikkien keskisuurten ja suurten yritysten omistajuutta ja sen vaikutuksia. Nyt toteutamme vastaavan hankkeen pienten yritysten osalta vuoden 2006 yritysrekisterin vuositietojen pohjalta. Yrityksenne on valikoitunut Tilastokeskuksessa viime marraskuussa tehtyyn 2000:n pienen yrityksen otokseen. Pienen yrityksen kriteerinä on alle 50:n henkilön henkilöstö.

Sivun kääntöpuolella olevien kysymysten tiedot yhdistetään myöhemmin Tilastokeskuksessa yritysten rakennetilastoihin ja ne palvelevat tutkimustarpeiden lisäksi yritystaloustiedon käyttäjiä ja elinkeinopolitiikkaa. Edellä mainittujen tutkimustemme tuloksia käytettiin keväällä 2007 mm. hallitusneuvottelujen taustamateriaalina ja niitä on julkaistu Tilastokeskuksen julkaisuissa, Taloustaito- ja Liiketalous- lehdissä sekä Perheyritysten liiton kotisivulla.

Toivomme saavamme Teiltä arvokkaat vastauksenne, jotka ovat tutkimuksemme perusta. Jokainen vastaus on tästä syystä erittäin tärkeä.

Tutkimus on täysin luottamuksellinen. Tarkastelemme tuloksia tilastollisin menetelmin, eivätkä yksittäisen yrityksen tiedot tule mitenkään esille. Vastauksenne voitte lähettää myös sähköpostitse osoitteella antti.kirmanen@jyu.fi tai puhelimitse numeroon…

Etukäteen arvokkaasta vastauksestanne kiittäen!

Jyväskylässä 1.1. 2009

Professori Matti Koiranen, Jyväskylän yliopisto
Professori Juha Kansikas, Jyväskylän yliopisto
Tutkija Kalevi Tourunen, Jyväskylän yliopisto
Opiskelija Antti Kirmanen, Jyväskylän yliopisto

Survey (Translation from Finnish to English)

Your firm's name at the end of year 2006:

Was your firm a family business at the end of the year 2006?

Family business in an enterprise run by a founding generation or an enterprise which have managed a succession. At least half of a firm should be owned by a one person or owned by a group of family members. At least one member of a family should act in a management position or at a board of directors.
Answer: Yes / No.

(If your firm was not a family business you do not have to answer for this question)

If your firm was a family firm at the end of the 2006, have you managed a succession before the end of the year 2006? In other words, was at least half of your family firm ownership transferred for the next generation?
Answer: Yes / No.

(If your firm was not a family business you do not have to answer for this question)

Has your firm been family business all the time between 2000 and 2006?
Answer: (a) founder generation family business (b) next generation family business or (c) both

27 The microeconomics of family business
Eduardo L. Giménez and José Antonio Novo

1 INTRODUCTION

During recent decades the academic research in the area of family business has grown notably. A wide variety of tools and approaches from different disciplines has illuminated our understanding of the distinctive features and problems faced by any family firm; and, more precisely, on the interaction among each family member's different goals and interests concerning the firm, whether as manager, owner, worker or potential heir.[1] In fact, many authors have claimed that building and improving the conceptual knowledge base is a priority in this field.[2]

With respect to economic theory, despite the significance of family firms even in developed economies, only a few works have been interested in unveiling the decision-making process concerning the family members interacting with and within the family business in an economic environment. One reason may be that, to tackle the family firm's features different theoretical frameworks are required, comprising, for instance, the classical consumer theory, the theory of the firm, the theory of human capital, financial economics or the agency theory of asymmetric information. In fact, the existing theoretical literature displays disparate analytical settings as the foundation of empirical works or focuses on a particular facet of the family business, but without a unified and comprehensive framework. Thus building and improving the conceptual knowledge base for the economic theory approach to study the family business may also be considered as a priority. In this work, we present a unified framework founded upon the standard microeconomics theory to analyze the family firm.

From an analytical point of view, the challenge for economic theory lies in analyzing the decision-making process that involves the family business as a complex mixture of the interaction and reciprocal influence among a heterogenous set of individuals, as the well-known three-circle model describes. The agents involved comprise not only the family members working for the firm, but also other family members, and even non-family members belonging to the ownership and/or management circles. A theoretical economic model must identify who takes each decision, as well as enumerate the idiosyncratic features concerning the different agents interacting with the firm, such as the heterogeneity among the family members (abilities, income, goals, involvement etc.) or the heterogeneous individual information set concerning the economic performance at the firm.

The analysis of this decision-making process must integrate the two distinctive features of family firms: first, the decisions in the family circle are jointly taken with the decisions in the firm circle; and second, the family ties among those members interacting within the firm circle may affect the decisions taken in the firm. In the former, the objectives of the family and those of the firm are closely linked, although in some cases not coincident and, as a result, a number of conflicts arises. An illustrative example is the pecuniary rents extracted from the firm by some family members. A formal model that specifies the individual motivations of the family members would clarify the disparity of results in the existing literature, which emphasizes that this first feature is the key to explain the non-maximizing behaviour of family firms with respect to non-family firms.

In the latter, the family ties affect those decisions concerning the firm that require a particular analytical treatment. For instance, a distinctive characteristic of any family firm concerns the desire to transfer the business to the family's next generation. In order to clearly understand the succession conflicts, the altruistic motivations of the family members must be formally depicted. A theoretical model that considers altruism would clarify the disparity of results in the existing literature: some authors have pointed to this feature as a cause of inefficiency and as a threat to the firm's survival; while others have emphasized that this characteristic is a source of competitive advantage with respect to non-family firms.

The purpose of this chapter is to integrate and systematize within a common analytical framework the formal contributions of the theoretical literature on family businesses. To this end, we study the family firm decisions by means of the standard microeconomic tools to articulate the dominant problems and conflicts in family businesses. In our opinion the systematic approach presented here can be useful for characterizing the distinctive features of family business with respect to non-family business, as well as to show some directions for future research in this microeconomic approach. Among these distinctive features of family business to be characterized, we can enumerate the following: (i) a single family displays a high degree of ownership of the firm; (ii) one member – or very few members – of the family (usually known as the owner-manager) is involved in the managerial activities of the firm; (iii) the owner (the family) or the manager (the owner-manager) of the firm exhibits a degree of altruism towards the family's children; that is, in formal terms, at the time of taking decisions concerning the firm the family children's present and future well-being is considered; (iv) the family firm provides amenity benefits to the owner or to the manager, whether in terms of social acknowledge or as providing a job for the family children; (v) a family business displays a higher productivity than a non-family firm, *ceteris paribus* – that is, the same level of inputs; and, (vi) a family firm is financially constrained to obtain external funds because it precludes outside investors from the firm.

The chapter is structured as follows. Section 2 presents a brief survey of the existing microeconomics literature on family business; the topics analyzed are reviewed in the following sections. Section 3 analyzes how the literature has approached the specific features of family firms by considering the owner-manager's decisions in both a static and dynamic framework. Section 4 studies family firms in terms of the principal–agent model and considers the succession decision in a scenario of altruism and succession commitment. Section 5 investigates whether explicit consideration of institutional legal settings (more specifically, the minority shareholders' legal protection) and the financial market's development affect the ownership and management decisions in family firms. Section 6 summarizes the main conclusions of the analysis and proposes some potential links between research in family business and some related topics of economic theory.

2   A REVIEW OF THE LITERATURE

The main contributions of the microeconomics literature in the family business field can be organized according to their primary analytical focus. We identify three sets of works which deal with some of the defining characteristics of family firms. The first one studies family firms from the perspective of the concentration of ownership and control of the firm by a single individual. In particular, a number of works have analyzed the compatibility and potential conflicts in the decision-making process among the two simultaneous optimization processes resulting from such a concentration, namely the firm's profit maximization and the family's welfare maximization. The second one uses the agency theory approach to study the relationships among the family members interacting within the family. At the same time, this approach takes into account the implications of some specific characteristics of the founder's preferences – more specifically, his altruistic motivations and the desire to transfer the business to his heir. The third group of contributions focuses on the role of those characteristics of the firm's environment that are exogenous to the firm, such as institutional (legal and financial) imperfections, that affect the firm's decisions concerning ownership and governance mechanisms. We briefly review each set of works in the following paragraphs.

We begin with the group of academic works that makes use of a narrow definition of the family firm based exclusively on two dimensions: firm ownership and control. A family firm is understood in terms of a stereotype of a single economic agent called the owner-manager – that is, a firm in which ownership and control are restricted to a single decision-maker. The setting of the analysis presents an individual who is playing two roles simultaneously: he is both the family welfare maximizer and the firm profit maximizer. Despite its restricted view, the analysis includes a basic feature of family firms: the potential conflicts that arise when family's and firm's goals diverge. Thus, by restricting the extent and variety of family firms, this literature has provided some intuitions and clarified several issues. A first issue concerns the incompatibility of simultaneous maximizing of decision-making in the family and in the firm as a possible source of inefficiency. This incompatibility stems from the existence of non-pecuniary arguments in the family's welfare, for example amenity benefits, which are generated at the expense of the firm (see Feinberg, 1975, 1980, 1982; Olsen, 1973, 1977; Hannan, 1982 in a static framework; James, 1999 in a dynamic one). A second issue has to do with the conceptual boundaries of the owner-manager's income, which is composed of both the imputed wages from his managerial services in the firm and the perceived dividends derived from firm profits (see Graaff, 1950–51; Ng, 1974; Schlesinger, 1981; Lapan et al., 1988). This issue is closely related to another one, which consists of the way in which the imputed wage is determined. The alternative option to an exogenous wage is the consideration of a 'market' formed by the family's supply of labor and the family firm's demand for labor to determine the payment to the owner-manager managerial services in the firm. An important point here has to do with the possible specificity of the managerial services developed by the owner-manager and, then, their substitutability. The controversy generated in the works around these two issues was solved by Hannan (1982), who explicitly considers that the owner-manager's wage is not invariant, but changes with respect to the level of non-pecuniary benefits that he obtains from the firm. Both variables, wage and non-pecuniary profits, are jointly determined by the same set of preferences: those of the owner-manager. A third issue studies the timing of the business-operating family's deci-sion of bringing in the designated successor, both in the context of perfect financial markets and borrowing constraints in a dynamic context (see Kimhi, 1997). Finally, a fourth issue is the study of specific characteristics related to family firms, such as the intensity of labor, growth and control, which can be found in the literature in a static (Galve-Górriz et al., 1996, 2003, Sec. 2.2) and dynamic framework (Galve-Górriz et al., 2003, Sec. 2.3; James, 1999).

In Section 3 we follow the work of Hannan (1982) to study the role of the non-pecuniary benefits in the family's welfare by developing a simple static microeconomic model that characterizes the double role played by the founder deciding simultaneously at the family and firm levels. Then we extend the framework to a dynamic setting follow-ing James (1999).

The second microeconomics approach to the realm of family business deals with the family ties among those members interacting within the family firm, and how these interac-tions and the variety of individual motivations account for the survival of the family firm. A family firm is understood in terms of the mutual interaction of a family member who takes the production and managerial decisions concerning the firm (the owner-manager) and other family members who work for the firm. Agency problems arise from this relation-ship among family members with different goals. The setting of analysis is the principal–agent model. Contrary to the wide set of applications to the theory of the firm, the number of contributions that employs this approach in the area of family firms is very low. Chami (2001) and Galve-Górriz et al. (2003, Sec. 1.6), which are closely related to Schulze et al. (2001, 2002, 2003) posed in a non-microeconomic approach, are the only exceptions. These works studied the relationship between a founder and his son (and possible successor) interacting within the firm. These contributions deal with the influence of altruistic motiva-tions, whether parental or two-sided, on the relationship between a founder and his child interacting within the firm in both a static and a two-period model, which also considers that the child succeeds the parent and inherits the business. Note that this is a limited scope of the interactions within a family firm, and consequently further efforts are needed in order to cover a wider set of problems and situations by including more complex structures of families and firms. Yet it should be noted that the concept of family firm implicit in this approach is broader than the one previously mentioned in the first group of works. Here, two additional elements are present in the analysis: first, the generational dimension of family firms which can be found in the parent child relationship; and second, the values and family commitment – in the form of loyalty or altruism – or the desire to maintain ownership and control inside the family. Having in mind this restricted setting, this literature has provided a number of intuitions concerning this relationship.

We present a simplified and unified framework in Section 2 that summarizes the main findings of this approach. A well-known result in the literature of the agency theory, the interaction inside the firm of the principal (the manager) and the agent (the worker), results in an inefficient outcome for the firm. This interaction inside a family firm might result in a different outcome. The existence of parental altruism of the founder towards his children, however, is not enough for the survival of family firms. Thus we investigate the conditions that explicitly consider two-sided altruism – that is, a parent altruistic towards his child, and a child altruistic towards her parent – or succession commitments and a qualified heir account for the survival of the family firm.

The third group of works includes some papers devoted to studying the role of institutional imperfections both in the family firm's decisions as well as in the ownership structure and governance structures of the firm. We focus on two types of imperfections: legal environment and financial constraints. With respect to the former, Burkart et al. (2003) deals with the characteristics of the legal environment (particularly the legal protection of minority shareholders) as a determinant factor in the founder's decisions on succession, professionalizing the firm and preserving firm control and ownership. With respect to the latter, Kimhi (1997), Bhattacharya and Ravikumar (2001) and Castañeda (2006) have analyzed the influence of the development of capital markets on the evolution of family firms by means of a dynamic model of economic growth. The main argument in this case is that the quantity and quality of external financing sources have a crucial role in family firm ownership, size and length of life. Note again that this group of works considers family firms in narrow terms in order to focus the analysis on variables which are exogenous to the firm. However, by restricting the extent and variety of family firms this literature has provided some intuitions concerning the relevance of the institutional imperfections to the family firm.

In Section 5 we summarize the main contributions of this third group of papers by unifying them in a simplified version of Burkart et al. (2003).

The review of this section concerning the basic features developed in the literature has shown that the three approaches can be considered to be complementary, because all deal with the same issues, but from different perspectives. Two of them are internal perspectives, one related to the conflicts among the basic goals of each of the two systems that compose family firms, and the other related to the role of the interactions of the family members. The third one is an external perspective that deals with the influence of environmental factors. However, as will be explained in the following sections, greater analytical efforts are required in order to cover broader definitions of family firms, and to deal with a wider variety of questions.

3   THE OWNER-MANAGER AS A UTILITY MAXIMIZER

The distinctive characteristic of the family firm is that decisions in the family are taken jointly with decisions in the firm. The goals pursued by the former may be closely linked to the objectives of the latter, yet they need not to be coincident. Thus some decisions are aimed to achieve some particular family goals at the expense of the firm. This trade-off has been studied formally in the early literature on family firms.

A number of works have analyzed the decisions taken by the family intertwined with those taken in the firm in a standard microeconomics setting. Next, we present a common framework developed in this literature. There are two agents: a family, represented by the owner-manager, and the firm.

The family is represented by a single individual, denoted as the owner-manager, who is the owner and the only worker of the firm, and who also runs the business alone.[3] As is common in microeconomic theory, this single individual is fully characterized by three elements: the set of commodities that exists for the owner-manager; his endowments; and his preferences represented by a utility function. First, the owner-manager's endowment consists of three elements: an exogenous wealth W; an amount of available time T that can be devoted to labor or leisure activities, denoted to by n and l respectively; and, as he is the owner of the firm, all the shares belongs to him, $\theta = 1$. Second, the owner-manager's welfare is enhanced by devoting time to leisure activities, l, and consuming goods purchased in the market, $\mathbf{c}$. In addition, he may increase welfare by consuming goods only provided by the family firm, $\mathbf{b}$, a vector of goods whose quantity finally consumed results from the decisions taken in the family firm. We consider that there exist two types of these goods. One type is the non-pecuniary goods, denoted by $\mathbf{B}$, those goods that involve an expenditure or a cost for the firm and have to do with several kinds of goods that the manager can enjoy when running the company, which may or may not have a productive motivation in the firm (e.g. travelling and diverse luxury articles are typical examples).[4] The other type is the purely amenity goods (see e.g. Demsetz and Lehn, 1985), denoted by $\mathbf{A}$, those goods that do not come at the expense of the firm's profits and are derived from the mere existence of the decisions taken when running the firm (e.g. feeling for the business, emotional attachment, personal reputation and standing in society, or social, political and cultural influence in general).[5] We will assume that the individual's preferences can be represented by a twice-differentiable, strictly quasi-concave, increasing, continuous utility function, $U(\mathbf{x})$ with $\mathbf{x} = (\mathbf{c}, l, \mathbf{b})$.

The firm is characterized by technical procedures that transform inputs into an output. The firm produces a single good y by combining a number of inputs $y = (y^1, y^2, y^3, \ldots, y^J) \in \mathfrak{R}^J_+$. These inputs may comprise labor N, human capital H – which includes management abilities – physical capital K and other inputs, whether fixed or variable, each represented by y^m, with $j = 1, \ldots, J$. In addition, the firm may provide some goods to the family that cannot be obtained outside the firm or purchased in any open market. These non-pecuniary goods, $\mathbf{B}$, may require to be purchased by the firm, and may be used as an input. The technology will be represented by a twice-differentiable, concave, strictly increasing, continuous production function $y = f(\mathbf{y})$. In a market economy the firm interacts with other firms in an economic environment both in the goods and the inputs markets. We will consider that this environment is competitive (the case of alternative market structures is left to the conclusions). Thus the firm will consider as exogenous both the price of the good produced, p^y, and the price of all other inputs purchased in the market, w^m.

Considering this simple theoretical setting, most of the literature has inquired whether the family and the firm are – or are not – utility and profit maximizers. Other works have been concerned with investment decisions in the family firm when providing non-pecuniary goods to the family. We cover these issues here in static and dynamic frameworks.

3.1   The Family Business in a Static Model

3.1.1   The basic model
In this section we present a static model that can be seen as an extension of different works found in the literature.[6] In this section we simplify the notation as follows. The family consumes only one consumption good, $\mathbf{c} = c$, that can be purchased at market price p^c, and only a non-pecuniary good is considered, $\mathbf{b} = B$; in addition, it has an exogenous monetary wealth endowment, that is $\mathbf{W} = W$. The firm produces among others, with labor, $y^1 = N$, and the non-pecuniary good, $y^2 = B$, as inputs.

We can consider the case of an owner-manager solving the problem simultaneously for the family and the firm given the prices of goods and inputs in a single period of time. He chooses the family's goods consumption, leisure and non-pecuniary consumption, and the firm's output and input factors that maximize the welfare of the family $U(c,l,B)$ subject to three conditions. First, the family's temporal constraint

$$n + l = T \tag{27.1}$$

second, the family's monetary constraint

$$p^c c = W + w^N n + \theta \pi(y, \mathbf{y}) \tag{27.2}$$

where p^c is the price of the consumption good and π represents the profits. Finally, the firm's profits are

$$\pi(y, \mathbf{y}) = p^y f(\mathbf{y}) - w^N B - \sum_{j=3}^{J} w^j y^j \tag{27.3}$$

where p^y is the price of the good produced by the family firm, and w^j the price of the input j with $j = 1, \ldots, J$.

Because the profits are not taken as exogenous to the owner-manager problem, the firm's profits (27.3) can be explicitly considered as part of the family income. Thus the family's monetary constraint (27.2) becomes

$$p^c c + w^B B = W + p^y f(n, B, y^3, \ldots, y^J) - \sum_{j=3}^{J} w^j y^j$$

The first-order conditions are the following:

$$\frac{p^c}{p^y} \frac{U_l(\mathbf{x})}{U_c(\mathbf{x})} = f_N(\mathbf{y}) = \frac{w^n}{p^y} \tag{27.4}$$

$$f_{y^j}(\mathbf{y}) = \frac{w^j}{p^y} \quad j = 3, \ldots J \tag{27.5}$$

$$f_B(\mathbf{y}) = \frac{w^B}{p^y} - \frac{p^c}{p^y} \frac{U_l(\mathbf{x})}{U_c(\mathbf{x})} \tag{27.6}$$

First, the optimal condition (27.4) refers to the labor decisions. The family sacrifices leisure to supply labor and then increase consumption, until the welfare lost by the last unit of foregone leisure equals the welfare gain for increasing consumption due to an increase in labor income. The firm demand for labor until the marginal productivity of the last unit of labor hired equals its costs of hiring. Note that both decisions, the family's supply and the firm's demand for labor, are compatible. Also observe that the owner-manager's imputed wage is found from the interaction between the family's supply of labor and the family firm's demand for labor, and it is not the exogenous 'wage rate that would be paid to a hired manager', 'that is, to an imperfect substitute of the family manager'.[7]

Second, the optimal condition (27.5) refers to the firm's demand for an input $j = 3, \ldots,$ J; that is, the input m is purchased (or hired) until the marginal productivity of its last unit equals its marginal costs. Because of the competitive (and partial equilibrium) setting assumed, the supply of any input m is exogenously given, which is infinitely elastic, as its price is constant.

Finally, the optimal condition (27.6) refers to the firm's demand for the non-pecuniary good. Observe that if non-pecuniary benefits do not enhance welfare, that is, $U_B(c,l,B) = 0$, the input B will be hired until the marginal productivity of its last unit equals its marginal costs. Then, as observed by Olsen (1973), 'the profit and utility are simultaneously maximized' (p. 393). Alternatively, when the non-pecuniary good increases welfare, the firm does not demand the non-pecuniary input until the marginal productivity of the last unit of non-pecuniary good purchased or hired equals its cost. It is important to realize that our framework allows us to show that, because the well-being of the family is directly affected by the decisions taken at the firm concerning the non-pecuniary good, an externality exists. This external effect is considered in the marginal rate of substitution, the last term on the right-hand side of (27.6). This entails that there exists an overprovision of the non-pecuniary good, because of the concavity of the production function, with respect to the case that the externality does not exist. Yet no inefficiency arises, because the family takes consumption and productive decisions simultaneously, and then internalizes all mutual external effects.

3.1.2 An extension: decisions on productive factors

In this section we extend the previous framework to consider the consequences of two distinctive features that affect family firms: the higher cost of capital and the higher productivity of labor in family firms with respect to non-family businesses. The former refers to the limited portfolio diversification and a higher cost of capital due to the higher risk premium faced by those firms displaying a concentration of ownership and decision-making process (see, e.g., Galve-Górriz et al., 2003, Sec. 2.2). The latter refers to the advantage of the family-controlled firms concerning the high family members' motivation, implication, specific knowledge and skills.

We present a static model that can be seen as an extension of Galve-Górriz et al. (1996, 2003, Sec. 2.2). The framework is the same as before, but the family does not play any role but to provide labor inelastically to the firm. This could be seen as considering $U(\mathbf{c},l,\mathbf{b}) = U(c,0,0)$, so maximizing the firm profits is independent of the family decisions. The firm produces with labor, $y^1 = N$, and capital, $y^2 = K$, as inputs.

The firm profits are given by (27.3), to find the first-order condition (27.5). We will distinguish family and non-family firms by the ownership structure, denoted by $\theta = 1$ and $\theta < 1$ respectively. Provided the cost of capital is higher in family firms than in non-family firms and the productivity of labor is higher in family firms, we can prove the following result:

Proposition 3.1.1   Labor intensity in family firms   Consider two firms, a family and a non-family business, differing in ownership structure and similar in size, that is, with the same number of workers. Then, the family firm will be more labor intensive than the non-family firm, that is,

$$\frac{K(\theta = 1)}{N(\theta = 1)} < \frac{K(\theta < 1)}{N(\theta < 1)}$$

The proof is simple. By dividing the first-order conditions for capital and labor, we find that $w^K(\theta)f_N(\mathbf{y};\theta) = w^N(\theta)f_K(\mathbf{y};\theta)$. The cost of capital and the productivity of labor are higher for the family firm than for non-family firms, $w^K(\theta = 1)f_N(\mathbf{y};\theta = 1) > w^K(\theta < 1)f_K(\mathbf{y};\theta < 1)$. Thus, as wages are competitively determined and equal for both firms, two firms with the same number of workers yield a higher productivity of capital for a family firm than for a non-family firm. Because the marginal productivity of capital is decreasing, the stock of capital will be lower for family firms than for non-family firms, $K^*(\theta = 1) < K^* (\theta < 1)$, and accordingly the labor intensity will be higher.

Moreover, as a straightforward consequence of this proposition, if the availability of capital were limited for family firms due to financial restrictions, the additional restriction $K \le \overline{K}$ would have to be included in the firm's problem. Thus:

Corollary 3.1.2   Consider two firms, a family and a non-family firm, similar in size, that is, with the same number of workers. In the case that the family firm faces a financial constraint, that is, $K^*(\theta = 1) \le \overline{K}$, then the family firm will be more labor intensive than the non-family firm:

$$\frac{K(\theta = 1)}{N(\theta = 1)} < \frac{K(\theta < 1)}{N(\theta < 1)}$$

In this case, the first-order condition for any input holds at (27.5), except for the capital, which becomes

$$p^y f_K(\mathbf{y};\theta = 1) = w^K(\theta = 1) \ge w^K(\theta < 1)$$

This entails that the productivity of capital for family firms is higher than where there is no capital restrictions, and then it follows that $K^* (\theta = 1) = \overline{K} \le K^*(\theta < 1)$.

This theoretical finding presents an empirical hypothesis to be tested, as it shows a positive relationship between the variations of the rate of return and the variations of the size in family firms, and a null relation for non-family firms; in other words, family firms tend to be characterized by a suboptimal size.[8] This relationship can also be found in our framework. The firm's profitability can be expressed as follows:[9]

$$R = \frac{p^y f(\mathbf{y}) - w^N N}{K}$$

It is a concave function because of the concavity of technology $f(\mathbf{y})$. Then, the variation in the firm's profitability under changes in capital is

$$\frac{dR(N^*)}{dK} = \frac{p^y f_K(\mathbf{y}) - R(N^*)}{K}$$

The term $p_y f_K(\mathbf{y}) - R(N^*)$ is the difference between marginal and average return on capital at the optimal labor level $N = N^*$. This difference may be positive, negative or zero, depending upon whether there are increasing, decreasing or constant returns to scale.

To illustrate this issue, assume that labor and capital are the only inputs and take the Cobb–Douglas production function, $f(\mathbf{y}) = A(\theta)K^\alpha N^\beta$. Then the above expression is equal to

$$p_y f_K(\mathbf{y}) - R(N^*) = (\alpha + \beta - 1)\frac{p_y f(\mathbf{y})}{K}$$

Under constant returns to scale ($\alpha + \beta = 1$) differences in productive efficiency will be proportionally translated into differences in profitability, that is, $dR(N^*)/dK = 0$. When dR/dK is positive, its value increases with $A(\theta)$, the level of efficiency as a function of the ownership structure of the firm (i.e. the intertwined firm's and family's specific level of efficiency). Therefore, to test for differences in efficiency among firms when only data on profitability are available, it can be tested for differences in the slope of the locus of size–rate of return combinations (see Galve-Górriz et al., 1996).

3.2   The Family Business in a Dynamic Model

3.2.1   The basic model

The fact that decisions in the family are simultaneously taken with decisions in the firm also allows the owner-manager to take intertemporal decisions seeking long-run family goals. This is the case when he has children and desires to transfer the family business after he retires. Whenever the owner is concerned about long-run goals, such as the well-being of his children, then the issue of the intertemporal compatibility between profit maximization of the business and utility maximization of the family arises again. In this section we analyze the effect of descendant altruism for the family firm decisions, that is, the existence of a non-pecuniary good that enhances family welfare as a result of leaving the company to his children, an issue that requires a dynamic model.

Next, we present a dynamic model that can be seen as an extension of James (1999). We simplify the notation as follows. The economic decisions are taken in two periods of time, denoted by $t = 1$ and $t = 2$. The family founds a firm at $t = 1$ by investing an amount of resources that will become the stock of physical capital K, and only produces at period $t = 2$ with a technology that makes use of labor and physical capital. We will assume that the marginal productivity of capital for small units of capital is extremely high, meaning that the first investments for producing the good yield high returns; that is, $\lim_{K_1 \to 0} f_K(\mathbf{y}) = +\infty$. Finally, after period $t = 2$, the capital suffers a depreciation $\delta \in [0,1]$, so that the capital stock at the end of period $t = 2$ is $K_2 = (1-\delta)K_1$.

The family consumes only one consumption good at each period, $\mathbf{c} = (c_1, c_2)$; the family is endowed with an initial wealth at each period $\mathbf{W} = (W_1, W_2)$; and the owner-manager enhances the family's welfare by consuming at each period, and by leaving the company to his children, a single non-pecuniary good at period 2,[10] that is, $\mathbf{b} = K_2$; thus $u(\mathbf{c}, K_2) \equiv U(\mathbf{c}, l, \mathbf{b})$.[11]

Finally, as regards the financial structure, we will assume that there exists a financial security z that can be purchased or sold at period $t = 1$ at a given price q, with an exogenous return $(1 + r)$ representing the gross market return.

This setting allows us to consider the case of an owner-manager solving simultaneously the intertemporal problem for the family and the firm given the prices of goods and inputs. He chooses the family's goods consumption, leisure and security, and the firm's output and input factors that maximize the welfare of the family $u(\mathbf{c},(1{-}\delta)K_1)$ subject to three conditions: the family's temporal constraint (1) at period $t = 2$; and the family's monetary constraints for the periods $t = 1$ and $t = 2$:

$$p_1^c c_1 + z + K_1 = W_1,$$

$$p_2^c c_2 = W_2 + (1 + \bar{r})z + w^N n + w^K K_1 + \theta\pi\,(y, \mathbf{y}) \tag{27.7}$$

where p_t^c is the price of the consumption good at period t. Finally, the firm's profits are

$$\pi\,(y, \mathbf{y}) = p^y f(\mathbf{y}) - w^N N - w^K K_1 - \sum_{j=3}^{J} w^j y^j \tag{27.8}$$

Because the profits are not taken as exogenous to the owner-manager problem, the firm's profits (27.8) can be explicitly considered as the family's income. Thus the period $t = 2$ family's monetary constraint (27.7) becomes

$$p_2^c c_2 = W_2 + (1 + \bar{r})z + p^y f(n, K_1, y^3, \ldots y^J) - \sum_{j=3}^{J} w^j y^j$$

The first-order conditions are the following:

$$\frac{p_2^c\, U_{c_1}(\mathbf{x})}{p_1^c\, U_{c_2}(\mathbf{x})} = (1 + \bar{r}) \tag{27.9}$$

$$\frac{(1 + \bar{r})}{p^y} - \frac{p_2^c}{p^y}(1 - \delta)\frac{U_K(\mathbf{x})}{U_{c_2}(\mathbf{x})} = f_K(\mathbf{y}) = \frac{w^K}{p^y} \tag{27.10}$$

$$f_{y^j}(\mathbf{y}) = \frac{w^j}{p^y} \qquad j = 1, 3, \ldots J$$

Additionally, as indicated, the owner-manager is the only worker and, as leisure offers him no welfare, he supplies inelastically all the time, $N = n = T$.

The intuitions provided by the optimal conditions are analogous to those of the previous section, except for the optimal condition (27.10), which refers to the productive investment decision, that is, the non-pecuniary good. For this input, the market return is higher than the productivity of capital. Because the well-being of the family is directly affected by the decisions taken in the firm concerning capital investment, an externality exists, but again no inefficiency arises.[12] The external effect is considered in the marginal rate of substitution, the second term of the left-hand side. This allows us to state the following result:

Proposition 3.2.1   Capital overinvestment in family firms with descendant altruism
Descendant altruism of the owner-manager, in terms of his preference for leaving the company to his children, leads to an overinvestment in the capital good in family firms with respect to non-family firms.

The proof is straightforward from (27.10) and the concavity of the production function. In other words, this result implies that 'investment in the firm by the proprietor will be higher than in the case of a non-family business' (James, 1999, p. 46).[13]

3.2.2   An extension: growth and firm control in family business

It is often argued that personal preferences concerning growth, risk and ownership-control may be the driving forces behind a 'peculiar financial logic' of family firms. As Gallo et al. (2004) point out, generally accepted principles of financial management establish that the ultimate objective of the financial function is to maximize the value of the company's stock in terms of the market price. However, in family firms 'the stock is not only its price, but it includes other considerations such as passing on a "tradition," offering job opportunities to family members, and staying in power for long periods of time' (p. 314). In this section we explore the effect of the existence of amenity benefits for the owner-manager concerning the control and growth of the family firm.

Here we extend the previous framework to consider that economic decisions are taken in infinite periods of time, denoted to by $t = 1, 2, 3, \ldots$. The dynamic model can be seen as an extension of Kimhi (1997), Bhattacharya et al. (2001), Galve-Górriz et al. (2003, Sec. 2.3) and Castañeda (2006). Now, the family does not play any role but to provide labor inelastically to the firm. The firm produces with a technology that makes use of labor, physical capital and, additionally, human capital. Concerning human capital, it is a business-specific component so it is reduced if the family owner leaves the firm. Concerning physical capital, the family's investment at each period t becomes productive at the following period $t + 1$, a process that involves a transaction cost represented by an increasing and convex adjustment cost function $\Phi(K_{t+1}/K_t; \theta)$, which depends on the ownership structure of the firm. In addition, physical capital suffers a full depreciation after the production process, that is, $\delta = 1$. We will assume that the marginal productivity of capital for small units of capital is extremely high; that is, $\lim_{K \to 0} f_K(y) = +\infty$.

The family is the owner of the initial given stock of capital K_1. The owner-manager consumes only one consumption good at each period, $\mathbf{c} = (c_1, c_2, \ldots)$; and the family's welfare is enhanced by consuming at each period. In addition, the family may (or may not) enhance welfare by consuming two goods provided by the firm: an amenity benefit concerning the degree of the ownership of the firm, $\mathbf{A} = \theta$; as well as the non-pecuniary good 'discounted value of the firm', $\mathbf{B} = V$; thus $b = (\theta, V)$. Finally, the utility function is defined as $u(\mathbf{c}, \mu\mathbf{b}) \equiv U(\mathbf{c}, l, \mathbf{b})$, with $\mu = 1$ or 0 depending on whether the amenity benefits are considered or not.

To conclude the setting, we will assume that there exists a financial security z that can be purchased or sold at period t at a given price q, with an exogenous return $(1 + r)$ at $t + 1$ representing the gross market return.

The owner-manager's budget constraint at any period t is

$$p_t^c c_t + [1 + \Phi((K_{t+1}/K_t); \theta)] K_{t+1} + z_t = w_t^N n_t + w_t^K K_t + \theta \pi_t(y_t, y_t) + (1 + \bar{r}) z_{t-1}$$

Consider the intertemporal budget constraint at the initial period $t = 1$:

$$\sum_{t=1}^{\infty} \frac{1}{(1+\bar{r})^{t-1}} \left[p_t^c c_t + \left[1 + \Phi\left(\frac{K_{t+1}}{K_t};\theta\right) \right] K_{t+1} \right] = \sum_{t=1}^{\infty} \frac{1}{(1+\bar{r})^{t-1}} [w_t^N n_t + w_t^K K_t + \pi_t(y_t, y_t)]$$

Now, consider the following consumption pattern for the family. At every period, the family consumes only the labor income, that is, $p_t^c c_t = w_t^N n_t$, so all returns are reinvested. Then, considering the intertemporal budget constraint, we can find the market value of the family firm as the discounted stream of future dividends at period $t = 1$. That is,

$$V_{t=1} = \sum_{t=1}^{\infty} \frac{1}{(1+\bar{r})^{t-1}} \left[w_t^K K_t + \pi_t(y_t, y_t) - \left(1 + \Phi\left(\frac{K_{t+1}}{K_t};\theta\right) \right) K_{t+1} \right]$$

$$= \sum_{t=1}^{\infty} \frac{K_t}{(1+\bar{r})^{t-1}} [R_t - I_t]$$

where $R_t(H_t) = [p_y^t f(y_t) - w_t^N n_t]/K_t$ is the firm's profitability at period t that depends on the business-specific input human capital, and $I_t = [1 + \Phi((K_{t+1}/K_t);\theta)]K_{t+1}/K_t$ is the investment rate at period t.

Now assume that the firm grows at a constant net rate g, so $K_t = (1 + g)^{t-1} K_1$. Considering the stationary case where the rate of return and investment rate are constant,

$$V^S(H,g) = \frac{R(H) - I(g;\theta)}{\bar{r} - g} K_1(1 + \bar{r}) \qquad (27.11)$$

This is the market value of the discounted stream of constant dividends at period $t = 1$. Observe that the investment $I(g;\theta)$ depends on the kind of ownership structure of the firm and it is an increasing and convex function of the constant growth rate, that is, $I(g;\theta) = [1 + \Phi(g;\theta)]g$.

This setting allows us to study two problems: how the ownership property affects the growth of family firms (as in Galve-Górriz et al., 2003, Sec. 2.3); and when to leave the firm management (as in Kimhi, 1997).

3.2.2.1   Growth and firm control   In this section, we analyze how the ownership property affects the growth of family firms; thus we will keep the human capital constant along the analysis, that is, $\bar{H}$. The key assumption here is that provided the owner family derives some amenity benefits from the firm, the degree of family control reduces the growth rate of the firm. That is, only if there are amenity benefits derived from ownership control, that is, $\mu = 1$, is the growth rate of capital negatively affected by family ownership control; so the growth rate depends on the ownership structure, $g(\theta)$ with $g'(\theta) < 0$. This constraint stems from the financial restrictions set on external funds to preclude investors outside the family firm (Galve-Górriz et al., 2003, Sec. 2.3, p. 54).

We consider two cases depending on whether non-pecuniary goods provided by the firms are included or not.

1. No good provided by the firm enhances welfare, that is, $\mu = 0$. Consider the case where no amenity benefit is provided to the family by the firm. Then the optimal growth rate of the firm g^* is found by differentiating (27.11), $dV^s(\overline{H}, g)/dg = 0$; that is,

$$V^s(\overline{H},g) = \frac{dI(g^*;\theta)}{dg} K_1 (1 + \overline{r})$$

    where $V^s(\overline{H},g^*) = (1 + \overline{r}) K_1 \lfloor R - I(g^*;\theta)/(\overline{r} - g^*) \rfloor$
    Note that as the second derivative,

$$\frac{\partial^2 V^s(\overline{H},g)}{\partial^2 g^2} = -\frac{\partial^2 I(g^*;\theta)}{\partial^2 g^2} = \frac{1}{\overline{r} - g} K_1 (1 + \overline{r})$$

    is negative, as the investment function is convex. So the growth rate g^* is a global maximum.
2. Goods provided by the firm enhance welfare, that is, $\mu = 1$. In this case, the growth rate of the physical capital, g, depends on the ownership property, θ. The owner-manager's problem is to choose the degree of control θ^* that maximizes his welfare, which is found from the first-order conditions

$$U_\theta(x) + U_V(x)\frac{dV^s(\overline{H},g(\theta))}{dg}\frac{dg(\theta)}{d\theta} = 0 \qquad (27.12)$$

    Then the optimal growth rate of the firm is $g(\theta^*)$. Now we can prove the following result (see also Galve-Górriz et al., (2003, p. 55).

Proposition 3.2.2 The market value of the family firm is increasing with the growth of the size of the firm evaluated at the optimal constant growth rate that maximizes the family welfare, that is, $dV^s(\overline{H},g(\theta^*))/dg > 0$.

To prove this proposition, remember that the welfare is increasing in the firm control and its market value, that is, U_θ, $U_V > 0$, and $dg(\theta)/d\theta < 0$. Thus to fulfill the identity (27.12), $dV^s(\overline{H}, g)/dg$ must be positive at the optimal growth rate $g(\theta^*)$.

A consequence of this proposition is that the concern for the control results in a family firm that displays a steady-state growth in which not all the opportunities are taken to create economic value along the growth path. This result can be summarized in the following corollary (see also Galve-Górriz et al., (2003, p. 55):

Corollary 3.2.3 Provided family firms consider ownership as an amenity benefit, that is, $\mu = 1$, then it is verified that:

(a) the ratio of the market value to the cost value of the productive asset will be lower in a family firm than in a non-family firm for a similar productive efficiency, that is, $V^s(\overline{H}, g(\theta^*))/K_1 < V^s(\overline{H}, g^*)/K_1$;
(b) the growth rate of a family business should be less than that of a non-family business for a similar productive efficiency, that is, $g(\theta^*) < g^*$;

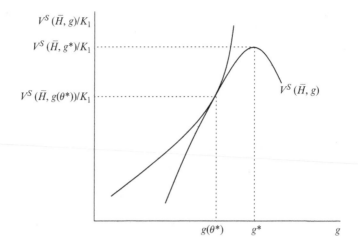

Note: Considering ownership as an amenity benefit entails that the value and the growth rate of family firms are lower than those of non-family firms.

Figure 27.1   Proof of Corollary 3.2.3

(c)   for a similar age, the average size of the family business must be less than that of the non-family business for a similar productive efficiency, that is, $K_t (g(\theta^*)) < K_t(g^*)$.

Proof   Part (a) is straightforward from Figure 27.1. This figure shows the growth rate and the market value of the firm are at their maximum without and with amenity benefit considerations by the owner-manager; that is, g^* and $V^s(\overline{H}, g^*)$, and $g(\theta^*)$ and $V^s(\overline{H}, g(\theta^*))$ respectively. Note that both $V^s(\overline{H}, g(\theta^*))/K_1 < V^s(\overline{H}, g^*)/K_1$ and $g(\theta^*) < g^*$ are lower, as stated in (a) and (b). Part (c) is straightforward from the lower growth rate of the physical capital in family firms, $g(\theta^*) < g^*$.

As a final comment, it is worth mentioning that in this section we have assumed a similar productive efficiency for family and non-family businesses. Yet, if the family firm takes its comparative advantage on motivation and control, then it will achieve a higher productive efficiency than a non-family firm. This means that conclusions from Corollary 3.2.3 must be drawn with caution. For instance, we can consider that the human capital of the family members associated with the firm is higher than in non-family businesses. Then the market value of a family firm may turn out to be higher than that of a non-family business, for example $V^s(\overline{\overline{H}}, g(\theta^*))/K_1 < V^s(\overline{H}, g^*)/K_1$ for a high enough $\overline{\overline{H}} > \overline{H}$. Also, the growth rate for family firms needs not be lower than that for non-family firms.

3.2.2.2   Leaving the family business   In this section, we analyze the owner-manager decision to leave the firm;[14] thus we will keep the growth rate of the physical capital constant throughout the analysis, that is, $\overline{g}$. There are two key assumption here (see Kimhi, 1997): (i) before inheriting the family firm, the successor (or future owner-manager) works outside the firm, accumulating an ever-increasing wealth $\eta\omega$ at a rate $(1 + g)\eta$ each period, which she will invest in the firm on her arrival; and (ii) at the time the owner-manager leaves the firm, it suffers a drop in productivity $\rho \in (0,1)$ that can be interpreted as a decrease in the human capital as a business-specific component associated with the firm[15, 16]

The dilemma faced by the owner-manager is the following. Leaving the firm to his outside successor reduces the market value of the family firm because of the drop of productivity, but it increases it because of the increase in the stock of physical capital. As the successor's accumulated wealth increases over time, there will exist a period t^* at which the costs of productivity are offset by the increase in the stock of capital. At this moment, the owner-manager leaves the firm. Note that at this period the stock of capital is $K_{t^*} = (1 + g)^{t^*-1}[K_1 + \eta^{t^*}\omega]$. So the problem is to find such a period by equalizing the family firm's market value:

$$V^S(H,\bar{g};K_1) = \frac{R(H) - I(g;\theta)}{\bar{r} - \bar{g}} K_1(1 + \bar{r})$$

$$= \frac{R(\rho H) - I(\bar{g};\theta)}{\bar{r} - \bar{g}}(1 + \bar{r})[K_1 + \eta^{t^*}\omega] = V^S(\rho H,\bar{g};K_1 + \eta^{t^*}\omega)$$

Then, operating and taking logarithms, we find the period t^* when the owner-manager leaves the firm:

$$t^*(\bar{g}) = Ln\left[\frac{R(H) - R(\rho H)}{R(\rho H) - I(\bar{g};\theta)} \frac{K_1}{\omega}\right]^{1/Ln\eta} \tag{27.13}$$

Note that the higher the productivity penalty, that is, the lower ρ, the more time the owner-manager leads the family firm.

4   FAMILY BUSINESS IN THE PRINCIPAL–AGENT MODEL

A second distinctive feature of the family firm concerns the relationship among the family members interacting within the firm. These members are linked by family ties that may affect the decisions taken in the firm. This may result in a variety of individual behavior, such as loyalty or shirking, which may benefit or damage the firm. A number of academic works have displayed this trade-off between the family and the business within a microeconomics model based on the theory of agency.

The basic version of the principal–agent model considers two economic agents: the informed party, whose information is relevant for the common welfare; and the uninformed party. This party will propose a 'take-it-or-leave it' contract and therefore request a 'yes or no' answer, giving all bargaining power to one of the parties. Salanié (1998) points out that the principal–agent game is a Stackelberg game, in which the leader – the one who proposes the contract – is called the principal and the follower – the party who just has to accept or reject the contract – is called the agent. Accordingly, the principal–agent model can be considered as a simplifying device that avoids the complexity of bargaining under asymmetric information.

In the context of the theory of the firm, agency problems arise from the separation of ownership and management, leading to a principal–agent relationship in which managers (i.e. the agent) may not make decisions that are in the best interest of the owner (i.e. the principal).

In relation to family firms, there are two opposing perspectives on the dimension of agency costs. One view asserts that these costs may be alleviated because the non-separation of ownership and management naturally aligns the owner-manager's interests.[17] Moreover, individual family members are engaged in altruistic behaviors wherein they subjugate their self-interests to the collective good of the family. Altruism is modelled in terms of preferences where the welfare of one individual is positively linked with the welfare of others. This provides a self-reinforcing incentive because efforts to maximize one's own utility allow the individual to simultaneously satisfy both other-regarding and self-regarding preferences. The alternative view argues that governance arrangements of family firms need not remove nor even reduce agency costs and, in fact, family firms might even suffer from specially high agency costs.[18] Agency relationships in family firms are distinctive because they are embedded in the parent–child relationships and therefore are characterized by altruism. This view considers that parents' altruism can cause a family firm's specific agency costs because it can induce parents to take inefficient decisions at the firm level. In this sense, they could be faced with a 'Samaritan's dilemma' in which their actions give beneficiaries incentives to take actions or make decisions that may harm their own welfare such as free-riding, shirking or remaining dependent upon their parents. In this section, we cover all these issues.

4.1   The Basic Model

The literature dealing with the conflict of interests between the family and the business based on the theory of agency considers the family as represented by two individuals: the owner of a firm, who also runs the business alone, and will be termed the owner-manager principal; and a family relative who works for the firm, who will be called the worker-agent.

4.1.1   The owner-manager principal
A family member, usually the parent, is the owner of the firm, and devotes all his time to managerial activities in the firm. Among these activities we find hiring labor and monitoring. His welfare may be enhanced by two elements. One is his own consumption of goods purchased in the market, c^p; the other is his relative's welfare, thus displaying 'descendant altruism'. The literature considers separability of preferences between both elements; also, the principal is assumed to be risk-neutral with respect to consumption, so preferences can be represented by a twice-differentiable, increasing, continuous utility function, $u_p(c^p)$. Thus his preferences will be represented by $U_p(c^p, \beta_p, \text{ll}_a) = u_p(c^p) + \beta_p \text{ll}_a$, where $\beta_p \geq 0$ is a parameter of descendant altruism, an intercohort discount factor; and ll_a is the welfare of the family relative working for the firm.

4.1.2   The worker-agent
There exists an additional family member – usually a child – who, if working for the firm, will devote all his time to working activities in exchange for a wage, w^N. Her welfare may

be also affected by three elements: it is increased by consuming goods purchased in the market, c^a, and by considering her relative's welfare, thus displaying 'ascendant altruism'; in addition, it is reduced by the effort e required at work, an unobservable variable to the manager principal. The literature considers separability of preferences between these elements. Thus her preferences will be represented by

$$U_a(c^a, e, \beta_a, \mathcal{U}_p) = u_a(c^a) - \mathcal{C}(e) + \beta_p \mathcal{U}_p$$

where $u_a(c^a)$ is a twice-differentiable, increasing, continuous utility function; $\mathcal{C}(e)$ is an increasing, strictly convex welfare cost function of effort, which will be assumed to be $\mathcal{C}(e) = (k/2)e^2$ with $k > 0$; $\beta_a \geq 0$ as a parameter of ascendant altruism, an intercohort discount factor; and $\mathcal{U}_p$ is the welfare of the family manager.

4.1.3 The firm

The firm produces a single good **y** by combining a number of inputs $\mathbf{y} \in \mathfrak{R}^J_+$, which comprise the worker-agent's effort e. The technology will be represented by a twice differentiable, concave, strictly increasing, continuous production function $y = f(\mathbf{y})$. In a market economy the firm interacts with other firms in an economic environment both in the good and the inputs markets. We will consider that this environment is competitive. Thus the firm will consider as exogenous both the price of the good produced, p^y, and the price of all other inputs purchased in the market, w^j with $j = 1, \ldots, J$.

For expositional purposes we focus on the simplest version of the model in which the principal–agent model can be treated as a leader–follower model. Obviously, variations in the characteristics of the utility functions (i.e. the degree of risk aversion of the agents, which we consider constant and equal to zero), the contract design (a lineal contract in our case), or the explicit consideration of uncertainty can lead us to different parametric results and even to the non-existence of optimal solutions.[19] Accordingly, the simplicity of our model is at no cost; for instance, issues concerning the risk sharing between the parent manager and the child worker concerning the firm's uncertainties cannot be explicitly considered. Yet, as will be shown, most of the basic qualitative results obtained in this section can be also found in the literature.

Next, we first present the efficient allocations as a benchmark in order to show that agency problems result in inefficient allocations. Then it is shown under what conditions altruism and succession commitments can either contribute to the survival of a family firm or threaten its continuity.

4.2 The Efficient Locations

If no agency problems exist, the principal will offer a wage and the agent will make enough effort to jointly maximize welfare. In this section, we briefly present those efficient allocations that will allow us to compare the magnitude of the inefficiency arising because of the presence of agency conflicts. In this section we will simplify the notation. Each family member consumes only one consumption good, $c^i = c^i$, and the utility function on consumption is linear, that is, $u_i(c^i) = c^i$ for $i = p, a$. The firm produces only with the worker's effort, $y^1 = e$, and we will assume a linear technology $f(e) = Ae$, where A represents the constant marginal productivity of effort.

To find the Pareto-optimal allocations, consider a social planner jointly maximizing a weighted principal's and agent's welfare:

$$\Pi = \alpha_p U_p(c^p,0,0) + \alpha_a U_a(c^p,e,0,0)\,^{20}$$

where α_i is the planner weight for the agent $i = p, a$. The planner chooses the level of effort and the output share that maximizes overall welfare subject to the production outcome $y = f(e)$, and the share of output among the agents $c^p = y(1-w)$ and $c^a = wy$, with $w, e \in [0,1]$. First-order conditions are the following:

$$e\lfloor\alpha_p A(1 - w) + \alpha_a(Aw - ke)\rfloor = 0$$

$$(w - 1)w\lfloor-\alpha_p Ae + \alpha_a Ae\rfloor = 0$$

The optimal allocations depend on the weight ratio α_p/α_a, as shown in the following result.

Proposition 4.2.1　Pareto-efficient allocations　Consider an environment as described. The Pareto-efficient allocations are the following:

1.　Case $\alpha_a \geq \alpha_p$. If both individuals are weighted the same, $\alpha_a = \alpha_p$, the optimal effort will be $\hat{e}=A/k$, the share is undefined $\hat{w} \in [0,1]$, and the overall welfare is $\hat{\Pi} = \alpha_p A^2/(2k)$.
　　The same allocation is achieved if the agent's welfare has a higher weight, $\alpha_a > \alpha_p$, except that all income is given to her, that is, $\hat{w} = 1$.
2.　Case $\alpha_p > \alpha_a$. If the principal's welfare has a higher weight, the optimal effort will be $\hat{e} = (\alpha_p / \alpha_a)A/k$, no output share is provided to the worker-agent, that is, $\hat{w} = 0$, *and the* overall welfare is $\hat{\Pi}=(\alpha_p^2/ \alpha_a)A^2/(2k)$.

4.3　The Agency Problems in Non-Family Business: The Inefficient Allocations

We consider the same environment as before but no altruism exists, so $\beta_a = \beta_p = 0$. Thus we turn to the case where the agency problem exists between a manager and a worker in non-family firms, or between the owner-manager of a family firm and a worker not belonging to the family.

The owner-manager principal hires labor activities. The timing of the labor hiring process is as follows. First, the owner-manager offers a wage contract, w; second, the worker-agent accepts the contract; then she decides the level of effort; and finally the firm's output is realized and wages are paid. We will consider that the wage perceived by the agent is proportional to the production, which is observable by both the manager and the child; that is, we consider that $w^N = wy$, where $0 < w < 1$. Note that, because wages paid are proportional to output, this entails that in the absence of ascendant altruism the agent will be better off, and accept a job offer if her effort falls into the interval $e \in[0,2A/k]$; otherwise, the worker-agent will receive strictly negative welfare and will not work for the firm, that is, $e = 0$.

As usual, the model is solved by backwards induction. The worker-agent first chooses her optimal level of effort by maximizing her welfare $U_a(c^a,e,0,0)$ subject to $c^a = wAe$. The first-order condition provides the supply function of effort, which depends on the wages received in compensation:

$$e(w) = w\frac{A}{k} \tag{27.14}$$

Note that the level of effort is proportional to the wages paid. Thus the incentives for increasing effort to the non-family worker-agent are guided only by wages.

Lemma 4.3.1   Work effort incentives in non-family firms   Consider the environment described without altruism, that is, $\beta_a = \beta_p = 0$. *Then* $\partial e/\partial w = A/k > 0$.

The owner-manager, as the principal, chooses the optimal wage that maximizes his welfare $U^p(c^p,0,0)$ subject to $c^a = (1-w)Ae$ and taking into consideration the optimal effort level chosen by the agent (27.14). Note that we can establish an analogy between the manager's revenue and the firm resulting profits, that is, $\pi(w,e) = u_p(c^p)$, which will be useful in the next subsections. The optimal wage is $w^*(\beta_p, \beta_a) = w^* (0,0)=1/2$, and then the optimal level of effort $e^* (0,0) = e(w^*(0,0)) = A/(2k)$.

As a consequence, the owner-manager's and the non-family worker-agent's welfare are $U_p(c^{p^*}(0,0),0,0) = A^2/(4k)$, and $U_a(c^{a^*}(0,0), e^*(0,0),0,0) = A^2/(8k)$ respectively, so the allocation is found to be inefficient from Proposition 4.2.1: the worker makes an inefficient effort, $e^*(0,0) < \hat{e}$, resulting in an overall lower welfare and lower firm profits, that is, $ll^*(0,0) = U_p(c^{p^*},0,0) + U_a(c^{a^*},e^*,0,0) < \mathcal{U}$ and $\pi(w^*(0,0),e^*(0,0)) < (w,e)$, respectively. The reason is that the worker-agent takes her decisions without taking into account the manager's welfare. The internalization of this external effect will be crucial to understanding why the agency problems might be mitigated within a family firm, resulting in a Pareto improvement allocation. This will be shown in the following sections.

4.4   The Agency Problem in a Family Business with Altruism

In this section we present a static model that can be seen as a non-stochastic version of Chami (2001) and Galve-Górriz et al. (2003, Sec. 1.6). We will consider two cases: first, the descendant altruism case with an altruistic parent and a selfish child who does not expect to inherit the business; and second, the two-sided altruistic case, which we could understand as the role of loyalty and trust. Finally, the last subsection extends the model to a two-period case in order to study the role of succession and inheriting the business.

4.4.1   One-sided altruism: descendant altruism
In this section, we analyze the case where the agency problem exists between the owner-manager and a family worker in a family firm, in which there exists only descendant altruism with an altruistic parent, that is, $\beta_p > 0$, and a selfish child who does not expect to inherit the business, that is, $\beta_a = 0$. The way altruism is modelled consists in considering that the parent is concerned with the overall welfare of the child, hence $ll_a = U_a(c^a,e,0,0)$ (see Chami, 2001, Sec. II).[21]

As usual, the model is solved by backwards induction. As in the previous section, the worker-agent first chooses her optimal level of effort by maximizing her welfare $U_a(c^a,e,0,0)$ subject to $c^a = wAe$, resulting in the supply function of effort (27.14), which depends on the wages received in compensation. Note that when there is no ascendant altruism, that is, $\beta_a = 0$, the child behaves as any other non-family worker, so her incentives for increasing effort are guided only by wages. This is shown in the following result, similar to Chami (2001, Lemma 1).

Lemma 4.4.1   Work effort incentives in family firms with no-ascendant altruism   Consider the environment with no ascendant altruism, that is, $\beta_a = 0$. Then $\partial e/\partial w = A/k > 0$.

The owner-manager, as the principal, chooses the optimal wage that maximizes his welfare $U_p(c^p,\beta_p,U_a(c^a,e,0,0)) = u_p(c^p) + \beta_p[u_a(c^a,e)-\mathfrak{C}(e)]$ subject to $c^p = (1-w)Ae$, $c^a = wAe$ and taking into consideration the optimal effort level supplied by the agent (27.14). Now, the optimal wage is $w^*(\beta_p,0) = 1/(2-\beta_p)$, and then the optimal level of effort $e^*(\beta_p,0) = e(w^*(\beta_p,0)) = A/[(2 - \beta_p)k]$. It is easy to see that, as a consequence of his altruistic motivations, the parent pays a higher wage to his child.

Proposition 4.4.2   Wages under one-sided altruism   Consider the environment with descendant but not ascendant altruism, that is, $\beta_p > 0$ and $\beta_a = 0$. In contrast to a non-family business, (family) workers receive a higher compensation wage in family firms, that is, $w^*(\beta_p,0) > w^*(0,0)$.

Observe that the child has no incentive to seek employment elsewhere, as she uses her parent's altruism to get paid more. This is the same result as Chami (2001, Prop. 2), but in a different environment.

Three comments are in order. First, note that in our simple model the child's effort is higher than a non-family employee's effort, that is, $e^*(\beta_p,0) > e^*(0,0)$. This contrasts with other results found in the literature (e.g. Chami, 2001, Sec. II, or Galve-Górriz et al., 2003, Sec. 1.6.2). In stochastic environments concerning uncertain productive outcome, for example a state-dependent wage resulting from a stochastic productivity parameter A and unobservable levels of effort, the parental altruism provides higher wage insurance to the child. Because of her opportunistic behavior, the child behaves as a free-rider at the firm – a kind of 'bad boy' (or, in our case, bad girl) – and the parent is contented with lower effort and lower income. Yet these works also found that descendant altruism increases the worker's compensation.

Second, despite inefficient, this result represents a Pareto improvement over the previous case, as both agents, the owner-manager and the worker, improve in welfare terms. That is, the owner-manager's welfare and the worker-agent's welfare are $U_p(c^{p*}(\beta_p,0),\beta_p,U_a) = A^2/[2(2-\beta_p)k]$ and $U_a(c^{a*}(\beta_p,0),e^*(\beta_p,0),0,0) = A^2/[2(2-\beta_p)^2k]$, respectively.

Finally, the firm's profits, $\pi(w^*(\beta_p,0), e^*(\beta_p,0)) = [A^2(1 - \beta_p)]/[(2 - \beta_p)^2k]$, are now lower than in the previous section when the principal was not altruistic towards the agent, as shown in the following result.

Proposition 4.4.3   Profits under one-sided altruism   Consider the environment with descendant but not ascendant altruism, that is, $\beta_p > 0$ and $\beta_a = 0$. In contrast to non-family businesses, profits are lower in family firms, that is, $\pi(w^*(\beta_p,0), e^*(\beta_p,0)) < \pi(w^*(0,0), e^*(0,0))$, jeoparadizing their own existence.

This result coincides with that found by Galve-Górriz et al. (2003, Sec. 1.6) in a different setting. From Section 3.1, the reason is already known. Note that hiring the child becomes a non-pecuniary good for the owner-manager $\mathbf{B} = \beta_p U_a$. Hence, as long as the owner-manager takes his decisions simultaneously with the decisions in the firm, this may allow him to divert some resources from the firm to achieve some of his own particular altruistic goals, in this case to improve his child's welfare. Yet this entails that descendant altruism may jeoparadize the existence of the firm in the long run. As Chami (2001, Sec. II) points out,

> unless the family business is operating in an imperfectly competitive market ... paternalism cannot be a reason for why family businesses continue to exist and compete with other business entities in the long run. For the family business to continue to survive in a competitive market, the family and the business are better off having the parent replace the child with another non-family employee. In this case altruism will be absent, and the parent can then make side transfers to the child without having the child influence the business profits directly through his effort level.

To sum up, to understand why a family business survives over time we must explore reasons other than parental altruism. The following two sections provide two possibilities suggested in the literature: trust and succession commitment.

4.4.2 Two-sided altruism: descendant and ascendant altruism

In this section, we analyze the case where the agency problem exists between the owner-manager and a family worker in a family firm, in which there exists descendant altruism for an altruistic parent, that is, $\beta_p > 0$, as well as ascendant altruism for an altruistic child, that is, $\beta_a > 0$, where the child is involved and identified with the goals of the family firm and the family. The way altruism is modelled consists in considering that each family member is concerned with the overall welfare of the other, hence $\mathfrak{U}_a = U_a(c^a,e,0,0)$ and $\mathfrak{U}_p = U_p(c^p,0)$ (see Chami, 2001, Sec. III). In this sense, following to Bernheim and Stark (1988) or Chami and Fullenkamp (2002), reciprocal altruism between individuals can be identified as trust when the weight on the other person's utility is close to unity.

As usual, the model is solved by backwards induction. As in the previous section, the worker-agent first chooses her optimal level of effort by maximizing her welfare $U_a(c^a,e,\beta_a,u_p(c^p)) = u_a(c^a,e) - \mathfrak{C}(c) + \beta_a u_p(c^p)$ subject to $c^a = wAe$ and $c^p = (1 - w)Ae$, resulting in a supply function of effort that depends on the wages received in compensation

$$e(w;\beta_a) = [w + \beta_a(1 - w)]\frac{A}{k} \tag{27.15}$$

Note that where ascendant altruism exists, that is, $\beta_a > 0$, the child's incentives for increasing effort are guided by wages and altruism.

Lemma 4.4.4 Work effort incentives with ascendant altruism   Consider the environment with ascendant altruism, that is, $\beta_a > 0$. Then, for any $w \in [0,1]$, $\partial e/\partial w = (1 - \beta_a)$ A/k for $\beta_a \in (0,1)$.

Note that this result is independent of the parent being altruistic. Moreover, where the child displays a high degree of altruism towards her parent, reducing her wage leads her to increased effort. This could lead to an opportunistic behavior by a non-altruistic manager parent.[22] The next result compares the work effort in family and non-family businesses.

Proposition 4.4.5   Work effort with ascendant altruism   Consider the environment with ascendant altruism, that is, $\beta_a > 0$. Receiving the same labor compensation, the child's effort is higher than a non-family employee's effort, that is, $e(w;\beta_a) > e(w;0)$ for any $w \in [0,1]$.

Note that this is the same result as Chami (2001, Prop. 3) in a different economic environment. The proof is straightforward, because $\partial e(w;\beta_a)/\partial\beta_a > 0$ for any given wage w. The more altruistic the child towards her parent, the greater her internalization of the impact of her own actions on her parent's welfare. As a result, the presence of agency conflicts between the manager and the worker is mitigated.

The owner-manager, as principal, chooses the optimal wage that maximizes his welfare, $U_p(c^p, \beta_p, U_a(c^a, e, 0, 0)) = u_p(c^p) + \beta_p[u_a(c^a, e) - \mathfrak{C}(e)]$ subject to $c^p = (1 - w)Ae$, $c^a = wAe$ and taking into consideration the optimal effort level chosen by the agent (27.15). The interaction of both forms of altruism results in an optimal wage share. Because the value of the wage share is restricted to the interval $w \in [0,1]$, this sets a bound on the available wage contract to be proposed by the manager. We will restrict our analysis to the case β_a, $\beta_p \in [0,1]$. In this case the optimal wage share is

$$w^*(\beta_p, \beta_a) = \begin{cases} \dfrac{1 - 2\beta_a + \beta_p\beta_a^2}{(1 - \beta_a)(2 - \beta_p - \beta_a\beta_p)}, & \text{if } \beta_a \leq \Omega(\beta_p) \\ 0, & \text{if } \beta_a > \Omega(\beta_p) \end{cases}$$

with $\Omega(\beta_p) = [1 - (1 - \beta_p)^{1/2}]/\beta_p$; and then the optimal level of effort is

$$e^*(\beta_p, \beta_a) = \begin{cases} \dfrac{1 - \beta_a\beta_p}{2 - \beta_p - \beta_a\beta_p}\dfrac{A}{k}, & \text{if } \beta_a \leq \Omega(\beta_p) \\ \beta_a\dfrac{A}{k}, & \text{if } \beta_a > \Omega(\beta_p) \end{cases}$$

Note that these optimal results depict all cases concerning the relationships between manager and workers, depicted in Figure 27.2: the paternalistic case, that is, one-sided descendant altruism, $\beta_p > 0$ and $\beta_a = 0$; the altruistic child case, that is, one-sided ascendant altruism, $\beta_p = 0$ and $\beta_a > 0$; the non-family business (or worker) case, that is, no altruism, $\beta_p = 0$ and $\beta_a = 0$; and the two-sided altruism, $\beta_p > 0$ and $\beta_a > 0$.

The findings for $\beta_a \geq \Omega(\beta_p)$ constitute the 'good boy' case (the 'good girl', in our example). The child will make a work effort in the firm even if there are no monetary incentives, that is, the area denoted by $w^* = 0$ in Figure 27.2. This effort to achieve the family firm goals without any compensation has been denoted in the literature as

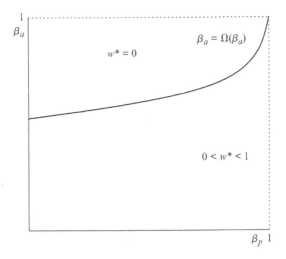

Note: One-sided altruism is also represented, both descendant – X-axis- or ascendant – Y-axis.

Figure 27.2   The wage contract under two-sided altruism, case β_a, $\beta_b \in [0,1]$

'loyalty'. This behavior happens even with non-descendant altruism, $\beta_p = 0$ (see Y-axis in Figure 27.2). Thus the child's ascendant altruism towards her parent, or the general goals and interests of the family, constitutes one of the mainstays of the efficiency of the family business.

To proceed with the analysis, we present the following result, similar to Chami (2001, Lemma 2). It shows how the optimal wage contract and effort are modified under different degrees of altruism.

Lemma 4.4.6   Optimal wage, work effort and profits under different degrees of altruism   Consider the environment with descendant and ascendant altruism, that is, β_a, $\beta_p \in [0,1]$. Then, for $\beta_a \le \Omega(\beta_p)$:

1.   *Different degrees of descendant altruism*

$$\frac{\partial w^* (\beta_p, \beta_a)}{\partial \beta_p} = \frac{1}{(2 - \beta_p - \beta_p\beta_a)^2} > 0$$

$$\frac{\partial e^* (\beta_p, \beta_a)}{\partial \beta_p} = \frac{1 - \beta_a}{(2 - \beta_p - \beta_p\beta_a)^2} \frac{A}{k} > 0$$

$$\frac{\partial \pi^* (\beta_p, \beta_a)}{\partial \beta_p} = \frac{-\beta_a}{(2 - \beta_p - \beta_p\beta_a)^2} \frac{A^2}{k} < 0$$

2.   Different degrees of ascendant altruism

$$\frac{\partial w^*(\beta_p,\beta_a)}{\partial \beta_a} = -\frac{2(1-\beta_p)(1-\beta_p\beta_a)}{(1-\beta_a)^2(2-\beta_p-\beta_p\beta_a)^2} < 0$$

$$\frac{\partial e^*(\beta_p,\beta_a)}{\partial \beta_a} = -\frac{\beta_p(1-\beta_p)}{(2-\beta_p-\beta_p\beta_a)^2}\frac{A}{k} < 0$$

$$\frac{\partial \pi^*(\beta_p,\beta_a)}{\partial \beta_a} = \frac{(1-\beta_p)^2 + (1-\beta_a\beta_p)^2 + (1-\beta_a\beta_p)\beta_p(1-\beta_a)}{(1-\beta_a)^2(2-\beta_p-\beta_p\beta_a)^4}\frac{A^2}{k} > 0$$

Three comments are in order. First, the higher degree of parental altruism β_p, the higher the wages paid by the manager, a result that extends to two-sided altruism the findings in Proposition 4.4.2 for one-sided altruism. In addition, observe that the child's effort is higher. This could be interpreted as the altruistic child's response to her parent's altruism. Yet in our model this also happened in the previous one-sided altruism case. The child, despite being altruistic with her parent, still reacts by increasing work effort under monetary incentives, as already noted in Lemma 4.4.4. As indicated before, this may not be the case in other models with uncertainty and other contract designs.

Second, the higher degree of ascendant altruism β_a, the lower are the wages paid by the family manager. This is interesting because the manager, despite being altruistic, may also display opportunistic behavior towards an altruistic worker, thus paying her child less. Thus the child faces a trade-off between putting in more work effort because of being more altruistic, or putting in less effort because of being paid less. This trade-off is displayed by differentiating the optimal condition (27.15)

$$\frac{\partial e(w^*(\beta_p,\beta_a);\beta_a)}{\partial \beta_a} = [1-w^*(\beta_p,\beta_a)]\frac{A}{k} + (1-\beta_a)\frac{\partial w^*(\beta_p,\beta_a)}{\partial \beta_a}\frac{A}{k}$$

so that the first term represents the positive altruistic motive, while the second term represents the negative compensating motive. In our simple model the latter offsets the former, thus resulting in a lower work effort.

Finally, concerning the firm's profits, note that profits decrease, the higher degree of parental altruism β_p for any degree of descendant altruism $\beta_a \in [0,1]$, a result that extends to two-sided altruism the findings of Proposition 4.4.3 for one-sided altruism. In addition, profits increase, the higher degree of the ascendant altruism of the child, β_a. Figure 27.2 shows that this entails that higher profits are found leftwards and upwards. The following result compares the amount of profits under two-sided altruism with respect to those achieved in the previous sections.

Proposition 4.4.7   Profits under two-sided altruism   Consider the environment with two-sided altruism, that is, β_p, $\beta_a \in [0,1]$. Then:

1.   *Non-sufficiently altruistic child case*   For $\beta_a < \Omega(\beta_p)$, profits are lower in family firms in contrast to non-family businesses, that is,

$$\pi(w^*(\beta_p, \beta_a), e^*(\beta_p, \beta_a)) < \pi(w^*(0,0), e^*(0,0))$$

2. *The 'good boy' (or 'good girl') case*   For $\beta_a \geq \Omega(\beta_p)$ profits are higher in family firms in contrast to non-family businesses, that is,

$$\pi(w^*(\beta_p, \beta_a), e^*(\beta_p, \beta_a)) = \beta_a A^2/k \geq \pi(w^*(0,0), e^*(0,0))$$

3. *The outstanding child case*   For $\beta_a = 1$ profits achieve their highest value,

$$\pi(w^*(\beta_p,1), e^*(\beta_p,1)) = (A/k) > \pi(w^*(\beta_p, \beta_p), e^*(\beta_p, \beta_p))$$

The first result is found in the bottom area of Figure 27.2. This is where the descendant altruism is too high, at least with respect to ascendant altruism. The parent extracts pecuniary benefits from hiring his child, then jeoparadizing the existence of the family firm. As indicated in the comments of Proposition 4.4.3, where the child is not sufficiently identified with the goals of the family, it is better for the manager to hire a non-family worker and then divert some resources from the firm to achieve some particular own altruistic goals in order that the firm may survive in the long run.

The second result is found in the upper area of Figure 27.2. For any given descendant altruism, $\beta_p \in [0,1]$, where the child's involvement with the goals of the family is so high that she works for no wage compensation, then the profits of the family are higher under two-sided altruism than in the case of non-family business. This 'good boy' case occurs when the child makes sufficient effort even if no descendant altruism exists, that is, $\beta_p = 0$ and $\beta_p \geq 1/2$. In this case, the non-altruistic manager undertakes opportunistic behavior by paying no wages in exchange for high effort from the worker.

In addition, note also that the higher the ascendant altruism, the more efficient allocation is found. In the third result, we state that in the case that $\beta_a = 1$, full efficiency is achieved, that is, $e^*(\beta_p,1) = e$, and the firm's profits $\pi(0, e^*(\beta_p,1))$ are the highest for any degree of descendant altruism $\beta_p \in [0,1]$.[23] This result is similar to Galve-Górriz et al.'s (2003, Sec. 1.6) finding in a different setting, although they found that only non-descendant altruism case is efficient, that is, $\beta_p = 0$ and $\beta_a = 1$, that is, the upper-left corner in Figure 27.2.

To sum up, Proposition 4.4.7 entails two important consequences for family businesses. First, two-sided altruism may explain the survival of the family firm over time, whenever there exists enough involvement of the child with the family firm. This is formalized by a relatively high degree of descendant altruism with respect to descendant altruism. And, second, it is pointed out that the existence of descendant altruism is not enough to keep the family firm out of trouble: a rude and tough family manager (i.e. lower β_p) may not turn low into high profits, at least for a range of low degrees of ascendant altruism (i.e. $\beta_a < 0.5$).

Note that it has been frequently argued that trust is a distinctive feature that separates successful family business from non-family ones or unsucceessful family businesses.[24] Our results could then explain why family businesses arise and succeed. In other words, under certain circumstances which have to do with the degree and intensity of reciprocal altruism, trust would provide the family business with a competitive edge versus other firms in the market.

4.5   Succession

In this section we study the owner's decision to transfer the family business to his child after he retires. We inquire whether the succession commitment along with descendant altruism accounts for family business survival, an issue that requires a dynamic model.

Next, we present a dynamic model with descendant altruism and a succession commitment, an extension of the previous framework to two periods that can be seen as an version of Chami (2001, Sec. IV). The economic decisions are taken in two periods of time, denoted to by $t = 1$ and $t = 2$. There exists descendant altruism for an altruistic parent, that is, $\beta_p > 0$, but there is no ascendant altruism for a child, that is, $\beta_a = 0$, who is not involved and identified with the goals of the family firm but with her owns goals for the future. The succession commitment consists in, at the beginning of period $t = 1$, the owner-manager faithfully promising a family member who works for the firm that she will be the owner of the family firm at period $t = 2$.

The parent and the child overlap at the first period. The owner-manager consumes only for one period of time, that is, $\mathbf{c}^p = (c^p, 0)$, while the worker-agent consumes one consumption good at each period, $\mathbf{c}^a = (c^a_1, c^a_2)$. Descendant altruism is modelled as before: the parent is concerned with the overall welfare of the child, hence $\mathit{U}_a = U_a(c^a, e, 0, 0)$. We also consider separability of preferences, so the worker-agent's preferences will be represented by $U_a(c^a, e, 0, 0) = u_a(c^a_1) + \gamma\, u_a(c^a_2) - \mathfrak{C}(e)$, where $u_a(c^a_t)$ is a twice-differentiable, increasing, continuous utility function for $t = 1, 2$; the cost function $\mathfrak{C}(e)$ is defined as before; and $\gamma < 1$ is a parameter of intertemporal preference discount factor. Note that the succession commitment is modelled by considering that the worker-agent considers that her future consumption depends on her present work effort decisions, so $\gamma > 0$.

Finally, at period $t = 1$ the firm produces only with the worker's effort, $y^1_1 = e$, and a linear technology $f_1(e) = A_1 e$; while at period $t = 2$ the firm produces with the same worker's effort as in period $t = 1$, $y^1_2 = e$, and a linear technology $f_2(e) = A_2 e$, where A_t represents the constant marginal productivity of effort for $t = 1, 2$.[25]

As usual, the model is solved by backwards induction. The worker-agent first chooses her optimal level of effort by maximizing her welfare $U_a(c^a, e, 0, 0) = u_a(c^a_1) + \gamma u_a(c^a_2) - \mathfrak{C}(e)$ subject to $c^a_1 = wA_1 e$ and $c^a_2 = A_2 e$, resulting in a supply function of effort that depends on the wages received in compensation

$$e(w; \beta_a, \beta_p, \gamma) = e(w; 0, \beta_p, \gamma) = w\frac{A_1}{k} + \frac{\gamma A_2}{k} \qquad (27.16)$$

Note that, as no ascendant altruism exists, that is, $\beta_a = 0$, the child behaves as any other non-family worker, so her incentives for increasing effort are only guided by wages, as already shown in Lemma 4.4.1. However, her effort is higher under the succession commitment, as the next result, similar to Chami (2001, Prop. 5), shows:

Proposition 4.5.1   Work effort with succession commitment   Consider the environment where the child expects to take over the family firm, that is, $\gamma > 0$. Receiving the same labor compensation, the child's effort is higher than that of any other worker who does not expect to inherit the family firm, that is, $e(w; \beta_p, 0, \gamma) > e(w; \beta_p, 0, 0)$ for any given $w \in [0,1]$ and any $\beta_p > 0$.

The proof is straightforward. Note that the child, being selfish, that is, $\beta_a = 0$, but expecting to inherit the business, $\gamma > 0$, makes a higher effort than a non-family employee and also higher than any other family worker who does not expect to inherit the business. Thus the succession commitment makes the difference. As a consequence, the presence of agency conflicts between the manager and a worker who will inherit the family firm is mitigated.

The owner-manager, as principal, chooses the optimal wage that maximizes his welfare $U_p(c^p, \beta_p, U_a(c^a, e, 0, 0)) = u_p(c^p) + \beta_p[u_a(c_1^a) + \gamma u_a(c_2^a) - \mathfrak{C}(e)]$ subject to $c^p = (1-w)Ae$, $c_1^a = wA_1e$, $c_2^a = A_2e$ and taking into consideration the optimal effort level chosen by the agent (27.16). Now, the optimal wage is

$$
w^*(\beta_p, 0, \gamma) = \begin{cases} \dfrac{1}{2 - \beta_p} - \dfrac{2\gamma A_2}{A_1} \dfrac{1 - \beta_p}{2 - \beta_p} & \text{if } 1 \geq \Psi(\psi, \beta_p) \\[2mm] 0, & \text{if } 1 \geq \Psi(\psi, \beta_p) \end{cases}
$$

with $\Psi(\psi, \beta_p) = \psi(1 - \beta_p)$ and $\psi = \gamma A_2/A_1$; and then the optimal level of effort is

$$
e^*(\beta_p, 0, \gamma) = \begin{cases} \dfrac{A_1 + \gamma A_2}{(2 - \beta_p)k} & \text{if } 1 \geq \Psi(\psi, \beta_p) \\[2mm] \dfrac{\gamma A_2}{k} & \text{if } 1 \geq \Psi(\psi, \beta_p) \end{cases}
$$

Next, we present the following result that shows how the optimal wage contract and effort are modified under different parameters.

Lemma 4.5.2 Optimal wage, work effort and profits under different value of the parameters Consider the environment with descendant altruism and succession, that is, $\beta_p > 0$, $\beta_a = 0$, and $\gamma > 0$. Then, for $1 \geq \Psi(\psi, \beta_p)$:

1. *Different degrees of descendant altruism*

$$
\frac{\partial w^*(\beta_p, 0, \gamma)}{\partial \beta_p} = \frac{1}{(2 - \beta_p)^2} \frac{A_1 + \gamma A_2}{A_1} > 0
$$

$$
\frac{\partial e^*(\beta_p, 0, \gamma)}{\partial \beta_p} = \frac{1 - \beta_a}{(2 - \beta_p)^2} \frac{A_1 + \gamma A_2}{k} > 0
$$

$$
\frac{\partial \pi^*(\beta_p, 0, \gamma)}{\partial \beta_p} = \frac{(2 - \beta_p)(A_1 + \gamma A_2)^2}{(2 - \beta_p)^4}(1 - 2\beta_p) \begin{cases} > 0 \text{ if } \beta_p < 1/2 \\ < 0 \text{ if } \beta_p > 1/2 \end{cases}
$$

2. *Different degrees of the intertemporal discount*

$$\frac{\partial w^*(\beta_p,0,\gamma)}{\partial \gamma} = -\frac{A_2(1 - \beta_p)}{A_1(2 - \beta_p)} < 0$$

$$\frac{\partial e^*(\beta_p,0,\gamma)}{\partial \gamma} = \frac{A_2}{k(2 - \beta_p)} > 0;$$

$$\frac{\partial \pi^*(\beta_p,0,\gamma)}{\partial \beta_p} = \frac{2\gamma(1 - \beta_p)(A_1 + \gamma A_2)}{k(2 - \beta_p)^2} > 0$$

3.   *Different degrees of the productivity at period* t = 2

$$\frac{\partial w^*(\beta_p,0,\gamma)}{\partial A_2} = -\frac{\gamma(1 - \beta_p)}{A_1(2 - \beta_p)} < 0$$

$$\frac{\partial e^*(\beta_p,0,\gamma)}{\partial A_2} = \frac{\gamma}{k(2 - \beta_p)} > 0$$

$$\frac{\partial \pi^*(\beta_p,0,\gamma)}{\partial A_2} = \frac{2A_2(1 - \beta_p)(A_1 + \gamma A_2)}{k(2 - \beta_p)^2} > 0$$

Four comments are in order. First, observe that the higher the degree of parental altruism β_p, the higher the wages paid by the manager. Recall that the child reacts by increasing working effort under monetary incentives, as already noted in Lemma 4.4.1.

Proposition 4.5.3   Wages under one-sided altruism and succession commitment   Consider the environment with descendant but not ascendant altruism, that is, $\beta_p > 0$ *and* $\beta_a = 0$, and a child's expectation to take over the firm. In contrast to a *family* worker who does not expect to inherit the firm, the child receives a lower compensation wage in family firms, that is, $w^*(\beta_p,0,\gamma) < w^*(\beta_p,0,0)$

It is easy to see that, as a consequence of the child's expectation to take over the family firm, the parent will reduce the incentive wage component; that is, the manager has opportunistic behavior at period $t = 1$ towards a worker who expects to take over the firm at $t = 2$. This wage is not as high as the one obtained whenever descendant altruism exists and the child will not inherit the firm; and it is not as low as the one received by a non-family worker. This finding is summarized in the following result.

Theorem 4.5.4   Wages and working effort under different scenarios of altruism and succession commitment   Consider the same environment considered without ascendant altruism, $\beta_a = 0$. Consider the following three scenarios: no altruism and no succession ($\beta_p = \gamma = 0$); descendant altruism and no succession ($\beta_p > 0$ and $\gamma = 0$); and descendant altruism and succession ($\beta_p > 0$ and $\gamma > 0$). Then it is verified that

$$w^*(\beta_p,0,0) > w^*(\beta_p,0,\gamma) > w^*(0,0,0)$$

and

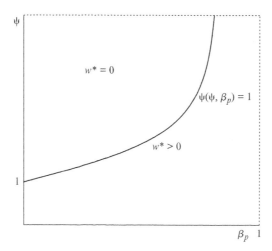

Note: $\psi = \gamma A_2/A_1$ represents the productivity ratio between period $t = 1$ and $t = 2$. Note that the descendant one-sided altruism is also represented on the X-axis.

Figure 27.3 *The wage contract under descendant altruism and succession commitment, case $\beta_a = 0$, $\beta_b \in [0,1]$ and $\gamma = 0$*

$$e^* (\beta_p,0,\gamma) > e^* (\beta_p,0,0) > e^* (0,0,0)$$

This result is not surprising if we realize that the contract offered by the manager to the worker is a payment at two periods of time: (i) a wage wA_1e at period $t = 1$; and (ii) the value of the outcome A_2e in period $t = 2$. Thus the discounted value of the income received by the worker who expects to inherit the family firm, $A_1ew + \gamma A_2e = [(A_1 + \gamma A_2)/(2-\beta)]^2/k$, will be higher than the income received by the other worker who has not such an expectation. Then she has incentives to increase work effort to obtain higher income.

Second, the child's effort is higher under a parental succession commitment. This could be interpreted as the child's response to her parent's altruism, but this need not be the case. As shown in the previous comment, the heir is not ascendant altruistic and the higher overall income received will be her only incentive to work harder.

Third, the higher the technological productivity at period $t = 2$, A_2, and the intertemporal discount factor, γ, the lower the wage and the higher the work effort. Note that the higher discounted future income, γA_2, the more the manager may display opportunistic behavior as he receives more income at period $t = 1$ in exchange for the promise of higher income for the worker at $t = 2$. Moreover, for a high enough valuation of future income or for a high enough productivity at $t = 2$, the worker might still work for the firm despite receiving no monetary compensation, $w^*(\beta_p,0,\gamma) = 0$ (see Figure 27.3).

Finally, concerning the firm's profits at period $t = 1$ note that profits increase for a low degree of parental altruism and decrease for a high enough degree of parental altruism β_p, a result that extends to the case of succession commitment the findings in Proposition 4.4.3 for one-sided altruism. In addition, profits increase the higher the degree of intertemporal discount parameter, and the more productive is technology at period $t = 2$. See Figure 27.3, which entails that higher profits are found higher up the graph. Note that the parameter $\psi = \gamma A_2/A_1$, the ratio of firm's productivity when the manager is the child to firm's productivity when the manager is the parent, can be interpreted as a degree of the smartness of the child, for instance her managerial abilities to run the firm. The following result compares the amount of profits under inheritance with respect to those achieved in previous sections.

Proposition 4.5.5   Profits under succession commitment   Consider the environment with descendant altruism and heritance, that is, $\beta_p > 0$, $\beta_a = 0$ and $\gamma > 0$. Then:

1. *The clumsy boy (or girl) case*   For $1 \geq \Psi(\psi, \beta_p)$ profits are lower in family firms in contrast to non-family businesses, that is,

$$\pi_1(0,0,0) > \pi_1(\beta_p,0,\gamma) > \pi_1(\beta_p,0,0)$$

2. *The smart child case*   For $1 \leq \Psi(\psi, \beta_p)$, profits are higher in family firms in contrast to non-family businesses and one-sided altruism, that is,

$$\pi_1(\beta_p,0,\gamma) > \pi_1(0,0,0) > \pi_1(\beta_p,0,0)$$

The first result is found in the bottom area of Figure 27.3. This is the case where descendant altruism is too high, or the heir is not smart enough to turn the family firm into a more productive business. The parent extracts pecuniary benefits from hiring his child, then jeopardizing the existence of the family firm. Analogously to the comments of Proposition 4.4.3, where the child is not enough qualified to run the firm, it is better if the manager hires a non-family worker and sells the firm on the market, or hires the family worker and hires a manager to run the firm in the future. Thus diverting some resources from the firm to achieve some particular own altruistic goals may allow the firm to survive in the long run.

The second result is found in the upper area of Figure 27.3. This is the case where the girl is clever enough to turn the family firm into a very productive business at period $t = 2$, so she is even interested in working for no wage compensation at period $t = 1$. Thus the profits of the family are higher under a succession commitment and a smart heir than in the case of the non-family business. This 'smart boy' case occurs when the child makes enough effort even if no descendant altruism exists, that is, $\beta_p = 0$ (see Y-axis in Figure 27.3). In this case, the non-altruistic manager undertakes opportunistic behavior by paying no wages in exchange for high effort of the worker.

To sum up, Proposition 4.5.5 is important as it means that the succession commitment may explain the survival of the family firm over time, whenever the heir is smart enough to turn the family firm into a more productive one. This is formalized by a relatively high ratio between the marginal productivities of work effort across periods, ψ. In addition, it is pointed out that the succession commitment itself is not enough to keep the family firm out of trouble. First, a rude and tough family manager (i.e. lowering β_p) may not turn low into high profits, at least for the case where the child is not very smart (i.e. $\psi < 1$). Second, firms with low altruistic owner-managers and clumsy heirs will survive only by professionalizing the firm.

5 THE ROLE OF INSTITUTIONAL IMPERFECTIONS

5.1 Legal Imperfections and the Professionalization of Family Business

There are several explanations for control preservation in a family firm that are based on aspects and variables that are external to the business. One of them is the prevailing legal system concerning shareholder protection.[26] Under some poor legal protection such a separation between ownership and control could become very costly, for example in terms of monitoring. This explanation is based on the possibility of expropriation that comes with control. The argument can be employed to study both the separation of ownership and management, and the professionalization decision in the family firm as two aspects of the same problem. In other words, the decision to maintain ownership can be influenced by the capacity of the professional manager to expropriate benefits: if legal protection is low, concentrated ownership and no separation of ownership and management is the natural outcome, which prevents profit diversion by non-family managers.

5.2 The Basic Model

This literature considers three agents: the owner of a firm, who also runs the business alone, termed the owner-manager; a non-family manager who can be hired to run the firm, called the professional manager; and the firm.

5.2.1 The owner-manager
The family is represented by a single individual, who is the owner of a firm, that is, $\theta = 1$, the only worker of the firm, and who also runs the business alone. He is endowed with managerial knowledge h^p and an amount of available time $T = 1$ that can be devoted to leisure or to the firm's related activities. His welfare is enhanced by devoting time to leisure activities, l^p, and consuming goods purchased in the market, $\mathbf{c}^p$. In addition, he may increase welfare by consuming purely amenity goods only provided by the family firm, $\mathbf{b} = \mathbf{A}$, derived from the mere existence or the decisions taken when running the firm, which does not involve any expense for the firm. The literature considers separability of preferences between these elements. Thus his preferences will be represented by $U_p(\mathbf{c}^p, l^p, \mathbf{A}) = u_p(\mathbf{c}^p, l^p) + \mathbf{A}$, where $u_p(\mathbf{c}^p, l^p)$ is a twice differentiable, increasing, concave, continuous utility function. Finally, in the case that a professional management from outside of the family is hired to run the firm, the owner-manager may still monitor her performance in the firm. We will assume that this activity incurs him a cost of leisure $C(m)$.[27]

5.2.2 The professional manager
This agent is endowed with managerial knowledge h^a and an amount of available time $T = 1$ that can be devoted to leisure or to labor. If hired, she will replace the owner-manager in the firm by devoting all her time to management activities in exchange for a wage. Her welfare is increased by consuming goods purchased in the market, $\mathbf{c}^a$, and leisure, h^a, and her preferences will be represented by a twice differentiable, strictly increasing, continuous utility function, $U_a(\mathbf{x}^a) = u_a(\mathbf{c}^a, l^a)$.

5.2.3   The firm

The firm produces a single good y by combining a number of inputs $\mathbf{y} \in \Re_+^J$, which comprise the management services H. The technology will be represented by a twice differentiable, concave, strictly increasing, continuous production function $y = f(\mathbf{y})$. In a market economy the firm interacts with other firms in an economic environment both in the goods and the inputs markets. We will assume that this environment is competitive. Thus the firm will consider as exogenous both the price of the good produced, p^y, and the price of all other inputs purchased in the market, w^j, with $j = 1, \ldots, J$.

Finally, the person who manages the firm chooses the level of expropriation, partially impeded by law, and, in the case of the professional manager, she is subject to monitoring by the firm's owners. This non-contractable expropriation decision can be modelled as a choice of the manager's private benefit share $\phi \in [0,1]$, such that dividends are a proportion $(1 - \phi)$ of the firm's profits. This expropriation is limited by legal shareholder protection: the law sets an upper bound $\bar{\phi} \in [0,1]$ on the fraction of revenues that can be diverted by the party in control. Stronger legal protection corresponds to lower value of $\bar{\phi}$. As in Burkart et al. (2003), this upper bound is irrespective of the form in which those benefits are enjoyed; that is, wages in excess of market value are already incorporated in this proportion.

5.3   The Separation of Ownership and Management

In this section, we present a model of separation of ownership and management based on Burkart et al. (2003). We will simplify the notation. The firm produces only with management services, that is, qualified labor, as the input, $y^1 = HN$, and we will assume a linear technology $f(HN) = AHN$, where A represents a technological parameter. Both managers may only consume one consumption good, $\mathbf{c}^i = c^i$, and their respective utility functions are linear on consumption and leisure, that is, $u^i(\mathbf{c}^i, l^i) = c^i + \varphi\,(l^i - T)$, with $i = a$ and p. Note that whoever manages the firm chooses the optimal labor decisions by devoting all their time to work, that is, $n^i = T(=1)$ for $i = a$ and p, so the disutility of the effort is represented by φT. The owner-manager's cost function of monitoring the professional manager, if hired, is $C(m) = (k/\varphi)m^2/2$ (see Pagano and Röell, 1998).

The model is static, but it comprises the following sub-periods. The owner-manager has to decide at date $t = 0$ whether to appoint a professional manager to run the firm or keep management in the family. Simultaneously he decides what fraction $1 - \theta$ of the shares to sell to dispersed shareholders and, if the founder appoints a professional, he also offers a wage, w^{HN}. At date $t = 1$ the professional manager accepts or rejects the offer to run the company. At date $t = 2$ the family, as a shareholder, decides the monitoring intensity m that reduces private benefit extraction in a proportion $m \in [0,1]$. At date $t = 3$ the firm generates revenues that depend on the identity of the manager. If control remains inside the family, total revenues generated are $y^p = f(h^p n^p) = Ah^p$; if a professional manager runs the firm, total revenues are $y^a = f(h^a n^a) = Ah^a$.

Following Burkart et al. (2003), professionalization questions arise when the founder or his heir are not the best manager, as otherwise there is no reason to sell equity and the family will naturally retain management. Next, we study two cases. First, the founder retains management and second, a manager is hired.

5.3.1 No separation of ownership and management

If ownership and management are not separated, the owner-manager keeps running the firm, that is, $n^a = 1$. At date $t = 3$, his decision on how to allocate the profits $\pi(y^p, h^p n^p)$ – defined as in (27.3) – is constrained to divert no more than $\overline{\phi}$ of the revenues as private benefits. Thus he will extract the legal upper bound $\overline{\phi}$. Absent a professional manager, there is neither date $t = 2$ monitoring nor a date $t = 1$ job acceptance decision. His decision at date $t = 0$ is concerned with the fraction of shares to sell to outside investors. The owner-manager maximizes his welfare $U^p(c^p, l^p, A)$ subject to the temporal constraint $l^p + n^p = T$ and $c^p = w^{HN} n^p + \theta(1 - \overline{\phi})\pi(y^p, h^p n^p) + (1 - \theta)\overline{\phi}\pi(y^p, h^p n^p) + B$. Note that $\theta(1 - \overline{\phi})\pi(y^p, h^p n^p)$ is the value of his date $t = 3$ block, and $(1 - \theta)\overline{\phi}\pi(y^p, h^p n^p)$ is the proceeds from selling $1 - \theta$ shares at date $t = 0$. Since diversion is efficient, the optimal ownership structure is indeterminate when ownership and management are separated, as shown in the following result.

Lemma 5.3.1 (Burkart et al. 2003, Lemma 1) For any $\overline{\phi} \in [0,1]$, $U^p(c^p(\theta^*), 0, A) = y_p - \varphi + A$ and $\theta^* \in [0,1]$.

To summarize, the case of no separation does not yield precise predictions, notably for the ownership structure.

5.3.2 Separation of ownership and management

As usual the model is solved by backwards induction. At date $t = 3$ total revenues under the professional manager are y^a, and the law stipulates that $(1 - \overline{\phi})\pi(y^a, h^a)$ must be paid out to shareholders as dividends. What fraction of the remaining $\overline{\phi}\pi(y^a, h^a n^a)$ is actually diverted depends on monitoring. At date 2 the owner-manager has to choose a monitoring intensity. For a given block θ and for a given wage rate w^{HN}, the owner-manager maximizes his welfare $U^p(c^p, l^p, 0)$, subject to $c^p = \theta\pi(y^a, h^a) + (m - \overline{\phi})y^a$, and the temporal constraint $l^p + C(m) = T$. Hence the optimal monitoring level is

$$m(\theta) = \min\left\{\overline{\phi}, \theta\frac{y^a}{k}\right\}$$

At date $t = 1$, the professional manager decides to run the firm by maximizing her welfare $U^a(c^a, l^a)$, subject to $c^a = w^{HN} n^a - (m - \overline{\phi})y^a$, and the temporal constraint $l^a + n^a = T$. Thus she will agree as long as $U^a(c^a(\theta, m), 1) \geq 0$, that is, if the sum of the wage and the private benefits exceeds her utility of effort. This participation constraint can be written as

$$m(\theta) = m(w^{HN}, \overline{\phi}) \equiv \overline{\phi} + \frac{w^{HN} - \varphi}{y^a}$$

Note that higher ownership concentration and better legal protection – that is, low $\overline{\phi}$ – make it more difficult to satisfy the professional manager's participation constraint, whereas higher wages make it easier. This is the basic trade-off when ownership and management are separated.

At date $t = 0$ the owner-manager chooses the ownership structure and the wage to maximize his welfare $U^p(c^p, T - C(m(\theta)), 0)$, subject to $c^p = \pi(y^a, h^a) + (m(\theta) - \bar{\phi})y^a$ and the professional manager's participation constraint $m(\theta) \in [0, m(w^{HN}, \bar{\phi})]$.

Note that if the owner-manager chooses an ownership structure such that $\bar{\phi} < \theta^* y^a/k$, then the professional manager is able to divert no private benefits, $m(\theta^*) = \bar{\phi}$; thus the owner-manager would have to offer a wage $w^{HN^*} = \varphi$ to induce her to accept the job. By choosing an ownership structure such that $\bar{\phi} > \theta^* y^a/k$, the owner-manager leaves some private benefits to the professional manager by monitoring less $m(\theta^*) = \theta^* y^a/k$. Inserting this level into the owner-manager's welfare yields $V^p(\theta, w^{HN}; \bar{\phi}, k)) \equiv U^p(c^p(\theta^*, m(\theta^*)), T - C(m(\theta^*)), 0)$ with $dV^p(\theta, w^{HN})/d\theta = (1 - \theta)(y^a)^2/k \geq 0$ and $dV^p(\theta, w^{HN})/dw^{HN} = -1 < 0$, provided the professional manager accepts the job, that is, $m(\theta^*) \leq \bar{m}$. This is the case whenever $y^a/k + \phi/y^a \leq \bar{\phi}$.

The following result summarizes the ownership and wages decisions of the owner-manager:

Lemma 5.3.2   (Burkart et al., 2003, Lemma 2)

(i)   Under strong legal protection, that is, $\bar{\phi} < \varphi\, y^a$, the owner-manager sells the firm $\theta^* = 0$, there is no monitoring $m(\theta^*) = 0$, the wage offer is $w^{HN^*} = \varphi - \bar{\phi}y^a$, and $V^p(\theta^*, w^{H^*}; \bar{\phi}) = y^a - \varphi$.

(ii)   Under moderate legal protection, that is, $\bar{\phi} \in [\frac{\varphi}{y^a}, \frac{\varphi}{y^a} + \frac{y^a}{k}]$, the wage offer is $w^* = 0$, there is some monitoring $m^* = m(0, \bar{\phi})$, the owner-manager sells $\theta^* = \frac{k}{y^a}(\bar{\phi} - \frac{\varphi}{y^a})$, and $V^p(\theta^*, 0, \bar{\phi}) = y^a - \varphi - \frac{k}{2}(\bar{\phi} - \frac{\varphi}{y^a})^2$.

(iii)   Under poor legal protection, that is, $y^a/k + \varphi/y^a \leq \bar{\phi}$, the owner-manager does not sell the firm, the monitoring level is $m(\theta^*) = y^a/k$, the wage offer is $w^{HN^*} = 0$ and $V^p(\theta^*, 0, \bar{\phi}) = y^a(1 - \bar{\phi}) + (\frac{y^a}{2k})^2$.

When legal protection is strong (case (i)), ownership is completely dispersed, no monitoring is undertaken and the professional manager is offered a wage that induces her to accept the job. When legal protection is moderate (case (ii)), the wage offered is reduced as the professional manager is able to divert some private benefits, and it is optimal to carry out some degree of monitoring to limit the size of these private benefits. Because of $V^p(\theta^*, w^{HN}; \bar{\phi}, k)$ decreases in $\bar{\phi}$ and k, less legal protection and a higher cost of monitoring entail a higher optimal level of monitoring. Finally, when legal protection is poor (case (iii)), the owner-manager cannot avoid leaving a private benefit to the professional manager, so a zero wage is offered, and full ownership of the firm is retained.

Summarizing, the fraction of shares that the founder decides to maintain is decreasing with the degree of legal protection, and the separation of ownership and management is more feasible as legal protection diminishes.

Next, we present the conditions under which the owner-manager chooses to hire a professional manager.

Proposition 5.3.3
1.   (Burkart et al., 2003, Prop. 1)
   (i)   If $y^p + \mathbf{A} > y^a$, then ownership and management is never separated; and
   (ii)   If $(y^a)^2/(2k) > y^p + \mathbf{A}$, then ownership and management are always separated.
2.   Under moderate legal protection, that is, $\bar{\phi} \in [\frac{\varphi}{y^a}, \frac{\varphi}{y^a} + \frac{y^a}{k}]$, the family retains manage-

ment only if the owner, manager's performance as a manager is notably better than the performance of the professional, that is, $y^p = y^a - \varphi - \frac{k}{2}(\overline{\phi} - \frac{\varphi}{y^a})^2$.

Note that as the amenity potential is important for the owner-manager, it increases the propensity for the 'no-separation' outcome that we obtained in the previous analysis.

5.4   Financial Imperfections

It is often argued that the development of financial markets has a decisive influence on the family business ownership, size and length of life. Thus in less developed financial markets it is more difficult to sell the firm and the sources of funding are more limited; then the firm lasts longer and, as it grows over time, it is bigger at the time of selling. In this section we explore the effect of the existence of financial restrictions on selling the firm concerning the control and growth of the family firm. The family firm owns and manages the firm until it is more profitable to sell the business.

In this section we extend the previous framework to consider that economic decisions are taken in infinite periods of time, denoted by $t = 1, 2, 3, \ldots$. The dynamic model is a simplified version of the extension of Kimhi (1997), Bhattacharya and Ravikumar (2001), Galve-Górriz et al. (2003, Sec. 2.3) and Castañeda (2006) presented in Section 3.2.2. We will follow Bhattacharya and Ravikumar (2001) and Castañeda (2006) and simplify the setting by assuming that (i) no adjustment costs exists, $\overline{\phi}\,() = 0$; (ii) no amenity benefits are considered, that is, $u(\mathbf{c}) \equiv U(\mathbf{c}, l, \mathbf{b})$;[28] (iii) the technology depends only on labor and physical capital to produce, and we will assume that it exhibits constant returns to scale, for example the Cobb–Douglas technology $f(y_t) = AK_t^{\alpha}N_t^{1-\alpha}$, with $\alpha \in (0,1]$; and (iv) the price of the financial security z is purchased at a price $q + \chi$, where $\chi \geq 0$ represents the degree of underdevelopment of the financial markets, so the higher χ, the less developed the capital markets so the more expensive (and difficult) it is to sell the firm (see Bhattacharya and Ravikumar 2001).

The owner-manager's budget constraint is affected by the ability to access the financial markets. Consider that at period t^* the firm is sold. Then the budget constraints are

$$p_t^c c_t + K_{t+1} = w_t^N n_t + w_t^K K_t + \theta \pi_t(y_t, \mathbf{y}_t), \text{ for } t = 1, \ldots, t^* - 1$$

$$p_{t^*}^c c_{t^*} + (q + \chi)z_{t^*} = w_{t^*}^N n_t + w_{t^*}^K K_{t^*} + \theta \pi_{t^*}(y_{t^*}, \mathbf{y}_{t^*}) \text{ and}$$

$$p_t^c c_t + z_t = (1 + \overline{r})z_t, \text{ for } t \geq t^*$$

Note that because of constant returns to scale there are no economic profits at each period, $\pi_t(y_t, \mathbf{y}_t) = 0$ for all t, and the factors are remunerated at marginal productivity, $w^N = (1 - \alpha)f_N(y)$ and $w^K = \alpha f_K(y)$. Finally, the owner-manager devotes all his time to labor.

The owner-manager problem is to decide when to switch from a marginal decreasing returns in capital technology to a AK technology, taking into account that the switch of technology involves a cost χ. The switch will be undertaken whenever the rate of return is higher for the AK technology, after considering the cost of changing. The balance growth path for the Cobb–Douglas technology is $k_{t+1} = \beta \alpha A k_t^{\alpha}$ for any $t < t^*$ converging to the steady-state stock of capital $K^s = (\beta \alpha A)^{1/(1-\alpha)}$, and for the linear technology it is $z_{t+1} = \beta(1+\bar{r})z_t$ for any $t > t^*$ (see Ljungqvist and Sargent 2000, Sec. 3.1.2). Then, at the period $t = t^*$, $(q + \chi)z_{t^*} = \beta \alpha A K^{\alpha}_{t^*-1}$. Accordingly, at period t^* the owner-manager would be indifferent between investing in capital K_{t^*} and buying the security z_{t^*} as both provide the same marginal productivity. This means that the family firm accumulates capital until it reaches a threshold

$$\bar{K}(\chi) = \left((q + \chi)\frac{\alpha^2 A}{1 + \bar{r}} \right)^{1/(1-\alpha)}$$

beyond which it is profitable to switch the technology. Note that this threshold is a decreasing function of the development of the financial restriction, that is, $\partial \bar{K}/\partial \chi > 0$.

The following results can be proved. First, we show the conditions required to guarantee that the firm will be sold, a result similar to that of Battacharya et al (2001, Lemma 2).

Lemma 5.4.1   Consider the family firm that faces an imperfect financial market. There exists a degree of underdevelopment $\hat{\chi}$ of the financial market such that the firm will never be sold, that is, $K^S < K(\hat{\chi})$. Conversely, if $K^S > K(\hat{\chi})$, then there exists a finite period $t^*(\hat{\chi})$ at which the business is sold.

Second, we show the conditions such that the firm has a greater size under underdeveloped financial markets, a result similar to that of Battacharya et al (2001, Prop. 4).

Proposition 5.4.2   Consider the same family firm operating in different economies that display different degrees of imperfect financial markets. Then the family firm that faces higher degrees of financial market imperfections lasts longer, that is, $t^*(\chi_1) > t^*(\chi_2)$ for $\chi_1 > \chi_2$, and, at the time of selling, the family business is larger, that is, $\bar{K}(\chi_1) > \bar{K}(\chi_2)$.

The proof is straightforward.

As a final comment, it is interesting to realize that the finding that financial constraints delay the sale of the family firm that turns out to be a large business (Battacharya et al. 2001, Sec. III) contrasts with the opposite results found in Kimhi (1997, Sec. 3): the financial constraints bring forward the departure of the owner-manager from the family firm that turns out to be a small business. The difference stems from the assumption that funds for capital accumulation of the family firm come from internal sources in the former, and external sources in the latter (see Section 3.2.2). In Kimhi's model, the family firm has access to financial funds – unlike in Battacharya and Ravikumar model – but there exists a borrowing constraint $K_{t+1} \leq (q + \chi)z_t$ as in Evans and Jovanovic (1989). The existence of this restriction results in the firm growing at a lower rate, $\bar{g} < g$, and then a decrease in the firm's investment and the family business is smaller at the time the owner family leaves the firm, that is, $K(\bar{g}) < K(g)$. This means that as the borrowing constraint gets tighter, the family firm needs financial funds provided by the successor when inheriting the firm, so the transfer of the earlier that is, $t^*(g) < t^*(\bar{g})$ (see equation (27.13)).

6 CONCLUDING REMARKS

This chapter presents an analytical framework that surveys and, at the same time, unifies the microeconomic literature of family firms. We identify three sets of works: the first studies the family firm under an owner-manager who simultaneously maximizes the firm's profits and the family's welfare; the second uses the agency theory approach to study the relationships among the family members interacting within the family; and the third deals with the influence of legal and financial imperfections on the family firm's decisions. Although this literature is scarce and limited in scope, the application of microeconomic tools has been found useful to characterize the particular features of family businesses compared to non-family businesses, as well as to explain under what conditions some distinctive features of family firms hold.

Some of the most important of these particular features of family business are: (i) a single family displays a high degree of ownership of the firm; (ii) one member – or very few members – of the family (usually known as the owner-manager) is involved in the managerial activities of the firm; (iii) the owner (the family) or the manager (the owner-manager) of the firm exhibits a degree of altruism towards the family's children; that is, in formal terms at the time of taking decisions concerning the firm the family children's present and future well-being is considered; (iv) the family firm provides amenity benefits to the owner or to the manager, whether in terms of social acknowledge or to provide a job for the family children; (v) a family business displays a higher productivity than a non-family firm, *ceteris paribus* – that is, the same level of inputs – and, (vi) a family firm is financially constrained to obtain external funds because it precludes outside investors from the firm. In our opinion the contributions systematized in Section 3 include these distinctive features related to the productivity of labor, the cost of capital, the growth rate and the optimal size, among others, and provide the theoretical support for empirical research on the specificities of family firms compared with non-family firms. This framework also allowed us to explain non-pecuniary benefits in terms of an externality derived from the fact that the well-being of the family is directly affected by the decisions taken in the firm. In this sense, we show that the founder's particular own altruistic goals can be understood as a type of non-pecuniary benefits.

The principal–agent approach, studied in Section 4, has revealed that survival of family firms depends on the existence of two-sided altruism or on the existence of a succession plan for a smart family heir. The analysis shows that paternalistic altruism may jeopardize the existence of the firm in the long run. In this framework a succession commitment can explain the survival of family firms over time, depending on the quality of the heir. Some of the results obtained in the principal–agent section need to be replicated using more sophisticated formal models which include, among others, the role of the temporal dimension and of uncertainty about some of the key variables of the decision-making process. For instance, one of the most obvious aspects to be taken into account is the founder's uncertainty about being alive in the near future. The temporal dimension has to be included in the analysis in order to understand how the family and the firm take decisions and interact through stages over time.

The approach based on institutional imperfections, reviewed in Section 5, provides a partial analysis that establishes the conditions that determine the decisions of selling and professionalizing the firm, depending on the legal protection of minority shareholders and the development of financial markets. In the former, the fraction of shares that the founder decides to maintain is decreasing with the degree of legal protection, and the separation of ownership and management is more likely as legal protection diminishes. In the case of financial imperfections the results show that the family firm that faces higher degrees of financial market imperfections lasts longer.

A number of limitations of the analysis and directions for future research can be drawn. Most of the literature surveyed in this chapter has made use of a quite narrow definition of family business, which is implicit in the owner-manager stereotype, in the 'imperfections approach' and even in the principal–agent approach. In this sense, greater efforts are needed in the microeconomics approach to cover broader definitions of family firms. This includes the consideration of the higher complexity of the family ties in terms of multiple family owners and members with different and even contradictory goals, as well as an explicit definition of the variables and processes that characterize the family member's involvement, such as values and trust. This will be shown useful in analyzing family businesses in a broader perspective to explain emotional costs, personal commitment, loyalty, among many others that are typical notions in the stewardship perspective. In this sense, an open area of theoretical research is the role of non-economic motivations and goals of the family firm's owners – for instance in aspects such as personal commitment, long-term planning, human resources practices, human capital intergenerational transfer, successor training or internal monitoring mechanisms, among many others. As Chrisman et al. (2010) point out, non-economic goals are essential to explain family firms' behavior because they can either exacerbate or mitigate many of their typical conflicts.

With respect to the agency theory approach, as Greenwood (2003) remarks, one important limitation in the context of the family firm lies in the binary treatment of power in principal–agent models: the principal has power and the agent does not. This could be misleading because power and influence in family business can be dispersed among several family members. Thus children frequently do have power or capacity to manipulate or persuade their parents to relax the criteria to which the contract was originally tied. Moreover, altruism itself can make it difficult for parents to enforce their plans (in particular commitment on announced punishments), both in the case of indulgent parents and in the case that children have the capacity to take actions that can threaten the welfare of the family and the firm alike (Schulze et al., 2003). Changed circumstances that influence family welfare can cause parents to unilaterally alter existing agreements (e.g. in Bergstrom's (1989) case of the prodigal son). In our opinion the theory of contracts could be applied to a deeper extent than our simple principal–agent model presented in Section 4 in order to take into consideration informational asymmetries among family members, and particularly in the founder–successor relationship. In this sense, not only moral hazard problems are relevant. Adverse selection and signalling approaches should also be addressed when dealing with questions related to the succession decision, the process of incorporation of family members to the firm and professionalization.

Finally, microeconomic theory provides a wide variety of instruments and frameworks that are ready to use in the analysis of the characteristics and specificities of family firms. It is not a question of a limited or simplistic view of the microeconomic models, but a question of building more complete and complex models to tackle a wider set of specific characteristics and problems for family businesses. In our opinion intergenerational family transfers are among the most obvious of these, concerning the myriad of dimensions of influence that the family exerts on the firm, such as cultural transmission, knowledge and technology transfers and human capital accumulation.

ACKNOWLEDGMENTS

The authors are grateful for the useful comments and advice of the editors and an anonymous reviewer for their help that extended the scope of the analysis and improved the exposition of the chapter. The authors would like to thank the Galician Association of Family Business (AGEF), Caixanova, Inditex, the Spanish Family Enterprise Institute (IEF) and the Xunta de Galicia (Proyect 10PXIB137153PR) for financial support.

NOTES

1. A comprehensive survey on methodologies and issues can be found in Wortman (1994) or Sharma (2004).
2. See for example Wortman (1994), Chrisman et al. (2003) or Poutziouris et al. (2006).
3. Alternatively, Ng (1974) and Feinberg (1975) consider that the managerial services can be hired outside the family, and the hired manager is a perfect substitute for the owner-manager himself, who is just as efficient in the managerial role as the owner-manager and zero cost of monitoring is needed. However, see Olsen (1977, Sec. III) for a theoretical and empirical critique of this external option. This market option is not important for the problem studied here, as pointed out by Hannan (1982).
4. Feinberg (1975) gives some extreme examples, such as 'pretty (but inefficient) secretaries, lavish offices, and discrimination by race, sex, or religion in employment decisions' (p. 131).
5. 'The satisfaction a father may derive from having his son work in the family enterprises, or . . . the effect of prejudice on the part of the employer (owner-manager) toward one of his employees' (Olsen 1977, p. 1390). These amenity potentials also comprise social, political and cultural influence.
6. See Feinberg (1975), Olsen (1977), Hannan (1982) and Formby and Millner (1985). See also Graaff (1950–51), Ng (1973), Ng (1974) and Lapan and Brown (1988) in the case that no amenity benefits are considered, i.e. $U(\mathbf{c},l,\mathbf{b}) = u(\mathbf{c},l)$.
7. This issue has already been noticed by Hannan (1982), contrary with most of the literature, for example Olsen (1973, 1977), Ng (1974), Feinberg (1975, 1980, 1982), Schlesinger (1981), and Fomby and Millner (1985).
8. See Galve-Górriz et al. (1996, 2003) for an empirical analysis of these issues.
9. Note that the firm's profitability, R, the accounting profits per unit of capital, equals w^K, the unitary cost of the physical capital, only in the case of constant returns to scale.
10. Our treatment differs from that given by James (1999) for this non-pecuniary good. James assigns as a non-pecuniary good a function of the return of the company at the period $t = 2$.
11. James (1999) additionally assumes that the utility function is separable between periods $U(\mathbf{c},l,\mathbf{b}) = u(c_2)$ $+ \beta u(c_2, K_2)$, with $\beta \in (0,1]$.
12. Observe that in the case where no externality exists, for example $u(c, K_2) = u(\mathbf{c},0)$, the rate of return paid by both assets, capital and the financial security, must be the same, that is, $w^K = (1 + r)$.
13. James (1999) considers that the non-pecuniary good is the return of the firm at period $t = 2$, that is $b = \theta\pi(y,\mathbf{y})$ in our terminology, instead of the remaining stock of capital at the end of period $t = 2$, θK_2. Note that James's is a rather strange depiction of altruism. The profits are part of the family's period 2 income, see (27.7), which is completely consumed – but also 'this return of the company is also included in the proprietor's utility function' (p. 46). We can only interpret James's non-pecuniary benefits as that the owner-manager is proud to leave his children a firm yielding a certain level of profits, and in the expectation that the firm will keep providing this amount of profits in the future. Yet we believe that leaving the ownership of the firm, that is, $\theta K_1(1-\delta)$, to his children is what really enhances the owner-manager's welfare.
14. The issue of how financial restrictions affect the owner-manager's decision to leave the firm will be taken up in Section 5.4.

15. Kimhi (1997) considers that the human capital is concave in age. The declining pattern of human capital will only exacerbate the results presented in this section.
16. Kimhi (1997) presents a model for the decision of the business-operating family to bring in the designated successor. Note that in this specification the succession process has not been planned. First, there has been no training: the young successor's human capital is lower than the owner-manager's, because no transmission of the firm culture has occurred as the successor worked outside the firm before inheriting it. Second, there are no complementarities between the old owner-manager and the heir owner-manager: the owner-manager leaves the firm. This turns out to be a strange theory of intergenerational succession in the small family business. Instead, it looks as if a sudden unfortunate event requires the heir to take charge of the firm.
17. This view can be inferred from Jensen and Meckling(1976) and Fama and Jensen (1983).
18. This perspective can be found in Chami (2001), Schultze et al. (2001, 2002, 2003), Salas (2000) or Galve-Górriz et al. (2003).
19. For a complete description of the principal–agent model, see Salanié (1998) or Macho-Stadler and Pérez-Castrillo (1997). The application to family firms can be found in Chami (2001) and Galve-Górriz et al. (2003, Sec. 1.6).
20. Observe that considering altruism affects only the individual weights.
21. Although the assumption $\beta_i \in [0,1]$ is common in the literature, it could also be considered the possibility of a very generous and charitable parent by letting $\beta_p > 1$; that is, the parent values the child's welfare more than his own welfare. This happens, for instance, when the founder is willing to give up present welfare in order to increase the future profits of the family firm. This possibility is studied in Galve-Górriz et al. (2003, Sec. 1.6) by considering two different parameters of altruism on the child's welfare: one referring to her welfare on consumption $\beta_p^c = 1$, and the other referring to her cost of effort $\beta_p^{C(e)} \geq 1$. This may stem from the disparate results found in the Galve-Górriz et al. contribution, some of them the opposite of those obtained in this section. However, considering two altruistic parameters for the same individual seems to be an odd formulation of altruism.
22. Note that an increase in the degree of ascendant altruism beyond that of considering her parent's welfare more important than hers, that is, $\beta_a \geq 1$, reduces effort. Yet this does not mean that this is an equilibrium outcome, as a corner wage offer may result optimally, for example $w = 0$. This case falls outside Lemma 4.4.4 as $\beta_a \geq 1$.
23. Despite beyond the scope of this section, note that for a higher degree of altruism, that is, $\beta_a > 1$, the child will not make any additional effort as her wages must be further reduced, according to Lemma 4.4.4, which is not possible.
24. See, for example, Gersick et al. (1997), Davies (1997) or Sundaramurthy (2008), among others.
25. Note that, in this formulation, the worker decides to make the same work effort in both periods. Despite its oddness, we follow Chami's formulation. Anyway, this could make sense under a reinterpretation of the model by considering the role of the successor. For example, the child could decide different levels of work effort in each period but both decisions could be connected, allowing for some kind of accumulation of knowledge, experience effect or acquisition of managerial abilities. On this interpretation, it would be easy to understand our assumption that the productivity of the effort A differs across periods, unlike Chami's assumption that it is constant.
26. Obviously, national fiscal laws (more specifically, inheritance and capital gains taxes) influence the decisions on firm intergenerational transmission. This subject is beyond the scope of this chapter.
27. Note that this cost is associated with a utility loss. The alternative possibility of attaching this cost to the firm would involve the problem of specifying how the decision is taken: it would be a fixed cost for the firm, yet to be decided by the family.
28. Bhattacharya and Ravikumar (2001) assume $u(c) = \sum_{t=1}^{\infty} \beta^t Lnc_t$, with $\beta \in (0,1)$.

REFERENCES

Bergstrom, T.C. (1989), 'A fresh look at the Rotten Kid theorem – and other household mysteries', *Journal of Political Economy*, **97**, 1138–59.
Bernheim, D. and Stark, O. (1988), 'Altruism within the family reconsidered: do nice guys finish last?', *American Economic Review*, **78**, 1034–45.
Bhattacharya, U. and Ravikumar, B. (2001), 'Capital markets and the evolution of family business', *Journal of Business*, **74**(2), 187–219.
Burkart, M., Panunzi, F. and Shleifer, A. (2003), 'Family Firms', *The Journal of Finance*, **58**(5), 2167–201.
Castañeda, G. (2006), 'Economic growth and concentrated ownership in stock markets', *Journal of Economic Behavior and Organization*, **59**, 249–86.

Chami, R. (2001), 'What is different about family businesses?', International Monetary Fund Working Paper, 01/70.

Chami, R. and Fullenkamp, C. (2002), 'Trust and efficiency', *Journal of Banking and Finance*, **26**, 1785–809.

Chrisman, J.J., Chua, J.H. and Steier, Ll. (2003), 'An introduction to theories of family business', *Journal of Business Venturing*, **18**, 441–8.

Chrisman, J., Kellermanns, F., Chan, K. and Liano, K. (2010), 'Intellectual foundations of current research in family business: an identification and review of 25 influential articles', *Family Business Review*, **23**(1), 9–26.

Davies, P.W.F. (1997), *Current Issues in Business Ethics*, New York; Routledge.

Demsetz, H. and Lehn, K. (1985), 'The structure of corporate ownership: causes and consequences', *Journal of Political Economy*, **93**(6), 1155–77.

Evans, D.S. and Jovanovic, B. (1989), 'An estimated model of entrepreneurial choice under liquidity constraints', *Journal of Political Economy*, **97**(4), 808–27.

Fama, E. and Jensen, M. (1983), 'Separation of ownership and control', *Journal of Law and Economics*, **26**, 301–25.

Feinberg, R.M. (1975), 'Profit maximization vs. utility maximization', *Southern Economic Journal*, **42**(1), 130–31.

Feinberg, R.M. (1980), 'On the consistency of non-profit-maximizing behaviour with perfect competition', *Southern Economic Journal*, **48**(2), 513–16.

Feinberg, R.M. (1982), 'On the equivalence of profit maximization and utility maximization by an owner-manager: reply', *Southern Economic Journal*, **49**(2), 260–61.

Formby, J.P. and Millner, E.L. (1985), 'The convergence of utility and profit maximization', *Southern Economic Journal*, **51**(4), 1174–85.

Galve-Górriz, C. and Salas-Fumas, V. (1996), 'Ownership structure and firm performance: some empirical evidence from Spain', *Managerial and Decision Economics*, **17**, 575–86.

Galve-Górriz, C. and Salas-Fumas, V. (2003), *La empresa familiar en España. Fundamentos económicos y resultados*, Bilbao: Fundación BBVA.

Gallo, M.A., Tàpies, J. and Cappuyns, K. (2004), 'Comparison of family and nonfamily business: financial logic and personal preferences', *Family Business Review*, **4**, 303–18.

Gersick, K.E., Davis, J.A., Hampton, M.M. and Lansberg, I. (1997), *Generation to generation: Life Cycles of the Family Business*, Boston, MA: Harvard Business School Press.

Graaff, J. (1950–51), 'Income effects and the theory of the firm', *Review of Economic Studies*, **18**(2), 79–86.

Greenwood, R. (2003), 'Commentary on 'Toward a theory of agency and altruism in family firms', *Journal of Business Venturing*, **18**, 491–94.

Hannan, Timothy H. (1982), 'On the equivalence of profit maximization and utility maximization by an owner-manager: comment', *Southern Economic Journal*, **49**(2), 255–9.

James, H.S. Jr (1999), 'Owner as a manager, extended horizons and the family firm', *International Journal of the Economics of Business*, **6**(1), 441–55.

Jensen, M.C. and Meckling, W.H. (1976), 'Theory of the firm: managerial behavior agency costs and ownership structure', *Journal of Financial Economics*, **3**, 305–60.

Kimhi, A. (1997), 'Intergenerational succession in small family business: borrowing constraints and optimal timing of succession', *Small Business Economics*, **9**, 309–18.

Lapan, G.E. and Brown, D.M. (1988), 'Utility maximization, individual production and market equilibrium', *Southern Economic Journal*, **55** (2), 374–89.

Ljungqvist, L. and Sargent, T.J. (2000), *Recursive Macroeconomic Theory*, 2nd edn, Cambridge, MA: MIT Press.

Macho-Stadler, I. and Pérez-Castrillo, D. (1997), *An Introduction to the Economics of Information: Incentives and Contracts*, Oxford: Oxford University Press.

Ng, Y. (1974), 'Utility and profit maximization by an owner-manager: towards a general analysis', *Journal of Industrial Economics*, **23**(2), 97–108.

Olsen, E.O. Jr (1973), 'Utility and profit maximization by an owner-manager', *Southern Economic Journal*, **39**(3), 389–95.

Olsen, E.O. Jr (1977), 'Utility and profit maximization by an owner-manager: a correction', *Southern Economic Journal*, **43**(3), 1390–93.

Pagano, M., and Röell, A. (1998), 'The choice of stock ownership structure: agency costs, monitoring and the decision to go public', *Quarterly Journal of Economics* **113**, 187–225.

Poutziouris, P., Smyrnios, K. and Klein, S. (2006), 'Introduction: the business of researching family enterprises', in P. Poutziouris, K. Smyrnios, and S. Klein, (eds) *Handbook of Research in Family Business*, Cheltenham, UK and Northampton, MA, USA: Edward Elgar, pp. 1–8.

Salanié, B. (1998), *The Economics of Contracts. A Primer*, Cambridge, MA: MIT Press.

Salas, V. (2000), 'La cultura en las organizaciones', *Cuadernos de Economía y Dirección de la Empresa*, **7**, 341–69.

Schlesinger, H. (1981), 'A note on the consistency of non-profit-maximizing behaviour with perfect competition', *Southern Economic Journal*, **48**(2), 513–16.

Schulze, W., Lubatkin, M.H. and Dino, R.N. (2002), 'Altruism, agency, and the competitiveness of family firms', *Managerial and Decision Economics*, **23**, 247–59.

Schulze, W., Lubatkin, M.H. and Dino, R.N. (2003), 'Toward a theory of agency and altruism in family firms', *Journal of Business Venturing*, **18**, 473–90.

Schulze, W., Lubatkin, M.H., Dino, R.N. and Buchholtz, A.K. (2001), 'Agency relationships in family firms: theory and evidence', *Organization Science*, **12**(2), 99–116.

Sundaramurthy, C. (2008), 'Sustaining trust within family businesses', *Family Business Review*, **21** (1), 89–102.

Wortman, M. (1994), 'Theoretical foundations for family-owned business: a conceptual and research based paradigm', *Family Business Review*, **7**(1), 3–27.

APPENDIX: VARIABLES

Family

W	exogenous monetary wealth endowment
W_t	exogenous monetary wealth endowment at period $t = 1, 2$
ω	heir's exogenous monetary wealth endowment at period $t = 1$
w	share of output among agents
η	growth rate of the heir's exogenous monetary wealth endowment
θ	family firm's share ($\theta \in [0,1]$)
$\theta = 1$	a family firm
$\theta < 1$	a non-family firm
T	owner-manager's amount of available time
n	owner-manager's labor time
l	owner-manager's leisure time
l^i	agent i's leisure time
$C()$	owner-manager's time cost function of monitoring
k	owner-manager's time cost of monitoring parameter
φ	owner-manager's time cost of monitoring parameter
m	owner-manager's monitoring intensity
h^i	agent i's managerial knowledge
$\mathbf{c}$	owner-manager's consumption vector
c^p	owner-manager's consumption vector
c^a	worker's consumption vector
w	share of output among agents
c	owner-manager's consumption good
c_t	the parent's consumption good at period $t = 1, 2$
c^i	agent i's consumption good
$\mathbf{b}$	owner-manager's consumption goods vector only provided by the firm $\mathbf{b} = (\mathbf{A},\mathbf{B})$
$\mathbf{A}$	purely amenity goods
$\mathbf{B}$	non-pecuniary goods that can be used by the firm as input
B	a non-pecuniary good
$U()$	owner-manager's continuous utility function
$U_p()$	the parent's continuous utility function
$u_p()$	the parent's continuous utility function on the consumption good
$\mathcal{U}_a$	welfare of the family relative working for the firm
$U_a()$	worker's continuous utility function
$u_a()$	worker's continuous utility function for the consumption good
$\mathcal{U}_p$	welfare of the family manager
$\mathcal{U}$	social planner welfare function
$\mathcal{U}^*$	social welfare level at the decentralized allocation
$\hat{\mathcal{U}}$	social welfare level at the efficient allocation
$\mathcal{C}()$	worker's welfare cost function of effort
$k > 0$	worker's welfare cost of effort parameter
$\mathbf{x}$	arguments that provide welfare to the owner-manager ($\mathbf{x} = (\mathbf{c},l,\mathbf{b})$)

x^i	arguments that provide welfare to the agent x^i ($x^i = (c^i, l^i, b^i)$)
$\beta_p \geq 0$	parent's descendant altruism preference parameter
$\beta_a \geq 0$	worker's ascendant altruism preference parameter
$\mu = 0,1$	preference parameter representing whether **b** are considered (=1) or not (=0)
γ	intertemporal preference discount factor parameter
α_i	social planner weight for agent i
$\Omega()$	a function of altruistic parameters
$\Psi()$	a function of preference and technological parameters
ϕ	manager's private benefit share
$\underline{\phi}$	legal shareholder protection

Firm

y	commodity produced by the firm
y^j	input j used by the firm
$\mathbf{y}$	vector of inputs used by the firm $\mathbf{y} = (y^1, y^2, y^3, \ldots, y^J)$
J	number of inputs used by the firm
N	labor input
H	human capital input
ρ	penalty on the firm's human capital input after succession
K	physical capital input
K_t	physical capital input at period $t = 1, 2$
g	physical capital constant net growth rate
δ	depreciation rate of physical capital, $\delta \in [0,1]$
e	worker's effort input
$f()$	the technology of the firm
$f_t()$	the technology of the firm at period t
$f_{yj}()$	marginal productivity of input y^j
A	marginal productivity of effort
A_t	marginal productivity of effort at period t
$\pi()$	profit function of the firm
$\pi_t()$	profit function of the firm at period t
V	discounted value of the firm
$V^s()$	discounted value of the firm in steady state
$\Phi(\cdot; \theta)$	adjustment cost function of changing the input capital
R	firm's profitability
R_t	firm's profitability at period t
I_t	investment rate at period t
t^*	period of time that the owner-manager leaves or sells the family firm

Prices

p^y	competitive price of the output produced by the firm
w^j	competitive price of the input j used by the firm
w^N	wages
w^K	rate of return on capital

w^B	competitive price of the non-pecuniary input used by the firm
p^c	market price of the consumption good
$p^c{}_t$	market price of the consumption good at period t

Financial Securities

z	family holdings of a financial security
z_t	family holdings of a financial security at period t
q	price of the financial security z
q_t	price of the financial security at period t
r	exogenous return of a financial security z
$\chi \geq 0$	degree of underdevelopment of the financial markets.

PART X

BROAD-BASED ISSUES IN FAMILY FIRMS

28 Reputational capital in family firms: understanding uniqueness from the stakeholder point of view
Anna Blombäck and Isabel C. Botero

REALIZING FAMILY FIRM UNIQUENESS THROUGH BRANDING

The development and maintenance of competitive advantage is a continuous struggle for companies. In a time when competition is fierce and the rapid advances in technology enable consumers to easily access information about products and organizations, companies face the challenge of creating a coherent perception about who they are and the advantages that they offer to consumers (Einwiller and Will, 2002). Brand management (or branding) is one way of achieving such coherence (Hulberg, 2006). In recent years scholars have begun to use the branding framework to understand how family businesses market themselves in ways that enable differentiation between family businesses and other types of organizations (Blombäck and Ramírez-Pasillas, 2012; Craig et al., 2008, Litchfield, 2008).

To date, most research that explores family firm uniqueness concentrates on understanding resources that are based on intra-organizational features, which derive from the interaction between family and business. 'Familiness' (Habbershon and Williams, 1999) and different forms of family capital (Sirmon and Hitt, 2003) are examples of such unique resources. In this chapter we suggest that the uniqueness of family businesses can also come from resources that are external to the firm. In line with this perspective, we rely on the brand management literature to explore new ways to understand family firms' uniqueness. In particular, we argue that by recognizing and exploring the perceptions that external stakeholders have about family firms and their products, as well as how family businesses communicate family involvement, scholars and practitioners will be able to further understand the unique characteristics and resources of family businesses. To frame our discussion and add to the ongoing debate about different forms of family business capital, we build on previous work in reputational capital (Petrick et al., 1999; Suh and Amine, 2007). Reputational capital is a term used to describe 'the residual value of the company's intangible assets over and above its stock of patents and know-how' (Fombrun et al., 2000, p.87). It represents the benefits a company can gain from being known in general as a credible, responsible, trustworthy and reliable actor (Fombrun, 1996). Drawing on past research on reputational capital, we contend that family businesses as a group hold a common reputation. This common reputation is often associated with perceptions about family firms as being good and responsible citizens. Thus these perceptions form the basis for reputational capital of family firms. With this in mind, we believe that brand management is an important process to consider and understand in order for family businesses to highlight their uniqueness and gain competitive advantage.

To achieve our goal we have structured this chapter the following way. In the first section, we introduce the concepts of brand and brand management, specifically outlining key concepts and the value of applying a brand strategy. In the second section we review research that integrates family business and the brand management framework. In this section we summarize the extant literature on branding and family firms. In the third and final section we discuss the contributions of branding research to our understanding of family business characteristics, resources, values and uniqueness. We add to the existing family business capital construct by describing the notion of a reputational capital of family firms. We also provide some ideas on future directions for family business and brand management research.

UNDERSTANDING BRANDS AND BRAND MANAGEMENT

In the last 100 years changes in technology and availability of products and services have altered the way customers and organizations obtain and share information (Kotler et al., 2009). As availability of options for consumers has increased, organizations need to make sure that they highlight the unique benefits of their products and services to consumers. In line with these developments, the meaning and role of brands and brand management has changed over time from a sign of identification to a sign of differentiation and bearer of added value to the organization and its products (de Chernatony and McDonald, 1998, Riezebos, 2003). Today, brands are recognized as both the means to obtain a competitive edge and the element that helps influence customers in their buying behavior (Kotler et al., 2009).

Literature in marketing and communication has emphasized the strategic importance of brands and brand management to create unique and favorable impressions in the minds of consumers about companies and their products (Anisimova, 2007; Balmer and Gray, 2003; Hulberg, 2006). In a general sense, a brand can be defined as a 'name, term, sign, symbol, or design, or combination of them which is intended to identify the goods or services of one seller or group of sellers and to differentiate them from those of competitors' (Kotler, 1991, p. 442). The components that help stakeholders identify and differentiate the brand are referred to as brand identities (Keller, 1993) or brand elements (Keller, 2008; Keller et al., 2008; Riezebos, 2003) and help create competitive advantage by highlighting desired characteristics of the brand. On the other hand, the term brand management is used to describe the process and efforts that organizations and individuals engage in to obtain and maintain differentiation and a feasible image among stakeholders in order to achieve positive business performance (Kotler et al., 2009; LaForet, 2009; Riezebos, 2003). Brands and brand management are developed because of the perception that they can provide positive outcomes for an organization or a person.

The Value of Brands

Research exploring the importance of brands highlights the valuable role they play for customers (Keller, 1993) and the advantages for the brand owner (de Chernatony and McWilliam, 1989). From the customer's point of view, the value of a brand is tied to the bundle of information that they represent (LaForet, 2009). Brands have both functional (e.g. they help in the selection of products and in the identification of products that customers trust) and psychosocial (e.g. the brand as a means to buyer's identity, or the brand as a way to maintain connections with important groups) advantages for customers. As a consequence of the brand's ability to connect to and influence consumer behavior, successful brands help an organization achieve good performance (Da Silva and Alwi, 2006; Erdem and Swait, 2004; Esch et al., 2006; Gammoh et al., 2006).

From the brand owner's (i.e. organization's) perspective the benefits of brands and their management can be seen through the impact that they have on company performance. Riezebos (2003) suggests that benefits can be grouped based on the financial, strategic and managerial implications of the brand to the organization. Financial benefits of brands include the ability of a brand owner to add value to the firm and obtain more sales if the positioning of a brand is successful. In instances in which a brand is strong enough to have loyal customers, it can maintain a stable market share and, thus, secure future income (Chaudhuri and Holbrook, 2001). The strategic benefits of brands include having a strong position in relation to retailers, new market entrants and the labor market (Riezebos, 2003). When brands achieve a strong reputation among consumers, a pull effect is created, which allows the brand owner to gain a stronger position in the negotiation with retailers (Keller et al., 2008) and the recruitment of high-quality applicants (Cable and Turban, 2001; Turban and Cable, 2003). Finally, managerial benefits of a brand include the advantages a previous well-developed and positioned brand offers a company when they seek to launch new product offers (Riezebos, 2003). The idea is that when a company already has a strong brand in the market it can develop brand extensions (i.e. using an established brand name to introduce a new product; Keller, 2008) that allow the potential to reduce cost for launching and improve the chance of reaching successful sales for new product offers.

Brand Equity

In general, the value of a brand for both consumers and organizations is based on the sources of differentiation it creates. However, to achieve differentiation, brands must represent something of added value to the consumer or to the brand owner (i.e. the organization or individual). Brand equity is the term used to describe and compute the value of a brand. Generally speaking, brand equity can be can be calculated either as a financial benefit (i.e. the amount of financial benefit that a brand represents to a company; Keller et al., 2008; Riezebos, 2003) or behavior benefit (i.e. the value a brand holds based on the responses of consumers to the brand; LaForet, 2009). For the purpose of this chapter we are particularly interested in the second form of brand equity.

Based on the behavioral approach, positive brand equity results from favorable attitudes of customers when they identify a brand. These attitudes are the result of consumer's knowledge about a brand (i.e. what they have learned, felt, seen and heard about a brand as a result of their experiences over time) and what they remember from about the brand (Keller, 2008). There are two types of information that are relevant when developing knowledge about a brand: awareness and image. Brand awareness refers to the likelihood that a brand will come to mind given a certain need (i.e. strength of brand in memory). Awareness is based on the recognition that an individual has of a brand and the ability to recall the brand from memory (Keller, 1993). On the other hand, brand image represents the cognitive summary of impressions related to a brand and their translation into a set of associations (Keller, 1993). In general, the type, the favorability, the strength and the uniqueness of associations are the important factors in determining brand equity (Keller, 1993). As a result, building positive brand equity requires that consumers are both aware of and have a general positive impression of the branded entity. It is only under these conditions that brand owners will find value in their brands.

The Practice of Brand Management

As mentioned earlier, brand management describes the effort by brand owners to develop positive brand equity (Jones, 2005; Keller, 1993). Therefore the primary aim of brand management is to achieve brand identification and to establish favorable, strong and unique associations with audiences (Keller, 1993; Kotler et al., 2009). Strategic brand management (i.e. the process of converting brand responses to customer loyalty and relationships; Kotler et al., 2009) is a way to achieve this purpose. Although strategic brand management also involves decisions about price, place, product, range of brands and brand extensions, for the purpose of this chapter we focus on the cognitive component of brand management (i.e. what brand managers can do to create recognition and positive feelings toward a brand).

The first step of strategic brand management is to plan the brand's identity (Aaker and Joachimsthaler, 2000; De Chernatony, 1999; Kapferer, 1992). As defined by Aaker and Joachimsthaler (2000, p. 43), brand identity 'is a set of associations that the brand strategist aspires to create or maintain.' To ensure a consistent brand message, brand managers must maintain focus on the brand identity while planning marketing communications and marketing programs that support the aspired brand meaning (Keller, 1993). Once the brand identity has been determined, it is also necessary to identify and select fundamental brand elements like the brand name, logotype, packaging or other identifying trademarks (Keller, 1993). Following this, the strategic component of brand management begins. This process starts when organizations try to develop a positive brand by using inductive or deductive inferences in the branding process (Riezebos, 2003).

Inductive inferences rely on brand associations that are formed through direct encounters with the brand and exposure to planned communications for the brand. From this inductive approach there are several important tools (e.g. advertising, direct or event marketing and sales promotion) in brand management. In this approach, the brand manager needs to consider basic questions of what, where, how and when to communicate with audiences, whether the messages support the brand's identity and how they might influence brand knowledge (Keller et al., 2008). This enables the development of a strong brand.

Deductive inferences, on the other hand, rely on brand associations that are formed by connecting the brand in question to other brands or entities, which have established images (Riezebos, 2003). The goal from this approach is to achieve a transfer of image in which associations are deduced from a source to a target (Gwinner, 1997). We refer to this as the leveraging of secondary brand associations (Keller, 1993; Keller et al., 2008). Secondary brand associations can be developed in several ways. For example, a brand's meaning can be influenced by collaborating with other brands (using a celebrity as endorser for the brand, including and revealing a renowned ingredient brand, or collaborating with another product brand in terms of new product offers or in distribution), by referencing quality, awards, country of origin, by sponsorship, and/or through the use of corporate endorsement (Keller et al., 2008; Riezebos, 2003). The deductive inference can be used to enforce and complement the brand's current image (Keller et al., 2008).

In the section above, we have introduced some of the basic elements of a brand management process. We recognize, though, that each branding process is different and agree that the involvement of consumers can neither be excluded nor generalized. With this is mind, in the next section we explore how branding has been examined in the area of family business.

BRANDING AND FAMILY BUSINESS

One of the primary focuses in family business research is to understand how family firms differ from non-family firms and what are the unique characteristics that family businesses possess. One of the approaches used in the last decade to understand and highlight the uniqueness of family firms focuses on brand management. Researchers use the branding framework presented above to understand the attitudes and associations towards the expression 'family business' (Blombäck, 2009).

The exploration of branding in family firms has primarily focused on two lines of research. The first line has explored the perceptions that non-family stakeholders have about family firms and their brands. The second approach has explored what family businesses do to manage the family brand and the benefits that this management brings to the family firm. In the subsections below we summarize these two approaches.

Stakeholder Perceptions of Family Firm Brands

One of the assumptions in the research on branding and family firms is that customers often have positive associations with family-owned brands (Blombäck, 2006, 2009; Craig et al., 2008; Frost, 2008). The belief is that family-owned brands are emblems of success and prestige that lead customers to trust products that come from family firms (Frost, 2008). Thus family firms are in a unique position that allows them to leverage their family ownership to build sustainable competitive advantage (Poza, 2010; Ward, 1997). In general, the research exploring stakeholder perceptions of family brands can be divided into three areas: effects of family ownership on perceptions of customer service; effects of family ownership on perceptions of quality of products and services; and effects of family ownership on attractiveness to work for family firms.

In the area of customer service, the work of Lyman (1991) and Cooper and colleagues (2005) highlights that family firms differ from non-family firms in the type of customer service experience they offer. In particular, family businesses that can create and maintain superior customer service enjoy the competitive advantage brought by customer loyalty, good will and perceptions of trustworthiness (Biberman, 2001). As a result, customer service in family firms is often perceived as better than those of non-family organizations.

A second set of studies has explored stakeholders' perceptions of brands that allude to family firm ownership and aim to better understand the image the brand holds for consumers. In a set of three studies Litchfield (2008) explored whether using the term 'family-owned business' in messages to consumers could create strategic advantage for an organization. Her results suggest that participants had both positive and negative perceptions about family-owned businesses. On the positive side, respondents associated the term family business with high-quality products and services, while on the negative side the term family business was associated with internal conflict in firms. In general, perceptions about services offered by family-owned businesses were positive and this was significantly related to intention to buy from a family-owned business. Carrigan and Buckley (2008) also conducted in-depth interviews with 19 consumers about their perceptions of family businesses. Similar to the work of Litchfield (2008), they found that participants had positive perceptions about family firms and higher expectations about their services and products. Thus they concluded that family ownership played an important role in purchasing behaviors, and should be promoted in communications to external stakeholders. In a separate study, Orth and Green (2009) designed an experiment in which participants were exposed either to a description of a grocery store that was family owned or a national chain. Results from this study indicated that consumers viewed family firms as more trustworthy and they were more satisfied with their services. Thus Orth and Green concluded that family ownership could work as a source of competitive advantage in the case of grocery stores. Finally, the work of Okoroafo and Koh (2009) explored the impact of family business marketing activities on consumers' purchase intention. Results from the study suggested that promotion of family ownership was positively related to purchasing intentions.

A third set of studies has explored the perceptions that stakeholders have about the family brand and how it affects attractiveness to and intentions to work for family firms. In this area, the research from Covin (1994) suggests that participants in her study had a strong preference for working in family firms, especially when this firm was part of their own family. In particular, those that were more attracted to family firms indicated a stronger need for jobs that provide variety of duties and activities, and were more likely to be females. Additionally, findings from a study conducted by Michael-Tsabari and colleagues (2008) suggests that when applicants for managerial positions are asked about their perceptions of family firms they tend to have negative associations about work experiences in family firms and are less likely to express interest in working for them. On the other hand, in a study conducted in the USA, Botero et al. (2009a) found that there was no difference in perceptions of attractiveness and willingness to work for family and non-family firms in non-managerial positions. Although perceptions of organizational prestige, image and job security predicted attractiveness to a firm, there were no differences in the perceptions of these characteristics between family and non-family firms. Botero et al. (2009b) conducted a similar study in China and found that, in general, participants had positive perceptions about family firms and working for family firms, and these positive perceptions were positively associated to attractiveness to working in family firms.

When these three sets of studies are taken together, they suggest that references to family in brand management can influence consumers in their perceptions about the quality of customer relations, quality of product and quality of service of family businesses. Given the positive associations identified, we believe that referencing family associations when branding family firms can have positive effects for businesses that focus on services and products. On the other hand, the effects referencing family to attract applicants and promote working for a family firm have mixed results and future research should explore whether there is a strategic advantage of highlighting the family association when recruiting employees into family firms. We now turn to summarizing research on how family firms manage the family brand.

Managing the Family Firm Brand

As mentioned earlier, one of the purposes of brand management is to develop positive associations in the mind of consumers. In the case of family businesses, one of the ways in which a positive image transfer is expected to occur is through secondary brand associations. Secondary brand associations represent links in the mind of the consumers that arise because of past experiences with a company of similar characteristics or other similar attributes. Thus mentioning that a company is a family firm or is family owned can serve as a way for the consumer to associate some characteristics of family firms with the organization that is trying to brand itself. This action is believed to help distinguish a family business from other organizations. In general, it is believed that making associations to the family can act as important brand elements that can establish and provide recognition for a brand entity and add meaning to the brand in the stakeholders' minds.

In the case of family firms, the term 'family business' can be thought of as an element of the brand that is used to elicit positive associations with the firm and the products it creates. In this case, organizations use the term 'family business' in their communication because they believe that it is perceived as a positive feature of the organization and it will help prime consumers to think about families. This priming helps create positive associations in the mind of stakeholders. In turn, these positive associations add value to the organization. Blombäck (2009) argues that the explicit choice to present family involvement as a feature of a firm can be compared to other references like geographic origin ('we are an American company'), company philosophy ('we are a socially responsible company'), or company age ('75 years in business'). In all these cases, the choice to add a reference suggests that this information reveals important characteristics about the business to stakeholders.

Considering that past research has found that people have positive associations with the term 'family business' (Carrigan and Buckley, 2008; Litchfield, 2008; Orth and Green, 2009), referencing that the organization is a family firm is expected to affect stakeholders in a positive way. It is important to note that future interactions between the client and the organization will be determined by the experience of the customer during the first interaction. Thus it is expected that the family business reference works as a secondary brand that helps the customer establish a fuller picture of a company in the market and adds to the value proposition perceived among stakeholders (Blombäck, 2009). It is important to note that although the assumption is that consumers have positive associations with the term 'family business', it is also possible that if the customer has had a bad experience with a family firm, the consumer will have formed a negative association with the term 'family business', resulting in no added value to the organizations that brand themselves as a family firm.

In the last five years different studies looking at how family businesses communicate their uniqueness to external stakeholders have been conducted. These studies use branding as a framework to explain how family firms can differentiate themselves from other organizations. A first set of studies by Blombäck (2006) and Blombäck and Ramírez-Pasillas (2012) claim that the explicit references of family business ownership in communications from family firms can be interpreted as the promotion of a corporate category brand (i.e. the family business brand). They argue that mentioning that an organization is a family firm can be considered a brand and, consequently, expressions referring to family should not be overlooked as possible important keys for corporate brand management. In these projects 14 CEOs or vice CEOs were interviewed by the researchers and asked why they used the expression 'family business' in their external communication, what the expression meant to them, and whether they believed that family firms had special characteristics. Their results revealed that some of the organizations referenced family ownership as part of their planned strategic communication while others did it without consciously planning for it. Blombäck and colleagues also suggest that reference to family ownership comes in different forms. While some referenced ownership in the name (e.g. Mary & Sons), others mention it as part of a description of time (e.g. in the same family for the last 30 years), by highlighting the number of generations that have been part of the business (e.g. fifth generation), or by saying that they are family owned (e.g. we are a family company).

The work of Craig et al. (2008) has also investigated how the promotion of family-based brand identity influences competitive orientation (customer versus product) and performance in family firms. In their project, they contacted 218 leaders from family firms and asked whether their organizations promoted family ownership as a characteristic of the firm to customers, suppliers and to their financiers, and which communication medium they used to promote family ownership to others (i.e. letterhead, websites, cars or others). Additionally, they collected information about financial performance and explored how promotion of family ownership was related to financial performance. In their results they found that communicating a family-based brand identity (i.e. creating perceptions of trust and consistency in the minds of customers) rendered positive effects in terms of financial performance. In particular, firms in which leaders reported that the organization focused on customers and promoted that they were family owned to suppliers, customers and financiers were more likely to perform better (i.e. after tax return on total sales and total assets, market growth and sales growth) than those firms that did not communicate that their family ownership. It is important to note that Craig et al. (2008) did not focus specifically on the nature of the brand involved, or the family component's position relative to other brand elements. While past research has shown the advantages of referencing family ownership, in a recent study Morgan (2009) found that very few family firms in the USA were likely to reference family ownership using their web pages (13 per cent in home page and 35 per cent in the 'about us' page).

When taken together, the results of these three areas suggest that referencing family ownership can reflect positively in better sales and growth (Craig et al., 2008). In a similar way, indicating that an organization is family owned helps highlight the owner's identification with the family (Blombäck and Ramírez-Pasillas, 2012). And, finally, although there have been positive results from creating secondary associations to the family firm brand, it seems that not many family firms are taking advantage of highlighting the family association (Morgan, 2009).

After summarizing the research in branding and family firms, we now explain how we see the contribution of this line of research in helping researchers and practitioners understand and strategically use the uniqueness of family firms. We do this in the next section.

CONTRIBUTION OF BRANDING TO THE FAMILY BUSINESS FIELD

As highlighted by Sharma (2004), the ultimate goal of family business research is to improve the functioning of family firms. She highlights that to be able to achieve this goal, scholars need to create and disseminate knowledge that is useful for scholars and practitioners alike. Therefore in this section we want to highlight what we see as the main contributions from the current research on branding in the family context and some areas for future research.

Contributions from Branding to the Family Business Field

Organizations have two types of resources that play an important role in their ability to gain competitive advantage: company skills (i.e. what the company can do) and assets (i.e. what the company owns; Aaker, 1989; Hall, 1992; Petrick et al., 1999). While skills are by definition intangible, assets can be both tangible (e.g. machinery and facilities) and intangible (e.g. patents and registered designs) (Hall, 1992). We believe that branding offers a contribution to the family business field that focuses on both skills (i.e. emphasizing how companies can differentiate themselves among customers) and intangible assets (i.e. pointing to the potential value of stakeholder perceptions). The branding perspective adds to the existing discourse on family business resources because it enables the distinction of a kind of uniqueness that has not yet been highlighted. This uniqueness is based on the associations that can be added to an organization through referencing family ownership. This implies a combination of an existing family business reputation (intangible asset) and the ability to promote family ownership in a suitable way (skill). Research into associations between image and attitude reveals uniqueness beyond that which happens inside the family business. That is, this research allows us to explore intangible assets that are not directly managed by the company. Below we summarize the research on the unique resources of family firms and explain where we believe branding is adding to our understanding of family firms.

Research exploring the unique resources of family firms has primarily focused on the resources that are based on intra-organizational features (Blombäck, 2009). In the family business literature these resources have been labeled 'familiness' (Habbershon and Williams, 1999; Sirmon and Hitt, 2003). As defined by Habbershon and Williams (1999), familiness represents a unique bundle of resources that are the product of the interaction between the family and the business. To identify these unique resources family business researchers have primarily used the principles of the resource-based view (RBV) theory of the firm (Sharma, 2004). Based on this theory, family businesses are said to perform better than other businesses because they have resources that are unique, valuable, rare and difficult to imitate (Anderson and Reeb, 2003; Castillo and Wakefield, 2007; Dibrell and Craig, 2006; McConaughy et al., 2001; Miller et al., 2008; Westhead and Howorth, 2006).

Sirmon and Hitt (2003) present a theoretical model in which they describe five unique and salient characteristics that differentiate family from non-family businesses. They describe these unique factors as different forms of capital. First, they present Human capital as a major strength. They suggest that family firms have an advantage over other types of organizations because they can acquire a great deal of their human capital from the family, and this can enable the transfer of tacit knowledge (Lane and Lubatkin, 1998). Social capital, on the other hand, describes the networks of relationships between individuals or between organizations (Burt, 1997). For family firms, the strength of social capital lies on the resources (both actual and potential) that are embedded, available and derived from these networks (Nahapiet and Ghoshal, 1998). Third is patient financial capital, which suggests that family firms are able to pursue more creative and innovative strategies because the family often has the financial means to invest in thinking about the long term, and not having to worry about short-term success (Sirmon and Hitt, 2003). Survivability capital, the fourth type of capital, describes the personal resources that family members are willing to loan, contribute or share for the benefit of the family business especially in hard times (Haynes et al., 1999). Lastly, governance structure and costs capital suggests that family firms have an advantage over other types of firms because their structures and family bonds reduce governance cost (Sirmon and Hitt, 2003).

In recent years an additional form of capital unique to family businesses has been discussed: family capital or family social capital. Hoffman et al. (2006) argue that family capital is a special form of social capital that is limited to family relationships. Family capital has its origin in the relationships between family members and manifests itself through the restrictions on and expectations about certain behavior and responsibilities, which the established bonds and norms of the family imply (Arrègle et al., 2007; Pearson et al., 2008). This family capital gives rise to social control and trust within the family, which provides fertile ground for competitive advantage (Hoffman et al., 2006). In addition, family social capital is believed to affect the development of organizational social capital through the effects that family has on the structure and relationships that organizations form with individuals and other organizations (Arrègle et al., 2007).

This short summary shows how research on the unique features of family firms has primarily focused on internal characteristics, which emerge from the combination of family and business factors. We believe that, although this internal focus is important, much can be learned from an external and perceptual focus. In particular, we perceive that a resource that has not been explored is the perceptions that stakeholders have about family firms. This asset is different from the others because, rather than being internal to the firm, it is held externally and organizations have the choice of exploiting it or not. We maintain that the branding literature provides a means to understand these external assets that can enhance our understanding of the uniqueness of family firms. In the next section we develop our ideas.

Projecting Family Business: A Reputational Resource

In the above section we identified the unique characteristics of family firms that enable a favorable position in regard to several types of capital. The discussion indicates that family firms achieve some of these particular resources simply by 'being family business'. That is, the human and social capital, which derives from the overlap of family, ownership and management, and ties between family members. Meanwhile, the patient financial capital, survivability capital and the governance structure and costs reflect that family firms achieve particular resources by behaving in a certain way, that is, 'acting like family business'. The introduction of brand management to family business research reveals another potential resource, which only appears as a result of the 'projecting of family business'. Given that a key to successful branding is the ability to differentiate and create strong associations, we propose that referencing family ownership creates a distinction that reflects a reputational resource. Revealing that an organization is a family business and highlighting any positive associations that family ownership brings to mind for consumers can help leverage this reputational resource. To better explain what we mean by reputational resource we need to first define what is reputation and how branding and reputation are related.

Reputation can be defined as an asset and intangible resource (Hall, 1992). Scholars refer to corporate reputation as 'a perceptual representation of a company's past actions and future prospects that describes the firm's overall appeal to all of its key constituents when compared with other leading rivals' (Fombrun, 1996, p. 72). Thus a company's reputation can vary from good to bad, and stakeholders do not need a direct experience with the company to know of a company's reputation. Reputation, then, is a concept that points to an aggregate of associations or images towards the entity in question. It is a collective judgment of a firm that relies on the merge of the firm's communication efforts and stakeholders' interpretations of these communication efforts (Fombrun and Shanley, 1990; DiMaggio and Powell, 1983). Essentially, reputation is an outcome of the stakeholders' combined assessment of a firm's being credible, trustworthy, reliable and responsible (Fombrun, 1996). That is, reputation concerns both what a company has been known to do in the past and what it can be assumed to do in the future. Scholars normally elaborate on reputation as something that reflects one particular organization. Relying on this framework, we suggest that family businesses as a group can also maintain a common reputation. Previous research on family business and branding supports this notion.

Building on this idea, we think that using a branding approach to explore family business allows researchers to consider how each family business communicates its uniqueness. At the same time this approach can help understand how a firm's communication efforts can build a unique corporate brand image and use the general reputation for family businesses as a secondary brand association. Therefore, in situations in which stakeholders have positive perceptions about family ownership, referencing this ownership in marketing and communication efforts will allow companies to tap into the reputation that family firms have as a group and link it to their corporate or product brand image, representing a form of secondary brand associations (Keller et al., 2008) and allowing for the development of a family business reputational capital.

Petrick and colleagues (1999) define reputational capital as 'that portion of the excess market value that can be attributed to the perception of the firm as a responsible domestic and global corporate citizen' (p. 60). Given this definition, reputational capital is an example of the financial value of intangible assets (Fombrun et al., 2000). In line with our previous description of brand equity, we believe that viewing reputation as an asset and source of capital requires us to recognize that there is a value in reputation that goes further than the mere recognition of a company.

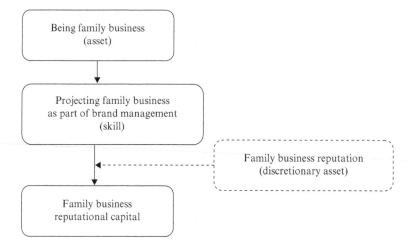

Figure 28.1   Family business reputational capital – a result of being and projecting family ownership

Fombrun (1996) describes reputational capital as 'a form of intangible wealth that is closely related to what accountants call "goodwill" and marketers term "brand equity"' (p. 11). Thus reputational capital represents the ability to charge premium prices, reduce marketing costs, attract good employees, and overcome crises as a result of the firm being generally held in high esteem among stakeholders. Therefore, rather than viewing the reputation of family business as a judgment, we see it as an asset that can be employed by companies if they choose to do so (Barnett et al., 2006). As shown in Figure 28.1, the fact that firms can choose to reference their family ownership and thereby highlight any positive reputation linked to family business can be seen as an additional unique resource associated with being a family firm. We believe that, in this sense, family brand references or association enable competitive advantage, because in this sense this association or reference is valuable, rare, difficult to imitate and non-substitutable (Barney, 1991).

   To summarize, we believe that exploring the uniqueness of family firms using a branding framework helps researchers and practitioners better understand the uniqueness that emerges from the perceptions that external stakeholders have about family firms. We argue that these perceptions can represent another form of capital for family firms. Building on previous work in the area of reputation, we refer to this asset as family business reputational capital. Our arguments are based on the belief that reputation is similar to brand equity in the sense that it comprises perceptions of the company and, therefore, its chances to be successful in the future. However, we argue that reputation is a useful construct in the context of family business in that it can function as a joint and discretionary asset that family-owned companies can choose to use as they engage in brand management. By applying this framework to family business, we highlight how family-owned companies can take advantage of an existing reputation through secondary brand associations, thereby communicating uniqueness and possibly gaining competitive advantage. In other words, we argue that brand management represents a means to gain family business reputational capital, which ultimately feeds into the company's brand equity.

   Finally, an important part of our line of reasoning is that the inclusion of reputation and brand management into our understanding of family firms outlines external audiences as active publics in the creation of family firm uniqueness. This suggests a shift in focus from exploring uniqueness that resides solely in internal dimensions of family-owned enterprises to a view that includes external dimensions to explain significant family business values.

FUTURE RESEARCH AND CONCLUSIONS

To conclude this chapter, we would like to identify some areas for future research to continue enhancing our understanding of the unique resources that result from referencing family ownership in the branding process. We here present a number of concerns that need further exploration, involving family business and brand management based on our discussion about reputational capital. Like other resources, reputation does not guarantee unconditional rewards. Depending on the context and circumstances, the benefits of referencing family ownership will vary and there may also be downsides to this practice. Consequently, we want to highlight the need for research in several areas to better understand when the family business reputation can translate into benefits (i.e. reputational capital) for family firms.

The first area for future research that we highlight is the need for intercultural understanding of branding in family firms. In particular, one area that needs research includes how referencing family ownership might work differently based on the country in which this association is highlighted. It may be that the association of firms and families, and the reputation of family businesses, differs depending on what country we consider. Thus, in some countries associations to family firms might be related to positive connotations and expectations, while in other countries this might not be the case. Similarly, the effect of family firm references might differ between countries, depending on the recognition of and attention paid to the family business format in each country. Given this, we believe that there is a need to better understand how people in different countries perceive family firms and family firm associations.

A second area that also needs exploration is whether firms from different industries reference their family ownership in different ways and in which industries these references might bring positive benefits for the organizations. Anecdotal evidence suggests that companies in certain industries are more likely to reference their family ownership than others. The food industry, for example, is one example where many organizations communicate their family association. Thus there might be some industries in which ties to family would influence consumers and their purchase intentions, while in other industries this might not be the case. The understanding of the relationship between industry and referencing family ownership can also help researchers better understand whether using the family business for secondary brand associations is related to what the company is selling, to the importance of family business, or a matter of tradition.

To complement our previous idea, we also suggest that it is important to analyze different types of customers. A common division of customers in marketing literature is that between private consumers (business-to-consumer markets) and professional buyers (business-to-business markets). While both groups, for example, rely on previous experiences and impressions for decision-making in situations of uncertainty, there are also differences in their buying behavior. Business-to-business markets more commonly involve team purchasing, precise product requirements and a search for long-term relationships (Ford et al., 2002). Moreover, in the business-to-consumer context, the purpose of buying normally relates to home and family life, which is not the case in business-to-business contexts. Therefore, to learn more about the potential of family business in brand management we suggest research initiatives that investigate whether the chances to reap the family business reputational capital among customers varies depending on whether they are acting as private individuals or as professional buyers.

However, people do not only pay attention to firms as customers. Bearing in mind that people approach companies for different reasons (as customers, suppliers, competitors, investors, employees, neighbors), we also raise the question of whether individuals' objectives for interacting with a certain company impact the role of family business reputation. That is, if we acknowledge that in any given market there is such a thing as a family business reputation, which is made up of customer, employee, community and investor images (Fombrun, 1996, p. 37), does this reputation – good or bad, weak or strong – affect all constituent parties of a given company in the same way? Given this, we suggest that more research needs to be conducted to be able to better understand when reputational capital can be sought and give leverage.

In regard to the outcome of family business reputational capital for single firms, there are a number of opportunitites for further research on a theoretical level. For example, it would be highly interesting to explore whether the family business reputational capital reduces transactional costs for the organization. In particular, it would be useful to understand whether companies that, by branding their family business character, are able to reach such reputational capital, spend fewer resources in building trust with their stakeholders and in maintaining their relationships with them. In this case, aspects of agency theory could be applied to help us better understand the benefits of reputational capital for family firms. From a transgenerational entrepreneurship perspective, it would be interesting to explore whether family business reputational capital influences companies' tendency to maintain a strong family involvement in the business, or even survive. Finally, an issue related to selection that would be of interest to explore is whether the existence of family firm reputational capital influences the decision-making processes of consumers and external stakeholders. That is, is this reputational capital used as a heuristic in making decisions about family firms?

Concluding Thoughts

Brand management has developed over a number of years and is now an established research area in the marketing literature. However, much remains to be understood regarding the meaning, importance and management of brands in relation to various types of markets, organizations and offers. The aim of this chapter was to elaborate on how family business research can evolve further by using this brand management perspective. We believe that, so far, researchers have not thoroughly applied an internal marketing and branding perspective to the referencing of family ownership. Thus, linking to the corporate identity and culture discourses, we believe that a distinction is feasible between the influence of family business in brand management towards internal and external stakeholders. We introduce the idea of family business reputation capital as a way in which family businesses can leverage their family association to obtain financial, strategic and managerial benefits from secondary brand association. Finally, we also lay the foundation for further research that can help scholars and practitioners understand and leverage the strategic advantage of being a family firm.

REFERENCES

Aaker, D.A. (1989), 'Managing assets and skills: the key to a sustainable competitive advantage', *California Management Review*, 91–106.

Aaker, D.A. and Joachimsthaler, E. (2000), *Brand Leadership*, New York: The Free Press.

Andersson, R.A. and Reeb, D.M. (2003), 'Founding-family ownership and firm performance: evidence from the S&P 500', *The Journal of Finance*, **58**(3), 1301–28.

Anisimova, T.A. (2007), 'The effects of corporate brand attributes on attitudinal and behavioural consumer loyalty', *Journal of Consumer Marketing*, **24**(7), 395–405.

Arrègle, J.-L., Hitt, M.A., Sirmon, D.G. and Very, P. (2007), 'The development of organizational social capital: attributes of family firms', *Journal of Management Studies*, **44**(1), 73–95.

Balmer, J.M.T. and Gray, E.R. (2003), 'Corporate brands: what are they? What of them?', *European Journal of Marketing*, **37**(7/8), 972–97.

Barnett, M.L., Jermier, J.M. and Lafferty, B.A. (2006), 'Corporate reputation: the definitional landscape', *Corporate Reputation Review*, **9**(1), 26–38.

Barney, J. (1991), 'Firm resources and sustained competitive advantage', *Journal of Management*, **17**(1), 99–120.

Biberman, J. (2001), 'The little shop that could', *Family Business Magazine*, **12**(1), 23.

Blombäck, A. (2006), 'The family business concept as an element in corporate branding', paper presented at 2nd workshop on Family Firm Management Research, Nice, France, June.

Blombäck, A. (2009), 'Family business – a secondary brand in corporate brand management', CeFEO Working Paper series, 2009:1, Jönköping International Business School.

Blombäck, A. and Ramírez-Pasillas, M. (2012), 'Exploring the logics of corporate brand identity formation', *Corporate Communications – An International Journal*, **17**(1), 7–28.

Botero, I.C., McKenna, T., Morgan, B., Zartman, W., Fediuk, T.A. and Faber, A. (2009a), 'Attracting non-family employees into family businesses: the effects of mentioning whether an organization is family-owned or not on organizations' perceived attractiveness', paper presented at the 9th Annual International Family Enterprise Research Academy.

Botero, I.C., Stuart-Doig, L.P., Min, J. and Zweifel, K. (2009b), 'Perceptions of family firms and their effects on organizational attractiveness: an international approach', paper presented at the 9th Annual International Family Enterprise Research Academy.

Burt, R.S. (1997), 'The contingent value of social capital', *Administrative Science Quarterly*, 42(2), 339–65.

Cable, D.M., and Turban, D.B. (2001), 'Establishing the dimensions, sources, and value of job seekers' employer knowledge during recruitment', in G.R. Ferris (ed.), *Research in Personnel and Human Resource Management*, Vol. 20, Oxford: Elsevier Science, pp. 115–63.

Carrigan, M. and Buckley, J. (2008), 'What is so special about family business? An exploratory study of UK and Irish consumer experiences of family businesses', *International Journal of Consumer Studies*, **32**, 656–66.

Castillo, J. and Wakefield, M.W. (2007), 'An exploration of firm performance factors in family businesses: do families value only the "bottom line"', *Journal of Small Business Strategy*, **17**(2), 37–51.

Chaudhuri, A. and Holbrook, M.B. (2001), 'The chain of effects from brand trust and brand affect to brand performance: the role of brand loyalty', *Journal of Marketing*, **65**, 81–93.

Cooper, M.J., Upton, N. and Seaman, S. (2005), 'Customer relationship management: a comparative analysis of family and nonfamily business practices', *Journal of Small Business Management*, **43**(3), 242–56.

Covin, T.J. (1994), 'Profiling preference for employment in family firms', *Family Business Review*, **7**(3), 287–96.

Craig, J.B., Dibrell, C. and Davis, P.S. (2008), 'Leveraging family-based brand identity to enhance firm competitiveness and performance in family businesses', *Journal of Small Business Management*, **46**(3), 351–71.

Da Silva, R.V. and Alwi, S.F.S. (2006), 'Cognitive, affective attributes and conative, behavioural responses in retail corporate branding', *Journal of Product and Brand Management*, **15**(5), 293–305.

de Chernatony, L. (1999), 'Brand management through narrowing the gap between brand identity and brand reputation', *Journal of Marketing Management*, **15**(103), 157–80.

de Chernatony, L. and McDonald, M. (1998), *Creating Powerful Brands in Consumer, Service and Industrial Markets*, Oxford: Butterworth Heinemann.

de Chernatony, L. and McWilliam, G. (1989), 'The varying nature of brands as assets', *International Journal of Advertising*, **8**, 339–49.

Dibrell, C. and Craig, J.B. (2006), 'The natural environment, innovation, and firm performance: a comparative study', *Family Business Review*, **19**(4), 275–88.

DiMaggio, P.J. and Powell, W.W. (1983), 'The iron cage revisited: institutional isomorphism and collective rationality in organizational fields', *American Sociological Review*, **48**(2), 147–60.

Einwiller, S. and Will, M. (2002), 'Towards an integrated approach to corporate branding – An empirical study', *Corporate Communications*, **7**(2), 100–109.

Erdem, T. and Swait, J. (2004), 'Brand credibility, brand consideration, and choice', *Journal of Consumer Research*, **31**, 191–98.

Esch, F.-R., Langner, T., Schmitt, B.H. and Geus, P. (2006), 'Are brands forever? How brand knowledge and relationships affect current and future purchases', *The Journal of Product and Brand Management*, **15**(2), 98–104.

Fombrun, C.J. (1996), *Reputation: Realizing Value from the Corporate Image*, Cambridge, MA: Harvard Business School Press.

Fombrun, C.J., Gardberg, N.A. and Barnett, M.L. (2000), 'Opportunity platforms and safety nets: corporate citizenship and reputational risk', *Business and Society Review*, **105**(1), 85–106.

Fombrun, C.J. and Shanley, M. (1990), 'What's in a name? Reputation building and corporate strategy', *The Academy of Management Journal*, **33**(2), 233–58

Ford, D., Berthon, P., Brown, S., Gadde, L.-E., Håkansson, H., Naudé, P., Ritter, T. and Snehota, I. (2002), *The Business Marketing Course – Managing in Complex Networks*, Chichester, UK: John Wiley and Sons.

Frost, R. (2008), 'Family-owned brands: a sustainable legacy?', *brandchannel.com*, retrieved from http://www.brandchannel.com/start1.asp?fa_id=438.

Gammoh, B.S., Voss, K.E. and Chakraborty, G. (2006), 'Consumer evaluation of brand alliance signals', *Psychology and Marketing*, **23**(6), 465–86.

Gwinner, K. (1997), 'A model of image creation and image transfer in event sponsorship', *International Marketing Review*, **14**(3), 145–58.

Habbershon, T.G. and Williams, M.L. (1999), 'A resource-based framework for assessing the strategic advantages of family firms', *Family Business Review*, **12**(1), 1–25.

Hall, R. (1992), 'The strategic analysis of intangible resources', *Strategic Management Journal*, **13**(2), 135–44.

Haynes, G.W., Walker, R., Rowe, B.R. and Hong, G.-S. (1999), 'The intermingling of business and family finances in family-owned businesses', *Family Business Review*, **12**, 225–39.

Hoffman, J., Hoelscher, M. and Sorenson, R. (2006), 'Achieving sustained competitive advantage: a family capital theory', *Family Business Review*, **19**(2), 135–45.

Hulberg, J. (2006), 'Integrating corporate branding and sociological paradigms: a literature study', *Brand Management*, **14**(1/2), 60–73.

Jones, R. (2005), 'Finding sources of brand value: developing a stakeholder's model of brand equity', *Journal of Brand Management*, **13**(1), 10–32.

Kapferer, J.N. (1992), *Strategic Brand Management*, London: Kogan Page.

Keller, K.L. (1993), 'Conceptualizing, measuring, and managing customer-based brand equity', *Journal of Marketing*, **57**(1), 1–22.

Keller, K.L. (2008), *Strategic Brand Management: Building, Measuring, and Managing Brand Equity*, 3rd edn, Upper Saddle River, NJ: Pearson Prentice Hall.

Keller, K.L., Apéria, T. and Georgson, M. (2008), *Strategic Brand Management: A European Perspective*, Harlow, UK: Pearson Education Limited.

Kotler, P.H. (1991), *Marketing Management: Analysis, Planning, and Control*, 8th edn, Englewood Cliffs, NJ: Prentice Hall.

Kotler, P.H., Keller, K.L., Brady, M., Goodman, M. and Hansen, T. (2009), *Marketing Management* (European edn), Harlow, UK: Pearson Education Limited.

LaForet, S. (2009), *Managing Brands – A Contemporary Perspective*, Maidenhead, UK: McGraw-Hill Education.

Lane P.J. and Lubatkin, M. (1998), 'Relative absorptive capacity and interorganizational learning', *Strategic Management Journal*, **19**(8): 461–77.

Litchfield, S.R. (2008), 'Corporate branding: the case of the family firm', unpublished Master's thesis, Illinois State University, Normal.

Lyman, A. (1991), 'Customer service: does family ownership make a difference?', *Family Business Review*, **4**(3), 303–24.

McConaugby, D.L., Matthews, C.H., and Fialko, A.S. (2001), 'Founding family controlled firms: performance, risk, and value', *Journal of Small Business Management*, **39**(1), 31–49.

Michael-Tsabari, N., Lavee, Y. and Hareli, S. (2008), 'Stereotypes of family businesses and their role in choosing a workplace', paper presented at the 8th Annual IFERA Conference.

Miller, D., Le Breton-Miller, I. and Scholnick, B. (2008), 'Stewardship vs. stagnation: an empirical comparison of small family and non-family businesses', *The Journal of Management Studies*, **45**(1), 51–78.

Morgan, B.D. (2009), 'Branding the "family business" concept: what type of family businesses reference that they are a family firm when communicating through their web pages?', unpublished Master's thesis, Illinois State University, Normal.

Nahapiet, J. and Ghoshal, S. (1998), 'Social capital, intellectual capital and the organizational advantage', *Academy of Management Review*, **23**(2), 242–66.

Okoroafo, S.C. and Koh, A. (2009), 'The impact of marketing activities of family owned businesses on consumer purchase intentions', *International Journal of Business and Management*, **4**(10), 3–13.

Orth, U.R., and Green, M.T. (2009), 'Consumer loyalty to family versus non-family business: the roles of store image, trust and satisfaction', *Journal of Retailing and Consumer Services*, **16**, 248–59.

Pearson, A., Carr, J.C., and Shaw, J.C. (2008), 'Toward a theory of familiness: a social capital perspective', *Entrepreneurship Theory and Practice*, **32**(6), 949–69.

Petrick, J.A., Scherer, R.F., Brodzinski, J.D., Quinn, J.F. and Ainina, M.F. (1999), 'Global leadership skills and reputational capital: Intangible resources for sustainable competitive advantage', *Academy of Management Executive*, **13**(1), 58–69.

Poza, E.J. (2010), *Family Business*, 3rd edn, Mason, OH: Cenegade Learning.

Riezebos, R. (2003), *Brand Management – A Theoretical and Practical Approach*, Harlow, UK: Pearson Education.

Sharma, P. (2004), 'An overview of the field of family business studies: current status and directions for the future', *Family Business Review*, **17**(1), 1–36.

Sirmon, D.G. and Hitt, M.A. (2003), 'Managing resources: linking unique resources, management, and wealth creation in family firms', *Entrepreneurship Theory and Practice*, **27**(4), 339–58.

Suh, T. and Amine, L.S. (2007), 'Defining and managing reputational capital in global markets', *The Journal of Marketing Theory and Practice*, **15**(3), 205–17.

Turban, D.B. and Cable, D.M. (2003), 'Firm reputation and applicant pool characteristics', *Journal of Organizational Behavior*, **24**(6), 733–51.

Ward, J.L. (1997), 'Growing the family business – special challenges and best practices', *Family Business Review*, **10**(4), 323–37.

Westhead, P. and Howorth, C. (2006), 'Ownership and management issues associated with family firm performance and company objectives', *Family Business Review*, **19**(4), 301–16.

29 A study of innovation activities and the role played by ownership structure in Spanish industrial companies

Álvaro Gómez Vieites, Francisco Negreira del Río, Jesús Negreira del Río and José Luis Calvo González

1 INTRODUCTION

The ownership structure of firms has been considered as one of the factors determining the level of investment in R&D (Baysinger et al., 1991; Lee and O'Neil, 2003; Chen, 2009). In the field of family business this study has been conducted from different perspectives: family businesses have been identified as sources of technological innovation and economic development (Astrachan, 2003; Astrachan et al., 2003; Zahra, 2005), while other authors have analyzed the dynamics of evolution of ownership and its type in its effect on investment in R&D activities (Lee and O'Neil, 2003; Tribo et al., 2007).

Moreover, the relationships between firms' characteristics, innovation behavior and business performance have been studied by many authors. In fact, one of the first references in economic literature related to econometric analysis of R&D activities is Griliches's R&D capital stock model (Griliches, 1979). This model stresses that R&D activities enhance innovations and these foster firm performance. Griliches's model includes the typical productive factors and, additionally, it incorporates another one named 'technological capital', depending on R&D firms' expenditure, universities' R&D and technological centers' activities. This production function has been used in several later studies (Griliches and Mairesse, 1983; Acs et al., 1992; Audretsch, 1998; Porter and Stern, 1999).

Nevertheless, Griliches's model does not consider all the activities included in innovation, which is a multidimensional and interactive process (Kline and Rosenberg, 1986). R&D is only a part of innovation expenses, from the birth of the idea to complete development, and approaching innovation activity by exclusively R&D expenditures involves underestimation, especially in small firms and traditional industries (Calvo, 2000, 2006). In fact, Calvo (2006), in a study employing Spanish manufacturing firms, found that three-quarters of process innovation firms did not have R&D personnel and more than a half of product innovative firms did not spend on R&D.

At the same time, numerous models have been proposed to study the relationships between innovation behavior and firms' performance. Hurley and Hult (1998) analyze innovation activities considering that some structural and process characteristics (size, resources, age, planning, development and control of activities, information management and so on) influence innovation capacity. Moreover, cultural characteristics (market orientation, participative decision process and so on) affect innovation receptiveness. The

Figure 29.1   Camisón's model (1999)

innovation capacity, its receptiveness and structural process, and cultural characteristics determine firm's competitive advantage.

Other authors such as Greene et al. (1999) or Floyd and Wooldridge (1999) emphasize the relevance of organizational resources. These authors suggest that firms' innovative projects are the result of an accumulation of resources, generating new ones, especially knowledge.

In Spain, Camisón (1999) maintains that firms' competitive advantage is based on resources (especially intangibles) and capacities that are difficult to imitate by other firms. He proposes a model (Figure 29.1) where organizational characteristics influence innovation behavior, and this affects firms' performance.

2   THEORETICAL BACKGROUND: THE ROLE OF FAMILY IN BUSINESS, R&D AND INNOVATION

Two different and well-known models support the relationship between family ownership and management behavior, and their effects on family firms' innovation and R&D investments: agency theory (Jensen and Meckling, 1976) and stewardship theory (Donaldson, 1990a, 1990b; Barney, 1990).

Agency theory justifies the development of corporate governance (Williamson, 1985) in relation to ownership's need to monitor and control the manager. The board of directors monitors the CEO's behavior to ensure that his performance is always committed to the owner's interests. The task of monitoring the manager is not just the responsibility of the president, but it becomes a critical role of independent directors (Fama, 1980; Zahra and Pearce, 1989). Anderson and Reeb (2003) found that the most valuable privately held firms are those in which independent directors balance family representation on the board. This dual approach of developing an effective board of directors (Ward, 1991) through a clear distinction between the figures of the president and CEO and the incorporation of independent directors (Nash, 1988; Schulze et al., 2001) is also mentioned in Chen's work (2009), which suggests a positive correlation between the two characteristics of government and increased investment in R&D.

Furthermore, agency costs can be reduced as a consequence of involvement of the owners in governance and management, and this fact has contributed to qualifying family business as one of the most efficient forms of government organization (Kang, 2000). Anderson and Reeb (2003) found that among the companies in the S&P 500, many family firms had had better financial and market performance than non-family companies, which is consistent with the notion that family ownership reduces managers' opportunism. This approach could explain that, despite their lower level of R&D investment, family businesses can be more efficient in the management of resources and could achieve similar results in innovation compared to non-family firms with higher levels of R&D investment (Chen, 2009).

In fact, Chen (2009) focused on the relationship between family ownership, independence of the board and investment in R&D on a sample of Taiwanese companies, finding a negative correlation between family-owned company and investment in R&D. Chen's study suggests that a high percentage of the company's capital in the hands of family owners is a factor that could inhibit R&D activities with a long-term perspective, due to risk aversion.

DeAngelo and DeAngelo (2000) have documented how family shareholders in publicly traded companies obtain private benefits through special dividends, excessive incentive schemes and partly related transactions. Faccio et al. (2001) show that without external oversight, shareholders such as the members of the founding families tend to expropriate wealth from the firm at the expense of minority shareholders. One consequence of this negative practice may be the reduction in R&D investment in the long term compared to non-family-owned firms.

The professionalization of corporate governance in family business may have an additional effect during the succession process for the next generation, with a positive impact on the company's innovative abilities (McCann et al., 2001). In a successful succession process the next generation must have developed some critical characteristics, and one of them is the innovative spirit (Litz and Kleysen, 2001). According to a study carried out by Naldi et al. (2007), increased formalization and external monitoring in family business may lead to a risk-taking behavior that leads to better outcomes in terms of financial performance, but, at the same time, this formalization and external monitoring may stifle the entrepreneurial activities that give rise to the opportunities of developing new risky projects.

In a parallel approach, stewardship theory looks at advantages and disadvantages in a family-owned company. According to this theory, the agent is intrinsically motivated towards the collective benefit of the company. This attitude can be especially prevalent in family firms in which the leaders are members of the family or are closely linked to it. These executives share the company's mission, serve its employees and shareholders, and are motivated to act in the best way for the owner family and the organization (Miller and Le Breton-Miller, 2005). This attitude can generate precursors to distinctive capabilities and greater financial returns. However, not all types of family-owned companies will show 'stewardship' in their owners or agents (Miller & Le Breton-Miller, 2006).

These companies, according to the hypothesis proposed by Miller and Le Breton-Miller (2006), could have an advantage if they have a family CEO: leaders who belong to the family (his or her name being part of the business for generations) can act positively as 'stewards': there is a long-term commitment, better management of company resources and optimum management of the company's capabilities in the investment projection. As the authors show, the fact that the family CEO has a prolonged stay in the executive position generates a cumulative growth of capacity. This is a different point of view from that provided under the agency perspective, not opposite but complementary, and it could also justify the higher level of efficiency identified in the use of R&D investment in family firms versus those that do not have this kind of ownership structure (Chen, 2009).

A negative relationship between family ownership and R&D and innovation could be sustained by risk aversion. A greater risk aversion in family firms could be supported by the idea that the manager must not jeopardize the family's wealth accumulated over generations, and this perception is increased in those cases where the manager is at the same time the firm's owner. So they prefer not to undertake risk actions such as innovation.

Naldi et al. (2007) found that even if family firms do take risks as part of their entrepreneurial activities, they do it to a lesser extent than do non-family firms. In a previous work, Zahra (2005) had found that the length of a CEO's tenure is negatively associated with entrepreneurial risk taking; nevertheless his research found that the higher the number of generations from the same owner family that are active in the company, the higher the firm's focus on innovation.

Gómez-Mejía et al. (2007) faced this approach with a complementary dimension: family firms are concerned also with their 'socio-emotional wealth'. By 'socio-emotional wealth' these authors refer to non-financial aspects of the firm that meet the family's affective needs, such as identity, the ability to exercise family influence, and the perpetuation of the family dynasty.

Finally, Craig and Moores (2006) consider family business as a primary organizational type (according to traditional criteria usually used in innovation research as industry, sector, structure and/or strategy), and examine innovation longitudinally in respect to organizational life stage. The results found by these authors suggest that linkages between established family firms and innovation may be substantially stronger than currently assumed by many authors. In fact, other authors have proposed that family firms can be very innovative and aggressive in their markets (Aronoff, 1998).

3 A NEW MODEL PROPOSED TO STUDY INNOVATION IN FAMILY BUSINESS

The model proposed in this chapter introduces ownership structure in order to explain R&D activities and innovation. In doing so, first we include it in a set of several factors (contingent factors such as size and age; human and organizational resources; financial resources; as well as other aspects such as cooperation with other firms and agents, and or course ownership structure) that affect the development of R&D activities; afterwards, we employ those R&D activities, ownership structure again, information management and technological resources to influence innovation results; finally we estimate the way innovation results together with R&D activities and information management can help to improve firm's performance.

The most distinguishing feature of the model is versatility, breaking the linear structure estimation of the relationship between R&D, innovation and business performance. In our model there is a more flexible design, as represented in Figure 29.2.

The main hypothesis that support the proposed model are listed in Box 29.1

The justification for the different variables included in our model and their relationships are explained in the following sections, taking into account their references in the literature.

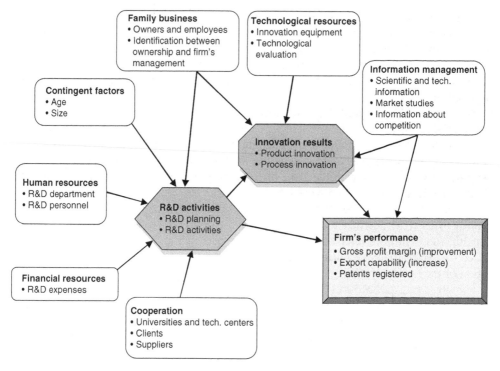

Figure 29.2   Model proposed by the authors

BOX 29.1   MAIN HYPOTHESES OF THE MODEL

Contingent factors (age and size) positively affect R&D activities
Human and organizational resources positively influence R&D activities
Financial resources directed to R&D activities have a positive effect on R&D
    activities
Cooperation with other agents generates a positive effect on R&D activities
Family business carries out fewer R&D activities than non-family business
Family business gets less innovation results than non-family business
Technological resources and the use of new technologies positively affect
    innovation results
Information management has a positive effect on innovation results
Information management has a positive effect on firm's performance
External or internal R&D activities and their planning have a positive effect on
    innovation results
External or internal R&D activities and their planning have a positive effect on
    firm's performance
Inovation results have a positive effect on firm's performance

3.1 Family-Owned Businesses and Innovation

In Section 2 we discussed the relationship between family-owned business and R&D and innovation activities. Different arguments have been put forward. In our model we support Chen's (2009) position, assuming that a family business carries out fewer R&D activities than non-family ones.

3.2 Contingent Factors: Company's Size and Age

The relationship between size and innovation has been studied by many researchers (Mansfield, 1981; Pavitt, 1984; Audretsch and Acs, 1987, 1990, and 1991; Moch and Morse, 1997; Calvo, 2000, among others), without having reached a consensus.

Thus, on one side a large group of authors notes that the firm size positively affects its innovative behavior (Moch and Morse, 1977; Dewar and Dutton, 1986). In contrast, other authors, such as Mohr (1969) or Audretsch and Acs (1987), support the existence of a negative relationship between size and innovation.

In this chapter we adopt an eclectic position, because although we believe that there is a positive relationship between size and R&D activities, we make no assumption, on its direct effect on innovation. We suggest that size influences R&D activities, as these activities require substantial investment, but at the same time we assume that small firms are able to compete on an equal footing in terms of innovation. In fact, small businesses may make innovations despite not having carried out systematic R&D activities, as is acknowledged by the *Oslo Manual* (OECD and Eurostat, 2005) and has been contrasted through empirical evidence.

Regarding company's age, some authors (Hurley and Hult, 1998) consider age as a contingent factor that influences the behavior of an innovative organization. In fact, taking into account that technological processes are cumulative, a company's experience is a factor that contributes positively to innovative results.

In this chapter we also defend this position, including in our model the contribution of organizational learning and experience gained by the organization.

3.3 Human and Organizational Resources

As Hurley and Hult (1998) defend in their work, human and organizational resources of a company directly affect its ability to innovate. In numerous works the authors include variables related to personnel dedicated to R&D and other organizational issues: centralization, specialization, formalization (Dewar and Dutton, 1986) or related to the development of human resources (Smith, 2004).

In our study we also try to specifically analyze the role of human and organizational resources related to R&D within the company. To do this we consider two factors: the existence of an R&D department within the company and personnel engaged in R&D activities.

3.4   Financial Resources

One of the most common indicators used to evaluate the commitment of an organization to R&D is the level of expenditure dedicated to this activity (Griliches, 1979, 1995; Calvo, 2006; and many others).

Given this background, the proposed model also includes the role of financial resources to support R&D in the company.

3.5   Collaboration with Other Agents

Since innovation is essentially conceived as an interactive learning process, many authors, such as Narula and Dunning (1997), argue that collaborative activities between different agents of a National Innovation System have great importance in achieving economies of scale, avoiding duplication of efforts and promoting the dissemination of the results of innovation.

Other studies have shown that cooperation in R&D usually bring significant benefits to businesses (Hagedoorn 1993, 1995; Hagedoorn and Narula, 1996; Narula and Dunning, 1997).

Therefore, taking into account the theoretical framework and previous references, we also consider the importance of collaboration between the company and other actors in explaining its ability to develop R&D.

3.6   Technology Resources

Following the initial approach of Hurley and Hult (1998) and other authors such as Arnold and Thuriaux (1997), and taking into account the methodology proposed by the *Oslo Manual* (OECD and Eurostat, 2005), we also include in our model two variables related to the technology available in the company as a key factor in explaining its innovative capacity: the acquisition of new technological equipment to support innovation, and the effort devoted to the analysis of new technologies and technological change.

3.7   Information and Knowledge Management

In a global, complex and very dynamic economy, companies must pay much more attention to a growing number of information sources in order to be prepared for changing conditions in markets, launch of new products and technologies, and an increasing competence all over the world.

Freeman (1994) suggests that innovation should be seen as an interactive process in which a company acquires knowledge through its own experience in the design, development, production and marketing of new products, constantly learning from its relationships with various external sources: customers, suppliers and other organizations such as universities, technological institutes, consultants and so on

Other authors, such as Pavitt (1984), include in their analysis the role played by information management to carry out innovations, distinguishing between internal and external sources (customers, suppliers, scientific and technological studies, market surveys etc.).

Considering all these previous references and theoretical background, we introduce in our model the role of information management as an element that could be of particular importance in the innovative behavior of the company. This is done using three factors related to information management: the procurement of scientific and technical information services; conducting market research; and obtaining information on competitors' activities and strategies.

3.8   R&D Activities

Given the framework of the *Frascati Manual* (OECD, 2002) and the *Oslo Manual* (OECD and Eurostat, 2005), R&D activities are included within the list of activities considered necessary for technological innovation.

Moreover, the interactive model proposed by Kline and Rosenberg (1986) considers R&D activities as a tool that can be used to solve problems occurring during the processes of innovation, being able to enter the process at any phase.

Therefore our model includes the role played by R&D activities as a key factor that can contribute positively to success in obtaining innovation, but R&D is not a requirement or prerequisite for success in the innovation process, as was suggested in the linear model of innovation.

In our work we also analyze the direct impact R&D activities can have on business results, as these activities could contribute to the achievement of radical innovations that provide greater competitive advantage (Mansfield et al., 1981; Mansfield, 1986; Narver and Slater, 1990; Acs et al., 2002).

The construct included in our model to take into account the role of R&D is defined by two variables: R&D activities by themselves (both internal and external); and systematic planning of these activities by the company.

3.9   Innovation Results

Our model includes a construct devoted to innovation results, distinguishing between product innovations and process innovations. This element depends not only on the R&D activities carried out by the company, but also other factors related to the technology incorporated by the company or to information management.

Furthermore, in accordance with the contributions of major authors who have analyzed the processes of innovation, it is considered that these innovations have a positive impact on organizational performance (Schumpeter, 1934; Nelson and Winter, 1977; Freeman, 1975, 1982; Pavitt 1984; Dosi et al., 1988; Arthur, 1994; OECD and Eurostat, 2005, etc.).

3.10   Business Performance

In the model proposed in this chapter, business performance is determined using three indicators: the share of exports in turnover; the improvement in gross profit margin (Narver and Slater, 1990; among others); and patents obtained by the company (Griliches, 1979, 1990; Mansfield et al., 1981; Mansfield, 1986).

In fact, the weight of exports can be considered as a factor that could explain the company's ability to compete in an open and globalized market.

4   DATA, VARIABLES AND METHODOLOGY FOR THE MODEL'S VALIDATION

The sample used in our study was taken from the Survey of Business Strategy (SBS)[1], which is a firm-level panel data set of Spanish manufacturing firms. The survey is compiled by the SEPI Foundation; it is random and stratified according to the industry sector and firm size.

The aim of the SBS is to document the evolution of the characteristics of and the strategies used by Spanish firms, and therefore it provides information on markets, customers, products, employment, outcome results, corporate strategy, human resources and technological activities. In our study we used data from the 2008 year survey, with a total number of 1999 valid samples.

The main variables obtained from these samples are included in Table 29.1[2]:

The model we propose here defines five constructs – latent variables built up from observed variables – affecting R&D activities: contingent factors obtained from the observed variables age (AEMP2) and size (TEMPRE3); human resources achieved using

Table 29.1   Main values of the sample

Variable	Total	Family-run businesses	Non family-run businesses
Number of firms	1999	1001	998
Business turnover (mean)	€53 149 893	€14 052 012	€92 842 569
Gross profit margin (share of business turnover)	67.77%	84.21%	51.27%
Export volume (share)	19.25%	12.64%	26.01%
Number of employees (mean)	222.91	72.98	373.28
R&D activities (share of firms)	35.47%	23.18%	47.80%
Planning R&D activities (share)	21.71%	13.49%	29.96%
Product innovation (share of firms)	18.01%	13.59%	22.44%
Process innovation (share of firms)	34.12%	28.27%	39.98%
Patents (share)	4.00%	3.60%	4.41%
R&D department (share of firms)	21.01%	12.69%	29.36%
R&D personnel (mean per firm)	2.02%	1.93%	2.10%
Equipment acquisition to support innovation	19.41%	16.18%	22.65%
Technological evaluation (share)	20.91%	16.48%	25.35%
R&D expenses (share of business turnover)	38.20%	41.98%	36.03%
Services of scientific and technological exploration	18.81%	15.08%	22.55%
Market studies (share)	15.31%	10.39%	20.24%
Information about competitors	16.96%	14.79%	19.14%
Cooperation with universities and tech. centers (share of firms)	22.51%	15.48%	29.56%
Cooperation with clients (share of firms)	16.76%	9.69%	23.85%
Cooperation with suppliers (share of firms)	19.41%	11.99%	26.85%

Source: Compiled by the authors.

two variables: R&D department (DCT2) and R&D personnel (EMPIDT3); financial resources, defined by R&D expenses (IDV3); cooperation, including three variables; cooperation with universities and research centers (CUTC2); cooperation with clients (CTCL2); and cooperation with suppliers (CTPR2); and family-run business, obtained from two observed variables, percentage of employees that are members of the owner family (PAFAM2) and identification between property and firm's management (IEPCN2).

The 'R&D activities' construct is attained using two variables: systematic R&D planning (PAI2) and R&D activities (AID3). They affect innovation results as well as firm's performance.

'Innovation results' is another latent variable obtained from two experiential variables: product innovation (IP2) and process innovation (IPR2). It depends on four constructs: R&D activities; family-run business; information management; and incorporated technological resources. This last latent variable is built up using two observed variables: innovation equipment acquisition (ADBEM2) and technological evaluation (SICYT4).

'Information management' is a new latent variable achieved from three information variables: scientific and technological surveillance (SICYT2); market studies (EMYM2); and information about competitors' activities (IPC3).

Finally, firms' performance is the last construct, defined as a latent variable obtained from three observed variables: gross profit margin (MBE2); firms' export capability (VEXPOR3); and firms' patents (PATESP3). We assume that firm's performance can be explained by R&D activities, innovation results and information management constructs.

The proposed model establishes multiple relationships between endogenous and exogenous variables, taking into account, at the same time, that there are several interactions between dependent and independent variables. Therefore the analysis technique is that of structural equations model (Hair et al., 1998), as a way to run multiple regressions between variables and latent variables.

In a structural equations model (SEM) we combine a predictive approach, typical of classic econometric techniques, with a psychometric methodology, applying factorial analysis to obtain latent variables (non-observed variables named constructs) from observed ones. Therefore, in a SEM we consider two types of model:

1. A model of measure applying factorial analysis. With this model we can observe the consistency and strength of theoretical constructs. Those constructs can be composed by reflective or formative indicators (Fornell, and Larcker, 1981). In our model, all of them, with the exception of R&D activities, are generated from formative variables.
2. A structural model to analyze the causality interactions between independent constructs (exogenous) and dependent ones (endogenous).

LISREL and AMOS among others are the most popular SEM software packages, and they are covariance-based with a maximum likelihood (ML) estimation. More recently, partial least squares (PLS) has begun to be used as a second-generation multivariate analysis method especially recommended for research in the business administration area, since it is usual in this field to find one or more of the next conditions: the theory is not well built; the measures are not fully developed; data do not have normal distributions (sometimes the distribution is even unknown) or several variables are ordinal, categorical or dummies. The objective of the PLS technique is latent variable prediction and it is not covariance-based but variance-based. PLS estimates model parameters to maximize the variance explained for all the endogenous constructs in the model, and to do this it uses an iterative algorithm that consists of a series of ordinary least squares (OLS) analyses.

In recent years many management researchers have used PLS since, compared to covariance-based methods, it offers many benefits with respect to distribution requirements, types of variables, sample size and the model's complexity to be tested. Nevertheless, the main drawback of PLS is its predictive and exploratory nature.

Since the theoretical model proposed in our work is exploratory and we essentially use Boolean and categorical variables without any previous assumption about data distribution, we apply the PLS technique to the structural equations model.

In PLS, reflective indicators are determined by the construct and they covariate. That is why we should employ factorial loads to evaluate those constructs. On the contrary, constructs based on formative indicators are a function of those items, and they do not need to be correlated. Latent variables with formative indicators have to be analyzed using their weights.

Therefore, if we want to evaluate a PLS model, we should follow two stages:

1. *Study of validity and reliability of the model of measure*   In this first stage it is necessary to analyze if theoretical concepts (approached by constructs) are correctly measured by observed variables.
2. *Evaluation of structural model*   In this second stage we study the relationships between constructs. So we should focus on the following:
    (a) Estimate the share of endogenous variables' variance explained by exogenous constructs.
    (b) Evaluate the influence of independent variables in dependent variables' variance.

5   DISCUSSION OF RESULTS AND MODEL VALIDATION

As we have said, we employ the PLS technique to estimate the proposed structural equations model.

First, we present regression weights and factorial loads for different constructs, since in order to evaluate the model we need to employ loads for reflective indicators and weights for formative variables (Table 29.2).

Regression coefficients (path values) between exogenous constructs (independents) and endogenous ones (dependent) are included in Table 29.3.

5.1   Validation of the Measurement Model

In order to evaluate the consistency of the measurement model we propose the following tests:

Table 29.2   Constructs' weights and factorial loads

Construct	Type of construct	Variable	Type of variable	Weight	Load
Cont. fact.	Independent			inward	
		TEMPRE3	Formative	0.976	0.998
		AEMP2	Formative	0.064	0.401
Human res.	Independent			inward	
		DCT2	Formative	0.730	0.951
		EMPIDT3	Formative	0.382	0.805
Tech. res.	Independent			inward	
		SICYT4	Formative	0.621	0.762
		ADBEM2	Formative	0.663	0.795
Fin. res.	Independent			outward	
		IDV2	Formative	1.000	1.000
Inf. mgmt	Independent			inward	
		EMYM2	Formative	0.460	0.744
		IPC3	Formative	0.062	0.154
		SICYT2	Formative	0.721	0.899
R&D	Dependent			outward	
		AID3	Reflective	0.555	0.929
		PAI2	Reflective	0.527	0.921
Cooperation	Independent			inward	
		CUCT2	Formative	0.392	0.784
		CTCL2	Formative	0.247	0.805
		CTPR2	Formative	0.544	0.908
Innovation	Dependent			inward	
		IP2	Formative	0.617	0.831
		IPR2	Formative	0.596	0.818
Firm's perf.	Dependent			inward	
		VEXPOR3	Formative	0.800	0.872
		MBE2	Formative	0.195	0.206
		PATESP3	Formative	0.454	0.588
Family business	Independent			inward	
		PAFAM2	Formative	0.748	0.952
		IEPCN2	Formative	0.367	0.784

5.1.1   Reflective indicators

1. *Liability of each item*, evaluating its factorial load. Carmines and Zeller (1979) establish the criterion that loads should be bigger than 0.707. In our case, R&D variables satisfy this restriction since R&D activities (AID3) = 0.929 and R&D planning (PAI2) = 0.921.
2. *Composite reliability*, used to test internal consistency. The criterion implies that the expression

$$\rho_c = \frac{\left(\sum \lambda_i\right)^2}{\left(\sum \lambda_i\right)^2 + \sum_i \text{var}(\varepsilon_i)}$$

Table 29.3   Path values

Path (β)	Cont. fact.	Human res.	Tech. res.	Fin. res.	Inf. mgmt	R&D	Coopera-tion	Innova-tion	Firm's. perf.	Family Bus.
Cont. fact.										
Human res.										
Tech. res.										
Fin. res.										
Inf. mgmt										
R&D	0.160	0.518			0.080		0.314			−0.010
Cooperation										
Innovation			0.354		0.094	0.311				−0.028
Firm's perf.					0.087	0.385		0.110		
Family business										

should be bigger than 0.7, where λ_i is the standardized load of indicator i and ε_i is measurement error. In our case the value obtained for the R&D construct is 0.922.

3. *Convergent validity*   In this case we use average variance extracted (AVE) proposed by Fornell and Larcker (1981), and according to these authors the value of the expression

$$AVE = \frac{\sum \lambda_t^{2i}}{\sum \lambda_i^2 + \sum_i \mathrm{var}(\varepsilon_i)}$$

should be bigger than 0.5, since more than 50 percent of construct variance should be explained by its variables. In our study the R&D construct reaches the value 0.773, fulfilling this criterion.

5.1.2   Formative indicators

1. *Multicollinearity*   First we should avoid a multicollinearity problem. Therefore we calculate an inflation variance factor (IVF) demanding a value smaller than 5 for all indicators. The results obtained in our study satisfy this criterion.
2. *Discriminate validity*   To test differences between constructs we employ two criteria: first we test that *AVE* should be bigger than any other correlation between variables (Fornell and Larcker, 1981). To do so, we substitute the diagonal of correlation matrix for the root square of *AVE*, and the diagonal should be bigger than any other cell in the same row or column. All the variables satisfy this first criterion, as we can see Table 29.4.

In the second criterion to test discriminate analysis we analyze if a construct shares more variance with its own indicators rather than with other variables, using the cross-loading table (Table 29.5), where the diagonal also should be bigger than any other cell in the same row or column:

According to this second criterion, we can observe that three variables, AEMP2

Table 29.4   Discriminate analysis and correlation matrix

Discriminate analysis	Cont. fact.	Human res.	Tech. res.	Fin. res.	Inf. mgmt	R&D	Coopera-tion	Innova-tion	Firm perf.	Family bus.
Cont. fact	0.761									
Human res	0.446	0.881								
Tech. res.	0.398	0.442	0.779							
Fin. res.	−0.119	0.158	0.097	1.000						
Inf. Mgmt	0.367	0.430	0.305	0.075	0.680					
R&D	0.539	0.828	0.495	0.172	0.414	0.925				
Cooperation	0.485	0.713	0.508	0.095	0.428	0.771	0.834			
Innovation	0.373	0.465	0.542	0.007	0.335	0.533	0.509	0.825		
Firm perf.	0.469	0.447	0.287	0.041	0.283	0.479	0.428	0.344	0.619	
Family business	−0.557	−0.245	−0.196	0.070	−0.184	−0.301	−0.255	−0.207	−0.296	0.872

(age of company), IPC3 (information about competitors) and MBE2 (gross margin) present problems with the discriminate analysis.

5.2   Validation of the Structural Model

To analyze and validate the structural model we have to test the two following criteria:

1. The share of the variance of each dependent construct explained by independent variables (R^2) should have a value bigger than 0.1, a criterion that is satisfied by all the dependent constructs, as is shown in Table 29.6.
2. Independent variables' contribution to explained variance of dependent variables should be significant, and for the study of this feature Falk and Miller (1992) proposed the following criterion: they suggested an empirical rule where predictor variable should explain at least 1.5 percent of the variance. According to this criterion, we can observe that all the independent variables satisfy this feature (Table 29.7).

Taking into account these results, we can observe that the most influent variable in R&D activities construct is human and organizational resources (explaining 42.89 percent of variance), followed by cooperation with other agents (24.21 percent); in the innovation results construct the most relevant factor is technological resources (19.19 percent of variance), followed by R&D activities (16.58 percent); and for the firm's performance construct the most important variable is R&D activities, with a 18.44 percent of variance, followed by innovation (3.78 percent).

Consequently, we can now examine the hypotheses we formulated and check them. Using the non-parametric technique bootstrap, we can estimate the accuracy of predictions (Chin, 1998), obtaining the results shown in Table 29.8.

Therefore, the main results of our study are included in Figure 29.3.

Finally, in order to measure the predictive capacity of dependent constructs we have used the Stone–Geiser test (Geisser, 1975; Stone, 1974), calculating the Q^2 value

Table 29.5 Cross-loading table

	Cont. Fact.	Human Res.	Tech. Res.	Fin. Res.	Inf. Mgmt.	R&D	Cooperation	Innovation	F. P.	Family Bus.
TEMPRE3	0.9982	0.4424	0.3973	0.5012	0.3523	0.5425	0.4835	0.3732	0.4680	-0.5561
AEMP2	**0.4003**	0.2086	0.1540	0.1958	0.1729	0.2176	0.1920	0.1326	0.2142	-0.2168
DCT2	0.4376	0.9457	0.4226	-0.6888	0.3811	0.7807	0.6840	0.4432	0.4000	-0.2403
EMPIDT3	0.2575	0.7074	0.2835	0.5787	0.3226	0.5742	0.4732	0.3059	0.3411	-0.1673
SICYT4	0.3609	0.4857	0.7619	0.4374	0.3397	0.5121	0.5441	0.4129	0.2874	-0.1384
ADBEM2	0.2621	0.2113	0.7951	0.2377	0.1359	0.2632	0.2562	0.4309	0.1639	-0.2998
IDV3	0.5018	0.7551	0.4291	1.0000	0.3623	0.9294	0.7109	0.4859	0.4756	-0.2998
EMYM2	0.2002	0.2389	0.1727	0.2180	0.5744	0.2288	0.2102	0.1953	0.1319	-0.1060
IPC3	0.1177	0.0637	0.0577	0.0764	**0.1417**	0.0822	0.0213	0.0473	0.0420	-0.0867
SICYT2	0.2085	0.2684	0.1837	0.2483	0.7034	0.2595	0.2866	0.2326	0.1826	-0.0998
AID3	0.5359	0.7606	0.4469	0.9751	0.3714	0.9477	0.7290	0.5019	0.4841	-0.3149
PAI2	0.4592	0.7707	0.4691	0.7043	0.3709	0.8978	0.6956	0.4831	0.4005	-0.2392
CUCT2	0.4370	0.5673	0.3945	0.5501	0.4020	0.6032	0.7819	0.4209	0.3548	-0.2215
CTCL2	0.3648	0.5936	0.3789	0.5935	0.2753	0.6236	0.8083	0.3795	0.3503	-0.2086
CTPR2	0.4103	0.6326	0.4773	0.6406	0.3390	0.7004	0.9078	0.4592	0.3733	-0.2144
IP2	0.2799	0.4552	0.3809	0.4508	0.2983	0.4939	0.4615	0.8305	0.3048	-0.1511
IPR2	0.3357	0.3083	0.5150	0.3491	0.2357	0.3837	0.3754	0.8187	0.2606	-0.1919
VEXPOR3	0.2597	0.2602	0.1167	0.3634	0.1155	0.2726	0.2297	0.1357	0.6342	-0.1880
MBE2	0.0081	0.0363	0.0261	0.0519	0.0516	0.0438	0.0415	0.0451	**0.0587**	-0.0069
PATESP3	0.1884	0.2716	0.1911	0.2397	0.1674	0.2623	0.2366	0.2677	0.5807	-0.0823
PAFAM2	-0.5196	-0.2315	-0.1967	-0.2846	-0.1703	-0.2849	-0.2352	-0.2065	-0.2856	0.9524
IEPCN2	-0.4579	-0.1952	-0.1322	-0.2369	-0.1317	-0.2516	-0.2152	-0.1447	-0.2272	0.7836

Table 29.6   Variance of each dependent construct explained by independent variables

R&D	0.773
Innovation	0.395
Firm's performance	0.247

Table 29.7   Independent variables' contribution to dependent variables' explained variance

	'R&D' construct		
Constructs	Path	Correlation	% explained variance
Contingent factors	0.160	0.539	8.62
Human resources	0.518	0.828	42.89
Financial resources	0.080	0.172	1.38
Cooperation	0.314	0.771	24.21
Family business	−0.010	−0.301	0.30
		R^2	0.774

	'Innovation' construct		
Constructs	Path	Correlation	% explained variance
R&D	0.311	0.533	16.58
Tech. resources	0.354	0.542	19.19
Inf. management	0.094	0.335	3.15
Family business	−0.028	−0.207	0.58
		R^2	0.395

	'Firm's performance' construct		
Constructs	Path	Correlation	% explained variance
R&D	0.385	0.479	18.44
Innovation	0.110	0.344	3.78
Inf. management	0.087	0.283	2.46
		R^2	0.247

(cross-validated redundancy) for every dependent construct. According to this test, if Q^2 value is bigger than 0, then the model has predictive relevance for that variable. In our study we can observe that all the dependent constructs satisfy this criterion (Table 29.9).

6   CONCLUSIONS

In this chapter we have proposed a model to analyze the role of ownership structure in R&D and innovation activities and how these, together with other variables, affect a firm's results. Its main characteristic is versatility, since it is possible to model flexible relationships between different elements affecting R&D, innovation results and their

Table 29.8   Hypotheses and accuracy of predictions

Contingent factors (age and size) positively affect R&D activities	$p < 0.001$
Human and organizational resources positively influence R&D activities	$p < 0.001$
Financial resources directed to R&D activities have a positive effect on R&D activities	$p < 0.01$
Cooperation with other agents generates a positive effect on R&D activities	$p < 0.001$
Family business carries out fewer R&D activities than non-family business	Checked and hypothesis not accepted
Family business get less innovation results than non-family business	$p < 0.05$
Technological resources and the use of new technologies positively affect innovation results	$p < 0.001$
Information management has a positive effect on innovation results	$p < 0.001$
Information management has a positive effect on firm's performance	$p < 0.001$
External or internal R&D activities and their planning have a positive effect on innovation results	$p < 0.001$
External or internal R&D activities and their planning have a positive effect on firm's performance	$p < 0.001$
Innovation results have a positive effect on firm's performance	$p < 0.001$

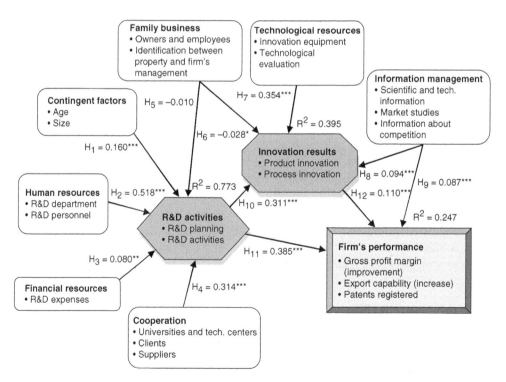

Figure 29.3   Main results of the study

Table 29.9   Stone–Geisser test

R&D	0.649
Innovation	0.189
Firm's performance	0.008

effects on business performance, by applying structural equations models and PLS techniques.

By means of a structural equations model it is possible to combine predictive techniques of classical econometric multiple regression (examining dependence relationships between variables) with the psychometric approach, based on the measurement of latent variables (not directly observed) through multiple variables observed (indicators), using a factor analysis technique in this second case. At the same time, PLS is considered as a second-generation multivariate analysis technique that is particularly appropriate for research projects in the field of business administration.

Our model explains how several factors (contingent factors such as size and age; human and organizational resources; financial resources; as well as other aspects such as cooperation with other firms and agents, and ownership structure) affect the development of R&D activities; how those R&D activities, ownership structure, information management and technological resources influence innovation results; and the way innovation results together with R&D activities and information management can help to improve the performance of Spanish industrial firms.

The results confirm the validity of our theoretical proposal, both the model of measure and the structural model. We have reached satisfactory outcomes, fulfilling all PLS requirements, using a sample of 1999 Spanish industrial companies obtained from the 2008 year Survey of Business Strategy.

Unless we have found a negative correlation between family-run business and R&D, this relationship is very weak and the hypothesis can not be accepted if we take into account the results of the PLS technique. In the case of innovation activities we accept the hypothesis of a negative correlation between family-run business and innovation results.

In the same way, when we evaluate R&D planning and activities in Spanish industrial companies we can reveal that the most important factors are human resources, followed by cooperation with other agents. In reference to firms' innovation, both process and product, we have proved that technological resources is the most relevant factor, followed by R&D activities.

Finally, in our study we also have shown that R&D activities, innovation results and information management have a very positive contribution to a firm's economic performance.

This study has important academic and practical implications. From an academic point of view, this research first evaluates in a broad perspective the role of several factors and firms' resources in the firm's innovativeness and performance. And from a practitioner's point of view, this research has shown that family-run businesses are less engaged in innovation activities, despite the importance of innovation as a key factor of success in today's global markets. And so managers, owners and policy-makers should be aware that family-run business could change this situation and strongly focus on innovation activities if they want to remain competitive.

7   LIMITATIONS AND FUTURE RESEARCH

In this study we decided to classify a company as a 'family-run business', taking into account the positive answer to the question 'Is the company controlled by the owner family?', and so we worked with a total number of 1001 'family-run business' out of 1999 Spanish industrial firms. This criterion is consistent with the definition of 'family-run business' as firms that are controlled by a family group through a clear majority of ordinary voting shares, the family is represented on the management team and the leading representative of the family perceives the business to be a family firm (Westhead and Cowling, 1999).

In our sample this group of companies is characterized by having a small size (measured by turnover and number of employees), clearly below the average shown for non-family companies (see Table 29.1), and this smaller size could have had a negative influence on firms' innovativeness.

Moreover, and also from a strictly descriptive point of view, the gross profit margin of these companies is relatively higher than in the case of non-family firms, and this fact could indicate that family managers effectively have an aversion to risk which leads them to protect the short-term returns of the company as a guarantee of their personal wealth, instead of investing in R&D and innovation, whose long-term returns are not strong enough to overcome the agency costs of family ownership (Schulze et al., 2001). This conclusion is coincident with that found by Naldi et al. (2007): even if family firms do take risks when they are engaged in entrepreneurial activities, they do to a lesser extent than non-family firms.

In our study we used a very well-known and reliable Spanish database for management research, but it has a limitation regarding the number of variables related to family firms' characteristics, so this study based on our exploratory model could be complemented in the future with other source of data that could provide more appropriate proxies for family business variables of interest.

At this point, further research regarding the cross effects of size, ownership and governance structure of the firm and their impact on innovativeness and firm's performance will be necessary in order to try to verify Chen's (2009) proposal about the potentially positive effect that a high percentage of independent directors could have on the innovation in family firms, at least in small to medium-sized companies, which could be compatible with Baysinger et al.'s (1991) findings in large firms, where the presence of independent directors is positively related to R&D spending.

ACKNOWLEDGMENT

We are very grateful to SEPI Foundation for the data set employed in this study.

NOTES

1. SBS: http://www.funep.es/esee/en/einfo_que_es.asp.
2. A complete description of these variables can be found in the Appendix.

REFERENCES

Acs, Z.J., Anselin, L. and Varga, A. (2002), 'Patents and innovations counts as measures of regional production of new knowledge', *Research Policy*, **31**, 1069–85.

Acs, Z., Audretsch, D. Feldman, M. (1992), 'Real effect of academic research: comment', *The American Economic Review*, **82**(1), 363–7.

Anderson, R. and Reeb, D. (2003), 'Founding family ownership and firm performance: evidence from the S&P 500'. *Journal of Finance*, **58**, 1301–28.

Arnold, E. and Thuriaux, B. (1997), 'Developing firms' technological capabilities', Report for the OECD, Brighton, Technopolis.

Aronoff, C.E. (1998), 'Megatrends in family business', *Family Business Review*, **11**(3), 181–6.

Arthur, B. (1994), *Increasing returns and path dependence in the economy*, Ann Arbor, MI: University of Michigan Press.

Astrachan, J.H. (2003), 'Commentary on the special issue: the emergence of a field', *Journal of Business Venturing*, **18**, 567–73.

Astrachan, J.H., Zahra, S.A. and Sharma, P. (2003), *'Family-sponsored Ventures*, Kansas City, MO: Kauffman Foundation.

Audretsch, D.B. (1998), 'Agglomeration and the location of innovative activity', *Oxford Review of Economic Policy*, **14**(2), 18–29.

Audretsch, D.B. and Acs, Z.J. (1987), 'Innovation, market structure and firm size', *Review of Economics and Statistics*, **69**(4), 567–75.

Audretsch, D.B and Acs, Z.J. (1991), 'Innovation and size at the firm level', in D.B. Audretsch (ed.), *Entrepreneurship, Innovation and Economic Growth*, Cheltenham, UK and Northampton, MA, USA: Edward Elgar, 2006, pp. 26–31.

Barney, J.B. (1990), 'The debate between traditional management theory and organizational economics: substantive differences or intergroup conflict?', *Academy of Management Review*, **15**, 382–93.

Baysinger, B., Kosnik, R. and Turk, T. (1991), 'Effects of board and ownership structure on corporate R&D strategy', *Academy of Management Journal*, **34**(1), 205–14.

Calvo, J.L. (2000), 'Una caracterización de la innovación tecnológica en los sectores manufactureros españoles: algunos datos', *Economía Industrial*, no. 331, 139–50.

Calvo, J.L. (2006), '¿Son las actividades de I+D una buena aproximación a la Innovación Tecnológica?', *Economía Industrial*, no. 358, 173–84.

Camisón, C. (1999), 'Sobre cómo medir las competencias distintivas: un examen empírico de la fiabilidad y validez de los modelos multi-item para la medición de los activos intangibles', First International Conference, Management Related Theory and Research: An Iberoamerican Perspective, The Iberoamerican Academy of Management.

Carmines, E.G. and Zeller, R.A. (1979), *Reliability and Validity Assessment*, London: Sage.

Chen, H.L. (2009), 'Family ownership, board independence, and R&D investment', *Family Business Review*, **22**(4), 347–62.

Chin, W.W. (1998), 'The partial least squares approach to structural equation modelling', in G.A. Marcoulides (ed.)', *Modern Methods for Business Research*, Mahwah, NJ: Lawrence Erlbaum, pp. 295–336.

Craig, J.B.L. and Moores, K. (2006), 'A 10-year longitudinal investigation of strategy, systems and environment on innovation in family firms', *Family Business Review*, **19**(1), 1–10.

Deangelo, H. and Deangelo, L. (2000), 'Controlling stockholders and the disciplinary role of corporate payout policy: a study of the Times Mirror Company', *Journal of Financial Economics*, **56**, 153–207.

Dewar, R.D. and Dutton, J.E. (1986), 'The adoption of radical and incremental innovations: an empirical analysis', *Management Science*, **32**(11), 1422–33.

Donaldson, L. (1990a), 'The ethereal hand: organizational economics and management theory', *Academy of Management Review*, **15**, 369–81.

Donaldson, L. (1990b), 'A rational basis for criticisms of organizational economics: a reply to Barney', *Academy of Management Review*, **15**, 394–401.

Dosi, G., Freeman, C., Nelson, R.R., Silverberg, G. and Soete, L. (1988), *Technology Change and Economic Theory*, London: Pinter Publishers.

Faccio, M. Lang, L. and Young, L. (2001), 'Dividends and expropriation', *American Economic Review*, **91**, 54–78.

Falk, R.F. and Miller, N.B. (1992), *A Primer for Soft Modelling*, Akron, OH: The University of Akron.

Fama, E.F. (1980), 'Agency problems and the theory of the firm', *Journal of Political Economy*, **88**, 288–307.

Floyd, S.W. and Wooldridge, B. (1999), 'Knowledge creation and social networks in corporate entrepreneurship: the renewal of organizational capability', *Entrepreneurship Theory and Practice*, **23**(3), 123–43.

Fornell, C. and Larcker, D.F. (1981), 'Evaluating structural equation models with unobservable variables and measurement error', *Journal of Marketing Research*, **18**, February, 39–50.

Freeman, C. (1975), *Teoría Económica de la Innovación Industrial*, Madrid: Alianza Editorial.

Freeman, C. (1982), *The Economics of Industrial Innovation*, 2nd edn, London: Frances Printer.

Freeman, C. (1994), 'The economics of technical change', Cambridge *Journal of Economics*, **18**(5), 463–514.

Geisser, S. (1975), 'The predictive sample reuse method with applications', *Journal of the American Statistical Association*, **70**, 320–28.

Gómez-Mejía, L., Takács Haynes, K., Núñez-Níckel, M., Jocobson, K and Moyano-Fuentes, J. (2007), 'Socioemotional wealth and business risks in family-controlled firms: evidence from spanish olive oil mills', *Administrative Science Quarterly*, **52**, 106–37.

Greene, P.G., Brush, C.G. and Hart, M.M. (1999), 'The corporate venture champion: a resource-based approach to role and process', *Entrepreneurship, Theory and Practice*, **23**(3), 103–22.

Griliches, Z. (1979), 'Issues in assessing the contribution of R&D to productivity growth', *Bell Journal of Economics*, **10** (Spring), 92–116.

Griliches, Z. (1990), 'Patent statistics as economic indicators: a survey', *Journal of Economic Literature*, **XXVIII**, December, 1661–707.

Griliches, Z. and Mairesse, J. (1983), 'Comparing productivity growth: an exploration of French and U.S. industrial and firm data', *European Economic Review*, **21**, 89–119.

Hagedoorn, J. (1993), 'Understanding the rationale of strategic technology partnering: interorganizational modes of cooperation and sectorial differences', *Strategic Management Journal*, **14**, 371–85.

Hagedoorn, J. (1995), 'Strategic technology partnering during the 1980's. Trends, networks, and corporate patterns in non-core technologies', *Research Policy*, **24**, 207–31.

Hagedoorn, J. and Narula, R. (1996), 'Choosing organizational modes of strategic technology partnering: interorganizational modes of cooperation and sectorial differences', *Strategic Management Journal*, **14**(5), 371–85.

Hair, J., Anderson, R., Tatham, R. and Black, W. (1998), *Multivariate Data Analysis*, Upper Saddle River, NJ: Prentice Hall International.

Hurley, R.F. and HULT, G.T. (1998), 'Innovation, market orientation and organization learning: an integration and empirical examination', *Journal of Marketing*, **62** (July), 42–54.

Jensen, M.C. and Meckling, W.H. (1976), 'Theory of the firm: managerial behavior, agency costs, and ownership structure', *Journal of Financial Economics*, **3**, 305–60.

Kang, D. (2000), 'The impact or family ownership on perfomance in public organizations: a study of the U.S. Fortune 500, 1982–1994', 2000 Academy of Management Meetings, Toronto, Canada.

Kline, S.J. and Rosenberg, N. (1986), 'An overview of innovation', in R. Landau and N. Rosenberg (eds), *The Positive Sum Strategy: Harnessing Technology for Economic Growth*, Washington, DC: National Academy Press, pp. 275–305.

Lee, P.M. and O'Neil, H.M. (2003), 'Ownership structures and R&D investments of US and Japanese firms: agency and stewardship perspectives', *Academic of Management Journal*, **46**, 212–25.

Litz, R.A. and Kleysen, R.F. (2001), 'Your old men shall dream dreams, young men shall see visions: toward a theory of family firms innovation with help from the Bobbeck family', *Family Business Review*, **14**(4), 335–51.

Mccann, J.E. III, Leon-Guerrero, A.Y. and Haley, J.D. Jr (2001), 'Strategic goals and practices of innovative family businesses', *Journal of Small Business Management*, **39**(1), 50–59.

Mansfield, E. (1981), 'Composition of R&D expenditures, relationship to size of firm, concentration and innovative output', *Review of Economics and Statistics*, vol. 63, 610–615.

Mansfield, E. (1986), 'Patents and innovations: an empirical study', *Management Science*, **32**(2), 173–81.

Mansfield, E., Schwartz, M. and Wagner, S. (1981), 'Imitation costs and patents: an empirical study', *The Economic Journal*, **91**, 907–18.

Miller, D. and Le Breton-Miller, I. (2005), '*Managing for the Long Run: Lessons in Competitive Advantages from Great Family Business*', Boston, MA: Harvard Business School Press.

Miller, D. and Le Breton-Miller, I. (2006), 'Family governance and firm perfomance: agency, stewardship, and capabilities', *Family Business Review*, **19**(1), 73–87.

Moch, M.K. and Morse, E.V. (1997), 'Size, centralization and organizational adoption of innovations', *American Sociological Review*, **42**, 716–25.

Mohr, L.B. (1969), 'Determinants of innovation in organizations'. *American Political Science Review* **63**, 111–26.

Naldi, L., Nordqvist, M., Sjöberg, K. and Wiklund, J. (2007), 'Entrepreneurial orientation, risk taking, and perfomance in family firms', *Family Business Review*, **XX**(1), 33–47.

Narula, R. and Dunning, J. (1997), 'Explaining international R&D alliances and the role of governments', MERIT Working Paper Series 97–011.

Narver, J.C. and Slater, S.F. (1990), 'The effect of a market orientation on business profitability', *Journal of Marketing*, **54**, 20–35.

Nash, J.M. (1988), 'Boards of privately-held companies: their responsibility and structure'. *Family Business Review*, **1**(3), 263–369.

Nelson, R.R. and Winter, S.G. (1977), 'In search of a useful theory of innovation', *Research Policy*, **6**(1), 36–77.

OECD (2002), *Frascati Manual: Proposed Standard Practice for Survey of Research and Experimental Development*, The Measurement of Scientific and Technological Activities, Paris: OECD.

OECD & Eurostat (2005), *Oslo Manual, Guidelines for Collecting and Interpreting Innovation Data*, The measurement of Scientific and Technological Activities, 3rd edn, Paris: OECD and Eurostat.

Pavitt, K. (1984), 'Sectorial patterns of technical change: towards a taxonomy and a theory', *Research Policy*, **13**(6), 343–73.

Porter, M. E. and Stern, S. (1999), 'Measuring the ideas production function: evidence from the international patent output', NBER Working Paper 7891.

Schulze, W.S., Lubatkin, M.H., Dino, R.D. and Buchholtz, A.K. (2001), 'Agency relationships in family firms', *Organization Science*, **12**, 99–116.

Schumpeter, J.A. (1934), *The Theory of Economic Development*, Cambridge, MA: Harvard University Press.

Smith, K. (2005), 'Measuring innovation', in J. Fageberg, D.C. Mowery and R.R. Nelson (eds), *The Oxford Handbook of Innovation*, Oxford: Oxford University Press, pp. 148–77.

Stone, M. (1974), 'Cross-validatory choice and assessment of statistical predictions', *Journal of the Royal Statistical Society*, **36**, 111–47.

Tribo, J.A., Berrone, P. and Surroca, J. (2007), 'Do the type and number of blockholders influence R&D investments? New evidence from Spain', *Corporate Governance: An International Review*, **15**(5), 828–42.

Ward, J.L. (1991), *Creating Effective Boards for Private Enterprises. Meeting the Challenges of Continuity and Competition*, San Francisco, CA: Jossey-Bass.

Westhead, P. and Cowling, M. (1999), 'Family firm research: the need for a methodological rethink', *Entrepreneurship Theory and Practice*, **23**(1), 31–56.

Williamson, O. (1985), 'Corporate Governance: assessing corporate performance by boardroom attributes', *Journal of Business Research*, **6**, 203–20.

Zahra, S.A. (2005), 'Entrepreneurial risk taking in family firms'. *Family Business Review*, **18**, 23–40.

Zahra, S.A. and Pearce, J.A. (1989), 'Boards of directors and corporate financial performance: a review and integrative model', *Journal of Management*, **15**, 291–334.

APPENDIX: VARIABLES

This appendix contains a detailed description of all the variables included in the proposed model.

Variable [ADBEM2] is a Boolean variable that shows if the firm has acquired specific machinery or new equipment to support innovation activities during the period under review.

Variable [AEMP2] is firm's age. This variable takes its different values according to Table 29A.1.

Variable [AID3] is a Boolean variable that shows if the firm has performed R&D activities during the period under review.

Variable [CTCL2] is a Boolean variable that shows if the firm has established cooperation agreements with clients during the period under review.

Variable [CTPR2] is a Boolean variable that shows if the firm has established cooperation agreements with suppliers during the period under review.

Variable [CUCT2] is a Boolean variable that shows if the firm has established cooperation agreements with universities and technological centers.

Variable [DCT2] is a Boolean variable that indicates the presence of an R&D department inside the firm.

Variable [EMPIDT3] is a variable that represents the weight of R&D personnel in relation to the firm's total number of employees, and it takes its different values according to Table 29A.2.

Variable [EMYM2] is a Boolean variable that shows if the firm has carried out market research during the period under review.

Variable [IDV3] is a variable used to represent firm's total expenditure on R&D (both

Table 29A.1   Variable [AEMP2]

Value	Description
0.8	Created before 1940
0.6	From 1940 to 1959
0.4	From 1960 to 1975
0.2	From 1976 to 1985
0.0	1986 and later

Table 29A.2   Variable [EMPIDT3]

Value	R&D personnel
1.0	More than 10%
0.8	Between 5% and 10%
0.6	Between 2% and 5%
0.4	Between 1% and 2%
0.2	Between 0% and 1%
0.0	0%

Table 29A.3   Variable [IDV3]

Value	R&D expenditure
1.0	More than 3% of total income
0.8	Between 2% and 3% of total income
0.6	Between 1% and 2% of total income
0.4	Between 0.5% and 1% of total income
0.2	Between 0% and 0.5% of total income
0.0	0%

Table 29A.4   Variable [MBE2]

Value	Margin
1.00	More than 25%
0.75	Between 15% and 25%
0.50	Between 5% and 15%
0.25	Between 0% and 5%
0.00	0%

internal and external) during the period under review, as a percentage of total income, and it takes its different values according to Table 29A.3.

Variable [IEPCN2] is a Boolean variable that shows if there is identification between ownership and firm's management in the firm.

Variable [IP2] is a Boolean variable that shows if the firm has successfully adopted some product innovations during the period under review.

Variable [IPC3] is used to represent the firm's effort to obtain information about its competitors regarding their prices and/or sales volumes. It takes its value on a scale ranging from 0 (no information) to 1 (detailed and current information about competitors).

Variable [IPR2] is a Boolean variable that shows if the firm has successfully adopted some process innovations during the period under review.

Variable [MBE2] is used to analyze the firm's gross profit margin, according to Table 29A.4.

Variable [PAFAM2] represents the percentage of the firm's employees who are members of the owner family.

Variable [PAI2] is a Boolean variable that shows if the firm has planned in a systematic way its R&D activities during the period under review.

Variable [PATESP3] shows if patents or other types of intellectual property have been granted to the firm during the period under review.

Variable [SICYT2] is a Boolean variable that shows if the firm has carried out scientific and technique information surveillance during the period under review.

Variable [SICYT4] is a Boolean variable that represents the firm's effort to evaluate new technologies and technological change during the period under review, on a scale ranging from 0 to 1.

Table 29A.5   Variable [TEMPRE3]

Value	Description
0.17	Fewer than 20 employees
0.33	Between 21 and 50 employees
0.50	Between 51 and 100 employees
0.67	Between 101 and 200 employees
0.83	Between 201 and 500 employees
1.00	More than 500 employees

Table 29A.6   Variable [VEXPOR3]

Value	Export sales
1.0	More than 40% of total income
0.8	Between 20% and 40% of total income
0.6	Between 10% and 20% of total income
0.4	Between 5% and 10% of total income
0.2	Between 0% and 5% of total income
0.0	0% of total income

Variable [TEMPRE3] is used to represent the firm's size (taking into account the total number of employees), according to Table 29A.5.

Variable [VEXPOR3] is used to represent the firm's export capability, according to Table 29A.6 that depends upon export sales percentage.

30 Acquisition and diversification behaviour in large family firms
Alexandra Dawson and Giovanni Valentini

INTRODUCTION

In this chapter we focus on the acquisition and diversification behaviour of large family firms. A number of conceptual and empirical articles have been written on this topic; however, they have reached contrasting conclusions. For example, Miller et al. (2010) focused on the scale (volume) and scope (diversification) of acquisitions by family firms and found that they acquire less and diversify more than non-family firms. Miller et al. (2010) explained these results by taking into account family firms' business and portfolio risk preferences. However, other studies have reached different conclusions. For example, Gómez-Mejía et al. (2010) concluded that on average family firms diversify less than non-family firms in order to preserve the affect-related value of the firm or socio-emotional wealth.

Based on a sample of 100 of the largest Italian firms, 38 of which are family firms, we find that being a family firm does not affect acquisition propensity, but that this behaviour is linked to other variables such as being public, more profitable, and larger. This finding differs from prior studies (e.g. Miller et al., 2010), most of which have found that family firms acquire less than non-family firms. Furthermore, we find that family firms are more likely to make acquisitions in non-correlated sectors. Prior research on diversification has reached contradictory results; therefore our study is in line with some prior work (e.g. Ducassy and Prevot, 2010; Miller et al., 2010) but not with other work (Gómez-Mejía et al., 2010).

The rest of the chapter is structured as follows. First, we review the literature on acquisitions and diversification by family firms and propose two hypotheses. Second, we present the empirical research design. Third, we illustrate the results of our study. Fourth, we discuss findings in light of recent research. Last, we present concluding remarks, including limitations of our study, future research directions and implications for practitioners.

LITERATURE REVIEW AND HYPOTHESIS DEVELOPMENT

Acquisition Behaviour

The literature presents opposing arguments with regard to acquisition behaviour of family firms. On the one hand, the prevailing view has been based on an agency theory lens. Scholars have argued that concentrated ownership in family firms should reduce the ability of managers to make opportunistic acquisitions, through reduced information asymmetries and greater monitoring by the owners (Jensen, 1986; Miller et al., 2010). There are also other arguments in favour of family firms' reduced acquisition behaviour. Miller et al. (2010) explained the lower acquisition volume by family firms compared to non-family firms through the owning family's business risk preference. Business risk involves identifying and pursuing entrepreneurial opportunities by rearranging existing resources and acquiring new ones in ways that create an advantage. Pursuing such opportunities involves risk because their duration and payoff are difficult to predict (Zahra, 2005). Acquisitions involve taking risks, because they require venturing into the unknown, committing a relatively large portion of assets, and (often) incurring heavy debt (Baird and Thomas, 1985). Family firms frequently have limited human and financial resources, because of their concern for preserving family control and avoiding external monitoring (Schulze et al., 2001). This is expected to lead to risk-averse strategies (Miller et al., 2010) in which acquisitions are avoided because executives are not competent enough, there are insufficient funds, or owners are unwilling to dilute equity (Ward, 2004). Families may also avoid the potential disruption caused by acquisitions because they want to preserve the firm for future generations (Casson, 1999) or maintain the stability of their relationships with suppliers, customers and the local community (Miller and Le Breton-Miller, 2005).

Whilst some scholars have argued – in support of the view presented above – that family firms take fewer risks than non-family firms (see, e.g. Morck and Yeung, 2003; Gómez-Mejía et al., 2007; Naldi et al. 2007), others have maintained that, instead, they are less risk averse (Litz, 1995; Aldrich and Cliff, 2003; Rogoff and Heck, 2003). Memili et al. (2010) found that family ownership positively influences risk taking, because family firm leaders want to grow their business in view of succession and can benefit from flexibility and greater responsiveness to changes in the business environment thanks to centralized decision-making among family members. Zellweger (2007) also argued against the view that high concentration of ownership results in risk-averse strategic behaviour and maintained that long-term-oriented firms, such as family firms, often seek investment projects that are more risky and/or less profitable because they tend to invest in long-term projects, given their interest in transferring the business to future generations (James, 1999). These arguments suggest that family firms might be more engaged in acquisition behaviour.

In this chapter, we take the prevailing view that is based on an agency theory perspective. A majority of studies, not only in the management and entrepreneurship fields, but also in finance, accounting and other social sciences literature, supports this view, according to which family firms are risk averse (Gómez-Mejía et al., 2007). Risky investments, such as acquisitions, can have negative outcomes with significant personal and financial implications for the owning family, which often has an undiversified personal investment portfolio (Eisenmann, 2002; Fama and Jensen, 1983). Therefore,

Hypothesis 1 Family firms are less likely to make corporate acquisitions than non-family firms.

Diversification Behaviour

As with acquisition behaviour, there are also theoretical arguments both for and against diversification by family firms. A firm is diversified when it produces for several markets.

Whilst firms can diversify in several ways, for example developing new business areas internally or engaging in joint ventures with other firms, here we focus on diversification activity that is related to acquisitions (Besanko et al., 2004).

On the one side, there are arguments based on agency theory, according to which there is a negative relationship between the existence of a block of controlling shareholders and the level of diversification (Amihud and Lev, 1981; Berger and Ofek, 1995; Ducassy and Prevot, 2010). Whilst diversification may be advantageous for managers because it allows them to reduce personal risk, develop their reputation and influence, and increase their remuneration (Amihud and Lev, 1981; Jensen, 1986; Shleifer and Vishny, 1986), it may also lead to a reduction in the share value for shareholders (Berger and Ofek, 1995). Several studies have confirmed this view. In their analysis of S&P 500 firms, Anderson and Reeb (2003) considered whether founding families try to reduce firm-specific risk through their diversification decisions. They concluded that family firms experience less diversification than non-family firms. Carney and Gedajlovic (2002) reached similar conclusions in their study of Hong Kong firms, although they suggested that diversification may occur at the level of family estate, or private holding company. Gómez-Mejía et al. (2010) found that family firms diversify less both domestically and internationally than non-family firms. They explained these findings through family firm owners' tendency to preserve the socio-emotional wealth of their firm, that is the non-financial aspects that satisfy family members' affective needs such as preserving the identity, influence and values of the family (Gómez-Mejía et al., 2007). Gómez-Mejía et al. (2010) argued that family firms are willing to accept more concentrated business risk and, therefore, threats to their firm's financial success if this can help them prevent the loss of socio-emotional wealth.

On the other side, there are arguments for greater diversification by family firms. The ownership of the firm's equity often constitutes a significant portion of a family's wealth over the long term, and having a business with a diversified portfolio of assets may reduce risk (Carney and Gedajlovic, 2002; Ward, 2004). As family ownership becomes more dispersed, younger family members may be given different spheres of activity without jeopardizing the core business (Landes, 2006; Ward, 2004) and reducing potential conflict (Carney and Gedajlovic, 2002). Other reasons for diversifying include being able to operate in more dynamic business environments than the existing one (Carney, 2005), and not having to integrate acquired businesses into the core one, thus avoiding potential disruption or conflict (Miller and Le Breton-Miller, 2005). In line with these arguments, Miller et al. (2010) found that family ownership is associated with the diversification of acquisitions and explained it through family owners' desire to reduce portfolio risk by retaining control of their firms for offspring and maintaining their wealth in a concentrated from. Similarly, Ducassy and Prevot (2010) found that French family firms diversify more than non-family firms in order to spread risk across different sectors.

The theory and evidence on diversification are mixed. Here, in line with the first hypothesis presented above, we take the latter view, according to which family firms tend to be risk averse. Therefore;

Hypothesis 2   Family firms are more likely to diversify than non-family firms.

RESEARCH DESIGN

Sample

We tested the two hypotheses on a sample of 100 Italian family firms. We identified the firms using Amadeus, a database of comparable financial information for public and private companies across Europe. First, we ordered all Italian firms by turnover in 2004, the most recent year for which consolidated financial statements were available. Second, we excluded all those companies that operated in the financial intermediation sector, which includes activities such as banking, leasing, insurance and pension funding, because the accounting of this type of business is subject to distinct regulations and their balance sheet structures differ from those of other types of firms.[1] Third, we excluded firms that had any missing financial data, including information on employees, turnover, total assets, cash flow and return on assets (ROA), for the period 2000–2004. Finally, we chose the top 100 firms for which we had complete data. This procedure took us down to position number 229 (Table 30.1).

Variables

After identifying the 100 firms in our sample, we obtained financial and other data from Amadeus. Specifically, we selected the following information:

- Sector, according to the NACE classification, that is the statistical classification of economic activities in the European Union.
- Type of firm: family firm or non-family firm. Following standard criteria in the literature, a firm is considered a family firm if one or more families linked by kinship, close affinity or solid alliances directly or indirectly hold(s) a sufficiently large share of the voting capital to control major decisions. This means that the dominant family (or families) either hold(s) (directly or indirectly) more than 50 per cent of the equity capital or exhibits control over the strategic decisions of the company without possessing a majority of the equity capital, considering all available information, such as the composition of the board, top executives, and voting power (see Astrachan and Shanker, 2003; Corbetta and Minichilli, 2005).
- Foreign capital: if the company is a subsidiary of a foreign corporation or not.
- Quoted: if the company is listed on the Italian market or not.
- Financial data for the time period 2000–2004: number of employees, turnover, total assets, cash flow and return on assets (ROA). We also calculated capital intensity of the company (K/L) as the ratio between total assets (capital) and number of employees (labour).

Source of Information on Acquisitions

All information on acquisitions carried out by the firms in the sample was retrieved from the Zephyr database, which includes deal information on M&A, IPO, private equity and venture capital deals. We included acquisitions in which the acquirer obtained a majority stake in the target firm. Table 30.2 shows the number of acquisitions in each year as well

Table 30.1 Sample of 100 firms used in the study (number indicates position in the Amadeus database by 2004 turnover size) *

1	Eni	4	Enel	6	Enel Distribuzione	7	**Fiat Auto**
9	**Tim**	12	Finmeccanica	13	Poste Italiane	14	**Erg**
18	**Riva Fire**	20	Enel Trade	22	Tamoil Italia	26	**Ilva**
31	**Italcementi**	32	Autogerma	35	**Esselunga**	38	Total Italia
39	Saipem	42	**Api**	43	GS	45	Agipfuel
46	**Mediaset**	49	**Autogrill**	58	**Impregilo**	61	**Buzzi Unicem**
63	Ssc	65	Bmw Italia	68	**Publitalia '80**	69	Lucchini
70	Sma	71	**Rti**	72	Ford Italia	76	Rizzoli
81	Rete Base 2001	82	**Sata**	83	Sevel	85	Pignone
87	**Cremonini**	90	STMicroelectronics	91	Coop Adriatica	92	AEM
93	Citroen Italia	94	**Tel. It. Sparkle**	95	Nestlè Italia	96	**Benetton Group**
97	**Ferrero and Co.**	102	**Mondadori Editore**	106	Hera	107	Michelin Italia
108	Hp Italiana	109	**Mossi and Ghisolfi**	110	**Ferrari**	111	Peugeot Italia
118	**Case New Holland**	123	Iper Montebello	125	**Fiat Powertrain**	127	**Bennet**
130	**Perfetti Van Melle**	134	**Pirelli Pneumatici**	135	Edison Energia	139	**Giorgio Armani**
140	**De Longhi**	143	Mediamarket	144	Benind	148	Shell Italia
149	Lloyd Triestino	154	Asm Brescia	156	**Lottomatica**	157	Sipra
160	Ericsson Telecomunicazioni	162	Agricola 3 Valli	163	Eurospin Italia	164	Comifar Distribuzione
166	Sacmi Coop.	171	Coop Lombardia	172	**L'Espresso**	175	Conad Del Tirreno
177	**Costa Crociere**	179	Unicoop Tirreno	180	Gruppo Coin	181	**Merloni Termosanitari**
183	**Aia**	187	Alcatel Italia	190	**Danieli and Co.**	192	Lucchini Piombino
193	Abbott	200	Aspiag Service	201	GlaxoSmithKline	203	**Bracco**
206	**Davide Campari**	208	Fma	211	**Diesel**	212	Egl Italia
216	Technip Italy	219	Serono	221	Samsung Italia	222	Coop Nordest
223	**Feralpi Holding**	226	Aem Torino	228	Consorzio Coop	229	Gruppo Miroglio

Note: * Family firms are in bold.

Table 30.2   Acquisitions by the firms in the sample, 2001–2004

Year	Number of majority-stake acquisitions	Number (percentage) of acquisitions (100% stake)
2001	19	11 (58)
2002	18	14 (78)
2003	27	20 (74)
2004	13	6 (46)
TOTAL	77	51 (66)

as the number of acquisitions in which 100 per cent of the target firm was purchased (in parentheses is the number of such acquisitions as a percentage of total acquisitions in that year).

We combined the information on acquisitions with the data collected for the 100 firms in the sample. We included two more variables: the geographical origin of the target company (Italian or foreign) and the sector of the acquired company (according to NACE).

RESULTS

Descriptive Analysis

This section contains descriptive statistics on the sample of 100 Italian companies. Table 30.3 includes information on the target firms, by sector (same versus different sector as acquirer) and country (Italian versus foreign). Data show that 56 per cent of target companies are Italian (44 per cent are foreign) and that 62 per cent are in a different sector from the acquirer (38 per cent are in the same sector). When the target company is Italian, there appears to be a tendency to acquire in a different sector, whilst when the target company is foreign, there appears to be a tendency to acquire in the same sector.

We considered whether the acquiring and target firms were family firms or non-family firms and whether they were publicly listed or not (Table 30.4). In the sample, 38 firms (38 per cent) were family firms. Of these, 14 (37 per cent) were listed on the stock market and 24 (63 per cent) were not. Sixty-two firms (62 per cent) in the sample were non-family firms. Of these, 13 (21 per cent) were listed on the stock market and 49 (78 per cent) were not. With regard to subsidiaries, only one was listed on the Italian stock market. Overall, only 27 firms in the sample (27 per cent) were publicly traded (14 family firms and 13 non-family firms).

In terms of sector distribution, two sectors dominate (Table 30.5): wholesale and retail trade/repair of motor vehicles, motorcycles and personal and household goods (26 firms in the sample, or 26 per cent) and real-estate, renting and business activities (12 firms in the sample, or 12 per cent).

In terms of financial data, 41 firms (41 per cent) had turnover that ranged between €1 billion and €2 billion and 29 firms (29 per cent) had turnover below €1 billion (Fig. 30.1).

Family firms in the sample were on average smaller than non-family firms, as indicated

Table 30.3 Characteristics of target firms

	Same sector (%)	Different sector (%)	Total (%)
Italian	10 (13)	33 (43)	43 (56)
Foreign	19 (25)	15 (19)	34 (44)
Total	29 (38)	48 (62)	77 (100)

Table 30.4 Characteristics of acquiring firms

Acquirer		Family firm		Non-family firm	
		Yes	No	Yes	No
Acquirer listed					
Target listed	Yes	0	1	1	19
	No	14	23	12	30
Subtotal		14	24	13	49
Total			38		62

Table 30.5 Sector of acquiring firms

Sector	Number of acquiring firms
Wholesale and retail trade; repair of motor vehicles, motorcycles and personal and household goods	26
Real estate, renting and business activities	12
Transport, storage and communication	6
Manufacture of basic metals and fabricated metal products	5
Manufacture of transport equipment	5
Electricity, gas and water supply	5
Construction	5
Manufacture of food products, beverages and tobacco	4
Manufacture of coke, refined petroleum products and nuclear fuel	4
Manufacture of machinery and equipment	4
Manufacture of electrical and optical equipment	4
Manufacture of chemicals, chemical products and man-made fibres	3
Hotels and restaurants	3
Mining and quarrying of energy producing materials	2
Manufacture of textiles and textile products	2
Manufacture of pulp, paper and paper products; publishing and printing	2
Manufacture of rubber and plastic products	2
Public administration and defence; compulsory social security	2
Other community, social and personal service activities	2
Agriculture, hunting and forestry	1
Manufacture of other non-metallic mineral products	1
Total number of acquiring firms	100

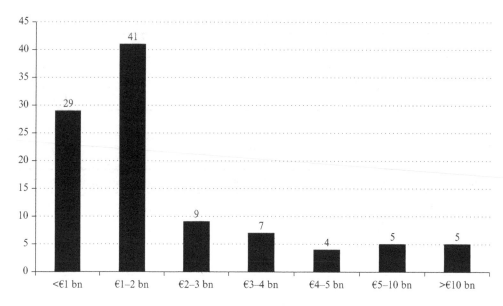

Figure 30.1   Acquiring firms by turnover

Table 30.6   Comparison between family firms and non-family firms

	Family firms	Non-family firms
Average no. of employees	5827	8649
Average turnover (× 1000)	€2439995	€3492677
Average capital intensity (×1000)	€523	€877
Average no. of acquisitions by firm	0.605	0.871

by average turnover, number of employees and capital intensity. They also made fewer acquisitions (see Table 30.6).

Statistical Analysis

In order to test the first hypothesis – whether family firms are less likely to make acquisitions than non-family firms – we used a logit panel data model (for variables, see Table 30.7; we used log-transformed variables for employees, turnover and capital intensity). Table 30.8 shows the results of the regression, which was performed by entering all variables except assets (which was excluded because the variable was highly correlated with turnover).

Results show that the variable *family* is not significant, indicating that family firms are not statistically different from non-family firms in their likelihood to make acquisitions. Thus Hypothesis 1 is rejected.

Four other variables, however, are significant: *listed* (whether the firm is listed on the stock market), *ROA*, number of *employees* and *capital intensity*. This indicates that

Table 30.7 Variables

Label	Values
Acquisition yes/no	0 = no acquisition in a year
	1 = one or more acquisitions in a year
At least one acquisition	0 = no acquisition over entire period
	1 = one or more acquisitions over entire period
Assets	Total assets/liabilities (€)
Cash flow	Cash flow (€)
Sector	0 = no acquisitions
	1 = same sector for acquirer and target
	2 = similar sector for acquirer and target (same first two
	numbers in NACE Rev. 1.1 code)
	3 = different sector for acquirer and target
Employees	Number of employees
Family	0 = non-family firm; 1 = family firm
Turnover	Turnover (€)
Foreigncap	0 = firm without foreign capital
	1 = firm owned by/part of multinational
K/L	Capital intensity measured as capital over labour ratio
	(assets/employees)
Listed	0 = listed on stock exchange; 1 = not listed on stock exchange
Number of acquisitions	Number of acquisitions in a year
ROA	Return on assets (%)
Sector	Sector of acquiring firm
Year	Year of acquisition

Table 30.8 Regression results: likelihood of acquisition

Acquisition yes/no	Coefficient	Standard error	p-value
Cash flow	−0.00007	0.00024	–
Family	0.08965	0.61738	–
Foreigncap	−0.41223	0.92369	–
Listed	1.63470	0.50798	***
ROA	0.10528	0.03764	***
Log employees	1.18055	0.42202	***
Log turnover	−0.53104	0.38527	–
Log K/L	0.88858	0.51157	*
Year dummy	Included		
Sector dummy	Included		
Model significance	**		

Note: $* p < 0.1; ** p < 0.05; *** p < 0.01$.

Table 30.9   Regression results: number of acquisitions

Number of acquisitions	Coefficient	Standard error	*p*-value
Cash flow	−0.00022	0.00015	–
Family	−0.49077	0.54716	–
Foreigncap	−0.05808	0.66656	–
Listed	1.83651	0.45972	***
ROA	0.07909	0.03163	**
Log employees	0.59661	0.18094	***
Log *K/L*	0.67039	0.36980	*
Year dummy	Included		
Sector dummy	Included		
Model significance	***		

Note: * $p < 0.1$; ** $p < 0.05$; *** $p < 0.01$.

publicly quoted firms and larger firms are more likely to make acquisitions, regardless of their ownership.

We also wanted to find out whether firm ownership had an effect on the number of acquisitions made. In order to do so, we used a negative binomial distribution for the panel data described above, seeing that *number of acquisitions* is a discrete variable. Table 30.9 shows the results of this second regression. Once again, the variable *family* is not significant, indicating that ownership does not affect the number of acquisitions made. As previously, variables that are significantly associated with the number of acquisitions are *listed* (whether the firm is listed on the stock market), *ROA*, number of *employees* and *capital intensity*.

Regressions with *family* as the only predictor and *at least one acquisition* as dependent variable did not produce any significant results.

In order to test the second hypothesis – whether family firms are more likely to diversify than non-family firms – we considered the observations in our database for which there had been at least one acquisition and used an ordered probit regression model. As illustrated in Table 30.10, two variables are significant: *foreigncap* and, for the first time, *family*. This indicates that family firms, as well as multinational firms, are more likely to diversify than local firms and non-family firms. Thus Hypothesis 2 is accepted.

DISCUSSION

Our results indicate that family or non-family ownership does not affect the likelihood of making acquisitions, nor the number of acquisitions made. In other words, we did not find family firms to be different from non-family firms in their acquisition behaviour. This result differs from several prior studies, for example Miller et al. (2010).

Instead, what makes a difference, in our sample of firms, is whether the (family or non-family) firm is listed on the stock market and its size. Thus public companies and larger companies are more likely to make acquisitions. Public companies have access to publicly

Table 30.10   Regression results: sector of acquiring and acquired firms

Number of acquisitions	Coefficient	Standard error	p-value
Cash flow	−0.00021	0.00025	–
Family	2.30191	1.25464	*
Foreigncap	2.92842	1.26593	**
Listed	−0.87508	0.68176	–
ROA	−0.04411	0.04352	–
Log employees	0.66728	0.83990	–
Log turnover	−0.96500	0.60161	–
Log K/L	−0.80540	0.96185	–
Year dummy	Included		
Sector dummy	Included		
Model significance	***		

Note: $* p < 0.1; ** p < 0.05; *** p < 0.01.$

traded equity to offer in an acquisition and their managers can benefit from acquisitions, for example by gaining in prestige and by seeing their compensation and perks increase as they manage larger companies (Bargeron et al., 2008). Furthermore, public companies have non-family managers and board members with business skills and external networks that can make acquisitions more likely (Blumentritt et al., 2007; Hillman and Dalziel, 2003). Larger firm are more likely to make acquisitions thanks to their greater resources and assets. Firm size is associated with the use of multiple financial institutions, access to debt and the employment of diverse financial products (Gallo and Vilaseca, 1996; Romano et al., 2000). Thus these conditions, rather than the type of ownership, are associated with acquisition behaviour.

Where we did find family firms to be significantly different from non-family firms is in their diversification behaviour. Our results suggest that family firms are more risk averse than non-family firms, as indicated by their tendency to make their acquisitions in unrelated sectors. This confirms that family firms try to protect the family wealth by spreading the portfolio of assets (Carney and Gedajlovic, 2002).

Three key considerations emerge from this study. First, our sample includes private and public firms, unlike several other studies which have focused solely on public companies. In order to get a better picture of the population of family firms, it is appropriate also to take into account private firms (Shanker and Astrachan, 1996), many of which avoid becoming listed. Furthermore, our definition of family firm – that is, a firm in which the family holds more than 50 per cent of the equity capital or exhibits control over the strategic decisions of the company without possessing a majority of the equity capital – allows us to capture a sample that is representative of family firms in which family members are involved in owning and running the business (Miller et al., 2008).

Second, our study suggests that acquisition behaviour is associated not with ownership of the firm (family or non-family) but with size. Again, this can be explained by our choice of sample. Whereas in other studies non-family firms were on average two times larger than non-family firms – see, for example, Anderson and Reeb (2003) for their US-based comparison of family and non-family firms, and Ducassy and Prevot (2010) for their French-based study – in our sample the two types of firms are closer in size (non-family firms are 40 per cent larger by turnover than family firms). Therefore our choice of sample should allow us to capture differences in ownership rather than differences in size, which may have been at play in prior studies, explaining why we do not find differences in acquisition behaviour between family and non-family firms. This implies that larger family firms engage in acquisition behaviour in order to continue building and growing the business. Thanks to their entrepreneurial spirit, these firms are proactive and innovative, thereby playing an important role in employment creation, technological innovation and economic progress (Miller, 1983; Zahra, 2005; Zahra et al., 2004). They do so regardless of family or non-family ownership; in other words these firms behave as large firms and not as family (or non-family) firms.

Third, we find that, when they do acquire, family firms are more risk averse than non-family firms and we see this because they diversify more. Previous studies help explain this. George et al. (2005) observed that internal owners are more risk averse than external owners, such as venture capitalists and institutional investors. Naldi et al. (2007) concluded that, although family firms may take risks while engaged in entrepreneurial activities, they take fewer risks than non-family firms. Our finding is in line with Miller et al. (2010), who explained the tendency to diversify more through family owners' desire to reduce portfolio risk. Our finding may also be influenced by the national context. In their study of French firms, Ducassy and Prevot (2010) attributed their finding that family firms diversify more than non-family firms to the civil-law legal system that characterizes much of Western European countries, including Italy. Unlike the USA or the UK, this is associated with relatively poor protection of minority shareholders, concentrated ownership, presence of large family shareholders in public firms (Faccio and Lang, 2002; La Porta et al., 1999; Sraer and Thesmar, 2007). These external conditions may induce family firms to be more risk averse in their acquisitions by spreading risk across different sectors.

CONCLUDING REMARKS

The acquisition and diversification behaviour of family firms is receiving a great deal of scholarly attention, as witnessed by several recent studies (e.g. Gómez-Mejía et al., 2010; Miller et al., 2010). However, whilst most studies, which have been based on agency theory, have concluded that family firms make fewer acquisitions than non-family firms – see, for example, Miller et al., 2010 – studies about diversification behaviour have been less conclusive – for example, Miller et al. (2010) found that family firms diversify more than non-family firms, whereas Gómez-Mejía et al. (2010) found the opposite. This study contributes to extending research on family firms. In particular, we have analysed the acquisition and diversification behaviour of large family firms. In line with some previous studies, we hypothesized that family firms acquire less and diversify more than non-family firms because they are more risk averse. This is because they have limited human and financial resources, want to preserve family control for future generations, avoid external monitoring, and maintain the stability of their relationships with suppliers, customers and the local community (Casson, 1999; Miller and Le Breton-Miller, 2005;

Schulze et al., 2001; Ward, 2004). Our sample consisted of 100 of the largest Italian firms for the period 2000–2004. These firms, 38 per cent of which were family firms, carried out a total of 77 acquisitions over the period. Unlike previous studies, we considered both private and public firms, which are more representative of the population of family firms. We found that family or non-family ownership does not affect acquisition propensity, but that this propensity is linked to other variables such as being larger and more profitable, as well as being publicly listed. Therefore our study suggests that size, rather than ownership, is associated with acquisition behaviour. Furthermore, we found that family firms are more likely to make acquisitions in non-correlated sectors, indicating that they are more risk averse than non-family firms.

This study has limitations, which can also indicate future research opportunities. First, we limited our analysis to large firms. Whilst this offers the advantage of allowing greater access to financial information, it would be interesting to extend the analysis to small and medium family firms in order to generalize our results. Second, our sample focuses on one country. Whilst most studies suffer from the same limitation, cross-country studies would enable researchers to identify whether individual countries have specificities in terms of acquisition or diversification behaviour. Indeed, previous studies have suggested that national context may matter, as indicated above (Ducassy and Prevot, 2010).

Future research should also take into account further factors reflecting the fact that family firms are not a homogeneous group of firms (Westhead and Howorth 2007), allowing us to deepen our understanding of their acquisition and diversification behaviour. For example, Miller et al. (2010) considered degrees of family ownership and found that the percentage of equity held by family members is inversely related to the number and dollar volume of acquisitions. Other studies have also taken into account different generations controlling the family firm (e.g. Cater and Justis, 2009; Cruz and Nordqvist, 2012). Finally, future studies should also consider the role of the external environment. For example, Casillas et al. (2010) found that, in hostile environments, family firms become less risk averse, and Schulze et al. (2003) concluded that, during periods of high growth, family boards are more willing to use debt when ownership is either concentrated in the hands of a controlling owner or dispersed among many owners (as in a cousin consortium), and less willing to use debt when ownership is divided into similar proportions (as in a sibling partnership).

With regard to family firm practitioners, this study indicates that family firms' acquisition behaviour is not associated with the type of ownership. Therefore strategies and policies aimed at encouraging family firms to grow, engage in activities that can increase profitability, and improve the likelihood of becoming public would be in a better position to encourage acquisition behaviour. Our study also suggests that diversification behaviour is associated with risk aversion, which may be explained by national context. This may be partly a cultural factor, and partly explained by the level of protection of minority shareholders. Policy makers may want to address this, seeing that diversification requires greater managerial complexity with different resources and competences (Ducassy and Prevot, 2010; Markides and Williamson, 1994), which may actually increase the risk that family firms are engaging in.

NOTE

1. We used the statistical classification of economic activities in the European Union, abbreviated as NACE (derived from the French *Nomenclature statistique des activités économiques dans la Communauté européenne*). In this study, we adopted the NACE Rev 1.1 classification (a revised version of the classification, introduced in 2002).

REFERENCES

Aldrich, H.E. and Cliff, J.E. (2003), 'The pervasive effects of family on entrepreneurship: toward a family embeddedness perspective', *Journal of Business Venturing*, **18**(5), 573–96.

Amihud, Y. and Lev, B. (1981), 'Risk reduction as a managerial motive for conglomerate mergers', *Bell Journal of Economics*, **12**, 605–17.

Anderson, R.C. and Reeb, D.M. (2003), 'Founding-family ownership, corporate diversification, and firm leverage', *Journal of Law & Economics*, **46**(2), 653–80.

Astrachan, J.H. and Shanker, M.C. (2003), 'Family businesses' contribution to the U.S. economy: a closer look'. *Family Business Review*, **16**(3), 211–19.

Baird, I.S. and Thomas, H. (1985), 'Toward a contingency model of strategic risk taking', *Academy of Management Reviews*, **10**(2), 230–43.

Bargeron, L.L., Schlingemann, F.P., Stulz, R.M. and Zutter, C.J. (2008), 'Why do private acquirers pay so little compared to public acquirers?', *Journal of Financial Economics*, **9**(3), 375–90.

Berger, P.G. and Ofek, E. (1995), 'Diversification's effect on firm value', *Journal of Financial Economics*, **37**(1), 39–65.

Besanko, D., Dranove, D., Shanley, M. and Schaefer (2004), *Economics of Strategy*, New York: Wiley.

Blumentritt, T.P., Keyt, A.D. and Astrachan, J.H. (2007), 'Creating an environment for successful non-family CEOs: an exploratory study of good principles', *Family Business Review*, **20**, 321–55.

Carney, M. (2005), 'Corporate governance and competitive advantage in family-controlled firms', *Entrepreneurship Theory and Practice*, **29**(3), 249–65.

Carney, M. and Gedajlovic, E. (2002), 'The coupling of ownership and control and the allocation of financial resources: evidence from Hong Kong', *Journal of Management Studies*, **39**(1), 123–46.

Casillas, J.C., Moreno, A.M. and Barbero, J.L. (2010), 'A configurational approach of the relationship between entrepreneurial orientation and growth of family firms', *Family Business Review*, **23**(1), 27–44.

Casson, M. (1999), 'The economics of the family firm', *Scandinavian Economics History Review*, **47**, 10–23.

Cater, J.J. and Justis, R.T. (2009), 'The development of successors from followers to leaders in small family firms', *Family Business Review*, **22**(2), 109–24.

Corbetta, G. and Minichilli, A. (2005), 'Il governo delle imprese italiane quotate a controllo familiare: i risultati di una ricerca esplorativa'. *Economia & Management*, **6**, 59–77.

Cruz, C. and Nordqvist, M. (2012), 'Entrepreneurial orientation in family firms: a generational perspective', *Small Business Economics*, **38**(1), 33–49.

Ducassy, I. and Prevot, F. (2010), 'The effects of family dynamics on diversification strategy: empirical evidence from French companies', *Journal of Family Business Strategy*, **1**(4), 224–35.

Eisenmann, T.R. (2002), 'The effects of CEO equity ownership and firm diversification on risk taking', *Strategic Management Journal*, **23**(6), 513–34.

Faccio, M. and Lang, M.H.P. (2002), 'The ultimate ownership of Western European corporations', *Journal of Financial Economics*, **65**(3), 365–95.

Fama, E.F. and Jensen, M.C. (1983), 'Separation of ownership and control', *Journal of Law and Economics*, **26**, 301–25.

Gallo, M.A. and Vilaseca, A. (1996), 'Finance in family business', *Family Business Review*, **9**(4), 387–401.

George, G., Wiklund, J. and Zahra, S.A. (2005), 'Ownership and the internationalization of small firms', *Journal of Management*, **31**(2), 210–33.

Gómez-Mejía, L., Haynes, K., Nez-Nickel, M., Jacobson, K. and, Moyano-Fuentes, J. (2007), 'Socioemotional wealth and business risks in family-controlled firms: evidence from Spanish olive oil mills', *Administrative Science Quarterly*, **52**(1), 106–37.

Gómez-Mejía, L., Makri, M. and Kintana, M. L. (2010), 'Diversification decisions in family-controlled firms', *Journal of Management Studies*, **47**(2), 223–52.

Hillman, A.J. and Dalziel, T. (2003), 'Boards of directors and firm performance: integrating agency and resource dependence perspectives', *Academy of Management Review*, **28**(3), 383–96.

James, H.S. (1999), 'Owners as manager, extended horizons and the family firm', *International Journal of the Economics of Business*, **6**(1), 41–55.

Jensen, M.C. (1986), 'Agency costs of free cash flow, corporate finance and takeovers', *American Economic Review*, **76**, 323–9.

Landes, D. (2006), *Dynasties: Fortunes and Misfortunes of the World's Great Family Businesses*, New York: Viking.

La Porta, R., Lopez-de-Silanes, F. and Shleifer, A. (1999), 'Corporate ownership around the world', *Journal of Finance*, **54**, 471–517.

Litz, R.A. (1995), 'The family business: toward definitional clarity', *Family Business Review*, **8**(2), 71–81.

Markides, C. and Williamson, P. (1994), 'Related diversification, core competences and corporate performance', *Strategic Management Journal*, **15**, 149–65.

Memili, E., Eddleston, K.A., Kellermanns, F.W., Zellweger, T.M. and Barnett, T. (2010), 'The critical path to family firm success through entrepreneurial risk taking and image', *Journal of Family Business Strategy*, **1**(4), 200–209.

Miller, D. (1983), 'The correlates of entrepreneurship in three types of firms', *Management Science*, **29**, 770–91.

Miller, D. and Le-Breton-Miller, I. (2005), *Managing for the Long Run: Lessons in Competitive Advantage from Great Family Businesses*, Boston, MA: Harvard Business School Press.

Miller, D., Le Breton-Miller, I. and Scholnick, B. (2008), 'Stewardship vs. stagnation: an empirical comparison of small family and non-family businesses', *Journal of Management Studies*, **45**(1), 51–78.

Miller, D., Le Breton-Miller, I. and Lester, R. (2010), 'Family ownership and acquisition behaviour in publicly-traded companies', *Strategic Management Journal*, **31**(2), 201–23.

Morck, R. and Yeung, B. (2003), 'Agency problems in large family business groups', *Entrepreneurship Theory and Practice*, **27**(4), 367–82.

Naldi, L., Nordqvist, M., Sjöberg, K. and Wiklund, J. (2007), 'Entrepreneurial orientation, risk taking, and performance in family firms', *Family Business Review*, **20**(1), 33–47.

Rogoff, E.G. and Heck, R.K.Z. (2003), 'Evolving research in entrepreneurship and family business: recognizing family as the oxygen that feeds the fire of entrepreneurship', *Journal of Business Venturing*, **18**(5), 559–66.

Romano, C.A., Tanewski, G.A. and Smyrnios, K.X. (2000), 'Capital structure decision making: a model for family business', *Family Business Review*, **16**, 285–310.

Schulze, W.S., Lubatkin, M.H. and Dino, R.N. (2003), 'Exploring the agency consequences of ownership dispersion among the directors of private firms', *Academy of Management Journal*, **46**(2), 179–94.

Schulze, W.S., Lubatkin, M.H., Dino, R.N. and Buchholtz, A.K. (2001), 'Agency relationships in family firms: theory and evidence', *Organization Science*, **12**(2), 99–116.

Shanker, M.C. and Astrachan, J.H. (1996), 'Myths and realities: family businesses' contribution to the U.S. economy. A framework for assessing family business statistics', *Family Business Review*, **9**(2), 107–23.

Shleifer, A. and Vishny, R. (1986), 'Large shareholders and corporate control', *Journal of Political Economy*, **94**, 461–88.

Sraer, D. and Thesmar, D. (2007), 'Performance and behaviour of family firms: evidence from the French stock market', *Journal of the European Economic Association*, **5**(4), 709–51.

Ward, J. (2004), *Perpetuating the Family Business*, Marietta, GA: Family Enterprise Publishers.

Westhead, P. and Howorth, C. (2007), '"Types" of private family firms: an exploratory conceptual and empirical analysis', *Entrepreneurship & Regional Development*, **19**, 405–31.

Zahra, S.A. (2005), 'Entrepreneurial risk taking in family firms', *Family Business Review*, **18**(1), 23–40.

Zahra, S.A., Hayton, J.C. and Salvato, C. (2004), 'Entrepreneurship in family vs. non-family firms: a resource-based analysis of the effect of organizational culture', *Entrepreneurship Theory and Practice*, **28**(4), 363–81.

Zellweger, T. (2007), 'Time horizon, costs of equity capital, and generic investment strategies of firms', *Family Business Review*, **20**(1), 1–15.

31 Emotional dimensions within the family business: towards a conceptualization
Rania Labaki, Nava Michael-Tsabari and Ramona Kay Zachary

INTRODUCTION

For over two decades, there has been a growing research interest in the role of emotions in organizations (Rafaeli et al., 2007; Rafaeli and Sutton, 1987). Emotions have been found to influence critical organizational outcomes such as job performance, decision-making, creativity, turnover, prosocial behavior, teamwork, negotiation and leadership (Barsade and Gibson, 2007), to the degree that recently scholars referred to an 'affective revolution' taking place in organizational behavior (Barsade et al., 2003).

In the family business field, emotions were mainly attributed to the family system (Carlock and Ward, 2001; Fleming, 2000; Kepner, 1983; Whiteside and Brown, 1991), which is the least studied part of the family business phenomena (Dyer, 2003; Rogoff and Heck, 2003). But in recent years, more and more scholars have called for the study of emotions within the family business (Astrachan and Jaskiewicz, 2008; Brundin, Florin-Samuelsson and Melin, 2008; Van den Heuval et al., 2007) and suggested their own emotional constructs specific to the family business, such as emotional ownership (Bjornberg and Nicholson, 2008), family and business emotional cohesion (Pieper, 2007), emotional returns and costs (Astrachan and Jaskiewicz, 2008), and emotional value (Zellweger and Astrachan, 2008). By limiting the analysis to their own constructs, scholars restrict generalizability of their findings and add to the complexity and confusion of the notion of emotions in the family business field. In addition, at the opposite of the organizational behavior field, emotions in the family business field have been mainly studied from the family point of view (Carlock and Ward, 2001), whereas the business is also a highly emotional arena.

To overcome these gaps in research, our chapter aims to offer a comprehensive framework for studying emotions in the family business. We look systematically at the relevance of studying emotions in family businesses and enhance our understanding of their influence in the family business context. We wish to set the ground for future studies on emotions by presenting a first analytical literature review that establishes the theoretical scope, constructs and definitions of emotions in this field. Our state-of-the-art review captures the contributions and limitations of the main research studies on emotions in the family business as presented in Table 31.1.

We maintain that a systems view is necessary to understand the emotions rooted in each family and business system as well as their interfaces and their evolution from one system to another. We propose using Bowen's family systems theory, the social exchange theory and the emotional dissonance theory as possible and appropriate theoretical frameworks to study emotions in the family business. In addition, we contribute to the

Table 31.1   *Research studies on emotions within the family business field*

Citation	Type of paper	Subsystem	Type of emotion	Samples	Hypotheses	Findings
			The family system			
(1) Sharma (2004)	Theoretical	Family	Emotional capital	N/A	N/A	Typology of 4 types of family businesses along the family and the business axis: low/high emotional capital – low/high financial capital
(2) Kets de Vries et al. (2007)	Theoretical	Family	N/A	N/A	N/A	N/A
(3) Brundin and Sharma (2010)	Theoretical – conference paper	Family	Emotional messiness	N/A	N/A	Suggested construct of emotional messiness caused by different charged events or issues
			The family and business systems			
(4) Pieper (2007)	Dissertation, qualitative	Family + business (ownership)	Family emotional cohesion and business emotional cohesion	8 multi-generational family businesses in Germany	N/A	4 types of cohesion mechanisms to assure longevity of FB: family/business emotional cohesion and family/business financial cohesion
(5) Bjornberg and Nicholson (2008)	Empirical	Family + business (ownership)	Emotional ownership (EO)	600 next-generation members from 67 countries	N/A	EO comes from involvement and personal career investment in the business, an adaptive flexible family, having support structures. EO is culturally and gender influenced

Table 31.1 (continued)

Citation	Type of paper	Subsystem	Type of emotion	Samples	Hypotheses	Findings
The family and business systems (continued)						
(6) Pieper and Astrachan (2008)	Theoretical	Family + business (ownership)	Family emotional cohesion and business emotional cohesion	N/A	N/A	N/A
(7) Collins et al. (2010)	Theoretical – conference paper	Family + business	Emotional labor	Emotional labor in a well-known UK family business	N/A	N/A
The business system						
(8) Goss (2005)	Theoretical	Business (entrepren-eurship)	Emotional energy	N/A	N/A	N/A
(9) Brundin and Melin (2006)	Empirical	Business	Confidence and frustration, emotional energy	2 in-depth field studies with 2 CEOs of private SMEs	Emotions and display of emotions influence strategizing	Emotions can work either as driving or as counteracting forces in strategizing; the crucial point is whether the emotions experienced and displayed conform
(10) Brundin et al. (2008)	Empirical	Business	Displayed emotions: frustration, worry, bewilderment, confidence and satisfaction	91 employees from 31 small firms	Emotions displayed by managers influence employees' willingness to act entrepreneurially	Managers' displays of confidence and satisfaction enhance employees' willingness to act entrepreneurially while displays of frust-ration, worry and bewil-derment diminish it

736

	Type	Field	Concept	Sample	Finding	Detail
(11) Goss (2007)	Theoretical	Business (entrepreneurship)	Emotional energy (EE)	N/A	N/A	A model that encompasses social interaction, emotion and cognition to explain entrepreneurial behavior, especially in the family firm
(12) Gómez-Mejía et al. (2007)	Empirical	Business (ownership)	Socio-emotional wealth	1237 Spanish family-owned olive oil firms, during 1944–88	To avoid losing their socio-emotional wealth, family firms are willing to accept a significant risk to their performance, yet avoid risky business decisions that might aggravate the risk	To avoid losing their socio-emotional wealth, family firms are willing to accept a significant risk to their performance, yet avoid risky business decisions that might aggravate the risk
(13) Van den Heuvel et al. (2007)	Empirical – conference paper	Business	Empathy	191 family member CEOs of Belgian and Dutch SMEs	The higher the family CEO's empathy level, the more importance he will place on family-oriented goals; the presence of an external board attenuates this relationship	Family CEO's level of empathic concern has a positive influence on the importance of family-oriented goals, but the presence of an external board attenuates this relationship
(14) Brundin et al. (2008)	Theoretical – conference paper	Business (ownership)	Emotions	N/A	N/A	N/A
(15) Brundin and Nordqvist (2008)	Empirical	Business	Emotions, emotional energy	A case study of a Swedish privately held firm	Emotions play a role in boardroom dynamics	Emotions are sources of energy that play a role depending on the interpretations that board members assign to them. Emotions can be viewed as long term and have an impact as power and status energizers

737

Table 31.1 (continued)

Citation	Type of paper	Subsystem	Type of emotion	Samples	Hypotheses	Findings
			The business system (continued)			
(16) Danes et al. (2008)	Theoretical	Family/business/ community	Emotional capital	N/A	N/A	N/A
(17) Zellweger et al. (2008)	Empirical – conference paper	Business (ownership)	Socioemotional wealth	69 CEOs of Swiss family firms	There is a positive relationship between the desire for transgenerational sustainability of the firm and the family owner's valuation of the firm	Transgenerational sustainability expectations influence the CEO's valuations of firm value
(18) Zellweger and Astrachan (2008)	Theoretical	Business (ownership)	Emotional value (EV), emotional costs and emotional benefits	N/A	N/A	N/A
(19) Astrachan and Jaskiewicz (2008)	Theoretical	Business (ownership)	Emotional costs (EC) and emotional returns (ER)	N/A	N/A	N/A
(20) Cardon et al. (2005, 2009)	Theoretical	Business (entrepre- neurship)	Passion	N/A	N/A	General framework of passion in entrepreneurship

738

	Type	Field	Construct	Sample	Focus	Findings
(21) Zampetakis et al. (2009)	Empirical	Business (entrepre-neurship)	Emotional intelligence (EI)	280 undergraduate students	Relationships among EI, creativity, proactivity and attitudes towards entrepreneurship and entrepreneurial intent	Creativity and proactivity fully mediated the positive effect of trait EI on attitudes towards entrepreneurship. Attitudes towards entrepreneurship fully mediated the effects of creativity and proactivity on entrepreneurial intent
(22) Pachulia and Henderson (2009)	Empirical – unpublished thesis	Business	Emotional intelligence (EI)	35 owner-managers of small Swedish high-tech industry	Owner's EI can predict entrepreneurial orientation (EI)	Hypothesis rejected

existing literature on emotions and organizational behavior because we suggest transposing existing theoretical frameworks from the organizational behavior field to the family business field on the one hand, and on the other hand, enriching the theories of emotions by shedding light on an original and complex organizational setting, that is the family business.

The chapter opens with an introduction to emotions in general and looks at the relevance of studying emotions in the family business from both a systems and a dynamic perspective. It then presents a critical overview of the family business literature on emotions and builds on selected theories in the social sciences field while highlighting their potential contributions to the family business field. This leads to focusing the analysis on emotional evolvement (EE) throughout the stages of the family business life span with a series of suggested propositions. Finally, the chapter concludes with the implications, limitations and future research orientations that derive from our analysis.

THE NATURE OF EMOTIONS: CONCEPTS AND DEFINITIONS

'What is an emotion?' (James, 1884) – this question was first formulated in the psychology field by William James over a hundred years ago and is still a current issue for the research community. Indeed, the first challenge researchers have to face when dealing with emotions is that of delineating their content and boundaries. Despite the conceptual debate among different disciplines – mainly philosophy, psychology and neurobiology – a consensus exists regarding the complexity of emotions.

Etymologically speaking, 'emotion' is derived from Latin *emovēre*, to remove or displace, and from Middle French, *émouvoir*, to stir up. Emotions thus emerge because of a stimulus. Among general definitions, *The Merriam Webster Dictionary* defines emotion as a state of feeling or a conscious mental reaction (such as anger or fear), subjectively experienced as strong feeling, usually directed toward a specific object, and typically accompanied by physiological and behavioral changes in the body.

Several terms have been often used to refer to emotions. Affect is a general term that encompasses a wide range of discrete emotions, moods and negative or positive dispositional affects (Barsade and Gibson, 2007). These terms differ in the way they relate to different dimensions such as intensity, physiological, cognitive or behavioral expressions, duration, cause and complexity. Emotions are elicited by a specific target or cause, often include physiological dimensions and action sequences, and are relatively intense and short lived (Frijda, 1986; Lazarus, 1991). Moods are more diffuse, take the form of a general positive or negative feeling, and tend not to be focused on a particular cause (Frijda, 1986; Tellegen, 1985). Dispositional affect is a personality trait referring to a person's relatively stable, underlying tendency to experience positive and negative moods and emotions (Watson and Petre, 1990).

Primary emotions can be perceived as being discrete, including joy, love, anger, fear, sadness, disgust and surprise, but their precise number and identity varies among scholars (Barsade and Gibson, 2007). Moods and dispositional affects are however often defined on a continuum, such as along two main axes of pleasant or unpleasant and high- or -low-energy attributes (Russell, 1980).

The range of approaches to define and study emotions in organizations is wide

(Barsade and Gibson, 2007) and beyond the scope of this chapter. Three main levels of analysis of emotions can be distinguished. Whereas the research focus was primarily on the antecedents and consequences of individual affect, only scarce research focused on emotions on the interpersonal level (Hareli and Rafaeli, 2008; Rafaeli et al., 2007). The collective level of emotion in work groups or in organizations was defined as combinations of individual-level affective factors that group members possess as well as group or contextual-level factors that define or shape the affective experience of the group (Kelly and Barsade, 2001).

Hence, there are three main directions of research on emotions: meta concepts such as emotional intelligence; regulation of individual emotions; and group emotion (Barsade and Gibson, 2007). We will now look at the study of emotions in the family business field so far. We will address the subject of emotions by looking at its relevance to family businesses, critically reviewing all the literature that has dealt with it so far and suggesting new directions for future studies.

THE RELEVANCE OF EMOTIONS TO THE STUDY OF FAMILY BUSINESS

Emotions have gained only little attention in family business studies. Although most researchers distinguish family businesses from their non-family counterparts based on the family component, only few researchers explicitly included emotional characteristics of the family in their family business definition (Carsrud, 1994). In addition, most studies used to attribute emotions to the family rather than to the business system (Carlock and Ward, 2001; Fleming, 2000; Kepner, 1983; Whiteside and Brown, 1991), although an emotional relationship exists between the family members and their business (Shepherd, 2003). It is therefore important to enlarge our understanding of emotions in the family business by exploring how the family business literature deals with emotions in each of the family and business systems.

We build upon the premise according to which both the family and the business are emotional and rational organizations to a certain extent. We do not link *a priori* emotion to the family and rationality to the business, although we observe that the family business literature predominantly does so. As Steier (2003) notes, exchange in the family rarely has a pure economic motive and, as a consequence, leads to behavior that differs from 'pure economic rationality' in the sense of Simon (1955). We believe in the same vein as Steier (2003) in a continuum of family altruistic rationality and business economic rationality that makes it possible to position each system, especially as they differ according to the cultural setting. The family can thus be sometimes viewed as a long-term institution that grants economic survival rather than a nexus of emotional well-being.

The dual approach to the family business that was dominant in earlier literature describes a model of two separate entities of business and family in terms of structure, goals and tasks (Carlock and Ward, 2001; Tagiuri and Davis, 1996; Whiteside and Brown, 1991). This duality tends to encourage contrast and radicalization of the two systems' characteristics, and supports the stereotypical view of each (Whiteside and Brown, 1991). This shows itself in definitions such as '[A] family business is a unique form of business organization since it involves the overlap of a system structured on rational economic principles with a system organized and driven by emotions' (Kets-de-Vries et al., 2007, p. 26).

The identification of the family as an organization with emotional characteristics influenced the earlier approaches seeking to separate the family from the business operations in the name of 'right' and 'professional' management while the family was seen as contributing to the 'irrationality' of the business function (Denison et al., 2004; Hollander and Elman, 1988; Kepner, 1983; Nordqvist, 2005; Whiteside and Brown, 1991). As stated by Whiteside and Brown (1991, p. 384), 'Since the purpose of business was to be logical and profit making, the emotional aspects of the family were an interference that needed to be excluded'. Hollander and Elman (1988, p. 146) noted: 'Many writers . . . advocated placing the firm's interests before the family's interests and condemned family emotional processes as the prime source of contamination'. This may imply that up until recently the family business field, with its focus on the business subsystem (Chua et al., 2003; Dyer, 2003), referred to emotions mainly as the opposite of finance (Astrachan and Jaskiewicz, 2008; Zellweger and Astrachan, 2008), as being irrational (Hollander and Elman, 1988), as having a possibly negative influence on the family business as a whole (Astrachan and Jaskiewicz, 2008; Brundin, Florin-Samuelsson, and Melin, 2008; Hollander and Elman, 1988), and did not look into their characteristics and mechanisms.

Emotions may be considered as part of the family's resources according to Hobfoll's definition used by Danes et al.: '[O]bjects, personal characteristics, conditions, or energies that are valued in their own right, or that are valued because they act as conduits to the protection or achievement of valued goals (Hobfoll, 1989)' (Danes et al., 2008, p. 246).

Two contributions within the family business field in recent years led to a change in the way emotions are perceived: moving from a dual to a holistic view of the family firm (Pieper and Klein, 2007), and empirical findings showing that the family influences the financial performance of the family business (Anderson and Reeb, 2003; Olson et al., 2003; Villalonga and Amit, 2006). This has allowed for a change in the conceptual and theoretical approaches of family businesses, while occurring simultaneously with the rise of interest in emotions in the more general organizational behavior literature.

In updated models like the sustainable family business theory (SFBT), the family and the business are equal and overlapping systems moving simultaneously towards mutual existence, when success in one system leads to success in the other, and in the same way problems or changes in one manifest in problems or changes in the other (Danes et al., 2008; Heck et al., 2006). The mechanisms of the family that might 'carry' emotions apply also to the business in terms of roles, rules, and/or forms of social and human capital.

The second contribution concerns the influence of the business family on the organization. Studies that show that family businesses financially outperform non-family businesses (Anderson and Reeb, 2003; Villalonga and Amit, 2006) highlight a series of competitive advantages. This leads to new definitions valuing for the first time non-economic components (Chrisman et al., 2003). The concept of familiness is presented as the unique bundle of resources a family business has due to systematic interaction between the family, the individuals constituting it, and the business (Chrisman et al., 2003; Habbershon et al., 2006; Habbershon and Williams, 1999). It has received significant attention from family business scholars trying to understand its components and essence (Sharma, 2008). Current studies define familiness as a positive influence of family involvement in the firm, but their scope of analysis is restricted to social capital theory and constructs (Ensley and Pearson, 2005), the resource-based view (RBV) (Irava, 2009), and organizational identity theory (Zellweger et al., 2010) while excluding existing theories on emotions.

Although there was a risk that it might become an obscure umbrella concept, at this point in time familiness is seen as a combination of social, human, financial and physical capital resources resulting from interactions between family and business systems (Ensley and Pearson, 2005; Habbershon and Williams, 1999; Sharma, 2008). Emotions would therefore be part of the human capital: '[H]uman capital refers to the knowledge, technical abilities, emotional strength or carrying capability, and intellectual capital of family and nonfamily members' (Sharma, 2008, p. 974).

We will look into emotions within the family and the business systems and their interfaces – the influences that may transfer from one system into another – and the context of the family business as a whole encompassing its environment (Pieper and Klein, 2007). Ownership includes the family and/or non family members that own the business while the family system includes all family members. We consider therefore ownership issues as part of the business system.

THE FAMILY SYSTEM

Definition

Many scholars recognize the controversy surrounding the definition of the 'family' in general (Walsh, 2003), and the lack of clarity regarding the family in business in particular (Winter et al., 1998). Only few family business scholars have presented a definition of 'the family' in their research (Klein, 2000; Winter et al., 1998). Building on a literature review of basic definitions in multiple disciplinary fields (Labaki, 1999, pp. 14–19), we suggest viewing the family as 'a group of people related by blood, alliance and adoption' while maintaining that its relationships characteristics are not only financial, political and informational, but also emotional (Labaki, 2005).

Current State of Family Business Literature

The family remains the missing variable in family business research (Dyer, 2003; Rogoff and Heck, 2003). In particular, the dynamics and characteristics of the family that owns the business have been only little researched (Chua et al., 2003; Dyer, 2003; Winter et al., 1998). When researchers do refer to the family, the majority look at the influence of the family on the business rather than the characteristics of the family itself (Kepner, 1983; Rogoff and Heck, 2003; Sten, 2007; Uhlaner, 2006).

Every family business reflects the family behind it; hence no family business can be understood without understanding its family (Fukuyama, 1999). Emotions play an important role in describing the healthy business family (Fukuyama, 1999). While most research on emotions in the family business is based on anecdotal evidence, we could not find a direct study of the business family's emotions in the literature. The family business literature looks mainly into the characteristics of the business family to define its influence on the business (Uhlaner, 2006). Emotions are discussed indirectly when referring to several phenomena that influence the business, such as family conflicts (Beehr et al., 1997; Danes et al., 1999; Kaye, 1996; Kellermanns and Eddleston, 2007; Lee and Rogoff, 1996; Levinson, 1971), relationships (Kaye, 1996), and culture (Danes et al., 2008; Dyer, 1986).

Whereas Danes et al. (1999) did not look directly into negative emotions, they studied predictors of tensions in the family as well as in the business, and their connection to achievement of family and business goals. Kaye (1996) explored the sustained family conflict cycle and noted that motivations and emotions in this cycle can be varied and complex.

Cramton (1993) studied the entrepreneurial phase of the family business using the life-cycle perspective that stems from Bowen's family systems theory (Bowen, 1978). The changing emotional relationships within the owning family provided a better explanation for the story of a business creation than the one suggested by traditional theories of entrepreneurship (Cramton, 1993). This is an example of the positive influence that emotions in the business family may have on the family business itself.

Most researchers, however, referred to a negative connotation of emotions in business families such as anxiety during the critical stage of succession (Dunn, 1999), guilt and emotional unavailability (Kets-de-Vries, 1993), conflicts (Eddleston and Kellermanns, 2007; Kaye, 1996), rivalry (Friedman, 1991), and discrete emotions like jealousy (Astrachan and Jaskiewicz, 2008; Davis and Harveston, 1999; Dyer, 2003).

Bowen's Family Systems Theory as a Proposed Theoretical Perspective

Despite the focus of social psychology and family therapy on emotions, few references in the family business literature build on these fields to cast light on the emotions of the family in business. Among the predominant theoretical contributions lies Bowen's family systems theory, which has been considered as the most comprehensive theory in family therapy (Nichols and Schwartz, 2006).

Bowen's theory is especially relevant to family businesses because it deals with the emotional forces that operate in the family over the years in recurrent patterns. We inherit styles of differentiation from our parents, choose our mates according to our own level of differentiation, and incorporate our children into our emotional atmosphere (Bowen, 1978). Hence emotional patterns are transferred from generation to generation (Bowen, 1978; Nichols and Schwartz, 2006).

This fundamental assumption has relevant implications for business families that encourage a culture of connections between generations and a long-term view. Normative expectations in a business family include a strong set of family values and history which are passed on to the next generations (Denison et al., 2004; Rothstein, 1992). A historical perspective can help explain current emotional functioning in the family because some patterns are reproduced across generations, and allow for predictions of emotional functioning for next generations. As a theory that looks into the long-term development and function of emotional patterns within families, Bowen's theory can be applied as a rich framework to the study of the business family emotions.

THE BUSINESS SYSTEM

Emotions in Organizations

Relative to the family system predominantly viewed as embedded in emotions, the business has been considered a purely rational system aimed at generating goods and services that provide financial and social interests for the family and other stakeholders (Carlock and Ward, 2001; Kepner, 1983). Although organizational behavior researchers have acknowledged the role of emotions in the business, most family business researchers still consider the business system as emotionless.

After being widely researched in the 1930s, affect in organizations knew a faded interest for about half a century (Barsade et al., 2003). There are two notable exceptions to the long neglect of 'feelings at work' during these decades: research on job satisfaction and stress at work (Rafaeli et al., in press). Hochschild's (1983) book on emotional labor is believed to be the starting point for the modern research on emotion (Fisher and Ashkanasy, 2000). Building on the case of flight attendants, Hochschild (1983) described how '[T]he emotional style of offering the service is part of the service itself', and when they have been asked to help, the airlines compete in the marketplace: 'flight attendants have been asked to hand out commercial love at an ever faster rate, to more people in the same amount of time' (Hochschild, 1983, p. 5).

Hochschild (1983) inspired management scholars to focus attention on emotional expression as part of the work role (Rafaeli and Sutton, 1987; Sutton and Rafaeli, 1988). Towards the end of the twentieth century, affect in organizations was taken up so intensely that an 'affective revolution' in organizational psychology research has been proclaimed (Barsade et al., 2003; Rafaeli et al., in press).

Economic behavior and most early decision-making models were based on the notion that economic decisions follow a rational and systematic pattern (Simon, 1945, 1978). Emotions were regarded as interference with rationality, as judgment mistakes, errors to be minimized, repaired or simply ignored and not regarded as intrinsic to decision-making (Fineman, 2003). The growing attention to emotions in organizations in recent years looked at emotions as an integral and inseparable part of organizational life (Ashforth and Humphrey, 1995), and started referring to the 'emotional organization' (Fineman, 2003).

In the organizational behavior literature, emotions have been found to be connected to many individual and organizational outcomes: positive moods and emotions are associated with an increase in work performance measures including higher income, enhanced negotiating ability and performing discretionary acts for the benefit of the organization (Barsade and Gibson, 2007). Positive affect can facilitate the efficient and flexible use of new information, which increases the effectiveness of decision-making, and influences creativity positively (Barsade and Gibson, 2007). Overall, there is strong support for the connection between positive emotions and prosocial behaviors (Barsade and Gibson, 2007). Negotiators with positive moods tend to be more cooperative and come to more agreements that enhance joint gains (Barsade, 2002). Positive moods induce more innovative problem-solving strategies, which are connected to more integrative ('win–win') solutions (Carnevale and Isen, 1986). In a broader perspective, negative and positive emotional dissonance have been found to increase customer satisfaction (Pugh, 2001) but to worsen job satisfaction (Lewig and Dollard, 2003; Morris and Feldman, 1996; Rutner et al., 2008), increase emotional exhaustion (Rutner et al., 2008), lead to job burnout (Erickson and Ritter, 2001) and lower organizational commitment (Abraham, 1999).

Current State of Family Business Literature

Recently, there has been a growing research interest in the aspects of family businesses that are beyond the sole pursuit of performance towards more focus on non-economic activities which are intertwined with individual emotions (Klein and Kellermanns, 2008). Researchers suggest that family businesses would appear to be especially rich contexts in which emotions influence processes and behavior (Van den Heuval et al., 2007). As family businesses are located at the intersection of the family and the business systems, they offer pronounced characteristics to learn about non-economic behavior and its outcomes in a business environment (Klein and Kellermanns, 2008).

Entrepreneurship is also a research area that has investigated emotions (Baron, 2008; Brundin et al., 2008b; Cardon et al., 2005; Goss, 2005, 2007; Pachulia and Henderson, 2009; Zampetakis et al., 2009). Recent studies view entrepreneurship as a form of social action rather than as a systemic function and suggest looking specifically at the emotions involved from an entrepreneur's perspective (Goss, 2005, 2007) and offer a framework to study them (Cardon et al., 2005; Goss, 2007).

Brundin et al. (2008b) measured employees' willingness to act entrepreneurially and showed that displaying different emotions by managers influenced their employees' behavior. Specifically, displays of confidence and satisfaction with an entrepreneurial project enhance the employees' willingness to act entrepreneurially, whereas displays of frustration, worry and bewilderment, respectively, diminish it (Brundin et al., 2008b).

Goss (2007) suggests capitalizing on the widely recognized developments in studying emotions in social sciences and develops a model of entrepreneurial behavior that links social interaction, emotion and cognition.

Given this overview, it is possible to note a growing interest in empirical studies that look directly at emotions and their influence within the business organization of a family business.

As for the ownership component of the family business, it refers mainly to the family voting shares or voting power over a trust (Ward and Dolan, 1998). This entails a direct influence of the shareholders over the management, which – in a simplistic hypothesis of insignificant agency problems – further justifies including ownership into the business system. Studies that looked into emotions in ownership generally define 'emotional' as standing for human or psychological processes linked to voting shares rather than to emotions as they are studied in the research of affect.

It seems that in the family business literature emotions are defined more by either what they are *not*: when a variable is *not* financial (Astrachan and Jaskiewicz, 2008; Pieper and Astrachan, 2008; Zellweger and Astrachan, 2008), *not* rational (Whiteside and Brown, 1991), or *not* easy to explain and define (Gómez-Mejía et al., 2007), and by connecting them to other constructs such as cohesion, possessions, capital, values and costs (Astrachan and Jaskiewicz, 2008; Pieper, 2007; Pieper and Astrachan, 2008).

In recent years several empirical studies started looking into the link between emotions and organizational outcomes in family businesses. Van den Heuval et al. (2007) measured empathy levels of family CEOs and their influence on the importance of family-oriented goals. They claim that not only emotions related to empathy play a role in the conduct of family businesses, but that other emotions such as fear, anger, jealousy and loyalty should be studied as well (Van den Heuval et al., 2007).

Brundin and Melin (2006) studied the dynamics of emotions as an important part of strategizing. They looked at the emotions of confidence and frustration as displayed by two CEOs during an in-depth field study. Their conclusion is that emotions exert an influence as driving or as counteracting forces, depending on how the emotions are displayed and interpreted over time. The crucial point according to this study is whether conformity between emotional experiences and emotional displays actually exists.

Brundin and Nordqvist (2008) looked into the role of emotions in boardroom dynamics. They realized that emotions are sources of energy that play a role depending on the interpretations that board members assign to them. Emotions can also be viewed as long term and impact power and status energizers.

Therefore, there has been a growing interest in the emotional aspects of ownership in family business over recent years. This led researchers to call for including emotions in ownership and business processes (Brundin et al., 2008s) and suggested several emotional constructs like emotional capital (Sharma, 2004), emotional ownership (Bjornberg and Nicholson, 2008), emotional returns and costs (Astrachan and Jaskiewicz, 2008), emotional value (Zellweger and Astrachan, 2008), family and business emotional cohesion (Pieper, 2007; Pieper and Astrachan, 2008) and socio-emotional wealth (Gómez-Mejía et al., 2007).

Gómez-Mejía et al. (2007) argue that family businesses are willing to protect their socio-emotional wealth even at the cost of significant risk to their performance. The definition of socio-emotional wealth in this study is however not operational, nor has it been directly measured (Zellweger and Astrachan, 2008), but rather implied by the results. Zellweger et al. (2008) suggest that the central aspect of socio-emotional wealth is transgenerational sustainability, beside other aspects of tradition, status and family legacy. While their study shows that the desire to keep the business for the next generations influences the value that owners ascribe to their firms, it is still a long way from defining the emotional aspects of the ownership subsystem.

Pieper (2007) and Pieper and Astrachan (2008) study the mechanisms that assure long-term family business survival, and look into cohesion as a necessary condition for family business success and sustainability. They identify four cohesion constructs: business financial cohesion, family financial cohesion, and also family emotional cohesion and business emotional cohesion. Among the dimensions of family emotional cohesion as measured in Pieper's (2007) qualitative study are disappointment, fear and jealousy, which are part of discrete emotions. However, the definition of *family emotional cohesion* does not refer to emotions, but rather to a process of attachment and bonding that satisfies needs for security and affiliation (Pieper and Astrachan, 2008). This is evident in the following example of family emotional cohesion from this study: '[Despite all criticism that I used to have for the business] I think the bonding to the family – wherein my grandmother, who meant a lot to me, certainly plays an important role – this attachment has always been there subliminally. It reduced the distance; there has always been a certain sense of belonging' (Pieper and Astrachan, 2008, p. 5).

Bjornberg and Nicholson (2008) define emotional ownership (EO) as what psychologists call 'identification' (Bjornberg and Nicholson, 2008, p. 3). So, like the former family and business emotional cohesion construct, this too is a psychological construct which refers to the interpersonal and cognitive processes of attachment and identification and not directly to emotions. More than that, when they tried to connect EO to positive and negative feelings of family members towards the business, results indicated that EO is not compromised by having feelings about the firm (Bjornberg and Nicholson, 2008).

Sharma (2004) describes a possible typology of family firms in terms of family and business dimensions. She assumes that good business performance indicates high financial capital while good family performance 'indicates firms with high cumulative emotional capital' (Sharma, 2004, p. 6). Whereas there is no clear definition for this kind of emotional capital, some explanations are provided – as when emotional capital is high it is synonymous with family harmony and warm hearts, and when it is low it denotes tension or failed family relationships. Emotional capital stands parallel to financial capital in the business, as a kind of familial currency. Families with high levels of emotional and financial capital '[E]njoy high cumulative stocks of both financial and emotional capital that may help sustain the family and business through turbulent economic and emotional times' (Sharma, 2004, p. 7).

Zellweger and Astrachan (2008) use financial theories of possession attachment and endowment literature to define the emotional value (EV) of owning a firm. They propose a research framework to measure EV that includes perceived emotional benefits and costs from ownership. As seen in previous suggested emotional constructs within ownership, these costs and benefits relate more to psychological and/or social characteristics of family business ownership, and less to emotional ones.

Astrachan and Jaskiewicz (2008) suggest a valuation formula of a family business from an owner's perspective that addresses emotional costs and returns. In this model, 'emotional' stands for non-financial components. While the non-financial aspects of the family business include emotional dimensions, the term 'emotional' is used to capture *all* possible components of psychological, behavioral, social and cognitive aspects.

To sum up this review of the existing literature on emotions in the business system, it is clear that scholars tend to use emotional aspects now more often than previously. But these new constructs are either not well defined, or encompass many social, psychological and behavioral aspects, and not only emotional ones. It seems that whatever is not purely rational and financially related falls into the emotional domain.

We suggest focusing on the emotional side of ownership as defined in the research of affect. This means looking into different discrete emotions like jealousy, anger or love and their influence on different aspects within ownership like governance or control mechanisms, and elaborating on the first findings of positive and negative feelings to influence ownership issues (Bjornberg and Nicholson, 2008). Moreover, we suggest looking into group emotions and positive/negative affect that have been studied in organizations and applying them to the family business field. We will now look into the interfaces between the family and the business systems and suggest a possible theoretical approach for the mechanism of transference between these systems.

THE OVERLAP BETWEEN THE FAMILY SYSTEM AND THE BUSINESS SYSTEM

Current State of Family Business Literature

The discussion about the interfaces between the family and business systems has evolved during the last decade. The overlap area between the business and the family was first perceived as a possible source of conflict (Miller et al., 1999), or a factor that needs to be effectively managed in order to succeed in the family business (Danes et al., 2008; Sharma, 2004). The current search for the unique resources and capabilities that the family brings into the business (Habbershon and Williams, 1999) transformed the interface between the family and the firm into a synergetic and symbiotic connection between the two systems that is necessary in order for the family business to survive the competitive market of the twenty-first century (Chua et al., 2003).

The two systems of family and business interaction and emotions may transfer from one system to another. This is suggested at the group level, like other resources that the family brings to the business or ownership since '[F]amily and business interact by exchanging resources across their boundaries' (Danes et al., 2008, pp. 244–5). At the individual level, the mechanism designed to link the systems should be explained by an appropriate theoretical framework, such as the exchange theory from the family research field (Pieper, 2007).

The Exchange Theory as a Proposed Theoretical Perspective

The exchange theory is based on basic behaviorist and economics ideas – the assumption is that social structural patterns are a reflection of individuals' economic motives (Sabatelli and Shehan, 1993) and the paradigm explores the interplay of economic and social factors in family life (Ruben, 1998). Emotions are one component of socio-emotional and symbolic resources and returns (Bagarozzi, 1993; Ruben, 1998; Sabatelli and Shehan, 1993). For example, love is thought of as one out of six types of resources (Sabatelli and Shehan, 1993). Emotions are not only components of resources and/or rewards, but can also be the results of exchanges. Individuals in inequitable exchanges feel more distressed than equitably treated individuals: an under-benefited individual may feel anger while an over-benefited may feel guilt (Longmore and Demaris, 1997).

The exchange theory is widely used to explain marital relationships, and it may have special relevance to the family business field. The two systems of family and business coexist side by side, with cost and reward calculations in each system, and the overlap between them could lead towards an utilitarian calculation of costs in one system and rewards in another, and vice versa (Michael-Tsabari and Lavee, 2008). This could lead to implementing the exchange theory not only between the family members in their marital and personal relationships, but also across the systems of family and business. Emotional costs and emotional rewards need not come only from one system – an individual can invest in one system and get his or her reward in the other. We offer the exchange theory as a valuable theory for future family business studies on the transference of emotions from one system to the other.

The Role of Culture in Shaping Family Business Emotions

Recent and open-systems approaches incorporate the surrounding environment within family business models (Danes et al., 2008; Pieper and Klein, 2007). The integration of this perspective helps to understand how the business and the environment interact and allows comparisons across different cultures or nations (Pieper and Klein, 2007). Wortman (1994) refers to the differences between family businesses in varying types of contexts, including local, multicultural and global ones. Hence we suggest looking into cultural factors that may influence emotions in the family business.

Hofstede's (2001) study was the first to introduce cultural differences across nations (Hofstede, 1993). The idea that cultural differences may influence emotions in the family business is demonstrated in Brundin and Nordqvist's (2008) note in their study of emotions in the boardroom, suggesting that emotions, given the Swedish context of the company, may be different in other contexts. Bjornberg and Nicholson (2008) found that emotional ownership (EO) is especially strong in Latin cultures, suggesting a cultural difference in terms of EO intensity between family firms in different cultures.

Sharma and Manikutty (2005) refer to the contextual culture of a family business when they suggest a frame to study divestment decisions. They do not directly include emotions in their model, but their interest is to understand the role of social and psychological pressures on these decisions, as part of the non-rational impacts on divestment (Chrisman et al., 2005).

The cultural dimension of collectivism–individualism, to which several scholars referred in their studies of family businesses (Alwuhaibi, 2009; Chrisman et al., 2005), has been recognized by researchers of emotions as having significant implications for shaping emotional experiences across cultures (Markus and Kitayama, 1991). In recent decades, research has shown that cultures exert considerable influence over emotion (Matsumoto, 1993). In individualistic cultures, ego-focused emotions such as anger, frustration and pride will be more frequently expressed. In these cultures, people will attend more to these feelings and act on the basis of them (Markus and Kitayama, 1991).

In contrast, in the collectivistic cultures, other-focused emotions such as sympathy, feelings of interpersonal communication and shame will be more frequently expressed (Markus and Kitayama, 1991). Many collectivistic cultures have well-developed strategies that render them experts in avoiding the expression of negative emotions like anger. The differences between expressing and regulating emotions in different cultures, and the findings concerning anger and negative emotions in particular, show the importance of including the cultural context when studying the role of emotions in the family business.

After examining the systems of the family firm, their interfaces and their environmental culture, we will look at the family business from a dynamic perspective. In order to do so, we will incorporate the theory of emotional dissonance and use it to suggest one possible dynamic perspective of the family business, and the emotions' evolvement over time. Our claim is that existing theories from social sciences, like the emotional dissonance theory, can be fruitful in studying emotions within family businesses. More in-depth analysis based on the full development of this theory and others should be part of future studies to explain the family business phenomena.

A DYNAMIC PERSPECTIVE OF EMOTIONS IN FAMILY BUSINESSES

The basic aim and characteristic of emotional experience is emotional expression (Andersen and Guerrero, 1998). Understanding the influence of emotions in the family business system requires taking into account how and why key family members express or not their emotions. Beyond potential differences in the families' cultural perspectives that explain families encouraging or not the expression of emotions, it is important to analyze the potential gap between expressed and experienced emotions of family members, and its effects. The theory of emotional dissonance (ED) (Abraham, 1998b; Morris and Feldman, 1996; Zerbe, 2000) is useful to complement this analysis.[1]

Emotional Dissonance: A Brief Overview

Emotional dissonance, also called emotive dissonance, derives from the concept of cognitive dissonance and stems from the emotional labor theory.[2] Emotional labor is a process of emotion management whereby individuals control their emotions by displaying what is perceived as 'acceptable' (Ashforth and Humphrey, 1993; Hochschild, 1983). The ED is a process that originates from the conflict between expressed and experienced emotions (Abraham, 1998a) and leads to suppressing felt but undesired emotions (neutral, positive or negative), while expressing unfelt emotions (neutral, positive or negative) instead (Hochschild, 1983).

The organizational behavior literature studied the expression of emotions of employees who work in specific industry sectors and positions, mainly services industries, where they are expected to display predefined emotions. Scholars studied the emotional dissonance of flight attendants and bill collectors (Hochschild, 1983), convenience store clerks (Sutton and Rafaeli, 1988), medical representatives (Mishra and Bhatnagar, 2009), IT professionals (Rutner et al., 2008), police detectives (Stenross and Kleinman, 1989), Disney employees (Van Maanen and Kunda, 1989), call centre workers (Lewig and Dollard, 2003), who are required to comply with external demands of displaying neutral, positive or negative emotions in order to influence the clients' feelings and satisfaction, leading to organizational performance. However, no research has yet investigated in depth emotional dissonance in the family business.

Emotional Dissonance Characteristics in the Family Business

Although family business researchers did not coin the expression ED, they presented some evidence of existing ED. Tagiuri and Davis (1996) observed that all family members do not express their emotions in a similar manner. Hubler (1999) noted that the most involved family members do not express their feelings and desires. When emotions (love or hate) arise from the unconscious to the conscious, family members must decide whether to express them or not. Some families publicly prohibit the expression of conflict to avoid embarrassing situations (Tagiuri and Davis, 1996). Some family members are psychologically strictly prohibited from explicit conflicts with others, leading to prohibiting the expression of feelings and even the exclusion of a feeling (Tagiuri and Davis, 1996). Kepner (1983) characterizes the expression of emotions in some families in business as resigned, inhibited or ritualized. While other families easily express negative emotions, some families encourage both the expression of positive and negative emotions that are appropriate to the context (Kepner, 1983).

This discrepancy between experienced and expressed emotions can be either thought of as a spontaneous or automatic process – such as emotional harmony (Ashforth and Humphrey, 1993) or as passive deep acting (Hochschild, 1983), either as an intentional process designed to abide by certain occupational (Hochschild, 1979), behavioural (Sutton, 1991) and organizational norms (Rafaeli and Sutton, 1989). In both cases, it aims at attaining a positive outcome that is beneficial to all parties involved in the emotional process.

No scholar to date has explicitly studied ED of family members in the family business systems, the nature of family business norms regarding emotional expression, and the outcomes of ED. In the family business, we maintain that there are ED norms designed by family members to conform to both family and business objectives. For example, family members may seek to protect the family and business systems' reputation through prohibiting the expression of negative emotions that would put the family business at stake, and to serve the individual interests of family members. Some families fear that an open discussion of critical issues – such as inheritance and succession – would serve only to fuel unpleasant comparisons among the heirs that could destroy the fabric of the family (Lansberg, 1988). Hence, in opposition to other businesses, we suggest that in the family business the desired norms of emotional expression may stem not only from the business system but also from the family system. Family members are impelled to comply both with organizationally desired emotions and family desired emotions. Given the overlap between both systems, one can suppose that these norms should not be conflicting but congruent. To better understand the existing norms and influence of ED in the family business, it is important to consider the evolution of the family and business life spans.

Toward a Conceptualization of 'Emotional Evolvement' (EE) in the Family Business

The family and business systems evolve over the family business life span leading to a change in the ED norms to meet the evolving challenges of each system. Conflicting objectives between family and business systems at some stages of the life span might make the gap between norms of desirability in the family and the business narrower or wider, and make the ED evolve across the life cycle as well. Given the characteristics of the family business interfaces described previously, emotional experience can be transferred from one system to another. Emotions follow a cycle with reciprocal influences among the participants (Hareli and Rafaeli, 2008). In a family business, the individual family members' experience of emotions can be transmitted to other family members, and contribute to create a collective emotional climate (emotional contagion) that influences the business positively or negatively. This influence may, however, depend on the extent of ED.

Emotions are not static as they emerge and evolve given more or less critical events in each family business system (succession, divorce, illness, family or business loss, economic downturn etc.) (Dunn, 1999; Gersick et al., 1997; Post and Robins, 1993; Rosenblatt et al., 1985; Shepherd, 2003). The evolution of emotions refers mainly to a change in the intensity and importance of emotions, and the consequent gap between the expressed and experienced ones, that is ED. Depending on the level of analysis (individual, interpersonal, group or organizational), this evolution might affect organizational and behavioral outcomes, such as efficiency of decision-making, social and financial performance, family health and satisfaction.

In the family business, despite the fact that emotional communication has been scarcely studied, researchers tend to converge towards the idea that the expression of emotions leads to positive effects on family and business performance. The communication of emotions is considered as central to the development, maintenance and change of relations (Dillard, 1998). These emotions were found to affect mainly the relations within the family business (Mustakallio, 2002). An inability to communicate emotions is associated with conflicting relations, whereas emotional expression is associated with relationship satisfaction (Gaelick et al., 1985). The degree of emotional expression of family members promotes or hinders the balance of family ties (Olson, 2000).

On the other hand, the expression of emotions like love has positive effects such as motivation, cemented loyalty and increasing trust among family members (Tagiuri and Davis, 1996). However, according to these authors, the absence of emotional expression has negative effects. The feelings of hatred combined with a sense of guilt severely complicate the relations within the family business. The denial of negative feelings results in the exclusion of discussions on natural differences of opinion and leads to obscure expressions of hostility in the form of mistrust, avoidance of other family members, refusal of emotional support and escalating conflicts in the business. Accordingly, the lack of emotional expression between family members may affect family ties and relationships at work and thus seriously affect the family business.

According to Hubler (1999), the absence of emotional expression in the family is an indicator of a weak and inefficient communication. Active and non-active family members may communicate indirectly, which creates a triangle that deteriorates the quality of family ties (Bowen, 1978; Hubler, 1999). Thus the expression of negative emotions can be regarded as useful in better addressing problems and solving them on a direct basis (Kepner, 1983).

We suggest reconciling the extreme approaches sustaining the good or bad effects of positive and negative emotions' expression through the concept of ED, that is focusing on the existing gap between felt and expressed emotions, whether these emotions are positive or negative. In addition, transposing this analysis to the family business needs to consider several possible issues: At which stages of the life span are emotions more or less critical? How does ED evolve over the life span and impact the family and business outcomes? What is the difference between day-to-day ED and ED during critical events?

Given the complexity of the family business, we propose to analyze ED in three different life span stages of the family business as outlined by Gersick et al. (1997), although we are conscious that it conveys a restricted and simplistic analysis. The first stage relates to a young founding family that starts up a business. The second stage refers to a siblings' partnership involved in the expansion of the business. The third stage relates to a cousins' consortium in a mature business.

First stage of the family business life span
The first stage of the family business life span coincides with the start-up phase of the business system, a founder's controlling ownership (business system) and a young family in business (family system) (Gersick et al., 1997). The founder–entrepreneur generally

starts the business by creating a product or service that corresponds to his/her own internal desires and needs, to express subjective conceptions of beauty, emotion or some aesthetic ideal (Cova and Svanfeldt, 1993). In the business system, the founder brings to the management his/her individual propensities, values and operating rules, which in turn stem from his/her development and history (Kelly et al., 2000). At this stage, the degree of the founder's centrality is known to be relatively high. The critical emotions are mainly rooted in the founder, who, due to his/her central position, may transmit them through emotional contagion to the other organizational actors. By doing so, the founder's emotions might impact his/her motivation and others' motivation to make the entrepreneurial business successful as explained herein.

We suggest that the extent of ED highly differs between the founder and other family members at this stage. This difference might be explained by the centrality of the founder who mainly inspires the norms of ED. Whereas the ED of the founder is relatively weak during the first stage of the family business life cycle, the ED of other family members is supposed to be relatively higher and to comply with the norms that are implicitly derived from the founder's characteristics. Additional explanations can be found in the research work on entrepreneurial emotions. Although the existing studies do not refer directly to ED, the issues of the founder's centrality in the emotional set-up, the gap between experienced and expressed emotions, and the mechanism of emotional contagion are often addressed.

For example, Cardon et al. (2005) offer a framework for studying emotions in entrepreneurship. They propose the notion of entrepreneurial passion as the enduring emotional meta-experience that the entrepreneur consciously attributes to the venture and that is characterized by a quite intense discrete emotion (Cardon et al., 2005, p. 6). They investigate why passion matters in entrepreneurial effectiveness and discuss the essential role that emotional regulation plays in converting strong affective experiences into drivers of entrepreneurial behavior.

Given the frequently reported emotional expression at the entrepreneurial stage and its outcomes, we suggest a series of possible propositions.

Proposition 1a   In the first family business life stage, the founder predominates the emotional dimension within the family and business systems.

Proposition 1b   In the first family business life stage, emotional norms mainly emerge from the founder's characteristics rather than family and business characteristics.

Proposition 1c   In the first family business life stage, the emotional dissonance of the founder is relatively weak as compared with the emotional dissonance of other family members.

Proposition 1e   In the first family business life stage, the mechanism of emotional contagion from the founder to other family members begins to develop and is carried over to the next family business life stages.

As soon as the founder approaches retirement and as the passing of the baton to the second generation is being prepared, many new issues which are emotionally loaded in both the business and the family emerge, such as business challenges, identity preservation and succession issues.

Second stage of the family business life span

At the second stage, emotions become more diffuse and encompass more family members. They also touch upon a wider variety of issues in both the business and the family systems. The second stage of the family business life span, known as the siblings' partnership stage, is considered by the literature as a fertile ground for rivalries that infect family ties between the 'newcomers' in the business sphere (Casson, 1999; Davis and Herrera, 1998; Harvey and Evans, 1994; Kenyon-Rouvinez and Ward, 2004), while increasing the risk of business failure.

At this stage, the emotional norms not only stem from the founder but also relate to the family and the business. The family norms of emotional expression are designed to regulate family behavior. These norms are functional in ensuring that relationships within the family are guided by personal caring rather than economic opportunism (Lansberg, 1988). The same norms within the family system can be transposed to the business system and serve to discourage discussions of critical business-related issues. Some emotionally charged issues can hence be prohibited from being displayed in order to maintain the family harmony.[3] These issues may include succession, economic and financial matters, such as estate or succession planning and inheritance, since an open discussion about them may denote self-interest and mistrust (Lansberg, 1988).

Lansberg (1988) reports a case of a family business where children are actively discouraged from engaging in discussions about the future of the family business while the founder's spouse is playing the role of 'emotional guardian of the family', constantly shielding the family from the emotionally upsetting issues of succession.

In addition to succession, identity forms an important emotionally rooted component. For members of a family business, the firm may not only be a source of income but also a context for family activity and the embodiment of family pride and identity (Meyer and Zucker, 1989, p. 78).

Family pride, personal sacrifice, loyalty and reputation are valuable factors which influence business operations, especially their continuity during periods of hardship (Donnelley, 1964). As Donnelley (1964, p. 97) observes, 'Reinforced and perpetuated by family pride, identification and tradition, the unity of purpose between the family and the business represents a factor in the success of many family firms.'

Hence, family members may be impelled to not display their felt emotions in order to preserve the reputation of the family and consequently of the business, and vice versa. This implies that the ED of all family members would increase at the second stage of the family business life span – as compared with the first stage of the life span where differences in ED exist between the founder and other family members – in order to allow for the survival of the business and for the harmony of the family, at least in the short run.

Given the evolution of emotional expression at the second stage of the life span in terms of members involved, norms and intensity, we suggest a series of possible propositions.

Proposition 2a   In the second family business life stage, emotions are more diffuse and encompass multiple family members.

Proposition 2b   In the second family business life stage, family and business norms of emotional expression regulate emotional dissonance.

Proposition 2c   In the second family business life stage, sibling rivalries are more likely to occur and affect family ties, increasing the risk of business failure.

Proposition 2d   In the second family business life stage, strong emotional expression is more likely prohibited in order to maintain family harmony.

Third stage of the family business life span
The potential for conflicting relationships is increased as long as the family spans many generations and the family business moves from the founder's controlled business to the cousins' consortium (Gersick et al., 1997; Mustakallio et al., 2002; Ward and Dolan, 1998), mainly exacerbated by the emotions of the different cousins' branches. While not documented in the literature yet, ED may evolve in different directions – growing, declining or remaining stable. This opens up an interesting avenue for future studies that should take into account one important variable, the formal family and business governance structures which are mostly set up at this stage of the family business. Effective governance encourages social interaction and communication among family members (Mustakallio, 2002; Mustakallio et al., 2002), hence leading to lower their ED. At the third stage, the implicit family and business emotional norms may prove to be less effective in adjusting the ED of family members. Family businesses have then to find the way to survive and build different formal governance systems in order to handle their ED more effectively. Building upon these insights, we suggest a series of possible propositions.

Proposition 3a   In the third family business life stage, the possibility of conflicting relationships increases in likelihood.

Proposition 3b   In the third family business life stage, weak family relationships are generally associated with high emotional dissonance for all family members.

Proposition 3c   In the third family business life stage, the relationship between family relationships' quality and emotional dissonance is moderated by the cultural context.

Proposition 3d   In the third family business life stage, effective formal governance systems regulate emotional dissonance among family members.

In sum, we suggest that ED differs given the life-cycle span and the roles of family members involved in the family business. It does not necessarily continuously grow from the first stage to the third stage of the life span. It may follow an inverted U curve – that is, ED is relatively low for the key family member represented by the founder–entrepreneur during the first stage where ED norms are mainly inspired by the founder (Propositions 1a through 1d), expands to more family members and turns into higher at the second stage where ED norms are inspired both by the family and the business (Propositions 2a through 2d), and has two extreme tendencies at the third stage depending on the efficiency of formal governance structures and the cultural context (Propositions 3a through 3d): ED would be either very heightened or very weakened. Each extreme would then have different outcomes. The first extreme, as the cousins show openly their emotions and discontent, may be harmful for the business – if not managed appropriately. It is important for the family business to maintain a balance according to the context – such as increasing the level of ED above the one present at the second stage to reduce conflicts and allow for the survival of the business. On the other hand, very high ED can be harmful for the family, since weak communication has been reported to lead to low family cohesion and adaptability (Labaki, 2007).

CONCLUSIONS AND FUTURE RESEARCH DIRECTIONS

In the family business literature to date, emotions have been partly conceptualized and analyzed with a focus on the family system. It is this chapter's contention that this perspective may have prevented us from fully examining the nature of emotions in the family business and from exploring their influence on the family and the business systems.

By suggesting a first and more in-depth analysis of emotions in the family business, the contributions of our chapter are twofold:

- *Conceptual*   By focusing on the construct of emotions, which has not been given much of attention in the family business field, we bring together the main theoretical and empirical studies that explored this construct in the family business, and suggest several ways of incorporating emotions into the understanding of family business behavior.
- *Theoretical*   By suggesting and adopting several theories from the social and organizational fields, we contribute to building a theory of the family business from one side and broadening the scope of these theories towards new implementations in the family business setting from the other.

Since this chapter is a first dynamic description of emotions within and across family business systems, we used several simplistic assumptions to outline the topic and set the stage for the analysis. Emotions play a role in many systems, stages and critical events, and have several outcomes. The stages of the life-cycle span that we build upon to suggest our preliminary propositions are questionable since the family business does not necessarily follow a linear and three-stage evolution from the founder's controlling ownership to the cousin's consortium (Labaki, 2007). The scope of the current analysis does not allow for a deeper look at separate phenomena, which should be the concern of future research. These studies should include a more refined analysis of the different stages of the family business life span.

We suggested mainly the exchange theory from the family and marital relationships field and the emotional dissonance theory from organizational behavior field to explain the stages, mechanisms and behaviors related to emotions. Other theories may be relevant and could provide further knowledge and understanding.

These limitations open up new avenues for research. In order to discuss the place and contribution of emotions, emotional constructs and emotional theories, there is a need to define emotions as theoretically and practically separate from other constructs (psychological, behavioral, social or cognitive). As the tendency of research on emotions within the organizational field moves into emotions at the group level and the different mechanisms that operate at this level (emotional cycles, emotional contagion etc.), the family business can benefit from incorporating this perspective. The affective culture of the family system, of the business system and of the whole complex phenomena can be studied.

In addition, since emotions can be analyzed at three different levels – mega constructs, individual emotions and regulation of emotions – future research should inquire about the level of analysis to gain a better understanding of the individuals within the family business and their behavior within the systems. The interfaces of the systems and the relationship with the cultural environment may show unique characteristics of family businesses and therefore contribute to other theories of families and/or organizational behavior.

Lastly, the refinement of emotional evolvement and its propositions within and over the stages of the family business life span is now possible. Further, we are posed to embark on more developed research studies in the future on emotions in both the family and the business systems.

NOTES

1. Other emotions theories might enlighten our knowledge of family business emotions. We will not discuss them in depth but we will use some of their insights: the affective events theory (Weiss and Cropanzano, 1996), emotion regulation theory (Gross, 1998, 1999), emotional contagion theory (Côté and Morgan, 2002; Pugh, 2001), intergroup emotions theory (Mackie et al., 2000; Smith, 1993).
2. We choose to focus on emotional dissonance, among other important dimensions of emotional labor, since emotional dissonance is the most relevant and most connected to emotional consequences (Lewig and Dollard, 2003; Morris and Feldman, 1996; Rutner et al., 2008).
3. For example, Lansberg explains that Western cultures have norms regulating family behavior that discourage parents and offspring from openly discussing the future of the family beyond the lifetime of the parents (Lansberg, 1988).

REFERENCES

Abraham, R. (1998), 'Emotional dissonance in organizations: antecedents, consequences, and moderators', *Genetic, Social, and General Psychology Monographs*, **124**(2), 229–46.
Abraham, R. (1999), 'The impact of emotional dissonance on organizational commitment and intention to turnover', *The Journal of Psychology*, **133**(4), 441–55.
Alwuhaibi, S.A. (2009), 'A cultural perspective on the impact of family and society on the competitive advantage of organizations and nations', unpublished dissertation, Mississipi State University, Mississipi.
Andersen, P.A. and Guerrero, L.K. (1998), *Handbook of Communication and Emotion: Research, Theory, Applications and Contexts*, USA: Academic Press.
Anderson, R.C. and Reeb, D.M. (2003), 'Founding family ownership and firm performance: evidence from the S&P 500', *The Journal of Finance*, **58**(3), 1301–28.
Ashforth, B.E. and Humphrey, R.H. (1993), 'Emotional labor in service roles: the influence of identity', *Academy of Management Review*, **18**(1), 88–115.
Ashforth, B.E. and Humphrey, R.H. (1995), 'Emotion in the workplace: a reappraisal', *Human Relations*, **48**(2), 97–126.
Astrachan, J.H. and Jaskiewicz, P. (2008), 'Emotional returns and emotional costs in privately held family businesses: advancing traditional business valuation', *Family Business Review*, **21**(2), 139–49.
Bagarozzi, D.A. (1993), 'Clinical uses of social exchange principles', in P.G. Boss, W.J. Doherty, R. LaRossa,

W.R. Schumm and S.K. Steinmetz (eds), *Sourcebook of Family Theories and Methods: A Contextual Approach*, New York: Plenum, pp.412–17.

Baron, R.A. (2008), 'The role of affect in the entrepreneurial process', *Academy of Management Review*, **33**(2), 328–40.

Barsade, S.G. (2002), 'The ripple effect: emotional contagion and its influence on group behavior', *Administrative Science Quarterly*, **47**(4), 644–75.

Barsade, S.G., Brief, A.P. and Sapataro, S.E. (2003), 'The affective revolution in organizational behavior: the emergence of a paradigm', in J. Greenberg (ed.), *Organizational Behavior: The Art of the Science*, London: Lawrence Erlbaum, pp.3–50.

Barsade, S.G. and Gibson, D. (2007), 'Why does affect matter in organizations?', *Academy of Management Perspectives*, **21**(1), 36–59.

Beehr, A., Drexler, J.A.J. and Faulkner, S. (1997), 'Working in small family businesses: empirical comparisons to non-family businesses', *Journal of Organizational Behavior*, **18**(3), 297–312.

Bjornberg, A. and Nicholson, N. (2008), *Emotional Ownership: The Critical Pathway Between the Next Generation and the Family Firm*, London: The Institute for Family Business.

Bowen, M. (1978), *Family Therapy in Clinical Practice* (2004 edn), Lanham, MD: Rowman & Littlefield Publishers.

Brundin, E. and Melin, L. (2006), 'Unfolding the dynamics of emotions: how emotion drives or counteracts strategizing', *International Journal of Work Organization and Emotion*, **1**(3), 277–98.

Brundin, E. and Nordqvist, M. (2008), 'Beyond facts and figures: the role of emotions in boardroom dynamics', *Corporate Governance*, **16**(4), 326–41.

Brundin, E., Florin-Samuelsson, E. and Melin, L. (2008a), 'The family ownership logic: core characteristics of family-controlled businesses, CeFEO Working Paper Series, Center for Family Enterprise and Ownership Jönköping International Business School.

Brundin, E., Patzelt, H. and Shepherd, D.A. (2008b), 'Managers' emotional displays and employees' willingness to act entrepreneurially', *Journal of Business Venturing*, **23**, 221–43.

Cardon, M.S., Wincent, J., Singh, J. and Drnovsek, M. (2005), 'Entrepreneurial passion: the nature of emotions in entrepreneurship', paper presented at the Academy of Management, Honolulu.

Cardon, M.S., Wincent, J., Singh, J. and Drnovsek, M. (2009), 'The nature and experience of entrepreneurial passion', *Academy of Management Review*, **34**(3), 511–32.

Carlock, R.S. and Ward, J.L. (2001), *Strategic Planning for the Family Business*, New York: Palgrave.

Carnevale, P.J.D. and Isen, A.M. (1986), 'The influence of positive affect and visual access on the discovery of integrative solutions in bilateral negotiation', *Organizational Behavior and Human Decision Processes*, **37**, 1–13.

Carsrud, A.L. (1994), 'Meanderings of a resurrected psychologist or, lessons learned in creating a family business program', *Entrepreneurship Theory and Practice*, **19**(1), 39–48.

Casson, M. (1999), 'The economics of the family firm', *Scandinavian Economic History Review*, **47**(1), 10–23.

Chrisman, J.J., Chua, J.H. and Sharma, P. (2003), 'Current trends and future directions in family business management studies: toward a theory of the family firm', available at <http://www.usasbe.org/knowledge/whitepapers/index.asp>, Coleman White Paper Series.

Chrisman, J.J., Chua, J.H. and Sharma, P. (2005), 'Trends and directions in the development of a strategic management theory of the family firm', *Entrepreneurship Theory and Practice*, **29**(5), 555–75.

Chua, J.H., Chrisman, J.J. and Steier, L.P. (2003), 'Extending the theoretical horizons of family business research', *Entrepreneurship Theory and Practice*, **27**(4), 331–8.

Côté, S. and Morgan, L.M. (2002), 'A longitudinal analysis of the association between emotion regulation, job satisfaction, and intentions to quit', *Journal of Organizational Behavior*, **23**(8), 947–63.

Cova, B. and Svanfeldt, C. (1993), 'Societal innovations and the postmodern aestheticization of everyday life', *International Journal of Research in Marketing*, **10**(3), 297–310.

Cramton, C.D. (1993), 'Is rugged individualism the whole story? Public and private accounts of a firm's founding', *Family Business Review*, **6**(3), 233–61.

Danes, S.M., Lee, J., Stafford, K. and Heck, R.K.Z. (2008), 'The effects of ethnicity, families and culture on entrepreneurial experience: an extension of Sustainable Family Business Theory', *Journal of Developmental Entrepreneurship*, **13**(3), 229–68.

Danes, S.M., Zuiker, V., Kean, R. and Arbuthnot, J. (1999), 'Predictors of family business tensions and goal achievement', *Family Business Review*, **12**(3), 241–52.

Davis, J.A. and Herrera, R.M. (1998), 'The social psychology of family shareholder dynamics', *Family Business Review*, **11**(3), 253–60.

Davis, P.S. and Harveston, P.D. (1999), 'In the founder's shadow: conflict in the family firm', *Family Business Review*, **12**(4), 311–23.

Denison, D., Leif, C. and Ward, J.L. (2004), 'Culture in family-owned enterprises: recognizing and leveraging unique strengths', *Family Business Review*, **17**(1), 61–70.

Dillard, P.J. (1998), 'The role of affect in communication, biology, and social relationships', in P.A. Andersen and L.K. Guenero (eds), *Handbook of Communication and Emotion: Research, Theory, Applications and Contexts*, San Diego, CA: Academic Press, pp. xvii–xxxii.

Donnelley, R.G. (1964), 'The family business', *Harvard Business Review*, **42**(4), 93–105.

Dunn, B. (1999), 'The family factor: the impact of family relationship dynamics on business-owning families during transitions', *Family Business Review*, **12**(1), 41–60.

Dyer, W.G. (1986), *Cultural Change in Family Firms*, San Francisco, CA and London: Jossey-Bass.

Dyer, W.G. (2003), 'The family: the missing variable in organizational research', *Entrepreneurship Theory and Practice*, **27**(4), 401–16.

Eddleston, K.A. and Kellermanns, F.W. (2007), 'Destructive and productive family relationships: a stewardship theory perspective', *Journal of Business Venturing*, **22**, 545–65.

Ensley, M.D. and Pearson, A.W. (2005), 'An exploratory comparison of the behavioral dynamics of top management teams in family and nonfamily new ventures: cohesion, conflict, potency, and consensus', *Entrepreneurship Theory and Practice*, **29**(3), 267–84.

Erickson, R.J. and Ritter, C. (2001), 'Emotional Labor, burnout, and inauthenticity: does gender matter?', *Social Psychology Quarterly*, **64**(2), 146–63.

Fineman, S. (2003), *Understanding Emotion at Work*, London: Sage Publications.

Fisher, C.D. and Ashkanasy, N.M. (2000), 'The emerging role of emotions in work life: an introduction', *Journal of Organizational Behavior*, **21**(2), 123–9.

Fleming, Q.J. (2000), *Keep the Family Baggage out of the Family Business*, New York: Fireside.

Friedman, S.D. (1991), 'Sibling relationships and intergenerational succession in family firms', *Family Business Review*, **4**(1), 3–20.

Frijda, N.H. (1986), *The Emotions*, Cambridge: Cambridge University Press.

Fukuyama, F. (1999), *The Great Disruption: Human Nature and the Reconstitution of Social Order*, New York: Free Press.

Gaelick, L., Bodenhausen, G.V. and Wyer, R.S., Jr (1985), 'Emotional communication in close relationships', *Journal of Personality and Social Psychology*, **49**(5), 1246–65.

Gersick, K., Davis, J., Hampton, M.M. and Lansberg, I. (1997), *Generation to Generation: Lifecycles of the Family Business*, Boston, MA: Harvard Business School Press.

Gómez-Mejía, L.R., Haynes, K.T., Núñez-Nickel, M., Jacobson, K.J.L. and Moyano-Fuentes, J. (2007), 'Socioemotional wealth and business risks in family-controlled firms: evidence from Spanish olive oil mills', *Administrative Science Quarterly*, **52**(1), 106–37.

Goss, D. (2005), 'Schumpeter's legacy? Interaction and emotions in the sociology of entrepreneurship', *Entrepreneurship Theory and Practice*, **29**(2), 205–18.

Goss, D. (2007), 'Enterprise ritual: a theory of entrepreneurial emotion and exchange', *British Journal of Management*, **18**, 1–18.

Gross, J. (1998), 'The emerging field of emotion regulation: an integrative review', *Review of General Psychology*, **2**, 271–99.

Gross, J. (1999), 'Emotion regulation: past, present, future', *Cognition & Emotion*, **13**(5), 551–73.

Habbershon, T.G. and Williams, M.L. (1999), 'A resource-based framework for assessing the strategic advantages of family firms', *Family Business Review*, **12**(1), 1–25.

Habbershon, T.G., Williams, M. and MacMillan, I.C. (2006), 'A unified systems perspective of family firm performance', in P.Z. Poutziouris, K.X. Smyrnios and S.B. Klein (eds), *Handbook of Research on Family Business*, Cheltenham, UK and Northampton, MA, USA: Edward Elgar, pp. 67–79.

Hareli, S. and Rafaeli, A. (2008), 'Emotion cycles: on the social influence of emotion in organizations', *Research in Organizational Behavior*, **28**, 35–59.

Harvey, M. and Evans, R.E. (1994), 'Family business and multiple levels of conflict', *Family Business Review*, **7**(4), 331–48.

Heck, R.K.Z., Danes, S.M., Fitzgerald, M.A., Haynes, G.W., Jasper, C.R., Schrank, H.L. et al. (2006), 'The family's dynamic role within family business entrepreneurship', in P.Z. Poutziouris, K.X. Smyrnios and S.B. Klein (eds), *Handbook of Research on Family Business*, Cheltenham, UK and Northampton, MA, USA: Edward Elgar, pp. 80–105.

Hochschild, A.R. (1979), 'Emotion work, feeling rules, and social structure', *American Journal of Sociology*, **85**(3), 551–75.

Hochschild, A.R. (1983), *The Managed Heart: Commercialization of Human Feeling*, Berkeley, CA: University of California Press.

Hofstede, G. (1993), 'Cultural constraints in management theories', *The Executive*, **7**(1), 81–94.

Hofstede, G. (2001), *Culture's Consequences*, 2nd edn, Thousand Oaks, CA: Sage Publications.

Hollander, B.S. and Elman, N.S. (1988), 'Family-owned businesses: an emerging field of inquiry', *Family Business Review*, **1**(2), 145–64.

Hubler, T. (1999), 'Ten most prevalent obstacles to family-business succession planning', *Family Business Review*, **12**(2), 117–21.

Irava, W.J. (2009), 'Familiness qualities, entrepreneurial orientation and long-term performance advantage', Bond University, Queensland Australia.

James, W. (1884), 'What is an emotion?', *Mind*, **9**(34), 188–205.

Kaye, K. (1996), 'When the family business is a sickness', *Family Business Review*, **9**(4), 347–68.

Kellermanns, F.W. and Eddleston, K.A. (2007), 'A family perspective on when conflict benefits family firm performance', *Journal of Business Research*, **60**(10), 1048–57.

Kelly, J.R. and Barsade, S.G. (2001), 'Mood and emotions in small groups and work teams', *Organizational Behavior and Human Decision Processes*, **86**(1), 99–130.

Kelly, L.M., Athanassiou, N. and Crittenden, W.F. (2000), 'Founder centrality and strategic behavior in the family-owned firm', *Entrepreneurship Theory and Practice*, **25**, 27–42.

Kenyon-Rouvinez, D. and Ward, J.L. (2004), *Les entreprises familiales*, Paris: PUF.

Kepner, E. (1983), 'The family and the firm: a coevolutionary perspective', *Organizational Dynamics*, **12**(1), 57–70.

Kets-de-Vries, M.F.R. (1993), 'The dynamics of family controlled firms: the good and the bad news', *Organizational Dynamics*, **21**, 59–71.

Kets-de-Vries, M.F.R., Carlock, R.S. and Florent-Treacy, E. (2007), '*Family Business on the Couch: A Psychological Perspective*, Chichester, UK: John Wiley & Sons.

Klein, S.B. (2000), 'Family businesses in Germany: significance and structure', *Family Business Review*, **13**(3), 157–81.

Klein, S.B. and Kellermanns, F.W. (2008), 'Editor's note: understanding the non economic-motivated behavior in family firms: an introduction', *Family Business Review*, **21**, 121–5.

Labaki, R. (1999), 'Atténuation ou renforcement des liens familiaux dans les entreprises familiales', Unpublished dissertation, University of Montesquieu Bordeaux IV, Bordeaux.

Labaki, R. (2005), 'The family relationship factor: its theoretical contribution to family business performance', paper presented at the 6th FBN-IFERA World Academic Research Forum, Brussels.

Labaki, R. (2007), 'Contribution à la connaissance des liens familiaux dans les entreprises familiales françaises cotées: Renforcement versus atténuation', unpublished PhD dissertation, University of Montesquieu Bordeaux IV, Bordeaux.

Lansberg, I. (1988), 'The succession conspiracy', *Family Business Review*, **1**(2), 119–43.

Lazarus, R.S. (1991), *Emotion & Adaptation*, New York: Oxford University Press.

Lee, M.-S. and Rogoff, E.G. (1996), 'Research note: comparison of small business with family participation versus small businesses without family participation: an investigation of differences in goals, attitudes and family/business conflict', *Family Business Review*, **9**(4), 423–37.

Levinson, H. (1971), 'Conflicts that plague family businesses', *Harvard Business Review*, **49**, 90–98.

Lewig, K.A. and Dollard, M.F. (2003), 'Emotional dissonance, emotional exhaustion and job satisfaction in call centre workers', *European Journal of Work and Organizational Psychology*, **12**(4), 366–92.

Longmore, M.A. and Demaris, A. (1997), 'Perceived inequity and depression in intimate relationships: the moderating effect of self-esteem', *Social Psychology Quarterly*, **60**(2), 172–84.

Mackie, D.M., Devos, T. and Smith, E.R. (2000), 'Intergroup emotions: explaining offensive action tendencies in an intergroup context', *Journal of Personality & Social Psychology*, **79**(4), 602–16.

Markus, H.R. and Kitayama, S. (1991), 'Culture and the self: implications for cognition, emotion, and motivation', *Psychological Review*, **98**(2), 224–53.

Matsumoto, D. (1993), 'Ethnic differences in affect intensity, emotion judgments, display rules attitudes and self-reported emotional expression in an American sample', *Motivation and Emotion*, **17**(2), 107–23.

Meyer, M.W. and Zucker, L.G. (1989), *Permanently Failing Organizations*, Newbury Park, CA: Sage.

Michael-Tsabari, N. and Lavee, Y. (2008), 'The circumplex model in family research and its implementation to family businesses', paper presented at the International Family Enterprise Research Academy meeting.

Miller, N.J., Fitzgerald, M.A., Winter, M. and Paul, J. (1999), 'Exploring the overlap of family and business demands: household and family business managers' adjustment strategies', *Family Business Review*, **12**(3), 253–68.

Mishra, S.K. and Bhatnagar, D. (2009), 'Linking emotional dissonance and organizational identification to turnover intention and well-being', paper presented at the Academy of Management Proceedings.

Morris, J.A. and Feldman, D.C. (1996), 'The dimensions, antecedents and consequences of emotional labor', *Academy of Management Review*, **21**(4), 986–1010.

Mustakallio, M. (2002), 'Contractual and relational governance in family firms: effects on strategic decision-making quality and firm performance', University of Technology, Helsinki.

Mustakallio, M., Autio, E. and Zahra, S.A. (2002), 'Relational and contractual governance in family firms: effects on strategic decision making', *Family Business Review*, **15**(3), 205–22.

Nichols, M.P. and Schwartz, R.C. (2006), *Family Therapy: Concepts and Methods*, 7th edn, Boston, MA: Pearson Education, Inc.

Nordqvist, M. (2005), 'Familiness in top management teams: commentary on Ensley and Pearson's "An exploratory comparison of the behavioral dynamics of top management teams in family and nonfamily new ventures: cohesion, conflict, potency, and consensus"', *Entrepreneurship Theory and Practice*, **29**(3), 285–91.

Olson, D.H. (2000), 'Circumplex model of marital and family systems', *Journal of Family Therapy*, **22**, 144–67.

Olson, P.D., Zuiker, V.S., Danes, S.M., Stafford, K., Heck, R.K.Z. and Duncan, K.A. (2003), 'The impact of the family and the business on family business sustainability', *Journal of Business Venturing*, **18**, 639–66.

Pachulia, G. and Henderson, L. (2009), 'The relationship between emotional intelligence and entrepreneurial orientation', unpublished Master thesis within Business Administration: Entrepreneurship, Jönköping University.

Pieper, T.M. (2007), *Mechanisms to Assure Long-Term Family Business Survival: A Study of the Dynamics of Cohesion in Multigenerational Family Business Families*, Frankfurt am Main: Peter Lang.

Pieper, T.M. and Astrachan, J.H. (2008), *Mechanisms to Assure Family Business Cohesion: Guidelines for Family Business Leaders and Their Families*, Kennesaw, GA: Cox Family Enterprise Center, Coles College of Business, Kennesaw State University.

Pieper, T.M. and Klein, S.B. (2007), 'The bulleye: a systems approach to modeling family firms', *Family Business Review*, **20**(4), 301–19.

Post, J.M. and Robins, R.S. (1993), 'The captive king and his captive court: the psychopolitical dynamics of the disabled leader and his inner circle', *Family Business Review*, **6**(2), 203–21.

Pugh, S.D. (2001), 'Service with a smile: emotional contagion in the service encounter', *Academy of Management Journal*, **44**(5), 1018–27.

Rafaeli, A., Semmer, N. and Tschan, F. (2007), 'Emotion in work settings', in K. Scherer and D. Sander (eds), *Oxford Companion to Emotion and the Affective Sciences*, Oxford: Oxford University Press.

Rafaeli, A. and Sutton, R.I. (1987), 'Expression of emotion as part of the work role', *The Academy of Management Review*, **13**(1), 23–37.

Rafaeli, A. and Sutton, R. (1989), 'The expression of emotion in organizational life', in L.L. Cummings and B.M. Staw (eds), *Research in Organizational Behavior*, Vol. 11, Greenwich, CT: JAI Press, pp. 1–42.

Rogoff, E.G. and Heck, R.K.Z. (2003), 'Evolving research in entrepreneurship and family business: recognizing family as the oxygen that feeds the fire of entrepreneurship', *Journal of Business Venturing*, **18**(5), 559–66.

Rosenblatt, P., De Mik, L., Anderson, R.M. and Johnson, P.A. (1985), *The Family in Business: Understanding and Dealing with the Challenges Entrepreneurial Families Face*, San Francisco, CA: Jossey-Bass.

Rothstein, J. (1992), 'Don't judge a book by its cover: a reconsideration of eight assumptions about Jewish family businesses', *Family Business Review*, **5**(4), 397–411.

Ruben, D.H. (1998), 'Social exchange theory: dynamics of a system governing the dysfunctional family and guide to assessment', *Journal of Contemporary Psychotherapy*, **28**(3), 307–25.

Russell, J.A. (1980), 'A circumplex model of affect', *Journal of Personality and Social Psychology*, **39**, 1161–78.

Rutner, P.S., Hardgrave, B.C. and McKnight, D.H. (2008), 'Emotional dissonance and the information technology professional', *MIS Quarterly*, **32**(3), 635–52.

Sabatelli, R.M. and Shehan, C.L. (1993), 'Exchange and resource theories', in P.G. Boss, W.J. Doherty, R. LaRossa, W.R. Schumm and S.K. Steinmetz (eds), *Sourcebook of Family Theories and Methods: A Contextual Approach*, New York: Plenum, pp. 385–411.

Sharma, P. (2004), 'An overview of the field of family business studies: current status and directions for the future', *Family Business Review*, **17**(1), 1–36.

Sharma, P. (2008), 'Commentary: familiness: capital stocks and flows between family and business', *Entrepreneurship Theory and Practice*, **32**(6), 971–77.

Sharma, P. and Manikutty, S. (2005), 'Strategic divestments in family firms: role of family structure and community culture', *Entrepreneurship Theory and Practice*, **29**, 293–311.

Shepherd, D.A. (2003), 'Learning from business failure: propositions of grief recovery for the self-employed', *Academy of Management Review*, **28**(2), 318–28.

Simon, H.A. (1945), *Administrative Behaviour: A Study of Decision-making Processes in Administrative Organizations*, 4th edn, New York: Free Press.

Simon, H.A. (1955), 'A behavioral model of rational choice', *The Quarterly Journal of Economics*, **69**(1), 99–118.

Simon, H.A. (1978), 'Rationality as process and as product of thought', *American Economic Review*, **68**(2), 1–16.

Smith, E.R. (1993), 'Social identity and social emotions: toward new conceptualizations of prejudice', in D.M. Mackie and D.L. Hamilton (eds), *Affect, Cognition, and Stereotyping: Interactive Processes in Group Perception*, San Diego, CA: Academic Press, pp. 297–315.

Steier, L. (2003), 'Variants of agency contracts in family-financed ventures as a continuum of familial altruistic and market rationalities', *Journal of Business Venturing*, **18**(5), 597–618.

Sten, J. (2007), 'What is a business family?', *Electronic Journal of Family Business Studies*, **1**(2), 168–85.

Stenross, B. and Kleinman, S. (1989), 'The highs and lows of emotional labor: detectives' encounters with criminals and victims', *Journal of Contemporary Ethnography*, **17**, 435–52.

Sutton, R.I. (1991), 'Maintaining norms about expressed emotions: the case of bill collectors', *Administrative Science Quarterly*, **36**(2), 245–68.

Sutton, R.I. and Rafaeli, A. (1988), 'Untangling the relationship between displayed emotions and organizational sales: the case of convenience stores', *Academy of Management Journal*, **31**, 461–87.

Tagiuri, R. and Davis, J. (1996), 'Bivalent attributes of the family firm', *Family Business Review*, **9**(2), 199–208.

Tellegen, A. (1985), 'Stuctures of mood and personality and their relevance to assessing anxiety, with an emphasis on self-report', in A.H. Tuma and J.D. Maser (eds), *Anxiety and the Anxiety Disorders*, Hillsdale, NJ: Erlbaum, pp. 681–706.

Uhlaner, L.M. (2006), 'Business family as a team: underlying force for sustained competitive advantage', in P.Z. Poutziouris, K.X. Smyrnios and S.B. Klein (eds), *Handbook of Research on Family Business*, Cheltenham, UK and Northampton, MA, USA: Edward Elgar, pp. 125–44.

Van den Heuvel, J., Goel, S., Van Gils, A. and Voordeckers, W. (2007), 'Family businesses as emotional arenas: the influence of family CEO's empathy and external monitoring on the importance of family goals', Research Center for Innovation and Entrepreneurship (KIZOK), University of Hasselt, Netherlands.

Van Maanen, J. and Kunda, G. (1989), 'Real feelings: emotional expression and organizational culture', in L.L. Cummings and B.M. Staw (eds), *Research in Organizational Behavior*, Vol. 11, Greenwich, CT: JAI Press, pp. 43–104.

Villalonga, B. and Amit, R. (2006), 'How do family ownership, control and management affect firm value?', *Journal of Financial Economics*, **80**, 385–417.

Walsh, F. (2003), *Normal Family Process*, New York: Guilford.

Ward, J.L. and Dolan, C. (1998), 'Defining and describing family business ownership configurations', *Family Business Review*, **11**(4), 305–10.

Watson, T.J. and Petre, P. (1990), *Father, Son & Co.: My Life at IBM and Beyond*, New York: Bantam Books.

Weiss, H.M. and Cropanzano, R. (1996), 'Affective events theory: a theoretical discussion of the structure, causes and consequences of affective experiences at work', *Research in Organizational Behavior*, **18**, 1–74.

Whiteside, M.F. and Brown, F.H. (1991), 'Drawbacks of a dual systems approach to family firms: can we expand our thinking?', *Family Business Review*, **4**(4), 383–95.

Winter, M., Fitzgerald, M.A., Heck, R.K.Z., Haynes, G. and Danes, S. (1998), 'Revisiting the study of family businesses: methodological challenges, dilemmas, and alternative approaches', *Family Business Review*, **11**(3), 239–52.

Wortman, M.S. (1994), 'Theoretical foundations for family-owned business: a conceptual and research-based paradigm', *Family Business Review*, **7**(1), 3–27.

Zampetakis, L.A., Kafetsios, K., Bouranta, N., Dewett, T. and Moustakis, V.S. (2009), 'On the relationship between emotional intelligence and entrepreneurial attitudes and intentions', *International Journal of Entrepreneurial Behaviour & Research*, **15**(6), 595–618.

Zellweger, T.M. and Astrachan, J.H. (2008), 'On the emotional value of owning a firm', *Family Business Review*, **21**(4), 347–63.

Zellweger, T.M., Eddleston, K.A. and Kellermanns, F.W. (2010), 'Exploring the concept of familiness: introducing family firm identity', *Journal of Family Business Strategy*, **1**(1), 54–63.

Zerbe, W.J. (2000), 'Emotional dissonance and employee well-being', in N. Ashkanasy, C. Hartel and W.J. Zerbe (eds), *Emotions in the Workplace: Research, Theory, and Practice*, Westport, CT: Quorum Books, pp. 189–214.

Index

Titles of publications are shown in *italics*.